EIGHTY SIXTH EDITION

SINCE 1912

WHO'S WHO
IN BASEBALL
2001

Official Lifetime Records
Of Major League Players

Executive Editor
Norman MacLean

Editor
Bill Shannon

Associate Editor
Pete Palmer

Graphic Designer
Rory S. Slifkin

Editorial Assistant
Alex MacLean

WHO'S WHO IN BASEBALL is published annually by Who's Who in Baseball Magazine Co., Inc., 1115 Broadway, New York, New York 10010. Single copy price: $6.95. Submissions of manuscripts, illustrations and/or photographs must be accompanied by a stamped, self-addressed envelope. The publisher assumes no responsibility for unsolicited material. Copyright © 2001 by Who's Who in Baseball Magazine Co., Inc. All rights reserved under International and Pan American Copyright Conventions. Reproduction in whole or in part without written permission of the publisher is strictly prohibited. Printed in U.S.A.

BATTERS

ABBOTT, JEFFREY WILLIAM (JEFF)
Born, Atlanta, Georgia, August 17, 1972.
Bats Right. Throws Right. Height, 6 feet, 2 inches. Weight, 190 pounds.

Year Club	Lea	Pos	G	AB	R	H	2B	3B	HR	RBI	SB	Avg
1994 White Sox	Gulf Coast	OF	4	15	4	7	1	0	1	3	2	.46
1994 Hickory	So.Atl.	OF	63	224	47	88	16	6	6	48	2	.39:
1995 Pr William	Carolina	OF	70	264	41	92	16	0	4	47	7	.34'
1995 Birmingham	Southern	OF	55	197	25	63	11	1	3	28	1	.32
1996 Nashville	A.A.	OF	113	440	64	143	27	1	14	60	12	.32|
1997 Nashville	A.A.	OF	118	465	88	152	35	3	11	63	12	.32
1997 Chicago	A.L.	OF	19	38	8	10	1	0	1	2	0	.26:
1998 Chicago	A.L.	OF	89	244	33	68	14	1	12	41	3	.27'
1999 Charlotte	Int.	OF	66	277	42	88	24	1	9	37	2	.31
1999 Chicago a	A.L.	OF	17	57	5	9	0	0	2	6	1	.15
2000 Chicago b	A.L.	OF	80	215	31	59	15	1	3	29	2	.27'
Major League Totals		4 Yrs.	205	554	77	146	30	2	18	78	6	.26|
Division Series												
2000 Chicago	A.L.	OF	1	1	0	0	0	0	0	0	0	.00|

a On disabled list from May 30 to June 28 and August 1 to 10, 1999.
b Traded to Florida Marlins for outfielder Julio Ramirez, December 10, 2000.

ABBOTT, KURT THOMAS
Born, Zanesville, Ohio, June 2, 1968.
Bats Right. Throws Right. Height, 6 feet. Weight, 170 pounds.

Year Club	Lea	Pos	G	AB	R	H	2B	3B	HR	RBI	SB	Avg
1989 So. Oregon	Northwest	SS	5	10	2	1	0	0	0	1	1	.10|
1989 Scottsdale Athletics	Ariz.	SS-2B-3B	36	155	27	42	5	3	0	25	0	.27'
1990 Madison	Midwest	SS-2B-3B	104	362	38	84	18	0	0	28	21	.232
1991 Modesto	California	SS	58	216	36	55	8	2	3	25	6	.255
1991 Huntsville	Southern	SS	53	182	18	46	6	1	-0	11	6	.253
1992 Tacoma	P.C.	SS	11	39	2	6	1	0	0	1	1	.154
1992 Huntsville	Southern	SS	124	452	64	115	14	5	9	52	16	.254
1993 Tacoma	P.C.	SS	133	480	75	153-	36	11	12	79	19	.31º
1993 Oakland a	A.L.	OF-SS-2B	20	61	11	15	1	0	3	9	2	.24º
1994 Florida	N.L.	SS	101	345	41	86	17	3	9	33	3	.24º
1995 Charlotte	Int.	SS	5	-18	3	5	0	0	1	3	1	.27º
1995 Florida b	N.L.	SS	120	420	60	107	18	7	17	60	4	.255
1996 Charlotte	Int.	SS-2B-3B	18	69	20	26	10	1	5	11	2	.37º
1996 Florida c	N.L.	SS-3B-2B	109	320	37	81	18	7	8	33	3	.253
1997 Florida d	N.L.	2B-OF-SS-3B	94	252	35	69	18	2	6	30	3	.274
1998 Edmonton	P.C.	SS	7	25	5	10	2	0	2	4	0	.40º
1998 Oakland	A.L.	SS-OF-3B	35	123	17	33	7	1	2	9	2	.26º
1998 Colorado e-f-g	N.L.	OF-2B-SS-3B	42	71	9	18	6	0	3	15	0	.254
1999 Colorado h-i	N.L.	2B-1B-OF-SS	96	286	41	78	17	2	8	41	3	.273
2000 Norfolk	Int.	SS	2	4	1	1	0	0	0	0	0	.250
2000 New York j-k	N.L.	SS-2B-3B-OF	79	157	22	34	7	1	6	12	1	.217
Major League Totals		8 Yrs.	696	2035	273	521	109	23	62	242	21	.256
Division Series												
1997 Florida	N.L.	2B	3	8	0	2	0	0	0	0	0	.250
2000 New York	N.L.	SS	1	2	0	0	0	0	0	0	0	.000
Division Series Totals			4	10	0	2	0	0	0	0	0	.200
Championship Series												
1997 Florida	N.L.	2B	2	8	0	3	1	0	0	0	0	.375
2000 New York	N.L.	SS	2	3	0	0	0	0	0	0	0	.000
Championship Series Totals			4	11	0	3	1	0	0	0	0	.273
World Series Record												
1997 Florida	N.L.	DH	3	3	0	0	0	0	0	0	0	.00º
2000 New York	N.L.	SS	5	8	0	2	1	0	0	0	0	.250
World Series Totals			8	11	0	2	1	0	0	0	0	.182

a Traded to Florida Marlins for outfielder Kerwin Moore, December 20, 1993.
b On disabled list from April 25 to May 6, 1995.
c On disabled list from May 6 to June 13, 1996.
d Traded to Oakland A's for Pitcher Eric Ludwich December 21, 1997.

2

e On disabled list from March 31 to April 16, 1998.
f Traded to Colorado Rockies for player to be named later, June 9, 1998.
g Oakland Athletics received pitcher Ara Petrosian to complete trade, June 18, 1998.
h On disabled list from May 23 to June 7 and July 23 to August 7, 1999.
i Filed for free agency, November 1, 1999. Signed with New York Mets organization, January 26, 2000.
j On disabled list from June 30 to July 26, 2000.
k Not offered 2001 contract, November 2, 2000, signed with Atlanta Braves organization, December 14, 2000.

ABREU, BOB KELLY

Born, Aragua, Venezuela, March 11, 1974.
Bats Left. Throws Right. Height, 6 feet. Weight, 160 pounds.

Year	Club	Lea	Pos	G	AB	R	H	2B	3B	HR	RBI	SB	Avg
1991 Astros	Gulf Coast	OF-SS	56	183	21	55	7	3	0	20	10	.301
1992 Asheville	So. Atl.	OF	135	480	81	140	21	4	8	48	15	.292
1993 Osceola	Fla.St.	OF	129	474	62	134	21	17	5	55	10	.283
1994 Jackson	Texas	OF	118	400	61	121	25	9	16	73	12	.303
1995 Tucson	P.C.	OF-2B	114	415	72	126	24	17	10	75	16	.304
1996 Tucson	P.C.	OF	132	484	86	138	14	16	13	68	24	.285
1996 Houston	N.L.	OF	15	22	1	5	1	0	0	1	0	.227
1997 Jackson	Texas	OF	3	12	2	2	1	0	0	0	0	.167
1997 New Orleans	A.A.	OF	47	194	25	52	9	4	2	22	7	.268
1997 Houston a-b-c	N.L.	OF	59	188	22	47	10	2	3	26	7	.250
1998 Philadelphia	N.L.	OF	151	497	68	155	29	6	17	74	19	.312
1999 Philadelphia	N.L.	OF	152	546	118	183	35	*11	20	93	27	.335
2000 Philadelphia	N.L.	OF	154	576	103	182	42	10	25	79	28	.316
Major League Totals		5 Yrs.	531	1829	312	572	117	29	65	273	81	.313
Division Series													
1997 Houston	N.L.	PH	3	3	0	1	0	0	0	0	1	.333

a On disabled list from May 25 to July 1, 1997.
b Selected in expansion draft by Tampa Bay Devil Rays, November 18, 1997.
c Traded to Philadelphia Phillies for infielder Kevin Stocker, November 19, 1997.

AGBAYANI, BENNY PETER

Born, Honolulu, Hawaii, December 28, 1971.
Bats Right. Throws Right. Height, 6 feet. Weight, 225 pounds.

Year	Club	Lea	Pos	G	AB	R	H	2B	3B	HR	RBI	SB	Avg
1993 Pittsfield	N.Y.-Penn.	OF	51	167	26	42	6	3	2	22	7	.251
1994 St. Lucie	Fla.St.	OF	119	411	72	115	13	5	5	63	8	.280
1995 St. Lucie	Fla.St.	DH-OF	44	155	24	48	9	3	2	29	8	.310
1995 Binghamton	Eastern	OF	88	295	38	81	11	2	1	26	12	.275
1996 Binghamton	Eastern	OF	21	53	7	9	1	0	2	8	1	.170
1996 Norfolk	Int.	OF-1B	99	331	43	92	13	9	7	56	14	.278
1997 Norfolk	Int.	OF	127	468	90	145	24	2	11	51	29	.310
1998 Norfolk	Int.	OF-1B	90	322	43	91	20	5	11	53	16	.283
1998 New York	N.L.	OF	11	15	1	2	0	0	0	0	0	.133
1999 Norfolk	Int.	OF	28	101	21	36	8	1	8	32	5	.356
1999 New York	N.L.	OF	101	276	42	79	18	3	14	42	6	.286
2000 New York	N.L.	OF	119	350	59	101	19	1	15	60	5	.289
Major League Totals		3 Yrs.	231	641	102	182	37	4	29	102	11	.284
Division Series													
1999 New York	N.L.	OF	4	10	1	3	1	0	0	1	0	.300
2000 New York	N.L.	OF	4	15	1	5	1	0	1	1	0	.333
Division Series Totals			8	25	2	8	2	0	1	2	0	.320
Championship Series													
1999 New York	N.L.	OF	4	7	2	1	0	0	0	0	1	.143
2000 New York	N.L.	OF	5	17	0	6	2	0	0	3	0	.353
Championship Series Totals			9	24	2	7	2	0	0	3	1	.292
World Series Record													
2000 New York	N.L.	OF	5	18	2	5	2	0	0	2	0	.278

ALEXANDER, MANUEL DEJESUS (MANNY)

Born, San Pedro de Marcoris, Dominican Republic, March 20, 1971.
Bats Right. Throws Right. Height, 5 feet, 10 inches. Weight, 165 pounds.

Year	Club	Lea	Pos	G	AB	R	H	2B	3B	HR	RBI	SB	Avg
1988				Played in Dominican Summer League									
1989 Bluefield	Appal.	SS	65	*274	49	*85	13	2	2	34	19	.310
1990 Wausau a	Midwest	SS	44	152	16	27	3	1	0	11	8	.178

3

Year	Club	Lea	Pos	G	AB	R	H	2B	3B	HR	RBI	SB	Avg
1991 Frederick	Carolina		SS	134	548	*81	*143	17	3	3	42	47	.261
1991 Hagerstown	Eastern		SS	3	9	3	3	1	0	0	2	0	.333
1992 Hagerstown	Eastern		SS	127	499	70	129	22	8	2	41	43	.259
1992 Rochester	Int.		SS	6	24	3	7	1	0	0	3	2	.292
1992 Baltimore	A.L.		SS	4	5	1	1	0	0	0	0	0	.200
1993 Rochester	Int.		SS	120	471	55	115	23	8	6	51	19	.244
1993 Baltimore	A.L.		PR	3	0	1	0	0	0	0	0	0	.000
1994 Rochester b	Int.		SS-2B	111	426	63	106	23	6	6	39	30	.249
1995 Baltimore	A.L.		2B-SS-3B	94	242	35	57	9	1	3	23	11	.236
1996 Baltimore	A.L.		SS-2B-3B-OF	54	68	6	7	0	0	0	4	3	.103
1997 St. Lucie c-d	Fla. St.		SS	1	4	0	1	0	0	0	0	0	.250
1997 New York-Chicago e	N.L.		SS-2B-3B	87	248	37	66	12	4	3	22	13	.266
1998 Chicago	N.L.		SS-2B-3B-OF	108	264	34	60	10	1	5	25	4	.227
1999 Chicago	N.L.		SS-3B-2B-OF	90	177	17	48	11	2	0	15	4	.271
2000 Boston g-h	A.L.		3B-SS-2B	101	194	30	41	4	3	4	19	2	.211
Major League Totals			8 Yrs.	541	1198	161	280	46	11	15	108	37	.234
Division Series													
1996 Baltimore	A.L.		DH	3	0	2	0	0	0	0	0	0	.000
1998 Chicago	N.L.		SS	2	5	0	0	0	0	0	0	0	.000
Division Series Totals				5	5	2	0	0	0	0	0	0	.000

a On disabled list from April 26 to July 23, 1990.
b On disabled list from March 25 to May 2, 1994.
c Traded to New York Mets with infielder Scott McClain for pitcher Hector Ramirez, March 22, 1997.
d On disabled list from June 11 to July 10 and July 25 to August 11, 1997.
e Sent to Chicago Cubs as player to be named later for pitcher Mel Rojas, pitcher Turk Wendell and outfielder Brian McRae, August 14, 1997.
f Traded to Boston Red Sox for outfielder Damon Buford, December 11, 1999.
g On disabled list from September 29 to October 29, 2000.
h Filed for free agency, October 30, 2000.

ALFONZO, EDGARDO ANTONIO
Born, Santa Teresa, Venezuela, August 11, 1973.
Bats Right. Throws Right. Height, 5 feet, 11 inches. Weight, 185 pounds.

Year	Club	Lea	Pos	G	AB	R	H	2B	3B	HR	RBI	SB	Avg
1991 Mets	Gulf Coast		2B-SS-3B	54	175	29	58	8	4	0	27	6	.331
1992 St. Lucie	Fla. St.		2B-SS	4	5	0	0	0	0	0	0	0	.000
1992 Pittsfield	N.Y.-Penn.		SS	74	298	41	106	13	5	1	44	7	.356
1993 St. Lucie	Fla. St.		SS	128	494	75	145	18	3	11	86	26	.294
1994 Binghamton	Eastern		SS-2B-1B	127	498	89	146	34	2	15	75	14	.293
1995 New York a	N.L.		3B-2B-SS	101	335	26	93	13	5	4	41	1	.278
1996 New York	N.L.		2B-3B-SS	123	368	36	96	15	2	4	40	2	.261
1997 New York	N.L.		3B-SS-2B	151	518	84	163	27	2	10	72	11	.315
1998 New York b	N.L.		3B-SS	144	557	94	155	28	2	17	78	8	.278
1999 New York	N.L.		2B	158	628	123	191	41	1	27	108	9	.304
2000 New York	N.L.		2B	150	544	109	176	40	2	25	94	3	.324
Major League Totals			6 Yrs.	827	2950	472	874	164	14	87	433	34	.296
Division Series													
1999 New York	N.L.		2B	4	16	6	4	1	0	3	6	0	.250
2000 New York	N.L.		2B	4	18	1	5	2	0	1	5	0	.278
Division Series Totals				8	34	7	9	3	0	4	11	0	.265
Championship Series													
1999 New York	N.L.		2B	6	27	2	6	4	0	0	1	0	.222
2000 New York	N.L.		2B	5	18	5	8	1	1	0	4	0	.444
Championship Series Totals				11	45	7	14	5	1	0	5	0	.311
World Series Record													
2000 New York	N.L.		2B	5	21	1	3	0	0	0	1	0	.143

a On disabled list from August 11 to September 1, 1995.
b On disabled list from May 4 to May 19, 1998.

ALICEA, LUIS RENE
Born, Santurce, Puerto Rico, July 29, 1965.
Bats Both. Throws Right. Height, 5 feet, 9 inches. Weight, 177 pounds.

Year	Club	Lea	Pos	G	AB	R	H	2B	3B	HR	RBI	SB	Avg
1986 Erie	N.Y.-Penn.		2B	47	163	40	46	6	1	3	18	27	.282
1986 Arkansas	Texas		2B	25	68	8	16	3	0	0	3	0	.235
1987 Arkansas	Texas		2B	101	337	57	91	14	3	4	47	13	.270

Year Club	Lea	Pos	G	AB	R	H	2B	3B	HR	RBI	SB	Avg
1987 Louisville	A.A.	2B	29	105	18	32	10	2	2	20	4	.305
1988 Louisville	A.A.	2B-SS	49	191	21	53	11	6	1	21	8	.277
1988 St. Louis	N.L.	2B	93	297	20	63	10	4	1	24	1	.212
1989 Louisville	A.A.	2B	124	412	53	102	20	3	8	48	13	.248
1990 St. Petersburg a	Fla. St.	2B-3B	29	95	14	22	1	4	0	12	9	.232
1990 Arkansas	Texas	2B-3B	14	49	11	14	3	1	0	4	2	.286
1990 Louisville	A.A.	2B-3B	25	92	10	32	6	3	0	10	0	.348
1991 Louisville	A.A.	2B	31	112	26	44	6	3	4	16	5	.393
1991 St. Louis b	N.L.	2B-3B-SS	56	68	5	13	3	0	0	0	0	.191
1992 Louisville	A.A.	2B	20	71	11	20	8	0	0	6	0	.282
1992 St. Louis c	N.L.	2B-SS	85	265	26	65	9	11	2	32	2	.245
1993 St. Louis	N.L.	2B-OF-3B	115	362	50	101	19	3	3	46	11	.279
1994 St. Louis d-e	N.L.	2B-OF	88	205	32	57	12	5	5	29	4	.278
1995 Boston f	A.L.	2B	132	419	64	113	20	3	6	44	13	.270
1996 St. Louis g-h-i-j	N.L.	2B	129	380	54	98	26	3	5	42	11	.258
1997 Anaheim k-l	A.L.	2B-3B	128	388	59	98	16	7	5	37	22	.253
1998 Texas	A.L.	2B-3B-OF	101	259	51	71	15	3	6	33	4	.274
1999 Texas m	A.L.	2B-3B-OF	68	164	33	33	10	0	3	17	2	.201
2000 Texas n	A.L.	2B-3B-SS	139	540	85	159	25	8	6	63	1	.294
Major League Totals	11 Yrs.		1134	3347	479	871	165	47	42	367	71	.260
Division Series												
1995 Boston	A.L.	2B	3	10	1	6	1	0	1	1	1	.600
1996 St. Louis	N.L.	2B	3	11	1	2	2	0	0	0	0	.182
1998 Texas	A.L.	PH	1	1	0	0	0	0	0	0	0	.000
Division Series Totals			7	22	2	8	3	0	1	1	1	.364
Championship Series												
1996 St. Louis	N.L.	2B	5	8	0	0	0	0	0	0	0	.000

a On disabled list from April 6 to June 4, 1990.
b On disabled list from April 25 to May 25, 1991.
c On disabled list from June 1 to July 6, 1992.
d Traded to Boston Red Sox for pitcher Nate Minchey and outfielder Jeff McNeely, December 7, 1994.
e Became restricted free agent under Major League Baseball implemented labor proposal, December 23, 1994.
f Signed with Boston Red Sox, April 7, 1995.
g Waived by Boston Red Sox, March 12, 1996.
h Signed with St. Louis Cardinals, March 17, 1996.
i Filed for free agency, October 31, 1996.
j Signed with Anaheim Angels organization, January 20, 1997.
k Filed for free agency, October 30, 1997.
l Signed with Texas Rangers, December 11, 1997.
m Filed for free agency, October 28, 1999, re-signed with Texas Rangers, December 7, 1999.
n Filed for free agency, October 31, 2000.

ALOMAR (VELAZQUEZ), ROBERTO

Born, Salinas, Puerto Rico, February 5, 1968.
Bats Both. Throws Right. Height, 6 feet. Weight, 185 pounds.

Year Club	Lea	Pos	G	AB	R	H	2B	3B	HR	RBI	SB	Avg
1985 Charleston	So. Atl.	2B-SS	*137	*546	89	160	14	3	0	54	36	.293
1986 Reno	Calif.	2B	90	356	53	123	16	4	4	49	14	*.346
1987 Wichita	Texas	SS-2B	130	536	88	171	41	4	12	68	43	.319
1988 Las Vegas	P.C.	2B	9	37	5	10	1	0	2	14	3	.270
1988 San Diego	N.L.	2B	143	545	84	145	24	6	9	41	24	.266
1989 San Diego	N.L.	2B	158	623	82	184	27	1	7	56	42	.295
1990 San Diego a	N.L.	2B-SS	147	586	80	168	27	5	6	60	24	.287
1991 Toronto	A.L.	2B	161	637	88	188	41	11	9	69	53	.295
1992 Toronto	A.L.	2B	152	571	105	177	27	8	8	76	49	.310
1993 Toronto	A.L.	2B	153	589	109	192	35	6	17	93	55	.326
1994 Toronto	A.L.	2B	107	392	78	120	25	4	8	38	19	.306
1995 Toronto b	A.L.	2B	130	517	71	155	24	7	13	66	30	.300
1996 Baltimore	A.L.	2B	153	588	132	193	43	4	22	94	17	.328
1997 Baltimore c	A.L.	2B	112	412	64	137	23	2	14	60	9	.333
1998 Baltimore d-e	A.L.	2B	147	588	86	166	36	1	14	56	18	.282
1999 Cleveland	A.L.	2B	159	563	*138	182	40	3	24	120	37	.323
2000 Cleveland	A.L.	2B	155	610	111	189	40	2	19	89	39	.310
Major League Totals	13 Yrs.		1877	7221	1228	2196	412	60	170	918	416	.304
Division Series												
1996 Baltimore	A.L.	2B	4	17	2	5	0	0	1	4	0	.294
1997 Baltimore	A.L.	2B	4	10	1	3	2	0	0	2	0	.300
1999 Cleveland	A.L.	2B	5	19	4	7	4	0	0	3	2	.368
Division Series Totals			13	46	7	15	6	0	1	9	2	.326

Year Club	Lea	Pos	G	AB	R	H	2B	3B	HR	RBI	SB	Avg
Championship Series												
1991 Toronto . . . . .A.L.		2B	5	19	3	9	0	0	0	4	2	.474
1992 Toronto . . . . .A.L.		2B	6	26	4	11	1	0	2	4	5	.423
1993 Toronto . . . . .A.L.		2B	6	24	3	7	1	0	0	4	4	.292
1996 Baltimore . . . . .A.L.		2B	5	23	2	5	2	0	0	1	0	.217
1997 Baltimore . . . . .A.L.		2B	6	22	2	4	0	0	1	2	0	.182
Championship Series Totals			28	114	14	36	4	0	3	15	11	.316
World Series Record												
1992 Toronto . . . . .A.L.		2B	6	24	3	5	1	0	0	0	2	.208
1993 Toronto . . . . .A.L.		2B	6	25	5	12	2	1	0	6	4	.480
World Series Totals			12	49	8	17	3	1	0	6	6	.347

a Traded to Toronto Blue Jays with outfielder Joe Carter for shortstop Tony Fernandez and first baseman Fred McGriff, December 5, 1990.
b Filed for free agency, October 30, 1995. Signed with Baltimore Orioles, December 21, 1995.
c On disabled list from July 30 to August 26, 1997.
d On disabled list from July 19 to August 4, 1998.
e Filed for free agency, October 26, 1998, signed with Cleveland Indians, November 24, 1998.

ALOMAR (VELAZQUEZ), SANTOS JR. (SANDY)

Born, Salinas, Puerto Rico, June 18, 1966.
Bats Right. Throws Right. Height, 6 feet, 5 inches. Weight, 215 pounds.

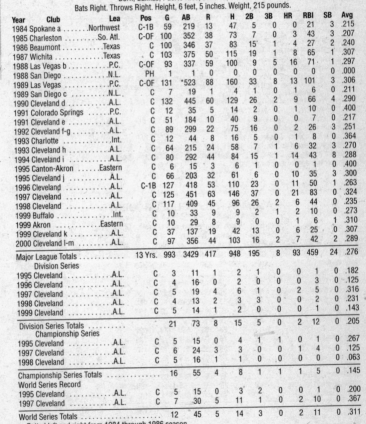

Year Club	Lea	Pos	G	AB	R	H	2B	3B	HR	RBI	SB	Avg
1984 Spokane a . . . . . . .Northwest		C-1B	59	219	13	47	5	0	0	21	3	.215
1985 Charleston . . . . .So. Atl.		C-OF	100	352	38	73	7	0	3	43	3	.207
1986 Beaumont . . . . .Texas		C	100	346	37	83	15	1	4	27	2	.240
1987 Wichita . . . . .Texas		C	103	375	50	115	19	1	8	65	1	.307
1988 Las Vegas b . . . . .P.C.		C-OF	93	337	59	100	9	5	16	71	1	.297
1988 San Diego . . . . .N.L.		PH	1	1	0	0	0	0	0	0	0	.000
1989 Las Vegas . . . . .P.C.		C-OF	131	*523	88	160	33	8	13	101	3	.306
1989 San Diego c . . . . .N.L.		C	7	19	1	4	1	0	1	6	0	.211
1990 Cleveland d . . . . .A.L.		C	132	445	60	129	26	2	9	66	4	.290
1991 Colorado Springs . . . . . .P.C.		C	12	35	5	14	2	0	1	10	0	.400
1991 Cleveland e . . . . .A.L.		C	51	184	10	40	9	0	0	7	0	.217
1992 Cleveland f-g . . . . .A.L.		C	89	299	22	75	16	0	2	26	3	.251
1993 Charlotte . . . . .Int.		C	12	44	8	16	5	0	1	8	0	.364
1993 Cleveland h . . . . .A.L.		C	64	215	24	58	7	1	6	32	3	.270
1994 Cleveland i . . . . .A.L.		C	80	292	44	84	15	1	14	43	8	.288
1995 Canton-Akron . . . . . .Eastern		C	6	15	3	6	1	0	0	1	0	.400
1995 Cleveland j . . . . .A.L.		C	66	203	32	61	6	0	10	35	3	.300
1996 Cleveland . . . . .A.L.		C-1B	127	418	53	110	23	0	11	50	1	.263
1997 Cleveland . . . . .A.L.		C	125	451	63	146	37	0	21	83	0	.324
1998 Cleveland . . . . .A.L.		C	117	409	45	96	26	2	6	44	0	.235
1999 Buffalo . . . . .Int.		C	10	33	9	9	2	1	2	10	0	.273
1999 Akron . . . . .Eastern		C	10	29	8	9	0	0	1	6	1	.310
1999 Cleveland k . . . . .A.L.		C	37	137	19	42	13	0	6	25	0	.307
2000 Cleveland l-m . . . . .A.L.		C	97	356	44	103	16	2	7	42	2	.289
Major League Totals	13 Yrs.		993	3429	417	948	195	8	93	459	24	.276
Division Series												
1995 Cleveland . . . . .A.L.		C	3	11	1	2	1	0	0	1	0	.182
1996 Cleveland . . . . .A.L.		C	4	16	0	2	0	0	0	3	0	.125
1997 Cleveland . . . . .A.L.		C	5	19	4	6	1	0	2	5	0	.316
1998 Cleveland . . . . .A.L.		C	4	13	2	3	3	0	0	2	0	.231
1999 Cleveland . . . . .A.L.		C	5	14	1	2	0	0	0	1	0	.143
Division Series Totals			21	73	8	15	5	0	2	12	0	.205
Championship Series												
1995 Cleveland . . . . .A.L.		C	5	15	0	4	1	1	0	1	0	.267
1997 Cleveland . . . . .A.L.		C	6	24	3	3	0	0	1	4	0	.125
1998 Cleveland . . . . .A.L.		C	5	16	1	1	0	0	0	0	0	.063
Championship Series Totals			16	55	4	8	1	1	1	5	0	.145
World Series Record												
1995 Cleveland . . . . .A.L.		C	5	15	0	3	2	0	0	1	0	.200
1997 Cleveland . . . . .A.L.		C	7	30	5	11	1	0	2	10	0	.367
World Series Totals			12	45	5	14	3	0	2	11	0	.311

a Batted left and right from 1984 through 1986 season.
b On disabled list from August 14 to September 16, 1988.
c Traded to Cleveland Indians with infielder Carlos Baerga and outfielder Chris James for outfielder Joe Carter, December 7, 1989.
d Selected Rookie of the Year in American League for 1990.

e On disabled list from May 15 to June 17 and July 29 to end of 1991 season.
f On disabled list from May 1 to May 18, 1992.
g Suspended three games by American League for June 8 mound charging from July 29 to August 2, 1992.
h On disabled list May 1 to August 7, 1993.
i On disabled list from April 24 to May 11, 1994.
j On disabled list from April 25 to June 29, 1995.
k On disabled list from May 11 to September 6, 1999.
l On disabled list from April 19 to May 7, 2000.
m Filed for free agency, October 27, 2000, signed with Chicago White Sox, December 18, 2000.

ALOU, MOISES ROJAS
Born, Atlanta, Georgia, July 3, 1966.
Bats Right. Throws Right. Height, 6 feet, 3 inches. Weight, 190 pounds.

Year	Club	Lea	Pos	G	AB	R	H	2B	3B	HR	RBI	SB	Avg
1986 Watertown	N.Y.-Penn.	OF	69	254	30	60	9	*8	6	35	14	.236
1987 Macon a	So. Atl.	OF	4	8	1	1	0	0	0	0	0	.125
1987 Watertown	N.Y.-Penn.	OF	39	117	20	25	6	2	4	18	6	.214
1988 Augusta	So. Atl.	OF	105	358	58	112	23	5	7	62	24	.313
1989 Salem	Carolina	OF	86	321	50	97	29	2	14	53	12	.302
1989 Harrisburg	Eastern	OF	54	205	36	60	5	2	3	19	8	.293
1990 Buff.-Indianap.	A.A.	OF	90	326	44	86	5	6	5	37	13	.264
1990 Harrisburg	Eastern	OF	36	132	19	39	12	2	3	22	7	.295
1990 Pitts.-Montreal b	N.L.	OF	16	20	4	4	0	1	0	0	0	.200
1991 Montreal c	N.L.					INJURED—Did Not Play							
1992 Montreal d	N.L.	OF	115	341	53	96	28	2	9	56	16	.282
1993 Montreal e	N.L.	OF	136	482	70	138	29	6	18	85	17	.286
1994 Montreal	N.L.	OF	107	422	81	143	31	5	22	78	7	.339
1995 Montreal f	N.L.	OF	93	344	48	94	22	0	14	58	4	.273
1996 Montreal g-h	N.L.	OF	143	540	87	152	28	2	21	96	9	.281
1997 Florida i	N.L.	OF	150	538	88	157	29	5	23	115	9	.292
1998 Houston	N.L.	OF	159	584	104	182	34	5	38	124	11	.312
1999 Houston j	N.L.					INJURED—Did Not Play							
2000 Houston k	N.L.	OF	126	454	82	161	28	2	30	114	3	.355
Major League Totals		9 Yrs.	1045	3725	617	1127	229	28	175	726	76	.303
Division Series												
1997 Florida	N.L.	OF	3	14	1	3	1	0	0	1	0	.214
1998 Houston	N.L.	OF	4	16	0	3	0	0	0	0	0	.188
Division Series Totals			7	30	1	6	1	0	0	1	0	.200
Championship Series												
1997 Florida	N.L.	OF	5	15	0	1	1	0	0	5	0	.067
World Series Record												
1997 Florida	N.L.	OF	7	28	6	9	2	0	3	9	1	.321

a On disabled list from March 31 to April 18, 1987.
b Traded to Montreal Expos organization to complete August 8 trade in which Pittsburgh Pirates acquired pitcher Zane Smith for pitcher Scott Ruskin, shortstop Willie Greene and player to be named, August 16, 1990.
c On disabled list from March 19 to end of 1991 season.
d On disabled list from July 7 to July 27, 1992.
e On disabled list from September 18 to end of 1993 season.
f On disabled list from August 19 to September 5 and September 11 to October 2, 1995.
g On disabled list from July 8 to July 23, 1996.
h Signed as free agent with Florida Marlins, December 12, 1996.
i Traded to Houston Astros for pitcher Oscar Henriquez, pitcher Manuel Barrios and player to be named later, November 11, 1997. Florida Marlins received pitcher Mark Johnson on December 16, 1997.
j On disabled list from April 3 to October 4, 1999.
k On disabled list from April 27 to May 13, 2000.

ANDERSON, BRADY KEVIN
Born, Silver Spring, Maryland, January 18, 1964.
Bats Left. Throws Left. Height, 6 feet, 1 inch. Weight, 195 pounds.

Year	Club	Lea	Pos	G	AB	R	H	2B	3B	HR	RBI	SB	Avg
1985 Elmira	N.Y.-Penn.	OF	71	215	36	55	7	*6	5	21	13	.256
1986 Winter Haven	Fla. St.	OF	126	417	86	133	19	11	12	87	44	.319
1987 New Britain a	Eastern	OF	52	170	30	50	4	3	6	35	7	.294
1987 Pawtucket	Int.	OF	23	79	18	30	4	0	2	8	2	.380
1988 Pawtucket	Int.	OF	49	167	27	48	6	1	4	19	8	.287
1988 Boston-Balt. b	A.L.	OF	94	325	31	69	13	4	1	21	10	.212
1989 Rochester	Int.	DH	21	70	14	14	1	2	1	8	2	.200
1989 Baltimore	A.L.	OF	94	266	44	55	12	2	4	16	16	.207
1990 Hagerstown	Eastern	DH	9	34	8	13	0	2	1	5	2	.382
1990 Baltimore c	A.L.	OF	89	234	24	54	5	2	3	24	15	.231

7

Year	Club	Lea	Pos	G	AB	R	H	2B	3B	HR	RBI	SB	Avg
1991	Rochester	Int.	OF	7	26	5	10	3	0	0	2	4	.385
1991	Baltimore d	A.L.	OF	113	256	40	59	12	3	2	27	12	.230
1992	Baltimore	A.L.	OF	159	623	100	169	28	10	21	80	53	.271
1993	Baltimore e	A.L.	OF	142	560	87	147	36	8	13	66	24	.262
1994	Baltimore	A.L.	OF	111	453	78	119	25	5	12	48	31	.263
1995	Baltimore	A.L.	OF	143	554	108	145	33	10	16	64	26	.262
1996	Baltimore	A.L.	OF	149	579	117	172	37	5	50	110	21	.297
1997	Baltimore f-g	A.L.	OF	151	590	97	170	39	7	18	73	18	.288
1998	Baltimore h	A.L.	OF	133	479	84	113	28	3	18	51	21	.236
1999	Baltimore	A.L.	OF	150	564	109	159	28	5	24	81	36	.282
2000	Baltimore	A.L.	OF	141	506	89	130	26	0	19	50	16	.257
Major League Totals	13 Yrs.			1669	5989	1008	1561	322	64	201	711	299	.261
Division Series													
1996	Baltimore	A.L.	OF	4	17	3	5	0	0	2	4	0	.294
1997	Baltimore	A.L.	OF	4	17	3	6	1	0	1	4	1	.353
Divisional Series Totals			8	34	6	11	1	0	3	8	1	.324
Championship Series													
1996	Baltimore	A.L.	OF	5	21	5	4	1	0	1	1	0	.190
1997	Baltimore	A.L.	OF	6	25	5	9	2	0	2	3	2	.360
Championship Series Totals			11	46	10	13	3	0	3	4	2	.283

a On disabled list from June 5 to July 20, 1987.
b Traded to Baltimore Orioles with pitcher Curt Schilling for pitcher Mike Boddicker, July 29, 1988.
c On disabled list from June 8 to July 20, 1990.
d On disabled list from May 28 to June 14, 1991.
e On disabled list from June 23 to July 8, 1993.
f Filed for free agency, October 27, 1997.
g Re-signed with Baltimore Orioles, December 5, 1997.
h On disabled list from April 20 to May 8, 1998.

ANDERSON, GARRET JOSEPH
Born, Los Angeles, California, June 30, 1972.
Bats Left. Throws Left. Height, 6 feet, 3 inches. Weight, 190 pounds.

Year	Club	Lea	Pos	G	AB	R	H	2B	3B	HR	RBI	SB	Avg
1990	Mesa Angels	Arizona	OF	32	127	5	27	2	0	0	14	3	.213
1990	Boise	Northwest	OF	25	83	11	21	3	1	1	8	0	.253
1991	Quad City	Midwest	OF	105	392	40	102	22	2	2	42	5	.260
1992	Palm Springs	California	OF	81	322	46	104	15	2	1	62	1	.323
1992	Midland	Texas	OF	39	146	16	40	5	0	2	19	2	.274
1993	Vancouver	P.C.	OF-1B	124	467	57	137	34	4	4	71	3	.293
1994	Vancouver	P.C.	OF-1B	123	505	75	162	42	6	12	102	3	.321
1994	California	A.L.	OF	5	13	0	5	0	0	0	1	0	.385
1995	Vancouver	P.C.	OF	14	61	9	19	7	0	0	12	0	.311
1995	California	A.L.	OF	106	374	50	120	19	1	16	69	6	.321
1996	California	A.L.	OF	150	607	79	173	33	2	12	72	7	.285
1997	Anaheim	A.L.	OF	154	624	76	189	36	3	8	92	10	.303
1998	Anaheim	A.L.	OF	156	622	62	183	41	7	15	79	8	.294
1999	Anaheim	A.L.	OF	157	620	88	188	36	2	21	80	3	.303
2000	Anaheim	A.L.	OF	159	647	92	185	40	3	35	117	7	.286
Major League Totals	7 Yrs.			887	3507	447	1043	205	18	107	510	41	.297

ARIAS, ALEJANDRO (ALEX)
Born, New York, New York, November 20, 1967.
Bats Right. Throws Right. Height, 6 feet, 3 inches. Weight, 185 pounds.

Year	Club	Lea	Pos	G	AB	R	H	2B	3B	HR	RBI	SB	Avg
1987	Wytheville	Appal.	SS-3B	61	233	41	69	7	0	0	24	16	.296
1988	Charleston, WV ...	So. Atl.	SS-3B-2B	127	472	57	122	12	1	0	33	41	.258
1989	Peoria	Midwest	SS	*136	506	74	140	10	*11	2	64	31	.277
1990	Charlotte	Southern	SS	119	419	55	103	16	3	4	38	12	.246
1991	Charlotte	Southern	SS	134	488	69	134	26	0	4	47	23	.275
1992	Iowa	A.A.	SS-2B	106	409	52	114	23	3	5	40	14	.279
1992	Chicago a	N.L.	SS	32	99	14	29	6	0	0	7	0	.293
1993	Florida	N.L.	2B-3B-SS	96	249	27	67	5	1	2	20	1	.269
1994	Florida	N.L.	SS-3B	59	113	4	27	5	0	0	15	0	.239
1995	Florida	N.L.	SS-3B-2B	94	216	22	58	9	2	3	26	1	.269
1996	Florida	N.L.	3B-SS-1B-2B	100	224	27	62	11	2	3	26	2	.277
1997	Florida b-c-d	N.L.	3B-SS	74	93	13	23	2	0	1	11	0	.247
1998	Philadelphia	N.L.	SS-3B-2B	56	133	17	39	8	0	1	16	2	.293

Year	Club	Lea	Pos	G	AB	R	H	2B	3B	HR	RBI	SB	Avg
1999 Philadelphia .......N.L.		N.L.	SS-3B-2B	118	347	43	105	20	1	4	48	2	.303
2000 Philadelphia e .....N.L.		N.L.	SS-3B-2B	70	155	17	29	9	0	2	15	1	.187
Major League Totals			9 Yrs.	699	1629	184	439	75	6	16	184	9	.269
Division Series													
1997 Florida ...........N.L.		N.L.	PH	1	1	1	1	0	0	0	1	0	1.000
Championship Series													
1997 Florida ...........N.L.		N.L.	3B	3	1	0	1	0	0	0	0	0	1.000
World Series Record													
1997 Florida ...........N.L.		N.L.	3B-DH	2	1	1	0	0	0	0	0	0	.000

a Traded to Florida Marlins with third baseman Gary Scott for pitcher Greg Hibbard, November 17, 1992.
b On disabled list from June 14 to July 2, 1997.
c Designated for assignment by Florida Marlins, December 8, 1997.
d Signed with Philadelphia Phillies, December 27, 1997.
e Filed for free agency, October 30, 2000, signed with San Diego Padres, December 13, 2000.

AURILIA, RICHARD SANTO (RICH)
Born, Brooklyn, New York, September 2, 1971.
Bats Right. Throws Right. Height, 6 feet. Weight, 170 pounds.

Year	Club	Lea	Pos	G	AB	R	H	2B	3B	HR	RBI	SB	Avg
1992 Butte ....Pioneer		Pioneer	SS	59	202	37	68	11	3	3	30	13	.337
1993 Charlotte ....Fla. St.		Fla. St.	SS	122	440	80	136	16	5	5	56	15	.309
1994 Tulsa ....Texas		Texas	SS	129	458	67	107	18	6	12	57	10	.234
1995 Shreveport ....Texas		Texas	SS	64	226	29	74	17	1	4	42	10	.327
1995 Phoenix ............P.C.		P.C.	SS	71	258	42	72	12	0	5	34	2	.279
1995 San Francisco .....N.L.		N.L.	SS	9	19	4	9	3	0	2	4	1	.474
1996 Phoenix ............P.C.		P.C.	SS-2B	7	30	9	13	7	0	0	4	1	.433
1996 San Francisco a ......N.L.		N.L.	SS-2B	105	318	27	76	7	1	3	26	4	.239
1997 Phoenix .............P.C.		P.C.	SS	8	34	9	10	2	0	1	5	2	.294
1997 San Francisco .........N.L.		N.L.	SS	46	102	16	28	8	0	5	19	1	.275
1998 San Francisco b .....N.L.		N.L.	SS	122	413	54	110	27	2	9	49	3	.266
1999 San Francisco .........N.L.		N.L.	SS	152	558	68	157	23	1	22	80	2	.281
2000 San Francisco .........N.L.		N.L.	SS	141	509	67	138	24	2	20	79	1	.271
Major League Totals			6 Yrs.	575	1919	236	518	92	6	61	257	12	.270
Division Series													
2000 San Francisco .........N.L.		N.L.	SS	4	15	0	2	1	0	0	0	0	.133

a On disabled list from September 24 to September 30, 1996.
b On disabled list from July 4 to July 20, 1998.

AUSMUS, BRADLEY DAVID (BRAD)
Born, New Haven, Connecticut, April 14, 1969.
Bats Right. Throws Right. Height, 5 feet, 11 inches. Weight, 190 pounds.

Year	Club	Lea	Pos	G	AB	R	H	2B	3B	HR	RBI	SB	Avg
1988 Oneonta ........N.Y.-Penn.		N.Y.-Penn.	C	2	4	0	1	0	0	0	0	0	.250
1988 Sarasota Yankees ....Gulf C.		Gulf C.	C	43	133	22	34	2	0	0	15	5	.256
1989 Oneonta ........N.Y.-Penn.		N.Y.-Penn.	C-3B	52	165	29	43	6	0	1	18	6	.261
1990 Prince William .....Carolina		Carolina	C	107	364	46	86	12	2	0	27	2	.236
1991 Prince William .....Carolina		Carolina	C	63	230	28	70	14	3	2	30	17	.304
1991 Albany ....Eastern		Eastern	C	67	229	36	61	9	2	1	29	14	.266
1992 Albany ....Eastern		Eastern	C	5	18	0	3	0	1	0	1	2	.167
1992 Columbus a ....Int.		Int.	C-OF	111	364	48	88	14	3	2	35	19	.242
1993 Colorado Springs b .....P.C.		P.C.	C-OF	76	241	31	65	10	4	2	33	10	.270
1993 San Diego ..........N.L.		N.L.	C	49	160	18	41	8	1	5	12	2	.256
1994 San Diego ..........N.L.		N.L.	C-1B	101	327	45	82	12	1	7	24	5	.251
1995 San Diego ..........N.L.		N.L.	C-1B	103	328	44	96	16	4	5	34	16	.293
1996 San Diego c .........N.L.		N.L.	C	50	149	16	27	4	0	1	13	1	.181
1996 Detroit d ...........A.L.		A.L.	C	75	226	30	56	12	0	4	22	3	.248
1997 Houston ............N.L.		N.L.	C	130	425	45	113	25	1	4	44	14	.266
1998 Houston e ..........N.L.		N.L.	C	128	412	62	111	10	4	6	45	10	.269
1999 Detroit ............A.L.		A.L.	C	127	458	62	126	25	6	9	54	12	.275
2000 Detroit f ...........A.L.		A.L.	C-1B-2B-3B	150	523	75	139	25	3	7	51	11	.266
Major League Totals			8 Yrs.	913	3008	397	791	137	20	48	299	74	.263
Division Series													
1997 Houston .............N.L.		N.L.	C	2	5	1	2	1	0	0	2	0	.400
1998 Houston .............N.L.		N.L.	C	4	9	0	2	0	0	0	0	0	.222
Division Series Totals				6	14	1	4	1	0	0	2	0	.286

a Selected by Colorado Rockies from New York Yankees organization in expansion draft, November 17, 1992.

b Traded by Colorado Rockies to San Diego Padres with pitcher Doug Bochtler and player to be named for pitchers Greg W. Harris and Bruce Hurst, July 26; San Diego Padres acquired pitcher Andy Ashby to complete trade, July 28, 1993.
c Traded to Detroit Tigers with infielder Andujar Cedeno for catcher John Flaherty and infielder Chris Gomez, June 18, 1996.
d Traded to Houston Astros with pitcher C.J. Nitkowski, pitcher Jose Lima, pitcher Trever Miller and infielder Daryle Ward for outfielder Brian Hunter, infielder Orlando Miller, pitcher Todd Jones and pitcher Doug Brocail, December 10, 1996.
e Traded to Detroit Tigers with pitcher C.J. Nitkowski for pitcher Dean Crow, pitcher Mark Persails, pitcher Brian Powell, catcher Paul Bako and infielder Carlos Villalobos, January 14, 1999.
f Traded to Houston Astros with pitcher Doug Brocail and pitcher Nelson Cruz for pitcher Chris Holt, outfielder Roger Cedeno and catcher Mitch Meluskey, December 11, 2000.

AVEN, DAVID BRUCE (BRUCE)
Born, Orange, Texas, March 4, 1972.
Bats Right. Throws Right. Height, 5 feet, 9 inches. Weight, 180 pounds.

Year	Club	Lea	Pos	G	AB	R	H	2B	3B	HR	RBI	SB	Avg
1994 Watertown	.........N.Y.-Penn.		OF	61	220	49	73	14	5	5	33	12	.332
1995 Kinston	.............Carolina		OF	130	479	70	125	23	5	23	69	15	.261
1996 Canton-Akrn	........Eastern		OF	131	481	91	143	31	4	23	79	22	.297
1996 Buffalo	................A.A.		OF	3	9	5	6	0	0	1	2	0	.667
1997 Buffalo	................A.A.		OF	121	432	69	124	27	3	17	77	10	.287
1997 Cleveland	...............A.L.		OF	13	19	4	4	1	0	0	2	0	.211
1998 Buffalo a	................Int.		DH	5	15	4	3	1	0	1	1	3	.200
1999 Florida b	................N.L.		OF	137	381	57	110	19	2	12	70	3	.289
2000 Nashville	...............P.C.		OF	3	10	1	3	1	0	0	3	0	.300
2000 Albuquerque	...........P.C.		OF	9	32	7	9	1	0	0	3	0	.281
2000 Pittsburgh-Los Angeles c-d	N.L.		OF	81	168	20	42	11	0	7	29	2	.250
Major League Totals	....		3 Yrs.	231	568	81	156	31	2	19	101	5	.275

a Claimed on waivers by Florida Marlins, October 20, 1998.
b Traded to Pittsburgh Pirates for outfielder Brant Brown, December 13, 1999.
c On disabled list from June 30 to July 17, 2000.
d Traded to Los Angeles Dodgers for player to be named later, August 6, 2000.

BAGWELL, JEFFREY ROBERT
Born, Boston, Massachusetts, May 27, 1968.
Bats Right. Throws Right. Height, 6 feet, 195 pounds.

Year	Club	Lea	Pos	G	AB	R	H	2B	3B	HR	RBI	SB	Avg
1989 Sarasota Red Sox	....Gulf C.		3B	5	19	3	6	1	0	0	3	0	.316
1989 Winter Haven	.......Fla. St.		3B	64	210	27	65	13	2	2	19	1	.310
1990 New Britain a	.......Eastern		3B	136	481	63	*160	*34	7	4	61	5	.333
1991 Houston b	...........N.L.		1B	156	554	79	163	26	4	15	82	7	.294
1992 Houston	.............N.L.		1B	*162	586	87	160	34	6	18	96	10	.273
1993 Houston	.............N.L.		1B	142	535	76	171	37	4	20	88	13	.320
1994 Houston c	............N.L.		1B-OF	110	400	*104	147	32	2	39	*116	15	.368
1995 Jackson	............Texas		1B	4	12	0	2	0	0	0	0	0	.167
1995 Houston d	............N.L.		1B	114	448	88	130	29	0	21	87	12	.290
1996 Houston	.............N.L.		1B	*162	568	111	179	*48	2	31	120	21	.315
1997 Houston	.............N.L.		1B	*162	566	109	162	40	2	43	135	31	.286
1998 Houston e	............N.L.		1B	147	540	124	164	33	1	34	111	19	.304
1999 Houston	.............N.L.		1B	*162	562	*143	171	35	0	42	126	30	.304
2000 Houston	.............N.L.		1B	159	590	*152	183	37	1	47	132	9	.310
Major League Totals	....		10 Yrs.	1476	5349	1073	1630	351	22	310	1093	167	.305
Division Series													
1997 Houston	.............N.L.		1B	3	12	0	1	0	0	0	0	0	.083
1998 Houston	.............N.L.		1B	4	14	0	2	0	0	0	4	0	.143
1999 Houston	.............N.L.		1B	4	13	3	2	0	0	0	0	0	.154
Division Series Totals	....			11	39	3	5	0	0	0	4	0	.128

a Traded by Boston Red Sox to Houston Astros for pitcher Larry Andersen, August 31, 1990.
b Selected Rookie of the Year in National League for 1991.
c Selected Most Valuable Player in National League for 1994.
d On disabled list from July 31 to September 1, 1995.
e On disabled list from May 13 to May 28, 1998.

BAINES, HAROLD DOUGLASS
Born, Easton, Maryland, March 15, 1959.
Bats Left. Throws Left. Height, 6 feet, 2 inches. Weight, 195 pounds.

Year	Club	Lea	Pos	G	AB	R	H	2B	3B	HR	RBI	SB	Avg
1977 Appleton	.........Midwest		OF	69	222	37	58	11	2	5	29	2	.261
1978 Knoxville	.........Southern		OF-1B	137	502	70	138	16	6	13	72	3	.275

Year	Club	Lea	Pos	G	AB	R	H	2B	3B	HR	RBI	SB	Avg
1979 Iowa	A.A.		OF	125	466	87	139	25	8	22	87	5	.298
1980 Chicago	A.L.		OF	141	491	55	125	23	6	13	49	2	.255
1981 Chicago	A.L.		OF	82	280	42	80	11	7	10	41	6	.286
1982 Chicago	A.L.		OF	161	608	89	165	29	8	25	105	10	.271
1983 Chicago	A.L.		OF	156	596	76	167	33	2	20	99	7	.280
1984 Chicago	A.L.		OF	147	569	72	173	28	10	29	94	1	.304
1985 Chicago	A.L.		OF	160	640	86	198	29	3	22	113	1	.309
1986 Chicago	A.L.		OF	145	570	72	169	29	2	21	88	2	.296
1987 Chicago a	A.L,		OF	132	505	59	148	26	4	20	93	0	.293
1988 Chicago	A.L.		OF	158	599	55	166	39	1	13	81	0	.277
1989 Chicago-Texas b	A.L.		OF	146	505	73	156	29	1	16	72	0	.309
1990 Texas-Oakland c	A.L.		OF	135	415	52	118	15	1	16	65	0	.284
1991 Oakland	A.L.		DH	141	488	76	144	25	1	20	90	0	.295
1992 Oakland d-e	A.L.		DH-OF	140	478	58	121	18	0	16	76	1	.253
1993 Bowie	Eastern		DH	2	6	0	0	0	0	0	0	0	.000
1993 Baltimore f-g	A.L.		DH	118	416	64	130	22	0	20	78	0	.313
1994 Baltimore h	A.L.		DH	94	326	44	96	12	1	16	54	0	.294
1995 Baltimore i	A.L.		DH	127	385	60	115	19	1	24	63	0	.299
1996 Chicago j-k	A.L.		DH	143	495	80	154	29	0	22	95	3	.311
1997 Chicago-Balt. l-m-n ..	A.L.		DH-OF	137	452	55	136	23	0	16	67	0	.301
1998 Baltimore o	A.L.		DH	104	293	40	88	17	0	9	57	0	.300
1999 Baltimore-Cleveland p	A.L.		DH	135	430	62	134	18	1	25	103	1	.312
2000 Baltimore-Chicago r-s	A.L.		DH	96	283	26	72	13	0	11	39	0	.254
Major League Totals			21 Yrs.	2798	9824	1296	2855	487	49	384	1622	34	.291
Division Series													
1997 Baltimore	A.L.		DH	2	5	2	2	0	0	1	1	0	.400
1999 Cleveland	A.L.		DH	4	14	1	5	0	0	1	4	0	.357
2000 Chicago	A.L.		DH	2	4	1	1	1	0	0	0	0	.250
Division Series Totals				8	23	4	8	1	0	2	5	0	.348
Championship Series													
1983 Chicago	A.L.		OF	4	16	0	2	0	0	0	0	0	.125
1990 Oakland	A.L.		DH	4	14	2	5	1	0	0	3	1	.357
1992 Oakland	A.L.		DH	6	25	6	11	2	0	1	4	0	.440
1997 Baltimore	A.L.		DH	6	17	1	6	0	0	1	2	0	.353
Championship Series Totals				20	72	9	24	3	0	2	9	1	.333
World Series Record													
1990 Oakland	A.L.		DH	3	7	1	1	0	0	1	2	0	.143

a On disabled list from April 7 to May 8, 1987.
b Traded to Texas Rangers with infielder Fred Manrique for infielder Scott Fletcher, outfielder Sam Sosa and pitcher Wilson Alvarez, July 29, 1989.
c Traded to Oakland Athletics for two players to be named, August 29; Texas Rangers acquired pitchers Joe Bitker and Scott Chiamparino to complete trade, September 4, 1990.
d Filed for free agency, October 27, 1992; re-signed with Oakland Athletics, December 18, 1992.
e Traded to Baltimore Orioles for pitchers Bobby Chouinard and Allen Plaster, January 14, 1993.
f On disabled list from May 5 to May 27, 1993.
g Filed for free agency, November 1; re-signed with Baltimore Orioles, December 2, 1993.
h Filed for free agency, October 14; re-signed with Baltimore Orioles, December 23, 1994.
i signed with Chicago White Sox, December 11, 1995.
j Filed for free agency, November 18, 1996.
k Signed with Chicago White Sox, January 10, 1997.
l Traded to Baltimore Orioles for player to be named later, July 29, 1997. Chicago White Sox received infielder Juan Bautista to complete trade, August 18, 1997.
m Filed for free agency, October 29, 1997.
n Re-signed by Baltimore Orioles, December 20, 1997.
o On disabled list from July 11 to August 4, 1998.
p Traded to Cleveland Indians for pitcher Juan Aracena and player to be named later, August 27, 1999. Baltimore Orioles received pitcher Jimmy Hamilton to complete trade, August 31, 1999.
q Filed for free agency, October 29, 1999, signed with Baltimore Orioles, December 9, 1999.
r Traded to Chicago White Sox with catcher Charles Johnson for catcher Brook Fordyce, pitcher Miguel Felix, pitcher Juan Figueroa and pitcher Jason Lakman, July 29, 2000.
s Filed for free agency, November 3, 2000, signed with Chicago White Sox organization, January 8, 2001.

BAKO, GABOR PAUL (PAUL)

Born, Lafayette, Louisiana, June 20, 1972.
Bats Left. Throws Right. Height, 6 feet, 2 inches. Weight, 205 pounds.

Year	Club	Lea	Pos	G	AB	R	H	2B	3B	HR	RBI	SB	Avg
1993 Billings	Pioneer		C-1B	57	194	34	61	11	0	4	30	5	.314
1994 Winston-Sal	Carolina		C	90	289	29	59	9	1	3	26	2	.204
1995 Winston-Sal	Carolina		C	82	249	29	71	11	2	7	27	3	.285
1996 Chattanooga	Southern		C	110	360	53	106	27	0	8	48	1	.294
1997 Indianapolis a	A.A.		C	104	321	34	78	14	1	8	43	0	.243

11

Year Club	Lea	Pos	G	AB	R	H	2B	3B	HR	RBI	SB	Avg
1998 Toledo	.Int.	C	13	48	5	14	3	1	1	6	0	.292
1998 Detroit b	.A.L.	C	96	305	23	83	12	1	3	30	1	.272
1999 New Orleans	.P.C.	C	12	47	2	9	3	1	1	4	0	.191
1999 Houston	.N.L.	C	73	215	16	55	14	1	2	17	1	.256
2000 Houston-Florida-Atlanta c-d-e	N.L.	C-1B	81	221	18	50	10	1	2	20	0	.226
Major League Totals .... 3 Yrs.			250	741	57	188	36	3	7	67	2	.254
Division Series												
2000 Atlanta	.N.L.	C	2	1	0	0	0	0	0	0	0	.000

a Traded by Cincinnati Reds to Detroit Tigers with pitcher Donne Wall for outfielder Melvin Nieves, November 11, 1997.
b Traded to Houston Astros with pitcher Dean Crow, pitcher Mark Persails, pitcher Brian Powell and infielder Carlos Villalobos for pitcher C.J. Nitkowski and catcher Brad Ausmus, January 14, 1999.
c Traded to Florida Marlins for player to be named later, April 11, 2000.
d Houston Astros received cash to complete trade, October 10, 2000.
e Claimed on waivers by Atlanta Braves, July 21, 2000.

BARKER, GLEN F.
Born, Albany, New York, May 10, 1971.
Bats Both. Throws Right. Height, 5 feet, 10 inches. Weight, 180 pounds.

Year Club	Lea	Pos	G	AB	R	H	2B	3B	HR	RBI	SB	Avg
1993 Niagara Fls	N.Y.-Penn.	OF	72	253	49	55	11	4	5	23	37	.217
1994 Fayetteville	.So.Atl.	OF	74	267	38	61	13	5	1	30	41	.228
1994 Lakeland	.Fla.St.	OF	28	104	10	19	5	1	2	6	5	.183
1995 Jacksnville	Southern	OF	133	507	74	121	26	4	10	49	39	.239
1996 Fayetteville	.So.Atl.	OF	37	132	23	38	1	0	1	9	20	.288
1996 Toledo	.Int.	OF	24	80	13	20	2	1	0	2	6	.250
1996 Jacksnville	Southern	OF	43	120	9	19	2	1	0	8	6	.158
1997 Toledo	.Int.	OF	21	47	9	9	1	0	1	3	6	.191
1997 Lakeland	.Fla.St.	OF	13	57	9	18	4	0	1	11	7	.316
1997 Jacksnville	Southern	OF	69	257	47	72	8	4	6	29	•17	.280
1998 Jacksnville a	Southern	OF	110	453	95	127	29	6	6	54	31	.280
1999 Houston b	.N.L.	OF	81	73	23	21	2	0	1	11	17	.288
2000 New Orleans	.P.C.	OF	26	107	15	29	5	0	2	10	11	.271
2000 Houston	.N.L.	OF	84	67	18	15	2	1	2	6	9	.224
Major League Totals .... 2 Yrs.			165	140	41	36	4	1	3	17	26	.257
Division Series												
1999 Houston	.N.L.	OF	2	3	1	0	0	0	0	0	1	.000

a Selected by Houston Astros from Detroit Tigers in Rule V draft, December 14, 1998.
b On disabled list from August 24 to September 8, 1999.

BARNES, JOHN DELBERT
Born, San Diego, California, April 24, 1976.
Bats Right. Throws Right. Height, 6 feet, 2 inches. Weight, 176 pounds.

Year Club	Lea	Pos	G	AB	R	H	2B	3B	HR	RBI	SB	Avg
1996 Red Sox	Gulf Coast	OF	30	101	9	28	4	0	1	17	4	.277
1997 Michigan	Midwest	OF	130	490	80	149	19	5	6	73	19	.304
1998 Trenton	Eastern	OF	100	380	53	104	18	0	14	36	3	.274
1998 New Britain a	Eastern	OF	20	71	9	19	4	1	0	8	1	.268
1999 New Britain	Eastern	OF	129	452	62	119	21	1	13	58	10	.263
2000 Salt Lake	.P.C.	OF	120	441	107	161	37	6	13	87	7	.365
2000 Minnesota	.A.L.	OF	11	37	5	13	4	0	0	2	0	.351

a Traded to Minnesota Twins by Boston Red Sox with pitcher Matt Kinney and pitcher Joe Thomas for pitcher Greg Swindell and infielder Orlando Merced, July 31, 1998.

BARRETT, MICHAEL PATRICK
Born, Atlanta, Georgia, October 22, 1976.
Bats Right. Throws Right. Height, 6 feet, 3 inches. Weight, 185 pounds.

Year Club	Lea	Pos	G	AB	R	H	2B	3B	HR	RBI	SB	Avg
1995 Expos	Gulf Coast	SS-3B	50	183	22	57	13	4	0	19	7	.311
1995 Vermont	N.Y.-Penn.	DH-SS	3	10	0	1	0	0	0	1	0	.100
1996 Delmarva	.So.Atl.	C-3B	129	474	57	113	29	4	4	62	5	.238
1997 Wst Plm Bch	.Fla.St.	C	119	423	52	120	30	0	8	61	7	.284
1998 Harrisburg	.Eastern	C-3B	120	453	78	145	32	2	19	87	7	.320
1998 Montreal	.N.L.	C-3B	8	23	3	7	2	0	1	2	0	.304
1999 Ottawa	.Int.	3B	2	7	1	3	0	0	0	2	0	.429
1999 Montreal a	.N.L.	3B-C-SS	126	433	53	127	32	3	8	52	0	.293

12

Year	Club	Lea	Pos	G	AB	R	H	2B	3B	HR	RBI	SB	Avg
2000 Ottawa ....Int.			3B	31	120	21	43	7	0	2	19	1	.358
2000 Montreal .............N.L.			3B-C	89	271	28	58	15	1	1	22	0	.214
Major League Totals			3 Yrs.	223	727	84	192	49	4	10	76	0	.264

a On disabled list from June 23 to July 11, 1999.

BATISTA, LEOCADIO FRANCISCO (TONY)

Born, Puerto Plata, Dominican Republic, December 9, 1973.
Bats Right. Throws Right. Height, 6 feet. Weight,180 pounds.

Year	Club	Lea	Pos	G	AB	R	H	2B	3B	HR	RBI	SB	Avg
1992 Athletics ....Arizona			2B-SS-OF	45	167	32	41	6	2	0	22	1	.246
1993 Athletics ....Arizona			3B-2B-SS	24	104	21	34	6	2	2	17	6	.327
1993 Tacoma ..............P.C.			SS	4	12	1	2	1	0	0	1	0	.167
1994 Modesto ....California			SS-2B	119	466	91	131	26	3	17	68	7	.281
1995 Huntsville ....Southern			SS-2B	120	419	55	107	23	1	16	61	7	.255
1996 Edmonton ............P.C.			SS	57	205	33	66	17	4	8	40	2	.322
1996 Oakland ..............A.L.			2B-3B-SS	74	238	38	71	10	2	6	25	7	.298
1997 Edmonton ............P.C.			SS	33	124	25	39	10	1	3	21	2	.315
1997 Oakland a-b ..........A.L.			SS-3B-2B	68	188	22	38	10	1	4	18	2	.202
1998 Arizona ..............N.L.			2B-SS-3B	106	293	46	80	16	1	18	41	1	.273
1999 Arizona ..............N.L.			SS	44	144	16	37	5	0	5	21	2	.257
1999 Toronto c ............A.L.			SS	98	375	61	107	25	1	26	79	2	.285
2000 Toronto ..............A.L.			3B	154	620	96	163	32	2	41	114	5	.263
Major League Totals			5 Yrs.	544	1858	279	496	98	7	100	298	19	.267

a On disabled list from August 27 to September 12, 1997.
b Selected in expansion draft by Arizona Diamondbacks, November 18, 1997.
c Traded to Toronto Blue Jays with pitcher John Frascatore for pitcher Dan Plesac, June 12, 1999.

BAUTISTA, DANIEL (DANNY)

Born, Santo Domingo, Dominican Republic, May 24, 1972.
Bats Right. Throws Right. Height, 5 feet, 11 inches. Weight,170 pounds.

Year	Club	Lea	Pos	G	AB	R	H	2B	3B	HR	RBI	SB	Avg
1990 Bristol ....Appal.			OF	27	95	9	26	3	0	2	12	2	.274
1991 Fayetteville a ....So.Atl.			OF	69	234	21	45	6	4	1	30	7	.192
1992 Fayetteville ....So.Atl.			OF	121	453	59	122	22	0	5	52	18	.269
1993 London ....Eastern			OF	117	424	55	121	21	1	6	48	28	.285
1993 Detroit ...............A.L.			OF	17	61	6	19	3	0	1	9	3	.311
1994 Toledo ....Int.			OF	27	98	7	25	7	0	2	14	2	.255
1994 Detroit b .............A.L.			OF	31	99	12	23	4	1	4	15	1	.232
1995 Toledo ....Int.			OF	18	58	6	14	3	0	0	4	1	.241
1995 Detroit ...............A.L.			OF	89	271	28	55	9	0	7	27	4	.203
1996 Detroit ...............A.L.			OF	25	64	12	16	2	0	2	8	1	.250
1996 Atlanta c .............N.L.			OF	17	20	1	3	0	0	0	1	0	.150
1997 Richmond ....Int.			OF	46	170	28	48	10	3	2	28	1	.282
1997 Atlanta d .............N.L.			OF	64	103	14	25	3	2	3	9	2	.243
1998 Greenville ....Southern			OF	2	6	1	2	0	0	1	2	0	.333
1998 Atlanta e .............N.L.			OF	82	144	17	36	11	0	3	17	1	.250
1999 Calgary ..............P.C.			OF	38	135	25	43	8	1	8	28	3	.319
1999 Florida f .............N.L.			OF	70	205	32	59	10	1	5	24	3	.288
2000 Florida-Arizona g .....N.L.			OF	131	351	54	100	20	7	11	59	6	.285
Major League Totals			8 Yrs.	526	1318	176	336	62	11	36	169	21	.255
Division Series													
1997 Atlanta ..............N.L.			OF	3	3	0	1	0	0	0	2	0	.333
1998 Atlanta ..............N.L.			OF	2	2	0	1	1	0	0	0	0	.500
Division Series Totals				5	5	0	2	1	0	0	2	0	.400
Championship Series													
1997 Atlanta ..............N.L.			OF	2	4	0	1	0	0	0	0	0	.250
1998 Atlanta ..............N.L.			OF	5	5	0	0	0	0	0	0	0	.000
Championship Series Totals ...				7	9	0	1	0	0	0	0	0	.111

a On disabled list from May 24 to July 10, 1991.
b On disabled list from June 8 to July 31, 1994.
c Traded to Atlanta Braves for outfielder Anton French, May 31, 1996.
d On disabled list from March 23 to April 23, 1997.
e On disabled list from April 17 to May 7 and August 25 to September 17, 1998.
f Released by Atlanta Braves, March 31, 1999. Signed with Florida Marlins organization, April 8, 1999.
g Traded to Arizona Diamondbacks for infielder Andy Fox, June 9, 2000.

BECKER, RICHARD GODHARD (RICH)

Born, Aurora, Illinois, February 1, 1972.
Bats Left. Throws Right. Height, 5 feet, 10 inches. Weight, 180 pounds.

Year	Club	Lea	Pos	G	AB	R	H	2B	3B	HR	RBI	SB	Avg
1990 Elizabethton	.........Appal.		OF	56	194	54	56	5	1	6	24	18	.289
1991 Kenosha	..........Midwest		OF	130	494	100	132	38	3	13	53	19	.267
1992 Visalia	.........California		OF	136	506	*118	160	37	2	15	82	29	.316
1993 Nashville	.........Southern		OF	138	516	93	148	25	7	15	66	29	.287
1993 Minnesota a	.........A.L.		OF	3	7	3	2	2	0	0	0	1	.286
1994 Salt Lake City	.........P.C.		OF	71	282	64	89	21	3	2	38	7	.316
1994 Minnesota b	..........A.L.		OF	28	98	12	26	3	0	1	8	6	.265
1995 Salt Lake	.............P.C.		OF	36	123	26	38	7	0	6	28	6	.309
1995 Minnesota	............A.L.		OF	106	392	45	93	15	1	2	33	8	.237
1996 Minnesota	..........A.L.		OF	148	525	92	153	31	4	12	71	19	.291
1997 Minnesota c	..........A.L.		OF	132	443	61	117	22	3	10	45	17	.264
1998 New York	.............N.L.		OF	49	100	15	19	4	2	3	10	3	.190
1998 Baltimore d-e	.........A.L.		OF	79	113	22	23	1	0	3	11	2	.204
1999 Milwaukee f	.............N.L.		OF	89	139	15	35	5	2	5	16	5	.252
1999 Oakland g	............A.L.		OF	40	125	21	33	3	0	1	10	3	.264
2000 Oakland-Detroit h-i	.....A.L.		OF	115	285	59	69	14	0	8	39	2	.242
Major League Totals	....	8 Yrs.		789	2227	345	570	100	12	45	243	66	.256

a On disabled list from September 13 to end of 1993 season.
b On disabled list from April 29 to May 17, 1994.
c Traded to New York Mets for outfielder Alex Ochoa, December 14, 1997.
d Claimed on waivers by Baltimore Orioles, June 16, 1998.
e Released by Baltimore Orioles, December 9, 1998. Signed with Milwaukee Brewers, January 11, 1999.
f Traded to Oakland Athletics for player to be named later, August 18, 1999.
   Milwaukee Brewers received pitcher Carl Dale to complete trade, August 20, 1999.
g Not offered contract, December 21, 1999, re-signed with Oakland Athletics, December 29, 1999.
h Released by Oakland Athletics, May 6, 2000, signed with Detroit Tigers, May 10, 2000.
i Filed for free agency, October 30, 2000.

BELL, DAVID MICHAEL

Born, Cincinnati, Ohio, September 14, 1972.
Bats Right. Throws Right. Height, 5 feet, 10 inches. Weight,170 pounds.

Year	Club	Lea	Pos	G	AB	R	H	2B	3B	HR	RBI	SB	Avg
1990 Indians	......Gulf Coast		3B	30	111	18	29	5	1	0	13	1	.261
1990 Burlington	.......Appal.		3B	12	42	4	7	1	1	0	2	2	.167
1991 Columbus	.....So.Atl.		3B	136	491	47	113	24	1	5	63	3	.230
1992 Kinston	.......Carolina		3B	123	464	52	117	17	2	6	47	2	.252
1993 Canton-Akrn	....Eastern		3B-2B	129	483	69	141	20	2	9	60	3	.292
1994 Charlotte	........Int.		3B-SS-2B	134	481	66	141	17	4	18	88	2	.293
1995 Cleveland	.........A.L.		3B	2	2	0	0	0	0	0	0	0	.000
1995 Buffalo	.........A.A.		3B-SS-2B	70	254	34	69	11	1	8	34	0	.272
1995 Louisville	.........A.A.		2B	18	76	9	21	3	1	1	9	4	.276
1995 St. Louis a	.........N.L.		2B-3B	39	144	13	36	7	2	2	19	1	.250
1996 Louisville	.........A.A.		2B-3B-SS	42	136	9	24	5	1	0	7	1	.176
1996 St. Louis	.........N.L.		3B-2B-SS	62	145	12	31	6	0	1	9	1	.214
1997 Arkansas	........Texas		3B-2B	9	32	3	7	2	0	1	3	1	.219
1997 Louisville	.........A.A.		2B-3B-SS	6	22	3	5	0	0	1	4	0	.227
1997 St. Louis b	.........N.L.		3B-2B-SS	66	142	9	30	7	2	1	12	1	.211
1998 St. Louis	.........N.L.		3B-2B	4	9	0	2	1	0	0	0	0	.222
1998 Cleveland-Seattle c-d	A.L.		2B-3B-1B-SS	128	420	48	115	29	2	10	49	0	.274
1999 Seattle	.........A.L.		2B-1B-SS	157	597	92	160	31	2	21	78	7	.268
2000 Seattle	..........A.L.		3B-2B-1B-SS	133	454	57	112	24	2	11	47	2	.247
Major League Totals	....	6 Yrs.		591	1913	231	486	105	10	46	214	12	.254
Division Series													
2000 Seattle	.........A.L.		3B	3	11	0	4	1	0	0	1	0	.364
Championship Series													
2000 Seattle	.........A.L.		3B-2B	5	18	0	4	0	0	0	0	0	.222

a Traded to St. Louis Cardinals with catcher Pepe Manuel and pitcher Rock Heiserman for pitcher Ken Hill, July 27, 1995.
b On disabled list from April 29 to June 30, 1997.
c Claimed on waivers by Cleveland Indians, April 14, 1998.
d Traded to Seattle Mariners for infielder Joey Cora, August 31, 1998.

BELL, DEREK NATHANIEL

Born, Tampa, Florida, December 11, 1968.
Bats Right. Throws Right. Height, 6 feet, 2 inches. Weight, 215 pounds.

Year	Club	Lea	Pos	G	AB	R	H	2B	3B	HR	RBI	SB	Avg
1987 St. Catharines	. . . N.Y.-Penn.	OF	74	273	46	72	11	3	10	42	12	.264
1988 Myrtle Beach	. . . . . . So. Atl.	OF	91	352	55	121	29	5	12	60	18	*.344
1988 Knoxville a	. . . . . . Southern	OF	14	52	5	13	3	1	0	4	2	.250
1989 Knoxville	. . . . Southern	OF	136	513	72	124	22	6	16	75	15	.242
1990 Syracuse b	. . . . Int.	OF	109	402	57	105	13	5	7	56	21	.261
1991 Syracuse	. . . . Int.	OF	119	457	*89	*158	22	*12	13	*93	27	*.346
1991 Toronto	. . . . A.L.	OF	18	28	5	4	0	0	0	1	3	.143
1992 Dunedin	. . . . Fla. St.	OF	7	25	7	6	2	0	0	4	3	.240
1992 Toronto c-d	. . . . A.L.	OF	61	161	23	39	6	3	2	15	7	.242
1993 San Diego	. . . . N.L.	OF-3B	150	542	73	142	19	1	21	72	26	.262
1994 San Diego e-f	. . . . N.L.	OF	108	434	54	135	20	0	14	54	24	.311
1995 Houston	. . . . N.L.	OF	112	452	63	151	21	2	8	86	27	.334
1996 Houston	. . . . N.L.	OF	158	627	84	165	40	3	17	113	29	.263
1997 New Orleans	. . . . A.A.	OF	5	13	0	2	0	0	0	1	1	.154
1997 Houston g	. . . . N.L.	OF	129	493	67	136	29	3	15	71	15	.276
1998 Houston	. . . . N.L.	OF	156	630	111	198	41	2	22	108	13	.314
1999 Houston h-i	. . . . N.L.	OF	128	509	61	120	22	0	12	66	18	.236
2000 New York j	. . . . N.L.	OF-P	144	546	87	145	31	1	18	69	8	.266
Major League Totals	. . . .	10 Yrs.	1164	4422	628	1235	229	15	129	655	170	.279
Divisional Series												
1997 Houston	. . . . N.L.	OF	3	13	0	0	0	0	0	0	0	.000
1998 Houston	. . . . N.L.	OF	4	16	1	2	0	0	1	1	0	.125
1999 Houston	. . . . N.L.	OF	2	3	0	1	0	0	0	0	0	.333
2000 New York	. . . . N.L.	OF	1	1	0	0	0	0	0	0	0	.000
Division Series Totals	. . . .		10	33	1	3	0	0	1	1	0	.091

a On disabled list from July 30 to September 1, 1988.
b On disabled list from June 13 to June 21 and July 2 to July 12, 1990.
c On disabled list from April 9 to May 8, 1992.
d Traded to San Diego Padres with outfielder Stoney Briggs for outfielder Darrin Jackson, March 30, 1993.
e Suspended five games by National League for April 30 mound charging from July 14 to July 18, 1994.
f Traded to Houston Astros with outfielder Phil Plantier, shortstop Ricky Gutierrez, pitchers Pedro Martinez and Doug Brocail and infielder Craig Shipley for third baseman Ken Caminiti, shortstop Andujar Cedeño, outfielder Steve Finley, pitcher Brian Williams, first baseman Roberto Petagine and player to be named, December 28, 1994.San Diego received pitcher Sean Fesh to complete trade, May 1, 1995
g On disabled list from May 14 to June 13, 1997.
h On disabled list from August 17 to September 1, 1999.
i Traded to New York Mets with pitcher Mike Hampton for pitcher Octavio Dotel, outfielder Roger Cedeno and pitcher Kyle Kessel, December 23, 1999.
j Filed for free agency, October 41, 2000, signed with Pittsburgh Pirates, December 10, 2000.

BELL, JAY STUART

Born, Eglin Air Force Base, Florida, December 11, 1965.
Bats Right. Throws Right. Height, 6 feet, 1 inch. Weight, 185 pounds.

Year	Club	Lea	Pos	G	AB	R	H	2B	3B	HR	RBI	SB	Avg
1984 Elizabethton	. . . . Appal.	SS	66	245	43	54	12	1	6	30	4	.220
1985 Visalia a	. . . . California	SS	106	376	56	106	16	6	9	59	10	.282
1985 Waterbury	. . . . Eastern	SS	29	114	13	34	11	2	1	14	3	.298
1986 Waterbury	. . . . Eastern	SS	138	494	*88	137	28	4	7	74	10	.277
1986 Cleveland	. . . . A.L.	2B	5	14	3	5	2	0	1	4	0	.357
1987 Buffalo	. . . . A.A.	SS-2B	110	362	71	94	15	4	17	60	6	.260
1987 Cleveland	. . . . A.L.	SS	38	125	14	27	9	1	2	13	2	.216
1988 Colorado Springs	. . . . . . P.C.	SS	49	181	35	50	12	2	7	24	3	.276
1988 Cleveland b	. . . . A.L.	SS	73	211	23	46	5	1	2	21	4	.218
1989 Buffalo	. . . . A.A.	SS-3B	86	298	49	85	15	3	10	54	12	.285
1989 Pittsburgh	. . . . N.L.	SS	78	271	33	70	13	3	2	27	5	.258
1990 Pittsburgh	. . . . N.L.	SS	159	583	93	148	28	7	7	52	10	.254
1991 Pittsburgh	. . . . N.L.	SS	157	608	96	164	32	8	16	67	10	.270
1992 Pittsburgh	. . . . N.L.	SS	159	632	87	167	36	6	9	55	7	.264
1993 Pittsburgh	. . . . N.L.	SS	154	604	102	187	32	9	9	51	16	.310
1994 Pittsburgh	. . . . N.L.	SS	110	424	68	117	35	4	9	45	2	.276
1995 Pittsburgh	. . . . N.L.	SS-3B	138	530	79	139	28	4	13	55	2	.262
1996 Pittsburgh c	. . . . N.L.	SS	151	527	65	132	29	3	13	71	6	.250
1997 Kansas City d	. . . . A.L.	SS-3B	153	573	89	167	28	3	21	92	10	.291
1998 Arizona	. . . . N.L.	SS-2B	155	549	79	138	29	5	20	67	3	.251
1999 Arizona	. . . . N.L.	2B-SS	151	589	132	170	32	6	38	112	7	.289
2000 Arizona	. . . . N.L.	2B	149	565	87	151	30	6	18	68	7	.267

Year	Club	Lea	Pos	G	AB	R	H	2B	3B	HR	RBI	SB	Avg
Major League Totals			15 Yrs.	1830	6805	1050	1828	368	66	180	800	91	.269
Division Series													
1999 Arizona	.N.L.		2B	4	14	3	4	1	0	0	3	0	.286
Championship Series													
1990 Pittsburgh	.N.L.		SS	6	20	3	5	1	0	1	1	0	.250
1991 Pittsburgh	.N.L.		SS	7	29	2	12	2	0	1	1	0	.414
1992 Pittsburgh	.N.L.		SS	7	29	3	5	2	0	1	4	0	.172
Championship Series Totals				20	78	8	22	5	0	3	6	0	.282

a Traded by Minnesota Twins to Cleveland Indians organization with pitchers Curt Wardle and Rich Yett, and outfielder Jim Weaver for pitcher Bert Blyleven, August 1, 1985.
b Traded to Pittsburgh Pirates organization for shortstop Felix Fermin, March 25, 1989.
c Traded with infielder Jeff King to Kansas City Royals for pitchers Jeff Granger, Jeff Martin, Jeff Wallace and third baseman Joe Randa, December 14, 1996.
d Filed for free agency, November 3, 1997, Signed with Arizona Diamondbacks, November 17, 1997.

BELLE, ALBERT JOJUAN

Born, Shreveport, Louisiana, August 25, 1966.
Bats Right. Throws Right. Height, 6 feet, 2 inches. Weight, 200 pounds.

Year	Club	Lea	Pos	G	AB	R	H	2B	3B	HR	RBI	SB	Avg
1987 Kinston	.Carolina		OF	10	37	5	12	2	0	3	9	0	.324
1988 Waterloo	.Midwest		OF	9	28	2	7	1	0	1	2	0	.250
1988 Kinston	.Carolina		OF	41	153	21	46	16	0	8	39	2	.301
1989 Canton	.Eastern		OF	89	312	48	88	20	0	20	69	8	.282
1989 Cleveland	.A.L.		OF	62	218	22	49	8	4	7	37	2	.225
1990 Cleveland	.A.L.		OF	9	23	1	4	0	0	1	3	0	.174
1990 Colorado Spgs. a-b ...	.P.C.		OF	24	96	16	33	3	1	5	19	4	.344
1990 Canton	.Eastern		OF	9	32	4	8	1	0	0	3	0	.250
1991 Colorado Springs	.P.C.		OF	16	61	9	20	3	2	2	16	1	.328
1991 Cleveland c	.A.L.		OF	123	461	60	130	31	2	28	95	3	.282
1992 Cleveland d	.A.L.		DH-OF	153	585	81	152	23	1	34	112	8	.260
1993 Cleveland e	.A.L.		OF	159	594	93	172	36	3	38	*129	23	.290
1994 Cleveland f	.A.L.		OF	106	412	90	147	35	2	36	101	9	.357
1995 Cleveland	.A.L.		OF	143	546	*121	173	*52	1	*50	*126	5	.317
1996 Cleveland g-h	.A.L.		OF	158	602	124	187	38	3	48	*148	11	.311
1997 Chicago	.A.L.		OF	161	634	90	174	45	1	30	116	4	.274
1998 Chicago i	.A.L.		OF	*163	609	113	200	48	2	49	152	6	.328
1999 Baltimore	.A.L.		OF	161	610	108	181	36	1	37	117	17	.297
2000 Baltimore	.A.L.		OF	141	559	71	157	37	1	23	103	0	.281
Major League Totals			12 Yrs.	1539	5853	974	1726	389	21	381	1239	88	.295
Division Series													
1995 Cleveland	.A.L.		OF	3	11	3	3	1	0	1	3	0	.273
1996 Cleveland	.A.L.		OF	4	15	2	3	0	0	2	6	1	.200
Division Series Totals				7	26	5	6	1	0	3	9	1	.231
Championship Series													
1995 Cleveland	.A.L.		OF	5	18	1	4	1	0	1	1	0	.222
World Series Record													
1995 Cleveland	.A.L.		OF	6	17	4	4	0	0	2	4	0	.235

a Suspended five games by team from June 2 to June 7, 1990.
b On disabled list from June 7 to August 23, 1990.
c Suspended six games by American League for May 1 throwing ball at fan from July 12 to July 17, 1991.
d Suspended three games by American League for May 4 mound charging from August 4 to August 7, 1992.
e Suspended three games by American League for May 13 mound charging from June 4 to June 6, 1993.
f Suspended seven games by American League for July 17 suspected corked bat from August 1 to August 7, 1994.
g Filed for free agency, October 28, 1996.
h Signed with Chicago White Sox, November 19, 1996.
i Filed for free agency, October 27, 1998, signed with Baltimore Orioles, December 1, 1998.

BELLIARD, RONALD (RONNIE)

Born, Bronx, New York, July 4, 1975.
Bats Right. Throws Right. Height, 5 feet, 8 inches. Weight,180 pounds.

Year	Club	Lea	Pos	G	AB	R	H	2B	3B	HR	RBI	SB	Avg
1994 Brewers	.Arizona		2B-3B-SS	39	143	32	42	7	3	0	27	7	.294
1995 Beloit	.Midwest		2B-3B	130	461	76	137	28	5	13	76	16	.297
1996 El Paso	.Texas		2B	109	416	73	116	20	8	3	57	26	.279
1997 Tucson	.P.C.		2B-SS	118	443	80	125	35	4	4	55	10	.282
1998 Louisville	.Int.		2B-SS	133	507	114	163	36	7	14	73	32	.321

Year	Club	Lea	Pos	G	AB	R	H	2B	3B	HR	RBI	SB	Avg
1998 Milwaukee	....	N.L.	2B	8	5	0	1	0	0	0	0	0	.20
1999 Louisville	....	Int.	2B	29	108	14	26	4	0	1	8	12	.241
1999 Milwaukee	....	N.L.	2B-3B-SS	124	457	60	135	29	4	8	58	4	.295
2000 Milwaukee	....	N.L.	2B	152	571	83	150	30	9	8	54	7	.263
Major League Totals	....		3 Yrs.	284	1033	144	286	59	13	16	112	11	.277

BELLINGER, CLAYTON DANIEL (CLAY)

Born, Oneonta, New York, November 18, 1968.
Bats Right. Throws Right. Height, 6 feet, 3 inches. Weight, 195 pounds.

Year	Club	Lea	Pos	G	AB	R	H	2B	3B	HR	RBI	SB	Avg
1989 Everett	......	Northwest	SS	51	185	29	37	8	1	4	16	3	.200
1990 Clinton	......	Midwest	SS-3B	109	383	52	83	17	4	10	48	13	.217
1991 San Jose	.....	California	SS	105	368	65	95	29	2	8	62	13	.258
1992 Shreveport	......	Texas	SS	126	433	45	90	18	3	13	50	7	.208
1993 Phoenix	....	P.C.	3B-SS-1B	122	407	50	104	20	3	6	49	7	.256
1994 Phoenix	....	P.C.	OF-SS-1B-3B	106	337	48	90	15	1	7	50	6	.267
1995 Phoenix a	....	P.C.	SS-3B-OF-2B	97	277	34	76	16	1	2	32	3	.274
1996 Rochester b	......	Int.	SS-1B-2B	125	459	68	138	34	4	15	78	8	.301
1997 Columbus c	......	Int.	3B-OF-SS	111	416	55	114	31	3	12	59	10	.274
1998 Columbus d	....	Int.	1B-SS-3B-2B	115	397	35	89	20	2	9	40	5	.224
1999 Columbus	....	Int.	3B	40	141	19	33	10	1	2	14	6	.234
1999 New York	....	A.L.	3B-1B-OF-2B	32	45	12	9	2	0	1	2	1	.200
2000 Columbus	....	Int.	1B	8	28	3	9	2	0	0	2	1	.321
2000 New York	....	A.L.	OF-2B-3B-1B	98	184	33	38	8	2	6	21	5	.207
Major League Totals	....		2 Yrs.	130	229	45	47	10	2	7	23	6	.205
Division Series													
1999 New York	....	A.L.	DH	1	0	0	0	0	0	0	0	0	.000
2000 New York	....	A.L.	OF	2	1	0	1	1	0	0	1	0	1.000
Division Series Totals	....			3	1	0	1	1	0	0	1	0	1.000
Championship Series													
1999 New York	....	A.L.	DH-SS	3	1	0	0	0	0	0	0	0	.000
2000 New York	....	A.L.	OF	5	0	0	0	0	0	0	0	0	.000
Championship Series Totals	..			8	1	0	0	0	0	0	0	0	.000
World Series Record													
2000 New York	....	A.L.	OF	4	0	0	0	0	0	0	0	0	.000

a Filed for free agency from San Francisco Giants, October 16, 1995, signed with Baltimore Orioles, November 22, 1995.
b Filed for free agency October 15, 1996, signed with New York Yankees, November 4, 1996.
c Filed for free agency October 17, 1997, re-signed with New York Yankees, October 23, 1997.
d Filed for free agency October 16, 1998, re-signed with New York Yankees, November 19, 1998.

BELTRAN, CARLOS IVAN

Born, Manati, Puerto Rico, April 24, 1977.
Bats Both. Throws Right. Height, 6 feet. Weight, 175 pounds.

Year	Club	Lea	Pos	G	AB	R	H	2B	3B	HR	RBI	SB	Avg
1995 Royals	....	Gulf Coast	OF	52	180	29	50	9	0	0	23	5	.278
1996 Lansing	......	Midwest	OF	11	42	3	6	2	0	0	0	1	.143
1996 Spokane	....	Northwest	OF	59	215	29	58	8	3	7	29	10	.270
1997 Wilmington	......	Carolina	OF	120	419	57	96	15	4	11	46	17	.229
1998 Wilmington	......	Carolina	OF	52	192	32	53	14	0	5	32	11	.276
1998 Wichita	....	Texas	OF	47	182	50	64	13	3	14	44	7	.352
1998 Kansas City	....	A.L.	OF	14	58	12	16	5	3	0	7	3	.276
1999 Kansas City a	......	A.L.	OF	156	663	112	194	27	7	22	108	27	.293
2000 GC Royals	....	Gulf Coast	PH	1	4	3	2	1	0	1	1	0	.500
2000 Wilmington	......	Carolina	OF	3	13	2	4	0	1	2	6	0	.308
2000 Omaha	....	P.C.	OF	5	18	4	6	1	0	2	2	1	.333
2000 Kansas City b	....	A.L.	OF	98	372	49	92	15	4	7	44	13	.247
Major League Totals	....		3 Yrs.	268	1093	173	302	47	14	29	159	43	.276

a Selected Rookie of the Year in American League for 1999.
b On disabled list from July 4 to September 3, 2000.

BELTRE, ADRIAN
Born, Santo Domingo, Dominican Republic, April 7, 1978.
Bats Right. Throws Right. Height, 5 feet, 11 inches. Weight, 200 pounds.

Year	Club	Lea	Pos	G	AB	R	H	2B	3B	HR	RBI	SB	Avg
1995	La-S.Doming	....Dominican	3B	62	218	56	67	15	3	8	40	2	.307
1996	Savannah	........So.Atl.	3B-2B	68	244	48	75	14	3	16	59	4	.307
1996	San Berndno a	....California	3B	63	238	40	62	13	1	10	40	3	.261
1997	Vero Beach	........Fla.St.	3B-OF	123	435	95	138	24	2	26	104	25	.317
1998	San Antonio	........Texas	3B	64	246	49	79	21	2	13	56	20	.321
1998	Los Angeles	........N.L.	3B-SS	77	195	18	42	9	0	7	22	3	.215
1999	Los Angeles	........N.L.	3B	152	538	84	148	27	5	15	67	18	.275
2000	Los Angeles b	........N.L.	3B-SS	138	510	71	148	30	2	20	85	12	.290
Major League Totals			3 Yrs.	367	1243	173	338	66	7	42	174	33	.272

a On disabled list from June 25 to July 2, 1996.
b On disabled list from May 28 to June 16, 2000.

BENARD, MARVIN LARRY
Born, Bluefields, Nicaragua, January 20, 1970.
Bats Left. Throws Left. Height, 5 feet, 9 inches. Weight, 183 pounds.

Year	Club	Lea	Pos	G	AB	R	H	2B	3B	HR	RBI	SB	Avg
1992	Everett	........Northwest	OF	64	161	31	38	10	2	1	17	17	.236
1993	Clinton	..........Midwest	OF	112	349	44	105	14	2	5	50	42	.301
1994	Shreveport	........Texas	OF	125	454	66	143	32	3	4	48	24	.315
1995	Phoenix	..............P.C.	OF	111	378	70	115	14	6	6	32	10	.304
1995	San Francisco	........N.L.	OF	13	34	5	13	2	0	1	4	1	.382
1996	Phoenix	..............P.C.	OF	4	19	2	7	0	0	0	4	1	.368
1996	San Francisco	........N.L.	OF	135	488	89	121	17	4	5	27	25	.248
1997	Phoenix	..............P.C.	OF	17	60	14	20	5	0	0	5	4	.333
1997	San Francisco	........N.L.	OF	84	114	13	26	4	0	1	13	3	.228
1998	San Francisco	........N.L.	OF	121	286	41	92	21	1	3	36	11	.322
1999	San Francisco	........N.L.	OF	149	562	100	163	36	5	16	64	27	.290
2000	San Francisco	........N.L.	OF	149	560	102	147	27	6	12	55	22	.262
Major League Totals			6 Yrs.	651	2044	350	562	107	16	38	199	89	.275
Division Series													
1997	San Francisco	........N.L.	PH	2	2	0	0	0	0	0	0	0	.000
2000	San Francisco	........N.L.	OF	4	14	0	1	0	0	0	1	0	.071
Division Series Totals				6	16	0	1	0	0	0	1	0	.063

BENJAMIN, MICHAEL PAUL
Born, Euclid, Ohio, November 22, 1965.
Bats Right. Throws Right. Height, 6 feet. Weight, 169 pounds.

Year	Club	Lea	Pos	G	AB	R	H	2B	3B	HR	RBI	SB	Avg
1987	Fresno	......California	SS	64	212	25	51	6	4	6	24	6	.241
1988	Shreveport	......Texas	SS	89	309	48	73	19	5	6	37	14	.236
1988	Phoenix	..........P.C.	SS	37	106	13	18	4	1	0	6	2	.170
1989	Phoenix	..........P.C.	SS-2B	113	363	44	94	17	6	3	36	10	.259
1989	San Francisco	........N.L.	SS	14	6	6	1	0	0	0	0	0	.167
1990	Phoenix	..........P.C.	SS	118	415	61	104	21	7	5	39	13	.251
1990	San Francisco	........N.L.	SS	22	56	7	12	3	1	2	3	1	.214
1991	Phoenix	..........P.C.	SS	64	226	34	46	13	2	6	31	3	.204
1991	San Francisco	........N.L.	SS-3B	54	106	12	13	3	0	2	8	3	.123
1992	Phoenix	..........P.C.	SS-2B	31	108	15	33	9	2	0	17	3	.306
1992	San Francisco a	....N.L.	SS-3B	40	75	4	13	2	1	1	3	1	.173
1993	San Jose	.....California	2B-SS	2	8	1	0	0	0	0	0	0	.000
1993	San Francisco b	...N.L.	2B-SS-3B	63	146	22	29	7	0	4	16	0	.199
1994	San Francisco	........N.L.	SS-2B-3B	38	62	9	16	5	1	1	9	5	.258
1995	San Francisco c	....N.L.	3B-SS-2B	68	186	19	41	6	0	3	12	11	.220
1996	Clearwater d	....Fla.St.	SS	8	23	3	4	1	0	0	0	1	.174
1996	Scranton-WB	....Int.	SS	4	13	2	5	2	0	0	4	0	.385
1996	Philadelphia e-f	....N.L.	SS-2B	35	103	13	23	5	1	4	13	3	.223
1997	Pawtucket	......Int.	SS-3B-2B	33	105	12	26	4	1	4	12	4	.248
1997	Boston g-h	........A.L.	3B-SS-2B-1B	49	116	12	27	9	1	0	7	2	.233
1998	Boston i	........A.L.	2B-SS-3B-1B	124	349	46	95	23	0	4	39	3	.272
1999	Pittsburgh j	......N.L.	SS-2B-3B	110	368	42	91	26	7	1	37	10	.247
2000	Pittsburgh	......N.L.	3B-SS-2B-1B	93	233	28	63	18	2	2	19	5	.270
Major League Totals			12 Yrs.	710	1806	220	424	107	14	24	166	44	.235
Division Series													
1998	Boston	..............A.L.	2B-1B	4	11	1	1	0	0	0	0	0	.091

a On disabled list from March 31 to June 5, 1992.
b On disabled list from July 8 to August 6, 1993.
c Traded to Philadelphia for pitcher Jeff Juden, October 6, 1995.
d On disabled list from April 1 to April 26 and July 20 to September 30, 1996.
e Filed for free agency, October 8, 1996.
f Signed with Boston Red Sox organization, February 1, 1997.
g Filed for free agency, October 27, 1997.
h Re-signed with Boston Red Sox, November 21, 1997.
i Filed for free agency, October 26, 1998, signed with Pittsburgh Pirates, November 17, 1998.
j On disabled list from July 23 to August 11, 1999.

BERG, DAVID SCOTT

Born, Roseville, California, September 3, 1970.
Bats Right. Throws Right. Height, 5 feet, 11 inches. Weight, 185 pounds.

Year	Club	Lea	Pos	G	AB	R	H	2B	3B	HR	RBI	SB	Avg
1993	Elmira	N.Y.-Penn.	3B-2B-OF	75	281	37	74	13	1	4	28	7	.263
1994	Kane County	Midwest	3B-2B-OF	121	437	80	117	27	8	9	53	8	.268
1995	Brevard Cty	Fla.St.	SS-3B-2B	114	382	71	114	18	1	3	39	9	.298
1996	Portland	Eastern	SS-3B-1B	109	414	64	125	28	5	9	73	17	.302
1997	Charlotte	Int.	SS-2B-3B	117	424	76	125	26	6	9	47	16	.295
1998	Florida	N.L.	2B-3B-SS	81	182	18	57	11	0	2	21	3	.313
1999	Florida	N.L.	SS-2B-3B-OF	109	304	42	87	18	1	3	25	2	.286
2000	Brevard County	Fla.St.	2B	3	11	2	3	0	0	0	2	0	.273
2000	Florida a	N.L.	SS-3B-2B	82	210	23	53	14	1	1	21	3	.252
Major League Totals				3 Yrs.	272	696	83	197	43	2	6	67	8	.283

a On disabled list from April 2 to April 24, 2000.

BERGERON, PETER FRANCIS

Born, Greenfield, Massachusetts, November 9, 1977.
Bats Left. Throws Right. Height, 6 feet, 2 inches. Weight, 185 pounds.

Year	Club	Lea	Pos	G	AB	R	H	2B	3B	HR	RBI	SB	Avg
1996	Yakima	Northwest	OF	61	232	36	59	5	3	5	21	13	.254
1997	Savannah	So.Atl.	OF	131	492	89	138	18	5	5	36	32	.280
1997	San Berndno	California	OF	2	8	1	2	0	0	0	1	2	.250
1998	San Antonio	Texas	OF	109	416	81	132	17	8	8	54	33	.317
1998	Harrisburg a	Eastern	OF	34	134	22	33	8	4	0	9	8	.246
1999	Ottawa	Int.	OF	58	194	36	61	12	3	3	20	14	.314
1999	Harrisburg	Eastern	OF	42	162	29	53	14	2	4	18	9	.327
1999	Montreal	N.L.	OF	16	45	12	11	2	0	0	1	0	.244
2000	Montreal	N.L.	OF	148	518	80	127	25	7	5	31	11	.245
Major League Totals				2 Yrs.	164	563	92	138	27	7	5	32	11	.245

a Traded by Los Angeles Dodgers with infielder Wilton Guerrero, infielder Jonathan Tucker and pitcher Ted Lilly to Montreal Expos for infielder Mark Grudzielanek, pitcher Carlos Perez and outfielder Hiram Bocachica, July 31, 1998.

BERKMAN, WILLIAM LANCE (LANCE)

Born, Waco, Texas, February 10, 1976.
Bats Both. Throws Right. Height, 6 feet, 1 inch. Weight, 205 pounds.

Year	Club	Lea	Pos	G	AB	R	H	2B	3B	HR	RBI	SB	Avg
1997	Kissimmee	Fla.St.	OF	53	184	31	54	10	0	12	35	2	.293
1998	Jackson	Texas	OF	122	425	82	130	34	0	24	89	6	.306
1998	New Orleans	P.C.	OF	17	59	14	16	4	0	6	13	0	.271
1999	New Orleans	P.C.	OF	64	226	42	73	20	0	8	49	7	.323
1999	Houston a	N.L.	OF-1B	34	93	10	22	2	0	4	15	5	.237
2000	New Orleans	P.C.	OF	31	112	18	37	4	2	6	27	4	.330
2000	Houston	N.L.	OF-1B	114	353	76	105	28	1	21	67	6	.297
Major League Totals				2 Yrs.	148	446	86	127	30	1	25	82	11	.285

a On disabled list from April 13 to May 14, 1999.

BICHETTE, ALPHONSE (DANTE)

Born, West Palm Beach, Florida, November 18, 1963.
Bats Right. Throws Right. Height, 6 feet, 3 inches. Weight, 225 pounds.

Year	Club	Lea	Pos	G	AB	R	H	2B	3B	HR	RBI	SB	Avg
1984	Salem	Northwest	1B-OF-3B	64	250	27	58	9	2	4	30	6	.232
1985	Quad City	Midwest	OF-1B	137	547	58	145	28	4	11	78	25	.265
1986	Palm Springs	Calif.	OF-3B	68	290	39	79	15	0	10	73	2	.272

19

Year Club	Lea	Pos	G	AB	R	H	2B	3B	HR	RBI	SB	Avg
1986 Midland ....Texas	OF-3B	62	243	43	69	16	2	12	36	3	.284
1987 Edmonton a ..........P.C.	OF	92	360	54	108	20	3	13	50	3	.300
1988 Edmonton ............P.C.	OF	132	509	64	136	29	*10	14	81	7	.267
1988 California ............A.L.	OF	21	46	1	12	2	0	0	8	0	.261
1989 Edmonton ............P.C.	OF	61	226	39	55	11	2	11	40	4	.243
1989 California ............A.L.	OF	48	138	13	29	7	0	3	15	3	.210
1990 California b ..........A.L.	OF	109	349	40	89	15	1	15	53	5	.255
1991 Milwaukee ...........A.L.	OF-3B	134	445	53	106	18	3	15	59	14	.238
1992 Milwaukee c .........A.L.	OF	112	387	37	111	27	2	5	41	18	.287
1993 Colorado ............N.L.	OF	141	538	93	167	43	5	21	89	14	.310
1994 Colorado d ..........N.L.	OF	*116	*484	74	147	33	2	27	95	21	.304
1995 Colorado e ..........N.L.	OF	139	579	102	*197	38	2	*40	*128	13	.340
1996 Colorado f ..........N.L.	OF	159	633	114	198	39	3	31	141	31	.313
1997 Colorado ............N.L.	OF	151	561	81	173	31	2	26	118	6	.308
1998 Colorado ............N.L.	OF	161	662	97	*219	48	2	22	122	14	.331
1999 Colorado g ..........N.L.	OF	151	593	104	177	38	2	34	133	6	.298
2000 Cincinnati ..........N.L.	OF	125	461	67	136	27	2	16	76	5	.295
2000 Boston h ............A.L.	DH	30	114	13	33	5	0	7	14	0	.289
Major League Totals	13 Yrs.	1597	5990	889	1794	371	26	262	1092	150	.299
Division Series											
1995 Colorado ............N.L.	OF	4	17	6	10	3	0	1	3	0	.588

a On disabled list from May 6 to June 23, 1987.
b Traded to Milwaukee Brewers for designated hitter Dave Parker, March 14, 1991.
c Traded to Colorado Rockies for outfielder Kevin Reimer, November 17, 1992.
d Declared restricted free agent under Major League Baseball implemented labor proposal, December 23, 1994.
e Re-signed with Colorado Rockies, April 6, 1995.
f Had reconstructive knee surgery, October, 1996.
g Traded to Cincinnati Reds for outfielder Jeffrey Hammonds, pitcher Stan Belinda and cash, October 30, 1999.
h Traded to Boston Red Sox for pitcher Chris Reitsma and pitcher John Curtice, August 31, 2000.

BIGGIO, CRAIG ALAN
Born, Smithtown, New York, December 14, 1965.
Bats Right. Throws Right. Height, 5 feet, 11 inches. Weight, 180 pounds.

Year Club	Lea	Pos	G	AB	R	H	2B	3B	HR	RBI	SB	Avg
1987 Asheville ....So. Atl.	C	64	216	59	81	17	2	9	49	31	.375
1988 Tucson .............P.C.	C	77	281	60	90	21	4	3	39	19	.320
1988 Houston ...........N.L.	C	50	123	14	26	6	1	3	5	6	.211
1989 Houston ...........N.L.	C-OF	134	443	64	114	21	2	13	60	21	.257
1990 Houston ...........N.L.	C-OF	150	555	53	153	24	2	4	42	25	.276
1991 Houston ...........N.L.	C-2B-OF	149	546	79	161	23	4	4	46	19	.295
1992 Houston ...........N.L.	2B	*162	613	96	170	32	3	6	39	38	.277
1993 Houston ...........N.L.	2B	155	610	98	175	41	5	21	64	15	.287
1994 Houston ...........N.L.	2B	114	437	88	139	*44	5	6	56	*39	.318
1995 Houston a-b ........N.L.	2B	141	553	*123	167	30	2	22	77	33	.302
1996 Houston ...........N.L.	2B	*162	605	113	174	24	4	15	75	25	.288
1997 Houston ...........N.L.	2B	*162	619	*146	191	37	8	22	81	47	.309
1998 Houston ...........N.L.	2B	160	646	123	210	*51	2	20	88	50	.325
1999 Houston ...........N.L.	2B-OF	160	639	123	188	*56	0	16	73	28	.294
2000 Houston c ..........N.L.	2B	101	377	67	101	13	5	8	35	12	.268
Major League Totals	13 Yrs.	1800	6766	1187	1969	402	43	160	741	358	.291
Division Series											
1997 Houston ...........N.L.	2B	3	12	0	1	0	0	0	0	0	.083
1998 Houston ...........N.L.	2B	4	11	3	2	1	0	0	1	0	.182
1999 Houston ...........N.L.	2B	4	19	1	2	0	0	0	0	0	.105
Division Series Totals		11	42	4	5	1	0	0	1	0	.119

a Filed for free agency, November 12, 1995.
b Re-signed with Houston Astros, December 14, 1995.
c On disabled list from August 2 to November 5, 2000.

BLANCO, HENRY RAMON
Born, Caracas, Venezuela, August 29, 1971.
Bats Right. Throws Right. Height, 5 feet, 11 inches. Weight, 170 pounds.

Year Club	Lea	Pos	G	AB	R	H	2B	3B	HR	RBI	SB	Avg
1990 Dodgers ....Gulf Coast	3B	60	178	23	39	8	0	1	19	7	.219
1991 Vero Beach ....Fla.St.	3B-SS	5	7	0	1	0	0	0	0	0	.143
1991 Great Falls ....Pioneer	3B-1B	62	216	35	55	7	1	5	28	3	.255
1992 Bakersfield ......California	3B	124	401	42	94	21	2	5	52	10	.234
1993 San Antonio ....Texas	3B-1B-SS	117	374	33	73	19	1	10	42	3	.195

Year	Club	Lea	Pos	G	AB	R	H	2B	3B	HR	RBI	SB	Avg
1994	San Antonio	Texas	3B-1B-P	132	405	36	93	23	2	6	38	6	.230
1995	San Antonio	Texas	3B-C	88	302	37	77	18	4	12	48	1	.255
1995	Albuquerque	P.C.	3B-1B-OF	29	97	11	22	4	1	2	13	0	.227
1996	San Antonio	Texas	C-3B	92	307	39	82	14	1	5	40	2	.267
1996	Albuquerque	P.C.	C	2	6	1	1	0	0	0	0	0	.167
1997	Albuquerque	P.C.	C-1B-OF	91	294	38	92	20	1	6	47	7	.313
1997	Los Angeles	N.L.	1B-3B	3	5	1	2	0	0	1	1	0	.400
1998	San Berndno	California	C	7	19	5	6	1	0	2	3	1	.316
1998	Albuquerque a	P.C.	C	48	134	19	36	11	0	4	23	2	.269
1999	Colorado b	N.L.	C-OF	88	263	30	61	12	3	6	28	1	.232
2000	Indianapolis	Int.	PH	1	3	1	1	1	0	0	0	0	.333
2000	Milwaukee c	N.L.	C	93	284	29	67	24	0	7	31	0	.236
Major League Totals			3 Yrs.	184	552	60	130	36	3	14	60	1	.236

a Filed for free agency, October 16, 1998, signed with Colorado Rockies organization, November 23, 1998.
b Traded to Milwaukee Brewers with pitcher Jamey Wright and pitcher Justin Miller for infielder Jeff Cirillo and pitcher Scott Karl, December 13, 1999.
c On disabled list from April 15 to May 1, 2000.

BLUM, GEOFFREY E. (GEOFF)

Born, Redwood City, California, April 26, 1973.
Bats Both. Throws Right. Height, 6 feet, 3 inches. Weight, 193 pounds.

Year	Club	Lea	Pos	G	AB	R	H	2B	3B	HR	RBI	SB	Avg
1994	Vermont	N.Y.-Penn.	SS	63	241	48	83	15	1	3	38	5	.344
1995	Wst Plm Bch	Fla.St.	2B-SS-3B	125	457	54	120	20	2	1	62	6	.263
1996	Harrisburg	Eastern	2B-SS-1B-OF	120	396	47	95	22	2	1	41	6	.240
1997	Ottawa	Int.	2B-SS-3B	118	407	59	101	21	2	3	35	14	.248
1998	Ottawa	Int.	2B-SS	8	23	1	4	0	0	0	1	0	.174
1998	Expos	Gulf Coast	2B	5	18	0	3	1	1	0	1	0	.167
1998	Jupiter	Fla.St.	2B-3B-SS	17	58	13	16	6	0	0	5	1	.276
1998	Harrisburg	Eastern	3B-2B-2B	39	139	25	43	12	3	6	21	2	.309
1999	Ottawa	Int.	SS	77	268	43	71	14	1	10	37	6	.265
1999	Montreal a	N.L.	SS-2B	45	133	21	32	7	2	8	18	1	.241
2000	Montreal	N.L.	3B-SS-2B-1B	124	343	40	97	20	2	11	45	1	.283
Major League Totals			2 Yrs.	169	476	61	129	27	4	19	63	2	.271

a On disabled list from May 21 to June 15, 1999.

BOGAR, TIMOTHY PAUL

Born, Indianapolis, Indiana, October 28, 1966.
Bats Right. Throws Right. Height, 6 feet, 2 inches. Weight, 198 pounds.

Year	Club	Lea	Pos	G	AB	R	H	2B	3B	HR	RBI	SB	Avg
1987	Little Falls	N.Y.-Penn.	SS-2B	58	205	31	48	9	0	0	23	2	.234
1988	Columbia	So. Atl.	2B-SS	45	142	19	40	4	2	3	21	5	.282
1988	St. Lucie	Fla. St.	2B-SS-3B	76	236	34	65	7	1	2	30	9	.275
1989	Jackson	Texas	SS	112	406	44	108	13	5	4	45	8	.266
1990	Tidewater a	Int.	SS	33	117	10	19	2	0	0	4	1	.162
1991	Williamsport	Eastern	3B-2B-1B-SS	63	243	33	61	12	2	2	25	13	.251
1991	Tidewater	Int.	SS-2B-3B-1B-OF-C	65	218	23	56	11	0	1	23	1	.257
1992	Tidewater b	Int.	2B-SS-3B-1B	129	481	54	134	32	1	5	38	7	.279
1993	New York c	N.L.	SS-3B-2B	78	205	19	50	13	0	3	25	0	.244
1994	Norfolk	Int.	3B-2B	5	19	0	2	0	0	0	1	0	.105
1994	New York d	N.L.	3B-1B-SS-2B	50	52	5	8	0	0	2	5	1	.154
1995	New York	N.L.	3B-1B-SS-2B	78	145	17	42	7	0	1	21	1	.290
1996	New York	N.L.	1B-3B-SS-2B	91	89	17	19	4	0	0	6	1	.213
1997	Houston e-f	N.L.	SS-3B-1B	97	241	30	60	14	4	4	30	4	.249
1998	Houston g	N.L.	SS-2B-3B	79	156	12	24	4	1	1	8	2	.154
1999	Houston	N.L.	SS-3B-2B	106	309	44	74	16	2	4	31	3	.239
2000	Houston h	N.L.	SS-2B-P-3B	110	304	32	63	9	2	7	33	1	.207
Major League Totals			8 Yrs.	689	1501	176	340	67	9	22	159	13	.227
Division Series													
1999	Houston	N.L.	SS	2	4	0	3	1	0	0	1	0	.750

a On disabled list from May 18 to May 29 and June 14 to end of 1990 season.
b Record of 0-0 in one game as pitcher.
c On disabled list from August 15 to September 1, 1993.
d On disabled list from May 6 to June 9, 1994.
e Traded to Houston Astros for infielder Luis Lopez, March 31, 1997.
f On disabled list from September 5 to September 29, 1997.

h Filed for free agency, October 30, 2000.

BONDS, BARRY LAMAR
Born, Riverside, California, July 24, 1964.
Bats Left. Throws Left. Height, 6 feet, 1 inch. Weight, 185 pounds.

Year	Club	Lea	Pos	G	AB	R	H	2B	3B	HR	RBI	SB	Avg
1985	Prince William	Carolina	OF	71	254	49	76	16	4	13	37	15	.299
1986	Pittsburgh	N.L.	OF	113	413	72	92	26	3	16	48	36	.223
1986	Hawaii	P.C.	OF	44	148	30	46	7	2	7	37	16	.311
1987	Pittsburgh	N.L.	OF	150	551	99	144	34	9	25	59	32	.261
1988	Pittsburgh	N.L.	OF	144	538	97	152	30	5	24	58	17	.283
1989	Pittsburgh	N.L.	OF	159	580	96	144	34	6	19	58	32	.248
1990	Pittsburgh a	N.L.	OF	151	519	104	156	32	3	33	114	52	.301
1991	Pittsburgh	N.L.	OF	153	510	95	149	28	5	25	116	43	.292
1992	Pittsburgh b-c-d	N.L.	OF	140	473	*109	147	36	5	34	103	39	.311
1993	San Francisco e	N.L.	OF	159	539	129	181	38	4	*46	*123	29	.336
1994	San Francisco	N.L.	OF	112	391	89	122	18	1	37	81	29	.312
1995	San Francisco	N.L.	OF	*144	506	109	149	30	7	33	104	31	.294
1996	San Francisco	N.L.	OF	158	517	122	159	27	3	42	129	40	.308
1997	San Francisco	N.L.	OF	159	532	123	155	26	5	40	101	37	.291
1998	San Francisco	N.L.	OF	156	552	120	167	44	7	37	122	28	.303
1999	San Francisco f	N.L.	OF	102	355	91	93	20	2	34	83	15	.262
2000	San Francisco	N.L.	OF	143	480	129	147	28	4	49	106	11	.306
Major League Totals			15 Yrs.	2143	7456	1584	2157	451	69	494	1405	471	.289
Division Series													
1997	San Francisco	N.L.	OF	3	12	0	3	2	0	0	2	1	.250
2000	San Francisco	N.L.	OF	4	17	2	3	1	1	0	1	1	.176
Division Series Totals				7	29	2	6	3	1	0	3	2	.207
Championship Series													
1990	Pittsburgh	N.L.	OF	6	18	4	3	0	0	0	1	2	.167
1991	Pittsburgh	N.L.	OF	7	27	1	4	1	0	0	0	3	.148
1992	Pittsburgh	N.L.	OF	7	23	5	6	1	0	1	2	1	.261
Championship Series Totals				420	68	10	13	2	0	1	3	6	.191

a Selected Most Valuable Player in National League for 1990.
b On disabled list from June 15 to July 3, 1992.
c Selected Most Valuable Player in National League for 1992.
d Filed for free agency, October 26; signed with San Francisco Giants, December 6, 1992.
e Selected Most Valuable Player in National League for 1993.
f On disabled list from April 18 to June 9, 1999.

BONILLA, ROBERTO MARTIN ANTONIO (BOBBY)
Born, New York, New York, February 23, 1963.
Bats Both. Throws Right. Height, 6 feet, 3 inches. Weight, 240 pounds.

Year	Club	Lea	Pos	G	AB	R	H	2B	3B	HR	RBI	SB	Avg
1981	Brad. Pirates	Gulf C.	1B-C-3B	22	69	6	15	5	0	0	7	2	.217
1982	Brad. Pirates	Gulf C.	1B	47	167	20	38	3	0	5	26	2	.228
1983	Alexandria	Carolina	OF-1B	*136	504	88	129	19	7	11	59	28	.256
1984	Nashua	Eastern	OF-1B	136	484	74	128	19	5	11	71	15	.264
1985	Prince Wm. a-b	Carol.	1B-3B	39	130	15	34	4	1	3	11	1	.262
1986	Chicago c	A.L.	OF-1B	75	234	27	63	10	2	2	26	4	.269
1986	Pittsburgh	N.L.	OF-1B-3B	63	192	28	46	6	2	1	17	4	.240
1987	Pittsburgh	N.L.	3B-OF-1B	141	466	58	140	33	3	15	77	3	.300
1988	Pittsburgh	N.L.	3B	159	584	87	160	32	7	24	100	3	.274
1989	Pittsburgh	N.L.	3B-1B-OF	*163	616	96	173	37	10	24	86	8	.281
1990	Pittsburgh	N.L.	OF-3B-1B	160	625	112	175	39	7	32	120	4	.280
1991	Pittsburgh d	N.L.	OF-3B-1B	157	577	102	174	*44	6	18	100	2	.302
1992	New York e-f	N.L.	OF-1B	128	438	62	109	23	0	19	70	4	.249
1993	New York	N.L.	OF-3B-1B	139	502	81	133	21	3	34	87	3	.265
1994	New York	N.L.	3B	108	403	60	117	24	1	20	67	1	.290
1995	New York	N.L.	3B-OF-1B	80	317	49	103	25	4	18	53	0	.325
1995	Baltimore g	A.L.	OF-3B	61	237	47	79	12	4	10	46	0	.333
1996	Baltimore h-i	A.L.	OF-1B-3B	159	595	107	171	27	5	28	116	1	.287
1997	Florida	N.L.	3B-1B	153	562	77	167	39	3	17	96	6	.297
1998	Florida-Los Angeles j-k-l	N.L.	3B-OF	100	333	39	83	11	1	11	45	1	.249
1999	Norfolk	Int.	DH	3	13	1	3	0	0	1	0	0	.231
1999	New York m-n	N.L.	OF-1B	60	119	12	19	5	0	4	18	0	.160
2000	Atlanta o	N.L.	OF-3B	114	239	23	61	13	3	5	28	0	.255

22

Year	Club	Lea	Pos	G	AB	R	H	2B	3B	HR	RBI	SB	Avg
Major League Totals...........	15 Yrs.		2020	7039	1067	1973	401	61	282	1152	44	.280
Division Series													
1996 Baltimore ...........A.L.		OF	4	15	4	3	0	0	2	5	0	.200
1997 Florida .............N.L.		3B	3	12	1	4	0	0	1	3	0	.333
1999 New York ............N.L.		PH	2	1	1	0	0	0	0	0	0	.000
2000 Atlanta .............N.L.		OF	3	2	0	0	0	0	0	0	0	.000
Division Series Totals..........			12	30	6	7	0	0	3	8	0	.233
Championship Series													
1990 Pittsburgh ...........N.L.		OF-3B	6	21	0	4	1	0	0	1	0	.190
1991 Pittsburgh ...........N.L.		OF	7	23	2	7	2	0	0	1	0	.304
1996 Baltimore ...........A.L.		OF	5	20	1	1	0	0	1	2	0	.050
1997 Florida .............N.L.		3B	6	23	3	6	1	0	0	4	0	.261
1999 New York ...........N.L.		PH	3	3	0	1	0	0	0	0	0	.333
Championship Series Totals......			27	90	6	19	4	0	1	8	0	.211
World Series Record													
1997 Florida .............N.L.		3B	7	29	5	6	1	0	1	3	0	.207

a On disabled list from March 25 to July 19, 1985.
b Drafted by Chicago White Sox from Pittsburgh Pirates organization, December 10, 1985.
c Traded to Pittsburgh Pirates for pitcher Jose DeLeon, July 23, 1986.
d Filed for free agency, October 28; signed with New York Mets, December 2, 1991.
e Suspended two games by National League for June 24 contact with umpire from July 27 to July 28, 1992.
f On disabled list from August 2 to August 19, 1992.
g Traded to Baltimore Orioles with player to be named later for outfielder Alex Ochoa and outfielder Damon Buford, July 28, 1995. Baltimore Orioles received pitcher Jimmy Williams to complete trade, August 16, 1995.
h Filed for free agency, November 18, 1996.
i Signed with Florida Marlins, November 22, 1996.
j Traded to Los Angeles Dodgers with outfielder Gary Sheffield, outfielder Jim Eisenreich, catcher Charles Johnson and pitcher Manuel Barrios for catcher Mike Piazza and infielder Todd Zeile, May 15, 1998.
k On disabled list from March 31 to April 12 and June 18 to July 3 and July 15 to August 5, 1998.
l Traded to New York Mets for pitcher Mel Rojas, November 11, 1998.
m On disabled list from May 11 to May 31 and July 3 to September 1, 1999.
n Released by New York Mets, January 3, 2000. Signed with Atlanta Braves organization, January 28, 2000.
o Filed for free agency, October 31, 2000, signed with St. Louis Cardinals, January 5, 2001.

BOONE, AARON JOHN
Born, LaMesa, California, March 9, 1973.
Bats Right. Throws Right. 6 feet, 2 inches. Weight, 190 pounds.

Year	Club	Lea	Pos	G	AB	R	H	2B	3B	HR	RBI	SB	Avg
1994 Billings ....Pioneer		3B-1B-SS	67	256	48	70	15	5	7	55	6	.273
1995 Chattanooga .....Southern		3B	23	66	6	15	3	0	0	3	2	.227
1995 Winston-Sal .....Carolina		3B	108	395	61	103	19	1	14	50	11	.261
1996 Chattanooga .....Southern		3B-SS	136	548	86	158	44	7	17	95	21	.288
1997 Indianapolis ........A.A.		3B-SS-2B	131	476	79	138	30	4	22	75	12	.290
1997 Cincinnati ...........N.L.		3B-2B	16	49	5	12	1	0	0	5	1	.245
1998 Indianapolis ....Int.		3B-2B-SS	87	332	56	80	18	1	7	38	17	.241
1998 Cincinnati ...........N.L.		3B-2B-SS	58	181	24	51	13	2	2	28	6	.282
1999 Indianapolis ....Int.		3B	11	41	6	14	2	1	0	7	2	.341
1999 Cincinnati ...........N.L.		3B-SS	139	472	56	132	26	5	14	72	17	.280
2000 Cincinnati a ..........N.L.		3B-SS	84	291	44	83	18	0	12	43	6	.285
Major League Totals	4 Yrs.		297	993	129	278	58	7	28	148	30	.280

a On disabled list from July 10 to October 3, 2000.

BOONE, BRET ROBERT
Born, El Cajon, California, April 6, 1969.
Bats Right. Throws Right. Height, 5 feet, 10 inches. Weight, 180 pounds.

Year	Club	Lea	Pos	G	AB	R	H	2B	3B	HR	RBI	SB	Avg
1990 Peninsula ....Carolina		2B	74	255	42	68	13	2	8	38	5	.267
1991 Jacksonville .....Southern		2B	*139	475	64	121	10	1	19	75	9	.255
1992 Calgary ..............P.C.		2B	118	439	73	138	26	5	13	73	17	.314
1992 Seattle .............A.L.		2B-3B	33	129	15	25	4	0	4	15	1	.194
1993 Calgary ..............P.C.		2B	71	274	48	91	18	3	8	56	3	.332
1993 Seattle a ...........A.L.		2B	76	271	31	68	12	2	12	38	2	.251
1994 Cincinnati ...........N.L.		2B-3B	108	381	59	122	25	2	12	68	3	.320
1995 Cincinnati ...........N.L.		2B	138	513	63	137	34	2	15	68	5	.267
1996 Cincinnati b .........N.L.		2B	142	520	56	121	21	3	12	69	3	.233
1997 Indianapolis ........A.A.		2B	3	7	1	2	1	0	0	1	1	.286
1997 Cincinnati ...........N.L.		2B	139	443	40	99	25	1	7	46	5	.223
1998 Cincinnati c .........N.L.		2B	157	583	76	155	38	1	24	95	6	.266

Year	Club	Lea	Pos	G	AB	R	H	2B	3B	HR	RBI	SB	Avg
1999 Atlanta d	....	N.L.	2B	152	608	102	153	38	1	20	63	14	.252
2000 San Diego e-f	....	N.L.	2B	127	463	61	116	18	2	19	74	8	.251
Major League Totals	....		9 Yrs.	1072	3911	503	996	215	14	125	536	47	.255
Division Series													
1995 Cincinnati	....	N.L.	2B	3	10	4	3	1	0	1	1	1	.300
1999 Atlanta	....	N.L.	2B	4	19	3	9	1	0	0	1	1	.474
Division Series Totals	....			7	29	7	12	2	0	1	2	2	.414
Championship Series													
1995 Cincinnati	....	N.L.	2B	4	14	1	3	0	0	0	0	0	.214
1999 Atlanta	....	N.L.	2B	6	22	2	4	1	0	0	1	2	.182
Championship Series Totals	.....			10	36	3	7	1	0	0	1	2	.194
World Series Record													
1999 Atlanta	....	N.L.	2B	4	13	1	7	4	0	0	3	0	.538

a Traded to Cincinnati Reds with pitcher Erik Hanson for pitcher Bobby Ayala and catcher Dan Wilson, November 2, 1993.
b On disabled list from April 1 to April 16, 1996.
c Traded to Atlanta Braves with pitcher Mike Remlinger for pitcher Denny Neagle, outfielder Michael Tucker and pitcher Rob Bell, November 10, 1998.
d Traded to San Diego Padres with outfielder Ryan Klesko and pitcher Jason Shiell for infielder Wally Joyner, infielder Quilvio Veras and outfielder Reggie Sanders, December 22, 1999.
e On disabled list from August 27 to October 1, 2000.
f Not offered 2001 contract, October 30, 2000, signed with Seattle Mariners, December 23, 2000.

BORDICK, MICHAEL TODD
Born, Marquette, Michigan, July 21, 1965.
Bats Right. Throws Right. Height, 5 feet, 11 inches. Weight, 175 pounds.

Year	Club	Lea	Pos	G	AB	R	H	2B	3B	HR	RBI	SB	Avg
1986 Medford	.....	Northwest	SS	46	187	30	48	3	1	0	19	6	.257
1987 Modesto	.....	California	SS	133	497	73	133	17	0	3	75	8	.268
1988 Huntsville	.....	Southern	2B-SS-3B	*132	481	48	130	13	2	0	38	7	.270
1989 Tacoma	....	P.C.	2B-SS	136	487	55	117	17	1	1	43	4	.240
1990 Tacoma	....	P.C.	SS	111	348	49	79	16	1	2	30	3	.227
1990 Oakland	....	A.L.	3B-SS-2B	25	14	0	1	0	0	0	0	0	.071
1991 Tacoma	....	P.C.	SS	26	81	15	22	4	1	2	14	0	.272
1991 Oakland	....	A.L.	SS-2B-3B	90	235	21	56	5	1	0	21	3	.238
1992 Oakland	....	A.L.	2B-SS	154	504	62	151	19	4	3	48	12	.300
1993 Oakland	....	A.L.	SS-2B	159	546	60	136	21	2	3	48	10	.249
1994 Oakland	....	A.L.	SS-2B	114	391	38	99	18	4	2	37	7	.253
1995 Modesto	.....	California	SS	1	2	0	0	0	0	0	0	0	.000
1995 Oakland a	....	A.L.	SS	126	428	46	113	13	0	8	44	11	.264
1996 Oakland b-c	....	A.L.	SS	155	525	46	126	18	4	5	54	5	.240
1997 Baltimore	....	A.L.	SS	153	509	55	120	19	1	7	46	0	.236
1998 Baltimore	....	A.L.	SS	151	465	59	121	29	1	13	51	6	.260
1999 Baltimore	....	A.L.	SS	160	631	93	175	35	7	10	77	14	.277
2000 Baltimore	....	A.L.	SS	100	391	70	116	22	1	16	59	6	.297
2000 New York d-e	......	N.L.	SS	56	192	18	50	8	0	4	21	3	.260
Major League Totals	....		11 Yrs.	1443	4831	568	1264	207	25	71	506	77	.262
Division Series													
1997 Baltimore	....	A.L.	SS	4	10	4	4	1	0	0	4	0	.400
2000 New York	....	N.L.	SS	4	12	3	2	0	0	0	0	0	.167
Division Series Totals	....			8	22	7	6	1	0	0	4	0	.273
Championship Series													
1992 Oakland	....	A.L.	SS-2B	6	19	1	1	0	0	0	0	1	.053
1997 Baltimore	....	A.L.	SS	6	19	0	3	1	0	0	2	0	.158
2000 New York	....	N.L.	SS	5	13	2	1	0	0	0	0	0	.077
Championship Series Totals	.			17	51	3	5	1	0	0	2	1	.098
World Series Record													
1990 Oakland	....	A.L.	SS	3	0	0	0	0	0	0	0	0	.000
2000 New York	....	N.L.	SS	4	8	0	1	0	0	0	0	0	.125
World Series Totals	....			7	8	0	1	0	0	0	0	0	.125

a On disabled list from May 8 to May 27, 1995.
b Filed for free agency, October 28, 1996.
c Signed with Baltimore Orioles, December 12, 1996.
d Traded to New York Mets for infielder Melvin Mora, infielder Mike Kinkade, pitcher Pat Gorman and pitcher Leslie Brea, July 28, 2000.
e Filed for free agency, October 27, 2000, signed with Baltimore Orioles, December 20, 2000.

BRADLEY, MILTON OBELLE

Born, Harbor City, Florida, April 15, 1978.
Bats Both. Throws Right. Height, 6 feet. Weight, 180 pounds.

Year	Club	Lea	Pos	G	AB	R	H	2B	3B	HR	RBI	SB	Avg
1996 Expos	Gulf Coast	OF	32	112	18	27	7	1	1	12	7	.241
1997 Expos	Gulf Coast	OF	9	25	6	5	2	0	1	2	2	.200
1997 Vermont	N.Y.-Penn.	OF	50	200	29	60	7	5	3	30	7	.300
1998 Jupiter	Fla.St.	OF	67	261	55	75	14	1	5	34	17	.287
1998 Cape Fear	So.Atl.	OF	75	281	54	85	21	4	6	50	13	.302
1999 Harrisburg	Eastern	OF	86	346	62	114	22	5	12	50	14	.329
2000 Ottawa	Int.	OF	88	342	58	104	20	1	6	29	10	.304
2000 Montreal	N.L.	OF	42	154	20	34	8	1	2	15	2	.221

BRAGG, DARREN WILLIAM

Born, Waterbury, Connecticut, September 7, 1969.
Bats Left. Throws Right. Height, 5 feet, 9 inches. Weight, 180 pounds.

Year	Club	Lea	Pos	G	AB	R	H	2B	3B	HR	RBI	SB	Avg
1991 Peninsula	Carolina	OF-2B	69	237	42	53	14	0	3	29	21	.224
1992 Peninsula a	Carolina	OF-2B	135	428	83	117	25	5	9	58	44	.273
1993 Jacksonville b	Southern	OF	131	451	74	119	26	3	11	46	19	.264
1994 Calgary	P.C.	OF	126	500	112	175	33	6	17	85	28	.350
1994 Seattle	A.L.	OF	8	19	4	3	1	0	0	2	0	.158
1995 Tacoma	P.C.	OF	53	212	24	65	13	3	4	31	10	.307
1995 Seattle	A.L.	OF	52	145	20	34	5	1	3	12	9	.234
1996 Tacoma	P.C.	OF	20	71	17	20	8	0	3	8	1	.282
1996 Seattle-Boston c	A.L.	OF	127	417	74	109	26	2	10	47	14	.261
1997 Boston	OF-3B	153	513	65	132	35	2	9	57	10	.257
1998 Boston d	A.L.	OF	129	409	51	114	29	3	8	57	5	.279
1999 St. Louis d-e	N.L.	OF	93	273	38	71	12	1	6	26	3	.260
2000 Colorado f	N.L.	OF	71	149	16	33	7	1	3	21	4	.221
Major League Totals		7 Yrs.	633	1925	268	496	115	10	39	222	45	.258
Division Series													
1998 Boston	A.L.	OF	3	12	0	1	0	0	0	0	0	.083

a Record of 0-0 in one game as pitcher.
b Record of 0-0 in one game as pitcher.
c Traded to Boston Red Sox for pitcher Jamie Moyer, July 30, 1996.
d Not offered 1999 contract, December 21, 1998. Signed with St. Louis Cardinals, January 12, 1999.
d On disabled list from August 3 to November 3, 1999.
e Released by St. Louis Cardinals, December 16, 1999, signed with Colorado Rockies organization, December 21, 1999.
   Signed with Colorado Rockies organization, February 2, 2000.
f Filed for free agency, July 26, 2000.

BRANYAN, RUSSELL OLES

Born, Warner Robins, Georgia, December 19, 1975.
Bats Left. Throws Right. Height, 6 feet, 3 inches. Weight, 195 pounds.

Year	Club	Lea	Pos	G	AB	R	H	2B	3B	HR	RBI	SB	Avg
1994 Burlington	Appal.	3B	55	171	21	36	10	0	5	13	4	.211
1995 Columbus	So.Atl.	3B	76	277	46	71	8	6	19	55	1	.256
1996 Columbus	So.Atl.	3B	130	482	102	129	20	4	40	106	7	.268
1997 Kinston	Carolina	3B	83	297	59	86	26	2	27	75	3	.290
1997 Akron	Eastern	3B	41	137	26	32	4	0	12	30	0	.234
1998 Akron	Eastern	3B	43	163	35	48	11	3	16	46	1	.294
1998 Cleveland a	A.L.	3B	1	4	0	0	0	0	0	0	0	.000
1999 Buffalo	Int.	3B	110	395	51	82	11	1	30	67	8	.208
1999 Cleveland	A.L.	3B	11	38	4	8	2	0	1	6	0	.211
2000 Buffalo	Int.	3B	64	229	46	56	9	2	21	60	1	.245
2000 Cleveland	A.L.	OF-3B	67	193	32	46	7	2	16	38	0	.238
Major League Totals		3 Yrs.	79	235	36	54	9	2	17	44	0	.230

a On disabled list from April 23 to May 11 and May 16 to August 15, 1998.

BROGNA, RICO JOSEPH

Born, Turners Falls, Massachusetts, April 18, 1970.
Bats Left. Throws Left. Height, 6 feet, 2 inches. Weight, 202 pounds.

Year	Club	Lea	Pos	G	AB	R	H	2B	3B	HR	RBI	SB	Avg
1988 Bristol	Appal.	1B-OF	60	209	37	53	11	2	7	33	3	.254
1989 Lakeland	Fla. St.	1B	128	459	47	108	20	7	5	51	2	.235
1990 London	Eastern	1B	137	488	70	128	21	3	*21	*77	1	.262

25

Year	Club	Lea	Pos	G	AB	R	H	2B	3B	HR	RBI	SB	Avg
1991 London	Eastern	1B-OF	77	293	40	80	13	1	13	51	0	.273
1991 Toledo	Int.	1B	41	132	13	29	6	1	2	13	2	.220
1992 Toledo	Int.	1B	121	387	45	101	19	4	10	58	1	.261
1992 Detroit	A.L.	1B	9	26	3	5	1	0	1	3	0	.192
1993 Toledo a	Int.	1B	129	483	55	132	30	3	11	59	7	.273
1994 Norfolk	Int.	1B	67	258	33	63	14	5	12	37	1	.244
1994 New York	N.L.	1B	39	131	16	46	11	2	7	20	1	.351
1995 New York	N.L.	1B	134	495	72	143	27	2	22	76	0	.289
1996 New York b-c	N.L.	1B	55	188	18	48	10	1	7	30	0	.255
1997 Philadelphia	N.L.	1B	148	543	68	137	36	4	20	81	12	.252
1998 Philadelphia	N.L.	1B	153	565	77	150	36	3	20	104	7	.265
1999 Philadelphia	N.L.	1B	157	619	90	172	29	4	24	102	8	.278
2000 Clearwater	Fla.St.	1B	7	32	2	7	1	0	0	2	0	.219
2000 Philadelphia	N.L.	1B	38	129	12	32	14	0	1	13	1	.248
2000 Boston d-e-f	A.L.	1B	43	56	8	11	3	0	1	8	0	.196

Major League Totals		8 Yrs.	776	2752	364	744	167	13	103	437	29	.270

a Traded by Detroit Tigers to New York Mets organization for first baseman Alan Zinter, March 31, 1994.
b On disabled list from June 20 to September 30, 1996.
c Traded to Philadelphia Phillies for pitcher Ricardo Jordan and pitcher Toby Borland, November 27, 1996.
d On disabled list from May 11 to July 20, 2000.
e Claimed on waivers by Boston Red Sox, August 3, 2000.
f Filed for free agency, October 31, 2000, signed with Atlanta Braves, December 14, 2000.

BROSIUS, SCOTT DAVID
Born, Hillsboro, Oregon, August 15, 1966.
Bats Right. Throws Right. Height, 6 feet, 1 inch. Weight, 185 pounds.

Year	Club	Lea	Pos	G	AB	R	H	2B	3B	HR	RBI	SB	Avg
1987 Medford	Northwest	SS-3B-2B	65	255	34	73	18	1	3	49	5	.286
1988 Madison	Midwest	SS-3B-OF-1B	132	504	82	153	28	2	9	58	13	.304
1989 Huntsville	Southern	2B-3B-SS-1B	128	461	68	125	22	2	7	60	4	.271
1990 Huntsville	Southern	SS-2B-3B	*142	547	94	*162	*39	2	23	88	12	.296
1990 Tacoma	P.C.	2B	3	7	2	1	0	1	0	0	0	.143
1991 Tacoma	P.C.	3B-SS-2B	65	245	28	70	16	3	8	31	4	.286
1991 Oakland	A.L.	2B-OF-3B	36	68	9	16	5	0	2	4	3	.235
1992 Tacoma	P.C.	3B	63	236	29	56	13	0	9	31	8	.237
1992 Oakland a	A.L.	OF-3B-1B-SS	38	87	13	19	2	0	4	13	3	.218
1993 Tacoma	P.C.	3B-OF-2B-1B-SS	56	209	38	62	13	2	8	41	8	.297
1993 Oakland	A.L.	OF-1B-3B-SS	70	213	26	53	10	1	6	25	6	.249
1994 Oakland b	A.L.	3B-OF-1B-2B	96	324	31	77	14	1	14	49	2	.238
1995 Oakland	A.L.	3B-OF-1B-2B	123	388	69	102	19	2	17	46	4	.263
1996 Edmonton	P.C.	3B	8	8	5	5	1	0	0	0	0	.625
1996 Oakland c	A.L.	3B-1B-OF	114	428	73	130	25	0	22	71	7	.304
1997 Modesto	California	3B	2	3	1	1	0	0	0	1	0	.333
1997 Oakland d-e	A.L.	3B-SS-OF	129	479	59	97	20	1	11	41	9	.203
1998 New York f	A.L.	3B-1B-OF	152	530	86	159	34	0	19	98	11	.300
1999 Tampa	Fla.St.	3B	0	3	0	1	0	0	0	0	0	.333
1999 New York g	A.L.	3B	133	473	64	117	26	1	17	71	9	.247
2000 Tampa	Fla.St.	3B	2	4	0	1	0	0	0	0	0	.250
2000 New York h	A.L.	3B-1B-OF	135	470	57	108	20	0	16	64	0	.230

Major League Totals		10 Yrs.	1026	3461	487	878	175	6	128	482	54	.254

Division Series

Year	Club	Lea	Pos	G	AB	R	H	2B	3B	HR	RBI	SB	Avg
1998 New York	A.L.	3B	3	10	1	4	0	0	1	3	0	.400
1999 New York	A.L.	3B	3	10	0	1	1	0	0	1	0	.100
2000 New York	A.L.	3B	5	17	0	3	1	0	0	1	0	.176
Division Series Totals			11	37	1	8	2	0	1	5	0	.216

Championship Series

Year	Club	Lea	Pos	G	AB	R	H	2B	3B	HR	RBI	SB	Avg
1998 New York	A.L.	3B	6	20	2	6	1	0	1	6	0	.300
1999 New York	A.L.	3B	5	18	3	4	0	1	2	3	0	.222
2000 New York	A.L.	3B	6	18	2	4	0	0	0	0	0	.222
Championship Series Totals			17	56	7	14	1	1	3	9	0	

World Series Record

Year	Club	Lea	Pos	G	AB	R	H	2B	3B	HR	RBI	SB	Avg
1998 New York	A.L.	3B	4	17	3	8	0	0	2	6	0	.471
1999 New York	A.L.	3B	4	16	2	6	1	0	0	1	0	.375
2000 New York	A.L.	3B	5	13	2	4	0	0	1	3	0	.308
World Series Totals			13	46	7	18	1	0	3	10	0	.391

a On disabled list from April 18 to May 10 and July 17 to August 3, 1992.
b On disabled list from June 8 to June 26, 1994.
c On disabled list from May 5 to June 25, 1996.

d On disabled list from August 7 to August 29, 1997.
e Sent to New York Yankees as player to be named later for pitcher Kenny Rogers, November 18, 1997.
f Filed for free agency, October 27, 1998, re-signed with New York Yankees, November 9, 1998.
g On disabled list from April 14 to April 29, 1999.
h On disabled list from April 4 to April 24, 2000.

BROWN, ADRIAN DEMOND

Born, McComb, Mississippi, February 7, 1974.
Bats Both. Throws Right. Height, 6 feet. Weight, 175 pounds.

Year	Club	Lea	Pos	G	AB	R	H	2B	3B	HR	RBI	SB	Avg
1992 Pirates	Gulf Coast	OF-1B	39	121	11	31	2	2	0	12	8	.256
1993 Lethbridge	Pioneer	OF	69	282	47	75	12	9	3	27	22	.266
1994 Augusta	So.Atl.	OF	79	308	41	80	17	1	1	18	19	.260
1995 Augusta	So.Atl.	OF	76	287	64	86	15	4	4	31	25	.300
1995 Lynchburg	Carolina	OF	54	215	30	52	5	2	1	14	11	.242
1996 Lynchburg	Carolina	OF	52	215	39	69	9	3	4	25	18	.321
1996 Carolina	Southern	OF	84	341	48	101	11	3	3	25	27	.296
1997 Carolina	Southern	OF	37	145	29	44	4	4	2	15	9	.303
1997 Calgary	P.C.	OF	62	248	53	79	10	1	1	19	20	.319
1997 Pittsburgh	N.L.	OF	48	147	17	28	6	0	1	10	8	.190
1998 Nashville	P.C.	OF	85	311	58	90	12	5	3	27	25	.289
1998 Pittsburgh	N.L.	OF	41	152	20	43	4	1	0	5	4	.283
1999 Nashville	P.C.	OF	17	56	10	18	3	1	0	4	6	.321
1999 Pittsburgh	N.L.	OF	116	226	34	61	5	2	4	17	5	.270
2000 Altoona	Eastern	OF	2	5	1	0	0	0	0	0	0	.000
2000 Nashville	P.C.	OF	8	26	3	6	1	0	0	2	3	.231
2000 Pittsburgh a	N.L.	OF	104	308	64	97	18	3	4	28	13	.315
Major League Totals		4 Yrs.	309	833	135	229	33	6	9	60	30	.275

a On disabled list from June 13 to July 3 and from July 6 to August 6, 2000.

BROWN, BRANT MICHAEL

Born, Porterville, California, June 22, 1971.
Bats Left. Throws Right. Height, 6 feet, 3 inches. Weight, 220 pounds.

Year	Club	Lea	Pos	G	AB	R	H	2B	3B	HR	RBI	SB	Avg
1992 Peoria	Midwest	1B	70	248	28	68	14	0	3	27	3	.274
1993 Daytona	Fla.St.	1B-OF	75	266	26	91	8	7	3	33	8	.342
1993 Orlando a	Southern	1B	28	111	17	35	11	3	4	23	2	.315
1994 Orlando	Southern	1B-OF	127	470	54	127	30	6	5	37	11	.270
1995 Orlando	Southern	1B-OF	121	446	67	121	27	4	6	53	8	.271
1996 Iowa	A.A.	1B	94	342	48	104	25	3	10	43	6	.304
1996 Chicago	N.L.	1B	29	69	11	21	1	0	5	9	3	.304
1997 Iowa	A.A.	OF-1B	71	256	51	77	19	3	16	51	6	.301
1997 Chicago	N.L.	OF-1B	46	137	15	32	7	1	5	15	2	.234
1998 Iowa	P.C.	OF-1B	3	11	1	4	0	0	0	0	0	.364
1998 Chicago b-c	N.L.	OF-1B	124	347	56	101	17	7	14	48	4	.291
1999 Pittsburgh d	N.L.	OF-1B	130	341	49	79	20	3	16	58	3	.232
2000 Florida-Chicago e-f	N.L.	OF-1B	95	162	11	28	7	0	5	16	3	.173
Major League Totals		5 Yrs.	424	1056	142	261	52	11	45	146	15	.247
Division Series													
1998 Chicago	N.L.	PH	1	1	0	0	0	0	0	0	0	.000

a On disabled list from April 10 to April 25, 1993.
b On disabled list from June 26 to July 25, 1998.
c Traded to Pittsburgh Pirates for pitcher Jon Leiber, December 14, 1998.
d Traded to Florida Marlins for outfielder Bruce Aven, December 13, 1999.
e Traded to Chicago Cubs for pitcher Chuck Smith, June 9, 2000.
f Filed for free agency, October 10, 2000.

BUFORD, DAMON JACKSON

Born, Baltimore, Maryland, June 12, 1970.
Bats Right. Throws Right. Height, 5 feet, 10 inches. Weight, 170 pounds.

Year	Club	Lea	Pos	G	AB	R	H	2B	3B	HR	RBI	SB	Avg
1990 Wausau	Midwest	OF	41	160	31	48	7	2	1	14	15	.300
1991 Frederick	Carolina	OF-3B	133	505	71	138	25	6	8	54	50	.273
1992 Hagerstown	Eastern	OF	101	373	53	89	17	3	1	30	41	.239
1992 Rochester	Int.	OF	45	155	29	44	10	2	1	12	23	.284
1993 Rochester	Int.	OF	27	116	24	33	6	1	1	4	10	.284

27

Year	Club	Lea	Pos	G	AB	R	H	2B	3B	HR	RBI	SB	Avg
1993 Baltimore	A.L.	OF	53	79	18	18	5	0	2	9	2	.228
1994 Baltimore	A.L.	OF	4	2	2	1	0	0	0	0	0	.500
1994 Rochester	Int.	OF	111	452	89	122	21	4	16	66	31	.270
1995 Baltimore	A.L.	OF	24	32	6	2	0	0	0	2	3	.063
1995 Rochester	Int.	OF	46	188	40	58	12	3	4	18	17	.309
1995 New York a-b	N.L.	OF	44	136	24	32	5	0	4	12	7	.235
1996 Texas c	A.L.	OF	90	145	30	41	9	0	6	20	8	.283
1997 Texas d	A.L.	OF	122	366	49	82	18	0	8	39	18	.224
1998 Boston e	A.L.	OF-2B-3B	86	216	37	61	14	4	10	42	5	.282
1999 Boston f-g	A.L.	OF	91	297	39	72	15	2	6	38	9	.242
2000 Chicago	N.L.	OF	150	495	64	124	18	3	15	48	4	.251
Major League Totals		8 Yrs.	664	1768	269	433	84	9	51	210	56	.245
Division Series												
1996 Texas	A.L.	PR	2	0	0	0	0	0	0	0	0	.000
1998 Boston	A.L.	OF-DH	3	1	2	0	0	0	0	0	0	.000
1999 Boston	A.L.	OF	1	3	0	0	0	0	0	0	0	.000
Division Series Totals			6	4	2	0	0	0	0	0	0	.000
Championship Series												
1999 Boston	A.L.	OF	4	5	1	2	0	0	0	0	1	.400

a Traded to New York Mets with outfielder Alex Ochoa for infielder Bobby Bonilla and player to be named later, July 28, 1995.
b Baltimore Orioles received pitcher Jimmy Williams to complete trade, August 17, 1995.
c Traded to Texas Rangers for outfielder Terrell Lowery, January 25, 1996.
d Traded to Boston Red Sox with catcher Jim Leyritz for pitcher Aaron Sele and catcher Bill Haselman and pitcher Mark Brandenburg, November 6, 1997.
e On disabled list from May 18 to June 3 and August 27 to September 11, 1998.
f On disabled list from August 6 to August 23, 1999.
g Traded to Chicago Cubs for infielder Manny Alexander, December 11, 1999.

BUHNER, JAY CAMPBELL
Born, Louisville, Kentucky, August 13, 1964.
Bats Right. Throws Right. Height, 6 feet, 3 inches. Weight, 210 pounds.

Year	Club	Lea	Pos	G	AB	R	H	2B	3B	HR	RBI	SB	Avg
1984 Watertown a	N.Y.-Penn.	OF	65	229	43	74	16	3	9	*58	3	.323
1985 Ft. Lauderdale	Fla. St.	OF	117	409	65	121	18	10	11	76	6	.296
1986 Ft. Lauderdale b	Fla. St.	OF	36	139	24	42	9	1	7	31	1	.302
1987 Columbus	Int.	OF	134	502	83	140	23	1	*31	85	4	.279
1987 New York	A.L.	OF	7	22	0	5	2	0	0	1	0	.227
1988 Columbus	Int.	OF	38	129	26	33	5	0	8	18	1	.256
1988 New York-Seattle c	A.L.	OF	85	261	36	56	13	1	13	38	1	.215
1989 Calgary	P.C.	OF	56	196	43	61	12	1	11	45	4	.311
1989 Seattle d	A.L.	OF	58	204	27	56	15	1	9	33	1	.275
1990 Calgary	P.C.	OF	13	34	6	7	1	0	2	5	0	.206
1990 Seattle e	A.L.	OF	51	163	16	45	12	0	7	33	2	.276
1991 Seattle	A.L.	OF	137	406	64	99	14	4	27	77	0	.244
1992 Seattle	A.L.	OF	152	543	69	132	16	3	25	79	0	.243
1993 Seattle	A.L.	OF	158	563	91	153	28	3	27	98	2	.272
1994 Seattle f.............	A.L.	OF	101	358	74	100	23	4	21	68	0	.279
1995 Seattle g	A.L.	OF	126	470	86	123	23	0	40	121	0	.262
1996 Seattle	A.L.	OF	150	564	107	153	29	0	44	138	0	.271
1997 Seattle	A.L.	OF	157	540	104	131	18	2	40	109	0	.243
1998 Tacoma	P.C.	OF	2	4	2	2	2	0	0	2	0	.500
1998 Seattle h	A.L.	OF	72	244	33	59	7	1	15	45	0	.242
1999 Seattle i-j............	A.L.	OF-1B	87	266	37	59	11	0	14	38	0	.222
2000 Seattle k-l	A.L.	OF	112	364	50	92	20	0	26	82	0	.253
Major League Totals		14 Yrs.	1453	4968	794	1263	231	19	308	960	6	.254
Division Series												
1995 Seattle	A.L.	OF	5	24	2	11	1	0	1	3	0	.458
1997 Seattle	A.L.	OF	4	13	2	3	0	0	2	2	0	.231
2000 Seattle	A.L.	OF	2	5	1	1	0	0	1	1	0	.200
Division Series Totals			11	42	5	15	1	0	4	6	0	.357
Championship Series												
1995 Seattle	A.L.	OF	6	23	5	7	2	0	3	5	0	.304
2000 Seattle	A.L.	OF	4	11	0	2	0	0	0	0	0	.182
Championship Series Totals			10	34	5	9	2	0	3	5	0	.265

a Traded by Pittsburgh Pirates to New York Yankees organization with infielder Dale Berra and pitcher Alfonso Pulido for outfielder Steve Kemp, infielder Tim Foli and cash, December 20, 1984.
b On disabled list from April 11 to July 27, 1986.

c Traded to Seattle Mariners with pitcher Rick Balabon and player to be named for first baseman Ken Phelps, July
  21; Seattle acquired pitcher Troy Evers to complete deal, October 12, 1988.
d On disabled list from June 29 to August 19, 1989.
e On disabled list from March 31 to June 1 and June 17 to August 23, 1990.
f Filed for free agency, October 14; re-signed with Seattle Mariners, December 21, 1994.
g On disabled list from June 6 to June 22, 1995.
h On disabled list from April 7 to June 11 and September 8 to September 28, 1998.
i On disabled list from May 19 to July 15, 1999.
j Filed for free agency, November 11, 1999, re-signed with Seattle Mariners, December 6, 1999.
k On disabled list from August 17 to August 31, 2000.
l Filed for free agency, November 10, 2000, re-signed with Seattle Mariners, December 7, 2000.

BURKS, ELLIS RENA

Born, Vicksburg, Mississippi, September 11, 1964.
Bats Right. Throws Right. Height, 6 feet, 2 inches. Weight, 205 pounds.

Year	Club	Lea	Pos	G	AB	R	H	2B	3B	HR	RBI	SB	Avg
1983 Elmira	N.Y.-Penn.	OF	53	174	30	42	9	0	2	23	9	.241
1984 Winter Haven	Fla. St.	OF	112	375	52	96	15	4	6	43	29	.256
1985 New Britain	Eastern	OF	133	476	66	121	25	7	10	61	17	.254
1986 New Britain	Eastern	OF	124	462	70	126	20	3	14	55	31	.273
1987 Pawtucket	Int.	OF	11	40	11	9	3	1	3	6	1	.225
1987 Boston	A.L.	OF	133	558	94	152	30	2	20	59	27	.272
1988 Boston a	A.L.	OF	144	540	93	159	37	5	18	92	25	.294
1989 Pawtucket	Int.	OF	5	21	4	3	1	0	0	0	0	.143
1989 Boston b	A.L.	OF	97	399	73	121	19	6	12	61	21	.303
1990 Boston	A.L.	OF	152	588	89	174	33	8	21	89	9	.296
1991 Boston	A.L.	OF	130	474	56	119	33	3	14	56	6	.251
1992 Boston c-d	A.L.	OF	66	235	35	60	8	3	8	30	5	.255
1993 Chicago e	A.L.	OF	146	499	75	137	24	4	17	74	6	.275
1994 Colorado Springs	P.C.	OF	2	8	4	4	1	0	1	2	0	.500
1994 Colorado f	N.L.	OF	42	149	33	48	8	3	13	24	3	.322
1995 Colorado Springs	P.C.	OF	8	29	9	9	2	1	2	6	0	.310
1995 Colorado g	N.L.	OF	103	278	41	74	10	6	14	49	7	.266
1996 Colorado	N.L.	OF	156	613	*142	211	45	8	40	128	32	.344
1997 Colorado h	N.L.	OF	119	424	91	123	19	2	32	82	7	.290
1998 Colorado-San Fran i-j	N.L.	OF	142	504	76	147	28	6	21	76	11	.292
1999 San Francisco k	N.L.	OF	120	390	73	110	19	0	31	96	7	.282
2000 San Francisco l-m	N.L.	OF	122	393	74	135	21	5	24	96	5	.344
Major League Totals		14 Yrs.	1672	6044	1045	1770	334	61	285	1012	171	.293
Division Series													
1995 Colorado	N.L.	OF	2	6	1	2	1	0	0	2	0	.333
2000 San Francisco	N.L.	OF	4	13	2	3	1	0	1	4	0	.231
Division Series Totals			6	19	3	5	2	0	1	6	0	.263
Championship Series													
1988 Boston	A.L.	OF	4	17	2	4	1	0	0	1	0	.235
1990 Boston	A.L.	OF	4	15	1	4	2	0	0	0	1	.267
1993 Chicago	A.L.	OF	6	23	4	7	1	0	1	3	0	.304
Championship Series Totals			14	55	7	15	4	0	1	4	1	.273

a On disabled list from March 27 to April 12, 1988.
b On disabled list from June 16 to August 1, 1989.
c On disabled list from June 25 to end of 1992 season.
d Not offered 1993 contract, December 18, 1992; signed with Chicago White Sox, January 4, 1993.
e Filed for free agency, October 27; signed with Colorado Rockies, November 30, 1993.
f On disabled list from May 18 to July 31, 1994.
g On disabled list from April 25 to May 5, 1995.
h On disabled list from June 28 to July 29, 1997.
i Traded to San Francisco Giants for outfielder Darryl Hamilton and pitcher Jim Stoops, July 31, 1998. Colorado
  Rockies received pitcher Jason Brester to complete trade, August 17, 1998.
j Filed for free agency, November 2, 1998, re-signed with San Francisco Giants, November 12, 1998.
k On disabled list from June 9 to June 26, 1999.
l On disabled list from May 9 to May 23, 2000.
m Filed for free agency, October 30, 2000, signed with Cleveland Indians, November 20, 2000.

BURNITZ, JEROMY NEAL

Born, Westminster, California, April 15, 1969.
Bats Left. Throws Right. Height, 6 feet. Weight, 190 pounds.

Year	Club	Lea	Pos	G	AB	R	H	2B	3B	HR	RBI	SB	Avg
1990 Pittsfield	N.Y.-Penn.	OF	51	173	37	52	6	5	6	22	12	.301
1990 St. Lucie	Fla. St.	OF	11	32	6	5	1	0	0	3	1	.156
1991 Williamsport	Eastern	OF	135	457	80	103	16	10	31	85	31	.225

Year Club	Lea	Pos	G	AB	R	H	2B	3B	HR	RBI	SB	Avg
1992 Tidewater ....Int.		OF	121	445	56	108	21	3	8	40	30	.243
1993 Norfolk ....Int.		OF	65	255	33	58	15	3	8	44	10	.227
1993 New York ...........N.L.		OF	86	263	49	64	10	6	13	38	3	.243
1994 New York ...........N.L.		OF	45	143	26	34	4	0	3	15	1	.238
1994 Norfolk a ....Int.		OF	85	314	58	75	15	5	14	49	18	.239
1995 Buffalo ...........A.A.		OF	128	443	72	126	26	7	19	85	13	.284
1995 Cleveland ..........A.L.		OF	9	7	4	4	1	0	0	0	0	.571
1996 Cleveland-Milwaukee,b ..A.L.		OF	94	200	38	53	14	0	9	40	4	.265
1997 Milwaukee ..........A.L.		OF	153	494	85	139	37	8	27	85	20	.281
1998 Milwaukee ..........N.L.		OF	161	609	92	160	28	1	38	125	7	.263
1999 Milwaukee c .........N.L.		OF	130	467	87	126	33	2	33	103	7	.270
2000 Milwaukee ..........N.L.		OF	161	564	91	131	29	2	31	98	6	.232
Major League Totals		8 Yrs.	839	2747	472	711	156	19	154	504	48	.259

a Traded by New York Mets to Cleveland Indians with pitcher Joe Roa for pitchers Jerry DiPoto and Paul Byrd and player to be named, November 18; New York Mets acquired second baseman Jesus Azuaje to complete trade, December 6, 1994.
b Traded to Milwaukee Brewers for infielder Kevin Seitzer, August 31, 1996.
c On disabled list from July 18 to August 20, 1999.

BURRELL, PATRICK B. (PAT)

Born, Eureka Springs, Arkansas, October 10, 1976.
Bats Right. Throws Right. Height, 6 feet, 4 inches. Weight, 230 pounds.

Year Club	Lea	Pos	G	AB	R	H	2B	3B	HR	RBI	SB	Avg
1998 Clearwater ....Fla.St.		1B	37	132	29	40	7	1	7	30	2	.303
1999 Scranton-WB ....Int.		1B	9	33	4	5	0	0	1	4	0	.152
1999 Reading ....Eastern		1B	117	417	84	139	28	6	28	90	3	.333
2000 Scranton-WB ....Int.		OF	40	143	31	42	15	1	4	25	1	.294
2000 Philadelphia ..........N.L.		1B-OF	111	408	57	106	27	1	18	79	0	.260

BUSH, HOMER GILES

Born, East St. Louis, Illinois, November 12, 1972.
Bats Right. Throws Right. Height, 5 feet, 11 inches. Weight, 180 pounds.

Year Club	Lea	Pos	G	AB	R	H	2B	3B	HR	RBI	SB	Avg
1991 Padres ....Arizona		3B	32	127	16	41	3	2	0	16	11	.323
1992 Chston-Sc ....So. Atl.		2B	108	367	37	86	10	5	0	18	14	.234
1993 Waterloo ....Midwest		2B	130	472	63	152	19	3	5	51	39	.322
1994 Rancho Cuca .....California		2B	39	161	37	54	10	3	0	16	9	.335
1994 Wichita ....Texas		2B	59	245	35	73	11	4	3	14	20	.298
1995 Memphis ....Southern		2B	108	432	53	121	12	5	5	37	34	.280
1996 Las Vegas ...........P.C.		2B	32	116	24	42	11	1	2	3	3	.362
1997 Las Vegas ...........P.C.		2B	38	155	25	43	10	1	3	14	5	.277
1997 Columbus a ....Int.		2B	74	275	36	68	10	3	2	26	12	.247
1997 New York ...........A.L.		2B	10	11	2	4	0	0	0	0	3	.364
1998 New York ...........A.L.		2B-3B-SS	45	71	17	27	3	0	1	5	6	.380
1999 Dunedin ....Fla.St.		2B	0	14	3	5	2	0	0	0	1	.357
1999 Toronto b-c ..........A.L.		2B-SS	128	485	69	155	26	4	5	55	32	.320
2000 Toronto d ............A.L.		2B	76	297	38	64	8	0	1	18	9	.215
Major League Totals		4 Yrs.	259	864	126	250	37	4	7	81	47	.289
Division Series												
1998 New York ...........A.L.		DH	1	0	0	0	0	0	0	0	1	.000
Championship Series												
1998 New York ...........A.L.		DH	2	0	1	0	0	0	0	0	1	.000
World Series Record												
1998 New York ...........A.L.		DH	2	0	0	0	0	0	0	0	0	.000

a Traded to New York Yankees with pitcher Hideki Irabu and player to be named later for outfielder Ruben Rivera, pitcher Rafael Medina and cash, May 30, 1997. New York Yankees received outfielder Vernon Maxwell to complete trade, June 9, 1997.
b Traded to Toronto Blue Jays with pitcher David Wells and pitcher Graeme Lloyd for pitcher Roger Clemens, February 18, 1999.
c On disabled list from April 11 to May 14, 1999.
d On disabled list from May 22 to June 5 and July 31 to November 2, 2000.

CABRERA, JOLBERT ALEXIS
Born, Cartagena, Colombia, December 8, 1972.
Bats Right. Throws Right. Height, 6 feet. Weight, 177 pounds.

Year	Club	Lea	Pos	G	AB	R	H	2B	3B	HR	RBI	SB	Avg
1990 Montreal	....Dominican		SS	29	115	31	36	3	2	0	12	14	.313
1991 Sumter	........So.Atl.		SS	101	324	33	66	4	0	1	20	10	.204
1992 Albany	........So.Atl.		SS-OF	118	377	44	86	9	2	0	23	22	.228
1993 Burlington	....Midwest		SS	128	507	62	129	24	2	0	38	31	.254
1994 Wst Plm Bch	....Fla.St.		SS	83	266	32	54	4	0	0	13	7	.203
1994 San Berndno	..California		SS-OF	30	109	14	27	5	1	0	11	2	.248
1994 Harrisburg	....Eastern		SS	3	2	0	0	0	0	0	0	0	.000
1995 Wst Plm Bch	....Fla.St.		SS-2B-3B	103	357	62	102	23	2	1	25	19	.286
1995 Harrisburg	....Eastern		SS	9	35	4	10	2	0	0	1	3	.286
1996 Harrisburg	....Eastern		SS-OF-3B	107	354	40	85	18	2	3	29	10	.240
1997 Harrisburg	....Eastern		2B-SS-OF	48	171	28	43	9	0	2	11	5	.251
1997 Ottawa	...........Int.		3B-2B-SS-OF	68	191	28	54	10	4	0	12	15	.283
1998 Buffalo	...........Int.		SS-OF-2B	129	494	94	157	24	1	10	45	25	.318
1998 Cleveland a	.......A.L.		SS	1	2	0	0	0	0	0	0	0	.000
1999 Buffalo	...........Int.		OF	71	279	44	74	13	4	0	27	20	.265
1999 Cleveland	.........A.L.		OF-2B	30	37	6	7	1	0	0	0	3	.189
2000 Buffalo	...........Int.		OF	20	74	18	25	6	1	3	11	2	.338
2000 Cleveland	........A.L.		OF-2B-SS	100	175	27	44	3	1	2	15	6	.251
Major League Totals			3 Yrs.	131	214	33	51	4	1	2	15	9	.238

a Filed for free agency from Montreal Expos, October 17, 1997, signed with Cleveland Indians, January 20, 1998.

CABRERA, ORLANDO LUIS
Born, Cartagena, Colombia, November 2, 1974.
Bats Right. Throws Right. Height, 5 feet, 11 inches. Weight, 165 pounds.

Year	Club	Lea	Pos	G	AB	R	H	2B	3B	HR	RBI	SB	Avg
1994 Expos	.........Gulf Coast		2B-SS-OF	22	73	13	23	4	1	0	11	6	.315
1995 Wst Plm Bch	.......Fla. St.		SS	3	5	0	1	0	0	0	0	0	.200
1995 Vermont	.......N.Y.-Penn.		2B-SS	65	248	37	70	12	5	3	33	15	.282
1996 Delmarva	.......So. Atl.		SS-2B	134	512	86	129	28	4	14	65	51	.252
1997 Wst Plm Bch	.......Fla. St.		SS-2B	69	279	56	77	19	2	5	26	32	.276
1997 Harrisburg	.......Eastern		SS-2B	35	133	34	41	13	2	5	20	7	.308
1997 Ottawa	..........Int.		SS-2B	31	122	17	32	5	2	2	14	8	.262
1997 Montreal	............N.L.		SS-2B	16	18	4	4	0	0	0	2	1	.222
1998 Ottawa	............Int.		SS-2B	66	272	31	63	9	4	0	26	19	.232
1998 Montreal	............N.L.		SS-2B	79	261	44	73	16	5	3	22	6	.280
1999 Montreal a	............N.L.		SS	104	382	48	97	23	5	8	39	2	.254
2000 Ottawa	............Int.		SS	2	6	1	4	0	0	0	0	1	.667
2000 Montreal b	............N.L.		SS-2B	125	422	47	100	25	1	13	55	4	.237
Major League Totals			4 Yrs.	324	1083	143	274	64	11	24	118	13	.253

a On disabled list from August 9 to October 13, 1999.
b On disabled list from July 15 to August 14, 2000.

CAIRO, MIGUEL JESUS
Born, Anaco, Venezuela, May 4, 1974.
Bats Right. Throws Right. Height, 6 feet. Weight, 160 pounds.

Year	Club	Lea	Pos	G	AB	R	H	2B	3B	HR	RBI	SB	Avg
1992 Dodgers	.......Gulf Coast		SS-3B	21	76	10	23	5	2	0	9	1	.303
1992 Vero Beach	.........Fla. St.		2B-SS	36	125	7	28	0	0	0	7	5	.224
1993 Vero Beach	.........Fla. St.		2B-SS-3B	90	346	50	109	10	1	1	23	23	.315
1994 Bakersfield	......California		2B-SS	133	533	76	155	23	4	2	48	44	.291
1995 San Antonio a-b	......Texas		2B-SS	107	435	53	121	20	1	1	41	33	.278
1996 Syracuse	..............Int.		2B-3B-SS	120	465	71	129	14	4	3	48	27	.277
1996 Toronto c	............A.L.		2B	9	27	5	6	2	0	0	1	0	.222
1997 Iowa	................A.A.		2B-SS	135	569	82	159	35	4	5	46	40	.279
1997 Chicago d	..............N.L.		2B-SS	16	29	7	7	1	0	0	1	0	.241
1998 Tampa Bay	..........A.L.		2B	150	515	49	138	26	5	5	46	19	.268
1999 St.Petersburg	.......Fla.St.		2B	3	13	2	5	0	0	0	0	1	.385
1999 Orlando	.........Southern		2B	3	13	1	5	2	0	0	1	0	.385
1999 Tampa Bay e	.........A.L.		2B	120	465	61	137	15	5	3	36	22	.295
2000 Tampa Bay d	.........A.L.		2B	119	375	49	98	18	2	1	34	28	.261
Major League Totals			5 Yrs.	414	1411	171	386	62	12	9	118	69	.274

a Traded to Seattle Mariners with infielder Willie Otanez for third baseman Mike Blowers, November 29, 1995.
b Traded to Toronto Blue Jays with pitcher Bill Risley for pitchers Edwin Hurtado and Paul Menhart, December 18, 1995.

c On disabled list, May 27 to June 5, 1996.
d Selected in expansion draft by Tampa Bay Devil Rays, November 18, 1997.
e On disabled list from April 24 to May 17 and July 26 to August 11, 1999.
d Released by Tampa Bay Devil Rays, November 27, 2000.

CAMERON, MICHAEL TERRANCE
Born, La Grange, Georgia, January 8, 1973.
Bats Right. Throws Right. Height, 6 feet, 2 inches. Weight, 190 pounds.

Year	Club	Lea	Pos	G	AB	R	H	2B	3B	HR	RBI	SB	Avg
1991 White Sox	Gulf Coast	OF	44	136	20	30	3	0	0	11	13	.221
1992 Utica	N.Y.-Penn.	OF	28	87	15	24	1	4	2	12	3	.276
1992 South Bend	Midwest	OF	35	114	19	26	8	1	1	9	2	.228
1993 South Bend	Midwest	OF	122	411	52	98	14	5	0	30	19	.238
1994 Pr William	Carolina	OF	131	468	86	116	15	17	6	48	22	.248
1995 Birmingham	Southern	OF	107	350	64	87	20	5	11	60	21	.249
1995 Chicago	A.L.	OF	28	38	4	7	2	0	1	2	0	.184
1996 Birmingham	Southern	OF	123	473	120	142	34	12	28	77	39	.300
1996 Chicago	A.L.	OF	11	11	1	1	0	0	0	0	0	.091
1997 Nashville	A.A.	OF	30	120	21	33	7	3	6	17	4	.275
1997 Chicago	A.L.	OF	116	379	63	98	18	3	14	55	23	.259
1998 Chicago a	A.L.	OF	141	396	53	83	16	5	8	43	27	.210
1999 Cincinnati	N.L.	OF	146	542	93	139	34	9	21	66	38	.256
2000 Seattle b	A.L.	OF	155	543	96	145	28	4	19	78	24	.267
Major League Totals		6 Yrs.	597	1909	310	473	98	21	63	244	112	.248
Division Series													
2000 Seattle	A.L.	OF	3	12	2	3	0	0	0	2	1	.250
Championship Series													
2000 Seattle	A.L.	OF	6	18	3	2	0	0	0	1	1	.111

a Traded to Cincinnati Reds for infielder Paul Konerko, November 11, 1998.
b Traded to Seattle Mariners with pitcher Brett Tomko, infielder Antonio Perez and pitcher Jake Meyer for outfielder Ken Griffey, February 10, 2000.

CAMINITI, KENNETH GENE
Born, Hanford, California, April 21, 1963.
Bats Both. Throws Right. Height, 6 feet. Weight, 200 pounds.

Year	Club	Lea	Pos	G	AB	R	H	2B	3B	HR	RBI	SB	Avg
1985 Osceola	Fla.St.	3B	126	468	83	133	26	9	4	73	14	.284
1986 Columbus	Southern	3B	137	513	82	154	29	3	12	82	5	.300
1987 Columbus	Southern	3B	95	375	66	122	25	2	15	69	11	.325
1987 Houston	N.L.	3B	63	203	10	50	7	1	3	23	0	.246
1988 Tucson	P.C.	3B	109	416	54	113	24	7	5	66	13	.272
1988 Houston	N.L.	3B	30	83	5	15	2	0	1	7	0	.181
1989 Houston	N.L.	3B	161	585	71	149	31	3	10	72	4	.255
1990 Houston	N.L.	3B	153	541	52	131	20	2	4	51	9	.242
1991 Houston	N.L.	3B	152	574	65	145	30	3	13	80	4	.253
1992 Houston a	N.L.	3B	135	506	68	149	31	2	13	62	10	.294
1993 Houston	N.L.	3B	143	543	75	142	31	0	13	75	8	.262
1994 Houston b	N.L.	3B	111	406	63	115	28	2	18	75	4	.283
1995 San Diego	N.L.	3B	143	526	74	159	33	0	26	94	12	.302
1996 San Diego c-d	N.L.	3B	146	546	109	178	37	2	40	130	11	.326
1997 San Diego e	N.L.	3B	137	486	92	141	28	0	26	90	11	.290
1998 San Diego f-g	N.L.	3B	131	452	87	114	29	0	29	82	6	.252
1999 New Orleans	P.C.	3B	6	20	6	7	4	0	0	3	0	.350
1999 Houston h	N.L.	3B	78	273	45	78	11	1	13	56	6	.286
2000 Houston i-j	N.L.	3B	59	208	42	63	13	0	15	45	3	.303
Major League Totals		14 Yrs.	1642	5932	858	1629	331	16	224	942	88	.275
Division Series													
1996 San Diego	N.L.	3B	4	10	3	3	0	0	3	3	0	.300
1998 San Diego	N.L.	3B	4	14	2	2	0	0	0	0	0	.143
1999 Houston	N.L.	3B	4	17	3	8	0	0	3	8	0	.471
Division Series Totals			12	41	8	13	0	0	6	11	0	.317
Championship Series													
1998 San Diego	N.L.	3B	6	22	3	6	0	0	2	4	0	.273
World Series Record													
1998 San Diego	N.L.	3B	4	14	1	2	1	0	0	1	0	.143

a On disabled list from April 19 to May 11, 1992.
b Traded to San Diego Padres with outfielder Steve Finley, shortstop Andujar Cedeño, pitcher Brian Williams, first baseman Roberto Petagine and player to be named for outfielders Derek Bell and Phil Plantier, shortstop Ricky

Gutierrez, pitchers Pedro Martinez and Doug Brocail and infielder Craig Shipley, December 28, 1994. San Diego received pitcher Sean Fesh to complete trade, May 1, 1995.
c Selected Most Valuable Player in National League for 1996.
d Underwent rotator cuff surgery right arm, November 1996.
e On disabled list from May 12 to May 27, 1997.
f On disabled list from May 2 to May 23, 1998.
g Filed for free agency, October 23, 1998, signed with Houston Astros, November 15, 1998.
h On disabled list from May 22 to August 16, 1999.i On disabled list from June 16 to October 1, 2000.
j Not offered 2001 contract, October 18, 2000, signed with Texas Rangers, December 10, 2000.

CANIZARO, JASON KYLE (JAY)

Born, Beaumont, Texas, July 4, 1973.
Bats Right. Throws Right. Height, 5 feet, 9 inches. Weight, 170 pounds.

Year	Club	Lea	Pos	G	AB	R	H	2B	3B	HR	RBI	SB	Avg
1993 Giants	Arizona		2B-SS	49	180	34	47	10	6	3	41	12	.261
1994 San Jose	California	2B-SS-3B-OF	126	464	77	117	16	2	15	69	12	.252
1995 Shreveport	Texas		2B-SS	126	440	83	129	25	7	12	60	16	.293
1996 Phoenix	P.C.		2B-SS-3B	102	363	50	95	21	2	7	64	14	.262
1996 San Francisco	N.L.		2B-SS	43	120	11	24	4	1	2	8	0	.200
1997 Phoenix	P.C.		2B-3B	23	81	12	16	7	0	2	12	2	.198
1997 Shreveport	Texas		2B-SS-3B	50	176	36	45	9	0	11	38	2	.256
1998 Shreveport	Texas		2B	83	281	47	63	7	1	12	32	5	.224
1998 Fresno	P.C.		2B-OF-SS	45	106	23	24	6	2	6	14	0	.226
1999 Fresno	P.C.		2B	105	364	76	102	20	2	26	78	16	.280
1999 San Francisco a	N.L.		2B	12	18	5	8	2	0	1	9	1	.444
2000 Salt Lake	P.C.		2B	27	101	21	36	9	2	6	32	4	.356
2000 Minnesota	A.L.		2B	102	346	43	93	21	1	7	40	4	.269
Major League Totals			3 Yrs.	157	484	59	125	27	2	10	57	5	.258

a On disabled list from July 10 to August 15, 1999.

CANSECO (CAPAS), JOSE

Born, Havana, Cuba, July 2, 1964.
Bats Right. Throws Right. Height, 6 feet, 4 inches. Weight, 240 pounds.

Year	Club	Lea	Pos	G	AB	R	H	2B	3B	HR	RBI	SB	Avg
1982 Miami	Fla. St.		OF	6	9	0	1	0	0	0	0	0	.111
1982 Idaho Falls	Pioneer		OF-3B	28	57	13	15	3	0	2	7	3	.263
1983 Madison	Midwest		OF	34	88	8	14	4	0	3	10	2	.159
1983 Medford	Northwest		OF	59	197	34	53	15	2	11	40	6	.269
1984 Modesto	Calif.		OF	116	410	61	113	21	2	15	73	10	.276
1985 Huntsville a	Southern		OF	58	211	47	67	10	2	25	80	0	.318
1985 Tacoma	P.C.		OF	60	233	41	81	16	1	11	47	5	.348
1985 Oakland	A.L.		OF	29	96	16	29	3	0	5	13	1	.302
1986 Oakland b	A.L.		OF	157	600	85	144	29	1	33	117	15	.240
1987 Oakland	A.L.		OF	159	630	81	162	35	3	31	113	15	.257
1988 Oakland c	A.L.		OF	158	610	120	187	34	0	*42	*124	40	.307
1989 Huntsville	Southern		OF	9	29	2	6	0	0	0	3	1	.207
1989 Oakland d	A.L.		OF	65	227	40	61	9	1	17	57	6	.269
1990 Oakland e	A.L.		OF	131	481	83	132	14	2	37	101	19	.274
1991 Oakland	A.L.		OF	154	572	115	152	32	1	*44	122	26	.266
1992 Oakland-Texas f-g	A.L.		OF	119	439	74	107	15	0	26	87	6	.244
1993 Texas h-i	A.L.		OF	60	231	30	59	14	1	10	46	6	.255
1994 Texas j	A.L.		DH	111	429	88	121	19	2	31	90	15	.282
1995 Pawtucket	Int.		DH	2	6	1	1	0	0	0	1	0	.167
1995 Boston k-l-m	A.L.		DH-OF	102	396	64	121	25	1	24	81	4	.306
1996 Pawtucket n	Int.		DH	2	5	0	1	0	0	0	0	0	.200
1996 Boston o	A.L.		DH-OF	96	360	68	104	22	1	28	82	3	.289
1997 Oakland p-q-r	A.L.		DH-OF	108	388	56	91	19	0	23	74	8	.235
1998 Toronto s	A.L.		DH-OF	151	583	98	138	26	0	46	107	29	.237
1999 Tampa Bay t	A.L.		DH-OF	113	430	75	120	18	1	34	95	3	.279
2000 Tampa Bay-N.Y. u-v-w	A.L.		DH-OF	98	329	47	83	18	0	15	49	2	.252
Major League Totals			16 Yrs.	1811	6801	1140	1811	332	14	446	1358	198	.266
Division Series													
1995 Boston	A.L.		DH-OF	3	13	0	0	0	0	0	0	0	.000
Championship Series													
1988 Oakland	A.L.		OF	4	16	4	5	1	0	3	4	1	.313
1989 Oakland	A.L.		OF	5	17	1	5	0	0	1	3	0	.294
1990 Oakland	A.L.		OF	4	11	3	2	0	0	0	1	2	.182
Championship Series Totals				413	44	8	12	1	0	4	8	3	.273

33

Year	Club	Lea	Pos	G	AB	R	H	2B	3B	HR	RBI	SB	Avg
	World Series Record												
1988 Oakland	A.L.	OF	5	19	1	1	0	0	1	5	1	.053
1989 Oakland	A.L.	OF	4	14	5	5	0	0	1	3	1	.357
1990 Oakland	A.L.	OF	4	12	1	1	0	0	1	2	0	.083
2000 New York x	A.L.	PH	1	1	0	0	0	0	0	0	0	.000
World Series Totals			14	46	7	7	0	0	3	10	2	.152

a On disabled list from May 14 to June 3, 1985.
b Selected Rookie of the Year in American League for 1986.
c Selected Most Valuable Player in American League for 1988.
d On disabled list from March 23 to July 13, 1989.
e On disabled list from June 8 to June 23, 1990.
f On disabled list from July 1 to July 16, 1992.
g Traded to Texas Rangers for outfielder Ruben Sierra, pitchers Jeff Russell and Bobby Witt, and cash, August 31, 1992.
h Record of 0-0 in one game as pitcher.
i On disabled list from June 25 to end of 1993 season.
j Traded to Boston Red Sox for outfielder Otis Nixon and third baseman Luis Ortiz, December 9, 1994.
k On disabled list from May 15 to June 20, 1995.
l Filed for free agency, October 30, 1995.
m Re-signed with Boston Red Sox December 8, 1995.
n On disabled list from April 24 to May 9 and July 26 to September 17, 1996.
o Traded to Oakland for pitcher John Wasdin, January 27, 1997.
p On disabled list from August 1 to August 20 and August 27 to September 29, 1997.
q Filed for free agency, October 31, 1997.
r Signed as free agent with Toronto Blue Jays, February 4, 1998.
s Filed for free agency, October 22, 1998. Signed with Tampa Bay Devil Rays, December 10, 1998.
t On disabled list from July 10 to August 20, 1999.
u On disabled list from May 25 to July 17, 2000.
v Claimed on waivers by New York Yankees, August 7, 2000.
w Not offered 2001 contract, November 9, 2000.
x Signed with California Angels, January 23, 2001.

CASANOVA, RAUL

Born, Humacao, Puerto Rico, August 23, 1972.
Bats Both. Throws Right. Height, 6 feet. Weight, 192 pounds.

Year	Club	Lea	Pos	G	AB	R	H	2B	3B	HR	RBI	SB	Avg
1990 Mets	Gulf Coast	C	23	65	4	5	0	0	0	1	0	.077
1991 Mets	Gulf Coast	C	32	111	19	27	4	2	0	9	3	.243
1991 Kingsport	Appal.	C	5	18	0	1	0	0	0	0	0	.056
1992 Columbia	So.Atl.	C	5	18	2	3	0	0	0	1	0	.167
1992 Kingsport a	Appal.	C	42	137	25	37	9	1	4	27	3	.270
1993 Waterloo	Midwest	C-3B	76	227	32	58	12	0	6	30	0	.256
1994 Rancho Cuca	California	C	123	471	83	160	27	2	23	120	1	.340
1995 Memphis	Southern	C	89	306	42	83	18	0	12	44	4	.271
1996 Jacksnville	Southern	C	8	30	5	10	2	0	4	9	0	.333
1996 Toledo	Int.	C	49	161	23	44	11	0	8	28	0	.273
1996 Detroit b-c	A.L.	C	25	85	6	16	1	0	4	9	0	.188
1997 Toledo	Int.	C	12	41	1	8	0	0	1	3	0	.195
1997 Detroit	A.L.	C	101	304	27	74	10	1	5	24	1	.243
1998 Toledo	Int.	C	50	171	17	44	8	0	7	26	0	.257
1998 Detroit d	A.L.	C	16	42	4	6	2	0	1	3	0	.143
1999 Toledo	Int.	C	44	160	21	33	9	0	6	23	0	.206
1999 Lakeland	Fla.St.	C	4	12	3	6	2	0	1	6	0	.500
1999 GC Tigers e	Gulf Coast	C	2	5	1	4	0	0	1	1	0	.800
2000 Indianapolis	Int.	PH	20	73	10	21	2	0	5	12	0	.288
2000 Milwaukee f-g-h	N.L.	C	86	231	20	57	13	3	6	36	1	.247
Major League Totals	4 Yrs.		228	662	57	153	26	4	16	72	2	.231

a Sent by New York Mets to San Diego Padres to complete trade for infielder Tony Fernandez, December 14, 1992.
b Traded to Detroit Tigers with pitcher Richie Lewis and outfielder Melvin Nieves for outfielder Todd Steverson, pitcher Sean Bergman and pitcher Cade Gaspar, March 22, 1996.
c On disabled list from June 19 to August 13, 1996.
d On disabled list from April 25 to May 27 and July 21 to September 28, 1998.
e Filed for free agency, October 15, 1999, signed with Colorado Rockies organization, December 15, 1999.
f Released by Colorado Rockies, March 24, 2000.
g Signed with Milwaukee Brewers organization, March 24, 2000.
h Outrighted by Milwaukee Brewers, May 4, 2000, re-signed with Milwaukee Brewers, December 7, 2000.

CASEY, SEAN THOMAS
Born, Willingboro, New Jersey, July 2, 1974.
Bats Left. Throws Right. Height, 6 feet, 4 inches. Weight, 215 pounds.

Year	Club	Lea	Pos	G	AB	R	H	2B	3B	HR	RBI	SB	Avg
1995 Watertown	.....N.Y.-Penn.	1B	55	207	26	68	18	0	2	37	3	.329
1996 Kinston	.........Carolina	1B	92	344	62	114	31	3	12	57	1	.331
1997 Akron	............Eastern	1B	62	241	38	93	19	1	10	66	0	.386
1997 Buffalo	...............A.A.	DH-1B	20	72	12	26	7	0	5	18	0	.361
1997 Cleveland a	..........A.L.	1B	6	10	1	2	0	0	0	1	0	.200
1998 Indianapols	...........Int.	1B	27	95	14	31	8	1	1	13	0	.326
1998 Cincinnati b-c	........N.L.	1B	96	302	44	82	21	1	7	52	1	.272
1999 Cincinnati	...........N.L.	1B	151	594	103	197	42	3	25	99	0	.332
2000 Cincinnati d	...........N.L.	1B	133	480	69	151	33	2	20	85	1	.315
Major League Totals			4 Yrs.	386	1386	217	432	96	6	52	237	2	.312

a On disabled list from April 4 to June 8, 1997.
b Traded to Cincinnati Reds for pitcher Dave Burba, March 30, 1998.
c On disabled list from April 3 to May 5, 1998.
d On disabled list from April 2 to April 18, 2000.

CASTILLA (SORIA), VINICIO (VINNY)
Born, Oaxaca, Mexico, July 4, 1967.
Bats Right. Throws Right. Height, 6 feet, 1 inch. Weight, 180 pounds.

Year	Club	Lea	Pos	G	AB	R	H	2B	3B	HR	RBI	SB	Avg
1987 Saltillo	.........Mexican	3B	13	27	0	5	2	0	0	1	0	.185
1988 Saltillo-Monclova	.....Mex.	SS-3B	50	124	22	30	2	2	5	18	1	.242
1989 Saltillo a	.........Mexican	SS	128	462	70	142	25	13	10	58	11	.307
1990 Sumter	...........So. Atl.	SS	93	339	47	91	15	2	9	53	2	.268
1990 Greenville	.......Southern	SS	46	170	20	40	5	1	4	16	4	.235
1991 Greenville	.......Southern	SS	66	259	34	70	17	3	7	44	0	.270
1991 Richmond	............Int.	SS	67	240	25	54	7	4	7	36	1	.225
1991 Atlanta	..............N.L.	SS	12	5	1	1	0	0	0	0	0	.200
1992 Richmond	............Int.	SS	127	449	49	113	29	1	7	44	1	.252
1992 Atlanta b	............N.L.	3B-SS	9	16	1	4	1	0	0	1	0	.250
1993 Colorado c	............N.L.	SS	105	337	36	86	9	7	9	30	2	.255
1994 Colorado Springs	.....P.C.	3B-2B-SS	22	78	13	19	6	1	1	11	0	.244
1994 Colorado	..N.L.SS-2B-3B-1B	52	130	16	43	11	1	3	18	2	.331
1995 Colorado	...........N.L.	3B-SS	139	527	82	163	34	2	32	90	2	.309
1996 Colorado	...........N.L.	3B	160	629	97	191	34	0	40	113	7	.304
1997 Colorado	...........N.L.	3B	159	612	94	186	25	2	40	113	2	.304
1998 Colorado	...........N.L.	3B-SS	*162	645	108	206	28	4	46	144	5	.319
1999 Colorado d	...........N.L.	3B	158	615	83	169	24	1	33	102	2	.275
2000 Durham	............Int.	3B	2	8	1	3	1	0	1	3	0	.375
2000 Tampa Bay e	...........A.L.	3B	85	331	22	73	9	1	6	42	1	.221
Major League Totals			10 Yrs.	1041	3847	540	1122	175	18	209	653	23	.292
Division Series													
1995 Colorado	........N.L.	3B	4	15	3	7	1	0	3	6	0	.467

a Sold by Saltillo Sarape Makers of Mexican League to Atlanta Braves organization, March 19, 1990.
b Selected by Colorado Rockies in expansion draft, November 17, 1992.
c On disabled list from May 22 to June 4, 1993.
d Traded to Tampa Bay Devil Rays for pitcher Rolando Arrojo and infielder Aaron Ledesma, December 13, 1999.
e On disabled list from March 25 to April 10 and June 14 to July 2 and July 30 to September 3, 2000.

CASTILLO, ALBERTO TERRERO
Born, San Juan De La Maguana, Dominican Republic, February 10, 1970.
Bats Right. Throws Right. Height, 6 feet. Weight, 185 pounds.

Year	Club	Lea	Pos	G	AB	R	H	2B	3B	HR	RBI	SB	Avg
1987 Kingsport	.........Appal.	C-P	7	9	1	1	0	0	0	0	1	.111
1988 Mets	.........Gulf Coast	C	22	68	7	18	4	0	0	10	2	.265
1988 Kingsport	.........Appal.	C	24	75	7	22	3	0	1	14	0	.293
1989 Kingsport	.........Appal.	C-1B	27	74	15	19	4	0	3	12	2	.257
1989 Pittsfield	.......N.Y.-Penn.	C	34	123	13	29	8	0	1	13	2	.236
1990 Columbia	.........So.Atl.	C	30	103	8	24	4	3	1	14	1	.233
1990 Pittsfield	.......N.Y.-Penn.	C-OF-1B	58	187	19	41	8	1	4	24	3	.219
1990 St. Lucie	............Fla.St.	C	3	11	4	4	0	0	1	3	0	.364
1991 Columbia	.........So.Atl.	C	90	267	35	74	20	3	3	47	6	.277
1992 St. Lucie	.........Fla.St.	C	60	162	11	33	6	0	3	17	0	.204
1993 St. Lucie	..........Fla.St.	C	105	333	37	86	21	0	5	42	0	.258
1994 Binghamton	.......Eastern	C-1B	90	315	33	78	14	0	7	42	1	.248
1995 Norfolk	..............Int.	C	69	217	23	58	13	1	4	31	2	.267

35

Year	Club	Lea	Pos	G	AB	R	H	2B	3B	HR	RBI	SB	Avg
1995 New York	...........N.L.	C	13	29	2	3	0	0	0	0	1	.103
1996 Norfolk	...............Int.	C	113	341	34	71	12	1	11	39	2	.208
1996 New York	...........N.L.	C	6	11	1	4	0	0	0	0	0	.364
1997 Norfolk	...............Int.	C-OF	34	83	4	18	1	0	1	8	1	.217
1997 New York	...........N.L.	C	35	59	3	12	1	0	0	7	0	.203
1998 Norfolk	...............Int.	C-OF	21	49	4	9	2	0	1	6	0	.184
1998 New York a-b	...N.L.	C	38	83	13	17	4	0	2	7	0	.205
1999 St. Louis c	...........N.L.	C	93	255	21	67	8	0	4	31	0	.263
2000 Toronto	...........A.L.	C	66	185	14	39	7	0	1	16	0	.211
Major League Totals	....	6 Yrs.	251	622	54	142	20	0	7	61	1	.228

a Filed for free agency, October 16, 1998, signed with Philadelphia Phillies organization, October 29, 1998.
b Selected by St. Louis Cardinals in Rule V draft, December 14, 1998.
c Traded to Toronto Blue Jays with pitcher Lance Painter and pitcher Matt DeWitt for pitcher Pat Hentgen and pitcher Paul Spoljaric, November 11, 1999.

CASTILLO, LUIS ANTONIO
Born, San Pedro De Macoris, Dominican Republic, September 12, 1975.
Bats Both. Throws Right. Height, 5 feet, 11 inches. Weight, 145 pounds.

Year	Club	Lea	Pos	G	AB	R	H	2B	3B	HR	RBI	SB	Avg
1993 Florida	.........Dominican	SS	69	266	48	75	7	1	4	31	9	.282
1994 Marlins	.........Gulf Coast	2B-SS	57	216	49	57	8	0	0	16	31	.264
1995 Kane County	......Midwest	2B	89	340	71	111	4	4	0	23	41	.326
1996 Portland	.......Eastern	2B	109	420	83	133	15	7	1	35	51	.317
1996 Florida	.............N.L.	2B	41	164	26	43	2	1	1	8	17	.262
1997 Florida	.............N.L.	2B	75	263	27	63	8	0	0	8	16	.240
1997 Charlotte	.............Int.	2B	37	130	25	46	5	0	0	5	8	.354
1998 Charlotte	.............Int.	2B	100	381	74	109	11	2	0	15	41	.286
1998 Florida	.............N.L.	2B	44	153	21	31	3	2	1	10	3	.203
1999 Florida	.............N.L.	2B	128	487	76	147	23	4	0	28	50	.302
2000 Calgary	.............P.C.	2B	4	13	4	4	1	1	0	0	1	.308
2000 Florida a	.............N.L.	2B	136	539	101	180	17	3	2	17	*62	.334
Major League Totals	....	5 Yrs.	424	1606	251	464	53	10	4	71	148	.289

a On disabled list from April 16 to May 5, 2000.

CASTRO, JUAN GABRIEL
Born, Los Mochis, Mexico, June 20, 1972.
Bats Right. Throws Right. Height, 5 feet, 10 inches. Weight, 165 pounds.

Year	Club	Lea	Pos	G	AB	R	H	2B	3B	HR	RBI	SB	Avg
1991 Great Falls	.....Pioneer	SS-2B	60	217	36	60	4	2	1	27	7	.276
1992 Bakersfield	...California	SS	113	446	56	116	15	4	4	42	14	.260
1993 San Antonio	.....Texas	SS-2B	118	424	55	117	23	8	7	41	12	.276
1994 San Antonio	.....Texas	SS	123	445	55	128	25	4	4	44	4	.288
1995 Albuquerque	......P.C.	SS-2B	104	341	51	91	18	4	3	43	4	.267
1995 Los Angeles	.......N.L.	3B-SS	11	4	0	1	0	0	0	0	0	.250
1996 Albuquerque	......P.C.	3B-SS-2B	17	56	12	21	4	2	1	8	1	.375
1996 Los Angeles	.......N.L.	SS-3B-2B-OF	70	132	16	26	5	3	0	5	1	.197
1997 Albuquerque	......P.C.	SS-2B	27	101	11	31	5	2	2	11	1	.307
1997 Los Angeles a	.....N.L.	SS-2B-3B	40	75	3	11	3	1	0	4	0	.147
1998 Los Angeles	.......N.L.	SS-2B-3B	89	220	25	43	7	0	2	14	0	.195
1999 Albuquerque	......P.C.	SS	116	423	52	116	25	4	7	51	2	.274
1999 Los Angeles	.......N.L.	2B-SS	2	1	0	0	0	0	0	0	0	.000
2000 Louisville	.........Int.	SS	19	60	9	19	5	1	2	10	0	.317
2000 Cincinnati b-c	...N.L.	SS-2B-3B	82	224	20	54	12	2	4	23	0	.241
Major League Totals	....	6 Yrs.	294	656	64	135	27	6	6	46	1	.206
Division Series													
1996 Los Angeles	.......N.L.	2B	2	5	0	1	1	0	0	1	0	.200

a On disabled list from June 5 to August 2, 1997.
b Traded to Cincinnati Reds for player to be named later, April 1, 2000.
c Los Angeles Dodgers received pitcher Kenny Kutz to complete trade, June 7, 2000.

CATALANOTTO, FRANK JOHN
Born, Smithtown, New York, April 27, 1974.
Bats Left. Throws Right. Height, 6 feet. Weight, 170 pounds.

Year	Club	Lea	Pos	G	AB	R	H	2B	3B	HR	RBI	SB	Avg
1992 Bristol	...........Appal.	2B-1B	21	50	6	10	2	0	0	4	0	.200
1993 Bristol	...........Appal.	2B	55	199	37	61	9	5	3	22	3	.307

Year	Club	Lea	Pos	G	AB	R	H	2B	3B	HR	RBI	SB	Avg
1994 Fayettevlle	So. Atl.	2B	119	458	72	149	24	8	3	56	4	.325
1995 Jacksnville	Southern	2B	134	491	66	111	19	5	8	48	13	.226
1996 Jacksnville	Southern	2B	132	497	105	148	34	6	17	67	15	.298
1997 Toledo	Int.	2B-3B-OF	134	500	75	150	32	3	16	68	12	.300
1997 Detroit	A.L.	2B	13	26	2	8	2	0	0	3	0	.308
1998 Toledo	Int.	1B-2B	28	105	20	35	6	3	4	28	0	.333
1998 Detroit	A.L.	2B-1B-3B	89	213	23	60	13	2	6	25	3	.282
1999 Detroit a	A.L.	1B-2B-3B	100	286	41	79	19	0	11	35	3	.276
2000 Oklahoma	P.C.	2B	3	11	2	3	0	0	0	1	0	.273
2000 Texas b	A.L.	2B-1B-OF	103	282	55	82	13	2	10	42	6	.291
Major League Totals		4 Yrs.	305	807	121	229	47	4	27	105	12	.284

a Traded to Texas Rangers with pitcher Justin Thompson, pitcher Francisco Cordero, pitcher Alan Webb, outfielder Gabe Kapler and catcher Bill Haselman for outfielder Juan Gonzalez, pitcher Danny Patterson and catcher Greg Zaun, November 2, 1999.

b On disabled list from April 22 to May 14, 2000.

CEDENO, ROGER LEANDRO

Born, Valencia, Venezuela, August 16, 1974.
Bats Both. Throws Right. Height, 6 feet, 1 inch. Weight, 165 pounds.

Year	Club	Lea	Pos	G	AB	R	H	2B	3B	HR	RBI	SB	Avg
1992 Great Falls	Pioneer	OF	69	256	60	81	6	5	2	27	40	.316
1993 San Antonio	Texas	OF	122	465	70	134	12	8	4	30	28	.288
1993 Albuquerque	P.C.	OF	6	18	1	4	1	1	0	4	0	.222
1994 Albuquerque	P.C.	OF	104	383	84	123	18	5	4	49	30	.321
1995 Albuquerque	P.C.	OF	99	367	67	112	19	9	2	44	23	.305
1995 Los Angeles	N.L.	OF	40	42	4	10	2	0	0	3	1	.238
1996 Albuquerque	P.C.	OF	33	125	16	28	2	3	1	10	6	.224
1996 Los Angeles	N.L.	OF	86	211	26	52	11	1	2	18	5	.246
1997 Albuquerque	P.C.	OF	29	113	21	40	4	4	2	9	5	.354
1997 Los Angeles a	N.L.	OF	80	194	31	53	10	2	3	17	9	.273
1998 Vero Beach	Fla.St.	OF	6	21	5	9	0	1	1	6	1	.429
1998 Los Angeles b-c	N.L.	OF	105	240	33	58	11	1	2	17	8	.242
1999 New York d	N.L.	OF-2B	155	453	90	142	23	4	4	36	66	.313
2000 New Orleans	P.C.	OF	6	20	2	7	0	1	0	3	1	.350
2000 Houston e-f	N.L.	OF	74	259	54	73	2	5	6	26	25	.282
Major League Totals		6 Yrs.	540	1399	238	388	59	13	17	117	114	.277
Division Series												
1999 New York	N.L.	OF	4	7	1	2	0	0	0	2	1	.286
Championship Series												
1999 New York	N.L.	OF	5	12	2	6	1	0	0	1	2	.500

a On disabled list from April 1 to April 21 and August 26 to September 29, 1997.

b On disabled list from March 31 to April 24, 1998.

c Traded to New York Mets with catcher Charles Johnson for catcher Todd Hundley and pitcher Arnie Gooch, December 1, 1998.

d Traded to Houston Astros with pitcher Octavio Dotel and pitcher Kyle Kessel for pitcher Mike Hampton and outfielder Derek Bell, December 23, 1999.

e On disabled list from May 26 to August 17, 2000.

f Traded to Detroit Tigers with pitcher Chris Holt and catcher Mitch Meluskey for catcher Brad Ausmus, pitcher Doug Brocail and pitcher Nelson Cruz, December 11, 2000.

CHAVEZ, ERIC CESAR

Born, Los Angeles, California, December 7, 1977.
Bats Left. Throws Right. Height, 6 feet, 1 inch. Weight, 195 pounds.

Year	Club	Lea	Pos	G	AB	R	H	2B	3B	HR	RBI	SB	Avg
1997 Visalia	California	3B	134	520	67	141	30	3	18	100	13	.271
1998 Huntsville	Southern	3B	88	335	66	110	27	1	22	86	12	.328
1998 Edmonton	P.C.	3B	47	194	38	63	18	0	11	40	2	.325
1998 Oakland	A.L.	3B	16	45	6	14	4	1	0	6	1	.311
1999 Oakland a	A.L.	3B-SS	115	356	47	88	21	2	13	50	1	.247
2000 Oakland	A.L.	3B-SS	153	501	89	139	23	4	26	86	2	.277
Major League Totals		3 Yrs.	284	902	142	241	48	7	39	142	4	.267
Division Series												
2000 Oakland	A.L.	3B	5	21	4	7	3	0	0	4	0	.333

a On disabled list from August 21 to September 19, 1999.

CHRISTENSON, RYAN ALAN
Born, Redlands, California, March 28, 1974.
Bats Right. Throws Right. Height, 5 feet, 11 inches. Weight, 175 pounds.

Year	Club	Lea	Pos	G	AB	R	H	2B	3B	HR	RBI	SB	Avg
1995	Sou Oregon	Northwest	OF	49	158	14	30	4	1	1	16	5	.190
1996	Sou Oregon	Northwest	OF	36	136	31	39	11	0	5	21	8	.287
1996	W Michigan	Midwest	OF-3B	33	122	21	38	2	2	2	18	2	.311
1997	Visalia	California	OF	83	308	69	90	18	8	13	54	20	.292
1997	Huntsville	Southern	OF	29	120	39	44	9	3	2	18	5	.367
1997	Edmonton	P.C.	OF	16	49	12	14	2	2	2	5	2	.286
1998	Edmonton	P.C.	OF	22	88	17	23	6	1	1	7	4	.261
1998	Oakland	A.L.	OF	117	370	56	95	22	2	5	40	5	.257
1999	Vancouver	P.C.	OF	33	128	30	44	8	1	1	16	7	.344
1999	Oakland	A.L.	OF	106	268	41	56	12	1	4	24	7	.209
2000	Oakland	A.L.	OF	121	129	31	32	2	2	4	18	1	.248
Major League Totals			3 Yrs.	344	767	128	183	36	5	13	82	13	.239
Division Series													
2000	Oakland	A.L.	OF	2	2	0	1	0	0	0	1	0	.500

CIRILLO, JEFFREY HOWARD
Born, Pasadena, California, September 23, 1969.
Bats Right. Throws Right. Height, 6 feet, 2 inches. Weight, 190 pounds.

Year	Club	Lea	Pos	G	AB	R	H	2B	3B	HR	RBI	SB	Avg
1991	Helena	Pioneer	3B-OF	*70	286	60	100	16	2	10	51	3	.350
1992	Stockton	California	3B	7	27	2	6	1	0	0	5	0	.222
1992	Beloit	Midwest	3B-2B	126	444	65	135	27	3	9	71	21	.304
1993	El Paso	Texas	2B-3B	67	249	53	85	16	2	9	41	2	.341
1993	New Orleans	A.A.	3B-2B-SS	58	215	31	63	13	2	3	32	2	.293
1994	New Orleans	A.A.	3B-2B-SS	61	236	45	73	18	2	10	46	4	.309
1994	Milwaukee	A.L.	3B-2B	39	126	17	30	9	0	3	12	0	.238
1995	Milwaukee	A.L.	3B-2B-1B-SS	125	328	57	91	19	4	9	39	7	.277
1996	Milwaukee	A.L.	3B-1B-2B	158	566	101	184	46	5	15	83	4	.325
1997	Milwaukee	A.L.	3B	154	580	74	167	46	2	10	82	4	.288
1998	Milwaukee	N.L.	3B-1B	156	604	97	194	31	1	14	68	10	.321
1999	Milwaukee a	N.L.	3B	157	607	98	198	35	1	15	88	7	.326
2000	Colorado	N.L.	3B	157	598	111	195	53	2	11	115	3	.326
Major League Totals			7 Yrs.	946	3409	555	1059	239	15	77	487	35	.311

a Traded to Colorado Rockies with pitcher Scott Karl for catcher Henry Blanco, pitcher Jamey Wright and pitcher Justin Miller, December 13, 1999.

CLARK, ANTHONY CHRISTOPHER (TONY)
Born, Newton, Kansas, June 15, 1972.
Bats Both. Throws Right. Height, 6 feet, 7 inches. Weight, 240 pounds.

Year	Club	Lea	Pos	G	AB	R	H	2B	3B	HR	RBI	SB	Avg
1990	Bristol	Appal.	OF	25	73	2	12	2	0	1	8	0	.164
1991	Niagara Falls a	N.Y.-Penn.					INJURED—Did Not Play						
1992	Niagara Falls b	N.Y.-Penn.	OF	27	85	12	26	9	0	5	17	1	.306
1993	Lakeland c	Fla. St.	OF	36	117	14	31	4	14	1	22	0	.265
1994	Trenton	Eastern	1B	107	394	50	110	25	0	21	86	0	.279
1994	Toledo	Int.	1B	25	92	10	24	4	0	2	13	2	.261
1995	Toledo	Int.	1B	110	405	50	98	17	2	14	63	0	.242
1995	Detroit	A.L.	1B	27	101	10	24	5	1	3	11	0	.238
1996	Toledo	Int.	1B	55	194	42	58	7	1	14	36	1	.299
1996	Detroit	A.L.	1B	100	376	56	94	14	0	27	72	0	.250
1997	Detroit	A.L.	1B	159	580	105	160	28	3	32	117	1	.276
1998	Detroit	A.L.	1B	157	602	84	175	37	0	34	103	3	.291
1999	Toledo	Int.	1B	1	3	0	0	0	0	0	0	0	.000
1999	Detroit d	A.L.	1B	143	536	74	150	29	0	31	99	2	.280
2000	Toledo	Int.	1B	6	22	1	2	1	0	1	2	0	.091
2000	Detroit e	A.L.	1B	60	208	32	57	14	0	13	37	0	.274
Major League Totals			6 Yrs.	646	2403	361	660	127	4	140	439	6	.275

a On disabled list from May 30 to June 17; transferred to temporary inactive list from June 17 to end of 1991 season.
b On temporary inactive list from August 17 to end of 1992 season.
c On disabled list from August 24 to end of 1993 season.
d On disabled list from May 26 to June 10, 1999.
e On disabled list from May 13 to June 11 and July 15 to August 31 and September 17 to November 6, 2000.

CLARK, WILLIAM NUSCHLER, JR.

Born, New Orleans, Louisiana, March 13, 1964.
Bats Left. Throws Left. Height, 6 feet, 1 inch. Weight, 196 pounds.

Year	Club	Lea	Pos	G	AB	R	H	2B	3B	HR	RBI	SB	Avg
1985	Fresno	California	1B-OF	65	217	41	67	14	0	10	48	11	.309
1986	San Francisco a	N.L.	1B	111	408	66	117	27	2	11	41	4	.287
1986	Phoenix	P.C.	DH	6	20	3	5	0	0	0	1	1	.250
1987	San Francisco	N.L.	1B	150	529	89	163	29	5	35	91	5	.308
1988	San Francisco	N.L.	1B	*162	575	102	162	31	6	29	*109	9	.282
1989	San Francisco	N.L.	1B	159	588	*104	196	38	9	23	111	8	.333
1990	San Francisco	N.L.	1B	154	600	91	177	25	5	19	95	8	.295
1991	San Francisco	N.L.	1B	148	565	84	170	32	7	29	116	4	.301
1992	San Francisco	N.L.	1B	144	513	69	154	40	1	16	73	12	.300
1993	San Francisco b-c	N.L.	1B	132	491	82	139	27	2	14	73	2	.283
1994	Texas	A.L.	1B	110	389	73	128	24	2	13	80	5	.329
1995	Texas	A.L.	1B	123	454	85	137	27	3	16	92	0	.302
1996	Tulsa	Texas	1B	3	9	3	2	0	0	0	0	0	.222
1996	Texas d	A.L.	1B	117	436	69	124	25	1	13	72	2	.284
1997	Texas	A.L.	1B	110	393	56	128	29	1	12	51	0	.326
1998	Texas f	A.L.	1B	149	554	98	169	41	1	23	102	1	.305
1999	Baltimore g	A.L.	1B	77	251	40	76	15	0	10	29	2	.303
2000	Baltimore h-i	A.L.	1B	79	256	49	77	15	1	9	28	4	.301
2000	St. Louis j	N.L.	1B	51	171	29	59	15	1	12	42	1	.345
Major League Totals			15 Yrs.	1976	7173	1186	2176	440	47	284	1205	67	.303
Division Series													
1996	Texas	A.L.	1B	4	16	1	2	0	0	0	0	0	.125
1998	Texas	A.L.	1B	3	11	0	1	0	0	0	0	0	.091
2000	St. Louis	N.L.	1B	3	12	3	3	0	0	1	4	0	.250
Division Series Totals				10	39	4	6	0	0	1	4	0	.154
Championship Series													
1987	San Francisco	N.L.	1B	7	25	3	9	2	0	1	3	1	.360
1989	San Francisco	N.L.	1B	5	20	8	13	3	1	2	8	0	.650
2000	St. Louis	N.L.	1B	5	17	3	7	2	0	1	1	0	.412
Championship Series Totals				17	62	14	29	7	1	4	12	1	.468
World Series Record													
1989	San Francisco	N.L.	1B	4	16	2	4	1	0	0	0	0	.250

a On disabled list from June 4 to July 24, 1986.
b On disabled list from August 26 to September 10, 1993.
c Filed for free agency, October 25; signed with Texas Rangers, November 22, 1993.
d On disabled list from June 8 to June 23 and June 30 to July 16 and July 17 to August 4, 1996.
e On disabled list from April 1 to April 18 and August 25 to September 29, 1997.
f Filed for free agency, November 5, 1998, signed with Baltimore Orioles, December 5, 1998.
g On disabled list from April 19 to May 25 and August 14 to October 13, 1999.
h On disabled list from May 3 to May 17, 2000.
i Traded to St. Louis Cardinals for infielder Jose Leon, July 31, 2000.
j Announced retirement, November 2, 2000.

CLAYTON, ROYCE SPENCER

Born, Burbank, California, January 2, 1970.
Bats Right. Throws Right. Height, 6 feet. Weight, 183 pounds.

Year	Club	Lea	Pos	G	AB	R	H	2B	3B	HR	RBI	SB	Avg
1988	Everett	Northwest	SS	60	212	35	55	4	0	3	29	10	.259
1989	Clinton	Midwest	SS	104	385	39	91	13	3	0	24	28	.236
1989	San Jose	California	SS	28	92	5	11	2	0	0	4	10	.120
1990	San Jose	California	SS	123	460	80	123	15	10	7	71	33	.267
1991	Shreveport	Texas	SS	126	485	84	136	22	8	5	68	36	.280
1991	San Francisco	N.L.	SS	9	26	0	3	1	0	0	2	0	.115
1992	Phoenix	P.C.	SS	48	192	30	46	6	2	3	18	15	.240
1992	San Francisco	N.L.	SS-3B	98	321	31	72	7	4	4	24	8	.224
1993	San Francisco	N.L.	SS	153	549	54	155	21	5	6	70	11	.282
1994	San Francisco	N.L.	SS	108	385	38	91	14	6	3	30	23	.236
1995	San Francisco a	N.L.	SS	138	509	56	124	29	3	5	58	24	.244
1996	St. Louis	N.L.	SS	129	491	64	136	20	4	6	35	33	.277
1997	St. Louis	N.L.	SS	154	576	75	153	39	5	9	61	30	.266
1998	St. Louis	N.L.	SS	90	355	59	83	19	1	4	29	19	.234
1998	Texas b-c-d-e	A.L.	SS	52	186	30	53	12	1	5	24	5	.285
1999	Oklahoma	P.C.	SS	2	7	1	1	0	0	0	1	0	.143
1999	Texas f	A.L.	SS	133	465	69	134	21	5	14	52	8	.288
2000	Texas g	A.L.	SS	148	513	70	124	21	5	14	54	11	.242
Major League Totals			10 Yrs.	1212	4376	546	1128	204	39	70	439	172	.258

Year	Club	Lea	Pos	G	AB	R	H	2B	3B	HR	RBI	SB	Avg
	Division Series												
1996 St. Louis	...........N.L.		SS	2	6	1	2	0	0	0	0	0	.333
1998 Texas	...............A.L.		SS	3	9	0	2	0	0	0	0	0	.22
1999 Texas	...............A.L.		SS	3	10	0	0	0	0	0	0	0	.000
Division Series Totals	....			8	25	1	4	0	0	0	0	0	.160
	Championship Series												
1996 St. Louis	...........N.L.		SS	5	20	4	7	0	0	0	0	1	.350

a Traded from San Francisco Giants to St. Louis Cardinals for pitchers Allen Watson, Rich DeLucia, and Doug Creek, December 14, 1995.

b On disabled list from June 24 to July 9, 1998.

c Traded to Texas Rangers with pitcher Todd Stottlemyre for pitcher Darren Oliver, infielder Fernando Tatis and player to be named later, July 31, 1998.

d St. Louis Cardinals received infielder Mark Little to complete trade, August 9, 1998.

e Filed for free agency, October 23, 1998, re-signed with Texas Rangers, November 30, 1998.

f On disabled list from May 1 to May 21, 1999.

g Traded to Chicago White Sox for pitcher Aaron Myette and pitcher Brian Schmack, December 14, 2000.

COLBRUNN, GREGORY JOSEPH

Born Fontana, California, July 26, 1969.
Bats Right. Throws Right. Height, 6 feet. Weight, 200 pounds.

Year	Club	Lea	Pos	G	AB	R	H	2B	3B	HR	RBI	SB	Avg
1988 Rockford	.........Midwest		C	115	417	55	111	18	2	7	46	5	.266
1989 West Palm Beach	....Fla. St.		C	59	228	20	54	8	0	0	25	3	.237
1989 Jacksonville	......Southern		C	55	178	21	49	11	1	3	18	0	.275
1990 Jacksonville	......Southern		C	125	458	57	138	29	1	13	76	1	.301
1991 Indianapolis a	.........A.A.		INJURED—Did Not Play										
1992 Indianapolis	...........A.A.		1B	57	216	32	66	19	1	11	48	1	.306
1992 Montreal b	..............N.L.		1B	52	168	12	45	8	0	2	18	3	.268
1993 West Palm Beach	....Fla. St.		1B	8	31	6	12	2	1	1	5	0	.387
1993 Ottawa	..............Int.		1B	6	22	4	6	1	0	0	8	1	.273
1993 Montreal c-d	..........N.L.		1B	70	153	15	39	9	0	4	23	4	.255
1994 Edmonton	...........P.C.		1B	7	17	2	4	0	0	1	2	0	.235
1994 Brevard City	........Fla. St.		1B	7	11	3	6	2	0	1	2	0	.545
1994 Florida e	.............N.L.		1B	47	155	17	47	10	0	6	31	1	.303
1995 Florida	..............N.L.		1B	138	528	70	146	22	1	23	89	11	.277
1996 Florida f-g-h	..........N.L.		1B	141	511	60	146	26	2	16	69	4	.286
1997 Minnesota i	...........A.L.		1B	70	217	24	61	14	0	5	26	1	.281
1997 Atlanta j-k	...........N.L.		1B	28	54	3	15	3	0	2	9	0	.278
1998 Colorado-Atlanta m-n-o	.N.L.		1B-OF-C	90	166	18	51	11	2	3	23	4	.307
1999 Arizona	..............N.L.		1B-3B	67	135	20	44	5	3	5	24	1	.326
2000 Arizona	..............N.L.		1B-3B	116	329	48	103	22	1	15	57	0	.313
Major League Totals	....	9 Yrs.		819	2416	287	697	130	9	81	369	29	.288
	Division Series												
1997 Atlanta	.............N.L.		PH	1	1	0	1	0	0	0	2	0	1.000
1998 Atlanta	.............N.L.		PH	2	2	0	0	0	0	0	0	0	.000
1999 Arizona	.............N.L.		1B	2	5	1	2	1	0	1	2	0	.400
Division Series Totals	....			5	8	1	3	1	0	1	4	0	.375
	Championship Series												
1997 Atlanta	.............N.L.		PH	3	3	0	2	0	0	0	0	0	.667
1998 Atlanta	.............N.L.		PH	6	6	0	2	0	0	0	0	0	.333
Championship Series Totals	......			9	9	0	4	0	0	0	0	0	.444

a On disabled list from March 28 to end of 1991 season.

b On disabled list from August 2 to August 18, 1992.

c On disabled list from April 4 to April 23 and July 19 to end of 1993 season.

d Claimed on waivers by Florida Marlins, October 7, 1993.

e On disabled list from April 9 to May 27 and July 15 to July 30, 1994.

f On disabled list from July 24 to August 8, 1996.

g Florida declined to offer a 1997 contract, December 20, 1996.

h Signed with Minnesota Twins organization, January 24, 1997.

i Traded to Atlanta Braves for player to be named later, August 14, 1997.

j Minnesota Twins received outfielder Marc Lewis to complete trade, October 1, 1997.

k Filed for free agency, October 23, 1997.

l Signed with Colorado Rockies organization, December 23, 1997.

m Traded to Atlanta Braves for pitcher David Cortes, pitcher Mike Porzio and player to be named later, July 30, 1998.

n Colorado Rockies received pitcher Anthony Briggs to complete trade, September 9, 1998.

o Filed for free agency, October 23, 1998, signed with Arizona Diamondbacks, November 11, 1998.

CONINE, JEFFREY GUY

Born, Tacoma, Washington, June 27, 1966.
Bats Right. Throws Right. Height, 6 feet, 1 inch. Weight, 220 pounds.

Year Club	Lea	Pos	G	AB	R	H	2B	3B	HR	RBI	SB	Avg
1988 Baseball City ....Fla. St.		1B-3B	118	415	63	112	23	9	10	59	26	.272
1989 Baseball City ....Fla. St.		1B	113	425	89	116	12	7	14	60	32	.273
1990 Memphis ....Southern		1B-3B	137	487	89	156	37	8	15	95	21	.320
1990 Kansas City ...........A.L.		1B	9	20	3	5	2	0	0	2	0	.250
1991 Omaha a .............A.A.		1B-OF	51	171	23	44	9	1	3	15	0	.257
1992 Omaha .............A.A.		1B-OF	110	397	69	120	24	5	20	72	4	.302
1992 Kansas City b .........A.L.		OF-1B	28	91	10	23	5	2	0	9	0	.253
1993 Florida ..............N.L.		OF-1B	*162	595	75	174	24	3	12	79	2	.292
1994 Florida ..............N.L.		OF-1B	115	451	60	144	27	6	18	82	1	.319
1995 Florida ..............N.L.		OF-1B	133	483	72	146	26	2	25	105	2	.302
1996 Florida ..............N.L.		OF-1B	157	597	84	175	32	2	26	95	1	.293
1997 Florida c ............N.L.		1B-OF	151	405	46	98	13	1	17	61	2	.242
1998 Omaha .............P.C.		OF	2	9	0	0	0	0	0	0	0	.000
1998 Kansas City d .........A.L.		OF-1B	93	309	30	79	26	0	8	43	3	.256
1999 Baltimore e-f .........A.L.		1B-OF-3B	139	444	54	129	31	1	13	75	0	.291
2000 Baltimore ...........A.L.		3B-1B-OF	119	409	53	116	20	2	13	46	4	.284
Major League Totals		10 Yrs.	1106	3804	487	1089	206	19	132	597	15	.286

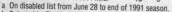

Division Series
1997 Florida .............N.L.		1B	3	11	3	4	1	0	0	0	0	.364

Championship Series
1997 Florida .............N.L.		1B	6	18	1	2	0	0	0	1	0	.111

World Series Record
1997 Florida .............N.L.		1B	6	13	1	3	0	0	0	2	0	.231

a On disabled list from June 28 to end of 1991 season.
b Selected by Florida Marlins in expansion draft, November 17, 1992.
c Traded to Kansas City Royals for pitcher Blaine Mull, November 21, 1997.
d On disabled list from March 31 to May 5 and July 27 to August 19, 1998.
e Traded to Baltimore Orioles for pitcher Chris Fussell, April 2, 1999.
f Filed for free agency, November 5, 1999. Re-signed with Baltimore Orioles, December 16, 1999.

COOMER, RONALD BRYAN

Born, Crest Hill, Illinois, November 18, 1966.
Bats Right. Throws Right. Height, 5 feet, 11 inches. Weight, 195 pounds.

Year Club	Lea	Pos	G	AB	R	H	2B	3B	HR	RBI	SB	Avg
1987 Medford .....Northwest		3B-1B-P	45	168	23	58	10	2	1	26	1	.345
1988 Modesto .....California		DH-3B-1B	131	495	67	138	23	2	17	85	2	.279
1989 Madison ......Midwest		3B-1B	61	216	28	69	15	0	4	28	0	.319
1990 Huntsville ...Southern		2B-1B-3B	66	194	22	43	7	0	3	27	3	.222
1991 Birmingham ..Southern		3B-1B-2B	137	505	81	129	27	5	13	76	0	.255
1992 Vancouver ........P.C.		3B	86	262	29	62	10	0	9	40	3	.237
1993 Birmingham ..Southern		3B-1B	69	262	44	85	18	0	13	50	1	.324
1993 Nashville .........A.A.		3B	59	211	34	66	19	0	13	51	1	.313
1994 Albuquerque .....P.C.		3B-2B	127	535	89	181	34	6	22	123	4	.338
1995 Albuquerque .....P.C.		3B-1B	85	323	54	104	23	2	16	76	5	.322
1995 Minnesota a ......A.L.		1B-3B-OF	37	101	15	26	3	1	5	19	0	.257
1996 Minnesota .......A.L.		1B-OF-3B	95	233	34	69	12	1	12	41	3	.296
1997 Minnesota .......A.L.		3B-1B-OF	140	523	63	156	30	2	13	85	4	.298
1998 Minnesota .......A.L.		3B-1B-OF	137	529	54	146	22	1	15	72	2	.276
1999 Minnesota .......A.L.		1B-3B-OF	127	467	53	123	25	1	16	65	2	.263
2000 Minnesota b ......A.L.		1B-3B	140	544	64	147	29	1	16	82	2	.270
Major League Totals		6 Yrs.	676	2397	283	667	121	7	77	364	13	.278

a Traded to Minnesota Twins with pitcher Jose Parra and pitcher Greg Hansell for pitcher Kevin Tapani and pitcher Mark Guthrie, July 31, 1995. Minnesota received outfielder Chris Latham to complete trade, October 30, 1995.
b Not offered 2001 contract, December 21, 2000, signed with Chicago Cubs, January 10, 2001.

CORA, JOSE ALEXANDER (ALEX)

Born, Caguas, Puerto Rico, October 18, 1975.
Bats Left. Throws Right. Height, 6 feet. Weight, 180 pounds.

Year Club	Lea	Pos	G	AB	R	H	2B	3B	HR	RBI	SB	AVG
1996 Vero Beach ....Fla.St.		SS-OF	61	214	26	55	5	4	0	26	5	.257
1997 San Antonio ......Texas		SS	127	448	52	105	20	4	3	48	12	.234
1998 Albuquerque .........P.C.		SS-2B	81	299	42	79	16	6	5	45	10	.264
1998 Los Angeles .........N.L.		SS-2B	29	33	1	4	0	1	0	0	0	.121
1999 Albuquerque .........P.C.		SS	80	302	51	93	11	7	4	37	9	.308
1999 Los Angeles a ........N.L.		SS-2B	11	30	2	5	1	0	0	3	0	.167
2000 Albuquerque .........P.C.		SS	30	110	18	41	8	3	0	20	5	.373

Year Club	Lea	Pos	G	AB	R	H	2B	3B	HR	RBI	SB	Avg
2000 Los Angeles .........N.L.		SS-2B	109	353	39	84	18	6	4	32	4	.238
Major League Totals		3 Yrs.	149	416	42	93	19	7	4	35	4	.224

a On disabled list from March 25 to June 27, 1999.

CORDERO, WILFRED NIEVA

Born, Mayaguez, Puerto Rico, October 3, 1971.
Bats Right. Throws Right. Height, 6 feet, 2 inches. Weight, 190 pounds.

Year Club	Lea	Pos	G	AB	R	H	2B	3B	HR	RBI	SB	Avg
1988 Jamestown ......N.Y.-Penn.		SS	52	190	18	49	3	0	2	22	3	.258
1989 West Palm Beach ....Fla. St.		SS	78	289	37	80	12	2	6	29	2	.277
1989 Jacksonville ......Southern		SS	39	121	9	26	6	1	3	17	1	.215
1990 Jacksonville ......Southern		SS	131	444	63	104	18	4	7	40	9	.234
1991 Indianapolis a .........A.A.		SS	98	360	48	94	16	4	11	52	9	.261
1992 Indianapolis b .........A.A.		SS	52	204	32	64	11	1	6	27	6	.314
1992 Montreal .............N.L.		SS-2B	45	126	17	38	4	1	2	8	0	.302
1993 Montreal .............N.L.		SS-3B	138	475	56	118	32	2	10	58	12	.248
1994 Montreal .............N.L.		SS	110	415	65	122	30	3	15	63	16	.294
1995 Montreal c ............N.L.		SS-OF	131	514	64	147	35	2	10	49	9	.286
1996 Red Sox ......Gulf Coast		DH-2B	3	10	1	3	0	0	1	3	0	.300
1996 Pawtucket ....Int.		2B	4	10	2	3	1	0	1	2	0	.300
1996 Boston d ...........A.L.		2B-1B	59	198	29	57	14	0	3	37	2	.288
1997 Boston e ...........A.L.		OF-2B	140	570	82	160	26	3	18	72	1	.281
1998 Birmingham ......Southern		1B	11	35	6	10	2	0	2	11	0	.286
1998 Chicago f-g .........A.L.		1B-OF	96	341	58	91	18	2	13	49	2	.26
1999 Akron ....Eastern		OF	3	11	2	4	2	0	0	0	0	.364
1999 Cleveland h-i .........A.L.		OF	54	194	35	58	15	0	8	32	2	.2997
2000 Pittsburgh ...........N.L.		OF	89	348	46	98	24	3	16	51	1	.282
2000 Cleveland j ..........A.L.		OF	38	148	18	39	11	2	0	17	0	.264
Major League Totals		9 Yrs.	900	3329	470	928	209	18	95	436	45	.279
Division Series												
1999 Cleveland ............A.L.		DH-OF	3	9	3	5	0	0	1	2	0	.556

a On disabled list from July 31 to end of 1991 season.
b On disabled list from May 12 to June 11 and July 7 to July 20, 1992.
c Traded to the Boston Red Sox with pitcher Bryan Eversgerd for pitcher Rheal Cormier, first baseman Ryan McGuire and pitcher Shane Bennett, January 10, 1996.
d On disabled list from May 21 to August 12, 1996.
e Released by Boston Red Sox, September 28, 1997.
f Signed with Chicago White Sox, March 23, 1998.
g Filed for free agency, November 3, 1998. Signed with Cleveland Indians, February 3, 1999.
h On disabled list from June 9 to September 8, 1999.
i Filed for free agency, October 29, 1999. Signed with Pittsburgh Pirates, December 14, 1999.
j Traded to Cleveland Indians for outfielder Alex Ramirez and infielder Enrique Wilson, July 28, 2000.

COUNSELL, CRAIG JOHN

Born, South Bend, Indiana, August 21, 1970.
Bats Left. Throws Right. Height, 6 feet. Weight, 170 pounds.

Year Club	Lea	Pos	G	AB	R	H	2B	3B	HR	RBI	SB	Avg
1992 Bend ....Northwest		2B-SS	18	61	11	15	6	1	0	8	1	.246
1993 Central Val ......California		SS	131	471	79	132	26	3	5	59	14	.280
1994 New Haven ....Eastern		SS-2B	83	300	47	84	20	1	5	37	4	.280
1995 Colo Sprngs .........P.C.		SS	118	399	60	112	22	6	5	53	10	.281
1995 Colorado ...........N.L.		SS	3	1	0	0	0	0	0	0	0	.000
1996 Colo Sprngs .........P.C.		2B-3B-SS	25	75	17	18	3	0	2	10	4	.240
1997 Colo Sprngs .........P.C.		2B-SS	96	376	77	126	31	6	5	63	12	.335
1997 Colorado-Florida a .....N.L.		2B	52	164	20	49	9	2	1	16	1	.299
1998 Florida b ............N.L.		2B	107	335	43	84	19	5	4	40	3	.251
1999 Florida-Los Angeles c-d .N.L.		2B-SS	87	174	24	38	7	0	0	11	1	.218
2000 Tucson .............P.C.		2B	50	198	45	69	14	3	3	27	4	.348
2000 Arizona e ............N.L.		2B-3B-SS	67	152	23	48	8	1	2	11	3	.316
Major League Totals		5 Yrs.	316	826	110	219	43	8	7	78	8	.265
Division Series												
1997 Florida ..............N.L.		2B	3	5	0	2	1	0	0	1	0	.400
Championship Series												
1997 Florida ..............N.L.		2B	5	14	0	6	0	0	0	2	0	.429
World Series Record												
1997 Florida ..............N.L.		2B	7	22	4	4	1	0	0	2	1	.182

a Traded to Florida Marlins for pitcher Mark Hutton, July 27, 1997.
b On disabled list from August 4 to September 28, 1998.
c Traded to Los Angeles Dodgers for player to be named later, June 15, 1999.
  Florida Marlins received pitcher Ryan Moskau to complete trade, July 15, 1999.
d Outrighted by Los Angeles Dodgers, November 24, 1999. Signed with Arizona Diamondbacks organization, March 17, 2000.

COX, CHARLES STEVEN (STEVE)

Born, Delano, California, October 31, 1974.
Bats Left. Throws Right. Height, 6 feet, 4 inches. Weight, 225 pounds.

Year	Club	Lea	Pos	G	AB	R	H	2B	3B	HR	RBI	SB	Avg
1992	Athletics	Arizona	1B	52	184	30	43	4	1	1	35	2	.234
1993	Sou Oregon a	Northwest	1B	15	57	10	18	4	1	2	16	0	.316
1994	W Michigan	Midwest	1B-OF	99	311	37	75	19	2	6	32	2	.241
1995	Modesto	California	1B	132	483	95	144	29	3	30	110	5	.298
1996	Huntsville	Southern	1B	104	381	59	107	21	1	12	61	2	.281
1997	Edmonton b	P.C.	1B	131	467	84	128	34	1	15	93	1	.274
1998	Durham c	Int.	1B-OF	119	431	64	110	23	2	13	67	3	.255
1999	Durham	Int.	1B	134	534	107	182	49	4	25	127	3	.341
1999	Tampa Bay	A.L.	1B-OF	6	19	0	4	1	0	0	0	0	.211
2000	Tampa Bay	A.L.	OF-1B	116	318	44	90	19	1	11	35	1	.283
Major League Totals			2 Yrs.	122	337	44	94	20	1	11	35	1	.279

a On disabled list from July 23 to September 1, 1993.
b Selected in expansion draft by Tampa Bay Devil Rays, November 18, 1997.
c On disabled list from April 12 to 26, 1998.

CRESPO (CLAUSIO), FELIPE JAVIER

Born, Rio Piedras, Puerto Rico, March 5, 1973.
Bats Both. Throws Right. Height, 5 feet, 11 inches. Weight, 195 pounds.

Year	Club	Lea	Pos	G	AB	R	H	2B	3B	HR	RBI	SB	Avg
1991	Medicine Hat	Pioneer	2B	49	184	40	57	11	4	4	31	6	.310
1992	Myrtle Bch	So.Atl.	2B	81	263	43	74	14	3	1	29	7	.281
1993	Dunedin	Fla.St.	2B	96	345	51	103	16	8	6	39	18	.299
1994	Knoxville a	Southern	3B-2B	129	502	74	135	30	4	8	49	20	.269
1995	Syracuse a	Int.	2B	88	347	56	102	20	5	13	41	12	.294
1996	Dunedin	Fla.St.	2B	9	34	3	11	1	0	2	6	1	.324
1996	Syracuse	Int.	2B-OF-3B-1B	98	355	53	100	25	0	8	58	10	.282
1996	Toronto b	A.L.	2B-3B-1B	22	49	6	9	4	0	0	4	1	.184
1997	Syracuse	Int.	OF-2B-1B-3B	80	290	53	75	12	0	12	26	7	.259
1997	Toronto	A.L.	3B-2B	12	28	3	8	0	1	1	5	0	.286
1998	Toronto	A.L.	OF-2B-3B-1B	66	130	11	34	8	1	1	5	4	.262
1999	Fresno c-d	P.C.	1B	112	385	98	128	27	5	24	84	17	.332
2000	San Francisco	N.L.	OF-1B-2B	89	131	17	38	6	1	4	29	3	.290
Major League Totals			4 Yrs.	189	338	37	89	18	3	6	53	8	.263
Division Series													
2000	San Francisco	N.L.	PH	4	4	0	1	0	0	0	0	0	.250

a On disabled list from May 26 to July 2, 1995.
b On disabled list from April 1 to April 14, 1996.
c Released March 17, 1999, signed with San Francisco Giants, April 27, 1999.
d Filed for free agency, October 15, 1999, re-signed with San Francisco Giants, October 29, 1999.

CRUZ, DEIVI

Born, Bani, Dominican Republic, November 6, 1975.
Bats Right. Throws Right. Height, 5 feet, 11 inches. Weight, 160 pounds.

Year	Club	Lea	Pos	G	AB	R	H	2B	3B	HR	RBI	SB	Avg
1993	Giants	Arizona	3B-SS-1B	29	82	8	28	3	0	0	15	3	.341
1994	Giants	Arizona	SS-3B	18	53	10	16	8	0	0	5	0	.302
1995	Burlington	Midwest	2B-3B-SS	16	58	2	8	1	0	1	9	1	.138
1995	Bellingham	Northwest	3B-2B	62	223	32	66	17	0	3	28	6	.296
1996	Burlington a-b	Midwest	SS-3B	127	517	72	152	27	2	9	64	12	.294
1997	Detroit	A.L.	SS	147	436	35	105	26	0	2	40	3	.241
1998	Lakeland	Fla.St.	SS	2	9	0	0	0	0	0	0	0	.000
1998	Toledo	Int.	SS	2	9	1	1	1	0	0	2	0	.111
1998	Detroit c	A.L.	SS	135	454	52	118	22	3	5	45	3	.260
1999	Detroit	A.L.	SS	155	518	64	147	35	0	13	58	1	.284
2000	Detroit	A.L.	SS	156	583	68	176	46	5	10	82	1	.302

Year	Club	Lea	Pos	G	AB	R	H	2B	3B	HR	RBI	SB	Avg
Major League Totals			4 Yrs.	593	1991	219	546	129	8	30	225	8	.274

a Selected by Los Angeles Dodgers in Rule V draft, December 9, 1996.
b Traded to Detroit Tigers with outfielder Juan Hernandez for infielder Jeff Berblinger, December 9, 1996.
c On disabled list from March 31 to April 27, 1998.

CRUZ, JOSE L.

Born, Arroyo, Puerto Rico, April 19, 1974.
Bats Both. Throws Right. Height, 6 feet. Weight, 190 pounds.

Year	Club	Lea	Pos	G	AB	R	H	2B	3B	HR	RBI	SB	Avg
1995 Everett	Northwest		OF	3	11	6	5	0	0	0	2	1	.455
1995 Riverside	California		OF	35	144	34	37	7	1	7	29	3	.257
1996 Lancaster	California		OF	53	203	38	66	17	1	6	43	7	.325
1996 Port City	Southern		OF	47	181	39	51	10	2	3	31	5	.282
1996 Tacoma	P.C.		OF	22	76	15	18	1	2	6	15	1	.237
1997 Tacoma	P.C.		OF	50	190	33	51	16	2	6	30	3	.268
1997 Seattle-Toronto a	A.L.		OF	104	395	59	98	19	1	26	68	7	.248
1998 Syracuse	Int.		OF	40	141	29	42	14	1	7	23	8	.298
1998 Toronto	A.L.		OF	105	352	55	89	14	3	11	42	11	.253
1999 Syracuse	Int.		OF	31	103	17	19	3	1	3	14	5	.184
1999 Toronto b	A.L.		OF	106	349	63	84	19	3	14	45	14	.241
2000 Toronto	A.L.		OF	*162	603	91	146	32	5	31	76	15	.242
Major League Totals			4 Yrs.	477	1699	268	417	84	12	82	231	47	.245

a Traded to Toronto Blue Jays for pitchers Mike Timlin and Paul Spoljaric, July 31, 1997.
b On disabled list from June 24 to July 9, 1999.

CUMMINGS, MIDRE ALMERIC

Born, St.Croix, Virgin Islands, October 14, 1971.
Bats Left. Throws Right. Height, 6 feet. Weight, 196 pounds.

Year	Club	Lea	Pos	G	AB	R	H	2B	3B	HR	RBI	SB	Avg
1990 Twins	Gulf Coast		OF	47	177	28	56	3	4	5	28	14	.316
1991 Kenosha	Midwest		OF	106	382	59	123	20	4	4	54	28	.322
1992 Salem a	Carolina		OF	113	420	55	128	20	5	14	75	23	.305
1993 Carolina	Southern		OF	63	237	33	70	17	2	6	26	5	.295
1993 Buffalo	A.A.		OF	60	232	36	64	12	1	9	21	5	.276
1993 Pittsburgh	N.L.		OF	13	36	5	4	1	0	0	3	0	.111
1994 Buffalo	A.A.		OF	49	183	23	57	14	4	2	22	5	.311
1994 Pittsburgh b	N.L.		OF	24	86	11	21	4	0	1	12	0	.244
1995 Calgary	P.C.		OF	45	159	19	44	9	1	1	16	1	.277
1995 Pittsburgh c	N.L.		OF	59	152	13	37	7	1	2	15	1	.243
1996 Pittsburgh	N.L.		OF	24	85	11	19	3	1	3	7	0	.224
1996 Calgary	P.C.		OF	97	368	60	112	24	3	8	55	6	.304
1997 Pittsburgh-Philadelphia d	N.L.		OF	115	314	35	83	22	6	4	31	2	.264
1998 Boston e-f-g	A.L.		DH-OF	67	120	20	34	8	0	5	15	3	.283
1999 Salt Lake	P.C.		OF	69	261	50	84	19	4	13	68	4	.322
1999 New Britain	Eastern		OF	24	93	28	35	7	0	2	15	3	.376
1999 Minnesota h	A.L.		OF	16	38	1	10	0	0	1	9	2	.263
2000 Minnesota-Boston i-j . .	A.L.		OF	98	206	29	57	10	0	4	24	0	.277
Major League Totals			8 Yrs.	416	1037	125	265	55	8	20	116	8	.256
Division Series													
1998 Boston	A.L.		PH	3	3	0	0	0	0	0	0	0	.000

a Traded by Minnesota Twins with pitcher Denny Neagle to Pittsburgh Pirates for pitcher John Smiley, March 17, 1992.
b On disabled list from April 21 to June 6, 1994.
c On disabled list from June 17 to July 1, 1995.
d Claimed on waivers by Philadelphia Phillies, July 8, 1997.
e Released by Philadelphia Phillies, February 24, 1998, signed with Cincinnati Reds organization, February 27, 1998.
f Claimed on waivers by Boston Red Sox, March 19, 1998.
g On disabled list from July 29 to September 7, 1998.
h Released by Boston Red Sox, March 30, 1999, signed with Minnesota Twins, December 1, 1999.
i Traded to Boston Red Sox for infielder Hector De Los Santos, August 31, 2000.
j Filed for free agency, October 14, 2000, signed with Arizona Diamondbacks, December 15, 2000.

CURTIS, CHAD DAVID

Born, Marion, Indiana, November 6, 1968.
Bats Right. Throws Right. Height, 5 feet, 10 inches. Weight, 175 pounds.

Year	Club	Lea	Pos	G	AB	R	H	2B	3B	HR	RBI	SB	Avg
1989 Mesa Angels		Arizona	2B-OF	32	122	30	37	4	4	3	20	17	.303
1989 Quad City		Midwest	OF	23	78	7	19	3	0	2	11	7	.244
1990 Quad City		Midwest	2B-OF	*135	*492	87	*151	28	1	14	65	64	.307
1991 Edmonton		.P.C.	3B-OF-2B	115	431	81	136	28	7	9	61	46	.316
1992 California		.A.L.	OF	139	441	59	114	16	2	10	46	43	.259
1993 California		.A.L.	OF-2B	152	583	94	166	25	3	6	59	48	.285
1994 California		.A.L.	OF	114	453	67	116	23	4	11	50	25	.256
1995 Detroit a		.A.L.	OF	144	586	96	157	29	3	21	67	27	.268
1996 Detroit b		.A.L.	OF	104	400	65	105	20	1	10	37	16	.262
1996 Los Angeles c-d		.N.L.	OF	43	104	20	22	5	0	2	9	2	.212
1997 Akron e		Eastern	OF	4	18	5	7	1	0	3	6	0	.389
1997 Cleveland-New York f		.A.L.	OF	115	349	59	99	22	1	15	55	12	.284
1998 New York		.A.L.	OF	151	456	79	111	21	1	10	56	21	.243
1999 New York g		.A.L.	OF	96	195	37	51	6	0	5	24	8	.262
2000 Texas		.A.L.	OF	108	335	48	91	25	1	8	48	3	.272
Major League Totals	9 Yrs.			1166	3902	624	1032	192	16	98	451	205	.264
Division Series													
1996 Los Angeles		.N.L.	OF	1	2	0	0	0	0	0	0	0	.000
1997 New York		.A.L.	OF	4	6	0	1	0	0	0	0	0	.167
1998 New York		.A.L.	OF	3	3	1	2	1	0	0	0	1	.667
1999 New York		.A.L.	OF	3	3	1	0	0	0	0	0	0	.000
Division Series Totals				11	14	2	3	1	0	0	0	1	.214
Championship Series													
1998 New York		.A.L.	OF	2	4	0	0	0	0	0	0	0	.000
1999 New York		.A.L.	OF-DH	3	6	1	0	0	0	0	0	1	.000
Championship Series Totals				5	10	1	0	0	0	0	0	1	.000
World Series Record													
1999 New York		.A.L.	OF	3	6	3	2	0	0	2	2	0	.333

a Traded to Detroit Tigers for outfielder Tony Phillips, April 13, 1995.
b Traded to Los Angeles Dodgers for pitcher Joey Eischen and pitcher John Cummings, July 31, 1996.
c Filed for free agency, October 15, 1996.
d Signed with Cleveland Indians December 18, 1996.
e Traded to New York Yankees for pitcher Dave Weathers, June 9, 1997.
f On disabled list from May 14 to June 9, 1997.
g Traded to Texas Rangers for pitcher Sam Marsonek and pitcher Brandon Knight, December 13, 1999.

DAMON, JOHNNY DAVID

Born, Fort Riley, Kansas, November 5, 1973.
Bats Left. Throws Left. Height, 6 feet. Weight, 175 pounds.

Year	Club	Lea	Pos	G	AB	R	H	2B	3B	HR	RBI	SB	Avg
1992 Royals		Gulf Coast	OF	50	192	58	67	12	9	4	24	23	.349
1992 Baseball City		Fla. St.	OF	1	1	0	0	0	0	0	0	0	.000
1993 Rockford		Midwest	OF	127	511	82	148	25	13	5	50	59	.290
1994 Wilmington		Carolina	OF	119	472	96	149	25	13	6	75	44	.316
1995 Wichita		Texas	OF	111	423	83	145	15	9	16	54	26	.343
1995 Kansas City		.A.L.	OF	47	188	32	53	11	5	3	23	7	.282
1996 Kansas City		.A.L.	OF	145	517	61	140	22	5	6	50	25	.271
1997 Kansas City		.A.L.	OF	146	472	70	130	12	8	8	48	16	.275
1998 Kansas City		.A.L.	OF	161	642	104	178	30	10	18	66	26	.277
1999 Kansas City		.A.L.	OF	145	583	101	179	39	9	14	77	36	.307
2000 Kansas City a		.A.L.	OF	159	655	*136	214	42	10	16	88	*46	.327
Major League Totals	6 Yrs.			803	3057	504	894	156	47	65	352	156	.292

a Traded to Oakland Athletics with infielder Mark Ellis and player to be named later for pitcher Roberto Hernandez, catcher A.J. Hinch, outfielder Angel Berroa and cash, January 8, 2001.

DAUBACH, BRIAN MICHAEL

Born, Belleville, Illinois, February 11, 1972.
Bats Left. Throws Right. Height, 6 feet, 1 inch. Weight, 201 pounds.

Year	Club	Lea	Pos	G	AB	R	H	2B	3B	HR	RBI	SB	Avg
1990 Mets		Gulf Coast	1B	45	152	26	41	8	4	1	19	2	.270
1991 Kingsport		Appal.	1B	65	218	30	53	9	1	7	42	1	.243
1992 Pittsfield		N.Y.-Penn.	1B	72	260	26	63	15	2	2	40	4	.242
1993 Capital Cty		So.Atl.	DH-1B-OF	102	379	50	106	19	3	7	72	6	.280

45

Year Club	Lea	Pos	G	AB	R	H	2B	3B	HR	RBI	SB	Avg
1994 St. Lucie ....Fla.St.		1B	129	450	52	123	30	2	6	74	14	.273
1995 Binghamton ....Eastern		1B-3B	135	469	61	115	25	2	10	72	6	.245
1995 Norfolk ....Int.		1B	2	7	0	0	0	0	0	0	0	.000
1996 Norfolk ....Int.		1B	17	54	7	11	2	0	0	6	1	.204
1996 Binghamton a ......Eastern		1B-3B	122	436	80	129	24	1	22	76	7	.296
1997 Charlotte ....Int.		1B	136	461	66	128	40	2	21	93	1	.278
1998 Charlotte ....Int.		OF-1B	140	497	102	157	45	4	35	124	9	.316
1998 Florida b-c ..........N.L.		1B	10	15	0	3	1	0	0	3	0	.200
1999 Pawtucket ....Int.		DH	9	31	4	9	2	0	1	6	0	.290
1999 Boston ..............A.L.		1B-OF-3B	110	381	61	112	33	3	21	73	0	.294
2000 Boston ..............A.L.		1B-OF-3B	142	495	55	123	32	2	21	76	1	.248
Major League Totals	3 Yrs.		262	891	116	238	66	5	42	152	1	.267
Division Series												
1999 Boston ..........A.L.		DH-1B	4	16	3	4	2	0	1	3	0	.250
Championship Series												
1999 Boston ..........A.L.		DH-1B	5	17	2	3	1	0	1	3	0	.176

a Filed for free agency from New York Mets, October 15, 1996, signed with Florida Marlins organization, November 7, 1996.
b Filed for free agency, October 17, 1997, re-signed with Florida Marlins organization, January 8, 1998.
c Released by Florida Marlins, November 19,1998, signed with Boston Red Sox, December 18, 1998.

DAVIS, ERIC KEITH

Born, Los Angeles, California, May 29, 1962.
Bats Right. Throws Right. Height, 6 feet, 3 inches. Weight, 185 pounds.

Year Club	Lea	Pos	G	AB	R	H	2B	3B	HR	RBI	SB	Avg
1980 Eugene ....Northwest		SS-2B	33	73	12	16	1	0	1	11	0	.219
1981 Eugene ....Northwest		OF	62	214	*67	69	10	4	11	39	*40	.322
1982 Cedar Rapids ......Midwest		OF	111	434	80	120	20	5	15	56	53	.276
1983 Waterbury ....Eastern		OF	89	293	56	85	13	1	15	43	39	.290
1983 Indianapolis ..........A.A.		OF	19	77	18	23	4	0	7	19	9	.299
1984 Wichita ..............A.A.		OF	52	194	42	61	9	5	14	34	27	.314
1984 Cincinnati a ..........N.L.		OF	57	174	33	39	10	1	10	30	10	.224
1985 Cincinnati ............N.L.		OF	56	122	26	30	3	3	8	18	16	.246
1985 Denver ..............A.A.		OF	64	206	48	57	10	2	15	38	35	.277
1986 Cincinnati ............N.L.		OF	132	415	97	115	15	3	27	71	80	.277
1987 Cincinnati ............N.L.		OF	129	474	120	139	23	4	37	100	50	.293
1988 Cincinnati ............N.L.		OF	135	472	81	129	18	3	26	93	35	.273
1989 Cincinnatti b ..........N.L.		OF	131	462	74	130	14	2	34	101	21	.281
1990 Cincinnatti c ..........N.L.		OF	127	453	84	118	25	2	24	86	21	.260
1991 Cincinnatti d-e ........N.L.		OF	89	285	39	67	10	0	11	33	14	.235
1992 Los Angeles f-g ......N.L.		OF	76	267	21	61	8	1	5	32	19	.228
1993 Los Angeles h ........N.L.		OF	108	376	57	88	17	0	14	53	33	.234
1993 Detroit ..............A.L.		OF	23	75	14	19	1	1	6	15	2	.253
1994 Detroit i-j ............A.L.		OF	37	120	19	22	4	0	3	13	5	.183
1995			RETIRED - Did Not Play									
1996 Cincinnatti l-m-n ......N.L.		OF-1B	129	415	81	119	20	0	26	83	23	.287
1997 Baltimore o ..........A.L.		OF	42	158	29	48	11	0	8	25	6	.304
1998 Baltimore p ..........A.L.		OF	131	452	81	148	29	1	28	89	7	.327
1999 St. Louis q ..........N.L.		OF	58	191	27	49	9	2	5	30	5	.257
2000 St. Louis r ..........N.L.		OF	92	254	38	77	14	0	6	40	1	.303
Major League Totals	16 Yrs.	1552	5165	921	1398	232	23	278	912	348	.271
Division Series												
1997 Baltimore ............A.L.		OF	3	9	0	2	0	0	0	2	0	.222
2000 St. Louis ............N.L.		OF	2	4	0	0	0	0	0	0	0	.000
Division Series Totals			5	13	0	2	0	0	0	2	0	.154
Championship Series												
1990 Cincinnatti ...........N.L.		OF	6	23	2	4	1	0	0	2	0	.174
1997 Baltimore ............A.L.		OF-DH	6	13	1	2	0	0	1	1	0	.154
2000 St. Louis ............N.L.		OF	4	10	1	2	1	0	0	1	0	.200
Championship Series Totals			16	46	4	8	2	0	1	4	0	.174
World Series Record												
1990 Cincinnati ............N.L.		OF	4	14	3	4	0	0	1	5	0	.286

a On disabled list from August 16 to September 1, 1984.
b On disabled list from May 3 to May 18, 1989.
c On disabled list from April 25 to May 19, 1990.
d On disabled list from June 12 to June 27 and July 31 to August 26, 1991.
e Traded to Los Angeles Dodgers with pitcher Kip Gross for pitchers Tim Belcher and John Wetteland, November 27, 1991.

f On disabled list from May 23 to June 19 and August 5 to August 25, 1992.
g Filed for free agency, November 3; re-signed with Los Angeles Dodgers, December 1, 1992.
h Traded to Detroit Tigers for player to be named, August 31; Los Angeles Dodgers acquired pitcher John DeSilva to complete trade, September 7, 1993.
i On disabled list from May 23 to July 19 and July 27 to end of 1994 season.
j Filed for free agency, October 17, 1994.
k Signed with Cincinnati Reds organization, January 2, 1996.
l On disabled list from May 26 to June 10, 1996.
m Filed for free agency, October 28, 1996.
n Signed with Baltimore Orioles, December 19, 1996.
o On disabled list from May 26 to September 15, 1997.
p Filed for free agency, October 27, 1998, signed with St. Louis Cardinals, November 19, 1998.
q On disabled list from June 28 to November 8, 1999.
r Filed for free agency, November 2, 2000, signed with San Francisco Giants, December 23, 2000.

DAVIS, RUSSELL STUART

Born, Birmingham, Alabama, September 13, 1969.
Bats Right. Throws Right. Height, 6 feet. Weight, 170 pounds.

Year	Club	Lea	Pos	G	AB	R	H	2B	3B	HR	RBI	SB	Avg
1988 Sarasota Yankees	Gulf C.		3B	58	213	33	49	11	3	2	30	6	.230
1989 Fort Lauderdale	Fla. St.		3B	48	147	8	27	5	1	2	22	3	.184
1989 Oneonta	N.Y.-Penn.		3B	65	236	33	68	7	5	7	42	3	.288
1990 Prince William	Carolina		3B	137	510	55	127	*37	3	16	71	3	.249
1991 Albany	Eastern		3B	135	473	57	103	23	3	8	58	3	.218
1992 Albany	Eastern		3B	132	491	77	140	23	4	22	71	3	.285
1993 Columbus	Int.		3B	113	424	63	108	24	1	26	83	1	.255
1994 Columbus	Int.		3B-1B	117	416	76	115	30	2	25	69	3	.276
1994 New York	A.L.		3B	4	14	0	2	0	0	0	1	0	.143
1995 Columbus	Int.		3B-1B	20	76	12	19	4	1	2	15	0	.250
1995 New York a	A.L.		3B-1B	40	98	14	27	5	2	2	12	0	.276
1996 Seattle b	A.L.		3B	51	167	24	39	9	0	5	18	2	.234
1997 Seattle c	A.L.		3B	119	420	57	114	29	1	20	63	6	.271
1998 Seattle	A.L.		3B-OF	141	502	68	130	30	1	20	82	4	.259
1999 Seattle d	A.L.		3B-SS	124	432	55	106	17	1	21	59	3	.245
2000 San Francisco	N.L.		3B-1B	80	180	27	47	5	0	9	24	0	.261
Major League Totals			7 Yrs.	559	1813	245	465	95	5	77	259	15	.256
Division Series													
1995 New York	A.L.		3B	2	5	0	1	0	0	0	0	0	.200
2000 San Francisco	N.L.		PH	2	2	0	0	0	0	0	0	0	.000
Division Series Totals				4	7	0	1	0	0	0	0	0	.143

a Traded to Seattle Mariners with pitcher Sterling Hitchcock for first baseman Tino Martinez, pitcher Jeff Nelson and pitcher Jim Mecir, December 7, 1995.
b On disabled list from June 8 to September 30, 1996.
c On disabled list from August 25 to September 26, 1997.
d Not offered contract, December 21, 1999. Signed with San Francisco Giants organization, January 24, 2000.

DE LA ROSA, TOMAS

Born, LaVictoria, Dominican Republic, January 28, 1978.
Bats Right. Throws Right. Height, 5 feet, 10 inches. Weight, 165 pounds.

Year	Club	Lea	Pos	G	AB	R	H	2B	3B	HR	RBI	SB	Avg
1996 Expos	Gulf Coast		SS	54	187	35	47	7	1	0	21	8	.251
1996 Vermont	N.Y.-Penn.		SS	3	8	1	2	0	0	0	1	0	.250
1997 Wst Plm Bch	Fla.St.		SS	4	9	1	2	0	0	0	2	2	.222
1997 Vermont	N.Y.-Penn.		SS	69	271	46	72	14	6	2	40	19	.266
1998 Jupiter	Fla.St.		SS-3B	117	390	56	98	22	1	3	43	27	.251
1999 Harrisburg	Eastern		SS	135	467	70	122	22	3	6	43	28	.261
2000 Ottawa	Int.		SS	103	340	27	69	10	1	1	36	10	.203
2000 Montreal	N.L.		SS	32	66	7	19	3	1	2	9	2	.288

DELGADO (HERNANDEZ), CARLOS JUAN

Born, Aguadilla, Puerto Rico, June 25, 1972.
Bats Left. Throws Right. Height, 6 feet, 3 inches. Weight, 220 pounds.

Year	Club	Lea	Pos	G	AB	R	H	2B	3B	HR	RBI	SB	Avg
1989 St. Catharines	N.Y.-Penn.		DH-C	31	89	9	16	5	0	0	11	0	.180
1990 St. Catharines	N.Y.-Penn.		C	67	228	30	64	13	0	6	39	2	.281
1991 Myrtle Beach	So. Atl.		C	132	441	72	126	18	2	18	70	9	.286
1991 Syracuse	Int.		C	1	3	0	0	0	0	0	0	0	.000

Year	Club	Lea	Pos	G	AB	R	H	2B	3B	HR	RBI	SB	Avg
1992 Dunedin	Fla. St.	C	133	485	83	*157	*30	2	*30	*100	2	.324
1993 Knoxville	Southern	C	140	468	91	142	28	0	*25	*102	10	.303
1993 Toronto	A.L.	C	2	1	0	0	0	0	0	0	0	.000
1994 Toronto	A.L.	OF-C	43	130	17	28	2	0	9	24	1	.215
1994 Syracuse	Int.	DH-C-1B	85	307	52	98	11	0	19	58	1	.319
1995 Syracuse	Int.	1B-OF	91	333	59	106	23	4	22	74	0	.318
1995 Toronto	A.L.	OF-1B	37	91	7	15	3	0	3	11	0	.165
1996 Toronto	A.L.	DH-1B	138	488	68	132	28	2	25	92	0	.270
1997 Toronto	A.L.	1B	153	519	79	136	42	3	30	91	0	.262
1998 Dunedin	Fla.St.	1B	4	16	4	5	1	0	2	7	0	.313
1998 Syracuse	Int.	1B	2	7	4	4	2	0	1	6	0	.571
1998 Toronto a	A.L.	1B	142	530	94	155	43	1	38	115	3	.292
1999 Toronto	A.L.	1B	152	573	113	156	39	0	44	134	1	.272
2000 Toronto	A.L.	1B	*162	569	115	196	*57	1	41	137	0	.344
Major League Totals			8 Yrs.	829	2901	493	818	214	7	190	604	5	.282

a On disabled list from March 31 to April 24, 1998.

DELGADO (DURAN), WILSON
Born, San Cristobal, Dominican Republic, July 15, 1975.
Bats Both. Throws Right. Height, 5 feet, 11 inches. Weight, 165 pounds.

Year	Club	Lea	Pos	G	AB	R	H	2B	3B	HR	RBI	SB	Avg
1993 Seattle	Dominican	SS	60	171	19	50	8	0	0	26	5	.292
1994 Mariners	Arizona	SS-2B	39	149	30	56	5	4	0	10	13	.376
1994 Appleton	Midwest	SS	9	31	2	6	0	0	0	0	0	.194
1995 Port City	Southern	SS	13	41	3	8	4	0	0	1	0	.195
1995 Wisconsin	Midwest	SS	19	70	13	17	3	0	0	7	3	.243
1995 Burlington	Midwest	SS	93	365	52	113	20	3	5	37	9	.310
1995 San Jose a	California	SS	1	2	1	0	0	0	0	0	0	.000
1996 San Jose	California	SS	121	462	59	124	19	6	2	54	8	.268
1996 Phoenix	P.C.	SS	12	43	1	6	0	1	0	1	0	.140
1996 San Francisco	N.L.	SS	6	22	3	8	0	0	0	2	1	.364
1997 Phoenix	P.C.	SS-2B	119	416	47	120	22	4	9	59	9	.288
1997 San Francisco	N.L.	2B-SS	8	7	1	1	1	0	0	0	0	.143
1998 Fresno	P.C.	SS	127	512	87	142	22	2	12	63	9	.277
1998 San Francisco	N.L.	SS	10	12	1	2	1	0	0	1	0	.167
1999 Fresno	P.C.	SS	57	213	28	64	10	3	1	33	4	.300
1999 San Francisco	N.L.	SS-2B	35	71	7	18	2	1	0	3	1	.254
2000 N.Y.-Kansas City b-c	A.L.	2B-SS-3B	64	128	21	33	2	0	1	11	2	.258
Major League Totals			5 Yrs.	123	240	33	62	6	1	1	17	4	.258

a Traded by Seattle Mariners with pitcher Shawn Estes to San Francisco Giants for pitcher Salomon Torres, May 21, 1995.
b Traded to New York Yankees for infielder Juan Melo, March 23, 2000.
c Traded to Kansas City Royals for infielder Nick Ortiz, August 11, 2000.

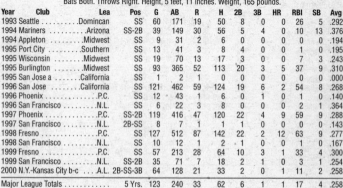

DESHIELDS, DELINO LAMONT
Born, Seaford, Delaware, January 15, 1969.
Bats Left. Throws Right. Height, 6 feet, 1 inch. Weight, 175 pounds.

Year	Club	Lea	Pos	G	AB	R	H	2B	3B	HR	RBI	SB	Avg
1987 Bradenton Expos	Gulf C.	SS	31	111	17	24	5	2	1	4	16	.216
1987 Jamestown	N.Y.-Penn.	SS	34	96	16	21	1	2	1	5	14	.219
1988 Rockford	Midwest	SS	129	460	97	116	26	6	12	46	59	.252
1989 Jacksonville	Southern	SS	93	307	55	83	10	6	3	35	37	.270
1989 Indianapolis	A.A.	SS	47	181	29	47	8	4	2	14	16	.260
1990 Montreal a	N.L.	2B	129	499	69	144	28	6	4	45	42	.289
1991 Montreal	N.L.	2B	151	563	83	134	15	4	10	51	56	.238
1992 Montreal	N.L.	2B	135	530	82	155	19	8	7	56	46	.292
1993 Montreal b-c	N.L.	2B	123	481	75	142	17	7	2	29	43	.295
1994 Los Angeles d	N.L.	2B-SS	89	320	51	80	11	3	2	33	27	.250
1995 Los Angeles	N.L.	2B	127	425	66	109	18	3	8	37	39	.256
1996 Los Angeles e	N.L.	2B	154	581	75	130	12	8	5	41	48	.224
1997 St. Louis	N.L.	2B	150	572	92	169	26	*14	11	58	55	.295
1998 Arkansas	Texas	2B	4	13	1	2	0	0	0	0	0	.154
1998 St. Louis f-g	N.L.	2B-1B	117	420	74	122	21	8	7	44	26	.290
1999 Bowie	Eastern	2B	4	15	2	4	1	0	0	0	0	.267
1999 Baltimore h	A.L.	2B	96	330	46	87	11	2	6	34	11	.264
1999 Frederick	Carolina	2B	2	8	1	1	0	0	1	2	0	.125

48

Year	Club	Lea	Pos	G	AB	R	H	2B	3B	HR	RBI	SB	Avg
1999 Delmarva	So.Atl.	2B	2	7	1	2	0	0	1	2	0	.286
2000 Baltimore	A.L.	2B-OF	151	561	84	166	43	5	10	86	37	.296
Major League Totals		11 Yrs.	1422	5282	797	1438	221	68	72	514	430	.272
Division Series												
1995 Los Angeles	N.L.	2B	3	12	1	3	0	0	0	0	0	.250
1996 Los Angeles	N.L.	2B	2	4	0	0	0	0	0	0	0	.000
Division Series Totals			5	16	1	3	0	0	0	0	0	.188

a On disabled list from June 16 to July 12, 1990.
b On disabled list from August 12 to September 11, 1993.
c Traded to Los Angeles Dodgers for pitcher Pedro Martinez, November 19, 1993.
d On disabled list from May 26 to June 19, 1994.
e Filed for free agency, October 29, 1996, signed with St. Louis Cardinals, November 20, 1996.
f On disabled list from July 5 to Agust 10, 1998.
g Filed for free agency, October 23, 1998, signed with Baltimore Orioles, December 4, 1998.
h On disabled list from March 26 to April 11 and June 20 to July 23 and October 1 to October 13, 1999.

DIAZ, EINAR ANTONIO

Born, Chiriqui, Panama, December 28, 1972.
Bats Right. Throws Right. Height, 5 feet, 10 inches. Weight, 165 pounds.

Year	Club	Lea	Pos	G	AB	R	H	2B	3B	HR	RBI	SB	Avg
1991 Cleveland	Dominican	SS	62	239	35	67	6	3	1	29	10	.280
1992 Burlington	Appal.	3B-SS	52	178	19	37	3	0	1	14	2	.208
1993 Burlington	Appal.	C-3B	60	231	40	69	15	3	5	33	7	.299
1993 Columbus	So.Atl.	C	1	5	0	0	0	0	0	0	0	.000
1994 Columbus	So.Atl.	C-3B	120	491	67	137	23	2	16	71	4	.279
1995 Kinston	Carolina	C-3B	104	373	46	98	21	0	6	43	3	.263
1996 Canton-Akrn	Eastern	C-3B	104	395	47	111	26	2	3	35	3	.281
1996 Cleveland	A.L.	C	4	1	0	0	0	0	0	0	0	.000
1997 Buffalo	A.A.	C-3B	109	336	40	86	18	2	3	31	2	.256
1997 Cleveland	A.L.	C	5	7	1	1	1	0	0	1	0	.143
1998 Buffalo	Int.	C	115	415	62	130	21	3	8	63	3	.313
1998 Cleveland	A.L.	C	17	48	8	11	1	0	2	9	0	.229
1999 Cleveland	A.L.	C	119	392	43	110	21	1	3	32	11	.281
2000 Cleveland	A.L.	C-3B	75	250	29	68	14	2	4	25	4	.272
Major League Totals		5 Yrs.	220	698	81	190	37	3	9	67	15	.272
Division Series												
1999 Cleveland	A.L.	C	2	1	0	0	0	0	0	0	0	.000
Championship Series												
1998 Cleveland	A.L.	C	5	4	0	0	0	0	0	0	0	.000

DIFELICE, MICHAEL WILLIAM

Born, Philadelphia, Pennsylvania, May 28, 1969.
Bats Right. Throws Right. Height, 6 feet, 2 inches. Weight, 205 pounds.

Year	Club	Lea	Pos	G	AB	R	H	2B	3B	HR	RBI	SB	Avg
1991 Hamilton	N.Y.-Penn.	C	43	157	10	33	5	0	4	15	1	.210
1992 Hamilton	N.Y.-Penn.	C-1B	18	58	11	20	3	0	2	9	2	.345
1992 St.Pete	Fla.St.	C	17	53	0	12	3	0	0	4	0	.226
1993 Springfield	Midwest	C	8	20	5	7	1	0	0	3	0	.350
1993 St.Pete	Fla.St.	C	30	97	5	22	2	0	0	8	1	.227
1994 Arkansas	Texas	C	71	200	19	50	11	2	2	15	0	.250
1995 Arkansas	Texas	C	62	176	14	47	10	1	1	24	0	.267
1995 Louisville	A.A.	C	21	63	8	17	4	0	0	3	1	.270
1996 Louisville	A.A.	C	79	246	25	70	13	0	9	33	0	.285
1996 St. Louis	N.L.	C	4	7	0	2	1	0	0	2	0	.286
1997 Arkansas	Texas	C	1	3	0	1	1	0	0	0	0	.333
1997 Louisville	A.A.	C	1	4	1	1	0	0	1	1	0	.250
1997 St. Louis a	N.L.	C-1B	93	260	16	62	10	1	4	30	1	.238
1998 Tampa Bay	A.L.	C	84	248	17	57	12	3	3	23	0	.230
1999 Tampa Bay	A.L.	C	51	179	21	55	11	0	6	27	0	.307
2000 Tampa Bay	A.L.	C	60	204	23	49	13	1	6	19	0	.240
Major League Totals		5 Yrs.	292	898	77	225	47	5	19	101	1	.251

a Selected in expansion draft by Tampa Bay Devil Rays, November 18, 1997.

DREW, DAVID J. (J.D.)
Born, Tallahassee, Florida, November 20, 1975.
Bats Left. Throws Right. Height, 6 feet, 1 inch. Weight, 190 pounds.

Year Club	Lea	Pos	G	AB	R	H	2B	3B	HR	RBI	SB	Avg
1997 St. Paul	Northern	OF	44	170	51	58	6	1	18	50	5	.341
1998 St. Paul	Northern	OF	30	114	27	44	11	2	9	33	8	.386
1998 Arkansas	Texas	OF	19	67	18	22	3	1	5	11	2	.328
1998 Memphis	P.C.	OF	26	79	15	25	8	1	2	13	1	.316
1998 St. Louis	N.L.	OF	14	36	9	15	3	1	5	13	0	.417
1999 St. Louis a	N.L.	OF	104	368	72	89	16	6	13	39	19	.242
2000 St. Louis-b	N.L.	OF	135	407	73	120	17	2	18	57	17	.295
Major League Totals	3 Yrs.		253	811	154	224	36	9	36	109	36	.276
Division Series												
2000 St. Louis	N.L.	OF	2	6	1	1	0	0	0	0	2	.167
Championship Series												
2000 St. Louis	N.L.	OF	5	12	2	4	1	0	0	1	0	.333

a On disabled list from May 16 to June 17, 1999.
b On disabled list from July 8 to July 26, 2000.

DUCEY, ROBERT THOMAS (ROB)
Born, Toronto, Ontario, May 24, 1965.
Bats Left. Throws Right. Height, 6 feet, 2 inches. Weight, 185 pounds.

Year Club	Lea	Pos	G	AB	R	H	2B	3B	HR	RBI	SB	Avg
1984 Medicine Hat	Pioneer	OF-1B	63	235	49	71	10	3	12	49	13	.302
1985 Florence	So. Atl.	OF-1B	134	529	78	133	22	2	13	86	12	.251
1986 Ventura	California	OF-1B	47	178	36	60	11	3	12	38	17	.337
1986 Knoxville	Southern	OF	88	344	49	106	22	3	11	58	7	.308
1987 Syracuse	Int.	OF	100	359	62	102	14	10	10	60	7	.284
1987 Toronto	A.L.	OF	34	48	12	9	1	0	1	6	2	.188
1988 Syracuse	Int.	OF	90	317	40	81	14	4	7	42	7	.256
1988 Toronto	A.L.	OF	27	54	15	17	4	1	0	6	1	.315
1989 Syracuse	Int.	OF	10	29	0	3	0	1	0	3	0	.103
1989 Toronto a	A.L.	OF	41	76	5	16	4	0	0	7	-2	.211
1990 Syracuse	Int.	OF	127	438	53	117	32	7	7	47	14	.267
1990 Toronto	A.L.	OF	19	53	7	16	5	0	0	7	1	.302
1991 Syracuse	Int.	OF	72	266	53	78	10	3	8	40	5	.293
1991 Toronto	A.L.	OF	39	68	8	16	2	2	1	4	2	.235
1992 Toronto-Calif. b-c	A.L.	OF	54	80	7	15	4	0	0	2	2	.188
1993 Okla City	A.A.	OF	105	389	68	118	17	10	17	56	17	.303
1993 Texas	A.L.	OF	27	85	15	24	6	3	2	9	2	.282
1994 Texas	A.L.	OF	11	29	1	5	1	0	0	1	0	.172
1994 Okla City d-e	A.A.	OF	115	403	69	108	27	9	17	65	9	.268
1995 Nippon	Japan Pac.	OF	117	425	61	106	19	4	25	61	7	.249
1996 Nippon	Japan Pac.	OF	120	427	68	105	17	5	26	59	3	.246
1997 Tacoma f	P.C.	OF	23	74	8	24	8	0	0	11	0	.324
1997 Seattle g-h	A.L.	OF	76	143	25	41	15	2	5	10	3	.287
1998 Seattle i-j	A.L.	OF	97	217	30	52	18	2	5	23	4	.240
1999 Philadelphia	N.L.	OF	104	188	29	49	10	2	8	33	2	.261
2000 Toronto	A.L.	OF	5	13	2	2	1	0	0	1	0	.154
2000 Philadelphia k-l-m	N.L.	OF	112	152	24	30	4	1	6	25	1	.197
Major League Totals	12 Yrs.		646	1206	180	292	75	13	28	134	22	.242
Division Series												
1997 Seattle	A.L.	OF	2	4	0	2	0	0	0	1	0	.500

a On disabled list from June 9 to September 2, 1989.
b Traded to California Angels with catcher Greg Myers for pitcher Mark Eichhorn, July 30, 1992.
c Refused assignment to minor leagues and became free agent, November 9; signed with Texas Rangers org
December 18, 1992.
d Released by Texas Rangers, October 14, 1994.
e Signed with Nippon Ham Fighters (Japan), February 18, 1995.
f Signed with Seattle Mariners organization, January 22, 1997.
g On disabled list from August 3 to August 21, 1997.
h Re-signed with Seattle Mariners, December 11, 1997.
i On disabled list from March 31 to April 20, 1998.
j Not offered 1999 contract, December 21, 1998. Signed with Philadelphia Phillies, December 22, 1998.
k Traded to Toronto Blue Jays for player to be named later, July 26, 2000.
l Philadelphia Phillies received pitcher John Sneed to complete trade, July 31, 2000.
m Sent to Philadelphia Phillies as player to be named later for infielder Mickey Morandini, August 7, 2000.

DUNSTON, SHAWON DONNELL

Born, Brooklyn, New York, March 21, 1963.
Bats Right. Throws Right. Height, 6 feet, 1 inch. Weight, 180 pounds.

Year Club	Lea	Pos	G	AB	R	H	2B	3B	HR	RBI	SB	Avg
1982 Sarasota Cubs Gulf Coast		SS-3B	53	190	27	61	11	0	2	28	32	.321
1983 Quad Cities a	..Midwest	SS	117	455	65	141	17	8	4	62	58	.310
1984 Midland	...Texas	SS	73	298	44	98	13	3	3	34	11	.329
1984 Iowa	..........A.A.	SS	61	210	25	49	11	1	7	27	9	.233
1985 Chicago	.........N.L.	SS	74	250	40	65	12	4	4	18	11	.260
1985 Iowa	..........A.A.	SS	73	272	24	73	9	6	2	28	17	.268
1986 Chicago	.........N.L.	SS	150	581	66	145	37	3	17	68	13	.250
1987 Iowa	..........A.A.	SS	5	19	1	8	1	0	0	2	1	.421
1987 Chicago b	.......N.L.	SS	95	346	40	85	18	3	5	22	12	.246
1988 Chicago	.........N.L.	SS	155	575	69	143	23	6	9	56	30	.249
1989 Chicago	.........N.L.	SS	138	471	52	131	20	6	6	60	19	.278
1990 Chicago	.........N.L.	SS	146	545	73	143	22	8	17	66	25	.262
1991 Chicago	.........N.L.	SS	142	492	59	128	22	7	12	50	21	.260
1992 Chicago c	.........N.L.	SS	18	73	8	23	3	1	0	2	2	.315
1993 Chicago d	.......N.L.	SS	7	10	3	4	2	0	0	2	0	.400
1994 Chicago	.........N.L.	SS	88	331	38	92	19	0	11	35	3	.278
1995 Chicago e	.......N.L.	SS	127	477	58	141	30	6	14	69	10	.296
1996 San Francisco f-g-h .N.L.		SS	82	287	27	86	12	2	5	25	8	.300
1997 Chicago-Pitt i-j-k .. .N.L.		SS-OF	132	490	71	147	22	5	14	57	32	.300
1998 Cleveland	..........A.L.	2B-SS-OF	62	156	26	37	11	3	3	12	9	.237
1998 San Francisco l-m-n N.L.		SS-OF-2B	36	51	10	9	2	0	3	8	0	.176
1999 St. Louis-N.Y. o-p-q .N.L.		OF-1B-SS-3B	104	243	35	78	11	3	5	41	10	.321
2000 St. Louis r	......N.L.	OF-SS-1B-3B	98	216	28	54	11	2	12	43	3	.250
Major League Totals	....	16 Yrs.	1654	5594	703	1511	277	59	140	634	208	.270
Division Series												
1999 New York	........,N.L.	OF	4	6	0	1	0	0	0	0	0	.167
2000 St. Louis	.........N.L.	PH	1	1	0	1	0	0	0	0	0	1.000
Division Series Totals	....		5	7	0	2	0	0	0	0	0	.286
Championship Series												
1989 Chicago	.........N.L.	SS	5	19	2	6	0	0	0	0	1	.316
1999 New York	........N.L.	OF	5	7	1	1	0	0	0	0	1	.143
2000 St. Louis	.........N.L.	OF	4	6	1	2	1	0	0	0	0	.333
Championship Series Totals	.....		14	32	5	9	1	0	0	0	2	.281

a On disabled list from May 31 to June 10, 1983.
b On disabled list from June 16 to August 21, 1987.
c On disabled list from May 5 to end of 1992 season.
d On disabled list from March 29 to September 1, 1993.
e Filed for free agency, November 12, 1995. Signed with San Francisco Giants, January 8, 1996.
f On disabled list from April 24 to May 13 and August 5 to September 30, 1996.
g Filed for free agency, November 18, 1996.
h Signed with Chicago Cubs, December 2, 1996.
i On disabled list from June 9 to June 24, 1997.
j Sold to Pittsburgh Pirates, August 31, 1997.
k Filed for free agency, October 28, 1997.
l Signed with Cleveland Indians, February 16, 1998.
m Traded to San Francisco Giants with pitcher Jose Mesa and pitcher Alvin Morman for pitcher Steve Reed and outfielder Jacob Cruz, July 24, 1998.
n Filed for free agency, October 23, 1998. Signed with St. Louis Cardinals, February 17, 1999.
o On disabled list from June 23 to July 9, 1999.
p Traded to New York Mets for infielder Craig Paquette, July 31, 1999.
q Filed for free agency, October 29, 1999. Signed with St. Louis Cardinals organization, February 3, 2000.
r Filed for free agency, October 27, 2000, signed with San Francisco Giants, December 8, 2000.

DURAZO, ERUBIEL CARDENAS

Born, Hermosillo, Mexico, January 23, 1974.
Bats Left. Throws Right. Height, 6 feet, 3 inches. Weight, 225 pounds.

Year Club	Lea	Pos	G	AB	R	H	2B	3B	HR	RBI	SB	Avg
1997 Monterrey	.......Mexican	1B-OF	110	358	47	101	21	10	8	61	3	.282
1998 Monterrey	.......Mexican	1B	119	420	84	147	32	2	19	98	4	.350
1999 Arizona	..............N.L.	1B	52	155	31	51	4	2	11	30	1	.329
2000 AR Diamondbacks ...Arizona		1B	2	5	2	3	0	0	1	2	0	.600
2000 Tucson	..............P.C.	1B	13	43	9	18	6	0	3	10	0	.419
2000 Arizona a	............N.L.	1B	67	196	35	52	11	0	8	33	1	.265
Major League Totals	....	2 Yrs.	119	351	66	103	15	2	19	63	2	.293
Division Series												
1999 Arizona	..............N.L.	1B	2	7	1	1	0	0	1	1	0	.143

a On disabled list from May 30 to June 23 and June 27 to July 12 and August 20 to October 2, 2000.

DURHAM, RAY
Born, Charlotte, North Carolina, November 30, 1971.
Bats Both. Throws Right. Height, 5 feet, 8 inches. Weight, 170 pounds.

Year	Club	Lea	Pos	G	AB	R	H	2B	3B	HR	RBI	SB	Avg
1990	Sarasota White Sox	Gulf C.	2B	35	116	18	32	3	3	0	13	23	.276
1991	Sarasota White Sox	Gulf C.	2B	6	23	3	7	1	0	0	4	5	.304
1991	Utica	N.Y.-Penn.	2B	39	142	29	36	2	7	0	17	12	.254
1992	Sarasota White Sox	Gulf C.	DH	5	13	3	7	2	0	0	2	1	.538
1992	Sarasota a	Fla. St.	2B	57	202	37	55	6	3	0	7	28	.272
1993	Birmingham	Southern	2B	137	528	83	143	22	10	3	37	39	.271
1994	Nashville	A.A.	2B	133	527	89	156	33	*12	16	66	34	.296
1995	Chicago	A.L.	2B	125	471	68	121	27	6	7	51	18	.257
1996	Chicago	A.L.	2B	156	557	79	153	33	5	10	65	30	.275
1997	Chicago	A.L.	2B	155	634	106	172	27	5	11	53	33	.271
1998	Chicago	A.L.	2B	158	635	126	181	35	8	19	67	36	.285
1999	Chicago	A.L.	2B	153	612	109	181	30	8	13	60	34	.296
2000	Chicago	A.L.	2B	151	614	121	172	35	9	17	75	25	.280
Major League Totals			6 Yrs.	898	3523	609	980	187	41	77	371	176	.278
Division Series													
2000	Chicago	A.L.	2B	3	10	2	2	1	0	1	1	0	.200

a On disabled list from June 16 to July 9, 1992.

DYE, JERMAINE TERRELL
Born, Oakland, California, January 28, 1974.
Bats Right. Throws Right. Height, 6 feet, 4 inches. Weight, 210 pounds.

Year	Club	Lea	Pos	G	AB	R	H	2B	3B	HR	RBI	SB	Avg
1993	Braves	Gulf Coast	OF-3B	31	124	17	43	14	0	0	27	5	.347
1993	Danville	Appal.	OF	25	94	6	26	6	1	2	12	4	.277
1994	Macon	So.Atl.	OF	135	506	73	151	41	4	15	98	19	.298
1995	Greenville	Southern	OF	104	403	50	115	26	4	15	71	4	.285
1996	Richmond	Int.	OF	36	142	25	33	7	1	6	19	3	.232
1996	Atlanta	N.L.	OF	98	292	32	82	16	0	12	37	1	.281
1997	Omaha	A.A.	OF	39	144	21	44	6	0	10	25	0	.306
1997	Kansas City a-b	A.L.	OF	75	263	26	62	14	0	7	22	2	.236
1998	Omaha	P.C.	OF-1B	41	157	29	47	6	0	12	35	7	.299
1998	Kansas City c	A.L.	OF	60	214	24	50	5	1	5	23	2	.234
1999	Kansas City	A.L.	OF	158	608	96	179	44	8	27	119	2	.294
2000	Kansas City	A.L.	OF	157	601	107	193	41	2	33	118	2	.321
Major League Totals			5 Yrs.	548	1978	285	566	120	11	84	319	7	.286
Division Series													
1996	Atlanta	N.L.	OF	3	11	1	2	0	0	1	1	1	.182
Championship Series													
1996	Atlanta	N.L.	OF	7	28	2	6	1	0	0	4	0	.214
World Series Record													
1996	Atlanta	N.L.	OF	5	17	0	2	0	0	0	1	0	.118

a Traded to Kansas City Royals with pitcher Jamie Walker for infielder Keith Lockhart and outfielder Michael Tucker, March 27, 1997.

b On disabled list from April 17 to May 3 and July 3 to August 13, 1997.

c On disabled list from March 31 to May 8 and September 1 to September 28, 1998.

EASLEY, JACINTO (DAMION)
Born, New York, New York, November 11, 1969.
Bats Right. Throws Right. Height, 5 feet, 11 inches. Weight, 185 pounds.

Year	Club	Lea	Pos	G	AB	R	H	2B	3B	HR	RBI	SB	Avg
1989	Bend	Northwest	SS	36	131	34	39	5	1	4	21	9	.298
1990	Quad City	Midwest	SS-3B	103	365	59	100	19	3	10	56	25	.274
1991	Midland	Texas	SS	127	452	73	115	24	4	6	57	23	.254
1992	Edmonton	P.C.	SS-3B	108	429	61	124	18	3	3	44	26	.289
1992	California	A.L.	3B-SS	47	151	14	39	5	0	1	12	9	.258
1993	California a	A.L.	2B-3B	73	230	33	72	13	2	2	22	6	.313
1994	California b	A.L.	3B-2B	88	316	41	68	16	1	6	30	4	.215
1995	California	A.L.	2B-SS	114	357	35	77	14	2	4	35	5	.216
1996	Midland	Texas	3B-SS	4	14	1	6	2	0	0	2	1	.429
1996	Vancouver c	P.C.	SS-2B-3B	12	48	13	15	2	1	2	8	4	.313
1996	California-Detroit d	A.L.	SS-2B-3B-OF	49	112	14	30	2	0	4	17	3	.268
1997	Detroit	A.L.	2B-SS	151	527	97	139	37	3	22	72	28	.264
1998	Detroit	A.L.	2B-SS	153	594	84	161	38	2	27	100	15	.271
1999	Detroit	A.L.	2B-SS	151	549	83	146	30	1	20	65	11	.266
2000	Toledo	Int.	2B	4	13	3	3	1	0	1	4	0	.231

Year Club	Lea	Pos	G	AB	R	H	2B	3B	HR	RBI	SB	Avg
2000 Detroit e . . . . .A.L.		2B	126	464	76	120	27	2	14	58	13	.259
Major League Totals	9 Yrs.		952	3300	477	852	182	13	100	411	94	.258

a On disabled list from June 19 to July 4 and July 28 to end of 1993 season.
b On disabled list from May 30 to June 17, 1994.
c On disabled list from April 1 to May 10, 1996.
d Traded to Detroit Tigers for pitcher Greg Gohr, July 31, 1996.
e On disabled list from April 10 to April 24 and May 9 to June 1, 2000.

EDMONDS, JAMES PATRICK

Born, Fullerton, California, June 27, 1970.
Bats Left. Throws Left. Height, 6 feet, 1 inch. Weight, 190 pounds.

Year Club	Lea	Pos	G	AB	R	H	2B	3B	HR	RBI	SB	Avg
1988 Bend . . . . .Northwest		OF	35	122	23	27	4	0	0	13	4	.221
1989 Quad City a . . . . . .Midwest		OF	31	92	11	24	4	0	1	4	1	.261
1990 Palm Springs . . . .California		OF	91	314	36	92	18	6	3	56	5	.293
1991 Palm Springs b-c . .California		OF-1B	60	187	28	55	15	1	2	27	2	.294
1992 Midland . . . . .Texas		OF	70	246	42	77	15	2	8	32	3	.313
1992 Edmonton . . . . .P.C.		OF	50	194	37	58	15	2	6	36	3	.299
1993 Vancouver d . . . . .P.C.		OF	95	356	59	112	28	4	9	74	6	.315
1993 California . . . . .A.L.		OF	18	61	5	15	4	1	0	4	0	.246
1994 California . . . . .A.L.		OF-1B	94	289	35	79	13	1	5	37	4	.273
1995 California . . . . .A.L.		OF	141	558	120	162	30	4	33	107	1	.290
1996 Lk Elsinore e . . . . .California		OF	5	15	4	6	2	0	1	4	0	.400
1996 California . . . . .A.L.		OF	114	431	73	131	28	3	27	66	4	.304
1997 Anaheim f . . . . .A.L.		OF-1B	133	502	82	146	27	0	26	80	5	.291
1998 Anaheim . . . . .A.L.		OF	154	599	115	184	42	1	25	91	7	.307
1999 Lake Elsinore . . . .California		DH	5	19	4	8	2	0	0	3	2	.421
1999 Anaheim g . . . . .A.L.		OF-1B	55	204	34	51	17	2	5	23	5	.250
2000 St. Louis h . . . . .N.L.		OF-1B	152	525	129	155	25	0	42	108	10	.295
Major League Totals	8 Yrs.		861	3169	593	923	186	12	163	516	36	.291
Division Series												
2000 St. Louis . . . . .N.L.		OF	3	14	5	8	4	0	2	7	1	.571
Championship Series												
2000 St. Louis . . . . .N.L.		OF	5	22	1	5	1	0	1	5	0	.227

a On disabled list from June 19 to end of 1989 season.
b Record of 0-0 in one game as pitcher.
c On disabled list from April 10 to May 7 and July 23 to end of 1991 season.
d On disabled list from June 29 to July 19, 1993.
e On disabled list from May 26 to June 10 and June 12 to July 18, 1996.
f On disabled list from July 31 to August 16, 1997.
g On disabled list from March 30 to August 2, 1999.
h Traded to St. Louis Cardinals for pitcher Kent Bottenfield and infielder Adam Kennedy, March 23, 2000.

ENCARNACION, JUAN DE DIOS

Born, Las Matas De Faran, Dominican Republic, March 8, 1976.
Bats Right. Throws Right. Height, 6 feet, 2 inches. Weight, 160 pounds.

Year Club	Lea	Pos	G	AB	R	H	2B	3B	HR	RBI	SB	Avg
1994 Fayetteville . . . . .So. Atl.		OF	24	83	6	16	1	1	1	4	1	.193
1994 Bristol . . . . .Appal.		OF	54	197	16	49	7	1	4	31	9	.249
1994 Lakeland . . . . .Fla. St.		OF	3	6	1	2	0	0	0	0	0	.333
1995 Fayetteville . . . . .So. Atl.		OF	124	457	62	129	31	7	16	72	5	.282
1996 Lakeland . . . . .Fla. St.		OF	131	499	54	120	31	2	15	58	11	.240
1997 Jacksonville . . . . . . .Southern		OF	131	493	91	159	31	4	26	90	17	.323
1997 Detroit . . . . .A.L.		OF	11	33	3	7	1	1	1	5	3	.212
1998 Lakeland . . . . .Fla.St.		OF	4	16	4	4	0	1	0	4	4	.250
1998 Toledo . . . . .Int.		OF	92	356	55	102	17	3	8	41	24	.287
1998 Detroit a . . . . .A.L.		OF	40	164	30	54	9	4	7	21	7	.329
1999 Detroit . . . . .A.L.		OF	132	509	62	130	30	6	19	74	33	.255
2000 Detroit . . . . .A.L.		OF	141	547	75	158	25	6	14	72	16	.289
Major League Totals	4 Yrs.		324	1253	170	349	65	17	41	172	59	.279

a On disabled list from March 31 to April 29, 1998.

ERSTAD, DARIN CHARLES

Born, Jamestown, North Dakota, June 4, 1974.
Bats Left. Throws Left. Height, 6 feet, 2 inches. Weight, 195 pounds.

Year Club	Lea	Pos	G	AB	R	H	2B	3B	HR	RBI	SB	Avg
1995 Angels . . . . .Arizona		OF	4	18	2	10	1	0	0	1	1	.556
1995 Lk Elsinore . . . . . . .California		OF	25	113	24	41	7	3	5	24	3	.363

Year	Club	Lea	Pos	G	AB	R	H	2B	3B	HR	RBI	SB	Avg
1996 Vancouver	............P.C.		OF-1B	85	351	63	107	22	5	6	41	11	.305
1996 California	...........A.L.		OF	57	208	34	59	5	1	4	20	3	.284
1997 Anaheim	..........A.L.		1B-OF	139	539	99	161	34	4	16	77	23	.299
1998 Anaheim a	..........A.L.		OF-1B	133	537	84	159	39	3	19	82	20	.296
1999 Anaheim b	...........A.L.		1B-OF	142	585	84	148	22	5	13	53	13	.253
2000 Anaheim	...........A.L.		OF-1B	157	*676	121	*240	39	6	25	100	28	.355
Major League Totals	....	5 Yrs.		628	2545	422	767	139	19	77	332	87	.301

a On disabled list from August 4 to August 19, 1998.
b On disabled list from August 11 to August 26, 1999.

ESTALELLA, ROBERT M. (BOBBY)

Born, Hialeah, Florida, August 23, 1974.
Bats Right. Throws Right. Height, 6 feet, 1 inch. Weight, 200 pounds.

Year	Club	Lea	Pos	G	AB	R	H	2B	3B	HR	RBI	SB	Avg
1993 Martinsvlle	.........Appal.		C	35	122	14	36	11	0	3	19	0	.295
1993 Clearwater	.........Fla.St.		C	11	35	4	8	0	0	0	4	0	.229
1994 Spartanburg	........So.Atl.		C	86	299	34	65	19	1	9	41	0	.217
1994 Clearwater	.........Fla.St.		C	13	46	3	12	1	0	2	9	0	.261
1995 Clearwater	.........Fla.St.		C	117	404	61	105	24	1	15	58	0	.260
1995 Reading	.........Eastern		C	10	34	5	8	1	0	2	9	0	.235
1996 Reading	.........Eastern		C	111	365	48	89	14	2	23	72	2	.244
1996 Scranton-WB	.........Int.		C	11	36	7	9	3	0	3	8	0	.250
1996 Philadelphia	.........N.L.		C	7	17	5	6	0	0	2	4	1	.353
1997 Scranton-WB	.........Int.		C	123	433	63	101	32	0	16	65	3	.233
1997 Philadelphia	.........N.L.		C	13	29	9	10	1	0	4	9	0	.345
1998 Scranton-WB	.........Int.		C	76	242	49	68	14	1	17	49	0	.281
1998 Philadelphia	.........N.L.		C	47	165	16	31.	6	1	8	20	0	.188
1999 Clearwater	.........Fla.St.		C	8	26	3	11	3	0	1	8	0	.423
1999 Scranton-WB	.........Int.		C	110	386	58	89	23	2	15	62	4	.231
1999 Philadelphia a-b	.........N.L.		C	9	18	2	3	0	0	0	1	0	.167
2000 San Francisco	.........N.L.		C	106	299	45	70	22	3	14	53	3	.234
Major League Totals	....	5 Yrs.		182	528	77	120	29	4	28	87	4	.227
Division Series													
2000 San Francisco	........N.L.		C	4	12	1	1	0	0	0	1	0	.083

a On disabled list from March 27 to April 29, 1999.
b Traded to San Francisco Giants for pitcher Chris Brock, December 12, 1999.

EUSEBIO, RAUL ANTONIO BARE

Born, San Jose de Los Llamos, Dominican Republic, April 27, 1967.
Bats Right. Throws Right. Height, 6 feet, 2 inches. Weight, 180 pounds.

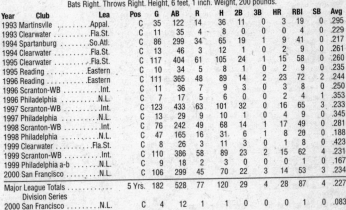

Year	Club	Lea	Pos	G	AB	R	H	2B	3B	HR	RBI	SB	Avg
1985 Sarasota Astros	.....Gulf C.		C	1	1	0	0	0	0	0	0	0	.000
1986	....				Played in Dominican Summer League								
1987 Sarasota Astros	.....Gulf C.		C-1B	42	125	26	26	1	2	1	15	8	.208
1988 Osceola	..........Fla. St.		C-OF	118	392	45	96	6	3	0	40	20	.245
1989 Columbus	........Southern		C	65	203	20	38	6	1	0	18	7	.187
1989 Osceola	..........Fla. St.		C	52	175	22	50	6	3	0	30	5	.286
1990 Columbus a	.....Southern		C	92	318	36	90	18	0	4	37	6	.283
1991 Tucson	..............P.C.		C	5	20	5	8	1	0	0	2	1	.400
1991 Jackson	...........Texas		C	66	222	27	58	8	3	2	31	3	.261
1991 Houston	..............N.L.		C	10	19	4	2	1	0	0	0	0	.105
1992 Jackson	...........Texas		C	94	339	33	104	9	3	5	44	1	.307
1993 Tucson b	...........P.C.		C	78	281	39	91	20	1	1	43	1	.324
1994 Houston	..............N.L.		C	55	159	18	47	9	1	5	30	0	.296
1995 Houston	..............N.L.		C	113	368	46	110	21	1	6	58	0	.299
1996 Tucson c	...........P.C.		C	15	53	8	22	4	0	0	14	0	.415
1996 Houston	..............N.L.		C	58	152	15	41	7	2	1	19	0	.270
1997 Houston	..............N.L.		C	60	164	12	45	2	0	1	18	0	.274
1998 Houston	..............N.L.		C	66	182	13	46	6	1	1	36	1	.253
1999 Houston d-e	..............N.L.		C	103	323	31	88	15	0	4	33	0	.272
2000 Houston	..............N.L.		C	74	218	24	61	18.	0	7	33	0	.280
Major League Totals	....	8 Yrs.		539	1585	163	440	79	5	25	227	1	.278
Division Series													
1997 Houston	..............N.L.		C	1	3	1	2	0	0	0	0	1	.667
1998 Houston	..............N.L.		C	1	3	0	1	1	0	0	0	0	.333
1999 Houston	..............N.L.		C	4	15	2	4	0	0	1	3	0	.267
Division Series Totals	....			6	21	3	7	1	0	1	3	1	.333

On disabled list from August 5 to end of 1990 season.
On disabled list from August 24 to end of 1993 season.
On disabled list from May 8 to June 17 and June 22 to August 7, 1996.
On disabled list from July 30 to August 15, 1999.
Filed for free agency, October 28, 1999, re-signed with Houston Astros, November 29, 1999.

EVERETT, CARL EDWARD
Born, Tampa, Florida, June 3, 1970.
Bats Both. Throws Right. Height, 6 feet. Weight, 190 pounds.

Year Club	Lea	Pos	G	AB	R	H	2B	3B	HR	RBI	SB	Avg
90 Tampa Yankees	Gulf C.	OF	48	185	28	48	8	5	1	14	15	.259
91 Greensboro	So. Atl.	OF	123	468	96	127	18	0	4	40	28	.271
92 Fort Lauderdale	Fla. St.	OF	46	183	30	42	8	2	2	9	11	.230
92 Prince William a	Carolina	OF	6	22	7	7	0	0	4	9	1	.318
93 High Desert	California	OF	59	253	48	73	12	6	10	52	24	.289
93 Florida	N.L.	OF	11	19	0	2	0	0	0	0	1	.105
93 Edmonton	P.C.	OF	35	136	28	42	13	4	6	16	12	.309
94 Edmonton	P.C.	OF	78	321	63	108	17	2	11	47	16	.336
94 Florida b-c	N.L.	OF	16	51	7	11	1	0	2	6	4	.216
95 Norfolk	Int.	OF-SS	67	260	52	78	16	4	6	35	12	.300
95 New York	N.Y.	OF	79	289	48	75	13	1	12	54	2	.260
96 New York d	N.L.	OF	101	192	29	46	8	1	1	16	6	.240
97 New York e	N.L.	OF	142	443	58	110	28	3	14	57	17	.248
98 Houston	N.L.	OF	133	467	72	138	34	4	15	76	14	.296
99 Houston f-g	N.L.	OF	123	464	86	151	33	3	25	108	27	.325
00 Boston	A.L.	OF	137	496	82	149	32	4	34	108	11	.300
Major League Totals		8 Yrs.	742	2421	382	682	149	16	103	425	82	.282
Division Series												
98 Houston	N.L.	OF	4	13	1	2	0	0	0	0	0	.154
99 Houston	N.L.	OF	4	15	2	2	0	0	0	1	0	.133
Division Series Totals			8	28	3	4	0	0	0	1	0	.143

Selected by Florida Marlins from New York Yankees organization in expansion draft, November 17, 1992.
On disabled list from July 23 to August 10, 1994.
Traded to New York Mets for second baseman Quilvio Veras, November 29, 1994.
On disabled list from April 12 to April 27, 1996.
Traded to Houston Astros for pitcher John Hudek, December 22, 1997.
On disabled list from July 16 to August 6, 1999.
Traded to Boston Red Sox for infielder Adam Everett and pitcher Greg Miller, December 15, 1999.

FEBLES, CARLOS MANUEL
Born, El Seibo, Dominican Republic, May 24, 1976.
Bats Right. Throws Right. Height, 5 feet, 11 inches. Weight, 170 pounds.

Year Club	Lea	Pos	G	AB	R	H	2B	3B	HR	RBI	SB	Avg
94 Kc/Colorado	Dominican	2B	56	184	38	61	9	3	2	37	12	.332
95 Royals	Gulf Coast	2B	54	188	40	53	13	5	3	20	16	.282
96 Lansing	Midwest	2B-SS	102	363	84	107	23	5	5	43	30	.295
97 Wilmington	Carolina	2B	122	438	78	104	27	6	3	29	49	.237
98 Wichita	Texas	2B	126	432	110	141	28	9	14	52	51	.326
98 Kansas City	A.L.	2B	11	25	5	10	1	2	0	2	2	.400
99 Kansas City a	A.L.	2B	123	453	71	116	22	9	10	53	20	.256
00 GC Royals	Gulf Coast	2B	1	3	0	1	1	0	0	0	1	.333
00 Wichita	Texas	2B	4	15	2	2	0	0	0	1	2	.133
00 Omaha	P.C.	2B	11	42	6	9	4	0	1	5	3	.214
00 Kansas City b	A.L.	2B	100	339	59	87	12	1	2	29	17	.257
Major League Totals		3 Yrs.	234	817	135	213	35	12	12	84	39	.261

On disabled list from August 21 to September 17, 1999.
On disabled list from June 5 to July 17 and August 14 to September 1, 2000.

FELIZ, PEDRO JULIO
Born, Azua, Dominican Republic, April 27, 1977.
Bats Right. Throws Right. Height, 6 feet, 1 inch. Weight, 180 pounds.

Year Club	Lea	Pos	G	AB	R	H	2B	3B	HR	RBI	SB	Avg
94 Giants	Arizona	3B	38	119	7	23	0	0	0	3	2	.193
95 Bellingham	Northwest	3B-1B	43	113	14	31	2	1	0	16	1	.274
96 Burlington	Midwest	3B-1B	93	321	36	85	12	2	5	36	5	.265
97 Bakersfield	California	3B	135	515	59	140	25	4	14	56	5	.272

55

Year	Club	Lea	Pos	G	AB	R	H	2B	3B	HR	RBI	SB	Avg
1998 Shreveport	Texas	3B	100	364	39	96	23	2	12	50	0	.264
1998 Fresno	P.C.	3B	3	7	1	3	1	0	1	3	0	.429
1999 Shreveport	Texas	3B	131	491	52	124	24	6	13	77	4	.253
2000 Fresno	P.C.	3B	128	503	85	150	34	2	33	105	1	.298
2000 San Francisco	N.L.	3B	8	7	1	2	0	0	0	0	0	.286

FICK, ROBERT CHARLES JOHN (ROB)

Born, Torrance, California, March 15, 1974.
Bats Left. Throws Right. Height, 6 feet, 1 inch. Weight, 189 pounds.

Year	Club	Lea	Pos	G	AB	R	H	2B	3B	HR	RBI	SB	Avg
1996 Jamestown	N.Y.-Penn.	C	43	133	18	33	6	0	1	14	3	.248
1997 W Michigan	Midwest	1B-C-3B	122	463	100	158	50	3	16	90	13	.341
1998 Jacksnville	Southern	C-1B-OF	130	515	101	164	47	6	18	114	8	.318
1998 Detroit	A.L.	C-1B	7	22	6	8	1	0	3	7	1	.364
1999 West Michigan	Midwest	1B	3	11	2	3	0	0	0	0	1	.273
1999 Toledo	Int.	1B	14	48	11	15	0	1	2	8	1	.313
1999 GC Tigers	Gulf Coast	1B	3	9	2	3	1	0	0	2	1	.333
1999 Detroit a	A.L.	C	15	41	6	9	0	0	3	10	1	.220
2000 Toledo	Int.	1B	17	68	5	10	5	0	1	7	1	.147
2000 Detroit b	A.L.	1B-C	66	163	18	41	7	2	3	22	2	.252
Major League Totals	3 Yrs.	88	226	30	58	8	2	9	39	4	.257

a On disabled list from March 31 to September 7, 1999.
b On disabled list from July 6 to August 31, 2000.

FINLEY, STEVEN ALLEN

Born, Union City, Tennessee, May 12, 1965.
Bats Left. Throws Left. Height, 6 feet, 2 inches. Weight, 180 pounds.

Year	Club	Lea	Pos	G	AB	R	H	2B	3B	HR	RBI	SB	Avg
1987 Newark	N.Y.-Penn.	OF	54	222	40	65	13	2	3	33	26	.293
1987 Hagerstown	Carolina	OF	15	65	9	22	3	2	1	5	7	.338
1988 Hagerstown	Carolina	OF	8	28	2	6	2	0	0	3	4	.214
1988 Charlotte	Southern	OF	10	40	7	12	4	2	1	6	2	.300
1988 Rochester	Int.	OF	120	456	61	*143	19	7	5	54	20	*.314
1989 Hagerstown	Southern	OF	11	48	11	20	3	1	0	7	4	.417
1989 Rochester	Int.	OF	7	25	2	4	0	0	0	2	3	.160
1989 Baltimore a	A.L.	OF	81	217	35	54	5	2	2	25	17	.249
1990 Baltimore b	A.L.	OF	142	464	46	119	16	4	3	37	22	.256
1991 Houston	N.L.	OF	159	596	84	170	28	10	8	54	34	.285
1992 Houston	N.L.	OF	*162	607	84	177	29	13	5	55	44	.292
1993 Houston c	N.L.	OF	142	545	69	145	15	*13	8	44	19	.266
1994 Jackson	Texas	OF	5	13	3	4	0	0	0	1	1	.308
1994 Houston d-e	N.L.	OF	94	373	64	103	16	5	11	33	13	.276
1995 San Diego	N.L.	OF	139	562	104	167	23	8	10	44	36	.297
1996 San Diego	N.L.	OF	161	655	126	195	45	9	30	95	22	.298
1997 Mobile	Southern	DH	1	4	1	2	0	0	1	2	0	.500
1997 Rancho Cuca	California	DH-OF	4	14	3	4	0	0	2	3	1	.286
1997 San Diego f	N.L.	OF	143	560	101	146	26	5	28	92	15	.261
1998 San Diego g	N.L.	OF	159	619	92	154	40	6	14	67	12	.249
1999 Arizona	A.L.	OF	156	590	100	156	32	10	34	103	8	.264
2000 Arizona	N.L.	OF	152	539	100	151	27	5	35	96	12	.280
Major League Totals	12 Yrs.	1690	6327	1005	1737	302	90	188	745	254	.275

Division Series

Year	Club	Lea	Pos	G	AB	R	H	2B	3B	HR	RBI	SB	Avg
1996 San Diego	N.L.	OF	3	12	0	1	0	0	0	1	1	.083
1998 San Diego	N.L.	OF	4	10	2	1	1	0	0	1	0	.100
1999 Arizona	N.L.	OF	4	13	0	5	1	0	0	5	0	.385
Division Series Totals			11	35	2	7	2	0	0	7	1	.200

Championship Series

Year	Club	Lea	Pos	G	AB	R	H	2B	3B	HR	RBI	SB	Avg
1998 San Diego	N.L.	OF	6	21	3	7	1	0	0	2	1	.333

World Series Record

Year	Club	Lea	Pos	G	AB	R	H	2B	3B	HR	RBI	SB	Avg
1998 San Diego	N.L.	OF	3	12	0	1	1	0	0	0	1	.083

a On disabled list from April 4 to April 21 and July 30 to September 1, 1989.
b Traded to Houston Astros with pitchers Pete Harnisch and Curt Schilling for first baseman Glenn Davis, January 10, 1991.
c On disabled list from April 25 to May 14, 1993.
d On disabled list from June 13 to July 3, 1994.
e Traded to San Diego Padres with third baseman Ken Caminiti, shortstop Andujar Cedeño, pitcher Brian Williams, first baseman Roberto Petagine and player to be named for outfielders Derek Bell and Phil Plantier, pitchers Doug

Brocail and Pedro Martinez, shortstop Ricky Gutierrez and infielder Craig Shipley, December 28, 1994. San Diego received pitcher Sean Fesh to complete trade, May 1, 1995.
f On disabled list from April 20 to May 6, 1997.
g Filed for free agency, October 26, 1998, signed with Arizona Diamondbacks, December 7, 1998.

FLAHERTY, JOHN TIMOTHY
Born, New York, New York, October 21, 1967.
Bats Right. Throws Right. Height, 6 feet, 1 inch. Weight, 195 pounds.

Year	Club	Lea	Pos	G	AB	R	H	2B	3B	HR	RBI	SB	Avg
1988 Elmira	N.Y.-Penn.	C	46	162	17	38	3	0	3	16	2	.235
1989 Winter Haven	Fla. St.	C-1B	95	334	31	87	14	2	4	28	1	.260
1990 Pawtucket	Int.	C-3B	99	317	35	72	18	0	4	32	1	.227
1990 Lynchburg	Carolina	C	1	4	0	0	0	0	0	1	0	.000
1991 New Britain	Eastern	C	67	225	27	65	9	0	3	18	0	.289
1991 Pawtucket	Int.	C	45	156	18	29	7	0	3	13	0	.186
1992 Pawtucket	Int.	C	31	104	11	26	3	0	0	7	0	.250
1992 Boston	A.L.	C	35	66	3	13	2	0	0	2	0	.197
1993 Pawtucket	Int.	C	105	365	29	99	22	0	6	35	0	.271
1993 Boston a	A.L.	C	13	25	3	3	2	0	0	2	0	.120
1994 Toledo	Int.	C	44	151	20	39	10	2	7	17	3	.258
1994 Detroit	A.L.	C	34	40	2	6	1	0	0	4	0	.150
1995 Detroit	A.L.	C	112	354	39	86	22	1	11	40	0	.243
1996 Detroit	A.L.	C	47	152	18	38	12	0	4	23	1	.250
1996 San Diego b	N.L.	C	72	264	22	80	12	0	9	41	2	.303
1997 San Diego c	N.L.	C	129	439	38	120	21	1	9	46	4	.273
1998 Durham	Int.	C	6	23	1	3	1	0	0	2	0	.130
1998 Tampa Bay d	A.L.	C	91	304	21	63	11	0	3	24	0	.207
1999 Tampa Bay	A.L.	C	117	446	53	124	19	0	14	71	0	.278
2000 Tampa Bay	A.L.	C	109	394	36	103	15	0	10	39	0	.261
Major League Totals		9 Yrs.	759	2484	235	636	117	2	60	292	7	.256

a Traded to Detroit Tigers for catcher Rich Rowland, April 1, 1994.
b Traded to San Diego Padres with infielder Chris Gomez for catcher Brad Ausmus and infielder Andujar Cedeno, June 18, 1996.
c Traded to Tampa Bay Devil Rays for pitcher Brian Boehringer and infielder Andy Sheets, November 19, 1997
d On disabled list from May 26 to June 20, 1998.

FLETCHER, DARRIN GLEN
Born, Elmhurst, Illinois, October 3, 1966.
Bats Left. Throws Right. Height, 6 feet, 1 inch. Weight, 198 pounds.

Year	Club	Lea	Pos	G	AB	R	H	2B	3B	HR	RBI	SB	Avg
1987 Vero Beach	Fla. St.	C	43	124	13	33	7	0	0	15	0	.266
1988 San Antonio	Texas	C	89	279	19	58	8	0	1	20	2	.208
1989 Albuquerque	P.C.	C	100	315	34	86	16	1	5	44	1	.273
1989 Los Angeles	N.L.	C	5	8	1	4	0	0	1	2	0	.500
1990 Albuquerque	P.C.	C	105	350	58	102	23	1	13	65	1	.291
1990 Los Angeles-Phil. a	N.L.	C	11	23	3	3	1	0	0	1	0	.130
1991 Scranton	Int.	C-1B	90	306	39	87	13	1	8	50	1	.284
1991 Philadelphia b	N.L.	C	46	136	5	31	8	0	1	12	0	.228
1992 Indianapolis	A.A.	C	13	51	2	13	2	0	1	9	0	.255
1992 Montreal c	N.L.	C	83	222	13	54	10	2	2	26	0	.243
1993 Montreal	N.L.	C	133	396	33	101	20	1	9	60	0	.255
1994 Montreal	N.L.	C	94	285	28	74	18	1	10	57	0	.260
1995 Montreal	N.L.	C	110	350	42	100	21	1	11	45	0	.286
1996 Montreal	N.L.	C	127	394	41	105	22	0	12	57	0	.266
1997 Montreal d-e-f	N.L.	C	96	310	39	86	20	1	17	55	1	.277
1998 Toronto g	A.L.	C	124	407	37	115	23	1	9	52	0	.283
1999 Syracuse	Int.	C	4	15	0	4	0	0	0	0	0	.267
1999 Toronto h	A.L.	C	115	412	48	120	26	0	18	80	0	.291
2000 Toronto i	A.L.	C	122	416	43	133	19	1	20	58	1	.320
Major League Totals		12 Yrs.	1066	3359	333	926	188	8	110	505	2	.276

a Traded to Philadelphia Phillies for pitcher Dennis Cook, September 13, 1990.
b Traded to Montreal Expos with cash for pitcher Barry Jones, December 9, 1991.
c On disabled list from May 12 to June 15, 1992.
d On disabled list from June 18 to July 3, 1997.
e Filed for free agency, October 27, 1997.
f Signed with Toronto Blue Jays, November 26, 1997.
g On disabled list from May 30 to June 14, 1998.
h On disabled list from May 1 to June 1, 1999.
i On disabled list from June 11 to July 3, 2000.

FLOYD, CORNELIUS CLIFFORD (CLIFF)
Born, Chicago, Illinois, December 5, 1972.
Bats Left. Throws Right. Height, 6 feet 4 inches. Weight, 220 pounds.

Year	Club	Lea	Pos	G	AB	R	H	2B	3B	HR	RBI	SB	Avg
1991	Bradenton Expos	....Gulf C.	1B	56	214	35	56	9	3	6	30	13	.262
1992	Albany	...........So. Atl.	OF-1B	134	516	83	157	24	*16	16	*97	32	.304
1992	West Palm Beach	...Fla. St.	OF	1	4	0	0	0	0	0	1	0	.000
1993	Harrisburg	.........Eastern	1B-OF	101	380	82	125	17	4	*26	*101	31	.329
1993	Ottawa	..............Int.	1B	32	125	12	30	2	2	2	18	2	.240
1993	Montreal	...............N.L.	1B	10	31	3	7	0	0	1	2	0	.226
1994	Montreal	...............N.L.	1B-OF	100	334	43	94	19	4	4	41	10	.281
1995	Montreal a	...........N.L.	1B-OF	29	69	6	9	1	0	1	8	3	.130
1996	Ottawa	...............Int.	OF-3B	20	76	7	23	3	1	1	8	2	.303
1996	Montreal	...............N.L.	OF-1B	117	227	29	55	15	4	6	26	7	.242
1997	Charlotte	.............Int.	OF-1B	39	131	27	48	10	0	9	33	7	.366
1997	Florida b-c	............N.L.	OF-1B	61	137	23	32	9	1	6	19	6	.234
1998	Florida	.................N.L.	OF	153	588	85	166	45	3	22	90	27	.282
1999	Calgary	..............P.C.	OF	9	31	6	12	1	0	3	8	0	.387
1999	Florida d	............N.L.	OF	69	251	37	76	19	1	11	49	5	.303
2000	Florida e	............N.L.	OF	121	420	75	126	30	0	22	91	24	.300
Major League Totals			8 Yrs.	660	2057	301	565	138	13	73	326	82	.275
World Series Record													
1997	Florida	.............N.L.	DH	4	2	1	0	0	0	0	0	0	.000

a On disabled list from May 16 to September 11, 1995.
b Traded to Florida Marlins for pitcher Dustin Hermanson and outfielder Joe Orsulak, March 26, 1997.
c On disabled list from May 9 to May 24 and June 21 to September 1, 1997.
d On disabled list from March 30 to April 27 and June 20 to September 7, 1999.
e On disabled list from July 29 to August 28, 2000.

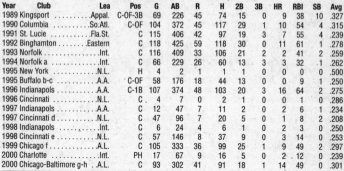

FORDYCE, BROOK ALEXANDER
Born, New London, Connecticut, May 7, 1970.
Bats Right. Throws Right. Height, 6 feet, 1 inch. Weight, 185 pounds.

Year	Club	Lea	Pos	G	AB	R	H	2B	3B	HR	RBI	SB	Avg
1989	Kingsport	.........Appal.	C-OF-3B	69	226	45	74	15	0	9	38	10	.327
1990	Columbia	..........So.Atl.	C-OF	104	372	45	117	29	1	10	54	4	.315
1991	St. Lucie	..........Fla.St.	C	115	406	42	97	19	3	7	55	4	.239
1992	Binghamton	.......Eastern	C	118	425	59	118	30	0	11	61	1	.278
1993	Norfolk	..............Int.	C	116	409	33	106	21	2	2	41	2	.259
1994	Norfolk a	..............Int.	C	66	229	26	60	13	3	3	32	1	.262
1995	New York	...............N.L.	H	4	2	1	1	1	0	0	0	0	.500
1995	Buffalo b-c	...........A.A.	C-OF	58	176	18	44	13	0	0	9	1	.250
1996	Indianapols	..........A.A.	C-1B	107	374	48	103	20	3	16	64	2	.275
1996	Cincinnati	..............N.L.	C	4	7	0	2	1	0	0	1	0	.286
1997	Indianapols	...........A.A.	C	12	47	7	11	2	0	2	6	1	.234
1997	Cincinnati d	...........N.L.	C	47	96	7	20	5	0	1	8	2	.208
1998	Indianapols	...............Int.	C	6	24	4	6	1	0	2	3	0	.250
1998	Cincinnati e	.............N.L.	C	57	146	8	37	9	0	3	14	0	.253
1999	Chicago f	...............A.L.	C	105	333	36	99	25	1	9	49	2	.297
2000	Charlotte	...............Int.	PH	17	67	9	16	5	0	2	12	0	.239
2000	Chicago-Baltimore g-h	.A.L.	C	93	302	41	91	18	1	14	49	0	.301
Major League Totals			6 Yrs.	310	886	93	250	59	2	27	121	4	.282

a On disabled list from June 19 to July 2 and July 18 to August 30, 1994.
b Claimed on waivers by Cleveland Indians, May 15, 1995.
c Filed for free agency, October 16, 1995, signed with Cincinnati Reds organization, December 7, 1995.
d On disabled list from July 16 to August 5, 1997.
e On disabled list from July 13 to August 12, 1998.
f Traded to Chicago White Sox for pitcher Jake Meyer, March 25, 1999.
g On disabled list from March 25 to May 22, 2000.
h Traded to Baltimore Orioles with pitcher Miguel Felix, pitcher Juan Figueroa and pitcher Jason Lakman for designated hitter Harold Baines and catcher Charles Johnson, July 29, 2000.

FOX, ANDREW JUNIPERO (ANDY)
Born, Sacramento, California, January 12, 1971.
Bats Left. Throws Right. Height, 6 feet, 4 inches. Weight, 205 pounds.

Year	Club	Lea	Pos	G	AB	R	H	2B	3B	HR	RBI	SB	Avg
1989	Yankees	.....Gulf Coast	3B	40	141	26	35	9	2	3	25	6	.248
1990	Greensboro	.....So.Atl.	3B	134	455	68	99	19	4	9	55	26	.218
1991	Pr William	.....Carolina	3B	126	417	60	96	22	2	10	46	15	.230

Year	Club	Lea	Pos	G	AB	R	H	2B	3B	HR	RBI	SB	Avg
1992 Pr William	Carolina		3B-SS	125	473	75	113	18	3	7	42	28	.239
1993 Albany	Eastern		3B	65	236	44	65	16	1	3	24	12	.275
1994 Albany	Eastern		3B-SS-2B	121	472	75	105	20	3	11	43	22	.222
1995 Norwich	Eastern		SS	44	175	23	36	3	5	5	17	8	.206
1995 Columbus	Int.		3B-SS-OF-2B	82	302	61	105	16	6	9	37	22	.348
1996 New York	A.L.		2B-3B-SS-OF	113	189	26	37	4	0	3	13	11	.196
1997 Columbus	Int.		3B-2B-SS-OF	95	318	66	87	11	4	6	33	28	.274
1997 New York	A.L.		3B-2B-SS-OF	22	31	13	7	1	0	0	1	2	.226
1998 Arizona a	N.L.		2B-0F-3B-1B	139	502	67	139	21	6	9	44	14	.277
1999 Arizona b	N.L.		SS-3B	99	274	34	70	12	2	6	33	4	.255
2000 El Paso	Texas		3B	4	15	3	6	2	0	0	4	1	.400
2000 Tucson	P.C.		2B	3	13	1	3	0	1	0	3	0	.231
2000 Arizona-Florida c-d	N.L.		SS-3B-OF-2B	100	250	29	58	8	2	4	20	10	.232
Major League Totals			5 Yrs.	473	1246	169	311	46	10	22	111	41	.250
Division Series													
1996 New York	A.L.		DH-PR	2	0	0	0	0	0	0	0	0	.000
1997 New York	A.L.		2B	2	0	0	0	0	0	0	0	0	.000
1999 Arizona	N.L.		SS	1	3	0	0	0	0	0	0	0	.000
Division Series Totals				5	3	0	0	0	0	0	0	0	.000
Championship Series													
1996 New York	A.L.		PR	2	0	0	0	0	0	0	0	0	.000
World Series													
1996 New York	A.L.		2B-3B	4	0	1	0	0	0	0	0	0	.000

a Traded to Arizona Diamondbacks for pitcher Marty Janzen and pitcher Todd Erdos, March 8, 1998.
b On disabled list from August 28 to September 12, 1999.
c On disabled list from March 23 to April 16, 2000.
d Traded to Florida Marlins for outfielder Danny Bautista, June 9, 2000.

FRANCO, MATTHEW NEIL

Born, Santa Monica, California, August 19, 1969.
Bats Left. Throws Right. Height, 6 feet, 2 inches. Weight, 210 pounds.

Year	Club	Lea	Pos	G	AB	R	H	2B	3B	HR	RBI	SB	Avg
1987 Wytheville	Appal.		3B-1B-2B	62	202	25	50	10	1	1	21	4	.248
1988 Wytheville	Appal.		3B-1B-OF	20	79	14	31	9	1	0	16	0	.392
1988 Geneva	N.Y.-Penn.		3B-1B	44	164	19	42	2	0	3	21	2	.256
1989 Chston-Wv	So. Atl.		3B-1B-OF	109	377	42	102	16	1	5	48	2	.271
1989 Peoria	Midwest		3B	16	58	4	13	4	0	0	9	0	.224
1990 Peoria	Midwest		1B-3B	123	443	52	125	33	2	6	65	4	.282
1991 Winston-Sal	Carolina		1B-3B-SS	104	307	47	66	12	1	4	41	4	.215
1992 Charlotte	Southern		3B-1B-OF	108	343	35	97	18	3	2	31	3	.283
1993 Orlando	Southern		1B-3B	68	237	31	75	20	1	7	37	3	.316
1993 Iowa	A.A.		1B-OF-2B	62	199	24	58	17	4	5	29	4	.291
1994 Iowa	A.A.		1B-3B-OF	128	437	63	121	32	4	11	71	3	.277
1995 Iowa	A.A.		3B-1B-C	121	455	51	128	28	5	6	58	1	.281
1995 Chicago	N.L.		2B-1B-3B	16	17	3	5	1	0	0	1	0	.294
1996 Norfolk a	Int.		3B-1B	133	508	74	164	40	2	7	81	5	.323
1996 New York	N.L.		3B-1B	14	31	3	6	1	0	1	2	0	.194
1997 Norfolk	Int.		OF-1B-3B	7	26	5	7	2	0	0	0	0	.269
1997 New York	N.L.		3B-1B-OF	112	163	21	45	5	0	5	21	1	.276
1998 Norfolk	Int.		3B-OF-1B	5	19	2	7	1	0	0	1	2	.368
1998 New York b	N.L.		3B-OF-1B	103	161	20	44	7	2	1	13	0	.273
1999 New York	N.L.		1B-OF-3B-P	120	132	18	31	5	0	4	21	0	.235
2000 Norfolk	Int.		3B	14	51	3	7	1	0	0	1	0	.137
2000 New York C	N.L.		1B-3B-OF-2B	101	134	9	32	4	0	2	14	0	.239
Major League Totals			6 Yrs.	468	638	74	163	23	2	13	72	1	.255
Division Series													
1999 New York	N.L.		PH	1	0	0	0	0	0	0	0	0	.000
Championship Series													
1999 New York	N.L.		PH	5	2	1	1	1	0	0	0	0	.500
2000 New York	N.L.		1B	2	3	0	0	0	0	0	0	0	.000
Championship Series Totals				7	5	1	1	1	0	0	0	0	.200
World Series Record													
2000 New York	N.L.		1B	1	1	0	0	0	0	0	0	0	.000

a Traded by Chicago Cubs to New York Mets for a player-to-be-named later, April 8, 1996. Chicago received pitcher Chris DeWitt, June 11, 1996.
b On disabled list from June 29 to July 14, 1998.
c Not offered 2001 contract, December 19, 2000.

FRIAS, HANLEY
Born, Villa Altagracia, Dominican Republic, December 5, 1973.
Bats Both. Throws Right. Height, 6 feet. Weight, 160 pounds.

Year	Club	Lea	Pos	G	AB	R	H	2B	3B	HR	RBI	SB	Avg
1991 Texas	Domincan		-SS	63	234	34	58	11	7	0	18	25	.248
1992 Rangers	Gulf Coast		2B-SS	58	205	37	50	9	2	0	28	28	.244
1993 Chston-Sc	So.Atl.		2B-OF-SS	132	473	61	109	20	4	4	37	27	.230
1994 High Desert	California		SS	124	452	70	115	17	6	3	59	37	.254
1995 Charlotte	Fla.St.		SS	33	120	23	40	6	3	0	14	8	.333
1995 Tulsa	Texas		SS	93	360	44	101	18	4	0	27	14	.281
1996 Tulsa	Texas		SS	134	505	73	145	24	12	2	41	9	.287
1997 Okla City	A.A.		SS	132	484	64	128	17	4	5	46	35	.264
1997 Texas a	A.L.		SS-2B	14	26	4	5	1	0	0	1	0	.192
1998 Tucson	P.C.		SS-3B-2B	63	253	32	73	10	4	1	21	16	.289
1998 Arizona	N.L.		2B-3B-SS	15	23	4	3	0	1	1	2	0	.130
1999 Tucson	P.C.		3B	23	80	15	24	3	0	0	6	3	.300
1999 Arizona	N.L.		SS-2B	69	150	27	41	3	2	1	16	4	.273
2000 Arizona	N.L.		SS-2B-3B	75	112	18	23	5	0	2	6	2	.205
Major League Totals			4 Yrs.	173	311	53	72	9	3	4	25	6	.232
Division Series													
1999 Arizona	N.L.		SS	4	7	0	0	0	0	0	0	0	.000

a Selected in expansion draft by Arizona Diamondbacks, November 18, 1997.

FRYE, JEFFREY DUSTIN (JEFF)
Born, Oakland, California, August 31, 1966.
Bats Right. Throws Right. Height, 5 feet, 9 inches. Weight, 165 pounds.

Year	Club	Lea	Pos	G	AB	R	H	2B	3B	HR	RBI	SB	Avg
1988 Butte	Pioneer		2B-SS	55	185	47	53	7	1	0	14	16	.286
1989 Gastonia	So.Atl.		2B	125	464	85	145	26	3	1	40	33	.313
1990 Charlotte	Fla.St.		2B	131	503	77	137	16	7	0	50	29	.272
1991 Tulsa	Texas		2B	131	503	92	152	32	11	4	41	15	.302
1992 Okla City	A.A.		2B	87	337	64	101	26	2	2	28	11	.300
1992 Texas	A.L.		2B	67	199	24	51	9	1	1	12	1	.256
1993 Texas a	A.L.		INJURED - did not play										
1994 Okla City	A.A.		2B	17	68	7	19	3	0	1	5	2	.279
1994 Texas b	A.L.		2B-3B	57	205	37	67	20	3	0	18	6	.327
1995 Texas c	A.L.		2B	90	313	38	87	15	2	4	29	3	.278
1996 Okla City	A.A.		2B-SS-OF-3B	49	181	25	43	10	0	1	18	10	.238
1996 Boston d-e	A.L.		2B-OF-SS	105	419	74	120	27	2	4	41	18	.286
1997 Boston	A.L.		2B-3B-OF	127	404	56	126	36	2	3	51	19	.312
1998 Boston f	A.L.		INJURED - did not play										
1999 Boston g	A.L.		2B-3B-SS	41	114	14	32	3	0	1	12	2	.281
1999 GC Red Sox	Gulf Coast		2B	6	20	4	8	1	0	0	1	0	.400
1999 Pawtucket	Int.		2B	3	9	0	3	0	0	0	2	0	.333
2000 Boston	A.L.		2B-OF-3B	69	239	35	69	13	0	1	13	1	.289
2000 Colorado h-i	N.L.		2B-3B	37	87	14	31	6	0	0	3	4	.356
Major League Totals			7 Yrs.	593	1980	292	583	129	10	14	179	54	.294

a On disabled list from March 27 to October 1, 1993.
b On disabled list from June 9 to 24, 1994.
c On disabled list from June 3 to 18 and June 21 to July 6, 1995.
d Not offered 1996 contract, December 20, 1995, re-signed with Texas Rangers organization, March 25, 1996.
e Released by Texas Rangers, June 5, 1996, signed with Boston Red Sox, June 6, 1996.
f On disabled list from March 13 to October 1, 1998.
g On disabled list from June 16 to September 1, 1999.
h Traded to Colorado Rockies with pitcher Brian Rose, pitcher John Wasdin and pitcher Jeff Taglienti for pitcher Rolando Arrojo, pitcher Rick Croushore and infielder Mike Lansing, July 27, 2000.
i Filed for free agency, October 30, 2000, signed with Toronto Blue Jays, December 11, 2000.

FRYMAN, DAVID (TRAVIS)
Born, Lexington, Kentucky, April 25, 1969.
Bats Right. Throws Right. Height, 6 feet, 1 inch. Weight, 194 pounds.

Year	Club	Lea	Pos	G	AB	R	H	2B	3B	HR	RBI	SB	Avg
1987 Bristol	Appal.		SS	67	248	25	58	9	0	2	20	6	.234
1988 Fayetteville	So. Atl.		SS	123	411	44	96	17	4	0	47	18	.234
1989 London	Eastern		SS	118	426	52	113	*30	1	9	56	5	.265
1990 Toledo	Int.		SS	87	327	38	84	22	2	10	53	4	.257
1990 Detroit	A.L.		3B-SS	66	232	32	69	11	1	9	27	3	.297
1991 Detroit	A.L.		3B-SS	149	557	65	144	36	3	21	91	12	.259
1992 Detroit	A.L.		SS-3B	161	*659	87	175	31	4	20	96	8	.266

Year	Club	Lea	Pos	G	AB	R	H	2B	3B	HR	RBI	SB	Avg
1993 Detroit	A.L.		SS-3B	151	607	98	182	37	5	22	97	9	.300
1994 Detroit	A.L.		3B	114	*464	66	122	34	5	18	85	2	.263
1995 Detroit	A.L.		3B	144	567	79	156	21	5	15	81	4	.275
1996 Detroit	A.L.		3B-SS	157	616	90	165	32	3	22	100	4	.268
1997 Detroit a-b	A.L.		3B	154	595	90	163	27	3	22	102	16	.274
1998 Cleveland	A.L.		3B-SS	146	557	74	160	33	2	28	96	10	.287
1999 Akron	Eastern		DH	4	12	4	3	0	0	1	4	0	.250
1999 Buffalo	Int.		3B	3	11	1	2	0	0	1	2	0	.182
1999 Cleveland c			3B	85	322	45	82	16	2	10	48	2	.255
2000 Cleveland	A.L.		3B-1B	155	574	93	184	38	4	22	106	1	.321
Major League Totals			11 Yrs.	1482	5750	819	1602	316	37	209	929	71	.279
Division Series													
1998 Cleveland	A.L.		3B	4	13	1	2	1	0	0	0	1	.154
1999 Cleveland	A.L.		3B	5	15	2	4	0	0	1	4	1	.267
Division Series Totals				9	28	3	6	1	0	1	4	2	.214
Championship Series													
1998 Cleveland	A.L.		3B	6	23	2	4	0	0	0	0	1	.174

a Traded to Arizona Diamondbacks for third baseman Joe Randa, infielder Gabe Alvarez and pitcher Matt Drews, November 19, 1997.
b Traded to Cleveland Indians with pitcher Tom Martin for infielder Matt Williams, December 1, 1997.
c On disabled list from June 6 to June 25 and July 4 to September 2, 1999.

FULLMER, BRADLEY RYAN (BRAD)

Born, Chatsworth, California, January 17, 1975.
Bats Left. Throws Right. Height, 6 feet, 1 inch. Weight 185 pounds.

Year	Club	Lea	Pos	G	AB	R	H	2B	3B	HR	RBI	SB	Avg
1995 Albany	So. Atl.		DH-3B-1B	123	468	69	151	38	4	8	67	10	.323
1996 Wst Plm Bch	Fla. St.		OF-1B	102	380	52	115	29	1	5	63	4	.303
1996 Harrisburg	Eastern		OF-1B	24	98	11	27	4	1	4	14	0	.276
1997 Harrisburg	Eastern		1B-OF-3B	94	357	60	111	24	2	19	62	6	.311
1997 Ottawa	Int.		1B-OF	24	91	13	27	7	0	3	17	1	.297
1997 Montreal	N.L.		1B-OF	19	40	4	12	2	0	3	8	0	.300
1998 Montreal	N.L.		1B	140	505	58	138	44	2	13	73	6	.273
1999 Ottawa	Int.		1B	39	142	31	45	9	0	11	32	2	.317
1999 Montreal	N.L.		1B	100	347	38	96	34	2	9	47	2	.277
2000 Toronto a-b	A.L.		DH-1B	133	482	76	142	29	1	32	104	3	.295
Major League Totals			4 Yrs.	392	1374	176	388	109	5	57	232	11	.282

a Traded to Texas Rangers for infielder Lee Stevens, March 16, 2000.
b Traded to Toronto Blue Jays for infielder David Segui, March 16, 2000.

FURCAL, RAFAEL

Born, Loma De Cabrera, Dominican Republic, August 24, 1980.
Bats Both. Throws Right. Height, 5 feet, 10 inches. Weight, 150 pounds.

Year	Club	Lea	Pos	G	AB	R	H	2B	3B	HR	RBI	SB	Avg
1997 Braves	Gulf Coast		2B-OF	50	190	31	49	5	4	1	9	15	.258
1998 Danville	Appal.		2B	66	268	56	88	15	4	0	23	60	.328
1999 Myrtle Beach	Carolina		SS	43	184	32	54	9	3	0	12	23	.293
1999 Macon	So.Atl.		SS	83	335	73	113	15	1	1	29	73	.337
2000 Greenville	Southern		SS	3	10	1	2	0	0	1	3	0	.200
2000 Atlanta a-b	N.L.		SS-2B	131	455	87	134	20	4	4	37	40	.295
Division Series													
2000 Atlanta	N.L.		SS	3	11	2	1	0	0	0	0	1	.091

a On disabled list from June 13 to June 28, 2000.
b Selected Rookie of the Year in National League for 2000.

GALARRAGA, ANDRES JOSE

Born, Caracas, Venezuela, June 18, 1961.
Bats Right. Throws Right. Height, 6 feet, 3 inches. Weight, 235 pounds.

Year	Club	Lea	Pos	G	AB	R	H	2B	3B	HR	RBI	SB	Avg
1979 W. Palm Beach	Fla. St.		1B	7	23	3	3	0	0	0	1	0	.130
1979 Calgary	Pioneer		1B-3B-C	42	112	14	24	3	1	4	16	1	.214
1980 Calgary	Pioneer		1B-3B-C-OF	59	190	27	50	11	4	4	22	3	.263
1981 Jamestown	N.Y.-Penn.		C-OF-3B	47	154	24	40	5	4	6	26	0	.260
1982 W. Palm Beach	Fla. St.		1B-OF	105	338	39	95	20	2	14	51	2	.281
1983 W. Palm Beach	Fla. St.		1B	104	401	55	116	18	3	10	66	7	.289

Year Club	Lea	Pos	G	AB	R	H	2B	3B	HR	RBI	SB	Avg
1984 Jacksonville . . .Southern		1B	143	533	81	154	28	4	27	87	2	.289
1985 Indianapolis . . . . . . .Int.		1B-OF	121	439	*75	118	15	8	25	87	3	.269
1985 Montreal . . . . .N.L.		1B	24	75	9	14	1	0	2	4	1	.187
1986 Montreal a . . . . .N.L.		1B	105	321	39	87	13	0	10	42	6	.305
1987 Montreal . . . . .N.L.		1B	147	551	72	168	40	3	13	90	7	.305
1988 Montreal . . . . .N.L.		1B	157	609	99	*184	*42	8	29	92	13	.302
1989 Montreal . . . . .N.L.		1B	152	572	76	147	30	1	23	85	12	.257
1990 Montreal . . . . .N.L.		1B	155	579	65	148	29	0	20	87	10	.256
1991 Montreal b-c . . . . . .N.L.		1B	107	375	34	82	13	2	9	33	5	.219
1992 Louisville . . . . .A.A.		1B	11	34	3	6	0	1	2	3	1	.176
1992 St. Louis d-e . . . . . .N.L.		1B	95	325	38	79	14	2	10	39	5	.243
1993 Colorado f-g . . . . . .N.L.		1B	120	470	71	174	35	4	22	98	2	*.370
1994 Colorado h . . . . . . .N.L.		1B	103	417	77	133	21	0	31	85	8	.319
1995 Colorado . . . . .N.L.		1B	143	554	89	155	29	3	31	106	12	.280
1996 Colorado . . . . .N.L.		1B-3B	159	626	119	190	39	3	*47	*150	18	.304
1997 Colorado i-j . . . . . .N.L.		1B	154	600	120	191	31	3	41	*140	15	.318
1998 Atlanta . . . . .N.L.		1B	153	555	103	169	27	1	44	121	7	.305
1999 Atlanta k . . . . .N.L.		ILLNESS - Did Not Play										
2000 Atlanta l . . . . .N.L.		1B	141	494	67	149	25	1	28	100	3	.302
Major League Totals		15 Yrs.	1915	7123	1078	2070	389	31	360	1272	124	.291
Division Series												
1995 Colorado . . . . .N.L.		1B	4	18	1	5	1	0	0	2	0	.278
1998 Atlanta . . . . .N.L.		1B	3	12	1	3	0	0	0	0	0	.250
2000 Atlanta . . . . .N.L.		1B	3	10	1	2	1	0	0	1	0	.200
Division Series Totals			10	40	3	10	2	0	0	3	0	.250
Championship Series												
1998 Atlanta . . . . .N.L.		1B	6	21	1	2	0	0	1	4	0	.095

a On disabled list from July 10 to September 4, 1986.
b On disabled list from May 26 to July 4, 1991.
c Traded to St. Louis Cardinals for pitcher Ken Hill, November 25, 1991.
d On disabled list from April 8 to May 22, 1992.
e Filed for free agency, October 27; signed with Colorado Rockies, November 17, 1992.
f On disabled list from May 10 to May 28 and July 25 to August 19, 1993.
g Filed for free agency, October 25; re-signed with Colorado Rockies, December 6, 1993.
h On disabled list from July 26 to end of 1994 season.
i Filed for free agency, October 27, 1997.
j Signed by Atlanta Braves, November 20, 1997.
k On disabled list from April 3 to November 1, 1999.
l Filed for free agency, October 30, 2000, signed with Texas Rangers, December 8, 2000.

GANT, RONALD EDWIN

Born, Victoria, Texas, March 2, 1965.
Bats Right. Throws Right. Height, 6 feet. Weight, 172 pounds.

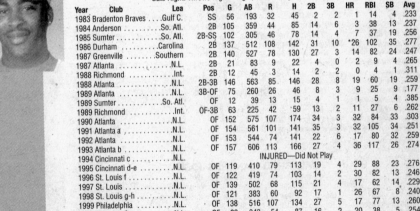

Year Club	Lea	Pos	G	AB	R	H	2B	3B	HR	RBI	SB	Avg
1983 Bradenton Braves . . . .Gulf C.		SS	56	193	32	45	2	2	1	14	4	.233
1984 Anderson . . . . .So. Atl.		2B	105	359	44	85	14	6	3	38	13	.237
1985 Sumter . . . . .So. Atl.		2B-SS	102	305	46	78	14	4	7	37	19	.256
1986 Durham . . . . .Carolina		2B	137	512	108	142	31	10	*26	102	35	.277
1987 Greenville . . . . . . .Southern		2B	140	527	78	130	27	3	14	82	24	.247
1987 Atlanta . . . . .N.L.		2B	21	83	9	22	4	0	2	9	4	.265
1988 Richmond . . . . .Int.		2B	12	45	.3	14	2	2	0	4	1	.311
1988 Atlanta . . . . .N.L.		2B-3B	146	563	85	146	28	8	19	60	19	.259
1989 Atlanta . . . . .N.L.		3B-OF	75	260	26	46	8	3	9	25	9	.177
1989 Sumter . . . . .So. Atl.		OF	12	39	13	15	4	1	1	5	4	.385
1989 Richmond . . . . .Int.		OF-3B	63	225	42	·59	13	2	11	27	6	.262
1990 Atlanta . . . . .N.L.		OF	152	575	107	174	34	3	32	84	33	.303
1991 Atlanta a . . . . .N.L.		OF	154	561	101	141	35	3	32	105	34	.251
1992 Atlanta . . . . .N.L.		OF	153	544	74	141	22	6	17	80	32	.259
1993 Atlanta b . . . . .N.L.		OF	157	606	113	166	27	4	36	117	26	.274
1994 Cincinnati c . . . . .N.L.		INJURED—Did Not Play										
1995 Cincinnati d-e . . . . . . .N.L.		OF	119	410	79	113	19	4	29	88	23	.276
1996 St. Louis f . . . . .N.L.		OF	122	419	74	103	14	2	30	82	13	.246
1997 St. Louis . . . . .N.L.		OF	139	502	68	115	21	4	17	62	14	.229
1998 St. Louis g-h . . . . . . .N.L.		OF	121	383	60	92	17	1	26	67	8	.240
1999 Philadelphia . . . . .N.L.		OF	138	516	107	134	27	5	17	77	13	.260
2000 Philadelphia . . . . .N.L.		OF	89	343	54	87	16	2	20	38	5	.254
2000 Anaheim i-j . . . . .A.L.		OF	34	82	15	19	3	1	6	16	1	.232
Major League Totals		13 Yrs.	1620	5847	972	1499	275	46	292	910	234	.256
Division Series												
1995 Cincinnati . . . . .N.L.		OF	3	13	3	3	0	0	1	2	0	.231

Year	Club	Lea	Pos	G	AB	R	H	2B	3B	HR	RBI	SB	Avg
1996 St. Louis	N.L.	OF	3	10	3	4	1	0	1	4	2	.400
Division Series Totals			6	23	6	7	1	0	2	6	2	.304
Championship Series												
1991 Atlanta	N.L.	OF	7	27	4	7	1	0	1	3	7	.259
1992 Atlanta	N.L.	OF	7	22	5	4	0	0	2	6	1	.182
1993 Atlanta	N.L.	OF	6	27	4	5	3	0	0	3	0	.185
1995 Cincinnati	N.L.	OF	4	16	1	3	0	0	0	1	0	.188
1996 St. Louis	N.L.	OF	7	25	3	6	1	0	2	4	0	.240
Championship Series Totals			31	117	17	25	5	0	5	17	8	.214
World Series Record												
1991 Atlanta	N.L.	OF	7	30	3	8	0	1	0	4	1	.267
1992 Atlanta	N.L.	OF	4	8	2	1	1	0	0	0	2	.125
World Series Totals			411	38	5	9	1	1	0	4	3	.237

a Suspended one game by National League for July 4 umpire bumping, July 31, 1991.
b Released, March 15; signed with Cincinnati Reds, June 21, 1994.
c On disabled list from June 21 to end of 1994 season.
d Filed for free agency, November 12, 1995.
e Signed with St. Louis Cardinals, December 25, 1995.
f On disabled list from May 11 to June 14, 1996.
g On disabled list from June 21 to July 11, 1998.
h Traded to Philadelphia Phillies with pitcher Jeff Brantley, pitcher Cliff Politte and cash for pitcher Ricky Bottalico and pitcher Garrett Stephenson, November 19, 1998.
i Traded to Anaheim Angels for pitcher Kent Bottenfield, July 30, 2000.
j Filed for free agency, October 30, 2000, signed with Colorado Rockies, December 10, 2000.

GARCIAPARRA, ANTHONY NOMAR (NOMAR)

Born, Whittier, Calif., July 23, 1973.
Bats Right. Throws Right. Height, 6 feet. Weight, 167 pounds.

Year	Club	Lea	Pos	G	AB	R	H	2B	3B	HR	RBI	SB	Avg
1994 Sarasota	Fla.St.	SS	28	105	20	31	8	1	1	16	5	.295
1995 Trenton	Eastern	SS	125	513	77	137	20	8	8	47	35	.267
1996 Red Sox	Gulf Coast	SS	5	14	4	4	2	1	0	5	0	.286
1996 Pawtucket	Int.	SS	43	172	40	59	15	2	16	46	3	.343
1996 Boston	A.L.	SS-2B	24	87	11	21	2	3	4	16	5	.241
1997 Boston a	A.L.	SS	153	*684	122	*209	44	*11	30	98	22	.306
1998 Boston b	A.L.	SS	143	604	111	195	37	8	35	122	12	.323
1999 Boston	A.L.	SS	135	532	103	190	42	4	27	104	14	* .357
2000 Boston c	A.L.	SS	140	529	104	197	51	3	21	96	5	* .372
Major League Totals	5 Yrs.		595	2436	451	812	176	29	117	436	58	.333
Division Series												
1998 Boston	A.L.	SS	4	15	4	5	1	0	3	11	0	.333
1999 Boston	A.L.	SS	5	12	6	5	2	0	2	4	0	.417
Division Series Totals			9	27	10	10	3	0	5	15	0	.370
Championship Series												
1999 Boston	A.L.	SS	5	20	2	8	2	0	2	5	1	.400

a Selected Rookie of the Year in American League for 1997.
b On disabled list from May 9 to May 28, 1998.
c On disabled list from May 12 to May 26, 2000.

GIAMBI, JASON GILBERT

Born, West Covina, California, January 8, 1971.
Bats Left. Throws Right. Height, 6 feet, 2 inches. Weight, 200 pounds.

Year	Club	Lea	Pos	G	AB	R	H	2B	3B	HR	RBI	SB	Avg
1992 South Oregon	Northwest	3B	13	41	9	13	3	0	3	13	1	.317
1993 Modesto	California	3B	89	313	72	91	16	2	12	60	2	.291
1994 Huntsville	Southern	3B-1B	56	193	31	43	9	0	6	30	0	.223
1994 Tacoma	P.C.	3B-1B-SS	52	176	28	56	20	0	4	38	1	.318
1995 Edmonton	P.C.	3B-1B	55	190	34	65	26	1	3	41	0	.342
1995 Oakland	A.L.	3B-1B	54	176	27	45	7	0	6	25	2	.256
1996 Oakland	A.L.	1B-OF-3B	140	536	84	156	40	1	20	79	0	.291
1997 Oakland	A.L.	OF-1B	142	519	66	152	41	2	20	81	0	.293
1998 Oakland	A.L.	1B	153	562	92	166	28	0	27	110	2	.295
1999 Oakland	A.L.	1B-3B	158	575	115	181	36	1	33	123	1	.315
2000 Oakland a	A.L.	1B	152	510	108	170	29	1	43	137	2	.333
Major League Totals	6 Yrs.		799	2878	492	870	181	5	149	555	7	.302
Division Series												
2000 Oakland	A.L.	1B	5	14	2	4	0	0	0	1	1	.286

a Selected Most Valuable Player in American League for 2000.

GIAMBI, JEREMY DEAN

Born, San Jose, California, September 30, 1974.
Bats Left. Throws Right. Height, 6 feet. Weight, 185 pounds.

Year	Club	Lea	Pos	G	AB	R	H	2B	3B	HR	RBI	SB	Avg
1996 Spokane	. . . .Northwest		OF	67	231	58	63	17	0	6	39	22	.273
1997 Lansing	. . . . .Midwest		OF	31	116	33	39	11	1	5	21	5	.336
1997 Wichita	. . . . .Texas		OF-1B	74	268	50	86	15	1	11	52	4	.321
1998 Omaha	. . . . .P.C.		OF-1B	96	325	68	121	21	2	20	66	8	.372
1998 Kansas City	. . . . . .A.L.		OF	18	58	6	13	4	0	2	8	0	.224
1999 Omaha	. . . . .P.C.		OF	35	127	31	44	5	1	12	28	1	.346
1999 Kansas City a	. . . . . .A.L.		DH-1B-OF	90	288	34	82	13	1	3	34	0	.285
2000 Sacramento	. . . . . . .P.C.		OF	8	31	8	11	2	0	2	8	1	.355
2000 Oakland b-c	. . . . . .A.L.		OF-1B	104	260	42	66	10	2	10	50	0	.254
Major League Totals	. . . .		3 Yrs.	212	606	82	161	27	3	15	92	0	.266
Division Series													
2000 Oakland	. . . . .A.L.		OF-DH	4	9	1	3	0	0	0	1	0	.333

a On disabled list from April 5 to May 15, 1999.
b Traded to Oakland Athletics for pitcher Brett Laxton, February 18, 2000.
c On disabled list from August 22 to September 7, 2000.

GIL, ROMAR (BENJI)

Born, Tijuana, Mexico, October 6, 1972.
Bats Right. Throws Right. Height, 6 feet, 2 inches. Weight, 180 pounds.

Year	Club	Lea	Pos	G	AB	R	H	2B	3B	HR	RBI	SB	Avg
1991 Butte	. . . . .Pioneer		SS	32	129	25	37	4	3	2	15	9	.287
1992 Gastonia	. . . .So.Atl.		SS-OF	132	482	75	132	21	1	9	55	26	.274
1993 Texas	. . . . .A.L.		SS	22	57	3	7	0	0	0	2	1	.123
1993 Tulsa	. . . . .Texas		SS	101	342	45	94	9	1	17	59	20	.275
1994 Okla City	. . . . . . .A.A.		SS	139	487	62	121	20	6	10	55	14	.248
1995 Texas	. . . . .A.L.		SS	130	415	36	91	20	3	9	46	2	.219
1996 Charlotte	. . . . . . .Fla.St.		SS	11	31	2	8	6	0	1	7	0	.258
1996 Okla City	. . . . . . .A.A.		SS	84	292	32	65	15	1	6	28	4	.223
1996 Texas a	. . . . .A.L.		SS	5	5	0	2	0	0	0	1	0	.400
1997 Texas a	. . . . .A.L.		SS	110	317	35	71	13	2	5	31	1	.224
1998 Calgary b	. . . . .P.C.		SS-OF	128	460	80	114	24	5	14	69	11	.248
1999 Calgary c	. . . . .P.C.		SS	116	412	74	115	29	1	17	64	17	.279
2000 Anaheim d	. . . . , .A.L.		SS-2B-1B	110	301	28	72	14	1	6	23	10	.239
Major League Totals	. . . .		5 Yrs.	377	1095	102	243	47	6	20	103	14	.222

a Traded to Chicago White Sox for pitcher Alan Levine and pitcher Larry Thomas, December 19, 1997.
b Selected by Florida Marlins in Rule V draft, December 14, 1998.
c Filed for free agency, October 15, 1999.
d Signed with Anaheim Angels organization, February 1, 2000.

GILES, BRIAN STEPHEN

Born, El Cajon, California, January 21, 1971.
Bats Left. Throws Left. Height, 5 feet, 11 inches. Weight, 195 pounds.

Year	Club	Lea	Pos	G	AB	R	H	2B	3B	HR	RBI	SB	Avg
1989 Burlington	. . . . .Appal.		OF	36	129	18	40	7	0	0	20	6	.310
1990 Watertown	. . . . .N.Y.-Penn.		OF	70	246	44	71	15	2	1	23	11	.289
1991 Kinston	. . . . .Carolina		OF	125	394	71	122	14	0	4	47	19	.310
1992 Canton-Akrn	. . . . . .Eastern		OF	23	74	6	16	4	0	0	3	3	.216
1992 Kinston	. . . . .Carolina		OF	42	140	28	37	5	1	3	18	3	.264
1993 Canton-Akrn	. . . . . .Eastern		OF	123	425	64	139	17	6	8	64	18	.327
1994 Charlotte	. . . . .Int.		OF	128	434	74	136	18	3	16	58	8	.313
1995 Buffalo	. . . . .A.A.		OF	123	413	67	128	18	8	15	67	7	.310
1995 Cleveland	. . . . .A.L.		OF	6	9	6	5	0	0	1	3	0	.556
1996 Buffalo	. . . . .A.A.		OF	83	318	65	100	17	6	20	64	1	.314
1996 Cleveland	. . . . .A.L.		DH-OF	51	121	26	43	14	1	5	27	3	.355
1997 Cleveland	. . . . .A.L.		OF	130	377	62	101	15	3	17	61	13	.268
1998 Buffalo	. . . . .Int.		OF	13	46	5	11	2	0	2	7	0	.239
1998 Cleveland a-b	. . . . . .A.L.		OF	112	350	56	94	19	0	16	66	10	.269
1999 Pittsburgh	. . . . .N.L.		OF	141	521	109	164	33	3	39	115	6	.315
2000 Pittsburgh	. . . . .N.L.		OF	156	559	111	176	37	7	35	123	6	.315
Major League Totals	. . . .		6 Yrs.	596	1937	370	583	118	14	113	395	38	.301
Division Series													
1996 Cleveland	. . . . .A.L.		PH	1	1	0	0	0	0	0	0	0	.000
1997 Cleveland	. . . . .A.L.		OF	3	7	0	1	0	0	0	0	0	.143
1998 Cleveland	. . . . .A.L.		OF-DH	3	10	1	2	1	0	0	0	0	.200

Year	Club	Lea	Pos	G	AB	R	H	2B	3B	HR	RBI	SB	Avg
Division Series Totals				7	18	1	3	1	0	0	0	0	.167
Championship Series													
1997 Cleveland		.A.L.	OF	6	16	1	3	3	0	0	0	0	.188
1998 Cleveland		.A.L.	OF	4	12	0	1	0	0	0	0	0	.083
Championship Series Totals				10	28	1	4	3	0	0	0	0	.143
World Series Record													
1997 Cleveland		.A.L.	OF	5	4	1	2	1	0	0	2	0	.400

a On disabled list from June 1 to July 7, 1998.
b Traded to Pittsburgh Pirates for pitcher Ricardo Rincon, November 18, 1998.

GILKEY, OTIS (BERNARD)
Born, St. Louis, Missouri, September 24, 1966.
Bats Right. Throws Right. Height, 6 feet. Weight, 190 pounds.

Year	Club	Lea	Pos	G	AB	R	H	2B	3B	HR	RBI	SB	Avg
1985 Erie	N.Y.-Penn.	OF	*77	*294	57	60	9	1	7	27	34	.204
1986 Savannah	So. Atl.	OF	105	374	64	88	15	4	6	36	32	.235
1987 Springfield a	Midwest	OF	46	162	30	37	5	0	0	9	18	.228
1988 Springfield	Midwest	OF	125	492	84	120	19	6	6	36	54	.244
1989 Arkansas	Texas	OF	131	500	*104	139	25	3	6	57	*53	.278
1990 Louisville	A.A.	OF	132	499	83	147	26	8	3	46	45	.295
1990 St. Louis	N.L.	OF	18	64	11	19	5	2	1	3	6	.297
1991 Louisville	A.A.	OF	11	41	5	6	2	0	0	2	1	.146
1991 St. Louis b	N.L.	OF	81	268	28	58	7	2	5	20	14	.216
1992 St. Louis	N.L.	OF	131	384	56	116	19	4	7	43	18	.302
1993 St. Louis c	N.L.	OF-1B	137	557	99	170	40	5	16	70	15	.305
1994 St. Louis	N.L.	OF	105	380	52	96	22	1	6	45	15	.253
1995 Louisville d	A.A.	OF	2	6	3	2	1	0	1	1	0	.333
1995 St. Louis	N.L.	OF	121	480	73	143	33	4	17	69	12	.298
1996 New York e	N.L.	OF	153	571	108	181	44	3	30	117	17	.317
1997 New York	N.L.	OF	145	518	85	129	31	1	18	78	7	.249
1998 New York-Arizona f-g-h	N.L.	OF	111	365	41	85	15	0	5	33	9	.233
1999 Arizona	N.L.	OF	94	204	28	60	16	1	8	39	2	.294
2000 Arizona	N.L.	OF	38	73	6	8	1	0	2	6	0	.110
2000 Boston i-j	A.L.	OF	36	91	11	21	5	1	1	9	0	.231
Major League Totals		11 Yrs.	1170	3955	598	1086	238	24	116	532	115	.275
Division Series													
1999 Arizona	N.L.	OF	2	6	0	0	0	0	0	0	0	.000

a On disabled list from May 29 to end of 1987 season.
b On disabled list from June 14 to July 11, 1991.
c On disabled list from April 29 to May 14, 1993.
d On disabled list from June 28 to July 17, 1995.
e Traded to New York Mets for pitcher Eric Ludwick, pitcher Erik Hiljus and outfielder Yudith Ozorio, January 22, 1996.
f On disabled list from April 26 to May 12, 1998.
g Traded to Arizona Diamondbacks with pitcher Nelson Figueroa and cash for pitcher Willie Blair, catcher Jorge Fabregas and player to be named later, July 31, 1998.
h New York Mets received cash to complete trade, September 3, 1998.
i Released by Arizona Diamondbacks, June 27, 2000, signed with Boston Red Sox, July 4, 2000.
j Filed for free agency, October 30, 2000, signed with St. Louis Cardinals organization, January 5, 2001.

GINTER, KEITH MICHAEL
Born, Norwalk, California, May 5, 1976.
Bats Right. Throws Right. Height, 5 feet, 10 inches. Weight, 190 pounds.

Year	Club	Lea	Pos	G	AB	R	H	2B	3B	HR	RBI	SB	Avg
1998 Auburn	N.Y.-Penn.	2B	71	241	55	76	22	1	8	41	10	.315
1999 Jackson	Texas	2B	9	34	9	13	1	0	1	6	0	.382
1999 Kissimmee	Fla.St.	2B	103	376	66	99	15	4	13	46	9	.263
2000 Round Rock	Texas	2B	125	462	108	154	30	3	26	92	24	.333
2000 Houston	N.L.	2B	5	8	3	2	0	0	1	3	0	.250

GIRARDI, JOSEPH ELLIOTT
Born, Peoria, Illinois, October 14, 1964.
Bats Right. Throws Right. Height, 5 feet, 11 inches. Weight, 195 pounds.

Year	Club	Lea	Pos	G	AB	R	H	2B	3B	HR	RBI	SB	Avg
1986 Peoria a	Midwest	C	68	230	36	71	13	1	3	28	6	.309
1987 Winston-Salem	Carolina	C	99	364	51	102	9	8	8	46	9	.280

Year	Club	Lea	Pos	G	AB	R	H	2B	3B	HR	RBI	SB	Avg
1988 Pittsfield b	Eastern		C-OF	104	357	44	97	14	1	7	41	7	.272
1989 Iowa	A.A.		C	32	110	12	27	4	2	2	11	3	.245
1989 Chicago	N.L.		C	59	157	15	39	10	0	1	14	2	.248
1990 Chicago	N.L.		C	133	419	36	113	24	2	1	38	8	.270
1991 Iowa	A.A.		C	12	36	3	8	1	0	0	4	2	.222
1991 Chicago c	N.L.		C	21	47	3	9	2	0	0	6	0	.191
1992 Chicago d	N.L.		C	91	270	19	73	3	1	1	12	0	.270
1993 Colorado Springs	P.C.		C	8	31	6	15	1	1	1	6	1	.484
1993 Colorado e	N.L.		C	86	310	35	90	14	5	3	31	6	.290
1994 Colorado f	N.L.		C	93	330	47	91	9	4	4	34	3	.276
1995 Colorado g	N.L.		C	125	462	63	121	17	2	8	55	3	.262
1996 New York h-i	A.L.		C	124	422	55	124	22	3	2	45	13	.294
1997 New York	A.L.		C	112	398	38	105	23	1	1	50	2	.264
1998 New York	A.L.		C	78	254	31	70	11	4	3	31	2	.276
1999 New York j	A.L.		C	65	209	23	50	16	1	2	27	3	.239
2000 Chicago	N.L.		C	106	363	47	101	15	1	6	40	1	.278
Major League Totals			12 Yrs.	1093	3641	412	986	166	24	32	383	43	.271
Division Series													
1995 Colorado	N.L.		C	4	16	0	2	0	0	0	0	0	.125
1996 New York	A.L.		C	4	9	1	2	0	0	0	0	0	.222
1997 New York	A.L.		C	5	15	2	2	0	0	0	0	0	.133
1998 New York	A.L.		C	2	7	0	3	0	0	0	0	0	.429
1999 New York	A.L.		C	2	6	0	0	0	0	0	0	0	.000
Division Series Totals				17	53	3	9	0	0	0	0	0	.170
Championship Series													
1989 Chicago	N.L.		C	4	10	1	1	0	0	0	0	0	.100
1996 New York	A.L.		C	4	12	1	3	0	1	0	0	0	.250
1998 New York	A.L.		C	3	8	2	2	0	0	0	0	0	.250
1999 New York	A.L.		C	3	8	0	2	0	0	0	0	0	.250
Championship Series Totals				14	38	4	8	0	1	0	0	0	.211
World Series													
1996 New York	A.L.		C	4	10	1	2	0	1	0	1	0	.200
1998 New York	A.L.		C	2	6	0	0	0	0	0	0	0	.000
1999 New York	A.L.		C	2	7	1	2	0	0	0	0	0	.286
World Series Totals				8	23	2	4	0	1	0	1	0	.174

a On disabled list from August 27 to end of 1986 season.
b On disabled list from August 8 to end of 1988 season.
c On disabled list from April 17 to August 5, 1991.
d Selected by Colorado Rockies in expansion draft, November 17, 1992.
e On disabled list from June 5 to August 11, 1993.
f On disabled list from July 11 to July 26, 1994.
g Traded to New York Yankees for pitcher Mike DeJean and player to be named, November 20, 1995. Colorado Rockies received pitcher Steve Shoemaker to complete trade, December 6, 1995.
h Filed for free agency, November 4, 1996.
i Re-signed with New York Yankees, December 3, 1996.
j Filed for free agency, November 5, 1999. Signed with Chicago Cubs, December 15, 1999.

GLANVILLE, DOUGLAS METUNWA

Born, Hackensack, New Jersey, August 25, 1970.
Bats Right. Throws Right. Height, 6 feet, 2 inches. Weight, 175 pounds.

Year	Club	Lea	Pos	G	AB	R	H	2B	3B	HR	RBI	SB	Avg
1991 Geneva	N.Y.-Penn.		OF	36	152	29	46	8	0	2	12	17	.303
1992 Winston-Sal	Carolina		OF	120	485	72	125	18	4	4	36	32	.258
1993 Daytona	Fla. St.		OF	61	239	47	70	10	1	2	21	18	.293
1993 Orlando	Southern		OF	73	296	42	78	14	4	9	40	15	.264
1994 Orlando	Southern		OF	130	483	53	127	22	2	5	52	26	.263
1995 Iowa	A.A.		OF	112	419	48	113	16	2	4	37	13	.270
1996 Iowa	A.A.		OF	90	373	53	115	23	3	3	34	15	.308
1996 Chicago	N.L.		OF	49	83	10	20	5	1	1	10	2	.241
1997 Chicago a	N.L.		OF	146	474	79	142	22	5	4	35	19	.300
1998 Philadelphia	N.L.		OF	158	*678	106	189	28	7	8	49	23	.279
1999 Philadelphia	N.L.		OF	150	628	101	204	38	6	11	73	34	.325
2000 Philadelphia	N.L.		OF	154	637	89	175	27	6	8	52	31	.275
Major League Totals			5 Yrs.	657	2500	385	730	120	25	32	219	109	.292

a Traded to Philadelphia Phillies for second baseman Mickey Morandini, December 23, 1997.

GLAUS, TROY

Born, Newport Beach, California, August 3, 1976.
Bats Right. Throws Right. Height, 6 feet, 5 inches. Weight, 220 pounds.

Year	Club	Lea	Pos	G	AB	R	H	2B	3B	HR	RBI	SB	Avg
1998 Midland	Texas		3B	50	188	51	58	11	2	19	51	4	.309
1998 Vancouver	P.C.		3B	59	219	33	67	16	0	16	42	3	.306
1998 Anaheim	A.L.		3B	48	165	19	36	9	0	1	23	1	.218
1999 Anaheim	A.L.		3B	154	551	85	132	29	0	29	79	5	.240
2000 Anaheim	A.L.		3B-SS	159	563	120	160	37	1	*47	102	14	.284
Major League Totals			3 Yrs.	361	1279	224	328	75	1	77	204	20	.256

GONZALEZ, ALEXANDER (ALEX)

Born, Cagua, Venezuela, February 15, 1977.
Bats Right. Throws Right. Height, 6 feet. Weight, 170 pounds.

Year	Club	Lea	Pos	G	AB	R	H	2B	3B	HR	RBI	SB	Avg
1994 Florida	Dominican		SS	66	282	39	67	9	5	4	39	5	.238
1995 Brevard Cty	Fla.St.		SS	17	59	6	12	2	1	0	8	1	.203
1995 Marlins	Gulf Coast		SS	53	187	30	55	7	4	2	30	11	.294
1996 Marlins	Gulf Coast		SS	10	41	6	16	3	0	0	6	1	.390
1996 Kane County	Midwest		SS	4	10	2	2	0	0	0	0	0	.200
1996 Portland	Eastern		SS	11	34	4	8	0	1	0	1	0	.235
1997 Portland	Eastern		SS	133	449	69	114	16	4	19	65	4	.254
1998 Charlotte	Int.		SS	108	422	71	117	20	10	10	51	4	.277
1998 Florida	N.L.		SS	25	86	11	13	2	0	3	7	0	.151
1999 Florida	N.L.		SS	136	560	81	155	28	8	14	59	3	.277
2000 Brevard County	Fla.St.		SS	4	17	1	2	0	0	0	2	1	.118
2000 Florida a	N.L.		SS	109	385	35	77	17	4	7	42	7	.200
Major League Totals			3 Yrs.	270	1031	127	245	47	12	24	108	10	.238

a On disabled list from July 28 to August 31, 2000.

GONZALEZ, ALEXANDER SCOTT

Born, Miami, Florida, April 8, 1973.
Bats Right. Throws Right. Height, 6 feet. Weight, 182 pounds.

Year	Club	Lea	Pos	G	AB	R	H	2B	3B	HR	RBI	SB	Avg
1991 Charlotte Blue Jays	Gulf C.		SS	53	191	29	40	5	4	0	10	7	.209
1992 Myrtle Beach	So. Atl.		SS	134	535	82	145	22	9	10	62	26	.271
1993 Knoxville	Southern		SS	142	561	*93	162	29	7	16	69	38	.289
1994 Toronto a	A.L.		SS	15	53	7	8	3	1	0	1	3	.151
1994 Syracuse	Int.		SS	110	437	69	124	22	4	12	57	23	.284
1995 Toronto	A.L.		SS-3B	111	367	51	89	19	4	10	42	4	.243
1996 Toronto	A.L.		SS	147	527	64	124	30	5	14	64	16	.235
1997 Toronto b	A.L.		SS	126	426	46	102	23	2	12	35	15	.239
1998 Toronto	A.L.		SS	158	568	70	136	28	1	13	51	21	.239
1999 Toronto c	A.L.		SS	38	154	22	45	13	0	2	12	4	.292
2000 Syracuse	Int.		SS	1	5	0	0	0	0	0	0	0	.000
2000 Toronto d-e	A.L.		SS	141	527	68	133	31	2	15	69	4	.252
Major League Totals			7 Yrs.	736	2622	328	637	147	15	66	274	67	.243

a On disabled list from April 29 to May 27, 1994.
b On disabled list from August 14 to September 14, 1997.
c On disabled list from May 17 to November 3, 1999.
d On disabled list from July 7 to July 21, 2000.
e Filed for free agency, October 30, 2000, re-signed with Toronto Blue Jays, December 10, 2000.

GONZALEZ (VAZQUEZ), JUAN ALBERTO

Born, Vega Baja, Puerto Rico, October 16, 1969.
Bats Right. Throws Right. Height, 6 feet, 3 inches. Weight, 215 pounds.

Year	Club	Lea	Pos	G	AB	R	H	2B	3B	HR	RBI	SB	Avg
1986 Sarasota Rangers	Gulf C.		OF	60	*233	24	56	4	1	0	36	7	.240
1987 Gastonia	So. Atl.		OF	127	509	69	135	21	2	14	74	9	.265
1988 Charlotte a	Fla. St.		OF	77	277	25	71	14	3	8	43	5	.256
1989 Texas	A.L.		OF	24	60	6	9	3	0	1	7	0	.150
1990 Oklahoma City	A.A.		OF	128	496	78	128	29	4	*29	*101	2	.258
1990 Texas	A.L.		OF	25	90	11	26	7	1	4	12	0	.289
1991 Texas b	A.L.		OF	142	545	78	144	34	1	27	102	4	.264
1992 Texas	A.L.		OF	155	584	77	152	24	2	*43	109	0	.260
1993 Texas	A.L.		OF	140	536	105	166	33	1	*46	118	4	.310

Year	Club	Lea	Pos	G	AB	R	H	2B	3B	HR	RBI	SB	Avg
1994 Texas	.A.L.		OF	107	422	57	116	18	4	19	85	6	.275
1995 Texas c	.A.L.		DH-OF	90	352	57	104	20	2	27	82	0	.295
1996 Texas d-e	.A.L.		OF	134	541	89	170	33	2	47	144	2	.314
1997 Texas f	.A.L.		DH-OF	133	533	87	158	24	3	42	131	0	.296
1998 Texas g	.A.L.		OF	154	606	110	193	*50	2	45	*157	2	.318
1999 Texas h	.A.L.		OF	144	562	114	183	36	1	39	128	3	.326
2000 Detroit i	.A.L.		OF	115	461	69	133	30	2	22	67	1	.289
Major League Totals		12 Yrs.	1363	5292	860	1554	312	21	362	1142	22	.294	
Division Series													
1996 Texas	.A.L.		OF	4	16	5	7	0	0	5	9	0	.438
1998 Texas	.A.L.		OF	3	12	1	1	1	0	0	0	0	.083
1999 Texas	.A.L.		OF	3	11	1	2	0	0	1	1	0	.182
Division Series Totals			10	39	7	10	1	0	6	10	0	.256	

a On disabled list from April 27 to June 17, 1988.
b On disabled list from March 30 to April 26, 1991.
c On disabled list from April 25 to June 1 and July 27 to August 16, 1995.
d Selected Most Valuable Player in American League for 1996.
e On disabled list from May 8 to June 1, 1996.
f On disabled list from April 1 to May 2, 1997.
g Selected Most Valuable Player in American League for 1998.
h Traded to Detroit Tigers with pitcher Danny Patterson and catcher Greg Zaun for pitcher Justin Thompson, pitcher Francisco Cordero, pitcher Alan Webb, outfielder Gabe Kapler, catcher Bill Haselman and infielder Frank Catalanotto, November 2, 1999.
i Filed for free agency, November 1, 2000, signed with Cleveland Indians, January 9, 2001.

GONZALEZ, LUIS EMILIO
Born, Tampa, Florida, September 3, 1967.
Bats Left. Throws Right. Height, 6 feet, 2 inches. Weight, 180 pounds.

Year	Club	Lea	Pos	G	AB	R	H	2B	3B	HR	RBI	SB	Avg
1988 Asheville	.So. Atl.		3B	31	115	13	29	7	1	2	14	2	.252
1988 Auburn	.N.Y.-Penn.		3B	39	157	32	49	10	3	5	27	2	.312
1989 Osceola a	.Fla. St.		DH	86	287	46	82	16	7	6	38	2	.286
1990 Columbus	.Southern		1B-3B	138	495	86	131	30	6	*24	89	27	.265
1990 Houston	.N.L.		3B-1B	12	21	1	4	2	0	0	0	0	.190
1991 Houston b	.N.L.		OF	137	473	51	120	28	9	13	69	10	.254
1992 Tucson	.P.C.		OF	13	44	11	19	4	2	1	9	4	.432
1992 Houston c	.N.L.		OF	122	387	40	94	19	3	10	55	7	.243
1993 Houston	.N.L.		OF	154	540	82	162	34	3	15	72	20	.300
1994 Houston	.N.L.		OF	112	392	57	107	29	4	8	67	15	.273
1995 Houston-Chicago d-e	.N.L.		OF	133	471	69	130	29	8	13	69	6	.276
1996 Chicago f-g	.N.L.		OF-1B	146	483	70	131	30	4	15	79	9	.271
1997 Houston h-i	.N.L.		OF-1B	152	550	78	142	31	2	10	68	10	.258
1998 Detroit j	.A.L.		OF	154	547	84	146	35	5	23	71	12	.267
1999 Arizona	.N.L.		OF	153	614	112	*206	45	4	26	111	9	.336
2000 Arizona	.N.L.		OF	*162	618	106	192	47	2	31	114	2	.311
Major League Totals		11 Yrs.	1437	5096	750	1434	329	44	164	775	100	.281	
Division Series													
1997 Houston	.N.L.		OF	3	12	0	4	0	0	0	0	0	.333
1999 Arizona	.N.L.		OF	4	10	3	2	1	0	1	2	0	.200
Division Series Totals			7	22	3	6	1	0	1	2	0	.273	

a On disabled list from May 26 to July 5, 1989.
b On disabled list from August 29 to September 13, 1991.
c On disabled list from July 21 to August 5, 1992.
d Traded to Chicago Cubs with catcher Scott Servais for catcher Rick Wilkins, June 28, 1995.
e Was not offered contract by Chicago Cubs, December 20, 1995.
f Filed for free agency, October 28, 1996.
g Signed with Houston Astros, December 19, 1996.
h Filed for free agency, October 28, 1997.
i Signed with Detroit Tigers, December 9, 1997.
j Traded to Arizona Diamondbacks for outfielder Karim Garcia, December 28, 1998.

GONZALEZ, WIKLENMAN (WIKI)
Born, Aragua, Venezuela, May 17, 1974.
Bats Right. Throws Right. Height, 5 feet, 11 inches. Weight, 175 pounds.

Year	Club	Lea	Pos	G	AB	R	H	2B	3B	HR	RBI	SB	Avg
1992 Pittsburgh	.Dominican		C	63	190	20	48	6	1	3	33	4	.253
1993 Pittsburgh	.Dominican		C	69	244	47	73	10	3	7	47	24	.299
1994 Pirates	.Gulf Coast		C-1B-P	41	143	25	48	8	2	4	26	2	.336

Year	Club	Lea	Pos	G	AB	R	H	2B	3B	HR	RBI	SB	Avg
1995 Augusta	.........So.Atl.		C	84	278	41	67	17	0	3	36	5	.241
1996 Augusta a	.........So.Atl.		C	118	419	52	106	21	3	4	62	4	.253
1997 Rancho Cuca	.....California		DH-C	33	110	18	33	9	1	5	26	1	.300
1997 Mobile	.........Southern		C	47	143	15	39	7	1	4	25	1	.273
1998 Mobile	.........Southern		C	22	67	20	26	9	0	4	26	0	.388
1998 Rancho Cuca b	....California		C	75	292	51	84	24	2	10	59	0	.288
1999 Mobile	.........Southern		C	61	225	38	76	16	2	10	49	0	.338
1999 Las Vegas	.........P.C.		C	25	92	13	25	6	0	6	12	0	.272
1999 San Diego c	.........N.L.		C	30	83	7	21	2	1	3	12	0	.253
2000 San Diego	.........N.L.		C	95	284	25	66	15	1	5	30	1	.232
Major League Totals			2 Yrs.	125	367	32	87	17	2	8	42	1	.237

a Selected by San Diego Padres from Pittsburgh Pirates in Rule V draft, December 9, 1996.
b Filed for free agency, October 16, 1998, re-signed with San Diego Padres organization, October 23, 1998.
c On disabled list from May 24 to June 6, 1999.

GOODWIN, THOMAS JONES
Born, Fresno, California, July 27, 1968.
Bats Left. Throws Right. Height, 6 feet, 1 inch. Weight, 170 pounds.

Year	Club	Lea	Pos	G	AB	R	H	2B	3B	HR	RBI	SB	Avg
1989 Great Falls	........Pioneer		OF	63	240	55	74	12	3	2	33	*60	.308
1990 Bakersfield	.........California		OF	32	134	24	39	6	2	0	13	22	.291
1990 San Antonio	........Texas		OF	102	428	76	119	14	4	0	28	*60	.278
1991 Albuquerque	.........P.C.		OF	132	509	84	139	19	4	1	45	48	.273
1991 Los Angeles	.........N.L.		OF	16	7	3	1	0	0	0	0	1	.143
1992 Albuquerque	.........P.C.		OF	82	319	48	96	10	4	2	28	27	.301
1992 Los Angeles	.........N.L.		OF	57	73	15	17	1	1	0	3	7	.233
1993 Albuquerque	.........P.C.		OF	85	289	48	75	5	5	1	28	21	.260
1993 Los Angeles a	.........N.L.		OF	30	17	6	5	1	0	0	1	1	.294
1994 Kansas City	.........A.L.		OF	2	0	1	0	0	0	0	0	0	.000
1994 Omaha	.........A.A.		OF	113	429	67	132	17	7	2	34	*50	.308
1995 Kansas City	.........A.L.		OF	133	480	72	138	16	3	4	28	50	.287
1996 Kansas City	.........A.L.		OF	143	524	80	148	14	4	1	35	66	.282
1997 Kansas City-Texas b	.........A.L.		OF	150	574	90	149	26	6	2	39	50	.260
1998 Texas	.........A.L.		OF	154	520	102	151	13	3	2	33	38	.290
1999 Charlotte	.........Fla.St.		OF	2	11	2	4	1	0	0	0	0	.364
1999 Texas c-d	.........A.L.		OF	109	405	63	105	12	6	3	33	39	.259
2000 Colorado-Los Angeles e	.........N.L.		OF	147	528	94	139	11	9	6	58	55	.263
Major League Totals			10 Yrs.	941	3130	525	853	94	32	18	230	307	.273

Division Series

Year	Club	Lea	Pos	G	AB	R	H	2B	3B	HR	RBI	SB	Avg
1998 Texas	.........A.L.		OF	2	4	0	1	0	0	0	0	0	.250
1999 Texas	.........A.L.		OF	3	7	0	1	0	0	0	0	0	.143
Division Series Totals				5	11	0	2	0	0	0	0	0	.182

a Claimed on waivers by Kansas City Royals, January 6, 1994.
b Traded to Texas Rangers for infielder Dean Palmer, July 26, 1997.
c On disabled list from June 12 to June 27 and June 28 to August 6, 1999.
d Filed for free agency, October 28, 1999. Signed with Colorado Rockies, December 8, 1999.
e Traded to Los Angeles Dodgers for outfielder Todd Hollandsworth, outfielder Kevin Gibbs and pitcher Randey Dorame, July 31, 2000.

GRACE, MARK EUGENE
Born, Winston-Salem, North Carolina, June 28, 1964.
Bats Left. Throws Left. Height, 6 feet, 2 inches. Weight, 190 pounds.

Year	Club	Lea	Pos	G	AB	R	H	2B	3B	HR	RBI	SB	Avg
1986 Peoria	.........Midwest		1B	126	465	81	*159	30	4	15	95	6	*.342
1987 Pittsfield	.........Eastern		1B	123	453	81	151	29	8	17	*101	5	.333
1988 Iowa	.............A.A.		1B	21	67	11	17	4	0	0	14	1	.254
1988 Chicago	.............N.L.		1B	134	486	65	144	23	4	7	57	3	.296
1989 Chicago a	.............N.L.		1B	142	510	74	160	28	3	13	79	14	.314
1990 Chicago	.............N.L.		1B	157	589	72	182	32	1	9	82	15	.309
1991 Chicago	.............N.L.		1B	160	*619	87	169	28	5	8	58	3	.273
1992 Chicago	.............N.L.		1B	158	603	72	185	37	5	9	79	6	.307
1993 Chicago	.............N.L.		1B	155	594	86	193	39	4	14	98	8	.325
1994 Chicago b	.............N.L.		1B	106	403	55	120	23	3	6	44	0	.298
1995 Chicago c-d-e	.............N.L.		1B	143	552	97	180	*51	3	16	92	6	.326
1996 Chicago f	.............N.L.		1B	142	547	88	181	39	1	9	75	2	.331
1997 Chicago g	.............N.L.		1B	151	555	87	177	32	5	13	78	2	.319
1998 Chicago	.............N.L.		1B	158	595	92	184	39	3	17	89	4	.309

69

Year Club	Lea	Pos	G	AB	R	H	2B	3B	HR	RBI	SB	Avg
1999 Chicago ............N.L.		1B	161	593	107	183	44	5	16	91	3	.309
2000 Chicago h-i .........N.L.		1B	143	510	75	143	41	1	11	82	1	.280
Major League Totals		13 Yrs.	1910	7156	1057	2201	456	43	148	1004	67	.308
Division Series												
1998 Chicago ............N.L.		1B	3	12	0	1	0	0	0	1	0	.083
Championship Series												
1989 Chicago ............N.L.		1B	5	17	3	11	3	1	1	8	1	.647

a On disabled list from June 5 to June 23, 1989.
b Filed for free agency, October 17, 1994.
c Re-signed with Chicago Cubs, April 7, 1995.
d Filed for free agency, November 12, 1995.
e Re-signed with Chicago Cubs, December 19, 1995.
f On disabled list from June 11 to June 28, 1996.
g On disabled list from April 4 to April 19, 1997.
h On disabled list from May 11 to May 30, 2000.
i Filed for free agency, October 30, 2000, signed with Arizona Diamondbacks, December 8, 2000.

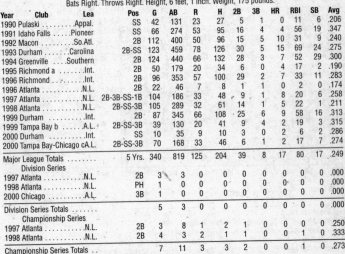

GRAFFANINO, ANTHONY (TONY)

Born, Amityville, New York, June 6, 1972.
Bats Right. Throws Right. Height, 6 feet, 1 inch. Weight, 175 pounds.

Year Club	Lea	Pos	G	AB	R	H	2B	3B	HR	RBI	SB	Avg
1990 Pulaski ....Appal.		SS	42	131	23	27	5	1	0	11	6	.206
1991 Idaho Falls .....Pioneer		SS	66	274	53	95	16	4	4	56	19	.347
1992 Macon ....So.Atl.		2B	112	400	50	96	15	5	10	31	9	.240
1993 Durham ....Carolina		2B-SS	123	459	78	126	30	5	15	69	24	.275
1994 Greenville ....Southern		2B	124	440	66	132	28	3	7	52	29	.300
1995 Richmond a ....Int.		2B	50	179	20	34	6	0	4	17	2	.190
1996 Richmond ....Int.		2B	96	353	57	100	29	2	7	33	11	.283
1996 Atlanta ..........N.L.		2B	22	46	7	8	1	1	0	2	0	.174
1997 Atlanta ..........N.L.	2B-3B-SS-1B		104	186	33	48	9	1	8	20	6	.258
1998 Atlanta ..........N.L.	2B-SS-3B		105	289	32	61	14	1	5	22	1	.211
1999 Durham ....Int.		2B	87	345	66	108	25	6	9	58	16	.313
1999 Tampa Bay b ......A.L.	2B-SS-3B		39	130	20	41	9	4	2	19	3	.315
2000 Durham ....Int.		SS	10	35	9	10	3	0	2	6	2	.286
2000 Tampa Bay-Chicago c	A.L.	2B-SS-3B	70	168	33	46	6	1	2	17	7	.274
Major League Totals		5 Yrs.	340	819	125	204	39	8	17	80	17	.249
Division Series												
1997 Atlanta ..........N.L.		2B	3	3	0	0	0	0	0	0	0	.000
1998 Atlanta ..........N.L.		PH	1	0	0	0	0	0	0	0	0	.000
2000 Chicago .........A.L.		3B	1	0	0	0	0	0	0	0	0	.000
Division Series Totals			5	3	0	0	0	0	0	0	0	.000
Championship Series												
1997 Atlanta ..........N.L.		2B	3	8	1	2	1	0	0	0	0	.250
1998 Atlanta ..........N.L.		2B	4	3	2	1	1	0	0	1	0	.333
Championship Series Totals ..			7	11	3	3	2	0	0	1	0	.273

a On disabled list from July 3 to September 1, 1995.
b Released by Atlanta Braves, March 31, 1999, signed with Tampa Bay Devil Rays organization, April 9, 1999.
c Traded to Chicago White Sox for pitcher Tanyon Sturtze, May 31, 2000.

GREEN, BERTRUM (SCARBOROUGH)

Born, Creve Coeur, Missouri, June 9, 1974.
Bats Both. Throws Right. Height, 5 feet, 10 inches. Weight, 170 pounds.

Year Club	Lea	Pos	G	AB	R	H	2B	3B	HR	RBI	SB	Avg
1993 Cardinals .....Arizona		SS	33	95	16	21	3	1	0	11	3	.221
1994 Johnson City .....Appal.	SS-OF-3B		54	199	32	48	5	0	0	11	22	.241
1995 Savannah ......So.Atl.		SS	132	429	48	98	7	6	1	25	26	.228
1996 St. Pete ......Fla.St.		OF	36	140	26	41	4	1	1	11	13	.293
1996 Arkansas ....Texas		OF	92	300	45	60	6	3	3	24	21	.200
1997 Arkansas ....Texas		OF	76	251	45	77	14	4	2	29	11	.307
1997 Louisville .......A.A.		OF	52	209	26	53	11	2	3	13	10	.254
1997 St. Louis ........N.L.		OF	20	31	5	3	0	0	0	1	0	.097
1998 Memphis .........P.C.		OF	26	81	11	16	5	0	0	2	1	.198
1998 Arkansas a .....Texas		OF	18	75	16	27	2	1	2	9	9	.360
1999 Oklahoma ........P.C.		OF	104	359	68	89	16	6	3	29	26	.248
1999 Texas ...........A.L.		OF	18	13	4	4	0	0	0	0	0	.308
2000 Oklahoma ........P.C.		OF	27	99	20	31	6	0	1	10	14	.313

70

Year Club	Lea	Pos	G	AB	R	H	2B	3B	HR	RBI	SB	Avg
2000 Texas b-c ........A.L.		OF	79	124	21	29	1	1	0	9	10	.234
Major League Totals		3 Yrs.	117	168	30	36	1	1	0	10	10	.214

a Claimed on waivers by Texas Rangers, September 8, 1998.
b Signed with Texas Rangers organization, February 4, 2000.
c Signed with Chicago Cubs organization, December 13, 2000.

GREEN, SHAWN DAVID

Born, Des Plaines, Illinois, November 10, 1972.
Bats Left. Throws Left. Height, 6 feet, 4 inches. Weight, 190 pounds.

Year Club	Lea	Pos	G	AB	R	H	2B	3B	HR	RBI	SB	Avg
1992 Dunedin ....Fla. St.		OF	114	417	44	114	21	3	1	49	22	.273
1993 Knoxville ....Southern		OF	99	360	40	102	14	2	4	34	4	.283
1993 Toronto ...........A.L.		OF	3	6	0	0	0	0	0	0	0	.000
1994 Syracuse ....Int.		OF	109	433	82	149	27	3	13	61	19	*.344
1994 Toronto ...........A.L.		OF	14	33	1	3	1	0	0	1	1	.091
1995 Toronto ...........A.L.		OF	121	379	52	109	31	4	15	54	1	.288
1996 Toronto ...........A.L.		OF	132	422	52	118	32	3	11	45	5	.280
1997 Toronto ...........A.L.		OF	135	429	57	123	22	4	16	53	14	.287
1998 Toronto ...........A.L.		OF	158	630	106	175	33	4	35	100	35	.278
1999 Toronto a .........A.L.		OF	153	614	134	190	*45	0	42	123	20	.309
2000 Los Angeles ........N.L.		OF	*162	610	98	164	44	4	24	99	24	.269
Major League Totals		8 Yrs.	878	3123	500	882	208	19	143	475	100	.282

a Traded to Los Angeles Dodgers with infielder Jorge Nunez for outfielder Raul Mondesi and pitcher Pedro Borbon, November 8, 1999.

GREENE, WILLIE LOUIS

Born, Milledgeville, Georgia, September 23, 1971.
Bats Left. Throws Right. Height, 5 feet, 11 inches. Weight, 184 pounds.

Year Club	Lea	Pos	G	AB	R	H	2B	3B	HR	RBI	SB	Avg
1989 Bradenton Pirates .Gulf C.		SS	23	86	17	24	3	3	5	11	4	.279
1989 Princeton ....Appal.		SS	39	136	22	44	6	4	2	24	4	.324
1990 Augusta ....So. Atl.		SS	86	291	59	75	12	4	11	47	7	.258
1990 Salem a ....Carolina		SS	17	60	9	11	1	1	3	9	0	.183
1990 Rockford ....Midwest		SS	11	35	4	14	3	0	0	2	2	.400
1991 W. Palm Beach b .Fla. St.		3B	99	322	46	70	9	3	12	43	9	.217
1992 Cedar Rapids .Midwest		3B	34	120	26	34	8	2	12	40	0	.283
1992 Chattanooga ..Southern		3B	96	349	47	97	19	2	15	66	9	.278
1992 Cincinnati .......N.L.		3B	29	93	10	25	5	2	2	13	0	.269
1993 Indianapolis ......A.A.		3B-SS	98	341	62	91	19	0	22	58	0	.267
1993 Cincinnati c .......N.L.		SS-3B	15	50	7	8	1	1	2	5	0	.160
1994 Indianapolis ......A.A.		3B-SS	114	435	77	124	24	1	23	80	8	.285
1994 Cincinnati ........N.L.		3B-OF	16	37	5	8	2	0	0	3	0	.216
1995 Indianapolis ......A.A.		3B-SS-OF	91	325	57	79	12	2	19	45	3	.243
1995 Cincinnati ........N.L.		3B	8	19	1	2	0	0	0	0	0	.105
1996 Cincinnati d .......N.L.		3B-OF-1B-2B	115	287	48	70	5	5	19	63	6	.244
1997 Cincinnati ......N.L.		3B-OF-1B-SS	151	495	62	125	22	1	26	91	6	.253
1998 Cincinnati .......N.L.		3B-OF-SS	111	356	57	96	18	1	14	49	6	.270
1998 Baltimore e f .....A.L.		OF	24	39	8	6	1	0	1	5	1	.154
1999 Syracuse ....Int.		OF	14	52	12	17	1	0	5	11	0	.327
1999 Toronto g .......A.L.		DH-3B-OF	81	226	22	46	7	0	12	41	0	.204
2000 Iowa ............P.C.		3B	6	17	4	5	2	0	1	4	1	.294
2000 Chicago h-i .......N.L.		3B	105	299	34	60	15	2	10	37	4	.201
Major League Totals		9 Yrs.	655	1902	254	446	76	12	86	307	17	.234

a Traded by Pittsburgh Pirates to Montreal Expos organization with pitcher Scott Ruskin and player to be named for pitcher Zane Smith, August 8; Montreal acquired outfielder Moises Alou to complete trade, August 16, 1990.
b Traded by Montreal Expos to Cincinnati Reds organization with outfielder Dave Martinez and pitcher Scott Ruskin for pitchers John Wetteland and Bill Risley, December 11, 1991.
c On disabled list from August 21 to end of 1993 season.
d On disabled list from June 27 to July 12, 1996.
e Traded to Baltimore Orioles for outfielder Jeffrey Hammonds, August 10, 1998.
f Not offered 1999 contract, December 21, 1998. Signed with Toronto Blue Jays, January 18, 1999.
g Outrighted by Toronto Blue Jays, October 7, 1999. Signed with Chicago Cubs, January 19, 2000.
h On disabled list from March 23 to April 25, 2000.
i Filed for free agency, October 11, 2000.

GREER, THURMAN CLYDE (RUSTY)
Born, Fort Rucker, Alabama, January 21, 1969.
Bats Left. Throws Left. Height, 6 feet. Weight, 190 pounds.

Year	Club	Lea	Pos	G	AB	R	H	2B	3B	HR	RBI	SB	Avg
1990 Butte	Pioneer		OF	62	226	48	78	12	6	10	50	9	.345
1991 Charlotte	Fla. St.		OF-1B	111	388	52	114	25	1	5	48	12	.294
1991 Tulsa	Texas		OF	20	64	12	19	3	2	3	12	2	.297
1992 Tulsa	Texas		1B-OF	106	359	47	96	22	4	5	37	2	.267
1993 Tulsa	Texas		1B	129	474	70	138	25	6	15	59	10	.291
1993 Oklahoma City	A.A.		OF	8	27	6	6	2	0	1	4	0	.222
1994 Oklahoma City	A.A.		OF-1B	31	111	18	35	12	1	3	13	1	.315
1994 Texas	A.L.		OF-1B	80	277	36	87	16	1	10	46	0	.314
1995 Texas	A.L.		OF-1B	131	417	58	113	21	2	13	61	3	.271
1996 Texas	A.L.		OF-1B	139	542	96	180	41	6	18	100	9	.332
1997 Texas	A.L.		OF	157	601	112	193	42	3	26	87	9	.321
1998 Texas	A.L.		OF	155	598	107	183	31	5	16	108	2	.306
1999 Texas	A.L.		OF	147	556	107	167	41	3	20	101	2	.300
2000 Tulsa	Texas		OF	2	7	0	1	0	0	0	1	0	.143
2000 Texas a	A.L.		OF	105	394	65	117	34	3	8	65	4	.297
Major League Totals		7 Yrs.		914	3385	581	1040	226	23	111	568	29	.307
Division Series													
1996 Texas	A.L.		OF	4	16	2	2	0	0	0	0	0	.125
1998 Texas	A.L.		OF	3	11	0	1	0	0	0	0	0	.091
1999 Texas	A.L.		OF	3	9	0	1	0	0	0	0	0	.111
Division Series Totals				10	36	2	4	0	0	0	0	0	.111

a On disabled list from April 13 to May 26, 2000.

GRIEVE, BENJAMIN
Born, Arlington, Texas, May 4, 1976.
Bats Left. Throws Right. Height, 6 feet, 4 inches. Weight, 220 pounds.

Year	Club	Lea	Pos	G	AB	R	H	2B	3B	HR	RBI	SB	Avg
1994 Sou Oregon	Northwest		OF	72	252	44	83	13	0	7	50	2	.329
1995 W. Michigan	Midwest		OF	102	371	53	97	16	1	4	62	11	.261
1995 Modesto	California		OF	28	107	17	28	5	0	2	14	2	.262
1996 Modesto	California		OF	72	281	61	100	20	1	11	51	8	.356
1996 Huntsville	Southern		OF	63	232	34	55	8	1	8	32	0	.237
1997 Huntsville	Southern		OF	100	372	100	122	29	2	24	108	5	.328
1997 Edmonton	P.C.		OF	27	108	27	46	11	1	7	28	0	.426
1997 Oakland	A.L.		OF	24	93	12	29	6	0	3	24	0	.312
1998 Oakland a	A.L.		OF	155	583	94	168	41	2	18	89	2	.288
1999 Oakland	A.L.		OF	148	486	80	129	21	0	28	86	4	.265
2000 Oakland b	A.L.		OF	158	594	92	166	40	1	27	104	3	.279
Major League Totals		4 Yrs.		485	1756	278	492	108	3	76	303	9	.280
Division Series													
2000 Oakland	A.L.		OF	5	17	1	2	0	0	0	2	0	.118

a Selected Rookie of the Year in American League for 1998.
b Traded to Tampa Bay Devil Rays with player to be named later for pitcher Cory Lidle and pitcher Roberto Hernandez, January 8, 2001.

GRIFFEY, GEORGE KENNETH, JR. (JUNIOR)
Born, Donora, Pennsylvania, November 21, 1969.
Bats Left. Throws Left. Height, 6 feet, 3 inches. Weight, 205 pounds.

Year	Club	Lea	Pos	G	AB	R	H	2B	3B	HR	RBI	SB	Avg
1987 Bellingham	Northwest		OF	54	182	43	57	9	1	14	40	13	.313
1988 San Bernardino a	California		OF	58	219	50	74	13	3	11	42	32	.338
1988 Vermont	Eastern		OF	17	61	10	17	5	1	2	10	4	.279
1989 Seattle b	A.L.		OF	127	455	61	120	23	0	16	61	16	.264
1990 Seattle	A.L.		OF	155	597	91	179	28	7	22	80	16	.300
1991 Seattle	A.L.		OF	154	548	76	179	42	1	22	100	18	.327
1992 Seattle c	A.L.		OF	142	565	83	174	39	4	27	103	10	.308
1993 Seattle	A.L.		OF-1B	156	582	113	180	38	3	45	109	17	.309
1994 Seattle	A.L.		OF	111	433	94	140	24	4	*40	90	11	.323
1995 Tacoma	P.C.		DH	1	3	0	0	0	0	0	0	0	.000
1995 Seattle d	A.L.		OF	72	260	52	67	7	0	17	42	4	.258
1996 Seattle e	A.L.		OF	140	545	125	165	26	2	49	140	16	.303
1997 Seattle f	A.L.		OF	157	608	*125	185	34	3	*56	*147	15	.304
1998 Seattle	A.L.		OF-1B	161	633	120	180	33	3	*56	146	20	.284

72

Year	Club	Lea	Pos	G	AB	R	H	2B	3B	HR	RBI	SB	Avg
1999 Seattle	A.L.		OF	160	606	123	173	26	3	*48	134	24	.285
2000 Cincinnati g	N.L.		OF	145	520	100	141	22	3	40	118	6	.271
Major League Totals		12 Yrs.	1680	6352	1163	1883	342	33	438	1270	173	.296	
Division Series													
1995 Seattle	A.L.		OF	5	23	9	9	0	0	5	7	1	.391
1997 Seattle	A.L.		OF	4	15	0	2	0	0	0	2	2	.133
Division Series Totals			9	38	9	11	0	0	5	9	3	.289	
Championship Series													
1995 Seattle	A.L.		OF	6	21	2	7	2	0	1	2	2	.333

a On disabled list from June 9 to August 15, 1988.
b On disabled list from July 24 to August 20, 1989.
c On disabled list from June 9 to June 25, 1992.
d On disabled list from May 27 to August 15, 1995.
e On disabled list from June 20 to July 13, 1996.1
f Selected Most Valuable Player in American League for 1997.
g Traded to Cincinnati Reds for pitcher Brett Tomko, outfielder Mike Cameron, infielder Antonio Perez and pitcher Jake Meyer, February 10, 2000.

GRISSOM, MARQUIS DEON

Born, Atlanta, Georgia, April 17, 1967.
Bats Right. Throws Right. Height, 5 feet, 11 inches. Weight, 190 pounds.

Year	Club	Lea	Pos	G	AB	R	H	2B	3B	HR	RBI	SB	Avg
1988 Jamestown	N.Y.-Penn.	OF	74	291	*69	94	14	7	8	39	23	.323	
1989 Jacksonville	Southern	OF	78	278	43	83	15	4	3	31	24	.299	
1989 Indianapolis	A.A.	OF	49	187	28	52	10	4	2	21	16	.278	
1989 Montreal	N.L.	OF	26	74	16	19	2	0	1	2	1	.257	
1990 Indianapolis	A.A.	OF	5	22	3	4	0	0	2	3	1	.182	
1990 Montreal a	N.L.	OF	98	288	42	74	14	2	3	29	22	.257	
1991 Montreal	N.L.	OF	148	558	73	149	23	9	6	39	*76	.267	
1992 Montreal	N.L.	OF	159	*653	99	180	39	6	14	66	*78	.276	
1993 Montreal	N.L.	OF	157	630	104	188	27	2	19	95	53	.298	
1994 Montreal b	N.L.	OF	110	475	96	137	25	4	11	45	36	.288	
1995 Atlanta c-d	N.L.	OF	139	551	80	142	23	3	12	42	29	.258	
1996 Atlanta	N.L.	OF	158	671	106	207	32	10	23	74	28	.308	
1997 Cleveland e-f-g	A.L.	OF	144	558	74	146	27	6	12	66	22	.262	
1998 Milwaukee	N.L.	OF	142	542	57	147	28	1	10	60	13	.271	
1999 Milwaukee	N.L.	OF	154	603	92	161	27	1	20	83	24	.267	
2000 Milwaukee	N.L.	OF	146	595	67	145	18	2	14	62	20	.244	
Major League Totals		12 Yrs.	1581	6198	906	1695	285	46	145	663	402	.273	
Division Series													
1995 Atlanta	N.L.	OF	4	21	5	11	2	0	3	4	2	.524	
1996 Atlanta	N.L.	OF	3	12	2	1	0	0	0	0	1	.083	
1997 Cleveland	A.L.	OF	5	17	3	4	0	1	0	0	0	.235	
Division Series Totals			12	50	10	16	2	1	3	4	3	.320	
Championship Series													
1995 Atlanta	N.L.	OF	4	19	2	5	0	1	0	0	0	.263	
1996 Atlanta	N.L.	OF	7	35	7	10	1	0	1	3	2	.286	
1997 Cleveland	A.L.	OF	6	23	2	6	0	0	1	4	3	.261	
Championship Series Totals			17	77	11	21	1	1	2	7	5	.273	
World Series Record													
1995 Atlanta	N.L.	OF	6	25	3	9	1	0	0	1	3	.360	
1996 Atlanta	N.L.	OF	6	27	4	12	2	1	0	5	1	.444	
1997 Cleveland	A.L.	OF	7	25	5	9	1	0	0	2	0	.360	
World Series Totals			19	77	12	30	4	1	0	8	4	.390	

a On disabled list from May 29 to June 30, 1990.
b Declared restricted free agent under Major League Baseball implemented labor proposal, December 23, 1994.
c Traded to Atlanta Braves for outfielder Roberto Kelly, outfielder Tony Tarasco and pitcher Esteban Yan, April 6, 1995.
d Signed with Atlanta Braves, April 25, 1995.
e Traded to Cleveland Indians with outfielder David Justice for outfielder Kenny Lofton and pitcher Alan Embree, March 25, 1997.
f On disabled list from April 20 to May 5, 1997.
g Traded to Milwaukee Brewers with pitcher Jeff Jodar for pitchers Ben McDonald, Mike Fetters and Ron Villone, December 8, 1997.

GRUDZIELANEK, MARK JAMES
Born, Milwaukee, Wisconsin, June 30, 1970.
Bats Right. Throws Right. Height, 6 feet, 1 inch. Weight, 185 pounds.

Year	Club	Lea	Pos	G	AB	R	H	2B	3B	HR	RBI	SB	Avg
1991 Jamestown	N.Y.-Penn.	SS	72	275	44	72	9	3	2	32	14	.262
1992 Rockford	Midwest	SS	128	496	64	122	12	5	5	54	25	.246
1993 West Palm Beach	Fla. St.	2B-SS-OF	86	300	41	80	11	6	1	34	17	.267
1994 Harrisburg	Eastern	SS-3B	122	488	92	157	37	3	11	66	32	.322
1995 Ottawa	Int.	SS	49	181	26	54	9	1	1	22	12	.298
1995 Montreal	N.L.	SS-3B-2B	78	269	27	66	12	2	1	20	8	.245
1996 Montreal	N.L.	SS	153	657	99	201	34	4	6	49	33	.306
1997 Montreal	N.L.	SS	156	*649	76	177	*54	3	4	51	25	.273
1998 Montreal-Los Angeles a	N.L.	SS	156	589	62	160	21	1	10	62	18	.272
1999 San Bernardino	California	SS	4	16	2	4	0	0	0	0	0	.250
1999 Los Angeles b	N.L.	SS	123	488	72	159	23	5	7	46	6	.326
2000 Los Angeles	N.L.	2B-SS	148	617	101	172	35	6	7	49	12	.279
Major League Totals		6 Yrs.	814	3269	437	935	179	21	35	277	102	.286

a Traded to Los Angeles Dodgers with outfielder Hiram Bocachica and pitcher Carlos Perez for infielder Wilton
Guerrero, outfielder Peter Bergeron, pitcher Ted Lilly and infielder Jonathan Tucker, July 31, 1998
b On disabled list from June 3 to July 6, 1999.

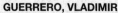

GUERRERO, VLADIMIR
Born, Nizao Bani, Dominican Republic, February 9, 1976.
Bats Right. Throws Right. Height, 6 feet, 2 inches. Weight, 195 pounds.

Year	Club	Lea	Pos	G	AB	R	H	2B	3B	HR	RBI	SB	Avg
1994 Montreal	DSL		25	92	34	39	11	0	12	35	5	.424
1994 Expos	Gulf Coast	OF	37	137	24	43	13	3	5	25	0	.314
1995 Albany	So.Atl.	OF	110	421	77	140	21	10	16	63	12	.333
1996 Wst Plm Bch	Fla.St.	OF	20	80	16	29	8	0	5	18	2	.363
1996 Harrisburg	Eastern	OF	118	417	84	150	32	8	19	78	17	.360
1996 Montreal	N.L.	OF	9	27	2	5	0	0	1	1	0	.185
1997 Wst. Plm. Bch	Fla. St.	OF	3	10	0	4	2	0	0	2	1	.400
1997 Montreal a	N.L.	OF	90	325	44	98	22	2	11	40	3	.302
1998 Montreal	N.L.	OF	159	623	108	202	37	7	38	109	11	.324
1999 Montreal	N.L.	OF	160	610	102	193	37	5	42	131	14	.316
2000 Montreal	N.L.	OF	154	571	101	197	28	11	44	123	9	.345
Major League Totals		5 Yrs.	572	2156	357	695	124	25	136	404	37	.322

a On disabled list from April 1 to May 2 and June 6 to June 21 and July 12 to July 27, 1997.

GUERRERO, WILTON
Born, Don Gregorio, Dominican Republic, October 24, 1974.
Bats Right. Throws Right. Height, 5 feet, 11 inches. Weight, 145 pounds.

Year	Club	Lea	Pos	G	AB	R	H	2B	3B	HR	RBI	SB	Avg
1993 Great Falls	Pioneer	SS	66	256	44	76	5	1	0	21	20	.297
1994 Vero Beach	Fla. St.	SS	110	402	55	118	11	4	1	32	23	.294
1995 San Antonio	Texas	SS	95	382	53	133	13	6	0	26	21	.348
1995 Albuquerque	P.C.	SS-OF	14	49	10	16	1	1	0	2	2	.327
1996 Albuquerque	P.C.	2B-SS	98	425	79	146	17	12	2	38	26	.344
1996 Los Angeles	N.L.	SS-2B	5	2	1	0	0	0	0	0	0	.000
1997 Albuquerque	P.C.	SS-2B	10	45	9	18	0	1	0	5	3	.400
1997 Los Angeles	N.L.	2B-SS	111	357	39	104	10	9	4	32	6	.291
1998 Albuquerque	P.C.	2B-OF	30	121	15	36	3	2	1	10	11	.298
1998 Los Angeles-Montreal a	N.L.	2B-SS-OF	116	402	50	114	14	9	2	27	8	.284
1999 Montreal	N.L.	2B-OF	132	315	42	92	15	7	2	31	7	.292
2000 Montreal b	N.L.	OF-2B	127	288	30	77	7	2	2	23	8	.267
Major League Totals		5 Yrs.	491	1364	162	387	46	27	10	113	29	.284

a Traded to Montreal Expos with outfielder Peter Bergeron, pitcher Ted Lilly and infielder Jonathan Tucker for infielder
Mark Grudzielanek, outfielder Hiram Bocachica and pitcher Carlos Perez, July 31, 1998
b Not offered 2001 contract, December 21, 2000, signed with Cincinnati Reds, January 9, 2001.

GUILLEN, CARLOS ALFONSO
Born, Maracay, Venezuela, September 30, 1975.
Bats Both. Throws Right. Height, 6 feet, 1 inch. Weight, 180 pounds.

Year	Club	Lea	Pos	G	AB	R	H	2B	3B	HR	RBI	SB	Avg
1993 Houston a	Dominican	SS	18	56	12	14	4	2	0	8	0	.250
1995 Astros	Gulf Coast	DH	30	105	17	31	4	2	2	15	17	.295

74

Year	Club	Lea	Pos	G	AB	R	H	2B	3B	HR	RBI	SB	Avg
1996 Quad City b	.......Midwest		SS	29	112	23	37	7	1	3	17	13	.330
1997 Jackson	............Texas		SS	115	390	47	99	16	1	10	39	6	.254
1997 New Orleans	.........A.A.		SS	3	13	3	4	1	0	0	0	0	.308
1998 New Orleans	.........P.C.		SS	100	374	67	109	18	4	12	51	3	.291
1998 Tacoma	..............P.C.		2B	24	92	8	21	1	1	1	4	1	.228
1998 Seattle c-d	..........A.L.		2B	10	39	9	13	1	1	0	5	2	.333
1999 Seattle e	.............A.L.		SS-2B	5	19	2	3	0	0	1	3	0	.158
2000 Tacoma	..............P.C.		3B	24	87	19	26	4	1	2	11	4	.299
2000 Seattle f	..............A.L.		3B-SS	90	288	45	74	15	2	7	42	1	.257
Major League Totals	....		3 Yrs.	105	346	56	90	16	3	8	50	3	.260
Division Series													
2000 Seattle	..............A.L.		PH	1	1	0	1	0	0	0	1	0	1.000
Championship Series													
2000 Seattle	..............A.L.		3B	2	5	1	1	0	0	1	2	0	.200

a On disabled list from June 1 to September 12, 1994.
b On disabled list from May 21 to September 11, 1996.
c Traded by Houston Astros to Seattle Mariners with pitcher Freddy Garcia and player to be named later for pitcher Randy Johnson, July 31, 1998.
d Seattle Mariners received pitcher John Halama to complete trade, October 1, 1998.
e On disabled list from April 11 to November 12, 1999.
f On disabled list from April 13 to April 27, 2000.

GUILLEN, JOSE MANUEL
Born, San Cristobal, Dominican Republic, May 17, 1976.
Bats Right. Throws Right. Height, 5 feet, 11 inches. Weight, 165 pounds.

Year	Club	Lea	Pos	G	AB	R	H	2B	3B	HR	RBI	SB	Avg
1994 Pirates	.........Gulf Coast		OF	30	110	17	29	4	1	4	11	2	.264
1995 Erie	.......N.Y.-Penn.		OF	66	258	41	81	17	1	12	46	1	.314
1995 Augusta	..........So. Atl.		OF	10	34	6	8	1	1	2	6	0	.235
1996 Lynchburg	......Carolina		OF	136	528	78	170	30	0	21	94	24	.322
1997 Pittsburgh	.........N.L.		OF	143	498	58	133	20	5	14	70	1	.267
1998 Pittsburgh	.........N.L.		OF	153	573	60	153	38	2	14	84	1	.267
1999 Pittsburgh a	.........N.L.		OF	40	120	18	32	6	0	1	18	3	.267
1999 Nashville	...........P.C.		OF	35	132	28	44	10	0	5	22	0	.333
1999 Durham	............Int.		OF	9	34	8	13	1	0	3	12	0	.382
1999 Tampa Bay	...........A.L.		OF	47	168	24	41	10	0	2	13	0	.244
2000 Durham	............Int.		OF	19	78	20	33	8	2	9	31	0	.423
2000 Tampa Bay b	.........A.L.		OF	105	316	40	80	16	5	10	41	3	.253
Major League Totals	....		4 Yrs.	488	1675	200	439	90	12	41	226	8	.262

a Traded to Tampa Bay Devil Rays with pitcher Jeff Sparks for catcher Joe Oliver and catcher Humberto Cota, July 23, 1999.
b On disabled list from March 28 to April 11, 2000.

GUILLEN (BARRIOS), OSWALDO JOSE (OZZIE)
Born, Oculare del Tuy, Venezuela, January 20, 1964.
Bats Left. Throws Right. Height, 5 feet, 11 inches. Weight, 164 pounds.

Year	Club	Lea	Pos	G	AB	R	H	2B	3B	HR	RBI	SB	Avg
1981 Bradenton	...Gulf Coast		SS-2B	55	189	26	49	4	1	0	16	8	.259
1982 Reno	........California		SS	130	528	*103	*183	33	4	2	54	25	.347
1983 Beaumont	.......Texas		SS	114	427	62	126	20	4	2	48	7	.295
1984 Las Vegas a	....P.C.		SS-2B	122	463	81	137	26	6	5	53	9	.296
1985 Chicago b	........A.L.		SS	150	491	71	134	21	9	1	33	7	.273
1986 Chicago	.........A.L.		SS	159	547	58	137	19	4	2	47	8	.250
1987 Chicago	.........A.L.		SS	149	560	64	156	22	7	2	51	25	.279
1988 Chicago	.........A.L.		SS	156	566	58	148	16	7	0	39	25	.261
1989 Chicago	.........A.L.		SS	155	597	63	151	20	8	1	54	36	.253
1990 Chicago	.........A.L.		SS	160	516	61	144	21	4	1	58	13	.279
1991 Chicago	.........A.L.		SS	154	524	52	143	20	3	3	49	21	.273
1992 Chicago c	.........A.L.		SS	12	40	5	8	4	0	0	7	1	.200
1993 Chicago	.........A.L.		SS	134	457	44	128	23	4	4	50	5	.280
1994 Chicago	.........A.L.		SS	100	365	46	105	9	5	1	39	5	.288
1995 Chicago	.........A.L.		SS	122	415	50	103	20	3	1	41	6	.248
1996 Chicago	.........A.L.		SS-OF	150	499	62	131	24	8	4	45	6	.263
1997 Chicago d-e	.........A.L.		SS	142	490	59	120	21	6	4	52	5	.245
1998 Baltimore	.........A.L.		SS-3B	12	16	2	1	0	0	0	0	0	.063
1998 Atlanta f-g-h	.....N.L.		SS-2B-1B-3B	83	264	35	73	15	1	1	22	1	.277
1999 Atlanta	..........N.L.		SS-3B-2B	92	232	21	56	10	0	1	20	4	.241

Year Club	Lea	Pos	G	AB	R	H	2B	3B	HR	RBI	SB	Avg
2000 Tampa Bay i-j . . . . . .A.L.		SS-3B-1B-2B	63	107	22	26	4	0	2	12	1	.243
Major League Totals		16 Yrs.	1993	6686	773	1764	275	69	28	619	169	.264
Division Series												
1998 Atlanta . . . . .N.L.		PH	1	1	0	0	0	0	0	0	0	.000
1999 Atlanta . . . . .N.L.		PH	1	1	0	0	0	0	0	0	0	.000
Division Series Totals			2	2	0	0	0	0	0	0	0	.000
Championship Series												
1993 Chicago . . . . .A.L.		SS	6	22	4	6	1	0	0	2	1	.273
1998 Atlanta . . . . .N.L.		SS	4	12	1	5	0	0	0	1	0	.417
1999 Atlanta . . . . .N.L.		SS	3	3	0	1	0	0	0	1	0	.333
Championship Series Totals . .			13	37	5	12	1	0	0	4	1	.324
World Series Record												
1999 Atlanta . . . . .N.L.		SS-DH	3	5	0	0	0	0	0	0	0	.000

a Traded by San Diego Padres to Chicago White Sox with pitchers Tim Lollar and Bill Long and infielder Luis Salazar for pitchers LaMarr Hoyt, Todd Simmons and Kevin Kristan, December 6, 1984.
b Selected Rookie of the Year in American League for 1985.
c On disabled list from April 21 to end of 1992 season.
d Filed for free agency, November 3, 1997.
e Signed with Baltimore Orioles organization, January 29, 1998.
f Released by Baltimore Orioles, May 1, 1998.
g Signed with Atlanta Braves, May 6, 1998.
h Filed for free agency, November 2, 1998, re-signed with Atlanta Braves, December 1, 1998.
i Released by Atlanta Braves, March 31, 2000, signed with Tampa Bay Devil Rays, April 5, 2000.
j Filed for free agency, November 9, 2000, signed with Tampa Bay Devil Rays organization, December 6, 2000.

GUTIERREZ, RICARDO

Born, Miami, Florida, May 23, 1970.
Bats Right. Throws Right. Height, 6 feet, 1 inch. Weight, 175 pounds.

Year Club	Lea	Pos	G	AB	R	H	2B	3B	HR	RBI	SB	Avg
1988 Bluefield . . . . . . .Appal.		SS	62	208	35	51	8	2	2	19	5	.245
1989 Frederick . . . . . .Carolina		SS	127	456	48	106	16	2	3	41	15	.232
1990 Hagerstown . . . .Eastern		SS	20	64	4	15	0	1	0	6	2	.234
1990 Frederick . . . . . .Carolina		SS	112	425	54	117	16	4	1	46	12	.275
1991 Hagerstown . . . .Eastern		SS	84	292	47	69	6	4	0	30	11	.236
1991 Rochester . . . . .Int.		SS-3B	49	157	23	48	5	3	0	15	4	.306
1992 Rochester a . . . . . . .Int.		2B-SS	125	431	54	109	9	3	0	41	14	.253
1992 Las Vegas . . . . . . .P.C.		2B-SS	3	6	0	1	0	0	0	1	0	.167
1993 Las Vegas . . . . . . .P.C.		2B-SS	5	24	4	10	4	0	0	4	4	.417
1993 San Diego . . . . . . .N.L.		SS-2B-OF-3B	133	438	76	110	10	5	5	26	4	.251
1994 San Diego b . . . . . .N.L.		SS-2B	90	275	27	66	11	2	1	28	2	.240
1995 Tucson . . . . .P.C.		SS	64	236	46	71	12	4	1	26	9	.301
1995 Houston . . . . .N.L.		SS-3B	52	156	22	43	6	0	0	12	5	.276
1996 Houston . . . . .N.L.		SS-3B-2B	89	218	28	62	8	1	1	15	6	.284
1997 New Orleans . . . . .A.A.		SS	7	27	2	5	1	0	0	4	0	.185
1997 Houston c . . . . . . .N.L.		SS-3B-2B	102	303	33	79	14	4	3	34	5	.261
1998 Houston d . . . . .N.L.		SS	141	491	55	128	24	3	2	46	13	.261
1999 Jackson . . . . .Texas		SS	4	12	4	4	1	0	0	1	0	.333
1999 New Orleans . . . . . .P.C.		SS	4	14	0	3	0	0	0	1	0	.214
1999 Houston d-e . . . .N.L.		SS-3B	85	268	33	70	7	5	1	25	2	.261
2000 Daytona . . . . . . .Fla.St.		SS	4	10	0	4	1	0	0	1	1	.400
2000 Chicago f . . . . .N.L.		SS	125	449	73	124	19	2	11	56	8	.276
Major League Totals		8 Yrs.	817	2598	347	682	99	22	24	242	45	.263
Division Series												
1997 Houston . . . . .N.L.		SS	3	8	0	1	0	0	0	0	0	.125
1998 Houston . . . . .N.L.		SS	4	10	1	3	0	0	0	0	1	.300
1999 Houston . . . . .N.L.		SS	3	10	0	0	0	0	0	0	0	.000
Division Series Totals			10	28	1	4	0	0	0	0	1	.143

a Traded by Baltimore Orioles to San Diego Padres organization to complete August 31 trade in which Baltimore acquired pitcher Craig Lefferts for pitcher Erik Schullstrom, September 4, 1992.
b Traded to Houston Astros with outfielders Derek Bell and Phil Plantier, pitchers Doug Brocail and Pedro Martinez and infielder Craig Shipley for third baseman Ken Caminiti, shortstop Andujar Cedeño, outfielder Steve Finley, pitcher Brian Williams, first baseman Roberto Petagine and player to be named, December 28, 1994. San Diego received pitcher Sean Fesh to complete trade, May 1, 1995
c On disabled list from April 1 to May 6, 1997.
d On disabled list from April 28 to June 7 and July 10 to August 9, 1999.
e Filed for free agency, October 28, 1999. Signed with Chicago Cubs, December 20, 1999.
f On disabled list from May 25 to June 22, 2000.

GUZMAN, CRISTIAN

Born, Santo Domingo, Dominican Republic, March 21, 1978.
Bats Both. Throws Right. Height, 6 feet. Weight, 180 pounds.

Year	Club	Lea	Pos	G	AB	R	H	2B	3B	HR	RBI	SB	Avg
1995 Yankees	....	Dominican	SS	46	160	24	43	6	5	3	20	11	.269
1996 Yankees	....	Gulf Coast	SS	42	170	37	50	8	2	1	21	7	.294
1997 Tampa	....	Fla.St.	SS	4	14	4	4	0	0	0	1	0	.286
1997 Greensboro	....	So.Atl.	SS	124	495	68	135	21	4	4	52	23	.273
1998 New Britain a	......	Eastern	SS	140	566	68	157	29	5	1	40	23	.277
1999 Minnesota b	....	A.L.	SS	131	420	47	95	12	3	1	26	9	.226
2000 Minnesota	....	A.L.	SS	156	631	89	156	25	*20	8	54	28	.247
Major League Totals	....		2 Yrs.	287	1051	136	251	37	23	9	80	37	.239

a Traded by New York Yankees to Minnesota Twins with pitcher Eric Milton, pitcher Danny Mota, outfielder Brian Buchanan and cash for infielder Chuck Knoblauch, February 6, 1998.

b On disabled list from May 27 to June 11, 1999.

GWYNN, ANTHONY KEITH (TONY)

Born, Los Angeles, California, May 9, 1960.
Bats Left. Throws Left. Height, 5 feet, 11 inches. Weight, 215 pounds.

Year	Club	Lea	Pos	G	AB	R	H	2B	3B	HR	RBI	SB	Avg
1981 Walla Walla	......	Northwest	OF	42	178	46	59	12	1	2	37	17	*.331
1981 Amarillo	....	Texas	OF	23	91	22	42	8	2	4	19	5	.462
1982 Hawaii	....	P.C.	OF	93	366	65	120	23	2	5	46	14	.328
1982 San Diego a	....	N.L.	OF	54	190	33	55	12	2	1	17	8	.289
1983 Las Vegas b	....	P.C.	OF	17	73	15	25	6	0	0	7	3	.342
1983 San Diego	....	N.L.	OF	86	304	34	94	12	2	1	37	7	.309
1984 San Diego	....	N.L.	OF	158	606	88	*213	21	10	5	71	33	*.351
1985 San Diego	....	N.L.	OF	154	622	90	197	29	5	6	46	14	.317
1986 San Diego	....	N.L.	OF	160	*642	*107	*211	33	7	14	59	37	.329
1987 San Diego	....	N.L.	OF	157	589	119	*218	36	13	7	54	56	*.370
1988 San Diego c	....	N.L.	OF	133	521	64	163	22	5	7	70	26	*.313
1989 San Diego	....	N.L.	OF	158	604	82	*203	27	7	4	62	40	*.336
1990 San Diego	....	N.L.	OF	141	573	79	177	29	10	4	72	17	.309
1991 San Diego	....	N.L.	OF	134	530	69	168	27	11	4	62	8	.317
1992 San Diego	....	N.L.	OF	128	520	77	165	27	3	6	41	3	.317
1993 San Diego	....	N.L.	OF	122	489	70	175	41	3	7	59	14	.358
1994 San Diego	....	N.L.	OF	110	419	79	*165	35	1	12	64	5	*.394
1995 San Diego	....	N.L.	OF	135	535	82	*197	33	1	9	90	17	*.368
1996 San Diego d	....	N.L.	OF	116	451	67	159	27	2	3	50	11	*.353
1997 San Diego	....	N.L.	OF	149	592	97	*220	49	2	17	119	12	*.372
1998 San Diego e	....	N.L.	OF	127	461	65	148	35	0	16	69	3	.321
1999 San Diego f	....	N.L.	OF	111	411	59	139	27	0	10	62	7	.338
2000 San Diego g-h	....	N.L.	OF	36	127	17	41	12	0	1	17	0	.323
Major League Totals	....		19 Yrs.	2369	9186	1378	3108	534	84	134	1121	318	.338
Division Series													
1996 San Diego	....	N.L.	OF	3	13	0	4	1	0	0	1	1	.308
1998 San Diego	....	N.L.	OF	4	15	1	3	2	0	0	2	0	.200
Division Series Totals	....			7	28	1	7	3	0	0	3	1	.250
Championship Series													
1984 San Diego	....	N.L.	OF	5	19	6	7	3	0	0	3	0	.368
1998 San Diego	....	N.L.	OF	6	26	1	6	1	0	0	2	0	.231
Championship Series Totals	......			11	45	7	13	4	0	0	5	0	.289
World Series Record													
1984 San Diego	....	N.L.	OF	5	19	1	5	0	0	0	0	1	.263
1998 San Diego	....	N.L.	OF	4	16	2	8	0	0	1	3	0	.500
World Series Totals	....			9	35	3	13	0	0	1	3	1	.371

a On disabled list from August 25 to September 10, 1982.

b On disabled list from March 26 to June 21, 1983.

c On disabled list from May 8 to May 28, 1988.

d On disabled list from July 2 to August 6, 1996.

e On disabled list from August 13 to September 1, 1998.

f On disabled list from May 22 to June 12 and June 20 to July 19, 1999.

g On disabled list from April 29 to May 14 and June 24 to October 1, 2000.

h Filed for free agency, October 31, 2000, re-signed with San Diego Padres, December 7, 2000.

HALTER, SHANE DAVID
Born, LaPlata, Maryland, November 8, 1969.
Bats Right. Throws Right. Height, 5 feet, 10 inches. Weight, 160 pounds.

Year	Club	Lea	Pos	G	AB	R	H	2B	3B	HR	RBI	SB	Avg
1991 Eugene	.....Northwest		SS	64	236	41	55	9	1	1	18	12	.233
1992 Appleton	.....Midwest		SS	80	313	50	83	22	3	3	33	21	.265
1992 Baseball Cy	.....Fla.St.		SS	44	117	11	28	1	0	1	14	5	.239
1993 Wilmington	....Carolina		SS	54	211	44	63	8	5	5	32	5	.299
1993 Memphis	.....Southern		SS	81	306	50	79	7	0	4	20	4	.258
1994 Memphis	.....Southern		SS	129	494	61	111	23	1	6	35	10	.225
1995 Omaha	...........A.A.		SS-2B	124	392	42	90	19	3	8	39	2	.230
1996 Charlotte	.........Int.		OF-2B-3B	16	41	3	12	1	0	0	4	0	.293
1996 Omaha	...........A.A.		OF-3B-SS-2B	93	299	43	77	24	0	3	33	7	.258
1997 Omaha	...........A.A.		3B-OF-2B-SS	14	49	10	13	1	1	2	9	0	.265
1997 Kansas City	.......A.L.		OF-2B-3B-SS	74	123	16	34	5	1	2	10	4	.276
1998 Omaha	...........P.C.		SS-1B-2B-3B	22	97	15	30	6	1	1	13	4	.309
1998 Kansas City	.......A.L.		SS-OF-3B-2B	86	204	17	45	12	0	2	13	2	.221
1999 Norfolk	..........Int.		SS	127	474	77	130	22	3	6	35	19	.274
1999 New York a	.......N.L.		OF-SS	7	0	0	0	0	0	0	0	0	.000
2000 Detroit b	........A.L.		3B-1B-SS-2B	105	238	26	62	12	2	3	27	5	.261
Major League Totals	....		4 Yrs.	272	565	59	141	29	3	7	50	11	.250

a Traded to New York Mets for outfielder Jonathan Guzman, March 22, 1999.
b Claimed on waivers by Detroit Tigers, March 13, 2000.

HAMMONDS, JEFFREY BRYAN
Born, Plainfield, New Jersey, March 5, 1971.
Bats Right. Throws Right. Height, 6 feet. Weight, 195 pounds.

Year	Club	Lea	Pos	G	AB	R	H	2B	3B	HR	RBI	SB	Avg
1993 Rochester	...........Int.		OF	36	151	25	47	9	1	5	23	6	.311
1993 Bowie	.....Eastern		OF	24	92	13	26	3	0	3	10	4	.283
1993 Baltimore a	.........A.L.		OF	33	105	10	32	8	0	3	19	4	.305
1994 Baltimore b	.........A.L.		OF	68	250	45	74	18	2	8	31	5	.296
1995 Bowie	.....Eastern		OF	9	31	7	12	3	1	1	11	3	.387
1995 Baltimore c	.........A.L.		OF	57	178	18	43	9	1	4	23	4	.242
1996 Rochester d	...........Int.		OF	34	125	24	34	4	2	3	19	3	.272
1996 Baltimore	...........A.L.		OF	71	248	38	56	10	1	9	27	3	.226
1997 Baltimore	...........A.L.		OF	118	397	71	105	19	3	21	55	15	.264
1998 Bowie	...........Eastern		OF	3	6	4	2	0	0	0	0	3	.333
1998 Baltimore	...........A.L.		OF	63	171	36	46	12	1	6	28	7	.269
1998 Cincinnati e-f	.........N.L.		OF	26	86	14	26	4	1	0	11	1	.302
1999 Cincinnati g	.........N.L.		OF	123	262	43	73	13	0	17	41	3	.279
2000 Colorado h-i	.........N.L.		OF	122	454	94	152	24	2	20	106	14	.335
Major League Totals	....		8 Yrs.	681	2151	369	607	117	11	88	341	56	.282
Division Series													
1997 Baltimore	............A.L.		OF	4	10	3	1	1	0	0	2	1	.100
Championship Series													
1997 Baltimore	............A.L.		OF	5	3	0	0	0	0	0	0	1	.000

a On disabled list from August 8 to September 1 and September 28 to end of 1993 season.
b On disabled list from May 4 to June 16, 1994.
c On disabled list from July 18 to September 3, 1995.
d On disabled list from August 16 to September 22, 1996.
e On disabled list from June 3 to July 11, 1998.
f Traded to Cincinnati Reds for infielder Willie Greene, August 10, 1998.
g Traded to Colorado Rockies with pitcher Stan Belinda and cash for outfielder Dante Bichette, October 30, 1999.
h On disabled list from April 4 to April 21, 2000.
i Filed for free agency, October 27, 2000, signed with Milwaukee Brewers, December 23, 2000.

HANSEN, DAVID ANDREW (DAVE)
Born, Long Beach, California, November 24, 1968.
Bats Left. Throws Right. Height, 6 feet. Weight, 195 pounds.

Year	Club	Lea	Pos	G	AB	R	H	2B	3B	HR	RBI	SB	Avg
1986 Great Falls	.....Pioneer		OF-3B-C-2B	61	204	39	61	7	3	1	36	9	.299
1987 Bakersfield	...California		3B-OF	132	432	68	113	22	1	3	38	4	.262
1988 Vero Beach	......Fla.St.		3B	135	512	68	149	28	6	7	81	2	.291
1989 San Antonio	....Texas		3B	121	464	72	138	21	4	6	52	3	.297
1989 Albuquerque	....P.C.		3B	6	30	6	8	1	0	2	10	0	.267
1990 Albuquerque	.....P.C.		3B-SS-OF	135	487	90	154	20	3	11	92	9	.316
1990 Los Angeles	.......N.L.		3B	5	7	0	1	0	0	0	1	0	.143

78

Year	Club	Lea	Pos	G	AB	R	H	2B	3B	HR	RBI	SB	Avg
1991 Albuquerque	.P.C.		3B-SS	68	254	42	77	11	1	5	40	4	.303
1991 Los Angeles	.N.L.		3B-SS	53	56	3	15	4	0	1	5	1	.268
1992 Los Angeles	.N.L.		3B	132	341	30	73	11	0	6	22	0	.214
1993 Los Angeles	.N.L.		3B	84	105	13	38	3	0	4	30	0	.362
1994 Los Angeles a	.N.L.		3B	40	44	3	15	3	0	0	5	0	.341
1995 Los Angeles	.N.L.		3B	100	181	19	52	10	0	1	14	0	.287
1996 Los Angeles	.N.L.		3B-1B	80	104	7	23	1	0	0	6	0	.221
1997 Chicago b-c	.N.L.		3B-1B-2B	90	151	19	47	8	2	3	21	1	.311
1998 Hanshin	.Japan Cent.		1B	121	400	42	101	13	1	11	55	0	.253
1999 Los Angeles d	.N.L.		1B-3B-OF	100	107	14	27	8	1	2	17	0	.252
2000 Los Angeles	.N.L.		1B-3B-OF	102	121	18	35	6	2	8	26	0	.289
Major League Totals		10 Yrs.		786	1217	126	326	54	5	25	147	2	.268
Division Series													
1995 Los Angeles	.N.L.		PH	3	3	0	2	0	0	0	0	0	.667
1996 Los Angeles	.N.L.		PH	2	2	0	0	0	0	0	0	0	.000
Division Series Totals				5	5	0	2	0	0	0	0	0	.400

a On disabled list from May 9 to May 28, 1994.
b Filed for free agency, November 27, 1996, signed with Chicago Cubs organization, January 22, 1997.
c Filed for free agency, October 27, 1997, signed with Hanshin Tigers (Japan Central), November 7, 1997.
d Played in Japan in 1998, signed as free agent by Los Angeles Dodgers, January 11, 1999.

HARRIS, LEONARD ANTHONY

Born, Miami, Florida, October 28, 1964.
Bats Left. Throws Right. Height, 5 feet, 10 inches. Weight, 220 pounds.

Year	Club	Lea	Pos	G	AB	R	H	2B	3B	HR	RBI	SB	Avg
1983 Billings	.Pioneer		3B	56	224	37	63	8	1	1	26	7	.281
1984 Cedar Rapids	.Midwest		3B	132	468	52	115	15	3	6	53	31	.246
1985 Tampa	.Fla. St.		3B	132	499	66	129	11	8	3	51	15	.259
1986 Vermont	.Eastern		3B	119	450	68	114	17	2	10	52	36	.253
1987 Nashville a	.A.A.		SS-3B	120	403	45	100	12	3	2	31	30	.248
1988 Glens Falls	.Eastern		2B	17	65	9	22	5	1	1	7	6	.338
1988 Nashville	.A.A.		2B	107	422	46	117	20	2	0	35	*45	.277
1988 Cincinnati	.N.L.		3B-2B	16	43	7	16	1	0	0	8	4	.372
1989 Nashville	.A.A.		2B	8	34	6	9	2	0	3	6	0	.265
1989 Cinc.-L.A. b	.N.L.		2B-3B-OF-SS	115	335	36	79	10	1	3	26	14	.236
1990 Los Angeles	.N.L.		3B-2B-OF-SS	137	431	61	131	16	4	2	29	15	.304
1991 Los Angeles	.N.L.		3B-2B-SS-OF	145	429	59	123	16	1	3	38	12	.287
1992 Los Angeles	.N.L.		2B-3B-OF-SS	135	347	28	94	11	0	0	30	19	.271
1993 Los Angeles c	.N.L.		2B-3B-SS-OF	107	160	20	38	6	1	2	11	3	.237
1994 Cincinnati	.N.L.		3B-1B-OF-2B	66	100	13	31	3	1	0	14	7	.310
1995 Cincinnati	.N.L.		3B-1B-OF-2B	101	197	32	41	8	3	2	16	10	.208
1996 Cincinnati d-e	.N.L.		OF-3B-1B-2B	125	302	33	86	17	2	5	32	14	.285
1997 Cincinnati	.N.L.		OF-2B-3B-1B	120	238	32	65	13	1	3	28	4	.273
1998 Cincinnati-N.Y. f-g	.N.L.		OF-3B-2B-1B	132	290	30	75	15	0	6	27	6	.259
1999 Colorado-Arizona h	.N.L.		2B-OF-3B	110	187	17	58	13	0	1	20	2	.310
2000 Arizona-New York i	.N.L.		3B-OF-1B-2B	112	223	31	58	7	4	4	26	13	.260
Major League Totals		13 Yrs.		1421	3282	399	895	136	18	31	305	123	.273
Division Series													
1999 Arizona	.N.L.		3B	2	2	0	0	0	0	0	0	0	.000
2000 New York	.N.L.		PH	2	2	1	0	0	0	0	0	1	.000
Division Series Totals				4	4	1	0	0	0	0	0	1	.000
Championship Series													
1995 Cincinnati	.N.L.		PH	3	2	0	2	0	0	0	0	1	1.000
2000 New York	.N.L.		PH	2	1	0	0	0	0	0	0	0	.000
Championship Series Totals				5	3	0	2	0	0	0	0	1	.667
World Series Record													
2000 New York	.N.L.		DH	3	4	1	0	0	0	0	0	0	.000

a Loaned by Cincinnati Reds to Detroit Tigers organization for 1987 season.
b Traded to LA Dodgers with outfielder Kal Daniels for pitcher Tim Leary and infielder Mariano Duncan, July 18, 1989.
c Released, October 8; signed with Cincinnati Reds, November 24, 1993.
d Filed for free agency, October 31, 1996.
e Re-signed with Cincinnati Reds, November 18, 1996.
f Traded to New York Mets for pitcher John Hudek, July 3, 1998.
g Filed for free agency, October 27, 1998, signed with Colorado Rockies, November 6, 1998.
h Traded to Arizona Diamondbacks for infielder Belvani Martinez, August 31, 1999.
i Traded to New York Mets for pitcher Bill Pulsipher, June 2, 2000.

HASELMAN, WILLIAM JOSEPH (BILL)
Born, Long Branch, New Jersey, May 25, 1966.
Bats Right. Throws Right. Height, 6 feet, 3 inches. Weight, 220 pounds.

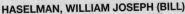

Year Club	Lea	Pos	G	AB	R	H	2B	3B	HR	RBI	SB	Avg
1987 Gastonia	So.Atl.	DH-C	61	235	35	72	13	1	8	33	1	.306
1988 Charlotte	Fla.St.	DH-C	122	453	56	111	17	2	10	54	8	.245
1989 Tulsa	Texas	C	107	352	38	95	17	2	7	36	5	.270
1990 Tulsa	Texas	C-1B-OF-3B	120	430	68	137	39	2	18	80	3	.319
1990 Texas	A.L.	C	7	13	0	2	0	0	0	3	0	.154
1991 Okla City	A.A.	C-OF-1B	126	442	57	113	22	2	9	60	10	.256
1992 Okla City	A.A.	OF-C	17	58	8	14	5	0	1	9	1	.241
1992 Calgary	P.C.	C-OF-1B	88	302	49	77	14	2	19	53	3	.255
1992 Seattle a-b	A.L.	C-OF	8	19	1	5	0	0	0	0	0	.263
1993 Seattle	A.L.	C-OF	58	137	21	35	8	0	5	16	2	.255
1994 Seattle	A.L.	C-OF	38	83	11	16	7	1	1	8	1	.193
1994 Calgary c	P.C.	C-1B	44	163	44	54	10	0	15	46	1	.331
1995 Boston	A.L.	C-1B-3B	64	152	22	37	6	1	5	23	0	.243
1996 Boston	A.L.	C-1B	77	237	33	65	13	1	8	34	4	.274
1997 Red Sox	Gulf Coast	DH	4	16	2	2	0	0	0	1	1	.125
1997 Trenton	Eastern	C	7	26	3	6	1	0	2	3	0	.231
1997 Boston d-e	A.L.	C	67	212	22	50	15	0	6	26	0	.236
1998 Texas f	A.L.	C	40	105	11	33	6	0	6	17	0	.314
1999 Detroit g	A.L.	C	48	143	13	39	8	0	4	14	2	.273
2000 Texas	A.L.	C	62	193	23	53	18	0	6	26	0	.275
Major League Totals			10 Yrs.	469	1294	157	335	81	3	41	167	9	.259
Division Series												
1995 Boston	A.L.	C	1	2	0	0	0	0	0	0	0	.000

a On disabled list from March 28 to May 4, 1992.
b Claimed on waivers by Seattle Mariners from Texas Rangers, May 29, 1992.
c Filed for free agency, October 15, 1994, signed with Boston Red Sox, November 7, 1994.
d On disabled list from June 30 to August 8, 1997.
e Traded to Texas Rangers with pitcher Aaron Sele and pitcher Mark Brandenburg for catcher Jim Leyritz and outfielder Damon Buford, November 6, 1997.
f Filed for free agency, October 23, 1998, signed with Detroit Tigers, December 14, 1998.
g Traded to Texas Rangers with pitcher Justin Thompson, pitcher Francisco Cordero, pitcher Alan Webb, outfielder Gabe Kapler and infielder Frank Catalanotto for outfielder Juan Gonzalez, pitcher Danny Patterson and catcher Greg Zaun, November 2, 1999.

HATTEBERG, SCOTT ALLEN
Born, Salem, Oregon, December 14, 1969.
Bats Left. Throws Right. Height, 6 feet, 1 inch. Weight, 195 pounds.

Year Club	Lea	Pos	G	AB	R	H	2B	3B	HR	RBI	SB	Avg
1991 Winter Havn	Fla. St.	C	56	191	21	53	7	3	1	25	1	.277
1991 Lynchburg	Carolina	C	8	25	4	5	1	0	0	2	0	.200
1992 New Britain	Eastern	C-1B	103	297	28	69	13	2	1	30	1	.232
1993 New Britain	Eastern	C	68	227	35	63	10	2	7	28	1	.278
1993 Pawtucket	Int.	C	18	53	6	10	0	0	1	2	0	.189
1994 New Britain	Eastern	C	20	68	6	18	4	1	1	9	0	.265
1994 Pawtucket	Int.	C	78	238	26	56	14	0	7	19	2	.235
1995 Pawtucket	Int.	C	85	251	36	68	15	1	7	27	2	.271
1995 Boston	A.L.	C	2	2	1	1	0	0	0	0	0	.500
1996 Pawtucket	Int.	C	90	287	52	77	16	0	12	49	1	.268
1996 Boston	A.L.	C	10	11	3	2	1	0	0	0	0	.182
1997 Boston	A.L.	C	114	350	46	97	23	1	10	44	0	.277
1998 Boston	A.L.	C	112	359	46	99	23	1	12	43	0	.276
1999 Sarasota	Fla.St.	C	1	1	0	1	0	0	0	1	0	1.000
1999 Pawtucket	Int.	C	10	34	3	6	2	0	0	4	0	.176
1999 GC Red Sox	Gulf Coast	C	6	15	4	6	2	0	1	6	0	.400
1999 Boston a	A.L.	C	30	80	12	22	5	0	1	11	0	.275
2000 Boston	A.L.	C-3B	92	230	21	61	15	0	8	36	0	.265
Major League Totals			6 Yrs.	360	1032	129	282	67	2	31	134	0	.273
Division Series												
1998 Boston	A.L.	C	3	9	0	1	0	0	0	0	0	.111
1999 Boston	A.L.	C	1	1	1	1	0	0	0	1	0	1.000
Division Series Totals				4	10	1	2	0	0	0	1	0	.200
Championship Series												
1999 Boston	A.L.	C	3	1	0	0	0	0	0	0	0	.000

a On disabled list from April 16 to May 7 and May 17 to August 16, 1999.

HAYES, CHARLES DEWAYNE
Born, Hattiesburg, Mississippi, May 29, 1965.
Bats Right. Throws Right. Height, 6 feet. Weight, 215 pounds.

Year	Club	Lea	Pos	G	AB	R	H	2B	3B	HR	RBI	SB	Avg
1983 Great Falls a	Pioneer		3B	34	111	9	29	4	2	0	9	1	.261
1984 Clinton	Midwest		3B	116	392	41	96	17	2	2	51	4	.245
1985 Fresno	California		3B	131	467	73	132	17	2	4	68	7	.283
1986 Shreveport	Texas		3B	121	434	52	107	23	2	5	45	1	.247
1987 Shreveport	Texas		3B	128	487	66	148	33	3	14	75	5	.304
1988 Phoenix	P.C.		OF-3B	131	492	71	151	26	4	7	71	4	.307
1988 San Francisco	N.L.		OF	7	11	0	1	0	0	0	0	0	.091
1989 Phoenix b	P.C.		3B-OF	61	229	25	65	15	1	7	27	0	.284
1989 Scranton	Int.		3B	7	27	4	11	3	1	1	3	0	.407
1989 S.F.-Philadelphia	N.L.		3B	87	304	26	78	15	1	8	43	3	.257
1990 Philadelphia	N.L.		3B-1B-2B	152	561	56	145	20	0	10	57	4	.258
1991 Philadelphia c	N.L.		3B-SS	142	460	34	106	23	1	12	53	3	.230
1992 New York d	A.L.		3B-1B	142	509	52	131	19	2	18	66	3	.257
1993 Colorado e	N.L.		3B-SS	157	573	89	175	*45	2	25	98	11	.305
1994 Colorado f	N.L.		3B	113	423	46	122	23	4	10	50	3	.288
1995 Philadelphia g-h-i	N.L.		3B	141	529	58	146	30	3	11	85	5	.276
1996 Pittsburgh	N.L.		3B	128	459	51	114	21	2	10	62	6	.248
1996 New York j	A.L.		3B	20	67	7	19	3	0	2	13	0	.284
1997 New York k	A.L.		3B-2B	100	353	39	91	16	0	11	53	3	.258
1998 San Francisco	N.L.		3B-1B	111	329	39	94	8	0	12	62	2	.286
1999 San Francisco l-m	N.L.		3B-1B-OF	95	264	33	54	9	1	6	48	3	.205
2000 Milwaukee n-o	N.L.		3B-1B	121	370	46	93	17	0	9	46	1	.251
Major League Totals	13 Yrs.			1516	5212	576	1369	249	16	144	736	47	.263
Division Series													
1996 New York	A.L.		3B	3	5	0	1	0	0	0	1	0	.200
1997 New York	A.L.		3B-2B	5	15	0	5	0	0	0	1	0	.333
Division Series Totals				8	20	0	6	0	0	0	2	0	.300
Championship Series													
1996 New York	A.L.		3B	4	7	0	1	0	0	0	0	0	.143
World Series													
1996 New York	A.L.		3B-1B	5	16	2	3	0	0	0	1	0	.188

a On disabled list from July 20 to end of 1983 season.
b Traded by San Francisco Giants to Philadelphia Phillies with pitchers Dennis Cook and Terry Mulholland for pitcher Steve Bedrosian and player to be named, June 18; San Francisco acquired infielder Rick Parker to complete trade, August 6, 1989.
c Traded to New York Yankees for pitcher Darrin Chapin, January 8, 1992.
d Selected by Colorado Rockies in expansion draft, November 17, 1992.
e Suspended three games by National League for June 15 fight from August 10 to August 12, 1993.
f Not offered 1995 contract, December 23, 1994.
g Signed with Philadelphia Phillies, April 6, 1995.
h Filed for free agency, November 12, 1995.
i Signed with Pittsburgh Pirates, December 28, 1995.
j Traded to New York Yankees for player to be named later, August 30, 1996.
k Traded to San Francisco Giants for outfielder Chris Singleton and pitcher Alberto Castillo, November 11, 1997.
l On disabled list from July 2 to July 21, 1999.
m Filed for free agency, November 2, 1999. Signed with New York Mets organization, January 19, 2000.
n Released by New York Mets, March 20, 2000, signed with Milwaukee Brewers organization, March 22, 2000.
o Filed for free agency, October 31, 2000, signed with Houston Astros organization, January 2, 2001.

HELTON, TODD LYNN
Born, Knoxville, Tennessee, August 20, 1973.
Bats Left. Throws Left. Height, 6 feet, 2 inches. Weight, 195 pounds.

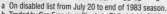

Year	Club	Lea	Pos	G	AB	R	H	2B	3B	HR	RBI	SB	Avg
1995 Asheville	So. Atl.		1B	54	201	24	51	11	1	1	15	1	.254
1996 New Haven	Eastern		1B	93	319	46	106	24	2	7	51	2	.332
1996 Colo Sprngs	P.C.		1B-OF	21	71	13	25	4	1	2	13	0	.352
1997 Colo Sprngs	P.C.		1B-OF	99	392	87	138	31	2	16	88	3	.352
1997 Colorado	N.L.		OF-1B	35	93	13	26	2	1	5	11	0	.280
1998 Colorado	N.L.		1B	152	530	78	167	37	1	25	97	3	.315
1999 Colorado	N.L.		1B	159	578	114	185	39	5	35	113	7	.320
2000 Colorado	N.L.		1B	160	580	138	*216	*59	2	42	*147	5	*.372
Major League Totals	4 Yrs.			506	1781	343	594	137	9	107	368	15	.334

HENDERSON, RICKEY HENLEY
Born, Chicago, Illinois, December 25, 1958.
Bats Right. Throws Left. Height, 5 feet, 10 inches. Weight, 190 pounds.

Year Club	Lea	Pos	G	AB	R	H	2B	3B	HR	RBI	SB	Avg
1976 Boise	Northwest	OF	46	140	34	47	13	2	3	23	29	.336
1977 Modesto	California	OF	134	481	120	166	18	4	11	69	*95	.345
1978 Jersey City	Eastern	OF	133	455	81	141	14	4	0	34	*81	.310
1979 Ogden	P.C.	OF	71	259	66	80	11	8	3	26	44	.309
1979 Oakland	A.L.	OF	89	351	49	96	13	3	1	26	33	.274
1980 Oakland	A.L.	OF	158	591	111	179	22	4	9	53	*100	.303
1981 Oakland	A.L.	OF	108	423	*89	*135	18	7	6	35	*56	.319
1982 Oakland	A.L.	OF	149	536	119	143	24	4	10	51	*130	.267
1983 Oakland	A.L.	OF	145	513	105	150	25	7	9	49	*108	.292
1984 Oakland a	A.L.	OF	142	502	113	147	27	4	16	58	*66	.293
1985 Ft. Lauderdale ...	Fla. St.	OF	3	6	5	1	0	1	0	3	1	.167
1985 New York b	A.L.	OF	143	547	*146	172	28	5	24	72	*80	.314
1986 New York	A.L.	OF	153	608	*130	160	31	5	28	74	*87	.263
1987 New York c	A.L.	OF	95	358	78	104	17	3	17	37	41	.291
1988 New York	A.L.	OF	140	554	118	169	30	2	6	50	*93	.305
1989 N.Y.-Oakland d-e ...	A.L.	OF	150	541	*113	148	26	3	12	57	*77	.274
1990 Oakland f	A.L.	OF	136	489	*119	159	33	3	28	61	*65	.325
1991 Oakland g	A.L.	OF	134	470	105	126	17	1	18	57	*58	.268
1992 Oakland h	A.L.	OF	117	396	77	112	18	3	15	46	48	.283
1993 Oakland-Toronto i-j ...	A.L.	OF	134	481	114	139	22	2	21	59	53	.289
1994 Oakland k	A.L.	OF	87	296	66	77	13	0	6	20	22	.260
1995 Oakland l-m	A.L.	OF	112	407	67	122	31	1	9	54	32	.300
1996 San Diego	N.L.	OF	148	465	110	112	17	2	9	29	37	.241
1997 San Diego n-o ...	N.L.	OF	88	288	63	79	11	0	6	27	29	.274
1997 Anaheim p-q ...	A.L.	DH-OF	32	115	21	21	3	0	2	7	16	.183
1998 Oakland r	A.L.	OF	152	542	101	128	16	1	14	57	*66	.236
1999 New York s	N.L.	OF	121	438	89	138	30	0	12	42	37	.315
2000 New York t	N.L.	OF	31	96	17	21	1	0	0	2	5	.219
2000 Seattle u	A.L.	OF	92	324	58	77	13	2	4	30	31	.238
Major League Totals		22 Yrs.	2856	10331	2178	2914	486	62	282	1052	1370	.282

Division Series

Year Club	Lea	Pos	G	AB	R	H	2B	3B	HR	RBI	SB	Avg
1981 Oakland	A.L.	OF	3	11	3	2	0	0	0	0	2	.182
1996 San Diego	N.L.	OF	3	12	2	4	0	0	0	1	0	.333
1999 New York	N.L.	OF	4	15	5	6	0	0	0	1	6	.400
2000 Seattle	A.L.	OF	3	5	3	2	0	0	0	0	1	.400
Division Series Totals			13	43	13	14	0	0	1	2	9	.326

Championship Series

Year Club	Lea	Pos	G	AB	R	H	2B	3B	HR	RBI	SB	Avg
1981 Oakland	A.L.	OF	3	11	0	4	2	1	0	1	2	.364
1989 Oakland	A.L.	OF	5	15	8	6	1	1	2	5	8	.400
1990 Oakland	A.L.	OF	4	17	1	5	0	0	0	3	2	.294
1992 Oakland	A.L.	OF	6	23	5	6	0	0	0	1	2	.261
1993 Toronto	A.L.	OF	6	25	4	3	2	0	0	0	2	.120
1999 New York	N.L.	OF	6	23	2	4	1	0	0	1	1	.174
2000 Seattle	A.L.	OF	3	9	2	2	1	0	0	1	0	.222
Championship Series Totals			33	123	22	30	7	2	2	12	17	.244

World Series Record

Year Club	Lea	Pos	G	AB	R	H	2B	3B	HR	RBI	SB	Avg
1989 Oakland	A.L.	OF	4	19	4	9	1	2	1	3	3	.474
1990 Oakland	A.L.	OF	4	15	2	5	2	0	1	1	3	.333
1993 Toronto	A.L.	OF	6	22	6	5	2	0	0	2	1	.227
World Series Totals			14	56	12	19	5	2	2	6	7	.339

a Traded to New York Yankees with pitcher Bert Bradley and cash for pitchers Jay Howell, Jose Rijo, Eric Plunk and Tim Birtsas and outfielder Stan Javier, December 5, 1984.

b On disabled list from March 30 to April 22, 1985.

c On disabled list from June 5 to June 29 and July 26 to September 1, 1987.

d Traded to Oakland Athletics for pitchers Eric Plunk and Greg Cadaret and outfielder Luis Polonia, June 21, 1989.

e Filed for free agency, November 2; re-signed with Oakland Athletics, November 28, 1989.

f Selected Most Valuable Player in American League for 1990.

g On disabled list from April 12 to April 27, 1991.

h On disabled list from May 28 to June 17 and June 30 to July 16, 1992.

i Traded to Toronto Blue Jays for pitcher Steve Karsay and player to be named, July 31; Oakland Athletics acquired outfielder Jose Herrera to complete trade, August 6, 1993.

j Filed for free agency, October 27; signed with Oakland Athletics, December 17, 1993.

k On disabled list from May 10 to May 27, 1994.

l Filed for free agency, October 30, 1995.

m Signed with San Diego Padres organization, December 29, 1995.

n On disabled list from May 9 to May 24, 1997.

o Traded to Anaheim Angels for pitcher Ryan Hancock, pitcher Steven Agosto and player to be named later, August 13, 1997. San Diego Padres received infielder George Arias to complete trade, August 19, 1997.

p Filed for free agency, October 27, 1997.
q Signed with Oakland Athletics, January 22, 1998.
r Filed for free agency, October 26, 1998. Signed with New York Mets, December 13, 1998.
s On disabled list from May 3 to May 22, 1999.
t Released by New York Mets, May 13, 2000, signed with Seattle Mariners, May 17, 2000.
u Not offered 2001 contract, November 2, 2000.

HERMANSEN, CHAD BRUCE

Born, Salt Lake City, Utah, September 10, 1977.
Bats Right. Throws Right. Height, 6 feet, 2 inches. Weight, 185 pounds.

Year	Club	Lea	Pos	G	AB	R	H	2B	3B	HR	RBI	SB	Avg
1995 Pirates	Gulf Coast		SS	24	92	14	28	10	1	3	17	0	.304
1995 Erie	N.Y.-Penn.		SS	44	165	30	45	8	3	6	25	4	.273
1996 Augusta	So.Atl.		SS	62	226	47	57	11	3	14	41	11	.252
1996 Lynchburg	Carolina		SS	66	251	40	69	11	3	10	46	5	.275
1997 Carolina	Southern		OF-SS-2B	129	487	87	134	31	4	20	70	18	.275
1998 Nashville	P.C.		OF-2B	126	458	81	118	26	5	28	78	21	.258
1999 Nashville	P.C.		OF	125	496	89	134	27	3	32	97	19	.270
1999 Pittsburgh	N.L.		OF	19	60	5	14	3	0	1	1	2	.233
2000 Nashville	P.C.		OF	78	294	47	66	12	1	11	38	16	.224
2000 Pittsburgh	N.L.		OF	33	108	12	20	4	1	2	8	0	.185
Major League Totals			2 Yrs.	52	168	17	34	7	1	3	9	2	.202

HERNANDEZ, CARLOS ALBERTO

Born, San Felix, Venezuela, May 24, 1967.
Bats Right. Throws Right. Height, 5 feet, 11 inches. Weight, 218 pounds.

Year	Club	Lea	Pos	G	AB	R	H	2B	3B	HR	RBI	SB	Avg
1985 Dodgers	Gulf Coast		3B-1B	22	49	3	12	1	0	0	6	0	.245
1986 Dodgers	Gulf Coast		C-3B	57	205	19	64	7	0	1	31	1	.312
1987 Bakersfield	California		C	48	162	22	37	6	1	3	22	8	.228
1988 Bakersfield	California		C	92	333	37	103	15	2	5	52	3	.309
1988 Albuquerque	P.C.		C	3	8	0	1	0	0	0	1	0	.125
1989 San Antonio	Texas		C	99	370	37	111	16	3	8	41	2	.300
1989 Albuquerque	P.C.		C	4	14	1	3	0	0	0	1	0	.214
1990 Albuquerque	P.C.		C	52	143	11	45	8	1	0	16	2	.315
1990 Los Angeles a	N.L.		C	10	20	2	4	1	0	0	1	0	.200
1991 Albuquerque	P.C.		C	95	345	60	119	24	2	8	44	5	.345
1991 Los Angeles	N.L.		C-3B	15	14	1	3	1	0	0	1	0	.214
1992 Los Angeles	N.L.		C	69	173	11	45	4	0	3	17	0	.260
1993 Los Angeles	N.L.		C	50	99	6	25	5	0	2	7	0	.253
1994 Los Angeles b	N.L.		C	32	64	6	14	2	0	2	6	0	.219
1995 Los Angeles	N.L.		C	45	94	3	14	1	0	2	8	0	.149
1996 Los Angeles	N.L.		C	13	14	1	4	0	0	0	0	0	.286
1996 Albuquerque c-d	P.C.		C-1B-3B	66	233	19	56	11	0	5	30	5	.240
1997 Rancho Cuca	California		C	1	4	0	1	0	0	0	0	0	.250
1997 Las Vegas	P.C.		C	3	10	1	4	0	0	1	5	0	.400
1997 San Diego e-f	N.L.		C-1B	50	134	15	42	7	1	3	14	0	.313
1998 San Diego g	N.L.		C-1B	129	390	34	102	15	0	9	52	2	.262
1999 San Diego h	N.L.	INJURED - did not play											
2000 San Diego-St. Louis i-j-k	N.L.		C-1B	75	242	23	62	15	0	3	35	2	.256
Major League Totals			10 Yrs.	488	1244	102	315	51	1	24	141	5	.253
Division Series													
1998 San Diego	N.L.		C	4	12	0	5	0	0	0	0	0	.417
2000 St. Louis	N.L.		C	3	11	3	3	0	0	1	1	0	.273
Division Series Totals				7	23	3	8	0	0	1	1	0	.348
Championship Series													
1998 San Diego	N.L.		C	6	18	2	6	2	0	0	0	0	.333
2000 St. Louis	N.L.		C	5	16	3	4	0	0	1	1	0	.250
Championship Series Totals				11	34	5	10	2	0	0	1	0	.294
World Series Record													
1998 San Diego	N.L.		C	4	10	0	2	0	0	0	0	0	.200

a On disabled list from May 27 to June 20, 1990.
b On disabled list from April 4 to 22, 1994.
c On disabled list from May 17 to June 14, 1996.
d Filed for free agency, October 15, 1996, signed with San Diego Padres organization, December 2, 1996.
e On disabled list from July 13 to August 15, 1997.
f Filed for free agency, October 31, 1997, re-signed with San Diego Padres, November 12, 1997.
g Filed for free agency, October 23, 1998, re-signed with San Diego Padres, December 2, 1998.

h On disabled list from March 29 to October 1, 1999.
i Traded to Seattle Mariners for catcher Carlos Maldonado, March 21, 2000.
j On disabled list from April 7 to April 21 and July 6 to July 27, 2000.
k Traded to St. Louis Cardinals with infielder Nathan Tebbs for pitcher Heathcliff Slocumb and outfielder Ben Johnson, July 31, 2000.

HERNANDEZ, JOSE ANTONIO

Born, Vega Alta, Puerto Rico, July 14, 1969.
Bats Right. Throws Right. Height, 6 feet. Weight, 180 pounds.

Year	Club	Lea	Pos	G	AB	R	H	2B	3B	HR	RBI	SB	Avg
1987 Sarasota Rangers	.Gulf C.		SS	24	52	5	9	1	1	0	2	2	.173
1988 Sarasota Rangers	.Gulf C.		3B-2B-SS-1B	55	162	19	26	7	1	1	13	4	.160
1989 Gastonia	.So. Atl.		3B-SS-2B-OF	91	215	35	47	7	6	1	16	9	.219
1990 Charlotte	.Fla. St.		SS-OF	121	388	43	99	14	7	1	44	11	.255
1991 Oklahoma City	.A.A.		SS	14	46	6	14	1	1	1	3	0	.304
1991 Tulsa	.Texas		SS	91	301	36	72	17	4	1	20	4	.239
1991 Texas a	.A.L.		SS-3B	45	98	8	18	2	1	0	4	0	.184
1992 Canton	.Eastern		SS	130	404	56	103	16	4	3	46	7	.255
1992 Cleveland	.A.L.		SS	3	4	0	0	0	0	0	0	0	.000
1993 Canton b	.Eastern		SS-3B	45	150	19	30	6	0	2	17	9	.200
1993 Orlando	.Southern		SS	71	263	42	80	8	3	8	33	8	.304
1993 Iowa	.A.A.		SS	6	24	3	6	1	0	0	3	0	.250
1994 Chicago	.N.L.		3B-SS-2B-OF	56	132	18	32	2	3	1	9	2	.242
1995 Chicago	.N.L.		SS-2B-3B	93	245	37	60	11	4	13	40	1	.245
1996 Chicago	.N.L.		SS-3B-2B-OF	131	331	52	80	14	1	10	41	4	.242
1997 Chicago	.N.L.		3B-SS-2B-OF	121	183	33	50	8	5	7	26	2	.273
1998 Chicago	.N.L.		3B-OF-SS-1B	149	488	76	124	23	7	23	75	4	.254
1999 Chicago-Atlanta c-d	.N.L.		SS-OF-1B	147	508	79	135	20	2	19	62	11	.266
2000 Indianapolis	.Int.		3B	2	9	2	3	0	0	2	3	0	.333
2000 Milwaukee e	.N.L.		3B-SS-OF	124	446	51	109	22	1	11	59	3	.244
Major League Totals			9 Yrs.	869	2435	354	608	102	24	84	316	27	.250
Division Series													
1998 Chicago	.N.L.		SS	2	7	1	2	0	0	0	0	0	.286
1999 Atlanta	.N.L.		SS	4	11	1	1	0	0	0	0	1	.091
Division Series Totals				6	18	2	3	0	0	0	0	1	.167
Championship Series													
1999 Atlanta	.N.L.		PH	2	2	0	1	0	0	0	2	0	.500
World Series Record													
1999 Atlanta	.N.L.		SS-DH	2	5	0	1	1	0	0	2	1	.200

a Claimed on waivers by Cleveland Indians from Texas Rangers, April 3, 1992.
b Traded by Cleveland Indians to Chicago Cubs organization for pitcher Heathcliff Slocumb, June 1, 1993.
c Traded to Atlanta Braves with pitcher Terry Mulholland for pitcher Micah Bowie, pitcher Ruben Quevedo and player to be named later, July 31, 1999. Chicago Cubs received pitcher Joey Nation to complete trade, August 24, 1999.
d Filed for free agency, November 5, 1999. Signed with Milwaukee Brewers, December 16, 1999.
e On disabled list from August 10 to August 31, 2000.

HERNANDEZ (MARIN), RAMON JOSE

Born, Caracas, Venezuela, May 20, 1976.
Bats Right. Throws Right. Height, 6 feet. Weight, 203 pounds.

Year	Club	Lea	Pos	G	AB	R	H	2B	3B	HR	RBI	SB	Avg
1994 Oakland	.Dominican		C	42	134	24	33	2	0	2	18	1	.246
1995 Athletics	.Arizona		C-1B-3B	48	143	37	52	9	6	4	37	6	.364
1996 W Michigan	.Midwest		C-1B	123	447	62	114	26	2	12	68	2	.255
1997 Visalia	.California		C-1B	86	332	57	120	21	2	15	85	2	.361
1997 Huntsville	.Southern		C-1B-3B	44	161	27	31	3	0	4	24	0	.193
1998 Huntsville	.Southern		DH-C-1B	127	479	83	142	24	1	15	98	4	.296
1999 Vancouver	.P.C.		C	77	291	38	76	11	3	13	55	1	.261
1999 Oakland a	.A.L.		C	40	136	13	38	7	0	3	21	1	.279
2000 Oakland	.A.L.		C	143	419	52	101	19	0	14	62	1	.241
Major League Totals			2 Yrs.	183	555	65	139	26	0	17	83	2	.250
Division Series													
2000 Oakland	.A.L.		C	5	16	3	6	2	0	0	3	0	.375

a On disabled list from July 26 to August 27, 1999.

HIDALGO, RICHARD JOSE

Born, Caracas, Venezuela, July 2, 1975.
Bats Right. Throws Right. Height, 6 feet, 3 inches. Weight, 190 pounds.

Year	Club	Lea	Pos	G	AB	R	H	2B	3B	HR	RBI	SB	Avg
1992 Astros	.........Gulf Coast	OF	51	184	20	57	7	3	1	27	14	.310
1993 Asheville	.........So. Atl.	OF	111	403	49	109	23	3	10	55	21	.270
1994 Quad City	.....Midwest	OF	124	476	68	139	47	6	12	76	12	.292
1995 Jackson	...........Texas	OF	133	489	59	130	28	6	14	59	8	.266
1996 Jackson	...........Texas	OF	130	513	66	151	34	2	14	78	11	.294
1997 New Orleans	.........A.A.	OF	134	526	74	147	37	5	11	78	6	.279
1997 Houston	..........N.L.	OF	19	62	8	19	5	0	2	6	1	.306
1998 New Orleans	.........P.C.	OF	10	24	0	4	2	0	0	1	0	.167
1998 Houston a	...........N.L.	OF	74	211	31	64	15	0	7	35	3	.303
1999 Houston b	...........N.L.	OF	108	383	49	87	25	2	15	56	8	.227
2000 Houston	...........N.L.	OF	153	558	118	175	42	3	44	122	13	.314
Major League Totals	....	4 Yrs.	354	1214	206	345	87	5	68	219	25	.284
Division Series												
1997 Houston	.............N.L.	OF	2	5	1	0	0	0	0	0	0	.000
1998 Houston	.............N.L.	OF	1	4	0	1	0	0	0	0	0	.250
Division Series Totals	....		3	9	1	1	0	0	0	0	0	.111

a On disabled list from May 30 to July 21, 1998.
b On disabled list from August 9 to October 4, 1999.

HIGGINSON, ROBERT LEIGH (BOBBY)

Born, Philadelphia, Pennsylvania, August 18, 1970.
Bats Left. Throws Right. Height, 5 feet, 11 inches. Weight, 180 pounds.

Year	Club	Lea	Pos	G	AB	R	H	2B	3B	HR	RBI	SB	Avg
1992 Niagara Falls	.....N.Y.-Penn.	OF	70	232	35	68	17	4	2	37	12	.293
1993 Lakeland	..........Fla. St.	OF	61	223	42	67	11	7	3	25	8	.300
1993 London	..........Eastern	OF	63	224	25	69	15	4	4	35	3	.308
1994 Toledo	.................Int.	OF	137	476	81	131	28	3	23	67	16	.275
1995 Detroit	.................A.L.	OF	131	410	61	92	17	5	14	43	6	.224
1996 Toledo a	.................Int.	OF	3	13	4	4	0	1	0	1	0	.308
1996 Detroit	.................A.L.	OF	130	440	75	141	35	0	26	81	6	.320
1997 Detroit b	.................A.L.	OF	146	546	94	163	30	5	27	101	12	.299
1998 Detroit	.................A.L.	OF	157	612	92	174	37	4	25	85	3	.284
1999 Detroit c	.................A.L.	OF	107	377	51	90	18	0	12	46	4	.239
2000 Detroit	.................A.L.	OF	154	597	104	179	44	4	30	102	15	.300
Major League Totals	....	6 Yrs.	825	2982	477	839	181	18	134	458	46	.281

a On disabled list from May 11 to June 7, 1996.
b On disabled list from June 11 to June 26, 1997.
c On disabled list from July 24 to August 24, 1999.

HILL, GLEN ALLEN

Born, Santa Cruz, California, March 22, 1965.
Bats Right. Throws Right. Height, 6 feet, 2 inches. Weight, 220 pounds.

Year	Club	Lea	Pos	G	AB	R	H	2B	3B	HR	RBI	SB	Avg
1983 Medicine Hat	......Pioneer	OF	46	133	26	34	3	4	6	27	4	.256
1984 Florence	...........So. Atl.	OF	129	440	75	105	19	5	16	64	30	.239
1985 Kinston	..........Carolina	OF	131	466	57	98	13	0	20	56	42	.210
1986 Knoxville	.........Southern	OF	141	*570	87	158	23	6	*31	97	18	.277
1987 Syracuse	.............Int.	OF	137	536	65	126	25	6	16	77	22	.235
1988 Syracuse	.............Int.	OF	51	172	21	40	7	0	4	19	7	.233
1988 Knoxville	.........Southern	OF	79	269	37	71	13	2	12	38	10	.264
1989 Syracuse	.............Int.	OF	125	483	86	155	31	15	21	72	21	.321
1989 Toronto	.............A.L.	OF	19	52	4	15	0	0	1	7	2	.288
1990 Toronto a	.............A.L.	OF	84	260	47	60	11	3	12	32	8	.231
1991 Tor.-Cleveland b	.......A.L.	OF	72	221	29	57	8	2	8	25	6	.258
1992 Canton	...........Eastern	OF	3	9	1	1	1	0	0	1	0	.111
1992 Cleveland c	.............A.L.	OF	102	369	38	89	16	1	18	49	9	.241
1993 Cleveland d	.........A.L.	OF	66	174	19	39	7	2	5	25	7	.224
1993 Chicago	..............N.L.	OF	31	87	14	30	7	0	10	22	1	.345
1994 Chicago e	.............N.L.	OF	89	269	48	80	12	1	10	38	19	.297
1995 San Francisco f-g	......N.L.	OF	132	497	71	131	29	4	24	86	25	.264
1996 Phoenix h	.............P.C.	OF	5	17	4	6	1	0	2	2	1	.353
1996 San Francisco	.............N.L.	OF	98	379	56	106	26	0	19	67	6	.280
1997 San Francisco i	........N.L.	OF	128	398	47	104	28	4	11	64	7	.261
1998 Seattle j	.............A.L.	OF	74	259	37	75	20	2	12	33	1	.290

Year	Club	Lea	Pos	G	AB	R	H	2B	3B	HR	RBI	SB	Avg
1998 Chicago k-l	..........N.L.		OF	48	131	26	46	5	0	8	23	0	.351
1999 Chicago m	..........N.L.		OF	99	253	43	76	9	1	20	55	5	.300
2000 Chicago n-o	..........N.L.		OF	64	168	23	44	4	1	11	29	0	.262
2000 New York	............A.L.		DH-OF	40	132	22	44	5	0	16	29	0	.333
Major League Totals			12 Yrs.	1146	3649	524	996	187	21	185	584	96	.273
Division Series													
1997 San Francisco .........N.L.			OF	3	7	0	0	0	0	0	0	0	.000
1998 Chicago ..............N.L.			OF	1	3	0	1	0	0	0	0	1	.333
2000 New York ............A.L.			DH	4	12	.1	1	0	0	0	2	0	.083
Division Series Totals				8	22	1	2	0	0	0	2	1	.091
Championship Series													
2000 New York ...........A.L.			PH	2	2	0	0	0	0	0	0	0	.000
World Series Record													
2000 New York ............A.L.			DH	3	3	0	0	0	0	0	0	0	.000

a On disabled list from July 6 to July 21, 1990.
b Traded to Cleveland Indians with outfielder Mark Whiten, pitcher Denis Boucher and player to be named for pitcher Tom Candiotti and outfielder Turner Ward, June 27; trade settled for cash, October 22, 1991.
c On disabled list from April 23 to May 22, 1992.
d Traded to Chicago Cubs for outfielder Candy Maldonado, August 19, 1993.
e Declared restricted free agent under Major League Baseball implemented labor proposal, December 23, 1994.
f Designated for assignment by Chicago Cubs, April 7, 1995.
g Signed with San Francisco Giants, April 9, 1995.
h On disabled list from May 27 to August 5, 1996.
i Filed for free agency, October 29, 1997.
j Signed with Seattle Mariners organization, Janaury 7, 1998.
k Claimed on waivers by Chicago Cubs, July 7, 1998.
l Filed for free agency, October 23, 1998, re-signed with Chicago Cubs, December 7, 1998.
m On disabled list from May 8 to May 23, 1999.
n On disabled list from March 20 to April 6, 2000.
o Traded to New York Yankees for pitcher Ben Ford and pitcher Ozwaldo Mairena, July 21, 2000.

HOCKING, DENNIS LEE

Born, Torrance, California, April 2, 1970.
Bats Both. Throws Right. Height, 5 feet, 10 inches. Weight, 180 pounds.

Year	Club	Lea	Pos	G	AB	R	H	2B	3B	HR	RBI	SB	Avg
1990 Elizabethton	....Appal.		SS-2B-3B	54	201	45	59	6	2	6	30	14	.294
1991 Kenosha	......Midwest		SS	125	432	72	110	17	8	2	36	22	.255
1992 Visalia	......California		SS	135	550	117	*182	34	9	7	81	38	.331
1993 Nashville	.....Southern		SS	107	409	54	109	9	4	8	50	15	.267
1993 Minnesota	.......A.L.		SS-2B	15	36	7	5	1	0	0	0	1	.139
1994 Salt Lake City	......P.C.		SS	112	394	61	110	14	6	5	57	13	.279
1994 Minnesota	.......A.L.		SS	11	31	3	10	3	0	0	2	2	.323
1995 Salt Lake	........P.C.		SS-2B	117	397	51	112	24	2	8	75	12	.282
1995 Minnesota	.......A.L.		SS	9	25	4	5	0	2	0	3	1	.200
1996 Salt Lake a	........P.C.		SS-OF-1B	37	130	18	36	6	2	3	22	2	.277
1996 Minnesota	.......A.L.		OF-SS-2B-1B	49	127	16	25	6	0	1	10	3	.197
1997 Minnesota	.......A.L.		SS-3B-OF-2B	115	253	28	65	12	4	2	25	3	.257
1998 Minnesota	.......A.L.		2B-SS-OF-3B	110	198	32	40	6	1	3	15	2	.202
1999 Minnesota	.......A.L.		SS-2B-OF-3B	136	386	47	103	18	2	7	41	11	.267
2000 Minnesota	.......A.L.		OF-2B-3B-SS	134	373	52	111	24	4	4	47	7	.298
Major League Totals			8 Yrs.	579	1429	189	364	70	13	17	143	30	.255

a On disabled list from April 1 to April 30 and May 30 to June 29 and July 31 to September 8, 1996.

HOLLANDSWORTH, TODD MATTHEW

Born, Dayton, Ohio, April 20, 1973.
Bats Left. Throws Left. Height, 6 feet, 2 inches. Weight, 195 pounds.

Year	Club	Lea	Pos	G	AB	R	H	2B	3B	HR	RBI	SB	Avg
1991 Dodgers	........Gulf Coast		OF	6	16	1	5	0	0	0	0	0	.313
1991 Yakima	.........Northwest		OF	56	203	34	48	5	1	8	33	11	.236
1992 Bakersfield	......California		OF	119	430	70	111	23	5	13	58	27	.258
1993 San Antonio	.........Texas		OF	126	474	57	119	24	9	17	63	24	.251
1994 Albuquerque	.........P.C.		OF	132	505	80	144	31	5	19	91	15	.285
1995 San Bernardino	...California		OF	1	2	0	1	0	0	0	0	0	.500
1995 Albuquerque	.........P.C.		OF	10	38	9	9	2	0	2	4	1	.237
1995 Los Angeles a	.........N.L.		OF	41	103	16	24	2	0	5	13	2	.233

Year	Club	Lea	Pos	G	AB	R	H	2B	3B	HR	RBI	SB	Avg
1996 Los Angeles b	N.L.	OF	149	478	64	139	26	4	12	59	21	.291
1997 Albuquerque	P.C.	OF	13	56	13	24	4	3	1	14	2	.429
1997 San Berndno	California	OF	2	8	1	2	0	1	0	2	0	.250
1997 Los Angeles c	N.L.	OF	106	296	39	73	20	2	4	31	5	.247
1998 Los Angeles d	N.L.	OF	55	175	23	47	6	4	3	20	4	.269
1999 San Bernardino	California	OF	4	13	3	5	2	0	0	3	0	.385
1999 Los Angeles e		OF-1B	92	261	39	74	12	2	9	32	5	.284
2000 Los Angeles-Colorado f-g	N.L.	OF	137	428	81	115	20	0	19	47	18	.269
Major League Totals	6 Yrs.		580	1741	262	472	86	12	52	202	55	.271
Division Series												
1995 Los Angeles	N.L.	OF	2	2	0	0	0	0	0	0	0	.000
1996 Los Angeles	N.L.	OF	3	12	1	4	3	0	0	1	0	.333
Division Series Totals			5	14	1	4	3	0	0	1	0	.286

a On disabled list from May 3 to July 7 and August 9 to September 12, 1995.
b Selected Rookie of the Year in National League for 1996.
c On disabled list from August 1 to August 16 and August 17 to September 6, 1997.
d On disabled list from June 5 to September 28, 1998.
e On disabled list from April 3 to April 23 and May 28 to June 19, 1999.
f Traded to Colorado Rockies with outfielder Kevin Gibbs and pitcher Randey Dorame for outfielder Tom Goodwin, July 31, 2000.
g Filed for free agency, October 27, 2000, signed with Colorado Rockies, November 16, 2000.

HOUSTON, TYLER SAM

Born, Las Vegas, Nevada, January 17, 1971.
Bats Left. Throws Right. Height, 6 feet, 2 inches. Weight, 212 pounds.

Year	Club	Lea	Pos	G	AB	R	H	2B	3B	HR	RBI	SB	Avg
1989 Idaho Falls	Pioneer	DH-C	50	176	30	43	11	0	4	24	4	.244
1990 Sumter	So.Atl.	C	117	442	58	93	14	3	13	56	6	.210
1991 Macon	So.Atl.	C	107	351	41	81	16	3	8	47	10	.231
1992 Durham	Carolina	C-3B-1B	117	402	39	91	17	1	7	38	5	.226
1993 Greenville	Southern	C-OF	84	262	27	73	14	1	5	33	5	.279
1993 Richmond	Int.	C	13	36	4	5	1	1	1	3	0	.139
1994 Richmond	Int.	1B-C-OF	97	312	33	76	15	2	4	33	3	.244
1995 Richmond	Int.	C-1B-OF-3B	103	349	41	89	10	3	12	42	3	.255
1996 Atlanta-Chicago a	N.L.	C-1B-3B-2B	79	142	21	45	9	1	3	27	3	.317
1997 Iowa	A.A.	3B-C	6	23	0	5	2	0	0	4	0	.217
1997 Rockford	Midwest	3B-C	2	6	1	3	1	0	0	1	0	.500
1997 Chicago b	N.L.	C-3B-1B-2B	72	196	15	51	10	0	2	28	1	.260
1998 Chicago c	N.L.	C-3B-1B	95	255	26	65	7	1	9	33	2	.255
1999 Chicago d	N.L.	3B-C-1B-OF	100	249	26	58	9	1	9	27	1	.233
1999 Cleveland e	A.L.	3B-C	13	27	2	4	1	0	1	3	0	.148
2000 Milwaukee f	N.L.	1B-3B-C	101	284	30	71	15	0	18	43	2	.250
Major League Totals	5 Yrs.		460	1153	120	294	51	3	42	161	9	.255
Division Series												
1998 Chicago	N.L.	C	3	6	1	1	0	0	1	1	0	.167

a Traded to Chicago Cubs for pitcher Ishmael Villegas, June 26, 1996.
b On disabled list from May 3 to May 19 and June 11 to July 11, 1997.
c On disabled list from May 26 to June 24, 1998.
d Traded to Cleveland Indians for pitcher Richard Negrette, August 31, 1999.
e Not offered contract, December 21, 1999. Signed with Milwaukee Brewers, January 17, 2000.
f On disabled list from May 15 to June 1, 2000.

HOWARD, THOMAS SYLVESTER

Born, Middletown, Ohio, December 11, 1964.
Bats Both. Throws Right. Height, 6 feet, 2 inches. Weight, 205 pounds.

Year	Club	Lea	Pos	G	AB	R	H	2B	3B	HR	RBI	SB	Avg
1986 Spokane	Northwest	OF	13	55	16	23	3	3	2	17	2	.418
1986 Reno	California	OF	61	223	35	57	7	3	10	39	10	.256
1987 Wichita	Texas	OF	113	401	72	133	27	4	14	60	26	.332
1988 Las Vegas	P.C.	OF	44	167	29	42	9	1	0	15	3	.251
1988 Wichita	Texas	OF	29	103	15	31	9	2	0	16	6	.301
1989 Las Vegas	P.C.	OF	80	303	45	91	18	3	3	31	22	.300
1990 San Diego	N.L.	OF	20	44	4	12	2	0	0	0	0	.273
1990 Las Vegas	P.C.	OF	89	341	58	112	26	8	5	51	27	.328
1991 Las Vegas	P.C.	OF	25	94	22	29	3	1	2	16	11	.309
1991 San Diego	N.L.	OF	106	281	30	70	12	3	4	22	10	.249
1992 San Diego	N.L.	OF	5	3	1	1	0	0	0	0	0	.333

Year	Club	Lea	Pos	G	AB	R	H	2B	3B	HR	RBI	SB	Avg
1992 Cleveland a-b .........A.L.			OF	117	358	36	99	15	2	2	32	15	.277
1993 Cleveland ............A.L.			OF	74	178	26	42	7	0	3	23	5	.236
1993 Cincinnati c ....•.......N.L.			OF	38	141	22	39	8	3	4	13	5	.277
1994 Cincinnati ............N.L.			OF	83	178	24	47	11	0	5	24	4	.264
1995 Cincinnati ............N.L.			OF	113	281	42	85	15	2	3	26	17	.302
1996 Chattanooga ......Southern			OF	8	30	4	10	1	0	1	2	1	.333
1996 Indianapolis ...........A.A.			OF	1	5	2	2	0	0	1	2	0	.400
1996 Cincinnati d ...........N.L.			OF	121	360	50	98	19	10	6	42	6	.272
1997 Houston ............N.L.			OF	107	255	24	63	16	1	3	22	1	.247
1998 Los Angeles e-f ......N.L.			OF	47	76	9	14	4	0	2	4	1	.184
1999 St. Louis g ..........N.L.			OF	98	195	16	57	10	0	6	28	1	.292
2000 Memphis .............P.C.			OF	17	34	7	9	2	0	0	5	0	.265
2000 St. Louis h ...........N.L.			OF-1B	86	133	13	28	4	1	6	28	1	.211
Major League Totals		11 Yrs.	1015	2483	297	655	123	22	44	264	66	.264	
Division Series													
1995 Cincinnati ............N.L.			OF	3	10	0	1	1	0	0	0	0	.100
1997 Houston ............N.L.			PH	2	1	0	0	0	0	0	0	0	.000
Division Series Totals				5	11	0	1	1	0	0	0	0	.091
Championship Series													
1995 Cincinnati ............N.L.			OF	4	8	0	2	1	0	0	1	0	.250

a Traded to Cleveland Indians for infielder Jason Hardtke and player to be named later, April 14, 1992.
b San Diego Padres received catcher Christopher Maffett to complete trade, July 10, 1992.
c Sent to Cincinnati Reds to complete trade for infielder Randy Milligan, August 20, 1993.
d Released by Cincinnati Reds, November 18, 1996, signed by Houston Astros, December 4, 1996.
e Filed for free agency, October 28, 1997, signed with Los Angeles Dodgers organization, January 16, 1998.
f Released by Los Angeles Dodgers, June 29, 1998, signed with St. Louis Cardinals organization, December 31, 1998.
g Filed for free agency, November 4, 1999. Re-signed with St. Louis Cardinals, December 21, 1999.
h Filed for free agency, November 2, 2000, signed with Pittsburgh Pirates organization, January 9, 2001.

HUBBARD, TRENIDAD AVIEL
Born, Chicago, Illinois, May 11, 1964.
Bats Right. Throws Right. Height, 5 feet, 8 inches. Weight, 180 pounds.

Year	Club	Lea	Pos	G	AB	R	H	2B	3B	HR	RBI	SB	Avg
1986 Auburn .....N.Y.-Penn.			2B-OF	70	242	42	75	12	1	1	32	35	.310
1987 Asheville ....So.Atl.			2B-OF-C	101	284	39	67	8	1	1	35	28	.236
1988 Osceola ....Fla.St.			2B-C-OF	130	446	68	116	15	11	3	65	44	.260
1989 Tucson ...........P.C.			OF-3B-C	21	50	3	11	2	0	0	2	3	.220
1989 Columbus ...Southern			2B-C-OF-3B	104	348	55	92	7	8	3	37	28	.264
1990 Tucson ..........P.C.			2B-3B-C	12	27	5	6	2	2	0	2	1	.222
1990 Columbus ...Southern			2B-OF-C-3B	95	335	39	84	14	4	4	35	17	.251
1991 Jackson ....Texas			2B-OF-1B-P	126	455	78	135	21	3	2	41	39	.297
1991 Tucson ..........P.C.			2B	2	4	0	0	0	0	0	0	0	.000
1992 Tucson a .........P.C.			2B-3B	115	420	69	130	16	4	2	33	34	.310
1993 Colo. Sprngs b .....P.C.			OF-2B-3B	117	439	83	138	24	8	7	56	33	.314
1994 Colo. Sprngs ......P.C.			OF	79	320	78	116	22	5	8	38	28	.363
1994 Colorado. c .......N.L.			OF	18	25	3	7	1	1	1	3	0	.280
1995 Colo. Sprngs .......P.C.			OF	123	480	102	163	29	7	12	66	37	.340
1995 Colorado ........N.L.			OF	24	58	13	18	4	0	3	9	2	.310
1996 Colo Sprngs .......P.C.			OF-2B-3B-C	50	188	41	59	15	5	6	16	6	.314
1996 Colorado-San Francisco													
d-e-f ................N.L.			OF	55	89	15	19	5	2	2	14	2	.213
1997 Cleveland ........A.L.			OF	7	12	3	3	1	0	0	0	2	.250
1997 Buffalo g-h ......A.A.			OF-3B	103	375	71	117	22	1	16	60	26	.312
1998 Albuquerque ......P.C.			OF	11	30	6	9	0	0	3	5	2	.300
1998 Los Angeles i .....N.L.			OF-3B	94	208	29	62	9	1	7	18	9	.298
1999 Albuquerque ......P.C.			OF	32	123	24	41	8	2	5	24	16	.333
1999 Los Angeles j ......N.L.			OF-C-2B	82	105	23	33	5	0	1	13	4	.314
2000 Atlanta ...........N.L.			OF	61	81	15	15	2	1	1	6	2	.185
2000 Baltimore k-l ......A.L.			OF	31	27	3	5	0	1	0	0	2	.185
Major League Totals		7 Yrs.	372	605	104	162	27	6	15	63	23	.268	
Division Series													
1995 Colorado ..........N.L.			PH	3	2	0	0	0	0	0	0	0	.000

a Filed for free agency, October 15, 1992, signed with Colorado Rockies organization, October 30, 1992.
b On disabled list from June 15 to June 14, 1993.
c Filed for free agency, October 15, 1993, re-signed with Colorado Rockies organization, November 14, 1994.
d Claimed on waivers by San Francisco Giants, August 21, 1996.
e On disabled list from September 13 to September 30, 1996.
f Traded to Cleveland Indians for pitcher Joe Roa as players to be named later in Matt Williams deal, December 16, 1996.
g Outrighted by Cleveland Indians, July 17, 1997.

h Filed for free agency, October 8, 1997, signed with Los Angeles Dodgers, December 3, 1997.
i On disabled list from May 15 to June 22, 1998.
j Filed for free agency, January 18, 2000, signed with Atlanta Braves organization, January 20, 2000.
k Traded to Baltimore Orioles with catcher Fernando Lunar and pitcher Luis Rivera for pitcher B.J. Surhoff and catcher Gabe Molina, July 31, 2000.
l Released by Baltimore Orioles, October 5, 2000.

HUFF, AUBREY L.
Born, Marion, Ohio, December 20, 1976.
Bats Left. Throws Right. Height, 6 feet, 4 inches. Weight, 220 pounds.

Year	Club	Lea	Pos	G	AB	R	H	2B	3B	HR	RBI	SB	Avg
1998 Chston-Sc	So.Atl.		3B	69	265	38	85	19	1	13	54	3	.321
1999 Orlando	Southern		3B	133	491	85	148	40	3	22	78	2	.301
2000 Durham	Int.		3B	108	408	73	129	36	3	20	76	2	.316
2000 Tampa Bay	A.L.		3B	39	122	12	35	7	0	4	14	0	.287

HUNDLEY, TODD RANDOLPH
Born, Martinsville, Virginia, May 27, 1969.
Bats Both. Throws Right. Height, 5 feet, 11 inches. Weight, 185 pounds.

Year	Club	Lea	Pos	G	AB	R	H	2B	3B	HR	RBI	SB	Avg
1987 Little Falls	N.Y.-Penn.		C	34	103	12	15	4	0	1	10	0	.146
1988 Little Falls	N.Y.-Penn.		C	52	176	23	33	8	0	2	18	1	.188
1988 St. Lucie	Fla. St.		C	1	1	0	0	0	0	0	0	0	.000
1989 Columbia	So. Atl.		C-OF	125	439	67	118	23	4	11	66	6	.269
1990 Jackson	Texas		C-3B	81	279	27	74	12	2	1	35	5	.265
1990 New York	N.L.		C	36	67	8	14	6	0	0	2	0	.209
1991 Tidewater a	Int.		C	125	454	62	124	24	4	14	66	1	.273
1991 New York	N.L.		C	21	60	5	8	0	1	1	7	0	.133
1992 New York	N.L.		C	123	358	32	75	17	0	7	32	3	.209
1993 New York	N.L.		C	130	417	40	95	17	2	11	53	1	.228
1994 New York	N.L.		C	91	291	45	69	10	1	16	42	2	.237
1995 New York b-c	N.L.		C	90	275	39	77	11	0	15	51	1	.280
1996 New York	N.L.		C	153	540	85	140	32	1	41	112	1	.259
1997 New York	N.L.		C	132	417	78	114	21	2	30	86	2	.273
1998 Mets	Gulf Coast		OF	1	2	0	0	0	0	0	0	0	.000
1998 St. Lucie	Fla.St.		OF	12	42	4	9	2	0	1	6	0	.214
1998 Norfolk	Int.		OF-C	10	30	9	13	1	0	4	15	0	.433
1998 New York d-e	N.L.		OF-C	53	124	8	20	4	0	3	12	1	.161
1999 Los Angeles	N.L.		C	114	376	49	78	14	0	24	55	3	.207
2000 Albuquerque	P.C.		PH	3	9	2	5	0	0	1	5	0	.556
2000 Los Angeles f-g	N.L.		C	90	299	49	85	16	0	24	70	0	.284
Major League Totals			11 Yrs.	1033	3224	438	775	148	7	172	522	14	.240

a On disabled list from June 29 to July 6, 1991.
b Signed with New York Mets, April 28, 1995.
c On disabled list from July 23 to October 2, 1995.
d On disabled list from March 31 to July 11 and August 28 to September 12, 1998.
e Traded to Los Angeles Dodgers with pitcher Arnie Gooch for catcher Charles Johnson and outfielder Roger Cedeno, December 1, 1998.
f On disabled list from May 31 to June 25 and July 17 to July 26, 2000.
g Filed for free agency, October 27, 2000, signed with Chicago Cubs, December 13, 2000.

HUNTER, BRIAN LEE
Born, Portland, Oregon, March 5, 1971.
Bats Right. Throws Right. Height, 6 feet, 4 inches. Weight, 180 pounds.

Year	Club	Lea	Pos	G	AB	R	H	2B	3B	HR	RBI	SB	Avg
1989 Kissimmee Astros	Gulf C.		OF	51	206	15	35	2	0	0	13	12	.170
1990 Asheville	So. Atl.		OF	127	444	84	111	14	6	0	16	45	.250
1991 Osceola	Fla. St.		OF	118	392	51	94	15	3	1	30	32	.240
1992 Osceola	Fla. St.		OF	131	489	62	146	18	9	1	62	39	.299
1993 Jackson	Texas		OF	133	523	84	154	22	5	10	52	*35	.294
1994 Tucson	P.C.		OF	128	513	*113	*191	28	9	10	51	*49	*.372
1994 Houston	N.L.		OF	6	24	2	6	1	0	0	0	2	.250
1995 Tucson	P.C.		OF	38	155	28	51	5	1	1	16	11	.329
1995 Jackson	Texas		OF	2	6	1	3	0	0	0	0	0	.500
1995 Houston	N.L.		OF	78	321	52	97	14	5	2	28	24	.302
1996 Tucson a	P.C.		OF	3	14	3	5	0	1	0	1	3	.357
1996 Houston b	N.L.		OF	132	526	74	145	27	2	5	35	35	.276

Year Club	Lea	Pos	G	AB	R	H	2B	3B	HR	RBI	SB	Avg
1997 Detroit	A.L.	OF	162	658	112	177	29	7	4	45	*74	.269
1998 Detroit	A.L.	OF	142	595	67	151	29	3	4	36	42	.254
1999 Detroit-Seattle c-d	A.L.	OF	139	539	79	125	13	6	4	34	*44	.232
2000 Colorado-Cincinnati e-f-g	N.L.	OF	104	240	47	64	5	1	1	14	20	.267
Major League Totals		7 Yrs.	763	2903	433	765	118	24	20	192	241	.264

a On disabled list from June 29 to July 27, 1996.
b Traded to Detroit Tigers with infielder Orlando Miller, pitcher Todd Jones and pitcher Doug Brocail for catcher Brad Ausmus, pitcher C.J. Nitkowski, pitcher Jose Lima, pitcher Trever Miller and infielder Daryle Ward, December 10, 1996.
c Traded to Seattle Mariners for player to be named later and player to be named later, April 28, 1999. Detroit Tigers received pitcher Andrew VanHekken to complete trade, June 27, 1999.
d On disabled list from July 12 to July 27, 1999.
e Released by Seattle Mariners, March 27, 2000, signed with Colorado Rockies, March 30, 2000.
f Traded to Cincinnati Reds for pitcher Robert Averette, August 6, 2000.
g Released by Cincinnati Reds, November 22, 2000, signed with Philadelphia Phillies, January 10, 2001.

HUNTER, BRIAN RONALD
Born, Torrance, California, March 4, 1968.
Bats Right. Throws Right. Height, 6 feet. Weight, 195 pounds.

Year Club	Lea	Pos	G	AB	R	H	2B	3B	HR	RBI	SB	Avg
1987 Pulaski	Appal.	1B-OF	65	251	38	58	10	2	8	30	3	.231
1988 Burlington	Midwest	1B-OF	117	417	58	108	17	0	22	71	7	.259
1988 Durham	Carolina	OF-1B	13	49	13	17	3	0	3	9	2	.347
1989 Greenville	Southern	OF-1B	124	451	57	114	19	2	19	82	5	.253
1990 Richmond	Int.	OF-1B	43	137	13	27	4	0	5	16	2	.197
1990 Greenville	Southern	OF-1B	88	320	45	77	13	1	14	55	3	.241
1991 Richmond	Int.	OF	48	181	28	47	7	0	10	30	3	.260
1991 Atlanta	N.L.	1B-OF	97	271	32	68	16	1	12	50	0	.251
1992 Atlanta	N.L.	1B-OF	102	238	34	57	13	2	14	41	1	.239
1993 Richmond	Int.	1B-OF	30	99	16	24	7	0	6	26	4	.242
1993 Atlanta a	N.L.	1B-OF	37	80	4	11	3	1	0	8	0	.138
1994 Pittsburgh-Cincinnati b-c-d	N.L.	1B-OF	85	256	34	60	16	1	15	57	0	.234
1995 Indianapolis	A.A.	OF-1B	9	36	7	13	5	0	4	11	0	.361
1995 Cincinnati e	N.L.	1B-OF	40	79	9	17	6	0	1	9	2	.215
1996 Tacoma	P.C.	OF-1B	25	92	19	32	6	1	7	24	1	.348
1996 Seattle f	A.L.	1B-OF	75	198	21	53	10	0	7	28	0	.268
1997 Indianapolis g-h	A.A.	1B-OF	139	506	74	142	36	4	21	85	9	.281
1998 St. Louis	N.L.	OF-1B	62	112	11	23	9	1	4	13	1	.205
1998 Calgary	P.C.	OF-1B	11	31	1	3	1	0	0	6	0	.097
1999 Atlanta i	N.L.	1B-OF	114	181	28	45	12	1	6	30	0	.249
2000 Richmond	Int.	1B	2	8	2	1	0	0	1	1	1	.125
2000 Atlanta-Philadelphia j-k	N.L.	1B-OF	87	140	14	30	5	0	8	23	0	.214
Major League Totals		9 Yrs.	699	1555	187	364	90	7	67	259	4	.234
Division Series												
1999 Atlanta	N.L.	1B	3	4	0	0	0	0	0	0	0	.000
Championship Series												
1991 Atlanta	N.L.	1B	5	18	2	6	2	0	1	4	0	.333
1992 Atlanta	N.L.	1B	3	5	1	1	0	0	0	0	0	.200
1999 Atlanta	N.L.	1B	6	10	1	1	0	0	0	2	1	.100
Championship Series Totals			14	33	4	8	2	0	1	6	1	.242
World Series Record												
1991 Atlanta	N.L.	1B-OF	7	21	2	4	1	0	1	3	0	.190
1992 Atlanta	N.L.	1B	4	5	0	1	0	0	0	2	0	.200
1999 Atlanta	N.L.	1B	2	4	0	1	0	0	0	0	0	.250
World Series Totals			13	30	2	6	1	0	1	5	0	.200

a Traded to Pittsburgh Pirates for player to named later, November 17, 1993.
b Atlanta Braves received infielder Jose Delgado to complete trade, June 6, 1994.
c Traded to Cincinnati Reds for player to be named later, July 27, 1994.
d Pittsburgh Pirates received outfielder Micah Franklin to complete trade, October 13, 1994.
e On disabled list from June 19 to July 24 and August 14 to September 1, 1995.
f Released March 8, 1996, signed with Seattle Mariners, May 4, 1996.
g Filed for free agency, October 8, 1995, signed with Cincinnati Reds organization, January 14, 1997.
h Filed for free agency, signed with St. Louis Cardinals organization, November 19, 1997.
i Filed for free agency, November 9, 1999, re-signed with Atlanta Braves organization, December 7, 1999.
j Claimed on waivers by Philadelphia Phillies, April 21, 2000.
k Filed for free agency, October 31, 2000, signed with Philadelphia Phillies organization, November 30, 2000.

HUNTER, TORII KEDAR

Born, Pine Bluff, Arkansas, July 18, 1975.
Bats Right. Throws Right. Height, 6 feet, 2 inches. Weight, 205 pounds.

Year	Club	Lea	Pos	G	AB	R	H	2B	3B	HR	RBI	SB	Avg
1993 Twins	Gulf Coast	OF	28	100	6	19	3	0	0	8	4	.190
1994 Fort Wayne	Midwest	OF	91	335	57	98	17	1	10	50	8	.293
1995 Fort Myers	Fla.St.	OF	113	391	64	96	15	2	7	36	7	.246
1996 Ft. Myers	Fla.St.	OF	4	16	1	3	0	0	0	1	1	.188
1996 New Britain	Eastern	OF	99	342	49	90	20	3	7	33	7	.263
1997 New Britain	Eastern	OF	127	471	57	109	22	2	8	56	8	.231
1997 Minnesota	A.L.	OF	1	0	0	0	0	0	0	0	0	.000
1998 New Britain	Eastern	OF	82	308	42	87	24	3	6	32	11	.282
1998 Salt Lake	P.C.	OF	26	92	15	31	7	0	4	20	2	.337
1998 Minnesota	A.L.	OF	6	17	0	4	1	0	0	2	0	.235
1999 Minnesota	A.L.	OF	135	384	52	98	17	2	9	35	10	.255
2000 Salt Lake	P.C.	OF	55	209	58	77	17	2	18	61	11	.368
2000 Minnesota	A.L.	OF	99	336	44	94	14	7	5	44	4	.280
Major League Totals		4 Yrs.	241	737	96	196	32	9	14	81	14	.266

HUSKEY, ROBERT LEON (BUTCH)

Born, Anadarko, Oklahoma, November 10, 1971.
Bats Right. Throws Right. Height, 6 feet, 3 inches. Weight, 244 pounds.

Year	Club	Lea	Pos	G	AB	R	H	2B	3B	HR	RBI	SB	Avg
1989 Mets	Gulf Coast	3B-1B	54	190	27	50	14	2	6	34	4	.263
1990 Kingsport	Appal.	3B	72	279	39	75	13	0	14	53	7	.269
1991 Columbia	So. Atl.	3B	134	492	88	141	27	5	26	99	22	.287
1992 St. Lucie	Fla. St.	3B	134	493	65	125	17	1	18	75	7	.254
1993 Binghamton	Eastern	3B-SS	139	526	72	132	23	1	25	98	11	.251
1993 New York	N.L.	3B	13	41	2	6	1	0	0	3	0	.146
1994 Norfolk	Int.	3B	127	474	59	108	23	3	10	57	16	.228
1995 Norfolk	Int.	3B-OF-1B	109	394	66	112	18	1	28	87	8	.284
1995 New York	N.L.	3B-OF	28	90	8	17	1	0	3	11	0	.189
1996 New York a	N.L.	1B-OF-3B	118	414	43	115	16	2	15	60	1	.278
1997 New York	N.L.	OF-1B-3B	142	471	61	135	26	2	24	81	8	.287
1998 Norfolk	Int.	DH	2	8	0	2	0	0	0	3	0	.250
1998 New York b-c	N.L.	OF	113	369	43	93	18	0	13	59	7	.252
1999 Seattle-Boston d-e	A.L.	OF-1B-3B	119	386	62	109	15	0	22	77	3	.282
2000 Salt Lake	P.C.	3B	2	9	2	3	0	0	2	5	0	.333
2000 Minnesota	A.L.	DH-OF-1B	64	215	22	48	13	0	5	27	0	.223
2000 Colorado f-g	N.L.	OF-1B	45	92	18	32	8	0	4	18	1	.348
Major League Totals		7 Yrs.	642	2078	259	555	98	4	86	336	21	.267
Division Series													
1999 Boston	A.L.	DH	2	5	0	1	0	0	0	0	0	.200
Championship Series													
1999 Boston	A.L.	DH	4	5	1	1	1	0	0	0	0	.200

a On disabled list from August 6 to September 1, 1996.
b On disabled list from August 3 to September 1, 1998.
c Traded to Florida Marlins for infielder Edgar Renteria, December 14, 1998.
d Traded to Boston Red Sox for pitcher Robert Ramsey, July 26, 1999.
e Not offered contract, December 21, 1999. Signed with Minnesota Twins organization, January 31, 2000.
f Traded to Colorado Rockies with infielder Todd Walker for infielder Todd Sears and cash, July 16, 2000.
g Not offered 2001 contract, December 21, 2000.

HUSON, JEFFREY KENT (JEFF)

Born, Scottsdale, Arizona, August 15, 1964.
Bats Left. Throws Right. Height, 6 feet, 3 inches. Weight, 180 pounds.

Year	Club	Lea	Pos	G	AB	R	H	2B	3B	HR	RBI	SB	Avg
1986 Burlington	Midwest	SS-3B-2B	133	457	85	132	19	1	16	72	32	.289
1986 Jacksnville	Southern	3B	1	4	0	0	0	0	0	0	0	.000
1987 Wst Plm Bch	Fla.St.	SS-2B-OF	131	455	54	130	15	4	1	53	33	.286
1988 Jacksnville	Southern	SS-2B-OF-3B	128	471	72	117	18	1	0	34	56	.248
1988 Montreal	N.L.	SS-2B-3B-OF	20	42	7	13	2	0	0	3	2	.310
1989 Indianapols	A.A.	SS-OF-2B	102	378	70	115	17	4	3	35	30	.304
1989 Montreal	N.L.	SS-3B-2B	32	74	1	12	5	0	0	2	3	.162
1990 Texas a	A.L.	SS-3B-2B	145	396	57	95	12	2	0	28	12	.240
1991 Okla City	A.A.	SS	2	6	0	3	1	0	0	0	0	.500
1991 Texas	A.L.	SS-2B-3B	119	268	36	57	8	3	2	26	8	.213
1992 Texas	A.L.	SS-2B-OF	123	318	49	83	14	3	4	24	18	.261
1993 Okla City	A.A.	3B-2B-SS-OF	24	76	11	22	5	0	1	10	1	.289

Year	Club	Lea	Pos	G	AB	R	H	2B	3B	HR	RBI	SB	Avg
1993 Texas	A.L.	SS-2B-3B	23	45	3	6	1	1	0	2	0	.133
1994 Okla City b ...	A.A.	2B-3B-OF	83	302	47	91	20	2	1	27	18	.301
1995 Rochester	.Int.	SS-2B	60	223	28	56	9	0	3	21	16	.251
1995 Baltimore	.A.L.	3B-2B-SS	66	161	24	40	4	2	1	19	5	.248
1996 Frederick	Carolina	OF	4	16	4	7	2	0	1	1	0	.438
1996 Bowie	Eastern	OF-3B	3	13	3	5	2	0	0	0	0	.385
1996 Rochester	.Int.	OF	2	8	0	2	0	0	0	1	0	.250
1996 Baltimore c ...	.A.L.	2B-3B-OF	17	28	5	9	1	0	0	2	0	.321
1996 Colo Sprngs	P.C.	2B-SS	14	61	10	18	4	0	0	8	6	.295
1997 Colo Sprngs d ...	.P.C.	3B-2B	9	20	3	7	3	0	1	5	0	.350
1997 Milwaukee e-f ...	.A.L.	2B-1B-OF-3B	84	143	12	29	3	0	0	11	3	.203
1998 Seattle g	.A.L.	2B-3B-1B-SS	31	49	8	8	1	0	1	4	1	.163
1998 Tucson h	.P.C.	SS-2B-3B-OF	27	82	7	25	4	1	1	12	0	.305
1999 Anaheim i	.A.L.	2B-SS-3B	97	225	21	59	7	1	0	18	10	.262
2000 Chicago k	.N.L.	3B-2B-SS-1B	70	130	19	28	7	1	0	11	2	.215
Major League Totals		12 Yrs.	827	1879	242	439	65	13	8	150	64	.234

a Traded to Texas Rangers for pitcher Drew Hall, April 2, 1990.
b Released by Texas Rangers, November 30, 1994, signed with Baltimore Orioles, December 31, 1994.
c Released by Baltimore Orioles, August 13, 1996, signed with Colorado Rockies organization, August 19,1996.
d Traded to Milwaukee Brewers for player to be named later, April 23, 1997.
e Filed for free agency, October 28, 1997, signed with Colorado Rockies organization, December 13, 1997.
f Selected by Seattle Mariners in Rule V draft, December 15, 1997.
g Released by Seattle Mariners, July 8, 1998, signed with Arizona Dimaondbacks organization, August 7, 1998.
h Filed for free agency, October 16, 1998, signed with Anaheim Angels organization, November 4, 1998.
i Filed for free agency, November 1, 1999. Signed with Chicago Cubs organization, January 14, 2000.
k Filed for free agency, October 31, 2000.

IBANEZ, RAUL JAVIER

Born, New York, New York, June 2, 1972.
Bats Left. Throws Right. Height, 6 feet, 2 inches. Weight, 210 pounds.

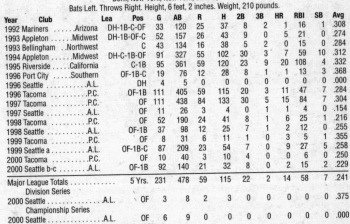

Year	Club	Lea	Pos	G	AB	R	H	2B	3B	HR	RBI	SB	Avg
1992 Mariners	Arizona	DH-1B-OF	33	120	25	37	8	2	1	16	1	.308
1993 Appleton	Midwest	DH-1B-OF-C	52	157	26	43	9	0	5	21	0	.274
1993 Bellingham ..Northwest		C	43	134	16	38	5	2	0	15	0	.284
1994 Appleton	Midwest	DH-C-1B-OF	91	327	55	102	30	3	7	59	10	.312
1995 Riverside	California	C-1B	95	361	59	120	23	9	20	108	4	.332
1996 Port City	Southern	OF-1B-C	19	76	12	28	8	1	1	13	3	.368
1996 Seattle	.A.L.	DH	4	5	0	0	0	0	0	0	0	.000
1996 Tacoma	.P.C.	OF-1B	111	405	59	115	20	3	11	47	7	.284
1997 Tacoma	.P.C.	OF	111	438	84	133	30	5	15	84	7	.304
1997 Seattle	.A.L.	OF	11	26	3	4	0	1	1	4	0	.154
1998 Tacoma	.P.C.	OF	52	190	24	41	8	1	6	25	1	.216
1998 Seattle	.A.L.	OF-1B	37	98	12	25	7	1	2	12	0	.255
1999 Tacoma	.P.C.	OF	8	31	6	11	1	0	3	5	1	.355
1999 Seattle a	.A.L.	OF-1B-C	87	209	23	54	7	0	9	27	5	.258
2000 Tacoma	.P.C.	OF	10	40	3	10	4	0	0	6	0	.250
2000 Seattle b-c	.A.L.	OF-1B	92	140	21	32	8	0	2	15	2	.229
Major League Totals		5 Yrs.	231	478	59	115	22	2	14	58	7	.241
Division Series													
2000 Seattle	.A.L.	OF	3	8	2	3	0	0	0	0	0	.375
Championship Series													
2000 Seattle	.A.L.	OF	6	9	0	0	0	0	0	0	0	.000

a On disabled list from May 18 to June 3, 1999.
b On disabled list from August 7 to August 21, 2000.
c Not offered 2001 contract, December 21, 2000.

JACKSON, DAMIAN JACQUES

Born, Los Angeles, California, August 16, 1973.
Bats Right. Throws Right. Height, 5 feet, 10 inches. Weight, 160 pounds.

Year	Club	Lea	Pos	G	AB	R	H	2B	3B	HR	RBI	SB	Avg
1992 Burlington	Appal.	SS	62	226	32	56	12	1	0	23	29	.248
1993 Columbus	So.Atl.	SS	108	350	70	94	19	3	6	45	26	.269
1994 Canton-Akrn	Eastern	SS-OF	138	531	85	143	29	5	5	46	37	.269
1995 Canton-Akrn	Eastern	SS	131	484	67	120	20	2	3	34	40	.248
1996 Buffalo	.A.A.	SS	133	452	77	116	15	1	12	49	24	.257
1996 Cleveland	.A.L.	SS	5	10	2	3	2	0	0	1	0	.300
1997 Buffalo	.A.A.	SS-2B-OF	73	266	51	78	12	0	4	13	20	.293
1997 Cleveland	.A.L.	SS-2B	8	9	2	1	0	0	0	0	1	.111

Year	Club	Lea	Pos	G	AB	R	H	2B	3B	HR	RBI	SB	Avg
1997 Indianapols	A.A.	2B-SS	19	71	12	19	6	1	0	7	4	.268	
1997 Cincinnati a	N.L.	SS-2B	12	27	6	6	2	1	1	2	1	.222	
1998 Indianapols	Int.	SS-2B-OF	131	517	102	135	36	10	6	49	25	.261	
1998 Cincinnati	N.L.	SS-OF	13	38	4	12	5	0	0	7	2	.316	
1999 San Diego b	N.L.	SS-2B-OF	133	388	56	87	20	2	9	39	34	.224	
2000 San Diego	N.L.	SS-2B-OF	138	470	68	120	27	6	6	37	28	.255	
Major League Totals	5 Yrs.		309	942	138	229	56	9	16	86	66	.243	

a Traded to Cincinnati Reds with pitcher Jim Crowell, pitcher Scott Winchester and pitcher Danny Graves for pitcher John Smiley and infielder Jeff Branson, July 31, 1997.

b Traded to San Diego Padres with outfielder Reggie Sanders and pitcher Josh Harris for outfielder Greg Vaughn and outfielder Mark Sweeney, February 2, 1999.

JAVIER, STANLEY JULIAN

Born, San Francisco Macoris, Dominican Republic, September 1, 1965.
Bats Both. Throws Right. Height, 6 feet. Weight, 185 pounds.

Year	Club	Lea	Pos	G	AB	R	H	2B	3B	HR	RBI	SB	Avg
1981 Johnson City	Appal.	OF	53	144	30	36	5	4	3	19	2	.250	
1982 Johnson City	Appal.	OF	57	185	45	51	3	*4	8	36	11	.276	
1983 Greensboro	So. Atl.	OF	129	489	109	152	*34	6	12	77	33	.311	
1984 New York	A.L.	OF	7	7	1	1	0	0	0	0	0	.143	
1984 Nashville a	Southern	OF	76	262	40	76	17	4	7	38	17	.290	
1984 Columbus b	Int.	OF	32	99	12	22	3	1	0	7	1	.222	
1985 Huntsville	Southern	OF	140	486	105	138	22	8	9	64	61	.284	
1986 Tacoma	P.C.	OF-1B	69	248	50	81	16	2	4	51	18	.327	
1986 Oakland	A.L.	OF	59	114	13	23	8	0	0	8	8	.202	
1987 Tacoma	P.C.	OF	15	51	6	11	2	0	0	2	3	.216	
1987 Oakland c	A.L.	OF	81	151	22	28	3	1	2	9	3	.185	
1988 Oakland d	A.L.	OF	125	397	49	102	13	3	2	35	20	.257	
1989 Oakland e	A.L.	OF-1B-2B	112	310	42	77	12	3	1	28	12	.248	
1990 Oakland f	A.L.	OF	19	33	4	8	0	2	0	3	0	.242	
1990 Los Angeles	N.L.	OF	104	276	56	84	9	4	3	24	15	.304	
1991 Los Angeles	N.L.	OF-1B	121	176	21	36	5	3	1	11	7	.205	
1992 L.A.-Philadelphia g-h	N.L.	OF	130	334	42	83	17	1	1	29	18	.249	
1993 California i	N.L.	OF-1B-2B	92	237	33	69	10	4	3	28	12	.291	
1994 Oakland	A.L.	OF-1B-3B	109	419	75	114	23	0	10	44	24	.272	
1995 Oakland j	A.L.	OF-3B	130	442	81	123	20	2	8	56	36	.278	
1996 San Jose k	California	OF	3	5	1	2	0	0	0	1	0	.400	
1996 San Francisco k	N.L.	OF	71	274	44	74	25	0	2	22	14	.270	
1997 San Francisco l-m	N.L.	OF-1B	142	440	69	126	16	4	8	50	25	.286	
1998 San Francisco	N.L.	OF	135	417	63	121	13	5	4	49	21	.290	
1999 San Fran-Houston n-o	N.L.	OF	132	397	61	113	19	2	3	34	16	.285	
2000 Seattle	A.L.	OF-1B	105	342	61	94	18	5	5	40	4	.275	
Major League Totals	16 Yrs.		1674	4766	737	1276	211	39	53	470	235	.268	
Division Series													
1997 San Francisco	N.L.	OF	3	12	2	5	1	0	0	1	1	.417	
1999 Houston	N.L.	OF	4	11	1	3	0	0	0	0	0	.273	
2000 Seattle	A.L.	OF	3	6	0	1	0	0	0	1	0	.167	
Division Series Totals			10	29	3	9	1	0	0	2	1	.310	
Championship Series													
1988 Oakland	A.L.	OF	2	4	0	2	0	0	0	1	0	.500	
1989 Oakland	A.L.	OF	1	2	0	0	0	0	0	0	0	.000	
2000 Seattle	A.L.	OF	4	14	0	1	0	0	0	1	0	.071	
Championship Series Totals			7	20	0	3	0	0	0	2	0	.150	
World Series Record													
1988 Oakland	A.L.	OF	3	4	0	2	0	0	0	2	0	.500	
1989 Oakland	A.L.	OF	1	0	0	0	0	0	0	0	0	.000	
World Series Totals			4	4	0	2	0	0	0	2	0	.500	

a Traded by St. Louis Cardinals to New York Yankees with shortstop Bobby Meacham for outfielder Bob Helsom and pitchers Marty Mason and Steve Fincher, December 14, 1982.

b Traded by New York Yankees to Oakland A's with pitchers Jay Howell, Jose Rijo, Eric Plunk and Tim Birtsas for outfielder Rickey Henderson and pitcher Bert Bradley, December 5, 1984.

c On disabled list from August 3 to September 1, 1987.

d On disabled list from August 18 to September 5, 1988.

e On disabled list from July 9 to July 24, 1989.

f Traded to Los Angeles Dodgers for second baseman Willie Randolph, May 11, 1990.

g Traded to Philadelphia Phillies for pitcher Steve Searcy and player to be named, July 2; Los Angeles Dodgers acquired outfielder Julio Peguero to complete trade, July 28, 1992.

h Filed for free agency, October 27, 1992; signed with California Angels organization, January 15, 1993.

i Filed for free agency, October 28; signed with Oakland Athletics, December 7, 1993.
j Filed for free agency, November 12, 1995; signed by San Francisco Giants, December 8, 1995.
k On disabled list from April 13 to April 29 and July 17 to September 30, 1996.
l Filed for free agency, October 28, 1997.
m Re-signed with San Francisco Giants, November 26, 1997.
n Traded to Houston Astros for pitcher Joe Messman, August 31, 1999.
o Filed for free agency, October 28, 1999. Signed with Seattle Mariners, December 20, 1999.

JENKINS, GEOFFREY SCOTT (GEOFF)

Born, Olympia, Washington, July 21, 1974.
Bats Left. Throws Right. Height, 6 feet, 1 inch. Weight, 205 pounds.

Year	Club	Lea	Pos	G	AB	R	H	2B	3B	HR	RBI	SB	Avg
1995 Helena	Pioneer	OF	7	28	2	9	0	1	0	9	0	.321
1995 Stockton	California	OF	13	47	13	12	2	0	3	12	2	.255
1995 El Paso	Texas	OF	22	79	12	22	4	2	1	13	3	.278
1996 El Paso	Texas	DH	22	77	17	22	5	4	1	11	1	.286
1996 Stockton a	California	DH-OF	37	138	27	48	8	4	3	25	3	.348
1997 Tucson b	P.C.	OF-SS	93	347	44	82	24	3	10	56	0	.236
1998 Louisville	Int.	OF	55	215	38	71	10	4	7	52	1	.330
1998 Milwaukee	N.L.	OF	84	262	33	60	12	1	9	28	1	.229
1999 Milwaukee	N.L.	OF	135	447	70	140	43	3	21	82	5	.313
2000 Milwaukee c	N.L.	OF	135	512	100	155	36	4	34	94	11	.303
Major League Totals	3 Yrs.		354	1221	203	355	91	8	64	204	17	.291

a On disabled list from May 8 to July 13, 1996.
b On disabled list from July 4 to August 11, 1997.
c On disabled list from May 6 to May 28, 2000.

JETER, DEREK SANDERSON

Born, Pequannock, New Jersey, June 26, 1974.
Bats Right. Throws Right. Height, 6 feet, 3 inches. Weight, 175 pounds.

Year	Club	Lea	Pos	G	AB	R	H	2B	3B	HR	RBI	SB	Avg
1992 Tampa Yankees	Gulf C.	SS	47	173	19	35	10	0	3	25	2	.202
1992 Greensboro	So. Atl.	SS	11	37	4	9	0	0	1	4	0	.243
1993 Greensboro	So. Atl.	SS	128	515	85	152	14	11	5	71	18	.295
1994 Tampa	Fla. St.	SS	69	292	61	96	13	8	0	39	28	.329
1994 Albany	Eastern	SS	34	122	17	46	7	2	2	13	12	.377
1994 Columbus	Int.	SS	35	126	25	44	7	1	3	16	10	.349
1995 Columbus	Int.	SS	123	486	96	154	27	9	2	45	20	.317
1995 New York a	A.L.	SS	15	48	5	12	4	1	0	7	0	.250
1996 New York a	A.L.	SS	157	582	104	183	25	6	10	78	14	.314
1997 New York	A.L.	SS	159	654	116	190	31	7	10	70	23	.291
1998 Columbus	Int.	SS	1	5	2	2	2	0	0	0	0	.400
1998 New York b	A.L.	SS	149	626	*127	203	25	8	19	84	30	.324
1999 New York	A.L.	SS	158	627	134	219	37	9	24	102	19	.349
2000 Tampa	Fla.St.	SS	1	3	2	2	1	0	0	0	0	.667
2000 New York c	A.L.	SS	148	593	119	201	31	4	15	73	22	.339
Major League Totals	6 Yrs.		786	3130	605	1008	153	35	78	414	108	.322
Division Series													
1996 New York	A.L.	SS	4	17	2	7	1	0	0	1	0	.412
1997 New York	A.L.	SS	5	21	6	7	1	0	2	2	1	.333
1998 New York	A.L.	SS	3	9	0	1	0	0	0	0	0	.111
1999 New York	A.L.	SS	3	11	3	5	1	1	0	0	0	.455
2000 New York	A.L.	SS	5	19	1	4	0	0	0	2	0	.211
Division Series Totals			20	77	12	24	3	1	2	5	1	.312
Championship Series													
1996 New York	A.L.	SS	5	24	5	10	2	0	1	1	2	.417
1998 New York	A.L.	SS	6	25	3	5	1	1	0	2	3	.200
1999 New York	A.L.	SS	5	20	3	7	1	0	1	3	0	.350
2000 New York	A.L.	SS	6	22	6	7	0	0	2	5	1	.318
Championship Series Totals			22	91	17	29	4	1	4	11	6	.319
World Series													
1996 New York	A.L.	SS	6	20	5	5	0	0	0	1	1	.250
1998 New York	A.L.	SS	4	17	4	6	0	0	0	1	0	.353
1999 New York	A.L.	SS	4	17	4	6	1	0	0	1	3	.353
2000 New York	A.L.	SS	5	22	6	9	2	1	2	2	0	.409
World Series Totals			19	76	19	26	3	1	2	5	4	.342

a Selected Rookie of the Year in American League for 1996.
b On disabled list from June 4 to June 19, 1998.
c On disabled list from May 12 to May 26, 2000.

JOHNSON, CHARLES EDWARD

Born, Fort Pierce, Florida, July 20, 1971.
Bats Right. Throws Right. Height, 6 feet, 2 inches. Weight, 215 pounds.

Year	Club	Lea	Pos	G	AB	R	H	2B	3B	HR	RBI	SB	Avg
1993	Kane County	Midwest	C	135	488	74	134	29	5	19	94	9	.275
1994	Portland	Eastern	C	132	443	64	117	29	1	*28	80	4	.264
1994	Florida	N.L.	C	4	11	5	5	1	0	1	4	0	.455
1995	Portland	Eastern	C	2	7	0	0	0	0	0	0	0	.000
1995	Florida a	N.L.	C	97	315	40	79	15	1	11	39	0	.251
1996	Florida b	N.L.	C	120	386	34	84	13	1	13	37	1	.218
1997	Florida	N.L.	C	124	416	43	104	26	1	19	63	0	.250
1998	Florida-Los Angeles c-d-e	N.L.	C	133	459	44	100	18	0	19	58	0	.218
1999	Baltimore	A.L.	C	135	426	58	107	19	1	16	54	0	.251
2000	Baltimore-Chicago f-g	A.L.	C	128	421	76	128	24	0	31	91	2	.304
Major League Totals			7 Yrs.	741	2434	300	607	116	4	110	346	3	.249
Division Series													
1997	Florida	N.L.	C	3	8	5	2	1	0	1	2	0	.250
2000	Chicago	A.L.	C	3	9	0	3	0	0	0	0	0	.333
Division Series Totals				6	17	5	5	1	0	1	2	0	.294
Championship Series													
1997	Florida	N.L.	C	6	17	1	2	2	0	0	5	0	.118
World Series Record													
1997	Florida	N.L.	C	7	28	4	10	0	0	1	3	0	.357

a On disabled list from August 9 to September 1, 1995.
b On disabled list from July 28 to September 1, 1996.
c Traded to Los Angeles Dodgers with outfielder Gary Sheffield, outfielder Jim Eisenreich, infielder Bobby Bonilla and pitcher Manuel Barrios for catcher Mike Piazza and infielder Todd Zeile, May 15, 1998.
d Traded to New York Mets with outfielder Roger Cedeno for catcher Todd Hundley and pitcher Arnie Gooch, December 1, 1998.
e Traded to Baltimore Orioles for pitcher Armando Benitez, December 1, 1998.
f Traded to Chicago White Sox with designated hitter Harold Baines for catcher Brook Fordyce, pitcher Miguel Felix, pitcher Juan Figueroa and pitcher Jason Lakman, July 29, 2000.
g Filed for free agency, October 30, 2000, signed with Florida Marlins, December 18, 2000.

JOHNSON, MARK LANDON

Born, Wheat Ridge, Colorado, September 12, 1975.
Bats Left. Throws Right. Height, 6 feet. Weight, 185 pounds.

Year	Club	Lea	Pos	G	AB	R	H	2B	3B	HR	RBI	SB	Avg
1994	White Sox	Gulf Coast	C	32	87	10	21	5	0	0	14	1	.241
1995	Hickory	So.Atl.	C	107	319	31	58	9	0	2	17	3	.182
1996	South Bend	Midwest	C	67	214	29	55	14	3	2	27	3	.257
1996	Pr William	Carolina	C	18	58	9	14	3	0	0	3	0	.241
1997	Winston-Sal	Carolina	C	120	375	59	95	27	4	4	46	4	.253
1998	Birmingham	Southern	C-1B	117	382	68	108	17	3	9	59	4	.283
1998	Chicago	A.L.	C	7	23	2	2	0	2	0	1	0	.087
1999	Chicago	A.L.	C	73	207	27	47	11	0	4	16	3	.227
2000	Chicago	A.L.	C	75	213	29	48	11	0	3	23	3	.225
Major League Totals			3 Yrs.	155	443	58	97	22	2	7	40	6	.219

JOHNSON, WILLIAM RUSSELL (RUSS)

Born, Baton Rouge, Louisiana, February 22, 1973.
Bats Right. Throws Right. Height, 5 feet, 10 inches. Weight, 185 pounds.

Year	Club	Lea	Pos	G	AB	R	H	2B	3B	HR	RBI	SB	Avg
1995	Jackson	Texas	SS	132	475	65	118	16	2	9	53	10	.248
1996	Jackson	Texas	SS	132	496	86	154	24	5	15	74	9	.310
1997	New Orleans	A.A.	3B-SS	122	445	72	123	16	6	4	49	7	.276
1997	Houston	N.L.	3B-2B	21	60	7	18	1	0	2	9	1	.300
1998	New Orleans	P.C.	3B-2B-SS	122	453	95	140	28	2	7	52	11	.309
1998	Houston	N.L.	3B-2B	8	13	2	3	1	0	0	0	1	.231
1999	New Orleans	P.C.	2B	22	77	17	27	6	0	1	12	1	.351
1999	Houston	N.L.	3B-2B-SS	83	156	24	44	10	0	5	23	2	.282
2000	Houston	N.L.	SS-3B-2B	26	45	4	8	0	0	0	3	1	.178
2000	Tampa Bay a	A.L.	3B-2B-SS	74	185	28	47	8	0	2	17	4	.254
Major League Totals			4 Yrs.	212	459	65	120	20	0	9	52	9	.261
Division Series													
1997	Houston	N.L.	PH	1	1	0	0	0	0	0	0	0	.000

95

Year	Club	Lea	Pos	G	AB	R	H	2B	3B	HR	RBI	SB	Avg
1999 Houston	.........N.L.		PH	2	1	0	1	1	0	0	0	0	1.000
Division Series Totals ...				3	2	0	1	1	0	0	0	0	.500

a Traded to Tampa Bay Devil Rays for pitcher Marc Valdes, May 27, 2000.

JONES, ANDRUW RUDOLF
Born, Curacao, Neth. Antilles, April 23, 1977.
Bats Right. Throws Right. Height, 6 feet, 1 inch. Weight, 185 pounds.

Year	Club	Lea	Pos	G	AB	R	H	2B	3B	HR	RBI	SB	Avg
1994 Braves	.........Gulf Coast	OF	27	95	22	21	5	1	2	10	5	.221
1994 Danville	...........Appal.	OF	36	143	20	48	9	2	1	16	16	.336
1995 Macon	.......So.Atl.	OF	139	537	104	149	41	5	25	100	56	.277
1996 Durham	.........Carolina	OF	66	243	65	76	14	3	17	43	16	.313
1996 Greenville	.......Southern	OF	38	157	39	58	10	1	12	37	12	.369
1996 Richmond	............Int.	OF	12	45	11	17	3	1	5	12	2	.378
1996 Atlanta	.............N.L.	OF	31	106	11	23	7	1	5	13	3	.217
1997 Atlanta	.............N.L.	OF	153	399	60	92	18	1	18	70	20	.231
1998 Atlanta	.............N.L.	OF	159	582	89	158	33	8	31	90	27	.271
1999 Atlanta	.............N.L.	OF	162	592	97	163	35	5	26	84	24	.275
2000 Atlanta	.............N.L.	OF	161	*656	122	199	36	6	36	104	21	.303
Major League Totals		5 Yrs.	666	2335	379	635	129	21	116	361	95	.272
Division Series												
1996 Atlanta	.............N.L.	OF	3	0	0	0	0	0	0	0	0	.000
1997 Atlanta	.............N.L.	OF	3	5	1	0	0	0	0	1	0	.000
1998 Atlanta	.............N.L.	OF	3	9	2	0	0	0	0	1	2	.000
1999 Atlanta	.............N.L.	OF	4	18	1	4	1	0	0	2	0	.222
2000 Atlanta	.............N.L.	OF	3	9	3	1	0	0	1	1	0	.111
Division Series Totals			16	41	7	5	1	0	1	5	2	.122
Championship Series												
1996 Atlanta	.............N.L.	OF	5	9	3	2	0	0	1	3	0	.222
1997 Atlanta	.............N.L.	OF	5	9	0	4	0	0	0	1	0	.444
1998 Atlanta	.............N.L.	OF	6	22	3	6	0	0	1	2	1	.273
1999 Atlanta	.............N.L.	OF	6	23	5	5	0	0	0	1	0	.217
Championship Series Totals			22	63	11	17	0	0	2	7	1	.270
World Series												
1996 Atlanta	.............N.L.	OF	6	20	4	8	1	0	2	6	1	.400
1999 Atlanta	.............N.L.	OF	4	13	1	1	0	0	0	0	0	.077
World Series Totals			10	33	5	9	1	0	2	6	1	.27

JONES, JACQUE DEWAYNE
Born, San Diego, California, April 25, 1975.
Bats Left. Throws Right. Height, 5 feet, 10 inches. Weight, 175 pounds.

Year	Club	Lea	Pos	G	AB	R	H	2B	3B	HR	RBI	SB	Avg
1996 Ft. Myers	..........Fla.St.	OF	1	3	0	2	1	0	0	1	0	.667
1997 Ft. Myers	..........Fla.St.	OF	131	539	84	160	33	6	15	82	24	.297
1998 New Britain	.......Eastern	OF	134	518	78	155	39	3	21	85	18	.299
1999 Salt Lake	.............P.C.	OF	52	198	32	59	13	2	4	26	9	.298
1999 Minnesota	............A.L.	OF	95	322	54	93	24	2	9	44	3	.289
2000 Minnesota	............A.L.	OF	154	523	66	149	26	5	19	76	7	.285
Major League Totals		2 Yrs.	249	845	120	242	50	7	28	120	10	.286

JONES, LARRY WAYNE (CHIPPER)
Born, Deland, Florida, April 24, 1972.
Bats Both. Throws Right. Height, 6 feet, 3 inches. Weight, 185 pounds.

Year	Club	Lea	Pos	G	AB	R	H	2B	3B	HR	RBI	SB	Avg
1990 Bradenton Braves	....Gulf C.	SS	44	140	20	32	1	1	1	18	5	.229
1991 Macon	............So. Atl.	SS	136	473	*104	154	24	11	15	98	40	.326
1992 Durham	.........Carolina	SS	70	264	43	73	22	1	4	31	10	.277
1992 Greenville	.......Southern	SS	67	266	43	92	17	11	9	42	14	.346
1993 Richmond	............Int.	SS	139	536	97	174	31	12	13	89	23	.325
1993 Atlanta	.............N.L.	SS	8	3	2	2	1	0	0	0	0	.667
1994 Atlanta a	............N.L.		INJURED—Did Not Play									
1995 Atlanta	.............N.L.	3B-OF	140	524	87	139	22	3	23	86	8	.265
1996 Atlanta b	............N.L.	3B-SS-OF	157	598	114	185	32	5	30	110	14	.309

Year	Club	Lea	Pos	G	AB	R	H	2B	3B	HR	RBI	SB	Avg
997 Atlanta		N.L.	3B-OF	157	597	100	176	41	3	21	111	20	.295
998 Atlanta		N.L.	3B	160	601	123	188	29	5	34	107	16	.313
999 Atlanta c		N.L.	3B-SS	157	567	116	181	41	1	45	110	25	.319
000 Atlanta		N.L.	3B-SS	156	579	118	180	38	1	36	111	14	.311
Major League Totals			7 Yrs.	935	3469	660	1051	204	18	189	635	97	.303
Division Series													
995 Atlanta		N.L.	3B	4	18	4	7	2	0	2	4	0	.389
996 Atlanta		N.L.	3B	3	9	2	2	0	0	1	2	1	.222
997 Atlanta		N.L.	3B	3	8	3	4	0	0	1	2	1	.500
998 Atlanta		N.L.	3B	2	10	2	2	0	0	0	1	0	.200
999 Atlanta		N.L.	3B	4	13	2	3	0	0	0	1	0	.231
2000 Atlanta		N.L.	3B	3	12	2	4	1	0	0	1	0	.333
Division Series Totals				19	70	15	22	3	0	4	11	2	.314
Championship Series													
995 Atlanta		N.L.	3B	4	16	3	7	0	0	1	3	1	.438
996 Atlanta		N.L.	3B	7	25	6	11	2	0	0	4	1	.440
997 Atlanta		N.L.	3B	6	24	5	7	1	0	2	4	0	.292
998 Atlanta		N.L.	3B	6	24	2	5	1	0	0	1	0	.208
999 Atlanta		N.L.	3B	6	19	3	5	2	0	0	1	3	.263
Championship Series Totals				29	108	19	35	6	0	3	13	5	.324
World Series Record													
995 Atlanta		N.L.	3B	6	21	3	6	3	0	0	1	0	.286
996 Atlanta		N.L.	3B-SS	6	21	3	6	3	0	0	3	1	.286
999 Atlanta		N.L.	3B	4	13	2	3	0	0	1	2	0	.231
World Series Totals				16	55	8	15	6	0	1	6	1	.273

a On disabled list from March 20 to end of 1994 season.
b On disabled list from April 1 to April 6, 1996.
c Selected Most Valuable Player in National League for 1999.

JONES, TERRY LEE

Born, Birmingham, Alabama, February 15, 1971.
Bats Both. Throws Right. Height, 5 feet, 10 inches. Weight, 160 pounds.

Year	Club	Lea	Pos	G	AB	R	H	2B	3B	HR	RBI	SB	Avg
1993 Bend	Northwest		OF	33	138	21	40	5	4	0	18	16	.290
1993 Central Val	California		OF	21	73	16	21	1	0	0	7	5	.288
1994 Central Val	California		OF	129	536	94	157	20	1	2	44	44	.293
1995 New Haven	Eastern		OF	124	472	78	127	12	1	1	26	51	.269
1996 Colo Sprngs	P.C.		OF	128	497	75	143	7	4	0	33	26	.288
1996 Colorado	N.L.		OF	12	10	6	3	0	0	0	1	0	.300
1997 Colo Sprngs a	P.C.		OF	92	363	70	98	14	4	1	25	36	.270
1998 Ottawa	Int.		OF	81	278	36	66	3	4	0	21	35	.237
1998 Montreal	N.L.		OF	60	212	30	46	7	2	1	15	16	.217
1999 Ottawa	Int.		OF	88	332	49	87	17	2	0	23	30	.262
1999 Montreal b-c	N.L.		OF	17	63	4	17	1	1	0	3	1	.270
2000 Montréal d-e	N.L.		OF	108	168	30	42	8	2	0	13	7	.250
Major League Totals			4 Yrs.	197	453	70	108	16	5	1	32	24	.238

a Traded by Colorado Rockies to Montreal Expos for pitcher Dave Veres, December 10, 1997.
b On disabled list from April 21 to May 7, 1999.
c Filed for free agency, October 4, 1999, signed with Los Angeles Dodgers organization, October 28, 1999.
d Claimed on waivers by Montreal Expos, April 1, 2000.
e On disabled list from July 18 to August 3, 2000.

JORDAN, BRIAN O'NEAL

Born, Baltimore, Maryland, March 29, 1967.
Bats Right. Throws Right. Height, 6 feet, 1 inch. Weight, 205 pounds.

Year	Club	Lea	Pos	G	AB	R	H	2B	3B	HR	RBI	SB	Avg
1988 Hamilton a	N.Y.-Penn.		OF	19	71	12	22	3	1	4	12	3	.310
1989 St. Petersburg	Fla. St.		OF	11	43	7	15	4	1	2	11	0	.349
1990 Arkansas b	Texas		OF	16	50	4	8	1	0	0	0	0	.160
1990 St. Petersburg	Fla. St.		OF	9	30	3	5	0	1	0	1	0	.167
1991 Louisville	A.A.		OF	61	212	35	56	11	4	4	24	0	.264
1992 St. Louis c	N.L.		OF	55	193	17	40	9	4	5	22	7	.207
1992 Louisville	Int.		OF	43	155	23	45	3	1	4	16	13	.290
1993 Louisville	A.A.		OF	38	144	24	54	13	2	5	35	9	.375
1993 St. Louis	N.L.		OF	67	223	33	69	10	6	10	44	6	.309
1994 St. Louis d	N.L.		OF-1B	53	178	14	46	8	2	5	15	4	.258

<table>
<thead>
<tr><th>Year</th><th>Club</th><th>Lea</th><th>Pos</th><th>G</th><th>AB</th><th>R</th><th>H</th><th>2B</th><th>3B</th><th>HR</th><th>RBI</th><th>SB</th><th>Avg</th></tr>
</thead>
<tbody>
<tr><td>1995 St. Louis</td><td>.N.L.</td><td></td><td>OF</td><td>131</td><td>490</td><td>83</td><td>145</td><td>20</td><td>4</td><td>22</td><td>81</td><td>24</td><td>.296</td></tr>
<tr><td>1996 St. Louis e</td><td>.N.L.</td><td></td><td>OF-1B</td><td>140</td><td>513</td><td>82</td><td>159</td><td>36</td><td>1</td><td>17</td><td>104</td><td>22</td><td>.310</td></tr>
<tr><td>1997 Louisville</td><td>.A.A.</td><td></td><td>OF</td><td>6</td><td>20</td><td>1</td><td>3</td><td>0</td><td>0</td><td>0</td><td>2</td><td>0</td><td>.150</td></tr>
<tr><td>1997 St. Louis f</td><td>.N.L.</td><td></td><td>OF</td><td>47</td><td>145</td><td>17</td><td>34</td><td>5</td><td>0</td><td>0</td><td>10</td><td>6</td><td>.234</td></tr>
<tr><td>1998 St. Louis g</td><td>.N.L.</td><td></td><td>OF-3B</td><td>150</td><td>564</td><td>100</td><td>178</td><td>34</td><td>7</td><td>25</td><td>91</td><td>17</td><td>.316</td></tr>
<tr><td>1999 Atlanta</td><td>.N.L.</td><td></td><td>OF</td><td>153</td><td>576</td><td>100</td><td>163</td><td>28</td><td>4</td><td>23</td><td>115</td><td>13</td><td>.283</td></tr>
<tr><td>2000 Atlanta h</td><td>.N.L.</td><td></td><td>OF</td><td>133</td><td>489</td><td>71</td><td>129</td><td>26</td><td>0</td><td>17</td><td>77</td><td>10</td><td>.264</td></tr>
<tr><td>Major League Totals</td><td>9 Yrs.</td><td></td><td></td><td>929</td><td>3371</td><td>517</td><td>963</td><td>176</td><td>28</td><td>124</td><td>559</td><td>109</td><td>.286</td></tr>
<tr><td colspan="14">Division Series</td></tr>
<tr><td>1996 St. Louis</td><td>.N.L.</td><td></td><td>OF</td><td>3</td><td>12</td><td>4</td><td>4</td><td>0</td><td>0</td><td>1</td><td>3</td><td>1</td><td>.333</td></tr>
<tr><td>1999 Atlanta</td><td>.N.L.</td><td></td><td>OF</td><td>4</td><td>17</td><td>2</td><td>8</td><td>1</td><td>0</td><td>1</td><td>7</td><td>0</td><td>.471</td></tr>
<tr><td>2000 Atlanta</td><td>.N.L.</td><td></td><td>OF</td><td>3</td><td>11</td><td>1</td><td>4</td><td>1</td><td>0</td><td>0</td><td>4</td><td>0</td><td>.364</td></tr>
<tr><td>Division Series Totals</td><td></td><td></td><td></td><td>10</td><td>40</td><td>7</td><td>16</td><td>2</td><td>0</td><td>2</td><td>14</td><td>1</td><td>.400</td></tr>
<tr><td colspan="14">Championship Series</td></tr>
<tr><td>1996 St. Louis</td><td>.N.L.</td><td></td><td>OF</td><td>7</td><td>25</td><td>3</td><td>6</td><td>1</td><td>1</td><td>1</td><td>2</td><td>0</td><td>.240</td></tr>
<tr><td>1999 Atlanta</td><td>.N.L.</td><td></td><td>OF</td><td>6</td><td>25</td><td>3</td><td>5</td><td>0</td><td>0</td><td>2</td><td>5</td><td>0</td><td>.200</td></tr>
<tr><td>Championship Series Totals</td><td></td><td></td><td></td><td>13</td><td>50</td><td>6</td><td>11</td><td>1</td><td>1</td><td>3</td><td>7</td><td>0</td><td>.220</td></tr>
<tr><td colspan="14">World Series Record</td></tr>
<tr><td>1999 Atlanta</td><td>.N.L.</td><td></td><td>OF</td><td>4</td><td>13</td><td>1</td><td>1</td><td>0</td><td>0</td><td>0</td><td>1</td><td>0</td><td>.077</td></tr>
</tbody>
</table>

a Batted left and right during 1988 season.
b On disabled list from May 6 to May 17 and June 8 to end of 1990 season.
c On disabled list from May 25 to June 22, 1992.
d On disabled list from July 11 to end of 1994 season.
e On disabled list from April 1 to April 15, 1996.
f On disabled list from May 6 to June 13 and June 27 to August 10 and August 25 to September 29, 1997.
g Filed for free agency, October 22, 1998, signed with Atlanta Braves, November 23, 1998.
h On disabled list from April 4 to April 19, 2000.

JORDAN, KEVIN WAYNE

Born, San Francisco, California, October 9, 1969.
Bats Right. Throws Right. Height, 6 feet, 1 inch. Weight, 206 pounds.

<table>
<thead>
<tr><th>Year</th><th>Club</th><th>Lea</th><th>Pos</th><th>G</th><th>AB</th><th>R</th><th>H</th><th>2B</th><th>3B</th><th>HR</th><th>RBI</th><th>SB</th><th>Avg</th></tr>
</thead>
<tbody>
<tr><td>1990 Oneonta</td><td>.N.Y.-Penn.</td><td>2B</td><td>73</td><td>276</td><td>47</td><td>92</td><td>13</td><td>7</td><td>4</td><td>54</td><td>19</td><td>.333</td><td></td></tr>
<tr><td>1991 Ft. Lauderdale</td><td>.Fla. St.</td><td>2B-1B</td><td>121</td><td>448</td><td>61</td><td>122</td><td>25</td><td>5</td><td>4</td><td>53</td><td>14</td><td>.272</td><td></td></tr>
<tr><td>1992 Pr William</td><td>.Carolina</td><td>2B-3B</td><td>112</td><td>438</td><td>67</td><td>136</td><td>29</td><td>8</td><td>8</td><td>63</td><td>6</td><td>.311</td><td></td></tr>
<tr><td>1993 Albany a</td><td>.Eastern</td><td>2B</td><td>135</td><td>513</td><td>87</td><td>145</td><td>33</td><td>4</td><td>16</td><td>87</td><td>8</td><td>.283</td><td></td></tr>
<tr><td>1994 Scranton-WB</td><td>.Int.</td><td>2B-3B</td><td>81</td><td>314</td><td>44</td><td>91</td><td>22</td><td>1</td><td>12</td><td>57</td><td>0</td><td>.290</td><td></td></tr>
<tr><td>1995 Scranton-WB</td><td>.Int.</td><td>2B</td><td>106</td><td>410</td><td>61</td><td>127</td><td>29</td><td>4</td><td>5</td><td>60</td><td>3</td><td>.310</td><td></td></tr>
<tr><td>1995 Philadelphia</td><td>.N.L.</td><td>2B-3B</td><td>24</td><td>54</td><td>6</td><td>10</td><td>1</td><td>0</td><td>2</td><td>6</td><td>0</td><td>.185</td><td></td></tr>
<tr><td>1996 Philadelphia b</td><td>.N.L.</td><td>1B-2B-3B</td><td>43</td><td>131</td><td>15</td><td>37</td><td>10</td><td>0</td><td>3</td><td>12</td><td>2</td><td>.282</td><td></td></tr>
<tr><td>1997 Scranton-WB</td><td>.Int.</td><td>3B-2B-1B</td><td>7</td><td>30</td><td>5</td><td>9</td><td>2</td><td>2</td><td>0</td><td>2</td><td>2</td><td>.300</td><td></td></tr>
<tr><td>1997 Philadelphia</td><td>.N.L.</td><td>1B-3B-2B</td><td>84</td><td>177</td><td>19</td><td>47</td><td>8</td><td>0</td><td>6</td><td>30</td><td>0</td><td>.266</td><td></td></tr>
<tr><td>1998 Philadelphia</td><td>.N.L.</td><td>1B-3B-2B</td><td>112</td><td>250</td><td>23</td><td>69</td><td>13</td><td>0</td><td>2</td><td>27</td><td>0</td><td>.276</td><td></td></tr>
<tr><td>1999 Philadelphia</td><td>.N.L.</td><td>3B-2B-1B</td><td>120</td><td>347</td><td>36</td><td>99</td><td>17</td><td>3</td><td>4</td><td>51</td><td>0</td><td>.285</td><td></td></tr>
<tr><td>2000 Philadelphia c</td><td>.N.L.</td><td>2B-3B-1B</td><td>109</td><td>337</td><td>30</td><td>74</td><td>16</td><td>2</td><td>5</td><td>36</td><td>0</td><td>.220</td><td></td></tr>
<tr><td>Major League Totals</td><td>6 Yrs.</td><td></td><td>492</td><td>1296</td><td>129</td><td>336</td><td>65</td><td>5</td><td>22</td><td>162</td><td>2</td><td>.259</td><td></td></tr>
</tbody>
</table>

a Traded by New York Yankees to Philadelphia Phillies with pitchers Bobby Munoz and Ryan Karp for pitchers Terry Mulholland and Jeff Patterson, February 9, 1994.
b On disabled list from June 17 to end of 1996 season.
c Not offered 2001 contract, December 21, 2000.

JOYNER, WALLACE KEITH (WALLY)

Born, Atlanta, Georgia, June 16, 1962.
Bats Left. Throws Left. Height, 6 feet, 2 inches. Weight, 200 pounds.

<table>
<thead>
<tr><th>Year</th><th>Club</th><th>Lea</th><th>Pos</th><th>G</th><th>AB</th><th>R</th><th>H</th><th>2B</th><th>3B</th><th>HR</th><th>RBI</th><th>SB</th><th>Avg</th></tr>
</thead>
<tbody>
<tr><td>1983 Peoria</td><td>.Midwest</td><td>1B</td><td>54</td><td>192</td><td>25</td><td>63</td><td>16</td><td>2</td><td>3</td><td>33</td><td>1</td><td>.328</td></tr>
<tr><td>1984 Waterbury</td><td>.Eastern</td><td>1B-OF</td><td>134</td><td>467</td><td>81</td><td>148</td><td>24</td><td>7</td><td>12</td><td>72</td><td>0</td><td>.317</td></tr>
<tr><td>1985 Edmonton</td><td>.P.C.</td><td>1B</td><td>126</td><td>477</td><td>68</td><td>135</td><td>29</td><td>5</td><td>12</td><td>73</td><td>2</td><td>.283</td></tr>
<tr><td>1986 California</td><td>.A.L.</td><td>1B</td><td>154</td><td>593</td><td>82</td><td>172</td><td>27</td><td>3</td><td>22</td><td>100</td><td>5</td><td>.290</td></tr>
<tr><td>1987 California</td><td>.A.L.</td><td>1B</td><td>149</td><td>564</td><td>100</td><td>161</td><td>33</td><td>1</td><td>34</td><td>117</td><td>8</td><td>.285</td></tr>
<tr><td>1988 California</td><td>.A.L.</td><td>1B</td><td>158</td><td>597</td><td>81</td><td>176</td><td>31</td><td>2</td><td>13</td><td>85</td><td>8</td><td>.295</td></tr>
<tr><td>1989 California</td><td>.A.L.</td><td>1B</td><td>159</td><td>593</td><td>78</td><td>167</td><td>30</td><td>2</td><td>16</td><td>79</td><td>3</td><td>.282</td></tr>
<tr><td>1990 California a</td><td>.A.L.</td><td>1B</td><td>83</td><td>310</td><td>35</td><td>83</td><td>15</td><td>0</td><td>8</td><td>41</td><td>2</td><td>.268</td></tr>
<tr><td>1991 California b</td><td>.A.L.</td><td>1B</td><td>143</td><td>551</td><td>79</td><td>166</td><td>34</td><td>3</td><td>21</td><td>96</td><td>2</td><td>.301</td></tr>
<tr><td>1992 Kansas City</td><td>.A.L.</td><td>1B</td><td>149</td><td>572</td><td>66</td><td>154</td><td>36</td><td>2</td><td>9</td><td>66</td><td>11</td><td>.269</td></tr>
<tr><td>1993 Kansas City</td><td>.A.L.</td><td>1B</td><td>141</td><td>497</td><td>83</td><td>145</td><td>36</td><td>3</td><td>15</td><td>65</td><td>5</td><td>.292</td></tr>
<tr><td>1994 Kansas City c</td><td>.A.L.</td><td>1B</td><td>97</td><td>363</td><td>52</td><td>113</td><td>20</td><td>3</td><td>8</td><td>57</td><td>3</td><td>.311</td></tr>
<tr><td>1995 Kansas City d</td><td>.A.L.</td><td>1B</td><td>131</td><td>465</td><td>69</td><td>144</td><td>28</td><td>0</td><td>12</td><td>83</td><td>3</td><td>.310</td></tr>
</tbody>
</table>

Year Club Lea	Pos	G	AB	R	H	2B	3B	HR	RBI	SB	Avg
1996 Rancho Cuca. . . . . .California	1B	3	10	1	3	1	0	0	2	0	.300
1996 San Diego e . . . . .N.L.	1B	121	433	59	120	29	1	8	65	5	.277
1997 Las Vegas . . . . .P.C.	1B	3	8	1	2	0	0	0	1	0	.250
1997 San Diego f . . . . .N.L.	1B	135	455	59	149	29	2	13	83	3	.327
1998 San Diego . . . . .N.L.	1B	131	439	58	131	30	1	12	80	1	.298
1999 Las Vegas . . . . .P.C.	1B	6	17	4	4	0	0	0	2	0	.235
1999 San Diego g-h . . . . .N.L.	1B	110	323	34	80	14	2	5	43	0	.248
2000 Atlanta i-j . . . . .N.L.	1B	119	224	24	63	12	0	5	32	0	.281
Major League Totals	15 Yrs.	1980	6979	959	2024	404	25	201	1092	59	.290
Division Series											
1996 San Diego . . . . .N.L.	1B	3	9	0	1	0	0	0	0	0	.111
1998 San Diego . . . . .N.L.	1B	4	6	1	1	0	0	1	2	0	.167
2000 Atlanta . . . . .N.L.	PH	3	3	0	1	1	0	0	0	0	.333
Division Series Totals		10	18	1	3	1	0	1	2	0	.167
Championship Series											
1986 California . . . . .A.L.	1B	3	11	3	5	2	0	1	2	0	.455
1998 San Diego . . . . .N.L.	1B	6	16	3	5	0	0	0	2	0	.313
Championship Series Totals		9	27	6	10	2	0	1	4	0	.370
World Series Record											
1998 San Diego . . . . .N.L.	1B	3	8	0	0	0	0	0	0	0	.000

a On disabled list from July 12 to end of 1990 season.
b Filed for free agency, October 28; signed with Kansas City Royals, December 9, 1991.
c On disabled list from June 26 to July 14, 1994.
d Traded to San Diego Padres with pitcher Aaron Dorlarque for infielder/outfielder Bip Roberts and pitcher Bryan Wolff, December 21, 1995.
e On disabled list from June 2 to July 11, 1996.
f On disabled list from April 28 to May 13, 1997.
g On disabled list from May 17 to June 25, 1999.
h Traded to Atlanta Braves with infielder Quilvio Veras and outfielder Reggie Sanders for infielder Bret Boone, outfielder Ryan Klesko and pitcher Jason Shiell, December 22, 1999.
i Not offered 2001 contract, October 27, 2000.
j Signed with California Angels, January 23, 2001

JUSTICE, DAVID CHRISTOPHER
Born, Cincinnati, Ohio, April 14, 1966.
Bats Left. Throws Left. Height, 6 feet, 3 inches. Weight, 200 pounds.

Year Club Lea	Pos	G	AB	R	H	2B	3B	HR	RBI	SB	Avg
1985 Pulaski . . . . .Appal.	OF	66	204	39	50	8	0	*10	46	0	.245
1986 Sumter . . . . .So. Atl.	OF	61	220	48	66	16	0	10	61	10	.300
1986 Durham . . . . .Carolina	OF	67	229	47	64	9	1	12	44	2	.279
1987 Greenville . . . . . . .Southern	OF	93	348	38	79	12	4	6	40	3	.227
1988 Richmond . . . . .Int.	OF	70	227	27	46	9	1	8	28	4	.203
1988 Greenville . . . . . . .Southern	OF	58	198	34	55	13	1	9	37	6	.278
1989 Richmond . . . . .Int.	1B	115	391	47	102	24	3	12	58	12	.261
1989 Atlanta . . . . .N.L.	OF	16	51	7	12	3	0	1	3	2	.235
1990 Richmond . . . . .Int.	OF-1B	12	45	7	16	5	1	2	7	0	.356
1990 Atlanta a . . . . .N.L.	1B-OF	127	439	76	124	23	2	28	78	11	.282
1991 Macon . . . . .So. Atl.	OF	3	10	2	2	0	0	2	5	0	.200
1991 Atlanta b . . . . .N.L.	OF	109	396	67	109	25	1	21	87	8	.275
1992 Atlanta c . . . . .N.L.	OF	144	484	78	124	19	5	21	72	2	.256
1993 Atlanta . . . . .N.L.	OF	157	585	90	158	15	4	40	120	3	.270
1994 Atlanta . . . . .N.L.	OF	104	352	61	110	16	2	19	59	2	.313
1995 Atlanta d . . . . .N.L.	OF	120	411	73	104	17	2	24	78	4	.253
1996 Atlanta e . . . . .N.L.	OF	40	140	23	45	9	0	6	25	1	.321
1997 Cleveland f -g . . . . .A.L.	OF	139	495	84	163	31	1	33	101	3	.329
1998 Cleveland . . . . .A.L.	DH-OF	146	540	94	151	39	2	21	88	9	.280
1999 Cleveland . . . . .A.L.	OF	133	429	75	123	18	0	21	88	1	.287
2000 Cleveland-New York h-i . A.L.	OF	146	524	89	150	31	1	41	118	2	.286
Major League Totals	12 Yrs.	1381	4846	817	1373	246	20	276	917	48	.283
Division Series											
1995 Atlanta . . . . .N.L.	OF	4	13	2	3	0	0	0	0	0	.231
1997 Cleveland . . . . .A.L.	DH	5	19	3	5	2	0	1	2	0	.263
1998 Cleveland . . . . .A.L.	OF-DH	4	16	2	5	4	0	1	6	0	.313
1999 Cleveland . . . . .A.L.	OF	3	8	0	0	0	0	0	1	0	.000
2000 New York . . . . .A.L.	OF	5	18	2	4	0	0	1	1	0	.222
Division Series Totals		21	74	9	17	6	0	3	10	0	.230
Championship Series											
1991 Atlanta . . . . .N.L.	OF	7	25	4	5	1	0	1	2	0	.200
1992 Atlanta . . . . .N.L.	OF	7	25	5	7	1	0	2	6	0	.280
1993 Atlanta . . . . .N.L.	OF	6	21	2	3	1	0	0	4	0	.143

99

Year	Club	Lea	Pos	G	AB	R	H	2B	3B	HR	RBI	SB	Avg
1995 Atlanta	..............N.L.	OF	3	11	1	3	0	0	0	1	0	.274
1997 Cleveland	...........A.L.	DH	6	21	3	7	1	0	0	0	0	.333
1998 Cleveland	...........A.L.	DH-OF	6	19	2	3	0	0	1	2	0	.158
2000 New York	...........A.L.	OF	6	26	4	6	2	0	2	8	0	.231
Championship Series Totals			41	148	21	34	6	0	6	23	0	.230
World Series Record												
1991 Atlanta	..............N.L.	OF	7	27	5	7	0	0	2	6	2	.259
1992 Atlanta	..............N.L.	OF	6	19	4	3	0	0	1	3	1	.158
1995 Atlanta	..............N.L.	OF	6	20	3	5	1	0	1	5	0	.250
1997 Cleveland	...........A.L.	OF-DH	7	27	4	5	0	0	0	4	0	.185
2000 New York	...........A.L.	OF	5	19	1	3	2	0	0	3	0	.158
World Series Totals	....		31	112	17	23	3	0	4	21	3	.205

a Selected Rookie of the Year in National League for 1990.
b On disabled list from June 27 to August 20, 1991.
c On disabled list from April 12 to April 27, 1992.
d On disabled list from June 2 to June 17, 1995.
e On disabled list from May 16 to September 30, 1996.
f Traded to Cleveland Indians with outfielder Marquis Grissom for outfielder Kenny Lofton and pitcher Alan Embree, March 25, 1997.
g On disabled list from June 23 to July 10, 1997.
h Traded to New York Yankees for outfielder Ricky Ledee and player to be named later, June 29, 2000.
i Cleveland Indians received pitcher Zach Day to complete trade, July 24, 2000.

KAPLER, GABRIEL STEFAN (GABE)
Born, Hollywood, California, August 31, 1975.
Bats Right. Throws Right. Height, 6 feet, 2 inches. Weight, 190 pounds.

Year	Club	Lea	Pos	G	AB	R	H	2B	3B	HR	RBI	SB	Avg
1995 Jamestown	......N.Y.-Penn.	OF	63	236	38	68	19	4	4	34	1	.288
1996 Fayettevlle	.........So.Atl.	OF-3B	138	524	81	157	45	0	26	99	14	.300
1997 Lakeland	...........Fla.St.	OF	137	519	87	153	40	6	19	87	8	.295
1998 Jacksnville	.......Southern	OF-1B	139	547	113	176	47	6	28	146	6	.322
1998 Detroit	................A.L.	OF	7	25	3	5	0	1	0	0	2	.200
1999 Toledo	...............Int.	OF	14	54	11	17	6	2	3	14	0	.315
1999 Detroit a	...............A.L.	OF	130	416	60	102	22	4	18	49	11	.245
2000 Oklahoma	............P.C.	OF	3	9	3	3	0	0	0	0	0	.333
2000 Tulsa	...............Texas	OF	3	12	3	7	0	0	1	4	0	.583
2000 Texas b	..............A.L.	OF	116	444	59	134	32	1	14	66	8	.302
Major League Totals	....	3 Yrs.	253	885	122	241	54	6	32	115	21	.272

a Traded to Texas Rangers with pitcher Justin Thompson, pitcher Francisco Cordero, pitcher Alan Webb, catcher Bill Haselman and infielder Frank Catalanotto for outfielder Juan Gonzalez, pitcher Danny Patterson and catcher Greg Zaun, November 2, 1999.
b On disabled list from May 3 to June 8, 2000.

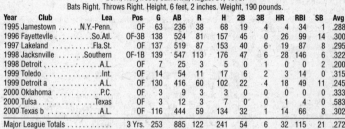

KARROS, ERIC PETER
Born, Hackensack, New Jersey, November 4, 1967.
Bats Right. Throws Right. Height, 6 feet, 4 inches. Weight, 216 pounds.

Year	Club	Lea	Pos	G	AB	R	H	2B	3B	HR	RBI	SB	Avg
1988 Great Falls	.........Pioneer	1B-3B	66	268	68	98	12	1	12	55	8	.366
1989 Bakersfield	......California	1B-3B	*142	545	86	*165	*40	1	15	86	18	.303
1990 San Antonio	.........Texas	1B	*131	509	91	*179	*45	2	18	78	8	*352
1991 Albuquerque	...........P.C.	1B	132	488	88	154	33	8	22	101	3	.316
1991 Los Angeles	..........N.L.	1B	14	14	0	1	1	0	0	1	0	.071
1992 Los Angeles a	.........N.L.	1B	149	545	63	140	30	1	20	88	2	.257
1993 Los Angeles	..........N.L.	1B	158	619	74	153	27	2	23	80	0	.247
1994 Los Angeles	..........N.L.	1B	111	406	51	108	21	1	14	46	2	.266
1995 Los Angeles	..........N.L.	1B	143	551	83	164	29	3	32	105	4	.298
1996 Los Angeles	..........N.L.	1B	154	608	84	158	29	1	34	111	8	.260
1997 Los Angeles	..........N.L.	1B	162	628	86	167	28	0	31	104	15	.266
1998 San Berndno	.....California	1B	4	15	3	4	1	0	0	1	0	.267
1998 Los Angeles b	.........N.L.	1B	139	507	59	150	20	1	23	87	7	.296
1999 Los Angeles	..........N.L.	1B	153	578	74	176	40	0	34	112	8	.304
2000 Los Angeles	..........N.L.	1B	155	584	84	146	29	0	31	106	4	.250
Major League Totals	....	10 Yrs.	1338	5040	658	1363	254	9	242	840	50	.270
Division Series												
1995 Los Angeles	..........N.L.	1B	3	12	3	6	1	0	2	4	0	.500
1996 Los Angeles	..........N.L.	1B	3	9	0	0	0	0	0	0	0	.000
Division Series Totals	....		6	21	3	6	1	0	2	4	0	.286

a Selected Rookie of the Year in National League for 1992.
b On disabled list from March 31 to April 24, 1998.

KENDALL, JASON DANIEL
Born, San Diego, California, June 26, 1974.
Bats Right. Throws Right. Height, 6 feet. Weight, 181 pounds.

Year	Club	Lea	Pos	G	AB	R	H	2B	3B	HR	RBI	SB	Avg
1992 Pirates	Gulf Coast	C	33	111	7	29	2	0	0	10	2	.261
1993 Augusta	So.Atl.	C	102	366	43	101	17	4	1	40	8	.276
1994 Salem	Carolina	C	101	371	68	118	19	2	7	66	14	.318
1994 Carolina	Southern	C	13	47	6	11	2	0	0	6	0	.234
1995 Carolina	Southern	C	117	429	87	140	26	1	8	71	10	.326
1996 Pittsburgh	N.L.	C	130	414	54	124	23	5	3	42	5	.300
1997 Pittsburgh	N.L.	C	144	486	71	143	36	4	8	49	18	.294
1998 Pittsburgh	N.L.	C	149	535	95	175	36	3	12	75	26	.327
1999 Pittsburgh a	N.L.	C	78	280	61	93	20	3	8	41	22	.332
2000 Pittsburgh	N.L.	C	152	579	112	185	33	6	14	58	22	.320
Major League Totals		5 Yrs.	653	2294	393	720	148	21	45	265	93	.314

a On disabled list from July 5 to November 17, 1999.

KENNEDY, ADAM THOMAS
Born, Riverside, California, January 10, 1976.
Bats Left. Throws Right. Height, 6 feet, 1 inch. Weight, 180 pounds.

Year	Club	Lea	Pos	G	AB	R	H	2B	3B	HR	RBI	SB	Avg
1997 New Jersey	N.Y.-Penn.	SS	29	114	20	39	6	3	0	19	9	.342
1997 Pr William	Carolina	SS	35	154	24	48	9	3	1	27	4	.312
1998 Pr William	Carolina	2B-SS	17	69	9	18	6	0	0	7	5	.261
1998 Arkansas	Texas	SS-2B	52	205	35	57	11	2	6	24	6	.278
1998 Memphis	P.C.	SS-2B	74	305	36	93	22	7	4	41	15	.305
1999 Memphis	P.C.	2B	91	367	69	120	22	4	10	63	20	.327
1999 St. Louis	N.L.	2B	33	102	12	26	10	1	1	16	0	.255
2000 Anaheim a	A.L.	2B	156	598	82	159	33	11	9	72	22	.266
Major League Totals		2 Yrs.	189	700	94	185	43	12	10	88	22	.264

a Traded to Anaheim Angels with pitcher Kent Bottenfield for outfielder Jim Edmonds, March 23, 2000.

KENT, JEFFREY FRANKLIN
Born, Bellflower, California, March 7, 1968.
Bats Right. Throws Right. Height, 6 feet, 1 inch. Weight, 185 pounds.

Year	Club	Lea	Pos	G	AB	R	H	2B	3B	HR	RBI	SB	Avg
1989 St. Catharines	N.Y.-Penn.	3B-SS	73	268	34	60	14	1	*13	37	5	.224
1990 Dunedin	Fla. St.	2B	132	447	72	124	32	2	16	60	17	.277
1991 Knoxville	Southern	2B	139	445	68	114	34	1	12	61	25	.256
1992 Toronto a	A.L.	3B-2B-1B	65	192	36	46	13	1	8	35	2	.240
1992 New York	N.L.	2B-3B-SS	37	113	16	27	8	1	3	15	0	.239
1993 New York	N.L.	2B-3B-SS	140	496	65	134	24	0	21	80	4	.270
1994 New York	N.L.	2B	107	415	53	121	24	5	14	68	1	.292
1995 New York b	N.L.	2B	125	472	65	131	22	3	20	65	3	.278
1996 New York c	N.L.	3B	89	335	45	97	20	1	9	39	4	.290
1996 Cleveland d	A.L.	1B-2B-3B	39	102	16	27	7	0	3	16	2	.265
1997 San Francisco	N.L.	2B-1B	155	580	90	145	38	2	29	121	11	.250
1998 San Francisco e	N.L.	2B-1B	137	526	94	156	37	3	31	128	9	.297
1999 San Francisco f	N.L.	2B-1B	138	511	86	148	40	2	23	101	13	.290
2000 San Francisco g	N.L.	2B-1B	159	587	114	196	41	7	33	125	12	.334
Major League Totals		9 Yrs.	1191	4329	680	1228	274	25	194	793	61	.284
Division Series												
1996 Cleveland	A.L.	2B-1B-3B	4	8	2	1	1	0	0	0	0	.125
1997 San Francisco	N.L.	2B-1B	3	10	2	3	0	0	2	2	0	.300
2000 San Francisco	N.L.	2B-1B	4	16	3	6	1	0	0	1	1	.375
Division Series Totals			11	34	7	10	2	0	2	3	1	.294

a Traded to New York Mets with player to be named for pitcher David Cone, August 27; New York acquired outfielder Ryan Thompson to complete trade, September 1, 1992.
b On disabled list from July 6 to July 21, 1995.
c Traded to Cleveland Indians with infielder Jose Vizcaino for infielder Carlos Baerga and infielder Alvaro Espinoza, July 29, 1996.
d Traded to San Francisco Giants with pitcher Julian Taverez, infielder Jose Vizcaino and player to be named later for infielder Matt Williams and player to be named later, November 13, 1996. San Francisco Giants received pitcher Joe Roa and Cleveland Indians received outfielder Trenidad Hubbard to complete trade, December 16, 1996.

e On disabled list from June 10 to July 10, 1998.
f On disabled list from August 3 to August 21, 1999.
g Selected Most Valuable Player in National League for 2000.

KLESKO, RYAN ANTHONY
Born, Westminster, California, June 12, 1971.
Bats Left. Throws Left. Height, 6 feet, 3 inches. Weight, 220 pounds.

Year	Club	Lea	Pos	G	AB	R	H	2B	3B	HR	RBI	SB	Avg
1989 Bradenton Braves	Gulf C.	1B	17	57	14	23	5	4	1	16	4	.404
1989 Sumter	So. Atl.	1B	25	90	17	26	6	0	1	12	1	.289
1990 Sumter	So. Atl.	1B	63	231	41	85	15	1	10	38	13	.368
1990 Durham	Carolina	1B	77	292	40	80	16	1	7	47	10	.274
1991 Greenville	Southern	1B	126	419	64	122	22	3	14	67	14	.291
1992 Richmond	Int.	1B	123	418	63	105	22	2	17	59	3	.251
1992 Atlanta	N.L.	1B	13	14	0	0	0	0	0	1	0	.000
1993 Richmond	Int.	1B-OF	98	343	59	94	14	2	22	74	4	.274
1993 Atlanta	N.L.	1B-OF	22	17	3	6	1	0	2	5	0	.353
1994 Atlanta	N.L.	OF-1B	92	245	42	68	13	3	17	47	1	.278
1995 Greenville	Southern	OF	4	13	1	3	0	0	1	4	0	.231
1995 Atlanta a	N.L.	OF-1B	107	329	48	102	25	2	23	70	5	.310
1996 Atlanta	N.L.	OF-1B	153	528	90	149	21	4	34	93	6	.282
1997 Atlanta	N.L.	OF-1B	143	467	67	122	23	6	24	84	4	.261
1998 Atlanta	N.L.	OF-1B	129	427	69	117	29	1	18	70	5	.274
1999 Atlanta b	N.L.	1B-OF	133	404	55	120	28	2	21	80	5	.297
2000 San Diego	N.L.	1B-OF	145	494	88	140	33	2	26	92	23	.283
Major League Totals		9 Yrs.	937	2925	462	824	173	20	165	542	49	.282
Division Series												
1995 Atlanta	N.L.	OF	4	15	5	7	1	0	0	1	0	.467
1996 Atlanta	N.L.	OF	3	8	1	1	0	0	1	1	1	.125
1997 Atlanta	N.L.	OF	3	8	2	2	1	0	1	1	0	.250
1998 Atlanta	N.L.	OF	3	11	1	3	0	0	1	4	0	.173
1999 Atlanta	N.L.	1B	4	12	3	4	0	0	0	1	0	.333
Division Series Totals			17	54	12	17	2	0	3	8	1	.315
Championship Series												
1995 Atlanta	N.L.	OF	4	7	0	0	0	0	0	0	0	.000
1996 Atlanta	N.L.	OF	6	16	1	4	0	0	1	3	0	.250
1997 Atlanta	N.L.	OF	5	17	2	4	0	0	2	4	0	.235
1998 Atlanta	N.L.	OF	5	12	2	1	0	0	0	1	0	.083
1999 Atlanta	N.L.	1B	4	8	1	1	0	0	1	1	0	.125
Championship Series Totals			24	60	6	10	0	0	4	9	0	.167
World Series Record												
1995 Atlanta	N.L.	OF-DH	6	16	4	5	0	0	3	4	0	.313
1996 Atlanta	N.L.	1B-DH	5	10	2	1	0	0	0	1	0	.100
1999 Atlanta	N.L.	1B	4	12	0	2	0	0	0	0	0	.167
World Series Totals			15	38	6	8	0	0	3	5	0	.211

a On disabled list from May 3 to May 18, 1995.
b Traded to San Diego Padres with infielder Bret Boone and pitcher Jason Shiell for infielder Wally Joyner, infielder Quilvio Veras and outfielder Reggie Sanders, December 22, 1999.

KNOBLAUCH, EDWARD CHARLES (CHUCK)
Born, Houston, Texas, July 7, 1968.
Bats Right. Throws Right. Height, 5 feet, 9 inches. Weight, 181 pounds.

Year	Club	Lea	Pos	G	AB	R	H	2B	3B	HR	RBI	SB	Avg
1989 Kenosha	Midwest	SS	51	196	29	56	13	1	2	19	9	.286
1989 Visalia	California	SS	18	77	20	28	10	0	0	21	4	.364
1990 Orlando	Southern	2B	118	432	74	125	23	6	2	53	23	.289
1991 Minnesota a	A.L.	2B-SS	151	565	78	159	24	6	1	50	25	.281
1992 Minnesota	A.L.	2B-SS	155	600	104	178	19	6	2	56	34	.297
1993 Minnesota	A.L.	2B-SS-OF	153	602	82	167	27	4	2	41	29	.277
1994 Minnesota	A.L.	2B-SS	109	445	85	139	*45	3	5	51	35	.312
1995 Minnesota	A.L.	2B-SS	136	538	107	179	34	8	11	63	46	.333
1996 Minnesota	A.L.	2B	153	578	140	197	35	*14	13	72	45	.341
1997 Minnesota-b	A.L.	2B-SS	156	611	117	178	26	10	9	58	62	.291
1998 New York	A.L.	2B	150	603	117	160	25	4	17	64	31	.265
1999 New York	A.L.	2B	150	603	120	176	36	4	18	68	28	.292
2000 Tampa	Fla.St.	2B	1	1	0	0	0	0	0	0	0	.000
2000 New York c	A.L.	2B	102	400	75	113	22	2	5	26	15	.283
Major League Totals		10 Yrs.	1415	5545	1025	1646	293	61	83	549	350	.297

Year	Club	Lea	Pos	G	AB	R	H	2B	3B	HR	RBI	SB	Avg
	Division Series												
1998 New York ...........A.L.			2B	3	11	0	1	0	0	0	0	0	.091
1999 New York ...........A.L.			2B	3	12	1	2	0	0	0	0	0	.167
2000 New York ...........A.L.			DH	3	9	1	3	0	0	0	1	1	.333
Division Series Totals				9	32	2	6	0	0	0	1	1	.188
	Championship Series												
1991 Minnesota ...........A.L.			2B	5	20	5	7	2	0	0	3	2	.350
1998 New York ...........A.L.			2B	6	25	4	5	1	0	0	0	0	.200
1999 New York ...........A.L.			2B	5	18	3	6	1	0	0	1	1	.333
2000 New York ...........A.L.			DH	6	23	3	6	2	0	0	2	0	.261
Championship Series Totals				22	86	15	24	6	0	0	6	3	.279
	World Series Record												
1991 Minnesota ...........A.L.			2B	7	26	3	8	1	0	0	2	4	.308
1998 New York ...........A.L.			2B	4	16	3	6	0	0	1	3	1	.375
1999 New York ...........A.L.			2B	4	16	5	5	1	0	1	3	1	.313
2000 New York ...........A.L.			DH	4	10	1	1	0	0	0	1	0	.100
World Series Totals				19	68	12	20	2	0	2	9	6	.294

a Selected Rookie of the Year in American League for 1991.
b Traded to New York Yankees for pitchers Eric Milton and Danny Mota, outfielder Brian Buchanan and infielder Cristian Guzman and reported $3 million, February 6, 1998.
c On disabled list from August 3 to August 31, 2000.

KONERKO, PAUL HENRY
Born, Providence, Rhode Island, March 5, 1976.
Bats Right. Throws Right. Height, 6 feet, 3 inches. Weight, 205 pounds.

Year	Club	Lea	Pos	G	AB	R	H	2B	3B	HR	RBI	SB	Avg
1994 Yakima ....Northwest			C	67	257	25	74	15	2	6	58	1	.288
1995 San Berndno .....California			C	118	448	77	124	21	1	19	77	3	.277
1996 San Antonio ....Texas			1B	133	470	78	141	23	2	29	86	1	.300
1996 Albuquerque .........P.C.			1B	4	14	2	6	0	0	1	2	0	.429
1997 Albuquerque .........P.C.	3B-1B-2B			130	483	97	156	31	1	37	127	2	.323
1997 Los Angeles .........N.L.			1B-3B	6	7	0	1	0	0	0	0	0	.143
1998 Albuquerque .........P.C.	OF-1B-3B			24	87	16	33	10	0	6	26	0	.379
1998 Indianapolis ....Int.			3B	39	150	25	49	8	0	8	39	1	.327
1998 Los Angeles-Cinc. a-b ...N.L.	1B-3B-OF			75	217	21	47	4	0	7	29	0	.217
1999 Chicago .............A.L.			1B-3B	142	513	71	151	31	4	24	81	1	.294
2000 Chicago .............A.L.			1B-3B	143	524	84	156	31	1	21	97	1	.298
Major League Totals	4 Yrs.			366	1261	176	355	66	5	52	207	2	.282
	Division Series												
2000 Chicago .............A.L.			1B	3	9	1	0	0	0	0	0	0	.000

a Traded to Cincinnati Reds with pitcher Dennis Reyes for pitcher Jeff Shaw, July 4, 1998.
b Traded to Chicago White Sox for outfielder Mike Cameron, November 11, 1998.

KOSKIE, CORDEL LEONARD (COREY)
Born, Anola, Manitoba, Canada, June 28, 1973.
Bats Left. Throws Right. Height, 6 feet, 3 inches. Weight, 215 pounds.

Year	Club	Lea	Pos	G	AB	R	H	2B	3B	HR	RBI	SB	Avg
1994 Elizabethton ....Appal.			3B	34	107	13	25	2	1	3	10	0	.234
1995 Ft. Wayne ....Midwest			3B	123	462	64	143	37	5	16	78	2	.310
1996 Ft. Myers a ....Fla.St.			3B	95	338	43	88	19	4	9	55	1	.260
1997 New Britain ....Eastern			3B	131	437	88	125	26	6	23	79	9	.286
1998 Salt Lake .............P.C.			3B	135	505	91	152	32	5	26	105	15	.301
1998 Minnesota ............A.L.			3B	11	29	2	4	0	0	1	2	0	.138
1999 Minnesota ............A.L.			3B-OF	117	342	42	106	21	0	11	58	4	.310
2000 Minnesota ............A.L.			3B	146	474	79	142	32	4	9	65	5	.300
Major League Totals	3 Yrs.			274	845	123	252	53	4	21	125	9	.298

a On disabled list from May 10 to May 28 and June 25 to July 4, 1996.

KOTSAY, MARK STEVEN
Born, Woodier, California, December 2, 1975.
Bats Left. Throws Left. Height, 6 feet. Weight, 180 pounds.

Year	Club	Lea	Pos	G	AB	R	H	2B	3B	HR	RBI	SB	Avg
1996 Kane County ......Midwest			OF	17	60	16	17	5	0	2	8	3	.283
1997 Florida .............N.L.			OF	14	52	5	10	1	1	0	4	3	.192

Year	Club	Lea	Pos	G	AB	R	H	2B	3B	HR	RBI	SB	Avg
1997 Portland	.........Eastern		OF	114	438	103	134	27	2	20	77	17	.306
1998 Florida	.............N.L.		OF-1B	154	578	72	161	25	7	11	68	10	.279
1999 Florida	.............N.L.		OF-1B	148	495	57	134	23	9	8	50	7	.271
2000 Florida	.............N.L.		OF-1B	152	530	87	158	31	5	12	57	19	.298
Major League Totals			4 Yrs.	468	1655	221	463	80	22	31	179	39	.280

KREUTER, CHAD MICHAEL

Born, Marin County, California, August 16, 1964.
Bats Both. Throws Right. Height, 6 feet, 2 inches. Weight, 195 pounds.

Year	Club	Lea	Pos	G	AB	R	H	2B	3B	HR	RBI	SB	Avg
1985 Burlington a	.......Midwest		C	69	199	25	53	10	0	4	26	3	.266
1986 Salem	...........Carolina		C	125	387	55	85	21	2	6	49	5	.220
1987 Charlotte	......Fla. St.		C	85	281	36	61	18	1	9	40	1	.217
1988 Tulsa	..............Texas		C	108	358	46	95	24	6	3	51	2	.265
1988 Texas	.............A.L.		C	16	51	3	14	2	1	1	5	0	.275
1989 Oklahoma City	.......A.A.		C	26	87	10	22	3	0	0	6	1	.253
1989 Texas	.............A.L.		C	87	158	16	24	3	0	5	9	0	.152
1990 Oklahoma City b	.....A.A.		C	92	291	41	65	17	1	7	35	0	.223
1990 Texas	.............A.L.		C	22	22	2	1	1	0	0	2	0	.045
1991 Oklahoma City	.......A.A.		C	24	70	14	19	6	0	1	12	2	.271
1991 Texas	.............A.L.		C	3	4	0	0	0	0	0	0	0	.000
1991 Tulsa c	............Texas		C	42	128	23	30	5	1	2	10	1	.234
1992 Detroit	...............A.L.		C	67	190	22	48	9	0	2	16	0	.253
1993 Detroit	..............A.L.		C-1B	119	374	59	107	23	3	15	51	2	.286
1994 Detroit d	.............A.L.		C-1B-OF	65	170	17	38	8	0	1	19	0	.224
1995 Tacoma	.............P.C.		C	15	48	6	14	5	0	1	11	0	.292
1995 Seattle e-f-g	.........A.L.		C	26	75	12	17	5	0	1	8	0	.227
1996 Chicago h-i	...........A.L.		C-1B	46	114	14	25	8	0	3	18	0	.219
1997 Chicago-Anaheim j-k-l	..A.L.		C-1B	89	255	25	59	9	2	5	21	0	.231
1998 Chicago-Anaheim m-n	.A.L.		C	96	252	27	63	10	1	2	33	1	.250
1999 Kansas City o	.........A.L.		C	107	324	31	73	15	0	5	35	0	.225
2000 Los Angeles	..........N.L.		C	80	212	32	56	13	0	6	28	1	.264
Major League Totals			13 Yrs.	823	2201	260	525	106	7	46	245	4	.239

a Batted righthanded only from 1985 through 1987 season.
b Batted righthanded only during 1990 season.
c Became free agent, October 15; signed with Detroit Tigers organization, December 17, 1991.
d Not offered 1995 contract, December 23, 1994.
e Signed with Seattle Mariners, April 8, 1995.
f On disabled list from June 19 to July 6, 1995.
g Became free agent, October 15, 1995; signed with Chicago White Sox organization, December 11, 1995.
h On disabled list from July 20 to September 30, 1996.
i Filed for free agency, October 14, 1996. Resigned with Chicago White Sox.
j Traded to Anaheim Angels with outfielder Tony Phillips for pitcher Chuck McElroy and catcher Jorge Fabregas, May 18, 1997.
k Filed for free agency, November 3, 1997.
l Signed with Florida Marlins organization, December 22, 1997.
m Sold to Anaheim, September 18, 1998.
n Filed for free agency, October 26, 1998. Signed with Kansas City Royals, December 14, 1998.
o Filed for free agency, October 29, 1999. Signed with Los Angeles Dodgers organization, January 20, 2000.

LAMB, MICHAEL ROBERT (MIKE)

Born, West Covina, California, August 9, 1975.
Bats Left. Throws Right. Height, 6 feet, 1 inch. Weight, 185 pounds.

Year	Club	Lea	Pos	G	AB	R	H	2B	3B	HR	RBI	SB	Avg
1997 Pulaski	...........Appal.		3B	60	233	59	78	19	3	9	47	7	.335
1998 Charlotte	...........Fla.St.		3B-1B	135	536	83	162	35	3	9	93	18	.302
1999 Oklahoma	............P.C.		3B	2	2	0	1	0	0	0	0	0	.500
1999 Tulsa	...............Texas		3B	137	544	98	176	51	5	21	100	4	.324
2000 Oklahoma	...........P.C.		3B	14	55	8	14	5	1	2	5	2	.255
2000 Texas	...............A.L.		3B	138	493	65	137	25	2	6	47	0	.278

LANKFORD, RAYMOND LEWIS (RAY)

Born, Modesto, California, June 5, 1967.
Bats Left. Throws Left. Height, 5 feet, 11 inches. Weight, 198 pounds.

Year	Club	Lea	Pos	G	AB	R	H	2B	3B	HR	RBI	SB	Avg
1987 Johnson City	........Appal.		OF	66	253	45	78	17	4	3	32	14	.308
1988 Springfield	........Midwest		OF	135	532	90	151	26	*16	11	66	33	.284

Year Club	Lea	Pos	G	AB	R	H	2B	3B	HR	RBI	SB	Avg
1989 Arkansas	Texas	OF	*134	498	98	*158	28	*12	11	98	38	.317
1990 Louisville	A.A.	OF	132	473	61	123	25	8	10	72	29	.260
1990 St. Louis	N.L.	OF	39	126	12	36	10	1	3	12	8	.286
1991 St. Louis	N.L.	OF	151	566	83	142	23	*15	9	69	44	.251
1992 St. Louis	N.L.	OF	153	598	87	175	40	6	20	86	42	.293
1993 St. Louis a	N.L.	OF	127	407	64	97	17	3	7	45	14	.238
1994 St. Louis b	N.L.	OF	109	416	89	111	25	5	19	57	11	.267
1995 St. Louis c	N.L.	OF	132	483	81	134	35	2	25	82	24	.277
1996 St. Louis	N.L.	OF	149	545	100	150	36	8	21	86	35	.275
1997 Pr William	Carolina	OF	4	13	3	4	1	0	0	4	1	.308
1997 St. Louis	N.L.	OF	133	465	94	137	36	3	31	98	21	.295
1998 St. Louis	N.L.	OF	154	533	94	156	37	1	31	105	26	.293
1999 St. Louis e	N.L.	OF	122	422	77	129	32	1	15	63	14	.306
2000 St. Louis	N.L.	OF	128	392	73	99	16	3	26	65	5	.253
Major League Totals	11 Yrs.		1397	4953	854	1366	307	48	207	768	244	.276
Division Series												
1996 St. Louis	N.L.	OF	1	2	1	1	0	0	0	0	0	.500
2000 St. Louis	N.L.	OF	3	10	2	2	1	0	0	3	0	.200
Division Series Totals			4	12	3	3	1	0	0	3	0	.250
Championship Series												
2000 St. Louis	N.L.	OF	5	12	1	4	1	0	0	1	0	.333

a On disabled list from June 24 to July 9, 1993.
b Declared restricted free agent under Major League Baseball implemented labor proposal, December 23, 1994.
c Re-signed with St. Louis Cardinals, May 18, 1995.
d On disabled list from April 1 to April 22, 1997.
e On disabled list from March 26 to April 24, 1999.

LANSING, MICHAEL THOMAS (MIKE)
Born, Rawlins, Wyoming, April 3, 1968.
Bats Right. Throws Right. Height, 6 feet. Weight, 180 pounds.

Year Club	Lea	Pos	G	AB	R	H	2B	3B	HR	RBI	SB	Avg
1990 Miami	Fla. St.	SS	61	207	20	50	5	2	2	11	15	.242
1991 Miami a	Fla. St.	SS-2B	104	384	54	110	20	7	6	55	29	.286
1992 Harrisburg	Eastern	SS	128	483	66	135	20	6	6	54	46	.280
1993 Montreal	N.L.	3B-SS-2B	141	491	64	141	29	1	3	45	23	.287
1994 Montreal	N.L.	2B-3B-SS	106	394	44	105	21	2	5	35	12	.266
1995 Montreal b	N.L.	2B-SS	127	467	47	119	30	2	10	62	27	.255
1996 Montreal	N.L.	2B-SS	159	641	99	183	40	2	11	53	23	.285
1997 Montreal c	N.L.	2B	144	572	86	161	45	2	20	70	11	.281
1998 Colorado	N.L.	2B-3B	153	584	73	161	39	2	12	66	10	.276
1999 Colorado d	N.L.	2B	35	145	24	45	9	0	4	15	2	.310
2000 Colorado	N.L.	2B	90	365	62	94	14	6	11	47	8	.258
2000 Boston e	A.L.	2B-3B	49	139	10	27	4	0	0	13	0	.194
Major League Totals	8 Yrs.		1004	3798	509	1036	231	17	76	406	116	.273

a Purchased by Montreal Expos from independent Miami Miracle, September 18, 1991.
b On disabled list from May 31 to June 15, 1995.
c Traded to Colorado Rockies for pitcher Jake Westbrook, pitcher John Nicholson and outfielder Mike Hamlin, November 18, 1997.
d On disabled list from May 21 to October 13, 1999.
e Traded to Boston Red Sox with pitcher Rolando Arrojo and pitcher Rick Croushore for pitcher Brian Rose, pitcher John Wasdin, pitcher Jeff Taglienti and infielder Jeff Frye, July 27, 2000.

LARKIN, BARRY LOUIS
Born, Cincinnati, Ohio, April 28, 1964.
Bats Right. Throws Right. Height, 6 feet. Weight, 196 pounds.

Year Club	Lea	Pos	G	AB	R	H	2B	3B	HR	RBI	SB	Avg
1985 Vermont	Eastern	SS	72	255	42	68	13	2	1	31	0	.267
1986 Denver	A.A.	SS-2B	103	413	67	136	31	10	10	51	19	.329
1986 Cincinnati	N.L.	SS-2B	41	159	27	45	4	3	3	19	8	.283
1987 Cincinnati a	N.L.	SS	125	439	64	107	16	2	12	43	21	.244
1988 Cincinnati	N.L.	SS	151	588	91	174	32	5	12	56	40	.296
1989 Nashville	A.A.	SS	2	5	2	5	1	0	0	0	0	1.000
1989 Cincinnati b	N.L.	SS	97	325	47	111	14	4	4	36	10	.342
1990 Cincinnati	N.L.	SS	158	614	85	185	25	6	7	67	30	.301
1991 Cincinnati c	N.L.	SS	123	464	88	140	27	4	20	69	24	.302
1992 Cincinnati d	N.L.	SS	140	533	76	162	32	6	12	78	15	.304
1993 Cincinnati e	N.L.	SS	100	384	57	121	20	3	8	51	14	.315

Year	Club	Lea	Pos	G	AB	R	H	2B	3B	HR	RBI	SB	Avg
1994 Cincinnati	N.L.		SS	110	427	78	119	23	5	9	52	26	.279
1995 Cincinnati f	N.L.		SS	131	496	98	158	29	6	15	66	51	.319
1996 Cincinnati	N.L.		SS	152	517	117	154	32	4	33	89	36	.298
1997 Cincinnati g	N.L.		SS	73	224	34	71	17	3	4	20	14	.317
1998 Cincinnati h	N.L.		SS	145	538	93	166	34	10	17	72	26	.309
1999 Cincinnati	N.L.		SS	161	583	108	171	30	4	12	75	30	.293
2000 Cincinnati i	N.L.		SS	102	396	71	124	26	5	11	41	14	.313
Major League Totals			15 Yrs.	1809	6687	1134	2008	361	70	179	834	359	.300
Division Series													
1995 Cincinnati	N.L.		SS	3	13	2	5	0	0	0	1	4	.385
Championship Series													
1990 Cincinnati	N.L.		SS	6	23	5	6	2	0	0	1	3	.261
1995 Cincinnati	N.L.		SS	4	18	1	7	2	1	0	0	1	.389
Championship Series Totals				10	41	6	13	4	1	0	1	4	.317
World Series Record													
1990 Cincinnati	N.L.		SS	4	17	3	6	1	1	0	1	0	.353

a On disabled list from April 13 to May 2, 1987.
b On disabled list from July 13 to September 1, 1989.
c On disabled list from May 18 to June 4, 1991.
d On disabled list from April 19 to May 8, 1992.
e On disabled list from August 5 to end of 1993 season.
f Selected Most Valuable Player in National League for 1995.
g On disabled list from June 17 to August 2 and September 1 to September 29, 1997.
h On disabled list from March 31 to April 7, 1998.
i On disabled list from April 22 to May 15, 2000.

LAWTON, MATTHEW

Born, Gulfport, Mississippi, November 3, 1971.
Bats Left. Throws Right. Height, 5 feet, 9 inches. Weight, 180 pounds.

Year	Club	Lea	Pos	G	AB	R	H	2B	3B	HR	RBI	SB	Avg
1992 Twins	Gulf Coast		2B	53	173	39	45	8	3	2	26	20	.260
1993 Ft. Wayne	Midwest		DH-OF	111	340	50	97	21	3	9	38	23	.285
1994 Ft. Myers	Fla. St.		OF	122	446	79	134	30	1	7	51	42	.300
1995 New Britain	Eastern		OF	114	412	75	111	19	5	13	54	26	.269
1995 Minnesota	A.L.		OF	21	60	11	19	4	1	1	12	1	.317
1996 Salt Lake	P.C.		OF	53	212	40	63	16	1	7	33	2	.297
1996 Minnesota	A.L.		OF	79	252	34	65	7	1	6	42	4	.258
1997 Minnesota	A.L.		OF	142	460	74	114	29	3	14	60	7	.248
1998 Minnesota	A.L.		OF	152	557	91	155	36	6	21	77	16	.278
1999 Ft.Myers	Fla.St.		OF	4	14	3	8	1	0	0	2	1	.571
1999 Twins	Gulf Coast		OF	1	4	0	1	0	0	0	1	0	.250
1999 Minnesota a	A.L.		OF	118	406	58	105	18	0	7	54	26	.259
2000 Minnesota	A.L.		OF	156	561	84	171	44	2	13	88	23	.305
Major League Totals			6 Yrs.	668	2296	352	629	138	13	62	333	77	.274

a On disabled list from June 9 to July 18, 1999.

LEDEE, RICARDO ALBERTO (RICKY)

Born, Ponce, Puerto Rico, November 22, 1973.
Bats Left. Throws Right. Height, 6 feet, 2 inches. Weight, 190 pounds.

Year	Club	Lea	Pos	G	AB	R	H	2B	3B	HR	RBI	SB	Avg
1990 Yankees	Gulf Coast		OF	19	37	5	4	2	0	0	1	2	.108
1991 Yankees	Gulf Coast		OF	47	165	22	44	6	2	0	18	3	.267
1992 Yankees	Gulf Coast		OF	52	179	25	41	9	2	2	23	1	.229
1993 Oneonta	N.Y.-Penn.		OF	52	192	32	49	7	6	8	20	7	.255
1994 Greensboro	So.Atl.		OF	134	484	87	121	23	9	22	71	10	.250
1995 Greensboro	So.Atl.		OF	89	335	65	90	16	6	14	49	10	.269
1996 Norwich	Eastern		OF	39	137	27	50	11	1	8	37	2	.365
1996 Columbus a	Int.		OF	96	358	79	101	22	6	21	64	6	.282
1997 Yankees	Gulf Coast		DH-OF	7	21	3	7	1	0	0	2	0	.333
1997 Columbus b	Int.		OF	43	170	38	52	12	1	10	39	4	.306
1998 Columbus	Int.		OF	96	360	70	102	21	1	19	41	7	.283
1998 New York	A.L.		OF	42	79	13	19	5	2	1	12	3	.241
1999 Columbus	Int.		OF	30	115	18	29	7	1	4	15	4	.252
1999 New York	A.L.		OF	88	250	45	69	13	5	9	40	4	.276
2000 N.Y.-Cleveland-Texas c-d-e	A.L.		OF	137	467	59	110	19	5	13	77	13	.236
Major League Totals			3 Yrs.	267	796	117	198	37	12	23	129	20	.249
Division Series													
1999 New York	A.L.		OF	3	11	1	3	2	0	0	2	0	.273

Year	Club	Lea	Pos	G	AB	R	H	2B	3B	HR	RBI	SB	Avg
Championship Series													
1998 New York ...........A.L.			OF-DH	3	5	0	0	0	0	0	0	0	.000
1999 New York ...........A.L.			OF	3	8	2	2	0	0	1	4	0	.250
Championship Series Totals				6	13	2	2	0	0	1	4	0	.154
World Series Record													
1998 New York ...........A.L.			OF	4	10	1	6	3	0	0	4	0	.600
1999 New York ...........A.L.			OF	3	10	0	2	1	0	0	1	0	.200
World Series Totals				7	20	1	8	4	0	0	5	0	.400

a On disabled list from April 6 to May 27, 1996.
b On disabled list from May 5 to May 16 and May 22 to August 4, 1997.
c Traded to Cleveland Indians with player to be named later for outfielder David Justice, June 29, 2000.
d Cleveland Indians received pitcher Zach Day to complete trade, July 24, 2000.
e Traded to Texas Rangers for infielder David Segui, July 28, 2000.

LEE, CARLOS

Born, Aguadulce, Panama, June 20, 1976.
Bats Right. Throws Right. Height, 6 feet, 2 inches. Weight, 200 pounds.

Year	Club	Lea	Pos	G	AB	R	H	2B	3B	HR	RBI	SB	Avg
1994 White Sox ....Gulf Coast			3B	29	56	6	7	1	0	0	1	0	.125
1995 Hickory ....So.Atl.			3B-SS	63	218	18	54	9	1	4	30	1	.248
1995 Bristol ....Appal.			3B-1B	67	269	43	93	17	1	7	45	17	.346
1996 Hickory ....So.Atl.			3B-1B	119	480	65	150	23	6	8	70	18	.313
1997 Winston-Sal ......Carolina			3B	139	546	81	173	50	4	17	82	11	.317
1998 Birmingham ....Southern			3B	138	549	77	166	33	2	21	106	11	.302
1999 Charlotte ....Int.			3B	25	94	16	33	5	0	4	20	2	.351
1999 Chicago ............A.L.			OF-1B	127	492	66	144	32	2	16	84	4	.293
2000 Chicago ............A.L.			OF	152	572	107	172	29	2	24	92	13	.301
Major League Totals	2 Yrs.			279	1064	173	316	61	4	40	176	17	.297
Division Series													
2000 Chicago .............A.L.			OF	3	11	0	1	1	0	0	1	0	.091

LEE, DERREK LEON

Born, Sacramento, California, September 6, 1975.
Bats Right. Throws Right. Height, 6 feet, 5 inches. Weight, 205 pounds.

Year	Club	Lea	Pos	G	AB	R	H	2B	3B	HR	RBI	SB	Avg
1993 Padres ....Arizona			1B	15	52	11	17	1	1	2	5	4	.327
1993 Rancho Cuca ....California			1B	20	73	13	20	5	1	1	10	0	.274
1994 Rancho Cuca ....California			3B-1B	126	442	66	118	19	2	8	53	18	.267
1995 Rancho Cuca ....California			1B	128	502	82	151	25	2	23	95	14	.301
1995 Memphis ....Southern			1B	2	9	0	1	0	0	0	1	0	.111
1996 Memphis ....Southern			1B-3B	134	500	98	140	39	2	34	104	13	.280
1997 Las Vegas ...........P.C.			1B	124	468	85	152	29	2	13	64	17	.325
1997 San Diego ...........N.L.			1B	22	54	9	14	3	0	1	4	0	.259
1998 Florida ............N.L.			1B	141	454	62	106	29	1	17	74	5	.233
1999 Calgary ............P.C.			1B	89	339	60	96	20	1	19	73	3	.283
1999 Florida ............N.L.			1B	70	218	21	45	9	1	5	20	2	.206
2000 Florida ............N.L.			1B	158	477	70	134	18	3	28	70	0	.281
Major League Totals	4 Yrs.			391	1203	162	299	59	5	51	168	7	.249

LEE, TRAVIS REYNOLDS

Born, San Diego, California, May 26, 1975.
Bats Left. Throws Right. Height, 6 feet, 3 inches. Weight, 205 pounds.

Year	Club	Lea	Pos	G	AB	R	H	2B	3B	HR	RBI	SB	Avg
1997 High Desert ......California			1B	61	226	63	82	18	1	18	63	5	.363
1997 Tucson .............P.C.			1B-OF	59	227	42	68	16	2	14	46	2	.300
1998 Arizona a ...........N.L.			1B	146	562	71	151	20	2	22	72	8	.269
1999 Arizona b ...........N.L.			1B-OF	120	375	57	89	16	2	9	50	17	.237
2000 El Paso ....Texas			1B	3	10	0	2	0	0	0	0	0	.200
2000 Tucson .............P.C.			1B	7	30	4	11	4	0	0	3	1	.367
2000 Arizona-Philadelphia c-d .N.L.			1B-OF	128	404	53	95	24	1	9	54	8	.235
Major League Totals	3 Yrs.			394	1341	181	335	60	5	40	176	33	.250

a On disabled list from July 25 to August 9, 1998.
b On disabled list from August 15 to September 10, 1999.
c On disabled list from May 25 to June 8, 2000.
d Traded to Philadelphia Phillies with pitcher Omar Daal, pitcher Vicente Padilla and pitcher Nelson Figueroa for pitcher Curt Schilling, July 26, 2000.

LEWIS, DARREN JOEL
Born, Berkeley, California, August 28, 1967.
Bats Right. Throws Right. Height, 6 feet. Weight, 189 pounds.

Year	Club	Lea	Pos	G	AB	R	H	2B	3B	HR	RBI	SB	Avg
1988 Scottsdale Athletics	. . . .	Ariz.	OF	5	15	8	5	3	0	0	4	4	.333
1988 Madison	. . . .	Midwest	OF	60	199	38	49	4	1	0	11	20	.246
1989 Modesto	. . . .	California	OF	129	503	74	150	23	5	4	39	27	.298
1989 Huntsville	. . . .	Southern	OF	9	31	7	10	1	1	1	7	0	.323
1990 Huntsville	. . . .	Southern	OF	71	284	52	84	11	3	3	23	21	.296
1990 Tacoma	. . . .	P.C.	OF	60	247	32	72	5	2	2	26	16	.291
1990 Oakland a	. . . .	A.L.	OF	25	35	4	8	0	0	0	1	2	.229
1991 Phoenix	. . . .	P.C.	OF	81	315	63	107	12	10	2	52	32	.340
1991 San Francisco	. . . . . .	N.L.	OF	72	222	41	55	5	3	1	15	13	.248
1992 Phoenix	. . . .	P.C.	OF	42	158	22	36	5	2	0	6	9	.228
1992 San Francisco	. . . . .	N.L.	OF	100	320	38	74	8	1	1	18	28	.231
1993 San Francisco b	. . . . . .	N.L.	OF	136	522	84	132	17	7	2	48	46	.253
1994 San Francisco	. . . . .	N.L.	OF	114	451	70	116	15	*9	4	29	30	.257
1995 San Francisco-Cin. c-d-e	.	N.L.	OF	132	472	66	118	13	3	1	24	32	.250
1996 Chicago	. . . .	A.L.	OF	141	337	55	77	12	2	4	53	21	.228
1997 Chicago f	. . . .	A.L.	OF	81	77	15	18	1	0	0	5	11	.234
1997 Los Angeles g-h	. . . . . .	N.L.	OF	26	77	7	23	3	1	1	10	3	.299
1998 Boston	. . . .	A.L.	OF	155	585	95	157	25	3	8	63	29	.268
1999 Boston	. . . .	A.L.	OF	135	470	63	113	14	6	2	40	16	.240
2000 GC Red Sox	. . . . .	Gulf Coast	OF	2	6	0	1	0	0	0	1	1	.167
2000 Boston i	. . . .	A.L.	OF	97	270	44	65	12	0	2	17	10	.241
Major League Totals	. . . .		11 Yrs.	1214	3838	582	956	125	35	26	323	241	.249
Division Series													
1995 Cincinnati	. . . .	N.L.	OF	3	3	0	0	0	0	0	0	0	.000
1998 Boston	. . . .	A.L.	OF	4	14	4	5	2	0	0	0	1	.357
1999 Boston	. . . .	A.L.	OF	4	16	5	6	1	0	0	2	1	.375
Division Series Totals	. . . .			11	33	9	11	3	0	0	2	2	.333
Championship Series													
1995 Cincinnati	. . . .	N.L.	OF	2	1	0	0	0	0	0	0	0	.000
1999 Boston	. . . .	A.L.	OF	5	17	2	2	1	0	0	1	1	.188
Championship Series Totals	. . . . . .			7	18	2	2	1	0	0	1	1	.111

a Traded to San Francisco Giants with player to be named for infielder Ernest Riles, December 4; San Francisco acquired pitcher Pedro Pena to complete trade, December 17, 1990.

b On disabled list from August 21 to September 4, 1993.

c Traded to Cincinnati Reds with pitcher Mark Portugal and pitcher Dave Burba for outfielder Deion Sanders, pitcher John Roper, pitcher Ricky Pickett, pitcher Scott Service and infielder David McCarty, July 21, 1995.

d Waived by Cincinnati Reds, December 1, 1995; claimed on waivers by Texas Rangers, December 6, 1995.

e Waiver claim rejected, became unrestricted free agent, December 11, 1995; signed with Chicago White Sox, December 12, 1995.

f Traded to Los Angeles Dodgers for player to be named later, August 27, 1997. Chicago White Sox received infielder Chad Fonville to complete trade, September 2, 1997.

g Filed for free agency, October 27, 1997.

h Signed as free agent with Boston Red Sox, December 23, 1997.

i On disabled list from June 29 to July 13, 2000.

LEWIS, MARK DAVID
Born, Hamilton, Ohio, November 30, 1969.
Bats Right. Throws Right. Height, 6 feet, 1 inch. Weight, 190 pounds.

Year	Club	Lea	Pos	G	AB	R	H	2B	3B	HR	RBI	SB	Avg
1988 Burlington	. . . .	Appal.	SS	61	227	39	60	13	1	7	43	14	.264
1989 Kinston a	. . . .	Carolina	SS	93	349	50	94	16	3	1	32	17	.269
1989 Canton	. . . .	Eastern	SS	7	25	4	5	1	0	0	1	0	.200
1990 Canton	. . . .	Eastern	SS	102	390	55	106	19	3	10	60	8	.272
1990 Colorado Springs	. . . . .	P.C.	SS	34	124	17	38	8	1	1	21	2	.306
1991 Colorado Springs	. . . . .	P.C.	SS-2B	46	179	29	50	10	3	2	31	3	.279
1991 Cleveland	. . . .	A.L.	2B-SS	84	314	29	83	15	1	0	30	2	.264
1992 Cleveland	. . . .	A.L.	SS-3B	122	413	44	109	21	0	5	30	4	.264
1993 Charlotte	. . . .	Int.	SS	126	507	93	144	30	4	17	67	9	.284
1993 Cleveland	. . . .	A.L.	SS	14	52	6	13	2	0	1	5	3	.250
1994 Charlotte	. . . .	Int.	SS-3B-3B	86	328	56	85	16	1	8	34	2	.259
1994 Cleveland b	. . . . . .	A.L.	SS-3B-2B	20	73	6	15	5	0	1	8	1	.205
1995 Cincinnati	. . . .	N.L.	3B-2B-SS	81	171	25	58	13	1	3	30	0	.339
1996 Detroit c	. . . .	A.L.	2B	145	545	69	147	30	3	11	55	6	.270
1997 San Francisco d-e-f	. . .	N.L.	3B-2B	118	341	50	91	14	6	10	42	3	.267
1998 Philadelphia g	. . . .	N.L.	2B	142	518	52	129	21	2	9	54	3	.249

Year Club	Lea	Pos	G	AB	R	H	2B	3B	HR	RBI	SB	Avg
1999 Cincinnati h ...........N.L.		3B-2B	88	173	18	44	16	0	6	28	0	.254
2000 Cincinnati ...........N.L.		3B	11	19	1	2	1	0	0	3	0	.105
2000 Baltimore i-j-k ........A.L.		3B-2B-SS	71	163	19	44	17	0	2	21	7	.270
Major League Totals		10 Yrs.	896	2782	319	735	155	13	48	306	29	.264
Division Series												
1995 Cincinnati ...........N.L.		3B	2	2	2	1	0	0	1	5	0	.500
1997 San Francisco .........N.L.		2B	1	5	0	3	0	0	0	1	0	.600
Division Series Totals			3	7	2	4	0	0	1	6	0	.571
Championship Series												
1995 Cincinnati ...........N.L.		3B	2	4	0	1	0	0	0	0	0	.250

a On disabled list from May 29 to June 20, 1989.
b Traded to Cincinnati Reds for infielder/outfielder Tim Costo, December 14, 1994.
c Traded to San Francisco Giants for 1B Jesus Ibarra, December 16, 1996.
d On disabled list from April 1 to April 13, 1997.
e San Francisco declined to offer contract, December 20, 1997.
f Signed with Philadelphia Phillies, December 23, 1997.
g Filed for free agency, October 26, 1998. Signed with Cincinnati Reds, December 12, 1998.
h Filed for free agency, October 29, 1999, re-signed with Cincinnati Reds, November 16, 1999.
i Claimed on waivers by Baltimore Orioles, April 25, 2000.
j On disabled list from July 21 to August 5, 2000.
k Filed for free agency, November 1, 2000.

LEYRITZ, JAMES JOSEPH (JIM)
Born, Lakewood, Ohio, December 27, 1963.
Bats Right. Throws Right. Height, 6 feet. Weight, 195 pounds.

Year Club	Lea	Pos	G	AB	R	H	2B	3B	HR	RBI	SB	Avg
1986 Oneonta a ...N.Y.-Penn.		C	23	91	12	33	3	1	4	15	1	.363
1986 Ft. Lauderdale ..Fla. St.		C	12	34	3	10	1	1	0	1	0	.294
1987 Ft. Lauderdale ...Fla. St.		C	102	374	48	115	22	0	6	51	2	.307
1988 Albany ....Eastern		C-3B	112	382	40	92	18	3	5	50	3	.241
1989 Albany ....Eastern		C-OF	114	375	53	118	18	2	10	66	2	*.315
1990 Columbus ....Int.		3B	59	204	36	59	11	1	8	32	4	.289
1990 New York .........A.L.		3B-OF-C	92	303	28	78	13	1	5	25	2	.257
1991 Columbus b ....Int.		C-3B-2B-SS	79	270	50	72	24	1	11	48	1	.267
1991 New York .........A.L.		3B-C-1B	32	77	8	14	3	0	0	4	0	.182
1992 New York A.L.C-1B-3B-OF-2B			63	144	17	37	6	0	7	26	0	.257
1993 New York .........A.L.		1B-OF-C	95	259	43	80	14	0	14	53	0	.309
1994 New York .........A.L.		C-1B	75	249	47	66	12	0	17	58	0	.265
1995 New York .........A.L.		C-1B	77	264	37	71	12	0	7	37	1	.269
1996 New York c .......A.L.		C-3B-1B	88	265	23	70	10	0	7	40	2	.264
1997 Ana.-Tex. d-e .....A.L.		C-1B	121	379	58	105	11	0	11	64	2	.277
1998 Boston .........A.L.		DH-C-1B	52	129	17	37	6	0	8	24	0	.287
1998 San Diego f ......N.L.		C-1B-3B-OF	62	143	17	38	10	0	4	18	0	.266
1999 San Diego g ......N.L.		C-1B-3B	50	134	17	32	5	0	8	21	0	.239
1999 Rancho Cucamonga												
California		DH	1	4	0	0	0	0	0	0	0	.000
1999 Las Vegas .......P.C.		1B	2	8	0	0	0	0	0	0	0	.000
1999 New York h .......A.L.		DH-1B-C-3B	31	66	8	15	4	1	0	5	0	.227
2000 New York ........A.L.		DH-C-1B	24	55	2	12	0	0	1	4	0	.218
2000 Los Angeles i-j ....N.L.		1B-OF-C	41	60	3	12	1	0	1	8	0	.200
Major League Totals		11 Yrs.	903	2527	325	667	107	2	90	387	7	.264
Division Series												
1995 New York .........A.L.		C	2	7	1	1	0	0	1	2	0	.143
1996 New York .........A.L.		C	2	3	0	0	0	0	0	0	0	.000
1998 San Diego ........N.L.		1B-C	4	10	3	4	0	0	3	5	0	.400
1999 New York .........A.L.		DH	2	2	0	0	0	0	0	1	0	.000
Division Series Totals			10	22	4	5	0	0	4	9	0	.227
Championship Series												
1996 New York .........A.L.		C-OF	3	8	1	2	0	0	1	2	0	.250
1998 San Diego .........N.L.		1B-C	5	12	1	2	0	0	1	4	0	.167
Championship Series Totals .			8	20	2	4	0	0	2	6	0	.200
World Series												
1996 New York .........A.L.		C	4	8	1	3	0	0	1	3	1	.375
1998 San Diego .........N.L.		1B-C-DH	4	10	0	0	0	0	0	0	0	.000
1999 New York .........A.L.		DH	2	1	1	1	0	0	1	2	0	1.000
World Series Totals			10	19	2	4	0	0	2	5	1	.211

a Batted left and right from 1986 through 1987 season.
b Suspended by New York Yankees organization from August 11 to August 15, 1991.

c Traded to California Angels for players to be named later, December 5, 1996.
d Traded to Texas Rangers with player to be named later for pitcher Ken Hill, July 29, 1997. Texas Rangers received infielder Rob Sasser to complete trade, October 31, 1997.
e Traded to Boston Red Sox with outfielder Damon Buford for pitchers Aaron Sele and catcher Bill Haselman and Mark Brandenburg, November 6, 1997.
f Traded to San Diego Padres for pitcher Carlos Reyes, catcher Mandy Romero and pitcher Dario Veras, June 21, 1998.
g On disabled list from June 23 to July 30, 1999.
h Traded to New York Yankees for pitcher Geraldo Padua, July 31, 1999.
i Traded to Los Angeles Dodgers for infielder Jose Vizcaino and cash, June 20, 2000.
j Filed for free agency, November 1, 2000.

LIEBERTHAL, MICHAEL SCOTT (MIKE)

Born, Glendale, California, January 18, 1972.
Bats Right. Throws Right. Height, 6 feet. Weight, 179 pounds.

Year Club	Lea	Pos	G	AB	R	H	2B	3B	HR	RBI	SB	Avg
1990 Martinsville	Appal.	C	49	184	26	42	9	0	4	22	2	.228
1991 Spartanburg	So. Atl.	C	72	243	34	74	17	0	0	31	1	.305
1991 Clearwater	Fla. St.	C	16	52	7	15	2	0	0	7	0	.288
1992 Reading	Eastern	C	86	309	30	88	16	1	2	37	4	.285
1992 Scranton a	Int.	C	16	45	4	9	1	0	0	4	0	.200
1993 Scranton	Int.	C	112	382	35	100	17	0	7	40	2	.262
1994 Scranton	Int.	C	84	296	23	69	16	0	1	32	1	.233
1994 Philadelphia	N.L.	C	24	79	6	21	3	1	1	5	0	.266
1995 Scranton-WB	Int.	C-3B	85	278	44	78	20	2	6	42	1	.281
1995 Philadelphia	N.L.	C	16	47	1	12	2	0	0	4	0	.255
1996 Philadelphia b	N.L.	C	50	166	21	42	8	0	7	23	0	.253
1997 Philadelphia	N.L.	C	134	455	59	112	27	1	20	77	3	.246
1998 Philadelphia c	N.L.	C	86	313	39	80	15	3	8	45	2	.256
1999 Philadelphia	N.L.	C	145	510	84	153	33	1	31	96	0	.300
2000 Philadelphia d	N.L.	C	108	389	55	108	30	0	15	71	2	.278
Major League Totals		7 Yrs.	563	1959	265	528	118	6	82	321	7	.270

a On disabled list from August 31 to end of 1992 season.
b On disabled list from August 22 to September 30, 1996.
c On disabled list from July 24 to September 2, 1998.
d On disabled list from July 18 to August 3 and September 11 to October 5, 2000.

LOCKHART, KEITH VIRGIL

Born, Whittier, California, November 10, 1964.
Bats Left. Throws Right. Height, 5 feet, 10 inches. Weight, 170 pounds.

Year Club	Lea	Pos	G	AB	R	H	2B	3B	HR	RBI	SB	Avg
1986 Billings	Pioneer	2B-3B	53	202	51	70	11	3	7	31	4	.347
1986 Cedar Rapids	Midwest	2B-3B	13	42	4	8	2	0	0	1	1	.190
1987 Cedar Rapids	Midwest	3B-2B	140	511	101	160	37	5	23	84	20	.313
1988 Chattanooga	Southern	3B-2B	139	515	74	137	27	3	12	67	7	.266
1989 Nashville	A.A.	2B	131	479	77	128	21	6	14	58	4	.267
1990 Nashville	A.A.	2B-3B-OF	126	431	48	112	25	4	9	63	8	.260
1991 Nashville	A.A.	3B-2B-OF	116	411	53	107	25	3	8	36	3	.260
1992 Tacoma	P.C.	2B-3B-SS	107	363	44	101	25	3	5	37	5	.278
1993 Louisville	A.A.	3B-2B-OF	132	467	66	140	24	3	13	68	3	.300
1994 San Diego	N.L.	3B-2B-SS-OF	27	43	4	9	0	0	2	6	1	.209
1994 Las Vegas a	P.C.	OF-SS-2B-3B	89	331	61	106	15	5	7	43	3	.320
1995 Omaha	A.A.	3B	44	148	24	56	7	1	5	19	1	.378
1995 Kansas City	A.L.	2B-3B	94	274	41	88	19	3	6	33	8	.321
1996 Kansas City	A.L.	2B-3B	138	433	49	118	33	3	7	55	11	.273
1997 Atlanta b-c	N.L.	2B-3B	96	147	25	41	5	3	6	32	2	.279
1998 Atlanta	N.L.	2B-3B	109	366	50	94	21	0	9	37	2	.257
1999 Atlanta	N.L.	2B-3B	108	161	20	42	3	1	1	21	3	.261
2000 Atlanta	N.L.	2B-3B	113	275	32	73	12	3	2	32	4	.265
Major League Totals		7 Yrs.	685	1699	221	465	93	13	33	216	29	.274
Division Series												
1997 Atlanta	N.L.	2B	2	6	0	0	0	0	0	0	0	.000
1998 Atlanta	N.L.	2B	3	12	2	4	0	0	0	0	0	.333
1999 Atlanta	N.L.	2B	3	1	0	0	0	0	0	0	0	.000
2000 Atlanta	N.L.	2B	3	8	0	1	0	0	0	0	0	.125
Division Series Totals			11	27	2	5	0	0	0	0	0	.185
Championship Series												
1997 Atlanta	N.L.	2B	5	16	4	8	1	1	0	3	0	.500
1998 Atlanta	N.L.	2B	6	17	2	4	1	1	0	0	0	.235
1999 Atlanta	N.L.	2B	3	5	0	2	0	1	0	1	0	.400

Year	Club	Lea	Pos	G	AB	R	H	2B	3B	HR	RBI	SB	Avg
Championship Series Totals				14	38	6	14	2	3	0	4	0	.368
World Series Record													
1999 Atlanta	.N.L.		2B-DH	4	7	1	1	0	0	0	0	0	.143

a Signed with Kansas City Royals, November 14, 1994.
b Traded to Atlanta Braves with outfielder Michael Tucker for outfielder Jermaine Dye and pitcher Jamie Walker, March 27, 1997.
c On disabled list from August 6 to August 22, 1997.

LOFTON, KENNETH
Born, East Chicago, Indiana, May 31, 1967.
Bats Left. Throws Left. Height, 6 feet. Weight, 180 pounds.

Year	Club	Lea	Pos	G	AB	R	H	2B	3B	HR	RBI	SB	Avg
1988 Auburn	.N.Y.-Penn.		OF	48	187	23	40	6	1	1	14	26	.214
1989 Auburn	.N.Y.-Penn.		OF	34	110	21	29	3	1	0	8	26	.264
1989 Asheville	.So. Atl.		OF	22	82	14	27	2	0	1	9	14	.329
1990 Osceola	.Fla. St.		OF	124	481	98	*159	15	5	2	35	62	.331
1991 Tucson	.P.C.		OF	130	545	93	*168	19	*17	2	50	40	.308
1991 Houston a	.N.L.		OF	20	74	9	15	1	0	0	0	2	.203
1992 Cleveland	.A.L.		OF	148	576	96	164	15	8	5	42	*66	.285
1993 Cleveland	.A.L.		OF	148	569	116	185	28	8	1	42	*70	.325
1994 Cleveland	.A.L.		OF	112	459	105	*160	32	9	12	57	*60	.349
1995 Cleveland b	.A.L.		OF	118	481	93	149	22	*13	7	53	*54	.310
1996 Cleveland	.A.L.		OF	154	*662	132	210	35	4	14	67	75	.317
1997 Atlanta c-d-e-f	.N.L.		OF	122	493	90	164	20	6	5	48	27	.333
1998 Cleveland	.A.L.		OF	154	600	101	169	31	6	12	64	54	.282
1999 Cleveland g	.A.L.		OF	120	465	110	140	28	6	7	39	25	.301
2000 Cleveland h	.A.L.		OF	137	543	107	151	23	5	15	73	30	.278
Major League Totals		10 Yrs.		1233	4922	959	1507	235	65	78	485	463	.306
Division Series													
1995 Cleveland	.A.L.		OF	3	13	1	2	0	0	0	0	0	.154
1996 Cleveland	.A.L.		OF	4	18	3	3	0	0	0	1	5	.167
1997 Atlanta	.N.L.		OF	3	13	2	2	1	0	0	0	0	.154
1998 Cleveland	.A.L.		OF	4	16	5	6	1	0	2	4	2	.475
1999 Cleveland	.A.L.		OF	5	16	5	2	1	0	0	1	2	.125
Division Series Totals				19	76	16	15	3	0	2	6	9	.197
Championship Series													
1995 Cleveland	.A.L.		OF	6	24	4	11	0	2	0	3	5	.458
1997 Atlanta	.N.L.		OF	6	27	3	5	0	1	0	1	1	.185
1998 Cleveland	.A.L.		OF	6	27	2	5	1	0	1	3	1	.185
Championship Series Totals				18	78	9	21	1	3	1	7	7	.269
World Series Record													
1995 Cleveland	.A.L.		OF	6	25	6	5	1	0	0	0	6	.200

a Traded to Cleveland Indians with infielder Dave Rohde for pitcher Willie Blair and catcher Ed Taubensee, December 10, 1991.
b On disabled list from July 17 to August 1, 1995.
c Traded to Atlanta Braves with pitcher Alan Embree for outfielder Marquis Grissom and outfielder David Justice, March 25, 1997.
d On disabled list from June 18 to July 5 and July 6 to July 28, 1997.
e Filed for free agency, October 28, 1997.
f Signed as free agent with Cleveland Indians, December 8, 1997.
g On disabled list from July 28 to August 14 and August 17 to September 1, 1999.
h On disabled list from April 27 to May 11, 2000.

LONG, TERRENCE DEON
Born, Montgomery, Alabama, February 29, 1976.
Bats Left. Throws Right. Height, 6 feet, 1 inch. Weight, 190 pounds.

Year	Club	Lea	Pos	G	AB	R	H	2B	3B	HR	RBI	SB	Avg
1994 Kingsport	.Appal.		OF-1B	60	215	39	50	9	2	12	39	9	.233
1995 Columbia	.So.Atl.		OF	55	178	27	35	1	2	2	13	8	.197
1995 Pittsfield	.N.Y.-Penn.		OF	51	187	24	48	9	4	4	31	11	.257
1996 Columbia a	.So.Atl.		OF	123	473	66	136	26	9	12	78	32	.288
1997 St. Lucie	.Fla.St.		OF	126	470	52	118	29	7	8	61	24	.251
1998 Binghamton	.Eastern		OF	130	455	69	135	20	10	16	58	23	.297
1999 Norfolk	.Int.		OF	78	304	41	99	20	4	7	47	14	.326
1999 Vancouver	.P.C.		OF	40	154	16	38	6	2	2	21	7	.247
1999 New York b	.N.L.		H	3	3	0	0	0	0	0	0	0	.000
2000 Sacramento	.P.C.		OF	15	60	11	24	6	0	3	15	0	.400

Year Club	Lea	Pos	G	AB	R	H	2B	3B	HR	RBI	SB	Avg
2000 Oakland .............A.L.		OF	138	584	104	168	34	4	18	80	5	.288
Major League Totals		2 Yrs.	141	587	104	168	34	4	18	80	5	.286
Division Series												
2000 Oakland .............A.L.		OF	5	19	2	3	0	0	1	1	0	.158

a On disabled list from May 15 to May 27, 1996.
b Traded to Oakland Athletics with pitcher Leoner Vasquez for pitcher Kenny Rogers, July 23, 1999.

LOPEZ, JAVIER TORRES (JAVY)
Born, Ponce, Puerto Rico, November 5, 1970.
Bats Right. Throws Right. Height, 6 feet, 3 inches. Weight, 185 pounds.

Year Club	Lea	Pos	G	AB	R	H	2B	3B	HR	RBI	SB	Avg
1988 Bradenton Braves ....Gulf C.		C	31	94	8	18	4	0	1	9	1	.191
1989 Pulaski ....Appal.		C	51	153	27	40	8	1	3	27	3	.261
1990 Burlington ....Midwest		C	116	422	48	112	17	3	11	55	0	.265
1991 Durham ....Carolina		C	113	384	43	94	14	2	11	51	10	.245
1992 Greenville ....Southern		C	115	442	64	142	28	3	16	69	7	.321
1992 Atlanta ...........N.L.		C	9	16	3	6	2	0	0	2	0	.375
1993 Richmond ....Int.		C	100	380	56	116	23	2	17	74	1	.305
1993 Atlanta ...........N.L.		C	8	16	1	6	1	1	1	2	0	.375
1994 Atlanta ...........N.L.		C	80	277	27	68	9	0	13	35	0	.245
1995 Atlanta ...........N.L.		C	100	333	37	105	11	4	14	51	0	.315
1996 Atlanta ...........N.L.		C	138	489	56	138	19	1	23	69	1	.282
1997 Atlanta a .........N.L.		C	123	414	52	122	28	1	23	68	1	.295
1998 Atlanta ...........N.L.		C	133	489	73	139	21	1	34	106	5	.284
1999 Atlanta b .........N.L.		C	65	246	34	78	18	1	11	45	0	.317
2000 Atlanta ...........N.L.		C	134	481	60	138	21	1	24	89	0	.287
Major League Totals		9 Yrs.	790	2761	343	800	130	10	143	467	7	.290
Division Series												
1995 Atlanta ...........N.L.		C	3	9	0	4	0	0	0	3	0	.444
1996 Atlanta ...........N.L.		C	2	7	1	2	0	0	1	1	1	.286
1997 Atlanta ...........N.L.		C	2	7	3	2	2	0	0	1	0	.286
1998 Atlanta ...........N.L.		C	2	7	1	2	0	0	1	1	0	.286
2000 Atlanta ...........N.L.		C	3	11	0	1	0	0	0	0	0	.091
Division Series Totals			12	41	5	11	2	0	2	6	1	.268
Championship Series												
1992 Atlanta ...........N.L.		C	1	1	0	0	0	0	0	0	0	.000
1995 Atlanta ...........N.L.		C	3	14	2	5	1	0	1	3	0	.357
1996 Atlanta ...........N.L.		C	7	24	8	13	5	0	2	6	1	.542
1997 Atlanta ...........N.L.		C	5	17	0	1	1	0	0	2	0	.059
1998 Atlanta ...........N.L.		C	6	20	2	6	0	0	1	1	0	.300
Championship Series Totals			22	76	12	25	7	0	4	12	1	.329
World Series Record												
1995 Atlanta ...........N.L.		C	6	17	1	3	2	0	1	3	0	.176
1996 Atlanta ...........N.L.		C	6	21	3	4	0	0	0	1	0	.190
World Series Totals			12	38	4	7	2	0	1	4	0	.184

a On disabled list from July 6 to July 22, 1997.
b On disabled list from June 21 to July 15 and July 25 to November 1, 1999.

LOPEZ, LUIS MANUEL
Born Cidra, Puerto Rico, September 4, 1970.
Bats Both. Throws Right. Height, 5 feet, 11 inches. Weight, 175 pounds.

Year Club	Lea	Pos	G	AB	R	H	2B	3B	HR	RBI	SB	Avg
1988 Spokane ....Northwest		SS	70	312	50	95	13	1	0	35	14	.304
1989 Chston-Sc ......So.Atl.		SS	127	460	50	102	15	1	1	29	12	.222
1990 Riverside .....California		SS	14	46	5	17	3	1	1	4	4	.370
1991 Wichita ....Texas		2B-SS	125	452	43	121	17	1	1	41	6	.268
1992 Las Vegas ........P.C.		SS-OF	120	395	44	92	8	8	1	31	6	.233
1993 Las Vegas ........P.C.		SS-2B	131	491	52	150	36	6	6	58	8	.305
1993 San Diego ........N.L.		2B	17	43	1	5	1	0	0	1	0	.116
1994 Las Vegas ........P.C.		2B	12	49	2	10	2	2	0	6	0	.204
1994 San Diego ........N.L.		SS-2B-3B	77	235	29	65	16	1	2	20	3	.277
1996 Las Vegas a .....P.C.		2B-SS	18	68	4	14	3	0	1	12	0	.206
1996 San Diego ........N.L.		SS-2B-3B	63	139	10	25	3	0	2	11	0	.180
1997 Norfolk b-c ....Int.		SS-2B	48	203	32	67	12	1	4	19	2	.330
1997 New York ........N.L.		SS-2B-3B	78	178	19	48	12	1	1	19	2	.270

Year Club	Lea	Pos	G	AB	R	H	2B	3B	HR	RBI	SB	Avg
1998 New York .........N.L.		2B-SS-3B-OF	117	266	37	67	13	2	2	22	2	.252
1999 New York d ......N.L.		SS-2B-3B	68	104	11	22	4	0	2	13	1	.212
2000 Milwaukee ........N.L.		SS-2B-3B	78	201	24	53	14	0	6	27	1	.264
Major League Totals	7 Yrs.		498	1166	131	285	63	4	15	113	9	.244
Division Series												
1996 San Diego		PR	1	0	0	0	0	0	0	0	0	.000

a On disabled list from April 1 to April 18 and July 31 to September 1, 1996.
b Traded to Houston Astros for pitcher Sean Runyan, March 16, 1997.
c Traded to New York Mets for infielder Tim Bogar, March 31, 1997.
d Traded to Milwaukee Brewers for pitcher Bill Pulsipher, January 21, 2000.

LORETTA, MARK DAVID
Born, Santa Monica, California, August 14, 1971.
Bats Right. Throws Right. Height, 6 feet. Weight, 175 pounds.

Year Club	Lea	Pos	G	AB	R	H	2B	3B	HR	RBI	SB	Avg
1993 Helena ....Pioneer		SS	6	28	5	9	1	0	1	8	0	.321
1993 Stockton .....California		SS-3B	53	201	36	73	4	1	4	31	8	.363
1994 El Paso ....Texas		SS-P	77	302	50	95	13	6	0	38	8	.315
1994 New Orleans ......A.A.		SS-2B	43	138	16	29	7	0	1	14	2	.210
1995 New Orleans ......A.A.		SS-3B-2B	127	479	48	137	22	5	7	79	8	.286
1995 Milwaukee ........A.L.		SS-2B	19	50	13	13	3	0	1	3	1	.260
1996 New Orleans ......A.A.		SS	19	71	10	18	5	1	0	11	1	.254
1996 Milwaukee ........A.L.		2B-3B-SS	73	154	20	43	3	0	1	13	2	.279
1997 Milwaukee ........A.L.		2B-SS-1B-3B	132	418	56	120	17	5	5	47	5	.287
1998 Milwaukee ........N.L.		1B-SS-3B-2B	140	434	55	137	29	0	6	54	9	.316
1999 Milwaukee ........N.L.		SS-1B-2B-3B	153	587	93	170	34	5	5	67	4	.290
2000 Indianapolis ....Int.		SS	10	25	6	6	1	0	0	5	0	.240
2000 Milwaukee a ......N.L.		SS-2B	91	352	49	99	21	1	7	40	0	.281
Major League Totals	6 Yrs.		608	1995	286	582	107	11	25	224	21	.292

a On disabled list from June 3 to August 17, 2000.

LOWELL, MICHAEL AVERETT (MIKE)
Born, San Juan, Puerto Rico, February 24, 1974.
Bats Right. Throws Right. Height, 6 feet, 4 inches. Weight, 195 pounds.

Year Club	Lea	Pos	G	AB	R	H	2B	3B	HR	RBI	SB	Avg
1995 Oneonta .....N.Y.-Penn.		3B	72	281	36	73	18	0	1	27	3	.260
1996 Greensboro .....So.Atl.		3B-SS-P	113	433	58	122	33	0	8	64	10	.282
1996 Tampa ....Fla.St.		3B	24	78	8	22	5	0	0	11	1	.282
1997 Norwich ....Eastern		3B-SS	78	285	60	98	17	0	15	47	2	.344
1997 Columbus ....Int.		3B-SS	57	210	36	58	13	1	15	45	2	.276
1998 Columbus ....Int.		3B-1B-SS	126	510	79	155	34	3	26	99	4	.304
1998 New York .........A.L.		3B	8	15	1	4	0	0	0	0	0	.267
1999 Calgary ..........P.C.		3B	24	83	11	26	3	0	2	9	0	.313
1999 Florida a-b .......N.L.		3B	97	308	32	78	15	0	12	47	0	.253
2000 Florida c .........N.L.		3B	140	508	73	137	38	0	22	91	4	.270
Major League Totals	3 Yrs.		245	831	106	219	53	0	34	138	4	.264

a Traded to Florida Marlins for pitcher Ed Yarnall, pitcher Mark Johnson and pitcher Todd Noel, February 1, 1999.
b On disabled list from March 26 to May 29, 1999.
c On disabled list from May 13 to May 28, 2000.

LUGO, JULIO CESAR
Born, Barahona, Dominican Republic, November 16, 1975.
Bats Right. Throws Right. Height, 6 feet. Weight, 165 pounds.

Year Club	Lea	Pos	G	AB	R	H	2B	3B	HR	RBI	SB	Avg
1995 Auburn .........N.Y.-Penn.		2B-SS-OF	59	230	36	67	6	3	1	16	17	.291
1996 Quad City ....Midwest		2B-3B-2B	101	393	60	116	18	2	10	50	24	.295
1997 Kissimmee ....Fla.St.		SS-2B-3B	125	505	89	135	22	14	7	61	35	.267
1998 Kissimmee ....Fla.St.		SS	128	509	81	154	20	14	7	62	51	.303
1999 Jackson a ....Texas		SS	116	445	77	142	24	5	10	42	25	.319
2000 New Orleans ..........P.C.		2B	24	101	22	33	4	1	3	12	12	.327
2000 Houston ............N.L.		SS-2B-OF	116	420	78	119	22	5	10	40	22	.283

a On disabled list from July 21 to 29, 1999.

MABRY, JOHN STEVEN
Born, Wilmington, Delaware, October 17, 1970.
Bats Left. Throws Right. Height, 6 feet, 4 inches. Weight, 195 pounds.

Year	Club	Lea	Pos	G	AB	R	H	2B	3B	HR	RBI	SB	Avg
1991 Hamilton	....N.Y.-Penn.		OF	49	187	25	58	11	0	1	31	9	.310
1991 Savannah	...So. Atl.		OF	22	86	10	20	6	1	0	8	1	.233
1992 Springfield	....Midwest		OF	115	438	63	115	13	6	11	57	2	.263
1993 Arkansas	.......Texas		OF	136	528	68	153	32	2	16	72	7	.290
1993 Louisville	.........A.A.		OF	4	7	0	1	0	0	0	1	0	.143
1994 Louisville	.........A.A.		OF	122	477	76	125	30	1	15	68	2	.262
1994 St. Louis	.........N.L.		OF	6	23	2	7	3	0	0	3	0	.304
1995 Louisville	.........A.A.		OF	4	12	0	1	0	0	0	0	0	.083
1995 St. Louis	.........N.L.		1B-OF	129	388	35	119	21	1	5	41	0	.307
1996 St. Louis	.........N.L.		1B-OF	151	543	63	161	30	2	13	74	3	.297
1997 St. Louis a	.........N.L.		OF-1B-3B	116	388	40	110	19	0	5	36	0	.284
1998 St. Louis b	........N.L.		OF-3B-1B	142	377	41	94	22	0	9	46	0	.249
1999 Seattle c	.........A.L.		OF-3B-1B	87	262	34	64	14	0	9	33	2	.244
2000 Tacoma	..........P.C.		1B	4	14	1	3	1	0	0	1	0	.214
2000 Seattle	..........A.L.		3B-OF-1B-P	48	103	18	25	5	0	1	7	0	.243
2000 San Diego d-e-f	....N.L.		OF-1B	48	123	17	28	8	0	7	25	0	.228
Major League Totals	....		7 Yrs.	727	2207	250	608	122	3	49	265	5	.275
Division Series													
1996 St. Louis	.........N.L.		1B	3	10	1	3	0	1	0	1	0	.300
Championship Series													
1996 St. Louis	.........N.L.		1B-OF	7	23	1	6	0	0	0	0	0	.261

a On disabled list from August 20 to September 24, 1997.
b Not offered 1999 contract, December 21, 1998. Signed with Seattle Mariners, December 30, 1998.
c On disabled list from August 14 to November 12, 1999.
d On disabled list from April 22 to May 11, 2000.
e Traded to San Diego Padres with pitcher Tom Davey for outfielder Al Martin, July 31, 2000.
f Filed for free agency, October 30, 2000, signed with St. Louis Cardinals organization, January 5, 2001.

MACIAS (SALAZAR), JOSE PRADO
Born, Panama City, Panama, January 25, 1974.
Bats Both. Throws Right. Height, 5 feet, 10 inches. Weight, 173 pounds.

Year	Club	Lea	Pos	G	AB	R	H	2B	3B	HR	RBI	SB	Avg
1992 Montreal	....Domincan		OF	61	198	58	58	5	1	2	23	41	.293
1993 Montreal	....Domincan		OF	64	211	60	66	12	1	4	26	38	.313
1994 Expos	......Gulf Coast		OF-2B-3B-P	31	104	23	28	8	2	1	6	4	.269
1995 Vermont	...N.Y.-Penn.		OF-2B-3B	53	176	24	42	4	2	0	9	11	.239
1996 Delmarva a	...So.Atl.		OF-2B-3B	116	369	64	91	13	4	1	33	38	.247
1997 Lakeland	......Fla.St.		2B-OF	122	424	54	113	18	2	2	21	10	.267
1998 Jacksnville	...Southern		2B	128	511	82	156	28	10	12	71	6	.305
1999 Toledo	...........Int.		2B	112	438	44	107	18	8	2	36	10	.244
1999 Detroit	..........A.L.		2B	5	4	2	1	0	0	1	2	0	.250
2000 Toledo	...........Int.		OF	33	130	19	30	5	0	0	8	2	.231
2000 Detroit	..........A.L.		2B-3B-OF-SS	73	173	25	44	3	5	2	24	2	.254
Major League Totals	....		2 Yrs.	78	177	27	45	3	5	3	26	2	.254

a Selected by Detroit Tigers from Montreal Expos in Rule V draft, December 9, 1996.

MAGADAN, DAVID JOSEPH
Born, Tampa, Florida, September 30, 1962.
Bats Left. Throws Right. Height, 6 feet, 3 inches. Weight, 205 pounds.

Year	Club	Lea	Pos	G	AB	R	H	2B	3B	HR	RBI	SB	Avg
1983 Columbia	.......S. Atlantic		1B	64	220	41	74	13	1	3	32	2	.336
1984 Lynchburg a	.......Carolina		1B	112	371	78	130	22	4	0	62	2	*.350
1985 Jackson	.............Texas		3B-1B	134	466	84	144	22	0	0	76	0	.309
1986 Tidewater	.............Int.		3B-1B	133	473	68	147	33	6	1	64	2	.311
1986 New York	.............N.L.		1B	10	18	3	8	0	0	0	3	0	.444
1987 New York b	...........N.L.		3B-1B	85	192	21	61	13	1	3	24	0	.318
1988 New York c	...........N.L.		1B-3B	112	314	39	87	15	0	1	35	0	.277
1989 New York	.............N.L.		1B-3B	127	374	47	107	22	3	4	41	1	.286
1990 New York	.............N.L.		1B-3B	144	451	74	148	28	6	6	72	2	.328
1991 New York	.............N.L.		1B	124	418	58	108	23	0	4	51	1	.258
1992 New York d-e	..........N.L.		3B-1B	99	321	33	91	9	1	3	28	1	.283
1993 Florida f	...............N.L.		3B-1B	66	227	22	65	12	0	4	29	0	.286
1993 Seattle g	...............A.L.		1B-3B	71	228	27	59	11	0	1	21	2	.259
1994 Florida h-i	............N.L.		3B-1B	74	211	30	58	7	0	1	17	0	.275
1995 Houston j-k	...........N.L.		3B-1B	127	348	44	109	24	0	2	51	2	.313

Year	Club	Lea	Pos	G	AB	R	H	2B	3B	HR	RBI	SB	Avg
1996 Daytona ....Fla. St.			3B	7	20	5	6	1	0	0	3	0	.300
1996 Iowa l ..............A.A.			3B	3	9	0	2	1	0	0	1	0	.222
1996 Chicago m-n .........N.L.			3B-1B	78	169	23	43	10	0	3	17	0	.254
1997 Oakland o-p .........A.L.			3B-1B	128	271	38	82	10	1	4	30	1	.303
1998 Oakland q-r .........A.L.			3B-1B	35	109	12	35	8	0	1	13	0	.321
1999 San Diego ..........N.L.			3B-1B	116	248	20	68	12	1	2	30	1	.274
2000 San Diego s-t ........N.L.			3B-1B-SS	95	132	13	36	7	0	2	21	0	.273
Major League Totals			15 Yrs.	1491	4031	504	1165	211	13	41	483	11	.289
Championship Series													
1988 New York ...........N.L.			PH	3	3	0	0	0	0	0	0	0	.000

a On disabled list from August 7 to September 10, 1984.
b On disabled list from March 29 to April 17, 1987.
c On disabled list from May 5 to May 20, 1988.
d On disabled list from August 9 to end of 1992 season.
e Filed for free agency, October 27; signed with Florida Marlins organization, December 8, 1992.
f Traded to Seattle Mariners for outfielder Henry Cotto and pitcher Jeff Darwin, June 27, 1993.
g Traded to Florida Marlins with cash for pitcher Jeff Darwin, November 9, 1993.
h On disabled list from March 29 to April 13 and July 21 to end of 1994 season.
i Filed for free agency, October 17, 1994.
j Signed with Houston Astros, April 13, 1995.
k Filed for free agency, October 30, 1995. Signed with Chicago Cubs, December 26, 1995.
l On disabled list from April 1 to April 15 and April 15 to June 1, 1996.
m Filed for free agency, November 18, 1996.
n Signed with Oakland A's organization, January 23, 1997.
o Filed for free agency, October 27, 1997.
p Re-signed with Oakland Athletics, November 12, 1997.
q On disabled list from May 16 to September 28, 1998.
r Filed for free agency, October 29, 1998. Signed with San Diego Padres, December 21, 1998.
s On disabled list from April 11 to April 29, 2000.
t Filed for free agency, October 27, 2000, re-signed with San Diego Padres, January 5, 2001.

MAGEE, WENDELL ERROL
Born, Hattiesburg, Mississippi, August 3, 1972.
Bats Right. Throws Right. Height, 6 feet. Weight, 225 pounds.

Year	Club	Lea	Pos	G	AB	R	H	2B	3B	HR	RBI	SB	Avg
1994 Batavia .........N.Y.-Penn.			OF	63	229	42	64	12	4	2	35	10	.279
1995 Clearwater ....Fla.St.			OF	96	388	67	137	24	5	6	46	7	.353
1995 Reading ....Eastern			OF	39	136	17	40	9	1	3	21	3	.294
1996 Reading ....Eastern			OF	71	270	38	79	15	5	6	30	10	.293
1996 Scranton-WB ....Int.			OF	44	155	31	44	9	2	10	32	3	.284
1996 Philadelphia ..........N.L.			OF	38	142	9	29	7	0	2	14	0	.204
1997 Philadelphia ..........N.L.			OF	38	115	7	23	4	0	1	9	1	.200
1997 Scranton-WB ....Int.			OF	83	294	39	72	20	1	10	39	4	.245
1998 Scranton-WB ....Int.			OF	126	507	86	147	30	7	24	72	7	.290
1998 Philadelphia ..........N.L.			OF	20	75	9	22	6	1	1	11	0	.293
1999 Scranton-WB ....Int.			OF	142	566	95	160	34	2	20	79	10	.283
1999 Philadelphia ..........N.L.			OF	12	14	4	5	1	0	2	5	0	.357
2000 Toledo ....Int.			OF	2	7	1	4	1	0	0	1	0	.571
2000 Detroit a-b .........A.L.			OF	91	186	31	51	4	2	7	31	1	.274
Major League Totals			5 Yrs.	199	532	60	130	22	3	13	70	2	.244

a Traded to Detroit Tigers for pitcher Bobby Sismondo, March 10, 2000.
b On disabled list from May 7 to May 28, 2000.

MARTIN, ALBERT LEE
Born, West Covina, California, November 24, 1967.
Bats Left. Throws Left. Height, 6 feet, 2 inches. Weight, 210 pounds.

Year	Club	Lea	Pos	G	AB	R	H	2B	3B	HR	RBI	SB	Avg
1985 Bradenton Braves ....Gulf C.			1B-OF	40	138	16	32	3	0	0	9	1	.232
1986 Idaho Falls ....Pioneer			OF-1B	63	242	39	80	17	*6	4	44	11	.331
1986 Sumter ....So. Atl.			1B	44	156	23	38	5	0	1	24	6	.244
1987 Sumter ....So. Atl.			OF-1B	117	375	59	95	18	5	12	64	27	.253
1988 Burlington ....Midwest			OF	123	480	69	134	21	3	7	42	40	.279
1989 Durham ....Carolina			OF	128	457	*84	124	26	3	9	48	27	.271
1990 Greenville ....Southern			OF	133	455	64	110	17	5	10	50	20	.242
1991 Greenville ....Southern			OF	86	301	38	73	13	3	7	38	19	.243
1991 Richmond a ....Int.			OF	44	151	20	42	11	1	5	18	11	.278
1992 Buffalo ..............A.A.			OF	125	420	85	128	16	*15	20	59	20	.305
1992 Pittsburgh ..........N.L.			OF	12	12	1	2	0	1	0	2	0	.167
1993 Pittsburgh ..........N.L.			OF	143	480	85	135	26	8	18	64	16	.281

Year	Club	Lea	Pos	G	AB	R	H	2B	3B	HR	RBI	SB	Avg
1994 Pittsburgh b	N.L.	OF	82	276	48	79	12	4	9	33	15	.286
1995 Pittsburgh	N.L.	OF	124	439	70	124	25	3	13	41	20	.282
1996 Pittsburgh	N.L.	OF	155	630	101	189	40	1	18	72	38	.300
1997 Carolina	Southern	OF	3	9	0	1	0	0	0	0	0	.111
1997 Pittsburgh c	N.L.	OF	113	423	64	123	24	7	13	59	23	.291
1998 Pittsburgh	N.L.	OF	125	440	57	105	15	2	12	47	20	.239
1999 Pittsburgh	N.L.	OF	143	541	97	150	36	8	24	63	20	.277
2000 San Diego	N.L.	OF	93	346	62	106	13	6	11	27	6	.306
2000 Seattle d-e	A.L.	OF	42	134	19	31	2	4	4	9	4	.231
Major League Totals	9 Yrs.	1032	3721	604	1044	193	44	122	417	162	.281		
Division Series													
2000 Seattle	A.L.	PH	1	1	0	0	0	0	0	0	0	.000
Championship Series													
2000 Seattle	A.L.	OF	4	11	2	2	2	0	0	0	0	.181

a Became free agent, October 15; signed with Pittsburgh Pirates organization, November 11, 1991.
b On disabled list from July 11 to end of 1994 season.
c On disabled list from May 22 to June 24, 1997.
d Traded to San Diego Padres for outfielder John Vander Wal, pitcher Jim Sak and pitcher Geraldo Padua, February 23, 2000.
e Traded to Seattle Mariners for infielder John Mabry and pitcher Tom Davey, July 31, 2000.

MARTINEZ, CONSTANTINO (TINO)
Born, Tampa, Florida, December 7, 1967.
Bats Left. Throws Right. Height, 6 feet, 2 inches. Weight, 210 pounds.

Year	Club	Lea	Pos	G	AB	R	H	2B	3B	HR	RBI	SB	Avg
1989 Williamsport	Eastern	1B	*137	*509	51	131	29	2	13	64	7	.257
1990 Calgary	P.C.	1B	128	453	83	145	28	1	17	93	8	.320
1990 Seattle	A.L.	1B	24	68	4	15	4	0	0	5	0	.221
1991 Calgary	P.C.	1B-3B	122	442	94	144	34	5	18	86	3	.326
1991 Seattle	A.L.	1B	36	112	11	23	2	0	4	9	0	.205
1992 Seattle	A.L.	1B	136	460	53	118	19	2	16	66	2	.257
1993 Seattle a	A.L.	1B	109	408	48	108	25	1	17	60	0	.265
1994 Seattle	A.L.	1B	97	329	42	86	21	0	20	61	1	.261
1995 Seattle b	A.L.	1B	141	519	92	152	35	3	31	111	0	.293
1996 New York	A.L.	1B	155	595	82	174	28	0	25	117	2	.292
1997 New York	A.L.	1B	158	594	96	176	31	2	44	141	3	.296
1998 New York	A.L.	1B	142	531	92	149	33	1	28	123	2	.281
1999 New York	A.L.	1B	159	589	95	155	27	2	28	105	3	.263
2000 New York	A.L.	1B	155	569	69	147	37	4	16	91	4	.258
Major League Totals	11 Yrs.	1312	4774	684	1303	262	15	229	889	17	.273		
Division Series													
1995 Seattle	A.L.	1B	5	22	4	9	1	0	1	5	0	.409
1996 New York	A.L.	1B	4	15	3	4	2	0	0	0	0	.267
1997 New York	A.L.	1B	5	18	1	4	1	0	1	4	0	.222
1998 New York	A.L.	1B	3	11	1	3	2	0	0	0	0	.273
1999 New York	A.L.	1B	3	11	2	2	0	0	0	0	0	.182
2000 New York	A.L.	1B	5	19	2	8	2	0	0	4	0	.421
Division Series Totals		25	96	13	30	8	0	2	13	0	.313		
Championship Series													
1995 Seattle	A.L.	1B	6	22	0	3	0	0	0	0	0	.136
1996 New York	A.L.	1B	5	22	3	4	1	0	0	0	0	.182
1998 New York	A.L.	1B	6	19	1	2	1	0	0	1	2	.105
1999 New York	A.L.	1B	5	19	3	5	1	0	1	3	0	.263
2000 New York	A.L.	1B	6	25	5	8	2	0	1	1	0	.320
Championship Series Totals		28	107	13	22	5	0	2	5	2	.206		
World Series													
1996 New York	A.L.	1B	6	11	0	1	0	0	0	0	0	.091
1998 New York	A.L.	1B	4	13	4	5	0	0	1	4	0	.385
1999 New York	A.L.	1B	4	15	3	4	0	0	1	5	0	.267
2000 New York	A.L.	1B	5	22	3	8	1	0	0	2	0	.364
World Series Totals		19	61	10	18	1	0	2	11	0	.295		

a On disabled list from August 13 to end of 1993 season.
b Traded to New York Yankees with pitchers Jeff Nelson and Jim Mecir for infielder Russ Davis and pitcher Sterling Hitchcock, November 7, 1995.

MARTINEZ, DAVID

Born, New York, New York, September 26, 1964.
Bats Left.-Throws Left. Height, 5 feet, 10 inches. Weight, 175 pounds.

Year	Club	Lea	Pos	G	AB	R	H	2B	3B	HR	RBI	SB	Avg
1983 Quad Cities	Midwest		OF	44	119	17	29	6	2	0	10	10	.244
1983 Geneva	N.Y.-Penn.		OF	64	241	35	63	15	2	5	33	16	.261
1984 Quad Cities a	Midwest		OF	12	41	6	9	2	2	0	5	3	.220
1985 Winston-Salem	Carolina		OF	115	386	52	132	14	4	5	54	38	*.342
1986 Iowa	A.A.		OF	83	318	52	92	11	5	5	32	42	.289
1986 Chicago	N.L.		OF	53	108	13	15	1	1	1	7	4	.139
1987 Chicago	N.L.		OF	142	459	70	134	18	8	8	36	16	.292
1988 Chicago-Montreal b	N.L.		OF	138	447	51	114	13	6	6	46	23	.255
1989 Montreal	N.L.		OF	126	361	41	99	16	7	3	27	23	.274
1990 Montreal c	N.L.		OF	118	391	60	109	13	5	11	39	13	.279
1991 Montreal d	N.L.		OF	124	396	47	117	18	5	7	42	16	.295
1992 Cincinnati e	N.L.		OF-1B	135	393	47	100	20	5	3	31	12	.254
1993 Phoenix	P.C.		OF	3	15	4	7	0	0	0	2	1	.467
1993 San Francisco f	N.L.		OF	91	241	28	58	12	1	5	27	6	.241
1994 San Francisco g	N.L.		OF-1B	97	235	23	58	9	3	4	27	3	.247
1995 Chicago h-i-j	A.L.		OF-1B-P	119	303	49	93	16	4	5	37	8	.307
1996 Chicago	A.L.		OF-1B	146	440	85	140	20	8	10	53	15	.318
1997 Chicago k	A.L.		OF-1B	145	504	78	144	16	6	12	55	12	.286
1998 Tampa Bay l-m	A.L.		OF-1B	90	309	31	79	11	0	3	20	8	.256
1999 Tampa Bay	A.L.		OF	143	514	79	146	25	5	6	66	13	.284
2000 Chicago n-o	N.L.		OF-1B	18	54	5	10	1	1	0	1	1	.185
2000 Tampa Bay-Texas-Toronto p-q	A.L.		OF-1B	114	403	55	115	18	4	5	46	7	.285
Major League Totals	15 Yrs.			1799	5558	762	1531	227	69	89	560	180	.275

a On disabled list from April 27 to end of 1984 season.
b Traded to Montreal Expos for outfielder Mitch Webster, July 14, 1988.
c Record of 0-0 in game one as pitcher.
d Traded to Cincinnati Reds with pitcher Scott Ruskin and shortstop Willie Greene for pitchers John Wetteland and Bill Risley, December 11, 1991.
e Filed for free agency, October 27; signed with San Francisco Giants, December 9, 1992.
f On disabled list from April 30 to June 4, 1993.
g Refused assignment to minor leagues and became free agent, October 14, 1994.
h Signed with Chicago White Sox, April 4, 1995.
i Filed for free agency, November 12, 1995.
j Re-signed with Chicago White Sox, November 14, 1995.
k Filed for free agency, October 27, 1997.
l Signed with Tampa Bay Devil Jays, December 4, 1997.
m On disabled list from July 22 to September 28, 1998.
n Traded to Chicago Cubs for pitcher Mark Guthrie and cash, May 12, 2000.
o Traded to Texas Rangers for pitcher Chuck Smith, June 9, 2000.
p Traded to Toronto Blue Jays for player to be named later, August 4, 2000.
q Filed for free agency, October 31, 2000, signed with Atlanta Braves, December 10, 2000.

MARTINEZ, EDGAR

Born, New York, New York, January 2, 1963.
Bats Right. Throws Right. Height, 5 feet, 11 inches. Weight, 190 pounds.

Year	Club	Lea	Pos	G	AB	R	H	2B	3B	HR	RBI	SB	Avg
1983 Bellingham	Northwest		3B	32	104	14	18	1	1	0	5	1	.173
1984 Wausau	Midwest		3B	126	433	72	131	32	2	15	66	11	.303
1985 Chattanooga	Southern		3B	111	357	43	92	15	5	3	47	1	.258
1985 Calgary	P.C.		3B	20	68	8	24	7	1	0	14	1	.353
1986 Chattanooga	Southern		3B	132	451	71	119	29	5	6	74	2	.264
1987 Calgary	P.C.		3B	129	438	75	144	31	1	10	66	3	.329
1987 Seattle	A.L.		3B	13	43	6	16	5	2	0	5	0	.372
1988 Calgary	P.C.		3B	95	331	63	120	19	4	8	64	9	*.363
1988 Seattle	A.L.		3B	14	32	0	9	4	0	0	5	0	.281
1989 Calgary	P.C.		3B-2B	32	113	30	39	11	0	3	20	2	.345
1989 Seattle	A.L.		3B	65	171	20	41	5	0	2	20	2	.240
1990 Seattle	A.L.		3B	144	487	71	147	27	2	11	49	1	.302
1991 Seattle	A.L.		3B	150	544	98	167	35	1	14	52	0	.307
1992 Seattle	A.L.		3B-1B	135	528	100	181	*46	3	18	73	14	*.343
1993 Jacksonville	Southern		DH	4	14	2	5	0	0	1	3	0	.357
1993 Seattle a	A.L.		DH-3B	42	135	20	32	7	0	4	13	0	.237
1994 Seattle b	A.L.		3B	89	326	47	93	23	1	13	51	6	.285
1995 Seattle	A.L.		DH-3B-1B	*145	511	121	182	*52	0	29	113	4	*.356
1996 Seattle c	A.L.		DH-1B-3B	139	499	121	163	52	2	26	103	3	.327
1997 Seattle	A.L.		DH-1B-3B	155	542	104	179	35	1	28	108	2	.330
1998 Seattle	A.L.		DH-1B	154	556	86	179	46	1	29	102	1	.322
1999 Seattle	A.L.		DH-1B	142	502	86	169	35	1	24	86	7	.337
2000 Seattle	A.L.		DH-1B	153	556	100	180	31	0	37	*145	3	.324

Year	Club	Lea	Pos	G	AB	R	H	2B	3B	HR	RBI	SB	Avg
Major League Totals			14 Yrs.	1540	5432	980	1738	403	14	235	925	43	.320
Division Series													
1995 Seattle		.A.L.	DH	5	21	6	12	3	0	2	10	0	.571
1997 Seattle		.A.L.	DH	4	16	2	3	0	0	2	3	0	.188
2000 Seattle		.A.L.	DH	3	11	2	4	1	0	1	2	0	.364
Division Series Totals			12	48	10	19	4	0	5	15	0	.396
Championship Series													
1995 Seattle		.A.L.	DH	6	23	0	2	0	0	0	0	1	.087
2000 Seattle		.A.L.	DH	6	21	2	5	1	0	1	4	0	.238
Championship Series Totals			12	44	2	7	1	0	1	4	1	.159

a On disabled list from April 3 to May 17, June 15 to July 21, and August 17 to end of 1993 season.
b On disabled list from April 16 to May 6, 1994.
c On disabled list from July 21 to August 12, 1996.

MARTINEZ (MATA), FELIX
Born, Nagua, Dominican Republic, May 18, 1974.
Bats Both. Throws Right. Height, 6 feet. Weight, 168 pounds.

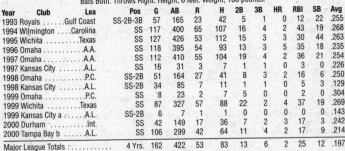

Year	Club	Lea	Pos	G	AB	R	H	2B	3B	HR	RBI	SB	Avg
1993 Royals ......Gulf Coast			SS-2B-3B	57	165	23	42	5	1	0	12	22	.255
1994 Wilmington ....Carolina			SS	117	400	65	107	16	4	2	43	19	.268
1995 Wichita ....Texas			SS	127	426	53	112	15	3	3	30	44	.263
1996 Omaha .........A.A.			SS	118	395	54	93	13	3	5	35	18	.235
1997 Omaha ..........A.A.			SS	112	410	55	104	19	4	2	36	21	.254
1997 Kansas City ......A.L.			SS	16	31	3	7	1	1	0	3	0	.226
1998 Omaha ..........P.C.			SS-2B	51	164	27	41	8	3	2	16	6	.250
1998 Kansas City ......A.L.			SS-2B	34	85	7	11	1	1	0	5	3	.129
1999 Omaha ..........P.C.			SS	8	23	2	7	5	0	0	2	0	.304
1999 Wichita ....Texas			SS	87	327	57	88	22	2	4	37	19	.269
1999 Kansas City a ......A.L.			SS-2B	6	7	1	1	0	0	0	0	0	.143
2000 Durham b ....Int.			SS	42	149	17	36	7	2	3	17	3	.242
2000 Tampa Bay .....A.L.			SS	106	299	42	64	11	4	2	17	9	.214
Major League Totals			4 Yrs.	162	422	53	83	13	6	2	25	12	.197

a Claimed on waivers by Philadelphia Phillies, October 6, 1999.
b Claimed on waivers by Tampa Bay Devil Rays, April 5, 2000.

MARTINEZ, RAMON E.
Born, Philadelphia, Pennsylvania, October 10, 1972.
Bats Right. Throws Right. Height, 6 feet, 1 inch. Weight, 170 pounds.

Year	Club	Lea	Pos	G	AB	R	H	2B	3B	HR	RBI	SB	Avg
1993 Royals ......Gulf Coast			2B-OF	37	97	16	23	5	0	0	9	3	.237
1993 Wilmington ....Carolina			2B-SS	24	75	8	19	4	0	0	6	1	.253
1994 Rockford .....Midwest			2B	6	18	3	5	0	0	0	3	1	.278
1994 Wilmington ....Carolina			2B	90	325	40	87	13	2	2	35	6	.268
1995 Wichita ....Texas			2B-SS	103	393	58	108	20	2	3	51	11	.275
1996 Omaha ..........A.A.			2B	85	320	35	81	12	3	6	41	3	.253
1996 Wichita a ....Texas			2B	26	93	16	32	4	1	1	8	4	.344
1997 Phoenix .........P.C.			2B-SS	18	57	6	16	2	0	1	7	1	.281
1997 Shreveport ......Texas			SS	105	404	72	129	32	4	5	54	4	.319
1998 Fresno ...........P.C.			2B-SS	98	364	58	114	21	2	14	60	0	.313
1998 San Francisco .....N.L.			2B	19	19	4	6	1	0	0	0	0	.316
1999 Fresno ...........P.C.			SS	29	114	13	37	7	1	2	17	2	.325
1999 San Francisco b ...N.L.			2B-SS-3B	61	144	21	38	6	0	5	19	1	.264
2000 San Francisco .....N.L.			SS-2B-1B-3B	88	189	30	57	13	2	6	25	3	.302
Major League Totals			3 Yrs.	168	352	55	101	20	2	11	44	4	.287
Division Series													
2000 San Francisco ......N.L.			2B-SS	2	6	0	2	0	0	0	0	0	.333

a Sent to San Francisco Giants by Kansas City Royals to complete trade in which Royals received pitcher Jamie Brewington, December 9, 1996.
b On disabled list from August 21 to September 5, 1999.

MATHENY, MICHAEL SCOTT (MIKE)
Born, Columbus, Ohio, September 22, 1970.
Bats Right. Throws Right. Height, 6 feet, 3 inches. Weight, 205 pounds.

Year	Club	Lea	Pos	G	AB	R	H	2B	3B	HR	RBI	SB	Avg
1991 Helena ....Pioneer			C	64	253	35	72	14	0	2	34	2	.285
1992 Stockton ....California			C	106	333	42	73	13	2	6	46	2	.219

118

Year	Club	Lea	Pos	G	AB	R	H	2B	3B	HR	RBI	SB	Avg
1993 El Paso	Texas	C	107	339	39	86	21	2	2	28	1	.254
1994 Milwaukee	A.L.	C	28	53	3	12	3	0	1	2	0	.226
1994 New Orleans	A.A.	C-1B	57	177	20	39	10	1	4	21	1	.220
1995 New Orleans	A.A.	C	6	17	3	6	2	0	3	4	0	.353
1995 Milwaukee	A.L.	C	80	166	13	41	9	1	0	21	2	.247
1996 New Orleans	A.A.	C	20	66	3	15	4	0	1	6	1	.227
1996 Milwaukee	A.L.	C	106	313	31	64	15	2	8	46	3	.204
1997 Milwaukee	A.L.	C-1B	123	320	29	78	16	1	4	32	0	.244
1998 Beloit	Midwest	C	2	8	1	2	1	0	0	2	0	.250
1998 Milwaukee a-b	N.L.	C	108	320	24	76	13	0	6	27	1	.237
1999 Toronto c	A.L.	C	57	163	16	35	6	0	3	17	0	.215
2000 St. Louis	N.L.	C-1B	128	417	43	109	22	1	6	47	0	.261
Major League Totals			7 Yrs.	630	1752	159	415	84	5	28	192	6	.237

a On disabled list from June 15 to July 13, 1998.
b Filed for free agency, December 21, 1998, signed with Toronto Blue Jays, December 23, 1998.
c Released by Toronto Blue Jays, November 17, 1999, signed with St. Louis Cardinals December 15, 1999.

MATOS, LUIS D.
Born, Bayamon, Puerto Rico, October 30, 1978.
Bats Right. Throws Right. Height, 6 feet. Weight, 180 pounds.

Year	Club	Lea	Pos	G	AB	R	H	2B	3B	HR	RBI	SB	Avg
1996 Orioles	Gulf Coast	OF	43	130	21	38	2	0	0	13	12	.292
1997 Delmarva	So.Atl.	OF	36	119	10	25	1	2	0	13	8	.210
1997 Bluefield	Appal.	OF	61	240	37	66	7	3	2	35	26	.275
1998 Delmarva	So.Atl.	OF	133	503	73	137	26	6	7	62	42	.272
1998 Bowie	Eastern	OF	5	19	2	5	0	0	1	3	1	.263
1999 Bowie	Eastern	OF	66	283	41	67	11	1	9	36	14	.237
1999 Frederick	Carolina	OF	68	273	40	81	15	1	7	41	27	.297
2000 Rochester	Int.	OF	11	35	2	6	1	0	0	0	2	.171
2000 Bowie	Eastern	OF	50	181	26	49	7	5	2	33	14	.271
2000 Baltimore	A.L.	OF	72	182	21	41	6	3	1	17	13	.225

MATTHEWS, GARY NATHANIEL JR.
Born, San Francisco, California, August 25, 1974.
Bats Both. Throws Right. Height, 6 feet, 3 inches. Weight, 200 pounds.

Year	Club	Lea	Pos	G	AB	R	H	2B	3B	HR	RBI	SB	Avg
1994 Spokane	Northwest	OF-2B	52	191	23	40	6	1	0	18	3	.209
1995 Clinton	Midwest	OF	128	421	57	100	18	4	2	40	28	.238
1996 Rancho Cuca	California	OF	123	435	65	118	21	11	7	54	7	.271
1997 Rancho Cuca	California	OF	69	268	66	81	15	4	8	40	10	.302
1997 Mobile	Southern	OF	28	90	14	22	4	1	2	12	3	.244
1998 Mobile	Southern	OF	72	254	62	78	15	4	7	51	11	.307
1999 Las Vegas	P.C.	OF	121	422	57	108	22	3	9	52	17	.256
1999 San Diego	N.L.	OF	23	36	4	8	0	0	0	7	2	.222
2000 Iowa	P.C.	OF	60	211	27	51	11	3	5	22	6	.242
2000 Chicago a	N.L.	OF	80	158	24	30	1	2	4	14	3	.190
Major League Totals			2 Yrs.	103	194	28	38	1	2	4	21	5	.196

a Traded to Chicago Cubs for pitcher Rodney Myers, March 23, 2000.

MAYNE, BRENT DANEM
Born, Loma Linda, California, April 19, 1968.
Bats Left. Throws Right. Height, 6 feet, 1 inch. Weight, 190 pounds.

Year	Club	Lea	Pos	G	AB	R	H	2B	3B	HR	RBI	SB	Avg
1989 Baseball City a	Fla. St.	C	7	24	5	13	3	1	0	8	0	.542
1990 Memphis	Southern	C	115	412	48	110	16	3	2	61	5	.267
1990 Kansas City	A.L.	C	5	13	2	3	0	0	0	1	0	.231
1991 Kansas City	A.L.	C	85	231	22	58	8	0	3	31	2	.251
1992 Kansas City	A.L.	C-3B	82	213	16	48	10	0	0	18	0	.225
1993 Kansas City	A.L.	C	71	205	22	52	9	1	2	22	3	.254
1994 Kansas City	A.L.	C	46	144	19	37	5	1	2	20	1	.257
1995 Kansas City b	A.L.	C	110	307	23	77	18	1	1	27	0	.251
1996 New York c	N.L.	C	70	99	9	26	6	0	1	6	0	.263
1997 Edmonton	P.C.	C	2	3	0	0	0	0	0	0	0	.000
1997 Oakland d-e	A.L.	C	85	256	29	74	12	0	6	22	1	.289
1998 San Francisco	N.L.	C	94	275	26	75	15	0	3	32	2	.273
1999 San Francisco f	N.L.	C	117	322	39	97	32	0	2	39	2	.301
2000 Colorado	N.L.	C-P	117	335	36	101	21	0	6	64	1	.301
Major League Totals			11 Yrs.	882	2400	243	648	136	3	26	282	12	.270

119

a On disabled list from July 24 to end of 1989 season.
b Traded to New York Mets for outfielder, Al Shirley, December 14, 1995.
c Signed with Seattle Mariners organization, January 11, 1997.
d Filed for free agency, October 30, 1997.
e Signed with San Francisco Giants, November 21, 1997.
f Filed for free agency, October 28, 1999, signed with Colorado Rockies, December 9, 1999.

Mc CARTY, DAVID ANDREW
Born, Houston, Texas, November 23, 1969.
Bats Right. Throws Right. Height, 6 feet, 5 inches. Weight, 215 pounds.

Year	Club	Lea	Pos	G	AB	R	H	2B	3B	HR	RBI	SB	Avg
1991	Visalia	California	OF	15	50	16	19	3	0	3	8	3	.380
1991	Orlando	Southern	OF	28	88	18	23	4	0	3	11	0	.261
1992	Orlando	Southern	OF-1B	129	456	75	124	16	2	18	79	6	.272
1992	Portland	P.C.	OF-1B	7	26	7	13	2	0	1	8	1	.500
1993	Portland	P.C.	OF-1B	40	143	42	55	11	0	8	31	5	.385
1993	Minnesota	A.L.	OF-1B	98	350	36	75	15	2	2	21	2	.214
1994	Minnesota	A.L.	1B-OF	44	131	21	34	8	2	1	12	2	.260
1994	Salt Lake	P.C.	OF-1B	55	186	32	47	9	3	3	19	1	.253
1995	Minnesota	A.L.	1B-OF	25	55	10	12	3	1	0	4	0	.218
1995	Indianapolis	A.A.	1B	37	140	31	47	10	1	8	32	0	.336
1995	Phoenix	P.C.	1B-OF	37	151	31	53	19	2	4	19	1	.351
1995	San Francisco a-b	N.L.	OF-1B	12	20	1	5	1	0	0	2	1	.250
1996	Phoenix	P.C.	OF-1B	6	25	4	10	1	1	1	7	0	.400
1996	San Francisco c	N.L.	1B-OF	91	175	16	38	3	0	6	24	2	.217
1997	Phoenix	P.C.	1B-OF	121	434	85	153	27	5	22	92	9	.353
1998	Tacoma	P.C.	OF-1B	108	398	73	126	30	2	11	52	9	.317
1998	Seattle d-e	A.L.	OF-1B	8	18	1	5	0	0	1	2	1	.278
1999	Toledo f	Int.	1B	132	466	85	125	24	3	31	77	6	.268
2000	Kansas City g	A.L.	1B-OF-SS	103	270	34	75	14	2	12	53	0	.278
Major League Totals			6 Yrs.	381	1019	119	244	44	7	22	118	8	.239

a Traded to Cincinnati Reds for pitcher John Courtright, June 8, 1995.
b Traded to San Francisco Giants with outfielder Deion Sanders, pitcher Ricky Pickett, pitcher Scott Service and pitcher John Roper for outfielder Darren Lewis, pitcher Mark Portugal and pitcher Dave Burba, July 21, 1995.
c On disabled list from June 6 to June 27, 1996.
d Traded to Seattle Mariners for outfielder Jalal Leach and outfielder Scott Smith, January 28, 1998.
e Filed for free agency, September 30, 1998, signed with Detroit Tigers organization, November 25, 1998.
f Filed for free agency, October 15, 1999, signed with Oakland Athletics, November 19, 1999.
g Sold to Kansas City Royals, March 24, 2000.

McEWING, JOSEPH EARL (JOE)
Born, Bristol, Pennsylvania, October 19, 1972.
Bats Right. Throws Right. Height, 5 feet, 10 inches. Weight, 170 pounds.

Year	Club	Lea	Pos	G	AB	R	H	2B	3B	HR	RBI	SB	Avg
1992	Cardinals	Arizona	OF-SS	55	211	55	71	4	2	0	13	23	.336
1993	Savannah	So.Atl.	OF	138	511	94	127	35	1	0	43	22	.249
1994	Madison	Midwest	OF	90	346	58	112	24	2	4	47	18	.324
1994	St. Pete	Fla.St.	OF-2B	50	197	22	49	7	0	1	20	8	.249
1995	St. Pete	Fla.St.	2B-OF	75	281	33	64	13	0	1	23	2	.228
1995	Arkansas	Texas	OF-2B	42	121	16	30	4	0	2	12	3	.248
1996	Arkansas	Texas	OF-2B	106	216	27	45	7	3	2	14	2	.208
1997	Arkansas	Texas	OF-2B-1B	103	263	33	68	6	3	4	35	2	.259
1998	Arkansas	Texas	OF-SS-P	60	223	45	79	21	4	9	46	4	.354
1998	Memphis	P.C.	OF-3B-2B-SS	78	329	52	110	30	7	6	46	11	.334
1998	St. Louis	N.L.	2B-OF	10	20	5	4	1	0	0	1	0	.200
1999	St. Louis	N.L.	2B-OF-3B-1B	152	513	65	141	28	4	9	44	7	.275
2000	Norfolk	Int.	OF	43	171	28	44	10	2	5	18	7	.257
2000	New York a	N.L.	OF-3B-2B-SS	87	153	20	34	14	1	2	19	3	.222
Major League Totals			3 Yrs.	249	686	90	179	43	5	11	64	10	.261
Division Series													
2000	New York	N.L.	OF-3B	4	1	0	1	0	0	0	0	0	1.000
Championship Series													
2000	New York	N.L.	OF-3B	4	0	2	0	0	0	0	0	0	.000
World Series Record													
2000	New York	N.L.	OF	3	1	1	0	0	0	0	0	0	.000

a Traded to New York Mets for pitcher Jesse Orosco, March 18, 2000.

McGRIFF, FREDERICK STANLEY (FRED)

Born, Tampa, Florida, October 31, 1963.
Bats Left. Throws Left. Height, 6 feet, 3 inches. Weight, 215 pounds.

Year	Club	Lea	Pos	G	AB	R	H	2B	3B	HR	RBI	SB	Avg
1981	Bradenton Yankees	Gulf C.	1B	29	81	6	12	2	0	0	9	0	.148
1982	Bradenton Yankees a	Gulf C.	1B	62	217	38.	59	11	1	*9	*41	0	.272
1983	Florence	So. Atl.	1B	33	119	26	37	3	1	7	26	3	.311
1983	Kinston	Carolina	1B	94	350	53	85	14	1	21	57	3	.243
1984	Knoxville	Southern	1B	56	189	29	47	13	2	9	25	0	.249
1984	Syracuse	Int.	1B	70	238	28	56	10	1	13	28	0	.235
1985	Syracuse b	Int.	1B	51	176	19	40	8	2	5	20	0	.227
1986	Syracuse	Int.	1B-OF	133	468	69	121	23	4	19	74	0	.259
1986	Toronto	A.L.	1B	3	5	1	1	0	0	0	0	0	.200
1987	Toronto	A.L.	1B	107	295	58	73	16	0	20	43	3	.247
1988	Toronto	A.L.	1B	154	536	100	151	35	4	34	82	6	.282
1989	Toronto	A.L.	1B	161	551	98	148	27	3	*36	92	7	.269
1990	Toronto c	A.L.	1B	153	557	91	167	21	1	35	88	5	.300
1991	San Diego	N.L.	1B	153	528	84	147	19	1	31	106	4	.278
1992	San Diego d	N.L.	1B	152	531	79	152	30	4	*35	104	8	.286
1993	San Diego-Atlanta e	N.L.	1B	151	557	111	162	29	2	37	101	5	.291
1994	Atlanta	N.L.	1B	113	424	81	135	25	1	34	94	7	.318
1995	Atlanta f-g	N.L.	1B	*144	528	85	148	27	1	27	93	3	.280
1996	Atlanta	N.L.	1B	159	617	81	182	37	1	28	107	7	.295
1997	Atlanta h	N.L.	1B	152	564	77	156	25	1	22	97	5	.277
1998	Tampa Bay	A.L.	1B	151	564	73	160	33	0	19	81	7	.284
1999	Tampa Bay	A.L.	1B	144	529	75	164	30	1	32	104	1	.310
2000	Tampa Bay	A.L.	1B	158	566	82	157	18	0	27	106	2	.277
Major League Totals		15 Yrs.		2055	7352	1176	2103	372	20	417	1298	70	.286

Division Series

Year	Club	Lea	Pos	G	AB	R	H	2B	3B	HR	RBI	SB	Avg
1995	Atlanta	N.L.	1B	4	18	4	6	0	0	2	6	0	.333
1996	Atlanta	N.L.	1B	3	9	1	3	1	0	1	3	0	.333
1997	Atlanta	N.L.	1B	3	9	4	2	0	0	0	1	0	.222
Division Series Totals				10	36	9	11	1	0	3	10	0	.306

Championship Series

Year	Club	Lea	Pos	G	AB	R	H	2B	3B	HR	RBI	SB	Avg
1989	Toronto	A.L.	1B	5	21	1	3	0	0	0	3	0	.143
1993	Atlanta	N.L.	1B	6	23	6	10	2	0	1	4	0	.435
1995	Atlanta	N.L.	1B	4	16	5	7	4	0	0	0	0	.438
1996	Atlanta	N.L.	1B	7	28	6	7	0	1	2	7	0	.250
1997	Atlanta	N.L.	1B	6	21	0	7	1	0	0	4	0	.333
Championship Series Totals				28	109	18	34	7	1	3	18	0	.312

World Series Record

Year	Club	Lea	Pos	G	AB	R	H	2B	3B	HR	RBI	SB	Avg
1995	Atlanta	N.L.	1B	6	23	5	6	2	0	2	3	1	.261
1996	Atlanta	N.L.	1B	6	20	4	6	0	0	2	6	0	.300
World Series Totals				12	43	9	12	2	0	4	9	1	.279

a Traded by New York Yankees to Toronto Blue Jays organization with outfielder Dave Collins and pitcher Mike Morgan for catcher-outfielder Tom Dodd and pitcher Dale Murray, December 9, 1982.
b On disabled list from June 5 to August 14, 1985.
c Traded to San Diego Padres with shortstop Tony Fernandez for outfielder Joe Carter and second baseman Roberto Alomar, December 5, 1990.
d Suspended four games by National League for June 18 mound charging and fighting, June 23 to June 26, 1992.
e Traded to Atlanta Braves for outfielders Melvin Nieves and Vince Moore and pitcher Donnie Elliott, July 18, 1993.
f Filed for free agency, November 12, 1995.
g Re-signed with Atlanta Braves, December 2, 1995.
h Traded to Tampa Bay Devil Rays for player to be named later, November 18, 1997. Atlanta Braves received cash to complete trade, April 1, 1998.

McGWIRE, MARK DAVID

Born, Claremont, California, October 1, 1963.
Bats Right. Throws Right. Height, 6 feet, 5 inches. Weight, 225 pounds.

Year	Club	Lea	Pos	G	AB	R	H	2B	3B	HR	RBI	SB	Avg
1984	Modesto	California	1B	16	55	7	11	3	0	1	1	0	.200
1985	Modesto	California	3B-1B	138	489	95	134	23	3	*24	*106	1	.274
1986	Tacoma	P.C.	3B	78	280	42	89	21	5	13	59	1	.318
1986	Huntsville	Southern	3B	55	195	40	59	15	0	10	53	3	.303
1986	Oakland	A.L.	3B	18	53	10	10	1	0	3	9	0	.189
1987	Oakland a	A.L.	1B-3B-OF	151	557	97	161	28	4	*49	118	1	.289
1988	Oakland	A.L.	1B-OF	155	550	87	143	22	1	32	99	0	.260
1989	Oakland b	A.L.	1B	143	490	74	113	17	0	33	95	1	.231
1990	Oakland	A.L.	1B	156	523	87	123	16	0	39	108	2	.235

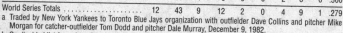

Year	Club	Lea	Pos	G	AB	R	H	2B	3B	HR	RBI	SB	Avg
1991 Oakland	A.L.	1B	154	483	62	97	22	0	22	75	2	.201
1992 Oakland c-d	A.L.	1B	139	467	87	125	22	0	42	104	0	.268
1993 Oakland e	A.L.	1B	27	84	16	28	6	0	9	24	0	.333
1994 Oakland f	A.L.	1B	47	135	26	34	3	0	9	25	0	.252
1995 Oakland g	A.L.	1B	104	317	75	87	13	0	39	90	1	.274
1996 Oakland h	A.L.	1B	130	423	104	132	21	0	*52	113	0	.312
1997 Oakland i	A.L.	1B	105	366	48	104	24	0	34	81	1	.284
1997 St. Louis	N.L.	1B	51	174	38	44	3	0	24	42	2	.253
1998 St. Louis	N.L.	1B	155	509	130	152	21	0	*70	147	1	.299
1999 St. Louis	N.L.	1B	153	521	118	145	21	0	*65	*147	0	.278
2000 St. Louis j	N.L.	1B	89	236	60	72	8	0	32	73	1	.305
Major League Totals		15 Yrs.	1777	5888	1119	1570	248	6	554	1350	12	.267
Division Series												
2000 St. Louis	N.L.	PH	3	2	1	1	0	0	1	1	0	.500
Championship Series												
1988 Oakland	A.L.	1B	4	15	4	5	0	0	1	3	0	.333
1989 Oakland	A.L.	1B	5	18	3	7	1	0	1	3	0	.389
1990 Oakland	A.L.	1B	4	13	2	2	0	0	0	2	0	.154
1992 Oakland	A.L.	1B	6	20	1	3	0	0	1	3	0	.150
2000 St. Louis	N.L.	PH	3	2	0	0	0	0	0	0	0	.000
Championship Series Totals			22	68	10	17	1	0	3	11	0	.250
World Series Record												
1988 Oakland	A.L.	1B	5	17	1	1	0	0	1	1	0	.059
1989 Oakland	A.L.	1B	4	17	0	5	1	0	0	1	0	.294
1990 Oakland	A.L.	1B	4	14	1	3	0	0	0	0	0	.214
World Series Totals			13	48	2	9	1	0	1	2	0	.188

a Selected Rookie of the Year in American League for 1987.
b On disabled list from April 10 to April 26, 1989.
c On disabled list from August 22 to September 11, 1992.
d Filed for free agency, October 26; re-signed with Oakland Athletics, December 24, 1992.
e On disabled list from May 14 to end of 1993 season.
f On disabled list from April 30 to June 18 and August 1 to end of 1994 season.
g On disabled list from July 18 to August 2 and August 5 to August 26, 1995.
h On disabled list from April 1 to April 23, 1996.
i Traded to St. Louis Cardinals for pitchers T.J. Mathews, Eric Ludwick and Blake Stein, July 31, 1997.
j On disabled list from July 7 to September 7, 2000.

McLEMORE, MARK TREMMELL
Born, San Diego, California, October 4, 1964.
Bats Both. Throws Right. Height, 5 feet, 11 inches. Weight, 207 pounds.

Year	Club	Lea	Pos	G	AB	R	H	2B	3B	HR	RBI	SB	Avg
1982 Salem	Northwest	2B-SS	55	165	42	49	6	2	0	25	14	.297
1983 Peoria	Midwest	2B-SS	95	329	42	79	7	3	0	18	15	.240
1984 Redwood	California	2B-SS	134	482	102	142	8	3	0	45	59	.295
1985 Midland a	Texas	2B-SS	117	458	80	124	17	6	2	46	31	.271
1986 Midland	Texas	2B	63	237	54	75	9	1	1	29	38	.316
1986 Edmonton	P.C.	2B	73	286	41	79	13	1	0	23	29	.276
1986 California	A.L.	2B	5	4	0	0	0	0	0	0	0	.000
1987 California	A.L.	2B-SS	138	433	61	102	13	3	3	41	25	.236
1988 Palm Springs	California	2B	11	44	9	15	3	1	0	6	3	.341
1988 Edmonton	P.C.	2B	12	45	7	12	3	0	0	6	1	.267
1988 California b	A.L.	2B-3B	77	233	38	56	11	2	2	16	13	.240
1989 Edmonton	P.C.	2B	114	430	60	105	13	2	2	34	26	.244
1989 California	A.L.	2B	32	103	12	25	3	1	0	14	6	.243
1990 Palm Springs	California	2B	6	22	3	6	0	0	0	2	0	.273
1990 Edm.-Colo. Spr.	P.C.	2B-SS-3B	23	93	15	25	4	0	1	10	5	.269
1990 Cal.-Cleveland c-d-e	A.L.	2B-SS	28	60	6	9	2	0	0	2	1	.150
1991 Houston	N.L.	2B	21	61	6	9	1	0	0	2	0	.148
1991 Tucson	P.C.	2B	4	14	2	5	1	0	0	0	0	.357
1991 Jackson f-g	Texas	2B	7	22	6	5	3	0	1	4	1	.227
1991 Rochester	Int.	2B-1B	57	228	32	64	11	4	1	28	12	.281
1992 Baltimore h	A.L.	2B	101	228	40	56	7	2	0	27	11	.246
1993 Baltimore	A.L.	OF-2B-3B	148	581	81	165	27	5	4	72	21	.284
1994 Baltimore i	A.L.	2B-OF	104	343	44	88	11	1	3	29	20	.257
1995 Texas	A.L.	OF-2B	129	467	73	122	20	5	5	41	21	.261
1996 Texas j-k	A.L.	2B-OF	147	517	84	150	23	4	5	46	27	.290
1997 Charlotte	Fla. St.	2B	2	7	1	4	1	0	0	3	1	.571
1997 Okla City	A.A.	2B	3	10	0	1	0	0	0	1	1	.100
1997 Texas l	A.L.	2B-OF	89	349	47	91	17	2	1	25	7	.261
1998 Texas m	A.L.	2B	126	461	79	114	15	1	5	53	12	.247

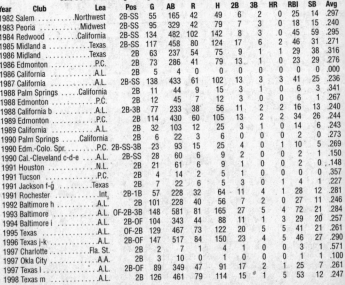

Year Club	Lea	Pos	G	AB	R	H	2B	3B	HR	RBI	SB	Avg
1999 Texas n	A.L.	2B-OF	144	566	105	155	20	7	6	45	16	.274
2000 Seattle	A.L.	2B-OF	138	481	72	118	23	1	3	46	30	.245
Major League Totals		15 Yrs.	1427	4887	748	1260	193	34	37	459	210	.258
Division Series												
1996 Texas	A.L.	2B	4	15	1	2	0	0	0	2	0	.133
1998 Texas	A.L.	2B	3	10	0	1	1	0	0	0	0	.100
1999 Texas	A.L.	2B	3	10	0	1	0	0	0	0	0	.100
2000 Seattle	A.L.	2B	3	9	1	1	0	0	0	0	0	.111
Division Series Totals			13	44	2	5	1	0	0	2	0	.114
Championship Series												
2000 Seattle	A.L.	2B	5	16	2	4	3	0	0	2	0	.250

a On disabled list from May 15 to May 27, 1985.
b On disabled list from May 24 to August 15, 1988.
c On disabled list from May 17 to August 14, 1990.
d Traded to Cleveland Indians organization to complete September 6, 1989 trade in which California Angels acquired catcher Ron Tingley, August 17, 1990.
e Released, December 13, 1990; signed with Houston Astros organization, January 31, 1991.
f On disabled list from May 9 to June 25, 1991.
g Released by Houston Astros, June 25; signed with Baltimore Orioles organization, July 5, 1991.
h Not offered 1993 contract, December 18, 1992; re-signed with Baltimore Orioles organization, January 8, 1993.
i Filed for free agency, October 17; signed with Texas Rangers, December 13, 1994.
j Filed for free agency, October 28, 1996.
k Re-signed with Texas Rangers, December 11, 1996.
l On disabled list from May 14 to June 12 and August 19 to September 29, 1997.
m On disabled list from June 7 to June 22, 1998.
n Filed for free agency, October 29, 1999. Signed with Seattle Mariners, December 20, 1999.

MEARES, PATRICK JAMES

Born, Salina, Kansas, September 6, 1968.
Bats Right. Throws Right. Height, 6 feet. Weight, 184 pounds.

Year Club	Lea	Pos	G	AB	R	H	2B	3B	HR	RBI	SB	Avg
1990 Kenosha	Midwest	3B-2B	52	197	26	47	10	2	4	22	2	.239
1991 Visalia	California	2B-3B-OF	89	360	53	109	21	4	6	44	15	.303
1992 Orlando a	Southern	SS	81	300	42	76	19	0	3	23	5	.253
1993 Portland	P.C.	SS	18	54	6	16	5	0	0	3	0	.296
1993 Minnesota	A.L.	SS	111	346	33	87	14	3	0	33	4	.251
1994 Minnesota b	A.L.	SS	80	229	29	61	12	1	2	24	5	.266
1995 Minnesota	A.L.	SS-OF	116	390	57	105	19	4	12	49	10	.269
1996 Minnesota	A.L.	SS-OF	152	517	66	138	26	7	8	67	9	.267
1997 Minnesota c	A.L.	SS	134	439	63	121	23	3	10	60	7	.276
1998 Minnesota d	A.L.	SS	149	543	56	141	26	3	9	70	7	.260
1999 Nashville	P.C.	SS	5	18	3	3	0	0	0	0	1	.167
1999 Pittsburgh e	N.L.	SS	21	91	15	28	4	0	0	7	0	.308
2000 Pittsburgh	N.L.	SS	132	462	55	111	22	2	13	47	1	.240
Major League Totals		8 Yrs.	895	3017	374	792	146	23	54	357	43	.263

a On disabled list from July 3 to July 28, 1992.
b On disabled list from June 22 to July 7, 1994.
c On disabled list from August 11 to August 26, 1997.
d Not offered 1999 contract, December 18, 1998. Signed with Pittsburgh Pirates, February 20, 1999.
e On disabled list from April 2 to April 23 and May 12 to September 21, 1999.

MELUSKEY, MITCHELL WADE (MITCH)

Born, Yakima, Washington, September 18, 1973.
Bats Both. Throws Right. Height, 6 feet. Weight, 185 pounds.

Year Club	Lea	Pos	G	AB	R	H	2B	3B	HR	RBI	SB	Avg
1992 Burlington	Appal.	C	43	126	23	29	7	0	3	16	3	.230
1993 Columbus	So.Atl.	C	101	342	36	84	18	3	3	47	1	.246
1994 Kinston	Carolina	C	100	319	36	77	16	1	3	41	3	.241
1995 Kinston	Carolina	C	8	29	5	7	5	0	0	2	0	.241
1995 Kissimmee a	Fla.St.	C	78	261	23	56	18	1	3	31	3	.215
1996 Kissimmee	Fla.St.	C	74	231	29	77	19	0	1	31	1	.333
1996 Jackson	Texas	C	38	134	18	42	11	0	0	21	0	.313
1997 Jackson	Texas	C	73	241	49	82	18	0	14	46	1	.340
1997 New Orleans	A.A.	C	51	172	22	43	7	0	3	21	0	.250
1998 New Orleans	P.C.	C-OF	121	397	76	140	41	0	17	71	2	.353
1998 Houston	N.L.	C	8	8	1	2	1	0	0	0	0	.250
1999 Houston b	N.L.	C	10	33	4	7	1	0	1	3	1	.212
2000 Houston c-d	N.L.	C-3B	117	337	47	101	21	0	14	69	1	.300
Major League Totals		3 Yrs.	135	378	52	110	23	0	15	72	2	.291

a Traded to Houston Astros by Cleveland Indians for outfielder Buck McNabb, April 27, 1995.
b On disabled list from April 26 to October 4, 1999.
c On disabled list from July 31 to August 17, 2000.
d Traded to Detroit Tigers with pitcher Chris Holt and outfielder Roger Cedeno for catcher Brad Ausmus, pitcher Doug Brocail and pitcher Nelson Cruz, December 11, 2000.

MENECHINO, FRANK

Born, Staten Island, New York, January 7, 1971.
Bats Right. Throws Right. Height, 5 feet, 9 inches. Weight, 175 pounds.

Year	Club	Lea	Pos	G	AB	R	H	2B	3B	HR	RBI	SB	Avg
1993	White Sox	Gulf Coast	2B	17	45	10	11	4	1	1	9	3	.244
1993	Hickory	So.Atl.	2B	50	178	35	50	6	3	4	19	11	.281
1994	South Bend	Midwest	2B	106	379	77	113	21	5	5	48	15	.298
1995	Pr William	Carolina	2B	137	476	65	124	31	3	6	58	6	.261
1996	Birmingham	Southern	2B	125	415	77	121	25	3	12	62	7	.292
1997	Nashville	A.A.	2B-3B-OF	37	113	20	26	4	0	4	11	3	.230
1997	Birmingham a	Southern	2B-3B	90	318	78	95	28	4	12	60	7	.299
1998	Edmonton	P.C.	2B	106	378	72	105	11	7	10	40	9	.278
1999	Vancouver	P.C.	3B	130	501	103	155	31	9	15	88	4	.309
1999	Oakland	A.L.	SS-3B	9	9	0	2	0	0	0	0	0	.222
2000	Sacramento	P.C.	SS	9	38	8	12	2	0	2	2	1	.316
2000	Oakland	A.L.	2B-SS-3B-P	66	145	31	37	9	1	6	26	1	.255
Major League Totals			2 Yrs.	75	154	31	39	9	1	6	26	1	.253
Division Series													
2000	Oakland	A.L.	2B	1	0	0	0	0	0	0	0	0	.000

a Selected by Oakland Athletics from Chicago White Sox in Rule V draft, December 15, 1997.

MIESKE, MATTHEW TODD

Born, Midland, Michigan, February 13, 1968.
Bats Right. Throws Right. Height, 6 feet. Weight, 185 pounds.

Year	Club	Lea	Pos	G	AB	R	H	2B	3B	HR	RBI	SB	Avg
1990	Spokane	Northwest	OF	*76	*291	*59	99	20	0	*12	*63	26	.340
1991	High Desert a	California	OF	133	492	108	*168	*36	6	15	119	39	*.341
1992	Denver	A.A.	OF	134	*524	80	140	29	11	19	77	13	.267
1993	New Orleans	A.A.	OF	60	219	36	57	14	2	8	22	6	.260
1993	Milwaukee	A.L.	OF	23	58	9	14	0	0	3	7	0	.241
1994	New Orleans	A.A.	OF	2	8	2	2	0	0	1	3	1	.250
1994	Milwaukee	A.L.	OF	84	259	39	67	13	1	10	38	3	.259
1995	Milwaukee	A.L.	OF	117	267	42	67	13	1	12	48	2	.251
1996	Milwaukee	A.L.	OF	127	374	46	104	24	3	14	64	1	.278
1997	Milwaukee b-c-d	A.L.	OF	84	253	39	63	15	3	5	21	1	.249
1998	Iowa	P.C.	OF	35	106	17	27	5	0	7	19	0	.255
1998	Chicago e	N.L.	OF	77	97	16	29	7	0	1	12	0	.299
1999	Seattle	A.L.	OF	24	41	11	15	0	0	4	7	0	.366
1999	Houston f	N.L.	OF	54	109	13	31	5	0	5	22	0	.284
2000	Tucson	P.C.	OF	6	25	2	6	2	0	1	3	0	.240
2000	Houston-Arizona g-h-i	N.L.	OF	73	89	10	16	1	2	2	7	0	.180
Major League Totals			8 Yrs.	663	1547	225	406	78	10	56	226	7	.262
Division Series													
1999	Houston	N.L.	OF	2	4	1	0	0	0	0	0	0	.000

a Traded by San Diego Padres to Milwaukee Brewers organization with pitcher Ricky Bones and infielder Jose Valentin for infielder Gary Sheffield and pitcher Geoff Kellogg, March 27, 1992.
b On disabled list from August 8 to September 2, 1997.
c Released by Milwaukee Brewers, December 22, 1997.
d Signed as free agent with Chicago Cubs, December 29, 1997.
e Claimed on waivers by Seattle Mariners, December 17, 1998.
f Traded to Houston Astros for pitcher Kevin Hodges, June 20, 1999.
g On disabled list from March 28 to April 12, 2000.
h Released by Houston Astros, August 18, 2000, signed with Arizona Diamondbacks organization, August 22, 2000.
i Filed for free agency, October 30, 2000.

MILLAR, KEVIN CHARLES

Born, Los Angeles, California, September 24, 1971.
Bats Right. Throws Right. Height, 6 feet, 1 inch. Weight, 195 pounds.

Year	Club	Lea	Pos	G	AB	R	H	2B	3B	HR	RBI	SB	Avg
1993	St. Paul	Northern	3B-2B	63	227	33	59	11	1	5	30	2	.260
1994	Kane County	Midwest	1B	135	477	75	144	35	2	19	93	3	.302
1995	Brevard Cty	Fla.St.	1B	129	459	53	132	32	2	13	68	4	.288

Year	Club	Lea	Pos	G	AB	R	H	2B	3B	HR	RBI	SB	Avg
1996 Portland	.........Eastern		1B-3B	130	472	69	150	32	0	18	86	6	.318
1997 Portland a	.........Eastern		1B-3B	135	511	94	175	34	2	32	131	2	.342
1998 Charlotte	.............Int.		3B-1B	14	46	14	15	3	0	4	15	1	.326
1998 Florida	..............N.L.		3B	2	2	1	1	0	0	0	0	0	.500
1999 Calgary	..............P.C.		OF	36	143	24	43	11	1	7	26	2	.301
1999 Florida	..............N.L.		1B-3B-OF	105	351	48	100	17	4	9	67	1	.285
2000 Florida	..............N.L.		1B-OF-3B	123	259	36	67	14	3	14	42	0	.259
Major League Totals	....		3 Yrs.	230	612	85	168	31	7	23	109	1	.275

a Filed for free agency, December 19, 1997, re-signed with Florida Marlins, December 21, 1997.

MILLER, DAMIAN DONALD
Born, LaCrosse, Wisconsin, October 13, 1969.
Bats Right. Throws Right. Height, 6 feet, 3 inches. Weight, 202 pounds.

Year	Club	Lea	Pos	G	AB	R	H	2B	3B	HR	RBI	SB	Avg
1990 Elizabethton	........Appal.		C	14	45	7	10	1	0	1	6	1	.222
1991 Kenosha	.........Midwest		C-1B-OF	80	267	28	62	11	1	3	34	3	.232
1992 Kenosha	.........Midwest		C	115	377	53	110	27	2	5	56	6	.292
1993 Ft. Myers	.........Fla. St.		C	87	325	31	69	12	1	1	26	6	.212
1993 Nashville	........Southern		C	4	13	0	3	0	0	0	0	0	.231
1994 Nashville	........Southern		C	103	328	36	88	10	0	8	35	4	.268
1995 Salt Lake	............P.C.		C-OF	83	295	39	84	23	1	3	41	2	.285
1996 Salt Lake	............P.C.		C-1B	104	385	54	110	27	1	7	55	1	.286
1997 Salt Lake	............P.C.		C	85	314	48	106	19	3	11	82	6	.338
1997 Minnesota a	.........A.L.		C	25	66	5	18	1	0	2	13	0	.273
1998 Tucson	..............P.C.		C	18	63	14	22	7	1	0	11	0	.349
1998 Arizona	.............N.L.		C-OF-1B	57	168	17	48	14	2	3	14	1	.286
1999 Arizona	.............N.L.		C	86	296	35	80	19	0	11	47	0	.270
2000 Arizona	.............N.L.		C-1B-SS	100	324	43	89	24	0	10	44	2	.275
Major League Totals	....		4 Yrs.	268	854	100	235	58	2	26	118	3	.275

a Selected in expansion draft by Arizona Diamondbacks, November 18, 1997.

MIRABELLI, DOUGLAS (DOUG)
Born, Kingman, Arizona, October 18, 1970.
Bats Right. Throws Right. Height, 6 feet, 1 inch. Weight, 205 pounds.

Year	Club	Lea	Pos	G	AB	R	H	2B	3B	HR	RBI	SB	Avg
1992 San Jose	.......California		C	53	177	30	41	11	1	0	21	1	.232
1993 San Jose	.......California		C	113	371	58	100	19	2	1	48	0	.270
1994 Shreveport	.........Texas		C-1B	85	255	23	56	8	0	4	24	3	.220
1995 Phoenix	..............P.C.		C	23	66	3	11	0	1	0	7	1	.167
1995 Shreveport a	.........Texas		C-1B	40	126	14	38	13	0	0	16	1	.302
1996 Phoenix	..............P.C.		C	14	47	10	14	7	0	0	7	0	.298
1996 Shreveport	.........Texas		C-1B	115	380	60	112	23	0	21	70	0	.295
1996 San Francisco	.........N.L.		C	9	18	2	4	1	0	0	1	0	.222
1997 Phoenix	..............P.C.		C	100	332	49	88	23	2	8	48	1	.265
1997 San Francisco	.........N.L.		C	6	7	0	1	0	0	0	0	0	.143
1998 Fresno	..............P.C.		C	85	265	45	69	12	2	13	53	2	.260
1998 San Francisco	.........N.L.		C	10	17	2	4	2	0	1	4	0	.235
1999 Fresno	..............P.C.		C	86	320	63	100	24	1	14	51	8	.313
1999 San Francisco	.........N.L.		C	33	87	10	22	6	0	1	10	0	.253
2000 San Francisco	.........N.L.		C	82	230	23	53	10	2	6	28	1	.230
Major League Totals	....		5 Yrs.	140	359	37	84	19	2	8	43	1	.234
Division Series													
2000 San Francisco	.........N.L.		C	1	2	0	0	0	0	0	0	0	.000

a On disabled list from May 16 to 23, 1995.

MOLINA, BENJAMIN JOSE (BEN)
Born, Rio Piedras, Puerto Rico, July 20, 1974.
Bats Right. Throws Right. Height, 5 feet, 11 inches. Weight, 200 pounds.

Year	Club	Lea	Pos	G	AB	R	H	2B	3B	HR	RBI	SB	Avg
1993 Angels	...........Arizona		DH-C	27	80	9	21	6	2	0	10	0	.262
1994 Cedar Rapds	......Midwest		C	48	171	14	48	8	0	3	16	1	.281
1995 Vancouver	..............P.C.		C	1	2	0	0	0	0	0	0	0	.000
1995 Cedar Rapds	......Midwest		C	39	133	15	39	9	0	4	17	1	.293
1995 Lk Elsinore	........California		C	27	96	21	37	7	2	2	12	0	.385
1996 Midland	.............Texas		C	108	365	45	100	21	2	8	54	0	.274
1997 Lk Elsinore	.......California		C	36	149	18	42	10	2	4	33	0	.282

Year	Club	Lea	Pos	G	AB	R	H	2B	3B	HR	RBI	SB	Avg
1997 Midland	...........Texas	DH-C	29	106	18	35	8	0	6	30	0	.330
1998 Midland	...........Texas	C	41	154	28	55	8	0	9	39	0	.357
1998 Vancouver	...........P.C.	C	49	184	13	54	9	1	1	22	1	.293
1998 Anaheim a	...........A.L.	C	2	1	0	0	0	0	0	0	0	.000
1999 Edmonton	...........P.C.	C	65	241	28	69	16	0	7	41	1	.286
1999 Anaheim b	...........A.L.	C	31	101	8	26	5	0	1	10	0	.257
2000 Anaheim	...........A.L.	C	130	473	59	133	20	2	14	71	1	.281
Major League Totals		3 Yrs.	163	575	67	159	25	2	15	81	1	.277

a On disabled list from May 13 to 22, 1998.
b On disabled list from June 4 to 14, 1999.

MONDESI, RAUL RAMON

Born, San Cristobal, Dominican Republic, March 12, 1971.
Bats Right. Throws Right. Height, 5 feet 11 inches. Weight, 202 pounds.

Year	Club	Lea	Pos	G	AB	R	H	2B	3B	HR	RBI	SB	Avg
1988-89	....					Played in Dominican Summer League							
1990 Great Falls	........Pioneer	OF	44	175	35	53	10	4	8	31	30	.303
1991 Bakersfield a	......California	OF	28	106	23	30	7	2	3	13	9	.283
1991 San Antonio	.........Texas	OF	53	213	32	58	11	5	5	26	8	.272
1991 Albuquerque	..........P.C.	OF	2	9	3	3	0	1	0	0	1	.333
1992 Albuquerque	..........P.C.	OF	35	138	23	43	4	7	4	15	2	.312
1992 San Antonio b	.......Texas	OF	18	68	8	18	2	2	2	14	3	.265
1993 Albuquerque	..........P.C.	OF	110	425	65	119	22	7	12	65	13	.280
1993 Los Angeles	.........N.L.	OF	42	86	13	25	3	1	4	10	4	.291
1994 Los Angeles c	.........N.L.	OF	112	434	63	133	27	8	16	56	11	.306
1995 Los Angeles	.........N.L.	OF	139	536	91	153	23	6	26	88	27	.285
1996 Los Angeles	.........N.L.	OF	157	634	98	188	40	7	24	88	14	.297
1997 Los Angeles	.........N.L.	OF	159	616	95	191	42	5	30	87	32	.310
1998 Los Angeles	.........N.L.	OF	148	580	85	162	26	5	30	90	16	.279
1999 Los Angeles d	.........N.L.	OF	159	601	98	152	29	5	33	99	36	.253
2000 Toronto e	............A.L.	OF	96	388	78	105	22	2	24	67	22	.271
Major League Totals		8 Yrs.	1012	3875	621	1109	212	39	187	585	162	.286
Division Series												
1995 Los Angeles	.........N.L.	OF	3	9	0	2	0	0	0	1	0	.222
1996 Los Angeles	.........N.L.	OF	3	11	0	2	2	0	0	1	0	.182
Division Series Totals			6	20	0	4	2	0	0	2	0	.200

a On disabled list from May 8 to July 5, 1991.
b On disabled list from May 8 to May 16, June 2 to June 16, June 24 to August 10, and August 24 to end of 1992 season.
c Selected Rookie of the Year in National League for 1994.
d Traded to Toronto Blue Jays with pitcher Pedro Borbon for outfielder Shawn Green and infielder Jorge Nunez, November 8, 1999.
e On disabled list from July 22 to September 19, 2000.

MORA, MELVIN

Born, Agua Negra, Venezuela, February 2, 1972.
Bats Right. Throws Right. Height, 5 feet, 10 inches. Weight, 160 pounds.

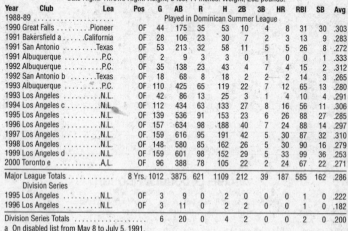

Year	Club	Lea	Pos	G	AB	R	H	2B	3B	HR	RBI	SB	Avg
1992 Astros	......Gulf Coast	OF-2B-3B	49	144	28	32	3	0	0	8	16	.222
1993 Asheville	.......So.Atl.	2B-OF-3B	108	365	66	104	22	2	2	31	20	.285
1994 Osceola	........Fla.St.	OF-3B-2B	118	425	57	120	29	4	8	46	24	.282
1995 Jackson	........Texas	OF-2B-3B	123	467	63	139	32	0	3	45	22	.298
1995 Tucson	...........P.C.	OF	2	5	3	3	0	1	0	1	1	.600
1996 Tucson	...........P.C.	3B-OF-2B	62	228	35	64	11	2	3	26	3	.281
1996 Jackson	........Texas	OF-2B-SS-3B	70	255	36	73	6	1	5	23	4	.286
1997 New Orleans	......A.A.	OF-3B-2B-SS	119	370	55	95	15	3	2	38	7	.257
1998 St. Lucie	........Fla.St.	2B-SS-OF	17	55	5	15	0	0	0	8	1	.273
1998 Norfolk a	..........Int.	3B-OF-2B	11	28	5	5	1	0	0	2	0	.179
1999 Norfolk	...........Int.	SS	82	304	55	92	17	2	8	36	18	.303
1999 New York b	........N.L.	OF-2B-3B-SS	66	31	6	5	0	0	0	1	2	.161
2000 Norfolk	...........Int.	OF	8	27	7	9	2	0	0	7	2	.333
2000 New York	..........N.L.	SS-OF-2B-3B	79	215	35	56	13	2	6	30	7	.260
2000 Baltimore c	.......A.L.	SS-2B	53	199	25	58	9	3	2	17	5	.291
Major League Totals		2 Yrs.	198	445	66	119	22	5	8	48	14	.267
Division Series												
1999 New York	.........N.L.	OF	3	1	1	0	0	0	0	0	0	.000

Year	Club	Lea	Pos	G	AB	R	H	2B	3B	HR	RBI	SB	Avg
Championship Series													
1999 New York	N.L.		OF	6	14	3	6	0	0	1	2	2	.429

a Filed for free agency from Houston Astros, October 17, 1997, signed with New York Mets, July 24, 1998.
b Filed for free agency, October 16, 1998, re-signed with New York Mets, February 2, 1999.
c Traded to Baltimore Orioles with infielder Mike Kinkade, pitcher Pat Gorman and pitcher Leslie Brea for infielder Mike Bordick, July 28, 2000.

MORANDINI, MICHAEL ROBERT (MICKEY)

Born, Kittanning, Pennsylvania, April 22, 1966.
Bats Left. Throws Right. Height, 5 feet, 11 inches. Weight, 180 pounds.

Year	Club	Lea	Pos	G	AB	R	H	2B	3B	HR	RBI	SB	Avg
1989 Spartanburg	So. Atl.	SS	63	231	43	78	19	1	1	30	9	.338
1989 Clearwater	Fla. St.	SS	17	63	14	19	4	1	0	4	1	.302
1989 Reading	Eastern	SS	48	188	39	66	12	1	5	29	5	.351
1990 Scranton	Int.	2B	138	502	77	131	24	*10	1	31	16	.261
1990 Philadelphia	N.L.	2B	25	79	9	19	4	0	1	3	3	.241
1991 Scranton	Int.	2B	12	46	7	12	4	0	1	9	2	.261
1991 Philadelphia	N.L.	2B	98	325	38	81	11	4	1	20	13	.249
1992 Philadelphia	N.L.	2B-SS	127	422	47	112	8	8	3	30	8	.265
1993 Philadelphia	N.L.	2B	120	425	57	105	19	9	3	33	13	.247
1994 Philadelphia	N.L.	2B	87	274	40	80	16	5	2	26	10	.292
1995 Philadelphia	N.L.	2B	127	494	65	140	34	7	6	49	9	.283
1996 Philadelphia a	N.L.	2B	140	539	64	135	24	6	3	32	26	.250
1997 Philadelphia b	N.L.	2B-SS	150	553	83	163	40	2	1	39	16	.295
1998 Chicago	N.L.	2B	154	582	93	172	20	4	8	53	13	.296
1999 Chicago c	N.L.	2B	144	456	60	110	18	5	4	37	6	.241
2000 Philadelphia d-e	N.L.	2B	91	302	31	76	13	3	0	22	5	.252
2000 Toronto f-g-h	A.L.	2B	35	107	10	29	2	1	0	7	1	.271
Major League Totals	11 Yrs.	1298	4558	597	1222	209	54	32	351	123	.268		
Division Series													
1998 Chicago	N.L.	2B	3	9	1	2	0	0	0	1	0	.222
Championship Series													
1993 Philadelphia	N.L.	2B	4	16	1	4	0	1	0	2	1	.250
World Series Record													
1993 Philadelphia	N.L.	2B	3	5	1	1	0	0	0	0	0	.200

a On disabled list from June 15 to June 30, 1996.
b Traded to Chicago Cubs for outfielder Doug Glanville, December 23, 1997.
c Filed for free agency, October 28, 1999. Signed with Montreal Expos organization, January 27, 2000.
d Sold to Philadelphia Phillies, March 28, 2000.
e On disabled list from May 13 to May 29, 2000.
f Traded to Toronto Blue Jays for player to be named later, August 6, 2000.
g Philadelphia Phillies received outfielder Rob Ducey to complete trade, August 7, 2000.
h Filed for free agency, October 31, 2000, signed with Toronto Blue Jays organization, December 6, 2000.

MORDECAI, MICHAEL HOWARD

Born, Birmingham, Alabama, December 13, 1967.
Bats Both. Throws Right. Height, 5 feet, 11 inches. Weight, 175 pounds.

Year	Club	Lea	Pos	G	AB	R	H	2B	3B	HR	RBI	SB	Avg
1989 Burlington	Midwest	SS-3B-2B	65	241	39	61	11	1	1	22	12	.253
1989 Greenville	Southern	3B-2B	4	8	0	3	0	0	0	1	0	.375
1990 Durham	Carolina	SS	72	271	42	76	11	7	3	36	10	.280
1991 Durham	Carolina	SS	109	397	52	104	15	2	4	42	30	.262
1992 Greenville	Southern	SS	65	222	31	58	13	1	4	31	9	.261
1992 Richmond	Int.	SS-2B-3B-OF	36	118	12	29	3	0	1	6	0	.246
1993 Richmond	Int.	2B-SS-3B-OF	72	205	29	55	8	1	2	14	10	.268
1994 Richmond	Int.	SS-1B-2B-3B	99	382	67	107	25	1	14	57	14	.280
1994 Atlanta	N.L.	SS	4	4	1	1	0	0	1	3	0	.250
1995 Atlanta	N.L.	2B-1B-SS	69	75	10	21	6	0	3	11	0	.280
1996 Richmond	Int.	SS	3	11	2	2	0	0	1	2	0	.182
1996 Atlanta a	N.L.	2B-3B-SS-1B	66	108	12	26	5	0	2	8	1	.241
1997 Richmond	Int.	2B-3B-SS	31	122	23	38	10	0	3	15	0	.311
1997 Atlanta b	N.L.	3B-2B-SS-1B	61	81	8	14	2	1	0	3	0	.173
1998 Jupiter	Fla.St.	2B-SS	2	8	0	0	0	0	0	0	0	.000
1998 Ottawa	Int.	SS-2B	6	22	2	5	2	0	0	1	0	.227
1998 Montreal c-d	N.L.	SS-2B-3B-1B	73	119	12	24	4	2	3	10	1	.202
1999 Montreal	N.L.	2B-SS-3B-1B	109	226	29	53	10	2	5	25	2	.235
2000 Montreal	N.L.	3B-SS-2B-1B	86	169	20	48	16	0	4	16	2	.284
Major League Totals	7 Yrs.	468	782	92	187	43	5	18	76	6	.239		

Year	Club	Lea	Pos	G	AB	R	H	2B	3B	HR	RBI	SB	Avg
	Division Series												
1995 Atlanta	.........N.L.		SS	2	3	1	2	1	0	0	2	0	.667
	Championship Series												
1995 Atlanta	.........N.L.		SS	2	2	0	0	0	0	0	0	0	.000
1996 Atlanta	.........N.L.		3B	4	4	1	1	0	0	0	0	0	.250
Championship Series Totals				6	6	1	1	0	0	0	0	0	.167
	World Series												
1995 Atlanta	.........N.L.		SS-DH	3	3	0	1	0	0	0	0	0	.333
1996 Atlanta	.........N.L.		PH	1	1	0	0	0	0	0	0	0	.000
World Series Totals				4	4	0	1	0	0	0	0	0	.250

a On disabled list from April 19 to May 11, 1996.
b Released by Atlanta Braves, December 22, 1997.
c Signed with Montreal Expos organization, January 16, 1998.
d On disabled list from June 24 to July 24, 1998.

MORRIS, WARREN RANDALL
Born, Alexandria, Louisiana, January 11, 1974.
Bats Left. Throws Right. Height, 5 feet, 11 inches. Weight, 190 pounds.

Year	Club	Lea	Pos	G	AB	R	H	2B	3B	HR	RBI	SB	Avg
1997 Charlotte	.........Fla.St.		2B-3B	128	494	78	151	27	9	12	75	16	.306
1997 Okla City	.............A.A.		2B	8	32	3	7	1	0	1	3	0	.219
1998 Tulsa	...............Texas		2B	95	390	59	129	22	5	14	73	12	.331
1998 Carolina a	.....Southern		2B	44	151	28	50	8	3	5	30	5	.331
1999 Pittsburgh	...........N.L.		2B	147	511	65	147	20	3	15	73	3	.288
2000 Pittsburgh	...........N.L.		2B	144	528	68	137	31	2	3	43	7	.259
Major League Totals		2 Yrs.	291	1039	133	284	51	5	18	116	10	.273	

a Traded by Texas Rangers to Pittsburgh Pirates with pitcher Todd Van Poppel for pitcher Esteban Loiaza, July 17, 1998.

MORRIS, WILLIAM HAROLD (HAL)
Born, Fort Rucker, Alabama, April 9, 1965.
Bats Left. Throws Left. Height, 6 feet, 4 inches. Weight, 210 pounds.

Year	Club	Lea	Pos	G	AB	R	H	2B	3B	HR	RBI	SB	Avg
1986 Oneonta	.......N.Y.-Penn.		1B	36	127	26	48	9	2	3	30	1	.378
1986 Albany	...........Eastern		1B	25	79	7	17	5	0	0	4	0	.215
1987 Albany	...........Eastern		1B	135	*530	65	*173	31	4	5	73	7	.326
1988 Columbus	............Int.		OF-1B	121	452	41	134	19	4	3	38	8	.296
1988 New York	..............A.L.		OF	15	20	1	2	0	0	0	0	0	.100
1989 Columbus	............Int.		1B-OF	111	417	70	136	24	1	17	66	5	*.326
1989 New York a	............A.L.		OF-1B	15	18	2	5	0	0	0	4	0	.278
1990 Nashville	.............A.A.		OF	16	64	8	22	5	0	1	10	4	.344
1990 Cincinnati	...........N.L.		1B-OF	107	309	50	105	22	3	7	36	9	.340
1991 Cincinnati	...........N.L.		1B-OF	136	478	72	152	33	1	14	59	10	.318
1992 Nashville	.............A.A.		1B	2	6	1	1	0	0	0	0	0	.167
1992 Cincinnati b	...........N.L.		1B	115	395	41	107	21	3	6	53	6	.271
1993 Indianapolis	...........A.A.		1B	3	13	4	6	0	1	1	5	0	.462
1993 Cincinnati c-d	.........N.L.		1B	101	379	48	120	18	0	7	49	2	.317
1994 Cincinnati	...........N.L.		1B	112	436	60	146	30	4	10	78	6	.335
1995 Indianapolis	...........A.A.		1B	2	5	2	2	0	0	0	1	0	.400
1995 Cincinnati e-f	.........N.L.		1B	101	359	53	100	25	2	11	51	1	.279
1996 Indianapolis g	.........A.A.		1B	1	4	1	2	1	0	1	1	0	.500
1996 Cincinnati	...........N.L.		1B	142	528	82	165	32	4	16	80	7	.313
1997 Cincinnati h-i-j	...........N.L.		1B	96	333	42	92	20	1	1	33	3	.276
1998 Kansas City k-l	.........A.L.		1B-OF	127	472	50	146	27	2	1	40	1	.309
1999 Cincinnati m	...........N.L.		1B-OF	80	102	10	29	9	0	0	16	0	.284
2000 Cincinnati	...........N.L.		1B-OF	59	63	9	14	2	1	2	6	0	.222
2000 Detroit n-o-p	.........A.L.		1B-OF	40	106	15	33	7	0	1	8	0	.311
Major League Totals		13 Yrs.	1246	3998	535	1216	246	21	76	513	45	.304	
	Division Series												
1995 Cincinnati	...........N.L.		1B	3	10	5	5	1	0	0	2	1	.500
	Championship Series												
1990 Cincinnati	...........N.L.		1B	5	12	3	5	1	0	0	1	0	.417
1995 Cincinnati	...........N.L.		1B	4	12	0	2	1	0	0	1	1	.167
Championship Series Totals				9	24	3	7	2	0	0	2	1	.292
	World Series Record												
1990 Cincinnati	...........N.L.		1B	4	14	0	1	0	0	0	2	0	.071

128

a Traded to Cincinnati Reds with pitcher Rodney Imes for pitcher Tim Leary and outfielder Van Snider, December 12, 1989.
b On disabled list from April 16 to May 17 and August 5 to August 21, 1992.
c On disabled list from March 31 to June 7, 1993.
d Suspended one game and fined by National League for March 30 brawl, August 10, 1993.
e On disabled list from June 18 to July 13, 1995.
f Filed for free agency November 12, 1995; re-signed with Cincinnati Reds, December 6, 1995.
g On disabled list from July 2 to July 17, 1996.
h On disabled list from August 2 to September 10 and September 24 to September 29, 1997.
i Filed for free agency, October 29, 1997.
j Signed with Kansas City Royals, December 22, 1997.
k On disabled list from May 8 to May 23, 1998.
l Filed for free agency, October 23, 1998. Signed with Cincinnati Reds, January 14, 1999.
m On disabled list from August 27 to September 25, 1999.
n Sold to Detroit Tigers, July 18, 2000.
o On disabled list from August 9 to September 4, 2000.
p Filed for free agency, November 1, 2000.

MOUTON, JAMES RALEIGH

Born, Denver, Colorado, December 29, 1968.
Bats Right. Throws Right. Height, 5 feet, 9 inches. Weight, 175 pounds.

Year	Club	Lea	Pos	G	AB	R	H	2B	3B	HR	RBI	SB	Avg
1991	Auburn	N.Y.-Penn.	2B	76	288	71	76	15	*10	2	40	*60	.264
1992	Osceola	Fla. St.	2B	133	507	*110	143	*30	6	11	62	*51	.282
1993	Tucson	P.C.	2B	134	546	*126	*172	42	12	16	92	40	.315
1994	Tucson	P.C.	OF	4	17	2	7	1	0	1	1	1	.412
1994	Houston	N.L.	OF	99	310	43	76	11	0	2	16	24	.245
1995	Tuscon	P.C.	OF	3	11	1	5	0	0	1	1	0	.455
1995	Houston a	N.L.	OF	104	298	42	78	18	2	4	27	25	.262
1996	Tucson	P.C.	OF	1	4	1	1	0	0	0	0	0	.250
1996	Houston	N.L.	OF	122	300	40	79	15	1	3	34	21	.263
1997	Houston	N.L.	OF	86	180	24	38	9	1	3	23	9	.211
1998	Las Vegas	P.C.	OF-2B	50	192	38	68	17	3	4	31	15	.354
1998	San Diego b-c	N.L.	OF	55	63	8	12	2	1	0	7	4	.190
1999	Montreal d	N.L.	OF	95	122	18	32	5	1	2	13	6	.262
2000	Milwaukee e	N.L.	OF	87	159	28	37	7	1	2	17	13	.233
Major League Totals			7 Yrs.	648	1432	203	352	67	7	16	137	102	.246

a On disabled list from June 12 to June 30, 1995.
b On disabled list from May 16 to June 1, 1998.
c Not offered 1999 contract, December 18, 1998. Signed with Montreal Expos organization, January 18, 1999.
d Filed for free agency, October 15, 1999. Signed with Milwaukee Brewers organization, December 13, 1999.
e Filed for free agency, October 30, 2000, signed with Milwaukee Brewers organization, December 7, 2000.

MUELLER, WILLIAM RICHARD (BILL)

Born, Maryland Heights, Missouri, March 17, 1971.
Bats Both. Throws Right. Height, 5 feet, 11 inches. Weight, 175 pounds.

Year	Club	Lea	Pos	G	AB	R	H	2B	3B	HR	RBI	SB	Avg
1993	Everett	Northwest	2B-SS	58	200	31	60	8	2	1	24	13	.300
1994	San Jose	California	3B-2B-SS	120	431	79	130	20	9	5	72	4	.302
1995	Shreveport	Texas	3B-2B	88	330	56	102	16	2	1	39	6	.309
1995	Phoenix	P.C.	3B-2B	41	172	23	51	13	6	2	19	0	.297
1996	Phoenix	P.C.	3B-SS-2B	106	440	73	133	14	6	4	36	2	.302
1996	San Francisco	N.L.	3B-2B	55	200	31	66	15	1	0	19	0	.330
1997	San Francisco a	N.L.	3B	128	390	51	114	26	3	7	44	4	.292
1998	San Francisco	N.L.	3B-2B	145	534	93	157	27	0	9	59	3	.294
1999	Fresno	P.C.	3B	3	12	3	5	0	1	0	6	0	.417
1999	San Francisco b	N.L.	3B-2B	116	414	61	120	24	0	2	36	4	.290
2000	San Francisco c	N.L.	3B-2B	153	560	97	150	29	4	10	55	4	.268
Major League Totals			5 Yrs.	597	2098	333	607	121	8	28	213	15	.289
Division Series													
1997	San Francisco	N.L.	3B	3	12	1	3	0	0	1	1	0	.250
2000	San Francisco	N.L.	3B	4	20	2	5	2	0	0	0	0	.250
Division Series Totals				7	32	3	8	2	0	1	1	0	.250

a On disabled list from June 30 to July 17, 1997.
b On disabled list from April 6 to May 17, 1999.
c Traded to Chicago Cubs for pitcher Tim Worrell, November 19, 2000.

MUNSON, ERIC WALTER
Born, San Diego, California, October 3, 1977.
Bats Left. Throws Right. Height, 6 feet, 3 inches. Weight, 220 pounds.

Year	Club	Lea	Pos	G	AB	R	H	2B	3B	HR	RBI	SB	Avg
1999 Lakeland	..........Fla.St.	DH	0	6	0	2	0	0	0	1	0	.333
1999 West Michigan	.....Midwest	1B	67	252	42	67	16	1	14	44	3	.266
2000 Jacksonville	......Southern	1B	98	365	52	92	21	4	15	68	5	.252
2000 Detroit	.............A.L.	1B	3	5	0	0	0	0	0	1	0	.000

MURRAY, CALVIN DUANE
Born, Dallas, Texas, July 30, 1971.
Bats Right. Throws Right. Height, 5 feet, 11 inches. Weight, 190 pounds.

Year	Club	Lea	Pos	G	AB	R	H	2B	3B	HR	RBI	SB	Avg
1993 Shreveport	.........Texas	OF	37	138	15	26	6	0	0	6	12	.188
1993 San Jose	.........California	OF	85	345	61	97	24	1	9	42	42	.281
1993 Phoenix	..............P.C.	OF	5	19	4	6	1	1	0	0	1	.316
1994 Shreveport	.........Texas	OF	129	480	67	111	19	5	2	35	33	.231
1995 Phoenix	..............P.C.	OF	13	50	8	9	1	0	4	10	2	.180
1995 Shreveport	.........Texas	OF	110	441	77	104	17	3	2	29	26	.236
1996 Shreveport	.........Texas	OF	50	169	32	44	7	0	7	24	6	.260
1996 Phoenix	..............P.C.	OF	83	311	50	76	16	6	3	28	12	.244
1997 Shreveport	.........Texas	OF	122	419	83	114	25	3	10	56	52	.272
1998 Shreveport	.........Texas	OF	88	337	63	104	22	5	8	39	34	.309
1998 Fresno	..............P.C.	OF	33	90	16	21	3	1	3	5	3	.233
1999 Fresno	..............P.C.	OF	130	548	122	183	31	7	23	73	42	.334
1999 San Francisco	.........N.L.	OF	15	19	1	5	2	0	0	5	1	.263
2000 San Francisco	.........N.L.	OF	108	194	35	47	12	1	2	22	9	.242
Major League Totals	....	2 Yrs.	123	213	36	52	14	1	2	27	10	.244
Division Series													
2000 San Francisco	.........N.L.	OF	3	5	0	1	0	0	0	0	0	.200

NEVIN, PHILLIP
Born, Fullerton, California, January 19, 1971.
Bats Right. Throws Right. Height, 6 feet, 2 inches. Weight, 185 pounds.

Year	Club	Lea	Pos	G	AB	R	H	2B	3B	HR	RBI	SB	Avg
1993 Tucson	..........P.C.	3B-OF	123	448	67	128	21	3	10	93	8	.286
1994 Tucson	..........P.C.	3B-OF	118	445	67	117	20	1	12	79	3	.263
1995 Tucson	..........P.C.	3B	62	223	31	65	16	0	7	41	2	.291
1995 Toledo	............Int.	OF	7	23	3	7	2	0	1	3	0	.304
1995 Houston	..........N.L.	3B	18	60	4	7	1	0	0	1	1	.117
1995 Detroit a	..........A.L.	OF	29	96	9	21	3	1	2	12	0	.219
1996 Jacksonville	...Southern	C-3B-OF	98	344	77	101	18	1	24	69	6	.294
1996 Detroit	..........A.L.	3B-OF-C	38	120	15	35	5	0	8	19	1	.292
1997 Lakeland	.....Fla. St.	1B-3B	3	9	3	5	1	0	1	4	0	.556
1997 Toledo	............Int.	1B-3B	5	19	1	3	0	0	1	3	0	.158
1997 Detroit b-c	........A.L.	OF-3B-1B	93	251	32	59	16	1	9	35	0	.235
1998 Anaheim	;.........A.L.	C-1B	75	237	27	54	8	1	8	27	0	.228
1999 Las Vegas	........P.C.	C	3	10	2	2	0	0	2	2	0	.200
1999 San Diego d-e	...N.L.	3B-C-OF-1B	128	383	52	103	27	0	24	85	1	.269
2000 San Diego	..........N.L.	3B	143	538	87	163	34	1	31	107	2	.303
Major League Totals	....	6 Yrs.	524	1685	226	442	94	4	82	286	5	.262

a Mike Henneman was traded to Houston Astros for player to be named later, August 10, 1995. Detroit Tigers received infielder Phil Nevin to complete trade, August 15, 1995.
b On disabled list from April 1 to April 16, 1997.
c Traded to Anaheim Angels with player to be named later for pitcher Nick Skuse, November 21, 1997.
d Traded to San Diego Padres with pitcher Keith Volkman for infielder Andy Sheets and outfielder Gus Kennedy, March 29, 1999.
e On disabled list from April 1 to April 16, 1999.

NIEVES, JOSE MIGUEL
Born, Guacara, Venezuela, June 16, 1975.
Bats Right. Throws Right. Height, 6 feet, 1 inch. Weight, 180 pounds.

Year	Club	Lea	Pos	G	AB	R	H	2B	3B	HR	RBI	SB	Avg
1994 Cubs/Sd a	...Dominican	2B	37	137	21	39	6	14	4	24	5	.285
1995 Williamsprt	.N.Y.-Penn.	SS-2B	69	276	46	59	13	1	4	44	11	.214
1996 Rockford	.....Midwest	SS-2B-3B	113	396	55	96	20	4	5	57	17	.242
1997 Daytona	........Fla.St.	SS-2B	85	331	51	91	20	1	4	42	16	.275

Year Club	Lea	Pos	G	AB	R	H	2B	3B	HR	RBI	SB	Avg
1998 West Tenn ....Southern		SS-2B	82	314	42	91	27	5	8	39	17	.290
1998 Chicago .........N.L.		SS	2	1	0	0	0	0	0	0	0	.000
1998 Iowa ............P.C.		SS	19	75	7	19	4	0	0	4	1	.253
1999 Iowa ............P.C.		SS	104	392	55	105	25	3	11	59	11	.268
1999 Chicago .........N.L.		SS	54	181	16	45	9	1	2	18	0	.249
2000 Daytona ....Fla.St.		3B	2	6	2	1	0	0	0	0	0	.167
2000 West Tenn ....Southern		3B	2	7	2	4	0	0	2	2	0	.571
2000 Iowa ............P.C.		3B	7	32	7	9	4	1	1	7	1	.281
2000 Chicago b .......N.L.		3B-SS-2B	82	198	17	42	6	3	5	24	1	.212
Major League Totals		3 Yrs.	138	380	33	87	15	4	7	42	1	.229

a Released by Milwaukee Brewers, October 19, 1993, signed with Chicago Cubs organization, June 30, 1994.
b On disabled list from May 31 to June 17, 2000.

NIXON, CHRISTOPHER TROTMAN (TROT)
Born, Durham, North Carolina, April 11, 1974.
Bats Left. Throws Right. Height, 6 feet, 1 inch. Weight, 195 pounds.

Year Club	Lea	Pos	G	AB	R	H	2B	3B	HR	RBI	SB	Avg
1994 Lynchburg ....Carolina		OF	71	264	33	65	12	6	12	43	10	.246
1995 Sarasota ....Fla.St.		OF	73	264	43	80	11	4	5	39	7	.303
1995 Trenton ....Eastern		OF	25	94	9	15	3	1	2	8	2	.160
1996 Trenton ....Eastern		OF	123	438	55	110	11	4	11	63	7	.251
1996 Boston .............A.L.		OF	2	4	2	2	1	0	0	0	1	.500
1997 Pawtucket ....Int.		OF	130	475	60	116	18	3	20	61	11	.244
1998 Pawtucket ....Int.		OF-1B	135	509	97	158	26	4	23	74	26	.310
1998 Boston .............A.L.		OF	13	27	3	7	1	0	0	0	0	.259
1999 Boston .............A.L.		OF	124	381	67	103	22	5	15	52	3	.270
2000 GC Red Sox .....Gulf Coast		OF	3	10	3	4	0	0	1	5	0	.400
2000 Boston a ...........A.L.		OF	123	427	66	118	27	8	12	60	8	.276
Major League Totals		4 Yrs.	262	839	138	230	51	13	27	112	12	.274
Division Series												
1998 Boston .............A.L.		OF	2	3	0	1	0	0	0	0	0	.333
1999 Boston .............A.L.		OF	5	14	5	3	3	0	0	6	0	.214
Division Series Totals			7	17	5	4	3	0	0	6	0	.235
Championship Series												
1999 Boston .............A.L.		OF	5	14	2	4	2	0	0	0	0	.286

a On disabled list from June 24 to July 24, 2000.

NORTON, GREGORY BLAKEMOOR (GREG)
Born, San Leandro, California, July 6, 1972.
Bats Both. Throws Right. Height, 6 feet, 1 inch. Weight, 190 pounds.

Year Club	Lea	Pos	G	AB	R	H	2B	3B	HR	RBI	SB	Avg
1993 White Sox ....Gulf Coast		3B	3	9	1	2	0	0	0	2	0	.222
1993 Hickory ....So.Atl.		3B-SS	71	254	36	62	12	2	4	36	0	.244
1994 South Bend ....Midwest		3B	127	477	73	137	22	2	6	64	5	.287
1995 Birmingham ......Southern		3B	133	469	65	117	23	2	6	60	19	.249
1996 Birmingham ......Southern		SS	76	287	40	81	14	3	8	44	5	.282
1996 Nashville ...........A.A.		SS-3B	43	164	28	47	14	2	7	26	2	.287
1996 Chicago .............A.L.		SS-3B	11	23	4	5	0	0	2	3	0	.217
1997 Nashville ...........A.A.		3B-SS-2B	114	414	82	114	27	1	26	76	3	.275
1997 Chicago .............A.L.		3B	18	34	5	9	2	2	0	1	0	.265
1998 Chicago .............A.L.		1B-3B-2B	105	299	38	71	17	2	9	36	3	.237
1999 Chicago .............A.L.		3B-1B	132	436	62	111	26	0	16	50	4	.255
2000 Charlotte ....Int.		3B	29	97	18	28	4	0	5	17	1	.289
2000 Chicago a ...........A.L.		3B-1B	71	201	25	49	6	1	6	28	1	.244
Major League Totals		5 Yrs.	337	993	134	245	51	5	33	118	8	.247

a Not offered 2001 contract, December 21, 2000, signed with Colorado Rockies, January 5, 2001.

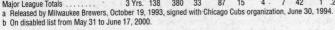

OCHOA, ALEX
Born, Miami Lakes, Florida, March 29, 1972.
Bats Right. Throws Right. Height, 6 feet. Weight, 185 pounds.

Year Club	Lea	Pos	G	AB	R	H	2B	3B	HR	RBI	SB	Avg
1991 Orioles ....Gulf Coast		OF	53	179	26	55	8	3	1	30	11	.307
1992 Kane County ......Midwest		OF	133	499	65	147	22	7	1	59	31	.295
1993 Frederick ....Carolina		OF	137	532	84	147	29	5	13	90	34	.276
1994 Bowie ....Eastern		OF	134	519	77	156	25	2	14	82	28	.301
1995 Rochester ....Int.		OF	91	336	41	92	18	2	8	46	17	.274

Year Club	Lea	Pos	G	AB	R	H	2B	3B	HR	RBI	SB	Avg
1995 Norfolk	Int.	OF	34	123	17	38	6	2	2	15	7	.309
1995 New York a	N.L.	OF	11	37	7	11	1	0	0	0	1	.297
1996 Norfolk	Int.	OF	67	233	45	79	12	4	8	39	5	.339
1996 New York	N.L.	OF	82	282	37	83	19	3	4	33	4	.294
1997 New York b	N.L.	OF	113	238	31	58	14	1	3	22	3	.244
1998 Minnesota c	A.L.	OF	94	249	35	64	14	2	2	25	6	.257
1999 Milwaukee d	N.L.	OF	119	277	47	83	16	3	8	40	6	.300
2000 Chattanooga	Southern	OF	4	16	3	3	2	0	1	2	1	.188
2000 Cincinnati e	N.L.	OF	118	244	50	77	21	3	13	58	9	.316
Major League Totals	6 Yrs.	537	1327	207	376	85	12	30	178	29	.283	

a Traded to New York Mets with outfielder Damon Buford for infielder Bobby Bonilla and player to be named later, July 28, 1995. Baltimore Orioles received pitcher Jimmy Williams to complete trade, August 16, 1995.
b Traded to Minnesota Twins for outfielder Rich Becker, December 14, 1997.
c Traded to Milwaukee Brewers for player to be named later, December 14, 1998. Minnesota Twins received outfielder Darrell Nicholas to complete trade, December 15, 1998.
d Traded to Cincinnati Reds for outfielder Mark Sweeney and player to be named later, January 14, 2000. Milwaukee Brewers received pitcher Gene Altman to complete trade, May 15, 2000.
e On disabled list from May 31 to June 15, 2000.

OFFERMAN (DONO), JOSE ANTONIO

Born, San Pedro de Macoris, Dominican Republic, November 8, 1968.
Bats Both. Throws Right. Height, 6 feet. Weight, 165 pounds.

Year Club	Lea	Pos	G	AB	R	H	2B	3B	HR	RBI	SB	Avg
1988 Great Falls	Pioneer	SS	60	251	75	83	11	5	2	28	*57	.331
1989 Bakersfield	California	SS	62	245	53	75	9	4	2	22	37	.306
1989 San Antonio	Texas	SS	68	278	47	80	6	3	2	22	32	.288
1990 Albuquerque	P.C.	SS	117	454	104	148	16	11	0	56	*60	.326
1990 Los Angeles	N.L.	SS	29	58	7	9	0	0	1	7	1	.155
1991 Albuquerque	P.C.	SS	76	289	58	86	8	4	0	29	32	.298
1991 Los Angeles	N.L.	SS	52	113	10	22	2	0	0	3	3	.195
1992 Los Angeles	N.L.	SS	149	534	67	139	20	8	1	30	23	.260
1993 Los Angeles	N.L.	SS	158	590	77	159	21	6	1	62	30	.269
1994 Los Angeles	N.L.	SS	72	243	27	51	8	4	1	25	2	.210
1994 Albuquerque	P.C.	SS	56	224	43	74	7	5	1	31	9	.330
1995 Los Angeles a	N.L.	SS	119	429	69	123	14	6	4	33	2	.287
1996 Kansas City	A.L.	1B-2B-SS-OF	151	561	85	170	33	8	5	47	24	.303
1997 Kansas City b	A.L.	2B	106	424	59	126	23	6	2	39	9	.297
1998 Kansas City c	A.L.	2B	158	607	102	191	28	*13	7	66	45	.315
1999 Boston	A.L.	2B-1B	149	586	107	172	37	*11	8	69	18	.294
2000 Boston d	A.L.	2B-1B	116	451	73	115	14	3	9	41	0	.255
Major League Totals	11 Yrs.	1259	4596	683	1277	200	65	39	422	157	.278	
Divisional Series												
1995 Los Angeles	N.L.	PR	1	0	0	0	0	0	0	0	0	.000
1999 Boston	A.L.	2B	5	18	4	7	1	0	1	6	0	.389
Division Series Totals			6	18	4	7	1	0	1	6	0	.389
Championship Series												
1999 Boston	A.L.	2B	5	24	4	11	0	1	0	2	1	.458

a Traded to Kansas City Royals for pitcher Billy Brewer, December 17, 1995.
b On disabled list from April 6 to April 29 and July 7 to July 22 and August 14 to September 6, 1997.
c Filed for free agency, October 23, 1998, signed with Boston Red Sox, November 13, 1998.
d On disabled list from May 25 to June 10 and July 30 to August 15, 2000.

O'LEARY, TROY FRANKLIN

Born, Compton, California, August 4, 1969.
Bats Left. Throws Left. Height, 6 feet. Weight, 190 pounds.

Year Club	Lea	Pos	G	AB	R	H	2B	3B	HR	RBI	SB	Avg
1987 Helena	Pioneer	OF	3	5	0	2	0	0	0	1	0	.400
1988 Helena	Pioneer	OF	67	203	40	70	11	1	0	27	10	.345
1989 Beloit	Midwest	OF	42	115	7	21	4	0	0	8	1	.183
1989 Helena	Pioneer	OF	68	263	54	89	16	3	11	56	9	.338
1990 Beloit	Midwest	OF	118	436	73	130	29	1	6	62	12	.298
1990 Stockton	California	OF	2	6	1	3	1	0	0	0	0	.500
1991 Stockton	California	OF	126	418	63	110	20	4	5	46	4	.263
1992 El Paso	Texas	OF	135	506	92	169	27	8	5	79	28	.334
1993 New Orleans	A.A.	OF-1B	111	388	65	106	32	1	7	59	6	.273
1993 Milwaukee	A.L.	OF	19	41	3	12	3	0	0	3	0	.293
1994 New Orleans	A.A.	OF-1B	63	225	44	74	18	5	8	43	10	.329
1994 Milwaukee	A.L.	OF	27	66	9	18	1	1	2	7	1	.273

Year	Club	Lea	Pos	G	AB	R	H	2B	3B	HR	RBI	SB	Avg
1995 Boston a	A.L.		OF	112	399	60	123	31	6	10	49	5	.308
1996 Boston	A.L.		OF	149	497	68	129	28	5	15	81	3	.260
1997 Boston	A.L.		OF	146	499	65	154	32	4	15	80	0	.309
1998 Boston	A.L.		OF	156	611	95	165	36	8	23	83	2	.270
1999 Boston	A.L.		OF	157	596	84	167	36	4	28	103	1	.280
2000 GC Red Sox	Gulf Coast		PH	3	8	3	6	1	0	0	1	0	.750
2000 Boston b	A.L.		OF	138	513	68	134	30	4	13	70	0	.261
Major League Totals	8 Yrs.			904	3222	452	902	197	32	106	476	12	.280
Division Series													
1998 Boston	A.L.		OF	4	16	0	1	0	0	0	0	0	.063
1999 Boston	A.L.		OF	5	20	4	4	0	0	2	7	0	.200
Division Series Totals				9	36	4	5	0	0	2	7	0	.139
Championship Series													
1999 Boston	A.L.		OF	5	20	2	7	3	0	0	1	0	.350

a Claimed on waivers by Boston Red Sox, April 14, 1995.
b On disabled list from June 18 to July 2, 2000.

OLERUD, JOHN GARRETT

Born, Bellevue, Washington, August 5, 1968.
Bats Left. Throws Left. Height, 6 feet, 5 inches. Weight, 218 pounds.

Year	Club	Lea	Pos	G	AB	R	H	2B	3B	HR	RBI	SB	Avg
1989 Toronto	A.L.		1B	6	8	2	3	0	0	0	0	0	.375
1990 Toronto	A.L.		1B	111	358	43	95	15	1	14	48	0	.265
1991 Toronto	A.L.		1B	139	454	64	116	30	1	17	68	0	.256
1992 Toronto	A.L.		1B	138	458	68	130	28	0	16	66	1	.284
1993 Toronto	A.L.		1B	158	551	109	200	*54	2	24	107	0	*.363
1994 Toronto	A.L.		1B	108	384	47	114	29	2	12	67	1	.297
1995 Toronto	A.L.		1B	135	492	72	143	32	0	8	54	0	.291
1996 Toronto a	A.L.		1B	125	398	59	109	25	0	18	61	1	.274
1997 New York b-c	N.L.		1B	154	524	90	154	34	1	22	102	0	.294
1998 New York	N.L.		1B	160	557	91	197	36	4	22	93	2	.354
1999 New York d	N.L.		1B	*162	581	107	173	39	4	19	96	3	.298
2000 Seattle	A.L.		1B	159	565	84	161	45	0	14	103	0	.285
Major League Totals	12 Yrs.			1555	5330	836	1595	367	11	186	865	8	.299
Division Series													
1999 New York	N.L.		1B	4	16	3	7	0	0	1	6	0	.438
2000 Seattle	A.L.		1B	3	10	2	3	0	0	1	2	0	.300
Division Series Totals				7	26	5	10	0	0	2	8	0	.385
Championship Series													
1991 Toronto	A.L.		1B	5	19	1	3	0	0	0	3	0	.158
1992 Toronto	A.L.		1B	6	23	4	8	2	0	1	4	0	.348
1993 Toronto	A.L.		1B	6	23	5	8	1	0	0	3	0	.348
1999 New York	N.L.		1B	6	27	4	8	0	0	2	6	0	.296
2000 Seattle	A.L.		1B	6	20	2	7	3	0	1	2	1	.350
Championship Series Totals				29	112	16	34	6	0	4	18	1	.304
World Series Record													
1992 Toronto	A.L.		1B	4	13	2	4	0	0	0	0	0	.308
1993 Toronto	A.L.		1B	5	17	5	4	1	0	1	2	0	.235
World Series Totals				9	30	7	8	1	0	1	2	0	.267

a Traded to New York Mets for RHP Robert Person December 21, 1996.
b Filed for free agency, October 27, 1997.
c Re-signed with New York Mets, November 24, 1997.
d Filed for free agency, October 29, 1999, signed with Seattle Mariners, December 7, 1999.

OLIVER, JOSEPH MELTON (JOE)

Born, Memphis, Tennessee, July 24, 1965.
Bats Right. Throws Right. Height, 6 feet, 3 inches. Weight, 210 pounds.

Year	Club	Lea	Pos	G	AB	R	H	2B	3B	HR	RBI	SB	Avg
1983 Billings	Pioneer		C-1B	56	186	21	40	4	0	4	28	1	.215
1984 Cedar Rapds	Midwest		C	102	335	34	73	11	0	3	29	2	.218
1985 Tampa	Fla.St.		C-1B	112	386	38	104	23	2	7	62	1	.269
1986 Vermont a	Eastern		C	84	282	32	78	18	1	6	41	2	.277
1987 Vermont	Eastern		C-1B	66	236	31	72	13	2	10	60	0	.305
1988 Nashville	A.A.		C	73	220	19	45	7	2	4	24	0	.205
1988 Chattanooga	Southern		C	28	105	9	26	6	0	3	12	0	.248
1989 Nashville	A.A.		C-1B	71	233	22	68	13	0	6	31	0	.292

133

Year Club	Lea	Pos	G	AB	R	H	2B	3B	HR	RBI	SB	Avg
1989 Cincinnati	N.L.	C	49	151	13	41	8	0	3	23	0	.272
1990 Cincinnati	N.L.	C	121	364	34	84	23	0	8	52	1	.231
1991 Cincinnati	N.L.	C	94	269	21	58	11	0	11	41	0	.216
1992 Cincinnati	N.L.	C-1B	143	485	42	131	25	1	10	57	2	.270
1993 Cincinnati	N.L.	C-1B-OF	139	482	40	115	28	0	14	75	0	.239
1994 Cincinnati b	N.L.	C	6	19	1	4	0	0	1	5	0	.211
1995 New Orleans	A.A.	C	4	13	0	1	1	0	0	0	0	.077
1995 Milwaukee c-d	A.L.	C-1B	97	337	43	92	20	0	12	51	2	.273
1996 Cincinnati e	N.L.	C-1B-OF	106	289	31	70	12	1	11	46	2	.242
1997 Indianapols	A.A.	C	2	9	1	3	0	0	1	1	0	.333
1997 Cincinnati f-g	N.L.	C-1B	111	349	28	90	13	0	14	43	1	.258
1998 Detroit-Seattle h	A.L.	C-1B	79	240	20	54	11	0	6	32	1	.225
1999 Durham	Int.	C	57	219	27	66	18	1	7	43	1	.301
1999 Pittsburgh i-j-k	N.L.	C	45	134	10	27	8	0	1	13	2	.201
2000 Tacoma	P.C.	PH	18	61	2	12	2	0	0	8	0	.197
2000 Seattle l-m	A.L.	C-1B	69	200	33	53	13	1	10	35	2	.265
Major League Totals		12 Yrs.	1059	3319	316	819	172	3	101	473	13	.247
Division Series												
2000 Seattle	A.L.	C	3	4	1	1	0	0	1	1	0	.250
Championship Series												
1990 Cincinnati	N.L.	C	5	14	1	2	0	0	0	0	0	.143
2000 Seattle	A.L.	C	4	6	0	1	0	0	0	0	0	.167
Championship Series Totals			9	20	1	3	0	0	0	0	0	.150
World Series Record												
1990 Cincinnati	N.L.	C	4	18	2	6	3	0	0	2	0	.333

a On disabled list from April 23 to May 6, 1986.
b On disabled list from April 12 to October 1, 1994.
c Released by Cincinnati Reds, November 3, 1994, signed with Milwaukee Brewers organization, March 24, 1995.
d On disabled list from July 14 to AUgust 15, 1995.
e Filed for free agency, October 31, 1995, signed with Cincinnati Reds, February 26, 1996.
f Filed for free agency, November 18, 1996, re-signed with Cincinnati Reds organization, February 8, 1997.
g Filed for free agency, October 30, 1997, signed with Detroit Tigers organization, December 22, 1997.
h Released by Detroit Tigers, July 15, 1998, signed with Seattle Mariners, July 22, 1998.
i Filed for free agency, October 27, 1998, signed with Tampa Bay Devil Rays organization, February 3, 1999.
j On disabled list from June 13 to 24, 1999.
k Traded to Pittsburgh Pirates with catcher Humberto Cota for outfielder Jose Guillen and pitcher Jeff Sparks, July 23, 1999.
l Filed for free agency, November 5, 1999, signed with Seattle Mariners organization, January 19, 2000.
m Filed for free agency, November 4, 2000, signed with New York Yankees, November 21, 2000.

O'NEILL, PAUL ANDREW
Born, Columbus, Ohio, February 25, 1963.
Bats Left. Throws Left. Height, 6 feet, 4 inches. Weight, 215 pounds.

Year Club	Lea	Pos	G	AB	R	H	2B	3B	HR	RBI	SB	Avg
1981 Billings	Pioneer	OF	66	241	37	76	7	2	3	29	6	.315
1982 Cedar Rapids	Midwest	OF	116	386	50	105	19	2	8	71	12	.272
1983 Tampa	Fla. St.	OF-1B	121	413	62	115	23	7	8	51	20	.278
1983 Waterbury	Eastern	OF	14	43	6	12	0	0	0	6	2	.279
1984 Vermont	Eastern	OF	134	475	70	126	31	5	16	76	29	.265
1985 Denver	A.A.	OF-1B	*137	*509	63	*155	*32	3	7	74	5	.305
1985 Cincinnati	N.L.	OF	5	12	1	4	1	0	0	1	0	.333
1986 Denver	A.A.	OF	55	193	20	49	9	2	5	27	1	.254
1986 Cincinnati	N.L.	PH	3	2	0	0	0	0	0	0	0	.000
1987 Nashville	A.A.	OF	11	37	12	11	0	0	3	6	1	.297
1987 Cincinnati	N.L.	OF	84	160	24	41	14	1	7	28	2	.256
1988 Cincinnati	N.L.	OF-1B	145	485	58	122	25	3	16	73	8	.252
1989 Nashville	A.A.	OF	4	12	1	4	0	0	0	0	1	.333
1989 Cincinnati a	N.L.	OF	117	428	49	118	24	2	15	74	20	.276
1990 Cincinnati	N.L.	OF	145	503	59	136	28	0	16	78	13	.270
1991 Cincinnati	N.L.	OF	152	532	71	136	36	0	28	91	12	.256
1992 Cincinnati b	N.L.	OF	148	496	59	122	19	1	14	66	6	.246
1993 New York	A.L.	OF	141	498	71	155	34	1	20	75	2	.311
1994 New York	A.L.	OF	103	368	68	132	25	1	21	83	5	*.359
1995 New York c	A.L.	OF	127	460	82	138	30	4	22	96	1	.300
1996 New York	A.L.	OF-1B	150	546	89	165	35	1	19	91	0	.302
1997 New York	A.L.	OF-1B	149	553	89	179	42	0	21	117	10	.324
1998 New York	A.L.	OF	152	602	95	191	40	2	24	116	15	.317
1999 New York	A.L.	OF	153	597	70	170	39	4	19	110	11	.285
2000 New York d	A.L.	OF	142	566	79	160	26	0	18	100	14	.283
Major League Totals		16 Yrs.	1916	6808	964	1969	418	20	260	1199	119	.289

Year	Club	Lea	Pos	G	AB	R	H	2B	3B	HR	RBI	SB	Avg
Division Series													
1995 New York ............A.L.			OF	5	18	5	6	0	0	0	3	6	0	.333
1996 New York ............A.L.			OF	4	15	0	2	0	0	0	0	0	.133
1997 New York ............A.L.			OF	5	19	5	8	2	0	2	7	0	.421
1998 New York ............A.L.			OF	3	11	1	4	2	0	1	1	0	.364
1999 New York ............A.L.			OF	3	8	2	2	0	0	0	0	0	.250
2000 New York ............A.L.			OF	5	19	4	4	1	0	0	0	0	.211
Division Series Totals				25	90	17	26	5	0	6	14	0	.289
Championship Series													
1990 Cincinnati ............N.L.			OF	5	17	1	8	3	0	1	4	1	.471
1996 New York ............A.L.			OF	4	11	1	3	0	0	1	2	0	.273
1998 New York ............A.L.			OF	6	25	6	7	2	0	1	3	2	.280
1999 New York ............A.L.			OF	5	21	2	6	0	0	0	1	0	.286
2000 New York ............A.L.			OF	6	20	0	5	0	0	0	5	0	.250
Championship Series Totals				26	94	10	29	5	0	3	15	3	.309
World Series Record													
1990 Cincinnati ............N.L.			OF	4	12	2	1	0	0	0	1	1	.108
1996 New York ............A.L.			OF	5	12	1	2	2	0	0	0	0	.167
1998 New York ............A.L.			OF	4	19	3	4	1	0	0	0	0	.211
1999 New York ............A.L.			OF	4	15	0	3	0	0	0	4	0	.200
2000 New York ............A.L.			OF	5	19	2	9	2	2	0	2	0	.474
World Series Totals				22	77	8	19	5	2	0	7	1	.247

a On disabled list from July 21 to September 1, 1989.
b Traded to New York Yankees with first baseman Joe DeBerry for outfielder Roberto Kelly, November 3, 1992.
c On disabled list from May 7 to May 23, 1995.
d Filed for free agency, November 10, 2000, re-signed with New York Yankees, November 16, 2000.

ORDAZ, LUIS JAVIER

Born, Maracaibo, Venezuela, August 12, 1975.
Bats Right. Throws Right. Height, 5 feet, 11 inches. Weight, 170 pounds.

Year	Club	Lea	Pos	G	AB	R	H	2B	3B	HR	RBI	SB	Avg
1993 Princeton ....Appal.		3B-SS-2B	57	217	28	65	9	7	2	39	3	.300
1994 Charlstn-Wv ....So.Atl.		SS	9	31	3	7	0	0	0	0	1	.226
1994 Princeton ....Appal.		SS-2B	60	211	33	52	12	3	0	12	7	.246
1995 Chston-Wv a ....So.Atl.		SS	112	359	43	83	14	7	2	42	12	.231
1996 St. Pete ....Fla.St.		SS	126	423	46	115	13	3	3	49	10	.272
1997 Arkansas ....Texas		SS	115	390	44	112	20	6	4	58	11	.287
1997 St. Louis .........N.L.		SS	12	22	3	6	1	0	0	1	3	.273
1998 Memphis .........P.C.		SS-2B	59	214	29	62	9	2	6	35	3	.290
1998 St. Louis b ........N.L.		SS-3B-2B	57	153	9	31	5	0	0	8	2	.203
1999 Memphis .........P.C.		SS	107	362	31	103	25	4	1	45	3	.285
1999 St. Louis c ....N.L.		SS-2B-3B	10	9	3	1	0	0	0	2	1	.111
2000 Kansas City d-e ....A.L.		SS-2B	65	104	17	23	2	0	0	11	4	.221
Major League Totals	4 Yrs.		144	288	32	61	8	0	0	22	10	.212

a Traded to St. Louis Cardinals by Cincinnati Reds with outfielder Miguel Mejias for outfielder Andre King, December 4, 1995.
b On disabled list from April 7 t o 16, 1998.
c Traded to Arizona Diamondbacks for outfielder Dante Powell, December 15, 1999.
d Released by Arizona Diamondbacks, April 3, 2000.
e Claimed on waivers by Kansas City Royals, April 5, 2000.

ORDONEZ, MAGGLIO

Born, Caracas, Venezuela, January 28, 1974.
Bats Right. Throws Right. Height, 5 feet, 11 inches. Weight, 170 pounds.

Year	Club	Lea	Pos	G	AB	R	H	2B	3B	HR	RBI	SB	Avg
1993 Hickory ....So. Atl.		OF	84	273	32	59	14	4	3	20	5	.216
1994 Hickory ....So. Atl.		OF	132	490	86	144	24	5	11	69	16	.294
1995 Pr William ....Carolina		OF	131	487	61	116	24	2	12	65	11	.238
1996 Birmingham ......Southern		OF	130	479	66	126	41	0	18	67	9	.263
1997 Nashville .............A.A.		OF	135	523	65	172	29	3	14	90	14	.329
1997 Chicago .............A.L.		OF	21	69	12	22	6	0	4	11	1	.319
1998 Chicago .............A.L.		OF	145	535	70	151	25	2	14	65	9	.282
1999 Chicago .............A.L.		OF	157	624	100	188	34	3	30	117	13	.301
2000 Chicago .............A.L.		OF	153	588	102	185	34	3	32	126	18	.315
\Major League Totals	4 Yrs.		476	1816	284	546	99	8	80	319	41	.301
Division Series													
2000 Chicago .............A.L.		OF	3	11	0	2	0	1	0	1	1	.182

ORDONEZ, REYNALDO (REY)
Born, Havana, Cuba, November 11, 1972.
Bats Right. Throws Right. Height, 5 feet, 9 inches. Weight, 159 pounds.

Year Club	Lea	Pos	G	AB	R	H	2B	3B	HR	RBI	SB	Avg
1993 St. Paul	Northern	SS-2B	15	60	10	17	4	0	0	7	3	.283
1994 St. Lucie	Fla. St.	SS	79	314	47	97	21	2	2	40	11	.309
1994 Binghamton	Eastern	SS	48	191	22	50	10	2	1	20	4	.262
1995 Norfolk	Int.	SS	125	439	49	94	21	4	2	50	11	.214
1996 New York	N.L.	SS	151	502	51	129	12	4	1	30	1	.257
1997 New York a	N.L.	SS	120	356	35	77	5	3	1	33	11	.216
1998 New York	N.L.	SS	153	505	46	124	20	2	1	42	3	.246
1999 New York	N.L.	SS	154	520	49	134	24	2	1	60	8	.258
2000 New York b	N.L.	SS	45	133	10	25	5	0	0	9	0	.188
Major League Totals	5 Yrs.		623	2016	191	489	66	11	4	174	23	.243
Division Series												
1999 New York	N.L.	SS	4	14	1	4	1	0	0	2	1	.286
Championship Series												
1999 New York	N.L.	SS	6	24	0	1	0	0	0	0	0	.042

a On disabled list from June 2 to July 11, 1997.
b On disabled list from May 30 to October 31, 2000.

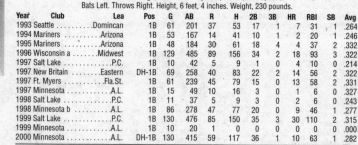

ORTIZ (ARIAS), DAVID AMERICO
Born, Santo Domingo, Dominican Republic, November 18, 1975.
Bats Left. Throws Right. Height, 6 feet, 4 inches. Weight, 230 pounds.

Year Club	Lea	Pos	G	AB	R	H	2B	3B	HR	RBI	SB	Avg
1993 Seattle	Domincan	1B	61	201	37	53	17	1	7	31	1	.264
1994 Mariners	Arizona	1B	53	167	14	41	10	1	2	20	1	.246
1995 Mariners	Arizona	1B	48	184	30	61	18	4	4	37	2	.332
1996 Wisconsin a	Midwest	1B	129	485	89	156	34	2	18	93	3	.322
1997 Salt Lake	P.C.	1B	10	42	5	9	1	0	4	10	0	.214
1997 New Britain	Eastern	DH-1B	69	258	40	83	22	2	14	56	2	.322
1997 Ft. Myers	Fla.St.	1B	61	239	45	79	15	0	13	58	2	.331
1997 Minnesota	A.L.	1B	15	49	10	16	3	0	1	6	0	.327
1998 Salt Lake	P.C.	1B	11	37	5	9	3	0	2	6	0	.243
1998 Minnesota b	A.L.	1B	86	278	47	77	20	0	9	46	1	.277
1999 Salt Lake	P.C.	1B	130	476	85	150	35	3	30	110	2	.315
1999 Minnesota	A.L.	1B	10	20	1	0	0	0	0	0	0	.000
2000 Minnesota	A.L.	DH-1B	130	415	59	117	36	1	10	63	1	.282
Major League Totals	4 Yrs.		241	762	117	210	59	1	20	115	2	.276

a Sent to Minnesota Twins by Seattle Mariners to complete trade for infielder Dave Hollins, September 13, 1996.
b On disabled list from May 10 to July 9, 1998.

ORTIZ (SANTOS), JOSE DANIEL
Born, Santo Domingo, Dominican Republic, June 13, 1977.
Bats Right. Throws Right. Height, 5 feet, 9 inches. Weight, 160 pounds.

Year Club	Lea	Pos	G	AB	R	H	2B	3B	HR	RBI	SB	Avg
1995 Oakland	Domincan	SS	61	217	45	65	12	2	9	41	14	.300
1996 Athletics	Arizona	SS	52	200	43	66	12	8	4	25	16	.330
1996 Modesto	California	2B	1	4	0	1	0	0	0	0	0	.250
1997 Modesto	California	SS-2B	128	497	92	122	25	7	16	58	22	.245
1998 Huntsville	Southern	2B-SS-OF	94	354	70	98	24	2	6	55	22	.277
1999 Vancouver	P.C.	SS	107	377	66	107	29	2	9	45	13	.284
2000 Sacramento	P.C.	2B	131	518	107	182	34	5	24	108	22	.351
2000 Oakland	A.L.	2B	7	11	4	2	0	0	0	1	0	.182

OWENS, ERIC BLAKE
Born, Danville, Virginia, February 3, 1971.
Bats Right. Throws Right. Height, 6 feet, 1 inch. Weight, 185 pounds.

Year Club	Lea	Pos	G	AB	R	H	2B	3B	HR	RBI	SB	Avg
1992 Billings	Pioneer	SS-3B	67	239	41	72	10	3	3	26	15	.301
1993 Winston-Sal	Carolina	SS	122	487	74	132	25	4	10	63	21	.271
1994 Chattanooga	Southern	3B-2B	134	523	73	133	17	3	3	36	38	.254
1995 Cincinnati	N.L.	3B	2	2	0	2	0	0	0	1	0	1.000
1995 Indianapols	A.A.	2B	108	427	86	134	24	8	12	63	33	.314
1996 Indianapols	A.A.	SS-3B-2B-OF	33	128	24	41	8	2	4	14	6	.320
1996 Cincinnati	N.L.	OF-2B-3B	88	205	26	41	6	0	0	9	16	.200

Year	Club	Lea	Pos	G	AB	R	H	2B	3B	HR	RBI	SB	Avg
1997 Cincinnati ........N.L.			OF-2B	27	57	8	15	0	0	0	3	3	.263
1997 Indianapolis ......A.A.			2B-SS-OF-3B	104	391	56	112	15	4	11	44	23	.286
1998 Louisville ....Int.			OF-3B	77	254	48	85	11	4	5	40	21	.335
1998 Milwaukee a-b-c ..N.L.			OF-2B	34	40	5	5	2	0	1	4	0	.125
1999 San Diego ........N.L.			OF-1B-3B-2B	149	440	55	117	22	3	9	61	33	.266
2000 San Diego ........N.L.			OF-2B	145	583	87	171	19	7	6	51	29	.293
Major League Totals	6 Yrs.			445	1327	181	351	49	10	16	129	81	.265

a Traded by Cincinnati Reds to Florida Marlins for a player to be named later, March 21, 1998. Reds received pitcher Jesus Martinez to complete trade, March 26, 1998.
b Purchased by Milwaukee Brewers, March 25, 1998.
c Filed for free agency, October 16, 1998, signed with San Diego Padres, December 10, 1998.

PALMEIRO, ORLANDO

Born, Hoboken, New Jersey, January 19, 1969.
Bats Left. Throws Right. Height, 5 feet, 11 inches. Weight, 155 pounds.

Year	Club	Lea	Pos	G	AB	R	H	2B	3B	HR	RBI	SB	Avg
1995 Vancouver ............P.C.			OF	107	398	66	122	21	4	0	47	16	.307
1995 California ............A.L.			OF	15	20	3	7	0	0	0	1	0	.350
1996 Vancouver ............P.C.			OF	62	245	40	75	13	4	0	33	7	.306
1996 California ............A.L.			OF	50	87	6	25	6	1	0	6	0	.287
1997 Anaheim a ............A.L.			OF	74	134	19	29	2	2	0	8	2	.216
1998 Vancouver ............P.C.			OF	43	140	21	42	13	3	1	29	3	.300
1998 Anaheim ............A.L.			OF	75	165	28	53	7	2	0	21	5	.321
1999 Anaheim ............A.L.			OF	109	317	46	88	12	1	1	23	5	.278
2000 Anaheim ............A.L.			OF	108	243	38	73	20	2	0	25	4	.300
Major League Totals	6 Yrs.			431	966	140	275	47	8	1	84	16	.285

a On disabled list from August 23 to September 7, 1997.

PALMEIRO, RAFAEL CORRALES

Born, Havana, Cuba, September 24, 1964.
Bats Left. Throws Left. Height 6 feet. Weight, 188 pounds.

Year	Club	Lea	Pos	G	AB	R	H	2B	3B	HR	RBI	SB	Avg
1985 Peoria ....Midwest			OF	73	279	34	83	22	4	5	51	9	.297
1986 Pittsfield ..../.....Eastern			OF	*140	509	66	*156	29	2	12	*95	15	.306
1986 Chicago ............N.L.			OF	22	73	9	18	4	0	3	12	1	.247
1987 Iowa ................A.A.			OF	57	214	36	64	14	3	11	41	4	.299
1987 Chicago ............N.L.			OF-1B	84	221	32	61	15	1	14	30	2	.276
1988 Chicago a ............N.L.			OF-1B	152	580	75	178	41	5	8	53	12	.307
1989 Texas ...........A.L.			1B	156	559	76	154	23	4	8	64	4	.275
1990 Texas ............A.L.			1B	154	598	72	*191	35	6	14	89	3	.319
1991 Texas ............A.L.			1B	159	631	115	203	*49	3	26	88	4	.322
1992 Texas ............A.L.			1B	159	608	84	163	27	4	22	85	2	.268
1993 Texas b ............A.L.			1B	160	597	*124	176	40	2	37	105	22	.295
1994 Baltimore ............A.L.			1B	111	436	82	139	32	0	23	76	7	.319
1995 Baltimore ............A.L.			1B	143	554	89	172	30	2	39	104	3	.310
1996 Baltimore ............A.L.			1B	162	626	110	181	40	2	39	142	8	.289
1997 Baltimore ............A.L.			1B	158	614	95	156	24	2	38	110	5	.254
1998 Baltimore c ............A.L.			1B	162	619	98	183	36	1	43	121	11	.296
1999 Texas ............A.L.			DH-1B	158	565	96	183	30	1	47	148	2	.324
2000 Texas ............A.L.			1B	158	565	102	163	29	3	39	120	2	.288
Major League Totals	15 Yrs.			2098	7846	1259	2321	455	36	400	1347	88	.296
Division Series													
1996 Baltimore ............A.L.			1B	4	17	4	3	1	0	1	2	0	.176
1997 Baltimore ............A.L.			1B	4	12	2	3	2	0	0	0	0	.250
1999 Texas ............A.L.			DH	3	11	0	3	0	0	0	0	0	.273
Division Series Totals				11	40	6	9	3	0	1	2	0	.225
Championship Series													
1996 Baltimore ............A.L.			1B	5	17	4	4	0	0	2	4	0	.235
1997 Baltimore ............A.L.			1B	6	25	3	7	2	0	1	2	0	.280
Championship Series Totals				11	42	7	11	2	0	3	6	0	.262

a Traded to Texas Rangers with pitchers Jamie Moyer and Drew Hall for infielders Curtis Wilkerson and Luis Benetiz, outfielder Pablo Delgado, and pitchers Mitch Williams, Paul Kilgus and Steve Wilson, December 5, 1988.
b Filed for free agency, October 25; signed with Baltimore Orioles, December 13, 1993.
c Filed for free agency, October 23, 1998, signed with Texas Rangers, December 1, 1998.

PALMER, DEAN WILLIAM
Born, Tallahassee, Florida, December 27, 1968.
Bats Right. Throws Right. Height, 6 feet, 2 inches. Weight, 195 pounds.

Year	Club	Lea	Pos	G	AB	R	H	2B	3B	HR	RBI	SB	Avg
1986	Sara. Rangers	Gulf C.	3B	50	163	19	34	7	1	0	12	6	.209
1987	Gastonia	So. Atl.	3B	128	484	51	104	16	0	9	54	5	.215
1988	Charlotte a	Fla. St.	3B	74	305	38	81	12	1	4	35	0	.266
1989	Tulsa	Texas	3B	133	498	82	125	31	5	*25	90	15	.251
1989	Texas	A.L.	3B-SS-OF	16	19	0	2	2	0	0	1	0	.105
1990	Tulsa	Texas	3B	7	24	4	7	0	1	3	9	0	.292
1990	Oklahoma City b	A.A.	3B-1B	88	316	33	69	17	4	12	39	1	.218
1991	Oklahoma City	A.A.	3B	60	234	45	70	11	2	22	59	4	.299
1991	Texas	A.L.	3B-OF	81	268	38	50	9	2	15	37	0	.187
1992	Texas	A.L.	3B	152	541	74	124	25	0	26	72	10	.229
1993	Texas	A.L.	3B-SS	148	519	88	127	31	2	33	96	11	.245
1994	Texas c	A.L.	3B	93	342	50	84	14	2	19	59	3	.246
1995	Texas d-e	A.L.	3B	36	119	30	40	6	0	9	24	1	.336
1996	Texas	A.L.	3B	154	582	98	163	26	2	38	107	2	.289
1997	Texas-Kansas City f-g-h	A.L.	3B	143	542	70	139	31	1	23	86	2	.256
1998	Kansas City i	A.L.	3B	152	572	84	159	27	2	34	119	8	.278
1999	Detroit	A.L.	3B	150	560	92	147	25	2	38	100	3	.262
2000	Detroit	A.L.	3B-1B	145	524	73	134	22	2	29	102	4	.256
Major League Totals		11 Yrs.		1270	4588	697	1169	218	15	264	803	44	.255

Division Series

Year	Club	Lea	Pos	G	AB	R	H	2B	3B	HR	RBI	SB	Avg
1996	Texas	A.L.	3B	4	19	3	4	1	0	1	2	0	.211

a On disabled list from July 4 to end of 1988 season.
b On disabled list from July 27 to August 5, 1990.
c On disabled list from April 30 to May 14, 1994.
d Signed with Texas Rangers, May 15, 1995.
e On disabled list from June 4 to September 22, 1995.
f Traded to Kansas City Royals for outfielder Tom Goodwin, July 26, 1997.
g Filed for free agency, October 27, 1997.
h Re-signed with Kansas City Royals December 15, 1997.
i Filed for free agency, October 23, 1998, signed with Detroit Tigers, November 13, 1998.

PAQUETTE, CRAIG HAROLD
Born, Long Beach, California, March 28, 1969.
Bats Right. Throws Right. Height, 6 feet. Weight, 190 pounds.

Year	Club	Lea	Pos	G	AB	R	H	2B	3B	HR	RBI	SB	Avg
1989	Sou Oregon	Northwest	3B-2B-SS	71	277	53	93	22	3	14	56	9	.336
1990	Modesto	California	3B	130	495	65	118	23	4	15	59	8	.238
1991	Huntsville a-b	Southern	3B-1B	102	378	50	99	18	1	8	60	0	.262
1992	Huntsville	Southern	3B	115	450	59	116	25	4	17	71	13	.258
1992	Tacoma	P.C.	3B	17	66	10	18	7	0	2	11	3	.273
1993	Tacoma	P.C.	3B-2B-SS	50	183	29	49	8	0	8	29	3	.268
1993	Oakland	A.L.	3B-OF	105	393	35	86	20	4	12	46	4	.219
1994	Oakland	A.L.	3B	14	49	0	7	2	0	0	0	1	.143
1994	Tacoma c	P.C.	3B	65	245	39	70	12	3	17	48	3	.286
1995	Oakland	A.L.	3B-OF-SS-1B	105	283	42	64	13	1	13	49	5	.226
1996	Omaha	A.A.	DH-3B-1B-OF	18	63	9	21	3	0	4	13	1	.333
1996	Kansas City d	A.L.	3B-OF-1B-SS	118	429	61	111	15	1	22	67	5	.259
1997	Kansas City	A.L.	3B-OF	77	252	26	58	15	1	8	33	2	.230
1997	Omaha e	A.A.	3B	23	91	9	28	6	0	3	20	0	.308
1998	Norfolk	Int.	3B-SS-OF	15	61	11	17	1	1	3	14	2	.279
1998	New York f-g	N.L.	3B-1B-OF	7	19	3	5	2	0	0	0	1	.263
1999	Norfolk	Int.	3B	70	283	40	77	20	3	15	54	3	.272
1999	St. Louis h-i	N.L.	OF-3B-2B-1B	48	157	21	45	6	0	10	37	1	.287
2000	St. Louis	N.L.	3B-OF-1B-2B	134	384	47	94	24	2	15	61	4	.245
Major League Totals		8 Yrs.		608	1966	235	470	97	9	80	293	23	.239

Division Series

Year	Club	Lea	Pos	G	AB	R	H	2B	3B	HR	RBI	SB	Avg
2000	St. Louis	N.L.	3B-OF	2	2	0	0	0	0	0	0	0	.000

Championship Series

Year	Club	Lea	Pos	G	AB	R	H	2B	3B	HR	RBI	SB	Avg
2000	St. Louis	N.L.	OF-3B	4	6	0	1	0	0	0	0	0	.167

a On disabled list from April 10 to May 5, 1991.
b On disabled list from June 1 to 11, 1991.
c On disabled list from July 18 to September 1, 1994.
d Released by Oakland Athletics, March 26, 1996, signed with Kansas City Royals organization, April 3, 1996.
e Filed for free agency, October 15, 1997, signed with New York Mets organization, December 23, 1997.
f On disabled list from May 7 to October 1, 1998.
g Filed for free agency, October 15, 1998, re-signed with New York Mets organization, December 18, 1998.
h On disabled list from April 22 to May 1, 1999.
i Traded to St. Louis Cardinals for infielder Shawon Dunston, July 31, 1999.

PATTERSON, DONALD COREY (COREY)
Born, Atlanta, Georgia, August 13, 1979.
Bats Left. Throws Right. Height, 5 feet, 10 inches. Weight, 175 pounds.

Year	Club	Lea	Pos	G	AB	R	H	2B	3B	HR	RBI	SB	Avg
1999 Lansing	....	Midwest	OF	112	475	94	152	35	17	20	79	33	.320
2000 West Tenn	....	Southern	OF	118	444	73	116	26	5	22	82	27	.261
2000 Chicago	....	N.L.	OF	11	42	9	7	1	0	2	2	1	.167

PAYTON, JASON LEE (JAY)
Born, Zanesville, Ohio, November 22, 1972.
Bats Right. Throws Right. Height, 5 feet, 10 inches. Weight, 185 pounds.

Year	Club	Lea	Pos	G	AB	R	H	2B	3B	HR	RBI	SB	Avg
1994 Pittsfield	....	N.Y.-Penn.	OF	58	219	47	80	16	2	3	37	10	.365
1994 Binghamton	....	Eastern	OF	8	25	3	7	1	0	0	1	1	.280
1995 Binghamton	....	Eastern	OF	85	357	59	123	20	3	14	54	16	.345
1995 Norfolk	....	Int.	OF	50	196	33	47	11	4	4	30	11	.240
1996 Mets	....	Gulf Coast	DH	3	13	3	5	1	0	1	2	1	.385
1996 Binghamton	....	Eastern	DH	4	10	0	2	0	0	0	2	0	.200
1996 St. Lucie	....	Fla.St.	DH	9	26	4	8	2	0	0	1	2	.308
1996 Norfolk a-b	....	Int.	DH-OF	55	153	30	47	6	3	6	26	10	.307
1998 St. Lucie	....	Fla.St.	OF	3	7	0	1	0	0	0	0	0	.143
1998 Norfolk	....	Int.	OF-1B	82	322	45	84	14	4	8	30	12	.261
1998 New York c	....	N.L.	OF	15	22	2	7	1	0	0	0	0	.318
1999 Norfolk	....	Int.	OF	38	144	27	56	13	2	8	35	2	.389
1999 St.Lucie	....	Fla.St.	OF	7	26	3	9	1	1	0	3	0	.346
1999 New York d-e	....	N.L.	OF	13	8	1	2	1	0	0	1	1	.250
2000 New York	....	N.L.	OF	149	488	63	142	23	1	17	62	5	.291
Major League Totals	....		3 Yrs.	177	518	66	151	25	1	17	63	6	.292
Division Series													
2000 New York	....	N.L.	OF	4	17	1	3	0	0	0	2	1	.176
Championship Series													
2000 New York	....	N.L.	OF	5	19	1	3	0	0	1	3	0	.158
World Series Record													
2000 New York	....	N.L.	OF	5	21	3	7	0	0	1	3	0	.333

a On disabled list from April 29 to July 3, 1996.
b On disabled list from April 3 to September 1, 1997.
c On disabled list from May 27 to June 15 and June 24 to July 20, 1998.
d On disabled list from March 21 to June 8, 1999.
e On disabled list from July 10 to August 19, 1999.

PEREZ, NEIFI NEFTALI
Born, Villa Mella, Dominican Republic, February 2, 1975.
Bats Both. Throws Right. Height, 6 feet. Weight, 176 pounds.

Year	Club	Lea	Pos	G	AB	R	H	2B	3B	HR	RBI	SB	Avg
1993 Bend	....	Northwest	SS-2B	75	296	35	77	11	4	3	32	19	.260
1994 Central Val	....	California	SS	134	506	64	121	16	7	1	35	9	.239
1995 Colo Spmgs	....	P.C.	SS	11	36	4	10	4	0	0	2	1	.278
1995 New Haven	....	Eastern	SS	116	427	59	108	28	3	5	43	5	.253
1996 Colo Spmgs	....	P.C.	SS	133	570	77	180	28	12	7	72	16	.316
1996 Colorado	....	N.L.	SS-2B	17	45	4	7	2	0	0	3	2	.156
1997 Colo Spmgs	....	P.C.	SS	68	303	68	110	24	3	8	46	8	.363
1997 Colorado	....	N.L.	SS-2B-3B	83	313	46	91	13	10	5	31	4	.291
1998 Colorado	....	N.L.	SS-C	*162	647	80	177	25	9	9	59	5	.274
1999 Colorado	....	N.L.	SS	157	*690	108	193	27	*11	12	70	13	.280
2000 Colorado	....	N.L.	SS	*162	651	92	187	39	11	10	71	3	.287
Major League Totals	....		5 Yrs.	581	2346	330	655	106	41	36	234	27	.279

PERRY, HERBERT EDWARD (HERB)
Born, Live Oak, Florida, September 15, 1969.
Bats Right. Throws Right. Height, 6 feet, 2 inches. Weight, 210 pounds.

Year	Club	Lea	Pos	G	AB	R	H	2B	3B	HR	RBI	SB	Avg
1991 Watertown	...	N.Y.-Penn.	DH	14	52	3	11	2	0	0	5	0	.212
1992 Kinston	......	Carolina	DH-1B-OF-3B	121	449	74	125	16	1	19	77	12	.278
1993 Canton-Akrn	....	Eastern	1B-3B-OF	89	327	52	88	21	1	9	55	7	.269
1994 Cleveland	....	A.L.	1B-3B	4	9	1	1	0	0	0	1	0	.111

Year	Club	Lea	Pos	G	AB	R	H	2B	3B	HR	RBI	SB	Avg
1994 Charlotte	Int.	1B-3B-OF	102	376	67	123	20	4	13	70	9	.327
1995 Buffalo	A.A.	1B	49	180	27	57	14	1	2	17	1	.317
1995 Cleveland	A.L.	1B-3B	52	162	23	51	13	1	3	23	1	.315
1996 Buffalo	A.A.	1B-3B-OF	40	151	21	51	7	1	5	30	4	.338
1996 Cleveland	A.L.	1B-3B	7	12	1	1	1	0	0	0	1	.083
1997 Cleveland a-b	A.L.	INJURED - Did Not Play										
1998 Durham	Int.	1B	5	17	1	5	4	0	0	1	0	.294
1998 Devil Rays	Gulf Coast	3B	8	26	1	3	0	0	0	1	0	.115
1998 St. Pete	Fla.St.	3B	2	8	1	1	0	0	0	0	0	.125
1999 Tampa Bay c	A.L.	3B-1B-OF	66	209	29	53	10	1	6	32	0	.254
2000 Tampa Bay-Chicago d	A.L.	3B-1B	116	411	71	124	30	1	12	62	4	.302
Major League Totals	5 Yrs.		245	803	125	230	54	3	21	118	6	.286
Division Series												
1995 Cleveland	A.L.	PH	1	1	0	0	0	0	0	0	0	.000
2000 Chicago	A.L.	3B	3	9	0	4	1	0	0	1	0	.444
Division Series Totals			4	10	0	4	1	0	0	1	0	.400
Championship Series												
1995 Cleveland	A.L.	1B	3	8	0	0	0	0	0	0	0	.000
World Series Record												
1995 Cleveland	A.L.	1B	3	5	0	0	0	0	0	0	0	.000

a On disabled list from March 26 to September 28, 1997.
b Selected in expansion draft by Tampa Bay Devil Rays, November 18, 1997.
c On disabled list from July 22 to September 1, 1999.
d Claimed on waivers by Chicago White Sox, April 21, 2000.

PETRICK, BENJAMIN WAYNE (BEN)

Born, Salem, Oregon, April 7, 1977.
Bats Right. Throws Right. Height, 6 feet. Weight, 195 pounds.

Year	Club	Lea	Pos	G	AB	R	H	2B	3B	HR	RBI	SB	Avg
1996 Asheville	So.Atl.	C	122	446	74	105	24	2	14	52	19	.235
1997 Salem	Carolina	C	121	412	68	102	23	3	15	56	30	.248
1998 New Haven	Eastern	C-OF	106	349	52	83	21	3	18	50	7	.238
1999 Carolina	Southern	C	20	68	18	21	5	1	4	22	3	.309
1999 Colorado Spgs	P.C.	C	84	282	56	88	16	5	19	64	9	.312
1999 Colorado	N.L.	C	19	62	13	20	3	0	4	12	1	.323
2000 Colorado Spgs	P.C.	PH	63	248	38	78	22	3	9	47	7	.315
2000 Colorado	N.L.	C	52	146	32	47	10	1	3	20	1	.322
Major League Totals	2 Yrs.		71	208	45	67	13	1	7	32	2	.322

PIATT, ADAM DAVID

Born, Chicago, Illinois, February 8, 1976.
Bats Right. Throws Right. Height, 6 feet, 2 inches. Weight, 195 pounds.

Year	Club	Lea	Pos	G	AB	R	H	2B	3B	HR	RBI	SB	Avg
1997 Sou Oregon	Northwest	3B-1B	57	216	63	63	9	1	13	35	19	.292
1998 Modesto	California	3B-SS-2B	133	500	91	144	40	3	20	107	20	.288
1999 Midland	Texas	3B	129	476	128	164	48	3	39	135	7	.345
1999 Vancouver	P.C.	3B	6	18	1	4	1	0	0	3	0	.222
2000 Sacramento	P.C.	OF	65	254	36	72	15	0	8	42	3	.283
2000 Oakland	A.L.	OF-3B-1B	60	157	24	47	5	5	5	23	0	.299
Division Series												
2000 Oakland	A.L.	OF	3	6	2	1	0	0	0	0	0	.167

PIAZZA, MICHAEL JOSEPH

Born, Norristown, Pennsylvania, September 4, 1968.
Bats Right. Throws Right. Height, 6 feet, 3 inches. Weight, 197 pounds.

Year	Club	Lea	Pos	G	AB	R	H	2B	3B	HR	RBI	SB	Avg
1989 Salem	Northwest	C	57	198	22	53	11	0	8	25	0	.268
1990 Vero Beach	Fla. St.	C-1B	88	272	27	68	20	0	6	45	0	.250
1991 Bakersfield	California	C-1B	117	448	71	124	27	2	29	80	0	.277
1992 San Antonio	Texas	C	31	114	18	43	11	0	7	20	0	.377
1992 Albuquerque	P.C.	C-1B	94	358	54	122	22	5	16	69	1	.341
1992 Los Angeles	N.L.	C	21	69	5	16	3	0	1	7	0	.232
1993 Los Angeles a	N.L.	C-1B	149	547	81	174	24	2	35	112	3	.318
1994 Los Angeles	N.L.	C	107	405	64	129	18	0	24	92	1	.319
1995 Los Angeles b	N.L.	C	112	434	82	150	17	0	32	93	1	.346

Year	Club	Lea	Pos	G	AB	R	H	2B	3B	HR	RBI	SB	Avg
1996 Los Angeles	....	N.L.	C	148	547	87	184	16	0	36	105	0	.336
1997 Los Angeles	....	N.L.	C	152	556	104	201	32	1	40	124	5	.362
1998 L.A.-Florida-N.Y. c-d-e	.	N.L.	C	151	561	88	184	38	1	32	111	1	.328
1999 New York f	....	N.L.	C	141	534	100	162	25	0	40	124	2	.303
2000 New York	....	N.L.	C	136	482	90	156	26	0	38	113	4	.324
Major League Totals	....		9 Yrs.	1117	4135	701	1356	199	4	278	881	17	.328
Division Series													
1995 Los Angeles	....	N.L.	C	3	14	1	3	1	0	1	1	0	.214
1996 Los Angeles	....	N.L.	C	3	10	1	3	0	0	0	2	0	.300
1999 New York	....	N.L.	C	2	9	0	2	0	0	0	0	0	.222
2000 New York	....	N.L.	C	4	14	1	3	1	0	0	0	0	.214
Division Series Totals	....			12	47	3	11	2	0	1	3	0	.234
Championship Series													
1999 New York	....	N.L.	C	6	24	1	4	0	0	1	4	0	.167
2000 New York	....	N.L.	C	5	17	7	7	3	0	2	4	0	.412
Championship Series Totals	......			11	41	8	11	3	0	3	8	0	.268
World Series Record													
2000 New York	....	N.L.	C-DH	5	22	3	6	2	0	2	4	0	.273

a Selected Rookie of the Year in National League for 1993.

b On disabled list from May 11 to June 4, 1995.

c Traded to Florida Marlins with infielder Todd Zeile for outfielder Gary Sheffield, outfielder Jim Eisenreich, catcher Charles Johnson, infielder Bobby Bonilla and pitcher Manuel Barrios, May 15, 1998.

d Traded to New York Mets for outfielder Preston Wilson, pitcher Ed Yarnall and player to be named later, May 22, 1998.

e Florida Marlins received pitcher Geoff Goetz to complete trade, July 3, 1998.

f On disabled list from April 10 to April 25, 1999.

PIERRE, JUAN D'VAUGHN

Born, Mobile, Alabama, August 14, 1977.
Bats Left. Throws Right. Height, 6 feet. Weight, 170 pounds.

Year	Club	Lea	Pos	G	AB	R	H	2B	3B	HR	RBI	SB	Avg
1998 Portland	....	Northwest	OF	64	264	55	93	9	2	0	30	38	.352
1999 Asheville	....	So.Atl.	OF	140	585	93	187	28	5	1	55	66	.320
2000 Carolina	....	Southern	OF	107	439	63	143	16	4	0	32	46	.326
2000 Colorado Spgs	......	P.C.	OF	4	17	3	8	0	1	0	1	1	.471
2000 Colorado	....	N.L.	OF	51	200	26	62	2	0	0	20	7	.310

POLANCO, PLACIDO ENRIQUE

Born, Santo Domingo, Dominican Republic, October 10, 1975.
Bats Right. Throws Right. Height, 5 feet, 10 inches. Weight, 168 pounds.

Year	Club	Lea	Pos	G	AB	R	H	2B	3B	HR	RBI	SB	Avg
1994 Cardinals	......	Arizona	SS-2B	32	127	17	27	4	0	1	10	4	.213
1995 Peoria	....	Midwest	SS-2B	103	361	43	96	7	4	2	41	7	.266
1996 St. Pete	....	Fla.St.	2B	137	540	65	157	29	5	0	51	4	.291
1997 Arkansas	....	Texas	2B	129	508	71	148	16	3	2	51	19	.291
1998 Memphis	....	P.C.	2B-SS	70	246	36	69	19	1	1	21	6	.280
1998 St. Louis	....	N.L.	SS-2B	45	114	10	29	3	2	1	11	2	.254
1999 Memphis	....	P.C.	2B	29	120	18	33	4	1	0	10	2	.275
1999 St. Louis	....	N.L.	2B-3B-SS	88	220	24	61	9	3	1	19	1	.277
2000 St. Louis a	....	N.L.	2B-3B-SS-1B	118	323	50	102	12	3	5	39	4	.316
Major League Totals	....		3 Yrs.	251	657	84	192	24	8	7	69	7	.292
Division Series													
2000 St. Louis	....	N.L.	3B	3	10	1	3	0	0	0	3	1	.300
Championship Series													
2000 St. Louis	....	N.L.	3B	4	5	0	1	0	0	0	0	0	.200

a On disabled list from July 1 to July 15, 2000.

POLONIA, LUIS ANDREW

Born, Santiago, Dominican Republic, October 12, 1964.
Bats Left. Throws Right. Height, 5 feet, 8 inches. Weight, 152 pounds.

Year	Club	Lea	Pos	G	AB	R	H	2B	3B	HR	RBI	SB	Avg
1984 Madison	....	Midwest	OF	135	528	103	162	21	10	8	64	55	.307
1985 Huntsville	......	Southern	OF	130	515	82	149	15	18	5	36	39	.289
1986 Tacoma	....	P.C.	OF	134	549	98	165	20	4	3	63	36	.301
1987 Tacoma	....	P.C.	OF	14	56	18	18	1	2	0	8	4	.321

141

Year	Club	Lea	Pos	G	AB	R	H	2B	3B	HR	RBI	SB	Avg
1987 Oakland	.............A.L.	OF	125	435	78	125	16	10	4	49	29	.287
1988 Tacoma	................P.C.	OF	65	254	58	85	13	5	2	27	31	.335
1988 Oakland	.............A.L.	OF	84	288	51	84	11	4	2	27	24	.292
1989 Oakland-New York a	...A.L.	OF	125	433	70	130	17	6	3	46	22	.300
1990 New York-California b	...A.L.	OF	120	403	52	135	7	9	2	35	21	.335
1991 California	............A.L.	OF	150	604	92	179	28	8	2	50	48	.296
1992 California	............A.L.	OF	149	577	83	165	17	4	0	35	51	.286
1993 California c	............A.L.	OF	152	576	75	156	17	6	1	32	55	.271
1994 New York	.........A.L.	OF	95	350	62	109	21	6	1	36	20	.311
1995 New York	...........A.L.	OF	67	238	37	62	9	3	2	15	10	.261
1995 Atlanta d	...........N.L.	OF	28	53	6	14	7	0	0	2	3	.264
1996 Rochester	.............Int.	OF	13	50	9	12	2	0	0	3	5	.240
1996 Baltimore	...........A.L.	OF	58	175	25	42	4	1	2	14	8	.240
1996 Atlanta e-f-g	.........N.L.	OF	22	31	3	13	0	0	0	2	1	.419
1997 Tigres h	.........Mexican	OF	110	408	105	154	29	5	7	59	48	.377
1998 Tigres i	..........Mexican	OF	86	357	82	136	15	14	9	63	36	.381
1999 Detroit j	.............A.L.	DH-OF	87	333	46	108	21	8	10	32	17	.324
2000 Detroit-New York k-l	....A.L.	OF	117	344	48	95	14	5	7	30	12	.276
Major League Totals	....		12 Yrs.	1379	4840	728	1417	189	70	36	405	321	.293
Division Series													
1995 Atlanta	.............N.L.	PH	3	3	0	1	0	0	0	2	1	.333
1996 Atlanta	............N.L.	PH	2	2	0	0	0	0	0	0	0	.000
2000 New York	............A.L.	PH	1	1	0	1	0	0	0	0	0	1.000
Division Series Totals	....			6	6	0	2	0	0	0	2	1	.333
Championship Series													
1988 Oakland	.............A.L.	OF	3	5	0	2	0	0	0	0	0	.400
1995 Atlanta	.............N.L.	OF	3	2	0	1	0	0	0	1	0	.500
1996 Atlanta	.............N.L.	PH	3	3	0	0	0	0	0	0	0	.000
2000 New York	............A.L.	PH	1	1	0	0	0	0	0	0	0	.000
Championship Series Totals	......			10	11	0	3	0	0	0	1	0	.273
World Series Record													
1988 Oakland	.............A.L.	OF	3	9	1	1	0	0	0	0	0	.111
1995 Atlanta	.............N.L.	OF	6	14	3	4	1	0	1	4	1	.286
1996 Atlanta	.............N.L.	PH	6	5	0	0	0	0	0	0	0	.000
2000 New York	............A.L.	PH	2	2	0	1	0	0	0	0	0	.500
World Series Totals	....			17	30	4	6	1	0	1	4	1	.200

a Traded to New York Yankees with pitcher Greg Cadaret and pitcher Eric Plunk for outfielder Rickey Henderson, June 21, 1989.
b Traded to California Angels for outfielder Claudell Washington and pitcher Rich Monteleone, April 29, 1990.
c Filed for free agency, October 27, 1993, signed with New York Yankees, December 20, 1993.
d Traded to Atlanta Braves for outfielder Troy Hughes, August 11, 1995.
e Filed for free agency, November 2, 1995, signed with Seattle Mariners, February 9, 1996.
f Released by Seattle Mariners, March 26, 1996, signed with Baltimore Orioles, April 22, 1996.
g Released by Baltimore Orioles, August 12, 1996, signed with Atlanta Braves, August 17, 1996.
h Filed for free agency, November 18, 1996, signed with Tampa Bay Devil Rays, March 11, 1997.
i Filed for free agency, October 16, 1998, signed with Detroit Tigers, December 18, 1998.
j Filed for free agency, November 4, 1999, re-signed with Detroit Tigers, November 10, 1999.
k Released by Detroit Tigers, July 31, 2000, signed with New York Yankees, August 3, 2000.
l Filed for free agency, October 30, 2000.

POSADA, JORGE RAFAEL
Born, Santurce, Puerto Rico, August 17, 1971.
Bats Both. Throws Right. Height, 6 feet, 2 inches. Weight, 205 pounds

Year	Club	Lea	Pos	G	AB	R	H	2B	3B	HR	RBI	SB	Avg
1991 Oneonta	........N.Y.-Penn	2B-C	71	217	34	51	5	5	4	33	6	.235
1992 Greensboro	........So. Atl.	DH-C-3B	101	339	60	94	22	4	12	58	11	.277
1993 Pr William	........Carolina	C-3B	118	410	71	106	27	2	17	61	17	.259
1993 Albany	...........Eastern	C	7	25	3	7	0	0	0	0	0	.280
1994 Columbus	.............Int.	C-OF	92	313	46	75	13	3	11	48	5	.240
1995 Columbus	.............Int.	C	108	368	60	94	32	5	8	51	4	.255
1995 New York	.............A.L.	C	1	0	0	0	0	0	0	0	0	.000
1996 Columbus	.............Int.	C-OF	106	354	76	96	22	6	11	62	3	.271
1996 New York	.............A.L.	C	8	14	1	1	0	0	0	0	0	.071
1997 New York	.............A.L.	C	60	188	29	47	12	0	6	25	1	.250
1998 New York	.............A.L.	C-1B	111	358	56	96	23	0	17	63	0	.268
1999 New York	.............A.L.	C-1B	112	379	50	93	19	2	12	57	1	.245
2000 New York	.............A.L.	C-1B	151	505	92	145	35	1	28	86	2	.287
Major League Totals	....		6 Yrs.	443	1444	228	382	89	3	63	231	4	.265

Year	Club	Lea	Pos	G	AB	R	H	2B	3B	HR	RBI	SB	Avg
	Division Series												
1995	New York	A.L.	C	1	0	1	0	0	0	0	0	0	.000
1997	New York	A.L.	C	2	2	0	0	0	0	0	0	0	.000
1998	New York	A.L.	C	1	2	1	0	0	0	0	0	0	.000
1999	New York	A.L.	C	1	4	0	1	1	0	0	0	0	.250
2000	New York	A.L.	C	5	17	2	4	2	0	0	1	0	.235
Division Series Totals				10	25	4	5	3	0	0	1	0	.200
	Championship Series												
1998	New York	A.L.	C	5	11	1	2	0	0	1	2	0	.182
1999	New York	A.L.	C	3	10	1	1	0	0	1	2	0	.100
2000	New York	A.L.	C	6	19	2	3	1	0	0	3	0	.158
Championship Series Totals				14	40	4	6	1	0	2	7	0	.150
	World Series Record												
1998	New York	A.L.	C	3	9	2	3	0	0	1	2	0	.333
1999	New York	A.L.	C	2	8	0	2	1	0	0	1	0	.250
2000	New York	A.L.	C	5	18	2	4	1	0	0	1	0	.222
World Series Totals				10	35	4	9	2	0	1	4	0	.257

PRATT, TODD ALAN

Born, Bellevue, Nebraska, February 9, 1967.
Bats Right. Throws Right. Height, 6 feet, 3 inches. Weight, 225 pounds.

Year	Club	Lea	Pos	G	AB	R	H	2B	3B	HR	RBI	SB	Avg
1985	Elmira	N.Y.-Penn.	C	39	119	7	16	1	1	0	5	0	.134
1986	Greensboro	So.Atl.	C-1B	107	348	63	84	16	0	12	56	0	.241
1987	Winter Haven	Fla.St.	C-1B-OF	118	407	57	105	22	0	12	65	0	.258
1988	New Britain a	Eastern	C-1B	124	395	41	89	15	2	8	49	1	.225
1989	New Britain	Eastern	C-1B	109	338	30	77	17	1	2	35	1	.228
1990	New Britain	Eastern	DH-C-1B	70	195	15	45	14	1	2	22	0	.231
1991	Pawtucket b-c	Int.	C-1B	68	219	27	64	16	0	11	41	0	.292
1992	Reading	Eastern	DH-C-1B	41	132	20	44	6	1	6	26	2	.333
1992	Scranton-WB	Int.	C-1B	41	125	20	40	9	1	7	28	1	.320
1992	Philadelphia	N.L.	C	16	46	6	13	1	0	2	10	0	.283
1993	Scranton-WB	Int.	C	3	9	1	2	1	0	0	1	0	.222
1993	Philadelphia	N.L.	C	33	87	8	25	6	0	5	13	0	.287
1994	Philadelphia	N.L.	C	28	102	10	20	6	1	2	9	0	.196
1995	Chicago	N.L.	C	25	60	3	8	2	0	0	4	0	.133
1995	Iowa d-e-f	A.A.	C-1B	23	58	3	19	1	0	0	5	0	.328
1996					Did Not Play								
1997	Norfolk	Int.	C	59	206	42	62	8	3	9	34	1	.301
1997	New York	N.L.	C	39	106	12	30	6	0	2	19	0	.283
1998	St. Lucie	Fla.St.	1B-C-OF	5	20	2	9	1	0	1	3	1	.450
1998	Mets	Gulf Coast	OF-C	2	4	1	1	0	0	0	0	0	.250
1998	Norfolk	Int.	DH-C-OF-1B	35	118	16	42	6	0	7	30	2	.356
1998	New York	N.L.	C-1B	41	69	9	19	9	1	2	18	0	.275
1999	New York	N.L.	C-1B-OF	71	140	18	41	4	0	3	21	2	.293
2000	New York	N.L.	C	80	160	33	44	6	0	8	25	0	.275
Major League Totals		8 Yrs.	333	770	99	200	40	2	24	119	2	.260		
	Division Series												
1999	New York	N.L.	C	3	8	2	1	0	0	1	1	0	.125
2000	New York	N.L.	C	1	1	0	0	0	0	0	0	0	.000
Division Series Totals				4	9	2	1	0	0	1	1	0	.111
	Championship Series												
1993	Philadelphia	N.L.	C	1	1	0	0	0	0	0	0	0	.000
1999	New York	N.L.	C	4	2	0	1	0	0	0	3	0	.500
Championship Series Totals				5	3	0	1	0	0	0	3	0	.333
	World Series Record												
2000	New York	N.L.	C	1	2	1	0	0	0	0	0	0	.000

a Selected by Cleveland Indians from Boston Red Sox in Rule V draft, December 7, 1987, returned, March 28, 1988.
b Filed for free agency, October 15, 1991, signed with Baltimore Orioles organization, November 13, 1991.
c Selected by Philadelphia Phillies in Rule V draft, December 9, 1991.
d Filed for free agency, December 23, 1994, signed with Chicago Cubs, April 8, 1995.
e Filed for free agency, October 16, 1995, signed with Seattle Mariners, January 14, 1996.
f Released by Seattle Mariners, March 27, 1996, signed with New York Mets, December 19, 1996.

QUINN, MARK DAVID

Born, LaMirada, California, May 21, 1974.
Bats Right. Throws Right. Height, 6 feet, 1 inch. Weight,175 pounds.

Year	Club	Lea	Pos	G	AB	R	H	2B	3B	HR	RBI	SB	Avg
1995 Spokane		Northwest	OF-3B	44	162	28	46	12	2	6	37	0	.284
1996 Lansing		Midwest	OF	113	437	63	132	23	3	9	71	14	.302
1997 Wilmington		Carolina	OF	87	299	51	92	22	3	16	71	3	.308
1997 Wichita		Texas	OF	26	96	26	36	13	0	2	19	1	.375
1998 Wichita		Texas	OF	100	372	82	130	26	6	16	84	4	.349
1999 Omaha		P.C.	OF	107	428	67	154	27	0	25	84	7	.360
1999 Kansas City		A.L.	OF	17	60	11	20	4	1	6	18	1	.333
2000 Omaha		P.C.	OF	13	61	8	23	5	0	3	13	0	.377
2000 Kansas City		A.L.	OF	135	500	76	147	33	2	20	78	5	.294
Major League Totals			2 Yrs.	152	560	87	167	37	3	26	96	6	.298

RAMIREZ, ALEXANDER RAMON (ALEX)

Born, Caracas, Venezuela, October 3, 1974.
Bats Right. Throws Right. Height, 5 feet, 11 inches. Weight, 180 pounds.

Year	Club	Lea	Pos	G	AB	R	H	2B	3B	HR	RBI	SB	Avg
1992 Cleveland		Domincan	OF	69	272	28	79	13	3	8	48	-17	.290
1993 Burlington		Appal.	OF	64	252	44	68	14	4	13	58	12	.270
1993 Kinston		Carolina	OF	3	12	0	2	0	0	0	1	0	.167
1994 Columbus		So.Atl.	OF	125	458	64	115	23	3	18	57	7	.251
1995 Bakersfield		California	OF	98	406	56	131	25	2	10	52	13	.323
1995 Canton-Akrn		Eastern	OF	33	133	15	33	3	4	1	11	3	.248
1996 Canton-Akrn		Eastern	OF	131	513	79	169	28	12	14	85	18	.329
1997 Buffalo		A.A.	OF	119	416	59	119	19	8	11	44	10	.286
1998 Buffalo		Int.	OF	121	521	94	156	21	8	34	103	6	.299
1998 Cleveland a		A.L.	OF	3	8	1	1	0	0	0	0	0	.125
1999 Buffalo		Int.	OF	75	305	50	93	20	2	12	50	5	.305
1999 Cleveland		A.L.	OF	48	97	11	29	6	1	3	18	1	.299
2000 Cleveland		A.L.	OF	41	112	13	32	5	1	5	12	1	.286
2000 Pittsburgh b-c		N.L.	OF-1B	43	115	13	24	6	1	4	18	1	.209
Major League Totals			3 Yrs.	135	332	38	86	17	3	12	48	3	.259

a On disabled list from May 21 to June 4, 1998.
b Traded to Pittsburgh Pirates with infielder Enrique Wilson for outfielder Wil Cordero, July 28, 2000.
c Sold to Yakult Swallows, November 1, 2000.

RAMIREZ (NIN), ARAMIS

Born, Santo Domingo, Dominican Republic, June 25, 1978.
Bats Right. Throws Right. Height, 6 feet, 1 inch. Weight, 190 pounds.

Year	Club	Lea	Pos	G	AB	R	H	2B	3B	HR	RBI	SB	Avg
1995 Pittsburgh		Domincan	3B	64	214	41	63	13	0	11	54	2	.294
1996 Erie		N.Y.-Penn.	3B	61	223	37	68	14	4	9	42	0	.305
1996 Augusta		So.Atl.	3B	6	20	3	4	1	0	1	2	0	.200
1997 Lynchburg		Carolina	3B	137	482	85	134	24	2	29	114	5	.278
1998 Nashville		P.C.	3B-SS	47	168	19	46	10	0	5	18	0	.274
1998 Pittsburgh a		N.L.	3B	72	251	23	59	9	1	6	24	0	.235
1999 Nashville		P.C.	3B	131	460	92	151	35	1	21	74	5	.328
1999 Pittsburgh		N.L.	3B	18	56	2	10	2	1	0	7	0	.179
2000 Nashville		P.C.	3B	44	167	28	59	12	2	4	26	2	.353
2000 Pittsburgh b		N.L.	3B	73	254	19	65	15	2	6	35	0	.256
Major League Totals			3 Yrs.	163	561	44	134	26	4	12	66	0	.239

a On disabled list from August 10 to September 4, 1998.
b On disabled list from August 29 to October 1, 2000.

RAMIREZ, MANUEL ARISTIDES (MANNY)

Born, Brooklyn, New York, May 30, 1972.
Bats Right. Throws Right. Height, 6 feet. Weight, 190 pounds.

Year	Club	Lea	Pos	G	AB	R	H	2B	3B	HR	RBI	SB	Avg
1991 Burlington		Appal.	OF	59	215	44	70	11	4	19	63	7	.326
1992 Kinston a		Carolina	OF	81	291	52	81	18	4	13	63	1	.278
1993 Canton		Eastern	OF	89	344	67	117	32	0	17	79	2	.340
1993 Charlotte		Int.	OF	40	145	38	46	12	0	14	36	1	.317
1993 Cleveland		A.L.	DH-OF	22	53	5	9	1	0	2	5	0	.170
1994 Cleveland		A.L.	OF	91	290	51	78	22	0	17	60	4	.269

Year	Club	Lea	Pos	G	AB	R	H	2B	3B	HR	RBI	SB	Avg
1995 Cleveland	A.L.		OF	137	484	85	149	26	1	31	107	6	.308
1996 Cleveland	A.L.		OF	152	550	94	170	45	3	33	112	8	.309
1997 Cleveland	A.L.		OF	150	561	99	184	40	0	26	88	2	.328
1998 Cleveland	A.L.		OF	150	571	108	168	35	2	45	145	5	.294
1999 Cleveland	A.L.		OF	147	522	131	174	34	3	44	*165	2	.333
2000 Akron	Eastern		PH	1	2	1	1	0	0	1	2	0	.500
2000 Buffalo	Int.		PH	5	11	5	5	1	0	3	7	0	.455
2000 Cleveland b-c	A.L.		OF	118	439	92	154	34	2	38	122	1	.351
Major League Totals			8 Yrs.	967	3470	665	1086	237	11	236	804	28	.313
Division Series													
1995 Cleveland	A.L.		OF	3	12	1	0	0	0	0	0	0	.000
1996 Cleveland	A.L.		OF	4	16	4	6	2	0	2	2	0	.375
1997 Cleveland	A.L.		OF	5	21	2	3	1	0	0	3	0	.143
1998 Cleveland	A.L.		OF	4	14	2	5	2	0	2	3	0	.357
1999 Cleveland	A.L.		OF	5	18	5	1	1	0	0	1	0	.056
Division Series Totals				21	81	14	15	6	0	4	9	0	.185
Championship Series													
1995 Cleveland	A.L.		OF	6	21	2	6	0	0	2	2	0	.286
1997 Cleveland	A.L.		OF	6	21	3	6	1	0	2	3	0	.286
1998 Cleveland	A.L.		OF	6	21	2	7	1	0	2	4	0	.333
Championship Series Totals				18	63	7	19	2	0	6	9	0	.302
World Series Record													
1995 Cleveland	A.L.		OF	6	18	2	4	0	0	1	2	1	.222
1997 Cleveland	A.L.		OF	7	26	3	4	0	0	2	6	0	.154
World Series Totals				13	44	5	8	0	0	3	8	1	.182

a On disabled list from July 10 to end of 1992 season.
b On disabled list from May 30 to July 12, 2000.
c Filed for free agency, October 27, 2000, signed with Boston Red Sox, December 13, 2000.

RANDA, JOSEPH GREGORY
Born, Milwaukee, Wisconsin, December 18, 1962.
Bats Right. Throws Right. Height, 5 feet, 11 inches. Weight, 190 pounds.

Year	Club	Lea	Pos	G	AB	R	H	2B	3B	HR	RBI	SB	Avg
1991 Eugene	Northwest		3B	72	275	53	93	20	2	11	59	6	.338
1992 Appleton	Midwest		3B	72	266	55	80	13	0	5	43	6	.301
1992 Baseball City	Fla. St.		3B-SS	51	189	22	52	7	0	1	12	4	.275
1993 Memphis	Southern		3B	131	505	74	149	31	5	11	72	8	.295
1994 Omaha	A.A.		3B	127	455	65	125	27	2	10	51	5	.275
1995 Omaha	A.A.		3B	64	233	33	64	10	2	8	33	2	.275
1995 Kansas City	A.L.		3B-2B	34	70	6	12	2	0	1	5	0	.171
1996 Omaha a	A.A.		3B	3	9	1	1	0	1	0	0	0	.111
1996 Kansas City b	A.L.		3B-2B-1B	110	337	36	102	24	1	6	47	13	.303
1997 Calgary	P.C.		3B	3	11	4	4	1	0	1	4	0	.364
1997 Pittsburgh c-d-e	N.L.		3B-2B	126	443	58	134	27	9	7	60	4	.302
1998 Detroit f-g	A.L.		3B-2B-1B	138	460	56	117	21	2	9	50	8	.254
1999 Kansas City	A.L.		3B	156	628	92	197	36	8	16	84	5	.314
2000 Kansas City	A.L.		3B	158	612	88	186	29	4	15	106	6	.304
Major League Totals			6 Yrs.	722	2550	336	748	139	24	54	352	36	.293

a On disabled list from May 5 to May 27, 1996.
b Traded to Pittsburgh Pirates with pitchers Jeff Granger, Jeff Martin and Jeff Wallace for infielders Jay Bell and Jeff King, December 14, 1996.
c On disabled list from June 28 to July 27, 1997.
d Selected on expansion draft by Arizona Diamondbacks, November 18, 1997.
e Traded to Detroit Tigers with infielder Gabe Alvarez and pitcher Matt Drews for infielder Travis Fryman, November 19, 1997.
f Traded to New York Mets for pitcher Willie Blair, December 4, 1998.
g Traded to Kansas City Royals for outfielder Juan Lebron, December 10, 1998.

REBOULET, JEFFREY ALLEN
Born, Dayton, Ohio, April 30, 1964.
Bats Right. Throws Right. Height, 6 feet. Weight, 169 pounds.

Year	Club	Lea	Pos	G	AB	R	H	2B	3B	HR	RBI	SB	Avg
1986 Visalia	California		SS	72	254	54	73	13	1	0	29	14	.287
1987 Orlando	Southern		SS-2B	129	422	52	108	15	1	1	35	9	.256
1988 Orlando	Southern		SS	125	439	57	112	24	2	4	41	18	.255
1988 Portland	P.C.		2B-SS	4	12	0	1	0	0	0	1	0	.083
1989 Portland	P.C.		SS-2B	26	65	9	16	1	0	0	3	2	.246

Year	Club	Lea	Pos	G	AB	R	H	2B	3B	HR	RBI	SB	Avg
1989 Orlando ......Southern			SS-2B	81	291	43	63	5	1	0	26	11	.216
1990 Orlando ......Southern			2B-SS-3B	97	287	43	66	12	2	2	28	10	.230
1991 Portland ............P.C.			SS-2B	134	391	50	97	27	3	3	46	2	.248
1992 Portland ..........P.C.			SS-3B	48	161	21	46	11	1	2	21	3	.286
1992 Minnesota ........A.L.			SS-3B-2B-OF	73	137	15	26	7	1	1	16	3	.190
1993 Minnesota ........A.L.			SS-3B-2B-OF	109	240	33	62	8	0	1	15	5	.258
1994 Minnesota ........A.L.			SS-2B-1B-3B	74	189	28	49	11	1	3	23	0	.259
1995 Minnesota ......A.L.			SS-3B-1B-2B	87	216	39	63	11	0	4	23	1	.292
1996 Minnesota a ......A.L.			SS-3B-2B-1B	107	234	20	52	9	0	0	23	4	.222
1997 Baltimore b ......A.L.			2B-SS-3B-OF	99	228	26	54	9	0	4	27	3	.237
1998 Baltimore .........A.L.			2B-SS-3B	79	127	20	31	6	0	1	8	0	.244
1999 Baltimore c ......A.L.			3B-2B-SS	99	154	25	25	4	0	0	4	1	.162
2000 Kansas City d ......A.L.			2B-3B-SS	66	182	29	44	7	0	0	14	3	.242
Major League Totals		9 Yrs.		793	1706	235	406	72	2	14	153	20	.238
Division Series													
1997 Baltimore .........A.L.			2B	2	5	1	1	0	0	1	1	0	.200
Championship Series													
1997 Baltimore .........A.L.			SS	1	2	1	0	0	0	0	0	0	.000

a Filed for free agency, October 4, 1996.
b Signed with Baltimore Orioles organization, January 30, 1997.
c Traded to Kansas City Royals for player to be named later, December 12, 1999.
d Filed for free agency, October 31, 2000.

REDMOND, MICHAEL PATRICK (MIKE)
Born, Seattle, Washington, May 5, 1971.
Bats Right. Throws Right. Height, 6 feet, 1 inch. Weight,185 pounds.

Year	Club	Lea	Pos	G	AB	R	H	2B	3B	HR	RBI	SB	Avg
1993 Kane County ......Midwest			C	43	100	10	20	2	0	0	10	2	.200
1994 Kane County ......Midwest			C	92	306	39	83	10	0	1	24	3	.271
1994 Brevard Cty ....Fla.St.			C	12	42	4	11	4	0	0	2	0	.262
1995 Portland ....Eastern			C-3B	105	333	37	85	11	1	3	39	2	.255
1996 Portland ....Eastern			C	120	394	43	113	22	0	4	44	3	.287
1997 Charlotte ....Int.			C	22	61	8	13	5	1	1	2	0	.213
1997 Marlins ....Gulf Coast			DH	16	55	7	19	3	0	0	5	2	.345
1997 Brevard Cty ....Fla.St.			DH-1B	5	17	2	0	0	0	0	0	0	.000
1998 Portland ....Eastern			C	8	28	7	9	4	0	1	7	0	.321
1998 Charlotte ....Int.			C	18	58	4	14	2	0	2	7	0	.241
1998 Florida ..............N.L.			C	37	118	10	39	9	0	2	12	0	.331
1999 Florida ..............N.L.			C	84	242	22	73	9	0	1	27	0	.302
2000 Florida ..............N.L.			C	87	210	17	53	8	1	0	15	0	.252
Major League Totals		3 Yrs.		208	570	49	165	26	1	3	54	0	.289

REED, JEFFREY SCOTT
Born, Joliet, Illinois, November 12, 1962.
Bats Left. Throws Right. Height, 6 feet, 2 inches. Weight, 190 pounds.

Year	Club	Lea	Pos	G	AB	R	H	2B	3B	HR	RBI	SB	Avg
1980 Elizabethton ....Appal.			C	65	225	39	64	15	1	1	20	2	.284
1981 Wisconsin Rapids ..Midwest			C	106	312	63	73	12	1	4	34	4	.234
1981 Orlando ....Southern			C	3	4	0	1	0	0	0	0	0	.250
1982 Visalia ....California			C	125	395	69	130	19	2	5	54	1	.329
1983 Orlando ....Southern			C	118	379	52	100	16	5	6	45	2	.264
1983 Toledo ....Int.			C	14	41	5	7	1	1	0	3	4	.171
1984 Minnesota ...........A.L.			C	18	21	3	3	3	0	0	1	1	.143
1984 Toledo ....Int.			C	94	301	30	80	16	3	3	35	1	.266
1985 Toledo ....Int.			C	122	404	53	100	15	3	5	36	1	.248
1985 Minnesota ...........A.L.			C	7	10	2	2	0	0	0	0	0	.200
1986 Minnesota ...........A.L.			C	68	165	13	39	6	1	2	9	1	.236
1986 Toledo a ....Int.			C	25	71	10	22	5	3	1	14	0	.310
1987 Montreal b ...........N.L.			C	75	207	15	44	11	0	1	21	0	.213
1987 Indianapolis ..........A.A.			C	5	17	0	3	0	0	0	0	0	.176
1988 Indianapolis ..........A.A.			C	8	22	1	7	3	0	0	1	0	.318
1988 Montreal-Cincinnati c ..N.L.			C	92	265	20	60	9	2	1	16	1	.226
1989 Cincinnati ...........N.L.			C	102	287	16	64	11	0	3	23	0	.223
1990 Cincinnati ...........N.L.			C	72	175	12	44	8	1	3	16	0	.251
1991 Cincinnati d .........N.L.			C	91	270	20	72	15	2	3	31	0	.267
1992 Nashville ............A.A.			C	14	25	1	6	1	0	1	2	0	.240

Year	Club	Lea	Pos	G	AB	R	H	2B	3B	HR	RBI	SB	Avg
1992 Cincinnati e-f		N.L.	C	15	25	2	4	0	0	0	2	0	.160
1993 San Jose	California		C	4	10	2	5	1	0	0	2	0	.500
1993 San Francisco g		N.L.	C	66	119	10	31	3	0	6	12	0	.261
1994 San Francisco		N.L.	C	50	103	11	18	3	0	1	7	0	.175
1995 San Francisco h-i		N.L.	C	66	113	12	30	2	0	0	9	0	.265
1996 Colorado		N.L.	C	116	341	34	97	20	1	8	37	2	.284
1997 Colorado j-k		N.L.	C	90	256	43	76	10	0	17	47	2	.297
1998 Colorado		N.L.	C	113	259	43	75	17	1	9	39	0	.290
1999 Colorado-Chicago l		N.L.	C-3B	103	256	29	66	16	2	3	28	1	.258
2000 Chicago m		N.L.	C	90	229	26	49	10	0	4	25	0	.214
Major League Totals			17 Yrs.	1234	3101	311	774	144	10	61	323	7	.250
Championship Series													
1990 Cincinnati		N.L.	C	4	7	0	0	0	0	0	0	0	.000

a Traded by Minnesota Twins to Montreal Expos with pitchers Yorkis Perez and Al Cardwood for pitcher Jeff Reardon and catcher Tom Nieto, February 3, 1987.
b On disabled list from April 20 to May 25, 1987.
c Traded to Cincinnati Reds with outfielder Herm Winningham and pitcher Randy St. Claire for outfielder Tracy Jones and pitcher Pat Pacillo, July 13, 1988.
d On disabled list from July 1 to July 19, 1991.
e On disabled list from April 26 to September 1, 1992.
f Filed for free agency, October 27, 1992; signed with San Francisco Giants organization, January 18, 1993.
g On disabled list from June 30 to August 3, 1993.
h Filed for free agency, November 12, 1995.
i Signed with Colorado Rockies, December 18, 1995.
j Filed for free agency, October 27, 1997.
k Re-signed with Colorado Rockies, November 18, 1997.
l Waived by Colorado Rockies, July 3, 1999, signed with Chicago Cubs, July 8, 1999.
m Filed for free agency, October 31, 2000.

REESE, CALVIN (POKEY)

Born, Columbia, South Carolina, June 10, 1973.
Bats Right. Throws Right. Height, 5 feet, 11 inches. Weight, 180 pounds.

Year	Club	Lea	Pos	G	AB	R	H	2B	3B	HR	RBI	SB	Avg
1991 Princeton	Appal.		SS-OF	62	231	30	55	8	3	3	27	10	.238
1992 Chston-Wv	So. Atl.		SS	106	380	50	102	19	3	6	53	19	.268
1993 Chattanooga	Southern		SS	102	345	35	73	17	4	3	37	8	.212
1994 Chattanooga	Southern		SS	134	484	77	130	23	4	12	49	21	.269
1995 Indianapolis	A.A.		SS	89	343	51	82	21	1	10	46	8	.239
1996 Indianapolis	A.A.		SS-3B	79	280	26	65	16	0	1	23	5	.232
1997 Indianapolis	A.A.		SS-2B	17	72	12	17	2	0	4	11	4	.236
1997 Cincinnati	N.L.		SS-2B-2B	128	397	48	87	15	0	4	26	25	.219
1998 Cincinnati a	N.L.		3B-SS-2B	59	133	20	34	2	2	1	16	3	.256
1999 Cincinnati	N.L.		2B-SS	149	585	85	167	37	5	10	52	38	.285
2000 Cincinnati	N.L.		2B	135	518	76	132	20	6	12	46	29	.255
Major League Totals			4 Yrs.	471	1633	229	420	74	13	27	140	95	.257

a On disabled list from July 31 to September 28, 1998.

RELAFORD, DESMOND LAMONT (DESI)

Born, Valdosta, Georgia, September 16, 1973.
Bats Both. Throws Right. Height, 5 feet, 8 inches. Weight, 155 pounds.

Year	Club	Lea	Pos	G	AB	R	H	2B	3B	HR	RBI	SB	Avg
1991 Mariners	Arizona		SS-2B	46	163	36	44	7	3	0	18	17	.270
1992 Peninsula	Carolina		SS	130	445	53	96	18	1	3	34	27	.216
1993 Jacksonville	Southern	SS-2B-3B	133	472	49	115	16	4	8	47	16	.244
1994 Jacksonville	Southern		SS	37	143	24	29	7	3	3	11	10	.203
1994 Riverside	California		SS	99	374	95	116	27	5	5	59	27	.310
1995 Port City	Southern		SS-2B	90	352	51	101	11	2	7	27	25	.287
1995 Tacoma	P.C.		2B-SS	30	113	20	27	5	1	2	7	6	.239
1996 Tacoma	P.C.		2B-SS	93	317	27	65	12	0	4	32	10	.205
1996 Scranton-WB	Int.		SS	21	85	12	20	4	1	1	11	7	.235
1996 Philadelphia a	N.L.		SS-2B	15	40	2	7	2	0	0	1	1	.175
1997 Scranton-WB	Int.		SS	131	517	82	138	34	4	9	53	29	.267
1997 Philadelphia	N.L.		SS	15	38	3	7	1	2	0	6	3	.184
1998 Philadelphia	N.L.		SS	142	494	45	121	25	3	5	41	9	.245
1999 Clearwater	Fla.St.		SS	2	7	1	2	0	0	0	1	0	.286
1999 Philadelphia b	N.L.		SS	65	211	31	51	11	2	1	26	4	.242
2000 Phil.-San Diego c-d-e	N.L.		SS	128	410	55	88	14	3	5	46	13	.215

Year	Club	Lea	Pos	G	AB	R	H	2B	3B	HR	RBI	SB	Avg
Major League Totals			5 Yrs.	365	1193	136	274	53	10	11	120	30	.230

a Traded by Seattle Mariners to Philadelphia Phillies for pitcher Terry Mulholland, July 31, 1996.
b On disabled list from June 17 to September 13, 1999.
c Traded to San Diego Padres for player to be named later, August 4, 2000.
d Philadelphia Phillies received infielder David Newhan to complete trade, August 7, 2000.
e Claimed on waivers by New York Mets, October 12, 2000.

RENTERIA, EDGAR ENRIQUE

Born, Barranquilla, Colombia, August 7, 1975.
Bats Right. Throws Right. Height, 6 feet, 1 inch. Weight, 172 pounds.

Year	Club	Lea	Pos	G	AB	R	H	2B	3B	HR	RBI	SB	Avg
1992 Marlins	Gulf Coast	SS	43	163	25	47	8	1	0	9	10	.288
1993 Kane County	Midwest	SS	116	384	40	78	8	0	1	35	7	.203
1994 Brevard Cty	Fla. St.	SS	128	439	46	111	15	1	0	36	6	.253
1995 Portland	Eastern	SS	135	508	70	147	15	7	7	68	30	.289
1996 Charlotte	Int.	SS	35	132	17	37	8	0	2	16	10	.280
1996 Florida a	N.L.	SS	106	431	68	133	18	3	5	31	16	.309
1997 Florida	N.L.	SS	154	617	90	171	21	3	4	52	32	.277
1998 Florida b-c	N.L.	SS	133	517	79	146	18	2	3	31	41	.282
1999 St. Louis	N.L.	SS	154	585	92	161	36	2	11	63	37	.275
2000 St. Louis	N.L.	SS	150	562	94	156	32	1	16	76	21	.278
Major League Totals		5 Yrs.	697	2712	423	767	125	11	39	253	147	.283
Division Series													
1997 Florida	N.L.	SS	3	13	1	2	0	0	0	1	0	.154
2000 St. Louis	N.L.	SS	3	10	5	2	0	0	0	0	2	.200
Division Series Totals			6	23	6	4	0	0	0	1	2	.174
Championship Series													
1997 Florida	N.L.	SS	6	22	4	5	1	0	0	0	1	.227
2000 St. Louis	N.L.	SS	5	20	4	6	1	0	0	4	3	.300
Championship Series Totals			11	42	8	11	2	0	0	4	4	.262
World Series Record													
1997 Florida	N.L.	SS	7	31	3	9	2	0	0	3	0	.290

a On disabled list from June 24 to July 11, 1996
b On disabled list from August 25 to September 9, 1998.
c Traded to New York Mets for outfielder Butch Huskey, December 14, 1998.

RICHARD, CHRISTOPHER (CHRIS)

Born, San Diego, California, June 7, 1974.
Bats Left. Throws Right. Height, 6 feet, 2 inches. Weight, 185 pounds.

Year	Club	Lea	Pos	G	AB	R	H	2B	3B	HR	RBI	SB	Avg
1995 New Jersey	N.Y.-Penn.	1B	75	284	36	80	14	3	3	43	6	.282
1996 St. Pete	Fla.St.	1B-OF	129	460	65	130	28	6	14	82	7	.283
1997 Arkansas	Texas	1B-OF	113	390	62	105	24	3	11	58	6	.269
1998 Pr William	Carolina	DH	8	30	5	8	2	0	0	1	1	.267
1998 Arkansas	Texas	1B	28	89	7	18	5	1	2	17	0	.202
1999 Arkansas	Texas	1B	133	442	78	130	26	3	29	94	7	.294
1999 Memphis	P.C.	1B	4	17	3	7	2	0	1	4	0	.412
2000 Memphis	P.C.	OF	95	375	64	104	24	0	16	75	9	.277
2000 St. Louis	N.L.	OF-1B	6	16	1	2	0	0	1	1	0	.125
2000 Baltimore a	A.L.	1B-OF	56	199	38	55	14	2	13	36	7	.276
Major League Totals		1 Yrs.	62	215	39	57	14	2	14	37	7	.265

a Traded to Baltimore Orioles with pitcher Mark Nussbeck for pitcher Mike Timlin, July 29, 2000.

RIOS, ARMANDO

Born, Santurce, Puerto Rico, September 13, 1971.
Bats Left. Throws Right. Height, 5 feet, 9 inches. Weight 180 pounds.

Year	Club	Lea	Pos	G	AB	R	H	2B	3B	HR	RBI	SB	Avg
1994 Clinton	Midwest	OF	119	407	67	120	23	4	8	60	16	.295
1995 San Jose	California	OF	128	488	76	143	34	3	8	75	51	.293
1996 Shreveport	Texas	OF	92	329	62	93	22	2	12	49	9	.283
1997 Shreveport	Texas	OF	127	461	86	133	30	6	14	79	17	.289
1998 Fresno	P.C.	OF-1B	125	445	85	134	23	1	26	103	17	.301
1998 San Francisco	N.L.	OF	12	7	3	4	0	0	2	3	0	.571
1999 Fresno	P.C.	OF	31	109	24	30	3	0	4	21	3	.275

Year Club	Lea	Pos	G	AB	R	H	2B	3B	HR	RBI	SB	Avg
1999 San Francisco a .......N.L.		OF	72	150	32	49	9	0	7	29	7	.327
2000 San Francisco .........N.L.		OF-1B	115	233	38	62	15	5	10	50	3	.266
Major League Totals		3 Yrs.	199	390	73	115	24	5	19	82	10	.295
Division Series												
2000 San Francisco .........N.L.		PH	2	2	0	1	0	0	0	0	0	.500

a On disabled list from June 22 to September 2, 1999.

RIPKEN, CALVIN EDWIN JR.

Born, Havre de Grace, Maryland, August 24, 1960.
Bats Right. Throws Right. Height, 6 feet, 4 inches. Weight, 220 pounds.

Year Club	Lea	Pos	G	AB	R	H	2B	3B	HR	RBI	SB	Avg
1978 Bluefield ....Appal.		SS	63	239	27	63	7	1	0	24	1	.264
1979 Miami ....Fla. St.		3B-SS-2B	105	393	51	119	*28	1	5	54	4	.303
1979 Charlotte ....Southern		3B	17	61	6	11	0	1	3	8	1	.180
1980 Charlotte ....Southern		2B-SS	*144	522	91	144	28	5	25	78	4	.276
1981 Rochester ....Int.		3B-SS	114	437	74	126	31	4	23	75	0	.288
1981 Baltimore ............A.L.		SS-3B	23	39	1	5	0	0	0	0	0	.128
1982 Baltimore a ..........A.L.		SS-3B	160	598	90	158	32	5	28	93	3	.264
1983 Baltimore b ..........A.L.		SS	*162	*663	*121	*211	*47	2	27	102	0	.318
1984 Baltimore ............A.L.		SS	*162	641	103	195	37	7	27	86	2	.304
1985 Baltimore ............A.L.		SS	161	642	116	181	32	5	26	110	2	.282
1986 Baltimore ............A.L.		SS	162	627	98	177	35	1	25	81	4	.282
1987 Baltimore ............A.L.		SS	*162	624	97	157	28	3	27	98	3	.252
1988 Baltimore ............A.L.		SS	161	575	87	152	25	1	23	81	2	.264
1989 Baltimore ............A.L.		SS	*162	646	80	166	30	0	21	93	3	.257
1990 Baltimore ............A.L.		SS	161	600	78	150	28	4	21	84	3	.250
1991 Baltimore c ..........A.L.		SS	*162	650	99	210	46	5	34	114	6	.323
1992 Baltimore ............A.L.		SS	*162	637	73	160	29	1	14	72	4	.251
1993 Baltimore ............A.L.		SS	*162	*641	87	165	26	3	24	90	1	.257
1994 Baltimore ............A.L.		SS	112	444	71	140	19	3	13	75	1	.315
1995 Baltimore ............A.L.		SS	144	550	71	144	33	2	17	88	0	.262
1996 Baltimore ............A.L.		SS-3B	*163	640	94	178	40	1	26	102	1	.278
1997 Baltimore ............A.L.		3B-SS	162	615	79	166	30	0	17	84	1	.270
1998 Baltimore ............A.L.		3B	161	601	65	163	27	1	14	61	0	.271
1999 Baltimore d ..........A.L.		3B	86	332	51	113	27	0	18	57	0	.340
2000 Baltimore e ..........A.L.		3B	83	309	43	79	16	0	15	56	0	.256
Major League Totals		20 Yrs.	2873	11074	1604	3070	587	44	417	1627	36	.277
Division Series												
1996 Baltimore ............A.L.		SS	4	18	2	8	3	0	0	2	0	.444
1997 Baltimore ............A.L.		3B	4	16	1	7	2	0	0	1	0	.438
Division Series Totals			8	34	3	15	5	0	0	3	0	.441
Championship Series												
1983 Baltimore ............A.L.		SS	4	15	5	6	2	0	0	1	0	.400
1996 Baltimore ............A.L.		SS	5	20	1	5	1	0	0	0	0	.250
1997 Baltimore ............A.L.		3B	6	23	3	8	2	0	1	3	0	.348
Championship Series Totals			15	58	9	19	5	0	1	4	0	.328
World Series Record												
1983 Baltimore ............A.L.		SS	5	18	2	3	0	0	0	1	0	.167

a Selected Rookie of the Year in American League for 1982.
b Selected Most Valuable Player in American League for 1983.
c Selected Most Valuable Player in American League for 1991.
d On disabled list from April 18 to May 13 and August 1 to September 1, 1999.
e On disabled list from June 28 to August 31, 2000.

RIVERA, RUBEN

Born, Chorrera, Panama, November 14, 1973.
Bats Right. Throws Right. Height, 6 feet, 3 inches. Weight, 200 pounds.

Year Club	Lea	Pos	G	AB	R	H	2B	3B	HR	RBI	SB	Avg
1992 Yankees ....Gulf Coast		OF	53	194	37	53	10	3	1	20	21	.273
1993 Oneonta ........N.Y.-Penn.		OF	55	199	45	55	7	6	13	47	12	.276
1994 Greensboro ....So. Atl.		OF	105	400	83	115	24	3	28	81	36	.287
1994 Tampa ....Fla. St.		OF	34	134	18	35	4	3	5	20	12	.261
1995 Norwich ....Eastern		OF	71	256	49	75	16	8	9	39	16	.293
1995 Columbus ....Int.		OF	48	174	37	47	8	2	15	35	8	.270
1995 New York .............A.L.		OF	5	1	0	0	0	0	0	0	0	.000
1996 Columbus ....Int.		OF	101	362	59	85	20	4	10	46	15	.235

Year Club	Lea	Pos	G	AB	R	H	2B	3B	HR	RBI	SB	Avg
1996 New York ...........A.L.		OF	46	88	17	25	6	1	2	16	6	.284
1997 Rancho Cuca ....California		DH	6	23	6	4	1	0	1	3	1	.174
1997 Las Vegas ...........P.C.		DH-1B	12	48	6	12	5	1	1	6	1	.250
1997 San Diego a-b ..........N.L.		OF	17	20	2	5	1	0	0	1	2	.250
1998 Las Vegas ...........P.C.		OF	30	104	9	15	3	0	3	11	4	.144
1998 San Diego ...........N.L.		OF	95	172	31	36	7	2	6	29	5	.209
1999 San Diego ...........N.L.		OF	147	411	65	80	16	1	23	48	18	.195
2000 Las Vegas ...........P.C.		OF	2	10	1	2	0	0	0	1	0	.200
2000 San Diego c .........N.L.		OF	135	423	62	88	18	6	17	57	8	.208
Major League Totals		6 Yrs.	445	1115	177	234	48	10	48	151	39	.210
Division Series												
1996 New York ............A.L.		OF	2	1	0	0	0	0	0	0	0	.000
1998 San Diego ............N.L.		OF	3	6	0	0	0	0	0	0	0	.000
Division Series Totals			5	7	0	0	0	0	0	0	0	.000
Championship Series												
1998 San Diego ............N.L.		OF	6	13	1	3	2	0	0	0	1	.231
World Series Record												
1998 San Diego ............N.L.		OF	3	5	1	4	2	0	0	1	0	.800

a Traded to San Diego Padres with pitcher Rafael Medina and cash for pitcher Hideki Irabu, infielder Homer Bush and player to be named later, May 30, 1997. New York Yankees received outfielder Vernon Maxwell to complete trade, June 9, 1997.
b On disabled list from April 1 to August 13, 1997.
c On disabled list from April 12 to May 4, 2000.

RODRIGUEZ, ALEXANDER EMMANUEL

Born, New York, New York, July 27, 1975.
Bats Right. Throws Right. Height, 6 feet, 3 inches. Weight, 190 pounds.

Year Club	Lea	Pos	G	AB	R	H	2B	3B	HR	RBI	SB	Avg
1994 Appleton ....Midwest		SS	65	248	49	79	17	6	14	55	16	.319
1994 Jacksonville ......Southern		SS	17	59	7	17	4	1	1	8	2	.288
1994 Seattle ..............A.L.		SS	17	54	4	11	0	0	0	2	3	.204
1994 Calgary ..............P.C.		SS	32	119	22	37	7	4	6	21	2	.311
1995 Tacoma ..............P.C.		SS	54	214	37	77	12	3	15	45	2	.360
1995 Seattle ..............A.L.		SS	48	142	15	33	6	2	5	19	4	.232
1996 Tacoma a ..........P.C.		SS	2	5	0	1	0	0	0	0	0	.200
1996 Seattle ..............A.L.		SS	146	601	*141	215	*54	1	36	123	15	*.358
1997 Seattle b ..........A.L.		SS	141	587	100	176	40	3	23	84	29	.300
1998 Seattle ..............A.L.		SS	161	*686	123	*213	35	5	42	124	46	.310
1999 Seattle c ..........A.L.		SS	129	502	110	143	25	0	42	111	21	.285
2000 Seattle d-e ...........A.L.		SS	148	554	134	175	34	2	41	132	15	.316
Major League Totals		7 Yrs.	790	3126	627	966	194	13	189	595	133	.309
Division Series												
1995 Seattle ..............A.L.		SS	1	1	1	0	0	0	0	0	0	.000
1997 Seattle ..............A.L.		SS	4	16	1	5	1	0	1	1	0	.313
2000 Seattle ..............A.L.		SS	3	13	0	4	0	0	0	2	0	.308
Division Series Totals			8	30	2	9	1	0	1	3	0	.300
Championship Series												
1995 Seattle ..............A.L.		PH	1	1	0	0	0	0	0	0	0	.000
2000 Seattle ..............A.L.		SS	6	22	4	9	2	0	2	5	1	.409
Championship Series Totals			7	23	4	9	2	0	2	5	1	.391

a On disabled list from April 22 to May 7, 1996.
b On disabled list from June 12 to June 27, 1997.
c On disabled list from April 7 to May 14, 1999.
d On disabled list from July 8 to July 23, 2000.
e Filed for free agency, October 30, 2000, signed with Texas Rangers, December 11, 2000.

RODRIGUEZ (LORENZO), HENRY ANDERSON

Born, Santo Domingo, Dominican Republic, November 8, 1967.
Bats Left. Throws Left. Height, 6 feet, 1 inch. Weight, 200 pounds.

Year Club	Lea	Pos	G	AB	R	H	2B	3B	HR	RBI	SB	Avg
1987 Sarasota Dodgers ....Gulf C.		1B	49	148	23	49	7	3	0	15	3	.331
1988 Santo Domingo ...Dom. Sum.		OF	19	21	9	8	2	0	0	10	4	.381
1988 Salem ....Northwest		1B	72	291	47	84	14	4	2	38	14	.289
1989 Vero Beach ....Fla. St.		1B	126	433	53	123	*33	1	10	73	7	.284
1989 Bakersfield ....California		1B	3	9	2	2	0	0	1	2	0	.222
1990 San Antonio ....Texas		OF	129	495	82	144	21	9	*28	*109	5	.291
1991 Albuquerque .........P.C.		OF-1B	121	446	61	121	22	5	10	67	4	.271
1992 Albuquerque .........P.C.		1B-OF	94	365	59	111	21	5	14	72	1	.304

Year	Club	Lea	Pos	G	AB	R	H	2B	3B	HR	RBI	SB	Avg
1992 Los Angeles	.........N.L.	OF-1B	53	146	11	32	7	0	3	14	0	.219
1993 Albuquerque	.........P.C.	1B-OF	46	179	26	53	13	5	4	30	1	.296
1993 Los Angeles	.........N.L.	OF-1B	76	176	20	39	10	0	8	23	1	.222
1994 Los Angeles	.........N.L.	OF-1B	104	306	33	82	14	2	8	49	0	.268
1995 Ottawa	.........Int.	DH	4	15	0	3	1	0	0	2	0	.200
1995 Los Angeles-Montreal a-b		OF-1B	45	138	13	33	4	1	2	15	0	.239
1996 Montreal	.............N.L.	OF-1B	145	532	81	147	42	1	36	103	2	.276
1997 Montreal c	.........N.L.	OF-1B	132	476	55	116	28	3	26	83	3	.244
1998 Chicago d-e	.........N.L.	OF	128	415	56	104	21	1	31	85	1	.251
1999 Chicago	.............N.L.	OF	130	447	72	136	29	0	26	87	2	.304
2000 Chicago-Florida f-g	.....N.L.	OF	112	367	47	94	21	1	20	61	1	.256
Major League Totals		9 Yrs.	925	3003	388	783	176	9	160	520	10	.261
Division Series												
1998 Chicago	.............N.L.	OF	3	7	0	1	1	0	0	0	0	.143

a Traded to Montreal Expos with infielder Jeff Treadway for outfielder Roberto Kelly and pitcher Joey Eischen, May 24, 1995.
b On disabled list from June 2 to October 2, 1995.
c Traded to Chicago Cubs for pitcher Miquel Batista, December 12, 1997.
d On disabled list from August 24 to September 8, 1998.
e Filed for free agency, October 23, 1998, re-signed with Chicago Cubs, December 2, 1998.
f Traded to Florida Marlins with cash for infielder Ross Gload and pitcher David Noyce, July 31, 2000.
g Filed for free agency, November 1, 2000.

RODRIGUEZ (TORRES), IVAN

Born, Vega Baja, Puerto Rico, November 30, 1971.
Bats Right. Throws Right. Height, 5 feet, 9 inches. Weight, 205 pounds.

Year	Club	Lea	Pos	G	AB	R	H	2B	3B	HR	RBI	SB	Avg
1989 Gastonia	.........So. Atl.	C	112	386	38	92	22	1	7	42	2	.238
1990 Charlotte	..........Fla. St.	C	109	408	48	117	17	7	2	55	1	.287
1991 Tulsa	...........Texas	C	50	175	16	48	7	2	3	28	1	.274
1991 Texas	..............A.L.	C	88	280	24	74	16	0	3	27	0	.264
1992 Texas a	..............A.L.	C	123	420	39	109	16	1	8	37	0	.260
1993 Texas	..............A.L.	C	137	473	56	129	28	4	10	66	8	.273
1994 Texas	..............A.L.	C	99	363	56	108	19	1	16	57	6	.298
1995 Texas	..............A.L.	C	130	492	56	149	32	2	12	67	0	.303
1996 Texas	..............A.L.	C	153	639	116	192	47	3	19	86	5	.300
1997 Texas	..............A.L.	C	150	597	98	187	34	4	20	77	7	.313
1998 Texas	..............A.L.	C	145	579	88	186	40	4	21	91	9	.321
1999 Texas b	..............A.L.	C	144	600	116	199	29	1	35	113	25	.332
2000 Texas c	..............A.L.	C	91	363	66	126	27	4	27	83	5	.347
Major League Totals		10 Yrs.	1260	4806	715	1459	288	24	171	704	65	.304
Division Series												
1996 Texas	..............A.L.	C	4	16	1	6	1	0	0	2	0	.375
1998 Texas	..............A.L.	C	3	10	0	1	0	0	0	1	0	.100
1999 Texas	..............A.L.	C	3	12	0	3	1	0	0	0	1	.250
Division Series Totals			10	38	1	10	1	0	0	3	1	.263

a On disabled list from June 6 to June 27, 1992.
b Selected Most Valuable Player in American League for 1999.
c On disabled list from July 25 to October 1, 2000.

ROLEN, SCOTT BRUCE

Born, Evansville, Indiana, April 4, 1975.
Bats Right. Throws Right. Height, 6 feet, 4 inches. Weight, 195 pounds.

Year	Club	Lea	Pos	G	AB	R	H	2B	3B	HR	RBI	SB	Avg
1993 Martinsvlle	.........Appal.	3B	25	80	8	25	5	0	0	12	3	.313
1994 Spartanburg	........So.Atl.	3B	138	513	83	151	34	5	14	72	6	.294
1995 Clearwater	..........Fla.St.	3B	66	238	45	69	13	2	10	39	4	.290
1995 Reading	..........Eastern	3B	20	76	16	22	3	0	3	15	1	.289
1996 Reading	..........Eastern	3B	61	230	44	83	22	2	9	42	8	.361
1996 Scranton-WB	..........Int.	3B	45	168	23	46	17	0	2	19	4	.274
1996 Philadelphia	.........N.L.	3B	37	130	10	33	7	0	4	18	0	.254
1997 Philadelphia a	.........N.L.	3B	156	561	93	159	35	3	21	92	16	.283
1998 Philadelphia	.........N.L.	3B	160	601	120	174	45	4	31	110	14	.290
1999 Philadelphia	.........N.L.	3B	112	421	74	113	28	1	26	77	12	.268
2000 Philadelphia b	.........N.L.	3B	128	483	88	144	32	6	26	89	8	.298
Major League Totals		5 Yrs.	593	2196	385	623	147	14	108	386	50	.284

a Selected Rookie of the Year in National League for 1997.
b On disabled list from May 24 to June 8, 2000.

ROLLINS, JAMES CALVIN (JIMMY)
Born, Oakland, California, November 27, 1978.
Bats Both. Throws Right. Height, 5 feet, 8 inches. Weight, 160 pounds.

Year	Club	Lea	Pos	G	AB	R	H	2B	3B	HR	RBI	SB	Avg
1996 Martinsvlle	.Appal.	SS	49	172	22	41	3	1	1	16	11	.238
1997 Piedmont	.So.Atl.	SS	139	560	94	151	22	8	6	59	46	.270
1998 Clearwater	.Fla.St.	SS	119	495	72	121	18	9	6	35	23	.244
1999 Reading	.Eastern	SS	133	532	81	145	21	8	11	56	24	.273
1999 Scranton-WB	.Int.	SS	4	13	0	1	1	0	0	0	1	.077
2000 Scranton-WB	.Int.	SS	133	470	67	129	28	11	12	69	24	.274
2000 Philadelphia	.N.L.	SS	14	53	5	17	1	1	0	5	3	.321

SAENZ, OLMEDO
Born, Chitre Herrera, Panama, October 8, 1970.
Bats Right. Throws Right. Height, 6 feet, 2 inches. Weight, 185 pounds.

Year	Club	Lea	Pos	G	AB	R	H	2B	3B	HR	RBI	SB	Avg
1991 Sarasota	.Fla.St.	3B	5	19	1	2	0	1	0	2	0	.105
1991 South Bend	.Midwest	3B	56	192	23	47	10	1	2	22	5	.245
1992 South Bend	.Midwest	3B-1B	132	493	66	121	26	4	7	59	16	.245
1993 South Bend	.Midwest	3B	13	50	3	18	4	1	0	7	1	.360
1993 Sarasota	.Fla.St.	3B	33	121	13	31	9	4	0	27	3	.256
1993 Birmingham	.Southern	3B	49	173	30	60	17	2	6	29	2	.347
1994 Chicago	.A.L.	3B	5	14	2	2	0	1	0	0	0	.143
1994 Nashville	.A.A.	3B	107	383	48	100	27	2	12	59	3	.261
1995 Nashville	.A.A.	3B	111	415	60	126	26	1	13	74	0	.304
1996 Nashville	.A.A.	3B	134	476	86	124	29	1	18	63	4	.261
1997 White Sox	.Gulf Coast	DH	2	1	0	1	1	0	0	0	0	1.000
1998 Calgary a-b	.P.C.	3B	124	466	89	146	29	0	29	102	3	.313
1999 Oakland c	.A.L.	3B-1B	97	255	41	70	18	0	11	41	1	.275
2000 Sacramento	.P.C.	PH	1	4	1	2	0	0	0	1	0	.500
2000 Oakland d	.A.L.	DH-3B-1B	76	214	40	67	12	2	9	33	1	.313
Major League Totals		3 Yrs.	178	483	83	139	30	3	20	74	2	.288
Division Series												
2000 Oakland	.A.L.	DH	4	13	1	3	0	0	1	4	0	.231

a Filed for free agency, October 17, 1997, re-signed with Chicago White Sox, January 25, 1998.
b Filed for free agency, October 16, 1998, signed with Oakland Athletics, November 13, 1998.
c On disabled list from July 26 to August 16, 1999.
d On disabled list from August 1 to September 18, 2000.

SALMON, TIMOTHY JAMES
Born, Long Beach, California, August 24, 1968.
Bats Right. Throws Right. Height, 6 feet, 3 inches. Weight, 220 pounds.

Year	Club	Lea	Pos	G	AB	R	H	2B	3B	HR	RBI	SB	Avg
1989 Bend	.Northwest	OF	55	196	37	48	6	5	6	31	2	.245
1990 Palm Springs	.California	OF	36	118	19	34	6	0	2	21	11	.288
1990 Midland	.Texas	OF	27	97	17	26	3	1	3	16	1	.268
1991 Midland	.Texas	OF	131	465	100	114	26	4	23	94	12	.245
1992 Edmonton	.P.C.	OF	118	409	*101	142	38	4	*29	*105	9	.347
1992 California	.A.L.	OF	23	79	8	14	1	0	2	6	1	.177
1993 California a	.A.L.	OF	142	515	93	146	35	1	31	95	5	.283
1994 California b	.A.L.	OF	100	373	67	107	18	2	23	70	1	.287
1995 California	.A.L.	OF	143	537	111	177	34	3	34	105	5	.330
1996 California	.A.L.	OF	156	581	90	166	27	4	30	98	4	.286
1997 Anaheim	.A.L.	OF	157	582	95	172	28	1	33	129	9	.296
1998 Anaheim c	.A.L.	DH-OF	136	463	84	139	28	1	26	88	0	.300
1999 Lake Elsinore	.California	DH	1	5	0	3	2	0	0	2	0	.600
1999 Anaheim d	.A.L.	OF	98	353	60	94	24	2	17	69	4	.266
2000 Anaheim	.A.L.	OF	158	568	108	165	36	2	34	97	0	.290
Major League Totals		9 Yrs.	1113	4051	716	1180	231	16	230	757	29	.291

a Selected Rookie of the Year in American League for 1993.
b On disabled list from July 18 to August 3, 1994.
c On disabled list from April 23 to May 9, 1998.
d On disabled list from May 4 to July 17, 1999.

SANCHEZ (GUADALUPE), REY FRANCISCO

Born, Rio Piedras, Puerto Rico, October 5, 1967.
Bats Right. Throws Right. Height, 5 feet, 9 inches. Weight, 170 pounds.

Year	Club	Lea	Pos	G	AB	R	H	2B	3B	HR	RBI	SB	Avg
1986	Sarasota Rangers	Gulf C.	SS	52	169	27	49	3	1	0	23	10	.290
1987	Gastonia	So. Atl.	SS	50	160	19	35	1	2	1	10	6	.219
1987	Butte	Pioneer	SS	49	189	36	69	10	6	0	25	22	.365
1988	Charlotte	Fla. St.	SS	128	418	60	128	6	5	0	38	29	.306
1989	Oklahoma City a	A.A.	SS	134	464	38	104	10	4	1	39	4	.224
1990	Iowa b	A.A.					INJURED—Did Not Play						
1991	Iowa	A.A.	SS	126	417	60	121	16	5	2	46	13	.290
1991	Chicago	N.L.	SS-2B	13	23	1	6	0	0	0	2	0	.261
1992	Iowa	A.A.	SS-2B	20	76	12	26	3	0	0	3	6	.342
1992	Chicago c	N.L.	SS-2B	74	255	24	64	14	3	1	19	2	.251
1993	Chicago	N.L.	SS	105	344	35	97	11	2	0	28	1	.282
1994	Chicago	A.L.	2B-SS-3B	96	291	26	83	13	1	0	24	2	.285
1995	Chicago d	N.L.	2B-SS	114	428	57	119	22	2	3	27	6	.278
1996	Iowa e	A.A.	SS	3	12	2	2	0	0	0	1	2	.167
1996	Chicago	N.L.	SS	95	289	28	61	9	0	1	12	7	.211
1997	Chicago f	N.L.	SS-2B-3B	97	205	14	51	9	0	1	12	4	.249
1997	New York g-h	A.L.	2B-SS	38	138	21	43	12	0	1	15	0	.312
1998	San Francisco i	N.L.	SS-2B	109	316	44	90	14	2	2	30	0	.285
1999	Kansas City j	A.L.	SS	134	479	66	141	18	6	2	56	11	.294
2000	Kansas City	A.L.	SS	143	509	68	139	18	2	1	38	7	.273
Major League Totals			10 Yrs.	1018	3277	384	894	140	18	12	263	40	.273
Division Series													
1997	New York	A.L.	2B	5	15	1	3	1	0	0	1	0	.200

a Traded by Texas Rangers to Chicago Cubs organization for infielder Bryan House, January 3, 1990.
b On disabled list from April 6 to end of 1990 season.
c On disabled list from May 6 to May 21, 1992.
d On disabled list from July 24 to August 9, 1995.
e On disabled list from June 5 to July 20 and August 11 to September 1, 1996.
f Traded to New York Yankees for pitcher Frisco Parotte, August 16, 1997.
g Filed for free agency, November 3, 1997.
h Signed with San Francisco Giants, January 22, 1998.
i Filed for free agency, November 5, 1998. Signed with Kansas City Royals, December 10, 1998.
j Filed for free agency, October 29, 1999, re-signed with Kansas City Royals, December 7, 1999.

SANDERS, REGINALD LAVERN (REGGIE)

Born, Florence, South Carolina, December 1, 1967.
Bats Right. Throws Right. Height, 6 feet, 1 inch. Weight, 180 pounds.

Year	Club	Lea	Pos	G	AB	R	H	2B	3B	HR	RBI	SB	Avg
1988	Billings	Pioneer	SS	17	64	11	15	1	1	0	3	10	.234
1989	Greensboro a	So. Atl.	SS	81	315	53	91	18	5	9	53	21	.289
1990	Cedar Rapids	Midwest	OF	127	466	89	133	21	4	17	63	40	.285
1991	Chattanooga	Southern	OF	86	302	50	95	15	8	8	49	15	.315
1991	Cincinnati b	N.L.	OF	9	40	6	8	0	0	1	3	1	.200
1992	Cincinnati c	N.L.	OF	116	385	62	104	26	6	12	36	16	.270
1993	Cincinnati	N.L.	OF	138	496	90	136	16	4	20	83	27	.274
1994	Cincinnati d	N.L.	OF	107	400	66	105	20	8	17	62	21	.262
1995	Cincinnati e	N.L.	OF	133	484	91	148	36	6	28	99	36	.306
1996	Indianapolis f	A.A.	OF	4	12	3	5	2	0	0	1	0	.417
1996	Cincinnati	N.L.	OF	81	287	49	72	17	1	14	33	24	.251
1997	Chattanooga	Southern	OF	3	11	3	6	1	1	1	3	0	.545
1997	Indianapolis	A.A.	OF	5	19	1	4	0	0	0	1	0	.211
1997	Cincinnati g	N.L.	OF	86	312	52	79	19	2	19	56	13	.253
1998	Cincinnati	N.L.	OF	135	481	83	129	18	6	14	59	20	.268
1999	San Diego h-i-j	N.L.	OF	133	478	92	136	24	7	26	72	36	.285
2000	Atlanta k-l	N.L.	OF	103	340	43	79	23	1	11	37	21	.232
Major League Totals			10 Yrs.	1041	3703	634	996	199	41	162	540	215	.269
Division Series													
1995	Cincinnati	N.L.	OF	3	13	3	2	1	0	1	2	2	.154
2000	Atlanta	N.L.	OF	3	9	0	0	0	0	0	0	0	.000
Division Series Totals				6	22	3	2	1	0	1	2	2	.091
Championship Series													
1995	Cincinnati	N.L.	OF	4	16	0	2	0	0	0	0	0	.125
2000	Atlanta	N.L.	OF	3	9	0	0	0	0	0	0	0	.000

a On disabled list from July 20 to end of 1989 season.
b On disabled list from August 26 to September 20, 1991.
c On disabled list from May 13 to May 28 and July 17 to August 2, 1992.

d Suspended five games and fined by National League for April 13 charging mound and inciting brawl from June 3 to June 8, 1994.
e On disabled list from June 1 to July 16, 1995.
f On disabled list from April 20 to May 22 and May 31 to June 15 and September 17 to September 30, 1996.
g On disabled list from April 19 to May 6 and May 24 to July 22, 1997.
h Traded to San Diego Padres with infielder Damian Jackson and pitcher Josh Harris for outfielder Greg Vaughn and outfielder Mark Sweeney, February 2, 1999.
i On disabled list from June 3 to June 18, 1999
j Traded to Atlanta Braves with infielder Wally Joyner and infielder Quilvio Veras for infielder Bret Boone, outfielder Ryan Klesko and pitcher Jason Shiell, December 22, 1999.
k On disabled list from April 30 to May 22 and July 28 to August 14, 2000.
l Filed for free agency, October 31, 2000, signed with Arizona Diamondbacks, January 5, 2001.

SANTANGELO, FRANK-PAUL (F.P.)

Born, Livonia, Michigan, October 24, 1967.
Bats Both. Throws Right. Height, 5 feet, 10 inches. Weight, 165 pounds.

Year Club	Lea	Pos	G	AB	R	H	2B	3B	HR	RBI	SB	Avg
1989 Jamestown	N.Y.-Penn	2B	2	6	0	3	1	0	0	0	1	.500
1989 West Palm Bch.	Fla. St.	DH-SS-2B-OF	57	173	18	37	4	0	0	14	3	.214
1990 West Palm Bch.	Fla. St.	SS-OF-2B	116	394	63	109	19	2	0	38	22	.277
1991 Harrisburg	Eastern	2B-OF-SS-3B	132	462	78	113	12	7	5	42	21	.245
1992 Indianapolis	A.A.	OF-2B-SS-3B	137	462	83	123	25	0	5	34	12	.266
1993 Ottawa	Int.	OF-SS-3B-2B	131	453	86	124	21	2	4	45	18	.274
1994 Ottawa	Int.	OF-2B-SS-3B	119	413	62	104	28	1	5	41	7	.252
1995 Ottawa	Int.	3B-2B-OF-SS	95	267	37	68	15	3	2	25	7	.255
1995 Montreal	N.L.	OF-2B	35	98	11	29	5	1	1	9	1	.296
1996 Montreal	N.L.	OF-3B-2B-SS	152	393	54	109	20	5	7	56	5	.277
1997 Montreal	N.L.	OF-3B-2B-SS	130	350	56	87	19	5	5	31	8	.249
1998 Ottawa	Int.	OF	2	8	1	2	0	0	0	1	0	.250
1998 Montreal a-b	N.L.	OF-2B-3B	122	383	53	82	18	0	4	23	7	.214
1999 San Francisco c	N.L.	OF-2B-3B-SS	113	254	49	66	17	3	3	26	12	.260
2000 San Bernardino	California	OF	7	19	2	9	2	1	0	1	1	.474
2000 Los Angeles d	N.L.	OF-2B	81	142	19	28	4	0	1	9	3	.197
Major League Totals		6 Yrs.	633	1620	242	401	83	14	21	154	36	.248

a On disabled list from July 16 to July 31, 1998.
b Not offered 1999 contract, December 18, 1998. Signed with San Francisco Giants, December 22, 1998.
c Not offered contract, December 21, 1999. Signed with Los Angeles Dodgers, January 7, 2000.
d On disabled list from July 17 to August 1 and August 23 to September 21, 2000.

SANTIAGO (RIVERA), BENITO

Born, Ponce, Puerto Rico, March 9, 1965.
Bats Right. Throws Right. Height, 6 feet, 1 inch. Weight, 185 pounds.

Year Club	Lea	Pos	G	AB	R	H	2B	3B	HR	RBI	SB	Avg
1983 Miami	Fla. St.	C	122	429	34	106	25	3	5	56	3	.247
1984 Reno	California	C	114	416	64	116	20	6	16	83	5	.279
1985 Beaumont a	Texas	C-1B-3B	101	372	55	111	16	6	5	52	12	.298
1986 Las Vegas	P.C.	C	117	436	55	125	26	3	17	71	19	.287
1986 San Diego	N.L.	C	17	62	10	18	2	0	3	6	0	.290
1987 San Diego b	N.L.	C	146	546	64	164	33	2	18	79	21	.300
1988 San Diego	N.L.	C	139	492	49	122	22	2	10	46	15	.248
1989 San Diego	N.L.	C	129	462	50	109	16	3	16	62	11	.236
1990 Las Vegas	P.C.	C	6	20	5	6	2	0	1	8	0	.300
1990 San Diego c	N.L.	C	100	344	42	93	8	5	11	53	5	.270
1991 San Diego	N.L.	C-OF	152	580	60	155	22	3	17	87	8	.267
1992 Las Vegas	P.C.	C	4	13	3	4	0	0	1	2	0	.308
1992 San Diego d-e	N.L.	C	106	386	37	97	21	0	10	42	2	.251
1993 Florida	N.L.	C-OF	139	469	49	108	19	6	13	50	10	.230
1994 Florida f	N.L.	C	101	337	35	92	14	2	11	41	1	.273
1995 Cincinnati g-h-i	N.L.	C-1B	81	266	40	76	20	0	11	44	2	.286
1996 Philadelphia j-k-l	N.L.	C-1B	136	481	71	127	21	2	30	85	2	.264
1997 Toronto m	A.L.	C	97	341	31	83	10	0	13	42	1	.243
1998 Dunedin	Fla. St.	DH-C	11	37	4	6	1	0	1	5	3	.162
1998 Syracuse	Int.	C	5	22	0	5	2	0	0	2	0	.227
1998 Toronto n-o	A.L.	C	15	29	3	9	5	0	0	4	0	.310
1999 Chicago p	N.L.	C-1B	109	350	28	87	18	3	7	36	1	.249
2000 Cincinnati q	N.L.	C	89	252	22	66	11	1	8	45	2	.262
Major League Totals		15 Yrs.	1556	5397	591	1406	242	29	178	722	81	.261

Year	Club	Lea	Pos	G	AB	R	H	2B	3B	HR	RBI	SB	Avg
	Division Series												
1995 Cincinnati	..........N.L.		C	3	9	2	3	0	0	1	3	0	.333
	Championship Series												
1995 Cincinnati	..........N.L.		C	4	13	0	3	0	0	0	0	0	.231

On disabled list from June 21 to July 2, 1985.
Selected Rookie of the Year in National League for 1987.
On disabled list from June 15 to August 10, 1990.
On disabled list from May 31 to July 11, 1992.
Filed for free agency, October 26; signed with Florida Marlins, December 16, 1992.
Filed for free agency, October 14, 1994.
Signed with Cincinnati Reds, April 17, 1995.
On disabled list from May 8 to July 4, 1995.
Filed for free agency, November 12, 1995.
Signed with Philadelphia Phillies, January 30, 1996.
Filed for free agency, November 18, 1996.
Signed with Toronto Blue Jays, December 9, 1996.
On disabled list from April 14 to April 29, 1997.
On disabled list from March 31 to September 3, 1998.
Filed for free agency, October 23, 1998. Signed with Chicago Cubs, December 9, 1998.
Not offered 2000 contract, October 27, 1999. Signed with Cincinnati Reds organization, February 24, 2000.
Filed for free agency, November 3, 2000.

SEFCIK, KEVIN JOHN

Born, Oak Lawn, Illinois, February 10, 1971.
Bats Right. Throws Right. Height, 5 feet, 10 inches. Weight, 175 pounds.

Year	Club	Lea	Pos	G	AB	R	H	2B	3B	HR	RBI	SB	Avg
1993 Batavia	........N.Y.-Penn.		2B-3B	74	281	49	84	24	4	2	28	20	.299
1994 Clearwater	........Fla. St.		3B-2B	130	516	83	147	29	8	2	46	30	.285
1995 Scranton-WB	.........Int.		2B	7	26	5	9	6	1	0	6	0	.346
1995 Reading	..........Eastern		SS-3B	128	508	68	138	18	4	4	46	14	.272
1995 Philadelphia	.........N.L.		3B	5	4	1	0	0	0	0	0	0	.000
1996 Scranton-WB	.........Int.		SS-2B	45	180	34	60	7	5	0	19	11	.333
1996 Philadelphia	.........N.L.		SS-3B	44	116	10	33	5	3	0	9	3	.284
1997 Scranton-WB	.........Int.		2B-3B-OF	29	123	19	41	11	2	1	7	5	.333
1997 Philadelphia	.........N.L.		2B-SS-3B	61	119	11	32	3	0	2	6	1	.269
1998 Philadelphia	.........N.L.		OF-3B-2B	104	169	27	53	7	2	3	20	4	.314
1999 Philadelphia	.........N.L.		OF-2B	111	209	28	58	15	3	1	11	9	.278
2000 Philadelphia a	.........N.L.		OF	99	153	15	36	6	2	0	10	4	.235
Major League Totals	....	6 Yrs.		424	770	92	212	36	10	6	56	21	.275

a Filed for free agency, November 10, 2000.

SEGUI, DAVID VINCENT

Born, Kansas City, Missouri, July 19, 1966.
Bats Both. Throws Left. Height, 6 feet, 1 inch. Weight, 202 pounds.

Year	Club	Lea	Pos	G	AB	R	H	2B	3B	HR	RBI	SB	Avg
1988 Hagerstown	.......Carolina		1B-OF	60	190	35	51	12	4	3	31	0	.268
1989 Frederick	.......Carolina		1B	83	284	43	90	19	0	10	50	2	.317
1989 Hagerstown	.......Eastern		1B	44	173	22	58	14	1	1	26	0	.324
1990 Rochester	.............Int.		1B	86	307	55	103	28	0	2	51	5	.336
1990 Baltimore	.............A.L.		1B	40	123	14	30	7	0	2	15	0	.244
1991 Rochester a	...........Int.		1B-OF	28	96	9	26	2	0	1	10	1	.271
1991 Baltimore	...........A.L.		1B-OF	86	212	15	59	7	0	2	22	1	.278
1992 Baltimore	...........A.L.		1B-OF	115	189	21	44	9	0	1	17	1	.233
1993 Baltimore b-c	........A.L.		1B	146	450	54	123	27	0	10	60	2	.273
1994 New York d	.........N.L.		1B-OF	92	336	46	81	17	1	10	43	0	.241
1995 New York-Montreal e	...N.L.		1B-OF	130	456	68	141	25	4	12	68	2	.309
1996 Montreal f	.............N.L.		1B	115	416	69	119	30	1	11	58	4	.286
1997 Montreal g-h-i	........N.L.		1B	125	459	75	141	22	3	21	68	1	.307
1998 Seattle	...............A.L.		1B-OF	143	522	79	159	36	1	19	84	3	.305
1999 Seattle-Toronto j-k-l	...A.L.		1B	121	440	57	131	27	3	14	52	1	.298
2000 Texas-Cleveland m-n-o	.A.L.		1B-OF	150	574	93	192	42	1	19	103	0	.334
Major League Totals	....	11 Yrs.		1263	4177	591	1220	249	14	121	590	15	.292

a On disabled list from April 15 to April 25, 1991.
b Suspended three games by American League for June 6 fight from August 16 to August 19, 1993.
c Traded to New York Mets for shortstop Kevin Daez and pitcher Tom Wegmann, March 27, 1994.
d On disabled list from June 20 to July 4, 1994.
e Traded to Montreal Expos for pitcher Reid Cornelius, June 8, 1995.
f On disabled list from July 4 to August 16, 1996.

g On disabled list from June 4 to June 21, 1997.
h Filed for free agency, October 28, 1997.
i Signed with Seattle Mariners, December 12, 1997.
j Traded to Toronto Blue Jays for pitcher Tom Davey and pitcher Steve Sinclair, July 28, 1999.
k On disabled list from August 8 to September 2, 1999.
l Filed for free agency, October 29, 1999, Accepted arbitration with Toronto Blue Jays, December 19, 1999.
m Traded to Texas Rangers for infielder Brad Fullmer, March 16, 2000.
n Traded to Cleveland Indians for outfielder Ricky Ledee, July 28, 2000.
o Filed for free agency, October 30, 2000, signed with Baltimore Orioles, December 21, 2000.

SEGUIGNOL, FERNANDO ALFREDO

Born, Bocas Del Toro, Panama, January 19, 1975.
Bats Both. Throws Right. Height, 6 feet, 5 inches. Weight, 190 pounds.

Year	Club	Lea	Pos	G	AB	R	H	2B	3B	HR	RBI	SB	Avg
1993 Yankees	Gulf Coast	OF-1B	45	161	16	35	3	3	2	20	2	.217
1994 Oneonta	N.Y.-Penn.	OF	73	266	36	77	14	9	2	32	4	.289
1995 Albany a	So.Atl.	OF	121	457	59	95	22	2	12	66	12	.208
1996 Delmarva	So.Atl.	OF	118	410	59	98	14	5	8	55	12	.239
1997 Wst Plm Bch	Fla.St.	1B-OF	124	456	70	116	27	5	18	83	5	.254
1998 Harrisburg	Eastern	1B-OF	80	281	54	81	13	0	25	69	6	.288
1998 Ottawa	Int.	OF-1B	32	109	16	28	8	0	6	16	0	.257
1998 Montreal b	N.L.	OF-1B	16	42	6	11	4	0	2	3	0	.262
1999 Ottawa	Int.	1B	87	312	54	89	17	3	23	74	3	.285
1999 Montreal c	N.L.	1B-OF	35	105	14	27	9	0	5	10	0	.257
2000 Ottawa	Int.	1B	41	141	20	39	16	0	8	31	1	.277
2000 Montreal	N.L.	1B-OF	76	162	22	45	8	0	10	22	0	.278
Major League Totals			3 Yrs.	127	309	42	83	21	0	17	35	0	.269

a Traded to Montreal Expos by New York Yankees with cash for pitcher John Wetteland, April 5, 1995.
b On disabled list from June 24 to July 17, 1998.
c On disabled list from July 11 to September 7, 1999.

SEXSON, RICHARD (RICHIE)

Born, Portland, Oregon, December 29, 1974.
Bats Right. Throws Right. Height, 6 feet, 6 inches. Weight, 205 pounds.

Year	Club	Lea	Pos	G	AB	R	H	2B	3B	HR	RBI	SB	Avg
1993 Burlington	Appal.	1B	40	97	11	18	3	0	1	5	1	.186
1994 Columbus	So.Atl.	1B	130	488	88	133	25	2	14	77	7	.273
1995 Kinston	Carolina	1B	131	494	80	151	34	0	22	85	4	.306
1996 Canton-Akron	Eastern	1B	133	518	85	143	33	3	16	76	2	.276
1997 Buffalo	A.A.	1B	115	434	57	113	20	2	31	88	5	.260
1997 Cleveland	A.L.	1B	5	11	1	3	0	0	0	0	0	.273
1998 Buffalo	Int.	OF-1B	89	344	58	102	20	1	21	74	1	.297
1998 Cleveland	A.L.	1B-OF	49	174	28	54	14	1	11	35	1	.310
1999 Cleveland	A.L.	1B-OF	134	479	72	122	17	7	31	116	3	.255
2000 Cleveland	A.L.	OF-1B	91	324	45	83	16	1	16	44	1	.256
2000 Milwaukee a-b	N.L.	1B	57	213	44	63	14	0	14	47	1	.296
Major League Totals			4 Yrs.	336	1201	190	325	61	9	72	242	6	.271
Division Series													
1998 Cleveland	A.L.	1B	3	2	0	0	0	0	0	0	0	.000
1999 Cleveland	A.L.	1B-OF	3	6	1	1	0	0	0	1	0	.167
Division Series Totals				6	8	1	1	0	0	0	1	0	.125
Championship Series													
1998 Cleveland	A.L.	1B	3	6	0	0	0	0	0	0	0	.000

a Traded to Milwaukee Brewers with pitcher Paul Rigdon, pitcher Kane Davis and player to be named later for pitcher Bob Wickman, pitcher Steve Woodard and pitcher Jason Bere, July 28, 2000.
b Milwaukee Brewers received infielder Marcus Scutaro to complete trade, August 30, 2000.

SHEFFIELD, GARY ANTONIAN

Born, Tampa, Florida, November 18, 1968.
Bats Right. Throws Right. Height, 5 feet, 11 inches. Weight, 190 pounds.

Year	Club	Lea	Pos	G	AB	R	H	2B	3B	HR	RBI	SB	Avg
1986 Helena	Pioneer	SS	57	222	53	81	12	2	15	71	14	.365
1987 Stockton	California	SS	129	469	84	130	23	3	17	*103	25	.277
1988 El Paso	Texas	SS	77	296	70	93	19	3	19	65	5	.314
1988 Denver	A.A.	3B-SS	57	212	42	73	9	5	9	54	8	.344
1988 Milwaukee	A.L.	SS	24	80	12	19	1	0	4	12	3	.238
1989 Denver a	A.A.	SS	7	29	3	4	1	1	0	0	0	.138

Year	Club	Lea	Pos	G	AB	R	H	2B	3B	HR	RBI	SB	Avg
1989 Milwaukee	....	A.L.	SS-3B	95	368	34	91	18	0	5	32	10	.247
1990 Milwaukee b	....	A.L.	3B	125	487	67	143	30	1	10	67	25	.294
1991 Milwaukee c-d	....	A.L.	3B	50	175	25	34	12	2	2	22	5	.194
1992 San Diego	....	N.L.	3B	146	557	87	184	34	3	33	100	5	*.330
1993 San Diego-Florida e-f	.	N.L.	3B	140	494	67	145	20	5	20	73	17	.294
1994 Portland	..........Eastern		OF	2	7	1	2	1	0	0	0	0	.286
1994 Florida g	....	N.L.	OF	87	322	61	89	16	1	27	78	12	.276
1995 Florida h	....	N.L.	OF	63	213	46	69	8	0	16	46	19	.324
1996 Florida	....	N.L.	OF	161	519	118	163	33	1	42	120	16	.314
1997 Florida i	....	N.L.	OF	135	444	86	111	22	1	21	71	11	.250
1998 Florida-Los Angeles j	.	N.L.	OF	130	437	73	132	27.	2	22	85	22	.302
1999 Los Angeles	....	N.L.	OF	152	549	103	165	20	0	34	101	11	.301
2000 Los Angeles	....	N.L.	OF	141	501	105	163	24	3	43	109	4	.325
Major League Totals	....	13 Yrs.		1449	5146	884	1508	265	19	279	916	160	.293
Division Series													
1997 Florida	....	N.L.	OF	3	9	2	5	1	0	1	1	1	.556
Championship Series													
1997 Florida	....	N.L.	OF	6	17	6	4	0	0	1	1	0	.235
World Series Record													
1997 Florida	....	N.L.	OF	7	24	4	7	1	0	1	5	0	.292

a On disabled list from July 14 to September 9, 1989.
b Suspended three games by American League for June 30 fight, August 31 to September 2, 1990.
c On disabled list from June 2 to July 3 and July 25 to end of 1991 season.
d Traded to San Diego Padres with pitcher Geoff Kellogg for pitcher Ricky Bones, infielder Jose Valentin and outfielder Matt Mieske, March 27, 1992.
e Suspended three games by National League for June 10 fight from July 9 to July 11, 1993.
f Traded to Florida Marlins with pitcher Rich Rodriguez for pitchers Trevor Hoffman, Andres Berumen and Jose Martinez, June 25, 1993.
g On disabled list from May 10 to May 25 and May 28 to June 11, 1994.
h On disabled list from June 11 to September 1, 1995.
i On disabled list from May 14 to May 29, 1997.
j Traded to Los Angeles Dodgers with outfielder Jim Eisenreich, catcher Charles Johnson, infielder Bobby Bonilla and pitcher Manuel Barrios for catcher Mike Piazza and infielder Todd Zeile, May 15, 1998.

SHUMPERT, TERRANCE (TERRY)

Born, Paducah, Kentucky, August 16, 1966.
Bats Right. Throws Right. Height, 5 feet, 11 inches. Weight, 185 pounds.

Year	Club	Lea	Pos	G	AB	R	H	2B	3B	HR	RBI	SB	Avg
1987 Eugene	.....Northwest		2B	48	186	38	54	16	1	4	21	16	.290
1988 Appleton	......Midwest		2B-OF	114	422	64	102	37	2	7	38	36	.242
1989 Omaha	....	A.A.	2B	113	355	54	88	29	2	4	22	23	.248
1990 Omaha	....	A.A.	2B	39	153	24	39	6	4	2	12	18	.255
1990 Kansas City	....	A.L.	2B	32	91	7	25	6	1	0	8	3	.275
1991 Kansas City	....	A.L.	2B	144	369	45	80	16	4	5	34	17	.217
1992 Omaha	....	A.A.	2B-SS	56	210	23	42	12	0	1	14	3	.200
1992 Kansas City	....	A.L.	2B-SS	36	94	6	14	5	1	1	11	2	.149
1993 Omaha	....	A.A.	2B	111	413	70	124	29	1	14	59	36	.300
1993 Kansas City	....	A.L.	2B	8	10	1	1	0	0	0	0	1	.100
1994 Kansas City a	.....	A.L.	2B-3B-SS	64	183	28	44	6	2	8	24	18	.240
1995 Boston	....	A.L.	2B-3B-SS	21	47	6	11	3	0	0	3	3	.234
1995 Pawtucket	....	Int.	3B-2B-OF	37	133	17	36	7	0	2	11	10	.271
1996 Iowa	....	A.A.	2B-3B-1B-SS	72	246	45	68	13	4	5	32	13	.276
1996 Chicago b-c	....	N.L.	3B-2B-SS	27	31	5	7	1	0	2	6	0	.226
1997 San Diego	....	N.L.	2B-OF-3B	13	33	4	9	3	0	1	6	0	.273
1997 Las Vegas	....	P.C.	3B-2B-SS	32	109	18	31	8	1	1	16	3	.284
1997 New Haven	.....	Eastern	2B	5	17	2	4	0	0	1	1	0	.235
1997 Colo Sprngs d	.....	P.C.	SS-2B-3B-OF	10	37	8	11	3	0	1	2	0	.297
1998 Colo Sprngs	.....	P.C.	2B-OF-3B	97	376	66	115	29	8	12	50	11	.306
1998 Colorado e	.....	N.L.	2B	23	26	3	6	1	0	1	2	0	.231
1999 Colorado Spgs	.....	P.C.	3B	29	80	15	30	8	1	6	17	3	.375
1999 Colorado f	....	N.L.	2B-OF-3B-SS	92	262	58	91	26	3	10	37	14	.347
2000 Colorado	....	N.L.	OF-2B-3B-SS	115	263	52	68	11	7	9	40	4	.259
Major League Totals	....	11 Yrs.		575	1409	214	356	78	18	37	171	66	.253

a Traded to Boston Red Sox for a player to be named later, December 13, 1994.
b Filed for free agency, October 6, 1995, signed with Chicago Cubs organization, March 12, 1996.
c Filed for free agency, October 15, 1996, signed with San Diego Padres organization, November 5, 1996.
d Released by San Diego Padres, August 5, 1997, signed with Colorado Rockies organization, August 13, 1997.
e Filed for free agency, October 15, 1998, re-signed with Colorado Rockies organization, December 15, 1998.
f Filed for free agency, October 29, 1999, re-signed with Colorado Rockies, December 15, 1999.

SINGLETON, CHRISTOPHER (CHRIS)
Born, Martinez, California, August 15, 1972.
Bats Left. Throws Right. Height, 6 feet, 2 inches. Weight, 195 pounds.

Year	Club	Lea	Pos	G	AB	R	H	2B	3B	HR	RBI	SB	Avg
1993 Everett	........Northwest	OF	58	219	39	58	14	4	3	18	14	.265
1994 San Jose	.California	OF	113	425	51	106	17	5	2	49	19	.249
1995 San Jose	........California	OF	94	405	55	112	13	5	2	31	33	.277
1996 Shreveport	..........Texas	OF	129	500	68	149	31	9	5	72	27	.298
1996 Phoenix	.............P.C.	OF	9	32	3	4	0	0	0	0	0	.125
1997 Shreveport a	.........Texas	OF	126	464	85	147	26	10	9	61	27	.317
1998 Columbus b	...........Int.	OF	121	413	55	105	17	10	6	45	9	.254
1999 Chicago	.............A.L.	OF	133	496	72	149	31	6	17	72	20	.300
2000 Chicago	.............A.L.	OF	147	511	83	130	22	5	11	62	22	.254
Major League Totals	....	2 Yrs.	280	1007	155	279	53	11	28	134	42	.277
Division Series													
2000 Chicago	............A.L.	OF	3	9	1	1	0	1	0	1	0	.111

a Traded by San Francisco Giants to New York Yankees with pitcher Alberto Castillo for infielder Charlie Hayes and cash, November 10, 1997.
b Traded by New York Yankees to Chicago White Sox for a player to be named later, December 6, 1998. Yankees received pitcher Rich Pratt to complete trade, January 10, 1999.

SMITH, MARK EDWARD
Born, Pasadena, California, May 7, 1970.
Bats Right. Throws Right. Height, 6 feet, 3 inches. Weight, 205 pounds.

Year	Club	Lea	Pos	G	AB	R	H	2B	3B	HR	RBI	SB	Avg
1991 Frederick	........Carolina	OF	38	148	20	37	5	1	4	29	1	.250
1992 Hagerstown	.......Eastern	OF	128	472	51	136	32	6	4	62	15	.288
1993 Rochester	.............Int.	OF	129	485	69	136	27	1	12	68	4	.280
1994 Baltimore	.............A.L.	OF	3	7	0	1	0	0	0	2	0	.143
1994 Rochester	.............Int.	OF	114	437	69	108	27	1	19	66	4	.247
1995 Rochester	.............Int.	OF	96	364	55	101	25	3	12	66	7	.277
1995 Baltimore	.............A.L.	OF	37	104	11	24	5	0	3	15	3	.231
1996 Rochester	.............Int.	OF	39	132	24	46	14	1	8	32	10	.348
1996 Baltimore	...........A.L.	OF	27	78	9	19	2	0	4	10	0	.244
1996 Frederick	.........Carolina	DH	1	1	0	0	0	0	0	0	0	.000
1996 Bowie a	..........Eastern	DH	6	22	1	2	0	0	1	2	0	.091
1997 Calgary	.............P.C.	OF	39	137	37	51	14	1	14	42	2	.372
1997 Carolina	........Southern	OF	3	12	5	5	1	0	3	4	0	.417
1997 Pittsburgh b-c-d	.......N.L.	OF-1B	71	193	29	55	13	1	9	35	3	.285
1998 Nashville	.........P.C.	OF-1B-3B	24	93	18	33	10	1	8	30	3	.355
1998 Pittsburgh e-f	.........N.L.	OF-1B	59	128	18	25	6	0	2	13	7	.195
1999 Yakult g	.......Japan Cent.	OF	98	293	38	96	11	1	20	55	3	.259
2000 Florida h-i	.........N.L.	OF	104	192	22	47	8	1	5	27	2	.245
Major League Totals	....	6 Yrs.	301	702	89	171	34	2	23	102	15	.244

a On disabled list from July 23 to September 30, 1996.
b Traded to San Diego Padres for catcher LeRoy McKinnis, January 9, 1997.
c Traded to to Pittsburgh Pirates with pitcher Hal Garrett for outfielder Trey Beamon and catcher Angel Encarnacion, March 29, 1997.
d On disabled list from May 23 to June 15, 1997.
e On disabled list from May 4 to May 19, 1998.
f Filed for free agency, September 29, 1998, signed with Yakult (Japan) for 1999.
g Returned from Japan, signed with Florida Marlins organization, December 14, 1999.
h On disabled list from May 11 to June 4, 2000.
i Filed for free agency, October 5, 2000, signed with Montreal Expos organization, November 17, 2000.

SNOW, JACK THOMAS (J.T.)
Born, Long Beach, California, February 26, 1968.
Bats Left. Throws Left. Height, 6 feet, 2 inches. Weight, 202 pounds.

Year	Club	Lea	Pos	G	AB	R	H	2B	3B	HR	RBI	SB	Avg
1989 Oneonta	........N.Y.-Penn.	1B	73	274	41	80	18	2	8	51	4	.292
1990 Prince William	.....Carolina	1B	*138	520	57	133	25	1	8	72	2	.256
1991 Albany	...........Eastern	1B	132	477	78	133	33	3	13	76	5	.279
1992 Columbus	...........Int.	1B-OF	135	492	81	154	26	4	15	78	3	*.313
1992 New York a	..........A.L.	1B	7	14	1	2	1	0	0	2	0	.143
1993 Vancouver	............P.C.	1B	23	94	19	32	9	1	5	24	0	.340
1993 California	............A.L.	1B	129	419	60	101	18	2	16	57	3	.241
1994 Vancouver	............P.C.	1B	53	189	35	56	13	2	8	43	1	.296
1994 California	............A.L.	1B	61	223	22	49	4	0	8	30	0	.220
1995 California	............A.L.	1B	143	544	80	157	22	1	24	102	2	.289

Year	Club	Lea	Pos	G	AB	R	H	2B	3B	HR	RBI	SB	Avg
1996 California b		A.L.	1B	155	575	69	148	20	1	17	67	1	.257
1997 San Francisco		N.L.	1B	157	531	81	149	36	1	28	104	6	.281
1998 San Francisco		N.L.	1B	138	435	65	108	29	1	15	79	1	.248
1999 San Francisco		N.L.	1B	161	570	93	156	25	2	24	98	0	.274
2000 San Francisco		N.L.	1B	155	536	82	152	33	2	19	96	1	.284
Major League Totals			9 Yrs.	1106	3847	553	1022	188	10	151	635	14	.266
Division Series													
1997 San Francisco		N.L.	1B	3	6	0	1	0	0	0	0	0	.167
2000 San Francisco		N.L.	1B	4	10	1	4	0	0	1	3	0	.400
Division Series Totals				7	16	1	5	0	0	1	3	0	.313

a Traded to California Angels with pitchers Jerry Nielsen and Russ Springer for pitcher Jim Abbott, December 6, 1992.
b Traded to San Francisco Giants for pitcher Allen Watson and pitcher Fausto Macey, November 27, 1996.

SOJO, LUIS BELTRAN

Born, Caracas, Venezuela, January 3, 1966.
Bats Right. Throws Right. Height, 5 feet, 11 inches. Weight, 174 pounds.

Year	Club	Lea	Pos	G	AB	R	H	2B	3B	HR	RBI	SB	Avg
1987 Myrtle Bch		So.Atl.	SS-2B-3B	72	223	23	47	5	4	2	15	5	.211
1988 Myrtle Bch		So.Atl.	SS	135	536	83	155	22	5	5	56	14	.289
1989 Syracuse		Int.	SS-2B	121	482	54	133	20	5	3	54	9	.276
1990 Syracuse		Int.	2B-SS	75	297	39	88	12	3	6	25	10	.296
1990 Toronto a-b		A.L.	2B-SS-OF-3B	33	80	14	18	3	0	1	9	1	.225
1991 California		A.L.	2B-SS-3B-OF	113	364	38	94	14	1	3	20	4	.258
1992 Edmonton		P.C.	3B-2B-SS	37	145	22	43	9	1	1	24	4	.297
1992 California		A.L.	2B-3B-SS	106	368	37	100	12	3	7	43	7	.272
1993 Toronto		A.L.	2B-SS-3B	19	47	5	8	2	0	0	6	0	.170
1993 Syracuse d		Int.	2B-OF-3B	43	142	17	31	7	2	1	12	2	.218
1994 Calgary		P.C.	SS-2B	24	102	19	33	9	3	1	18	5	.324
1994 Seattle e		A.L.	2B-SS-3B	63	213	32	59	9	2	6	22	2	.277
1995 Tacoma		P.C.	2B-SS	4	17	1	3	0	0	1	1	0	.176
1995 Seattle f		A.L.	SS-2B-OF	102	339	50	98	18	2	7	39	4	.289
1996 Seattle-New York g		A.L.	2B-3B-SS	95	287	23	63	10	1	1	21	2	.220
1997 New York h-i		A.L.	2B-SS-3B-1B	77	215	27	66	6	1	2	25	3	.307
1998 Tampa		Fla.St.	SS	3	9	1	2	0	0	0	0	0	.222
1998 Columbus		Int.	SS-2B	6	23	1	5	2	0	0	2	1	.217
1998 New York j		A.L.	SS-1B-2B-3B	54	147	16	34	3	1	0	14	1	.231
1999 New York		A.L.	3B-2B-SS-1B	49	127	20	32	6	0	2	16	1	.252
2000 Pittsburgh		N.L.	3B-2B	61	176	14	50	11	0	5	20	1	.284
2000 New York k-l-m-n		A.L.	2B-3B-1B-SS	34	125	19	36	7	1	2	17	1	.288
Major League Totals			11 Yrs.	806	2488	295	658	101	12	36	252	27	.264
Division Series													
1995 Seattle		A.L.	SS	5	20	0	5	0	0	0	3	0	.250
1996 New York		A.L.	2B	2	0	0	0	0	0	0	0	0	.000
2000 New York		A.L.	2B	5	16	2	3	2	0	0	5	0	.188
Division Series Totals				12	36	2	8	2	0	0	8	0	.222
Championship Series													
1995 Seattle		A.L.	SS	6	20	0	5	2	0	0	1	0	.250
1996 New York		A.L.	2B	3	5	0	1	0	0	0	0	0	.200
1998 New York		A.L.	1B	1	0	0	0	0	0	0	0	0	.000
1999 New York		A.L.	2B	2	1	0	0	0	0	0	0	0	.000
2000 New York		A.L.	2B-3B	6	23	1	6	1	0	0	2	0	.261
Championship Series Totals				18	49	1	12	3	0	0	3	0	.245
World Series Record													
1996 New York		A.L.	2B	5	5	0	3	1	0	0	1	0	.600
1999 New York		A.L.	2B	1	0	0	0	0	0	0	0	0	.000
2000 New York		A.L.	2B-3B	4	7	0	2	0	0	0	2	1	.286
World Series Totals				10	12	0	5	1	0	0	3	1	.417

a Traded to California Angels with outfielder Junior Felix and player named later for outfielder Devon White, pitcher Willie Fraser and player named later, December 2, 1990.
b California Angels received catcher Ken Rivers and Toronto Blue Jays received pitcher Marcus Moore to complete trade, December 4, 1990.
c Traded to Toronto Blue Jays for infielder Kelly Gruber and cash, December 8, 1992.
d On disabled list from May 10 to 30, 1993.
e Filed for free agency, October 15, 1993, signed with Seattle Mariners organization, January 10, 1994. On disabled list from June 7 to 23, 1995.
g Claimed on waivers by New York Yankees, August 22, 1996.
h On disabled list from August 15 to September 29, 1997.
i Filed for free agency, October 31, 1997, re-signed with New York Yankees, November 12, 1997.

SOSA, SAMUEL
Born, San Pedro de Macoris, Dominican Republic, November 12, 1968.
Bats Right. Throws Right. Height, 6 feet. Weight, 185 pounds.

Year	Club	Lea	Pos	G	AB	R	H	2B	3B	HR	RBI	SB	Avg
1986 Sarasota Rangers	....	Gulf C.	OF	61	229	38	63	*19	1	4	28	11	.275
1987 Gastonia	....	So. Atl.	OF	129	519	73	145	27	4	11	59	22	.279
1988 Charlotte	....	Fla. St.	OF	131	507	70	116	13	*12	9	51	42	.229
1989 Tulsa	....	Texas	OF	66	273	45	81	15	4	7	31	16	.297
1989 Oklahoma City a	......	A.A.	OF	10	39	2	4	2	0	0	3	4	.103
1989 Vancouver	....	P.C.	OF	13	49	7	18	3	0	1	5	2	.367
1989 Texas-Chicago		A.L.	OF	58	183	27	47	8	0	4	13	7	.257
1990 Chicago	....	A.L.	OF	153	532	72	124	26	10	15	70	32	.233
1991 Vancouver	....	P.C.	OF	32	116	19	31	7	2	3	19	9	.267
1991 Chicago b		A.L.	OF	116	316	39	64	10	1	10	33	13	.203
1992 Chicago c		N.L.	OF	67	262	41	68	7	2	8	25	15	.260
1992 Iowa	....	A.A.	OF	5	19	3	6	2	0	0	1	5	.316
1993 Chicago	....	N.L.	OF	159	598	92	156	25	5	33	93	36	.261
1994 Chicago d		N.L.	OF	105	426	59	128	17	6	25	70	22	.300
1995 Chicago e		N.L.	OF	*144	564	89	151	17	3	36	119	34	.268
1996 Chicago f		N.L.	OF	124	498	84	136	21	2	40	100	18	.273
1997 Chicago	....	N.L.	OF	162	642	90	161	31	4	36	119	22	.251
1998 Chicago g		N.L.	OF	159	643	*134	198	20	0	66	*158	18	.308
1999 Chicago	....	N.L.	OF	*162	625	114	180	24	2	63	141	7	.288
2000 Chicago	....	N.L.	OF	156	604	106	193	38	1	*50	138	7	.320
Major League Totals	....		12 Yrs.	1565	5893	947	1606	244	36	386	1079	231	.273
Division Series													
1998 Chicago	....	N.L.	OF	3	11	0	2	1	0	0	0	0	.182

a   Traded by Texas Rangers to Chicago White Sox organization with infielder Scott Fletcher and pitcher Wilson Alvarez for outfielder/designated hitter Harold Baines and infielder Fred Manrique, July 29, 1989.
b   Traded to Chicago Cubs with pitcher Ken Patterson for outfielder George Bell, March 30, 1992.
c   On disabled list from June 13 to July 27 and August 7 to September 16, 1992.
d   Declared restricted free agent under Major League Baseball implemented labor proposal, December 23, 1994.
e   Re-signed with Chicago Cubs, April 23, 1995.
f   On disabled list from August 21 to September 30, 1996.
g   Selected Most Valuable Player in National League for 1998.

SPENCER, MICHAEL SHANE (SHANE)
Born, Key West, Florida, February 20, 1972.
Bats Right. Throws Right. Height, 5 feet, 11 inches. Weight, 210 pounds.

Year	Club	Lea	Pos	G	AB	R	H	2B	3B	HR	RBI	SB	Avg
1990 Yankees	....	Gulf Coast	OF	42	147	20	27	4	0	0	7	11	.184
1991 Yankees	....	Gulf Coast	OF	41	160	25	49	7	0	0	30	9	.306
1991 Oneonta	....	N.Y.-Penn.	DH-OF	18	53	10	13	2	1	0	3	2	.245
1992 Greensboro	....	So.Atl.	OF-P	83	258	43	74	10	2	3	27	8	.287
1993 Greensboro	....	So.Atl.	OF-P	122	431	89	116	35	2	12	80	14	.269
1994 Tampa	....	Fla.St.	OF	90	334	44	97	22	3	8	53	5	.290
1995 Tampa	....	Fla.St.	OF	134	500	87	150	31	3	16	88	14	.300
1996 Norwich	....	Eastern	OF-1B-3B	126	450	70	114	19	0	29	89	4	.253
1996 Columbus	....	Int.	OF	9	31	7	11	4	0	3	6	0	.355
1997 Columbus	....	Int.	OF-3B	125	452	78	109	34	4	30	86	0	.241
1998 Columbus	....	Int.	OF-1B	87	342	66	110	29	1	18	67	1	.322
1998 New York	....	A.L.	OF-1B	27	67	18	25	6	0	10	27	0	.373
1999 Columbus	....	Int.	OF	14	50	17	18	2	0	2	10	0	.360
1999 New York a		A.L.	OF	71	205	25	48	8	0	8	20	0	.234
2000 New York b		A.L.	OF	73	248	33	70	11	3	9	40	1	.282
Major League Totals	....		3 Yrs.	171	520	76	143	25	3	27	87	1	.275
Division Series													
1998 New York	....	A.L.	OF	2	6	3	3	0	0	2	4	0	.500
Championship Series													
1998 New York	....	A.L.	OF	3	10	1	1	0	0	0	0	0	.100
1999 New York	....	A.L.	OF	3	9	1	1	0	0	0	0	0	.111
Championship Series Totals	.....			6	19	2	2	0	0	0	0	0	.105

Year	Club	Lea	Pos	G	AB	R	H	2B	3B	HR	RBI	SB	Avg
World Series Record													
1998 New York	...........A.L.		OF	1	3	1	1	1	0	0	0	0	.333

a On disabled list from July 3 to July 27, 1999.
b On disabled list from July 12 to November 12, 2000.

SPIERS, WILLIAM JAMES III

Born, Orangeburg, South Carolina, June 5, 1966.
Bats Left. Throws Right. Height, 6 feet, 2 inches. Weight, 190 pounds.

Year	Club	Lea	Pos	G	AB	R	H	2B	3B	HR	RBI	SB	Avg
1987 Helena	.......Pioneer		SS	6	22	4	9	1	0	0	3	2	.409
1987 Beloit	.......Midwest		SS	64	258	43	77	10	1	3	26	11	.298
1988 Stockton	.....California		SS	84	353	68	95	17	3	5	52	27	.269
1988 El Paso	.........Texas		SS	47	168	22	47	5	2	3	21	4	.280
1989 Denver	...........A.A.		SS	14	47	9	17	2	1	2	8	1	.362
1989 Milwaukee	.......A.L.		SS-3B-2B-1B	114	345	44	88	9	3	4	33	10	.255
1990 Denver	...........A.A.		SS	11	38	6	12	0	0	1	7	1	.316
1990 Milwaukee a	......A.L.		SS	112	363	44	88	15	3	2	36	11	.242
1991 Milwaukee	.......A.L.		SS-OF	133	414	71	117	13	6	8	54	14	.283
1992 Beloit	........Midwest		SS	16	55	9	13	3	0	0	7	4	.236
1992 Milwaukee b	.....A.L.		SS-2B-3B	12	16	2	5	2	0	0	2	1	.313
1993 Milwaukee c	......A.L.		2B-OF-SS	113	340	43	81	8	4	2	36	9	.238
1994 Milwaukee d	......A.L.		3B-SS-OF-1B	73	214	27	54	10	1	0	17	7	.252
1995 Norfolk	...........Int.		2B-3B	12	41	4	9	2	0	0	4	0	.220
1995 New York e-f-g	....N.L.		3B-2B	63	72	5	15	2	1	0	11	0	.208
1996 Houston h-i	......N.L.		3B-2B-1B-SS	122	218	27	55	10	1	6	26	7	.252
1997 Houston j-k	......N.L.		3B-SS-1B-2B	132	291	51	93	27	4	4	48	10	.320
1998 Houston	.......N.L.		3B-2B-1B-SS	123	384	66	105	27	4	4	43	11	.273
1999 Houston	.......N.L.		3B-OF-SS-2B	127	393	56	113	18	5	4	39	10	.288
2000 Houston l	.......N.L.		3B-SS-2B-OF	124	355	41	107	17	3	3	43	7	.301
Major League Totals	....		12 Yrs.	1248	3405	477	921	158	35	37	388	97	.270
Division Series													
1997 Houston	.........N.L.		3B	3	11	1	0	0	0	0	0	0	.000
1998 Houston	.........N.L.		3B	4	14	2	4	3	0	0	1	0	.286
1999 Houston	.............N.L.		OF	4	11	0	3	0	0	0	1	1	.273
Division Series Totals	....			11	36	3	7	3	0	0	2	1	.194

a On disabled list from April 1 to May 15, 1990.
b On disabled list from April 5 to September 2, 1992.
c Not offered 1994 contract, December 20; re-signed with Milwaukee Brewers, December 21, 1993.
d Claimed on waivers by New York Mets, October 25, 1994.
e On disabled list from May 15 to June 5 and June 26 to July 16, 1995.
f Filed for free agency, November 12, 1995.
g Signed with Houston Astros organization, January 9, 1996.
h Filed for free agency, November 14, 1996.
i Re-signed with Houston Astros, December 2, 1996.
j Filed for free agency, November 3, 1997.
k Re-signed with Houston Astros, November 25, 1997.
l Not offered 2001 contract, October 18, 2000.

SPIEZIO, SCOTT EDWARD

Born, Joliet, Illinois, September 21, 1972.
Bats Both. Throws Right. Height, 6 feet, 2 inches. Weight, 208 pounds.

Year	Club	Lea	Pos	G	AB	R	H	2B	3B	HR	RBI	SB	Avg
1993 Sou Oregon	......Northwest		3B-1B	31	125	32	41	10	2	3	19	0	.328
1993 Modesto	........California		3B-1B	32	110	12	28	9	1	1	13	1	.255
1994 Modesto	........California		3B-2B-SS	127	453	84	127	32	5	14	68	5	.280
1995 Huntsville	........Southern		3B-1B-2B	141	528	78	149	33	8	13	86	10	.282
1996 Edmonton	..............P.C.		3B-1B	140	523	87	137	30	4	20	91	6	.262
1996 Oakland	..............A.L.		3B	9	29	6	9	2	0	2	8	0	.310
1997 Sou Oregon	......Northwest		2B	2	9	1	5	0	0	0	2	0	.556
1997 Oakland a	.............A.L.		2B-3B	147	538	58	131	28	4	14	65	9	.243
1998 Edmonton	..............P.C.		2B	5	13	3	3	1	0	1	4	0	.231
1998 Oakland b	.............A.L.		2B	114	406	54	105	19	1	9	50	1	.259
1999 Vancouver	..............P.C.		2B	28	105	27	41	7	1	6	27	0	.390
1999 Oakland c	.............A.L.		2B-3B-1B	89	247	31	60	24	0	8	33	0	.243
2000 Anaheim	..............A.L.		DH-1B-3B-OF	123	297	47	72	11	2	17	49	1	.242
Major League Totals	....		5 Yrs.	482	1517	196	377	84	7	50	205	11	.249

a On disabled list from June 8 to June 25, 1997.
b On disabled list from June 15 to July 31, 1998.
c Not offered contract, December 21, 1999. Signed with Anaheim Angels, January 7, 2000.

SPRAGUE, EDWARD NELSON JR.
Born, Castro Valley, California, July 25, 1967.
Bats Right. Throws Right. Height, 6 feet, 2 inches. Weight, 210 pounds.

Year	Club	Lea	Pos	G	AB	R	H	2B	3B	HR	RBI	SB	Avg
1989 Dunedin	Fla. St.	3B	52	192	21	42	9	2	7	23	1	.219
1989 Syracuse	Int.	3B	86	288	23	60	14	1	5	33	0	.208
1990 Syracuse	Int.	3B-1B-C	*142	*519	60	124	23	5	20	75	4	.239
1991 Syracuse	Int.	C-3B	23	88	24	32	8	0	5	25	2	.364
1991 Toronto	A.L.	3B-1B-C	61	160	17	44	7	0	4	20	0	.275
1992 Syracuse	Int.	C-1B-3B	99	369	49	102	18	2	16	50	0	.276
1992 Toronto	A.L.	C-1B-3B	22	47	6	11	2	0	1	7	0	.234
1993 Toronto	A.L.	3B	150	546	50	142	31	1	12	73	1	.260
1994 Toronto	A.L.	3B-1B	109	405	38	97	19	1	11	44	1	.240
1995 Toronto a	A.L.	3B-1B	144	521	77	127	27	2	18	74	0	.244
1996 Toronto	A.L.	3B	159	591	88	146	35	2	36	101	0	.247
1997 Toronto b	A.L.	3B	138	504	63	115	29	4	14	48	0	.228
1998 Toronto-Oakland c-d	A.L.	3B-1B	132	469	57	104	25	0	20	58	1	.222
1999 Pittsburgh e-f	N.L.	3B	137	490	71	131	27	2	22	81	3	.267
2000 Boston g-h	A.L.	3B-1B	33	111	11	24	4	0	2	9	0	.216
2000 Rancho Cucamonga	California	2B	2	7	1	2	0	0	1	2	0	.286
2000 San Diego i	N.L.	1B-3B-OF-2B	73	157	19	41	12	0	10	27	0	.261
Major League Totals		10 Yrs.	1158	4001	497	982	218	12	150	542	6	.245
Championship Series												
1992 Toronto	A.L.	PH	2	2	0	1	0	0	0	0	0	.500
1993 Toronto	A.L.	3B	6	21	0	6	0	1	0	4	0	.286
Championship Series Totals			8	23	0	7	0	1	0	4	0	.304
World Series Record												
1992 Toronto	A.L.	1B	3	2	1	1	0	0	1	2	0	.500
1993 Toronto	A.L.	3B-1B	5	15	0	1	0	0	0	2	0	.067
World Series Totals			8	17	1	2	0	0	1	4	0	.118

a Signed with Toronto Blue Jays, April 28, 1995.
b On disabled list from September 4 to September 29, 1997.
c Traded to Oakland Athletics for pitcher Scott Rivette and cash, July 31, 1998.
d Filed for free agency, October 27, 1998. Signed with Pittsburgh Pirates, December 15, 1998.
e On disabled list from September 20 to October 4, 1999.
f Filed for free agency, October 29, 1999. Signed with San Diego Padres organization, February 3, 2000.
g Traded to Boston Red Sox for infielder Cesar Saba and pitcher Dennis Tankersley, June 30, 2000.
h Released by Boston Red Sox, August 23, 2000, signed with San Diego Padres organization, August 31, 2000.
i Filed for free agency, October 31, 2000, re-signed with San Diego Padres organization, December 7, 2000.

STAIRS, MATTHEW WADE (MATT)
Born, Fredericton, New Brunswick, Canada, February 27, 1969.
Bats Left. Throws Right. Height, 5 feet, 9 inches. Weight, 175 pounds.

Year	Club	Lea	Pos	G	AB	R	H	2B	3B	HR	RBI	SB	Avg
1989 Jamestown	N.Y.Penn.	2B-3B	14	43	8	11	1	0	1	5	1	.256
1989 West Palm Bch.	Fla. St.	3B-SS-2B	36	111	12	21	3	1	1	9	0	.189
1989 Rockford	Midwest	3B	44	141	20	40	9	2	2	14	5	.284
1990 West Palm Bch.	Fla. St.	3B-SS	55	183	30	62	9	3	3	30	15	.339
1990 Jacksonville	Southern	3B-OF-2B	79	280	26	71	17	0	3	34	5	.254
1991 Harrisburg	Eastern	2B-3B-OF	129	505	87	168	30	10	13	78	23	.333
1992 Montreal	N.L.	OF	13	30	2	5	2	0	0	5	0	.167
1992 Indianapolis	A.A.	OF	110	401	57	107	23	4	11	56	11	.267
1993 Ottawa a - b	Int.	OF	34	125	18	35	4	2	3	20	4	.280
1993 Montreal	N.L.	OF	6	8	1	3	1	0	0	2	0	.375
1994 New Britain	Eastern	OF-1B	93	317	44	98	25	2	9	61	10	.309
1995 Pawtucket	Int.	OF	75	271	40	77	17	0	13	56	3	.284
1995 Boston c	A.L.	OF	39	88	8	23	7	1	1	17	0	.261
1996 Edmonton	P.C.	DH-OF-1B	51	180	35	62	16	1	8	41	0	.344
1996 Oakland	A.L.	OF-1B	61	137	21	38	5	1	10	23	1	.277
1997 Oakland	A.L.	OF-1B	133	352	62	105	19	0	27	73	3	.298
1998 Oakland	A.L.	DH-OF-1B	149	523	88	154	33	1	26	106	8	.294
1999 Oakland	A.L.	OF-1B	146	531	94	137	26	3	38	102	2	.258
2000 Oakland d	A.L.	OF-1B	143	476	74	108	26	0	21	81	5	.227
Major League Totals		8 Yrs.	690	2145	350	573	119	6	123	409	19	.267
Division Series												
1995 Boston	A.L.	PH	1	1	F0	0	0	0	0	0	0	.000
2000 Oakland	A.L.	OF	3	9	0	1	1	0	0	0	0	.111
Division Series Totals			4	10	0	1	1	0	0	0	0	.100

a Released, June 8, 1993, played in Japan, re-signed by Montreal Expos organization, December 15, 1993.

b Traded to Boston Red Sox with pitcher Pete Young for player to be named later and cash, February 18, 1994.
c Filed for free agency, October 14, 1995, signed by Oakland Athletics organization, December 1, 1995.
d Traded to Chicago Cubs for pitcher Eric Ireland, November 20, 2000.

STANLEY, ROBERT MICHAEL (MIKE)

Born, Fort Lauderdale, Florida, June 25, 1963.
Bats Right. Throws Right. Height, 6 feet. Weight, 192 pounds.

Year	Club	Lea	Pos	G	AB	R	H	2B	3B	HR	RBI	SB	Avg
1985 Salem	Carolina	1B-C	4	9	2	5	0	0	0	3	0	.556
1985 Burlington	Midwest	C-1B-OF	13	42	8	13	2	0	1	6	0	.310
1985 Tulsa	Texas	C-1B-OF-2B	46	165	24	51	10	0	3	17	6	.309
1986 Tulsa	Texas	C-1B-3B	67	235	41	69	16	2	6	35	5	.294
1986 Texas	A.L.	3B-C-OF	15	30	4	10	3	0	1	1	1	.333
1986 Oklahoma City	A.A.	C-3B-1B	56	202	37	74	13	3	5	49	1	.366
1987 Oklahoma City	A.A.	C	46	182	43	61	8	3	13	54	2	.335
1987 Texas	A.L.	C-1B-OF	78	216	34	59	8	1	6	37	3	.273
1988 Texas a	A.L.	C-1B-3B	94	249	21	57	8	0	3	27	0	.229
1989 Texas b	A.L.	C-1B-3B	67	122	9	30	3	1	1	11	1	.246
1990 Texas c	A.L.	C-3B-1B	103	189	21	47	8	1	2	19	1	.249
1991 Texas d	A.L.	C-1B-3B-OF	95	181	25	45	13	1	3	25	0	.249
1992 New York	A.L.	C-1B	68	173	24	43	7	0	8	27	0	.249
1993 New York	A.L.	C	130	423	70	129	17	1	26	84	1	.305
1994 New York e	A.L.	C-1B	82	290	54	87	20	0	17	57	0	.300
1995 New York f	A.L.	C	118	399	63	107	29	1	18	83	1	.268
1996 Boston	A.L.	C	121	397	73	107	20	1	24	69	2	.270
1997 Boston-N.Y g-h-i	A.L.	DH-1B-C	125	347	61	103	25	0	16	65	0	.297
1998 Toronto-Boston k	A.L.	DH-1B-OF	145	497	74	127	25	0	29	79	3	.256
1999 Boston	A.L.	1B	136	427	59	120	22	0	19	72	0	.281
2000 Boston-Oakland l-m-n	A.L.	1B	90	282	33	67	12	0	14	46	0	.238
Major League Totals			15 Yrs.	1467	4222	625	1138	220	7	187	702	13	.270
Division Series													
1995 New York	A.L.	C	4	16	2	5	0	0	1	3	0	.313
1997 New York	A.L.	DH	2	4	1	3	1	0	0	1	0	.750
1998 Boston	A.L.	DH	4	15	1	4	0	0	0	0	0	.267
1999 Boston	A.L.	1B	5	20	4	10	2	1	0	2	0	.500
Division Series Totals				15	55	8	22	3	1	1	6	0	.400
Championship Series													
1999 Boston	A.L.	1B	5	18	1	4	0	0	0	1	0	.222

a On disabled list from July 23 to August 13, 1988.
b On disabled list from August 19 to September 2, 1989.
c Refused assignment to minor leagues and became free agent, October 27, 1990; re-signed with Texas Rangers organization, February 4, 1991.
d Refused assignment to minor leagues and became free agent, October 17, 1991; signed with New York Yankees organization, January 21, 1992.
e On disabled list from May 15 to May 29, 1994.
f Filed for free agency, November 12, 1995; signed with Boston Red Sox, December 14, 1995.
g Traded to New York Yankees with infielder Randy Brown for pitcher Tony Armas and player to be named later, August 13, 1997.
h Boston Red Sox received pitcher Jim Mecir to complete trade, September 29, 1997.
i Filed for free agency, October 27, 1997.
j Signed with Toronto Blue Jays, December 9, 1997
k Traded to Boston Red Sox for pitcher Peter Munro and pitcher Jay Yennaco, July 30, 1998.
l On disabled list from July 2 to July 22, 2000.
m Released by Boston Red Sox, July 31, 2000, signed with Oakland Athletics, August 4, 2000.
n Filed for free agency, October 30, 2000.

STEVENS, DE WAIN (LEE)

Born, Kansas City, Missouri, July 10, 1967.
Bats Left. Throws Left. Height, 6 feet, 4 inches. Weight, 226 pounds.

Year	Club	Lea	Pos	G	AB	R	H	2B	3B	HR	RBI	SB	Avg
1986 Salem	Northwest	OF-1B	72	267	45	75	18	2	6	47	13	.281
1987 Palm Sprngs	California	1B-OF	140	532	82	130	29	2	19	97	1	.244
1988 Midland	Texas	OF-1B	116	414	79	123	26	2	23	76	0	.297
1989 Edmonton	P.C.	1B-OF	127	446	72	110	29	9	14	74	5	.247
1990 Edmonton	P.C.	OF-1B	90	338	57	99	31	2	16	66	1	.293
1990 California	A.L.	1B	67	248	28	53	10	0	7	32	1	.214
1991 Edmonton	P.C.	OF-1B	123	481	75	151	29	3	19	96	3	.314
1991 California	A.L.	1B-OF	18	58	8	17	7	0	0	9	1	.293

163

Year	Club	Lea	Pos	G	AB	R	H	2B	3B	HR	RBI	SB	Avg
1992 California ............A.L.		A.L.	1B	106	312	25	69	19	0	7	37	1	.221
1993 Syracuse a-b-c-d-f .....Int.		Int.	OF-1B	116	401	61	106	30	1	14	66	2	.264
1994 Kintetsu ....Japan Pac.		Japan Pac.	OF-18	93	302	44	87	21	0	20	66	0	.288
1995 Kintetsu g ......Japan Pac.		Japan Pac.	1B-OF	129	476	54	117	*29	1	23	70	0	.246
1996 Okla City h-i ..........A.A.		A.A.	DH-1B-OF	117	431	84	140	37	2	32	94	3	.325
1996 Texas j ..............A.L.		A.L.	1B-OF	27	78	6	18	2	3	3	12	0	.231
1997 Texas ..............A.L.		A.L.	1B-OF	137	426	58	128	24	2	21	74	1	.300
1998 Oklahoma ...........P.C.		P.C.	DH-1B	3	12	2	4	0	0	1	1	0	.333
1998 Texas k ............A.L.		A.L.	DH-1B-OF	120	344	52	91	17	4	20	59	0	.265
1999 Texas ..............A.L.		A.L.	1B	146	517	76	146	31	1	24	81	2	.282
2000 Montreal l ............N.L.		N.L.	1B	123	449	60	119	27	2	22	75	0	.265
Major League Totals			8 Yrs.	744	2432	313	641	137	12	104	379	6	.264
Division Series													
1998 Texas ..............A.L.		A.L.	DH	1	3	0	0	0	0	0	0	0	.000
1999 Texas ..............A.L.		A.L.	1B	3	9	0	1	1	0	0	0	0	.111
Division Series Totals				4	12	0	1	1	0	0	0	0	.083

a Traded to Montreal Expos for pitcher Jeff Tuss, January 15, 1993.
b Released by Montreal Expos organization, March 30, 1993.
c Signed as free agent with Toronto Blue Jays organization, April 8, 1993.
d Filed for free agency, October 15, 1993.
e Signed with California Angels organization, October 25, 1993.
f Released by California Angels, November 16, 1993.
g Signed as a free agent with Cincinnati Reds organization, March 8, 1996.
h Released by Cincinnati Reds, March 25, 1996.
i Signed as free agent by Texas Rangers organization, April 4, 1996.
j On disabled list August 4 to September 1, 1996.
k On disabled list from August 8 to September 1, 1998.
l Traded to Montreal Expos for infielder Brad Fullmer, March 16, 2000.

STEWART, SHANNON HAROLD
Born, Cincinnati, Ohio, February 25, 1974.
Bats Right. Throws Right. Height, 6 feet, 1 inch. Weight, 194 pounds.

Year	Club	Lea	Pos	G	AB	R	H	2B	3B	HR	RBI	SB	Avg
1992 Blue Jays ....Gulf Coast		Gulf Coast	OF	50	172	44	40	1	0	1	11	32	.233
1993 St. Cathrnes .....N.Y.-Penn.		N.Y.-Penn.	DH-OF	75	301	53	84	15	2	3	29	25	.279
1994 Hagerstown ....So. Atl.		So. Atl.	OF	56	225	39	73	10	5	4	25	15	.324
1995 Knoxville ....Southern		Southern	OF	138	498	89	143	24	6	5	55	42	.287
1995 Toronto ..............A.L.		A.L.	OF	12	38	2	8	0	0	0	1	2	.211
1996 Syracuse ....Int.		Int.	OF	112	420	77	125	26	8	6	42	35	.298
1996 Toronto a ............A.L.		A.L.	OF	7	17	2	3	1	0	0	2	1	.176
1997 Syracuse ....Int.		Int.	OF	58	208	41	72	13	1	5	24	9	.346
1997 Toronto ..............A.L.		A.L.	OF	44	168	25	48	13	7	0	22	10	.286
1998 Toronto ..............A.L.		A.L.	OF	144	516	90	144	29	3	12	55	51	.279
1999 Toronto ..............A.L.		A.L.	OF	145	608	102	185	28	2	11	67	37	.304
2000 Dunedin ....Fla.St.		Fla.St.	OF	1	3	2	3	1	0	0	1	0	1.000
2000 Toronto b ............A.L.		A.L.	OF	136	583	107	186	43	5	21	69	20	.319
Major League Totals			6 Yrs.	488	1930	328	574	114	17	44	216	121	.297

a On disabled list May 13 to May 31, 1996.
b On disabled list from April 29 to May 13, 2000.

STINNETT, KELLY LEE
Born, Lawton, Oklahoma, February 4, 1970.
Bats Right. Throws Right. Height, 5 feet, 11 inches. Weight, 195 pounds.

Year	Club	Lea	Pos	G	AB	R	H	2B	3B	HR	RBI	SB	Avg
1990 Watertown ......N.Y.-Penn.		N.Y.-Penn.	C-1B	60	192	29	46	10	2	2	21	3	.240
1991 Columbus ....So. Atl.		So. Atl.	C-1B	102	384	49	101	15	1	14	74	4	.263
1992 Canton-Akrn ....Eastern		Eastern	C	91	296	37	84	10	0	6	32	7	.284
1993 Charlotte a ....Int.		Int.	C	98	288	42	79	10	3	6	33	0	.274
1994 New York ............N.L.		N.L.	C	47	150	20	38	6	2	2	14	2	.253
1995 New York b .........N.L.		N.L.	C	77	196	23	43	8	1	4	18	2	.219
1996 New Orleans .........A.A.		A.A.	C-3B	95	334	63	96	21	1	27	70	3	.287
1996 Milwaukee ...........A.L.		A.L.	C	14	26	1	2	0	0	0	0	0	.077
1997 Tucson ..............P.C.		P.C.	C-1B	64	209	50	67	15	3	10	43	1	.321
1997 Milwaukee c-d ........A.L.		A.L.	C	30	36	2	9	4	0	0	3	0	.250
1998 Arizona ..............N.L.		N.L.	C	92	274	35	71	14	1	11	34	0	.259
1999 Arizona ..............N.L.		N.L.	C	88	284	36	66	13	0	14	38	2	.232
2000 Arizona e ............N.L.		N.L.	C	76	240	22	52	7	0	8	33	0	.217
Major League Totals			7 Yrs.	424	1206	139	281	52	4	39	140	6	.233

Year	Club	Lea	Pos	G	AB	R	H	2B	3B	HR	RBI	SB	Avg
Division Series													
1999 Arizona		N.L.	C	4	14	1	2	1	0	0	0	0	.143

a Selected by New York Mets from Cleveland Indians organization in Rule V draft, December 13, 1993.
b Traded to Milwaukee Brewers for pitcher Cory Lidle, January 17, 1996.
c On disabled list from July 25 to August 31, 1997.
d Selected in expansion draft by Arizona Diamondbacks, November 18, 1997.
e Not offered 2001 contract, December 21, 2000, signed with Cincinnati Reds, January 9, 2001.

STOCKER, KEVIN DOUGLAS

Born, Spokane, Washington, February 13, 1970.
Bats Both. Throws Right. Height, 6 feet, 1 inches. Weight, 175 pounds.

Year	Club	Lea	Pos	G	AB	R	H	2B	3B	HR	RBI	SB	Avg
1991 Spartanburg	So. Atl.	SS	70	250	26	55	11	1	0	20	15	.220
1992 Clearwater	Fla. St.	SS	63	244	43	69	13	4	1	33	15	.283
1992 Reading	Eastern	SS	62	240	31	60	9	2	1	13	17	.250
1993 Scranton	Int.	SS	83	313	54	73	14	1	3	17	17	.233
1993 Philadelphia	N.L.	SS	70	259	46	84	12	3	2	31	5	.324
1994 Scranton	Int.	SS	4	13	1	4	1	0	0	2	0	.308
1994 Philadelphia a	N.L.	SS	82	271	38	74	11	2	2	28	2	.273
1995 Philadelphia	N.L.	SS	125	412	42	90	14	3	1	32	6	.218
1996 Scranton-WB	Int.	SS	12	44	5	10	3	0	2	6	1	.227
1996 Philadelphia	N.L.	SS	119	394	46	100	22	6	5	41	6	.254
1997 Philadelphia b	N.L.	SS	149	504	51	134	23	5	4	40	11	.266
1998 Tampa Bay c	A.L.	SS	112	336	37	70	11	3	6	25	5	.208
1999 Tampa Bay	A.L.	SS	79	254	39	76	11	2	1	27	9	.299
1999 St.Petersburg d	Fla.St.	SS	3	11	2	1	0	0	0	0	0	.091
2000 Tampa Bay-Anaheim e-f-g	A.L.	SS	110	343	41	75	20	4	2	24	1	.219
Major League Totals		8 Yrs.	846	2773	340	703	124	28	23	248	45	.254
Championship Series													
1993 Philadelphia	N.L.	SS	6	22	0	4	1	0	0	1	0	.182
World Series Record													
1993 Philadelphia	N.L.	SS	6	19	1	4	1	0	0	1	0	.211

a On disabled list from April 28 to June 1, 1994.
b Traded to Tampa Bay Devil Rays for outfielder Bob Abreu, November 19, 1997.
c On disabled list from August 30 to September 28, 1998.
d On disabled list from July 22 to November 9, 1999.
e Released by Tampa Bay Devil Rays, May 25, 2000, signed with Anaheim Angels, May 30, 2000.
f On disabled list from June 22 to July 6, 2000.
g Filed for free agency, October 31, 2000.

STYNES, CHRISTOPHER DESMOND

Born, Queens, New York, January 19, 1973.
Bats Right. Throws Right. Height, 5 feet, 9 inches. Weight, 170 pounds.

Year	Club	Lea	Pos	G	AB	R	H	2B	3B	HR	RBI	SB	Avg
1991 Blue Jays	Gulf Coast	3B	57	219	29	67	15	1	4	39	10	.306
1992 Myrtle Beach ...	So. Atl.	3B-2B	127	489	67	139	36	0	7	46	28	.284
1993 Dunedin	Fla. St.	3B	123	496	72	151	28	5	7	48	19	.304
1994 Knoxville	Southern	2B	136	545	79	173	32	4	8	79	28	.317
1995 Omaha	A.A.	2B-3B	83	306	51	84	12	5	9	42	4	.275
1995 Kansas City a	A.L.	2B	22	35	7	6	1	0	0	2	0	.171
1996 Omaha	A.A.	OF-3B-2B	72	284	50	101	22	2	10	40	7	.356
1996 Kansas City	A.L.	OF-2B-3B	36	92	8	27	6	0	0	6	5	.293
1997 Omaha	A.A.	2B-OF-3B	82	332	53	88	18	1	8	44	3	.265
1997 Indianapolis	A.A.	2B	21	86	14	31	8	0	1	17	4	.360
1997 Cincinnati b	N.L.	OF-2B-3B	49	198	31	69	7	1	6	28	11	.348
1998 Cincinnati	N.L.	OF-3B-2B-SS	123	347	52	88	10	1	6	27	15	.254
1999 Cincinnati	N.L.	2B-3B-OF	73	113	18	27	1	0	2	14	5	.239
2000 Cincinnati c	N.L.	3B-2B-OF	119	380	71	127	24	1	12	40	5	.334
Major League Totals		6 Yrs.	422	1165	187	344	49	3	26	117	41	.295

a Traded to Kansas City Royals with infielder Anthony Medrano and pitcher David Sinnes for pitcher David Cone, April 6, 1995.
b Traded to Cincinnati Reds with outfielder Jon Nunnally for pitcher Hector Carrasco and pitcher Scott Service, July 15, 1997.
c Traded to Boston Red Sox for infielder Donnie Sadler and outfielder Michael Coleman, November 16, 2000.

SURHOFF, WILLIAM JAMES (B.J.)

Born, Bronx, New York, August 4, 1964.
Bats Left. Throws Right. Height, 6 feet, 1 inch. Weight, 200 pounds.

Year Club	Lea	Pos	G	AB	R	H	2B	3B	HR	RBI	SB	Avg
1985 Beloit	Midwest	C	76	289	39	96	13	4	7	58	10	.332
1986 Vancouver	P.C.	C	116	458	71	141	19	3	5	59	21	.308
1987 Milwaukee	A.L.	C-3B-1B	115	395	50	118	22	3	7	68	11	.299
1988 Milwaukee	A.L.	C-3B-1B-SS-OF	139	493	47	121	21	0	5	38	21	.245
1989 Milwaukee	A.L.	C-3B	126	436	42	108	17	4	5	55	14	.248
1990 Milwaukee a	A.L.	C-3B	135	474	55	131	21	4	6	59	18	.276
1991 Milwaukee	A.L.	C-3B-OF-2B	143	505	57	146	19	4	5	68	5	.289
1992 Milwaukee	A.L.	C-1B-OF-3B	139	480	63	121	19	1	4	62	14	.252
1993 Milwaukee	A.L.	3B-OF-1B-C	148	552	66	151	38	3	7	79	12	.274
1994 El Paso	Texas	OF	3	12	2	3	1	0	0	0	0	.250
1994 New Orleans	A.A.	3B-1B-OF-C	5	19	3	6	2	0	0	1	0	.316
1994 Milwaukee b-c	A.L.	3B-C-1B-OF	40	134	20	35	11	2	5	22	0	.261
1995 Milwaukee d-e-f	A.L.	OF-1B-C	117	415	72	133	26	3	13	73	7	.320
1996 Baltimore	A.L.	3B-OF-1B	143	537	74	157	27	6	21	82	0	.292
1997 Baltimore	A.L.	OF-1B-3B	147	528	80	150	30	4	18	88	1	.284
1998 Baltimore g	A.L.	OF-1B	162	573	79	160	34	1	22	92	9	.279
1999 Baltimore	A.L.	OF-3B	*162	*673	104	207	38	-1	28	107	5	.308
2000 Baltimore b	A.L.	OF	103	411	56	120	27	0	13	57	7	.292
2000 Atlanta h	N.L.	OF	44	128	13	37	9	2	1	11	3	.289
Major League Totals		14 Yrs.	1863	6734	878	1895	359	38	160	961	127	.281
Division Series												
1996 Baltimore	A.L.	OF	4	13	3	5	0	0	3	5	0	.385
1997 Baltimore	A.L.	OF	3	11	0	3	1	0	0	2	0	.273
2000 Atlanta	N.L.	PH	2	2	0	1	0	0	0	0	0	.500
Division Series Totals			9	26	3	9	1	0	3	7	0	.346
Championship Series												
1996 Baltimore	A.L.	OF	5	15	0	4	0	0	0	2	0	.267
1997 Baltimore	A.L.	OF-1B	6	25	1	5	2	0	0	1	0	.200
Championship Series Totals			11	40	1	9	2	0	0	3	0	.225

a Suspended three games by American League for June 30 fight from August 24 to August 26, 1990.
b On disabled list from March 29 to April 16, April 20 to May 23, and July 7 to end of 1994 season.
c Filed for free agency, October 19, 1994.
d Signed with Milwaukee Brewers organization, April 8, 1995.
e Filed for free agency, November 12, 1995.
f Signed with Baltimore Orioles, December 20, 1995.
g Filed for free agency, October 26, 1998, resigned with Baltimore Orioles, December 4, 1998.
h Traded to Atlanta Braves with catcher Gabe Molina for catcher Fernando Lunar, outfielder Trenidad Hubbard and pitcher Luis Rivera, July 31, 2000.

SWEENEY, MARK PATRICK

Born, Framingham, Massachusetts, October 26, 1969.
Bats Left. Throws Right. Height, 6 feet, 1 inch. Weight, 195 pounds.

Year Club	Lea	Pos	G	AB	R	H	2B	3B	HR	RBI	SB	Avg
1991 Boise	Northwest	OF	70	234	45	66	10	3	4	34	9	.282
1992 Quad City	Midwest	OF	120	424	65	115	20	5	14	76	15	.271
1993 Palm Sprngs	California	OF-1B	66	245	41	87	18	3	3	47	9	.355
1993 Midland	Texas	OF	51	188	41	67	13	2	9	32	1	.356
1994 Midland	Texas	OF-1B	14	50	13	15	3	0	3	18	1	.300
1994 Vancouver	P.C.	DH-1B-OF	103	344	59	98	12	3	8	49	3	.285
1995 Vancouver	P.C.	OF-1B	69	226	48	78	14	2	7	59	3	.345
1995 Louisville	A.A.	1B	22	76	15	28	8	0	2	22	2	.368
1995 St. Louis a	N.L.	1B-OF	37	77	5	21	2	0	2	13	1	.273
1996 St. Louis b	N.L.	OF-1B	98	170	32	45	9	0	3	22	3	.265
1997 St. Louis-San Diego c	N.L.	OF-1B	115	164	16	46	7	0	2	23	2	.280
1998 San Diego	N.L.	OF-1B	122	192	17	45	8	3	2	15	1	.234
1999 Indianapolis	Int.	OF	86	311	66	100	17	1	12	51	3	.322
1999 Cincinnati d	N.L.	1B-OF	37	31	6	11	3	0	2	7	0	.355
2000 Indianapolis	Int.	1B	18	55	13	28	8	0	2	14	0	.509
2000 Milwaukee e-f-g-h	N.L.	OF-1B	71	73	9	16	6	0	1	6	0	.219
Major League Totals		6 Yrs.	480	707	85	184	35	3	12	86	7	.260
Division Series												
1996 St. Louis	N.L.	PH	1	1	0	1	0	0	0	0	0	1.000
1998 San Diego	N.L.	PH	2	1	0	0	0	0	0	0	0	.000
Division Series Totals			3	2	0	1	0	0	0	0	0	.500
Championship Series												
1996 St. Louis	N.L.	OF	5	4	1	0	0	0	0	0	0	.000

Year	Club	Lea	Pos	G	AB	R	H	2B	3B	HR	RBI	SB	Avg
1998 San Diego	.N.L.	PH	3	2	1	0	0	0	0	0	0	.000
Championship Series Totals				8	6	2	0	0	0	0	0	0	.000
World Series Record													
1998 San Diego	.N.L.	PH	3	3	0	2	0	0	0	1	0	.000

a Traded to St. Louis Cardinals organization by California Angels with player named later for pitcher John Habyan, July 8, 1995.
b St. Louis Cardinals received infielder Rod Correia to complete deal, January 31, 1996.
c Traded to San Diego Padres with pitcher Danny Jackson and pitcher Rich Batchelor for outfielder Phil Plantier, infielder Scott Livingstone and pitcher Fernando Valenzuela, June 14, 1997.
d Traded to Cincinnati Reds with outfielder Greg Vaughn for outfielder Reggie Sanders, infielder Damian Jackson and pitcher Josh Harris, February 2, 1999.
e Traded to Milwaukee Brewers with player named later for outfielder Alex Ochoa, January 14, 2000.
f Milwaukee Brewers received pitcher Gene Altman to complete trade, May 15, 2000.
g On disabled list from March 31 to May 6 and July 18 to August 14, 2000.
h Filed for free agency, October 5, 2000, signed with Milwaukee Brewers organization, January 3, 2001.

SWEENEY, MICHAEL JOHN (MIKE)
Born, Orange, California, July 22, 1973.
Bats Right. Throws Right. Height, 6 feet, 1 inch. Weight, 195 pounds.

Year	Club	Lea	Pos	G	AB	R	H	2B	3B	HR	RBI	SB	Avg
1991 Royals	.Gulf Coast	C-1B	38	102	8	22	3	0	1	11	1	.216
1992 Eugene	.Northwest	C	59	199	17	44	12	1	4	28	3	.221
1993 Eugene	.Northwest	C	53	175	32	42	10	2	6	29	1	.240
1994 Rockford	.Midwest	C	86	276	47	83	20	3	10	52	0	.301
1995 Wilmington	.Carolina	C-3B	99	332	61	103	23	1	18	53	6	.310
1995 Kansas City	.A.L.	C	4	4	1	1	0	0	0	0	0	.250
1996 Wichita	.Texas	DH-C	66	235	45	75	18	1	14	51	3	.319
1996 Omaha	.A.A.	C	25	101	14	26	9	0	3	16	0	.257
1996 Kansas City	.A.L.	C	50	165	23	46	10	0	4	24	1	.279
1997 Omaha	.A.A.	C	40	144	22	34	8	1	10	29	0	.236
1997 Kansas City	.A.L.	C	84	240	30	58	8	0	7	31	3	.242
1998 Kansas City	.A.L.	C	92	282	32	73	18	0	8	35	2	.259
1999 Kansas City	.A.L.	DH-1B-C	150	575	101	185	44	2	22	102	6	.322
2000 Kansas City	.A.L.	1B	159	618	105	206	30	0	29	144	8	.333
Major League Totals		6 Yrs.	539	1884	292	569	110	2	70	336	20	.302

TATIS, FERNANDO
Born, San Pedro De Macoris, Dominican Republic, January 1, 1975.
Bats Right. Throws Right. Height, 6 feet, 1 inch. Weight, 175 pounds.

Year	Club	Lea	Pos	G	AB	R	H	2B	3B	HR	RBI	SB	Avg
1994 Rangers	.Gulf Coast	3B-2B	60	212	34	70	10	2	6	32	21	.330
1995 Chston-Sc	.So. Atl.	3B	131	499	74	151	43	4	15	84	22	.303
1996 Charlotte	.Fla. St.	3B	85	325	46	93	25	0	12	53	9	.286
1996 Okla City	.A.A.	3B	2	4	0	2	1	0	0	0	0	.500
1997 Tulsa	.Texas	3B	102	382	73	120	26	1	24	61	17	.314
1997 Texas	.A.L.	3B	60	223	29	57	9	0	8	29	3	.256
1998 Texas	.A.L.	3B	95	330	41	89	17	2	3	32	6	.270
1998 St. Louis a	.N.L.	3B-SS	55	202	28	58	16	2	8	26	7	.287
1999 St. Louis	.N.L.	3B	149	537	104	160	31	2	34	107	21	.298
2000 Memphis	.P.C.	3B	3	9	0	0	0	0	0	0	0	.000
2000 St. Louis b-c	.N.L.	3B-1B	96	324	59	82	21	1	18	64	2	.253
Major League Totals		4 Yrs.	455	1616	261	446	94	7	71	258	39	.276
Championship Series													
2000 St. Louis	.N.L.	3B	5	13	1	3	2	0	0	2	0	.231

a Traded to St. Louis Cardinals with pitcher Darren Oliver and player to be named later for infielder Royce Clayton and pitcher Todd Stottlemyre, July 31, 1998. St. Louis Cardinals received infielder Mark Little to complete trade, August 9, 1998.
b On disabled list from April 30 to June 29, 2000.
c Traded to Montreal Expos with pitcher Britt Reames for pitcher Dustin Hermanson and pitcher Steve Kline, December 14, 2000.

TAUBENSEE, EDWARD KENNETH (EDDIE)
Born, Beeville, Texas, October 31, 1968.
Bats Left. Throws Right. Height, 6 feet, 4 inches. Weight, 205 pounds.

Year	Club	Lea	Pos	G	AB	R	H	2B	3B	HR	RBI	SB	Avg
1986 Sarasota Reds ...Gulf Coast		C	35	107	8	21	3	0	1	11	0	.196
1987 Billings	.Pioneer	C	55	162	24	43	7	0	5	28	2	.265

Year	Club	Lea	Pos	G	AB	R	H	2B	3B	HR	RBI	SB	Avg
1988 Greensboro	So. Atl.		C	103	330	36	85	16	1	10	41	8	.258
1988 Chattanooga	Southern		C	5	12	2	2	0	0	1	1	0	.167
1989 Cedar Rapids	Midwest		C	59	196	25	39	5	0	8	22	4	.199
1989 Chattanooga	Southern		C	45	127	11	24	2	0	3	13	0	.189
1990 Cedar Rapids a-b	Midwest		C	122	417	57	108	21	1	16	62	11	.259
1991 Colorado Springs	P.C.		C	91	287	53	89	23	3	13	39	0	.310
1991 Cleveland c	A.L.		C	26	66	5	16	2	1	0	8	0	.242
1992 Tucson	P.C.		C	20	74	13	25	8	1	1	10	0	.338
1992 Houston	N.L.		C	104	297	23	66	15	0	5	28	2	.222
1993 Houston	N.L.		C	94	288	26	72	11	1	9	42	1	.250
1994 Houston-Cincinnati d	N.L.		C	66	187	29	53	8	2	8	21	2	.283
1995 Cincinnati	N.L.		C-1B	80	218	32	62	14	2	9	44	2	.284
1996 Cincinnati	N.L.		C	108	327	46	95	20	0	12	48	3	.291
1997 Cincinnati	N.L.		C-OF-1B	108	254	26	68	18	0	10	34	0	.268
1998 Cincinnati	N.L.		C	130	431	61	120	27	0	11	72	1	.278
1999 Cincinnati	N.L.		C	126	424	58	132	22	2	21	87	0	.311
2000 Cincinnati e-f	N.L.		C	81	266	29	71	12	0	6	24	0	.267
Major League Totals		10 Yrs.		923	2758	335	755	149	8	91	408	11	.274

Championship Series

Year	Club	Lea	Pos	G	AB	R	H	2B	3B	HR	RBI	SB	Avg
1995 Cincinnati	N.L.		C	2	2	0	1	0	0	0	0	0	.500

a Drafted by Oakland Athletics from Cincinnati Reds organization, December 3, 1990.

b Claimed on waivers by Cleveland Indians from Oakland Athletics, April 4, 1991.

c Traded to Houston Astros with pitcher Willie Blair for outfielder Ken Lofton and infielder Dave Rohde, December 10, 1991.

d Traded to Cincinnati Reds for pitchers Ross Powell and Martin Lister, April 19, 1994.

e On disabled list from August 1 to October 3, 2000.

f Traded to Cleveland Indians for pitcher Jim Brower and pitcher Robert Pugmire, November 16, 2000.

TEJADA, MIGUEL ODALIS

Born, Bani, Dominican Republic, May 25, 1976.
Bats Right. Throws Right. Height, 5 feet, 10 inches. Weight, 170 pounds.

Year	Club	Lea	Pos	G	AB	R	H	2B	3B	HR	RBI	SB	Avg
1994 Oakland	Dominican		2B	74	218	51	64	9	1	18	62	13	.294
1995 Sou Oregon	Northwest		SS	74	269	45	66	15	5	8	44	19	.245
1996 Modesto	California		SS-3B	114	458	97	128	12	5	20	72	27	.279
1997 Huntsville	Southern		SS	128	502	85	138	20	3	22	97	15	.275
1997 Oakland	A.L.		SS	26	99	10	20	3	2	2	10	2	.202
1998 Edmonton	P.C.		SS	1	3	0	0	0	0	0	0	0	.000
1998 Huntsville	Southern		SS	15	52	9	17	6	0	2	7	1	.327
1998 Oakland a	A.L.		SS	105	365	53	85	20	1	11	45	5	.233
1999 Oakland	A.L.		SS	159	593	93	149	33	4	21	84	8	.251
2000 Oakland	A.L.		SS	160	607	105	167	32	1	30	115	6	.275
Major League Totals		4 Yrs.		450	1664	261	421	88	8	64	254	21	.253

a On disabled list from March 31 to May 20, 1998.

Division Series

Year	Club	Lea	Pos	G	AB	R	H	2B	3B	HR	RBI	SB	Avg
2000 Oakland	A.L.		SS	5	20	5	7	2	0	0	1	1	.350

THOMAS, FRANK EDWARD

Born, Columbus, Georgia, May 27, 1968.
Bats Right. Throws Right. Height, 6 feet, 5 inches. Weight, 257 pounds.

Year	Club	Lea	Pos	G	AB	R	H	2B	3B	HR	RBI	SB	Avg
1989 Sarasota White Sox	Gulf C.		1B	16	48	7	16	5	0	1	11	4	.333
1989 Sarasota	Fla. St.		1B	55	188	27	52	9	1	4	30	0	.277
1990 Birmingham	Southern		1B	109	353	84	114	27	5	18	71	7	.323
1990 Chicago	A.L.		1B	60	191	39	63	11	3	7	31	0	.330
1991 Chicago	A.L.		1B	158	559	104	178	31	2	32	109	1	.318
1992 Chicago	A.L.		1B	160	573	108	185	*46	2	24	115	6	.323
1993 Chicago a	A.L.		1B	153	549	106	174	36	0	41	128	4	.317
1994 Chicago b	A.L.		1B	113	399	*106	141	34	1	38	101	2	.353
1995 Chicago c	A.L.		1B	*145	493	102	152	27	0	40	111	3	.308
1996 Chicago c	A.L.		1B	141	527	110	184	26	0	40	134	1	.349
1997 Chicago d	A.L.		1B	146	530	110	184	35	0	35	125	1	*.347
1998 Chicago	A.L.		DH-1B	160	585	109	155	35	2	29	109	7	.265
1999 Chicago	A.L.		DH-1B	135	486	74	148	36	0	15	77	3	.305
2000 Chicago	A.L.		DH-1B	159	582	115	191	44	0	43	143	1	.328
Major League Totals		11 Yrs.		1530	5474	1083	1755	361	10	344	1183	29	.321

Year	Club	Lea	Pos	G	AB	R	H	2B	3B	HR	RBI	SB	Avg
	Division Series												
2000 Chicago	A.L.	DH-1B	3	9	0	0	0	0	0	0	0	.000
	Championship Series												
1993 Chicago	A.L.	1B	6	17	2	6	0	0	1	3	0	.353

a Selected Most Valuable Player in American League for 1993.
b Selected Most Valuable Player in American League for 1994.
c On disabled list from July 8 to July 30, 1996.
d On disabled list from June 7 to June 22, 1997.

THOME, JAMES HOWARD (JIM)
Born, Peoria, Illinois, August 27, 1970.
Bats Left. Throws Right. Height, 6 feet, 4 inches. Weight, 220 pounds.

Year	Club	Lea	Pos	G	AB	R	H	2B	3B	HR	RBI	SB	Avg
1989 Indians	Gulf Coast	SS-3B	55	186	22	44	5	3	0	22	6	.237
1990 Burlington	Appal.	3B	34	118	31	44	7	1	12	34	6	.373
1990 Kinston	Carolina	3B	33	117	19	36	4	1	4	16	4	.308
1991 Canton	Eastern	3B	84	294	47	99	20	2	5	45	8	.337
1991 Colorado Springs	.P.C.	3B	41	151	20	43	7	3	2	28	0	.285
1991 Cleveland	A.L.	3B	27	98	7	25	4	2	1	9	1	.255
1992 Colorado Springs	.P.C.	3B	12	48	11	15	4	1	2	14	0	.313
1992 Cleveland a	A.L.	3B	40	117	8	24	3	1	2	12	2	.205
1993 Charlotte	Int.	3B	115	410	85	136	21	4	25	*102	1	*.332
1993 Cleveland	A.L.	3B	47	154	28	41	11	0	7	22	2	.266
1994 Cleveland	A.L.	3B	98	321	58	86	20	1	20	52	3	.268
1995 Cleveland	A.L.	3B	137	452	92	142	29	3	25	73	4	.314
1996 Cleveland	A.L.	3B	151	505	122	157	28	5	38	116	2	.311
1997 Cleveland	A.L.	1B	147	496	104	142	25	0	40	102	1	.286
1998 Cleveland b	A.L.	1B	123	440	89	129	34	2	30	85	1	.293
1999 Cleveland	A.L.	1B	146	494	101	137	27	2	33	108	0	.277
2000 Cleveland	A.L.	1B	158	557	106	150	33	1	37	106	1	.269
Major League Totals		10 Yrs.	1074	3634	715	1033	214	17	233	685	17	.284
	Division Series												
1995 Cleveland	A.L.	3B	3	13	1	2	0	0	1	3	0	.154
1996 Cleveland	A.L.	3B	4	10	1	3	0	0	0	0	0	.300
1997 Cleveland	A.L.	1B	5	15	1	3	0	0	0	1	0	.200
1998 Cleveland	A.L.	1B-DH	4	15	2	2	0	0	2	2	0	.133
1999 Cleveland	A.L.	1B	5	17	7	6	0	0	4	10	0	.353
Division Series Totals			20	70	12	16	0	0	7	16	0	.229
	Championship Series												
1995 Cleveland	A.L.	3B	5	15	2	4	0	0	2	5	0	.267
1997 Cleveland	A.L.	1B	6	14	3	1	0	0	0	0	0	.071
1998 Cleveland	A.L.	1B-DH	6	23	4	7	0	0	4	8	0	.304
Championship Series Totals			17	52	9	12	0	0	6	13	0	.231
	World Series Record												
1995 Cleveland	A.L.	3B	6	19	1	4	1	0	1	2	0	.211
1997 Cleveland	A.L.	1B	7	28	8	8	0	1	2	4	0	.286
World Series Totals			13	47	9	12	1	1	3	6	0	.255

a On disabled list from March 28 to May 18 and May 29 to June 15, 1992.
b On disabled list from August 8 to September 16, 1998.

TRACY, ANDREW MICHAEL (ANDY)
Born, Bowling Green, Ohio, December 11, 1973.
Bats Left. Throws Right. Height, 6 feet, 3 inches. Weight, 220 pounds.

Year	Club	Lea	Pos	G	AB	R	H	2B	3B	HR	RBI	SB	Avg
1996 Vermont	N.Y.-Penn.	1B-3B	57	175	26	47	11	1	4	24	1	.269
1997 Cape Fear	So.Atl.	1B	59	210	31	63	9	2	8	43	6	.300
1998 Jupiter	Fla.St.	1B-3B	71	251	37	67	16	1	11	53	6	.267
1998 Harrisburg	Eastern	1B-OF	62	211	33	48	12	3	10	33	1	.227
1999 Harrisburg	Eastern	3B	134	493	96	135	26	2	37	128	6	.274
2000 Ottawa	Int.	1B	55	195	28	60	18	0	10	36	2	.308
2000 Montreal	N.L.	3B-1B	83	192	29	50	8	1	11	32	1	.260

TRAMMELL, THOMAS BUBBA
Born, Knoxville, Tennessee, November 6, 1971.
Bats Right. Throws Right. Height, 6 feet, 3 inches. Weight, 205 pounds.

Year Club	Lea	Pos	G	AB	R	H	2B	3B	HR	RBI	SB	Avg
1994 Jamestown	N.Y.-Penn.	OF	65	235	37	70	18	6	5	41	9	.298
1995 Lakeland	Fla. St.	OF	122	454	61	129	32	3	16	72	13	.284
1996 Jacksnville	Southern	OF	83	311	63	102	23	2	27	75	3	.328
1996 Toledo	Int.	OF	51	180	32	53	14	1	6	24	5	.294
1997 Toledo	Int.	OF	90	319	56	80	15	1	28	75	2	.251
1997 Detroit a	A.L.	OF	44	123	14	28	5	0	4	13	3	.228
1998 Durham	Int.	OF	57	217	46	63	12	0	16	48	6	.290
1998 Tampa Bay	A.L.	OF	59	199	28	57	18	1	12	35	0	.286
1999 Durham	Int.	OF	47	186	25	50	12	0	7	31	0	.269
1999 Tampa Bay	A.L.	OF	82	283	49	82	19	0	14	39	0	.290
2000 Tampa Bay	A.L.	OF	66	189	19	52	11	2	7	33	3	.275
2000 New York b-c	N.L.	OF	36	56	9	13	2	0	3	12	1	.232
Major League Totals	4 Yrs.		287	850	119	232	55	3	40	132	7	.273
Championship Series												
2000 New York	N.L.	PH	3	3	0	0	0	0	0	0	0	.000
World Series Record												
2000 New York	N.L.	OF	4	5	1	2	0	0	0	3	0	.400

a Selected in expansion draft by Tampa Bay Devil Rays, November 18, 1997.
b Traded to New York Mets with pitcher Rick White for outfielder Jason Tyner and pitcher Paul Wilson, July 28, 2000.
c Traded to San Diego Padres for pitcher Donne Wall, December 11, 2000.

TRUBY, CHRISTOPHER JOHN (CHRIS)
Born, Palm Springs, California, December 9, 1973.
Bats Right. Throws Right. Height, 6 feet, 2 inches. Weight, 190 pounds.

Year Club	Lea	Pos	G	AB	R	H	2B	3B	HR	RBI	SB	Avg
1993 Astros	Gulf Coast	3B-SS	57	215	30	49	10	2	1	24	16	.228
1993 Osceola	Fla.St.	3B	3	13	0	0	0	0	0	0	0	.000
1994 Quad City	Midwest	3B-1B	36	111	12	24	4	1	2	19	1	.216
1994 Auburn	N.Y.-Penn.	3B	73	282	56	91	17	6	7	61	20	.323
1995 Quad City	Midwest	3B-OF	118	400	68	93	23	4	9	64	27	.233
1996 Quad City	Midwest	1B-3B	109	362	45	91	15	3	8	37	6	.251
1997 Quad City	Midwest	3B	68	268	34	75	14	1	7	46	13	.280
1997 Kissimmee	Fla.St.	3B-1B-SS-2B	57	199	23	49	11	0	2	29	8	.246
1998 Kissimmee	Fla.St.	3B	52	212	36	66	16	1	14	48	6	.311
1998 Jackson	Texas	3B-1B	80	308	46	89	20	5	16	63	8	.289
1998 New Orleans	P.C.	3B	5	17	6	7	1	1	1	1	1	.412
1999 Jackson a	Texas	3B	124	464	78	131	21	3	28	87	20	.282
2000 New Orleans	P.C.	3B	64	268	31	76	11	3	2	30	6	.284
2000 Houston	N.L.	3B	78	258	28	67	15	4	11	59	2	.260

a On disabled list from April 26 to May 11, 1999.

TUCKER, MICHAEL ANTHONY
Born, S. Boston, Virginia, June 25, 1971.
Bats Left. Throws Right. Height, 6 feet, 2 inches. Weight, 185 pounds.

Year Club	Lea	Pos	G	AB	R	H	2B	3B	HR	RBI	SB	Avg
1993 Wilmington	Carolina	2B	61	239	42	73	14	2	6	44	12	.305
1993 Memphis	Southern	2B	72	244	38	68	7	4	9	35	12	.279
1994 Omaha	A.A.	OF	132	485	75	134	16	7	21	77	11	.276
1995 Omaha	A.A.	OF	71	275	37	84	18	4	4	28	11	.305
1995 Kansas City	A.L.	OF	62	177	23	46	10	0	4	17	2	.260
1996 Wichita a	Texas	OF-1B	6	20	4	9	1	3	0	7	0	.450
1996 Kansas City	A.L.	OF-1B	108	339	55	88	18	4	12	53	10	.260
1997 Atlanta b	N.L.	OF	138	499	80	141	25	7	14	56	12	.283
1998 Atlanta c	N.L.	OF	130	414	54	101	27	3	13	46	8	.244
1999 Cincinnati	N.L.	OF	133	296	55	75	8	5	11	44	11	.25
2000 Cincinnati	N.L.	OF-2B	148	270	55	72	13	4	15	36	13	.267
Major League Totals	6 Yrs.		719	1995	322	523	101	23	69	252	56	.262
Division Series												
1997 Atlanta	N.L.	OF	2	6	0	1	0	0	0	1	0	.167
1998 Atlanta	N.L.	OF	3	8	1	2	0	0	1	2	1	.250
Division Series Totals			5	14	1	3	0	0	1	3	1	.214
Championship Series												
1997 Atlanta	N.L.	OF	5	10	1	1	0	0	1	1	0	.100

Year	Club	Lea	Pos	G	AB	R	H	2B	3B	HR	RBI	SB	Avg
1998 Atlanta ............N.L.			OF	6	13	1	5	1	0	1	5	0	.385
Championship Series Totals				11	23	2	6	1	0	2	6	0	.261

a On disabled list from June 4 to June 21 and August 28 to September 30, 1996.
b Traded to Atlanta Braves with infielder Keith Lockhart for outfielder Jermaine Dye and pitcher Jamie Walker, March 27, 1997.
c Traded to Cincinnati Reds, with pitcher Denny Neagle and pitcher Rob Bell for infielder Bret Boone and pitcher Mike Remlinger, November 10, 1998.

VALENTIN, JOHN WILLIAM

Born, Mineola, New York, February 18, 1967.
Bats Right. Throws Right. Height, 6 feet. Weight, 180 pounds.

Year	Club	Lea	Pos	G	AB	R	H	2B	3B	HR	RBI	SB	Avg
1988 Elmira ..........N.Y.-Penn.			SS	60	207	18	45	5	1	2	16	5	.217
1989 Winter Haven ....Fla. St.			SS	55	215	27	58	13	1	3	18	4	.270
1989 Lynchburg ....Carolina			SS	75	264	47	65	7	2	8	34	5	.246
1990 New Britain ....Eastern			SS	94	312	20	68	18	1	2	31	1	.218
1991 New Britain ....Eastern			SS	23	81	8	16	3	0	0	5	1	.198
1991 Pawtucket a ....Int.			SS	100	329	52	87	22	4	9	49	0	.264
1992 Pawtucket ....Int.			SS	97	331	47	86	18	1	9	29	1	.260
1992 Boston .............A.L.			SS	58	185	21	51	13	0	5	25	1	.276
1993 Pawtucket ....Int.			SS	2	9	3	3	0	0	1	1	0	.333
1993 Boston b ............A.L.			SS	144	468	50	130	40	3	11	66	3	.278
1994 Pawtucket ....Int.			SS	5	18	2	6	0	0	1	2	0	.333
1994 Boston c ............A.L.			SS	84	301	53	95	26	2	9	49	3	.316
1995 Boston .............A.L.			SS	135	520	108	155	37	2	27	102	20	.298
1996 Boston d ............A.L.			SS-3B	131	527	84	156	29	3	13	59	9	.296
1997 Boston .............A.L.			2B-3B	143	575	95	176	47	5	18	77	7	.306
1998 Boston .............A.L.			3B-2B	153	588	113	145	44	1	23	73	4	.247
1999 Boston e ............A.L.			3B	113	450	58	114	27	1	12	70	0	.253
2000 Boston f ............A.L.			3B	10	35	6	9	1	0	2	2	0	.257
Major League Totals	9 Yrs.			971	3649	588	1031	264	17	120	523	47	.283
Division Series													
1995 Boston ..............A.L.			SS	3	12	1	3	1	0	1	2	0	.250
1998 Boston ..............A.L.			3B	4	15	5	7	1	0	0	0	0	.467
1999 Boston ..............A.L.			3B	5	22	6	7	2	0	3	12	0	.318
Division Series Totals				12	49	12	17	4	0	4	14	0	.347
Championship Series													
1999 Boston ..............A.L.			3B	5	23	3	8	2	0	1	5	0	.238

a On disabled list from August 9 to August 16, 1991.
b On disabled list from April 1 to April 20, 1993.
c On disabled list from May 4 to June 5, 1994.
d On disabled list from August 3 to August 18, 1996.
e On disabled list from June 26 to July 11 and August 31 to September 23, 1999.
f On disabled list from April 10 to May 18 and May 31 to November 12, 2000.

VALENTIN, JOSE ANTONIO

Born, Manati, Puerto Rico, October 12, 1969.
Bats Both. Throws Right. Height, 5 feet, 10 inches. Weight, 175 pounds.

Year	Club	Lea	Pos	G	AB	R	H	2B	3B	HR	RBI	SB	Avg
1987 Spokane ....Northwest			SS	70	244	52	61	8	2	2	24	8	.250
1988 Charleston, SC ......So. Atl.			SS	133	444	56	103	20	1	6	44	11	.232
1989 Riverside ....California			SS	114	381	40	74	10	5	10	41	8	.194
1989 Wichita ....Texas			SS-3B	18	49	8	12	1	0	2	5	1	.245
1990 Wichita a ....Texas			SS	11	36	4	10	2	0	0	2	2	.278
1991 Wichita b ....Texas			SS	129	447	73	112	22	5	17	68	8	.251
1992 Denver ............A.A.			SS	139	492	78	118	19	11	3	45	9	.240
1992 Milwaukee ............A.L.			2B-SS	4	3	1	0	0	0	0	1	0	.000
1993 New Orleans .........A.A.			SS-1B	122	389	56	96	22	5	9	53	9	.247
1993 Milwaukee ............A.L.			SS	19	53	10	13	1	2	1	7	1	.245
1994 Milwaukee ............A.L.			SS-2B-3B	97	285	47	68	19	0	11	46	12	.239
1995 Milwaukee ............A.L.			SS-3B	112	338	62	74	23	3	11	49	16	.219
1996 Milwaukee ............A.L.			SS	154	552	90	143	33	7	24	95	17	.259
1997 Beloit ....Midwest			SS	2	6	3	3	1	0	0	1	0	.500
1997 Milwaukee c ............A.L.			SS	136	494	58	125	23	1	17	58	19	.253
1998 Milwaukee ............N.L.			SS-1B	151	428	65	96	24	0	16	49	10	.224
1999 Louisville ....Int.			SS	6	20	6	5	0	0	3	3	0	.250
1999 Milwaukee d-e ........N.L.			SS	89	256	45	58	9	5	10	38	3	.227
2000 Chicago f ............A.L.			SS-OF	144	568	107	155	37	6	25	92	19	.273

171

Year	Club	Lea	Pos	G	AB	R	H	2B	3B	HR	RBI	SB	Avg
Major League Totals		9 Yrs.		906	2977	485	732	169	24	115	435	97	.246
Division Series													
2000 Chicago	.A.L.		SS	3	10	2	3	2	0	0	1	3	.300

a On disabled list from April 16 to May 1, and May 18 to end of 1990 season.
b Traded by San Diego Padres to Milwaukee Brewers organization with pitcher Ricky Bones and outfielder Matt Mieske for outfielder/infielder Gary Sheffield and pitcher Geoff Kellogg, March 27, 1992.
c On disabled list from April 14 to May 5, 1997.
d On disabled list from April 11 to June 16, 1999.
e Traded to Chicago White Sox with pitcher Cal Eldred for pitcher John Snyder and pitcher Jamie Navarro, January 12, 2000.
f Filed for free agency, October 30, 2000, re-signed with Chicago White Sox, November 22, 2000.

VANDER WAL, JOHN HENRY
Born, Grand Rapids, Michigan, April 29, 1966.
Bats Left. Throws Left. Height, 6 feet, 2 inches. Weight, 190 pounds.

Year	Club	Lea	Pos	G	AB	R	H	2B	3B	HR	RBI	SB	Avg
1987 Jamestown	N.Y.-Penn.	OF	18	69	24	33	12	3	3	15	3	.478
1987 West Palm Beach ...	Fla. St.	OF	50	189	29	54	11	2	2	22	8	.286
1988 West Palm Beach ...	Fla. St.	OF	-62	231	50	64	15	2	10	33	11	.277
1988 Jacksonville	Southern	OF	58	208	22	54	14	0	3	14	3	.260
1989 Jacksonville	Southern	OF	71	217	30	55	9	2	6	24	2	.253
1990 Jacksonville	Southern	OF	77	277	45	84	25	3	8	40	6	.303
1990 Indianapolis	A.A.	OF	51	135	16	40	6	0	2	14	0	.296
1991 Indianapolis	A.A.	OF	133	478	84	140	36	8	15	71	8	.293
1991 Montreal	N.L.	OF	21	61	4	13	4	1	1	8	0	.213
1992 Montreal	N.L.	OF-1B	105	213	21	51	8	2	4	20	3	.239
1993 Montreal a	N.L.	1B-OF	106	215	34	50	7	4	5	30	6	.233
1994 Colorado	N.L.	1B-OF	91	110	12	27	3	1	5	15	2	.245
1995 Colorado	N.L.	1B-OF	105	101	15	35	8	1	5	21	1	.347
1996 Colorado	N.L.	OF-1B	104	151	20	38	6	2	5	31	2	.252
1997 Colo Sprngs	P.C.	1B-OF	25	103	29	42	12	1	3	19	1	.408
1997 Colorado	N.L.	OF-1B	76	92	7	16	2	0	1	11	1	.174
1998 Colorado-San Diego -b-c	N.L.	OF-1B	109	129	21	36	13	1	5	20	0	.279
1999 San Diego	N.L.	OF-1B	132	246	26	67	18	0	6	41	2	.272
2000 Pittsburgh d	N.L.	OF-1B	134	384	74	115	29	0	24	94	11	.299
Major League Totals		10 Yrs.		983	1702	234	448	98	12	61	291	28	.263
Division Series													
1995 Colorado	N.L.	PH	4	4	0	0	0	0	0	0	0	.000
1998 San Diego	N.L.	PH	3	3	1	1	0	1	0	2	0	.333
Division Series Totals				7	7	1	1	0	1	0	2	0	.143
Championship Series													
1998 San Diego	N.L.	OF	3	7	1	3	0	0	1	2	0	.429
World Series Record													
1998 San Diego	N.L.	OF	4	5	0	2	1	0	0	0	0	.400

a Traded to Colorado Rockies for player to be named and cash, March 31; Montreal Expos acquired outfielder Ronnie Hall to complete trade, June 11, 1994.
b Traded to San Diego Padres for player to be named later and outfielder Kevin Buford, August 31, 1998.
   Colorado Rockies received pitcher Roberto Ramirez and outfielder Kevin Buford to complete trade, October 29, 1998.
c Filed for free agency, October 26, 1998. Re-signed with San Diego Padres, November 13, 1998.
d Traded to Pittsburgh Pirates with pitcher Jim Sak and pitcher Geraldo Padua for outfielder Al Martin, February 23, 2000.

VARITEK, JASON A.
Born, Rochester, Minnesota, April 11, 1972.
Bats Both. Throws Right. Height, 6 feet, 2 inches. Weight, 210 pounds.

Year	Club	Lea	Pos	G	AB	R	H	2B	3B	HR	RBI	SB	Avg
1995 Port City	Southern	C	104	352	42	79	14	2	10	44	0	.224
1996 Port City	Southern	C-3B-OF	134	503	63	132	34	1	12	67	7	.262
1997 Tacoma	P.C.	C	87	307	54	78	13	0	15	48	0	.254
1997 Pawtucket	Int.	C	20	66	6	13	5	0	1	5	0	.197
1997 Boston a	A.L.	C	1	1	0	1	0	0	0	0	0	1.000
1998 Boston	A.L.	C	86	221	31	56	13	0	7	33	2	.253
1999 Boston	A.L.	C	144	483	70	130	39	2	20	76	1	.269
2000 Boston	A.L.	C	139	448	55	111	31	1	10	65	1	.248
Major League Totals		4 Yrs.		370	1153	156	298	83	3	37	174	4	.258
Division Series													
1998 Boston	A.L.	C	1	4	0	1	0	0	0	1	0	.250
1999 Boston	A.L.	C	5	21	7	5	3	0	1	3	0	.238
Division Series Totals				6	25	7	6	3	0	1	4	0	.240

Year	Club	Lea	Pos	G	AB	R	H	2B	3B	HR	RBI	SB	Avg
	Championship Series												
1999 Boston	A.L.		C	5	20	1	4	1	1	1	1	0	.200

a Traded to Boston Red Sox with pitcher Derek Lowe for pitcher Heathcliff Slocumb, July 31, 1997.

VAUGHN, GREGORY LAMONT

Born, Sacramento, California, July 3, 1965.
Bats Right. Throws Right. Height, 6 feet. Weight, 205 pounds.

Year	Club	Lea	Pos	G	AB	R	H	2B	3B	HR	RBI	SB	Avg
1986 Helena	Pioneer	OF	66	258	64	75	13	2	16	54	23	.291
1987 Beloit	Midwest	OF	139	492	*120	150	31	6	*33	105	36	.305
1988 El Paso	Texas	OF	131	505	*104	152	*39	2	*28	*105	22	.301
1989 Denver	A.A.	OF	110	387	74	107	17	5	*26	*92	20	.276
1989 Milwaukee	A.L.	OF	38	113	18	30	3	0	5	23	4	.265
1990 Milwaukee a	A.L.	OF	120	382	51	84	26	2	17	61	7	.220
1991 Milwaukee	A.L.	OF	145	542	81	132	24	5	27	98	2	.244
1992 Milwaukee	A.L.	OF	141	501	77	114	18	2	23	78	15	.228
1993 Milwaukee	A.L.	OF	154	569	97	152	28	2	30	97	10	.267
1994 Beloit	Midwest	DH	2	6	1	1	0	0	0	0	0	.167
1994 Milwaukee b	A.L.	OF	95	370	59	94	24	1	19	55	9	.254
1995 Milwaukee	A.L.	DH	108	392	67	88	19	1	17	59	10	.224
1996 Milwaukee	A.L.	OF	102	375	78	105	16	0	31	95	5	.280
1996 San Diego c-d	N.L.	OF	43	141	20	29	3	1	10	22	4	.206
1997 San Diego	N.L.	OF	120	361	60	78	10	0	18	57	7	.216
1998 San Diego	N.L.	OF	158	573	112	156	28	4	50	119	11	.272
1999 Cincinnati e-f	N.L.	OF	153	550	104	135	20	2	45	118	15	.245
2000 Tampa Bay g	A.L.	OF	127	461	83	117	27	1	28	74	8	.254
Major League Totals	12 Yrs.	1504	5330	907	1314	246	21	320	956	107	.247
Division Series												
1996 San Diego	N.L.	OF	3	3	0	0	0	0	0	0	0	.000
1998 San Diego	N.L.	OF	4	15	2	5	1	0	1	1	0	.333
Division Series Totals		7	18	2	5	1	0	1	1	0	.278
Championship Series												
1998 San Diego	N.L.	OF	3	8	1	2	0	0	0	0	0	.250
World Series Record												
1998 San Diego	N.L.	OF-DH	4	15	3	2	0	0	2	4	0	.133

a On disabled list from May 27 to June 10, 1990.
b On disabled list from April 8 to April 27, 1994.
c Filed for free agency, October 28, 1996.
d Re-signed with San Diego Padres, December 13, 1996.
e Traded to Cincinnati Reds with outfielder Mark Sweeney for outfielder Reggie Sanders, infielder Damian Jackson and pitcher Josh Harris, February 2, 1999.
f Filed for free agency, October 28, 1999. Signed with Tampa Bay Devil Rays, December 13, 1999.
g On disabled list from June 15 to July 6, 2000.

VAUGHN, MAURICE SAMUEL (MO)

Born, Norwalk, Connecticut, December 15, 1967.
Bats Left. Throws Right. Height, 6 feet, 1 inch. Weight, 225 pounds.

Year	Club	Lea	Pos	G	AB	R	H	2B	3B	HR	RBI	SB	Avg
1989 New Britain	Eastern	1B	73	245	28	68	15	0	8	38	1	.278
1990 Pawtucket a	Int.	1B	108	386	62	114	26	1	22	72	3	.295
1991 Pawtucket	Int.	1B	69	234	35	64	10	0	14	50	2	.274
1991 Boston	A.L.	1B	74	219	21	57	12	0	4	32	2	.260
1992 Pawtucket	Int.	1B	39	149	15	42	6	0	6	28	1	.282
1992 Boston	A.L.	1B	113	355	42	83	16	2	13	57	3	.234
1993 Boston	A.L.	1B	152	539	86	160	34	1	29	101	4	.297
1994 Boston	A.L.	1B	111	394	65	122	25	1	26	82	4	.310
1995 Boston b	A.L.	1B	140	550	98	165	28	3	39	*126	11	.300
1996 Boston	A.L.	1B	161	635	118	207	29	1	44	143	2	.326
1997 Boston c	A.L.	1B	141	527	91	166	24	0	35	96	2	.315
1998 Boston d	A.L.	1B	154	609	107	205	31	2	40	115	0	.337
1999 Anaheim e	A.L.	1B	139	524	63	147	20	0	33	108	0	.281
2000 Anaheim	A.L.	1B	161	614	93	167	31	0	36	117	2	.272
Major League Totals	10 Yrs.	1346	4966	784	1479	250	10	299	977	30	.298
Division Series												
1995 Boston	A.L.	1B	3	14	0	0	0	0	0	0	0	.000
1998 Boston	A.L.	1B	4	17	3	7	2	0	2	7	0	.412
Division Series Totals		7	31	3	7	2	0	2	7	0	.226

a On disabled list from May 1 to June 5, 1990.
b Selected Most Valuable Player in American League for 1995.
c On disabled list from June 17 to July 10, 1997.
d Filed for free agency, October 23, 1998, signed with Anaheim Angels, November 25, 1998.
e On disabled list from April 7 to April 22, 1999.

VELARDE, RANDY LEE
Born, Midland, Texas, November 24, 1962.
Bats Right. Throws Right. Height, 6 feet. Weight, 192 pounds.

Year	Club	Lea	Pos	G	AB	R	H	2B	3B	HR	RBI	SB	Avg
1985 Niagara Fls.	.N.Y.-Penn.	OF-SS-2B-3B	67	218	28	48	7	3	1	16	8	.220
1986 Appleton	Midwest	SS-3B-OF	124	417	55	105	31	4	11	50	13	.252
1986 Buffalo a	.A.A.	SS	9	20	2	4	1	0	0	2	1	.200
1987 Albany	Eastern	SS	71	263	40	83	20	2	7	32	8	.316
1987 Columbus	.Int.	SS	49	185	21	59	10	6	5	33	8	.319
1987 New York	.A.L.	SS-2B	8	22	1	4	0	0	0	1	0	.182
1988 Columbus	.Int.	SS	78	293	39	79	23	4	5	37	7	.270
1988 New York	.A.L.	2B-SS-3B	48	115	18	20	6	0	5	12	1	.174
1989 Columbus	.Int.	SS-3B	103	387	59	103	26	3	11	53	3	.266
1989 New York b	.A.L.	3B-SS	33	100	12	34	4	2	2	11	0	.340
1990 New York	.A.L.	3B-SS-OF-2B	95	229	21	48	6	2	5	19	0	.210
1991 New York	.A.L.	3B-SS-OF	80	184	19	45	11	1	1	15	3	.245
1992 New York	.A.L.	SS-3B-OF-2B	121	412	57	112	24	1	7	46	7	.272
1993 Albany	Eastern	SS-OF	5	17	2	4	0	0	1	2	0	.235
1993 New York c	.A.L.	OF-SS-3B	85	226	28	68	13	2	7	24	2	.301
1994 New York d-e	.A.L.	SS-3B-OF-2B	77	280	47	78	16	1	9	34	4	.279
1995 New York f-g-h	.A.L.	2B-SS-OF-3B	111	367	60	102	19	1	7	46	5	.278
1996 California	.A.L.	2B-3B-SS	136	530	82	151	27	3	14	54	7	.285
1997 Anaheim i	.A.L.	PR	1	0	0	0	0	0	0	0	0	.000
1998 Lk Elsinore	.California	2B	5	20	6	11	2	1	1	7	1	.550
1998 Vancouver	.P.C.	2B	4	16	0	4	2	0	0	2	1	.250
1998 Anaheim j	.A.L.	2B	51	188	29	49	13	1	4	26	7	.261
1999 Anaheim-Oakland k	.A.L.	2B	156	631	105	200	25	7	16	76	24	.317
2000 Midland	.Texas	2B	5	16	4	2	0	0	1	1	0	.125
2000 Sacramento	.P.C.	2B	3	11	3	5	0	0	0	2	2	.455
2000 Oakland l-m	.A.L.	2B	122	485	82	135	23	0	12	41	9	.278
Major League Totals		14 Yrs.	1124	3769	561	1046	187	21	89	405	69	.278
Division Series												
1995 New York	.A.L.	2B-3B-OF	5	17	3	3	0	0	0	1	0	.176
2000 Oakland	.A.L.	2B	5	20	2	5	1	0	0	3	1	.250
Division Series Totals			10	37	5	8	1	0	0	4	1	.216

a Traded by Chicago White Sox to New York Yankees organization with pitcher Pete Filson for pitcher Scott Nielson and infielder Mike Soper, January 5, 1987.
b On disabled list from August 9 to August 29, 1989.
c On disabled list from June 6 to July 30, 1993.
d Filed for free agency, October 25, 1994; ruled ineligible by Player Relations Committee due to insufficient service time.
e Not offered 1995 contract, December 20, 1994.
f Re-signed with New York Yankees, April 11, 1995.
g Filed for free agency, November 12, 1995.
h Signed with California Angels, November 22, 1995.
i On disabled list from April 1 to September 1 and September 7 to September 29, 1997.
j On disabled list from March 31 to May 13 and May 15 to August 3, 1998.
k Traded to Oakland Athletics with pitcher Omar Olivares for pitcher Elvin Nina, outfielder Jeff DaVanon and outfielder Nathan Haynes, July 29, 1999.
l On disabled list from April 2 to May 7, 2000.
m Traded to Texas Rangers for pitcher Aaron Harang and pitcher Ryan Cullen, November 17, 2000.

VENTURA, ROBIN MARK
Born, Santa Maria, California, July 14, 1967.
Bats Left. Throws Right. Height, 6 feet, 1 inch. Weight, 198 pounds.

Year	Club	Lea	Pos	G	AB	R	H	2B	3B	HR	RBI	SB	Avg
1989 Birmingham	.Southern	3B	129	454	75	126	25	2	3	67	9	.278
1989 Chicago	.A.L.	3B	16	45	5	8	3	0	0	7	0	.178
1990 Chicago	.A.L.	3B-1B	150	493	48	123	17	1	5	54	1	.249
1991 Chicago	.A.L.	3B-1B	157	606	92	172	25	1	23	100	2	.284
1992 Chicago	.A.L.	3B-1B	157	592	85	167	38	1	16	93	2	.282
1993 Chicago	.A.L.	3B-1B	157	554	85	145	27	1	22	94	1	.262
1994 Chicago	.A.L.	3B-1B-SS	109	401	57	113	15	1	18	78	3	.282

Year	Club	Lea	Pos	G	AB	R	H	2B	3B	HR	RBI	SB	Avg
1995 Chicago	....	A.L.	3B-1B	135	492	79	145	22	0	26	93	4	.295
1996 Chicago	∶	A.L.	3B-1B	158	586	96	168	31	2	34	105	1	.287
1997 Nashville	....	A.A.	3B	5	15	3	6	1	0	2	5	0	.400
1997 Birmingham	......	Southern	3B	4	17	3	5	1	0	1	2	0	.294
1997 Chicago a	....	A.L.	3B	54	183	27	48	10	1	6	26	0	.262
1998 Chicago b	....	A.L.	3B	161	590	84	155	31	4	21	91	1	.263
1999 New York	....	N.L.	3B-1B	161	588	88	177	38	0	32	120	1	.301
2000 New York c	....	N.L.	3B-1B	141	469	61	109	23	1	24	84	3	.232
Major League Totals	....		12 Yrs.	1556	5599	807	1530	280	13	227	945	19	.273
Division Series													
1999 New York	....	N.L.	3B	4	14	1	3	2	0	0	1	0	.214
2000 New York	....	N.L.	3B	4	14	1	2	0	0	1	2	0	.143
Division Series Totals	....			8	28	2	5	2	0	1	3	0	.179
Championship Series													
1993 Chicago	....	N.L.	3B-1B	6	20	2	4	0	0	1	5	0	.200
1999 New York	....	N.L.	3B	6	25	2	3	1	0	0	1	0	.120
2000 New York	....	N.L.	3B	5	14	4	3	1	0	0	5	0	.214
Championship Series Totals	......			17	59	8	10	2	0	1	11	0	.169
World Series Record													
2000 New York	....	N.L.	3B	5	20	1	3	1	0	1	1	0	.150

a On disabled list from April 1 to July 24, 1997.
b Filed for free agency, October 23, 1998, signed with New York Mets, December 1, 1998.
c On disabled list from July 14 to July 28, 2000.

VERAS (PEREZ), QUILVIO ALBERTO
Born, Santo Domingo, Dominican Republic, April 3, 1971.
Bats Both. Throws Right. Height, 5 feet, 9 inches. Weight, 166 pounds.

Year	Club	Lea	Pos	G	AB	R	H	2B	3B	HR	RBI	SB	Avg
1990 Sarasota Mets	......	Gulf C.	2B	30	98	26	29	3	3	1	5	16	.296
1990 Kingsport	....	Appal.	2B	24	94	21	36	6	0	1	14	14	.383
1991 Kingsport	....	Appal.	2B	64	226	*54	76	11	4	1	16	*38	.336
1991 Pittsfield	....	N.Y.-Penn.	2B-SS	5	15	3	4	0	1	0	2	2	.267
1992 Columbia	....	So. Atl.	2B	117	414	97	132	24	10	2	40	*66	*.319
1993 Binghamton	....	Eastern	2B	128	444	87	136	19	7	2	51	52	.306
1994 Norfolk a	....	Int.	2B	123	457	71	114	22	4	0	43	40	.249
1995 Florida	....	N.L.	2B-OF	124	440	86	115	20	7	5	32	*56	.261
1996 Charlotte b	....	Int.	2B	28	104	22	34	5	2	2	8	8	.327
1996 Florida c	....	N.L.	2B	73	253	40	64	8	1	4	14	8	.253
1997 San Diego	....	N.L.	2B	145	539	74	143	23	1	3	45	33	.265
1998 San Diego	....	N.L.	2B	138	517	79	138	24	2	6	45	24	.267
1999 San Diego d-e	......	N.L.	2B	132	475	95	133	25	2	6	41	30	.280
2000 Atlanta f	....	N.L.	2B	84	298	56	92	15	0	3	37	25	.309
Major League Totals	....		6 Yrs.	696	2522	430	685	115	13	29	214	176	.272
Division Series													
1998 San Diego	....	N.L.	2B	4	15	1	2	0	0	0	0	0	.133
Championship Series													
1998 San Diego	....	N.L.	2B	6	24	2	6	1	0	0	2	0	.250
World Series Record													
1998 San Diego	....	N.L.	2B	4	15	3	3	2	0	0	1	0	.200

a Traded by New York Mets to Florida Marlins for outfielder Carl Everett, November 29, 1994.
b On disabled list from May 10 to June 21, 1996.
c Traded to San Diego Padres for pitcher Dustin Hermanson, November 21, 1996.
d On disabled list from August 8 to August 23, 1999.
e Traded to Atlanta Braves with infielder Wally Joyner and outfielder Reggie Sanders for infielder Bret Boone, outfielder Ryan Klesko and pitcher Jason Shiell, December 22, 1999
f On disabled list from July 15 to October 30, 2000.

VIDRO, JOSE ANGEL
Born, Mayaguez, Puerto Rico, August 27, 1974.
Bats Both. Throws Right. Height, 5 feet, 11 inches. Weight, 175 pounds.

Year	Club	Lea	Pos	G	AB	R	H	2B	3B	HR	RBI	SB	Avg
1992 Expos	......	Gulf Coast	2B	54	200	29	66	6	2	4	31	10	.330
1993 Burlington	....	Midwest	2B	76	287	39	69	19	0	2	34	3	.240
1994 Wst Plm Bch	...	Fla. St.	2B	125	465	57	124	30	2	4	49	8	.267
1995 Harrisburg	.....	Eastern	2B-SS-3B	64	246	33	64	16	2	4	38	3	.260
1995 Wst Plm Bch	....	Fla. St.	2B-SS-3B	44	163	20	53	15	2	3	24	0	.325
1996 Harrisburg	.....	Eastern	3B-2B-SS	126	452	57	117	25	3	18	82	3	.259

175

Year	Club	Lea	Pos	G	AB	R	H	2B	3B	HR	RBI	SB	Avg
1997	Ottawa	Int.	3B-2B	73	279	40	90	17	0	13	47	2	.323
1997	Montreal	N.L.	3B-2B	67	169	19	42	12	1	2	17	1	.249
1998	Ottawa	Int.	2B-3B	63	235	35	68	14	2	2	32	5	.289
1998	Montreal	N.L.	2B-3B	83	205	24	45	12	0	0	18	2	.220
1999	Montreal	N.L.	2B-1B-OF-3B	140	494	67	150	45	2	12	59	0	.304
2000	Montreal	N.L.	2B	153	606	101	200	51	2	24	97	5	.330
Major League Totals			4 Yrs.	443	1474	211	437	120	5	38	191	8	.296

VINA, FERNANDO

Born, Sacramento, California, April 16, 1969.
Bats Left. Throws Right. Height, 5 feet, 9 inches. Weight, 170 pounds.

Year	Club	Lea	Pos	G	AB	R	H	2B	3B	HR	RBI	SB	Avg
1991	Columbia	So.Atl.	2B	129	498	77	135	23	6	6	50	42	.271
1992	Tidewater	Int.	2B	11	30	3	6	0	0	0	2	0	.200
1992	St. Lucie a	Fla.St.	2B	111	421	61	124	15	5	1	42	36	.295
1993	Seattle	A.L.	2B-SS	24	45	5	10	2	0	0	2	6	.222
1993	Norfolk b	Int.	SS-2B-OF	73	287	24	66	6	4	4	27	16	.230
1994	New York	N.L.	2B-3B-SS-OF	79	124	20	31	6	0	0	6	3	.250
1994	Norfolk c-d-e	Int.	SS-2B	6	17	2	3	0	0	0	1	1	.176
1995	Milwaukee	A.L.	2B-SS-3B	113	288	46	74	7	7	3	29	6	.257
1996	Milwaukee	A.L.	2B	140	554	94	157	19	10	7	46	16	.283
1997	Stockton	California	2B	3	9	2	4	0	1	0	3	0	.444
1997	Tucson	P.C.	2B	6	19	3	9	3	0	1	5	0	.474
1997	Milwaukee f	A.L.	2B	79	324	37	89	12	2	4	28	8	.275
1998	Milwaukee	N.L.	2B	159	637	101	198	39	7	7	45	22	.311
1999	Beloit	Midwest	2B	2	10	1	2	1	0	0	0	0	.200
1999	Milwaukee g-h	N.L.	2B	37	154	17	41	7	0	1	16	5	.266
2000	St. Louis i-j	N.L.	2B	123	487	81	146	24	6	4	31	10	.300
Major League Totals			8 Yrs.	754	2613	401	746	116	32	26	203	76	.285
Division Series													
2000 St. Louis		N.L.	2B	3	13	3	4	0	0	1	3	0	.308
Championship Series													
2000 St. Louis		N.L.	2B	5	23	3	6	1	0	0	1	0	.261

a Selected by Seattle Mariners from New York Mets in Rule V draft, December 7, 1992.
b Returned to New York Mets, June 15, 1993.
c On disabled list from May 22 to June 6, 1994.
d On disabled list from August 30 to September 6, 1994.
e Sent to Milwaukee Brewers to complete trade for pitcher Doug Henry, December 22, 1994.
f On disabled list from April 20 to July 18, 1997.
g On disabled list from May 13 to May 25 and from June 4 to November 2, 1999.
h Traded to St. Louis Cardinals for pitcher Juan Acevedo and two players named later, December 20, 1999.
i Milwaukee Brewers received pitcher Matt Parker and catcher Eliezer Alfonso to complete trade, June 13, 2000.
j On disabled list from June 17 to July 3, 2000.

VIZCAINO (PIMENTAL), JOSE LUIS

Born, Palenque de San Cristobal, Dominican Republic, March 26, 1968.
Bats Both. Throws Right. Height, 6 feet, 1 inch. Weight, 180 pounds.

Year	Club	Lea	Pos	G	AB	R	H	2B	3B	HR	RBI	SB	Avg
1987	Sarasota Dodgers	Gulf C.	SS	49	150	26	38	5	1	0	12	8	.253
1988	Bakersfield	California	SS	122	433	77	126	11	4	0	38	13	.291
1989	Albuquerque	P.C.	SS	129	434	60	123	10	4	1	44	16	.283
1989	Los Angeles	N.L.	SS	7	10	2	2	0	0	0	0	0	.200
1990	Albuquerque	P.C.	2B-SS	81	276	46	77	10	2	2	38	13	.279
1990	Los Angeles a	N.L.	SS-2B	37	51	3	14	1	1	0	2	1	.275
1991	Chicago	N.L.	3B-SS-2B	93	145	7	38	5	0	0	10	2	.262
1992	Chicago b	N.L.	SS-3B-2B	86	285	25	64	10	4	1	17	3	.225
1993	Chicago c	N.L.	SS-3B-2B	151	551	74	158	19	4	4	54	12	.287
1994	New York d	N.L.	SS	103	410	47	105	13	3	3	33	1	.256
1995	New York e	N.L.	SS-2B	135	509	66	146	21	5	3	56	8	.287
1996	New York f	N.L.	2B	96	363	47	110	12	6	1	32	9	.303
1996	Cleveland g	A.L.	2B-SS	48	179	23	51	5	2	0	13	6	.285
1997	San Francisco h	N.L.	SS-2B	151	568	77	151	19	7	5	50	8	.266
1998	Los Angeles j	N.L.	SS	67	237	30	62	9	0	3	29	7	.262
1999	Los Angeles k	N.L.	SS-2B-3B-OF	94	266	27	67	9	0	1	29	2	.252
2000	Los Angeles	N.L.	SS-3B-2B-1B	40	93	9	19	2	1	0	4	1	.204
2000	New York l-m	A.L.	2B-3B-SS	73	174	23	48	8	1	0	10	5	.276
Major League Totals			12 Yrs.	1181	3841	460	1035	133	34	21	339	65	.269

Year	Club	Lea	Pos	G	AB	R	H	2B	3B	HR	RBI	SB	Avg
Division Series													
1996 Cleveland ..........A.L.			2B	3	12	1	4	2	0	0	1	0	.333
1997 San Francisco .........N.L.			SS	3	11	1	2	1	0	0	0	0	.182
2000 New York ...........A.L.			2B	1	0	-1	0	0	0	0	0	0	.000
Division Series Totals				7	23	3	6	3	0	0	1	0	.261
Championship Series													
2000 New York ...........A.L.			2B	4	2	3	2	1	0	0	2	2	1.000
World Series Record													
2000 New York ...........A.L.			2B	4	17	0	4	0	0	0	1	0	.235

a Traded to Chicago Cubs for infielder Greg Smith, December 14, 1990.
b On disabled list from April 20 to May 6 and August 26 to September 16, 1992.
c Traded to New York Mets for pitchers Anthony Young and Ottis Smith, March 30, 1994.
d Declared restricted free agent under Major League Baseball implemented labor proposal, December 23, 1994.
e Re-signed with New York Mets, April 28, 1995.
f Traded to Cleveland Indians with infielder Jeff Kent for infielder Carlos Baerga and infielder Alvaro Espinoza, July 29, 1996.
g Traded to San Francisco Giants with infielder Jeff Kent, pitcher Julian Taverez and player to be named later for infielder Matt Williams and player to be named later, November 13, 1996. San Francisco Giants received pitcher Joe Roa and Cleveland Indians received outfielder Trenidad Hubbard to complete trade, December 16, 1996.
h Filed for free agency, October 29, 1997.
i Signed with Los Angeles Dodgers December 8, 1997.
j On disabled list from June 22 to September 9, 1998.
k On disabled list from May 17 to June 4, 1999.
l Traded to New York Yankees with cash for catcher Jim Leyritz, June 20, 2000.
m Filed for free agency, November 1, 2000, signed with Houston Astros, November 20, 2000.

VIZQUEL, OMAR ENRIQUE

Born, Caracas, Venezuela, April 24, 1967.
Bats Both. Throws Right. Height, 5 feet, 9 inches. Weight, 165 pounds.

Year	Club	Lea	Pos	G	AB	R	H	2B	3B	HR	RBI	SB	Avg
1984 Butte a ....Pioneer			SS-2B	15	45	7	14	2	0	0	4	2	.311
1985 Bellingham .....Northwest			SS-2B	50	187	24	42	9	0	5	17	4	.225
1986 Wausau ....Midwest			SS-2B	105	352	60	75	13	2	4	28	19	.213
1987 Salinas ....California			SS-2B	114	407	61	107	12	8	0	38	25	.263
1988 Vermont ....Eastern			SS	103	375	54	95	18	2	2	35	30	.253
1988 Calgary ............P.C.			SS	33	107	10	24	2	3	1	12	2	.224
1989 Seattle ............A.L.			SS	143	387	45	85	7	3	1	20	1	.220
1989 Calgary ............P.C.			SS	7	28	3	6	2	0	0	3	0	.214
1990 San Bernardino ...California			SS	6	28	5	7	0	0	0	3	1	.250
1990 Calgary ............P.C.			SS	48	150	18	35	6	2	0	8	4	.233
1990 Seattle b ............A.L.			SS	81	255	19	63	3	2	2	18	4	.247
1991 Seattle ............A.L.			SS-2B	142	426	42	98	16	4	1	41	7	.230
1992 Seattle c ............A.L.			SS	136	483	49	142	20	4	0	21	15	.294
1992 Calgary ............P.C.			SS	6	22	0	6	1	0	0	2	0	.273
1993 Seattle d ............A.L.			SS	158	560	68	143	14	2	2	31	12	.255
1994 Charlotte ....Int.			SS	7	26	3	7	1	0	0	1	1	.269
1994 Cleveland e ............A.L.			SS	69	286	39	78	10	1	1	33	13	.273
1995 Cleveland ............A.L.			SS	136	542	87	144	28	0	6	56	29	.266
1996 Cleveland ............A.L.			SS	151	542	98	161	36	1	9	64	35	.297
1997 Cleveland ............A.L.			SS	153	565	89	158	23	6	5	49	43	.280
1998 Cleveland ............A.L.			SS	151	576	86	166	30	6	2	50	37	.288
1999 Cleveland ............A.L.			SS-OF	144	574	112	191	36	4	5	66	42	.333
2000 Cleveland ............A.L.			SS	156	613	101	176	27	3	7	66	22	.287
Major League Totals		12 Yrs.		1620	5809	835	1605	250	36	41	515	260	.276
Division Series													
1995 Cleveland ............A.L.			SS	3	12	2	2	1	0	0	4	1	.167
1996 Cleveland ............A.L.			SS	4	14	4	6	1	0	0	2	4	.429
1997 Cleveland ............A.L.			SS	5	18	3	9	0	0	0	1	4	.500
1998 Cleveland ............A.L.			SS	4	15	1	1	0	0	0	0	0	.067
1999 Cleveland ............A.L.			SS	5	21	3	5	1	1	0	3	0	.238
Division Series Totals				21	80	13	23	3	1	0	10	9	.287
Championship Series													
1995 Cleveland ............A.L.			SS	6	23	2	2	1	0	0	2	3	.087
1997 Cleveland ............A.L.			SS	6	25	1	1	0	0	0	0	0	.040
1998 Cleveland ............A.L.			SS	6	25	2	11	0	1	0	0	4	.440
Championship Series Totals				18	73	5	14	1	1	0	2	7	.192
World Series Record													
1995 Cleveland ............A.L.			SS	6	23	3	4	0	1	0	1	1	.174
1997 Cleveland ............A.L.			SS	7	30	5	7	2	0	0	1	5	.233
World Series Totals				13	53	8	11	2	1	0	2	6	.208

a Batted righthanded only from 1984 through 1988 season.
b On disabled list from April 7 to May 14, 1990.
c On disabled list from April 13 to May 11, 1992.
d Traded to Cleveland Indians for shortstop Felix Fermin and first baseman Reggie Jefferson, December 20, 1993.
e On disabled list from April 23 to June 13, 1994.

WALKER, LARRY KENNETH ROBERT

Born, Maple Ridge, British Columbia, December 1, 1966.
Bats Left. Throws Right. Height, 6 feet, 3 inches. Weight, 215 pounds.

Year	Club	Lea	Pos	G	AB	R	H	2B	3B	HR	RBI	SB	Avg
1985	Utica	N.Y.-Penn.	1B-3B	62	215	24	48	8	2	2	26	12	.223
1986	Burlington	Midwest	OF-3B	95	332	67	96	12	6	29	74	16	.289
1986	West Palm Beach	Fla. St.	OF	38	113	20	32	7	5	4	16	2	.283
1987	Jacksonville	Southern	OF	128	474	91	136	25	7	26	83	24	.287
1988	Montreal a	N.L.				INJURED—Did Not Play								
1989	Indianapolis	A.A.	OF	114	385	68	104	18	2	12	59	36	.270
1989	Montreal	N.L.	OF	20	47	4	8	0	0	0	4	1	.170
1990	Montreal	N.L.	OF	133	419	59	101	18	3	19	51	21	.241
1991	Montreal b	N.L.	OF-1B	137	487	59	141	30	2	16	64	14	.290
1992	Montreal	N.L.	OF	143	528	85	159	31	4	23	93	18	.301
1993	Montreal c	N.L.	OF-1B	138	490	85	130	24	5	22	86	29	.265
1994	Montreal d	N.L.	OF-1B	103	395	76	127	44	2	19	86	15	.322
1995	Colorado e	N.L.	OF	131	494	96	151	31	5	36	101	16	.306
1996	Salem	Carolina	DH	2	8	3	4	3	0	1	1	0	.500
1996	Colo Sprngs	P.C.	OF	3	11	2	4	0	0	2	8	0	.364
1996	Colorado f	N.L.	OF	83	272	58	75	18	4	18	58	18	.276
1997	Colorado g	N.L.	OF-1B	153	568	143	208	46	4	*49	130	33	.366
1998	Colorado h	N.L.	OF-2B-3B	130	454	113	165	46	3	23	67	14	*.363
1999	Colorado i	N.L.	OF	127	438	108	166	26	4	37	115	11	*.379
2000	Colorado j	N.L.	OF	87	314	64	97	21	7	9	51	5	.309
Major League Totals			12 Yrs.	1385	4906	950	1528	335	43	271	906	195	.311
Division Series													
1995	Colorado	N.L.	OF	4	14	3	3	0	0	1	3	1	.214

a On disabled list from March 28 to end of 1988 season.
b On disabled list from June 28 to July 13, 1991.
c On disabled list from May 30 to June 10, 1993.
d Filed for free agency, October 18, 1994.
e Signed with Colorado Rockies, April 8, 1995.
f On disabled list from June 10 to August 15, 1996.
g Selected Most Valuable Player in National League for 1997.
h On disabled list from June 18 to July 3, 1998.
i On disabled list from March 29 to April 14, 1999.
j On disabled list from May 11 to June 8 and August 20 to October 3, 2000.

WALKER, TODD ARTHUR

Born, Bakersfield, California, May 25, 1973.
Bats Left. Throws Right. Height, 6 feet. Weight, 170 pounds.

Year	Club	Lea	Pos	G	AB	R	H	2B	3B	HR	RBI	SB	Avg
1994	Ft. Myers	Fla.St.	2B	46	171	29	52	5	2	10	34	6	.304
1995	New Britain	Eastern	2B-3B	137	513	83	149	27	3	21	85	23	.290
1996	Salt Lake	P.C.	3B-2B	135	551	94	187	41	9	28	111	13	.339
1996	Minnesota	A.L.	3B-2B	25	82	8	21	6	0	0	6	2	.256
1997	Salt Lake	P.C.	3B	83	322	69	111	20	1	11	53	5	.345
1997	Minnesota	A.L.	3B-2B	52	156	15	37	7	1	3	16	7	.237
1998	Minnesota	A.L.	2B	143	528	85	167	41	3	12	62	19	.316
1999	Minnesota	A.L.	2B	143	531	62	148	37	4	6	46	18	.279
2000	Salt Lake	P.C.	2B	63	249	51	81	14	1	2	37	8	.325
2000	Minnesota	A.L.	2B	23	77	14	18	1	0	2	8	3	.234
2000	Colorado a	N.L.	2B	57	171	28	54	10	4	7	36	4	.316
Major League Totals			5 Yrs.	443	1545	212	445	102	12	30	174	53	.288

a Traded to Colorado Rockies with outfielder Butch Huskey for infielder Todd Sears and cash, July 16, 2000.

WARD, DARYLE LAMAR

Born, Lynwood, California, June 27, 1975.
Bats Left. Throws Right. Height, 6 feet, 2 inches. Weight, 240 pounds.

Year	Club	Lea	Pos	G	AB	R	H	2B	3B	HR	RBI	SB	Avg
1994	Bristol	Appal.	1B	48	161	17	43	6	0	5	30	4	.267
1995	Fayettevlle	So.Atl.	1B	137	524	75	149	32	0	14	106	1	.284

Year	Club	Lea	Pos	G	AB	R	H	2B	3B	HR	RBI	SB	Avg
1996 Toledo	Int.		1B	6	23	1	4	0	0	0	1	0	.174
1996 Lakeland a	Fla.St.		1B	128	464	65	135	29	4	10	68	1	.291
1997 Jackson	Texas		1B	114	422	72	139	25	0	19	90	4	.329
1997 New Orleans	A.A.		1B	14	48	4	18	1	0	2	8	0	.375
1998 New Orleans	P.C.		OF-1B	116	463	78	141	31	1	23	96	2	.305
1998 Houston	N.L.		##	4	3	1	1	0	0	0	0	0	.333
1999 New Orleans	P.C.		1B	61	241	56	85	15	1	28	65	1	.353
1999 Houston	N.L.		OF-1B	64	150	11	41	6	0	8	30	0	.273
2000 Houston	N.L.		OF-1B	119	264	36	68	10	2	20	47	0	.258
Major League Totals			3 Yrs.	187	417	48	110	16	2	28	77	0	.264
Division Series													
1999 Houston	N.L.		OF	3	7	1	1	0	0	1	1	0	.143

a Traded to Houston Astros by Detroit Tigers with catcher Brad Ausmus, pitcher Jose Lima, pitcher C.J. Nitkowski and pitcher Trever Miller for outfielder Brian Hunter, infielder Orlando Miller, pitcher Doug Brocail, pitcher Todd Jones and cash, December 10, 1996.

WEISS, WALTER WILLIAM (WALT)
Born, Tuxedo, New York, November 28, 1963.
Bats Both. Throws Right. Height, 6 feet. Weight, 175 pounds.

Year	Club	Lea	Pos	G	AB	R	H	2B	3B	HR	RBI	SB	Avg
1985 Pocatello	Pioneer		SS	40	158	19	49	9	3	0	21	6	.310
1985 Modesto	California		SS	30	122	17	24	4	1	0	7	3	.197
1986 Huntsville	Southern		SS	46	160	19	40	2	1	0	13	5	.250
1986 Madison	Midwest		SS	84	322	50	97	15	5	2	54	12	.301
1987 Huntsville	Southern		SS	91	337	43	96	16	2	1	32	23	.285
1987 Tacoma	P.C.		SS	46	179	35	47	4	3	0	17	8	.263
1987 Oakland	A.L.		SS	16	26	3	12	4	0	0	1	1	.462
1988 Oakland a	A.L.		SS	147	452	44	113	17	3	3	39	4	.250
1989 Modesto	California		SS	5	8	1	3	0	0	0	1	0	.375
1989 Tacoma	P.C.		SS	2	9	1	1	1	0	0	1	0	.111
1989 Oakland b	A.L.		SS	84	236	30	55	11	0	3	21	6	.233
1990 Oakland c	A.L.		SS	138	445	50	118	17	1	2	35	9	.265
1991 Oakland d	A.L.		SS	40	133	15	30	6	1	0	13	6	.226
1992 Tacoma	P.C.		SS	4	13	2	3	1	0	0	3	0	.231
1992 Oakland e-f	A.L.		SS	103	316	36	67	5	2	0	21	6	.212
1993 Florida g	N.L.		SS	158	500	50	133	14	2	1	39	7	.266
1994 Colorado	N.L.		SS	110	423	58	106	11	4	1	32	12	.251
1995 Colorado h-i	N.L.		SS	137	427	65	111	17	3	1	25	15	.260
1996 Colorado	N.L.		SS	155	517	89	146	20	2	8	48	10	.282
1997 Colorado j-k-l	N.L.		SS	121	393	52	106	23	5	4	38	5	.270
1998 Atlanta	N.L.		SS	96	347	64	97	18	2	0	27	7	.280
1999 Atlanta m	N.L.		SS	110	279	38	63	13	4	2	29	7	.226
2000 Atlanta m-n	N.L.		SS	80	192	29	50	6	2	0	18	1	.260
Major League Totals			14 Yrs.	1495	4686	623	1207	182	31	25	386	96	.258
Division Series													
1995 Colorado	N.L.		SS	4	12	1	2	0	0	0	0	1	.167
1998 Atlanta	N.L.		SS	3	13	2	2	0	0	0	0	0	.154
1999 Atlanta	N.L.		SS	3	6	1	1	0	0	0	0	0	.167
2000 Atlanta	N.L.		SS	1	3	0	2	1	0	0	2	0	.667
Division Series Totals				11	34	4	7	1	0	0	2	1	.206
Championship Series													
1988 Oakland	A.L.		SS	4	15	2	5	2	0	0	2	0	.333
1989 Oakland	A.L.		SS	4	9	2	1	1	0	0	0	1	.111
1990 Oakland	A.L.		SS	2	7	2	0	0	0	0	0	0	.000
1992 Oakland	A.L.		SS	3	6	1	1	0	0	0	0	2	.167
1998 Atlanta	N.L.		SS	4	15	0	3	0	0	0	0	1	.200
1999 Atlanta	N.L.		SS	6	21	2	6	2	0	0	1	2	.286
Championship Series Totals				23	73	9	16	5	0	0	4	6	.219
World Series Record													
1988 Oakland	A.L.		SS	5	16	1	1	0	0	0	0	1	.063
1989 Oakland	A.L.		SS	4	15	3	2	0	0	1	1	0	.133
1999 Atlanta	N.L.		SS	3	9	1	2	0	0	0	0	0	.333
World Series Totals				12	40	5	5	0	0	1	1	1	.125

a Selected Rookie of the Year in American League for 1988.
b On disabled list from May 18 to July 31, 1989.
c On disabled list from August 23 to September 7, 1990.
d On disabled list from April 15 to April 30 and June 7 to end of 1991 season.

e On disabled list from March 31 to June 6, 1992.
m On disabled list from June 7 to July 1, 1999.
f Traded to Florida Marlins for catcher Eric Helfand and player to be named, November 17; Oakland Athletics acquired pitcher Scott Baker to complete trade, November 20, 1992.
g Filed for free agency, October 25, 1993; signed with Colorado Rockies, January 7, 1994.
h Filed for free agency, November 12, 1995.
i Re-signed with Colorado Rockies, November 20, 1995.
j On disabled list from July 22 to August 8, 1997.
k Filed for free agency, October 27, 1997.
l Signed with Atlanta Braves, November 17, 1997.
m On disabled list from May 4 to May 20, 2000.
n Filed for free agency, October 30, 2000.

WELLS, VERNON M.
Born, Shreveport, Louisiana, December 8, 1978.
Bats Right. Throws Right. Height, 6 feet, 1 inch. Weight, 195 pounds.

Year	Club	Lea	Pos	G	AB	R	H	2B	3B	HR	RBI	SB	Avg
1997	St.Cathrnes	N.Y.-Penn.	OF	66	264	52	81	20	1	10	31	8	.307
1998	Hagerstown	So.Atl.	OF	134	509	86	145	35	2	11	65	13	.285
1999	Dunedin	Fla.St.	OF	0	265	43	91	16	2	11	43	13	.343
1999	Knoxville	Southern	OF	26	106	18	36	6	2	3	17	6	.340
1999	Syracuse	Int.	OF	33	129	20	40	8	1	4	21	5	.310
1999	Toronto	A.L.	OF	24	88	8	23	5	0	1	8	1	.261
2000	Syracuse	Int.	OF	127	493	76	120	31	7	16	66	23	.243
2000	Toronto	A.L.	OF	3	2	0	0	0	0	0	0	0	.000
Major League Totals			2 Yrs.	27	90	8	23	5	0	1	8	1	.256

WHITE, RONDELL BERNARD
Born, Milledgeville, Georgia, February 23, 1972.
Bats Right. Throws Right. Height, 6 feet, 1 inch. Weight, 205 pounds.

Year	Club	Lea	Pos	G	AB	R	H	2B	3B	HR	RBI	SB	Avg
1990	Bradenton Expos	Gulf Coast	OF	57	221	33	66	7	4	5	34	10	.299
1991	Sumter	So. Atl.	OF	123	465	80	122	23	6	13	68	50	.262
1992	West Palm Beach	Fla. St.	OF	111	450	80	142	10	12	4	41	42	.316
1992	Harrisburg	Eastern	OF	21	89	22	27	7	1	2	7	6	.303
1993	Ottawa	Int.	OF	37	150	28	57	8	2	7	32	10	.380
1993	Harrisburg	Eastern	OF-1B	91	373	72	122	16	10	12	52	21	.327
1993	Montreal	N.L.	OF	23	73	9	19	3	1	2	15	1	.260
1994	Ottawa	Int.	OF	42	169	23	46	7	0	7	18	9	.272
1994	Montreal	N.L.	OF	40	97	16	27	10	1	2	13	1	.278
1995	Montreal	N.L.	OF	130	474	87	140	33	4	13	57	25	.295
1996	Wst Plm Bch	Fla.St.	DH-OF	3	10	0	2	1	0	0	2	0	.200
1996	Expos	Gulf Coast	OF	3	12	3	3	0	0	2	4	1	.250
1996	Harrisburg a	Eastern	OF	5	20	5	7	1	0	3	6	1	.350
1996	Montreal	N.L.	OF	88	334	35	98	19	4	6	41	14	.293
1997	Montreal	N.L.	OF	151	592	84	160	29	5	28	82	16	.270
1998	Montreal b	N.L.	OF	97	357	54	107	21	2	17	58	16	.300
1999	Montreal c	N.L.	OF	138	539	83	168	26	6	22	64	10	.312
2000	Montreal-Chicago d-e	N.L.	OF	94	357	59	111	26	0	13	61	5	.311
Major League Totals			8 Yrs.	761	2823	427	830	167	23	103	391	88	.294

a On disabled list from April 28 to July 16, 1996.
b On disabled list from July 21 to September 28, 1998.
c On disabled list from June 14 to June 29 and July 2 to July 17, 1999.
d Traded to Chicago Cubs for pitcher Scott Downs, July 31, 2000.
e On disabled list from July 8 to August 5, 2000 and from August 27 to October 10, 2000.

WIDGER, CHRISTOPHER JON (CHRIS)
Born, Wilmington, Delaware, May 21, 1971.
Bats Right. Throws Right. Height, 6 feet, 3 inches. Weight, 195 pounds.

Year	Club	Lea	Pos	G	AB	R	H	2B	3B	HR	RBI	SB	Avg
1992	Bellingham	Northwest	C	51	166	28	43	7	2	5	30	8	.259
1993	Riverside	California	C-OF	97	360	44	95	28	2	9	58	5	.264
1994	Jacksonville	Southern	C-OF-1B	116	388	58	101	15	3	16	59	8	.260
1995	Tacoma	P.C.	C-OF	50	174	29	48	11	1	9	21	0	.276
1995	Seattle	A.L.	C-OF	23	45	2	9	0	0	1	2	0	.200
1996	Tacoma	P.C.	C	97	352	42	107	20	2	13	48	7	.304
1996	Seattle a	A.L.	C	8	11	1	2	0	0	0	0	0	.182

180

ear	Club	Lea	Pos	G	AB	R	H	2B	3B	HR	RBI	SB	Avg
997 Montreal	....	N.L.	C	91	278	30	65	20	3	7	37	2	.234
998 Montreal	....	N.L.	C	125	417	36	97	18	1	15	53	6	.233
999 Montreal	....	N.L.	C	124	383	42	101	24	1	14	56	1	.264
)00 Montreal	....	N.L.	C	86	281	31	67	17	2	12	34	1	.238
)00 Seattle b-c-d		A.L.	C-1B-OF	10	11	1	1	0	0	1	1	0	.091
Major League Totals	....		6 Yrs.	467	1426	143	342	79	7	50	183	10	.240
Division Series													
995 Seattle	....	A.L.	C	2	3	0	0	0	0	0	0	0	.000
Championship Series													
995 Seattle	....	A.L.	C	3	1	0	0	0	0	0	0	0	.000

Traded to Montreal Expos with pitcher Matt Wagner and pitcher Trey Moore for pitcher Jeff Fassero and pitcher Alex Pachecho, October 29, 1996.
On disabled list from May 25 to June 8, 2000.
Traded to Seattle Mariners for player to be named later, August 8, 2000.
Montreal Expos received outfielder Termal Sledge to complete trade, September 28, 2000.

WILLIAMS (FIGUEROA), BERNABE (BERNIE)
Born, San Juan, Puerto Rico, September 13, 1968.
Bats Both. Throws Right. Height, 6 feet, 2 inches. Weight, 200 pounds.

ear	Club	Lea	Pos	G	AB	R	H	2B	3B	HR	RBI	SB	Avg
986 Sarasota Yankees a	..Gulf C.		OF	61	230	*45	62	5	3	2	25	33	.270
987 Fort Lauderdale b	....Fla. St.		OF	25	71	11	11	3	0	0	4	9	.155
987 Oneonta	.......N.Y.-Penn.		OF	25	93	13	32	4	0	0	15	9	.344
988 Prince William c	....Carolina		OF	92	337	72	113	16	7	7	45	29	*.335
989 Albany	............Eastern		OF	91	314	63	79	11	8	11	42	26	.252
989 Columbus	...........Int.		OF	50	162	21	35	8	1	2	16	11	.216
990 Albany	............Eastern		OF	134	466	*91	131	28	5	8	54	*39	.281
991 Columbus	...........Int.		OF	78	306	52	90	14	6	8	37	9	.294
991 New York	............A.L.		OF	85	320	43	76	19	4	3	34	10	.238
392 Columbus	...........Int.		OF	95	363	68	111	23	9	8	50	20	.306
992 New York	............A.L.		OF	62	261	39	73	14	2	5	26	7	.280
993 New York d	............A.L.		OF	139	567	67	152	31	4	12	68	9	.268
994 New York	............A.L.		OF	108	408	80	118	29	1	12	57	16	.289
995 New York	............A.L.		OF	144	563	93	173	29	9	18	82	8	.307
996 New York e	............A.L.		OF	143	551	108	168	26	7	29	102	17	.305
997 New York f	............A.L.		OF	129	509	107	167	35	6	21	100	15	.328
998 Tampa	............Fla.St.		OF	1	2	0	1	1	0	0	0	0	.500
998 Norwich	...........Eastern		OF	3	11	6	6	2	0	2	5	0	.545
998 New York g-h	............A.L.		OF	128	499	101	169	30	5	26	97	15	*.339
999 New York	............A.L.		OF	158	591	116	202	28	6	25	115	9	.342
)00 New York	............A.L.		OF	141	537	108	165	37	6	30	121	13	.307
Major League Totals	....		10 Yrs.	1237	4806	862	1463	278	50	181	802	119	.304
Division Series													
995 New York	............A.L.		OF	5	21	8	9	2	0	2	5	1	.429
996 New York	............A.L.		OF	4	15	5	7	0	0	3	5	1	.467
997 New York	............A.L.		OF	5	17	3	2	1	0	0	1	0	.118
998 New York	............A.L.		OF	3	11	0	0	0	0	0	0	0	.000
999 New York	............A.L.		OF	3	11	2	4	1	0	1	6	0	.364
)00 New York	............A.L.		OF	5	20	3	5	3	0	0	1	0	.250
ivision Series Totals	....			25	95	21	27	7	0	6	18	2	.284
Championship Series													
996 New York	...........:A.L.		OF	5	19	6	9	3	0	2	6	1	.474
998 New York	............A.L.		OF	6	21	4	8	1	0	0	5	1	.381
999 New York	............A.L.		OF	5	20	3	5	1	0	1	2	1	.250
)00 New York	............A.L.		OF	6	23	5	10	1	0	1	3	1	.435
hampionship Series Totals	......			22	83	18	32	6	0	4	16	4	.386
World Series													
996 New York	............A.L.		OF	6	24	3	4	0	0	1	4	1	.167
998 New York	............A.L.		OF	4	16	2	1	0	0	1	3	0	.062
999 New York	............A.L.		OF	4	13	2	3	0	0	0	0	1	.231
)00 New York	............A.L.		OF	5	18	2	2	0	0	1	1	0	.111
World Series Totals	....			19	71	9	10	0	0	3	8	2	.141

Batted righthanded only from 1986 through 1988 season.
On disabled list from May 17 to June 17, 1987.
On disabled list from July 14 to end of 1988 season.
On disabled list from May 14 to June 7, 1993.
On disabled list from May 11 to May 26, 1996.
On disabled list from June 15 to July 2 and July 14 to August 1, 1997.

h Filed for free agency, October 26, 1998, re-signed with New York Yankees, November 25, 1998.

WILLIAMS, GERALD FLOYD (ICE)

Born, New Orleans, Louisiana, August 10, 1966.
Bats Right. Throws Right. Height, 6 feet, 2 inches. Weight, 190 pounds.

Year	Club	Lea	Pos	G	AB	R	H	2B	3B	HR	RBI	SB	Avg
1987 Oneonta	N.Y.-Penn.	OF	29	115	26	42	6	2	2	29	6	.365
1988 Prince William	Carolina	OF	54	159	20	29	3	0	2	18	6	.182
1988 Fort Lauderdale	Fla. St.	OF	63	212	21	40	7	2	2	17	4	.189
1989 Prince William	Carolina	OF	134	454	63	104	19	6	13	69	15	.229
1990 Fort Lauderdale	Fla. St.	OF	50	204	25	59	4	5	7	43	19	.289
1990 Albany	Eastern	OF	96	324	54	81	17	2	13	58	18	.250
1991 Albany	Eastern	OF	45	175	28	50	15	0	5	32	18	.286
1991 Columbus	Int.	OF	61	198	20	51	8	3	2	27	9	.258
1992 Columbus	Int.	OF	142	547	92	156	31	6	16	86	14	.285
1992 New York	A.L.	OF	15	27	7	8	2	0	3	6	2	.296
1993 Columbus	Int.	OF	87	336	53	95	19	6	8	38	29	.283
1993 New York	A.L.	OF	42	67	11	10	2	3	0	6	2	.149
1994 New York	A.L.	OF	57	86	19	25	8	0	4	13	1	.291
1995 New York	A.L.	OF	100	182	33	45	18	2	6	28	4	.247
1996 New York-Milwaukee a	A.L.	OF	125	325	43	82	19	4	5	34	10	.252
1997 Milwaukee b	A.L.	OF	155	566	73	143	32	2	10	41	23	.253
1998 Atlanta	N.L.	OF	129	266	46	81	19	2	10	44	11	.305
1999 Atlanta c	N.L.	OF	143	422	76	116	24	1	17	68	19	.275
2000 Tampa Bay	A.L.	OF	146	632	87	173	30	2	21	89	12	.274
Major League Totals		9 Yrs.	912	2573	395	683	154	16	76	329	84	.265
Division Series												
1995 New York	A.L.	OF	5	5	1	0	0	0	0	0	0	.000
1998 Atlanta	N.L.	OF	2	2	1	1	0	0	0	1	0	.500
1999 Atlanta	N.L.	OF	4	18	2	7	1	0	0	3	1	.389
Division Series Totals			11	25	4	8	1	0	0	4	1	.320
Championship Series												
1998 Atlanta	N.L.	OF	5	13	0	2	0	0	0	0	1	.154
1999 Atlanta	N.L.	OF	6	28	4	5	2	0	0	1	3	.179
Championship Series Totals			11	41	4	7	2	0	0	1	4	.171

a Traded to Milwaukee Brewers with pitcher Bob Wickman for pitcher Graeme Lloyd, pitcher Ricky Bones and player to be named later, August 23, 1996. New York Yankees received infielder Gabby Martinez to complete trade, November 5, 1996.
b Traded to Atlanta Braves for pitcher Chad Fox, December 11, 1997.
c Filed for free agency, November 3, 1999. Signed with Tampa Bay Devil Rays, December 19, 1999.

WILLIAMS, MATTHEW DERRICK

Born, Bishop, California, November 28, 1965.
Bats Right. Throws Right. Height, 6 feet, 2 inches. Weight, 216 pounds.

Year	Club	Lea	Pos	G	AB	R	H	2B	3B	HR	RBI	SB	Avg
1986 Everett	Northwest	SS	4	17	3	4	0	1	1	10	0	.235
1986 Clinton	Midwest	SS	68	250	32	60	14	3	7	29	3	.240
1987 Phoenix	P.C.	3B	56	211	36	61	15	1	6	37	6	.289
1987 San Francisco	N.L.	SS-3B	84	245	28	46	9	2	8	21	4	.188
1988 Phoenix	P.C.	3B	82	306	45	83	19	1	12	51	6	.271
1988 San Francisco	N.L.	3B-SS	52	156	17	32	6	1	8	19	0	.205
1989 Phoenix	P.C.	3B-SS	76	284	61	91	20	2	26	61	9	.320
1989 San Francisco	N.L.	3B-SS	84	292	31	59	18	1	18	50	1	.202
1990 San Francisco	N.L.	3B	159	617	87	171	27	2	33	*122	7	.277
1991 San Francisco	N.L.	3B-SS	157	589	72	158	24	5	34	98	5	.268
1992 San Francisco	N.L.	3B	146	529	58	120	13	5	20	66	7	.227
1993 San Francisco a	N.L.	3B	145	579	105	170	33	4	38	110	1	.294
1994 San Francisco	N.L.	3B	112	445	74	119	16	3	*43	96	1	.267
1995 San Jose	California	3B	4	11	2	2	0	0	1	2	0	.182
1995 San Francisco b-c	N.L.	3B	76	283	53	95	17	1	23	65	2	.336
1996 San Francisco d-e	N.L.	3B-1B-SS	105	404	69	122	16	1	22	85	1	.302
1997 Cleveland f	A.L.	3B	151	596	86	157	32	3	32	*105	12	.263
1998 Tucson	P.C.	3B	2	5	0	1	0	0	0	0	0	.200
1998 Arizona g	N.L.	3B	135	510	72	136	26	1	20	71	5	.267
1999 Arizona	N.L.	3B	154	627	98	190	37	2	35	142	2	.303
2000 El Paso	Texas	3B	5	13	3	6	2	0	0	1	0	.462
2000 High Desert	California	3B	2	8	1	3	0	0	1	1	0	.375

Year	Club	Lea	Pos	G	AB	R	H	2B	3B	HR	RBI	SB	Avg
2000 Arizona h	N.L.		3B	96	371	43	102	18	2	12	47	1	.275
Major League Totals	14 Yrs.			1656	6243	893	1677	292	33	346	1097	49	.269
Division Series													
1997 Cleveland	A.L.		3B	5	17	4	4	1	0	1	3	0	.235
1999 Arizona	N.L.		3B	4	16	3	6	1	0	0	0	0	.375
Division Series Totals				9	33	7	10	2	0	1	3	0	.303
Championship Series													
1989 San Francisco	N.L.		3B-SS	5	20	2	6	1	0	2	9	0	.300
1997 Cleveland	A.L.		3B	6	23	1	5	1	0	0	2	1	.217
Championship Series Totals				11	43	3	11	2	0	2	11	1	.256
World Series Record													
1989 San Francisco	N.L.		3B-SS	4	16	1	2	0	0	1	1	0	.125
1997 Cleveland	A.L.		3B	7	26	8	10	1	0	1	3	0	.385
World Series Totals				11	42	9	12	1	0	2	4	0	.286

a On disabled list from June 28 to July 14, 1993.
b Traded to Houston Astros for catcher Eddie Tucker, May 15, 1995.
c On disabled list from June 4 to August 19, 1995.
d On disabled list from August 5 to September 30, 1996.
e Traded to Cleveland Indians with player to be named later for infielder Jeff Kent, pitcher Julian Tavarez, infielder Jose Vizcaino and player to be named later, November 13, 1996. San Francisco Giants received pitcher Joe Roa and Cleveland Indians received outfielder Trinidad Hubbard to complete trade, December 16, 1996.
f Traded to Arizona Diamondbacks for infielder Travis Fryman and pitcher Tom Martin, December 1, 1997.
g On disabled list from July 18 to August 3, 1998.
h On disabled list from March 29 to May 22 and June 25 to July 12, 2000.

WILSON, DANIEL ALLEN
Born, Arlington Heights, Illinois, March 25, 1969.
Bats Right. Throws Right. Height, 6 feet, 3 inches. Weight, 190 pounds.

Year	Club	Lea	Pos	G	AB	R	H	2B	3B	HR	RBI	SB	Avg
1990 Charleston, WV	So. Atl.	C	32	113	16	28	9	1	2	17	0	.248
1991 Charleston, WV	So. Atl.	C	52	197	25	62	11	1	3	29	1	.315
1991 Chattanooga	Southern	C	81	292	32	75	19	2	2	38	2	.257
1992 Nashville	A.A.	C	106	366	27	92	16	1	4	34	1	.251
1992 Cincinnati	N.L.	C	12	25	2	9	1	0	0	3	0	.360
1993 Indianapolis	A.A.	C	51	191	18	50	11	1	0	17	1	.262
1993 Cincinnati a	N.L.	C	36	76	6	17	3	0	0	8	0	.224
1994 Seattle	A.L.	C	91	282	24	61	14	2	3	27	1	.216
1995 Seattle	A.L.	C	119	399	40	111	22	3	9	51	2	.278
1996 Seattle	A.L.	C	138	491	51	140	24	0	18	83	1	.285
1997 Seattle	A.L.	C	146	508	66	137	31	1	15	74	7	.270
1998 Seattle b	A.L.	C	96	325	39	82	17	1	9	44	2	.252
1999 Seattle	A.L.	C-1B	123	414	46	110	23	2	7	38	5	.266
2000 Everett	Northwest	PH	1	2	2	1	0	0	1	1	0	.500
2000 Tacoma	P.C.	PH	1	4	0	1	1	0	0	0	0	.250
2000 Seattle c	A.L.	C-1B-3B	90	268	31	63	12	0	5	27	1	.235
Major League Totals	9 Yrs.		851	2788	305	730	147	9	66	355	19	.262
Division Series												
1995 Seattle	A.L.	C	5	17	0	2	0	0	0	1	0	.118
1997 Seattle	A.L.	C	4	13	0	0	0	0	0	0	0	.000
2000 Seattle	A.L.	C	2	3	0	0	0	0	0	1	0	.000
Division Series Totals			11	33	0	2	0	0	0	2	0	.061
Championship Series												
1995 Seattle	A.L.	C	6	16	0	0	0	0	0	0	0	.000
2000 Seattle	A.L.	C	4	11	0	1	0	0	0	0	0	.091
Championship Series Totals			10	27	0	1	0	0	0	0	0	.037

a Traded to Seattle Mariners with pitcher Bobby Ayala for pitcher Erik Hanson and second baseman Bret Boone, November 2, 1993.
b On disabled list from July 20 to September 1, 1998.
c On disabled list from June 15 to July 13, 2000.

WILSON, ENRIQUE
Born, Santo Domingo, Dominican Republic, July 27, 1975.
Bats Both. Throws Right. Height, 5 feet, 11 inches. Weight, 160 pounds.

Year	Club	Lea	Pos	G	AB	R	H	2B	3B	HR	RBI	SB	Avg
1992 Twins	Gulf Coast	SS	13	44	12	15	1	0	0	8	3	.341
1993 Elizabethtn	Appal.	SS-3B	58	197	42	57	8	4	13	50	5	.289

Year	Club	Lea	Pos	G	AB	R	H	2B	3B	HR	RBI	SB	Avg
1994 Columbus a	So.Atl.	SS	133	512	82	143	28	12	10	72	21	.279
1995 Kinston	Carolina	SS-2B	117	464	55	124	24	7	6	52	18	.267
1996 Canton-Akrn	Eastern	SS-2B	117	484	70	147	17	5	5	50	23	.304
1996 Buffalo	A.A.	3B-SS	3	8	1	4	1	0	0	0	0	.500
1997 Buffalo	A.A.	SS-2B-3B	118	451	78	138	20	3	11	39	9	.306
1997 Cleveland	A.L.	SS-2B	5	15	2	5	0	0	0	1	0	.333
1998 Buffalo	Int.	2B-SS	56	221	40	62	13	0	4	23	8	.281
1998 Cleveland b	A.L.	2B-SS-3B	32	90	13	29	6	0	2	12	2	.322
1999 Cleveland	A.L.	3B-SS-2B	113	332	41	87	22	1	2	24	5	.262
2000 Nashville	P.C.	2B	2	7	0	2	0	0	0	1	0	.286
2000 Cleveland	A.L.	3B-2B-SS	40	117	16	38	9	0	2	12	2	.325
2000 Pittsburgh c-d	N.L.	3B-2B-SS	40	122	11	32	6	1	3	15	0	.262
Major League Totals	4 Yrs.		230	676	83	191	43	2	9	64	9	.283

Division Series

Year	Club	Lea	Pos	G	AB	R	H	2B	3B	HR	RBI	SB	Avg
1998 Cleveland	A.L.	2B	1	2	0	0	0	0	0	0	0	.000
1999 Cleveland	A.L.	2B	3	2	0	0	0	0	0	0	0	.000
Division Series Totals			4	4	0	0	0	0	0	0	0	.000

Championship Series

Year	Club	Lea	Pos	G	AB	R	H	2B	3B	HR	RBI	SB	Avg
1998 Cleveland	A.L.	2B	5	14	2	3	0	0	0	1	0	.214

a Traded by Minnesota Twins to Cleveland Indians to complete Shawn Bryant trade, February 21, 1994.
b On disabled list from April 4 to June 15, 1998.
c Traded to Pittsburgh Pirates with outfielder Alex Ramirez for outfielder Wil Cordero, July 28, 2000.
d On disabled list from July 14 to July 31, 2000.

WILSON, PRESTON JAMES RICHARD
Born, Bamberg, South Carolina, July 19, 1974.
Bats Right. Throws Right. Height, 6 feet, 2 inches. Weight, 193 pounds.

Year	Club	Lea	Pos	G	AB	R	H	2B	3B	HR	RBI	SB	Avg
1993 Kingsport	Appal.	3B	66	259	44	60	10	0	16	48	6	.232
1993 Pittsfield	N.Y.-Penn.	3B	8	29	6	16	5	1	1	12	1	.552
1994 Columbia	So.Atl.	3B	131	474	55	108	17	4	14	58	13	.228
1995 Columbia	So.Atl.	OF	111	442	70	119	26	5	20	61	20	.269
1996 St. Lucie a	Fla.St.	OF	23	85	6	15	3	0	1	7	1	.176
1997 St. Lucie	Fla.St.	OF	63	245	32	60	12	1	11	48	3	.245
1997 Binghamton	Eastern	OF-3B	70	259	37	74	12	1	19	47	7	.286
1998 Norfolk	Int.	OF	18	73	9	18	5	1	1	9	1	.247
1998 Charlotte	Int.	OF	94	356	71	99	25	3	25	77	14	.278
1998 New York-Florida b	N.L.	OF	22	51	7	8	2	0	1	3	1	.157
1999 Florida	N.L.	OF	149	482	67	135	21	4	26	71	11	.280
2000 Florida	N.L.	OF	161	605	94	160	35	3	31	121	36	.264
Major League Totals	3 Yrs.		332	1138	168	303	58	7	58	195	48	.266

a On disabled list from April 4 to April 29 and May 21 to July 13 and July 29 to September 8, 1996.
b Traded to Florida Marlins with pitcher Ed Yarnall and player to be named later for catcher Mike Piazza, May 22, 1998. Florida Marlins received pitcher Geoff Goetz to complete trade, July 3, 1998.
b Selected in expansion draft by Tampa Bay Devil Rays, November 18, 1997.

WOMACK, ANTHONY DARRELL (TONY)
Born, Chatham, Virginia, September 25, 1969.
Bats Left. Throws Right. Height, 5 feet, 9 inches. Weight, 160 pounds.

Year	Club	Lea	Pos	G	AB	R	H	2B	3B	HR	RBI	SB	Avg
1991 Welland	N.Y.-Penn.	SS-2B	45	166	30	46	3	0	1	8	26	.277
1992 Augusta	So. Atl.	SS-2B	102	380	62	93	8	3	0	18	50	.245
1993 Salem	Carolina	SS	72	304	41	91	11	3	2	18	28	.299
1993 Carolina	Southern	SS	60	247	41	75	7	2	0	23	21	.304
1993 Pittsburgh	N.L.	SS	15	24	5	2	0	0	0	0	2	.083
1994 Pittsburgh	N.L.	2B-SS	5	12	4	4	0	0	0	1	0	.333
1994 Buffalo	A.A.	SS-2B	106	421	40	93	9	2	0	18	41	.221
1995 Calgary	P.C.	2B-SS	30	107	12	30	3	1	0	6	7	.280
1995 Carolina	Southern	SS-2B	82	332	52	85	9	4	1	19	27	.256
1996 Calgary	P.C.	SS-2B-OF	131	506	75	152	19	11	1	47	37	.300
1996 Pittsburgh	N.L.	OF-2B	17	30	11	10	3	1	0	2	2	.333
1997 Pittsburgh	N.L.	2B-SS	155	641	85	178	26	9	6	50	60	.278
1998 Pittsburgh	N.L.	2B-OF-SS	159	655	85	185	26	7	3	45	*58	.282
1999 Tucson	P.C.	OF	4	16	1	4	1	0	0	1	3	.250
1999 Arizona a-b	N.L.	OF-2B-SS	144	614	111	170	25	10	4	41	*72	.277
2000 Arizona	N.L.	SS-OF	146	617	95	167	21	*14	7	57	45	.271
Major League Totals	7 Yrs.		641	2593	396	716	101	41	20	201	239	.276

ar	Club	Lea	Pos	G	AB	R	H	2B	3B	HR	RBI	SB	Avg
	Division Series												
99	Arizona .............N.L.		OF-SS	4	18	2	2	0	1	0	0	0	.111

Traded to Arizona Diamondbacks for outfielder Paul Welchard and player to be named later, February 26, 1999.
Pittsburgh Pirates received pitcher Jason Boyd to complete trade, August 25, 1999.
On disabled list from March 26 to April 12, 1999.

YOUNG, DMITRI DELL

Born, Vicksburg, Mississippi, November 11, 1973.
Bats Both. Throws Right. Height, 6 feet, 2 inches. Weight, 240 pounds.

ar	Club	Lea	Pos	G	AB	R	H	2B	3B	HR	RBI	SB	Avg
91	Johnson Cty ....Appal.		3B	37	129	22	33	10	0	2	22	2	.256
92	Springfield ....Midwest		3B	135	493	74	153	36	6	14	72	14	.310
93	St. Pete ....Fla.St.		3B-1B	69	270	31	85	13	3	5	43	3	.315
93	Arkansas ....Texas		1B-3B	45	166	13	41	11	2	3	21	4	.247
94	Arkansas ....Texas		OF-1B	125	453	53	123	33	2	8	54	0	.272
95	Arkansas ....Texas		OF	97	367	54	107	18	6	10	62	2	.292
95	Louisville ............A.A.		OF	2	7	3	2	0	0	0	0	0	.286
96	Louisville ............A.A.		1B	122	459	90	153	31	8	15	64	16	.333
96	St. Louis ............N.L.		1B	16	29	3	7	0	0	0	2	0	.241
97	Louisville ............A.A.		OF-1B	24	83	10	23	7	0	4	14	1	.277
97	St. Louis a-b-c-d ....N.L.		1B-OF	110	333	38	86	14	3	5	34	6	.258
98	Cincinnati ...........N.L.		OF-1B	144	536	81	166	48	1	14	83	2	.310
99	Cincinnati ...........N.L.		OF-1B	127	373	63	112	30	2	14	56	3	.300
00	Cincinnati ...........N.L.		OF-1B	152	548	68	166	37	6	18	88	0	.303
	Major League Totals			5 Yrs.	549	1819	253	537	129	12	51	263	11	.295
	Championship Series												
96	St. Louis .............N.L.		1B	4	7	1	2	0	1	0	2	0	.286

On disabled list from May 11 to May 29, 1997.
Traded to Cincinnati Reds for pitcher Jeff Brantley, November 10, 1997.
Selected in expansion draft by Tampa Bay Devil Rays, November 18, 1997.
Sent to Cincinnati Reds as player to be named later for outfielder Mike Kelly, November 18, 1997.

YOUNG, ERIC ORLANDO

Born, Jacksonville, Florida, November 26, 1966.
Bats Right. Throws Right. Height, 5 feet, 9 inches. Weight, 180 pounds.

ar	Club	Lea	Pos	G	AB	R	H	2B	3B	HR	RBI	SB	Avg
89	Kissimmee Dodgers ..Gulf C.		2B-3B-C	56	197	53	65	11	5	2	22	*41	.330
90	Vero Beach ....Fla. St.		2B-OF	127	460	*101	132	23	7	2	50	*76	.287
91	San Antonio ....Texas		2B-OF	127	461	82	129	17	4	3	35	*71	.280
91	Albuquerque .........P.C.		2B	1	5	0	2	0	0	0	0	0	.400
92	Albuquerque .........P.C.		2B-OF	94	350	61	118	16	5	3	49	28	.337
92	Los Angeles a ........N.L.		2B	49	132	9	34	1	0	1	11	6	.258
93	Colorado ............N.L.		2B-OF	144	490	82	132	16	8	3	42	42	.269
94	Colorado ............N.L.		OF-2B	90	228	37	62	13	1	7	30	18	.272
95	Colorado ............N.L.		2B-OF	120	366	68	116	21	*9	6	36	35	.317
96	New Haven ....Eastern		2B	3	15	0	1	0	0	0	0	0	.067
96	Salem ....Carolina		2B	3	10	2	3	3	0	0	0	2	.300
96	Colo Sprngs b .........P.C.		2B	7	23	4	6	1	1	0	3	0	.261
96	Colorado ............N.L.		2B	141	568	113	184	23	4	8	74	53	.324
97	Colorado-Los Angeles c .N.L.		2B	155	622	106	174	33	8	8	61	45	.280
98	Los Angeles d ........N.L.		2B	117	452	78	129	24	1	8	43	42	.285
99	San Bernardino ...California		2B	3	12	0	3	0	0	0	0	0	.250
99	Los Angeles e-f .......N.L.		2B	119	456	73	128	24	2	2	41	51	.281
00	Chicago .............N.L.		2B	153	607	98	180	40	2	6	47	54	.297
	Major League Totals			9 Yrs.	1088	3921	664	1139	195	35	49	385	346	.290
	Division Series												
95	Colorado .............N.L.		2B	4	16	3	7	1	0	1	2	1	.438

Selected by Colorado Rockies in expansion draft, November 17, 1992.
On disabled list from April 1 to April 22, 1996.
Traded to Los Angeles Dodgers for pitcher Pedro Astacio, August 18, 1997.
On disabled list from July 13 to July 31, 1998.
On disabled list from July 24 to August 13, 1999.
Traded to Chicago Cubs with pitcher Ismael Valdes for pitcher Terry Adams, pitcher Chad Ricketts and player to be named later, December 12, 1999. Los Angeles Dodgers received pitcher Brian Stephenson to complete trade, December 16, 1999.

YOUNG, KEVIN STACEY

Born, Alpena, Michigan, June 16, 1969.
Bats Right. Throws Right. Height, 6 feet, 3 inches. Weight, 221 pounds.

Year	Club	Lea	Pos	G	AB	R	H	2B	3B	HR	RBI	SB	Avg
1990	Welland	N.Y.-Penn.	3B	72	238	46	58	16	2	5	30	10	.24
1991	Salem	Carolina	3B	56	201	38	63	12	4	6	28	3	.31
1991	Carolina	Southern	3B-1B	75	263	36	90	19	6	3	33	9	.34
1991	Buffalo	A.A.	3B-1B	4	9	1	2	1	0	0	2	1	.22
1992	Buffalo	A.A.	3B-SS-1B	137	490	91	154	29	6	8	65	18	.31
1992	Pittsburgh	N.L.	3B-1B	10	7	2	4	0	0	0	4	1	.57
1993	Pittsburgh	N.L.	1B-3B	141	449	38	106	24	3	6	47	2	.23
1994	Pittsburgh	N.L.	1B-3B-OF	59	122	15	25	7	2	1	11	0	.20
1994	Buffalo	A.A.	3B-1B	60	228	26	63	14	5	5	27	6	.27
1995	Calgary	P.C.	3B-1B	45	163	24	58	23	1	8	34	6	.35
1995	Pittsburgh a-b	N.L.	3B-1B	56	181	13	42	9	0	6	22	1	.23
1996	Omaha	A.A.	1B-3B	50	186	29	57	11	1	13	46	3	.30
1996	Kansas City c-d	A.L.	3B-1B	55	132	20	32	6	0	8	23	3	.24
1997	Pittsburgh e	N.L.	1B-3B-OF	97	333	59	100	18	3	18	74	11	.30
1998	Pittsburgh	N.L.	1B	159	592	88	160	40	2	27	108	15	.27
1999	Pittsburgh	N.L.	1B	156	584	103	174	41	6	26	106	22	.29
2000	Pittsburgh	N.L.	1B	132	496	77	128	27	0	20	88	8	.25
Major League Totals			9 Yrs.	865	2896	415	771	172	16	112	483	63	.26

a Released by Pittsburgh Pirates, March 26, 1996.
b Signed as free agent with Kansas City organization, March 29, 1996.
c Released by Kansas City, November 20, 1996.
d Signed as free agent by Pittsburgh Pirates, December 19, 1996.
e On disabled list from August 3 to September 12, 1997.

ZAUN, GREGORY OWEN

Born, Glendale, California, April 14, 1971.
Bats Both. Throws Right. Height, 5 feet, 10 inches. Weight, 170 pounds.

Year	Club	Lea	Pos	G	AB	R	H	2B	3B	HR	RBI	SB	Avg
1990	Wausau	Midwest	C	37	100	3	13	0	1	1	7	0	.13
1990	Bluefield	Appal.	C-3B-SS-P	61	184	29	55	5	2	2	21	5	.29
1991	Kane County ...	Midwest	C	113	409	67	112	17	5	4	51	4	.27
1992	Frederick	Carolina	C-2B	108	383	54	96	18	6	6	52	3	.25
1993	Bowie	Eastern	C-2B-3B	79	258	25	79	10	0	3	38	4	.30
1993	Rochester a	Int.	C	21	78	10	20	4	2	1	11	0	.25
1994	Rochester	Int.	C	123	388	61	92	16	4	7	43	4	.23
1995	Rochester	Int.	C	42	140	26	41	13	1	6	18	0	.29
1995	Baltimore	A.L.	C	40	104	18	27	5	0	3	14	1	.26
1996	Baltimore	A.L.	C	50	108	16	25	8	1	1	13	0	.23
1996	Rochester	Int.	C	14	47	11	15	2	0	0	4	0	.31
1996	Florida b	N.L.	C	10	31	4	9	1	0	1	2	1	.29
1997	Florida	N.L.	C-1B	58	143	21	43	10	2	2	20	1	.30
1998	Florida c	N.L.	C-2B	106	298	19	56	12	2	5	29	5	.18
1999	Texas d-e	A.L.	C	43	93	12	23	2	1	1	12	1	.24
2000	Omaha	P.C.	PH	9	25	7	7	3	0	0	3	1	.28
2000	Kansas City f-g ...	A.L.	C-1B-2B	83	234	36	64	11	0	7	33	7	.27
Major League Totals			6 Yrs.	390	1011	126	247	49	6	20	123	16	.24
Championship Series													
1997	Florida	N.L.	C	1	0	0	0	0	0	0	0	0	.00
World Series Record													
1997	Florida	N.L.	C	2	2	0	0	0	0	0	0	0	.00

a On disabled list from June 17 to July 15, 1993.
b Sent to Florida Marlins to complete trade for pitcher Terry Mathews, August 23, 1996.
c Traded to Texas Rangers for player to be named later, November 23, 1998.
d Florida Marlins received cash to complete trade, April 15, 1999.
e Traded to Detroit Tigers with outfielder Juan Gonzalez and pitcher Danny Patterson for pitcher Justin Thompson, pitcher Francisco Cordero, pitcher Alan Webb, outfielder Gabe Kapler, catcher Bill Haselman and infielder Frank Catalanotto, November 2, 1999.
f Traded to Kansas City Royals for player to be named later, March 7, 2000.
g On disabled list from April 15 to May 28, 2000.

ZEILE, TODD EDWARD
Born, Van Nuys, California, September 9, 1965.
Bats Right. Throws Right. Height, 6 feet, 1 inch. Weight, 190 pounds.

Year	Club	Lea	Pos	G	AB	R	H	2B	3B	HR	RBI	SB	Avg
1986	Erie	N.Y.-Penn.	C	70	248	40	64	14	1	14	63	5	.258
1987	Springfield	Midwest	C	130	487	94	142	24	4	25	*106	1	.292
1988	Arkansas	Texas	C	129	430	95	117	33	2	19	75	6	.272
1989	Louisville	A.A.	C	118	453	71	131	26	3	19	85	0	.289
1989	St. Louis	N.L.	C	28	82	7	21	3	1	1	8	0	.256
1990	St. Louis	N.L.	C-3B-1B-OF	144	495	62	121	25	3	15	57	2	.244
1991	St. Louis	N.L.	3B	155	565	76	158	36	3	11	81	17	.280
1992	St. Louis	N.L.	3B	126	439	51	113	18	4	7	48	7	.257
1992	Louisville	A.A.	3B	21	74	11	23	4	1	5	13	0	.311
1993	St. Louis	N.L.	3B	157	571	82	158	36	1	17	103	5	.277
1994	St. Louis a	N.L.	3B	113	415	62	111	25	1	19	75	1	.267
1995	Louisville	A.A.	1B	2	8	0	1	0	0	0	0	0	.125
1995	St.L.-Chic. b-c-d-e	N.L.	3B-1B-OF	113	426	50	105	22	0	14	52	1	.246
1996	Philadelphia f	N.L.	3B-1B	134	500	61	134	24	0	20	80	1	.268
1996	Baltimore g-h	A.L.	3B	29	117	17	28	8	0	5	19	0	.239
1997	Los Angeles	N.L.	3B	160	575	89	154	17	0	31	90	8	.268
1998	Los Angeles-Florida	N.L.	3B-1B	106	392	59	108	18	2	13	66	3	.276
1998	Texas i-j	A.L.	3B	52	180	26	47	14	1	6	28	1	.261
1999	Texas k	A.L.	3B-1B	156	588	80	172	41	1	24	98	1	.293
2000	New York	N.L.	1B	153	544	67	146	36	3	22	79	3	.268
Major League Totals		12 Yrs.	1626	5889	789	1576	323	20	205	884	50	.268	

Division Series

Year	Club	Lea	Pos	G	AB	R	H	2B	3B	HR	RBI	SB	Avg
1996	Baltimore	A.L.	3B	4	19	2	5	1	0	0	0	0	.263
1998	Texas	A.L.	3B	3	9	0	3	0	0	0	0	0	.333
1999	Texas	A.L.	3B	3	10	0	1	0	0	0	0	0	.100
2000	New York	N.L.	1B	4	14	0	1	1	0	0	0	0	.071
Division Series Totals			14	52	2	10	2	0	0	0	0	.192	

Championship Series

Year	Club	Lea	Pos	G	AB	R	H	2B	3B	HR	RBI	SB	Avg
1996	Baltimore	A.L.	3B	5	22	3	8	0	0	3	5	0	.364
2000	New York	N.L.	1B	5	19	1	7	3	0	1	8	0	.368
Championship Series Totals			10	41	4	15	3	0	4	13	0	.366	

World Series Record

Year	Club	Lea	Pos	G	AB	R	H	2B	3B	HR	RBI	SB	Avg
2000	New York	N.L.	1B	5	20	1	8	2	0	0	1	0	.400

a Declared restricted free agent under Major League Baseball implemented labor proposal, December 23, 1994.
b Re-signed with St. Louis Cardinals, April 5, 1995.
c On disabled list from April 25 to May 9, 1995.
d Traded to Chicago Cubs for pitcher Mike Morgan, infielder Paul Torres and catcher Francisco Morales, June 16, 1995.
e Filed for free agency, November 12, 1995; signed with Philadelphia Phillies, December 23, 1995.
f Traded to Baltimore Orioles with outfielder Pete Incaviglia for pitcher Kevin Gallagher and infielder Pedro Santana, August 27, 1996.
g Filed for free agency, October 27, 1996.
h Signed with Los Angeles Dodgers, December 8, 1996.
i Traded to Florida Marlins with catcher Mike Piazza for outfielder Gary Sheffield, outfielder Jim Eisenreich, catcher Charles Johnson, infielder Bobby Bonilla and pitcher Manuel Barrios, May 15, 1998.
j Traded to Texas Rangers for infielder Jose Santos and pitcher Daniel DeYoung, July 31, 1998.
k Filed for free agency, October 28, 1999, signed with New York Mets, December 11, 1999.

ZULETA, JULIO ERNESTO (TAPIA)
Born, Panama City, Panama, March 28, 1975.
Bats Right. Throws Right. Height, 6 feet, 6 inches. Weight, 230 pounds.

Year	Club	Lea	Pos	G	AB	R	H	2B	3B	HR	RBI	SB	Avg
1993	Cubs	Gulf Coast	DH-C-OF	17	53	3	13	0	1	0	6	0	.245
1994	Huntington	Appal.	C	6	15	0	1	0	0	0	2	0	.067
1994	Cubs	Gulf Coast	C	30	100	11	31	1	0	0	8	5	.310
1995	Williamsprt	N.Y.-Penn.	C	30	75	9	13	3	1	0	6	0	.173
1996	Williamsprt	N.Y.-Penn.	1B	62	221	35	57	12	2	1	29	7	.258
1997	Rockford	Midwest	1B	119	430	59	124	30	5	6	77	5	.288
1998	Daytona	Fla.St.	1B	94	366	69	126	25	1	16	86	6	.344
1998	West Tenn	Southern	1B	40	139	18	41	9	0	2	20	0	.295
1999	West Tenn	Southern	1B	133	482	75	142	37	4	21	97	4	.295
2000	Iowa	P.C.	1B	107	392	76	122	25	1	26	94	5	.311
2000	Chicago	N.L.	1B-OF	30	68	13	20	8	0	3	12	0	.294

ABBOTT, PAUL DAVID

Born, Van Nuys, California, September 15, 1967.
Bats Right. Throws Right. Height, 6 feet, 3 inches. Weight, 185 pounds.

Year	Club	Lea	G	IP	W	L	Pct	SO	BB	H	ERA	SAVES
1985	Elizabethtn	Appal.	10	35	1	5	.167	34	32	33	6.94	0
1986	Kenosha	Midwest	25	98	6	10	.375	73	73	102	4.50	0
1987	Kenosha	Midwest	26	145⅓	13	6	.684	138	103	102	3.65	0
1988	Visalia	California	28	172⅓	11	9	.550	205	143	141	4.18	0
1989	Orlando	Southern	17	90⅔	9	3	.750	102	48	71	4.37	0
1990	Portland	P.C.	23	128⅓	5	14	.263	129	82	110	4.56	0
1990	Minnesota	A.L.	7	34⅔	0	5	.000	25	28	37	5.97	0
1991	Portland	P.C.	8	44	2	3	.400	40	28	36	3.89	0
1991	Minnesota	A.L.	15	47⅓	3	1	.750	43	36	38	4.75	0
1992	Portland	P.C.	7	46⅓	4	1	.800	46	31	30	2.33	0
1992	Minnesota	A.L.	6	11	0	0	.000	13	5	12	3.27	0
1993	Cleveland	A.L.	5	18⅓	0	1	.000	7	11	19	6.38	0
1993	Charlotte	Int.	4	19	0	1	.000	12	7	25	6.63	0
1993	Canton-Akrn a-b	Eastern	13	75⅓	4	5	.444	86	28	72	4.06	0
1994	Omaha	A.A.	15	57⅓	4	1	.800	48	45	57	4.87	0
1995	Iowa c-d	A.A.	46	115⅓	7	7	.500	127	64	104	3.67	0
1996	Las Vegas	P.C.	28	28	4	2	.667	37	12	27	4.18	7
1997	Mariners	Arizona	3	9⅔	0	0	.000	13	7	0	0.93	0
1997	Tacoma e	P.C.	17	93⅔	8	4	.667	117	29	80	4.13	0
1998	Mariners	Arizona	1	3	0	0	.000	6	0	1	0.00	0
1998	Tacoma	P.C.	3	15	1	0	1.000	20	5	9	1.20	0
1998	Seattle f-g	A.L.	4	24⅔	3	1	.750	22	10	24	4.01	0
1999	Tacoma	P.C.	2	14	1	1	.500	10	4	21	6.43	0
1999	Seattle	A.L.	25	72⅔	6	2	.750	68	32	50	3.10	0
2000	Seattle	A.L.	35	179	9	7	.563	100	80	164	4.22	0
Major League Totals	7 Yrs.		97	387⅔	21	17	.553	278	202	344	4.29	0
Division Series												
2000	Seattle	A.L.	1	5⅔	1	0	1.000	1	3	5	1.59	0
Championship Series												
2000	Seattle	A.L.	1	5	0	1	.000	3	3	3	5.40	0

a Released by Minnesota Twins, March 2, 1993, signed with Cleveland Indians, March 27, 1993.
b Filed for free agency, October 15, 1993, signed with Kansas City Royals organization, November 21, 1993.
c Released by Kansas City Royals, June 30, 1994, signed with Chicago Cubs organization, March 17, 1995.
d Filed for free agency, October 16, 1995, signed with San Diego Padres organization, November 29, 1995.
e Filed for free agency, October 15, 1996, signed with Seattle Mariners organization, January 9, 1997.
f Filed for free agency, October 17, 1997, re-signed with Seattle Mariners organization, January 15, 1998.
g Released by Seattle Mariners, December 14, 1998, re-signed with Seattle Mariners organization, January 21, 1999.

ACEVEDO, JUAN CARLOS

Born, Juarez, Mexico, May 5, 1970.
Bats Right. Throws Right. Height, 6 feet, 2 inches, Weight, 195 pounds.

Year	Club	Lea	G	IP	W	L	Pct	SO	BB	H	ERA	SAVES
1992	Bend	Northwest	1	2	0	0	.000	3	1	4	13.50	0
1992	Visalia	California	12	64⅔	3	4	.429	37	33	75	5.43	0
1993	Central Valley	California	27	118⅔	9	8	.529	107	58	119	4.40	0
1994	New Haven	Eastern	26	174⅔	17	6	.739	161	38	142	2.37	0
1995	Colorado a	N.L.	17	65⅔	4	6	.400	40	20	82	6.44	0
1995	Colorado Springs	P.C.	3	14⅔	1	1	.500	7	7	18	6.14	0
1995	Norfolk	Int.	2	3	0	0	.000	2	1	0	0.00	0
1996	Norfolk	Int.	19	102⅔	4	8	.333	83	53	116	5.96	0
1997	Norfolk	Int.	18	116⅔	6	6	.500	99	34	111	3.86	0
1997	New York	N.L.	25	47⅔	3	1	.750	33	22	52	3.59	0
1998	Memphis	P.C.	2	8⅔	0	0	.000	6	1	5	0.00	0
1998	St. Louis b-c	N.L.	50	98⅓	8	3	.727	56	29	83	2.56	15
1999	St. Louis d	N.L.	50	102⅓	6	8	.429	52	48	115	5.89	4
2000	Indianapolis	Int.	2	4	0	0	.000	4	0	3	0.00	0
2000	Milwaukee e	N.L.	62	82⅔	3	7	.300	51	31	77	3.81	0
Major League Totals	5 Yrs.		204	396⅔	24	25	.490	232	150	409	4.45	19

a Traded to New York Mets with pitcher Arnold Gooch for pitcher Bret Saberhagen and player to be named later, July 21, 1995. Colorado Rockies received pitcher David Swanson to complete trade, March 29, 1998.

b Traded to St. Louis Cardinals for pitcher Rigo Beltran, March 29, 1998.
c On disabled list from July 18 to August 16, 1998.
d Traded to Milwaukee Brewers with 2 players to be named later for infielder Fernando Vina, December 20, 1999.
e On disabled list from April 7 to April 29, 2000.

ADAMS, TERRY WAYNE

Born, Mobile, Alabama, March 6, 1973.
Bats Right. Throws Right. Height, 6 feet, 3 inches, Weight, 205 pounds.

Year	Club	Lea	G	IP	W	L	Pct	SO	BB	H	ERA	SAVES
1991 Huntington	Appal.	14	57²/₃	0	9	.000	52	62	67	5.77	0
1992 Peoria	Midwest	25	157	7	12	.368	96	86	144	4.41	0
1993 Daytona	Fla. St.	13	70²/₃	3	5	.375	35	43	78	4.97	0
1994 Daytona	Fla. St.	39	84¹/₃	9	10	.474	64	46	87	4.38	7
1995 Orlando	Southern	37	37²/₃	2	3	.400	26	16	23	1.43	19
1995 Iowa	A.A.	7	6¹/₃	0	0	.000	10	2	3	0.00	5
1995 Chicago	N.L.	18	18	1	1	.500	15	10	22	6.50	1
1996 Chicago	N.L.	69	101	3	6	.333	78	49	84	2.94	4
1997 Chicago	N.L.	74	74	2	9	.182	64	40	91	4.62	18
1998 Iowa	P.C.	3	4	0	0	.000	5	3	1	0.00	0
1998 Chicago	N.L.	63	72²/₃	7	7	.500	73	41	72	4.33	1
1999 West Tenn	Southern	2	2²/₃	0	0	.000	2	2	5	16.88	0
1999 Chicago a-b	N.L.	52	65	6	3	.667	57	28	60	4.02	13
2000 Los Angeles	N.L.	66	84¹/₃	6	9	.400	56	39	80	3.52	2
Major League Totals	6 Yrs.	342	415	25	35	.417	343	207	409	3.93	39

a On disabled list from March 26 to May 8 and June 19 to July 4, 1999.
b Traded to Los Angeles Dodgers with pitcher Chad Ricketts and player to be named later for infielder Eric Young and pitcher Ismael Valdes, December 12, 1999. Los Angeles Dodgers received pitcher Brian Stephenson to complete trade, December 16, 1999.

AGUILERA, RICHARD WARREN (RICK)

Born, San Gabriel, California, December 31, 1961.
Bats Right. Throws Right. Height, 6 feet, 5 inches. Weight, 203 pounds.

Year	Club	Lea	G	IP	W	L	Pct	SO	BB	H	ERA	SAVES
1983 Little Falls	N.Y.-Penn.	16	104	5	6	.455	84	26	*109	3.72	0
1984 Lynchburg	Carolina	13	88¹/₃	8	3	.727	101	28	72	2.34	0
1984 Jackson a	Texas	11	67	4	4	.500	71	19	68	4.57	0
1985 New York	N.L.	21	122¹/₃	10	7	.588	74	37	118	3.24	0
1985 Tidewater	Int.	11	79	6	4	.600	55	17	64	2.51	0
1986 New York	N.L.	28	141²/₃	10	7	.588	104	36	145	3.88	0
1987 Tidewater	Int.	3	13	1	1	.500	10	1	8	0.69	0
1987 New York b	N.L.	18	115	11	3	.786	77	33	124	3.60	0
1988 St. Lucie	Fla. St.	2	7	0	0	.000	5	1	8	1.29	0
1988 Tidewater	Int.	1	6	0	0	.000	4	1	1	1.50	0
1988 New York c	N.L.	11	24²/₃	0	4	.000	16	10	29	6.93	0
1989 New York d	N.L.	36	69¹/₃	6	6	.500	80	21	59	2.34	7
1989 Minnesota	A.L.	11	75²/₃	3	5	.375	57	17	71	3.21	0
1990 Minnesota	A.L.	56	65¹/₃	5	3	.625	61	19	55	2.76	32
1991 Minnesota	A.L.	63	69	4	5	.444	61	30	44	2.35	42
1992 Minnesota	A.L.	64	66²/₃	2	6	.250	52	17	60	2.84	41
1993 Minnesota	A.L.	65	72¹/₃	4	3	.571	59	14	60	3.11	34
1994 Minnesota	A.L.	44	44²/₃	1	4	.200	46	10	57	3.63	23
1995 Minnesota-Boston e-f-g	A.L.	52	55¹/₃	3	3	.500	52	13	46	2.60	32
1996 Ft. Myers h	Fla. St.	2	12	2	0	1.000	12	1	13	3.75	0
1996 Minnesota	A.L.	19	111¹/₃	8	6	.571	83	27	124	5.42	0
1997 Minnesota	A.L.	61	68¹/₃	5	4	.556	68	22	65	3.82	26
1998 Minnesota	A.L.	68	74¹/₃	4	9	.308	57	15	75	4.24	38
1999 Minnesota	A.L.	17	21¹/₃	3	1	.750	13	2	10	1.27	6
1999 Chicago i-j	N.L.	44	46¹/₃	6	3	.667	32	10	44	3.69	8
2000 Chicago k-l	N.L.	54	47²/₃	1	2	.333	38	18	47	4.91	29
Major League Totals	16 Yrs.	732	1291¹/₃	86	81	.515	1030	351	1233	3.57	318
Division Series											
1995 Boston	A.L.	1	0²/₃	0	0	.000	1	0	3	13.50	0
Championship Series											
1986 New York	N.L.	2	5	0	0	.000	2	2	2	0.00	0
1988 New York	N.L.	3	7	0	0	.000	4	2	1	1.29	0
1991 Minnesota	A.L.	3	3¹/₃	0	0	.000	3	0	1	0.00	3
Championship Series Totals	8	15¹/₃	0	0	.000	9	4	6	0.59	3

189

Year	Club	Lea	G	IP	W	L	Pct	SO	BB	H	ERA	SAVES
	World Series Record											
1986	New York	N.L.	2	3	1	0	1.000	4	1	8	12.00	0
1991	Minnesota	A.L.	4	5	1	1	.500	3	1	6	1.80	2
World Series Totals		.5		8	2	1	.667	7	2	14	5.63	2

a On disabled list from September 3 to September 14, 1984.
b On disabled list from May 30 to August 24, 1987.
c On disabled list from April 19 to June 19 and July 12 to September 7, 1988.
d Traded to Minnesota Twins with pitchers Dave West, Tim Drummond and Kevin Tapani and player to be named for pitcher Frank Viola, July 31; Minnesota acquired pitcher Jack Savage to complete trade, October 16, 1989.
e Traded to Boston Red Sox for pitcher Frank Rodriguez and player to be named later, July 6, 1995.
f Minnesota Twins received outfielder Jermane Johnson to complete trade, October 11, 1995.
g Filed for free agency, November 12, 1995; signed with Minnesota Twins, December 11, 1995.
h On disabled list from April 1 to April 20 and April 20 to June 11, 1996.
i Traded to Chicago Cubs with pitcher Scott Downs for pitcher Jason Ryan and pitcher Kyle Lohse, May 21, 1999.
j On disabled list from August 1 to August 25, 1999.
k On disabled list from September 18 to October 10, 2000.
l Filed for free agency, October 30, 2000.

ALFONSECA, ANTONIO

Born, LaRomana, Dominican Republic, April 16, 1972.
Bats Right. Throws Right. Height, 6 feet, 5 inches. Weight, 235 pounds.

Year	Club	Lea	G	IP	W	L	Pct	SO	BB	H	ERA	SAVES
1991	Expos	Gulf Coast	11	51	3	3	.500	38	25	46	3.88	0
1992	Expos	Gulf Coast	12	66	3	4	.429	62	35	55	3.68	0
1993	Jamestown a	N.Y.-Penn.	15	33²/₃	2	2	.500	29	22	31	6.15	1
1994	Kane County	Midwest	32	86¹/₃	6	5	.545	74	21	78	4.07	0
1995	Portland b	Eastern	19	96¹/₃	9	3	.750	75	42	81	3.64	0
1996	Charlotte c	Int.	14	71²/₃	4	4	.500	51	22	86	5.53	1
1997	Charlotte	Int.	46	58¹/₃	7	2	.778	45	20	58	4.32	7
1997	Florida	N.L.	17	25²/₃	1	3	.250	19	10	36	4.91	0
1998	Florida d	N.L.	58	70²/₃	4	6	.400	46	33	75	4.08	8
1999	Florida	N.L.	73	77²/₃	4	5	.444	46	29	79	3.24	21
2000	Florida	N.L.	68	70	5	6	.455	47	24	82	4.24	*45
Major League Totals	4 Yrs.		216	244	14	20	.412	158	96	272	3.95	74

	World Series Record											
1997	Florida	N.L.	3	6¹/₃	0	0	.000	5	1	6	0.00	0

a Drafted by Florida Marlins from Montreal Expos organization in Rule V draft, December 13, 1993.
b On disabled list May 15 to June 15, 1995.
c On disabled list July 12 to September 3, 1996.
d On disabled list from May 14 to May 31, 1998.

ALMANZA, ARMANDO N.

Born, ElPaso, Texas, October 26, 1972.
Bats Left. Throws Right. Height, 6 feet, 3 inches. Weight, 205 pounds.

Year	Club	Lea	G	IP	W	L	Pct	SO	BB	H	ERA	SAVES
1993	Cardinals	Arizona	20	42	4	1	.800	56	14	38	3.21	0
1993	Johnson Cty	Appal.	3	4¹/₃	1	1	.500	4	3	6	4.15	0
1994	Madison a	Midwest			INJURED - did not play							
1995	Savannah	So.Atl.	20	108	3	9	.250	72	40	108	3.92	0
1996	Peoria	Midwest	52	62	8	6	.571	67	32	50	2.76	0
1997	Pr William	Carolina	58	64²/₃	2	3	.400	83	32	38	1.67	36
1998	Arkansas	Texas	28	32²/₃	4	1	.800	46	18	27	3.31	8
1998	Memphis b-c	P.C.	31	35²/₃	3	1	.750	45	19	35	3.03	1
1999	Calgary	P.C.	15	17¹/₃	2	2	.500	20	18	29	10.90	0
1999	Portland	Eastern	10	11¹/₃	0	1	.000	20	4	5	3.97	0
1999	Florida d	N.L.	14	15²/₃	0	1	.000	20	9	8	1.72	0
2000	Florida	N.L.	67	46¹/₃	4	2	.667	46	43	38	4.86	0
Major League Totals	2 Yrs.		81	62	4	3	.571	66	52	46	4.06	0

a On disabled list from April 8 to September 1, 1994.
b On disabled list from July 10 to 21, 1998.
c Traded by St. Louis Cardinals to Florida Marlins with pitcher Braden Looper and infielder Pablo Ozuna for infielder Edgar Renteria, December 14, 1998.
d On disabled list from May 10 to June 2, 1999.

ALMANZAR, CARLOS MANUEL
Born, Santiago, Dominican Republic, November 6, 1973.
Bats Right. Throws Right. Height, 6 feet, 2 inches. Weight, 166 pounds.

Year	Club	Lea	G	IP	W	L	Pct	SO	BB	H	ERA	SAVES
1991	Toronto #1	Dominican	6	35$^{1/3}$	3	1	.750	20	11	36	2.80	0
1992	Toronto-East	Dominican	13	67	10	0	1.000	60	31	277	2.01	1
1993	Toronto	Dominican	16	69$^{1/3}$	5	2	.714	59	32	60	3.38	2
1994	Medicne Hat	Pioneer	14	84$^{2/3}$	7	4	.636	77	19	82	2.87	0
1995	Knoxville	Southern	35	126$^{1/3}$	3	12	.200	93	32	144	3.99	2
1996	Knoxville	Southern	54	94$^{2/3}$	7	8	.467	105	33	106	4.85	9
1997	Knoxville	Southern	21	25$^{2/3}$	1	1	.500	25	5	30	4.91	8
1997	Syracuse	Int.	32	51	5	1	.833	47	8	30	1.41	3
1997	Toronto	A.L.	4	3$^{1/3}$	0	1	.000	4	1	1	2.70	0
1998	Syracuse	Int.	30	50$^{2/3}$	3	6	.333	53	13	44	2.31	10
1998	Toronto a	A.L.	25	28$^{2/3}$	2	2	.500	20	8	34	5.34	0
1999	Las Vegas	P.C.	11	22$^{2/3}$	1	3	.250	18	8	32	9.53	0
1999	San Diego b	N.L.	28	37$^{1/3}$	0	0	.000	30	15	48	7.47	0
2000	Las Vegas	P.C.	4	6	0	0	.000	7	0	9	4.50	0
2000	San Diego	N.L.	62	69$^{2/3}$	4	5	.444	56	25	73	4.39	0
Major League Totals		.4 Yrs.	119	139	6	8	.429	110	49	156	5.37	0

a Traded to San Diego Padres with pitcher Woody Williams and outfielder Peter Tucci for pitcher Joey Hamilton, December 13, 1998.
b On disabled list from April 24 to May 27, 1999.

ANDERSON, BRIAN JAMES
Born, Portsmouth, Virginia, April 16, 1972.
Bats Left. Throws Left. Height, 6 feet 1 inch. Weight, 190 pounds.

Year	Club	Lea	G	IP	W	L	Pct	SO	BB	H	ERA	SAVES
1993	Midland	Texas	2	10$^{2/3}$	0	1	.000	9	0	16	3.38	0
1993	Vancouver	P.C.	2	8	0	1	.000	2	6	13	12.38	0
1993	California	A.L.	4	11$^{1/3}$	0	0	.000	4	2	11	3.97	0
1994	Lake Elsinore	California	2	12	0	1	.000	9	0	6	3.00	0
1994	California a	A.L.	18	101$^{2/3}$	7	5	.583	47	27	120	5.22	0
1995	Lake Elsinore	California	3	14	1	1	.500	13	1	10	1.93	0
1995	California b	A.L.	18	99$^{2/3}$	6	8	.429	45	30	110	5.87	0
1996	Buffalo	A.A.	19	128	11	5	.688	85	28	125	3.59	0
1996	Cleveland c	A.L.	10	51$^{1/3}$	3	1	.750	21	14	58	4.91	0
1997	Buffalo	A.A.	15	85$^{2/3}$	7	1	.875	60	15	78	3.05	0
1997	Cleveland d-e	A.L.	8	48	4	2	.667	22	11	55	4.69	0
1998	Arizona	N.L.	32	208	12	13	.480	95	24	221	4.33	0
1999	Tucson	P.C.	2	6$^{2/3}$	0	1	.000	8	1	9	5.40	0
1999	Arizona	N.L.	31	130	8	2	.800	75	28	144	4.57	1
2000	Arizona	N.L.	33	213$^{1/3}$	11	7	.611	104	39	226	4.05	0
Major League Totals		.8 Yrs.	154	863$^{1/3}$	51	38	.573	413	175	945	4.63	1

Division Series
| 1999 | Arizona | N.L. | 1 | 7 | 0 | 0 | .000 | 4 | 0 | 7 | 2.57 | 0 |

Championship Series
| 1997 | Cleveland | A.L. | 3 | 6$^{1/3}$ | 1 | 0 | 1.000 | 7 | 3 | 1 | 1.42 | 0 |

World Series Record
| 1997 | Cleveland | A.L. | 3 | 3$^{2/3}$ | 0 | 0 | .000 | 2 | 0 | 2 | 2.45 | 1 |

a On disabled list from May 7 to June 7, 1994.
b On disabled list from May 6 to June 20, 1995.
c Traded to Cleveland Indians for pitcher Jason Grimsley and pitcher Pep Harris, February 15, 1996.
d On disabled list from July 5 to August 12, 1997.
e Selected in expansion draft by Arizona Diamondbacks, November 18, 1997.

ANDERSON, JAMES DREW (JIMMY)
Born, Portsmouth, Virginia, January 22, 1976.
Bats Left. Throws Right. Height, 6 feet, 1 inch. Weight, 195 pounds.

Year	Club	Lea	G	IP	W	L	Pct	SO	BB	H	ERA	SAVES
1994	Pirates	Gulf Coast	10	56$^{1/3}$	5	1	.833	66	27	35	1.60	0
1995	Augusta	So.Atl.	14	76$^{2/3}$	4	2	.667	75	31	51	1.53	0
1995	Lynchburg	Carolina	10	52$^{1/3}$	1	5	.167	32	21	56	4.13	0
1996	Lynchburg	Carolina	11	65$^{1/3}$	5	3	.625	56	21	51	1.93	0
1996	Carolina	Southern	17	97	8	3	.727	79	44	92	3.34	0
1997	Carolina	Southern	4	24$^{2/3}$	2	1	.667	23	9	16	1.46	0
1997	Calgary	P.C.	21	103	7	6	.538	71	64	124	5.68	0
1998	Nashville a	P.C.	35	123$^{2/3}$	9	10	.474	63	72	144	5.02	0
1999	Nashville	P.C.	21	133$^{2/3}$	11	2	.846	93	41	153	3.84	0

191

Year	Club	Lea	G	IP	W	L	Pct	SO	BB	H	ERA	SAVES
1999 Pittsburgh	....	N.L.	13	29$\frac{1}{3}$	2	1	.667	13	16	25	3.99	0
2000 Nashville	....	P.C.	2	13	0	0	.000	7	4	18	4.15	0
2000 Altoona	....	Eastern	1	9	1	0	1.000	6	1	7	0.00	0
2000 Pittsburgh	....	N.L.	27	144	5	11	.313	73	58	169	5.25	0
Major League Totals	2 Yrs.		40	173$\frac{1}{3}$	7	12	.368	86	74	194	5.04	0

a On disabled list from July 5 to 12, 1998.

ANDERSON, MATTHEW JASON
Born, Louisville, Kentucky, August 17, 1976.
Bats Right. Throws Right. Height, 6 feet, 4 inches. Weight, 200 pounds.

Year	Club	Lea	G	IP	W	L	Pct	SO	BB	H	ERA	SAVES
1998 Lakeland	....	Fla.St.	17	26	1	0	1.000	34	8	18	0.69	3
1998 Jacksnville	....	Southern	13	15	1	0	1.000	11	5	7	0.60	10
1998 Detroit	....	A.L.	42	44	5	1	.833	44	31	38	3.27	4
1999 Toledo	....	Int.	24	38	0	4	.000	35	31	32	6.39	5
1999 Detroit	....	A.L.	37	38	2	1	.667	32	35	33	5.68	0
2000 Detroit	....	A.L.	69	74$\frac{1}{3}$	3	2	.600	71	45	61	4.72	1
Major League Totals	3 Yrs.		148	156$\frac{1}{3}$	10	4	.714	147	111	132	4.55	1

ANKIEL, RICHARD ALEXANDER (RICK)
Born, Fort Pierce, Florida, July 19, 1979.
Bats Left. Throws Right. Height, 6 feet, 1 inch. Weight, 210 pounds.

Year	Club	Lea	G	IP	W	L	Pct	SO	BB	H	ERA	SAVES
1998 Peoria	....	Midwest	7	35	3	0	1.000	41	12	15	2.06	0
1998 Pr William	....	Carolina	21	126	9	6	.600	181	38	91	2.79	0
1999 Arkansas	....	Texas	8	49$\frac{1}{3}$	6	0	1.000	75	16	25	0.91	0
1999 Memphis	....	P.C.	16	88$\frac{1}{3}$	7	3	.700	119	46	73	3.16	0
1999 St. Louis	....	N.L.	9	33	0	1	.000	39	14	26	3.27	1
2000 St. Louis	....	N.L.	31	175	11	7	.611	194	90	137	3.50	0
Major League Totals	2 Yrs.		40	208	11	8	.579	233	104	163	3.46	1
Division Series												
2000 St. Louis	....	N.L.	1	2$\frac{2}{3}$	0	0	.000	3	6	4	13.50	0
Championship Series												
2000 St. Louis	....	N.L.	2	1$\frac{1}{3}$	0	0	.000	2	5	1	20.25	0

APPIER, ROBERT (KEVIN)
Born, Lancaster, California, December 6, 1967.
Bats Right. Throws Right. Height, 6 feet, 2 inches. Weight, 195 pounds.

Year	Club	Lea	G	IP	W	L	Pct	SO	BB	H	ERA	SAVES
1987 Eugene	....	Northwest	15	77	5	2	.714	72	29	81	3.04	0
1988 Baseball City	....	Fla. St.	24	147$\frac{1}{3}$	10	9	.526	112	39	134	2.75	0
1988 Memphis	....	Southern	3	19$\frac{2}{3}$	2	0	1.000	18	7	11	1.83	0
1989 Omaha	....	A.A.	22	139	8	8	.500	109	42	141	3.95	0
1989 Kansas City	....	A.L.	6	21$\frac{2}{3}$	1	4	.200	10	12	34	9.14	0
1990 Omaha	....	A.A.	3	18	2	0	1.000	17	3	15	1.50	0
1990 Kansas City	....	A.L.	32	185$\frac{2}{3}$	12	8	.600	127	54	179	2.76	0
1991 Kansas City	....	A.L.	34	207$\frac{2}{3}$	13	10	.565	158	61	205	3.42	0
1992 Kansas City	....	A.L.	30	208$\frac{1}{3}$	15	8	.652	150	68	167	2.46	0
1993 Kansas City	....	A.L.	34	238$\frac{2}{3}$	18	8	.692	186	81	183	*2.56	0
1994 Kansas City a	....	A.L.	23	155	7	6	.538	145	63	137	3.83	0
1995 Kansas City b-c	....	A.L.	31	201$\frac{1}{3}$	15	10	.600	185	80	163	3.89	0
1996 Kansas City	....	A.L.	32	211$\frac{1}{3}$	14	11	.560	207	75	192	3.62	0
1997 Kansas City	....	N.L.	34	235$\frac{2}{3}$	9	13	.409	196	74	215	3.40	0
1998 Royals	....	Gulf Coast	1	3$\frac{1}{3}$	0	1	.000	2	1	3	2.70	0
1998 Lansing	....	Midwest	1	4	0	0	.000	5	0	4	2.25	0
1998 Wichita	....	Texas	1	6	0	1	.000	1	2	8	6.00	0
1998 Omaha	....	P.C.	6	32	3	2	.600	22	12	41	7.03	0
1998 Kansas City d	....	A.L.	3	15	1	2	.333	9	5	21	7.80	0
1999 Kansas City-Oakland e	....	A.L.	34	209	16	14	.533	131	84	230	5.17	0
2000 Oakland f-g	....	A.L.	31	195$\frac{1}{3}$	15	11	.577	129	*102	200	4.52	0
Major League Totals	12 Yrs.		324	2084$\frac{2}{3}$	136	105	.564	1633	759	1926	3.63	0
Division Series												
2000 Oakland	....	A.L.	2	10$\frac{1}{3}$	0	1	.000	13	6	10	3.48	0

eclared restricted free agent under Major League Baseball implemented labor proposal, December 23, 1994.
e-signed with Kansas City Royals, May 23, 1995.
n disabled list from July 16 to August 12, 1995.
n disabled list from March 31 to September 1, 1998.
raded to Oakland Athletics for pitcher Brad Rigby, pitcher Blake Stein and pitcher Jeff M. D'Amico, July 31, 1999.
n disabled list from April 25 to May 12, 2000.
led for free agency, October 31, 2000, signed with New York Mets, December 11, 2000.

ARMAS, ANTONIO JOSE (TONY)
Born, Puerto Piritu, Venezuela, April 29, 1978.
Bats Right. Throws Right. Height, 6 feet, 4 inches. Weight, 205 pounds.

Club	Lea	G	IP	W	L	Pct	SO	BB	H	ERA	SAVES
5 Yankees	Gulf Coast	5	14	0	1	.000	13	6	12	0.64	0
6 Oneonta	N.Y.-Penn.	3	15²/₃	1	1	.500	14	11	14	5.74	0
6 Yankees	Gulf Coast	8	45²/₃	4	1	.800	45	13	41	3.15	1
7 Greensboro	So.Atl.	9	51²/₃	5	2	.714	64	13	36	1.05	0
7 Tampa	Fla.St.	9	46	3	1	.750	26	16	43	3.33	0
7 Sarasota a-b	Fla.St.	3	17²/₃	2	1	.667	9	12	18	6.62	0
8 Jupiter	Fla.St.	27	153¹/₃	12	8	.600	136	59	140	2.88	0
9 Montreal	N.L.	1	6	0	1	.000	2	2	8	1.50	0
9 Harrisburg	Eastern	24	149²/₃	9	7	.563	106	55	123	2.89	0
0 Jupiter	Fla.St.	1	4²/₃	0	0	.000	8	0	4	0.00	0
0 Ottawa	Int.	4	19	1	2	.333	12	4	22	3.79	0
0 Montreal c	N.L.	17	95	7	9	.438	59	50	74	4.36	0
or League Totals . . . . 2 Yrs.		18	101	7	10	.412	61	52	82	4.19	0

raded to Boston Red Sox by New York Yankees with player to be named later for designated hitter Mike Stanley
nd infielder Randy Brown, August.13, 1997. Boston Red Sox received pitcher Jim Mecir to complete trade,
eptember 29, 1997.
ent to Montreal Expos as player to be named to complete trade for pitcher Pedro J. Martinez, December 18, 1997.
n disabled list from March 31 to April 27 and July 18 to September 3, 2000.

ARROJO, LUIS ROLANDO (ROLANDO)
Born, Santa Clara, Cuba, July 18, 1968.
Bats Right. Throws Right. Height, 6 feet, 4 inches. Weight, 215 pounds.

Club	Lea	G	IP	W	L	Pct	SO	BB	H	ERA	SAVES
7 St. Petesburg a . . .	Fla.St.	16	89¹/₃	5	6	.455	73	13	73	3.43	0
8 Tampa Bay b	A.L.	32	202	14	12	.538	152	65	195	3.56	0
9 St.Petersburg	Fla.St.	2	10	0	1	.000	10	1	11	4.50	0
9 Tampa Bay c-d	A.L.	24	140²/₃	7	12	.368	107	60	162	5.18	0
0 Colorado e	N.L.	19	101¹/₃	5	9	.357	80	46	120	6.04	0
0 Boston f	A.L.	13	71¹/₃	5	2	.714	44	22	67	5.05	0
or League Totals . . . . 3 Yrs.		88	515¹/₃	31	35	.470	383	193	544	4.70	0

layed in Cuba, 1986-1996.
n disabled list from September 21 to September 28, 1998.
n disabled list from May 25 to July 15, 1999.
raded to Colorado Rockies with infielder Aaron Ledesma for infielder Vinny Castilla, December 13, 1999.
n disabled list from April 21 to May 5, 2000.
raded to Boston Red Sox with pitcher Rick Croushore and infielder Mike Lansing for pitcher Brian Rose, pitcher
ohn Wasdin, pitcher Jeff Taglienti and infielder Jeff Frye, July 27, 2000.

ARROYO, BRONSON ANTHONY
Born, Key West, Florida, February 24, 1977.
Bats Right. Throws Right. Height, 6 feet, 5 inches. Weight, 180 pounds.

Club	Lea	G	IP	W	L	PCT	SO	BB	H	ERA	SAVES
5 Pirates	Gulf Coast	13	61¹/₃	5	4	.556	48	9	72	4.26	1
6 Augusta	So.Atl.	26	135²/₃	8	6	.571	107	36	123	3.52	0
7 Lynchburg	Carolina	24	160¹/₃	12	6	.750	121	33	154	3.31	0
8 Carolina a	Southern	23	127	9	8	.529	90	51	158	5.46	0
9 Nashville	P.C.	3	13	0	2	.000	11	10	22	10.38	0
9 Altoona	Eastern	25	153	15	4	.789	100	58	167	3.65	1
0 Nashville	P.C.	13	88²/₃	8	2	.800	52	25	82	3.65	0
0 Lynchburg	Carolina	1	7	0	0	.000	3	2	8	3.86	0
0 Pittsburgh	N.L.	20	71²/₃	2	6	.250	50	36	88	6.40	0

n disabled list from May 18 to June 7 and June 18 to July 4, 1998.

ASHBY, ANDREW JASON (ANDY)

Born, Kansas City, Missouri, July 11, 1967.
Bats Right. Throws Right. Height, 6 feet, 5 inches. Weight, 190 pounds.

Year	Club	Lea	G	IP	W	L	Pct	SO	BB	H	ERA	SAV
1986	Bend	Northwest	16	60	1	2	.333	45	34	56	4.95	
1987	Spartanburg	So. Atl.	13	64⅓	4	6	.400	52	38	73	5.60	
1987	Utica	N.Y.-Penn.	13	60	3	7	.300	51	36	56	4.05	
1988	Batavia a	N.Y.-Penn.	6	44⅔	3	1	.750	32	16	25	1.61	
1988	Spartanburg	So. Atl.	3	16⅔	1	1	.500	16	7	13	2.70	
1989	Spartanburg b	So. Atl.	17	106⅔	5	9	.357	100	49	95	2.87	
1989	Clearwater	Fla. St.	6	43⅔	1	4	.200	44	21	28	1.24	
1990	Reading	Eastern	23	139⅔	10	7	.588	94	48	134	3.42	
1991	Scranton	Int.	26	161⅓	11	11	.500	113	60	144	3.46	
1991	Philadelphia	N.L.	8	42	1	5	.167	26	19	41	6.00	
1992	Philadelphia c	N.L.	10	37	1	3	.250	24	21	42	7.54	
1992	Scranton d	Int.	7	33	0	3	.000	18	14	23	3.00	
1993	Colorado Springs	P.C.	7	41⅔	4	2	.667	35	12	45	4.10	
1993	Colorado-San Diego e	N.L.	32	123	3	10	.231	77	56	168	6.80	
1994	San Diego	N.L.	24	164⅓	6	11	.353	121	43	145	3.40	
1995	San Diego	N.L.	31	192⅔	12	10	.545	150	62	180	2.94	
1996	San Diego f	N.L.	24	150⅔	9	5	.643	85	34	147	3.23	
1997	San Diego g	N.L.	30	200⅔	9	11	.450	144	49	207	4.13	
1998	San Diego	N.L.	33	226⅔	17	9	.654	151	58	223	3.34	
1999	San Diego h-i	N.L.	31	206	14	10	.583	132	54	204	3.80	
2000	Philadelphia-Atlanta k-l-m	N.L.	31	199⅓	12	13	.480	106	61	216	4.92	
Major League Totals	10 Yrs.		254	1542⅓	84	87	.491	1016	457	1573	4.10	
Division Series												
1996	San Diego	N.L.	1	5⅓	0	0	.000	5	1	7	6.75	
1998	San Diego	N.L.	1	4	0	0	.000	4	1	6	6.75	
2000	Atlanta	N.L.	2	3⅔	0	0	.000	5	3	1	2.45	
Division Series Totals			4	13	0	0	.000	14	5	14	5.54	
Championship Series												
1998	San Diego	N.L.	2	13	0	0	.000	5	2	14	2.08	
World Series Record												
1998	San Diego	N.L.	1	2⅔	0	1	.000	1	1	10	13.50	

a On disabled list from March 31 to July 10, 1988.
b On disabled list from April 2 to April 26, 1989.
c On disabled list from April 27 to August 10, 1992.
d Selected by Colorado Rockies from Philadelphia Phillies organization in expansion draft, November 17, 1992.
e Traded to San Diego Padres to complete July 26 trade in which Colorado acquired pitchers Greg W. Harris and Bruce Hurst for catcher Brad Ausmus and pitcher Doug Bochtler for player to be named, July 28, 1993.
f On disabled list from June 6 to June 22 and June 29 to July 15 and July 27 to September 1, 1996.
g On disabled list from May 20 to June 15, 1997.
h On disabled list from June 7 to June 24, 1999.
i Traded to Philadelphia Phillies for pitcher Carlton Loewer, pitcher Steve Montgomery and pitcher Adam Eaton, November 10, 1999.
k On disabled list from June 12 to June 26, 2000.
l Traded to Atlanta Braves for pitcher Bruce Chen and pitcher Jim Osting, July 12, 2000.
m Filed for free agency, November 1, 2000, signed with Los Angeles Dodgers, December 6, 2000.

ASTACIO, PEDRO JULIO

Born, Hato Mayor, Dominican Republic, November 28, 1969.
Bats Right. Throws Right. Height, 6 feet, 2 inches. Weight, 190 pounds.

Year	Club	Lea	G	IP	W	L	Pct	SO	BB	H	ERA	SAV
1988	Santo Domingo	Dom. Sum.	8	47⅔	4	2	.667	20	18	43	2.08	
1989	Kissimmee Dodgers	Gulf C.	12	76⅔	7	3	.700	52	12	77	3.17	
1990	Vero Beach	Fla. St.	8	47	1	5	.167	41	23	54	6.32	
1990	Bakersfield	California	10	52	5	2	.714	34	15	46	2.77	
1991	Vero Beach	Fla. St.	9	59⅓	5	3	.625	45	8	44	1.67	
1991	San Antonio	Texas	19	113	4	11	.267	62	39	142	4.78	
1992	Albuquerque	P.C.	24	98⅔	6	6	.500	66	44	115	5.47	
1992	Los Angeles	N.L.	11	82	5	5	.500	43	20	80	1.98	
1993	Los Angeles	N.L.	31	186⅓	14	9	.609	122	68	165	3.57	
1994	Los Angeles	N.L.	23	149	6	8	.429	108	47	142	4.29	
1995	Los Angeles	N.L.	48	104	7	8	.467	80	29	103	4.24	
1996	Los Angeles	N.L.	35	211⅔	9	8	.529	130	67	207	3.44	
1997	Los Angeles-Col. a	N.L.	33	202½	12	10	.545	166	61	200	4.14	
1998	Colorado	N.L.	35	209⅓	13	14	.481	170	74	245	6.23	
1999	Colorado	N.L.	34	232	17	11	.607	210	75	258	5.04	
2000	Colorado	N.L.	32	196⅓	12	9	.571	193	77	217	5.27	
Major League Totals	9 Yrs.		282	1573	95	82	.537	1222	518	1617	4.44	

Year	Club	Lea	G	IP	W	L	Pct	SO	BB	H	ERA	SAVES
	Division Series											
1995 Los Angeles		N.L.	3	3⅓	0	0	.000	5	0	1	0.00	0
1996 Los Angeles		N.L.	1	1⅔	0	0	.000	1	0	0	0.00	0
Division Series Totals		4	5	0	0	.000	6	0	1	0.00	0	

a Traded to Colorado Rockies for infielder Eric Young, August 18, 1997.

AYBAR, MANUEL ANTONIO
Born, Bani, Dominican Republic, October 5, 1974.
Bats Right. Throws Right. Height, 6 feet, 1 inch. Weight, 165 pounds.

Year	Club	Lea	G	IP	W	L	Pct	SO	BB	H	ERA	SAVES
1994 Cardinals	Arizona	13	72⅓	6	1	.857	79	9	69	2.12	0	
1995 Savannah	So. Atl.	18	112⅔	3	8	.273	99	36	82	3.04	0	
1995 St. Pete	Fla. St.	9	48⅓	2	5	.286	43	16	42	3.35	0	
1996 Arkansas	Texas	20	121	8	6	.571	83	34	120	3.05	0	
1996 Louisville	A.A.	5	30⅔	2	2	.500	25	7	26	3.23	0	
1997 Louisville	A.A.	22	137	5	8	.385	114	45	131	3.48	0	
1997 St. Louis	N.L.	12	68	2	4	.333	41	29	66	4.24	0	
1998 Memphis	P.C.	13	83	10	0	1.000	63	17	62	2.60	0	
1998 St. Louis	N.L.	20	81⅓	6	6	.500	57	42	90	5.98	0	
1999 St. Louis a	N.L.	65	97	4	5	.444	74	36	104	5.47	3	
2000 Louisville	Int.	3	6⅔	0	2	.000	1	10	10	13.50	0	
2000 Colo.-Cinc.-Florida b-c-d	N.L.	54	79⅓	2	2	.500	45	35	74	4.31	0	
Major League Totals	4 Yrs.	151	325⅔	14	17	.452	217	142	334	5.06	3	

a Traded to Colorado Rockies with pitcher Jose Jimenez, pitcher Rich Croushore and infielder Brent Butler for pitcher
Darryl Kile and pitcher Dave Veres, November 16, 1999.
b Traded to Cincinnati Reds for pitcher Gabe White, April 7, 2000.
c On disabled list from July 2 to July 23, 2000.
d Traded to Florida Marlins for pitcher Jorge Cordova, July 25, 2000.

BALDWIN, JAMES JR.
Born, South Pipes, North Carolina, July 15, 1971.
Bats Right. Throws Right. Height, 6 feet, 3 inches. Weight, 210 pounds.

Year	Club	Lea	G	IP	W	L	Pct	SO	BB	H	ERA	SAVES
1990 Sarasota White Sox	Gulf C.	9	37⅓	1	6	.143	32	18	32	4.10	0	
1991 Sarasota White Sox	Gulf C.	6	34	3	1	.750	48	16	16	2.12	0	
1991 Utica	N.Y.-Penn.	7	37⅓	1	4	.200	23	27	40	5.30	0	
1992 South Bend	Midwest	21	137⅔	9	5	.643	137	45	118	2.42	0	
1992 Sarasota	Fla. St.	6	37⅔	1	2	.333	39	7	31	2.87	0	
1993 Birmingham	Southern	17	120	8	5	.615	107	43	*94	*2.25	0	
1993 Nashville	A.A.	10	69	5	4	.556	61	36	43	2.61	0	
1994 Nashville	A.A.	26	162	12	6	.667	*156	83	144	3.72	0	
1995 Chicago	A.L.	6	14⅔	0	1	.000	10	9	32	12.89	0	
1995 Nashville	A.A.	18	95⅓	5	9	.357	89	44	120	5.85	0	
1996 Nashville	A.A.	2	14	1	1	.500	15	4	5	0.64	0	
1996 Chicago	A.L.	28	169	11	6	.647	127	57	168	4.42	0	
1997 Chicago	A.L.	32	200	12	*15	.444	140	83	205	5.26	0	
1998 Chicago	A.L.	37	159	13	6	.684	108	60	176	5.32	0	
1999 Chicago	A.L.	35	199⅓	12	13	.480	123	81	219	5.10	0	
2000 Chicago	A.L.	29	178	14	7	.667	116	59	185	4.65	0	
Major League Totals	6 Yrs.	167	920	62	48	.564	624	349	985	5.09	0	
	Division Series											
2000 Chicago	A.L.	1	6	0	0	.000	2	3	3	1.50	0	

BATISTA, MIGUEL JEREZ
Born, Santo Domingo, Dominican Republic, February 19, 1971.
Bats Right. Throws Right. Height, 6 feet. Weight, 160 pounds.

Year	Club	Lea	G	IP	W	L	Pct	SO	BB	H	ERA	SAVES
1990 Expos	Gulf Coast	9	39⅓	4	3	.571	21	17	33	2.06	0	
1990 Rockford	Midwest	3	12⅓	0	1	.000	7	5	16	8.76	0	
1991 Rockford a	Midwest	23	133⅔	11	5	.688	90	57	126	4.04	0	
1992 Pittsburgh b	N.L.	1	2	0	0	.000	1	3	4	9.00	0	
1992 Wst Plm Bch	Fla. St.	24	135⅓	7	7	.500	92	54	130	3.79	0	
1993 Harrisburg	Eastern	26	141	13	5	.722	91	86	139	4.34	0	
1994 Harrisburg c-d-e	Eastern	3	11⅓	0	1	.000	5	9	8	2.38	0	

195

Year	Club	Lea	G	IP	W	L	Pct	SO	BB	H	ERA	SAVES
1995 Charlotte	Int.	34	116⅓	6	12	.333	58	60	118	4.80	0
1996 Charlotte	Int.	47	77	4	3	.571	56	39	93	5.38	4
1996 Florida f	N.L.	9	11⅓	0	0	.000	6	7	9	5.56	0
1997 Iowa	A.A.	31	122	9	4	.692	95	38	117	4.20	0
1997 Chicago g	N.L.	11	36⅓	0	5	.000	27	24	36	5.70	0
1998 Montreal	N.L.	56	135	3	5	.375	92	65	141	3.80	0
1999 Ottawa	Int.	3	8	0	1	.000	7	4	3	2.25	0
2000 Montreal i	N.L.	4	8⅓	0	1	.000	7	3	19	14.04	0
2000 Omaha	P.C.	18	28⅓	2	2	.500	27	7	35	6.04	0
2000 Kansas City j	A.L.	14	57	2	6	.250	30	34	66	7.74	0
Major League Totals ....6 Yrs.		134	384⅔	13	24	.351	258	194	421	5.24	1

a Drafted from Montreal Expos organization in Rule V draft by Pittsburgh Pirates, December 9, 1991.
b Returned to Montreal Expos by Pittsburgh Pirates, April 23, 1992.
c On disabled list April 14 to 30 and May 7 to September 26, 1994.
d Released by Montreal Expos, November 18, 1994.
e Signed as free agent by Florida Marlins organization, December 9, 1994.
f Claimed on waivers by Chicago Cubs, December 10, 1996.
g Traded to Montreal Expos for outfielder Henry Rodriguez, December 12, 1997.
h On disabled list from July 16 to August 10, 1999.
i Traded to Kansas City Royals for pitcher Brad Rigby, April 25, 2000.
j Filed for free agency, October 2, 2000, signed with Arizona Diamondbacks, November 15, 2000.

BECK, RODNEY ROY (ROD)

Born, Burbank, California, August 3, 1968.
Bats Right. Throws Right. Height, 6 feet, 1 inch. Weight, 236 pounds.

Year	Club	Lea	G	IP	W	L	Pct	SO	BB	H	ERA	SAVES
1986 Medford	Northwest	13	32⅔	1	3	.250	21	11	47	5.23	1
1987 Medford a	Northwest	17	92	5	8	.385	69	26	106	5.18	0
1988 Clinton	Midwest	28	177	12	7	.632	123	27	177	3.00	0
1989 San Jose	California	13	97⅓	11	2	*.846	88	26	91	2.40	0
1989 Shreveport	Texas	16	99	7	3	.700	74	16	108	3.55	0
1990 Shreveport	Texas	14	93	10	3	.769	71	17	85	2.23	0
1990 Phoenix	P.C.	12	76⅔	4	7	.364	43	18	100	4.93	0
1991 Phoenix	P.C.	23	52⅓	4	3	.571	38	13	56	2.02	6
1991 San Francisco	N.L.	31	52⅓	1	1	.500	38	13	53	3.78	1
1992 San Francisco	N.L.	65	92	3	3	.500	87	15	62	1.76	17
1993 San Francisco	N.L.	76	79⅓	3	1	.750	86	13	57	2.16	48
1994 San Francisco b	N.L.	48	48⅔	2	4	.333	39	13	49	2.77	28
1995 San Francisco	N.L.	60	58⅔	5	6	.455	42	21	60	4.45	33
1996 San Francisco	N.L.	63	62	0	9	.000	48	10	56	3.34	35
1997 San Francisco c-d	N.L.	73	70	7	4	.636	53	8	67	3.47	37
1998 Chicago	N.L.	*81	80⅓	3	4	.429	81	20	86	3.02	51
1999 Iowa	P.C.	2	2	0	0	.000	2	0	1	0.00	0
1999 Chicago	N.L.	31	30	2	4	.333	13	13	41	7.80	7
1999 Boston e-f	A.L.	12	14	0	1	.000	12	5	9	1.93	3
2000 Pawtucket	Int.	3	6	1	0	1.000	7	0	4	0.00	0
2000 Boston g	A.L.	34	40⅔	3	0	1.000	35	12	34	3.10	0
Major League Totals ....10 Yrs.		574	628	29	37	.439	534	143	574	3.20	260

Division Series

Year	Club	Lea	G	IP	W	L	Pct	SO	BB	H	ERA	SAVES
1997 San Francisco	N.L.	1	1⅓	0	0	.000	1	0	1	0.00	0
1998 Chicago	N.L.	1	1⅔	0	0	.000	1	2	5	16.20	0
1999 Boston	A.L.	2	2	0	0	.000	2	0	2	0.00	0
Division Series Totals		4	5	0	0	.000	4	2	8	5.40	0

Championship Series

Year	Club	Lea	G	IP	W	L	Pct	SO	BB	H	ERA	SAVES
1999 Boston	A.L.	2	0⅔	0	1	.000	1	0	2	27.00	0

a Traded by Oakland Athletics to San Francisco Giants organization for pitcher Charlie Korbel, March 23, 1988.
b On disabled list from April 6 to April 30, 1994.
c Filed for free agency, October 27, 1997.
d Signed as free agent with Chicago Cubs, January 15, 1998.
e On disabled list from May 17 to July 21, 1999.
f Traded to Boston Red Sox for pitcher Mark Guthrie and player to be named later, August 31, 1999. Chicago Cubs received infielder Cole Liniak to complete trade, September 1, 1999.
g On disabled list from March 20 to June 12 and June 28 to July 22, 2000.

BEIRNE, KEVIN PATRICK

Born, Houston, Texas, January 1, 1974.
Bats Left. Throws Right. Height, 6 feet, 4 inches. Weight, 210 pounds.

Year	Club	Lea	G	IP	W	L	Pct	SO	BB	H	ERA	SAVES
1995 White Sox	Gulf Coast		2	3²/₃	0	0	.000	3	1	2	2.45	2
1995 Bristol	Appal.		9	9	1	0	1.000	12	4	4	0.00	2
1995 Hickory	So.Atl.		3	4	0	0	.000	4	0	7	4.50	0
1996 South Bend	Midwest		26	145¹/₃	4	11	.267	110	60	153	4.15	0
1997 Winston-Sal	Carolina		13	82²/₃	4	4	.500	75	28	66	3.05	0
1997 Birmingham	Southern		13	75	6	4	.600	49	41	76	4.92	0
1998 Birmingham	Southern		26	167¹/₃	13	9	.591	153	87	142	3.44	0
1998 Calgary	P.C.		2	8	0	0	.000	6	4	12	4.50	0
1999 Charlotte a	Int.		20	113	5	5	.500	63	36	134	5.42	0
2000 Charlotte	Int.		7	33¹/₃	1	2	.333	28	7	39	3.51	0
2000 Chicago b	A.L.		29	49²/₃	1	3	.250	41	20	50	6.70	0

a On disabled list from August 6 to September 1, 1999.
b Traded to Toronto Blue Jays with pitcher Mike Sirotka, pitcher Mike Williams and outfielder Brian Simmons for pitcher David Wells and pitcher Matt DeWitt, January 14, 2001.

BELINDA, STANLEY PETER

Born, Huntington, Pennsylvania, August 6, 1966.
Bats Right. Throws Right. Height, 6 feet, 3 inches. Weight, 215 pounds.

Year	Club	Lea	G	IP	W	L	Pct	SO	BB	H	ERA	SAVES
1986 Bradenton Pirates	Gulf C.		17	20¹/₃	3	2	.600	17	2	23	2.66	7
1986 Watertown	N.Y.-Penn.		5	8	0	0	.000	5	2	5	3.38	2
1987 Macon	So. Atl.		50	82	6	4	.600	75	27	59	2.09	16
1988 Salem	Carolina		53	71²/₃	6	4	.600	63	32	54	2.76	14
1989 Harrisburg	Eastern		32	38²/₃	1	4	.200	33	25	32	2.33	13
1989 Buffalo	A.A.		19	28¹/₃	2	2	.500	28	13	13	0.95	9
1989 Pittsburgh	N.L.		8	10¹/₃	0	1	.000	10	2	13	6.10	0
1990 Buffalo	A.A.		15	23²/₃	3	1	.750	25	8	20	1.90	5
1990 Pittsburgh	N.L.		55	58¹/₃	3	4	.429	55	29	48	3.55	8
1991 Pittsburgh	N.L.		60	78¹/₃	7	5	.583	71	35	50	3.45	16
1992 Pittsburgh	N.L.		59	71¹/₃	6	4	.600	57	29	58	3.15	18
1993 Pittsburgh a	N.L.		40	42¹/₃	3	1	.750	30	11	35	3.61	19
1993 Kansas City	A.L.		23	27¹/₃	1	1	.500	25	6	30	4.28	0
1994 Kansas City b	A.L.		37	49	2	2	.500	37	24	47	5.14	1
1995 Sarasota	Fla. St.		1	2	0	0	.000	2	0	4	4.50	0
1995 Boston c-d	A.L.		63	69²/₃	8	1	.889	57	28	51	3.10	10
1996 Sarasota	Fla.St.		1	1	0	1	.000	1	1	6	45.00	0
1996 Pawtucket e	Int.		6	7²/₃	1	0	1.000	7	2	2	0.00	0
1996 Boston f-g	A.L.		31	28²/₃	2	1	.667	18	20	31	6.59	2
1997 Cincinnati	N.L.		84	99¹/₃	1	5	.167	114	33	84	3.71	1
1998 Cincinnati h	N.L.		40	61¹/₃	4	8	.333	57	28	46	3.23	1
1999 Indianapolis	Int.		10	11¹/₃	2	0	1.000	10	6	7	2.38	0
1999 Cincinnati i-j	N.L.		29	42²/₃	3	1	.750	40	18	42	5.27	2
2000 Colorado-Atlanta k-i	N.L.		56	46²/₃	1	3	.250	51	22	55	7.71	1
Major League Totals	12 Yrs.		585	685¹/₃	41	37	.526	622	285	590	4.15	79

Division Series

Year	Club	Lea	G	IP	W	L	Pct	SO	BB	H	ERA	SAVES
1995 Boston	A.L.		1	0¹/₃	0	0	.000	0	0	0	0.00	0

Championship Series

Year	Club	Lea	G	IP	W	L	Pct	SO	BB	H	ERA	SAVES
1990 Pittsburgh	N.L.		3	3²/₃	0	0	.000	4	0	3	2.45	0
1991 Pittsburgh	N.L.		3	5	1	0	1.000	4	3	0	0.00	0
1992 Pittsburgh	N.L.		2	1²/₃	0	0	.000	2	0	2	0.00	0
Championship Series Totals			8	10¹/₃	1	0	1.000	10	3	5	0.87	0

Traded to Kansas City Royals for pitchers John Lieber and Dan Miceli, July 31, 1993.
Not offered 1995 contract, December 23, 1994.
Signed with Boston Red Sox, April 9, 1995.
On disabled list from April 21 to May 6, 1995.
On disabled list from April 1 to April 6 and May 20 to July 26 and August 20 to September 30, 1996.
Filed for free agency, October 14, 1996.
Signed with Cincinnati Reds organization, December 20, 1996.
On disabled list from June 3 to July 9 and August 10 to September 28, 1998.
On disabled list from March 24 to June 25, 1999.
Traded to Colorado Rockies with outfielder Jeffrey Hammonds and cash for outfielder Dante Bichette, October 30, 1999.
Released by Colorado Rockies, July 25, 2000, signed with Atlanta Braves, July 29, 2000.
Released by Atlanta Braves, September 12, 2000.

BELL, ROBERT ALLEN (ROB)
Born, Newburgh, New York, January 17, 1977.
Bats Right. Throws Right. Height, 6 feet, 5 inches. Weight, 225 pounds.

Year	Club	Lea	G	IP	W	L	Pct	SO	BB	H	ERA	SAVES
1995 Braves	.........Gulf Coast		10	34	1	6	.143	33	14	38	6.88	0
1996 Eugene	.........Northwest		16	81	5	6	.455	74	29	89	5.11	0
1997 Macon	.............So.Atl.		27	146²/₃	14	7	.667	140	41	144	3.68	0
1998 Danville a	.........Carolina		28	178¹/₃	7	9	.438	197	46	169	3.28	0
1999 Chattanooga	.......Southern		12	72	3	6	.333	68	17	75	3.13	1
1999 GC Reds	.........Gulf Coast		2	8	0	0	.000	11	0	3	1.13	0
2000 Louisville	.............Int.		6	41	4	0	1.000	47	13	35	3.73	0
2000 Cincinnati	............N.L.		26	140¹/₃	7	8	.467	112	73	130	5.00	0

a Traded by Atlanta Braves to Cincinnati Reds with outfielder Michael Tucker and pitcher Denny Neagle for infielder Bret Boone and pitcher Mike Remlinger, November 10, 1998.

BENES, ALAN PAUL
Born, Evansville, Indiana, January 21, 1972.
Bats Right. Throws Right. Height, 6 feet, 5 inches. Weight, 215 pounds.

Year	Club	Lea	G	IP	W	L	Pct	SO	BB	H	ERA	SAVES
1993 Glens Falls	.......N.Y.-Penn.		7	37	0	4	.000	29	14	39	3.65	0
1994 Savannah	............So.Atl.		4	24¹/₃	2	0	1.000	24	7	21	1.48	0
1994 St. Pete	............Fla.St.		11	78¹/₃	7	1	.875	69	15	55	1.61	0
1994 Arkansas	.............Texas		13	87²/₃	7	2	.778	75	26	58	2.98	0
1994 Louisville	.............A.A.		2	15¹/₃	1	0	1.000	16	4	10	2.93	0
1995 Louisville	.............A.A.		11	56	4	2	.667	54	14	37	2.41	0
1995 St. Louis a	.............N.L.		3	16	1	2	.333	20	4	24	8.44	0
1996 St. Louis	.............N.L.		34	191	13	10	.565	131	87	192	4.90	0
1997 St. Louis b	.............N.L.		23	161²/₃	9	9	.500	160	68	128	2.89	0
1998 St. Louis c	.............N.L.	INJURED - did not play									
1999 Arkansas	.............Texas		2	4¹/₃	0	0	.000	0	1	6	6.23	0
1999 Potomac	.........Carolina		2	5	0	0	.000	2	4	1	1.80	0
1999 Memphis	.............P.C.		3	5²/₃	0	1	.000	3	2	8	3.18	0
1999 St. Louis d	.............N.L.		2	2	0	0	.000	2	0	2	0.00	0
2000 Memphis	.............P.C.		9	39¹/₃	1	2	.333	26	21	45	5.95	0
2000 St. Louis	.............N.L.		30	46	2	2	.500	26	23	54	5.67	0
Major League Totals	........5 Yrs.		92	416²/₃	25	23	.521	339	182	400	4.32	0
Championship Series												
1996 St. Louis	.............N.L.		2	6¹/₃	0	1	.000	5	2	3	2.84	0
2000 St. Louis	.............N.L.		1	8	1	0	1.000	5	3	6	2.25	0
Championship Series Totals	......		3	14¹/₃	1	1	.500	10	5	9	2.51	0

a On disabled list from May 3 to August 9, 1995.
b On disabled list from July 31 to September 29, 1997.
c On disabled list from March 22 to September 28, 1998.
d On disabled list from March 26 to September 5, 1999.

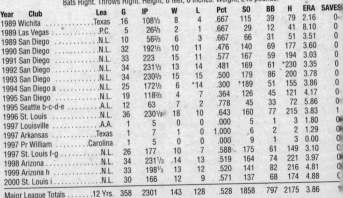

BENES, ANDREW CHARLES
Born, Evansville, Indiana, August 20, 1967.
Bats Right. Throws Right. Height, 6 feet, 6 inches. Weight, 240 pounds.

Year	Club	Lea	G	IP	W	L	Pct	SO	BB	H	ERA	SAVES
1989 Wichita	.............Texas		16	108¹/₃	8	4	.667	115	39	79	2.16	0
1989 Las Vegas	.............P.C.		5	26²/₃	2	1	.667	29	12	41	8.10	0
1989 San Diego	.............N.L.		10	56²/₃	6	3	.667	66	31	51	3.51	0
1990 San Diego	.............N.L.		32	192¹/₃	10	11	.476	140	69	177	3.60	0
1991 San Diego	.............N.L.		33	223	15	11	.577	167	59	194	3.03	0
1992 San Diego	.............N.L.		34	231¹/₃	13	14	.481	169	61	*230	3.35	0
1993 San Diego	.............N.L.		34	230²/₃	15	15	.500	179	86	200	3.78	0
1994 San Diego a	.............N.L.		25	172¹/₃	6	*14	.300	*189	51	155	3.86	0
1995 San Diego	.............N.L.		19	118²/₃	4	7	.364	126	45	121	4.17	0
1995 Seattle b-c-d-e	........A.L.		12	63	7	2	.778	45	33	72	5.86	0
1996 St. Louis	.............N.L.		36	230¹/₃	18	10	.643	160	77	215	3.83	1
1997 Louisville	.............A.A.		1	5	0	0	.000	5	1	3	1.80	0
1997 Arkansas	.............Texas		1	7	1	0	1.000	6	2	2	1.29	0
1997 Pr William	.........Carolina		1	5	0	0	.000	9	1	3	0.00	0
1997 St. Louis f-g	.............N.L.		26	177	10	7	.588	175	61	149	3.10	0
1998 Arizona	.............N.L.		34	231¹/₃	14	13	.519	164	74	221	3.97	0
1999 Arizona h	.............N.L.		33	198¹/₃	13	12	.520	141	82	216	4.81	0
2000 St. Louis i	.............N.L.		30	166	12	9	.571	137	68	174	4.88	0
Major League Totals	........12 Yrs.		358	2301	143	128	.528	1858	797	2175	3.86	1

Year	Club	Lea	G	IP	W	L	Pct	SO	BB	H	ERA	SAVES
	Division Series											
1995	Seattle	A.L.	2	11⅔	0	0	.000	8	9	10	5.40	0
1996	St. Louis	N.L.	1	7	0	0	.000	9	1	6	5.14	0
Division Series Totals			3	18⅔	0	0	.000	17	10	16	5.30	0
	Championship Series											
1995	Seattle	A.L.	1	2⅓	0	1	.000	3	2	6	23.14	0
1996	St. Louis	N.L.	3	15⅓	0	0	.000	9	3	19	5.28	0
Championship Series Totals			4	17⅔	0	1	.000	12	5	25	7.64	0

a Declared restricted free agent under Major League Baseball implemented labor proposal, December 23, 1994.
b Re-signed with San Diego Padres, April 5, 1995.
c Traded to Seattle Mariners with player to be named later for pitcher Ron Villone and outfielder Marc Newfield, July 31, 1995.
d Seattle Mariners received pitcher Greg Keagle to complete trade, September 16, 1995.
e Filed for free agency, November 12, 1995.
f On disabled list from April 1 to April 28, 1997.
g Filed for free agency, November 3, 1997. Signed with Arizona Diamondbacks, February 3, 1998.
h Filed for free agency, October 29, 1999. Signed with St. Louis Cardinals, January 7, 2000.
i On disabled list from August 15 to September 2, 2000.

BENITEZ, ARMANDO GERMAN

Born, Ramon Santana, Dominican Republic, November 3, 1972.
Bats Right. Throws Right. Height, 6 feet, 4 inches. Weight, 180 pounds.

Year	Club	Lea	G	IP	W	L	Pct	SO	BB	H	ERA	SAVES
1991	Sarasota Orioles	Gulf C.	14	36⅓	3	2	.600	33	11	35	2.72	0
1992	Bluefield	Appal.	25	31⅓	1	2	.333	37	23	35	4.31	5
1993	Albany	So. Atl.	40	53⅓	5	1	.833	83	19	31	1.52	14
1993	Frederick	Carolina	12	13⅔	3	0	1.000	29	4	7	0.66	4
1994	Bowie	Eastern	53	71⅔	8	4	.667	106	39	41	3.14	16
1994	Baltimore	A.L.	3	10	0	0	.000	14	4	8	0.90	0
1995	Rochester	Int.	17	21⅔	2	2	.500	37	7	10	1.25	8
1995	Baltimore	A.L.	44	47⅔	1	5	.167	56	37	37	5.66	2
1996	Orioles	Gulf Coast	1	2	1	0	1.000	5	0	1	0.00	0
1996	Bowie	Eastern	4	6	0	0	.000	8	0	7	4.50	0
1996	Rochester	Int.	2	4	0	0	.000	5	1	3	2.25	0
1996	Baltimore a	A.L.	18	14⅓	1	0	1.000	20	6	7	3.77	4
1997	Baltimore	A.L.	71	73⅓	4	5	.444	106	43	49	2.45	9
1998	Baltimore b	A.L.	71	68⅓	5	6	.455	87	39	48	3.82	22
1999	New York	N.L.	77	78	4	3	.571	128	41	40	1.85	22
2000	New York	N.L.	76	76	4	4	.500	106	38	39	2.61	41
Major League Totals	7 Yrs.		360	367⅔	19	23	.452	517	208	228	3.04	100
	Division Series											
1996	Baltimore	A.L.	3	4	2	0	1.000	6	2	1	2.25	0
1997	Baltimore	A.L.	3	3	0	0	.000	4	2	3	3.00	0
1999	New York	N.L.	2	2⅓	0	0	.000	2	1	2	0.00	0
2000	New York	N.L.	2	3	1	0	1.000	3	1	4	6.00	0
Division Series Totals			10	12⅓	3	0	1.000	15	6	10	2.92	0
	Championship Series											
1996	Baltimore	A.L.	3	2⅓	0	0	.000	2	3	3	7.71	1
1997	Baltimore	A.L.	4	3	0	2	.000	6	4	3	12.00	0
1999	New York	N.L.	5	6⅔	0	0	.000	9	2	3	1.35	1
2000	New York	N.L.	3	3	0	0	.000	2	2	3	0.00	1
Championship Series Totals			15	15	0	2	.000	19	11	12	4.20	3
	World Series Record											
2000	New York	N.L.	3	3	0	0	.000	2	2	3	3.00	1

a On disabled list from April 20 to August 26, 1996.
b Traded to New York Mets for catcher Charles Johnson, December 1, 1998.

BENSON, KRISTEN JAMES (KRIS)

Born, Kennesaw, Georgia, November 7, 1974.
Bats Right. Throws Right. Height, 6 feet, 4 inches. Weight, 190 pounds.

Year	Club	Lea	G	IP	W	L	Pct	SO	BB	H	ERA	SAVES
1997	Lynchburg	Carolina	10	59⅓	5	2	.714	72	13	49	2.58	0
1997	Carolina	Southern	14	68⅔	3	5	.375	66	32	81	4.98	0
1998	Nashville	P.C.	28	156	8	10	.444	129	50	162	5.37	0
1999	Pittsburgh	N.L.	31	196⅔	11	14	.440	139	83	184	4.07	0
2000	Pittsburgh	N.L.	32	217⅔	10	12	.455	184	86	206	3.85	0
Major League Totals	2 Yrs.		63	414⅓	21	26	.447	323	169	390	3.95	0

BERE, JASON PHILLIP
Born, Cambridge, Massachusetts, May 26, 1971
Bats Right. Throws Right. Height, 6 feet, 3 inches. Weight, 185 pounds.

Year	Club	Lea	G	IP	W	L	Pct	SO	BB	H	ERA	SAVES
1990	Sarasota White Sox	...Gulf C.	16	38	0	4	.000	41	19	26	2.37	1
1991	South Bend	........Midwest	27	163	9	12	.429	158	100	116	2.87	0
1992	Sarasota	...........Fla. St.	18	116	7	2	.778	106	34	84	2.41	0
1992	Birmingham	.......Southern	8	54	4	4	.500	45	20	44	3.00	0
1992	Vancouver	............P.C.	1	1	0	0	.000	2	0	2	0.00	0
1993	Nashville	..............A.A.	8	49⅓	5	1	.833	52	25	36	2.37	0
1993	Chicago	..............A.L.	24	142⅔	12	5	.706	129	81	109	3.47	0
1994	Chicago	..............A.L.	24	141⅔	12	2	*.857	127	80	119	3.81	0
1995	Nashville	..............A.A.	1	5⅓	1	0	1.000	7	2	6	3.38	0
1995	Chicago a	.............A.L.	27	137⅔	8	*15	.348	110	106	151	7.19	0
1996	White Sox	...Gulf Coast	1	3	0	1	.000	3	1	3	6.00	0
1996	Hickory	............So.Atl.	1	5	1	0	1.000	5	0	3	0.00	0
1996	Birmingham	.......Southern	1	4⅓	0	0	.000	5	4	4	4.15	0
1996	Nashville	..............A.A.	3	12⅔	0	0	.000	15	4	9	1.42	0
1996	Chicago b	..............A.L.	5	16⅔	0	1	.000	19	18	26	10.26	0
1997	White Sox	.......Gulf Coast	2	5	0	0	.000	5	0	2	0.00	0
1997	Hickory	............So. Atl.	1	3	0	0	.000	2	0	4	6.00	0
1997	Birmingham	.......Southern	2	7	0	1	.000	7	2	8	7.71	0
1997	Nashville	..............A.A.	4	19⅓	1	1	.500	13	7	23	5.59	0
1997	Chicago c	.............A.L.	6	28⅔	4	2	.667	21	17	20	4.71	0
1998	Chicago	..............A.L.	18	83⅔	3	7	.300	53	58	98	6.45	0
1998	Cincinnati d	...........N.L.	9	43⅔	3	2	.600	31	20	39	4.12	0
1999	Indianapolis	............Int.	5	17⅓	0	2	.000	8	19	25	10.19	0
1999	Louisville	..............Int.	5	26	2	1	.667	27	8	21	2.08	0
1999	Cincinnati-Milwaukee e-f-g	.N.L.	17	66⅔	5	0	1.000	47	50	79	6.07	0
2000	Milwaukee h-i	...........N.L.	20	115	6	7	.462	98	63	115	4.93	0
2000	Cleveland j	..............A.L.	11	54⅓	6	3	.667	44	26	65	6.63	0

Major League Totals	........8 Yrs.	161	830⅔	59	44	.573	679	519	821	5.28	0
Championship Series											
1993	Chicago	.............A.L.	1	2⅓	0	0	.000	3	2	5	11.57	0

a On disabled list from August 5 to August 20, 1995.
b On disabled list from April 22 to September 3 and September 14 to September 30, 1996.
c On disabled list from April 1 to August 19, 1997.
d Released by Chicago White Sox, July 16, 1998, signed with Cincinnati Reds organization, July 21, 1998.
e On disabled list from June 16 to August 3, 1999.
f Released by Cincinnati Reds, August 4, 1999, signed with Milwaukee Brewers organization, August 13, 1999.
g Filed for free agency, November 0, 1999, re-signed with Milwaukee Brewers, November 19, 1999.
h Traded to Cleveland Indians with pitcher Bob Wickman and pitcher Steve Woodard for infielder Richie Sexson, pitcher Paul Rigdon, pitcher Kane Davis and player to be named later, July 28, 2000.
i Milwaukee Brewers received infielder Marcus Scutaro to complete trade, August 30, 2000.
j Filed for free agency, October 31, 2000. signed with Chicago Cubs, December 14, 2000.

BERGMAN, SEAN FREDERICK
Born, Joliet, Illinois, April 11, 1970.
Bats Right. Throws Right. Height, 6 feet, 4 inches. Weight, 205 pounds.

Year	Club	Lea	G	IP	W	L	Pct	SO	BB	H	ERA	SAVES
1991	Niagara Falls	.....N.Y.-Penn.	15	84⅔	5	7	.417	77	42	87	4.46	0
1992	Lakeland	...........Fla. St.	13	83	5	2	.714	67	14	61	2.49	0
1992	London	...........Eastern	14	88⅓	4	7	.364	59	45	85	4.28	0
1993	Detroit	..............A.L.	9	39⅔	1	4	.200	19	23	47	5.67	0
1993	Toledo	................Int.	19	117	8	9	.471	91	53	124	4.38	0
1994	Toledo	................Int.	25	154⅔	11	8	.579	145	53	147	3.72	0
1994	Detroit	..............A.L.	3	17⅔	2	1	.667	12	7	22	5.60	0
1995	Toledo	................Int.	1	3	0	1	.000	4	0	4	6.00	0
1995	Detroit a	..............A.L.	28	135⅓	7	10	.412	86	67	169	5.12	0
1996	San Diego b	..............N.L.	41	113⅓	6	8	.429	85	33	119	4.37	0
1997	San Diego c	..........N.L.	44	99	2	4	.333	74	38	126	6.09	0
1998	Houston	.............N.L.	31	172	12	9	.571	100	42	183	3.72	0
1999	New Orleans	..........P.C.	3	6⅓	0	1	.000	2	2	9	9.95	0
1999	Houston-Atlanta d-e-f-g	.N.L.	25	105⅓	5	6	.455	44	29	135	5.21	0
2000	Minnesota h	..........A.L.	15	68	4	5	.444	35	33	111	9.66	0
2000	Calgary	...............P.C.	13	81⅔	4	3	.571	48	23	107	5.73	0

Major League Totals	........8 Yrs.	196	750⅓	39	47	.453	455	272	912	5.28	0

a On disabled list from June 26 to July 17, 1995.
b Traded to San Diego Padres with pitcher Cade Gaspar and outfielder Todd Steverson for outfielder Melvin Nieves, catcher Raul Casanova and pitcher Richie Lewis, March 22, 1996.
c Traded to Houston Astros for outfielder James Mouton, January 14, 1998.

On disabled list from June 27 to August 6, 1999.
Released by Houston Astros, August 31, 1999.
Signed with Atlanta Braves, September 5, 1999.
Claimed on waivers by Minnesota Twins, November 18, 1999.
Released by Minnesota Twins, June 20, 1999, signed with Tampa Bay Devil Rays organization, November 22, 2000.

BERNERO, ADAM G.

Born, San Jose, California, November 28, 1976.
Bats Right. Throws Right. Height, 6 feet, 4 inches. Weight, 205 pounds.

Year	Club	Lea	G	IP	W	L	Pct	SO	BB	H	ERA	SAVES
1999 West Michigan	.....Midwest		15	95^2/$_3$	8	4	.667	80	23	75	2.54	1
2000 Toledo	...............Int.		7	47^1/$_3$	3	1	.750	37	10	34	2.47	1
2000 Jacksonville	.......Southern		10	61^1/$_3$	2	5	.286	46	24	54	2.79	0
2000 Detroit	..............A.L.		12	34^1/$_3$	0	1	.000	20	13	33	4.19	0

BLAIR, WILLIAM ALLEN (WILLIE)

Born, Paintsville, Kentucky, December 18, 1965.
Bats Right. Throws Right. Height, 6 feet, 1 inch. Weight, 185 pounds.

Year	Club	Lea	G	IP	W	L	Pct	SO	BB	H	ERA	SAVES
1986 St. Catharines	....N.Y.-Penn.		21	53^2/$_3$	5	0	1.000	55	20	32	1.68	*12
1987 Dunedin	............Fla. St.		50	85^1/$_3$	2	9	.182	72	29	99	4.43	13
1988 Dunedin a	.........Fla. St.		4	6^2/$_3$	2	0	1.000	5	4	5	2.70	0
1988 Knoxville	.......Southern		34	102	5	5	.500	76	35	94	3.62	3
1989 Syracuse b	...........Int.		19	106^2/$_3$	5	6	.455	76	38	94	3.97	0
1990 Syracuse	.............Int.		3	19	0	2	.000	6	8	20	4.74	0
1990 Toronto c	.............A.L.		27	68^2/$_3$	3	5	.375	43	28	66	4.06	0
1991 Colorado Springs	.......P.C.		26	113^2/$_3$	9	6	.600	57	30	130	4.99	4
1991 Cleveland d	...........A.L.		11	36	2	3	.400	13	10	58	6.75	0
1992 Tucson	...............P.C.		21	53	4	4	.500	35	12	50	2.39	2
1992 Houston e	.........N.L.		29	78^2/$_3$	5	7	.417	48	25	74	4.00	0
1993 Colorado	............N.L.		46	146	6	10	.375	84	42	184	4.75	0
1994 Colorado f	..........N.L.		47	77^2/$_3$	0	5	.000	68	39	98	5.79	3
1995 San Diego g-h	.......N.L.		40	114	7	5	.583	83	45	112	4.34	0
1996 San Diego	..........N.L.		60	88	2	6	.250	67	29	80	4.60	1
1997 W Michigan	........Midwest		1	5	0	0	.000	7	0	1	0.00	0
1997 Toledo	...............Int.		1	7	0	0	.000	4	2	1	0.00	0
1997 Detroit i-j-k	..........A.L.		29	175	16	8	.667	90	46	186	4.17	0
1998 Arizona-New York l-m-n	.N.L.		34	175^1/$_3$	5	16	.238	92	61	188	4.98	0
1999 Detroit	.............A.L.		39	134	3	11	.214	82	44	169	6.85	0
2000 Detroit o	.............A.L.		47	156^2/$_3$	10	6	.625	74	35	185	4.88	0
Major League Totals	.......11 Yrs.		409	1250	59	82	.418	744	404	1400	4.93	4
Division Series												
1996 San Diego	............N.L.		1	2	0	0	.000	3	2	1	0.00	0

a On disabled list from April 8 to May 4, 1988.
b On disabled list from May 20 to June 28, 1989.
c Traded to Cleveland Indians for pitcher Alex Sanchez, November 6, 1990.
d Traded to Houston Astros with catcher Ed Taubensee for outfielder Kenny Lofton and infielder Dave Rohde, December 10, 1991.
e Selected by Colorado Rockies in expansion draft, November 17, 1992.
  Released, December 20, 1994.
g Signed with San Diego Padres organization, April 6, 1995.
h Not offered contract by San Diego Padres, December 20, 1995.
  On disabled list from May 5 to June 3, 1997.
  Filed for free agency, October 27, 1997.
k Signed as free agent with Arizona Diamondbacks, December 8, 1997.
  Traded to New York Mets with catcher Jorge Fabregas and player to be named later for outfielder Bernard Gilkey, pitcher Nelson Figueroa and cash, July 31, 1998.
m New York Mets received cash to complete trade, September 3, 1998.
n Traded to Detroit Tigers for infielder Joe Randa, December 4, 1998.
o Filed for free agency, November 3, 2000.

BOHANON, BRIAN EDWARD JR.

Born, Denton, Texas, August 1, 1968.
Bats Left. Throws Left. Height, 6 feet, 2 inches. Weight, 220 pounds.

Year	Club	Lea	G	IP	W	L	Pct	SO	BB	H	ERA	SAVES
1987 G.C. Rangers	.....Gulf Coast		5	21	0	2	.000	21	5	15	4.71	0
1988 Charlotte a	.........Fla. St.		2	6^2/$_3$	0	1	.000	9	5	6	5.40	0

Year	Club	Lea	G	IP	W	L	Pct	SO	BB	H	ERA	SAVES
1989 Charlotte b	Fla. St.	11	54^2/$_3$	0	3	.000	33	20	40	1.81	1
1989 Tulsa	Texas	11	73^2/$_3$	5	0	1.000	44	27	60	2.20	0
1990 Texas c	A.L.	11	34	0	3	.000	15	18	40	6.62	0
1990 Oklahoma City	A.A.	14	32	1	2	.333	22	8	35	3.66	1
1991 Charlotte	Fla. St.	2	11^2/$_3$	1	0	1.000	7	4	6	3.86	0
1991 Tulsa	Texas	2	11^2/$_3$	0	1	.000	6	11	9	2.31	0
1991 Oklahoma City	A.A.	7	46^1/$_3$	0	4	.000	37	15	49	2.91	0
1991 Texas d	A.L.	11	61^1/$_3$	4	3	.571	34	23	66	4.84	0
1992 Oklahoma City	A.A.	9	56	4	2	.667	24	15	53	2.73	0
1992 Texas e	A.L.	18	45^2/$_3$	1	1	.500	29	25	57	6.31	0
1992 Tulsa	Texas	6	28^1/$_3$	2	1	.667	25	9	25	1.27	0
1993 Oklahoma City	A.A.	2	7	0	1	.000	7	3	.7	6.43	0
1993 Texas f	A.L.	36	92^2/$_3$	4	4	.500	45	46	107	4.76	0
1994 Oklahoma City	A.A.	15	98^1/$_3$	5	10	.333	88	33	106	4.12	0
1994 Texas g	A.L.	11	37^1/$_3$	2	2	.500	26	8	51	7.23	0
1995 Detroit h-i	A.L.	52	105^2/$_3$	1	1	.500	63	41	121	5.54	1
1996 Toronto j-k	A.L.	20	22	0	1	.000	17	19	27	7.77	1
1996 Syracuse	Int.	31	58^1/$_3$	4	3	.571	38	17	56	3.86	0
1997 Norfolk	Int.	15	96	9	3	.750	84	32	88	2.63	0
1997 New York l-m-n	N.L.	19	94^1/$_3$	6	4	.600	66	34	95	3.82	0
1998 New York-Los Angeles o-p	N.L.	39	151^2/$_3$	7	11	.389	111	57	121	2.67	0
1999 Colorado	N.L.	33	197^1/$_3$	12	12	.500	120	92	236	6.20	0
2000 Colorado	N.L.	34	177	12	10	.545	98	79	181	4.68	0
Major League Totals	11 Yrs.	284	1019	49	52	.485	624	442	1102	5.00	2

a On disabled list from April 18 to end of 1988 season.
b On disabled list from March 31 to May 2, 1989.
c On disabled list from June 13 to July 19, 1990.
d On disabled list from April 8 to July 3, 1991.
e On disabled list from April 28 to May 12, 1992.
f On disabled list from June 8 to June 29, 1993.
g Not offered 1995 contract, December 23, 1994.
h Signed with Detroit Tigers organization, April 6, 1995.
i Waived by Detroit Tigers, October 16, 1995. Signed with Toronto Blue Jays organization, February 20, 1996.
j Outrighted by Toronto Blue Jays, May 31, 1996.
k Filed for free agency, October 3, 1996.
l Signed as free agent with New York Mets, December 18, 1996.
m Outrighted by New York Mets, May 6, 1997.
n Re-signed by New York Mets, December 19, 1997.
o Traded to Los Angeles Dodgers for pitcher Greg McMichael and cash, July 10, 1998.
p Filed for free agency, October 27, 1998, signed with Colorado Rockies, November 9, 1998.

BONES, RICARDO RICKY (RICKY)

Born, Salinas, Puerto Rico, April 7, 1969.
Bats Right. Throws Right. Height, 6 feet. Weight, 190 pounds.

Year	Club	Lea	G	IP	W	L	Pct	SO	BB	H	ERA	SAVES
1986 Spokane	Northwest	18	58	1	3	.250	46	29	63	5.59	0
1987 Chston-Sc	So.Atl.	26	170^1/$_3$	12	5	.706	130	45	183	3.65	0
1988 Riverside	California	25	175^1/$_3$	15	6	.714	129	64	162	3.64	0
1989 Wichita	Texas	24	136^1/$_3$	10	9	.526	88	47	162	5.74	0
1990 Wichita	Texas	21	137	6	4	.600	96	45	138	3.48	0
1990 Las Vegas	P.C.	5	36^1/$_3$	2	1	.667	25	10	45	3.47	0
1991 Las Vegas	P.C.	23	136^1/$_3$	8	6	.571	95	43	155	4.22	0
1991 San Diego	N.L.	11	54	4	6	.400	31	18	57	4.83	0
1992 Milwaukee a	A.L.	31	163^1/$_3$	9	10	.474	65	48	169	4.57	0
1993 Milwaukee	A.L.	32	203^2/$_3$	11	11	.500	63	63	222	4.86	0
1994 Milwaukee	A.L.	24	170^2/$_3$	10	9	.526	57	45	166	3.43	0
1995 Milwaukee	A.L.	32	200^1/$_3$	10	12	.455	77	83	218	4.63	0
1996 Milwaukee-New York b-c-d	A.L.	36	152	7	14	.333	63	68	184	6.22	0
1997 Cincinnati	N.L.	9	17^2/$_3$	0	1	.000	8	11	31	10.19	0
1997 Tucson	P.C.	8	42	5	0	1.000	22	8	40	2.79	0
1997 Kansas City e-f	A.L.	21	78^1/$_3$	4	7	.364	36	25	102	5.97	0
1998 Salt Lake	P.C.	8	47^1/$_3$	5	1	.833	41	19	41	3.42	0
1998 Omaha	P.C.	3	14^2/$_3$	1	2	.333	8	10	19	8.59	0
1998 Kansas City g-h-i	A.L.	32	53^1/$_3$	2	2	.500	38	24	49	3.04	1
1999 Baltimore j-k	A.L.	30	43^2/$_3$	0	3	.000	26	19	59	5.98	0
2000 Florida l-m	N.L.	56	77^1/$_3$	2	3	.400	59	27	94	4.54	0
Major League Totals	10 Yrs.	314	1214^1/$_3$	59	78	.431	523	431	1351	4.84	1

a Traded to Milwaukee Brewers with infielder Jose Valentin and outfielder Matt Mieske for infielder Gary Sheffield and pitcher Geoff Kellogg, March 27, 1992.

b Traded to New York Yankees with pitcher Graeme Lloyd and player to be named later for outfielder Gerald Williams and pitcher Bob Wickman, August 23, 1996.
c New York Yankees received infielder Gabby Martinez to complete trade, November 5, 1996.
d Filed for free agency, October 25, 1996, signed with Cincinnati Reds, December 10, 1996.
e Released by Cincinnati Reds, May 6, 1997, signed with Milwaukee Brewers organization, May 12, 1997.
f Sold to Kansas City Royals, June 26, 1997.
g Filed for free agency, November 4, 1997, signed by Minnesota Twins organization, January 6, 1998.
h Released by Minnesota Twins, May 22, 1998, signed with Kansas City Royals organization, May 26, 1998.
i Filed for free agency, October 29, 1998, signed with Baltimore Orioles, December 21, 1998.
j On disabled list from July 2 to July 17, 1999.
k Released by Baltimore Orioles, August 20, 1999, signed with Florida Marlins organization, December 22, 1999.
l On disabled list from May 6 to May 20, 2000.
m Filed for free agency, November 1, 2000.

BORBON, PEDRO FELIX

Born, Mao, Dominican Republic, November 15, 1967.
Bats Right. Throws Right. Height, 6 feet, 1 inch. Weight, 205 pounds.

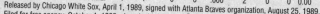

Year	Club	Lea	G	IP	W	L	Pct	SO	BB	H	ERA	SAVES
1988 White Sox a	Gulf Coast	16	74²/₃	5	3	.625	67	17	52	2.41	1
1990 Burlington	Midwest	14	97²/₃	11	3	.786	76	23	73	1.47	0
1990 Durham	Carolina	11	61¹/₃	4	5	.444	37	16	73	5.43	0
1991 Durham	Carolina	37	91	4	3	.571	79	35	85	2.27	5
1991 Greenville	Southern	4	29	0	1	.000	22	10	23	2.79	0
1992 Greenville	Southern	39	94	8	2	.800	79	42	73	3.06	3
1992 Atlanta	N.L.	2	1¹/₃	0	1	.000	1	1	2	6.75	0
1993 Richmond	Int.	52	76²/₃	5	5	.500	95	42	71	4.23	1
1993 Atlanta	N.L.	3	1²/₃	0	0	.000	2	3	3	21.60	0
1994 Richmond	Int.	59	80²/₃	3	4	.429	82	41	66	2.79	4
1995 Atlanta	N.L.	41	32	2	2	.500	33	17	29	3.09	2
1996 Greenville	Southern	1	1	0	0	.000	0	0	0	0.00	0
1996 Atlanta	N.L.	43	36	3	0	1.000	31	7	26	2.75	1
1998 Macon	So.Atl.	3	3	0	0	.000	3	1	4	9.00	0
1998 Greenville	Southern	16	19	0	2	.000	10	14	21	4.74	0
1998 Richmond b	Int.	20	23²/₃	0	1	.000	15	8	29	5.70	0
1999 Los Angeles c	N.L.	70	50²/₃	4	3	.571	33	29	39	4.09	1
2000 Toronto	A.L.	59	41²/₃	1	1	.500	29	38	45	6.48	1
Major League Totals ....6 Yrs.		218	163¹/₃	10	7	.588	129	95	144	4.41	5
Division Series											
1995 Atlanta	N.L.	1	1	0	0	.000	3	0	1	0.00	0
World Series Record											
1995 Atlanta	N.L.	1	1	0	0	.000	2	0	0	0.00	1

a Released by Chicago White Sox, April 1, 1989, signed with Atlanta Braves organization, August 25, 1989.
b Filed for free agency, October 1, 1998, signed with Los Angeles Dodgers, December 21, 1998.
c Traded to Toronto Blue Jays with outfielder Raul Mondesi for outfielder Shawn Green and infielder Jorge Nunez, November 8, 1999.

BOTTALICO, RICKY PAUL

Born, New Britain, Connecticut, August 26, 1969.
Bats Left. Throws Right. Height, 6 feet, 1 inch. Weight, 200 pounds.

Year	Club	Lea	G	IP	W	L	Pct	SO	BB	H	ERA	SAVES
1991 Martinsville	Appal.	7	33	3	2	.600	38	13	32	4.09	0
1991 Spartanburg	So. Atl.	2	15	2	0	1.000	11	2	4	0.00	0
1992 Spartanburg	So. Atl.	42	119²/₃	5	10	.333	118	56	94	2.41	13
1993 Clearwater	Fla. St.	13	19²/₃	1	0	1.000	19	5	19	2.75	4
1993 Reading	Eastern	49	72	3	3	.500	65	26	63	2.25	20
1994 Scranton	Int.	19	22¹/₃	3	1	.750	22	22	32	8.87	3
1994 Reading	Eastern	38	42²/₃	2	2	.500	51	10	29	2.53	22
1994 Philadelphia	N.L.	3	3	0	0	.000	3	1	3	0.00	0
1995 Philadelphia	N.L.	62	87²/₃	5	3	.625	87	42	50	2.46	1
1996 Philadelphia	N.L.	61	67²/₃	4	5	.444	74	23	47	3.19	34
1997 Philadelphia	N.L.	69	74	2	5	.286	89	42	68	3.65	34
1998 Scranton-WB	Int.	10	12¹/₃	0	1	.000	4	9	8	2.92	1
1998 Philadelphia a-b	N.L.	39	43¹/₃	1	5	.167	27	25	54	6.44	6
1999 St. Louis	N.L.	68	73¹/₃	3	7	.300	66	49	83	4.91	20
2000 Kansas City d	A.L.	62	72²/₃	9	6	.600	56	41	65	4.83	16
Major League Totals ....7 Yrs.		364	421²/₃	24	31	.436	402	223	370	4.01	111

a On disabled list from April 24 to July 1, 1998.

203

b Traded to St. Louis Cardinals with pitcher Garrett Stephenson for outfielder Ron Gant, pitcher Jeff Brantley, pitcher Cliff Politte and cash, November 19, 1998.
c Not offered contract, December 21, 1999, signed with Kansas City Royals, January 14, 2000.
d Filed for free agency, November 3, 2000, signed with Philadelphia Phillies, December 15, 2000.

BOTTENFIELD, KENT DENNIS

Born, Portland, Oregon, November 14, 1968.

Bats Both. Throws Right. Height, 6 feet, 3 inches. Weight, 225 pounds.

Year Club	Lea	G	IP	W	L	Pct	SO	BB	H	ERA	SAVES
1986 Bradenton Expos	Gulf C.	13	74⅓	5	6	.455	41	30	73	3.27	0
1987 Burlington	Midwest	27	161	9	13	.409	103	42	175	4.53	0
1988 West Palm Beach	Fla. St.	27	181	10	8	.556	120	47	165	3.33	0
1989 Jacksonville	Southern	25	138⅔	3	*17	.150	91	73	137	5.26	0
1990 Jacksonville	Southern	29	169	12	10	.545	121	67	158	3.41	0
1991 Indianapolis	A.A.	29	166⅓	8	15	.348	108	61	155	4.06	0
1992 Indianapolis	A.A.	25	152⅓	12	8	.600	111	58	139	3.43	0
1992 Montreal	N.L.	10	32⅓	1	2	.333	14	11	26	2.23	1
1993 Mont-Colorado a	N.L.	37	159⅔	5	10	.333	62	71	179	5.07	0
1994 Colo. Springs-Phoenix	P.C.	13	66	3	3	.500	28	22	65	3.68	0
1994 Colo.-San Fran. b-c-d	N.L.	16	26⅓	3	1	.750	15	10	33	6.15	1
1995 Toledo	Int.	27	136⅔	5	11	.313	68	55	148	4.54	1
1996 Iowa	A.A.	28	24⅔	1	2	.333	14	8	19	2.19	18
1996 Chicago	N.L.	48	61⅔	3	5	.375	33	19	59	2.63	1
1997 Chicago h-i	N.L.	64	84	2	3	.400	74	35	82	3.86	2
1998 St. Louis	N.L.	44	133⅔	4	6	.400	98	57	128	4.44	4
1999 St. Louis	N.L.	31	190⅓	18	7	.720	124	89	197	3.97	0
2000 Anaheim	A.L.	21	127⅔	7	8	.467	75	56	144	5.71	0
2000 Philadelphia j-k-l-m	N.L.	8	44	1	2	.333	31	21	41	4.50	0
Major League Totals 8 Yrs.		279	859⅔	44	44	.500	527	369	889	4.43	9

a Traded to Colorado Rockies for pitcher Butch Henry, July 17, 1993.
b On disabled list from March 27 to May 9, 1994.
c Refused assignment to minor leagues and became free agent, June 27; signed with San Francisco Giants, June 30, 1994.
d Released by San Francisco Giants, November 8, 1994.
e Signed as free agent with Detroit Tigers organization, April 3, 1995.
f Opted for free agency, October 16, 1995.
g Signed as free agent with Chicago Cubs organization, March 9, 1996.
h Released by Chicago Cubs, December 19, 1997.
i Signed with St. Louis Cardinals, January 6, 1998.
j Traded to Anaheim Angels with infielder Adam Kennedy for outfielder Jim Edmonds, March 23, 2000.
k On disabled list from June 6 to June 23, 2000.
l Traded to Philadelphia Phillies for outfielder Ron Gant, July 30, 2000.
m Filed for free agency, October 30, 2000, signed with Houston Astros, January 3, 2001.

BRANTLEY, JEFFREY HOKE (JEFF)

Born, Florence, Alabama, September 5, 1963.

Bats Right. Throws Right. Height, 5 feet, 11 inches. Weight, 190 pounds.

Year Club	Lea	G	IP	W	L	Pct	SO	BB	H	ERA	SAVES
1985 Fresno	California	14	94⅔	8	2	.800	85	37	83	3.33	0
1986 Shreveport	Texas	26	165⅔	8	10	.444	125	68	139	3.48	0
1987 Shreveport	Texas	2	11⅔	1	0	1.000	7	4	12	3.09	0
1987 Phoenix	P.C.	29	170⅓	6	11	.353	111	82	187	4.65	0
1988 Phoenix	P.C.	27	122⅔	9	5	.643	83	39	130	4.33	0
1988 San Francisco	N.L.	9	20⅔	0	1	.000	11	6	22	5.66	1
1989 Phoenix	P.C.	7	14⅓	1	1	.500	20	6	6	1.26	3
1989 San Francisco	N.L.	59	97⅓	7	1	.875	69	37	101	4.07	0
1990 San Francisco	N.L.	55	86⅔	5	3	.625	61	33	77	1.56	19
1991 San Francisco	N.L.	67	95⅓	5	2	.714	81	52	78	2.45	15
1992 San Francisco	N.L.	56	91⅔	7	7	.500	86	45	67	2.95	7
1993 San Francisco	N.L.	53	113⅔	5	6	.455	76	46	112	4.28	0
1994 Cincinnati a-b	N.L.	50	65⅓	6	6	.500	63	28	46	2.48	15
1995 Cincinnati	N.L.	56	70⅓	3	2	.600	62	20	53	2.82	28
1996 Cincinnati c	N.L.	66	71	1	2	.333	76	28	54	2.41	44
1997 Cincinnati d-e	N.L.	13	11⅔	1	1	.500	16	7	9	3.86	1
1998 Arkansas	Texas	2	1⅔	0	0	.000	3	1	0	0.00	0
1998 St. Louis f-g	N.L.	48	50⅔	0	5	.000	48	18	40	4.44	14
1999 Philadelphia h-i	N.L.	10	8⅔	1	2	.333	11	8	5	5.19.	5

Year	Club	Lea	G	IP	W	L	Pct	SO	BB	H	ERA	SAVES
2000 Scranton-WB	Int.	5	5	0	0	.000	4	1	3	3.60	0
2000 Clearwater	Fla.St.	5	6	2	0	1.000	5	3	5	3.00	0
2000 Philadelphia j-k	N.L.	55	55⅓	2	7	.222	57	29	64	5.86	23
Major League Totals	13 Yrs.	597	838⅓	43	45	.489	717	357	728	3.35	172

Division Series

Year	Club	Lea	G	IP	W	L	Pct	SO	BB	H	ERA	SAVES
1995 Cincinnati	N.L.	3	3	0	0	.000	2	0	5	6.00	1

Championship Series

Year	Club	Lea	G	IP	W	L	Pct	SO	BB	H	ERA	SAVES
1989 San Francisco	N.L.	3	5	0	0	.000	3	2	1	0.00	0
1995 Cincinnati	N.L.	2	2⅔	0	0	.000	1	2	0	0.00	0
Championship Series Totals		5	7⅔	0	0	.000	4	4	1	0.00	0

World Series Record

Year	Club	Lea	G	IP	W	L	Pct	SO	BB	H	ERA	SAVES
1989 San Francisco	N.L.	3	4⅓	0	0	.000	1	3	5	4.15	0

a Filed for free agency, December 20, 1993, signed with Cincinnati Reds, January 4, 1994.
b Filed for free agency, October 17, 1994, re-signed with Cincinnati Reds, October 28, 1994.
c On disabled list from April 1 to April 6, 1996.
d On disabled list from April 1 to April 15 and May 20 to September 29, 1997.
e Traded to St. Louis Cardinals for infielder Dmitri Young, November 10, 1997.
f On disabled list from March 31 to April 9, 1998.
g Traded to Philadelphia Phillies with outfielder Ron Gant, pitcher Cliff Politte and cash for pitcher Ricky Bottalico and pitcher Garrett Stephenson, November 19, 1998.
h On disabled list from April 29 to May 16, 1999 and May 24 to November 1, 1999.
i Filed for free agency, November 1, 1999, re-signed with Philadelphia Phillies, December 7, 1999.
j On disabled list from March 25 to May 3, 2000.
k Filed for free agency, October 31, 2000, signed with Texas Rangers organization, January 11, 2001.

BROCAIL, DOUGLAS KEITH

Born, Clearfield, Pennsylvania, May 16, 1967.
Bats Left. Throws Right. Height, 6 feet, 5 inches. Weight, 235 pounds.

Year	Club	Lea	G	IP	W	L	Pct	SO	BB	H	ERA	SAVES
1986 Spokane	Northwest	16	85	5	4	.556	77	53	85	3.81	0
1987 Charleston	So. Atl.	19	92⅓	2	6	.250	68	28	94	4.09	0
1988 Charleston	So. Atl.	22	107	8	6	.571	108	25	107	2.69	2
1989 Wichita	Texas	23	134⅔	5	9	.357	95	50	158	5.21	0
1990 Wichita a	Texas	12	52	2	2	.500	27	24	53	4.33	0
1991 Wichita	Texas	34	146⅓	10	7	.588	108	43	147	3.87	6
1992 Las Vegas	P.C.	29	172⅓	10	10	.500	103	63	187	3.97	0
1992 San Diego	N.L.	3	14	0	0	.000	15	5	17	6.43	0
1993 Las Vegas	P.C.	10	51⅓	4	2	.667	32	14	51	3.68	1
1993 San Diego b	N.L.	24	128⅓	4	13	.235	70	42	143	4.56	0
1994 Wichita	Texas	2	4	0	0	.000	2	1	3	0.00	0
1994 Las Vegas	P.C.	7	12⅔	0	0	.000	8	2	21	7.11	0
1994 San Diego c-d-e	N.L.	12	17	0	0	.000	11	5	21	5.82	0
1995 Tucson	P.C.	3	16⅓	1	0	1.000	16	4	18	3.86	0
1995 Houston	N.L.	36	77⅓	6	4	.600	39	22	87	4.19	1
1996 Jackson	Texas	2	4	0	0	.000	5	1	1	0.00	0
1996 Tucson	P.C.	5	7⅓	0	1	.000	4	1	12	7.36	0
1996 Houston f-g	N.L.	23	53	1	5	.167	34	23	58	4.58	0
1997 Detroit	A.L.	61	78	3	4	.429	60	36	74	3.23	2
1998 Detroit h	A.L.	60	62⅔	5	2	.714	55	18	47	2.73	0
1999 Detroit	A.L.	70	82	4	4	.500	78	25	60	2.52	2
2000 Detroit i-j	A.L.	49	50⅔	5	4	.556	41	14	57	4.09	0
Major League Totals	9 Yrs.	338	563	28	36	.438	403	190	564	3.87	5

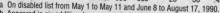

a On disabled list from May 1 to May 11 and June 8 to August 17, 1990.
b Appeared in six additional games as pinch runner.
c On disabled list from April 3 to June 29, 1994.
d Appeared in two additional games as pinch runner.
e Traded to Houston Astros with outfielders Phil Plantier and Derek Bell, shortstop Ricky Gutierrez, infielder Craig Shipley and pitcher Pedro Martinez for third baseman Ken Caminiti, shortstop Andujar Cedeño, outfielder Steve Finley, pitcher Brian Williams, first baseman Roberto Petagine and player to be named, December 28, 1994. San Diego received pitcher Sean Fesh to complete trade, May 1, 1995.
f On disabled list from May 11 to August 15, 1996.
g Traded to Detroit Tigers with outfielder Brian Hunter, infielder Orlando Miller and pitcher Todd Jones for catcher Brad Ausmus, pitcher C.J. Nitkowski, pitcher Jose Lima, pitcher Trever Miller and infielder Daryle Ward, December 10, 1996.
h On disabled list from August 9 to August 24, 1998.
i On disabled list from August 14 to August 31 and September 29 to November 6, 2000.
j Traded to Houston Astros with catcher Brad Ausmus and pitcher Nelson Cruz for pitcher Chris Holt, outfielder Roger Cedeno and catcher Mitch Meluskey, December 11, 2000.

BROCK, TERRENCE (CHRIS)
Born, Orlando, Florida, February 5, 1970.
Bats Right. Throws Right. Height, 6 feet. Weight, 175 pounds.

Year	Club	Lea	G	IP	W	L	Pct	SO	BB	H	ERA	SAVES
1992 Idaho Falls	Pioneer		15	78	6	4	.600	72	48	61	2.31	0
1993 Macon	So.Atl.		14	80	7	5	.583	92	33	61	2.70	0
1993 Durham	Carolina		12	79	5	2	.714	67	35	63	2.51	0
1994 Greenville	Southern		25	137⅓	7	6	.538	94	47	128	3.74	0
1995 Richmond	Int.		22	60	2	8	.200	43	27	68	5.40	0
1996 Richmond	Int.		26	150⅓	10	11	.476	112	61	137	4.67	0
1997 Richmond	Int.		20	118⅔	10	6	.625	83	51	97	3.34	0
1997 Atlanta a	N.L.		7	30⅔	0	0	.000	16	19	34	5.58	0
1998 Fresno	P.C.		17	115	11	3	.786	112	33	111	3.29	0
1998 San Francisco	N.L.		13	27⅔	0	0	.000	19	7	31	3.90	0
1999 San Francisco b-c	N.L.		19	106⅔	6	8	.429	76	41	124	5.48	0
2000 Philadelphia	N.L.		63	93⅓	7	8	.467	69	41	85	4.34	1
Major League Totals	4 Yrs.		102	258⅓	13	16	.448	180	108	274	4.91	1

a Filed for free agency, November 26, 1997, signed with San Francisco Giants, December 20, 1997.
b On disabled list from July 24 to October 5, 1999.
c Traded to Philadelphia Phillies for catcher Bobby Estalella, December 12, 1999.

BROWER, JAMES ROBERT (JIM)
Born, Edina, Minnesota, December 29, 1972.
Bats Right. Throws Right. Height, 6 feet, 2 inches. Weight, 205 pounds.

Year	Club	Lea	G	IP	W	L	Pct	SO	BB	H	ERA	SAVES
1994 Hudson Val	N.Y.-Penn.		4	19⅔	2	1	.667	15	6	14	3.20	0
1994 Charlstn-Sc	So.Atl.		12	78⅔	7	3	.700	84	26	52	1.72	0
1995 Charlotte	Fla.St.		27	173⅔	7	10	.412	110	62	170	3.89	0
1996 Charlotte	Fla.St.		23	145	9	8	.529	86	40	148	3.79	0
1996 Tulsa	Texas		5	33⅓	3	2	.600	16	10	35	3.78	0
1997 Tulsa	Texas		23	140	5	12	.294	103	42	156	5.21	0
1997 Okla City	A.A.		4	18⅔	2	1	.667	7	8	30	7.23	0
1998 Akron a	Eastern		23	155⅔	13	5	.722	91	38	142	3.01	0
1999 Buffalo	Int.		27	160	11	11	.500	76	59	164	4.72	0
1999 Cleveland b	A.L.		9	25⅔	3	1	.750	18	10	27	4.56	0
2000 Buffalo	Int.		16	101⅓	9	4	.692	68	24	99	3.11	0
2000 Cleveland c	A.L.		17	62	2	3	.400	32	31	80	6.24	0
Major League Totals	2 Yrs.		26	87⅔	5	4	.556	50	41	107	5.75	0

a Released by Texas Rangers, April 15, 1998, signed with Cleveland Indians organization, April 18, 1998.
b Filed for free agency, October 16, 1998, re-signed with Cleveland Indians organization, January 4, 1999.
c Traded to Cincinnati Reds with pitcher Robert Pugmire for catcher Eddie Taubensee, November 16, 2000.

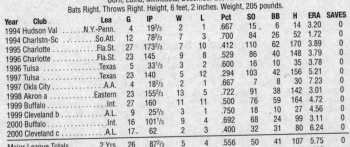

BROWN, JAMES (KEVIN)
Born, McIntyre, Georgia, March 14, 1965.
Bats Right. Throws Right. Height, 6 feet, 4 inches. Weight, 195 pounds.

Year	Club	Lea	G	IP	W	L	Pct	SO	BB	H	ERA	SAVES
1986 Sarasota Rangers	Gulf C.		3	6	0	0	.000	1	2	7	6.00	0
1986 Tulsa	Texas		3	10	0	0	.000	10	5	9	4.50	0
1986 Texas	A.L.		1	5	1	0	1.000	4	0	6	3.60	0
1987 Tulsa	Texas		8	42⅓	1	4	.200	25	18	53	7.29	0
1987 Oklahoma City	A.A.		3	24⅓	0	5	.000	9	17	32	10.73	0
1987 Charlotte	Fla. St.		6	36⅓	0	2	.000	21	17	33	2.72	0
1988 Tulsa	Texas		26	174⅓	12	10	.545	118	61	174	3.51	0
1988 Texas	A.L.		4	23⅓	1	1	.500	12	8	33	4.24	0
1989 Texas	A.L.		28	191	12	9	.571	104	70	167	3.35	0
1990 Texas a-b	A.L.		26	180	12	10	.545	88	60	175	3.60	0
1991 Texas	A.L.		33	210⅔	9	12	.429	96	90	233	4.40	0
1992 Texas	A.L.		35	*265⅔	*21	11	.656	173	76	*262	3.32	0
1993 Texas c-d	A.L.		34	233	15	12	.556	142	74	228	3.59	0
1994 Texas e	A.L.		26	170	7	9	.438	123	50	*218	4.82	0
1995 Baltimore f-g-h	A.L.		26	172⅓	10	9	.526	117	48	155	3.60	0
1996 Florida i	N.L.		32	233	17	11	.607	159	33	*187	*1.89	0
1997 Florida j-k	N.L.		33	237⅓	16	8	.667	205	66	214	2.69	0
1998 San Diego l-m	N.L.		36	257	18	7	.720	257	49	225	2.38	0
1999 Los Angeles	N.L.		35	252⅓	18	9	.667	221	59	210	3.00	0
2000 Los Angeles m	N.L.		33	230	13	6	.684	216	47	181	*2.58	0
Major League Totals	14 Yrs.		382	2660⅔	170	114	.599	1917	730	2494	3.21	0

Year	Club	Lea	G	IP	W	L	Pct	SO	BB	H	ERA	SAVES
	Division Series											
1997 Florida		N.L.	1	7	0	0	.000	5	0	4	1.29	0
1998 San Diego		N.L.	2	14²/₃	1	0	1.000	21	7	5	0.61	0
Division Series Totals			3	21²/₃	1	0	1.000	26	7	9	0.83	0
	Championship Series											
1997 Florida		N.L.	2	15	2	0	1.000	11	5	16	4.20	0
1998 San Diego		N.L.	2	10¹/₃	1	1	.500	12	4	5	2.61	0
Championship Series Totals			4	25¹/₃	3	1	.750	23	9	21	3.55	0
	World Series Record											
1997 Florida		N.L.	2	11	0	2	.000	6	5	15	8.18	0
1998 San Diego		N.L.	2	14¹/₃	0	1	.000	13	6	14	4.40	0
World Series Totals			4	25¹/₃	0	3	.000	19	11	29	6.04	0

a On disabled list from August 14 to August 29, 1990.
b Appeared in one additional game as pinch hitter.
c On disabled list from March 27 to April 11, 1993.
d Appeared in one additional game as pinch runner.
e Filed for free agency, October 21, 1994.
f Signed with Baltimore Orioles, April 8, 1995.
g Filed for free agency, November 12, 1995.
h Signed with Florida Marlins, December 22, 1995.
i On disabled list from May 13 to May 28, 1996.
j Pitched no-hit, no-run game against San Francisco Giants, winning 3-0, June 10, 1997.
k Traded to San Diego Padres for pitchers Steve Hoff and Rafael Medina and first baseman Derrek Lee, December 15, 1997.
l Filed for free agency, October 26, 1998. Signed with Los Angeles Dodgers, December 12, 1998.
m On disabled list from April 9 to April 24, 2000.

BUEHRLE, MARK A.
Born, St.Charles, Missouri, March 23, 1979.
Bats Left. Throws Right. Height, 6 feet, 2 inches. Weight, 200 pounds.

Year	Club	Lea	G	IP	W	L	PCT	SO	BB	H	ERA	SAVES
1999 Burlington		Midwest	20	98²/₃	7	4	.636	91	16	105	4.10	1
2000 Birmingham		Southern	16	118²/₃	8	4	.667	68	17	95	2.28	1
2000 Chicago		A.L.	28	51¹/₃	4	1	.800	37	19	55	4.21	0
	Division Series											
2000 Chicago		A.L.	1	0¹/₃	0	0	.000	1	0	2	0.00	0

BURBA, DAVID ALLEN
Born, Dayton, Ohio, July 7, 1966.
Bats Right. Throws Right. Height, 6 feet, 4 inches. Weight, 240 pounds.

Year	Club	Lea	G	IP	W	L	Pct	SO	BB	H	ERA	SAVES
1987 Bellingham		Northwest	5	23¹/₂	3	1	.750	24	3	20	1.93	0
1987 Salinas		California	9	54²/₃	1	6	.143	46	29	53	4.61	0
1988 San Bernardino		California	20	114	5	7	.417	102	54	106	2.68	0
1989 Williamsport		Eastern	25	156²/₃	11	7	.611	89	55	138	3.16	0
1990 Calgary a		P.C.	31	113²/₃	10	6	.625	47	45	124	4.67	2
1990 Seattle		A.L.	6	8	0	0	.000	4	2	8	4.50	0
1991 Calgary		P.C.	23	71¹/₃	6	4	.600	42	27	82	3.53	4
1991 Seattle b		A.L.	22	36²/₃	2	2	.500	16	14	34	3.68	1
1992 San Francisco		N.L.	23	70²/₃	2	7	.222	47	31	80	4.97	0
1992 Phoenix		P.C.	13	74¹/₃	5	5	.500	44	24	86	4.72	0
1993 San Francisco		N.L.	54	95¹/₃	10	3	.769	88	37	95	4.25	0
1994 San Francisco		N.L.	57	74	3	6	.333	84	45	59	4.38	0
1995 San Fran.-Cincinnati c		N.L.	52	106²/₃	10	4	.714	96	51	90	3.96	0
1996 Cincinnati		N.L.	34	195	11	13	.458	148	97	179	3.83	0
1997 Cincinnati d		N.L.	30	160	11	10	.524	131	73	157	4.72	0
1998 Cleveland e		A.L.	32	203²/₃	15	10	.600	132	69	210	4.11	0
1999 Cleveland		A.L.	34	220	15	9	.625	174	96	211	4.25	0
2000 Cleveland		A.L.	32	191¹/₃	16	6	.727	180	91	199	4.47	0
Major League Totals	11 Yrs.		376	1361¹/₃	95	70	.576	1100	606	1322	4.26	1
	Division Series											
1995 Cincinnati		N.L.	1	1	1	0	1.000	0	1	2	0.00	0
1998 Cleveland		A.L.	1	5¹/₃	1	0	1.000	4	2	4	5.06	0
1999 Cleveland		A.L.	1	4	0	0	.000	0	1	1	0.00	0
Division Series Totals			3	10¹/₃	2	0	1.000	4	4	7	2.61	0

Year	Club	Lea	G	IP	W	L	Pct	SO	BB	H	ERA	SAVES
Championship Series												
1995 Cincinnati	....	N.L.	2	3²/₃	0	0	.000	0	4	3	0.00	0
1998 Cleveland	....	A.L.	3	6	1	0	1.000	8	5	3	3.00	0
Championship Series Totals	......		5	9²/₃	1	0	1.000	8	9	6	1.86	0

a On disabled list from May 19 to June 2, 1990.
b Traded to San Francisco Giants with pitchers Bill Swift and Mike Jackson for outfielder Kevin Mitchell and pitcher Mike Remlinger, December 11, 1991.
c Traded to Cincinnati Reds with pitcher Mark Portugal and outfielder Darren Lewis for outfielder Deion Sanders, pitcher John Roper, pitcher Ricky Pickett, pitcher Scott Service and infielder David McCarty, July 21, 1995.
d On disabled list from August 7 to August 27, 1997.
e Traded to Cleveland Indians for infielder Sean Casey, March 30, 1998.

BURKETT, JOHN DAVID
Born, New Brighton, Pennsylvania, November 28, 1964.
Bats Right. Throws Right. Height, 6 feet, 2 inches. Weight, 211 pounds.

Year	Club	Lea	G	IP	W	L	Pct	SO	BB	H	ERA	SAVES
1983 Great Falls	....	Pioneer	13	50¹/₃	2	6	.250	38	30	73	6.26	0
1984 Clinton	....	Midwest	20	126²/₃	7	6	.538	83	38	120	4.33	0
1985 Fresno	....	California	20	109²/₃	7	4	.636	72	46	98	2.87	0
1986 Fresno	....	California	4	24²/₃	0	3	.000	14	8	34	5.47	0
1986 Shreveport	....	Texas	22	128²/₃	10	6	.625	73	42	99	2.66	0
1987 Shreveport	....	Texas	27	*177²/₃	*14	8	.636	126	53	181	3.34	0
1987 San Francisco	....	N.L.	3	6	0	0	000	5	3	7	4.50	0
1988 Shreveport	....	Texas	7	50²/₃	5	1	.833	34	18	33	2.13	0
1988 Phoenix	....	P.C.	21	114	5	11	.313	74	49	142	5.21	0
1989 Phoenix	....	P.C.	28	167²/₃	10	11	.476	105	59	197	5.05	0
1990 Phoenix	....	P.C.	3	23	2	1	.667	9	3	18	2.74	0
1990 San Francisco	....	N.L.	33	204	14	7	.667	118	61	201	3.79	1
1991 San Francisco	....	N.L.	36	206²/₃	12	11	.522	131	60	223	4.18	0
1992 San Francisco	....	N.L.	32	189²/₃	13	9	.591	107	45	194	3.84	0
1993 San Francisco	....	N.L.	34	231²/₃	*22	7	.759	145	40	224	3.65	0
1994 San Francisco a-b	.....	N.L.	25	159¹/₃	6	8	.429	85	36	176	3.62	0
1995 Florida c	....	N.L.	30	188¹/₃	14	14	.500	126	57	208	4.30	0
1996 Florida	....	N.L.	24	154	6	10	.375	108	42	154	4.32	0
1996 Texas d	....	A.L.	10	68²/₃	5	2	.714	47	16	75	4.06	0
1997 Okla City	....	A.A.	1	5	1	0	1.000	3	2	6	3.60	0
1997 Texas e	....	A.L.	30	189¹/₃	9	12	.429	139	30	240	4.56	0
1998 Texas	....	A.L.	32	195	9	13	.409	131	46	230	5.68	0
1999 Tulsa	....	Texas	2	6²/₃	0	1	.000	3	3	7	2.70	0
1999 Texas f-g	....	A.L.	30	147¹/₃	9	8	.529	96	46	184	5.62	0
2000 Atlanta i-j	....	N.L.	31	134¹/₃	10	6	.625	110	51	162	4.89	0
Major League Totals	....	12 Yrs.	350	2074¹/₃	129	107	.547	1348	533	2278	4.35	1
Division Series												
1996 Texas	....	A.L.	1	9	1	0	1.000	7	1	10	2.00	0
2000 Atlanta	....	N.L.	1	1¹/₃	0	0	.000	0	0	1	6.75	0
Division Series Totals	....		2	10¹/₃	1	0	1.000	7	1	11	2.61	0

a Traded to Texas Rangers for first baseman/outfielder Desi Wilson and shortstop Rich Aurelia, December 22, 1994.
b Declared restricted free agent under Major League Baseball implemented labor proposal, December 23, 1994.
c Signed with Florida Marlins, April 8, 1995.
d Traded to Texas Rangers for pitcher Ryan Dempster and player to be named later, August 8, 1996. Florida Marlins received pitcher Rick Helling to complete trade, September 3, 1996.
e On disabled list from August 5 to August 31, 1997.
f On disabled list from April 21 to May 9, 1999.
g Filed for free agency, November 1, 1999. Signed with Tampa Bay Devil Rays organization, January 17, 2000.
i Released by Tampa Bay Devil Rays, March 29, 2000, signed with Atlanta Braves, March 29, 2000.
j Filed for free agency, October 31, 2000, re-signed with Atlanta Braves, December 20, 2000.

BURNETT, ALLAN JAMES (A.J.)
Born, North Little Rock, Arkansas, January 3, 1977.
Bats Right. Throws Right. Height, 6 feet, 5 inches. Weight, 205 pounds.

Year	Club	Lea	G	IP	W	L	Pct	SO	BB	H	ERA	SAVES
1995 Mets	....	Gulf Coast	9	33²/₃	2	3	.400	26	23	27	4.28	0
1996 Kingsport	....	Appal.	12	58	4	0	1.000	68	54	31	3.88	0
1997 Mets	....	Gulf Coast	3	11¹/₃	0	1	.000	15	8	8	3.18	0
1997 Pittsfield	....	N.Y.-Penn.	9	44	3	1	.750	48	35	28	4.70	0
1998 Kane County a	......	Midwest	20	119	10	4	.714	186	45	74	1.97	0
1999 Portland	....	Eastern	26	120²/₃	6	12	.333	121	71	132	5.52	0

Year	Club	Lea	G	IP	W	L	Pct	SO	BB	H	ERA	SAVES
1999 Florida	N.L.	7	41⅓	4	2	.667	33	25	37	3.48	0
2000 Brevard County	Fla.St.	2	7⅓	0	0	.000	6	6	4	3.68	0
2000 Calgary	P.C.	1	5	0	0	.000	6	3	0	0.00	0
2000 Florida b	N.L.	13	82⅔	3	7	.300	57	44	80	4.79	0
Major League Totals ....2 Yrs.		20	124	7	9	.438	90	69	117	4.35	0

a Traded to Florida Marlins by New York Mets with pitcher Jesus Sanchez and outfielder Robert Stratton for pitcher Al Leiter and infielder Ralph Milliard, February 6, 1998.

b On disabled list from March 17 to July 19, 2000.

BYRD, PAUL GREGORY
Born, Louisville, Kentucky, December 3, 1970.
Bats Right. Throws Right. Height, 6 feet, 1 inches. Weight, 185 pounds.

Year	Club	Lea	G	IP	W	L	Pct	SO	BB	H	ERA	SAVES
1991 Kinston	Carolina	14	62⅔	4	3	.571	62	36	40	3.16	0
1992 Canton-Akron	Eastern	24	152⅓	14	6	.700	118	75	122	3.01	0
1993 Canton-Akron	Eastern	2	10	0	0	.000	8	3	7	3.60	0
1993 Charlotte	Int.	14	81	7	4	.636	54	30	80	3.89	0
1994 Canton-Akron a	Eastern	21	139⅓	5	9	.357	106	52	135	3.81	0
1994 Charlotte	Int.	9	36⅔	2	2	.500	15	11	33	3.93	1
1995 Norfolk	Int.	22	87	3	5	.375	61	21	71	2.79	6
1995 New York	N.L.	17	22	2	0	1.000	26	7	18	2.05	0
1996 Norfolk	Int.	5	7⅔	2	0	1.000	8	4	4	3.52	1
1996 New York b-c	N.L.	38	46⅔	1	2	.333	31	21	48	4.24	0
1997 Richmond	Int.	3	17	2	1	.667	14	1	14	3.18	0
1997 Atlanta	N.L.	31	53	4	4	.500	37	28	47	5.26	0
1998 Richmond	Int.	17	102⅓	5	5	.500	84	36	92	3.69	0
1998 Atlanta-Philadelphia d	N.L.	9	57	5	2	.714	39	18	45	2.68	0
1999 Philadelphia	N.L.	32	199⅔	15	11	.577	106	70	205	4.60	0
2000 Scranton-WB	Int.	3	26	2	0	1.000	10	6	20	1.73	0
2000 Philadelphia e-f	N.L.	17	83	2	9	.182	53	35	89	6.51	0
Major League Totals ....6 Yrs.		144	461⅓	29	28	.509	292	179	452	4.62	0

a Traded to New York Mets by Cleveland Indians with pitcher Dave Mlicki and pitcher Jerry DiPoto and player to be named later for outfielder Jeromy Burnitz and player Joe Roa, November 18, 1994. New York Mets received infielder Jesus Azuaje to complete trade, December 6, 1994.

b On disabled list from April 1 to June 9, 1996.

c Traded to Atlanta Braves with player to be named later for pitcher Greg McMichael, November 25, 1996. Atlanta Braves received pitcher Andy Zwirchitz to complete trade, June 1, 1997.

d Claimed on waivers by Philadelphia Phillies, August 10, 1998.

e On disabled list from July 27 to October 5, 2000.

f Filed for free agency, October 12, 2000.

CABRERA, JOSE ALBERTO
Born, Santiago, Dominican Republic, March 24, 1972.
Bats Right. Throws Right. Height, 6 feet. Weight, 200 pounds.

Year	Club	Lea	G	IP	W	L	Pct	SO	BB	H	ERA	SAVES
1991 Cleveland	Dominican	16	73⅓	6	4	.600	40	17	64	3.07	0
1992 Burlington	Appal.	13	92⅓	8	3	.727	79	18	74	1.75	0
1993 Columbus	So.Atl.	26	155⅓	11	6	.647	105	53	122	2.67	0
1994 Kinston	Carolina	24	133⅔	4	13	.235	110	43	134	4.44	0
1995 Canton-Akrn	Eastern	24	85	5	3	.625	61	21	83	3.28	0
1996 Bakersfield	California	7	41⅓	2	2	.500	52	21	40	3.92	0
1996 Kinston	Carolina	4	17⅔	1	1	.500	19	8	7	1.02	0
1996 Canton-Akrn	Eastern	15	62⅓	4	3	.571	40	17	78	5.63	0
1997 Buffalo	A.A.	5	15	3	0	1.000	11	7	8	1.20	0
1997 New Orleans	A.A.	31	46	2	2	.500	48	13	31	2.54	0
1997 Houston a	N.L.	12	15⅓	0	0	.000	18	6	6	1.17	0
1998 New Orleans	P.C.	5	5	0	0	.000	6	1	2	5.40	1
1998 Houston	N.L.	3	4⅓	0	0	.000	1	1	7	8.31	0
1999 New Orleans	P.C.	31	51	3	1	.750	41	12	34	2.82	7
1999 Houston	N.L.	26	29⅓	4	0	1.000	28	9	21	2.15	0
2000 New Orleans	P.C.	12	15⅓	0	1	.000	12	5	15	2.93	0
2000 Houston	N.L.	52	59⅓	2	3	.400	41	17	74	5.92	2
Major League Totals ....4 Yrs.		93	108⅓	6	3	.667	88	33	108	4.32	2
Division Series												
1999 Houston	N.L.	1	2	0	0	.000	6	0	2	0.00	0

a Traded by Cleveland Indians to Houston Astros for pitcher Alvin Morman, May 10, 1997.

CARPENTER, CHRISTOPHER JOHN
Born, Exeter, New Hampshire, April 27, 1975.
Bats Right. Throws Right. Height, 6 feet, 6 inches. Weight, 215 pounds.

Year	Club	Lea	G	IP	W	L	Pct	SO	BB	H	ERA	SAVES
1994 Medicne Hat	.Pioneer		15	84²/3	6	3	.667	80	39	76	2.76	0
1995 Dunedin	.Fla. St.		15	99¹/3	3	5	.375	56	50	83	2.17	0
1995 Knoxville	.Southern		12	64¹/3	3	7	.300	53	31	71	5.18	0
1996 Knoxville	.Southern		28	171¹/3	7	9	.438	150	91	161	3.94	0
1997 Syracuse	.Int.		19	120	4	9	.308	97	53	113	4.50	0
1997 Toronto	.A.L.		14	81¹/3	3	7	.300	55	37	108	5.09	0
1998 Toronto	.A.L.		33	175	12	7	.632	136	61	177	4.37	0
1999 St.Catnarines	.N.Y.-Penn.		1	4	0	0	.000	6	1	5	4.50	0
1999 Toronto a	.A.L.		24	150	9	8	.529	106	48	177	4.38	0
2000 Toronto	.A.L.		34	175¹/3	10	12	.455	113	83	204	6.26	0
Major League Totals	.4 Yrs.		105	581²/3	34	34	.500	410	229	666	5.04	0

a On disabled list from June 3 to June 28, 1999.

CARRASCO, HECTOR PACHECO PIPO (KING)
Born, San Pedro De Macoris, Dominican Republic, October 22, 1969.
Bats Right. Throws Right. Height, 6 feet, 2 inches. Weight, 175 pounds.

Year	Club	Lea	G	IP	W	L	Pct	SO	BB	H	ERA	SAVES
1988 Sarasota Mets	.Gulf C.		14	36²/3	0	2	.000	21	13	37	4.17	0
1989 Kingsport	.Appal.		12	53¹/3	1	6	.143	55	34	69	5.74	0
1990 Kingsport	.Appal.		3	6²/3	0	0	.000	5	1	8	4.05	0
1991 Pittsfield a	.N.Y.-Penn.		12	23¹/3	0	1	.000	20	21	25	5.40	1
1992 Asheville b	.So. Atl.		49	78¹/3	5	5	.500	67	47	66	2.99	8
1993 Kane County c	.Midwest		28	149	6	12	.333	127	76	153	4.11	6
1994 Cincinnati d	.N.L.		45	56¹/3	5	6	.455	41	30	42	2.24	6
1995 Cincinnati	.N.L.		64	87¹/3	2	7	.222	64	46	86	4.12	5
1996 Indianapolis	.A.A.		13	21	0	1	.000	17	13	18	2.14	0
1996 Cincinnati	.N.L.		56	74¹/3	4	3	.571	59	45	58	3.75	0
1997 Indianapols	.A.A.		3	4¹/3	0	0	.000	4	3	5	6.23	1
1997 Cincinnati e	.N.L.		38	51¹/3	1	2	.333	46	25	51	3.68	0
1997 Kansas City f	.A.L.		28	34²/3	1	6	.143	30	16	29	5.45	0
1998 Minnesota g	.A.L.		63	61²/3	4	2	.667	46	31	75	4.38	1
1999 Ft.Myers	.Fla.St.		1	2	0	0	.000	1	1	2	4.50	0
1999 Salt Lake	.P.C.		3	4¹/3	1	0	1.000	3	1	3	0.00	0
1999 Minnesota h	.A.L.		39	49	2	3	.400	35	18	48	4.96	1
2000 Minnesota-Boston i-j	.A.L.		69	78²/3	5	4	.556	64	38	90	4.69	1
Major League Totals	.7 Yrs.		402	493¹/3	24	33	.421	385	249	479	4.10	14
Championship Series												
1995 Cincinnati	.N.L.		1	1¹/3	0	0	.000	3	0	1	0.00	0

a Released by New York Mets, January 6; signed with Houston Astros organization, January 21, 1992.
b Traded by Houston Astros to Florida Marlins organization with pitcher Brian Griffiths for pitcher Tom Edens, November 17, 1992.
c Traded by Florida Marlins to Cincinnati Reds to complete March 27 trade in which Florida acquired pitcher Chris Hammond for infielder Gary Scott and player to be named, September 10, 1993.
d On disabled list from May 12 to June 1, 1994.
e Traded to Kansas City Royals with pitcher Scott Service for outfielder Jon Nunnally and outfielder Chris Stynes, July 15, 1997.
f Selected in expansion draft by Arizona Diamondbacks, November 18, 1997.
g Claimed on waivers by Minnesota Twins, March 25, 1998.
h On disabled list from April 3 to June 25, 1999.
i Traded to Boston Red Sox for outfielder Lew Ford, September 10, 2000.
j Filed for free agency, November 1, 2000.

CASTILLO, FRANK ANTHONY
Born, El Paso, Texas, April 1, 1969.
Bats Right. Throws Right. Height, 6 feet, 1 inch. Weight, 190 pounds.

Year	Club	Lea	G	IP	W	L	Pct	SO	BB	H	ERA	SAVES
1987 Wytheville	.Appal.		12	90¹/3	10	1	.909	83	21	86	2.29	0
1987 Geneva	.N.Y.-Penn.		1	6	1	0	1.000	6	1	3	0.00	0
1988 Peoria a	.Midwest		9	51	6	1	.857	58	10	25	0.71	0
1989 Winston-Sal	.Carolina		18	129¹/3	9	6	.600	114	24	118	2.51	0
1989 Charlotte	.Southern		10	68	3	4	.429	43	12	73	3.84	0
1990 Charlotte	.Southern		18	111¹/3	6	6	.500	112	27	113	3.88	0
1991 Iowa	.A.A.		4	25	3	1	.750	20	7	20	2.52	0
1991 Chicago b-c	.N.L.		18	111²/3	6	7	.462	73	33	107	4.35	0

Year	Club	Lea	G	IP	W	L	Pct	SO	BB	H	ERA	SAVES
1992 Chicago	N.L.	33	205⅓	10	11	.476	135	63	179	3.46	0
1993 Chicago	N.L.	29	141⅓	5	8	.385	84	39	162	4.84	0
1994 Daytona	Fla.St.	1	4	0	1	.000	1	0	7	4.50	0
1994 Orlando	Southern	1	7	1	0	1.000	2	1	4	1.29	0
1994 Iowa	A.A.	11	66	4	2	.667	64	10	57	3.27	0
1994 Chicago d-e	N.L.	4	23	2	1	.667	19	5	25	4.30	0
1995 Chicago	N.L.	29	188	11	10	.524	135	52	179	3.21	0
1996 Chicago	N.L.	33	182⅓	7	16	.304	139	46	209	5.28	0
1997 Chicago-Colorado f-g	N.L.	34	184⅓	12	12	.500	126	69	220	5.42	0
1998 Lakeland	Fla.St.	1	5	1	0	1.000	4	0	2	0.00	0
1998 Detroit h	A.L.	27	116	3	9	.250	81	44	150	6.83	1
1999 Nashville i-j-k	P.C.	19	119⅓	7	5	.583	90	32	139	4.68	0
2000 Toronto l-m	A.L.	25	138	10	5	.667	104	56	112	3.59	0
Major League Totals	9 Yrs.	232	1290	66	79	.455	896	407	1343	4.52	1

a On disabled list from April 1 to July 23, 1988.
b On disabled list from April 12 to June 6, 1991.
c On disabled list from August 11 to 27, 1991.
d On disabled list from March 20 to May 12, 1994.
e On disabled list from June 21 to July, 1994.
f Traded to Colorado Rockies for pitcher Matt Pool, July 15, 1997.
g Filed for free agency, October 30, 1997, signed with Detroit Tigers, December 11, 1997.
h On disabled list from March 31 to April 28, 1998.
i Filed for free agency, October 27, 1998, signed with Arizona Diamondbacks, January 12, 1999.
j Released by Arizona Diamondbacks, March 27, 1999, signed with Pittsburgh Pirates organization, April 20, 1999.
k Filed for free agency, October 15, 1999, signed with Toronto Blue Jays organization, December 21, 1999.
l On disabled list from August 14 to September 15, 2000.
m Filed for free agency, October 31, 2000, signed with Boston Red Sox, December 7, 2000.

CHEN, BRUCE KASTULO
Born, Panama City, Panama, June 19, 1977.
Bats Both. Throws Right. Height, 6 feet, 1 inch. Weight, 150 pounds.

Year	Club	Lea	G	IP	W	L	Pct	SO	BB	H	ERA	SAVES
1994 Braves	Gulf Coast	9	42⅔	1	4	.200	26	3	42	3.80	1
1995 Danville	Appal.	14	70⅓	4	4	.500	56	19	78	3.97	0
1996 Eugene	Northwest	11	35⅔	4	1	.800	55	14	23	2.27	0
1997 Macon	So.Atl.	28	146⅓	12	7	.632	182	44	120	3.51	0
1998 Greenville	Southern	24	139⅓	13	7	.650	164	48	106	3.29	0
1998 Richmond	Int.	4	24	2	1	.667	29	19	17	1.88	0
1998 Atlanta	N.L.	4	20⅓	2	0	1.000	17	9	23	3.98	0
1999 Richmond	Int.	14	78	6	3	.667	90	26	73	3.81	0
1999 Atlanta	N.L.	16	51	2	2	.500	45	27	38	5.47	0
2000 Richmond	Int.	1	6	1	0	1.000	6	1	5	0.00	0
2000 Atlanta-Philadelphia a	N.L.	37	134	7	4	.636	112	46	116	3.29	0
Major League Totals	3 Yrs.	57	205⅓	11	6	.647	174	82	177	3.90	0

a Traded to Philadelphia Phillies with pitcher Jim Osting for pitcher Andy Ashby, July 12, 2000.

CHRISTIANSEN, JASON SAMUEL
Born, Omaha, Nebraska, September 21, 1969.
Bats Right. Throws Left. Height, 6 feet, 5 inches. Weight, 230 pounds.

Year	Club	Lea	G	IP	W	L	Pct	SO	BB	H	ERA	SAVES
1991 Pirates	Gulf Coast	6	8	1	0	1.000	8	1	4	0.00	1
1991 Welland	N.Y.-Penn.	8	21⅓	0	1	.000	17	12	15	2.53	0
1992 Augusta	So. Atl.	10	20	1	0	1.000	21	8	12	1.80	2
1992 Salem	Carolina	38	50	3	1	.750	59	22	47	3.24	2
1993 Salem	Carolina	57	71⅓	1	1	.500	70	24	48	3.15	4
1993 Carolina	Southern	2	2⅔	0	0	.000	2	1	3	0.00	0
1994 Carolina	Southern	28	38⅔	2	1	.667	43	14	30	2.09	2
1994 Buffalo	A.A.	33	33⅔	3	1	.750	39	16	19	2.41	0
1995 Pittsburgh	N.L.	63	56⅓	1	3	.250	53	34	49	4.15	0
1996 Calgary	P.C.	2	11	1	0	1.000	10	1	9	3.27	0
1996 Pittsburgh	N.L.	33	44⅓	3	3	.500	38	19	56	6.70	0
1997 Carolina	Southern	8	15	0	1	.000	25	5	17	4.20	1
1997 Pittsburgh a	N.L.	39	33⅔	3	0	1.000	37	17	37	2.94	0
1998 Pittsburgh	N.L.	60	64⅔	3	3	.500	71	27	51	2.51	6
1999 Altoona	Eastern	2	3	0	0	.000	2	1	1	0.00	0
1999 Nashville	P.C.	2	2	0	0	.000	1	0	0	0.00	0
1999 Pittsburgh b	N.L.	39	37⅔	2	3	.400	35	22	26	4.06	3
2000 Pittsburgh-St. Louis c	N.L.	65	48	3	8	.273	53	27	41	5.06	1

Year	Club	Lea	G	IP	W	L	Pct	SO	BB	H	ERA	SAVES
Major League Totals ....6 Yrs.			299	284⅔	15	20	.429	287	146	260	4.17	10
Division Series												
2000 St. Louis	....	N.L.	1	0⅓	0	0	.000	0	0	0	0.00	0
Championship Series												
2000 St. Louis	....	N.L.	2	2	0	0	.000	1	0	0	0.00	0

a On disabled list from April 1 to June 28, 1997.

b On disabled list from May 7 to May 28 and July 29 to August 21 and August 23 to September 23, 1999.

c Traded to St. Louis Cardinals for infielder Jack Wilson, July 30, 2000.

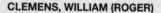

CLEMENS, WILLIAM (ROGER)

Born, Dayton, Ohio, August 4, 1962.
Bats Right. Throws Right. Height, 6 feet, 4 inches. Weight, 220 pounds.

Year	Club	Lea	G	IP	W	L	Pct	SO	BB	H	ERA	SAVES
1983 Winter Haven	....	Fla. St.	4	29	3	1	.750	36	0	22	1.24	0
1983 New Britain	....	Eastern	7	52	4	1	.800	59	12	31	1.38	0
1984 Pawtucket	....	Eastern	7	46⅔	2	3	.400	50	14	39	1.93	0
1984 Boston	....	A.L.	21	133⅓	9	4	.692	126	29	146	4.32	0
1985 Boston a	....	A.L.	15	98⅓	7	5	.583	74	37	83	3.29	0
1986 Boston	....	A.L.	33	254	*24	4	*.857	238	67	179	*2.48	0
1987 Boston c	....	A.L.	36	281⅔	*20	9	.690	256	83	248	2.97	0
1988 Boston	....	A.L.	35	264	18	12	.600	*291	62	217	2.93	0
1989 Boston	....	A.L.	35	253⅓	17	11	.607	230	93	215	3.13	0
1990 Boston d	....	A.L.	31	228⅓	21	6	.778	209	54	193	*1.93	0
1991 Boston e	....	A.L.	35	*271⅓	18	10	.643	*241	65	219	*2.62	0
1992 Boston	....	A.L.	32	246⅔	18	11	.621	208	62	203	*2.41	0
1993 Pawtucket	....	Int.	1	3⅔	0	0	.000	8	4	1	0.00	0
1993 Boston f	....	A.L.	29	191⅔	11	14	.440	160	67	175	4.46	0
1994 Boston	....	A.L.	24	170⅔	9	7	.563	168	71	124	2.85	0
1995 Sarasota	....	Fla. St.	1	4	0	0	.000	7	2	0	0.00	0
1995 Pawtucket	....	Int.	1	5	0	0	.000	5	3	1	0.00	0
1995 Boston g	....	A.L.	23	140	10	5	.667	132	60	141	4.18	0
1996 Boston h-i	....	A.L.	34	242⅔	10	13	.435	*257	106	216	3.63	0
1997 Toronto j	....	A.L.	34	*264	*21	7	.750	*292	68	204	*2.05	0
1998 Toronto k	....	A.L.	33	234⅔	*20	6	.769	*271	88	169	*2.65	0
1999 New York l-m	....	A.L.	30	187⅔	14	10	.583	163	90	185	4.60	0
2000 New York n	....	A.L.	32	204⅓	13	8	.619	188	84	184	3.70	0
Major League Totals ....17 Yrs.			512	3666⅔	260	142	.647	3504	1186	3101	3.07	0
Division Series												
1995 Boston	....	A.L.	1	7	0	0	.000	5	1	5	3.86	0
1999 New York	....	A.L.	1	7	1	0	1.000	2	2	3	0.00	0
2000 New York	....	A.L.	2	11	0	2	.000	10	8	13	8.18	0
Division Series Totals	....		4	25	1	2	.333	17	11	21	4.68	0
Championship Series												
1986 Boston	....	A.L.	3	22⅔	1	1	.500	17	7	22	4.37	0
1988 Boston	....	A.L.	1	7	0	0	.000	8	0	6	3.86	0
1990 Boston	....	A.L.	2	7⅔	0	1	.000	4	5	7	3.52	0
1999 New York	....	A.L.	1	2	0	1	.000	2	2	6	22.50	0
2000 New York	....	A.L.	1	9	1	0	1.000	15	2	1	0.00	0
Championship Series Totals	......		8	48⅓	2	3	.400	46	16	42	4.10	0
World Series Record												
1986 Boston	....	A.L.	2	11⅓	0	0	.000	11	6	9	3.18	0
1999 New York	....	A.L.	1	7⅔	1	0	1.000	4	2	4	1.17	0
2000 New York	....	A.L.	1	8	1	0	1.000	9	0	2	0.00	0
World Series Totals	....		4	27	2	0	1.000	24	8	15	1.67	0

a On disabled list from July 8 to August 3 and August 21 to end of 1985 season.

b Selected Most Valuable Player and Cy Young Award winner in American League for 1986.

c Selected Cy Young Award winner in American League for 1987.

d Suspended five games by American League for bumping and threatening umpire and refusing to leave dugout after ejection during Game Four, 1990 American League Championship Series, from April 26 to May 1, 1991.

e Selected Cy Young Award winner in American League for 1991.

f On disabled list from June 19 to July 16, 1993.

g On disabled list from April 16 to June 2, 1995.

h Filed for free agency, November 5, 1996.

i Signed with Toronto Blue Jays, December 13, 1996.

j Selected Cy Young Award Winner in American League for 1997.

k Selected Cy Young Award Winner in American League for 1998.

l Traded to New York Yankees for pitcher David Wells, pitcher Graeme Lloyd and infielder Homer Bush, February 18, 1999.

m On disabled list from April 28 to May 21, 1999.

n On disabled list from June 15 to July 1, 2000.

CLEMENT, MATTHEW PAUL

Born, McCandless Twsp., Pennsylvania, August 12, 1974.
Bats Right. Throws Right. Height, 6 feet, 3 inches. Weight, 190 pounds.

Year	Club	Lea	G	IP	W	L	Pct	SO	BB	H	ERA	SAVES
1994	Spokane	Northwest	2	7⅓	1	1	.500	4	11	8	6.14	0
1994	Padres	Arizona	13	67	8	5	.615	76	17	65	4.43	0
1995	Rancho Cuca	California	12	57⅓	3	4	.429	33	49	61	4.24	0
1995	Idaho Falls	Pioneer	14	81	6	3	.667	65	42	61	4.33	0
1996	Clinton	Midwest	16	96⅓	8	3	.727	109	52	66	2.80	0
1996	Rancho Cuca	California	11	56⅓	4	5	.444	75	26	61	5.59	0
1997	Rancho Cuca	California	14	101	6	3	.667	109	31	74	1.60	0
1997	Mobile	Southern	13	88	6	5	.545	92	32	83	2.56	0
1998	Las Vegas	P.C.	27	171⅔	10	9	.526	160	85	157	3.98	0
1998	San Diego	N.L.	4	13⅔	2	0	1.000	13	7	15	4.61	0
1999	San Diego	N.L.	31	180⅔	10	12	.455	135	86	190	4.48	0
2000	San Diego	N.L.	34	205	13	17	.433	170	*125	194	5.14	0
Major League Totals	3 Yrs.		69	399⅓	25	29	.463	318	218	399	4.82	0

COLON, BARTOLO

Born, Altamira, Dominican Republic, May 24, 1975.
Bats Right. Throws Right. Height, 6 feet. Weight, 185 pounds.

Year	Club	Lea	G	IP	W	L	Pct	SO	BB	H	ERA	SAVES
1994	Burlington	Appal.	12	66	7	4	.636	84	44	46	3.14	0
1995	Kinston	Carolina	21	128⅔	13	3	.813	152	39	91	1.96	0
1996	Canton-Akron	Eastern	13	62	2	2	.500	56	25	44	1.74	0
1996	Buffalo	A.A.	8	15	0	0	.000	19	8	16	6.00	0
1997	Buffalo	A.A.	10	56⅔	7	1	.875	54	23	45	2.22	0
1997	Cleveland	A.L.	19	94	4	7	.364	66	45	107	5.65	0
1998	Cleveland	A.L.	31	204	14	9	.609	158	79	205	3.71	0
1999	Cleveland	A.L.	32	205	18	5	.783	161	76	185	3.95	0
2000	Buffalo	Int.	1	5	1	0	1.000	4	0	6	1.80	0
2000	Cleveland a	A.L.	30	188	15	8	.652	212	98	163	3.88	0
Major League Totals	4 Yrs.		112	691	51	29	.637	597	298	660	4.09	0
Division Series												
1998	Cleveland	A.L.	1	5⅔	0	0	.000	3	3	5	1.59	0
1999	Cleveland	A.L.	2	9	0	1	.000	12	4	11	9.00	0
Division Series Totals			3	14⅔	0	1	.000	15	7	16	6.14	0
Championship Series												
1998	Cleveland	A.L.	1	9	1	0	1.000	3	4	4	1.00	0

a On disabled list from April 16 to May 11, 2000.

CONE, DAVID BRIAN

Born, Kansas City, Missouri, January 2, 1963.
Bats Left. Throws Right. Height, 6 feet, 1 inch. Weight, 190 pounds.

Year	Club	Lea	G	IP	W	L	Pct	SO	BB	H	ERA	SAVES
1981	Sarasota Royals	Gulf Coast	14	67	6	4	.600	45	33	52	2.55	0
1982	Charleston	So. Atl.	16	104⅔	9	2	.818	87	47	84	2.06	0
1982	Fort Myers	Fla. St.	10	72⅓	7	1	.875	57	25	56	2.12	0
1983	Jacksonville a	Southern					INJURED—Did Not Play					
1984	Memphis	Southern	29	178⅔	8	12	.400	110	114	162	4.28	0
1985	Omaha	A.A.	28	158⅔	9	15	.375	115	*93	157	4.65	0
1986	Omaha	A.A.	39	71	8	4	.667	63	25	60	2.79	14
1986	Kansas City b	A.L.	11	22⅔	0	0	.000	21	13	29	5.56	0
1987	Tidewater	Int.	3	11	0	1	.000	7	6	10	5.73	0
1987	New York c	N.L.	21	99⅓	5	6	.454	68	44	87	3.71	1
1988	New York	N.L.	35	231⅓	20	3	*.870	213	80	178	2.22	0
1989	New York	N.L.	34	219⅔	14	8	.636	190	74	183	3.52	0
1990	New York d	N.L.	31	211⅔	14	10	.583	*233	65	177	3.23	0
1991	New York	N.L.	34	232⅔	14	14	.500	*241	73	204	3.29	0
1992	New York e	N.L.	27	196⅔	13	7	.650	214	*82	162	2.88	0
1992	Toronto f	A.L.	8	53	4	3	.571	47	29	39	2.55	0
1993	Kansas City	A.L.	34	254	11	14	.440	191	114	205	3.33	0
1994	Kansas City g	A.L.	23	171⅔	16	5	.762	132	54	130	2.94	0
1995	Toronto-New York h-i-j	A.L.	30	*229⅓	18	8	.692	191	88	195	3.57	0
1996	Norwich	Eastern	2	10	0	0	.000	13	1	9	0.90	0
1996	New York k	A.L.	11	72	7	2	.778	71	34	50	2.88	0
1997	New York l	A.L.	29	195	12	6	.667	222	86	155	2.82	0
1998	New York	A.L.	31	207⅔	*20	7	.741	209	59	186	3.55	0

Year	Club	Lea	G	IP	W	L	Pct	SO	BB	H	ERA	SAVES
1999 New York m-n	A.L.	31	193⅓	12	9	.571	177	90	164	3.44	0
2000 New York o	A.L.	30	155	4	14	.222	120	82	192	6.91	0
Major League Totals	15 Yrs.	420	2745	184	116	.613	2540	1067	2336	3.40	1
Division Series											
1995 New York	A.L.	2	15⅔	1	0	1.000	14	9	15	4.60	0
1996 New York	A.L.	1	6	0	1	.000	8	2	8	9.00	0
1997 New York	A.L.	1	3⅓	0	0	.000	2	2	7	16.20	0
1998 New York	A.L.	1	5⅔	1	0	1.000	6	1	2	0.00	0
Divisional Series Totals		5	30⅔	2	1	.667	30	14	32	5.87	0
Championship Series											
1988 New York	N.L.	3	12	1	1	.500	9	5	10	4.50	0
1992 Toronto	A.L.	2	12	1	1	.500	9	5	11	3.00	0
1996 New York	A.L.	1	6	0	0	.000	5	5	5	3.00	0
1998 New York	A.L.	2	13	1	0	1.000	13	6	12	4.15	0
1999 New York	A.L.	1	7	1	0	1.000	9	3	7	2.57	0
2000 New York	A.L.	1	1	0	0	.000	0	0	0	0.00	0
Championship Series Totals		10	51	4	2	.667	45	24	45	3.53	0
World Series Record											
1992 Toronto	A.L.	2	10⅓	0	0	.000	8	8	9	3.48	0
1996 New York	A.L.	1	6	1	0	1.000	3	4	4	1.50	0
1998 New York	A.L.	1	6	0	0	.000	4	3	2	3.00	0
1999 New York	A.L.	1	7	1	0	1.000	4	5	1	0.00	0
2000 New York	A.L.	1	0⅓	0	0	.000	0	0	0	0.00	0
World Series Totals		6	29⅔	2	0	1.000	19	20	16	2.12	0

a On disabled list from April 8 to end of 1983 season.
b Traded to New York Mets with catcher Chris Jelic for pitchers Rick Anderson and Mauro Gozzo and catcher Ed Hearn, March 27, 1987.
c On disabled list from May 29 to August 13, 1987.
d Appeared in one additional game as pinch hitter.
e Traded to Toronto Blue Jays for infielder Jeff Kent and player to be named, August 27; New York Mets acquired outfielder Ryan Thompson to complete trade, September 1, 1992.
f Filed for free agency, October 30; signed with Kansas City Royals, December 8, 1992.
g Selected Cy Young Award winner in American League for 1994.
h Traded to Toronto Blue Jays for infielder Chris Stynes, infielder Anthony Medrano and pitcher David Sinnes, April 6, 1995.
i Traded to New York Yankees for pitcher Marty Janzen, pitcher Jason Jarvis and pitcher Mike Gordon, July 28, 1995.
j Filed for free agency, November 12, 1995. Resigned with New York Yankees, December 21, 1995.
k On disabled list from May 3 to September 2, 1996.
l On disabled list from August 18 to September 20, 1997.
m Pitched perfect no-hit, no-run game against Montreal Expos winning 6-0, July 18, 1999.
n Filed for free agency, November 3, 1999, re-signed with New York Yankees, December 6, 1999.
o Filed for free agency, November 7, 2000, signed with Boston Red Sox, January 11, 2001.

COOK, DENNIS BRYAN

Born, Dickinson, Texas, October 4, 1962.
Bats Left. Throws Left. Height, 6 feet, 3 inches. Weight, 185 pounds.

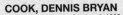

Year	Club	Lea	G	IP	W	L	Pct	SO	BB	H	ERA	SAVES
1985 Clinton	Midwest	13	83	5	4	.556	40	27	73	3.36	0
1986 Fresno	California	27	170	12	7	.632	*173	100	141	3.97	1
1987 Shreveport	Texas	16	105⅔	9	2	.818	98	20	94	2.13	0
1987 Phoenix	P.C.	12	62	2	5	.286	24	26	72	5.23	0
1988 Phoenix	P.C.	26	141⅓	11	9	.550	110	51	138	3.88	0
1988 San Francisco	N.L.	4	22	2	1	.667	13	11	9	2.86	0
1989 Phoenix a	P.C.	12	78	7	4	.636	85	19	73	3.12	0
1989 S. F.-Philadelphia	N.L.	23	121	7	8	.467	67	38	110	3.72	0
1990 Phil.-Los Angeles b-c	N.L.	47	156	9	4	.692	64	56	155	3.92	1
1991 San Antonio	Texas	7	50⅔	1	3	.250	45	10	43	2.49	0
1991 Albuquerque	P.C.	14	91⅔	7	3	.700	84	32	73	3.63	0
1991 Los Angeles d	N.L.	20	17⅔	1	0	1.000	8	7	12	0.51	0
1992 Cleveland	A.L.	32	158	5	7	.417	96	50	156	3.82	0
1993 Cleveland	A.L.	25	54	5	5	.500	34	16	62	5.67	0
1993 Charlotte e	Int.	12	42⅔	3	2	.600	40	6	46	5.06	0
1994 Chicago f	A.L.	38	33	3	1	.750	26	14	29	3.55	0
1995 Cleveland-Texas g	A.L.	46	57⅔	0	2	.000	53	26	63	4.52	2
1996 Texas h-i	A.L.	60	70⅓	5	2	.714	64	35	53	4.09	0
1997 Florida j	N.L.	59	62⅓	1	2	.333	63	28	64	3.90	0
1998 New York k	N.L.	73	68	8	4	.667	79	27	60	2.38	1
1999 New York	N.L.	71	63	10	5	.667	68	27	50	3.86	3

214

Year Club	Lea	G	IP	W	L	Pct	SO	BB	H	ERA	SAVES
2000 New York .............N.L.		68	59	6	3	.667	53	31	63	5.34	2
Major League Totals ....13 Yrs.		566	942	62	44	.585	688	366	886	3.90	9
Division Series											
1996 Texas ...............A.L.		2	$1\frac{1}{3}$	0	0	.000	0	1	0	0.00	0
1997 Florida ..............N.L.		2	3	1	0	1.000	3	1	0	0.00	0
1999 New York ............N.L.		1	$1\frac{2}{3}$	0	0	.000	1	1	1	0.00	0
2000 New York ............N.L.		2	$1\frac{1}{3}$	0	0	.000	1	2	0	0.00	0
Division Series Totals		7	$7\frac{1}{3}$	1	0	1.000	5	5	1	0.00	0
Championship Series											
1997 Florida ..............N.L.		2	$2\frac{1}{3}$	0	0	.000	2	0	0	0.00	0
1999 New York ............N.L.		3	$1\frac{1}{3}$	0	0	.000	1	2	1	0.00	0
2000 New York ............N.L.		1	1	0	0	.000	2	0	1	0.00	0
Championship Series Totals		6	$4\frac{2}{3}$	0	0	.000	5	2	2	0.00	0
World Series Record											
1997 Florida ..............N.L.		3	$3\frac{2}{3}$	1	0	1.000	5	1	1	0.00	0
2000 New York ............N.L.		3	$0\frac{2}{3}$	0	0	.000	1	3	1	0.00	0
World Series Totals		6	$4\frac{1}{3}$	1	0	1.000	6	4	2	0.00	0

a Traded by San Francisco Giants to Philadelphia Phillies with pitcher Terry Mulholland and third baseman/outfielder Charlie Hayes for pitcher Steve Bedrosian and player to be named, June 18; San Francisco acquired infielder Rich Parker to complete trade, August 6, 1989.
b Appeared in one additional game as pinch runner and five additional games as pinch hitter.
c Traded to Los Angeles Dodgers for catcher Darrin Fletcher, September 13, 1990.
d Traded to Cleveland Indians with pitcher Mike Christopher for pitcher Rudy Seanez, December 11, 1991.
e Refused assignment to minor leagues and became free agent, October 5, 1993; signed with Chicago White Sox organization, January 5, 1994.
f Claimed on waivers by Cleveland Indians, October 17, 1994.
g Traded to Texas Rangers for infielder Guillermo Mercedes, June 22, 1995.
h Filed for free agency, October 29, 1996.
i Signed with Florida Marlins, December 10, 1996.
j Traded to New York Mets for outfielder Fletcher Baines and pitcher Scott Comer, December 18, 1997.
k Filed for free agency, October 23, 1998, re-signed with New York Mets, November 18, 1998.

COOPER, BRIAN JOHN

Born, Hollywood, California, August 19, 1974.
Bats Right. Throws Right. Height, 6 feet, 1 inch. Weight, 175 pounds.

Year Club	Lea	G	IP	W	L	Pct	SO	BB	H	ERA	SAVES
1995 Boise ....Northwest		13	62	3	2	.600	66	22	60	3.92	1
1996 Lk Elsinore ......California		26	$162\frac{1}{3}$	7	9	.438	155	39	177	4.21	0
1997 Lk Elsinore ......California		17	117	7	3	.700	104	27	111	3.54	0
1998 Midland ....Texas		32	$161\frac{2}{3}$	8	10	.444	141	59	215	7.13	1
1999 Erie ....Eastern		22	158	10	5	.667	143	29	146	3.30	0
1999 Edmonton ...........P.C.		5	31	2	1	.667	32	10	30	3.77	0
1999 Anaheim ............A.L.		5	$27\frac{2}{3}$	1	1	.500	15	18	23	4.88	0
2000 Lake Elsinore ......California		1	7	0	0	.000	3	2	4	0.00	0
2000 Edmonton ...........P.C.		11	61	3	7	.300	37	18	87	7.23	1
2000 Anaheim ............A.L.		15	87	4	8	.333	36	35	105	5.90	0
Major League Totals ....2 Yrs.		20	$114\frac{2}{3}$	5	9	.357	51	53	128	5.65	0

CORDERO, FRANCISCO JAVIER

Born, Santo Domingo, Dominican Republic, August 11, 1977.
Bats Right. Throws Right. Height, 6 feet, 2 inches. Weight, 200 pounds.

Year Club	Lea	G	IP	W	L	Pct	SO	BB	H	ERA	SAVES
1994 Detroit ....Dominican		12	60	4	3	.571	36	27	65	3.90	0
1995 Fayetteville ....So.Atl.		4	20	0	3	.000	19	12	26	6.30	0
1995 Jamestown .....N.Y.-Penn.		15	88	4	7	.364	54	37	96	5.22	0
1996 Fayetteville ....So.Atl.		2	7	0	0	.000	7	6	2	2.57	0
1996 Jamestown .....N.Y.-Penn.		2	11	0	0	.000	10	2	5	0.82	0
1997 W Michigan ....Midwest		50	$54\frac{1}{3}$	6	1	.857	67	15	36	0.99	35
1998 Jacksonville ....Southern		17	$16\frac{2}{3}$	1	1	.500	18	9	19	4.86	8
1998 Lakeland ....Fla.St.		1	0	0	0	.000	0	0	1	0.00	0
1999 Jacksonville ....Southern		47	$52\frac{1}{3}$	4	1	.800	58	22	35	1.38	27
1999 Detroit a ............A.L.		20	19	2	2	.500	19	18	19	3.32	0
2000 Oklahoma ...........P.C.		3	$4\frac{1}{3}$	0	0	.000	5	3	7	4.15	0
2000 Texas ...............A.L.		56	$77\frac{1}{3}$	1	2	.333	49	48	87	5.35	0
Major League Totals ....2 Yrs.		76	$96\frac{1}{3}$	3	4	.429	68	66	106	4.95	0

a Traded to Texas Rangers with pitcher Justin Thompson, pitcher Alan Webb, outfielder Gabe Kapler, catcher Bill Haselman and infielder Frank Catalanotto for outfielder Juan Gonzalez, pitcher Danny Patterson and catcher Greg Zaun, November 2, 1999.

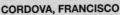

CORDOVA, FRANCISCO

Born, Veracruz, Mexico, April 26, 1972.
Bats Right. Throws Right. Height, 5 feet, 11 inches. Weight, 163 pounds.

Year	Club	Lea	G	IP	W	L	Pct	SO	BB	H	ERA	SAVES
1992	Mex. City Reds	Mex.	16	28	3	0	1.000	14	14	28	5.79	0
1993	Mex. City Reds	Mex.	43	106	9	2	.818	71	47	96	3.23	4
1994	Mex. City Reds	Mex.	41	150 1/3	15	4	.789	104	43	122	2.33	8
1995	Mex. City Reds	Mex.	27	125	13	0	1.000	88	42	131	3.10	4
1996	Pittsburgh a	N.L.	59	99	4	7	.364	95	20	103	4.09	12
1997	Pittsburgh b-c	N.L.	29	178 2/3	11	8	.579	121	49	175	3.63	0
1998	Pittsburgh	N.L.	33	220 1/3	13	14	.481	157	69	204	3.31	0
1999	Altoona	Eastern	2	9 2/3	1	1	.500	12	4	13	4.66	0
1999	Nashville	P.C.	2	12	2	0	1.000	7	1	10	0.75	0
1999	Pittsburgh d	N.L.	27	160 2/3	8	10	.444	98	59	166	4.43	0
2000	Pittsburgh e	N.L.	18	95	6	8	.429	66	38	107	5.21	0
Major League Totals	5 Yrs.		166	753 2/3	42	47	.472	537	235	755	3.96	12

a Signed by Pittsburgh Pirates as non-drafted free agent, January 18, 1996.
b Pitched first 9 innings of combined no-hitter (with Ricardo Rincon) against Houston Astros, winning 3-0 in 10 innings, July 12, 1997.
c On disabled list from August 22 to September 6, 1997.
d On disabled list from April 11 to May 19, 1999.
e On disabled list from May 5 to May 19 and July 5 to July 28 and August 9 to November 17, 2000.

CORMIER, RHEAL PAUL

Born, Moncton, New Brunswick, Canada, April 23, 1967.
Bats Left. Throws Right. Height, 5 feet, 10 inches. Weight, 185 pounds.

Year	Club	Lea	G	IP	W	L	Pct	SO	BB	H	ERA	SAVES
1989	St.Pete	Fla.St.	26	169 2/3	12	7	.632	122	33	141	2.23	0
1990	Arkansas	Texas	22	121 1/3	5	12	.294	102	30	133	5.04	0
1990	Louisville	A.A.	4	24	1	1	.500	9	3	18	2.25	0
1991	Louisville	A.A.	21	127 2/3	7	9	.438	74	31	140	4.23	0
1991	St. Louis	N.L.	11	67 2/3	4	5	.444	38	8	74	4.12	0
1992	Louisville	A.A.	1	4	0	1	.000	1	0	8	6.75	0
1992	St. Louis	N.L.	31	186	10	10	.500	117	33	194	3.68	0
1993	St. Louis	N.L.	38	145 1/3	7	6	.538	75	27	163	4.33	0
1994	Arkansas	Texas	2	9 1/3	1	0	1.000	11	0	9	1.93	0
1994	Louisville	A.A.	3	22	1	2	.333	13	8	21	4.50	0
1994	St. Louis	N.L.	7	39 2/3	3	2	.600	26	7	40	5.45	0
1995	Boston a	A.L.	48	115	7	5	.583	69	31	131	4.07	0
1996	Montreal b	N.L.	33	159 2/3	7	10	.412	100	41	165	4.17	0
1997	Montreal	N.L.	1	1 1/3	0	1	.000	0	1	4	33.75	0
1998	Akron c	Eastern	3	9 2/3	0	0	.000	6	2	15	6.52	0
1999	Boston d	A.L.	60	63 1/3	2	0	1.000	39	18	61	3.69	0
2000	Boston e	A.L.	64	68 1/3	3	3	.500	43	17	74	4.61	0
Major League Totals	9 Yrs.		293	846 1/3	43	42	.506	507	183	906	4.18	0
Division Series												
1995	Boston	A.L.	2	0 2/3	0	0	.000	2	1	2	13.50	0
1999	Boston	A.L.	2	4	0	0	.000	4	1	2	0.00	0
Division Series Totals			4	4 2/3	0	0	.000	6	2	4	1.93	0
Championship Series												
1999	Boston	A.L.	4	3 2/3	0	0	.000	4	3	3	0.00	0

a Traded to Boston Red Sox with outfielder Mark Whiten for infielder Scott Cooper, pitcher Cory Bailey and a player to be named later, April 8, 1995.
b Traded to Montreal Expos with pitcher Shayne Bennett and infielder Ryan McGuire for infielder Wil Cordero and pitcher Bryan Eversgerd, January 10, 1996.
c Filed for free agency, October 30, 1997, signed with Cleveland Indians organization, January 28, 1998.
d Filed for free agency, October 16, 1998, signed with Boston Red Sox organization, January 5, 1999.
e Filed for free agency, October 31, 2000, signed with Philadelphia Phillies, November 29, 2000.

CORNELIUS, JONATHAN REID (REID)

Born, Thomasville, Alabama, June 2, 1970.
Bats Right. Throws Right. Height, 6 feet. Weight, 200 pounds.

Year	Club	Lea	G	IP	W	L	Pct	SO	BB	H	ERA	SAVES
1989	Rockford	Midwest	17	84 1/3	5	6	.455	66	63	71	4.27	0
1990	Wst Plm Bch a	Fla.St.	11	56	2	3	.400	47	25	54	3.38	0
1991	Wst Plm Bch	Fla.St.	17	109 1/3	8	3	.727	81	43	79	2.39	0
1991	Harrisburg b-c	Eastern	3	18 2/3	2	1	.667	12	7	15	2.89	0
1992	Harrisburg d	Eastern	4	23	1	0	1.000	17	8	11	3.13	0
1993	Harrisburg	Eastern	27	157 2/3	10	7	.588	119	82	146	4.17	0

Year	Club	Lea	G	IP	W	L	Pct	SO	BB	H	ERA	SAVES
1994 Ottawa e	Int.	25	148	9	8	.529	87	75	149	4.38	0
1995 Ottawa	Int.	4	10²/₃	1	1	.500	7	5	16	6.75	0
1995 Norfolk	Int.	10	70¹/₃	7	0	1.000	43	19	57	0.90	0
1995 Montreal-New York f	N.L.	18	66²/₃	3	7	.300	39	30	75	5.53	0
1996 Buffalo g-h	A.A.	20	90	5	7	.417	62	49	101	5.60	0
1997 Portland	Eastern	6	33	5	0	1.000	24	17	32	2.73	0
1997 Charlotte i-j	Int.	22	130²/₃	12	5	.706	80	43	134	5.10	0
1998 Tucson	P.C.	19	94	4	7	.364	65	26	108	5.94	0
1998 Charlotte k-l	Int.	8	49¹/₃	3	2	.600	31	13	50	4.01	0
1999 Calgary	P.C.	27	172¹/₃	10	6	.625	135	68	184	4.49	1
1999 Florida m	N.L.	5	19¹/₃	1	0	1.000	12	5	16	3.26	0
2000 Calgary	P.C.	8	43¹/₃	2	5	.500	22	18	45	4.57	0
2000 Florida n	N.L.	22	125	4	10	.286	50	50	135	4.82	0
Major League Totals ...... .3 Yrs.		45	211	8	17	.320	101	85	226	4.91	0

a On disabled list from May 27 to August 2, 1990.
b On disabled list from May 20 to June 30, 1991.
c On disabled list from August 6 to September 1, 1991.
d On disabled list from April 27 to September 6, 1992.
e On disabled list from July 12 to 28, 1994.
f Traded to New York Mets for infielder David Segui, June 8, 1995.
g Traded to Cleveland Indians with outfielder Ryan Thompson for pitcher Mark Clark, March 31, 1996.
h On disabled list from April 16 to 28 and June 26 to July 28, 1996.
i Filed for free agency, October 15, 1996, signed with Florida Marlins organization, March 31, 1997.
j Filed for free agency, October 17, 1997, signed with Arizona Diamondbacks organization, November 24, 1997.
k Traded to Florida Marlins for player to be named later, July 24, 1998, Arizona Diamondbacks received outfielder Walt White to complete trade, October 29, 1998.
l Filed for free agency, October 16, 1998, signed with Anaheim Angels organization, November 16, 1998.
m Released by Anaheim Angels, March 20, 1999, signed with Florida Marlins organization, April 9, 1999.
n Outrighted by Florida Marlins, December 20, 2000.

CRABTREE, TIMOTHY LYLE

Born, Jackson, Michigan, October 13, 1969.
Bats Right. Throws Right. Height, 6 feet, 4 inches. Weight, 205 pounds.

Year	Club	Lea	G	IP	W	L	Pct	SO	BB	H	ERA	SAVES
1992 St. Catharines	N.Y.-Penn.	12	69	6	3	.667	47	22	45	1.57	0
1992 Knoxville	Southern	3	19	0	2	.000	13	4	14	0.95	0
1993 Knoxville	Southern	27	158²/₃	9	14	.391	67	59	178	4.08	0
1994 Syracuse	Int.	51	108	2	6	.250	58	49	125	4.17	2
1995 Syracuse	Int.	26	31²/₃	0	2	.000	22	12	38	5.40	5
1995 Toronto	A.L.	31	32	0	2	.000	21	13	30	3.09	0
1996 Toronto a	A.L.	53	67¹/₃	5	3	.625	57	22	59	2.54	1
1997 St. Catnarines	N.Y.-Penn.	2	3	0	0	.000	3	0	3	3.00	0
1997 Syracuse	Int.	3	3²/₃	0	0	.000	3	1	7	9.82	1
1997 Toronto b	A.L.	37	40²/₃	3	3	.500	26	17	65	7.08	2
1998 Texas c	A.L.	64	85¹/₃	6	1	.857	60	35	86	3.59	0
1999 Texas	A.L.	68	65	5	1	.833	54	18	71	3.46	0
2000 Texas	A.L.	68	80¹/₃	2	7	.222	54	31	86	5.15	2
Major League Totals .... .6 Yrs.		321	370²/₃	21	17	.553	272	136	397	4.05	5
Division Series											
1998 Texas	A.L.	2	4	0	0	.000	2	0	1	0.00	0
1999 Texas	A.L.	2	1²/₃	0	0	.000	1	1	1	5.40	0
Division Series Totals		4	5²/₃	0	0	.000	3	1	2	1.59	0

a On disabled list from August 16 to September 6, 1996.
b On disabled list from June 4 to August 4, 1997.
c Traded to Texas Rangers for catcher Kevin Brown, March 14, 1998.

CREEK, PAUL DOUGLAS (DOUG)

Born, Winchester, Virginia, March 1, 1969.
Bats Left. Throws Right. Height, 5 feet, 10 inches. Weight, 205 pounds.

Year	Club	Lea	G	IP	W	L	PCT	SO	BB	H	ERA	SAVES
1991 Hamilton	N.Y.-Penn.	9	38²/₃	3	2	.600	45	18	39	5.12	1
1991 Savannah	So.Atl.	5	28¹/₃	2	1	.667	32	17	24	4.45	0
1992 Springfield	Midwest	6	38¹/₃	4	1	.800	43	13	32	2.58	0
1992 St.Pete a	Fla.St.	13	73¹/₃	5	4	.556	63	37	57	2.82	0
1993 Arkansas	Texas	25	147²/₃	11	10	.524	128	48	142	4.02	0
1993 Louisville b	A.A.	2	14	0	0	.000	9	9	10	3.21	0
1994 Louisville	A.A.	7	26¹/₃	1	4	.200	16	23	37	8.54	0

Year Club	Lea	G	IP	W	L	Pct	SO	BB	H	ERA	SAVES
1994 Arkansas c	Texas	17	92	3	10	.231	65	36	96	4.40	0
1995 Arkansas	Texas	26	34$\frac{1}{3}$	4	2	.667	50	16	24	2.88	1
1995 Louisville	A.A.	26	30$\frac{2}{3}$	3	2	.600	29	21	20	3.23	0
1995 St. Louis d	N.L.	6	6$\frac{2}{3}$	0	0	.000	10	3	2	0.00	0
1996 San Francisco e	N.L.	63	48$\frac{1}{3}$	0	2	.000	38	32	45	6.52	0
1997 Phoenix	P.C.	25	129$\frac{2}{3}$	8	6	.571	137	66	140	4.93	0
1997 San Francisco f-g	N.L.	3	13$\frac{1}{3}$	1	2	.333	14	14	12	6.75	0
1998 Hanshin Tigers	J.P.L	7	28$\frac{2}{3}$	0	4	.000	24	25	23	5.65	0
1999 Iowa h	P.C.	25	130$\frac{2}{3}$	7	3	.700	140	62	116	3.79	0
1999 Chicago i	N.L.	3	6	0	0	.000	6	8	6	10.50	0
2000 Durham	Int.	10	18$\frac{1}{3}$	0	0	.000	22	14	10	1.96	0
2000 Tampa Bay j	A.L.	45	60$\frac{2}{3}$	1	3	.250	73	39	49	4.60	12000
Major League Totals	3 Yrs.	75	134	7	9	.438	103	45	142	5.04	0

a On disabled list from April 10 to May 21, 1992.
b On disabled list from July 25 to August 1, 1993.
c On disabled list from June 25 to July 10, 1994.
d Traded to San Francisco Giants with pitcher Allen Watson and pitcher Rich DeLucia for infielder Royce Clayton and player to be named later, December 14, 1995.
e St. Louis Cardinals received infielder Chris Wimmer to complete trade, January 16, 1996.
f Sold to Chicago White Sox, November 7, 1997.
g Sold to Hanshin Tigers (JPL), December 4, 1997.
h Signed with Chicago Cubs organization, January 29, 1999.
i Released by Chicago Cubs, September 13, 1999.
j Signed with Tampa Bay Devil Rays organization, February 1, 2000.

CRUZ, NELSON

Born, Puerto Plata, Dominican Republic, September 13, 1972.
Bats Right. Throws Right. Height, 6 feet, 1 inch. Weight, 160 pounds.

Year Club	Lea	G	IP	W	L	Pct	SO	BB	H	ERA	SAVES
1990 Montreal	Dominican	16	103$\frac{2}{3}$	9	2	.818	83	42	105	2.60	0
1991 Expos a	Gulf Coast	12	48$\frac{2}{3}$	2	4	.333	34	19	40	2.40	0
1995 Bristol	Appal.	1	1	0	0	.000	0	0	2	9.00	0
1995 Hickory	So.Atl.	44	66$\frac{2}{3}$	2	7	.222	68	15	65	2.70	9
1995 Pr William	Carolina	9	19$\frac{1}{3}$	2	1	.667	18	6	12	0.47	1
1996 Birmingham	Southern	37	149	6	6	.500	142	41	150	3.20	1
1997 Nashville	A.A.	21	123$\frac{1}{3}$	11	7	.611	93	31	139	5.11	0
1997 Chicago	A.L.	19	26$\frac{1}{3}$	0	2	.000	23	9	29	6.49	0
1998 Calgary b	P.C.	35	126$\frac{2}{3}$	10	6	.625	101	40	159	5.33	0
1999 Detroit	A.L.	29	66$\frac{2}{3}$	2	5	.286	46	23	74	5.67	0
2000 Toledo	Int.	11	52$\frac{1}{3}$	2	4	.333	39	17	54	4.82	0
2000 Detroit c-d	A.L.	27	41	5	2	.714	34	13	39	3.07	0
Major League Totals	3 Yrs.	75	134	7	9	.438	103	45	142	5.04	0

a Released by Montreal Expos, March 27, 1992, signed with Chicago White Sox, December 10, 1994.
b Filed for free agency, October 16, 1998, signed with Detroit Tigers, November 24, 1998.
c Traded to Oakland Athletics for infielder Jorge Velandia, August 30, 2000.
d Traded to Houston Astros with catcher Brad Ausmus and pitcher Doug Brocail for pitcher Chris Holt, outfielder Roger Cedeno and catcher Mitch Meluskey, December 11, 2000.

CUNNANE, WILLIAM JOSEPH (WILL)

Born, Suffern, New York, April 24, 1974.
Bats Right. Throws Right. Height, 6 feet, 2 inches. Weight, 175 pounds.

Year Club	Lea	G	IP	W	L	Pct	SO	BB	H	ERA	SAVES
1993 Marlins	Gulf Coast	16	66$\frac{2}{3}$	3	3	.500	64	8	75	2.70	2
1994 Kane County	Midwest	32	138$\frac{2}{3}$	11	3	.786	106	23	110	1.43	1
1995 Portland	Eastern	21	117$\frac{2}{3}$	9	2	.818	83	34	120	3.67	0
1996 Portland	Eastern	25	151$\frac{2}{3}$	10	12	.455	101	30	156	3.74	0
1997 San Diego	N.L.	54	91$\frac{1}{3}$	6	3	.667	79	49	114	5.81	0
1998 Las Vegas	P.C.	33	36	1	2	.333	30	19	45	5.25	4
1998 San Diego a	N.L.	3	3	0	0	.000	1	1	4	6.00	0
1999 Las Vegas	P.C.	28	36$\frac{2}{3}$	2	1	.667	54	16	30	0.98	0
1999 San Diego	N.L.	24	31	2	1	.667	22	12	34	5.23	0
2000 Las Vegas	P.C.	17	97$\frac{1}{3}$	7	4	.636	97	26	96	3.98	1
2000 San Diego	N.L.	27	38$\frac{1}{3}$	1	1	.500	34	21	35	4.23	0
Major League Totals	4 Yrs.	108	163$\frac{2}{3}$	9	5	.643	136	83	187	5.33	0

a On disabled list from March 31 to June 21, 1998.

DAAL (CORDERO), OMAR JESUS
Born, Maracaibo, Venezuela, March 1, 1972.
Bats Left. Throws Left. Height, 6 feet, 3 inches. Weight, 175 pounds.

Year	Club	Lea	G	IP	W	L	Pct	SO	BB	H	ERA	SAVES
1990-91				Played in Dominican Summer League								
1992 Albuquerque	.P.C.		12	10⅓	0	2	.000	9	11	14	7.84	0
1992 San Antonio	Texas		35	57⅓	2	6	.250	52	33	60	5.02	5
1993 Albuquerque	.P.C.		6	5⅓	1	1	.500	2	3	5	3.38	2
1993 Los Angeles	N.L.		47	35⅓	2	3	.400	19	21	36	5.09	0
1994 Albuquerque	.P.C.		11	34⅔	4	2	.667	28	16	38	5.19	1
1994 Los Angeles	N.L.		24	13⅔	0	0	.000	9	5	12	3.29	0
1995 Albuquerque	.P.C.		17	53⅓	2	3	.400	46	26	56	4.05	1
1995 Los Angeles a	N.L.		28	20.	4	0	1.000	11	15	29	7.20	0
1996 Montreal	N.L.		64	87⅓	4	5	.444	82	37	74	4.02	0
1997 Ottawa	Int.		2	8	0	1	.000	9	1	10	5.63	0
1997 Syracuse	Int.		5	33⅔	3	0	1.000	29	10	18	0.53	0
1997 Montreal	N.L.		33	30⅓	1	2	.333	16	15	48	9.79	1
1997 Toronto b-c	A.L.		9	27	1	1	.500	28	6	34	4.00	0
1998 Tucson	.P.C.		1	3	0	0	.000	4	1	3	3.00	0
1998 Arizona d	N.L.		33	162⅔	8	12	.400	132	51	146	2.88	0
1999 Arizona	N.L.		32	214⅔	16	9	.640	148	79	188	3.65	0
2000 Arizona-Philadelphia e	N.L.		32	167	4	*19	.174	96	72	208	6.14	0
Major League Totals ....8 Yrs.			302	758	40	51	.440	541	301	775	4.49	1
Division Series												
1999 Arizona	N.L.		1	4	0	1	.000	4	3	6	6.75	0

a Traded to Montreal Expos for pitcher Rick Clelland, December 15, 1995.
b Claimed on waivers by Toronto Blue Jays, July 24, 1997.
c Selected in expansion draft by Arizona Diamondbacks, November 18, 1997.
d On disabled list from June 22 to July 11, 1998.
e Traded to Philadelphia Phillies with infielder Travis Lee, pitcher Vicente Padilla and pitcher Nelson Figueroa for pitcher Curt Schilling, July 26, 2000.

D'AMICO, JEFFREY CHARLES (JEFF)
Born, St.Petersburg, Florida, December 27, 1975.
Bats Right. Throws Right. Height, 6 feet, 7 inches. Weight, 250 pounds.

Year	Club	Lea	G	IP	W	L	Pct	SO	BB	H	ERA	SAVES
1994 AR Brewers a	Arizona		INJURED - did not play									
1995 Beloit a	Midwest		21	132	13	3	.813	119	31	102	2.39	0
1996 El Paso	Texas		46	96	5	4	.556	76	13	89	3.19	0
1996 Milwaukee	A.L.		17	86	6	6	.500	53	31	88	5.44	0
1997 Beloit	Midwest		1	3	0	0	.000	7	1	0	0.00	0
1997 Milwaukee	A.L.		23	135⅔	9	7	.563	94	43	139	4.71	0
1998 Milwaukee b	A.L.		INJURED - did not play									
1999 Louisville	Int.		1	3⅓	0	0.	.000	1	2	6	13.50	0
1999 Huntsville	Southern		1	2	0	1	.000	2	2	6	36.00	0
1999 Beloit	Midwest		2	8	1	0	1.000	6	1	7	0.00	0
1999 Milwaukee c-d	N.L.		1	1	0	0	.000	1	0	1	0.00	0
2000 Indianapolis	Int.		6	31⅓	1	1	.500	20	11	25	3.16	0
2000 Milwaukee e	N.L.		23	162⅓	12	7	.632	101	46	143	2.66	0
Major League Totals ....4 Yrs.			64	385	27	20	.574	249	120	371	4.00	0

a On disabled list from June 24 to September 1, 1994.
b On disabled list from July 19 to September 2, 1997.
c On disabled list from January 14 to October 1, 1998.
d On disabled list from March 29 to September 24, 1999.
e On disabled list from June 6 to June 30, 2000.

DARENSBOURG, VICTOR
Born, Los Angeles, California, November 13, 1970.
Bats Left. Throws Right. Height, 5 feet, 10 inches. Weight, 165 pounds.

Year	Club	Lea	G	IP	W	L	Pct	SO	BB	H	ERA	SAVES
1992 Marlins	Gulf Coast		8	42	2	1	.667	37	11	28	0.64	2
1993 Kane County	Midwest		46	71⅓	9	1	.900	89	28	58	2.14	16
1993 High Desert	California		1	1	0	0	.000	1	0	1	0.00	0
1994 Portland	Eastern		34	149	10	7	.588	103	60	146	3.81	4
1995 Florida	N.L.		INJURED - Did Not Play									
1996 Brevard Cty	Fla.St.		2	3	0	0	.000	5	1	1	0.00	0
1996 Charlotte a	Int.		47	63⅓	1	5	.167	66	32	61	3.69	7
1997 Charlotte	Int.		27	24⅔	4	2	.667	21	15	22	4.38	2
1998 Florida	N.L.		59	71	0	0	.000	74	30	52	3.68	1

Year	Club	Lea	G	IP	W	L	Pct	SO	BB	H	ERA	SAVES
1999 Calgary	....	P.C.	9	11²/₃	0	0	.000	12	0	13	4.63	1
1999 Florida	....	N.L.	56	34²/₃	0	1	.000	16	21	50	8.83	0
2000 Florida	....	N.L.	56	62	5	3	.625	59	28	61	4.06	0
Major League Totals	....	3 Yrs.	171	167²/₃	5	11	.313	149	79	163	4.88	1

a On disabled list from April 4 to April 15, 1996.

DAVIS, DOUGLAS P. (DOUG)

Born, Sacramento, California, September 21, 1975.
Bats Right. Throws Right. Height, 6 feet, 3 inches. Weight, 185 pounds.

Year	Club	Lea	G	IP	W	L	Pct	SO	BB	H	ERA	SAVES
1996 Rangers	....	Gulf Coast	8	42²/₃	3	1	.750	49	26	28	1.90	0
1997 Rangers	....	Gulf Coast	4	21	3	1	.750	27	15	14	1.71	0
1997 Charlotte	....	Fla.St.	9	49¹/₃	5	3	.625	52	33	29	3.10	0
1998 Charlotte	....	Fla.St.	27	155¹/₃	11	7	.611	173	74	129	3.24	0
1999 Oklahoma	....	P.C.	13	78	7	0	1.000	74	31	77	3.00	0
1999 Tulsa	....	Texas	12	74¹/₃	4	4	.500	79	25	65	2.42	0
1999 Texas	....	A.L.	2	2²/₃	0	0	.000	3	0	12	33.75	0
2000 Oklahoma	....	P.C.	12	69²/₃	8	3	.727	53	34	62	2.84	0
2000 Texas	....	A.L.	30	98²/₃	7	6	.538	66	58	109	5.38	0
Major League Totals	....	2 Yrs.	32	101¹/₃	7	6	.538	69	58	121	6.13	0

DEJEAN, MICHEL DWAIN

Born, Baton Rouge, Louisiana, September 28, 1970.
Bats Right. Throws Right. Height, 6 feet, 2 inches. Weight, 205 pounds.

Year	Club	Lea	G	IP	W	L	Pct	SO	BB	H	ERA	SAVES
1992 Oneonta	....	N.Y.-Penn.	20	20²/₃	0	0	.000	20	3	12	0.44	16
1993 Greensboro	....	So. Atl.	20	18	2	3	.400	16	8	22	5.00	9
1994 Tampa	....	Fla. St.	34	34	0	2	.000	22	13	39	2.38	16
1994 Albany	....	Eastern	16	24²/₃	0	2	.000	13	15	22	4.38	4
1995 Norwich	....	Eastern	59	78¹/₃	5	5	.500	57	34	58	2.99	20
1996 New Haven a	....	Eastern	16	22¹/₃	0	0	.000	12	8	20	3.22	11
1996 Colo Sprngs	....	P.C.	30	40¹/₃	0	2	.000	31	21	52	5.13	1
1997 Colo Sprngs	....	P.C.	10	10	0	1	.000	9	7	17	5.40	4
1997 New Haven	....	Eastern	2	3	0	1	.000	2	2	3	6.00	0
1997 Colorado b	....	N.L.	55	67²/₃	5	0	1.000	38	24	74	3.99	2
1998 Colorado c	....	N.L.	59	74¹/₃	3	1	.750	27	24	78	3.03	2
1999 Colorado Spgs	....	P.C.	1	1	0	0	.000	0	0	1	0.00	0
1999 Colorado d	....	N.L.	56	61	2	4	.333	31	32	83	8.41	0
2000 Colorado Spgs	....	P.C.	12	14¹/₃	1	1	.500	12	4	15	2.51	0
2000 Colorado e	....	N.L.	54	53¹/₃	4	4	.500	34	30	54	4.89	0
Major League Totals	....	4 Yrs.	224	256¹/₃	14	9	.609	130	110	289	4.95	4

a Traded to Colorado Rockies with player to be named later for catcher Joe Girardi, November 20, 1995. Colorado Rockies received pitcher Steve Shoemaker to complete trade, December 6, 1995.
b On disabled list from July 18 to August 8, 1997.
c On disabled list from September 5 to September 28, 1998.
d On disabled list from August 14 to September 1, 1999.
e On disabled list from March 25 to April 27 and July 25 to August 14, 2000.

DE LOS SANTOS, VALERIO LORENZO

Born, Las Matas De Farfan, Dominican Republic, October 6, 1975.
Bats Left. Throws Right. Height, 6 feet, 4 inches. Weight, 185 pounds.

Year	Club	Lea	G	IP	W	L	Pct	SO	BB	H	ERA	SAVES
1993 Milwaukee	....	Dominican	19	63²/₃	1	7	.125	39	37	91	6.50	0
1994 Hou/Mil	....	Dominican	17	90¹/₃	7	6	.538	50	35	90	3.69	0
1995 Brewers	....	Arizona	14	82	4	6	.400	57	12	81	2.20	0
1996 Beloit	....	Midwest	33	164²/₃	10	8	.556	137	59	164	3.55	4
1997 El Paso	....	Texas	26	114¹/₃	6	10	.375	61	38	146	5.75	2
1998 El Paso	....	Texas	42	66²/₃	6	2	.750	62	25	81	3.92	10
1998 Louisville	....	Int.	5	5	0	0	.000	0	0	4	3.60	0
1998 Milwaukee	....	N.L.	13	21²/₃	0	0	.000	18	2	11	2.91	0
1999 Milwaukee a	....	N.L.	7	8¹/₃	0	1	.000	5	7	12	6.48	0
2000 Milwaukee	....	N.L.	66	73²/₃	2	3	.400	70	33	72	5.13	0
Major League Totals	....	3 Yrs.	86	103²/₃	2	4	.333	93	42	95	4.77	0

a On disabled list from April 20 to September 23, 1999.

DEMPSTER, RYAN SCOTT

Born, Sechelt, British Columbia, Canada, May 3, 1977.
Bats Right. Throws Right. Height, 6 feet, 2 inches. Weight, 195 pounds.

Year	Club	Lea	G	IP	W	L	Pct	SO	BB	H	ERA	SAVES
1995	Rangers	Gulf Coast	8	34⅓	3	1	.750	37	17	34	2.36	0
1995	Hudson Val	N.Y.-Penn.	1	5⅔	1	0	1.000	6	1	7	3.18	0
1996	Chston-Sc	So.Atl.	23	144⅓	7	11	.389	141	58	120	3.30	0
1996	Kane County a-b	Midwest	4	26⅓	2	1	.667	16	18	18	2.73	0
1997	Brevard Cty	Fla.St.	28	165⅓	10	9	.526	131	46	190	4.90	0
1998	Portland	Eastern	7	44⅔	4	3	.571	33	15	34	3.22	0
1998	Florida	N.L.	14	54⅔	1	5	.167	35	38	72	7.08	0
1998	Charlotte	Int.	5	33	3	1	.750	24	12	33	3.27	0
1999	Calgary	P.C.	5	30⅔	1	1	.500	29	10	30	4.99	0
1999	Florida	N.L.	25	147	7	8	.467	126	93	146	4.71	0
2000	Florida	N.L.	33	226⅓	14	10	.583	209	97	210	3.66	0
Major League Totals	3 Yrs.		72	428	22	23	.489	370	228	428	4.46	0

a Traded by Texas Rangers to Florida Marlins with player to be named later for pitcher John Burkett, August 8, 1996.
b Florida Marlins received pitcher Rick Helling to complete trade, September 3, 1996.

DESSENS, ELMER

Born, Hermosillo, Mexico, January 13, 1972.
Bats Right. Throws Right. Height, 6 feet. Weight, 190 pounds.

Year	Club	Lea	G	IP	W	L	Pct	SO	BB	H	ERA	SAVES
1993	Mexico a	Mexican	14	31	3	1	.750	16	5	31	2.32	2
1994	Mexico	Mexican	37	127⅔	11	4	.733	51	32	121	2.04	3
1995	Carolina	Southern	27	152	15	8	.652	68	21	170	2.49	0
1996	Calgary	P.C.	6	34⅓	2	2	.500	15	15	40	3.15	0
1996	Mexico	Mexican	7	50	7	0	1.000	17	10	44	1.26	0
1996	Carolina	Southern	5	11⅔	0	1	.000	7	4	15	5.40	0
1996	Pittsburgh b	N.L.	15	25	0	2	.000	13	4	40	8.28	0
1997	Mexico	Mexican	26	159⅓	16	5	.762	61	51	156	3.56	0
1997	Pittsburgh	N.L.	3	3⅓	0	0	.000	2	0	2	0.00	0
1998	Nashville	P.C.	6	30	3	1	.750	13	6	32	3.30	0
1998	Pittsburgh c-d	N.L.	43	74⅔	2	6	.250	43	25	90	5.67	0
1999	Yomiuri e	Japan Cent.	6	16⅓	0	1	.000	6	4	24	3.86	0
2000	Louisville	Int.	4	22⅔	2	0	1.000	14	7	24	3.18	0
2000	Cincinnati	N.L.	40	147⅓	11	5	.688	85	43	170	4.28	1
Major League Totals	4 Yrs.		101	250⅓	13	13	.500	143	72	302	5.03	1

a Loaned by Pittsburgh Pirates to Mexican League 1993, 1994, 1996 and 1997.
b On disabled list from July 31 to September 10, 1996.
c On disabled list from April 8 to April 24, 1998.
d Released by Pittsburgh Pirates, March 31, 1999, signed with Yomiuri Giants (JCL) for 1999.
e Signed with Cincinnati Reds, December 15, 1999.

DOTEL, OCTAVIO EDUARDO

Born, Santo Domingo, Dominican Republic, November 25, 1975.
Bats Right. Throws Right. Height, 6 feet. Weight, 175 pounds.

Year	Club	Lea	G	IP	W	L	Pct	SO	BB	H	ERA	SAVES
1993	Mets	Dominican	15	59⅓	6	2	.750	48	38	46	4.10	0
1994	Mets	Dominican	15	81⅓	5	0	1.000	95	31	84	4.32	0
1995	Mets	Gulf Coast	13	74⅓	7	4	.636	86	17	48	2.18	0
1995	St. Lucie	Fla.St.	3	8	1	0	1.000	9	4	10	5.63	0
1996	Columbia	So.Atl.	22	115⅓	11	3	.786	142	49	89	3.59	0
1997	Mets	Gulf Coast	3	9⅓	0	0	.000	7	2	9	0.96	1
1997	St. Lucie	Fla.St.	9	50	5	2	.714	39	23	44	2.52	0
1997	Binghamton	Eastern	12	55⅔	3	4	.429	40	38	66	5.98	0
1998	Binghamton	Eastern	10	68⅔	4	2	.667	82	24	41	1.97	0
1998	Norfolk	Int.	17	99	8	6	.571	118	43	82	3.45	0
1999	Norfolk	Int.	13	70⅓	5	2	.714	90	34	52	3.84	0
1999	New York a	N.L.	19	85⅓	8	3	.727	85	49	69	5.38	0
2000	Houston	N.L.	50	125	3	7	.300	142	61	127	5.40	16
Major League Totals	2 Yrs.		69	210⅓	11	10	.524	227	110	196	5.39	16
Division Series												
1999 New York	N.L.		1	0⅓	0	0	.000	0	2	1	54.00	0
Championship Series												
1999 New York	N.L.		1	3	1	0	1.000	5	2	4	3.00	0

a Traded to Houston Astros with outfielder Roger Cedeno and pitcher Kyle Kessel for pitcher Mike Hampton and outfielder Derek Bell, December 23, 1999.

DOWNS, SCOTT JEREMY
Born, Louisville, Kentucky, March 17, 1976.
Bats Left. Throws Right. Height, 6 feet, 2 inches. Weight, 180 pounds.

Year	Club	Lea	G	IP	W	L	Pct	SO	BB	H	ERA	SAVES
1997 Williamsprt		N.Y.-Penn.	5	23	0	2	.000	28	7	15	2.74	0
1997 Rockford		Midwest	5	36	3	0	1.000	43	8	17	1.25	0
1998 Daytona a		Fla.St.	27	161²/₃	8	9	.471	117	55	179	3.90	0
1999 New Britain		Eastern	6	19²/₃	0	0	.000	22	10	33	8.69	0
1999 West Tenn		Southern	13	80	8	1	.889	101	28	56	1.35	0
1999 Daytona		Fla.St.	7	48	5	0	1.000	41	11	41	1.88	0
1999 Ft.Myers b		Fla.St.	2	9²/₃	0	1	.000	9	6	7	0.00	0
2000 Chicago-Montreal c-d		N.L.	19	97	4	3	.571	63	40	122	5.29	0

a Sent by Chicago Cubs to Minnesota Twins as player to be named later for pitcher Mike Morgan, November 3, 1998.
b Traded to Chicago Cubs with pitcher Rick Aguilera for pitcher Jason Ryan and pitcher Kyle Lohse, May 21, 1999.
c Traded to Montreal Expos for outfielder Rondell White, July 31, 2000.
d On disabled list from August 9 to October 1, 2000.

DREIFORT, DARREN JAMES
Born, Wichita, Kansas, May 18, 1972.
Bats Right. Throws Right. Height, 6 feet, 2 inches. Weight, 205 pounds.

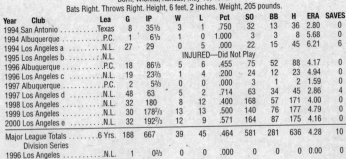

Year	Club	Lea	G	IP	W	L	Pct	SO	BB	H	ERA	SAVES
1994 San Antonio		Texas	8	35¹/₃	3	1	.750	32	13	36	2.80	0
1994 Albuquerque		P.C.	1	6¹/₃	1	0	1.000	3	3	8	5.68	0
1994 Los Angeles a		N.L.	27	29	0	5	.000	22	15	45	6.21	6
1995 Los Angeles b		N.L.			INJURED—Did Not Play							
1996 Albuquerque		P.C.	18	86¹/₃	5	6	.455	75	52	88	4.17	0
1996 Los Angeles c		N.L.	19	23²/₃	1	4	.200	24	12	23	4.94	0
1997 Albuquerque		P.C.	2	5²/₃	0	0	.000	3	1	2	1.59	0
1997 Los Angeles d		N.L.	48	63	5	2	.714	63	34	45	2.86	4
1998 Los Angeles		N.L.	32	180	8	12	.400	168	57	171	4.00	0
1999 Los Angeles		N.L.	30	178²/₃	13	13	.500	140	76	177	4.79	0
2000 Los Angeles e		N.L.	32	192²/₃	12	9	.571	164	87	175	4.16	0
Major League Totals		6 Yrs.	188	667	39	45	.464	581	281	636	4.28	10
Division Series												
1996 Los Angeles		N.L.	1	0²/₃	0	0	.000	0	0	0	0.00	0

a Appeared in one additional game as pinch hitter.
b On disabled list entire 1995 season.
c On disabled list from April 1 to May 16, 1996.
d On disabled list from May 12 to June 17, 1997.
e Filed for free agency, October 30, 2000, re-signed with Los Angeles Dodgers, December 11, 2000.

DURBIN, CHAD GRIFFIN
Born, Spring Valley, Illinois, December 3, 1977.
Bats Right. Throws Right. Height, 6 feet, 1 inch. Weight, 175 pounds.

Year	Club	Lea	G	IP	W	L	Pct	SO	BB	H	ERA	SAVES
1996 Royals		Gulf Coast	11	44¹/₃	3	2	.600	43	25	34	4.26	0
1997 Lansing		Midwest	26	144²/₃	5	8	.385	116	53	157	4.79	0
1998 Wilmington		Carolina	26	147²/₃	10	7	.588	162	59	126	2.93	0
1999 Wichita		Texas	28	157	8	10	.444	122	49	154	4.64	1
1999 Kansas City		A.L.	1	2¹/₃	0	0	.000	3	1	1	0.00	0
2000 Omaha		P.C.	12	72²/₃	4	4	.500	53	22	75	4.46	0
2000 Kansas City		A.L.	16	72¹/₃	2	5	.286	37	43	91	8.21	0
Major League Totals		2 Yrs.	17	74²/₃	2	5	.286	40	44	92	7.96	0

EATON, ADAM THOMAS
Born, Seattle, Washington, November 23, 1977.
Bats Right. Throws Right. Height, 6 feet, 2 inches. Weight, 190 pounds.

Year	Club	Lea	G	IP	W	L	Pct	SO	BB	H	ERA	SAVES
1997 Piedmont		So.Atl.	14	71¹/₃	5	6	.455	57	30	81	4.16	0
1998 Clearwater		Fla.St.	24	131²/₃	9	8	.529	89	47	152	4.44	0
1999 Clearwater a		Fla.St.	13	69	5	5	.500	50	24	81	3.91	0
1999 Reading		Eastern	12	77	5	4	.556	67	28	60	2.92	0
1999 Scranton-WB		Int.	3	21	1	1	.500	10	6	17	3.00	0

Year Club	Lea	G	IP	W	L	Pct	SO	BB	H	ERA	SAVES
2000 Mobile ....Southern		10	57	4	1	.800	58	18	47	2.68	1
2000 San Diego ...........N.L.		22	135	7	4	.636	90	61	134	4.13	0

a Traded by Philadelphia Phillies to San Diego Padres with pitcher Carlton Loewer and pitcher Steve Montgomery for pitcher Andy Ashby, November 10, 1999.

EILAND, DAVID WILLIAM
Born, Dade City, Florida, July 5, 1966.
Bats Right. Throws Right. Height, 6 feet, 3 inches. Weight, 205 pounds.

Year	Club	Lea	G	IP	W	L	Pct	SO	BB	H	ERA	SAVES
1987 Oneonta	N.Y.-Penn.	5	$29\frac{1}{3}$	4	0	1.000	16	3	20	1.84	0
1987 Ft.Laudrdle	Fla.St.	8	$62\frac{1}{3}$	5	3	.625	28	8	57	1.88	0
1988 Albany	Eastern	18	$119\frac{1}{3}$	9	5	.643	66	22	95	2.56	0
1988 New York	A.L.	3	$12\frac{2}{3}$	0	0	.000	7	4	15	6.39	0
1988 Columbus	Int.	4	$24\frac{1}{3}$	1	1	.500	13	6	25	2.59	0
1989 New York	A.L.	6	$34\frac{1}{3}$	1	3	.250	11	13	44	5.77	0
1989 Columbus	Int.	18	103	9	4	.692	45	21	107	3.76	0
1990 Columbus	Int.	27	$175\frac{1}{3}$	16	5	.762	96	32	155	2.87	0
1990 New York	A.L.	5	$30\frac{1}{3}$	2	1	.667	16	5	31	3.56	0
1991 Columbus	Int.	9	60	6	1	.857	18	7	54	2.40	0
1991 New York	A.L.	18	$72\frac{2}{3}$	2	5	.286	18	23	87	5.33	0
1992 San Diego	N.L.	7	27	0	2	.000	10	5	33	5.67	0
1992 Las Vegas a	P.C.	14	$63\frac{2}{3}$	4	5	.444	31	11	78	5.23	0
1993 San Diego	N.L.	10	$48\frac{1}{3}$	0	3	.000	14	17	58	5.21	0
1993 Charlotte	Int.	8	$35\frac{2}{3}$	1	3	.250	13	12	42	5.30	0
1993 Okla City b-c-d ...	A.A.	7	$35\frac{2}{3}$	3	1	.750	15	9	39	4.29	0
1994 Columbus e	Int.	26	$140\frac{2}{3}$	9	6	.600	84	33	141	3.58	0
1995 Columbus	Int.	19	109	8	7	.533	62	22	109	3.14	0
1995 New York f	A.L.	4	10	1	1	.500	6	3	16	6.30	0
1996 Louisville	A.A.	8	$24\frac{1}{3}$	0	1	.000	17	8	27	5.55	0
1996 Columbus g-h ...	Int.	15	$92\frac{1}{3}$	8	4	.667	76	13	77	2.92	0
1997 Yankees	Gulf Coast	2	7	1	0	1.000	5	0	12	9.00	0
1997 Tampa	Fla.St.	3	12	1	0	1.000	11	0	11	3.75	0
1997 Columbus i	Int.	13	$62\frac{1}{3}$	4	2	.667	43	14	80	6.64	0
1998 Durham	Int.	28	$171\frac{2}{3}$	13	5	.722	112	27	177	2.99	0
1998 Tampa Bay j	A.L.	1	$2\frac{2}{3}$	0	1	.000	1	3	6	20.25	0
1999 Durham	Int.	10	59	5	3	.625	46	9	60	3.36	0
1999 Tampa Bay k	A.L.	21	$80\frac{1}{3}$	4	8	.333	53	27	98	5.60	0
2000 Orlando	Southern	2	$11\frac{1}{3}$	1	0	1.000	8	1	7	1.59	0
2000 Durham	Int.	4	$13\frac{1}{3}$	2	1	.667	10	3	31	4.63	0
2000 Tampa Bay l-m ...	A.L.	17	$54\frac{2}{3}$	2	3	.400	17	18	77	7.24	0
Major League Totals ....10 Yrs.		92	373	12	27	.308	153	118	465	5.74	0

a Released by New York Yankees, January 19, 1992, signed by San Diego Padres, February 3, 1992.
b Filed for free agency, December 7, 1992, re-signed with San Diego Padres, February 28, 1993.
c Filed for free agency, May 27, 1993, signed with Cleveland Indians, May 29, 1993.
d Traded to Texas Rangers for pitcher Gerald Alexander and pitcher Allan Anderson, August 5, 1993.
e Filed for free agency, October 15, 1993, signed with New York Yankees, March 12, 1994.
f Filed for free agency, October 3, 1995, signed with St. Louis Cardinals, November 24, 1995.
g Released by St. Louis Cardinals, June 15, 1996, signed with New York Yankees organization, June 17, 1996.
h Filed for free agency, October 15, 1996, re-signed with New York Yankees, December 23, 1996.
i Filed for free agency, October 17, 1997, signed with Tampa Bay Devil Rays, December 16, 1997.
j Filed for free agency, October 16, 1998, re-signed with Tampa Bay Devil Rays, November 23, 1998.
k On disabled list from June 8 to June 23 and August 27 to September 11, 1999.
l On disabled list from May 24 to August 8, 2000.
m Filed for free agency, October 12, 2000, signed with Oakland Athletics organization, December 6, 2000.

ELARTON, VINCENT SCOTT (SCOTT)
Born, Lamar, Colorado, February 23, 1976.
Bats Right. Throws Right. Height, 6 feet, 7 inches. Weight, 240 pounds.

Year	Club	Lea	G	IP	W	L	Pct	SO	BB	H	ERA	SAVES
1994 Astros	Gulf Coast	5	28	4	0	1.000	28	5	9	0.00	0
1994 Quad City	Midwest	9	$54\frac{2}{3}$	4	1	.800	42	18	42	3.29	0
1995 Quad City	Midwest	26	$149\frac{2}{3}$	13	7	.650	112	71	149	4.45	0
1996 Kissimmee	Fla.St.	27	$172\frac{1}{3}$	12	7	.632	130	54	154	2.92	0
1997 Jackson	Texas	20	$133\frac{1}{3}$	7	4	.636	141	47	103	3.24	0
1997 New Orleans	A.A.	9	54	4	4	.500	50	17	51	5.33	0
1998 New Orleans	P.C.	14	92	9	4	.692	100	41	71	4.01	0

Year Club	Lea	G	IP	W	L	Pct	SO	BB	H	ERA	SAVES
1998 Houston ..............N.L.		28	57	2	1	.667	56	20	40	3.32	2
1999 Houston ..............N.L.		42	124	9	5	.643	121	43	111	3.48	1
2000 New Orleans ..........P.C.		2	12	1	0	1.000	12	4	3	0.75	0
2000 Round Rock ....Texas		1	6⅓	1	0	1.000	7	0	7	2.84	0
2000 Houston a .............N.L.		30	192⅔	17	7	.708	131	84	198	4.81	0
Major League Totals ....3 Yrs.		100	373⅔	28	13	.683	308	147	349	4.14	3
Division Series											
1998 Houston ..............N.L.		1	2	0	1	.000	3	1	1	4.50	0
1999 Houston ..............N.L.		2	2⅓	0	0	.000	3	1	4	3.86	0
Division Series Totals		3	4⅓	0	1	.000	6	2	5	4.15	0

a On disabled list from March 29 to April 22, 2000.

ELDRED, CALVIN JOHN
Born, Cedar Rapids, Iowa, November 24, 1967.
Bats Right. Throws Right. Height, 6 feet, 4 inches. Weight, 235 pounds.

Year Club	Lea	G	IP	W	L	Pct	SO	BB	H	ERA	SAVES
1989 Beloit ....Midwest		5	31⅓	2	1	.667	32	11	23	2.30	0
1990 Stockton ....California		7	50	4	2	.667	75	19	31	1.62	0
1990 El Paso ....Texas		19	110⅓	5	4	.556	93	47	126	4.49	0
1991 Denver ..............A.A.		29	*185	13	9	.591	*168	84	161	3.75	0
1991 Milwaukee ............A.L.		3	16	2	0	1.000	10	6	20	4.50	0
1992 Denver ..............A.A.		19	141	10	6	.625	99	42	122	3.00	0
1992 Milwaukee ............A.L.		14	100⅓	11	2	.846	62	23	76	1.79	0
1993 Milwaukee ............A.L.		36	*258	16	16	.500	180	91	232	4.01	0
1994 Milwaukee ............A.L.		25	179	11	11	.500	98	84	158	4.68	0
1995 Milwaukee a ..........A.L.		4	23⅔	1	1	.500	18	10	24	3.42	0
1996 New Orleans ...........A.A.		6	32⅓	2	2	.500	30	17	24	3.34	0
1996 Milwaukee b ..........A.L.		15	84⅔	4	4	.500	50	38	82	4.46	0
1997 Milwaukee ............A.L.		34	202	13	*15	.464	122	89	207	4.99	0
1998 Milwaukee c ..........N.L.		23	133	4	8	.333	86	61	157	4.80	0
1999 Huntsville ....Southern		2	12	0	1	.000	10	3	13	7.50	0
1999 Louisville ....Int.		4	18⅔	0	1	.000	21	10	19	5.30	0
1999 Milwaukee d-e .........N.L.		20	82	2	8	.200	60	46	101	7.79	0
2000 Charlotte ....Int.		2	5	0	1	.000	1	0	4	7.20	0
2000 Chicago f-g ...........A.L.		20	112	10	2	.833	97	59	103	4.58	0
Major League Totals ....10 Yrs.		194	1190⅔	74	67	.525	783	507	1160	4.52	0

a On disabled list from May 15 to October 2, 1995.
b On disabled list from April 1 to July 14, 1996.
c On disabled list from July 27 to September 28, 1998.
d On disabled list from March 29 to April 21 and July 2 to August 15, 1999.
e Traded to Chicago White Sox with infielder Jose Valentin for pitcher John Snyder and pitcher Jaime Navarro, January 12, 2000.
f On disabled list from July 15 to September 26, 2000.
g Filed for free agency, November 8, 2000, re-signed with Chicago White Sox, December 7, 2000.

EMBREE, ALAN DUANE
Born, Vancouver, Washington, January 23, 1970.
Bats Left. Throws Left. Height, 6 feet, 2 inches. Weight, 185 pounds.

Year Club	Lea	G	IP	W	L	Pct	SO	BB	H	ERA	SAVES
1990 Burlington ....Appal.		15	81⅔	4	4	.500	58	30	87	2.64	0
1991 Columbus ....So. Atl.		27	155⅓	10	8	.556	137	77	126	3.59	0
1992 Kinston ....Carolina		15	101	10	5	.667	115	32	89	3.30	0
1992 Canton-Akron ....Eastern		12	79	7	2	.778	56	28	61	2.28	0
1992 Cleveland ............A.L.		4	18	0	2	.000	12	8	19	7.00	0
1993 Canton-Akron ....Eastern		1	5⅓	0	0	.000	4	3	3	3.38	0
1994 Canton-Akron ....Eastern		30	157	9	16	.360	81	64	183	5.50	0
1995 Buffalo ...............A.A.		30	40⅔	3	4	.429	56	19	31	0.89	5
1995 Cleveland ............A.L.		23	24⅔	3	2	.600	23	16	23	5.11	1
1996 Buffalo ...............A.A.		20	34⅓	4	1	.800	46	14	26	3.93	5
1996 Cleveland ............A.L.		24	31	1	1	.500	33	21	30	6.39	0
1997 Atlanta b .............N.L.		66	46	3	1	.750	45	20	36	2.54	0
1998 Atlanta-Arizona c-d .....N.L.		55	53⅔	4	2	.667	43	23	56	4.19	1
1999 San Francisco ........N.L.		68	58⅔	3	2	.600	53	26	42	3.38	0
2000 San Francisco ........N.L.		63	60	3	5	.375	49	25	62	4.95	2
Major League Totals ....7 Yrs.		303	292	17	15	.531	258	139	268	4.41	4

Year	Club	Lea	G	IP	W	L	Pct	SO	BB	H	ERA	SAVES
Division Series												
1996 Cleveland	A.L.	3	1	0	0	.000	1	0	0	9.00	0
2000 San Francisco	N.L.	2	1²/₃	0	0	.000	0	0	0	0.00	0
Division Series Totals		5	2²/₃	0	0	.000	1	0	0	3.38	0
Championship Series												
1995 Cleveland	A.L.	1	0¹/₃	0	0	.000	1	0	0	0.00	0
1997 Atlanta	N.L.	1	1	0	0	.000	1	1	0	0.00	0
Championship Series Totals		2	1¹/₃	0	0	.000	2	1	0	0.00	0
World Series Record												
1995 Cleveland	A.L.	4	3¹/₃	0	0	.000	2	2	2	2.70	0

a On disabled list from August 1 to September 7, 1996.
b Traded to Atlanta Braves with outfielder Kenny Lofton for outfielder Marquis Grissom and outfielder David Justice, March 25, 1997.
c Traded to Arizona Diamondbacks for pitcher Russ Springer, June 22, 1998.
d Traded to San Francisco Giants for outfielder Dante Powell, November 10, 1998.

ERDOS, TODD MICHAEL

Born, Washington, Pennsylvania, November 21, 1973.
Bats Right. Throws Right. Height, 6 feet, 1 inch. Weight, 205 pounds.

Year	Club	Lea	G	IP	W	L	Pct	SO	BB	H	ERA	SAVES
1992 Padres	Arizona	12	57²/₃	3	4	.429	61	18	36	2.65	0
1992 Spokane	Northwest	2	13	1	0	1.000	11	5	9	0.69	0
1993 Waterloo	Midwest	11	47²/₃	1	9	.100	27	31	64	8.31	0
1993 Spokane	Northwest	16	90¹/₃	5	6	.455	64	53	73	3.19	0
1994 AR Padres a	Arizona					INJURED - Did Not Play					
1995 Rancho Cuca	California	1	2²/₃	0	0	.000	4	0	5	13.50	0
1995 Clinton	Midwest	5	5	0	0	.000	1	8	4	5.40	0
1995 Idaho Falls	Pioneer	32	41¹/₃	5	3	.625	48	30	34	3.48	1
1996 Rancho Cuca	California	55	67¹/₃	3	3	.500	82	37	63	3.74	17
1997 Mobile	Southern	55	59	1	4	.200	49	22	45	3.36	27
1997 San Diego b	N.L.	11	13²/₃	2	0	1.000	13	4	17	5.27	0
1998 Columbus	Int.	39	48²/₃	3	2	.600	50	20	52	4.62	16
1998 New York c-d	A.L.	2	2	0	0	.000	0	1	5	9.00	0
1999 Columbus	Int.	27	59	3	2	.600	53	25	70	6.56	0
1999 New York	A.L.	4	7	0	0	.000	4	4	5	3.86	0
2000 New York	A.L.	14	25	0	0	.000	18	11	31	5.04	1
2000 San Diego e-f	N.L.	22	29²/₃	0	0		16	17	32	6.67	1
Major League Totals	4 Yrs.	53	77¹/₃	2	0	1.00	5	3	9	0	5.7

a On disabled list from June 4 to September 1, 1994.
b Selected in expansion draft by Arizona Diamondbacks, November 18, 1997.
c Traded to New York Yankees with pitcher Marty Janzen for infielder Andy Fox, March 8, 1998.
d On disabled list from July 24 to September 1, 1998.
e Claimed on waivers by San Diego Padres, July 12, 2000.
   Outrighted by San Diego Padres, October 4, 2000.

ERICKSON, SCOTT GAVIN

Born, Long Beach, California, February 2, 1968.
Bats Right. Throws Right. Height, 6 feet, 4 inches. Weight, 222 pounds.

Year	Club	Lea	G	IP	W	L	Pct	SO	BB	H	ERA	SAVES
1989 Visalia	California	12	78²/₃	3	4	.429	59	22	79	2.97	0
1990 Orlando	Southern	15	101	8	3	.727	69	24	75	3.03	0
1990 Minnesota	A.L.	19	113	8	4	.667	53	51	108	2.87	0
1991 Minnesota a	A.L.	32	204	*20	8	.714	108	71	189	3.18	0
1992 Minnesota	A.L.	32	212	13	12	.520	101	83	197	3.40	0
1993 Minnesota b	A.L.	34	218²/₃	8	*19	.296	116	71	*266	5.19	0
1994 Minnesota c-d-e	A.L.	23	144	8	11	.421	104	59	173	5.44	0
1995 Minnesota-Baltimore f-g-h	A.L.	32	196¹/₃	13	10	.565	106	67	213	4.81	0
1996 Baltimore	A.L.	34	222¹/₃	13	12	.520	100	66	262	5.02	0
1997 Baltimore	A.L.	34	221²/₃	16	7	.696	131	61	218	3.69	0
1998 Baltimore	A.L.	36	*251¹/₃	16	13	.552	186	69	*284	4.01	0
1999 Baltimore	A.L.	34	230¹/₃	15	12	.556	106	*99	244	4.81	0
2000 Frederick	Carolina	1	6²/₃	0	0	.000	5	1	3	2.70	0
2000 Bowie	Eastern	1	7	0	0	.000	5	0	4	0.00	0
2000 Baltimore i	A.L.	16	92²/₃	5	8	.385	41	48	127	7.87	0
Major League Totals	11 Yrs.	326	2106¹/₃	135	116	.538	1152	745	2281	4.43	0

Year	Club	Lea	G	IP	W	L	Pct	SO	BB	H	ERA	SAVES
	Division Series											
1996	Baltimore	A.L.	1	6²/3	0	0	.000	6	2	6	4.05	0
1997	Baltimore	A.L.	1	6²/3	1	0	1.000	6	2	7	4.05	0
Divisional Series Totals			2	13¹/3	1	0	1.000	12	4	13	4.05	0
	Championship Series											
1991	Minnesota	A.L.	1	4	0	0	.000	2	5	3	4.50	0
1996	Baltimore	A.L.	2	11¹/3	0	1	.000	8	4	14	2.38	0
1997	Baltimore	A.L.	2	12²/3	1	0	1.000	6	1	15	4.26	0
Championship Series Totals			5	28	1	1	.500	16	10	32	3.54	0
	World Series Record											
1991	Minnesota	A.L.	2	10²/3	0	0	.000	5	4	10	5.06	0

a On disabled list from June 30 to July 15, 1991.
b On disabled list from April 2 to April 17, 1993.
c Pitched no-hit, no-run game against Milwaukee Brewers, winning 6-0, April 27, 1994.
d On disabled list from May 15 to May 31, 1994.
e Declared restricted free agent under Major League Baseball implemented labor proposal, December 23, 1994.
f Re-signed with Minnesota Twins, April 29, 1995.
g Traded to Baltimore Orioles for pitcher Scott Klingenbeck and player to be named later, July 7, 1995.
h Minnesota Twins received outfielder Kimera Bartee to complete trade, September 19, 1995.
i On disabled list from March 28 to May 3 and July 26 to October 31, 2000.

ESCOBAR, KELVIM JOSE
Born, LaGuaira, Venezuela, April 11, 1976.
Bats Right. Throws Right. Height, 6 feet, 1 inch. Weight, 205 pounds.

Year	Club	Lea	G	IP	W	L	Pct	SO	BB	H	ERA	SAVES
1994	Blue Jays	Gulf Coast	11	65	4	4	.500	64	18	56	2.35	0
1995	Medcine Hat	Pioneer	14	69¹/3	3	3	.500	75	33	66	5.71	0
1996	Dunedin	Fla. St.	18	110¹/3	9	5	.643	113	33	101	2.69	0
1996	Knoxville	Southern	10	54	3	4	.429	44	24	61	5.33	0
1997	Dunedin	Fla. St.	3	12	0	1	.000	16	3	16	3.75	0
1997	Knoxville	Southern	5	24¹/3	2	1	.667	31	16	20	3.70	0
1997	Toronto	A.L.	27	31	3	2	.600	36	19	28	2.90	14
1998	Syracuse	Int.	13	59²/3	2	2	.500	64	24	51	3.77	1
1998	Toronto a	A.L.	22	79²/3	7	3	.700	72	35	72	3.73	0
1999	Toronto	A.L.	33	174	14	11	.560	129	81	203	5.69	0
2000	Toronto	A.L.	43	180	10	15	.400	142	85	186	5.35	2
Major League Totals		4 Yrs.	125	464²/3	34	31	.523	379	220	489	5.04	16

a On disabled list from April 16 to May 6, 1998.

ESTES, AARON SHAWN (SHAWN)
Born, San Bernardino, California, February 18, 1973.
Bats Both. Throws Left. Height, 6 feet, 2 inches. Weight, 185 pounds.

Year	Club	Lea	G	IP	W	L	Pct	SO	BB	H	ERA	SAVES
1991	Bellingham	Northwest	9	34	1	3	.250	35	55	27	6.88	0
1992	Bellingham	Northwest	15	77	3	3	.500	77	45	84	4.32	0
1993	Appleton	Midwest	19	83¹/3	5	9	.357	65	52	108	7.24	0
1994	Mariners	Arizona	5	20	0	3	.000	31	6	16	3.15	0
1994	Appleton	Midwest	5	19²/3	0	2	.000	28	17	19	4.11	0
1995	Wisconsin	Midwest	2	10	0	0	.000	11	5	5	0.90	0
1995	Burlington	Midwest	4	15¹/3	0	0	.000	22	12	13	4.11	0
1995	San Jose	California	9	49²/3	5	2	.714	61	17	32	2.17	0
1995	Shreveport	Texas	4	22¹/3	2	0	1.000	18	10	14	2.01	0
1995	San Francisco a	N.L.	3	17¹/3	0	3	.000	14	5	16	6.75	0
1996	Phoenix	P.C.	18	110¹/3	9	3	.750	95	38	92	3.43	0
1996	San Francisco	N.L.	11	70	3	5	.375	60	39	63	3.60	0
1997	San Francisco b	N.L.	32	201	19	5	.792	181	*100	162	3.18	0
1998	Bakersfield	California	1	4¹/3	0	0	.000	5	1	3	0.00	0
1998	Fresno	P.C.	1	5	1	0	1.000	6	3	3	1.80	0
1998	San Francisco c	N.L.	25	149¹/3	7	12	.368	136	80	150	5.06	0
1999	San Francisco	N.L.	32	203	11	11	.500	159	112	209	4.92	0
2000	Fresno	P.C.	1	3	0	1	.000	2	2	5	9.00	0
2000	San Jose	California	1	7	1	0	1.000	11	1	2	0.00	0
2000	San Francisco d	N.L.	30	190¹/3	15	6	.714	136	108	194	4.26	0
Major League Totals		6 Yrs.	133	831	55	42	.567	686	444	794	4.30	0
	Divisional Series											
1997	San Francisco	N.L.	1	3	0	0	.000	3	4	5	15.00	0

Year	Club	Lea	G	IP	W	L	Pct	SO	BB	H	ERA	SAVES
2000 San Francisco	.........N.L.		1	3	0	0	.000	3	3	- 3	6.00	0
Division Series Totals	....		2	6	0	0	.000	6	7	8	10.50	0

a Traded to San Francisco Giants with infielder Wilson Delgado for pitcher Salomon Torres, May 20, 1995.
b On disabled list from April 1 to April 7, 1997.
c On disabled list from July 11 to September 4, 1998.
d On disabled list from March 29 to April 16, 2000.

ETHERTON, SETH MICHAEL
Born, Laguna Beach, California, October 17, 1976.
Bats Right. Throws Right. Height, 6 feet, 1 inch. Weight, 200 pounds.

Year	Club	Lea	G	IP	W	L	Pct	SO	BB	H	ERA	SAVES
1998 Midland	.........Texas		9	48$\frac{1}{3}$	1	5	.167	35	12	57	6.14	0
1999 Erie	.............Eastern		24	167$\frac{2}{3}$	10	10	.500	153	43	153	3.27	1
1999 Edmonton	............P.C.		4	21$\frac{1}{3}$	0	2	.000	19	6	25	5.48	0
2000 Edmonton	............P.C.		9	58$\frac{1}{3}$	3	2	.600	50	19	60	4.01	0
2000 Anaheim a-b	..........A.L.		11	60$\frac{1}{3}$	5	1	.833	32	22	68	5.52	0

a On disabled list from August 5 to October 31, 2000.
b Traded to Cincinnati Reds for infielder Wilmy Caceres, December 10, 2000.

FARNSWORTH, KYLE LYNN
Born, Wichita, Kansas, April 14, 1976.
Bats Right. Throws Right. Height, 6 feet, 4 inches. Weight, 205 pounds.

Year	Club	Lea	G	IP	W	L	Pct	SO	BB	H	ERA	SAVES
1995 Cubs	...........Gulf Coast		16	31	3	2	.600	18	11	22	0.87	1
1996 Rockford	.........Midwest		20	112	9	6	.600	82	35	122	3.70	0
1997 Daytona	.........Fla.St.		27	156$\frac{1}{3}$	10	10	.500	105	47	178	4.09	0
1998 West Tenn	.......Southern		13	81$\frac{1}{3}$	8	2	.800	73	21	70	2.77	0
1998 Iowa	..............P.C.		18	102$\frac{2}{3}$	5	9	.357	79	36	129	6.93	0
1999 Iowa	..............P.C.		6	39$\frac{1}{3}$	2	2	.500	29	9	38	3.20	0
1999 Chicago	..............N.L.		27	130	5	9	.357	70	52	140	5.05	0
2000 Iowa	..............P.C.		22	25$\frac{1}{3}$	0	2	.000	22	18	24	3.20	0
2000 Chicago	..............N.L.		46	77	2	9	.182	74	50	90	6.43	1
Major League Totals	.......2 Yrs.		73	207	7	18	.280	144	102	230	5.57	1

FASSERO, JEFFREY JOSEPH
Born, Springfield, Illinois, January 5, 1963.
Bats Left. Throws Left. Height, 6 feet, 1 inch. Weight, 195 pounds.

Year	Club	Lea	G	IP	W	L	Pct	SO	BB	H	ERA	SAVES
1984 Johnson City	.......Appal.		13	66$\frac{2}{3}$	4	7	.364	59	39	65	4.59	1
1985 Springfield	.......Midwest		29	119	4	8	.333	65	45	124	4.01	1
1986 St. Petersburg	......Fla. St.		26	*176	13	7	.650	112	56	156	2.45	0
1987 Arkansas	............Texas		28	151$\frac{1}{3}$	10	7	.588	118	67	168	4.10	0
1988 Arkansas	............Texas		70	78	5	5	.500	72	41	97	3.58	17
1989 Louisville	............A.A.		22	112	3	10	.231	73	47	136	5.22	0
1989 Arkansas a-b	........Texas		6	44	4	1	.800	38	12	32	1.64	0
1990 Canton c	.........Eastern		61	64$\frac{1}{3}$	5	4	.556	61	24	66	2.80	6
1991 Indianapolis	..........A.A.		18	18$\frac{1}{3}$	3	0	1.000	12	7	11	1.47	4
1991 Montreal	.............N.L.		51	55$\frac{1}{3}$	2	5	.286	42	17	39	2.44	8
1992 Montreal	.............N.L.		70	85$\frac{2}{3}$	8	7	.533	63	34	81	2.84	1
1993 Montreal	.............N.L.		56	149$\frac{2}{3}$	12	5	.706	140	54	119	2.29	1
1994 Montreal d	.............N.L.		21	138$\frac{2}{3}$	8	6	.571	119	40	119	2.99	0
1995 Montreal	.............N.L.		30	189	13	14	.481	164	74	207	4.33	0
1996 Montreal e	.............N.L.		34	231$\frac{2}{3}$	15	11	.577	222	55	217	3.30	0
1997 Seattle	............A.L.		35	234$\frac{1}{3}$	16	9	.640	189	84	226	3.61	0
1998 Seattle f	............A.L.		32	224$\frac{2}{3}$	13	12	.520	176	66	223	3.97	0
1999 Seattle-Texas g-h	.....A.L.		37	156$\frac{1}{3}$	5	14	.263	114	83	208	7.20	0
2000 Boston i-j	.............A.L.		38	130	8	8	.500	97	50	153	4.78	0
Major League Totals	.......10 Yrs.		404	1595$\frac{1}{3}$	100	91	.524	1326	557	1592	3.89	10
Division Series												
1997 Seattle	..............A.L.		1	8	1	0	1.000	3	4	3	1.13	0
1999 Texas	..............A.L.		1	1	0	0	.000	1	1	2	9.00	0
Division Series Totals	....		2	9	1	0	1.000	4	5	5	2.00	0

Drafted by Chicago White Sox from St. Louis Cardinals organization in minor league draft, December 5, 1989.
Released by Chicago White Sox, March 28; signed with Cleveland Indians organization, April 7, 1990.

c Became free agent, October 15, 1990; signed with Montreal Expos organization, January 3, 1991.
d On disabled list from July 24 to August 10, 1994.
e Traded to Seattle Mariners with pitcher Alex Pacheco for catcher Chris Widger, pitcher Matt Wagner and pitcher Trey Moore, October 29, 1996.
f On disabled list from March 31 to April 12, 1998.
g Traded to Texas Rangers for player to be named later, August 27, 1999.
h Filed for free agency, October 28, 1999. Signed with Boston Red Sox, December 22, 1999.
i On disabled list from June 19 to July 4, 2000.
j Filed for free agency, October 31, 2000, signed with Chicago Cubs, December 8, 2000.

FERNANDEZ, OSVALDO

Born, Holguin, Cuba, November 4, 1968.
Bats Right. Throws Right. Height, 6 feet, 2 inches. Weight, 190 pounds.

Year	Club	Lea	G	IP	W	L	Pct	SO	BB	H	ERA	SAVES
1996 San Francisco a	N.L.	30	171²/₃	7	13	.350	106	57	193	4.61	0
1997 Phoenix	P.C.	2	12	0	0	.000	4	3	10	3.00	0
1997 San Francisco b	N.L.	11	56¹/₃	3	4	.429	31	15	74	4.95	0
1998 San Francisco c-d	N.L.	INJURED - did not play									
1999 San Jose e	California	4	9	0	1	.000	5	2	6	6.00	0
2000 Louisville	Int.	10	56²/₃	6	1	.857	44	19	57	4.13	0
2000 Chattanooga	Southern	1	5²/₃	0	0	.000	1	3	11	12.71	0
2000 Cincinnati f	N.L.	15	79²/₃	4	3	.571	36	31	69	3.62	0

Major League Totals . . . . 3 Yrs. 56 307²/₃ 14 20 .412 173 103 336 4.42 0
a Signed with San Francisco Giants, January 16, 1996.
b On disabled list from May 20 to June 20 and June 26 to September 29, 1997.
c On disabled list from March 22 to October 15, 1998.
d Filed for free agency, December 18, 1998, re-signed with San Francisco Giants, January 4, 1999.
e Filed for free agency, October 15, 1999, signed with Cincinnati Reds organization, February 15, 2000.
f On disabled list from July 7 to August 31, 2000.

FETTERS, MICHAEL LEE

Born, Van Nuys, California, December 19, 1964.
Bats Right. Throws Right. Height, 6 feet, 4 inches. Weight, 215 pounds.

Year	Club	Lea	G	IP	W	L	Pct	SO	BB	H	ERA	SAVES
1986 Salem	Northwest	12	72	4	2	.667	72	51	60	3.38	0
1987 Palm Springs	California	19	116	9	7	.563	105	73	106	3.57	0
1988 Midland	Texas	20	114	8	8	.500	101	67	116	5.92	0
1988 Edmonton	P.C.	2	14	2	0	1.000	11	10	8	1.93	0
1989 Edmonton	P.C.	26	168	12	8	.600	144	72	160	3.80	0
1989 California	A.L.	1	3¹/₃	0	0	.000	4	1	5	8.10	0
1990 Edmonton	P.C.	5	27¹/₃	1	1	.500	26	13	22	0.99	0
1990 California	A.L.	26	67²/₃	1	1	.500	35	20	77	4.12	1
1991 Edmonton	P.C.	11	61	2	7	.222	43	26	65	4.87	0
1991 California a	A.L.	19	44²/₃	2	5	.286	24	28	53	4.84	0
1992 Milwaukee b	A.L.	50	62²/₃	5	1	.833	43	24	38	1.87	2
1993 Milwaukee	A.L.	45	59¹/₃	3	3	.500	23	22	59	3.34	0
1994 Milwaukee c	A.L.	42	46	1	4	.200	31	27	41	2.54	17
1995 Milwaukee d-e	A.L.	40	34²/₃	0	3	.000	33	20	40	3.38	22
1996 Milwaukee	A.L.	61	61¹/₃	3	3	.500	53	26	65	3.38	32
1997 Tucson	P.C.	2	1²/₃	0	0	.000	0	1	1	10.80	0
1997 Milwaukee f-g	A.L.	51	70¹/₃	1	5	.167	62	33	62	3.45	6
1998 Oakland-Anaheim h-i-j	A.L.	60	58²/₃	2	8	.200	43	25	62	4.30	5
1999 Rochester	Int.	4	3²/₃	0	0	.000	6	2	0	0.00	0
1999 Baltimore k-l	A.L.	27	31	1	0	1.000	22	22	35	5.81	0
2000 Los Angeles m	N.L.	51	50	6	2	.750	40	25	35	3.24	5

Major League Totals . . . . 12 Yrs. 473 589²/₃ 25 35 .417 413 273 572 3.59 90
a Traded to Milwaukee Brewers with pitcher Glenn Carter for pitcher Chuck Crim, December 10, 1991.
b On disabled list from May 3 to May 19, 1992.
c Declared restricted free agent under Major League Baseball implemented labor proposal, December 23, 1994
d Re-signed with Milwaukee Brewers, April 13, 1995.
e On disabled list from May 25 to June 9, 1995.
f On disabled list from April 4 to May 5, 1997.
g Traded to Cleveland Indians with pitcher Ben McDonald and pitcher Ron Villone for outfielder Marquis Grisso and pitcher Jeff Juden, December 8, 1997. Traded to Oakland Athletics for pitcher Steve Karsay, December 8, 199
h On disabled list from April 6 to April 26, 1998.
i Traded to Anaheim Angels for player to be named later and cash, August 10, 1998.
j Filed for free agency, October 26, 1998. Signed with Baltimore Orioles organization, February 4, 1999.

On disabled list from June 7 to September 1, 1999.
Filed for free agency, November 1, 1999. Signed with Los Angeles Dodgers organization, December 16, 1999.
On disabled list from May 4 to May 25, 2000.

FINLEY, CHARLES EDWARD (CHUCK)

Born, Monroe, Louisiana, November 26, 1962.
Bats Left. Throws Left. Height, 6 feet, 6 inches. Weight, 214 pounds.

Year	Club	Lea	G	IP	W	L	Pct	SO	BB	H	ERA	SAVES
'85	Salem	Northwest	18	29	3	1	.750	32	10	34	4.66	5
'86	Quad City	Midwest	10	12	1	0	1.000	16	3	4	0.00	6
'86	California	A.L.	25	46⅓	3	1	.750	37	23	40	3.30	0
'87	California	A.L.	35	90⅔	2	7	.222	63	43	102	4.67	0
'88	California	A.L.	31	194⅓	9	15	.375	111	82	191	4.17	0
'89	California a	A.L.	29	199⅔	16	9	.640	156	82	171	2.57	0
'90	California	A.L.	32	236	18	9	.667	177	81	210	2.40	0
'91	California	A.L.	34	227⅓	18	9	.667	171	101	205	3.80	0
'92	California b	A.L.	31	204⅓	7	12	.368	124	98	212	3.96	0
'93	California	A.L.	35	251⅓	16	14	.533	187	82	243	3.15	0
'94	California	A.L.	25	*183⅓	10	10	.500	148	71	178	4.32	0
'95	California c	A.L.	32	203	15	12	.556	195	93	192	4.21	0
'96	California	A.L.	35	238	15	16	.484	215	94	241	4.16	0
'97	Lk Elsinore	California	2	9	0	0	.000	12	4	5	2.00	0
'97	Anaheim d	A.L.	25	164	13	6	.684	155	65	152	4.23	0
'98	Anaheim	A.L.	34	223⅓	11	9	.550	212	109	210	3.39	0
'99	Anaheim e	A.L.	33	213⅓	12	11	.522	200	94	197	4.43	0
'00	Cleveland	A.L.	34	218	16	11	.593	189	101	211	4.17	0
Major League Totals	15 Yrs.		470	2893	181	151	.545	2340	1219	2755	3.76	0
Championship Series												
'86	California	A.L.	3	2	0	0	.000	1	0	1	0.00	0

On disabled list from August 22 to September 15, 1989.
On disabled list from April 7 to April 22, 1992.
Filed for free agency, November 12, 1995. Re-signed, January 4, 1996.
On disabled list from April 1 to April 15 and August 20 to September 29, 1997.
Filed for free agency, November 2, 1999. Signed with Cleveland Indians, December 16, 1999.

FLORIE, BRYCE BETTENCOURT

Born, Charleston, South Carolina, May 21, 1970.
Bats Right. Throws Right. Height, 6 feet. Weight, 185 pounds.

Year	Club	Lea	G	IP	W	L	Pct	SO	BB	H	ERA	SAVES
'88	Scottsdale Padres	Arizona	11	38⅓	4	5	.444	29	22	52	7.98	0
'89	Charleston, SC	So. Atl.	12	44	1	7	.125	22	42	54	6.95	0
'89	Spokane	Northwest	14	61	4	5	.444	50	40	79	7.08	0
'90	Waterloo	Midwest	14	65⅔	4	5	.444	38	37	60	4.39	0
'91	Waterloo	Midwest	23	133	7	6	.538	90	79	119	3.92	0
'92	High Desert	California	26	137⅔	9	7	.563	106	114	99	4.12	0
'92	Charleston, SC	So. Atl.	1	5	0	1	.000	5	0	5	1.80	0
'93	Wichita	Texas	27	154⅔	11	8	.579	133	100	128	3.96	0
'94	Las Vegas	P.C.	50	71⅔	2	5	.286	67	47	76	5.15	1
'94	San Diego	N.L.	9	9⅓	0	0	.000	8	3	8	0.96	0
'95	San Diego	N.L.	47	68⅔	2	2	.500	68	38	49	3.01	1
'96	San Diego a-b	N.L.	39	49⅓	2	2	.500	51	27	45	4.01	0
'96	Milwaukee	A.L.	15	19	0	1	.000	12	13	20	6.63	0
'97	Milwaukee c-d	A.L.	32	75	4	4	.500	53	42	74	4.32	0
'98	Toledo	Int.	1	4	0	0	.000	3	0	0	0.00	0
'98	Detroit e	A.L.	42	133	8	9	.471	97	59	141	4.80	0
'99	Lakeland	Fla.St.	1	3	0	0	.000	7	0	0	0.00	0
'99	Detroit-Boston f-g	A.L.	41	81⅓	4	1	.800	65	35	94	4.65	0
'00	Sarasota	Fla.St.	1	3	0	0	.000	2	1	3	0.00	0
'00	Trenton	Eastern	3	5	0	0	.000	11	2	2	0.00	0
'00	Boston h	A.L.	29	49⅓	0	4	.000	34	19	57	4.56	1
Major League Totals	7 Yrs.		254	485	20	23	.465	388	236	488	4.34	2

Traded to Milwaukee Brewers with pitcher Ron Villone and outfielder Marc Newfield for outfielder Greg Vaughn
and player to be named later, July 31, 1996.
San Diego Padres received outfielder Gerald Parent to complete trade, September 16, 1996.
On disabled list from August 21 to September 8, 1997.
Traded to Detroit Tigers with cash for pitcher Mike Myers, pitcher Rick Greene and infielder Santiago Perez,
November 21, 1997.

e On disabled list from June 23 to July 20, 1998.
f On disabled list from March 31 to May 6, 1999.
g Traded to Boston Red Sox for pitcher Mike Maroth, July 31, 1999.
h On disabled list from April 9 to June 18 and September 10 to November 12, 2000.

FORSTER, SCOTT CHRISTIAN
Born, Philadelphia, Pennsylvania, October 27, 1971.
Bats Right. Throws Right. Height, 6 feet, 1 inch. Weight, 194 pounds.

Year Club	Lea	G	IP	W	L	Pct	SO	BB	H	ERA	SAVE
1994 Vermont	N.Y.-Penn.	12	52²/₃	1	6	.143	39	34	38	3.25	0
1995 Wst Plm Bch	Fla.St.	26	146²/₃	6	11	.353	92	80	129	4.05	0
1996 Harrisburg	Eastern	28	176¹/₃	10	7	.588	97	67	164	3.78	0
1997 Harrisburg	Eastern	17	79¹/₃	3	6	.333	71	48	77	2.27	0
1998 Jupiter	Fla.St.	6	8	0	0	.000	7	5	9	9.00	0
1998 Harrisburg	Eastern	25	77²/₃	7	3	.700	54	47	90	4.87	0
1999 Ottawa	Int.	53	52¹/₃	0	4	.000	32	47	49	5.16	0
1999 Harrisburg	Eastern	2	5	0	0	.000	1	0	3	0.00	0
2000 Ottawa	Int.	23	31	1	0	1.000	22	22	24	2.32	0
2000 Montreal a	N.L.	42	32	0	1	.000	23	25	28	7.87	0

a Filed for free agency, October 15, 2000, signed with New York Mets, December 7, 2000.

FOULKE, KEITH CHARLES
Born, San Diego, California, October 19, 1972.
Bats Right. Throws Right. Height, 6 feet. Weight, 195 pounds.

Year Club	Lea	G	IP	W	L	Pct	SO	BB	H	ERA	SAVE
1994 Everett	Northwest	4	19¹/₃	2	0	1.000	22	3	17	0.93	0
1995 San Jose	California	28	177¹/₃	13	6	.684	168	32	166	3.50	0
1996 Shreveport	Texas	27	182²/₃	12	7	.632	129	35	149	2.76	0
1997 Phoenix	P.C.	12	76	5	4	.556	54	15	79	4.50	0
1997 Nashville	A.A.	1	4²/₃	0	0	.000	4	0	8	5.79	0
1997 San Francisco a	N.L.	11	44¹/₃	1	5	.167	33	18	60	8.26	0
1997 Chicago	A.L.	16	28²/₃	3	0	1.000	21	5	28	3.45	3
1998 Chicago b	A.L.	54	65¹/₃	3	2	.600	57	20	51	4.13	1
1999 Chicago	A.L.	67	105¹/₃	3	3	.500	123	21	72	2.22	9
2000 Chicago	A.L.	72	88	3	1	.750	91	22	66	2.97	34
Major League Totals .....4 Yrs.		220	332	13	11	.542	325	86	277	3.71	47
Division Series											
2000 Chicago	A.L.	2	2¹/₃	0	1	.000	2	2	4	11.57	0

a Traded to Chicago White Sox with infielder Mike Caruso, outfielder Brian Manning, pitcher Lorenzo Barcelo, pitcher Bob Howry and pitcher Ken Vining for pitcher Wilson Alvarez, pitcher Danny Darwin and pitcher Robert Hernandez, July 31, 1997.
b On disabled list from August 28 to September 28, 1998.

FRANCO, JOHN ANTHONY
Born, Brooklyn, New York, September 17, 1960.
Bats Left. Throws Left. Height, 5 feet, 10 inches. Weight, 185 pounds.

Year Club	Lea	G	IP	W	L	Pct	SO	BB	H	ERA	SAVE
1981 Vero Beach	Fla. St.	13	79	7	4	.636	60	41	78	3.53	0
1982 San Antonio	Texas	17	105¹/₃	10	5	.667	76	58	137	4.96	0
1982 Albuquerque	P.C.	5	27¹/₃	1	2	.333	24	15	41	7.24	0
1983 Albuquerque a	P.C.	11	15	0	0	.000	8	11	10	5.40	0
1983 Indianapolis	A.A.	23	115	6	10	.375	54	42	148	4.85	2
1984 Cincinnati	N.L.	54	79¹/₃	6	2	.750	55	36	74	2.61	4
1984 Wichita	A.A.	6	9¹/₃	1	0	1.000	11	4	8	5.79	0
1985 Cincinnati	N.L.	67	99	12	3	.800	61	40	83	2.18	12
1986 Cincinnati	N.L.	74	101	6	6	.500	84	44	90	2.94	29
1987 Cincinnati	N.L.	68	82	8	5	.615	61	27	76	2.52	32
1988 Cincinnati	N.L.	70	86	6	6	.500	46	27	60	1.57	*39
1989 Cincinnati b	N.L.	60	80²/₃	4	8	.333	60	36	77	3.12	32
1990 New York	N.L.	55	67²/₃	5	3	.625	56	21	66	2.53	*33
1991 New York	N.L.	52	55¹/₃	5	9	.357	45	18	61	2.93	30
1992 New York c	N.L.	31	33	6	2	.750	20	11	24	1.64	15
1993 New York d	N.L.	35	36¹/₃	4	3	.571	29	19	46	5.20	10
1994 New York e	N.L.	47	50	1	4	.200	42	19	47	2.70	*30

Year	Club	Lea	G	IP	W	L	Pct	SO	BB	H	ERA	SAVES
1995 New York f	...........N.L.		48	51 2/3	5	3	.625	41	17	48	2.44	29
1996 New York	...........N.L.		51	54	4	3	.571	48	21	54	1.83	28
1997 New York	...........N.L.		59	60	5	3	.625	53	20	49	2.55	36
1998 New York	...........N.L.		61	64 2/3	0	8	.000	59	29	66	3.62	38
1999 Binghamton	......Eastern		1	1 1/3	0	0	.000	1	0	0	0.00	0
1999 New York g	...........N.L.		46	40 2/3	0	2	.000	41	19	40	2.88	19
2000 New York h	...........N.L.		62	55 2/3	5	4	.556	56	26	46	3.40	4
Major League Totals	.......17 Yrs.		940	1097	82	74	.526	857	430	1007	2.68	420
Division Series												
1999 New York	...........N.L.		3	3 2/3	1	0	1.000	2	0	1	0.00	0
2000 New York	...........N.L.		2	2	0	0	.000	2	0	1	0.00	1
Division Series Totals	....		5	5 2/3	1	0	1.000	4	0	2	0.00	1
Championship Series												
1999 New York	...........N.L.		3	2 2/3	0	0	.000	3	1	3	3.38	0
2000 New York	...........N.L.		3	2 2/3	0	0	.000	2	2	3	6.75	0
Championship Series Totals	......		6	5 1/3	0	0	.000	5	3	6	5.06	0
World Series Record												
2000 New York	...........N.L.		4	3 1/3	1	0	1.000	1	0	3	0.00	0

a Traded by Los Angeles Dodgers to Cincinnati Reds organization with pitcher Brett Wise for infielder Rafael Landestoy, May 9, 1983.

b Traded to New York Mets with outfielder Don Brown for pitchers Randy Myers and Kip Gross, December 7, 1989.

c On disabled list from June 29 to August 1 and August 26 to end of 1992 season.

d On disabled list from April 17 to May 7 and August 3 to August 27, 1993.

e Filed for free agency, October 17, 1994.

f Re-signed with New York Mets, April 5, 1995.

g On disabled list from July 3 to September 4, 1999.

h Filed for free agency, October 31, 2000, re-signed with New York Mets, November 25, 2000.

FRASCATORE, JOHN VINCENT

Born, New York, N.Y., February 4, 1970.
Bats Right. Throws Right. Height, 6 feet, 1 inch. Weight, 210 pounds.

Year	Club	Lea	G	IP	W	L	Pct	SO	BB	H	ERA	SAVES
1991 Hamilton	........N.Y.-Penn.		30	30 1/3	2	7	.222	18	22	44	9.20	1
1992 Savannah	..........So. Atl.		50	58 2/3	5	7	.417	56	29	49	3.84	23
1993 Springfield	.........Midwest		27	157 1/3	7	12	.368	126	33	157	3.78	0
1994 Arkansas	...........Texas		12	78 1/3	7	3	.700	63	15	76	3.10	0
1994 St. Louis	...........N.L.		1	3 1/3	0	1	.000	2	2	7	16.20	0
1994 Louisville	...........A.A.		13	85	8	3	.727	58	33	82	3.39	0
1995 Louisville	...........A.A.		28	82	2	8	.200	55	34	89	3.95	5
1995 St. Louis	...........N.L.		14	32 2/3	1	1	.500	21	16	39	4.41	0
1996 Louisville	...........A.A.		36	156 1/3	6	13	.316	95	42	180	5.18	0
1997 St. Louis	...........N.L.		59	80	5	2	.714	58	33	74	2.48	0
1998 St. Louis	...........N.L.		69	95 2/3	3	4	.429	49	36	95	4.14	0
1999 Arizona a	...........N.L.		26	33	1	4	.200	15	12	31	4.09	0
1999 Toronto b	...........A.L.		33	37	7	1	.875	22	9	42	3.41	1
2000 Toronto c	...........A.L.		60	73	2	4	.333	30	33	87	5.42	0
Major League Totals	........6 Yrs.		262	354 2/3	19	17	.528	197	141	375	4.09	1

a Traded to Arizona Diamondbacks for pitcher Clint Sodowsky, March 30, 1999.

b Traded to Toronto Blue Jays with infielder Tony Batista for pitcher Dan Plesac, June 12, 1999.

c Designated for assignment by Toronto Blue Jays, January 15, 2001.

FULTZ, RICHARD AARON (AARON)

Born, Memphis, Tennessee, September 4, 1973.
Bats Left. Throws Right. Height, 6 feet. Weight, 196 pounds.

Year	Club	Lea	G	IP	W	L	Pct	SO	BB	H	ERA	SAVES
1992 Giants	.............Arizona		14	67 2/3	3	2	.600	72	33	51	2.13	0
1993 Clinton	..........Midwest		26	148	14	8	.636	144	64	132	3.41	0
1993 Ft. Wayne a	..........Midwest		1	4	0	0	.000	3	0	10	9.00	0
1994 Ft. Myers	.........Fla.St.		28	168 1/3	9	10	.474	132	60	193	4.33	0
1995 New Britain	.........Eastern		3	15	0	2	.000	12	9	11	6.60	0
1995 Ft. Myers	.........Fla.St.		21	122	3	6	.333	127	41	115	3.25	0
1996 San Jose b	.........California		36	104 2/3	9	5	.643	103	54	101	3.96	1
1997 Shreveport	..........Texas		49	70	6	3	.667	60	19	65	2.83	1
1998 Shreveport	..........Texas		54	62	5	7	.417	61	29	58	3.77	15
1998 Fresno c	.............P.C.		10	16	0	0	.000	13	2	22	5.06	0

Year	Club	Lea	G	IP	W	L	Pct	SO	BB	H	ERA	SAVES
1999 Fresno		P.C.	37	137⅓	9	8	.529	151	51	141	4.98	0
2000 San Francisco		N.L.	58	69⅓	5	2	.714	62	28	67	4.67	1
Division Series												
2000 San Francisco		N.L.	1	1⅓	0	1	.000	0	0	3	6.75	0

a Traded by San Francisco Giants to Minnesota Twins with infielder Andres Duncan and pitcher Greg Brummett for pitcher Jim Deshaies, August 28, 1993.

b Released by Minnesota Twins, April 1, 1996, signed with San Francisco Giants organization, April 4, 1996.

c Filed for free agency, October 16, 1998, re-signed with San Francisco Giants organization, October 23, 1998.

FUSSELL, CHRISTOPHER (CHRIS)
Born, Oregon, Ohio, May 19, 1976.
Bats Right. Throws Right. Height, 6 feet, 3 inches. Weight, 200 pounds.

Year	Club	Lea	G	IP	W	L	Pct	SO	BB	H	ERA	SAVES
1994 Orioles		Gulf Coast	14	56⅓	2	3	.400	65	24	53	4.15	0
1995 Bluefield		Appal.	12	65⅔	9	1	.900	98	32	37	2.19	0
1996 Frederick		Carolina	15	86⅓	5	2	.714	94	44	71	2.81	0
1997 Bowie		Eastern	19	82⅓	1	8	.111	71	58	102	7.11	0
1997 Frederick		Carolina	9	50	3	3	.500	54	31	42	3.96	0
1998 Bowie		Eastern	18	93	3	7	.300	84	52	87	4.26	0
1998 Rochester		Int.	10	58⅔	5	2	.714	51	28	50	3.99	0
1998 Baltimore		A.L.	3	9⅔	0	1	.000	8	9	11	8.38	0
1999 Omaha		P.C.	14	81⅓	10	3	.769	80	27	66	3.54	0
1999 Kansas City a		A.L.	17	56	0	5	.000	37	36	72	7.39	2
2000 GC Royals		Gulf Coast	2	3⅔	0	1	.000	6	2	6	2.45	0
2000 Omaha		P.C.	6	21⅔	1	1	.500	12	12	22	4.98	0
2000 Kansas City b		A.L.	20	70	5	3	.625	46	44	76	6.30	0
Major League Totals		3 Yrs.	40	135⅔	5	9	.357	91	89	159	6.90	2

a Traded to Kansas City Royals for infielder Jeff Conine, April 2, 1999.

b On disabled list from June 8 to August 7, 2000.

FYHRIE, MICHAEL EDWIN (MIKE)
Born, Long Beach, California, December 9, 1969.
Bats Right. Throws Right. Height, 6 feet, 2 inches. Weight, 190 pounds.

Year	Club	Lea	G	IP	W	L	Pct	SO	BB	H	ERA	SAVES
1991 Eugene		Northwest	21	39⅓	2	1	.667	45	19	42	2.52	5
1992 Baseball City		Fla.St.	26	162	7	13	.350	92	37	148	2.50	0
1993 Wilmington		Carolina	5	29⅓	3	2	.600	19	8	32	3.68	0
1993 Memphis		Southern	22	131⅓	11	4	.733	59	59	143	3.56	0
1994 Omaha		A.A.	18	85	6	5	.545	37	33	100	5.72	0
1994 Memphis		Southern	11	67	2	5	.286	38	17	67	3.22	0
1995 Wichita		Texas	17	74	3	2	.600	41	23	76	3.04	1
1995 Omaha		A.A.	14	60⅔	3	4	.429	39	14	71	4.45	0
1996 Norfolk		Int.	27	169	15	6	.714	103	33	150	3.04	0
1996 New York a-b-c		N.L.	2	2⅓	0	1	.000	0	3	4	15.43	0
1997 Chiba		Japan Pac.	8	43	3	4	.429	15	15	54	5.82	0
1998 Norfolk d		Int.	24	100⅓	3	7	.300	60	45	115	6.64	0
1999 Anaheim		A.L.	16	51⅔	0	4	.000	26	21	61	5.05	0
2000 Edmonton		P.C.	9	15⅔	2	1	.667	9	12	6	2.30	0
2000 Anaheim e		A.L.	32	52⅔	0	0	.000	43	15	54	2.39	0
Major League Totals		3 Yrs.	50	106⅔	0	5	.000	69	39	119	3.97	0

a Traded to New York Mets by Kansas City Royals for player to be named later, March 23, 1996.

b Sold to Chiba Lotte Marines (Japan Pacific), November 25, 1996.

c Played in Japan in 1997, signed as free agent by New York Mets, December 8, 1997.

d Filed for free agency, October 16, 1998, signed with Anaheim Angels organization, November 4, 1998.

e On disabled list from July 31 to September 3, 2000.

GAGNE, ERIC SERGE
Born, Montreal, Quebec, Canada, January 7, 1976.
Bats Right. Throws Right. Height, 6 feet, 2 inches. Weight, 195 pounds.

Year	Club	Lea	G	IP	W	L	Pct	SO	BB	H	ERA	SAVES
1996 Savannah		So.Atl.	23	115⅓	7	6	.538	131	43	94	3.28	0
1998 Vero Beach		Fla.St.	25	139⅔	9	7	.563	144	48	118	3.74	0
1999 San Antonio		Texas	26	167⅔	12	4	.750	185	64	122	2.63	0
1999 Los Angeles		N.L.	5	30	1	1	.500	30	15	18	2.10	0

Year	Club	Lea	G	IP	W	L	Pct	SO	BB	H	ERA	SAVES
2000 Albuquerque .........P.C.			9	55⅔	5	1	.833	59	15	56	3.88	0
2000 Los Angeles .........N.L.			20	101⅓	4	6	.400	79	60	106	5.15	0
Major League Totals ....2 Yrs.			25	131⅓	5	7	.417	109	75	124	4.45	0

GARCES, RICHARD

Born, Maracay, Venezuela, May 18, 1971.
Bats Right. Throws Right. Height, 6 feet. Weight, 215 pounds.

Year	Club	Lea	G	IP	W	L	Pct	SO	BB	H	ERA	SAVES
1988 Elizabethtn ....Appal.			17	59	5	4	.556	69	27	51	2.29	5
1989 Kenosha ....Midwest			24	142⅔	9	10	.474	84	62	117	3.41	0
1990 Visalia ....California			47	54⅔	2	2	.500	75	16	33	1.81	28
1990 Orlando ....Southern			15	17⅓	2	1	.667	22	14	17	2.08	8
1990 Minnesota ...........A.L.			5	5⅔	0	0	.000	1	4	4	1.59	2
1991 Portland .............P.C.			10	13	0	1	.000	13	8	10	4.85	3
1991 Orlando a ....Southern			10	16⅓	2	1	.667	17	14	12	3.31	0
1992 Orlando ....Southern			58	73⅓	3	3	.500	72	39	76	4.54	13
1993 Minnesota ...........A.L.			3	4	0	0	.000	3	2	4	0.00	0
1993 Portland .............P.C.			35	54	1	3	.250	48	64	70	8.33	0
1994 Nashville ....Southern			40	77⅓	4	5	.444	76	31	70	3.72	3
1995 Iowa .................A.A.			23	28⅓	0	2	.000	36	8	25	2.86	7
1995 Chicago-Florida b-c ....N.L.			18	24⅓	0	2	.000	22	11	25	4.44	0
1996 Pawtucket ....Int.			10	15⅔	4	0	1.000	13	5	10	2.30	0
1996 Boston d-e ...........A.L.			37	44	3	2	.600	55	33	42	4.91	0
1997 Boston ...............A.L.			12	13⅔	0	1	.000	12	9	14	4.61	0
1997 Pawtucket f ....Int.			26	31	2	1	.667	42	13	24	1.45	5
1998 Pawtucket ....Int.			7	8⅓	0	1	.000	10	2	6	5.40	3
1998 Boston ...............A.L.			30	46	1	1	.500	34	27	36	3.33	1
1998 Red Sox g-h ......Gulf Coast			7	11	0	0	.000	8	0	11	3.27	0
1999 Pawtucket ....Int.			21	27⅔	1	0	1.000	24	10	24	3.25	7
1999 Boston ...............A.L.			30	40⅔	5	1	.833	33	18	25	1.55	2
2000 Boston ...............A.L.			64	74⅔	8	1	.889	69	23	64	3.25	1
Major League Totals ....8 Yrs.			199	253	17	8	.680	229	127	214	3.38	6
Division Series												
1999 Boston ...............A.L.			2	2⅓	1	0	1.000	2	3	2	3.86	0
Championship Series												
1999 Boston ...............A.L.			2	3	0	0	.000	2	1	3	12.00	0

a On disabled list from May 17 to September 16, 1991.
b Filed for free agency, October 15, 1994, signed with Chicago Cubs organization, January 30, 1995.
c Claimed on waivers by Florida Marlins, August 9, 1995.
d Filed for free agency, October 16, 1995, signed with Boston Red Sox, April 25, 1996.
e Filed for free agency, October 16, 1995, signed with Boston Red Sox, April 25, 1996.
f On disabled list from July 25 to August 20 and August 24 to September 30, 1996.
g On disabled list from March 27 to April 27 and June 2 to June 23, 1997.
h On disabled list from April 14 to May 7 and July 1 to July 17 and August 3 to September 28, 1998.
h Released by Boston Red Sox, November 23, 1998, re-signed with Boston Red Sox organization, January 26, 1999.

GARCIA, FREDDY ANTONIO

Born, Caracas, Venezuela, October 6, 1976.
Bats Right. Throws Right. Height, 6 feet, 4 inches. Weight, 235 pounds.

Year	Club	Lea	G	IP	W	L	Pct	SO	BB	H	ERA	SAVES
1994 Hou/Mil ....Dominican			16	85	4	6	.400	68	38	80	5.29	0
1995 Astros ....Gulf Coast			11	58⅓	6	3	.667	58	14	60	4.47	0
1996 Quad City ....Midwest			13	60⅔	5	4	.556	50	27	57	3.12	0
1997 Kissimmee ....Fla.St.			27	179	10	8	.556	131	49	165	2.56	0
1998 Jackson ....Texas			19	119⅓	6	7	.462	115	58	94	3.24	0
1998 New Orleans ..........P.C.			2	14⅓	1	0	1.000	13	1	14	3.14	0
1998 Tacoma a ...........P.C.			5	32⅓	3	1	.750	30	13	30	3.86	0
1999 Seattle ..............A.L.			33	201⅓	17	8	.680	170	90	205	4.07	0
2000 Everett ....Northwest			2	10	0	0	.000	15	2	11	4.50	0
2000 Tacoma .............P.C.			1	7	1	0	1.000	11	2	5	2.57	0
2000 Seattle b ...........A.L.			21	124⅓	9	5	.643	79	64	112	3.91	0
Major League Totals ....2 Yrs.			54	325⅔	26	13	.667	249	154	317	4.01	0
Division Series												
2000 Seattle ..............A.L.			1	3⅓	0	0	.000	2	3	6	10.80	0
Championship Series												
2000 Seattle ..............A.L.			2	11⅔	2	0	1.000	11	4	10	1.54	0

a Traded by Houston Astros to Seattle Mariners with infielder Carlos Guillen and a player to be named later for pitcher Randy Johnson, July 31, 1998. Mariners received pitcher John Halama to complete trade, October 1, 1998.
b On disabled list from April 22 to July 6, 2000.

GARDNER, MARK ALLAN

Born, Los Angeles, California, March 1, 1962.
Bats Right. Throws Right. Height, 6 feet, 1 inch. Weight, 200 pounds.

Year	Club	Lea	G	IP	W	L	Pct	SO	BB	H	ERA	SAVES
1985	Jamestown	N.Y.-Penn.	3	13	0	0	.000	16	4	9	2.77	0
1985	West Palm Beach	Fla. St.	10	60²/₃	5	4	.556	44	18	54	2.37	0
1986	Jacksonville	Southern	29	168²/₃	10	11	.476	140	90	144	3.84	0
1987	Indianapolis	A.A.	9	46	3	3	.500	41	28	48	5.67	0
1987	Jacksonville	Southern	17	101	4	6	.400	78	42	101	4.19	0
1988	Indianapolis	A.A.	13	84¹/₃	4	2	.667	71	32	65	2.77	0
1988	Jacksonville	Southern	15	112¹/₃	6	3	.667	130	36	72	1.60	0
1989	Indianapolis	A.A.	24	163¹/₃	12	4	.750	*175	59	122	2.37	0
1989	Montreal	N.L.	7	26¹/₃	0	3	.000	21	11	26	5.13	0
1990	Montreal	N.L.	27	152²/₃	7	9	.438	135	61	129	3.42	0
1991	Indianapolis	A.A.	6	31	2	0	1.000	38	16	26	3.48	0
1991	Montreal a-b	N.L.	27	168¹/₃	9	11	.450	107	75	139	3.85	0
1992	Montreal c	N.L.	33	179²/₃	12	10	.545	132	60	179	4.36	0
1993	Omaha	A.A.	8	48¹/₃	4	2	.667	41	19	34	2.79	0
1993	Kansas City d-e	A.L.	17	91²/₃	4	6	.400	54	36	92	6.19	0
1994	Edmonton	P.C.	1	6	1	0	1.000	11	1	4	0.00	0
1994	Brevard City	Fla. St.	1	5	1	0	1.000	3	1	1	0.00	0
1994	Florida f-g	N.L.	20	92¹/₃	4	4	.500	57	30	97	4.87	0
1995	Florida h-i	N.L.	39	102¹/₃	5	5	.500	87	43	109	4.49	1
1996	San Jose j	California	1	5²/₃	0	0	.000	7	0	4	3.18	0
1996	San Francisco k	N.L.	30	179¹/₃	12	7	.632	145	57	200	4.42	0
1997	San Francisco	N.L.	30	180¹/₃	12	9	.571	136	57	188	4.29	0
1998	San Francisco l	N.L.	33	212	13	6	.684	151	65	203	4.33	0
1999	San Jose	California	2	10	1	0	1.000	13	3	10	4.50	0
1999	San Francisco m	N.L.	29	139	5	11	.313	86	57	142	6.47	0
2000	San Francisco n	N.L.	30	149	11	7	.611	92	42	155	4.05	0
Major League Totals	12 Yrs.		322	1673	94	88	.516	1203	594	1659	4.51	1
Division Series												
2000	San Francisco	N.L.	1	4¹/₃	0	1	.000	5	2	4	8.31	0

a On disabled list from April 2 to May 14, 1991.
b Pitched nine no-hit, no-run innings against Los Angeles Dodgers, losing 1-0 in tenth inning, July 26, 1991.
c Traded to Kansas City Royals with pitcher Doug Platt for catcher Tim Spehr and pitcher Jeff Shaw, December 9, 1992.
d On disabled list from July 7 to August 27, 1993.
e Released, December 8, 1993; signed with Florida Marlins organization, January 3, 1994.
f On disabled list from June 8 to June 25, 1994.
g Declared restricted free agent under Major League Baseball implemented labor proposal, December 23, 1994.
h Re-signed with Florida Marlins, April 4, 1995.
i Filed for free agency, October 4, 1995; signed with Florida Marlins organization, December 8, 1995.
j Signed with San Francisco Giants, March 29, 1996.
k On disabled list from July 3 to July 21, 1996.
l Filed for free agency, October 23, 1998, re-signed with San Francisco Giants, November 9, 1998.
m On disabled list from April 17 to May 9, 1999.
n Filed for free agency, October 31, 2000, re-signed with San Francisco Giants, December 7, 2000.

GARIBAY (BRAVO), DANIEL

Born, Maneadero, Mexico, February 14, 1973.
Bats Left. Throws Right. Height, 5 feet, 8 inches. Weight, 154 pounds.

Year	Club	Lea	G	IP	W	L	Pct	SO	BB	H	ERA	SAVES
1994	Tigres	Mexican	26	130	10	6	.625	68	86	147	4.85	0
1994	San Antonio a-b	Texas	3	0²/₃	0	1	.000	0	4	10	121.50	0
1995	Tigres	Mexican	21	45	2	0	1.000	26	29	49	6.40	0
1996	Tigres	Mexican	20	59²/₃	2	4	.333	36	32	64	4.98	0
1997	Tigres c	Mexican	26	159	13	8	.619	95	67	140	3.51	0
1998	Tigres	Mexican	26	155	10	2	.833	112	86	143	3.37	0
1999	Tigres d	Mexican	16	89	2	5	.286	59	56	91	5.06	0
2000	Iowa	P.C.	1	4¹/₃	0	0	.000	2	5	3	2.08	0
2000	Chicago	N.L.	30	74²/₃	2	8	.200	46	39	88	6.03	0

a Sold to Los Angeles Dodgers, March 1, 1992, loaned to Mexico City Tigers for 1993 and 1994.
b Sold to Mexico City Tigers, September 26, 1994.
c Sold to Tampa Bay Devil Rays, October 31, 1997, loaned to Mexico City Tigers for 1998 and 1999.
d Granted free agency October 15, 1999, signed with Chicago Cubs organization, November 14, 1999.

GARLAND, JON STEVEN

Born, Valencia, California, September 27, 1979.
Bats Right. Throws Right. Height, 6 feet, 6 inches. Weight, 205 pounds.

Year	Club	Lea	G	IP	W	L	Pct	SO	BB	H	ERA	SAVES
1997 Cubs	Arizona		10	40	3	2	.600	39	10	37	2.70	0
1998 Rockford	Midwest		19	107 1/3	4	7	.364	70	45	124	5.03	0
1998 Hickory a	So.Atl.		5	26 2/3	1	4	.200	19	13	36	5.40	0
1999 Winston-Salem	Carolina		19	119	5	7	.417	84	39	109	3.33	0
1999 Birmingham	Southern		7	39	3	1	.750	27	18	49	4.38	0
2000 Charlotte	Int.		16	103 2/3	9	2	.818	63	32	99	2.26	1
2000 Birmingham	Southern		1	6	0	0	.000	10	1	4	0.00	0
2000 Chicago b	A.L.		15	69 2/3	4	8	.333	42	40	82	6.46	0

a Traded by Chicago Cubs to Chicago White Sox for pitcher Matt Karcher, July 29, 1998.
b On disabled list from August 19 to September 2, 2000.

GLAVINE, THOMAS MICHAEL

Born, Concord, Massachusetts, March 25, 1966.
Bats Left. Throws Left. Height, 6 feet, 1 inch. Weight, 190 pounds.

Year	Club	Lea	G	IP	W	L	Pct	SO	BB	H	ERA	SAVES
1984 Bradenton Braves	Gulf C.		8	32 1/3	2	3	.400	34	13	29	3.34	0
1985 Sumter	So. Atl.		26	168 2/3	9	6	.600	174	73	*2.35		0
1986 Greenville	Southern		22	145 1/3	11	6	.647	114	70	129	3.41	0
1986 Richmond	Int.		7	40	1	5	.167	12	27	40	5.63	0
1987 Richmond	Int.		22	150 1/3	6	12	.333	91	56	142	3.35	0
1987 Atlanta	N.L.		9	50 1/3	2	4	.333	20	33	55	5.54	0
1988 Atlanta	N.L.		34	195 1/3	7	*17	.292	84	63	201	4.56	0
1989 Atlanta	N.L.		29	186	14	8	.636	90	40	172	3.68	0
1990 Atlanta a	N.L.		33	214 1/3	10	12	.455	129	78	232	4.28	0
1991 Atlanta b-c	N.L.		34	246 2/3	*20	11	.645	192	69	201	2.55	0
1992 Atlanta d	N.L.		33	225	*20	8	.714	129	70	197	2.76	0
1993 Atlanta	N.L.		36	239 1/3	*22	6	.786	120	90	236	3.20	0
1994 Atlanta e	N.L.		25	165 1/3	13	9	.591	140	70	173	3.97	0
1995 Atlanta	N.L.		29	198 2/3	16	7	.696	127	66	182	3.08	0
1996 Atlanta	N.L.		36	235 1/3	15	10	.600	181	85	222	2.98	0
1997 Atlanta	N.L.		33	240	14	7	.667	152	79	197	2.96	0
1998 Atlanta f	N.L.		33	229 1/3	*20	6	.769	157	74	202	2.47	0
1999 Atlanta	N.L.		35	234	14	11	.560	138	83	*259	4.12	0
2000 Atlanta	N.L.		35	241	*21	9	.700	152	65	222	3.40	0
Major League Totals	14 Yrs.		434	2900 2/3	208	125	.625	1811	965	2751	3.39	0
Division Series												
1995 Atlanta	N.L.		1	7	0	0	.000	3	1	5	2.57	0
1996 Atlanta	N.L.		1	6 2/3	1	0	1.000	7	3	5	1.35	0
1997 Atlanta	N.L.		1	6	1	0	1.000	4	5	4.50		0
1998 Atlanta	N.L.		1	7	0	0	.000	8	1	3	1.29	0
1999 Atlanta	N.L.		1	6	0	0	.000	6	3	5	3.00	0
2000 Atlanta	N.L.		1	2 1/3	0	1	.000	2	1	6	27.00	0
Division Series Totals			6	35	2	1	.667	30	14	29	4.11	0
Championship Series												
1991 Atlanta	N.L.		2	14	0	2	.000	11	6	12	3.21	0
1992 Atlanta	N.L.		2	7 1/3	0	2	.000	2	3	13	12.27	0
1993 Atlanta	N.L.		1	7	1	0	1.000	5	0	6	2.57	0
1995 Atlanta	N.L.		1	7	0	0	.000	5	2	7	1.29	0
1996 Atlanta	N.L.		2	13	1	1	.500	9	0	10	2.08	0
1997 Atlanta	N.L.		2	13 1/3	1	1	.500	9	11	13	5.40	0
1998 Atlanta	N.L.		2	11 1/3	0	2	.000	8	9	13	2.31	0
1999 Atlanta	N.L.		1	7	1	0	1.000	8	1	7	0.00	0
Championship Series Totals			13	80 1/3	4	8	.333	57	32	81	3.59	0
World Series Record												
1991 Atlanta	N.L.		2	13 1/3	1	1	.500	8	7	8	2.70	0
1992 Atlanta	N.L.		2	17	1	1	.500	8	4	10	1.59	0
1995 Atlanta	N.L.		2	14	2	0	1.000	11	6	4	1.29	0
1996 Atlanta	N.L.		1	7	0	1	.000	8	3	4	1.29	0
1999 Atlanta	N.L.		1	7	0	0	.000	3	0	7	5.14	0
World Series Totals			8	58 1/3	4	3	.571	38	20	33	2.16	0

a Appeared in one additional game as pinch runner.
b Appeared in one additional game as pinch hitter and one additional game as pinch runner.
c Selected Cy Young Award winner in National League for 1991.
d Appeared in two additional games as pinch hitter.
e Appeared in one additional game as pinch hitter.
f Selected Cy Young Award Winner in National League for 1998.

GLYNN, RYAN DAVID
Born, Portsmouth, Virginia, November 1, 1974.
Bats Right. Throws Right. Height, 6 feet, 3 inches. Weight,195 pounds.

Year	Club	Lea	G	IP	W	L	Pct	SO	BB	H	ERA	SAVES
1995	Hudson Val	N.Y.-Penn.	9	44	3	3	.500	21	16	56	4.70	0
1996	Chston-Sc	So.Atl.	19	121	8	7	.533	72	59	118	4.54	1
1997	Charlotte	Fla.St.	23	134	8	7	.533	96	44	148	4.97	1
1997	Tulsa	Texas	3	21$\frac{1}{3}$	1	1	.500	18	10	21	3.38	0
1998	Tulsa	Texas	26	157	9	6	.600	111	64	140	3.44	0
1999	Texas	A.L.	13	54$\frac{2}{3}$	2	4	.333	39	35	71	7.24	0
1999	Oklahoma	P.C.	16	90$\frac{1}{3}$	6	2	.750	55	36	81	3.39	0
2000	Oklahoma	P.C.	15	83$\frac{2}{3}$	4	2	.667	66	33	72	3.55	2
2000	Texas a	A.L.	16	88$\frac{2}{3}$	5	7	.417	33	41	107	5.58	0
Major League Totals	2 Yrs.		29	143$\frac{1}{3}$	7	11	.389	72	76	178	6.22	0

a On disabled list from July 2 to July 16 and August 12 to August 28, 2000.

GOMES, WAYNE MAURICE
Born, Hampton, Virginia, January 15, 1973.
Bats Right. Throws Right. Height, 6 feet. Weight, 215 pounds.

Year	Club	Lea	G	IP	W	L	Pct	SO	BB	H	ERA	SAVES
1993	Batavia	N.Y.-Penn.	5	7$\frac{1}{3}$	1	0	1.000	11	8	1	1.23	0
1993	Clearwater	Fla. St.	9	7$\frac{2}{3}$	0	0	.000	13	9	4	1.17	4
1994	Clearwater	Fla. St.	23	104$\frac{1}{3}$	6	8	.429	102	82	85	4.74	0
1995	Reading	Eastern	22	104$\frac{2}{3}$	7	4	.636	102	70	89	4.48	24
1996	Reading	Eastern	67	64$\frac{1}{3}$	0	4	.000	79	48	53	4.48	24
1997	Scranton-WB	Int.	26	38	3	1	.750	36	24	31	2.37	7
1997	Philadelphia	N.L.	37	42$\frac{2}{3}$	5	1	.833	24	24	45	5.27	0
1998	Philadelphia	N.L.	71	93$\frac{1}{3}$	9	6	.600	86	35	94	4.24	1
1999	Philadelphia	N.L.	73	74	5	5	.500	58	56	70	4.26	19
2000	Scranton-WB	Int.	3	4	0	0	.000	1	1	3	2.25	0
2000	Philadelphia a	N.L.	65	73$\frac{2}{3}$	4	6	.400	49	35	72	4.40	7
Major League Totals	4 Yrs.		246	283$\frac{2}{3}$	23	18	.561	217	150	281	4.44	27

a On disabled list from July 7 to August 7, 2000.

GOODEN, DWIGHT EUGENE (DOC)
Born, Tampa, Florida, November 16, 1964.
Bats Right. Throws Right. Height, 6 feet, 3 inches. Weight, 210 pounds.

Year	Club	Lea	G	IP	W	L	Pct	SO	BB	H	ERA	SAVES
1982	Kingsport	Appalachian	9	65$\frac{2}{3}$	5	4	.556	66	25	53	2.47	0
1982	Little Falls	N.Y.-Penn.	2	13	0	1	.000	18	3	11	4.15	0
1983	Lynchburg	Carolina	27	191	*19	4	.826	*300	*112	121	*2.50	0
1984	New York a	N.L.	31	218	17	9	.654	*276	73	161	2.60	0
1985	New York b	N.L.	35	*276$\frac{2}{3}$	*24	4	.857	*268	69	198	*1.53	0
1986	New York	N.L.	33	250	17	6	.739	200	80	197	2.84	0
1987	Lynchburg	Carolina	1	4	0	0	.000	3	2	2	0.00	0
1987	Tidewater	Int.	4	22	3	0	1.000	24	9	20	2.05	0
1987	New York c	N.L.	25	179$\frac{2}{3}$	15	7	.682	148	53	162	3.21	0
1988	New York	N.L.	34	248$\frac{1}{3}$	18	9	.667	175	57	242	3.19	0
1989	New York d	N.L.	19	118$\frac{1}{3}$	9	4	.692	101	47	93	2.89	1
1990	New York e	N.L.	34	232$\frac{2}{3}$	19	7	.731	223	70	229	3.83	0
1991	New York f	N.L.	27	190	13	7	.650	150	56	185	3.60	0
1992	New York g-h	N.L.	31	206	10	13	.435	145	70	197	3.67	0
1993	New York i	N.L.	29	208$\frac{2}{3}$	12	15	.444	149	61	188	3.45	0
1994	Norfolk	Int.	1	3	0	0	.000	4	1	0	0.00	0
1994	Binghamton	Eastern	1	5	1	0	1.000	4	1	2	0.00	0
1994	New York j-k-l	N.L.	7	41$\frac{1}{3}$	3	4	.429	40	15	46	6.31	0
1995 m				SUSPENDED—Did Not Play								
1996	New York n	A.L.	29	170$\frac{2}{3}$	11	7	.611	126	88	169	5.01	0
1997	Norwich	Eastern	3	18	3	0	1.000	14	5	13	3.00	0
1997	New York o-p-q	A.L.	20	106$\frac{1}{3}$	9	5	.643	66	53	116	4.91	0
1998	Buffalo	Int.	4	16	1	2	.333	18	7	23	9.00	0
1998	Cleveland r	A.L.	23	134	8	6	.571	83	51	135	3.76	0
1999	Akron	Eastern	1	3	0	0	.000	2	1	3	3.00	0
1999	Buffalo	Int.	1	3$\frac{2}{3}$	0	1	.000	3	3	6	2.45	0
1999	Cleveland s-t	A.L.	26	115	3	4	.429	88	67	127	6.26	0
2000	Houston	N.L.	1	4	0	0	.000	1	3	6	9.00	0
2000	GC Yankees	Gulf Coast	2	8	0	0	.000	12	1	3	0.00	0
2000	Tampa Bay-NY u-v-w	A.L.	26	101	6	5	.545	54	41	113	4.54	2

Year	Club	Lea	G	IP	W	L	Pct	SO	BB	H	ERA	SAVES
Major League Totals ...... 16 Yrs.			430	2800⅔	194	112	.634	2293	954	2564	3.51	3
Divisional Series												
1997 New York		A.L.	1	5⅔	0	0	.000	5	3	5	1.59	0
1998 Cleveland		A.L.	1	0⅓	0	0	.000	1	2	1	54.00	0
2000 New York		A.L.	1	1⅔	0	0	.000	1	1	4	21.60	0
Division Series Totals			3	7⅔	0	0	.000	7	6	10	8.22	0
Championship Series												
1986 New York		N.L.	2	17	0	1	.000	9	5	16	1.06	0
1988 New York		N.L.	3	18⅓	0	0	.000	20	8	10	2.95	0
1998 Cleveland		A.L.	1	4⅔	0	1	.000	3	3	3	5.79	0
2000 New York		A.L.	1	2⅓	0	0	.000	1	0	1	0.00	0
Championship Series Totals			7	42⅓	0	2	.000	33	16	30	2.34	0
World Series Record												
1986 New York		N.L.	2	9	0	2	.000	9	4	17	8.00	0

a Selected Rookie of the Year in National League for 1984.
b Selected Cy Young Award winner in National League for 1985.
c On disabled list from April 1 to June 5, 1987.
d On disabled list from July 2 to September 1, 1989.
e Appeared in one additional game as pinch runner.
f On disabled list from August 24 to end of 1991 season.
g On disabled list from July 18 to August 8, 1992.
h Appeared in two additional games as pinch hitter.
i Appeared in one additional game as pinch hitter.
j On disabled list from April 22 to June 9, 1994.
k Suspended 60 days by Commissioner's Office for violating drug aftercare program from July 28 to end of 1994 season and first 16 days of 1995 season; suspension extended to entire 1995 season for repeated violations of drug aftercare program, November 4, 1994.
l Filed for free agency, October 17, 1994.
m Signed with New York Yankees, October 16, 1995.
n Pitched no-hit, no-run game against Seattle Mariners, winning 2-0, May 14, 1996.
o On disabled list from April 6 to June 15, 1997.
p Filed for free agency, November 3, 1997.
q Signed as free agent with Cleveland Indians, December 8, 1997.
r On disabled list from March 31 to May 23, 1998.
s On disabled list from August 3 to August 31, 1999.
t Filed for free agency, November 4, 1999. Signed with Houston Astros organization, January 6, 2000.
u Sold to Tampa Bay Devil Rays, April 13, 2000.
v Released by Tampa Bay Devil Rays, May 25, 2000, signed with New York Yankees organization, June 11, 2000.
w Filed for free agency, November 10, 2000, re-signed with New York Yankees organization, December 7, 2000.

GORDON, THOMAS (FLASH)
Born, Sebring, Florida, November 18, 1967.
Bats Right. Throws Right. Height, 5 feet, 9 inches. Weight, 180 pounds.

Year	Club	Lea	G	IP	W	L	Pct	SO	BB	H	ERA	SAVES
1986 Sarasota Royals		Gulf C.	9	44	3	1	.750	47	23	31	1.02	0
1986 Omaha		A.A.	1	1⅓	0	0	.000	3	2	6	47.25	0
1987 Eugene		Northwest	15	72⅓	*9	0	*1.000	91	47	48	2.86	1
1987 Fort Myers		Fla. St.	3	13⅔	1	0	1.000	11	17	5	2.63	0
1988 Appleton		Midwest	17	118	7	5	.583	*172	43	69	2.06	0
1988 Memphis		Southern	6	47⅓	6	0	1.000	62	17	16	0.38	0
1988 Omaha		A.A.	3	20⅓	3	0	1.000	29	15	11	1.33	0
1988 Kansas City		A.L.	5	15⅔	0	2	.000	18	7	16	5.17	0
1989 Kansas City		A.L.	49	163	17	9	.654	153	86	122	3.64	1
1990 Kansas City		A.L.	32	195⅓	12	11	.522	175	99	192	3.73	0
1991 Kansas City		A.L.	45	158	9	14	.391	167	87	129	3.87	1
1992 Kansas City		A.L.	40	117⅔	6	10	.375	98	55	116	4.59	0
1993 Kansas City		A.L.	48	155⅔	12	6	.667	143	77	125	3.58	1
1994 Kansas City a-b		A.L.	24	155⅓	11	7	.611	126	87	136	4.35	0
1995 Kansas City c-d-e-f		A.L.	31	189	12	12	.500	119	89	204	4.43	0
1996 Boston		A.L.	34	215⅔	12	9	.571	171	105	249	5.59	0
1997 Boston		A.L.	42	182⅔	6	10	.375	159	78	155	3.74	11
1998 Boston		A.L.	73	79⅓	7	4	.636	78	25	55	2.72	*46
1999 Boston g		A.L.	21	17⅔	0	2	.000	24	12	17	5.60	11
2000 Boston h-i		A.L.	INJURED - did not play									
Major League Totals ...... 12 Yrs.			444	1645	104	96	.520	1431	807	1516	4.15	71
Division Series												
1998 Boston		A.L.	2	3	0	1	.000	1	4	4	9.00	0
1999 Boston		A.L.	2	2	0	0	.000	3	1	1	4.50	0
Division Series Totals			4	5	0	1	.000	4	5	5	7.20	0

Year	Club	Lea	G	IP	W	L	Pct	SO	BB	H	ERA	SAVES
	Championship Series											
1999 Boston		A.L.	3	2	0	0	.000	3	1	3	13.50	0

a Filed for free agency, October 17, 1994; ruled ineligible by Player Relations Committee due to insufficient service time.
b Declared restricted free agent under Major League Baseball implemented labor proposal, December 23, 1994.
c Re-signed with Kansas City Royals, April 28, 1995.
d On disabled list from May 8 to May 24, 1995.
e Filed for free agency, November 12, 1995.
f Signed with Boston Red Sox, December 21, 1995.
g On disabled list from April 18 to May 10 and June 12 to September 27, 1999.
h On disabled list from April 2 to October 30, 2000.
i Not offered 2001 contract, October 31, 2000, signed with Chicago Cubs, December 14, 2000.

GRAVES, DANIEL PETER

Born, Saigon, South Vietnam, August 7, 1973.
Bats Right. Throws Right. Height, 5 feet, 11 inches. Weight, 200 pounds.

Year	Club	Lea	G	IP	W	L	Pct	SO	BB	H	ERA	SAVES
1995 Kinston		Carolina	38	44	3	1	.750	46	12	30	0.82	21
1995 Canton-Akrn		Eastern	17	23 1/3	1	0	1.000	11	2	10	0.00	10
1995 Buffalo		A.A.	3	3	0	0	.000	2	1	5	3.00	0
1996 Buffalo		A.A.	43	79	4	3	.571	46	24	57	1.48	19
1996 Cleveland		A.L.	15	29 2/3	2	0	1.000	22	10	29	4.55	0
1997 Cleveland		A.L.	5	11 1/3	0	0	.000	4	9	15	4.76	0
1997 Buffalo		A.A.	19	43	2	3	.400	21	11	45	4.19	2
1997 Indianapols		A.A.	11	11 2/3	1	0	1.000	5	5	7	3.09	5
1997 Cincinnati a		N.L.	10	14 2/3	0	0	.000	7	11	26	6.14	0
1998 Indianapols		Int.	13	14	1	0	1.000	11	3	15	1.93	0
1998 Cincinnati		N.L.	62	81 1/3	2	1	.667	44	28	76	3.32	8
1999 Cincinnati		N.L.	75	111	8	7	.533	69	49	90	3.08	27
2000 Cincinnati		N.L.	66	91 1/3	10	5	.667	53	42	81	2.56	30
Major League Totals	5 Yrs.		233	339 1/3	22	13	.629	199	149	317	3.32	65

a Traded by Cleveland Indians to Cincinnati Reds with pitcher Jim Crowell, pitcher Scott Winchester and infielder Damian Jackson for pitcher John Smiley and infielder Jeff Branson, July 31, 1997.

GRIMSLEY, JASON ALAN

Born, Cleveland, Texas, August 7, 1967.
Bats Right. Throws Right. Height, 6 feet, 3 inches. Weight, 180 pounds.

Year	Club	Lea	G	IP	W	L	Pct	SO	BB	H	ERA	SAVES
1985 Bend		Northwest	6	11 1/3	0	1	.000	10	25	12	13.50	0
1986 Utica		N.Y.-Penn.	14	64 2/3	1	10	.091	46	77	63	6.40	0
1987 Spartanburg		So.Atl.	23	88 1/3	7	4	.636	98	54	59	3.16	0
1988 Clearwater		Fla.St.	16	101 1/3	4	7	.364	90	37	80	3.73	0
1988 Reading		Eastern	5	21 1/3	1	3	.250	14	13	20	7.17	0
1989 Reading		Eastern	26	172	11	8	.579	134	109	121	2.98	0
1989 Philadelphia		N.L.	4	18 1/3	1	3	.250	7	19	19	5.89	0
1990 Scr Wil-Bar		Int.	22	128 1/3	8	5	.615	99	78	111	3.93	0
1990 Philadelphia		N.L.	11	57 1/3	3	2	.600	41	43	47	3.30	0
1991 Philadelphia		N.L.	12	61	1	7	.125	42	41	54	4.87	0
1991 Scranton-WB		Int.	9	51 2/3	2	3	.400	43	37	48	4.35	0
1992 Tucson a		P.C.	26	124 2/3	8	7	.533	90	55	152	5.05	0
1993 Charlotte		Int.	28	135 1/3	6	6	.500	102	49	138	3.39	0
1993 Cleveland b		A.L.	10	42 1/3	3	4	.429	27	20	52	5.31	0
1994 Charlotte		Int.	10	71	7	0	1.000	60	17	58	3.42	0
1994 Cleveland		A.L.	14	82 2/3	5	2	.714	59	34	91	4.57	0
1995 Cleveland		A.L.	15	34	0	0	.000	25	32	37	6.09	1
1995 Buffalo		A.A.	10	68	5	3	.625	40	19	61	2.91	0
1996 Vancouver		P.C.	2	15	2	0	1.000	11	3	8	1.20	0
1996 California c		A.L.	35	130 1/3	5	7	.417	82	74	150	6.84	0
1997 Tucson		P.C.	36	85 1/3	5	10	.333	65	43	96	5.70	4
1997 Omaha d-e-f		A.A.	7	31	1	5	.167	22	29	36	6.68	0
1998 Buffalo g		Int.	52	88 2/3	6	3	.667	68	57	76	3.76	0
1999 New York h		A.L.	55	75	7	2	.778	49	40	66	3.60	1
2000 New York i		A.L.	63	96 1/3	3	2	.600	53	42	100	5.04	1
Major League Totals	9 Yrs.		219	597 1/3	28	29	.491	385	345	616	5.11	3
	Championship Series											
2000 New York		A.L.	2	1	0	0	.000	1	3	2	0.00	0
	World Series Record											
1999 New York		A.L.	1	2 1/3	0	0	.000	0	2	2	0.00	0

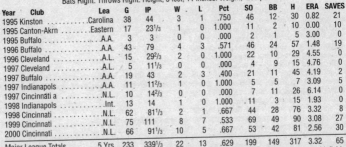

a Traded to Houston Astros for pitcher Curt Schilling, April 2, 1992.
b Filed for free agency, April 5, 1993, signed with Cleveland Indians, April 13, 1993.
c Traded to California Angels with pitcher Pep Harris for pitcher Brian Anderson, February 15, 1996.
d Filed for free agency, October 8, 1996, signed with Detroit Tigers, January 16, 1997.
e Released by Detroit Tigers, March 20, 1997, signed with Milwaukee Brewers, April 3, 1997.
f Traded to Kansas City Royals for pitcher Jamie Brewington, July 29, 1997.
g Filed for free agency, October 17, 1997, signed with Cleveland Indians organization, January 12, 1998.
h Filed for free agency, October 16, 1998, signed with New York Yankees organization, January 22, 1999.
i Released by New York Yankees, November 20, 2000.

GROOM, WEDSEL GARY JR. (BUDDY)

Born, Dallas, Texas, July 10, 1965.
Bats Left. Throws Left. Height, 6 feet, 2 inches. Weight, 200 pounds.

Year	Club	Lea	G	IP	W	L	Pct	SO	BB	H	ERA	SAVES
1987 Sarasota White Sox	...Gulf C.		4	12	1	0	1.000	8	2	12	0.75	1
1987 Daytona Beach	......Fla. St.		11	68	7	2	.778	29	33	60	3.59	0
1988 Tampa	............Fla. St.		27	*195	13	10	.565	118	51	181	2.54	0
1989 Birmingham	......Southern		26	167	13	8	.619	94	78	172	4.52	0
1990 Birmingham a	.....Southern		20	115	6	8	.429	66	48	135	5.07	0
1991 London	............Eastern		11	51²/₃	7	1	.875	39	12	51	3.48	0
1991 Toledo	................Int.		24	75	2	5	.286	49	25	75	4.32	1
1992 Toledo	................Int.		16	109¹/₃	7	7	.500	71	23	102	2.80	0
1992 Detroit	............A.L.		12	38²/₃	0	5	.000	15	22	48	5.82	1
1993 Toledo	................Int.		16	102	9	3	.750	78	30	98	2.74	0
1993 Detroit	............A.L.		19	36²/₃	0	2	.000	15	13	48	6.14	0
1994 Toledo	................Int.		5	4	0	0	.000	6	0	2	2.25	0
1994 Detroit	............A.L.		40	32	0	1	.000	27	13	31	3.94	1
1995 Toledo	................Int.		6	33	2	3	.400	24	4	31	1.91	0
1995 Detroit b-c	..........A.L.		23	40²/₃	1	3	.250	23	26	55	7.52	1
1995 Florida d-e	............N.L.		14	15	1	2	.333	12	6	26	7.20	0
1996 Oakland	............A.L.		72	77¹/₃	5	0	1.000	57	34	85	3.84	2
1997 Oakland	............A.L.		78	64²/₃	2	2	.500	45	24	75	5.15	3
1998 Oakland	............A.L.		75	57¹/₃	3	1	.750	36	20	62	4.24	0
1999 Oakland f	............A.L.		*76	46	3	2	.600	32	18	48	5.09	0
2000 Baltimore	............A.L.		70	59¹/₃	6	3	.667	44	21	63	4.85	4
Major League Totals	........9 Yrs.		479	467²/₃	21	21	.500	306	197	541	5.10	12

a Drafted by Detroit Tigers organization from Chicago White Sox organization in minor league draft, December 5, 1990.
b Traded to Florida Marlins for player to be named later, August 7, 1995.
c Detroit Tigers received pitcher Mike Myers to complete trade, August 9, 1995.
d Waived by Florida Marlins, October 4, 1995.
e Signed with Oakland Athletics organization, December 2, 1995.
f Filed for free agency, November 1, 1999. Signed with Baltimore Orioles, December 21, 1999.

GUARDADO, EDWARD ADRIAN

Born, Stockton, California, October 2, 1970.
Bats Right. Throws Left. Height, 6 feet. Weight, 193 pounds.

Year	Club	Lea	G	IP	W	L	Pct	SO	BB	H	ERA	SAVES
1991 Elizabethton	.........Appal.		14	92	8	4	.667	106	31	67	1.86	0
1992 Kenosha	...........Midwest		18	101	5	10	.333	103	30	106	4.37	0
1992 Visalia	..........California		7	49¹/₃	7	0	1.000	39	10	47	1.64	0
1993 Nashville	........Southern		10	65¹/₃	4	0	1.000	57	10	53	1.24	0
1993 Minnesota	...........A.L.		19	94²/₃	3	8	.273	46	36	123	6.18	0
1994 Salt Lake City	.........P.C.		24	151	12	7	.632	87	51	171	4.83	0
1994 Minnesota	...........A.L.		4	17	0	2	.000	8	4	26	8.47	0
1995 Minnesota	...........A.L.		51	91¹/₃	4	9	.308	71	45	99	5.12	2
1996 Minnesota	...........A.L.		*83	73²/₃	6	5	.545	74	33	61	5.25	4
1997 Minnesota	...........A.L.		69	46	0	4	.000	54	17	45	3.91	1
1998 Minnesota	...........A.L.		79	65²/₃	3	1	.750	53	28	66	4.52	0
1999 New Britain	........Eastern		3	4²/₃	0	0	.000	5	0	3	1.93	0
1999 Minnesota a	...........A.L.		63	48	2	5	.286	50	25	37	4.50	2
2000 Minnesota	...........A.L.		70	61²/₃	7	4	.636	52	25	55	3.94	9
Major League Totals	........8 Yrs.		438	498	25	38	.397	408	213	512	5.06	18

a On disabled list from May 22 to June 29, 1999.

GUTHRIE, MARK ANDREW

Born, Buffalo, New York, September 22, 1965.
Bats Both. Throws Left. Height, 6 feet, 4 inches. Weight, 206 pounds.

Year	Club	Lea	G	IP	W	L	Pct	SO	BB	H	ERA	SAVES
1987	Visalia	California	4	12	2	1	.667	9	5	10	4.50	0
1988	Visalia	California	25	171⅓	12	9	.571	182	86	169	3.31	0
1989	Orlando	Southern	14	96	8	3	.727	103	38	75	1.97	0
1989	Portland	P.C.	7	44⅓	3	4	.429	35	16	45	3.65	0
1989	Minnesota	A.L.	13	57⅓	2	4	.333	38	21	66	4.55	0
1990	Portland	P.C.	9	42⅓	1	3	.250	39	12	47	2.98	0
1990	Minnesota	A.L.	24	144⅔	7	9	.438	101	39	154	3.79	0
1991	Minnesota a	A.L.	41	98	7	5	.583	72	41	116	4.32	2
1992	Minnesota	A.L.	54	75	2	3	.400	76	23	59	2.88	5
1993	Minnesota b	A.L.	22	21	2	1	.667	15	16	20	4.71	0
1994	Minnesota	A.L.	50	51⅓	4	2	.667	38	18	65	6.14	1
1995	Minnesota	A.L.	36	42⅓	5	3	.625	48	16	47	4.46	0
1995	Los Angeles c	N.L.	24	19⅔	0	2	.000	19	9	19	3.66	0
1996	Los Angeles d-e	N.L.	66	73	2	3	.400	56	22	65	2.22	1
1997	Los Angeles	N.L.	62	69⅓	1	4	.200	42	30	71	5.32	1
1998	Los Angeles f	N.L.	53	54	2	1	.667	45	24	56	3.50	0
1999	Pawtucket	Int.	1	1	0	0	.000	1	0	0	0.00	0
1999	Boston	A.L.	46	46⅓	1	1	.500	36	20	50	5.83	2
1999	Chicago g-h	N.L.	11	12⅓	0	2	.000	9	4	7	3.65	0
2000	Chicago i	N.L.	19	18⅔	2	3	.400	17	10	17	4.82	0
2000	Tampa Bay-Toronto j-k	A.L.	57	52⅔	1	3	.250	46	27	53	4.61	0
Major League Totals	12 Yrs.		578	835⅔	38	46	.452	658	320	865	4.18	12
Division Series												
1995	Los Angeles	N.L.	3	1⅓	0	0	.000	1	1	2	6.75	0
1996	Los Angeles	N.L.	1	0⅓	0	0	.000	1	1	0	0.00	0
Division Series Totals		4		1⅔	0	0	.000	2	2	2	5.40	0
Championship Series												
1991	Minnesota	A.L.	2	2⅔	1	0	1.000	0	0	0	0.00	0
World Series Record												
1991	Minnesota	A.L.	4	4	0	1	.000	3	4	3	2.25	0

a Appeared in one additional game as pinch runner.
b On disabled list from May 29 to end of 1993 season.
c Traded to Los Angeles Dodgers with pitcher Kevin Tapani for pitcher Jose Parra, pitcher Greg Hansell and infielder Ron Coomer, July 31, 1995. Minnesota Twins received outfielder Chris Latham to complete trade, October 30, 1995.
d Filed for free agency, October 29, 1996.
e Re-signed with Los Angeles Dodgers, November 6, 1996.
f Filed for free agency, October 26, 1998. Signed with Boston Red Sox, December 19, 1998.
g On disabled list from July 4 to July 24, 1999.
h Traded to Chicago Cubs with player to be named later for pitcher Rod Beck, August 31, 1999. Chicago Cubs received infielder Cole Liniak to complete trade, September 1, 1999.
i Traded to Tampa Bay Devil Rays with cash for outfielder Dave Martinez, May 12, 2000.
j Traded to Toronto Blue Jays with pitcher Steve Trachsel for infielder Brent Abernathy and player to be named later, July 21, 2000.
k Filed for free agency, October 31, 2000, signed with Oakland Athletics, January 5, 2001.

GUZMAN, GERALDO MORENO

Born, Tenares, Dominican Republic, November 28, 1972.
Bats Right. Throws Right. Height, 6 feet, 2 inches. Weight, 180 pounds.

Year	Club	Lea	G	IP	W	L	Pct	SO	BB	H	ERA	SAVES
2000	Tucson a-b-c	P.C.	6	38	4	1	.800	44	10	23	1.42	1
2000	El Paso	Texas	17	50⅓	3	3	.500	53	22	47	3.75	0
2000	Arizona	N.L.	13	60⅓	5	4	.556	52	22	66	5.37	0

a Signed by Montreal Expos September 27, 1989, played in Dominican Summer League in 1990-92
b Released October 14, 1992, did not play from 1993 through 1998, played in Taiwan 1999
c Signed with Arizona Diamondbacks November 12, 1999.

HALAMA, JOHN THADEUZ

Born, Brooklyn, New York, February 22, 1972.
Bats Left. Throws Right. Height, 6 feet, 5 inches. Weight, 200 pounds.

Year	Club	Lea	G	IP	W	L	Pct	SO	BB	H	ERA	SAVES
1994	Auburn	N.Y.-Penn.	6	28	4	1	.800	27	5	18	1.29	1
1994	Quad City	Midwest	9	51⅓	3	4	.429	37	18	63	4.56	0
1995	Quad City	Midwest	55	62⅓	1	2	.333	56	22	48	2.02	2
1996	Jackson	Texas	27	162⅔	9	10	.474	110	59	151	3.21	0

Year	Club	Lea	G	IP	W	L	Pct	SO	BB	H	ERA	SAVES
1997	New Orleans	A.A.	26	171	13	3	.813	126	32	150	2.58	0
1998	New Orleans	P.C.	17	121	12	3	.800	86	16	118	3.20	0
1998	Houston a	N.L.	6	32⅓	1	1	.500	21	13	37	5.85	0
1999	Seattle	A.L.	38	179	11	10	.524	105	56	193	4.22	0
2000	Seattle	A.L.	30	166⅔	14	9	.609	87	56	206	5.08	0
Major League Totals		3 Yrs.	74	378	26	20	.565	213	125	436	4.74	0
	Championship Series											
2000	Seattle	A.L.	2	9⅓	0	0	.000	3	5	10	2.89	0

a Traded by Houston Astros to Seattle Mariners to complete trade in which Astros received pitcher Randy Johnson, October 1, 1998.

HALLADAY, HARRY LEROY (ROY)

Born, Denver, Colorado, May 14, 1977.
Bats Right. Throws Right. Height, 6 feet, 6 inches. Weight, 205 pounds.

Year	Club	Lea	G	IP	W	L	Pct	SO	BB	H	ERA	SAVES
1995	Blue Jays	Gulf Coast	10	50⅓	3	5	.375	48	16	35	3.40	0
1996	Dunedin	Fla.St.	27	164⅔	15	7	.682	109	46	158	2.73	0
1997	Knoxville	Southern	7	36⅔	2	3	.400	30	11	46	5.40	0
1997	Syracuse	Int.	22	125⅔	7	10	.412	64	53	132	4.58	0
1998	Syracuse	Int.	21	116⅓	9	5	.643	71	53	107	3.79	0
1998	Toronto	A.L.	2	14	1	0	1.000	13	2	9	1.93	0
1999	Toronto	A.L.	36	149⅓	8	7	.533	82	79	156	3.92	1
2000	Syracuse	Int.	11	73⅔	2	3	.400	38	21	85	5.50	0
2000	Toronto	A.L.	19	67⅔	4	7	.364	44	42	107	10.64	0
Major League Totals		3 Yrs.	57	231	13	14	.481	139	123	272	5.77	1

HAMILTON, JOHNS JOSEPH (JOEY)

Born, Statesboro, Georgia, September 9, 1970.
Bats Right. Throws Right. Height, 6 feet, 4 inches. Weight, 220 pounds.

Year	Club	Lea	G	IP	W	L	Pct	SO	BB	H	ERA	SAVES
1992	Charleston, SC	So. Atl.	7	34⅔	2	2	.500	35	4	37	3.38	0
1992	High Desert	California	9	49⅓	4	3	.571	43	18	46	2.74	0
1992	Wichita	Texas	6	34⅔	3	0	1.000	26	11	33	2.86	0
1993	Rancho Cucamonga	Calif.	2	11	1	0	1.000	6	2	11	4.09	0
1993	Wichita	Texas	15	90⅔	4	9	.308	50	36	101	3.97	0
1993	Las Vegas	P.C.	8	47	3	2	.600	33	22	49	4.40	0
1994	Las Vegas	P.C.	9	59⅓	3	5	.375	32	22	69	2.73	0
1994	San Diego	N.L.	16	108⅔	9	6	.600	61	29	98	2.98	0
1995	San Diego	N.L.	31	204⅓	6	9	.400	123	56	189	3.08	0
1996	San Diego	N.L.	34	211⅔	15	9	.625	184	83	206	4.17	0
1997	San Diego a	N.L.	31	192⅔	12	7	.632	124	69	199	4.25	0
1998	San Diego b	N.L.	34	217⅓	13	13	.500	147	*106	220	4.27	0
1999	Syracuse	Int.	3	12⅓	0	1	.000	9	5	15	5.11	0
1999	Toronto c	A.L.	22	98	7	8	.467	56	39	118	6.52	0
2000	Syracuse	Int.	6	39⅓	3	2	.600	17	12	41	3.66	0
2000	Toronto d	A.L.	6	33	2	1	.667	15	12	28	3.55	0
Major League Totals		7 Yrs.	174	1065⅔	64	53	.547	710	394	1058	4.07	0
	Division Series											
1996	San Diego	N.L.	1	6	0	1	.000	6	0	5	4.50	0
1998	San Diego	N.L.	2	3⅓	0	0	.000	3	2	1	0.00	0
Division Series Totals			3	9⅓	0	1	.000	9	2	6	2.89	0
	Championship Series											
1998	San Diego	N.L.	2	7⅓	0	1	.000	6	3	7	4.91	0
	World Series Record											
1998	San Diego	N.L.	1	1	0	0	.000	1	1	0	0.00	0

a On disabled list from April 24 to May 17, 1997.
b Traded to Toronto Blue Jays for pitcher Woody Williams, pitcher Carlos Almanzar and outfielder Peter Tucci, December 13, 1998.
c On disabled list from April 14 to May 24, 1999.
d On disabled list from March 21 to August 18, 2000.

HAMPTON, MICHAEL WILLIAM

Born, Brooksville, Florida, September 9, 1972.
Bats Right. Throws Left. Height, 5 feet, 10 inches. Weight, 190 pounds.

Year	Club	Lea	G	IP	W	L	Pct	SO	BB	H	ERA	SAVES
1990	Tempe Mariners	Arizona	14	64⅓	*7	2	.778	59	40	52	2.66	0
1991	San Bernardino	California	18	73⅔	1	7	.125	57	47	71	5.25	0

Year	Club	Lea	G	IP	W	L	Pct	SO	BB	H	ERA	SAVES
1991 Bellingham	.......Northwest		9	57	5	2	.714	65	26	32	1.58	0
1992 San Bernardino	....California		25	170	13	8	.619	132	66	163	3.12	0
1992 Jacksonville	.......Southern		2	101/3	0	1	.000	6	1	13	4.35	0
1993 Seattle		.A.L.	13	17	1	3	.250	8	17	28	9.53	1
1993 Jacksonville a	......Southern		15	871/3	6	4	.600	84	33	71	3.71	0
1994 Houston	/............N.L.		44	411/3	2	1	.667	24	16	46	3.70	0
1995 Houston b	............N.L.		24	1502/3	9	8	.529	115	49	141	3.35	0
1996 Houston	............N.L.		27	1601/3	10	10	.500	101	49	175	3.59	0
1997 Houston	............N.L.		34	223	15	10	.600	139	77	217	3.83	0
1998 Houston c	............N.L.		32	2112/3	11	7	.611	137	81	227	3.36	0
1999 Houston d	............N.L.		34	239	*22	4	*.846	177	101	206	2.90	0
2000 New York e	............N.L.		33	2172/3	15	10	.600	151	99	194	3.14	0
Major League Totals	........8 Yrs.		241	12602/3	85	53	.616	852	489	1234	3.44	1
Division Series												
1997 Houston	.............N.L.		1	42/3	0	1	.000	2	8	2	11.57	0
1998 Houston	.............N.L.		1	6	0	0	.000	2	1	2	1.50	0
1999 Houston	.............N.L.		1	7	0	0	.000	9	1	6	3.86	0
2000 New York	.............N.L.		1	51/3	0	1	.000	2	3	6	8.44	0
Division Series Totals	....		4	23	0	2	.000	15	13	16	5.87	0
Championship Series												
2000 New York	.............N.L.		2	16	2	0	1.000	12	4	9	0.00	0
World Series Record												
2000 New York	.............N.L.		1	6	0	1	.000	4	5	8	6.00	0

a Traded by Seattle Mariners to Houston Astros with outfielder Mike Felder for outfielder Eric Anthony, December 10, 1993.
b On disabled list from May 15 to June 13, 1995.
c On disabled list from June 16 to July 4, 1998.
d Traded to New York Mets with outfielder Derek Bell for pitcher Octavio Dotel, outfielder Roger Cedeno and pitcher Kyle Kessel, December 23, 1999.
e Filed for free agency, November 4, 2000, signed with Colorado Rockies, December 9, 2000.

HARNISCH, PETER THOMAS

Born, Commack, New York, September 23, 1966.
Bats Right. Throws Right. Height, 6 feet. Weight, 207 pounds.

Year	Club	Lea	G	IP	W	L	Pct	SO	BB	H	ERA	SAVES
1987 Bluefield	...........Appal.		9	522/3	3	1	.750	64	26	38	2.56	0
1987 Hagerstown	.......Carolina		4	20	1	2	.333	18	14	17	2.25	0
1988 Charlotte	........Southern		20	1321/3	7	6	.538	141	52	113	2.58	0
1988 Rochester	............Int.		7	581/3	4	1	.800	43	14	44	2.16	0
1988 Baltimore	............A.L.		2	13	0	2	.000	10	9	13	5.54	0
1989 Rochester	............Int.		12	871/3	5	5	.500	59	35	60	2.58	0
1989 Baltimore	............A.L.		18	1031/3	5	9	.357	70	64	97	4.62	0
1990 Baltimore a	............A.L.		31	1882/3	11	11	.500	122	86	189	4.34	0
1991 Houston	............N.L.		33	2162/3	12	9	.571	172	83	169	2.70	0
1992 Houston b	............N.L.		34	2062/3	9	10	.474	164	64	182	3.70	0
1993 Houston	............N.L.		33	2172/3	16	9	.640	185	79	171	2.98	0
1994 Tucson	............P.C.		1	5	0	0	.000	1	1	2	0.00	0
1994 Houston c-d-e-f	............N.L.		17	95	8	5	.615	62	39	100	5.40	0
1995 New York g-h	..........N.L.		18	110	2	8	.200	82	24	111	3.68	0
1996 St. Lucie	.......Fla.St.		2	13	1	0	1.000	12	0	11	2.77	0
1996 New York i	............N.L.		31	1942/3	8	12	.400	114	61	195	4.21	0
1997 Mets	...........Gulf Coast		1	3	0	0	.000	5	0	7	12.00	0
1997 St. Lucie	.......Fla. St.		2	12	1	0	1.000	7	4	5	3.00	0
1997 Norfolk	............Int.		3	162/3	1	1	.500	16	10	16	5.40	0
1997 New York j-k	..........N.L.		6	252/3	0	1	.000	12	11	35	8.06	0
1997 Milwaukee l-m	.......A.L.		4	14	1	1	.500	10	12	13	5.14	0
1998 Cincinnati	............N.L.		32	209	14	7	.667	157	64	176	3.14	0
1999 Cincinnati	............N.L.		33	1981/3	16	10	.615	120	57	190	3.68	0
2000 Louisville	............Int.		1	52/3	0	0	.000	6	0	6	3.18	0
2000 Cincinnati n	............N.L.		22	131	8	6	.571	71	46	133	4.74	0
Major League Totals	.......13 Yrs.		314	19232/3	110	100	.524	1351	699	1774	3.84	0

a Traded to Houston Astros with pitcher Curt Schilling and outfielder Steve Finley for first baseman Glenn Davis, January 10, 1991.
b Suspended three games by National League for June 24 blatantly throwing behind batter, July 7 to July 10, 1992.
c Appeared in one additional game as pinch runner.
d On disabled list from May 23 to June 30, 1994.
e Traded to New York Mets for one or two players to be named, November 28; Houston Astros acquired pitcher Andy Beckerman to complete trade, December 6, 1994.
f Not offered 1995 contract and became free agent, December 23, 1994.
g Re-signed with New York Mets, April 6, 1995.

h On disabled list from August 2 to October 2, 1995.
i On disabled list from April 1 to April 14, 1996.
j On disabled list from April 2 to August 5, 1997.
k Traded to Milwaukee Brewers for outfielder Donnie Moore, August 31, 1997.
l Filed for free agency, October 27, 1997.
m Signed as free agent with Cincinnati Reds, January 22, 1998.
n On disabled list from May 5 to June 28, 2000.

HASEGAWA, SHIGETOSHI

Born, Kobe, Japan, August 1, 1968.
Bats Right. Throws Right. Height, 5 feet, 11 inches. Weight, 160 pounds.

Year Club	Lea	G	IP	W	L	Pct	SO	BB	H	ERA	SAVES
1991 Orix a	Japan Pac.	28	185	12	9	.571	111	50	...	3.55	1
1992 Orix	Japan Pac.	24	143⅓	6	8	.428	86	51	...	3.27	1
1993 Orix	Japan Pac.	23	159⅔	12	6	.667	86	48	...	2.71	0
1994 Orix	Japan Pac.	25	156⅓	11	9	.550	86	46	...	3.11	1
1995 Orix	Japan Pac.	24	171	12	7	.632	91	51	...	2.89	0
1996 Orix	Japan Pac.	18	87⅔	4	6	.400	55	40	...	5.34	1
1997 Anaheim b	A.L.	50	116⅔	3	7	.300	83	46	118	3.93	0
1998 Anaheim	A.L.	61	97⅓	8	3	.727	73	32	86	3.14	5
1999 Anaheim	A.L.	64	77	4	6	.400	44	34	80	4.91	2
2000 Anaheim	A.L.	66	95⅔	10	5	.667	59	38	100	3.48	9
Major League Totals	4 Yrs.	241	386⅔	25	21	.543	259	150	384	3.82	16

a Selected Pacific League Rookie of the Year for 1991.
b Signed as free agent by Anaheim Angels, January 9, 1997.

HAWKINS, LA TROY

Born, Gary, Indiana, December 21, 1972.
Bats Right. Throws Right. Height, 6 feet, 5 inches. Weight, 195 pounds.

Year Club	Lea	G	IP	W	L	Pct	SO	BB	H	ERA	SAVES
1991 Twins	Gulf Coast	11	55	4	3	.571	47	26	62	4.75	0
1992 Twins	Gulf Coast	6	36⅓	3	2	.600	35	10	36	3.22	0
1992 Elizabethton	Appal.	5	26⅔	0	1	.000	36	11	21	3.38	0
1993 Ft. Wayne	Midwest	26	157⅓	15	5	.750	179	41	110	2.06	0
1994 Ft. Myers	Fla. St.	6	38⅔	4	0	1.000	36	6	32	2.33	0
1994 Nashville	Southern	11	73⅓	9	2	.818	53	28	50	2.33	0
1994 Salt Lake	P.C.	12	81⅔	5	4	.556	37	33	92	4.08	0
1995 Salt Lake	P.C.	22	144⅓	9	7	.563	74	40	150	3.55	0
1995 Minnesota	A.L.	6	27	2	3	.400	9	12	39	8.67	0
1996 Minnesota	A.L.	7	26⅓	1	1	.500	24	9	42	8.20	0
1996 Salt Lake	P.C.	20	137⅔	9	8	.529	99	31	138	3.92	0
1997 Salt Lake	P.C.	14	76	9	4	.692	53	16	100	5.45	0
1997 Minnesota	A.L.	20	103⅓	6	12	.333	58	47	134	5.84	0
1998 Minnesota	A.L.	33	190⅓	7	14	.333	105	61	227	5.25	0
1999 Minnesota	A.L.	33	174⅓	10	14	.417	103	60	238	6.66	0
2000 Minnesota	A.L.	66	87⅔	2	5	.286	59	32	85	3.39	14
Major League Totals	6 Yrs.	165	609	28	49	.364	358	221	765	5.76	14

HAYNES, JIMMY WAYNE

Born, LaGrange, Georgia, September 5, 1972.
Bats Right. Throws Right. Height, 6 feet, 4 inches. Weight, 175 pounds.

Year Club	Lea	G	IP	W	L	Pct	SO	BB	H	ERA	SAVES
1991 Orioles	Gulf Coast	14	62	3	2	.600	67	21	44	1.60	2
1992 Kane County	Midwest	24	144	7	11	.389	141	45	131	2.56	0
1993 Frederick	Carolina	27	172⅓	12	8	.600	174	61	139	3.03	0
1994 Rochester	Int.	3	13⅓	1	0	1.000	14	6	20	6.75	0
1994 Bowie	Eastern	25	173⅔	13	8	.619	177	46	154	2.90	0
1995 Rochester	Int.	26	167	12	8	.600	140	49	162	3.29	0
1995 Baltimore	A.L.	4	24	2	1	.667	22	12	11	2.25	0
1996 Rochester	Int.	5	28⅔	1	1	.500	24	18	31	5.65	0
1996 Baltimore	A.L.	26	89	3	6	.333	65	58	122	8.29	1
1997 Rochester	Int.	16	102	5	4	.556	113	55	89	3.44	0
1997 Edmonton	P.C.	5	29⅔	0	2	.000	24	11	36	4.85	0
1997 Oakland a	A.L.	13	73⅓	3	6	.333	65	40	74	4.42	0
1998 Oakland	A.L.	33	194⅓	11	9	.550	134	88	229	5.09	0
1999 Oakland b	A.L.	30	142	7	12	.368	93	80	158	6.34	0

Year	Club	Lea	G	IP	W	L	Pct	SO	BB	H	ERA	SAVES
2000 Milwaukee	....	.N.L.	33	199¹/₃	12	13	.480	88	100	228	5.33	0
Major League Totals	........6 Yrs.		139	722	38	47	.447	467	378	822	5.63	1

a Traded to Oakland Athletics with player to be named later for outfielder Geronimo Berroa, June 27, 1997. Oakland Athletics received pitcher Mark Seaver to complete trade, September 2, 1997.
b Traded to Milwaukee Brewers for pitcher Justin Miller as part of three-team deal, December 13, 1999.

HELLING, RICKY ALLEN (RICK)

Born, Devil's Lake, North Dakota, December 15, 1970.
Bats Right. Throws Right. Height, 6 feet, 3 inches. Weight, 220 pounds.

Year	Club	Lea	G	IP	W	L	Pct	SO	BB	H	ERA	SAVES
1992 Charlotte	....	.Fla. St.	3	19²/₃	1	1	.500	20	4	13	2.29	0
1993 Tulsa	....	.Texas	26	177¹/₃	12	8	.600	188	46	150	3.60	0
1993 Okla City	....	.A.A.	2	11	1	1	.500	17	3	5	1.64	0
1994 Texas	....	.A.L.	9	52	3	2	.600	25	18	62	5.88	0
1994 Okla City	....	.A.A.	20	132¹/₃	4	12	.250	85	43	153	5.78	0
1995 Texas	....	.A.L.	3	12¹/₃	0	2	.000	5	8	17	6.57	0
1995 Okla City	....	.A.A.	20	109²/₃	4	8	.333	80	41	132	5.33	0
1996 Okla City	....	.A.A.	23	140	12	4	.750	157	38	124	2.96	0
1996 Texas a	....	.A.L.	6	20¹/₃	1	2	.333	16	9	23	7.52	0
1996 Florida	....	.N.L.	5	27²/₃	2	1	.667	26	7	14	1.95	0
1997 Florida b	....	.N.L.	31	76	2	6	.250	53	48	61	4.38	0
1997 Texas	....	.A.L.	10	55	3	3	.500	46	21	47	4.58	0
1998 Texas	....	.A.L.	33	216¹/₃	*20	7	.741	164	78	209	4.41	0
1999 Texas	....	.A.L.	35	219¹/₃	13	11	.542	131	85	228	4.84	0
2000 Texas	....	.A.L.	35	217	16	13	.552	146	99	212	4.48	0
Major League Totals	........7 Yrs.		167	896	60	47	.561	612	373	873	4.65	0
Division Series												
1998 Texas	....	.A.L.	1	6	0	1	.000	9	1	8	4.50	0
1999 Texas	....	.A.L.	1	6¹/₃	0	1	.000	8	1	5	2.84	0
Division Series Totals	....		2	1 2¹/₃	0	2	.000	17	2	13	3.65	0

a Acquired by Florida Marlins, September 3, 1996, as player-to-be-named-later in trade which sent pitcher John Burkett to Texas Rangers for pitcher Ryan Dempster, August 8, 1996.
b Traded to Texas Rangers for pitcher Ed Vosberg, August 12, 1997.

HENRY, RICHARD DOUGLAS (DOUG)

Born, Sacramento, California, December 10, 1963.
Bats Right. Throws Right. Height, 6 feet, 4 inches. Weight, 205 pounds.

Year	Club	Lea	G	IP	W	L	Pct	SO	BB	H	ERA	SAVES
1986 Beloit	....	.Midwest	27	143¹/₃	7	8	.467	115	56	153	4.65	1
1987 Beloit	....	.Midwest	31	132²/₃	8	9	.471	106	51	145	4.88	2
1988 Stockton	....	.California	23	70²/₃	7	1	.875	71	31	46	1.78	7
1988 El Paso	....	.Texas	14	45²/₃	4	0	1.000	50	19	33	3.15	0
1989 El Paso a	....	.Texas	1	2	0	0	.000	2	3	3	13.50	0
1989 Stockton	....	.California	4	11	0	1	.000	9	3	9	0.00	0
1990 Stockton	....	.California	4	8	1	0	1.000	13	3	4	1.13	1
1990 El Paso	....	.Texas	15	30²/₃	1	0	1.000	25	11	31	2.93	9
1990 Denver	....	.A.A.	27	50²/₃	2	3	.400	54	27	46	4.44	8
1991 Denver	....	.A.A.	32	57²/₃	3	2	.600	47	20	47	2.18	14
1991 Milwaukee	....	.A.L.	32	36	2	1	.667	28	14	16	1.00	15
1992 Milwaukee	....	.A.L.	68	65	1	4	.200	52	24	64	4.02	29
1993 Milwaukee	....	.A.L.	54	55	4	4	.500	38	25	67	5.56	17
1994 El Paso	....	.Texas	6	8¹/₃	1	0	1.000	10	2	7	5.40	3
1994 New Orleans	....	.A.A.	10	14²/₃	1	0	1.000	10	10	5	1.84	3
1994 Milwaukee b-c	....	.A.L.	25	31¹/₃	2	3	.400	20	23	32	4.60	0
1995 New York	....	.N.L.	51	67	3	6	.333	62	25	48	2.96	4
1996 New York	....	.N.L.	58	75	2	8	.200	58	36	82	4.68	9
1997 San Francisco d-e	....	.N.L.	75	70²/₃	4	5	.444	69	41	70	4.71	3
1998 Houston	....	.N.L.	59	71	8	2	.800	59	35	55	3.04	2
1999 Jackson	....	.Texas	2	2	0	1	.000	3	1	2	4.50	0
1999 New Orleans	....	.P.C.	3	4	0	0	.000	3	3	4	4.50	0
1999 Houston f-g	....	.N.L.	35	40²/₃	2	3	.400	36	24	45	4.65	2
2000 Houston-San Fran. h-i	...	.N.L.	72	78¹/₃	4	4	.500	62	49	57	3.79	1
Major League Totals	........10 Yrs.		529	590	32	40	.444	484	296	536	3.95	82
Divisional Series												
1997 San Francisco	....	.N.L.	1	2	0	0	.000	2	3	1	0.00	0
1998 Houston	....	.N.L.	2	1²/₃	0	0	.000	1	0	2	5.40	0

Year Club	Lea	G	IP	W	L	Pct	SO	BB	H	ERA	SAVES
1999 Houston .............N.L.		2	3⅔	0	0	.000	2	3	1	0.00	0
2000 San Francisco .........N.L.		3	4	0	0	.000	1	3	1	2.25	0
Division Series Totals		8	11⅓	0	0	.000	6	9	5	1.59	0

a On disabled list from July 7 to August 10, 1989.
b On disabled list from March 29 to April 27, 1994.
c Traded to New York Mets for two players to be named, November 30; to complete trade, Milwaukee Brewers received catcher Javier Gonzalez on December 6 and infielder Fernando Vina on December 22, 1994.
d Filed for free agency, October 27, 1997.
e Signed with Houston Astros, November 26, 1997.
f On disabled list from May 10 to July 15, 1999.
g Filed for free agency, November 1, 1999, re-signed with Houston Astros, December 3, 1999.
h Traded to San Francisco Giants for pitcher Scott Linebrink, July 30, 2000.
i Filed for free agency, October 31, 2000, signed with Kansas City Royals, December 11, 2000.

HENTGEN, PATRICK GEORGE

Born, Detroit, Michigan, November 13, 1968.
Bats Right. Throws Right. Height, 6 feet, 2 inches. Weight, 200 pounds.

Year Club	Lea	G	IP	W	L	Pct	SO	BB	H	ERA	SAVES
1986 St. Catharines ....N.Y.-Penn.		13	40	0	4	.000	30	30	38	4.50	1
1987 Myrtle Beach ....So. Atl.		32	*188	11	5	.688	131	60	145	2.35	0
1988 Dunedin ....Fla. St.		31	151⅓	3	12	.200	125	65	139	3.45	0
1989 Dunedin ....Fla. St.		29	151⅓	9	8	.529	148	71	123	2.68	0
1990 Knoxville ....Southern		28	153⅓	9	5	.643	142	68	121	3.05	0
1991 Syracuse ....Int.		31	171	8	9	.471	*155	*90	146	4.47	0
1991 Toronto ..............A.L.		3	7⅓	0	0	.000	3	3	5	2.45	0
1992 Syracuse ....Int.		4	20⅓	1	2	.333	17	8	15	2.66	0
1991 Toronto a ...........A.L.		28	50⅓	5	2	.714	39	32	49	5.36	0
1993 Toronto .............A.L.		34	216⅓	19	9	.679	122	74	215	3.87	0
1994 Toronto .............A.L.		24	174⅔	13	8	.619	147	59	158	3.40	0
1995 Toronto .............A.L.		30	200⅔	10	14	.417	135	90	236	5.11	0
1996 Toronto b ...........A.L.		35	*265⅔	20	10	.667	177	94	238	3.22	0
1997 Toronto .............A.L.		35	*264	15	10	.600	160	71	253	3.68	0
1998 Toronto .............A.L.		29	177⅔	12	11	.522	94	69	208	5.17	0
1999 Toronto c ...........A.L.		34	199	11	12	.478	118	65	225	4.79	0
2000 St. Louis d ...........N.L.		33	194⅓	15	12	.556	118	89	202	4.72	0
Major League Totals .....10 Yrs.		285	1750	120	88	.577	1113	646	1789	4.21	0
Championship Series											
1993 Toronto ..............A.L.		1	3	0	1	.000	3	2	9	18.00	0
2000 St. Louis ............N.L.		1	3⅔	0	1	.000	2	5	7	14.73	0
Championship Series Totals		2	6⅔	0	2	.000	5	7	16	16.20	0
World Series Record											
1993 Toronto .............A.L.		1	6	1	0	1.000	6	3	5	1.50	0

a On disabled list from August 13 to September 29, 1992.
b Selected Cy Young Award Winner in American League for 1996.
c Traded to St. Louis Cardinals with pitcher Paul Spoljaric for catcher Alberto Castillo, pitcher Lance Painter and pitcher Matt DeWitt, November 11, 1999.
d Not offered 2001 contract, October 30, 2000, signed with Baltimore Orioles, December 19, 2000.

HEREDIA, FELIX

Born, Barahona, Dominican Republic, June 18, 1976.
Bats Left. Throws Left. Height, 6 feet. Weight, 160 pounds.

Year Club	Lea	G	IP	W	L	Pct	SO	BB	H	ERA	SAVES
1993 Marlins ....Gulf Coast		12	62	5	1	.833	53	11	50	2.47	0
1994 Kane County ....Midwest		24	68	4	5	.444	65	14	86	5.69	4
1995 Brevard Cty ....Fla. St.		34	95⅔	6	4	.600	76	36	101	3.57	1
1996 Portland ....Eastern		55	60	8	1	.889	42	15	48	1.50	5
1996 Florida .............N.L.		21	16⅔	1	1	.500	10	10	21	4.32	0
1997 Florida .............N.L.		56	56⅔	5	3	.625	54	30	53	4.29	0
1998 Florida-Chicago a .......N.L.		71	58⅔	3	3	.500	54	38	57	5.06	2
1999 Chicago .............N.L.		69	52	3	1	.750	50	25	56	4.85	1
2000 Chicago .............N.L.		74	58⅔	7	3	.700	52	33	46	4.76	2
Major League Totals ....5 Yrs.		291	242⅔	19	11	.633	220	136	233	4.71	5
Division Series											
1998 Chicago .............N.L.		1	0⅓	0	0	.000	0	2	0	54.00	0
Championship Series											
1997 Florida .............N.L.		2	3⅓	0	0	.000	4	2	3	5.40	0

Year	Club	Lea	G	IP	W	L	Pct	SO	BB	H	ERA	SAVES
	World Series Record											
1997 Florida	.N.L.	4	5⅓	0	0	.000	5	1	2	0.00	0	

a Traded to Chicago Cubs with infielder Eve Hoff for infielder Kevin Orie, pitcher Justin Speier and pitcher Todd Noel, July 31, 1998.

HEREDIA, GILBERT (GIL)

Born, Nogales, Arizona, October 26, 1965.
Bats Right. Throws Right. Height, 6 feet, 1 inch. Weight, 190 pounds.

Year	Club	Lea	G	IP	W	L	Pct	SO	BB	H	ERA	SAVES
1987 Everett	.Northwest	3	20	2	0	1.000	14	1	24	3.60	0	
1987 Fresno	.California	11	80²/₃	5	3	.625	60	23	62	2.90	0	
1988 San Jose	.California	27	206¹/₃	13	12	.520	121	46	216	3.49	0	
1989 San Luis	.Mexican	24	181	14	9	.609	125	35	183	2.98	0	
1989 Shreveport	.Texas	7	24²/₃	1	0	1.000	8	4	28	2.55	0	
1990 Phoenix	.P.C.	29	147	9	7	.563	75	37	159	4.10	1	
1991 Phoenix	.P.C.	33	140¹/₃	9	11	.450	75	28	155	2.82	1	
1991 San Francisco	.N.L.	7	33	0	2	.000	13	7	27	3.82	0	
1992 Phoenix	.P.C.	22	80²/₃	5	5	.500	37	13	83	2.01	1	
1992 Indianaplis	.A.A.	3	17²/₃	2	0	1.000	10	3	18	1.02	0	
1992 San Francisco-Montreal a	N.L.	20	44²/₃	2	3	.400	22	20	44	4.23	0	
1993 Ottawa	.Int.	16	102²/₃	8	4	.667	66	26	97	2.98	0	
1993 Montreal	.N.L.	20	57¹/₃	4	2	.667	40	14	66	3.92	2	
1994 Montreal	.N.L.	39	75¹/₃	6	3	.667	62	13	85	3.46	0	
1995 Montreal	.N.L.	40	119	5	6	.455	74	21	137	4.31	1	
1996 Okla City	.A.A.	6	9²/₃	0	0	.000	4	0	11	1.86	0	
1996 Texas b	.A.L.	44	73¹/₃	2	5	.286	43	14	91	5.89	1	
1997 Ottawa	.Int.	28	44	0	4	.000	41	9	50	4.70	0	
1997 Iowa c e	.A.A.	31	46²/₃	4	2	.667	30	9	54	3.86	1	
1998 Edmonton	.P.C.	29	144²/₃	10	8	.556	99	18	154	3.67	1	
1998 Oakland d f	.A.L.	8	42²/₃	3	3	.500	27	3	43	2.74	0	
1999 Oakland	.A.L.	33	200¹/₃	13	8	.619	117	34	228	4.81	0	
2000 Oakland	.A.L.	32	198²/₃	15	11	.577	101	66	214	4.12	0	
Major League Totals	.9 Yrs.	243	844¹/₃	50	43	.538	499	192	935	4.32	4	
	Division Series											
2000 Oakland	.A.L.	2	6¹/₃	1	1	.500	3	3	11	12.79	0	

a Claimed on waivers by Montreal Expos, August 18, 1992.
b Filed for free agency, December 20, 1995, signed with Texas Rangers, January 5, 1996.
c Released by Texas Rangers, November 13, 1996, signed with Montreal Expos organization, January 27, 1997.
d Traded to New York Mets for pitcher Juan Acevedo, March 29, 1997.
e Traded to Chicago Cubs for infielder Saul Bustos and outfielder David Jefferson, June 23, 1997.
f Filed for free agency, October 17, 1997, signed with Oakland Athletics, January 21, 1998.

HERGES, MATTHEW TYLER (MATT)

Born, Champaign, Illinois, April 1, 1970.
Bats Left. Throws Right. Height, 6 feet. Weight, 200 pounds.

Year	Club	Lea	G	IP	W	L	Pct	SO	BB	H	ERA	SAVES
1992 Yakima	.Northwest	27	44²/₃	2	3	.400	57	24	33	3.22	9	
1993 Bakersfield	.California	51	90¹/₃	2	6	.250	84	56	70	3.69	2	
1994 Vero Beach	.Fla.St.	48	111	8	9	.471	61	33	115	3.32	3	
1995 San Antonio	.Texas	19	27²/₃	0	3	.000	18	16	34	4.88	8	
1995 San Berndno	.California	22	51²/₃	5	2	.714	35	15	58	3.66	1	
1996 San Antonio	.Texas	30	83	3	2	.600	45	28	83	2.71	3	
1996 Albuquerque	.P.C.	10	34²/₃	4	1	.800	15	14	33	2.60	0	
1997 Albuquerque	.P.C.	31	85	0	8	.000	61	46	120	8.89	0	
1997 San Antonio	.Texas	4	15¹/₃	0	1	.000	12	10	22	8.80	0	
1998 San Antonio	.Texas	3	6	0	0	.000	3	2	3	0.00	0	
1998 Albuquerque	.P.C.	34	88¹/₃	3	5	.375	75	37	115	5.71	0	
1999 Albuquerque	.P.C.	21	131¹/₃	8	3	.727	88	47	135	4.73	0	
1999 Los Angeles a	.N.L.	17	24¹/₃	0	2	.000	18	8	24	4.07	0	
2000 Los Angeles	.N.L.	59	110²/₃	11	3	.786	75	40	100	3.17	1	
Major League Totals	.2 Yrs.	76	135	11	5	.688	93	48	124	3.33	1	

a Filed for free agency, October 15, 1998, re-signed by Los Angeles Dodgers organization, January 6, 1999.

HERMANSON, DUSTIN MICHAEL
Born, Springfield, Ohio, December 21, 1972.
Bats Right. Throws Right. Height, 6 feet, 3 inches. Weight, 195 pounds.

Year	Club	Lea	G	IP	W	L	Pct	SO	BB	H	ERA	SAVES
1994	Wichita	Texas	16	21	1	0	1.000	30	6	13	0.43	8
1994	Las Vegas	P.C.	7	7¹/₃	-0	0	.000	6	5	6	6.14	3
1995	Las Vegas	P.C.	31	36	0	1	.000	42	29	35	3.50	11
1995	San Diego	N.L.	26	31²/₃	3	1	.750	19	22	35	6.82	0
1996	Las Vegas	P.C.	42	46	1	4	.200	54	27	41	3.13	21
1996	San Diego a	N.L.	8	13²/₃	1	0	1.000	11	4	18	8.56	0
1997	Montreal b	N.L.	32	158¹/₃	8	8	.500	136	66	134	3.69	0
1998	Montreal c	N.L.	32	187	14	11	.560	154	56	163	3.13	0
1999	Montreal	N.L.	34	216¹/₃	9	14	.391	145	69	225	4.20	0
2000	Montreal d	N.L.	38	198	12	14	.462	94	75	226	4.77	4
Major League Totals		6 Yrs.	170	805	47	48	.495	559	292	801	4.17	4

a Traded to Florida Marlins for infielder Quilvio Veras, November 21, 1996.
b Traded to Montreal Expos with outfielder Joe Orsulak for infielder Cliff Floyd, March 26, 1997.
c On disabled list from May 15 to May 30, 1998.
d Traded to St. Louis Cardinals with pitcher Steve Kline for infielder Fernando Tatis and pitcher Britt Reames, December 14, 2000.

HERNANDEZ, EISLER LIVAN
Born, Villa Clara, Cuba, February 20, 1975.
Bats Right. Throws Right. Height, 6 feet, 2 inches. Weight, 220 pounds.

Year	Club	Lea	G	IP	W	L	Pct	SO	BB	H	ERA	SAVES
1996	Charlotte	Int.	10	49	2	4	.333	45	34	61	5.14	0
1996	Portland	Eastern	15	93¹/₃	9	2	.818	95	34	81	4.34	0
1996	Florida	N.L.	1	3	0	0	.000	2	2	3	0.00	0
1997	Portland	Eastern	1	4	0	0	.000	2	7	2	2.25	0
1997	Charlotte	Int.	14	81¹/₃	5	3	.625	58	38	76	3.98	0
1997	Florida	N.L.	17	96¹/₃	9	3	.750	72	38	81	3.18	0
1998	Florida	N.L.	33	234¹/₃	10	12	.455	162	104	*265	4.72	0
1999	Florida-San Francisco a	N.L.	30	199²/₃	8	12	.400	144	76	227	4.64	0
2000	San Francisco	N.L.	33	240	17	11	.607	165	73	*254	3.75	0
Major League Totals		5 Yrs.	114	773¹/₃	44	38	.537	545	293	830	4.19	0
Division Series												
1997	Florida	N.L.	1	4	0	0	.000	3	0	3	2.25	0
2000	San Francisco	N.L.	1	7²/₃	1	0	1.000	5	5	5	1.17	0
Division Series Totals			2	11²/₃	1	0	1.000	8	5	8	1.54	0
Championship Series												
1997	Florida	N.L.	2	10²/₃	2	0	1.000	16	2	5	0.84	0
World Series Record												
1997	Florida	N.L.	2	13²/₃	2	0	1.000	7	10	15	5.27	0

a Traded to San Francisco Giants for pitcher Jason Grilli and pitcher Nathan Bump, July 24, 1999.

HERNANDEZ, ORLANDO P. (EL DUQUE)
Born, Villa Clara, Cuba, October 11, 1965.
Bats Right. Throws Right. Height, 6 feet, 2 inches. Weight, 210 pounds.

Year	Club	Lea	G	IP	W	L	Pct	SO	BB	H	ERA	SAVES
1998	Tampa a	Fla.St.	2	9	1	1	.500	15	3	3	1.00	0
1998	Columbus	Int.	7	42¹/₃	6	0	1.000	59	17	41	3.83	0
1998	New York	A.L.	21	141	12	4	.750	131	52	113	3.13	0
1999	New York	A.L.	33	214¹/₃	17	9	.654	157	87	187	4.12	0
2000	Tampa	Fla.St.	1	4	0	0	.000	5	1	1	0.00	0
2000	New York b	A.L.	29	195²/₃	12	13	.480	141	51	186	4.51	0
Major League Totals		3 Yrs.	83	551	41	26	.612	429	190	486	4.00	0
Division Series												
1999	New York	A.L.	1	8	1	0	1.000	4	6	2	0.00	0
2000	New York	A.L.	2	7¹/₃	1	0	1.000	5	5	5	2.45	0
Division Series Totals			3	15¹/₃	2	0	1.000	9	11	7	1.17	0
Championship Series												
1998	New York	A.L.	1	7	1	0	1.000	6	2	3	0.00	0
1999	New York	A.L.	2	15	1	0	1.000	13	6	12	1.80	0
2000	New York	A.L.	2	15	2	0	1.000	14	8	13	4.20	0
Championship Series Totals			5	37	4	0	1.000	33	16	28	2.43	0
World Series Record												
1998	New York	A.L.	1	7	1	0	1.000	7	3	6	1.29	0

Year	Club	Lea	G	IP	W	L	Pct	SO	BB	H	ERA	SAVES
1999 New York	...........A.L.		1	7	1	0	1.000	10	2	1	1.29	0
2000 New York	...........A.L.		1	7$^1/_3$	0	1	.000	12	3	9	4.91	0
World Series Totals	....		3	21$^1/_3$	2	1	.667	29	8	16	2.53	0

a Signed with New York Yankees, March 7, 1998.
b On disabled list from July 14 to August 5, 2000.

HERNANDEZ, ROBERTO MANUEL

Born, Santurce, Puerto Rico, November 11, 1964.
Bats Right. Throws Right. Height, 6 feet, 4 inches. Weight, 235 pounds.

Year	Club	Lea	G	IP	W	L	Pct	SO	BB	H	ERA	SAVES
1986 Salem	..........Northwest		10	55	2	2	.500	38	42	57	4.58	0
1987 Quad City a	......Midwest		7	21	2	3	.400	21	12	24	6.86	1
1988 Quad City	......Midwest		24	164$^2/_3$	9	10	.474	114	48	157	3.17	0
1988 Midland	.............Texas		3	12$^1/_3$	0	2	.000	7	8	16	6.57	0
1989 Palm Springs	......California		7	42$^2/_3$	1	4	.200	33	16	49	4.64	0
1989 Midland b	...........Texas		12	64	2	7	.222	42	30	94	6.89	0
1989 South Bend	.......Midwest		4	24$^1/_3$	1	1	.500	17	17	19	3.33	0
1990 Birmingham	......Southern		17	108	8	5	.615	62	43	102	3.67	0
1990 Vancouver	...........P.C.		11	79$^1/_3$	3	5	.375	49	26	73	2.84	0
1991 Vancouver	...........P.C.		7	44$^2/_3$	4	1	.800	40	23	41	3.22	0
1991 Sarasota White Sox	...Gulf C.		1	6	0	0	.000	7	0	2	0.00	0
1991 Birmingham	......Southern		4	22$^2/_3$	2	1	.667	25	6	11	1.99	0
1991 Chicago	..............A.L.		9	15	1	0	1.000	6	7	8	7.80	0
1992 Vancouver	...........P.C.		9	20$^2/_3$	3	3	.500	23	11	13	2.61	2
1992 Chicago	.............A.L.		43	71	7	3	.700	68	20	45	1.65	12
1993 Chicago	.............A.L.		70	78$^2/_3$	3	4	.429	71	20	66	2.29	38
1994 Chicago	.............A.L.		45	47$^2/_3$	4	4	.500	50	19	44	4.91	14
1995 Chicago c	..........A.L.		60	59$^2/_3$	3	7	.300	84	28	63	3.92	32
1996 Chicago	.............A.L.		72	84$^2/_3$	6	5	.545	85	38	65	1.91	38
1997 Chicago d	............A.L.		46	48	5	1	.833	47	24	38	2.44	27
1997 San Francisco e-f	....N.L.		28	32$^2/_3$	5	2	.714	35	14	29	2.48	4
1998 Tampa Bay	...........A.L.		67	71$^1/_3$	2	6	.250	55	41	55	4.04	26
1999 Tampa Bay	...........A.L.		72	73$^1/_3$	2	3	.400	69	33	68	3.07	43
2000 Tampa Bay g-h	........A.L.		68	73$^1/_3$	4	7	.364	61	23	76	3.19	32
Major League Totals	....10 Yrs.		580	655$^1/_3$	42	42	.500	631	267	567	3.04	266
Divisional Series												
1997 San Francisco	.........N.L.		3	1$^1/_3$	0	1	.000	1	3	5	20.25	0
Championship Series												
1993 Chicago	.............A.L.		4	4	0	0	.000	1	0	4	0.00	1

a On disabled list from May 6 to May 21 and June 14 to August 14, 1987.
b Traded by California Angels to Chicago White Sox for outfielder Mark Davis, August 2, 1989.
c Signed with Chicago White Sox, April 28, 1995.
d Traded to San Francisco Giants with pitcher Wilson Alvarez and pitcher Danny Darwin for infielder Mike Caruso, outfielder Brian Manning, pitcher Lorenzo Barcelo, pitcher Keith Foulke, pitcher Bob Howry and pitcher Ken Vining, July 31, 1997.
e Filed for free agency, October 30, 1997.
f Signed with Tampa Bay Devil Rays, November 18, 1997.
g Traded to Oakland Athletics with pitcher Cory Lidle for outfielder Ben Grieve and player to be named later, January 8, 2001.
h Traded to Kansas City Royals with catcher A.J. Hinch, outfielder Angel Berroa and cash for outfielder Johnny Damon, infielder Mark Ellis and player to be named later, January 8, 2001.

HILL, KENNETH WADE

Born, Lynn, Massachusetts, December 14, 1965.
Bats Right. Throws Right. Height, 6 feet, 2 inches. Weight, 200 pounds.

Year	Club	Lea	G	IP	W	L	Pct	SO	BB	H	ERA	SAVES
1985 Gastonia	...........So. Atl.		15	69	3	6	.333	48	57	60	4.96	0
1986 Gastonia	...........So. Atl.		22	122$^1/_3$	9	5	.643	86	80	95	2.79	0
1986 Glens Falls a	.......Eastern		1	7	0	1	.000	4	6	4	5.14	0
1986 Arkansas	............Texas		3	18	1	2	.333	9	7	18	4.50	0
1987 Arkansas	............Texas		18	53$^2/_3$	3	5	.375	48	30	60	5.20	2
1987 St. Petersburg	.......Fla. St.		18	41	1	3	.250	32	17	38	4.17	2
1988 Arkansas	............Texas		22	115$^1/_3$	9	9	.500	107	50	129	4.92	0
1988 St. Louis b	............N.L.		4	14	0	1	.000	6	6	16	5.14	0
1989 Louisville	...............A.A.		3	18	0	2	.000	18	10	13	3.50	0
1989 St. Louis	...............N.L.		33	196$^2/_3$	7	*15	.318	112	*99	186	3.80	0
1990 Louisville	...............A.A.		12	85$^1/_3$	6	1	.857	104	27	47	1.79	0
1990 St. Louis	...............N.L.		17	78$^2/_3$	5	6	.455	58	33	79	5.49	0

Year	Club	Lea	G	IP	W	L	Pct	SO	BB	H	ERA	SAVES
1991	Louisville	A.A.	1	1	0	0	.000	2	0	0	0.00	0
1991	St. Louis c-d	N.L.	30	181⅓	11	10	.524	121	67	147	3.57	0
1992	Montreal	N.L.	33	218	16	9	.640	150	75	187	2.68	0
1993	Ottawa	Int.	1	4	0	0	.000	0	1	1	0.00	0
1993	Montreal e-f	N.L.	28	183⅔	9	7	.563	90	74	163	3.23	0
1994	Montreal g-h	N.L.	23	154⅔	*16	5	.762	85	44	145	3.32	0
1995	St. Louis	N.L.	18	110⅓	6	7	.462	50	45	125	5.06	0
1995	Cleveland i-j-k-l	A.L.	12	74⅔	4	1	.800	48	32	77	3.98	0
1996	Texas	A.L.	35	250⅔	16	10	.615	170	95	250	3.63	0
1997	Tulsa m	Texas	1	5	0	0	.000	3	1	2	0.00	0
1997	Texas-Anaheim n-o-p	A.L.	31	190	9	12	.429	106	*95	194	4.55	0
1998	Cedar Rapids	Midwest	2	7⅓	0	0	.000	6	1	7	1.23	0
1998	Lk Elsinore	California	1	4	0	0	.000	2	5	5	6.75	0
1998	Anaheim q	A.L.	19	103	9	6	.600	57	47	123	4.98	0
1999	Anaheim r	A.L.	26	128⅓	4	11	.267	76	76	129	4.77	0
2000	Lake Elsinore	California	1	4	0	0	.000	3	1	5	0.00	0
2000	Edmonton	P.C.	2	9⅔	0	0	.000	5	8	14	6.52	0
2000	Charlotte	Int.	1	4	0	0	.000	7	0	6	4.50	0
2000	Anaheim-Chicago s-t-u	A.L.	18	81⅔	5	8	.385	50	59	107	7.16	0
Major League Totals	13 Yrs.		327	1965⅔	117	108	.520	1179	847	1928	4.03	0
Division Series												
1995	Cleveland	A.L.	1	1⅓	1	0	1.000	2	0	1	0.00	0
1996	Texas	A.L.	1	6	0	0	.000	1	3	5	4.50	0
Division Series Totals	2			7⅓	1	0	1.000	3	3	6	3.68	0
Championship Series												
1995	Cleveland	A.L.	1	7	1	0	1.000	6	3	5	0.00	0
World Series Record												
1995	Cleveland	A.L.	2	7⅓	0	1	.000	1	4	7	4.26	0

a Traded by Detroit Tigers to St. Louis Cardinals organization with first baseman Mike Laga for catcher Mike Heath, August 10, 1986.
b On disabled list from March 26 to May 9, 1988.
c On disabled list from August 11 to September 1, 1991.
d Traded to Montreal Expos for first baseman Andres Galarraga, November 25, 1991.
e Appeared in one additional game as pinch hitter.
f On disabled list from June 26 to July 17, 1993.
g Appeared in one additional game as pinch hitter.
h Declared restricted free agent under Major League Baseball implemented labor proposal, December 23, 1994.
i Traded to St. Louis Cardinals for pitcher Bryan Eversgerd, pitcher Kirk Bollinger and outfielder Darond Stovall, April 5, 1995.
j Traded to Cleveland Indians for infielder David Bell, pitcher Rick Heiserman and catcher Pepe McNeal, July 27, 1995.
k Filed for free agency, November 12, 1995.
l Signed with Texas Rangers, December 23, 1995.
m On disabled list from May 1 to May 24, 1997.
n Traded to Anaheim Angels for catcher Jim Leyritz and player to be named later, July 29, 1997. Texas Rangers received infielder Rob Sasser to complete trade, October 31, 1997.
o Filed for free agency, November 7, 1997.
p Re-signed with Anaheim Angels, November 16, 1997.
q On disabled list from June 11 to August 28, 1998.
r On disabled list from July 1 to July 19 and August 15 to September 1, 1999.
s On disabled list from May 10 to June 27, 2000.
t Released by Anaheim Angels, August 7, 2000, signed with Chicago White Sox organization, August 18, 2000.
u Released by Chicago White Sox, August 30, 2000.

HITCHCOCK, STERLING ALEX

Born, Fayetteville, North Carolina, April 29, 1971.
Bats Left. Throws Left. Height, 6 feet, 1 inch. Weight, 192 pounds.

Year	Club	Lea	G	IP	W	L	Pct	SO	BB	H	ERA	SAVES
1989	Sarasota Yankees	Gulf C.	13	76⅔	*9	1	.900	*98	27	48	1.64	0
1990	Greensboro	So. Atl.	27	173⅓	12	12	.500	*171	60	122	2.91	0
1991	Prince William	Carolina	19	119⅓	7	7	.500	101	26	111	2.64	0
1992	Albany	Eastern	24	146⅔	6	9	.400	*155	42	116	2.58	0
1992	New York	A.L.	3	13	0	2	.000	6	6	23	8.31	0
1993	Oneonta	N.Y.-Penn.	1	1	0	0	.000	0	0	0	0.00	0
1993	Columbus a	Int.	16	76⅔	3	5	.375	85	28	80	4.81	0
1993	New York	A.L.	6	31	1	2	.333	26	14	32	4.65	0
1994	Albany	Eastern	1	5	1	0	1.000	7	0	4	1.80	0
1994	Columbus	Int.	10	50	3	4	.429	47	18	53	4.32	0
1994	New York	A.L.	23	49⅓	4	1	.800	37	29	48	4.20	2
1995	New York b	A.L.	27	168⅓	11	10	.524	121	68	155	4.70	0

Year Club	Lea	G	IP	W	L	Pct	SO	BB	H	ERA	SAVES
1996 Seattle c	A.L.	35	196²/₃	13	9	.591	132	73	245	5.35	0
1997 San Diego d	N.L.	32	161	10	11	.476	106	55	172	5.20	0
1997 San Diego	N.L.	70	81¹/₃	6	4	.600	111	24	59	2.66	37
1998 San Diego	N.L.	39	176¹/₃	9	7	.563	158	48	169	3.93	1
1999 San Diego e	N.L.	33	205²/₃	12	14	.462	194	76	202	4.11	0
2000 San Diego e	N.L.	11	65²/₃	1	6	.143	61	26	69	4.93	0
Major League Totals ...9 Yrs.		209	1067	61	62	.496	841	395	1115	4.69	3
Division Series											
1995 New York	A.L.	2	1²/₃	0	0	.000	1	2	2	5.40	0
1998 San Diego	N.L.	1	6	1	0	1.000	11	0	3	1.50	0
Division Series Totals		3	7²/₃	1	0	1.000	12	2	5	2.35	0
Championship Series											
1998 San Diego	N.L.	2	10	2	0	1.000	14	8	5	0.90	0
World Series Record											
1998 San Diego	N.L.	1	6	0	0	.000	7	1	7	1.50	0

a On disabled list from May 23 to July 21, 1993.
b Traded by New York Yankees to Seattle Mariners with infielder Russ Davis for pitchers Jeff Nelson and Jim Mecir and infielder Tino Martinez, December 7, 1995.
c Traded to San Diego Padres for pitcher Scott Sanders, December 6, 1996.
d On disabled list from June 6 to July 3, 1997.
e On disabled list from May 27 to October 12, 2000.

HOFFMAN, TREVOR WILLIAM

Born, Bellflower, California, October 13, 1967.
Bats Right. Throws Right. Height, 6 feet, 1 inch. Weight, 205 pounds.

Year Club	Lea	G	IP	W	L	Pct	SO	BB	H	ERA	SAVES
1991 Cedar Rapids	Midwest	27	33²/₃	1	1	.500	52	13	22	1.87	12
1991 Chattanooga	Southern	14	14	1	0	1.000	23	7	10	1.93	8
1992 Chattanooga	Southern	6	29²/₃	3	0	1.000	31	11	22	1.52	0
1992 Nashville a	A.A.	42	65¹/₃	4	6	.400	63	32	57	4.27	6
1993 Florida-San Diego b	N.L.	67	90	4	6	.400	79	39	80	3.90	5
1994 San Diego	N.L.	47	56	4	4	.500	68	20	39	2.57	20
1995 San Diego	N.L.	55	53¹/₃	7	4	.636	52	14	48	3.88	31
1996 San Diego	N.L.	70	88	9	5	.643	111	31	50	2.25	42
1997 San Diego	N.L.	70	81¹/₃	6	4	.600	111	24	59	2.66	*53
1998 San Diego	N.L.	66	73	4	2	.667	86	21	41	1.48	*53
1999 San Diego	N.L.	64	67¹/₃	2	3	.400	73	15	48	2.14	40
2000 San Diego	N.L.	70	72¹/₃	4	7	.364	85	11	61	2.99	43
Major League Totals ....8 Yrs.		509	581¹/₃	40	35	.533	665	175	426	2.72	271
Division Series											
1996 San Diego	N.L.	2	1²/₃	0	1	.000	2	1	3	10.80	0
1998 San Diego	N.L.	4	3	0	0	.000	4	1	3	0.00	2
Division Series Totals		6	4²/₃	0	1	.000	6	2	6	3.86	2
Championship Series											
1998 San Diego	N.L.	3	4¹/₃	1	0	1.000	7	2	2	2.08	1
World Series Record											
1998 San Diego	N.L.	1	2	0	1	.000	0	1	2	9.00	0

Record as Position Player

Year Club	Lea	Pos	G	AB	R	H	2B	3B	HR	RBI	SB	Avg
1989 Bellingham	Pioneer	SS	61	201	22	50	5	0	1	20	1	.249
1990 Charleston	So. Atl.	SS-3B	103	278	41	59	10	1	2	23	3	.212

a Selected by Florida Marlins from Cincinnati Reds organization in expansion draft, November 17, 1992.
b Traded to San Diego Padres with pitchers Andres Berumen and Jose Martinez for infielder Greg Sheffield and pitcher Rich Rodriguez, June 25, 1993.

HOLT, CHRISTOPHER (CHRIS)

Born, Dallas, Texas, September 18, 1971.
Bats Right. Throws Right. Height, 6 feet, 4 inches. Weight, 205 pounds.

Year Club	Lea	G	IP	W	L	Pct	SO	BB	H	ERA	SAVES
1992 Auburn	N.Y.-Penn.	14	83	2	5	.286	81	24	75	4.45	0
1993 Quad City	Midwest	26	186¹/₃	11	10	.524	176	54	162	2.27	0
1994 Jackson	Texas	26	167	10	9	.526	111	22	169	3.45	0
1995 Jackson	Texas	5	32¹/₃	2	2	.500	24	5	27	1.67	0
1995 Tucson	P.C.	20	118²/₃	5	8	.385	69	32	155	4.10	0
1996 Tucson	P.C.	28	186¹/₃	9	6	.600	137	38	209	3.72	0
1996 Houston	N.L.	4	4²/₃	0	1	.000	0	3	5	5.79	0

Year Club	Lea	G	IP	W	L	Pct	SO	BB	H	ERA	SAVES
1997 Houston .............N.L.		33	209²/₃	8	12	.400	95	61	211	3.52	0
1998 Kissimmee ....Fla.St.		1	4	0	1	.000	1	4	6	9.00	0
1999 Houston .............N.L.		32	164	5	13	.278	115	67	193	4.66	1
2000 Houston a ...........N.L.		34	207	8	16	.333	136	75	247	5.35	0
Major League Totals ....4 Yrs.		103	585¹/₃	21	42	.333	346	196	656	4.51	1
Division Series											
1999 Houston .............N.L.		1	0	0	0	.000	0	0	3	INF	0

a Traded to Detroit Tigers with outfielder Roger Cedeno and catcher Mitch Meluskey for catcher Brad Ausmus, pitcher Doug Brocail and pitcher Nelson Cruz, December 11, 2000.

HOLTZ, MICHAEL JAMES (MIKE)
Born, Arlington, Virginia, October 10, 1972.
Bats Left. Throws Right. Height, 5 feet, 9 inches. Weight, 172 pounds.

Year Club	Lea	G	IP	W	L	Pct	SO	BB	H	ERA	SAVES
1994 Boise ....Northwest		22	35	0	0	.000	59	11	22	0.51	11
1995 Lk Elsinore ....California		56	82²/₃	4	4	.500	101	23	70	2.29	3
1996 Midland ....Texas		33	41	1	2	.333	41	9	52	4.17	2
1996 California ............A.L.		30	29¹/₃	3	3	.500	31	19	21	2.45	0
1997 Anaheim .............A.L.		66	43¹/₃	3	4	.429	40	15	38	3.32	2
1998 Vancouver ...........P.C.		10	10¹/₃	0	0	.000	18	6	10	1.74	2
1998 Anaheim .............A.L.		53	30¹/₃	2	2	.500	29	15	38	4.75	1
1999 Edmonton ...........P.C.		20	27¹/₃	2	1	.667	39	11	20	2.30	0
1999 Anaheim a ...........A.L.		28	22¹/₃	2	3	.400	17	15	26	8.06	0
2000 Edmonton ...........P.C.		6	5	0	1	.000	1	1	5	10.80	0
2000 Anaheim .............A.L.		61	41	3	4	.429	40	18	37	5.05	0
Major League Totals ....5 Yrs.		238	166¹/₃	13	16	.448	157	82	160	4.49	3

a On disabled list from August 25 to September 10, 1999.

HOWRY, BOBBY DEAN (BOB)
Born, Phoenix, Arizona, August 4, 1973.
Bats Left. Throws Right. Height, 6 feet, 5 inches. Weight, 215 pounds.

Year Club	Lea	G	IP	W	L	Pct	SO	BB	H	ERA	SAVES
1994 Everett ....Northwest		5	19	0	4	.000	16	10	29	7.11	0
1994 Clinton ....Midwest		9	49¹/₃	1	3	.250	22	16	61	4.20	0
1995 San Jose ....California		27	165¹/₃	12	10	.545	107	54	171	3.54	0
1996 Shreveport ....Texas		27	156²/₃	10	8	.556	57	56	163	4.65	0
1997 Shreveport ....Texas		48	55	6	3	.667	43	21	58	4.91	22
1997 Birmingham a .....Southern		12	12²/₃	0	0	.000	3	3	16	2.84	2
1998 Calgary .............P.C.		23	31²/₃	1	2	.333	22	10	25	3.41	5
1998 Chicago .............A.L.		44	54¹/₃	0	3	.000	51	19	37	3.15	9
1999 Chicago .............A.L.		69	67²/₃	5	3	.625	80	38	58	3.59	28
2000 Chicago .............A.L.		65	71	2	4	.333	60	29	54	3.17	7
Major League Totals ....3 Yrs.		178	193	7	10	.412	191	86	149	3.31	44
Division Series											
2000 Chicago .............A.L.		2	2²/₃	0	0	.000	4	2	2	3.38	0

a Traded by San Francisco Giants to Chicago White Sox with infielder Mike Caruso, outfielder Brian Manning, pitcher Lorenzo Barcelo, pitcher Keith Foulke and pitcher Ken Vining for pitcher Wilson Alvare

HUDSON, TIMOTHY ADAM (TIM)
Born, Columbus, Georgia, July 14, 1975.
Bats Right. Throws Right. Height, 6 feet. Weight, 160 pounds.

Year Club	Lea	G	IP	W	L	Pct	SO	BB	H	ERA	SAVES
1997 Sou Oregon ......Northwest		8	28²/₃	3	1	.750	37	15	12	2.51	0
1998 Modesto ....California		8	37²/₃	4	0	1.000	48	18	19	1.67	0
1998 Huntsville ....Southern		22	134²/₃	10	9	.526	104	71	136	4.54	0
1999 Midland ....Texas		3	18	3	0	1.000	18	3	9	0.50	0
1999 Vancouver ...........P.C.		8	49	4	0	1.000	61	21	38	2.20	0
1999 Oakland .............A.L.		21	136¹/₃	11	2	.846	132	62	121	3.23	0
2000 Oakland .............A.L.		32	202¹/₃	*20	6	*.769	169	82	169	4.14	0
Major League Totals ....2 Yrs.		53	338²/₃	31	8	.795	301	144	290	3.77	0
Division Series											
2000 Oakland .............A.L.		1	8	0	1	.000	5	4	6	3.38	0

IRABU, HIDEKI
Born, Hyogo, Japan, May 5, 1969.
Bats Right. Throws Right. Height, 6 feet, 4 inches. Weight, 240 pounds.

Year Club	Lea	G	IP	W	L	Pct	SO	BB	H	ERA	SAVES
1988 Lotte ....Japan Pac.		14	39⅓	2	5	.286	21	15	30	3.69	1
1989 Lotte ....Japan Pac.		33	51	0	2	.000	50	27	37	3.53	9
1990 Lotte ....Japan Pac.		24	125⅔	8	5	.615	102	72	110	3.78	0
1991 Lotte ....Japan Pac.		24	100⅔	3	8	.273	79	70	110	6.88	0
1992 Chiba Lotte .....Japan Pac.		28	77	0	5	.000	55	37	78	3.88	0
1993 Chiba Lotte .....Japan Pac.		32	142⅓	8	7	.533	160	56	125	3.10	1
1994 Chiba Lotte .....Japan Pac.		27	207⅓	*15	10	.600	*239	94	170	3.04	0
1995 Chiba Lotte .....Japan Pac.		28	203	11	11	.500	*239	72	158	*2.53	0
1996 Chiba Lotte .....Japan Pac.		23	157⅓	12	6	.667	167	59	108	*2.40	0
1997 Tampa a-b ....Fla. St.		2	9	1	0	1.000	12	0	4	0.00	0
1997 Norwich ....Eastern		2	10	1	1	.500	9	0	13	4.50	0
1997 Columbus ....Int.		4	27	2	0	1.000	28	5	19	1.67	0
1997 New York ...........A.L.		13	53⅓	5	4	.556	56	20	69	7.09	0
1998 New York ...........A.L.		29	173	13	9	.591	126	76	148	4.06	0
1999 New York c .........A.L.		32	169⅓	11	7	.611	133	46	180	4.84	0
2000 Jupiter ....Fla.St.		2	8⅔	1	0	1.000	9	1	7	1.04	0
2000 Ottawa ....Int.		1	5⅔	0	1	.000	6	2	5	3.18	0
2000 Montreal d .........N.L.		11	54⅔	2	5	.286	42	14	77	7.24	0
Major League Totals ....4 Yrs.		85	450⅓	31	25	.554	357	156	474	5.10	0
Championship Series											
1999 New York ...........A.L.		1	4⅔	0	0	.000	3	0	13	13.50	0

a Rights acquired by San Diego Padres from Chiba Lotte Orions.
b Traded to New York Yankees by San Diego Padres with infielder Homer Bush, outfielder Gordon Amerson and
  player to be named later for outfielder Ruben Rivera, pitcher Rafael Medina and cash (reported to be $3 million),
  May 30, 1997. New York Yankees received outfielder Vernon Maxwell to complete trade, June 9, 1997.
c Traded to Montreal Expos for pitcher Jason Westbrook, player to be named later and player to be named later,
  December 22, 1999. New York Yankees received pitcher Ted Lilly (March 17, 2000) and pitcher Christian Parker
  (March 22, 2000) to complete trade.
d On disabled list from May 27 to July 25 and July 28 to October 1, 2000.

ISRINGHAUSEN, JASON DERIK
Born, Brighton, Illinois, September 7, 1972.
Bats Right. Throws Right. Height, 6 feet, 3 inches. Weight, 195 pounds.

Year Club	Lea	G	IP	W	L	Pct	SO	BB	H	ERA	SAVES
1992 Mets ....Gulf Coast		6	29	2	4	.333	25	17	26	4.34	0
1992 Kingsport ....Appal.		7	36	4	1	.800	24	12	32	3.25	0
1993 Pittsfield .........N.Y.-Penn.		15	90⅓	7	4	.636	104	28	68	3.29	0
1994 St. Lucie ....Fla.St.		14	101	6	4	.600	59	27	76	2.23	0
1994 Binghamton ....Eastern		14	92⅓	5	4	.556	69	23	78	3.02	0
1995 Binghamton ....Eastern		6	41	2	1	.667	59	12	26	2.85	0
1995 Norfolk ....Int.		12	87	9	1	.900	75	24	64	1.55	0
1995 New York ...........N.L.		14	93	9	2	.818	55	31	88	2.81	0
1996 New York a .........N.L.		27	171⅔	6	14	.300	114	73	190	4.77	0
1997 Mets ....Gulf Coast		1	4⅔	1	0	1.000	7	1	2	1.93	0
1997 St. Lucie ....Fla.St.		2	12	1	0	1.000	15	5	8	0.00	0
1997 Norfolk ....Int.		3	20	0	2	.000	17	8	20	4.05	0
1997 New York b .........N.L.		6	29⅔	2	2	.500	25	22	40	7.58	0
1998 New York c .........N.L.			INJURED - Did Not Play								
1999 New York ...........N.L.		13	39⅓	1	3	.250	31	22	43	6.41	1
1999 Oakland d ...........A.L.		20	25⅓	0	1	.000	20	12	21	2.13	8
2000 Oakland ...............A.L.		66	69	6	4	.600	57	32	67	3.78	33
Major League Totals ....5 Yrs.		146	428	24	26	.480	302	192	449	4.37	42
Division Series											
2000 Oakland .............A.L.		2	2	0	0	.000	3	0	1	0.00	1

a On disabled list from August 13 to September 1, 1996.
b On disabled list from March 24 to August 27, 1997.
c On disabled list from March 21 to September 28, 1998.
d Traded to Oakland Athletics with pitcher Greg McMichael for pitcher Billy Taylor, July 31, 1999.

JACKSON, MICHAEL RAY
Born, Houston, Texas, December 22, 1964.
Bats Right. Throws Right. Height, 6 feet. Weight, 223 pounds.

Year Club	Lea	G	IP	W	L	Pct	SO	BB	H	ERA	SAVES
1984 Spartanburg ....So. Atl.		14	80⅔	7	2	.778	77	50	53	2.68	0
1985 Peninsula ....Carolina		31	125⅓	7	9	.438	96	53	127	4.60	1

Year	Club	Lea	G	IP	W	L	Pct	SO	BB	H	ERA	SAVES
1986 Reading	Eastern		30	43⅓	2	3	.400	42	22	25	1.66	6
1986 Portland	P.C.		17	22⅔	3	1	.750	23	13	18	3.18	3
1986 Philadelphia	N.L.		9	13⅓	0	0	.000	3	4	12	3.38	0
1987 Maine	Int.		2	11	1	0	1.000	13	5	9	0.82	2
1987 Philadelphia a	N.L.		55	109⅓	3	10	.231	93	56	88	4.20	1
1988 Seattle	A.L.		62	99⅓	6	5	.545	76	43	74	2.63	4
1989 Seattle	A.L.		65	99⅓	4	6	.400	94	54	81	3.17	7
1990 Seattle	A.L.		63	77⅓	5	7	.417	69	44	64	4.54	3
1991 Seattle b	A.L.		72	88⅔	7	7	.500	74	34	64	3.25	14
1992 San Francisco	N.L.		67	82	6	6	.500	80	33	76	3.73	2
1993 San Francisco c	N.L.		*81	77⅓	6	6	.500	70	24	58	3.03	1
1994 San Francisco d-e	N.L.		36	42⅓	3	2	.600	51	11	23	1.49	4
1995 Chattanooga	Southern		3	3	0	0	.000	2	0	2	0.00	0
1995 Indianapolis	A.A.		2	2	0	0	.000	1	0	0	0.00	0
1995 Cincinnati f-g-h	N.L.		40	49	6	1	.857	41	19	38	2.39	2
1996 Seattle i-j	A.L.		73	72	1	1	.500	70	24	61	3.62	6
1997 Cleveland	A.L.		71	75	2	5	.286	74	29	59	3.24	15
1998 Cleveland	A.L.		69	64	1	1	.500	55	13	43	1.55	40
1999 Cleveland k	A.L.		72	68⅔	3	4	.429	55	26	60	4.06	39
2000 Philadelphia l-m	N.L.			INJURED - did not play								
Major League Totals 14 Yrs.			835	1017⅔	53	61	.465	905	414	801	3.26	138
Division Series												
1995 Cincinnati	N.L.		3	3⅔	0	0	.000	1	0	4	0.00	0
1997 Cleveland	A.L.		4	4⅓	1	0	1.000	5	1	3	0.00	0
1998 Cleveland	A.L.		3	4	0	0	.000	1	1	3	4.50	3
1999 Cleveland	A.L.		2	2	0	0	.000	1	1	2	4.50	0
Division Series Totals			12	14	1	0	1.000	8	3	12	1.93	3
Championship Series												
1995 Cincinnati	N.L.		3	2⅓	0	1	.000	1	4	5	23.14	0
1997 Cleveland	A.L.		5	4⅓	0	0	.000	7	1	1	0.00	0
1998 Cleveland	A.L.		1	1	0	0	.000	2	0	0	0.00	1
Championship Series Totals			9	7⅔	0	1	.000	10	5	6	7.04	0
World Series Record												
1997 Cleveland	A.L.		4	4⅔	0	0	.000	4	3	5	1.93	0

a Traded to Seattle Mariners with outfielders Glenn Wilson and Dave Brundage for outfielder Phil Bradley and pitcher Tom Fortugno, December 9, 1987.
b Traded to San Francisco Giants with pitchers Bill Swift and Dave Burba for outfielder Kevin Mitchell and pitcher Mike Remlinger, December 11, 1991.
c On disabled list from July 24 to August 9, 1993.
d On disabled list from June 17 to July 2 and July 7 to end of 1994 season.
e Filed for free agency, October 18, 1994.
f Signed with Cincinnati Reds, April 8, 1995.
g On disabled list from April 25 to June 5, 1995.
h Filed for free agency, November 12, 1995.
i Signed with Seattle Mariners, February 2, 1996.
j Filed for free agency, October 30, 1996. signed with Cleveland Indians, December 12, 1996.
k Filed for free agency, October 28, 1999, signed with Philadelphia Phillies, December 1, 1999.
l On disabled list from March 31 to October 5, 2000.
m Filed for free agency, October 14, 2000, signed with Houston Astros, December 14, 2000.

JAMES, MICHAEL ELMO (MIKE)

Born, Ft.Walton Beach, Florida, August 15, 1967.
Bats Right. Throws Right. Height, 6 feet, 4 inches. Weight, 215 pounds.

Year	Club	Lea	G	IP	W	L	PCT	SO	BB	H	ERA	SAVES
1988 Great Falls	Pioneer		14	67	7	1	.875	59	41	61	3.76	0
1989 Bakersfield	California		27	159⅔	11	8	.579	127	78	144	3.78	0
1990 San Antonio	Texas		26	157	11	4	.733	97	78	144	3.32	0
1991 San Antonio	Texas		15	89⅓	9	5	.643	74	51	88	4.53	0
1991 Albuquerque	P.C.		13	45	1	3	.250	39	30	51	6.60	0
1992 San Antonio	Texas		8	54	2	1	.667	52	20	39	2.67	0
1992 Albuquerque a	P.C.		18	46⅔	2	1	.667	33	22	55	5.59	1
1993 Albuquerque	P.C.		16	31⅓	1	0	1.000	32	19	38	7.47	2
1993 Vero Beach b-c	Fla.St.		30	60⅓	2	3	.400	60	33	54	4.92	5
1994 Vancouver	P.C.		37	91⅓	5	3	.625	66	34	101	5.22	8
1995 Lk Elsinore	California		5	5⅔	0	0	.000	8	3	9	9.53	0
1995 California d	A.L.		46	55⅔	3	0	1.000	36	26	49	3.88	1
1996 California	A.L.		69	81	5	5	.500	65	42	62	2.67	1
1997 Anaheim e	A.L.		58	62⅔	5	5	.500	57	28	69	4.31	7
1998 Anaheim f	A.L.		11	14	0	0	.000	12	7	10	1.93	0

<table>
<tr><th>Year</th><th>Club</th><th>Lea</th><th>G</th><th>IP</th><th>W</th><th>L</th><th>Pct</th><th>SO</th><th>BB</th><th>H</th><th>ERA</th><th>SAVES</th></tr>
<tr><td>1999 Edmonton . . . .</td><td>.P.C.</td><td>8</td><td>8 1/3</td><td>1</td><td>2</td><td>.333</td><td>3</td><td>2</td><td>16</td><td>8.64</td><td>0</td></tr>
<tr><td>1999 Lake Elsinore . . . . . .</td><td>California</td><td>3</td><td>9 1/3</td><td>0</td><td>0</td><td>.000</td><td>6</td><td>0</td><td>12</td><td>5.79</td><td>0</td></tr>
<tr><td>2000 Memphis . . . .</td><td>.P.C.</td><td>8</td><td>9 2/3</td><td>2</td><td>1</td><td>.667</td><td>8</td><td>4</td><td>6</td><td>0.93</td><td>0</td></tr>
<tr><td>2000 St. Louis g . . . .</td><td>N.L.</td><td>51</td><td>51 1/3</td><td>2</td><td>2</td><td>.500</td><td>41</td><td>24</td><td>40</td><td>3.16</td><td>2</td></tr>
<tr><td>Major League Totals . . . . .5 Yrs.</td><td></td><td>235</td><td>264 2/3</td><td>15</td><td>12</td><td>.556</td><td>211</td><td>127</td><td>230</td><td>3.37</td><td>11</td></tr>
<tr><td>Division Series</td><td></td><td></td><td></td><td></td><td></td><td></td><td></td><td></td><td></td><td></td><td></td></tr>
<tr><td>2000 St. Louis . . . .</td><td>N.L.</td><td>2</td><td>4 1/3</td><td>1</td><td>0</td><td>1.000</td><td>1</td><td>1</td><td>1</td><td>0.00</td><td>0</td></tr>
<tr><td>Championship Series</td><td></td><td></td><td></td><td></td><td></td><td></td><td></td><td></td><td></td><td></td><td></td></tr>
<tr><td>2000 St. Louis . . . .</td><td>N.L.</td><td>4</td><td>2 1/3</td><td>0</td><td>0</td><td>.000</td><td></td><td>1</td><td>5</td><td>15.43</td><td>0</td></tr>
</table>

a On disabled list from July 12 to August 26, 1992.
b On disabled list from July 2 to 9, 1993.
c Traded by Los Angeles Dodgers to California Angels for outfielder Reggie Williams, October 26, 1993.
d On disabled list from May 11 to June 1, 1995.
e On disabled list from July 3 to July 27, 1997.
f On disabled list from May 5 to September 28, 1998.
g On disabled list from May 26 to June 19, 2000.

JARVIS, KEVIN THOMAS

Born, Lexington, Kentucky, August 1, 1969.
Bats Left. Throws Right. Height, 6 feet, 2 inches. Weight, 200 pounds.

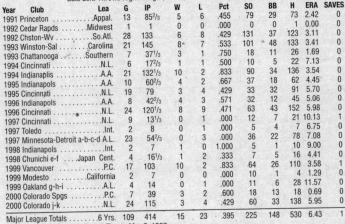

<table>
<tr><th>Year</th><th>Club</th><th>Lea</th><th>G</th><th>IP</th><th>W</th><th>L</th><th>Pct</th><th>SO</th><th>BB</th><th>H</th><th>ERA</th><th>SAVES</th></tr>
<tr><td>1991 Princeton . . . .</td><td>.Appal.</td><td>13</td><td>85 2/3</td><td>5</td><td>6</td><td>.455</td><td>79</td><td>29</td><td>73</td><td>2.42</td><td>0</td></tr>
<tr><td>1992 Cedar Rapds . . . . . .</td><td>Midwest</td><td>1</td><td>1</td><td>0</td><td>0</td><td>.000</td><td>0</td><td>0</td><td>1</td><td>0.00</td><td>0</td></tr>
<tr><td>1992 Chston-Wv . . . .</td><td>So.Atl.</td><td>28</td><td>133</td><td>6</td><td>8</td><td>.429</td><td>131</td><td>37</td><td>123</td><td>3.11</td><td>0</td></tr>
<tr><td>1993 Winston-Sal . . . .</td><td>Carolina</td><td>21</td><td>145</td><td>8</td><td>7</td><td>.533</td><td>101</td><td>48</td><td>133</td><td>3.41</td><td>0</td></tr>
<tr><td>1993 Chattanooga . . . . .</td><td>.Southern</td><td>7</td><td>37 1/3</td><td>3</td><td>1</td><td>.750</td><td>18</td><td>11</td><td>26</td><td>1.69</td><td>0</td></tr>
<tr><td>1994 Cincinnati . . . .</td><td>N.L.</td><td>6</td><td>17 2/3</td><td>1</td><td>1</td><td>.500</td><td>10</td><td>5</td><td>22</td><td>7.13</td><td>0</td></tr>
<tr><td>1994 Indianaplis . . . .</td><td>.A.A.</td><td>21</td><td>132 1/3</td><td>10</td><td>2</td><td>.833</td><td>90</td><td>34</td><td>136</td><td>3.54</td><td>0</td></tr>
<tr><td>1995 Indianapols . . . .</td><td>.A.A.</td><td>10</td><td>60 2/3</td><td>4</td><td>2</td><td>.667</td><td>37</td><td>18</td><td>62</td><td>4.45</td><td>0</td></tr>
<tr><td>1995 Cincinnati . . . .</td><td>N.L.</td><td>19</td><td>79</td><td>3</td><td>4</td><td>.429</td><td>33</td><td>32</td><td>91</td><td>5.70</td><td>0</td></tr>
<tr><td>1996 Indianapols . . . .</td><td>.A.A.</td><td>8</td><td>42 2/3</td><td>4</td><td>3</td><td>.571</td><td>32</td><td>12</td><td>45</td><td>5.06</td><td>0</td></tr>
<tr><td>1996 Cincinnati . . . .</td><td>N.L.</td><td>24</td><td>120 1/3</td><td>8</td><td>9</td><td>.471</td><td>63</td><td>43</td><td>152</td><td>5.98</td><td>0</td></tr>
<tr><td>1997 Cincinnati . . . .</td><td>N.L.</td><td>9</td><td>13 1/3</td><td>0</td><td>0</td><td>.000</td><td>12</td><td>7</td><td>21</td><td>10.13</td><td>1</td></tr>
<tr><td>1997 Toledo . . . .</td><td>.Int.</td><td>2</td><td>8</td><td>0</td><td>1</td><td>.000</td><td>5</td><td>4</td><td>7</td><td>6.75</td><td>0</td></tr>
<tr><td>1997 Minnesota-Detroit a-b-c-d</td><td>A.L.</td><td>23</td><td>54 2/3</td><td>0</td><td>3</td><td>.000</td><td>36</td><td>22</td><td>78</td><td>7.08</td><td>0</td></tr>
<tr><td>1998 Indianapols . . . .</td><td>.Int.</td><td>2</td><td>7</td><td>1</td><td>0</td><td>1.000</td><td>5</td><td>1</td><td>10</td><td>9.00</td><td>0</td></tr>
<tr><td>1998 Chunichi e-f . . . .</td><td>Japan Cent.</td><td>4</td><td>16 1/3</td><td>1</td><td>2</td><td>.333</td><td>7</td><td>5</td><td>16</td><td>4.41</td><td>0</td></tr>
<tr><td>1999 Vancouver . . . .</td><td>.P.C.</td><td>17</td><td>103</td><td>10</td><td>2</td><td>.833</td><td>64</td><td>26</td><td>110</td><td>3.58</td><td>1</td></tr>
<tr><td>1999 Modesto . . . .</td><td>California</td><td>2</td><td>7</td><td>0</td><td>0</td><td>.000</td><td>10</td><td>1</td><td>4</td><td>1.29</td><td>0</td></tr>
<tr><td>1999 Oakland g-h-i . . . .</td><td>.A.L.</td><td>4</td><td>14</td><td>0</td><td>1</td><td>.000</td><td>11</td><td>6</td><td>28</td><td>11.57</td><td>0</td></tr>
<tr><td>2000 Colorado Spgs . . . .</td><td>.P.C.</td><td>7</td><td>39</td><td>3</td><td>2</td><td>.600</td><td>18</td><td>13</td><td>18</td><td>0.69</td><td>0</td></tr>
<tr><td>2000 Colorado j-k . . . .</td><td>N.L.</td><td>24</td><td>115</td><td>3</td><td>4</td><td>.429</td><td>60</td><td>33</td><td>138</td><td>5.95</td><td>0</td></tr>
<tr><td>Major League Totals . . . . .6 Yrs.</td><td></td><td>109</td><td>414</td><td>15</td><td>23</td><td>.395</td><td>225</td><td>148</td><td>530</td><td>6.43</td><td>1</td></tr>
</table>

a Claimed on waivers by Detroit Tigers, May 2, 1997.
b Claimed on waivers by Minnesota Twins, May 9, 1997.
c Claimed on waivers by Detroit Tigers, June 17, 1997.
d On disabled list from June 25 to July 14, 1997.
e Released by Detroit Tigers, December 12, 1997, signed with Chunichi Dragons (JCL), January 23, 1998.
f Signed by Cincinnati Reds, August 27, 1998.
g Released by Cincinnati Reds, September 9, 1998, signed with Oakland Athletics organization, January 18, 1999.
h On disabled list from April 19 to June 4, 1999.
i Filed for free agency, October 8, 1999, signed with Colorado Rockies organization, December 1, 1999.
j On disabled list from July 28 to August 31, 2000.
k Not offered 2001 contract, December 21, 2000, signed with San Diego Padres, January 5, 2001.

JIMENEZ, JOSE

Born, San Pedro De Macoris, Dominican Republic, July 7, 1973.
Bats Right. Throws Right. Height, 6 feet, 3 inches. Weight, 170 pounds.

<table>
<tr><th>Year</th><th>Club</th><th>Lea</th><th>G</th><th>IP</th><th>W</th><th>L</th><th>Pct</th><th>SO</th><th>BB</th><th>H</th><th>ERA</th><th>SAVES</th></tr>
<tr><td>1992 Det/Stl . . . .</td><td>Dominican</td><td>18</td><td>48 2/3</td><td>3</td><td>2</td><td>.600</td><td>21</td><td>23</td><td>68</td><td>6.10</td><td>0</td></tr>
<tr><td>1993 Det/Stl . . . .</td><td>Dominican</td><td>12</td><td>56 1/3</td><td>3</td><td>5</td><td>.375</td><td>30</td><td>35</td><td>61</td><td>3.51</td><td>0</td></tr>
<tr><td>1994 Stl/Phil . . . .</td><td>Dominican</td><td>19</td><td>68 1/3</td><td>3</td><td>9</td><td>.250</td><td>54</td><td>30</td><td>54</td><td>2.77</td><td>3</td></tr>
<tr><td>1995 Johnson Cty . . . .</td><td>.Appal.</td><td>14</td><td>90 1/3</td><td>5</td><td>7</td><td>.417</td><td>85</td><td>25</td><td>81</td><td>3.49</td><td>0</td></tr>
<tr><td>1996 Peoria . . . .</td><td>Midwest</td><td>28</td><td>172 1/3</td><td>12</td><td>9</td><td>.571</td><td>129</td><td>53</td><td>158</td><td>2.92</td><td>0</td></tr>
<tr><td>1997 Pr William . . . .</td><td>Carolina</td><td>24</td><td>145 2/3</td><td>9</td><td>7</td><td>.563</td><td>81</td><td>42</td><td>128</td><td>3.09</td><td>0</td></tr>
<tr><td>1998 Arkansas . . . .</td><td>.Texas</td><td>26</td><td>179 2/3</td><td>15</td><td>6</td><td>.714</td><td>88</td><td>68</td><td>156</td><td>3.11</td><td>0</td></tr>
<tr><td>1998 St. Louis . . . .</td><td>N.L.</td><td>4</td><td>21 1/3</td><td>3</td><td>0</td><td>1.000</td><td>12</td><td>8</td><td>22</td><td>2.95</td><td>0</td></tr>
</table>

Year	Club	Lea	G	IP	W	L	Pct	SO	BB	H	ERA	SAVES
1999 Memphis	....	P.C.	4	26⅔	2	2	.500	18	9	30	3.04	0
1999 St. Louis a-b	....	N.L.	29	163	5	14	.263	113	71	173	5.85	0
2000 Colorado	....	N.L.	72	70⅓	5	2	.714	44	28	63	3.18	24
Major League Totals	....	3 Yrs.	105	255	13	16	.448	169	107	258	4.87	24

a Pitched no-hit, no-run game against Arizona Diamondbacks, June 25, 1999.

b Traded to Colorado Rockies with pitcher Manuel Aybar, pitcher Rich Croushore and infielder Brent Butler for pitcher Darryl Kile and pitcher Dave Veres, November 16, 1999.

JOHNSON, JASON MICHAEL

Born, Santa Barbara, California, October 27, 1973.
Bats Right. Throws Right. Height, 6 feet, 6 inches. Weight, 220 pounds.

Year	Club	Lea	G	IP	W	L	Pct	SO	BB	H	ERA	SAVES
1992 Pirates	....	Gulf Coast	5	7⅓	2	0	1.000	3	6	6	3.68	0
1993 Pirates	....	Gulf Coast	9	54	1	4	.200	39	14	48	2.33	0
1993 Welland	....	N.Y.-Penn.	6	35	1	5	.167	19	9	33	4.63	0
1994 Augusta	....	So. Atl.	20	102⅔	2	12	.143	69	32	119	4.03	0
1995 Augusta	....	So. Atl.	11	53⅔	3	5	.375	42	17	57	4.36	0
1995 Lynchburg	....	Carolina	10	55	1	4	.200	41	20	58	4.91	0
1996 Lynchburg	....	Carolina	15	44⅓	4	4	.200	27	12	56	6.50	0
1996 Augusta	....	So. Atl.	14	84	4	4	.500	83	25	82	3.11	0
1997 Lynchburg	....	Carolina	17	99⅓	8	4	.667	92	30	98	3.71	0
1997 Carolina	....	Southern	9	57⅓	3	3	.500	63	16	56	4.08	0
1997 Pittsburgh a	....	N.L.	3	6	0	0	.000	3	1	10	6.00	0
1998 Durham	....	Int.	2	12⅓	1	0	1.000	14	2	6	2.92	0
1998 Tampa Bay b	....	A.L.	13	60	2	5	.286	36	27	74	5.70	0
1999 Rochester	....	Int.	8	44⅓	4	2	.667	47	27	35	3.65	0
1999 Baltimore c	....	A.L.	22	115⅓	8	7	.533	71	55	120	5.46	0
2000 Rochester	....	Int.	8	55	3	1	.750	56	21	32	1.47	1
2000 Baltimore	....	A.L.	25	107⅔	1	10	.091	79	61	119	7.02	0
Major League Totals	....	4 Yrs.	63	289	11	22	.333	189	144	323	6.10	0

a Selected in expansion draft by Tampa Bay Devil Rays, November 18, 1997.

b On disabled list from July 4 to September 28, 1998.

c Traded to Baltimore Orioles for outfielder Danny Clyburn and player to be named later, March 29, 1999.

JOHNSON, MICHAEL KEITH (MIKE)

Born, Edmonton, Alberta, Canada, October 3, 1975.
Bats Left. Throws Right. Height, 6 feet, 2 inches. Weight, 175 pounds.

Year	Club	Lea	G	IP	W	L	Pct	SO	BB	H	ERA	SAVES
1993 Blue Jays	....	Gulf Coast	16	44⅓	0	2	.000	31	22	51	4.87	1
1994 Medcine Hat	....	Pioneer	9	36⅓	1	3	.250	8	22	48	4.46	0
1995 Blue Jays	....	Gulf Coast	3	15	0	2	.000	13	8	20	7.20	0
1995 Medcine Hat	....	Pioneer	19	49	4	1	.800	32	25	46	3.86	3
1996 Hagerstown a-b	......	So.Atl.	29	162⅔	11	8	.579	155	39	157	3.15	0
1997 Baltimore	....	A.L.	14	39⅔	0	1	.000	29	16	52	7.94	2
1997 Montreal c-d	....	N.L.	11	50	2	5	.286	28	21	54	5.94	0
1998 Harrisburg	....	Eastern	7	33⅔	3	2	.600	38	10	35	6.95	0
1998 Ottawa	....	Int.	18	109	4	9	.308	88	38	105	4.29	0
1998 Montreal	....	N.L.	2	7⅓	0	2	.000	4	2	16	14.73	0
1999 Ottawa	....	Int.	28	147⅓	6	12	.333	120	63	174	5.38	0
1999 Montreal	....	N.L.	3	8⅓	0	0	.000	6	7	12	8.64	0
2000 Ottawa	....	Int.	5	30	2	0	1.000	27	14	14	2.10	0
2000 Montreal	....	N.L.	41	101⅓	5	6	.455	70	53	107	6.39	0
Major League Totals	....	4 Yrs.	71	206⅔	7	14	.333	137	99	241	6.97	2

a Selected by San Francisco Giants from Toronto Blue Jays in Rule V draft, December 9, 1996.

b Sold to Baltimore Orioles, December 9, 1996.

c Traded to Montreal Expos for player to be named later, July 31, 1997.

d Baltimore Orioles received pitcher Everett Stull to complete trade, October 31, 1997.

JOHNSON, RANDALL DAVID (RANDY)

Born, Walnut Creek, California, September 10, 1964.
Bats Right. Throws Left. Height, 6 feet, 10 inches. Weight, 225 pounds.

Year	Club	Lea	G	IP	W	L	Pct	SO	BB	H	ERA	SAVES
1985 Jamestown	......	N.Y.-Penn.	8	27⅓	0	3	.000	21	24	29	5.93	0
1986 West Palm Beach	.....	Fla. St.	26	119⅔	8	7	.533	133	94	89	3.16	0

Year	Club	Lea	G	IP	W	L	Pct	SO	BB	H	ERA	SAVES
1987 Jacksonville	Southern	25	140	11	8	.579	*163	128	100	3.73	0	
1988 Indianapolis	A.A.	20	113⅓	8	7	.533	111	72	85	3.26	0	
1988 Montreal	N.L.	4	26	3	0	1.000	25	7	23	2.42	0	
1989 Montreal	N.L.	7	29⅔	0	4	.000	26	26	29	6.67	0	
1989 Indianapolis a	A.A.	3	18	1	1	.500	17	9	13	2.00	0	
1989 Seattle	A.L.	22	131	7	9	.438	104	70	118	4.40	0	
1990 Seattle b-c	A.L.	33	219⅔	14	11	.560	194	*120	174	3.65	0	
1991 Seattle	A.L.	33	201⅓	13	10	.565	228	*152	151	3.98	0	
1992 Seattle d	A.L.	31	210⅓	12	14	.462	*241	*144	154	3.77	0	
1993 Seattle	A.L.	35	255⅓	19	8	.704	*308	99	185	3.24	1	
1994 Seattle	A.L.	23	172	13	6	.684	*204	72	132	3.19	0	
1995 Seattle e	A.L.	30	214⅓	18	2	*.900	*294	65	159	*2.48	0	
1996 Everett	Northwest	1	2	0	0	.000	5	0	0	0.00	0	
1996 Seattle f	A.L.	14	61⅓	5	0	1.000	85	25	48	3.67	1	
1997 Seattle	A.L.	30	213	20	4	.833	291	77	147	2.28	0	
1998 Seattle	A.L.	23	160	9	10	.474	213	60	146	4.33	0	
1998 Houston g-h-i	N.L.	11	84⅓	10	1	.909	116	26	57	1.28	0	
1999 Arizona j	N.L.	35	*271⅔	17	9	.654	364	70	*207	*2.48	0	
2000 Arizona k	N.L.	35	248⅔	19	7	*.731	*347	76	202	2.64	0	
Major League Totals 13 Yrs.		366	2498⅔	179	95	.653	3040	1089	1932	3.19	2	
Division Series												
1995 Seattle	A.L.	2	10	2	0	1.000	16	6	5	2.70	0	
1997 Seattle	A.L.	2	13	0	2	.000	16	6	14	5.54	0	
1998 Houston	N.L.	2	14	0	2	.000	17	2	12	1.93	0	
1999 Arizona	N.L.	1	8⅓	0	1	.000	11	3	8	7.56	0	
Division Series Totals		7	45⅓	2	5	.286	60	17	39	4.17	0	
Championship Series												
1995 Seattle	A.L.	2	15⅓	0	1	.000	13	2	12	2.35	0	

a Traded by Montreal Expos to Seattle Mariners with pitchers Brian Holman and Gene Harris for pitcher Mark Langston and player to be named, May 25; Montreal acquired pitcher Mike Campbell to complete trade, July 31, 1989.
b Pitched no-hit, no-run game against Detroit Tigers, winning 2-0, June 2, 1990.
c Suspended three games by American League for June 30 fight from July 11 to July 13, 1990.
d On disabled list from June 11 to June 27, 1992.
e Selected Cy Young Award Winner in American League for 1995.
f On disabled list from May 13 to August 6 and August 27 to September 30, 1996.
g Traded to Houston Astros for infielder Carlos Guillen, pitcher Freddy Garcia and player to be named later, July 31, 1998.
h Seattle Mariners received pitcher John Halama to complete trade, October 1, 1998.
i Filed for free agency, October 28, 1998, signed with Arizona Diamondbacks, November 30, 1998.
j Selected Cy Young Award Winner in National League for 1999.
k Selected Cy Young Award Winner in National League for 2000.

JOHNSTONE, JOHN WILLIAM

Born, Liverpool, New York, November 25, 1968.
Bats Right. Throws Right. Height, 6 feet, 3 inches. Weight, 195 pounds.

Year	Club	Lea	G	IP	W	L	Pct	SO	BB	H	ERA	SAVES
1987 Kingsport	Appal.	17	29	1	1	.500	21	20	42	7.45	0	
1988 Mets	Gulf Coast	12	74	3	4	.429	57	25	65	2.68	0	
1989 Pittsfield	N.Y.-Penn.	15	104	11	2	.846	60	28	101	2.77	0	
1990 St. Lucie	Fla.St.	25	172⅔	15	6	.714	120	60	145	2.24	0	
1991 Williamsprt	Eastern	27	165⅓	7	9	.438	100	79	159	3.97	0	
1992 Binghamton a-b	Eastern	24	149⅓	7	7	.500	121	36	132	3.74	0	
1993 Edmonton	P.C.	30	144⅓	4	15	.211	126	59	167	5.18	4	
1993 Florida	N.L.	7	10⅔	0	2	.000	5	7	16	5.91	0	
1994 Edmonton	P.C.	29	42⅓	5	3	.625	43	9	46	4.46	4	
1994 Florida	N.L.	17	21⅓	1	2	.333	23	16	23	5.91	0	
1995 Florida c	N.L.	4	4⅔	0	0	.000	3	2	7	3.86	0	
1996 Houston	N.L.	9	13	1	0	1.000	5	5	17	5.54	0	
1996 Tucson d	P.C.	45	55⅓	3	3	.500	70	22	59	3.42	5	
1997 Phoenix	P.C.	38	38	0	3	.000	30	15	34	4.03	24	
1997 San Francisco	N.L.	13	18⅔	0	0	.000	15	7	15	3.38	0	
1997 Oakland e-f	A.L.	5	6⅓	0	0	.000	4	7	7	2.84	0	
1998 San Francisco	N.L.	70	88	6	5	.545	86	38	72	3.07	0	
1999 San Francisco	N.L.	62	65⅔	4	6	.400	56	20	48	2.60	3	
2000 San Jose	California	2	2	0	0	.000	3	0	4	9.00	0	
2000 Fresno	P.C.	1	2	0	0	.000	1	1	0	0.00	0	
2000 San Francisco g	N.L.	47	50	3	4	.429	37	13	64	6.30	0	
Major League Totals 8 Yrs.		234	278⅓	15	19	.441	234	115	269	4.01	3	

a On disabled list from June 24 to July 7, 1992.

b Selected in expansion draft by Florida Marlins from New York Mets, November 17, 1992.
c On disabled list from May 8 to September 30, 1995.
d Filed for free agency, September 30, 1996, signed with San Francisco Giants organization, December 17, 1996.
e Claimed on waivers by Oakland Athletics, August 7, 1997.
f Filed for free agency, August 31, 1997, signed with San Francisco Giants organization, September 1, 1997.
g On disabled list from July 18 to September 1, 2000.

JONES, DOUGLAS REID

Born, Covina, California, June 24, 1957.
Bats Right. Throws Right. Height, 6 feet, 2 inches. Weight, 195 pounds.

Year Club	Lea	G	IP	W	L	Pct	SO	BB	H	ERA	SAVES
1978 Newark a	N.Y.-Penn.	15	38	2	4	.333	27	15	49	5.21	2
1979 Burlington	Midwest	28	*190	10	10	.500	115	73	144	*1.75	0
1980 Stockton	California	11	76	6	2	.750	54	31	63	2.84	0
1980 Vancouver	P.C.	8	53	3	2	.600	28	15	52	3.23	0
1980 Holyoke	Eastern	8	62	5	3	.625	39	26	57	2.90	0
1981 El Paso	Texas	15	90	5	7	.417	62	28	121	5.80	0
1981 Vancouver	P.C.	10	80	5	3	.625	38	22	79	3.04	0
1982 Milwaukee	A.L.	4	2⅔	0	0	.000	1	1	5	10.13	0
1982 Vancouver	P.C.	23	106	5	8	.385	60	31	109	2.97	2
1983 Vancouver b	P.C.	3	7	0	1	.000	4	5	10	10.29	0
1984 Vancouver c	P.C.	3	8	1	0	1.000	2	3	0	10.13	0
1984 El Paso d	Texas	16	109⅓	6	8	.429	62	35	120	4.28	7
1985 Waterbury	Eastern	39	116	9	4	.692	113	36	123	3.65	0
1986 Maine	Int.	43	116⅓	5	6	.455	98	27	105	*2.09	9
1986 Cleveland	A.L.	11	18	1	0	1.000	12	6	18	2.50	1
1987 Buffalo	A.A.	23	61⅔	5	2	.714	61	12	49	2.04	7
1987 Cleveland	A.L.	49	91⅓	6	5	.545	87	24	101	3.15	8
1988 Cleveland	A.L.	51	83⅓	3	4	.429	72	16	69	2.27	37
1989 Cleveland	A.L.	59	80⅔	7	10	.412	65	13	76	2.34	32
1990 Cleveland	A.L.	66	84⅓	5	5	.500	55	22	66	2.56	43
1991 Cleveland	A.L.	36	63⅓	4	8	.333	48	17	87	5.54	7
1991 Colorado Springs e	P.C.	17	35⅔	2	2	.500	29	5	30	3.28	7
1992 Houston	N.L.	80	111⅔	11	8	.579	93	17	96	1.85	36
1993 Houston f	N.L.	71	85⅓	4	10	.286	66	21	102	4.54	26
1994 Philadelphia g	N.L.	47	54	2	4	.333	38	6	55	2.17	27
1995 Baltimore h-i-j	A.L.	52	46⅔	0	4	.000	42	16	55	5.01	22
1996 Chicago k-l	N.L.	28	32⅓	2	2	.500	26	7	41	5.01	2
1996 New Orleans	A.A.	13	24	0	3	.000	17	6	28	3.75	6
1996 Milwaukee m	A.L.	24	31⅔	5	0	1.000	34	13	31	3.41	1
1997 Milwaukee n-o-p	A.L.	75	80⅓	6	6	.500	82	9	62	2.02	36
1998 Milwaukee	N.L.	46	54	3	4	.429	43	11	65	5.17	12
1998 Cleveland q-r	A.L.	23	31⅓	1	2	.333	28	6	34	3.45	1
1999 Oakland	A.L.	70	104	5	5	.500	63	24	106	3.55	10
2000 Oakland s-t	A.L.	54	73⅓	4	2	.667	54	18	86	3.93	2
Major League Totals ....16 Yrs.		846	1128⅓	69	79	.466	909	247	1155	3.30	303
Division Series											
1998 Cleveland	A.L.	1	2⅔	0	0	.000	1	1	3	6.75	0
2000 Oakland	A.L.	2	1⅓	0	0	.000	1	0	1	0.00	0
Division Series Totals		3	4	0	0	.000	2	1	4	4.50	0

a On disabled list from June 20 to July 12, 1978.
b On disabled list from April 11 to September 1, 1983.
c On disabled list from April 25 to May 30, 1984.
d Became free agent, October 15, 1984; signed with Cleveland Indians organization, April 3, 1985.
e Not offered 1992 contract, December 20, 1991; signed with Houston Astros organization, January 24, 1992.
f Traded to Philadelphia Phillies with pitcher Jeff Juden for pitcher Mitch Williams, December 2, 1993.
j Filed for free agency, October 20, 1994.
h Signed with Baltimore Orioles, April 8, 1995.
i Not offered 1996 contract, November 1, 1995.
j Signed with Chicago Cubs, December 28, 1995.
k Released by Chicago Cubs, May 16, 1996.
l Filed for free agency, November 6, 1996.
m Signed with Milwaukee Brewers organization, December 7, 1996.
n On disabled list from July 16 to August 2, 1997.
o Filed for free agency, October 27, 1997.
p Re-signed with Milwaukee Brewers, November 18, 1997.
q Traded to Cleveland Indians for pitcher Eric Plunk, July 24, 1998.
r Filed for free agency, October 29, 1998. Signed with Oakland Athletics, January 11, 1999.
s On disabled list from March 23 to April 8, 2000.
t Filed for free agency, November 1, 2000.

JONES, ROBERT JOSEPH (BOBBY)

Born, Fresno, California, February 10, 1970.
Bats Right. Throws Right. height, 6 feet, 4 inches. Weight, 210 pounds.

Year	Club	Lea	G	IP	W	L	Pct	SO	BB	H	ERA	SAVES
1991	Columbia	So. Atl.	5	24⅓	3	1	.750	35	3	20	1.85	0
1992	Binghamton	Eastern	24	158	12	4	.750	143	43	118	1.88	0
1993	Norfolk	Int.	24	166	12	10	.545	126	32	149	3.63	0
1993	New York	N.L.	9	61⅔	2	4	.333	35	22	61	3.65	0
1994	New York	N.L.	24	160	12	7	.632	80	56	157	3.15	0
1995	New York	N.L.	30	195⅔	10	10	.500	127	53	209	4.19	0
1996	New York	N.L.	31	195⅔	12	8	.600	116	46	219	4.42	0
1997	New York	N.L.	30	193⅓	15	9	.625	125	63	177	3.63	0
1998	New York	N.L.	30	195⅓	9	9	.500	115	53	192	4.05	0
1999	Binghamton	Eastern	3	11⅔	1	2	.333	12	5	11	3.86	0
1999	Norfolk	Int.	2	11	2	0	1.000	8	3	11	2.45	0
1999	New York a	N.L.	12	59⅓	3	3	.500	31	11	69	5.61	0
2000	Norfolk	Int.	4	23⅔	2	0	1.000	19	4	31	5.32	0
2000	New York b-c	N.L.	27	154⅔	11	6	.647	85	49	171	5.06	0
Major League Totals		8 Yrs.	193	1215⅔	74	56	.569	714	353	1255	4.13	0
Division Series												
2000	New York	N.L.	1	9	1	0	1.000	5	2	1	0.00	0
Championship Series												
2000	New York	N.L.	1	4	0	0	.000	2	0	6	13.50	0
World Series Record												
2000	New York	N.L.	1	5	0	1	.000	3	3	4	5.40	0

a On disabled list from May 24 to September 10, 1999.
b On disabled list from April 17 to May 17, 2000.
c Filed for free agency, November 4, 2000.

JONES, TODD BARTON

Born, Marietta, Georgia, April 24, 1968.
Bats Left. Throws Right. Height, 6 feet, 3 inches. Weight, 200 pounds.

Year	Club	Lea	G	IP	W	L	Pct	SO	BB	H	ERA	SAVES
1989	Auburn	N.Y.-Penn.	11	49⅔	2	3	.400	71	42	47	5.44	0
1990	Osceola	Fla. St.	27	151⅓	12	10	.545	106	109	124	3.51	0
1991	Osceola	Fla. St.	14	72⅓	4	4	.500	51	35	69	4.35	0
1991	Jackson	Texas	10	55⅓	4	3	.571	37	39	51	4.88	0
1992	Jackson	Texas	61	66	3	7	.300	60	44	52	3.14	25
1992	Tucson	P.C.	3	4	0	1	.000	4	10	1	4.50	0
1993	Tucson	P.C.	41	48⅔	4	2	.667	45	31	49	4.44	12
1993	Houston	N.L.	27	37⅓	1	2	.333	25	15	28	3.13	2
1994	Houston	N.L.	48	72⅔	5	2	.714	63	26	52	2.72	5
1995	Houston	N.L.	68	99⅔	6	5	.545	96	52	89	3.07	15
1996	Tucson	P.C.	1	2	0	0	.000	0	2	1	0.00	0
1996	Houston a-b	N.L.	51	57⅓	6	3	.667	44	32	61	4.40	17
1997	Detroit	A.L.	68	70	5	4	.556	70	35	60	3.09	31
1998	Detroit	A.L.	65	63⅓	1	4	.200	57	36	58	4.97	28
1999	Detroit	A.L.	65	66⅓	4	4	.500	64	35	64	3.80	30
2000	Detroit	A.L.	67	64	2	4	.333	67	25	67	3.52	*42
Major League Totals		8 Yrs.	459	530⅔	30	28	.517	486	256	479	3.54	170

a On disabled list from July 19 to August 12 and August 18 to September 12, 1996.
b Traded to Detroit Tigers with outfielder Brian Hunter, infielder Orlando Miller and pitcher Doug Brocail for catcher Brad Ausmus, pitcher C.J. Nitkowski, pitcher Jose Lima, pitcher Trever Miller and infielder Daryle Ward, December 10, 1996.

KAMIENIECKI, SCOTT ANDREW

Born, Mount Clemens, Michigan, April 19, 1964.
Bats Right. Throws Right. Height, 6 feet. Weight, 195 pounds.

Year	Club	Lea	G	IP	W	L	Pct	SO	BB	H	ERA	SAVES
1987	Albany	Eastern	10	37	1	3	.250	19	33	41	5.35	0
1987	Prince William	Carolina	19	112⅓	9	5	.643	84	78	91	4.17	0
1988	Prince William	Carolina	15	100⅓	6	7	.462	72	50	115	4.40	0
1988	Fort Lauderdale	Fla. St.	12	77	3	6	.333	51	40	71	3.62	0
1989	Albany	Eastern	24	151	10	9	.526	*140	57	142	3.70	1
1990	Albany	Eastern	22	132	10	9	.526	99	61	113	3.20	0
1991	Columbus	Int.	11	76⅓	6	3	.667	58	20	61	2.36	0
1991	New York a	A.L.	9	55⅓	4	4	.500	34	22	54	3.90	0
1992	Fort Lauderdale	Fla. St.	1	7	1	0	1.000	3	0	8	1.29	0

Year	Club	Lea	G	IP	W	L	Pct	SO	BB	H	ERA	SAVES
1992 Columbus		Int.	2	13	1	0	1.000	12	4	6	0.69	0
1992 New York b		A.L.	28	188	6	14	.300	88	74	193	4.36	0
1993 Columbus		Int.	1	6	1	0	1.000	4	0	5	1.50	0
1993 New York		A.L.	30	154⅓	10	7	.588	72	59	163	4.08	1
1994 New York		A.L.	22	117⅓	8	6	.571	71	59	115	3.76	0
1995 Tampa		Fla. St.	1	5	1	0	1.000	2	1	6	1.80	0
1995 Columbus		Int.	1	6⅔	1	0	1.000	10	1	2	0.00	0
1995 New York c		A.L.	17	89⅔	7	6	.538	43	49	83	4.01	0
1996 Tampa		Fla. St.	3	23	2	1	.667	17	4	20	1.17	0
1996 New York d-e		A.L.	7	22⅔	1	2	.333	15	19	36	11.12	0
1996 Columbus f		Int.	5	30⅓	2	1	.667	27	8	33	5.64	0
1997 Baltimore g-h		A.L.	30	179⅓	10	6	.625	109	67	179	4.01	0
1998 Bowie		Eastern	3	11⅓	1	0	1.000	5	2	13	4.76	0
1998 Baltimore i		A.L.	12	54⅔	2	6	.250	25	26	67	6.75	0
1999 Frederick		Carolina	1	4	0	0	.000	3	1	0	0.00	0
1999 Bowie		Eastern	1	5	0	1	.000	1	0	6	3.60	0
1999 Rochester		Int.	4	23	1	2	.333	14	6	23	5.09	0
1999 Baltimore j-k		A.L.	43	56⅓	2	4	.333	39	29	52	4.95	2
2000 Cleveland l		A.L.	26	33⅓	1	3	.250	29	20	42	5.67	0
2000 Atlanta m		N.L.	26	24⅔	2	1	.667	17	22	22	5.47	2
Major League Totals		10 Yrs.	250	975⅔	53	59	.473	542	446	1006	4.52	5

Championship Series

Year	Club	Lea	G	IP	W	L	Pct	SO	BB	H	ERA	SAVES
1997 Baltimore		A.L.	2	8	1	0	1.000	5	2	4	0.00	0

Division Series

Year	Club	Lea	G	IP	W	L	Pct	SO	BB	H	ERA	SAVES
1995 New York		A.L.	1	5	0	0	.000	4	4	9	7.20	0

a On disabled list from August 3 to end of 1991 season.
b On disabled list from April 2 to April 29, 1992.
c On disabled list from May 6 to July 15, 1995.
d On disabled list from April 1 to April 24 and July 31 to September 30, 1996.
e Not offered contract by New York Yankees, December 21, 1996.
f Signed with Baltimore Orioles organization, January 22, 1997.
g Filed for free agency, October 30, 1997.
h Re-signed with Baltimore Orioles, December 5, 1997.
i On disabled list from April 25 to May 12 and May 23 to July 25 and August 22 to September 28, 1998.
j On disabled list from March 26 to May 8, 1999.
k Filed for free agency, November 2, 1999, signed with Cleveland Indians, December 2, 1999.
l Released by Cleveland Indians, June 30, 2000, signed with Atlanta Braves, July 5, 2000.
m Filed for free agency, October 31, 2000.

KARL, RANDALL SCOTT (SCOTT)

Born, Fontana, California, August 9, 1971.
Bats Left. Throws Left. Height, 6 feet, 2 inches. Weight, 195 pounds.

Year	Club	Lea	G	IP	W	L	Pct	SO	BB	H	ERA	SAVES
1992 Helena		Pioneer	9	61⅔	7	0	1.000	57	16	54	1.46	0
1993 El Paso		Texas	27	180	13	8	.619	95	35	172	2.45	0
1994 El Paso		Texas	8	54⅔	5	1	.833	51	15	44	2.96	0
1994 New Orleans		A.A.	15	89	5	5	.500	54	33	92	3.84	0
1995 New Orleans		A.A.	8	46⅓	3	4	.429	29	12	47	3.30	0
1995 Milwaukee		A.L.	25	124	6	7	.462	59	50	141	4.14	0
1996 Milwaukee		A.L.	32	207⅓	13	9	.591	121	72	220	4.86	0
1997 Milwaukee		A.L.	32	193⅓	10	13	.435	119	67	212	4.47	0
1998 Milwaukee		N.L.	33	192⅓	10	11	.476	102	66	219	4.40	0
1999 Milwaukee a		N.L.	33	197⅔	11	11	.500	74	69	246	4.78	0
2000 Colorado Spgs		P.C.	3	20⅔	0	3	.000	16	4	21	5.66	0
2000 Lake Elsinore		California	1	7	1	0	1.000	5	1	5	0.00	0
2000 Colorado b-c		N.L.	17	65⅔	2	3	.400	29	34	95	7.68	0
2000 Anaheim d		A.L.	6	21⅔	2	2	.500	9	12	31	6.65	0
Major League Totals		6 Yrs.	178	1002	54	56	.491	513	369	1164	4.81	0

a Traded to Colorado Rockies with infielder Jeff Cirillo for catcher Henry Blanco, pitcher Jamey Wright and pitcher Justin Miller, December 13, 1999. Miller was then traded to Oakland for pitcher Jimmy Haynes as part of a three-club deal, December 13, 1999.
b On disabled list from July 15 to August 4, 2000.
c Traded to Anaheim Angels for player to be named later, August 22, 2000.
d Filed for free agency, October 6, 2000, signed with San Diego Padres, December 1, 2000.

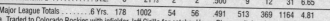

KARSAY, STEFAN ANDREW (STEVE)

Born, Flushing, New York, March 24, 1972.
Bats Right. Throws Right. Height, 6 feet, 3 inches. Weight, 210 pounds.

Year Club	Lea	G	IP	W	L	Pct	SO	BB	H	ERA	SAVES
1990 St.Cathrnes	N.Y.-Penn.	5	22²/₃	1	1	.500	25	12	11	0.79	0
1991 Myrtle Bch	So.Atl.	20	110²/₃	4	9	.308	100	48	96	3.58	0
1992 Dunedin	Fla.St.	16	85²/₃	6	3	.667	87	29	56	2.73	0
1993 Knoxville	Southern	19	104	8	4	.667	100	32	98	3.38	0
1993 Huntsville	Southern	2	14	0	0	.000	22	3	13	5.14	0
1993 Oakland a	A.L.	8	49	3	3	.500	33	16	49	4.04	0
1994 Oakland	A.L.	4	28	1	1	.500	15	8	26	2.57	0
1995 Oakland b	A.L.	INJURED - Did Not Play									
1996 Modesto	California	14	34	0	1	.000	31	1	35	2.65	0
1997 Oakland c	A.L.	24	132²/₃	3	12	.200	92	47	166	5.77	0
1998 Buffalo	Int.	16	79	6	4	.600	63	15	89	3.76	0
1998 Cleveland	A.L.	11	24¹/₃	0	2	.000	13	6	31	5.92	0
1999 Cleveland d	A.L.	50	78²/₃	10	2	.833	68	30	71	2.97	1
2000 Cleveland	A.L.	72	76²/₃	5	9	.357	66	25	79	3.76	20
Major League Totals ... 6 Yrs.		169	389¹/₃	22	29	.431	287	132	422	4.37	21
Division Series											
1999 Cleveland	A.L.	2	3	0	0	.000	3	1	5	9.00	0

a Traded to Oakland Athletics by Toronto Blue Jays with player to be named later for outfielder Rickey Henderson, August 1, 1993. Athletics received outfielder Jose Hernandez to complete trade, August 6. 1993.
b On disabled list from April 24 to October 10, 1995.
c Traded to Cleveland Indians for pitcher Mike Fetters, December 8, 1997.
d On disabled list from July 2 to July 26 and August 25 to September 22, 1999.

KILE, DARRYL ANDREW

Born, Garden Grove, California, December 2, 1968.
Bats Right. Throws Right. Height, 6 feet, 5 inches. Weight, 185 pounds.

Year Club	Lea	G	IP	W	L	Pct	SO	BB	H	ERA	SAVES
1988 Astros	Gulf C.	12	59²/₃	5	3	.625	54	33	48	3.17	0
1989 Columbus	Southern	20	125²/₃	11	6	.647	108	68	74	2.58	0
1989 Tucson	P.C.	6	25²/₃	2	1	.667	18	13	33	5.96	0
1990 Tucson a	P.C.	26	123¹/₃	5	10	.333	77	68	147	6.64	0
1991 Houston	N.L.	37	153²/₃	7	11	.389	100	84	144	3.69	0
1992 Tucson	P.C.	9	56¹/₃	4	1	.800	43	32	50	3.99	0
1992 Houston	N.L.	22	125¹/₃	5	10	.333	90	63	124	3.95	0
1993 Houston b	N.L.	32	171²/₃	15	8	.652	141	69	152	3.51	0
1994 Houston	N.L.	24	147²/₃	9	6	.600	105	*82	153	4.57	0
1995 Tucson	P.C.	4	24¹/₃	2	1	.667	15	12	29	8.51	0
1995 Houston	N.L.	25	127	4	12	.250	113	73	114	4.96	0
1996 Houston	N.L.	35	219	12	11	.522	219	97	233	4.19	0
1997 Houston c-d	N.L.	34	255²/₃	19	7	.731	205	94	208	2.57	0
1998 Colorado	N.L.	36	230¹/₃	13	*17	.433	158	96	257	5.20	0
1999 Colorado e	N.L.	32	190²/₃	8	13	.381	116	109	225	6.61	0
2000 St. Louis	N.L.	34	232¹/₃	20	9	.690	192	58	215	3.91	0
Major League Totals ... 10 Yrs.		311	1853¹/₃	112	104	.519	1439	825	1825	4.27	0
Division Series											
1997 Houston	N.L.	1	7	0	1	.000	4	2	2	2.57	0
2000 St. Louis	N.L.	1	7	1	0	.000	6	2	4	2.57	0
Division Series Totals		2	14	1	1	.500	10	4	6	2.57	0

a On disabled list from April 10 to April 20, 1990.
b Pitched no-hit game against New York Mets, winning 7-1, September 8, 1993.
c Filed for free agency, October 28, 1997.
d Signed with Colorado Rockies, December 5, 1997.
e Traded to St. Louis Cardinals with pitcher Dave Veres for pitcher Manuel Aybar, pitcher Jose Jimenez, pitcher Rich Croushore and infielder Brent Butler, November 16, 1999.

KIM, BYUNG-HYUN

Born, Kwangsan-Ku Songjungdong, South Korea, January 21, 1979.
Bats Right. Throws Right. Height, 5 feet, 11 inches. Weight, 176 pounds.

Year Club	Lea	G	IP	W	L	Pct	SO	BB	H	ERA	SAVES
1999 El Paso	Texas	10	21¹/₃	2	0	1.000	32	9	6	2.11	0
1999 Diamondbacks	Arizona	1	2	0	0	.000	2	1	1	0.00	0
1999 Tucson	P.C	11	30	4	0	1.000	40	15	21	2.40	1
1999 Arizona a	N.L.	25	27¹/₃	1	2	.333	31	20	20	4.61	1
2000 Tucson	P.C.	2	8¹/₃	0	0	.000	13	4	1	0.00	0

Year	Club	Lea	G	IP	W	L	Pct	SO	BB	H	ERA	SAVES
2000 Arizona		N.L.	61	70²/₃	6	6	.500	111	46	52	4.46	14
Major League Totals		2 Yrs.	86	98	7	8	.467	142	66	72	4.50	15

On disabled list from July 28 to September 10, 1999.

KLINE, STEVEN JAMES

Born, Sunbury, Pennsylvania, August 22, 1972.
Bats Both. Throws Left. Height, 6 feet, 2 inches. Weight, 200 pounds.

Year	Club	Lea	G	IP	W	L	Pct	SO	BB	H	ERA	SAVES
1993 Burlington		Appal.	2	7¹/₃	1	1	.500	4	2	11	4.91	0
1993 Watertown		N.Y.-Penn.	13	79	5	4	.556	45	12	77	3.19	0
1994 Columbus		So.Atl.	28	185²/₃	18	5	.783	174	36	175	3.01	0
1995 Canton-Akrn		Eastern	14	89¹/₃	2	3	.400	45	30	86	2.42	0
1996 Canton-Akrn		Eastern	25	146²/₃	8	12	.400	107	55	168	5.46	0
1997 Buffalo		A.A.	20	51¹/₃	3	3	.500	41	13	53	4.03	1
1997 Cleveland a		A.L.	20	26¹/₃	3	1	.750	17	13	42	5.81	0
1997 Montreal		N.L.	26	26¹/₃	1	3	.250	20	10	31	6.15	0
1998 Ottawa		Int.	2	2²/₃	0	0	.000	1	0	1	0.00	0
1998 Montreal		N.L.	78	71²/₃	3	6	.333	76	41	62	2.76	1
1999 Montreal b		N.L.	*82	69²/₃	7	4	.636	69	33	56	3.75	0
2000 Montreal c		N.L.	*83	82¹/₃	1	5	.167	64	27	88	3.50	14
Major League Totals		4 Yrs.	289	276¹/₃	15	19	.441	246	124	279	3.84	15

a Traded to Montreal Expos with player to be named later for pitcher Jeff Juden, July 31, 1997.
b On disabled list from April 11 to April 27, 1999.
c Traded to St. Louis Cardinals with pitcher Dustin Hermanson for infielder Fernando Tatis and pitcher Britt Reames, December 14, 2000.

KOCH, WILLIAM (BILLY)

Born, Rockville Centre, New York, December 14, 1974.
Bats Right. Throws Right. Height, 6 feet, 3 inches. Weight, 218 pounds.

Year	Club	Lea	G	IP	W	L	Pct	SO	BB	H	ERA	SAVES
1997 Dunedin		Fla.St.	3	21²/₃	0	1	.000	20	3	27	2.08	0
1998 Dunedin		Fla.St.	25	124²/₃	14	7	.667	108	41	120	3.75	0
1998 Syracuse		Int.	2	5²/₃	0	1	.000	9	5	9	14.29	0
1999 Syracuse		Int.	5	25²/₃	3	0	1.000	22	10	27	3.86	0
1999 Toronto		A.L.	56	63²/₃	0	5	.000	57	30	55	3.39	31
2000 Toronto		A.L.	68	78²/₃	9	3	.750	56	18	78	2.63	33
Major League Totals		2 Yrs.	124	142¹/₃	9	8	.529	117	48	133	2.97	64

KOHLMEIER, RYAN LYLE

Born, Salina, Kansas, June 25, 1977.
Bats Right. Throws Right. Height, 6 feet, 2 inches. Weight, 195 pounds.

Year	Club	Lea	G	IP	W	L	Pct	SO	BB	H	ERA	SAVES
1997 Bowie		Eastern	2	2²/₃	0	0	.000	5	2	0	0.00	1
1997 Delmarva		So.Atl.	50	74²/₃	2	2	.500	99	17	48	2.65	24
1998 Bowie		Eastern	42	50	4	4	.500	56	16	52	6.12	7
1998 Frederick		Carolina	9	9²/₃	1	2	.333	15	3	10	7.45	5
1999 Bowie		Eastern	55	62²/₃	3	7	.300	78	29	44	3.16	0
2000 Rochester		Int.	37	46²/₃	1	4	.200	49	16	33	2.51	0
2000 Baltimore		A.L.	25	26¹/₃	0	1	.000	17	15	30	2.39	13

LEITER, ALOIS TERRY (AL)

Born, Toms River, New Jersey, October 23, 1965.
Bats Left. Throws Left. Height, 6 feet, 3 inches. Weight, 215 pounds.

Year	Club	Lea	G	IP	W	L	Pct	SO	BB	H	ERA	SAVES
1984 Oneonta		N.Y.-Penn.	10	57	3	2	.600	48	26	52	3.63	0
1985 Oneonta		N.Y.-Penn.	6	38	3	2	.600	34	25	27	2.37	0
1985 Fort Lauderdale		Fla. St.	17	82	1	6	.143	44	57	87	6.48	0
1986 Fort Lauderdale		Fla. St.	22	117²/₃	4	8	.333	101	90	96	4.05	0
1987 Albany a		Eastern	15	78	3	3	.500	71	37	64	3.35	0
1987 Columbus		Int.	5	23¹/₃	1	4	.200	23	15	21	6.17	0
1987 New York		A.L.	4	22²/₃	2	2	.500	28	15	24	6.35	0

Year Club	Lea	G	IP	W	L	Pct	SO	BB	H	ERA	SAVES
1988 Columbus	Int.	4	13	0	2	.000	12	14	5	3.46	0
1988 New York b	A.L.	14	57⅓	4	4	.500	60	33	49	3.92	0
1989 New York-Toronto-c-d	A.L.	5	33⅓	1	2	.333	26	23	32	5.67	0
1989 Dunedin	Fla. St.	3	8	0	2	.000	4	5	11	5.63	0
1990 Dunedin	Fla. St.	6	24	0	0	.000	14	12	18	2.63	0
1990 Syracuse e	Int.	15	78	3	8	.273	69	68	59	4.62	0
1990 Toronto	A.L.	4	6⅓	0	0	.000	5	2	1	0.00	0
1991 Dunedin	Fla. St.	4	9⅔	0	0	.000	5	7	5	1.86	0
1991 Toronto f	A.L.	3	1⅔	0	0	.000	1	5	3	27.00	0
1992 Syracuse	Int.	27	163⅓	8	9	.471	108	64	159	3.86	0
1992 Toronto	A.L.	1	1	0	0	.000	0	2	1	9.00	0
1993 Toronto g	A.L.	34	105	9	6	.600	66	56	93	4.11	2
1994 Toronto h-i	A.L.	20	111⅔	6	7	.462	100	65	125	5.08	0
1995 Toronto j-k	A.L.	28	183	11	11	.500	153	*108	162	3.64	0
1996 Florida l	N.L.	33	215⅓	16	12	.571	200	*119	153	2.93	0
1997 Florida m-n	N.L.	27	151⅓	11	9	.550	132	91	133	4.34	0
1998 New York o	N.L.	28	193	17	6	.739	174	71	151	2.47	0
1999 New York	N.L.	32	213	13	12	.520	162	93	209	4.23	0
2000 New York	N.L.	31	208	16	8	.667	200	76	176	3.20	0
Major League Totals .... 14 Yrs.		264	1502⅔	106	79	.573	1307	759	1312	3.73	2
Division Series											
1997 Florida	N.L.	1	4	0	0	.000	3	3	7	9.00	0
1999 New York	N.L.	1	7⅔	0	0	.000	4	3	3	3.52	0
2000 New York	N.L.	1	8	0	0	.000	6	3	5	2.25	0
Division Series Totals		3	19⅔	0	0	.000	13	9	15	4.12	0
Championship Series											
1993 Toronto	A.L.	2	2⅔	0	0	.000	2	2	4	3.38	0
1997 Florida	N.L.	2	8⅓	0	1	.000	6	2	13	4.32	0
1999 New York	N.L.	2	7	0	1	.000	5	4	5	6.43	0
2000 New York	N.L.	1	7	0	0	.000	9	0	8	3.86	0
Championship Series Totals		7	25	0	2	.000	22	8	30	4.68	0
World Series Record											
1993 Toronto	A.L.	3	7	1	0	1.000	5	2	12	7.71	0
1997 Florida	N.L.	2	10⅔	0	0	.000	10	10	10	5.06	0
2000 New York	N.L.	2	15⅔	0	1	.000	16	6	12	2.87	0
World Series Totals		7	33⅓	1	1	.500	31	18	34	4.59	0

a On disabled list from May 1 to May 23, 1987.
b On disabled list from June 22 to July 26, 1988.
c Traded to Toronto Blue Jays for outfielder Jesse Barfield, April 30, 1989.
d On disabled list from May 11 to end of 1989 season.
e On disabled list from May 20 to June 13, 1990.
f On disabled list from April 22 to end of 1991 season.
g On disabled list from April 24 to May 9, 1993.
h On disabled list from June 9 to June 24, 1994.
i Declared restricted free agent under Major League Baseball implemented labor proposal, December 23, 1994.
j Signed with Toronto Blue Jays, April 28, 1995.
k Filed for free agency, November 12, 1995; signed with Florida Marlins, December 14, 1995.
l Pitched no-hit, no-run game against Colorado Rockies, May 11, 1996.
m On disabled list from May 1 to May 20 and August 13 to August 29, 1997.
n Traded to New York Mets with infielder Ralph Milliard for pitcher Jesus Sanchez, pitcher A. J. Burnett and outfielder Robert Stratton, February 6, 1998.
o On disabled list from June 27 to July 18, 1998.

LESKANIC, CURTIS JOHN
Born, Homestead, Pennsylvania, April 2, 1968.
Bats Right. Throws Right. Height, 6 feet. Weight, 180 pounds.

Year Club	Lea	G	IP	W	L	Pct	SO	BB	H	ERA	SAVES
1990 Kinston	Carolina	14	73⅓	6	5	.545	71	30	61	3.68	0
1991 Kinston a	Carolina	28	174⅓	*15	8	.652	*163	91	143	2.79	0
1992 Orlando	Southern	26	152⅔	9	11	.450	126	64	158	4.30	0
1992 Portland b	P.C.	5	15⅓	1	2	.333	14	8	16	9.98	0
1993 Wichita c	Texas	7	44⅓	3	2	.600	42	17	37	3.45	0
1993 Colorado Springs	P.C.	9	44⅓	4	3	.571	38	26	39	4.47	0
1993 Colorado	N.L.	18	57	1	5	.167	30	27	59	5.37	0
1994 Colorado Springs	P.C.	21	130⅓	5	7	.417	98	54	129	3.31	0
1994 Colorado	N.L.	8	22⅓	1	1	.500	17	10	27	5.64	0
1995 Colorado	N.L.	*76	98	6	3	.667	107	33	83	3.40	10
1996 Colo Sprngs	P.C.	3	3	0	0	:000	2	1	5	3.00	0
1996 Colorado d	N.L.	70	73⅔	7	5	.583	76	38	82	6.23	6
1997 Salem	Carolina	2	2⅓	0	0	.000	3	1	5	3.86	0

262

Year	Club	Lea	G	IP	W	L	Pct	SO	BB	H	ERA	SAVES
1997 Colo Sprngs	....	P.C.	10	19	0	0	.000	20	18	11	3.79	2
1997 Colorado e	....	N.L.	55	58⅓	4	0	1.000	53	24	59	5.55	2
1998 Colorado	....	N.L.	66	75⅔	6	4	.600	55	40	75	4.40	2
1999 Colorado f	....	N.L.	63	85	6	2	.750	77	49	87	5.08	0
2000 Milwaukee g	....	N.L.	73	77⅓	9	3	.750	75	51	58	2.56	12
Major League Totals .... 8 Yrs.			429	547⅓	40	23	.635	490	272	530	4.59	32
Division Series												
1995 Colorado	....	N.L.	3	3	0	1	.000	4	0	3	6.00	0

a Traded by Cleveland Indians to Minnesota Twins organization with pitcher Oscar Munoz, March 28, 1992.
b Selected by Colorado Rockies from Minnesota Twins organization in expansion draft, November 17, 1993.
c Loaned by Colorado Rockies to San Diego Padres organization from April 4 to May 20, 1993.
d On disabled list from May 30 to June 28, 1996.
e On disabled list from April 1 to April 12, 1997.
f Traded to Milwaukee Brewers for pitcher Mike Myers, November 17, 1999.
g On disabled list from May 12 to May 30, 2000.

LEVINE, ALAN BRIAN
Born, Park Ridge, Illinois, May 22, 1968.
Bats Left. Throws Right. Height, 6 feet, 3 inches. Weight, 180 pounds.

Year	Club	Lea	G	IP	W	L	Pct	SO	BB	H	ERA	SAVES
1991 Utica	....	N.Y.-Penn.	16	85	6	4	.600	83	26	75	3.18	1
1992 South Bend	....	Midwest	23	156⅔	9	5	.643	131	36	151	2.81	0
1992 Sarasota	....	Fla. St.	3	15⅔	0	2	.000	11	5	17	4.02	0
1993 Sarasota	....	Fla. St.	27	161⅓	11	8	.579	129	50	169	3.68	0
1994 Birmingham	....	Southern	18	114⅓	5	9	.357	94	44	117	3.31	0
1994 Nashville	....	A.A.	8	24	0	2	.000	24	11	34	7.87	0
1995 Nashville	....	A.A.	3	14	0	2	.000	14	7	20	5.14	0
1995 Birmingham	....	Southern	43	73	4	3	.571	68	25	61	2.34	7
1996 Nashville	....	A.A.	43	61⅔	4	5	.444	45	24	58	3.65	12
1996 Chicago	....	A.L.	16	18⅓	0	1	.000	12	7	22	5.40	0
1997 Nashville	....	A.A.	26	35⅓	1	1	.500	29	11	58	7.13	2
1997 Chicago a	....	A.L.	25	27⅓	2	2	.500	22	16	35	6.91	0
1998 Oklahoma	....	P.C.	12	53⅓	1	3	.250	30	17	51	4.72	1
1998 Texas	....	A.L.	30	58	0	1	.000	19	16	68	4.50	0
1999 Anaheim b	....	A.L.	50	85	1	1	.500	37	29	76	3.39	0
2000 Erie	....	Eastern	1	2	0	0	.000	0	0	3	0.00	0
2000 Anaheim c	....	A.L.	51	95⅓	3	4	.429	42	49	98	3.87	2
Major League Totals .... 5 Yrs.			172	284	6	9	.400	132	117	299	4.25	2

a Traded to Texas Rangers with pitcher Larry Thomas for infielder Benji Gil, December 19, 1997.
b Claimed on waivers by Anaheim Angels, April 3, 1999.
c On disabled list from July 31 to August 18, 2000.

LIDLE, CORY FULTON
Born, Hollywood, California, March 22, 1972.
Bats Right. Throws Right. Height, 5 feet, 11 inches. Weight, 175 pounds.

Year	Club	Lea	G	IP	W	L	PCT	SO	BB	H	ERA	SAVES
1991 Twins	....	Gulf Coast	4	4⅔	1	1	.500	5	0	5	5.79	0
1992 Elizabethtn	....	Appal.	19	43⅔	2	1	.667	32	21	40	3.71	6
1993 Pocatello a-b	....	Pioneer	17	106⅔	8	4	.667	91	54	104	4.13	1
1994 Stockton	....	California	25	42⅔	1	2	.333	38	13	60	4.43	4
1994 Beloit	....	Midwest	13	69	3	4	.429	62	11	65	2.61	0
1995 El Paso	....	Texas	45	109⅔	5	4	.556	78	36	126	3.36	2
1996 Binghamton c	....	Eastern	27	190⅓	14	10	.583	141	49	186	3.31	0
1997 Norfolk	....	Int.	7	42	4	2	.667	34	10	46	3.64	0
1997 New York d	....	N.L.	54	81⅔	7	2	.778	54	20	86	3.53	2
1998 High Desert	....	California	1	2⅔	0	0	.000	6	2	2	0.00	0
1998 Tucson e-f	....	P.C.	1	4⅔	0	0	.000	2	2	2	0.00	0
1999 St.Petersburg	....	Fla.St.	2	5	0	0	.000	0	2	2	0.00	0
1999 Durham	....	Int.	3	5⅔	0	0	.000	6	1	9	4.76	0
1999 Tampa Bay g	....	A.L.	5	5	1	0	1.000	4	2	8	7.20	0
2000 Durham	....	Int.	9	50	6	2	.750	44	8	52	2.52	0
2000 Tampa Bay h	....	A.L.	31	96⅔	4	6	.400	62	29	114	5.03	0
Major League Totals .... 3 Yrs.			90	183⅓	12	8	.600	120	51	208	4.42	2

a Released by Minnesota Twins, April 1, 1993, signed with Pocatello, Pioneer League, May 28, 1993.
b Sold to Milwaukee Brewers organization, September 17, 1993.
c Traded to New York Mets for catcher Kelly Stinnett, January 17, 1996.

d Selected in expansion draft by Arizona Diamondbacks, November 18, 1997.
e On disabled list from March 31 to October 1, 1998.
f Claimed on waivers by Tampa Bay Devil Rays, October 7, 1998.
g On disabled list from March 23 to September 18, 1999.
h Traded to Oakland Athletics with pitcher Roberto Hernandez for outfielder Ben Grieve and player to be named later, January 8, 2001.

LIEBER, JONATHAN RAY (JON)

Born, Council Bluffs, Iowa, April 2, 1970.
Bats Left. Throws Right. Height, 6 feet, 3 inches. Weight, 220 pounds.

Year	Club	Lea	G	IP	W	L	Pct	SO	BB	H	ERA	SAVES
1992	Eugene	Northwest	5	31	3	0	1.000	23	2	26	1.16	0
1992	Baseball City	Fla. St.	7	31	3	3	.500	19	8	45	4.65	0
1993	Wilmington	Carolina	17	114²/₃	9	3	.750	89	9	125	2.67	0
1993	Memphis-Carol. a	Southern	10	55	6	3	.667	45	16	71	5.07	0
1994	Carolina	Southern	3	21	2	0	1.000	21	2	13	1.29	0
1994	Buffalo	A.A.	3	21¹/₃	1	1	.500	21	1	16	1.69	0
1994	Pittsburgh	N.L.	17	108²/₃	6	7	.462	71	25	116	3.73	0
1995	Calgary	P.C.	14	77	1	5	.167	34	19	122	7.01	0
1995	Pittsburgh	N.L.	21	72²/₃	4	7	.364	45	14	103	6.32	0
1996	Pittsburgh	N.L.	51	142	9	5	.643	94	28	156	3.99	1
1997	Pittsburgh	N.L.	33	188¹/₃	11	14	.440	160	51	193	4.49	0
1998	Pittsburgh b	N.L.	29	171	8	14	.364	138	40	182	4.11	1
1999	Chicago c	N.L.	31	203¹/₃	10	11	.476	186	46	226	4.07	0
2000	Chicago	N.L.	35	*251	12	11	.522	192	54	248	4.41	0
Major League Totals	7 Yrs.		217	1137	60	69	.465	886	258	1224	4.32	2

a Traded by Kansas City Royals to Pittsburgh Pirates organization with pitcher Dan Miceli for pitcher Stan Belinda, July 31, 1993.

b On disabled list from August 21 to September 14, 1998.

c On disabled list from April 21 to May 8, 1999.

LIGTENBERG, KERRY DALE

Born, Rapid City, South Dakota, May 11, 1971.
Bats Right. Throws Right. Height, 6 feet, 2 inches. Weight, 185 pounds.

Year	Club	Lea	G	IP	W	L	Pct	SO	BB	H	ERA	SAVES
1994	Minneapolis	NCL	19	114¹/₃	5	5	.500	94	44	103	3.31	0
1995	Minneapolis	PRA	17	108²/₃	11	2	.846	100	26	101	2.73	0
1996	Durham	Carolina	49	59²/₃	7	4	.636	76	16	58	2.41	20
1997	Greenville	Southern	31	35¹/₃	3	1	.750	43	14	20	2.04	16
1997	Richmond	Int.	14	25	0	3	.000	35	2	21	4.32	1
1997	Atlanta	N.L.	15	15	1	0	1.000	19	4	12	3.00	1
1998	Atlanta	N.L.	75	73	3	2	.600	79	24	51	2.71	30
1999	Atlanta a	N.L.				INJURED - Did Not Play						
2000	Richmond	Int.	5	5²/₃	0	0	.000	7	4	0	0.00	0
2000	Atlanta	N.L.	59	52¹/₃	2	3	.400	51	24	43	3.61	12
Major League Totals	3 Yrs.		149	140¹/₃	6	5	.545	149	52	106	3.08	43
Division Series												
1998	Atlanta	N.L.	3	3¹/₃	0	0	.000	3	4	1	0.00	0
2000	Atlanta	N.L.	3	1²/₃	0	0	.000	3	1	0	5.40	0
Division Series Totals			6	5	0	0	.000	6	5	1	1.80	0
Championship Series												
1997	Atlanta	N.L.	2	3	0	0	.000	4	0	1	0.00	0
1998	Atlanta	N.L.	4	3²/₃	0	1	.000	5	2	3	7.36	0
Championship Series Totals			6	6²/₃	0	1	.000	9	2	4	4.05	0

a On disabled list from April 3 to November 1, 1999.

LIMA (RODRIGUEZ), JOSE DESIDERIO

Born, Santiago, Dominican Republic, September 30, 1972.
Bats Right. Throws Right. Height, 6 feet, 2 inches. Weight, 170 pounds.

Year	Club	Lea	G	IP	W	L	Pct	SO	BB	H	ERA	SAVES
1990	Bristol	Appal.	14	75¹/₃	3	8	.273	64	22	89	5.02	1
1991	Lakeland	Fla. St.	4	8²/₃	0	1	.000	5	2	16	10.38	0
1991	Fayetteville	So. Atl.	18	58	1	3	.250	60	25	53	4.97	0
1992	Lakeland	Fla. St.	25	151	5	11	.313	137	21	132	3.16	0
1993	London	Eastern	27	177	8	*13	.381	138	59	160	4.07	0
1994	Toledo	Int.	23	142¹/₃	7	9	.438	117	48	124	3.60	0

Year	Club	Lea	G	IP	W	L	Pct	SO	BB	H	ERA	SAVES
1994 Detroit	A.L.	3	6²/₃	0	1	.000	7	3	11	13.50	0	
1995 Lakeland	Fla. St.	4	21	3	1	.750	20	0	23	2.57	0	
1995 Toledo	Int.	11	74²/₃	5	3	.625	40	14	69	3.01	0	
1995 Detroit	A.L.	15	73²/₃	3	9	.250	37	18	85	6.11	0	
1996 Toledo	Int.	12	69	5	4	.556	57	12	93	6.78	0	
1996 Detroit a	A.L.	39	72²/₃	5	6	.455	59	22	87	5.70	3	
1997 Houston	N.L.	52	75	1	6	.143	63	16	79	5.28	2	
1998 Houston	N.L.	33	233¹/₃	16	8	.667	169	32	229	3.70	0	
1999 Houston	N.L.	35	246¹/₃	21	10	.677	187	44	256	3.58	0	
2000 Houston	N.L.	33	196¹/₃	7	16	.304	124	68	251	6.65	0	
Major League Totals	7 Yrs.	210	904	53	56	.486	646	203	998	4.87	5	
Division Series												
1997 Houston	N.L.	1	1	0	0	.000	1	1	0	0.00	0	
1999 Houston	N.L.	1	6²/₃	0	1	.000	4	2	9	5.40	0	
Division Series Totals		2	7²/₃	0	1	.000	5	3	9	4.70	0	

a Traded to Houston Astros with catcher Brad Ausmus, pitcher C.J. Nitkowski, pitcher Trever Miller and infielder Daryle Ward for outfielder Brian Hunter, infielder Orlando Miller, pitcher Todd Jones and pitcher Doug Brocail, December 10, 1996.

LIRA, ANTONIO FELIPE (FELIPE)
Born, Santa Teresa, Venezuela, April 26, 1972.
Bats Right. Throws Right. Height, 6 feet. Weight, 170 pounds.

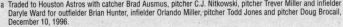

Year	Club	Lea	G	IP	W	L	Pct	SO	BB	H	ERA	SAVES
1990 Bristol	Appal.	13	78¹/₃	5	5	.500	71	16	70	2.41	1	
1990 Lakeland	Fla.St.	1	1²/₃	0	0	.000	4	3	3	5.40	0	
1991 Fayetteville a	So.Atl.	15	73¹/₃	5	5	.500	56	19	79	4.66	1	
1992 Lakeland	Fla.St.	32	109	11	5	.688	84	16	95	2.39	1	
1993 London	Eastern	22	152	10	4	.714	122	39	157	3.38	0	
1993 Toledo	Int.	5	31¹/₃	1	2	.333	23	11	32	4.60	0	
1994 Toledo	Int.	26	151¹/₃	7	12	.368	110	45	171	4.70	0	
1995 Detroit	A.L.	37	146¹/₃	9	13	.409	89	56	151	4.31	1	
1996 Detroit	A.L.	32	194²/₃	6	14	.300	113	66	204	5.22	0	
1997 Everett	Northwest	1	5	1	0	1.000	9	2	6	3.60	0	
1997 Tacoma	P.C.	3	21	2	0	1.000	17	5	21	3.43	0	
1997 Detroit-Seattle b	A.L.	28	110²/₃	5	11	.313	73	55	132	6.34	0	
1998 Tacoma	P.C.	20	129	6	8	.429	88	42	142	4.26	0	
1998 Seattle c	A.L.	7	15²/₃	1	0	1.000	16	5	22	4.60	0	
1999 Toledo	Int.	30	114	2	11	.154	70	35	163	6.71	0	
1999 Detroit d	A.L.	2	3¹/₃	0	0	.000	3	2	7	10.80	0	
2000 Ottawa	Int.	4	20	0	3	.000	10	3	24	4.95	0	
2000 Montreal e	N.L.	53	101²/₃	5	8	.385	51	36	129	5.40	1	
Major League Totals	6 Yrs.	159	572¹/₃	26	46	.361	345	220	645	5.25	1	

a On disabled list from April 10 to June 10, 1991.
b Traded to Seattle Mariners with pitcher Omar Olivares for pitcher Scott Sanders and pitcher Dean Crow, July 18, 1997.
c Filed for free agency, October 15, 1998, signed with Detroit Tigers organization, November 24, 1998.
d Filed for free agency, October 15, 1999, signed with Montreal Expos organization, February 16, 2000.
e Filed for free agency, October 4, 2000, signed with Montreal Expos organization, November 17, 2000.

LLOYD, GRAEME JOHN
Born, Victoria, Australia, April 9, 1967.
Bats Left. Throws Left. Height, 6 feet, 7 inches. Weight, 230 pounds.

Year	Club	Lea	G	IP	W	L	Pct	SO	BB	H	ERA	SAVES
1988 Myrtle Beach	So. Atl.	41	59²/₃	3	2	.600	43	30	71	3.62	2	
1989 Dunedin	Fla. St.	2	2²/₃	0	0	.000	0	1	6	10.13	0	
1989 Myrtle Beach a	So. Atl.	1	5	0	0	.000	3	0	5	5.40	0	
1990 Myrtle Beach	So. Atl.	19	49²/₃	5	2	.714	42	16	51	2.72	6	
1991 Dunedin	Fla. St.	50	60¹/₃	2	5	.286	39	25	54	2.24	24	
1991 Knoxville	Southern	2	1²/₃	0	0	.000	2	1	1	0.00	0	
1992 Knoxville b-c	Southern	49	92	4	8	.333	65	25	79	1.96	14	
1993 Milwaukee d-e	A.L.	55	63²/₃	3	4	.429	31	13	64	2.83	0	
1994 Milwaukee	A.L.	43	47	2	3	.400	31	15	49	5.17	3	
1995 Milwaukee f	A.L.	33	32	0	5	.000	13	8	28	4.50	4	
1996 Milwaukee-New York g	A.L.	65	56²/₃	2	6	.250	30	22	61	4.28	0	
1997 New York	A.L.	46	49	1	1	.500	26	20	55	3.31	1	
1998 New York h	A.L.	50	37²/₃	3	0	1.000	20	6	26	1.67	0	
1999 Toronto i-j	A.L.	74	72	5	3	.625	47	23	68	3.62	3	

Year	Club	Lea	G	IP	W	L	Pct	SO	BB	H	ERA	SAVES
2000 Montreal k		N.L.		INJURED - did not play								
Major League Totals	7 Yrs.		366	358	16	22	.421	198	107	351	3.62	11
Division Series												
1996 New York		A.L.	2	1	0	0	.000	0	0	1	0.00	0
1997 New York		A.L.	2	1⅓	0	0	.000	1	0	0	0.00	0
1998 New York		A.L.	1	0⅓	0	0	.000	0	0	0	0.00	0
Divisional Series Totals			5	2⅔	0	0	.000	1	0	1	0.00	0
Championship Series												
1996 New York		A.L.	2	1⅔	0	0	.000	1	0	0	0.00	0
1998 New York		A.L.	1	0⅔	0	0	.000	0	0	1	0.00	0
Championship Series Totals			3	2⅓	0	0	.000	1	0	1	0.00	0
World Series Record												
1996 New York		A.L.	4	2⅔	1	0	1.000	4	0	0	0.00	0
1998 New York		A.L.	1	0⅓	0	0	.000	0	0	0	0.00	0
World Series Totals			5	3	1	0	1.000	4	0	0	0.00	0

a On disabled list from June 29 to September 1, 1989.
b Drafted by Philadelphia Phillies from Toronto Blue Jays organization, December 7, 1992.
c Traded by Philadelphia Phillies to Milwaukee Brewers for pitcher John Trisler, December 8, 1992.
d On disabled list from August 20 to September 4, 1993.
e Suspended three games by American League, for participating in August 24 brawl while on disabled list, from September 5 to September 7, 1993.
f On disabled list from July 25 to September 10, 1995.
g Traded to New York Yankees with infielder Pat Listach for outfielder Gerald Williams and pitcher Bob Wickman. Yankees received pitcher Ricky Bones as a player-to-be-named-later, August 23, 1996. Listach was injured before trade and his deal was nullified when Yankees received infielder Gabby Martinez to complete transaction, November 5, 1996.
h On disabled list from April 23 to May 8, 1998.
i Traded to Toronto Blue Jays with pitcher David Wells and infielder Homer Bush for pitcher Roger Clemens, February 18, 1999.
j Filed for free agency, October 29, 1999. Signed with Montreal Expos, December 20, 1999.
k On disabled list from March 29 to November 13, 2000.

LOAIZA, ESTEBAN ANTONIO VEYNA

Born, Tijuana, Mexico, December 31, 1971.
Bats Right. Throws Right. Height, 6 feet, 4 inches. Weight, 190 pounds.

Year	Club	Lea	G	IP	W	L	Pct	SO	BB	H	ERA	SAVES
1991 Pirates		Gulf Coast	11	51⅔	5	1	.833	41	14	48	2.26	0
1992 Augusta		So. Atl.	26	143⅓	10	8	.556	123	60	134	3.89	0
1993 Salem		Carolina	17	109	6	7	.462	61	30	113	3.39	0
1993 Carolina		Southern	7	43	2	1	.667	40	12	39	3.77	0
1994 Carolina		Southern	24	154⅓	10	5	.667	115	30	169	3.79	0
1995 Pittsburgh		N.L.	32	172⅔	8	9	.471	85	55	205	5.16	0
1996 Calgary		P.C.	12	69⅓	3	4	.429	38	25	61	4.02	0
1996 Pittsburgh		N.L.	10	52⅔	2	3	.400	32	19	65	4.96	0
1997 Pittsburgh		N.L.	33	196⅓	11	11	.500	122	56	214	4.13	0
1998 Pittsburgh		N.L.	21	91⅔	6	5	.545	53	30	96	4.52	0
1998 Texas a		A.L.	14	79⅓	3	6	.333	55	22	103	5.90	0
1999 Oklahoma		P.C.	2	4⅓	0	0	.000	6	3	3	0.00	0
1999 Texas b		A.L.	30	120⅓	9	5	.643	77	40	128	4.56	0
2000 Texas-Toronto c		A.L.	34	199⅓	10	13	.435	137	57	228	4.56	1
Major League Totals	6 Yrs.		174	912⅓	49	52	.485	561	279	1039	4.72	1
Division Series												
1999 Texas		A.L.	1	7	0	1	.000	4	1	5	3.86	0

a Traded to Texas Rangers for pitcher Todd VanPoppel and infielder Warren Morris, July 17, 1998.
b On disabled list from May 12 to July 5, 1999.
c Traded to Toronto Blue Jays for pitcher Darwin Cubillan and infielder Mike Young, July 19, 2000.

LOISELLE, RICHARD FRANK

Born, Neenah, Wisconsin, January 12, 1972.
Bats Right. Throws Right. Height, 6 feet, 5 inches. Weight, 225 pounds.

Year	Club	Lea	G	IP	W	L	Pct	SO	BB	H	ERA	SAVES
1991 Padres		Arizona	12	61⅓	2	3	.400	47	26	72	3.52	0
1992 Chston-Sc		So.Atl.	19	97	4	8	.333	64	42	93	3.71	0
1993 Waterloo		Midwest	10	59⅓	1	5	.167	47	29	55	3.94	0
1993 Rancho Cuca		California	14	82⅔	5	8	.385	53	34	109	5.77	0
1994 Rancho Cuca		California	27	156⅔	9	10	.474	120	76	160	3.96	0
1995 Memphis		Southern	13	78⅔	6	3	.667	48	33	82	3.55	0

Year	Club	Lea	G	IP	W	L	Pct	SO	BB	H	ERA	SAVES
1995	Las Vegas	P.C.	8	27¹/3	2	2	.500	16	9	36	7.24	0
1995	Tucson a-b	P.C.	2	10¹/3	0	0	.000	4	4	8	2.61	0
1996	Jackson	Texas	16	98²/3	7	4	.636	65	27	107	3.47	0
1996	Tucson	P.C.	5	33¹/3	2	2	.500	31	11	28	2.43	0
1996	Calgary	P.C.	8	50²/3	2	2	.500	41	16	64	4.09	0
1996	Pittsburgh c	N.L.	5	20²/3	1	0	1.000	9	8	22	3.05	0
1997	Pittsburgh	N.L.	72	72²/3	1	5	.167	66	24	76	3.10	29
1998	Nashville	P.C.	4	5	0	0	.000	6	0	3	0.00	2
1998	Pittsburgh d	N.L.	54	55	2	7	.222	48	36	56	3.44	19
1999	Pittsburgh e	N.L.	13	15¹/3	3	2	.600	14	9	16	5.28	0
2000	GC Pirates	Gulf Coast	1	1	0	0	.000	2	0	0	0.00	0
2000	Altoona	Eastern	13	13²/3	0	1	.000	18	6	17	5.27	0
2000	Nashville	P.C.	4	4²/3	0	0	.000	3	2	2	0.00	0
2000	Pittsburgh f	N.L.	40	42¹/3	2	3	.400	32	30	43	5.10	0
Major League Totals	5 Yrs.		184	206	9	17	.346	169	107	213	3.76	48

a Traded by San Diego Padres to Houston Astros with pitcher Jeff Tabaka for outfielder Phil Plantier, July 19, 1995.
b On disabled list from August 2 to September 1, 1995.
c Traded to Pittsburgh Pirates for pitcher Danny Darwin, July 23, 1996.
d On disabled list from July 20 to August 17, 1998.
e On disabled list from May 8 to November 17, 1999.
f On disabled list from March 25 to May 21 and June 25 to August 2, 2000.

LOOPER, BRADEN LA VERN
Born, Weatherford, Oklahoma, October 28, 1974.
Bats Right. Throws Right. Height, 6 feet, 4 inches. Weight, 210 pounds.

Year	Club	Lea	G	IP	W	L	Pct	SO	BB	H	ERA	SAVES
1997	Pr William	Carolina	12	64¹/3	3	6	.333	58	25	71	4.48	0
1997	Arkansas	Texas	19	21¹/3	1	4	.200	20	7	24	5.91	5
1998	Memphis	P.C.	40	40²/3	2	3	.400	43	13	43	3.10	20
1998	St. Louis a	N.L.	4	3¹/3	0	1	.000	4	1	5	5.40	0
1999	Florida	N.L.	72	83	3	3	.500	50	31	96	3.80	0
2000	Florida	N.L.	73	67¹/3	5	1	.833	29	36	71	4.41	2
Major League Totals	3 Yrs.		149	153²/3	8	5	.615	83	68	172	4.10	2

a Traded to Florida Marlins with pitcher Armando Almanza and infielder Pablo Ozuna for infielder Edgar Renteria, December 14, 1998.

LOPEZ, ALBERT ANTHONY (ALBIE)
Born, Mesa, Arizona, August 18, 1971.
Bats Right. Throws Right. Height, 6 feet, 1 inch. Weight, 205 pounds.

Year	Club	Lea	G	IP	W	L	Pct	SO	BB	H	ERA	SAVES
1991	Burlington	Appal.	13	73¹/3	4	5	.444	81	23	61	3.44	0
1992	Columbus	So. Atl.	16	97	7	2	.778	117	33	80	2.88	0
1992	Kinston	Carolina	10	64	5	2	.714	44	26	56	3.52	0
1993	Canton	Eastern	16	110	9	4	.692	80	47	79	3.11	0
1993	Cleveland	A.L.	9	49²/3	3	1	.750	25	32	49	5.98	0
1993	Charlotte	Int.	3	12	1	0	1.000	7	2	8	2.25	0
1994	Charlotte	Int.	22	144	13	3	.813	105	42	136	3.94	0
1994	Cleveland	A.L.	4	17	1	2	.333	18	6	20	4.24	0
1995	Buffalo	A.A.	18	101¹/3	5	10	.333	82	51	101	4.44	0
1995	Cleveland	A.L.	6	23	0	0	.000	22	7	17	3.13	0
1996	Buffalo	A.A.	17	104²/3	10	2	.833	89	40	90	3.87	0
1996	Cleveland	A.L.	13	62	5	4	.556	45	22	80	6.39	0
1997	Akron	Eastern	1	1	0	0	.000	2	0	2	0.00	0
1997	Buffalo	A.A.	7	11¹/3	1	0	1.000	13	2	6	0.00	1
1997	Cleveland a-b	A.L.	37	76²/3	3	7	.300	63	40	101	6.93	0
1998	Durham	Int.	2	3	0	0	.000	2	1	4	0.00	0
1998	St. Pete	Fla.St.	1	1	0	1	.000	1	0	2	18.00	0
1998	Tampa Bay c	A.L.	54	79²/3	7	4	.636	62	32	73	2.60	1
1999	St.Petersburg	Fla.St.	2	3¹/3	0	0	.000	3	0	7	5.40	0
1999	Tampa Bay d	A.L.	51	64	3	2	.600	37	24	66	4.64	1
2000	Princeton	Appal.	1	0²/3	0	0	.000	1	0	0	0.00	0
2000	Tampa Bay	A.L.	45	185¹/3	11	13	.458	96	70	199	4.13	2
Major League Totals	8 Yrs.		219	557¹/3	33	33	.500	368	233	605	4.73	4

a On disabled list from July 2 to July 29 and August 14 to September 1, 1997.
b Selected in expansion draft by Tampa Bay Devil Rays, November 18, 1997.
c On disabled list from August 1 to August 26, 1998.
d On disabled list from May 12 to June 20, 1999.

LOWE, DEREK CHRISTOPHER

Born, Dearborn, Michigan, June 1, 1973.
Bats Right. Throws Right. Height, 6 feet, 6 inches. Weight, 170 pounds.

Year	Club	Lea	G	IP	W	L	Pct	SO	BB	H	ERA	SAVES
1991	Mariners	Arizona	12	71	5	3	.625	60	21	58	2.41	0
1992	Bellingham	Northwest	14	85²/₃	7	3	.700	66	22	69	2.42	0
1993	Riverside	California	27	154	12	9	.571	80	60	189	5.26	0
1994	Jacksnville	Southern	26	151¹/₃	7	10	.412	75	50	177	4.94	0
1995	Mariners	Arizona	2	9²/₃	1	0	1.000	11	2	5	0.93	0
1995	Port City	Southern	10	53¹/₃	1	6	.143	30	22	70	6.07	0
1996	Port City	Southern	10	65	5	3	.625	33	17	56	3.05	0
1996	Tacoma	P.C.	17	105	6	9	.400	54	37	118	4.54	0
1997	Tacoma	P.C.	10	57¹/₃	3	4	.429	49	20	53	3.45	0
1997	Pawtucket	Int.	6	30¹/₃	4	0	1.000	21	11	23	2.37	0
1997	Seattle-Boston a	A.L.	20	69	2	6	.250	52	23	74	6.13	0
1998	Boston	A.L.	63	123	3	9	.250	77	42	126	4.02	4
1999	Boston	A.L.	74	109¹/₃	6	3	.667	80	25	84	2.63	15
2000	Boston	A.L.	74	91¹/₃	4	4	.500	79	22	90	2.56	*42
Major League Totals		4 Yrs.	231	392²/₃	15	22	.405	288	112	374	3.67	61
Division Series												
1998	Boston	A.L.	2	4¹/₃	0	0	.000	2	1	3	2.08	0
1999	Boston	A.L.	3	8¹/₃	1	1	.500	7	1	6	4.32	0
Division Series Totals			5	12²/₃	1	1	.500	9	2	9	3.55	0
Championship Series												
1999	Boston	A.L.	3	6¹/₃	0	0	.000	7	2	6	1.42	0

a Traded to Boston Red Sox with catcher Jason Varitek for pitcher Heathcliff Slocumb, July 31, 1997.

LOWE, JONATHAN SEAN

Born, Dallas, Texas, March 29, 1971.
Bats Right. Throws Right. Height, 6 feet, 2 inches. Weight, 205 pounds.

Year	Club	Lea	G	IP	W	L	Pct	SO	BB	H	ERA	SAVES
1992	Hamilton	N.Y.-Penn.	5	28	2	0	1.000	22	14	14	1.61	0
1993	St.Pete	Fla.St.	25	132²/₃	6	11	.353	87	62	152	4.27	0
1994	St. Pete	Fla.St.	21	114	5	6	.455	92	37	119	3.47	0
1994	Arkansas	Texas	3	19¹/₃	2	1	.667	11	8	13	1.40	0
1995	Arkansas	Texas	24	129	9	8	.529	77	64	143	4.88	0
1996	Arkansas	Texas	6	33	2	3	.400	25	15	32	6.00	0
1996	Louisville	A.A.	25	115	8	9	.471	76	51	127	4.70	0
1997	Louisville	A.A.	26	131²/₃	6	10	.375	117	53	142	4.37	1
1997	St. Louis	N.L.	6	17¹/₃	0	2	.000	8	10	27	9.35	0
1998	Memphis	P.C.	25	153	12	8	.600	114	61	147	3.18	0
1998	St. Louis	N.L.	4	5¹/₃	0	3	.000	2	5	11	15.19	0
1999	Chicago a	A.L.	64	95²/₃	4	1	.800	62	46	90	3.67	0
2000	Charlotte	Int.	2	3	0	0	.000	1	1	5	3.00	0
2000	Chicago b	A.L.	50	70²/₃	4	1	.800	53	39	78	5.48	0
Major League Totals		4 Yrs.	124	189	8	7	.533	125	100	206	5.19	0

a Traded to Chicago White Sox for pitcher John Ambrose, February 9, 1999.
b On disabled list from July 29 to August 22, 2000.

MADDUX, GREGORY ALAN

Born, San Angelo, Texas, April 14, 1966.
Bats Right. Throws Right. Height, 6 feet. Weight, 175 pounds.

Year	Club	Lea	G	IP	W	L	Pct	SO	BB	H	ERA	SAVES
1984	Pikeville	Appalachian	14	85²/₃	6	2	.750	62	41	63	2.63	0
1985	Peoria	Midland	27	186	13	9	.591	125	52	176	3.19	0
1986	Pittsfield	Eastern	8	62²/₃	4	3	.571	35	15	49	2.69	0
1986	Iowa	A.A.	18	128¹/₃	10	1	*.909	65	30	127	3.02	0
1986	Chicago	N.L.	6	31	2	4	.333	20	11	44	5.52	0
1987	Iowa	A.A.	4	27²/₃	3	0	1.000	22	12	17	0.98	0
1987	Chicago a	N.L.	30	155³/₃	6	14	.300	101	74	181	5.61	0
1988	Chicago	N.L.	34	249	18	8	.692	140	81	230	3.18	0
1989	Chicago	N.L.	35	238¹/₃	19	12	.613	135	82	*242	2.95	0
1990	Chicago	N.L.	35	237	15	15	.500	144	71	*242	3.46	0
1991	Chicago	N.L.	39	*263	15	11	.577	198	66	232	3.35	0
1992	Chicago b-c	N.L.	35	*268	*20	11	.645	199	70	201	2.18	0
1993	Atlanta d	N.L.	36	*267	20	10	.667	197	52	228	*2.36	0
1994	Atlanta e	N.L.	25	*202	*16	6	.727	156	31	150	*1.56	0

Year	Club	Lea	G	IP	W	L	Pct	SO	BB	H	ERA	SAVES
1995 Atlanta f	....	N.L.	28	*209²/₃	*19	2	*.905	181	23	147	*1.63	0
1996 Atlanta	....	N.L.	35	245	15	11	.577	172	28	225	2.72	0
1997 Atlanta	....	N.L.	33	232²/₃	19	4	*.826	177	20	200	2.20	0
1998 Atlanta	....	N.L.	34	251	18	9	.667	204	45	201	*2.22	0
1999 Atlanta	....	N.L.	33	219¹/₃	19	9	.679	136	37	258	3.57	0
2000 Atlanta	....	N.L.	35	249¹/₃	19	9	.679	190	42	225	3.00	0
Major League Totals	.... 15 Yrs.		471	3318	240	135	.640	2350	733	2986	2.83	0
Division Series												
1995 Atlanta	....	N.L.	2	14	1	0	1.000	7	2	19	4.50	0
1996 Atlanta	....	N.L.	1	7	1	0	1.000	7	0	3	0.00	0
1997 Atlanta	....	N.L.	1	9	1	0	1.000	6	1	7	1.00	0
1998 Atlanta	....	N.L.	1	7	1	0	1.000	4	0	7	2.57	0
1999 Atlanta	....	N.L.	2	7	0	1	.000	5	5	10	2.57	0
2000 Atlanta	....	N.L.	1	4	0	1	.000	2	3	9	11.25	0
Division Series Totals	....		8	48	4	2	.667	31	11	55	3.19	0
Championship Series												
1989 Chicago	....	N.L.	2	7¹/₃	0	1	.000	5	4	13	13.50	0
1993 Atlanta	....	N.L.	2	12²/₃	1	1	.500	11	7	11	4.97	0
1995 Atlanta	....	N.L.	1	8	1	0	1.000	4	2	7	1.13	0
1996 Atlanta	....	N.L.	2	14¹/₃	1	1	.500	10	2	15	2.51	0
1997 Atlanta	....	N.L.	2	13	0	2	.000	16	4	9	1.38	0
1998 Atlanta	....	N.L.	2	6	0	1	.000	4	3	5	3.00	0
1999 Atlanta	....	N.L.	2	14	1	0	1.000	7	1	12	1.93	0
Championship Series Totals	......		13	75¹/₃	4	6	.400	57	23	72	3.58	1
World Series Record												
1995 Atlanta	....	N.L.	2	16	1	1	.500	8	3	9	2.25	0
1996 Atlanta	....	N.L.	2	15²/₃	1	1	.500	5	1	14	1.72	0
1999 Atlanta	....	N.L.	1	7	0	1	.000	5	3	5	2.57	0
World Series Totals	....		5	38²/₃	2	3	.400	18	7	28	2.09	0

a Appeared in two games as pinch hitter.
b Selected Cy Young Award winner in National League for 1992.
c Filed for free agency, October 26; signed with Atlanta Braves, December 9, 1992.
d Selected Cy Young Award winner in National League for 1993.
e Selected Cy Young Award winner in National League for 1994.
f Selected Cy Young Award Winner in National League for 1995.

MAGNANTE, MICHAEL ANTHONY

Born, Glendale, California, June 17, 1965.
Bats Left. Throws Left. Height, 6 feet, 1 inch. Weight, 190 pounds.

Year	Club	Lea	G	IP	W	L	Pct	SO	BB	H	ERA	SAVES
1988 Eugene	....	Northwest	3	16	1	1	.500	26	2	10	0.56	0
1988 Appleton	....	Midwest	9	47²/₃	3	2	.600	40	15	48	3.21	0
1988 Baseball City	....	Fla. St.	4	24	1	1	.500	19	8	19	4.13	0
1989 Memphis	....	Southern	26	157¹/₃	8	9	.471	118	53	137	3.66	0
1990 Omaha a	....	A.A.	13	76²/₃	2	5	.286	56	25	72	4.11	0
1991 Omaha	....	A.A.	10	65²/₃	6	1	.857	50	23	53	3.02	0
1991 Kansas City	....	A.L.	38	55	0	1	.000	42	23	55	2.45	0
1992 Kansas City b	....	A.L.	44	89¹/₃	4	9	.308	31	35	115	4.94	0
1993 Omaha	....	A.A.	33	105¹/₃	2	6	.250	74	29	97	3.67	2
1993 Kansas City	....	A.L.	7	35¹/₃	1	2	.333	16	11	37	4.08	0
1994 Kansas City c	....	A.L.	36	47	2	3	.400	21	16	55	4.60	0
1995 Omaha	....	A.A.	15	57	5	1	.833	38	13	55	2.84	0
1995 Kansas City	....	A.L.	28	44²/₃	1	1	.500	28	16	45	4.23	0
1996 Omaha	....	A.A.	1	3	1	0	1.000	6	0	3	0.00	0
1996 Kansas City d-e	....	A.L.	38	54	2	2	.500	32	24	58	5.67	0
1997 New Orleans	....	A.A.	17	24	2	3	.400	23	5	31	4.50	1
1997 Houston	....	N.L.	40	47²/₃	3	1	.750	43	11	39	2.27	1
1998 Houston f-g	....	N.L.	48	51²/₃	4	7	.364	39	26	56	4.88	2
1999 Anaheim h	....	A.L.	53	69¹/₃	5	2	.714	44	29	68	3.38	0
2000 Sacramento	....	P.C.	5	6²/₃	0	0	.000	4	1	6	4.05	0
2000 Oakland i	....	A.L.	55	39²/₃	1	1	.500	17	19	50	4.31	0
Major League Totals	.... 10 Yrs.		387	533²/₃	23	29	.442	313	210	578	4.11	3
Division Series												
1997 Houston	....	N.L.	2	2	0	0	.000	2	0	4	4.50	0
2000 Oakland	....	A.L.	2	3	0	0	.000	2	0	1	0.00	0
Division Series Totals	....		4	5	0	0	.000	4	0	5	1.80	0

a On disabled list from June 17 to end of 1990 season.
b On disabled list from July 2 to July 20, 1992.

c On disabled list from July 16 to July 31, 1994.
d On disabled list from May 19 to June 13, 1996.
e Waived by Kansas City Royals, October 3, 1996. Signed with Houston Astros organization, December 19, 1996.
f On disabled list from May 10 to May 25, 1998.
g Filed for free agency, October 23, 1998. Signed with Anaheim Angels, January 27, 1999.
h Filed for free agency, October 29, 1999, signed with Oakland Athletics, November 18, 1999.
i On disabled list from May 27 to June 26, 2000.

MAHOMES, PATRICK LAVON (PAT)

Born, Bryan, Texas, August 9, 1970.
Bats Right. Throws Right. Height, 6 feet, 4 inches. Weight, 210 pounds.

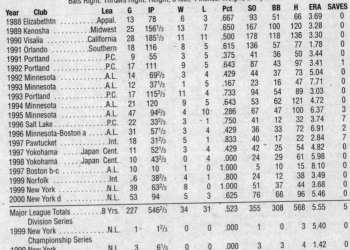

Year	Club	Lea	G	IP	W	L	Pct	SO	BB	H	ERA	SAVES
1988 Elizabethtn	....	Appal.	13	78	6	3	.667	93	51	66	3.69	0
1989 Kenosha	....	Midwest	25	156$\frac{1}{3}$	13	7	.650	167	100	120	3.28	0
1990 Visalia	....	California	28	185$\frac{1}{3}$	11	11	.500	178	118	136	3.30	0
1991 Orlando	....	Southern	18	116	8	5	.615	136	57	77	1.78	0
1991 Portland	....	P.C.	9	55	3	5	.375	41	36	50	3.44	0
1992 Portland	....	P.C.	17	111	9	5	.643	87	43	97	3.41	1
1992 Minnesota	....	A.L.	14	69$\frac{2}{3}$	3	4	.429	44	37	73	5.04	0
1993 Minnesota	....	A.L.	12	37$\frac{1}{3}$	1	5	.167	23	16	47	7.71	0
1993 Portland	....	P.C.	17	115$\frac{2}{3}$	11	4	.733	94	54	89	3.03	0
1994 Minnesota	....	A.L.	21	120	9	5	.643	53	62	121	4.72	0
1995 Minnesota	....	A.L.	47	94$\frac{2}{3}$	4	10	.286	67	47	100	6.37	3
1996 Salt Lake	....	P.C.	22	33$\frac{2}{3}$	3	1	.750	41	12	32	3.74	7
1996 Minnesota-Boston a	.....	A.L.	31	57$\frac{1}{3}$	3	4	.429	36	33	72	6.91	2
1997 Pawtucket	....	Int.	18	31$\frac{2}{3}$	5	1	.833	40	17	22	2.84	7
1997 Yokohama	....	Japan Cent.	11	52$\frac{1}{3}$	3	4	.429	42	25	54	4.82	0
1998 Yokohama	....	Japan Cent.	10	43$\frac{2}{3}$	0	4	.000	24	29	61	5.98	0
1997 Boston b-c	....	A.L.	10	10	1	0	1.000	5	10	15	8.10	0
1999 Norfolk	....	Int.	6	38$\frac{2}{3}$	4	1	.800	24	12	38	3.49	0
1999 New York	....	N.L.	39	63$\frac{2}{3}$	8	0	1.000	51	37	44	3.68	0
2000 New York d	....	N.L.	53	94	5	3	.625	76	66	96	5.46	0
Major League Totals	........8 Yrs.		227	546$\frac{2}{3}$	34	31	.523	355	308	568	5.55	5
Division Series												
1999 New York	....	N.L.	1	1$\frac{2}{3}$	0	0	.000	1	0	3	5.40	0
Championship Series												
1999 New York	....	N.L.	3	6$\frac{1}{3}$	0	0	.000	3	3	4	1.42	0

a Traded to Boston Red Sox for player to be named later, August 26, 1996. Minnesota Twins received pitcher Brian Looney to complete trade, December 17, 1996.
b Released by Boston Red Sox, June 27, 1997, signed with Yokohama Baystars (Japan Central), June 27, 1997.
c Played in Japan in 1997-98, signed as free agent by New York Mets, December 21, 1998.
d Not offered 2001 contract, December 19, 2000, signed with Texas Rangers organization, January 11, 2001.

MANTEI, MATTHEW BRUCE

Born, Tampa, Florida, July 7, 1973.
Bats Right. Throws Right. Height, 6 feet, 1 inch. Weight, 180 pounds.

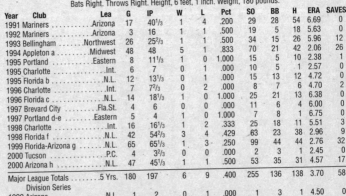

Year	Club	Lea	G	IP	W	L	Pct	SO	BB	H	ERA	SAVES
1991 Mariners	....	Arizona	17	40$\frac{1}{3}$	1	4	.200	29	28	54	6.69	0
1992 Mariners	....	Arizona	3	16	1	1	.500	19	5	18	5.63	0
1993 Bellingham	....	Northwest	26	25$\frac{2}{3}$	1	1	.500	34	15	26	5.96	12
1994 Appleton a	....	Midwest	48	48	5	1	.833	70	21	42	2.06	26
1995 Portland	....	Eastern	8	11$\frac{1}{3}$	1	0	1.000	15	5	10	2.38	1
1995 Charlotte	....	Int.	6	7	0	1	.000	10	5	1	2.57	0
1995 Florida b	....	N.L.	12	13$\frac{1}{3}$	0	1	.000	15	13	12	4.72	0
1996 Charlotte	....	Int.	7	7$\frac{2}{3}$	0	2	.000	8	7	6	4.70	2
1996 Florida c	....	N.L.	14	18$\frac{1}{3}$	1	0	1.000	25	21	13	6.38	0
1997 Brevard City	....	Fla.St.	4	6	0	0	.000	11	6	4	6.00	0
1997 Portland d-e	....	Eastern	5	4	1	0	1.000	7	8	1	6.75	0
1998 Charlotte	....	Int.	16	16$\frac{1}{3}$	1	2	.333	25	18	11	5.51	3
1998 Florida f	....	N.L.	42	54$\frac{2}{3}$	3	4	.429	63	23	38	2.96	9
1999 Florida-Arizona g	......	N.L.	65	65$\frac{1}{3}$	1	3	.250	99	44	44	2.76	32
2000 Tucson	....	P.C.	4	3$\frac{2}{3}$	0	0	.000	2	3	1	2.45	0
2000 Arizona h	....	N.L.	47	45$\frac{1}{3}$	1	1	.500	53	35	31	4.57	17
Major League Totals	........5 Yrs.		180	197	6	9	.400	255	136	138	3.70	58
Division Series												
1999 Arizona	....	N.L.	1	2	0	1	.000	1	3	1	4.50	0

a Selected by Florida Marlins from Seattle Mariners in Rule V draft, December 5, 1994.
b On disabled list from April 20 to June 18 and July 29 to September 1, 1995.
c On disabled list from June 19 to September 30, 1996.
d On disabled list from March 31 to September 30, 1997.

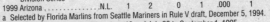

e Filed for free agency, December 21, 1997, re-signed with Florida Marlins organization, December 21, 1997.
f On disabled list from August 19 to September 4, 1998.
g Traded to Arizona Diamondbacks for pitcher Vladimir Nunez, pitcher Brad Penny and player to be named later, July 9, 1999. Florida Marlins received infielder Abraham Nunez to complete trade, December 13, 1999.
h On disabled list from April 2 to April 20 and May 5 to May 20, 2000.

MANZANILLO (ADAMS), JOSIAS

Born, San Pedro De Macoris, Dominican Republic, October 16, 1967.
Bats Right. Throws Right. Height, 6 feet. Weight, 190 pounds.

Year	Club	Lea	G	IP	W	L	Pct	SO	BB	H	ERA	SAVES
1983 Elmira	N.Y.-Penn.	12	38¹/₃	1	5	.167	19	20	52	7.98	0
1984 Elmira	N.Y.-Penn.	14	25²/₃	2	3	.400	15	26	27	5.26	1
1985 Greensboro	So.Atl.	7	12	1	1	.500	10	18	12	9.75	0
1985 Elmira	N.Y.-Penn.	19	39²/₃	2	4	.333	43	36	36	3.86	1
1986 Winter Havn	Fla.St.	23	142²/₃	13	5	.722	102	81	110	2.27	0
1987 New Britain a	Eastern	2	10	2	0	1.000	12	8	8	4.50	0
1988 New Britain b	Eastern		INJURED - Did Not Play								
1989 New Britain	Eastern	26	147²/₃	9	10	.474	93	85	129	3.66	0
1990 New Britain	Eastern	12	74	4	4	.500	51	37	66	3.41	0
1990 Pawtucket	Int.	15	82²/₃	4	7	.364	77	45	75	5.55	0
1991 New Britain	Eastern	7	49²/₃	2	2	.500	35	28	37	2.90	0
1991 Pawtucket	Int.	20	102²/₃	5	5	.500	65	53	109	5.61	0
1991 Boston	A.L.	1	1	0	0	.000	1	3	2	18.00	0
1992 Memphis	Southern	2	7¹/₃	0	2	.000	8	6	6	7.36	0
1992 Omaha c-d	A.A.	26	136¹/₃	7	10	.412	114	71	138	4.36	0
1993 Milwaukee	A.L.	10	17	1	1	.500	10	10	22	9.53	1
1993 New Orleans	A.A.	1	1	0	1	.000	3	0	1	9.00	0
1993 Norfolk	Int.	14	84	1	5	.167	79	25	82	3.11	0
1993 New York e	N.L.	6	12	0	0	.000	11	9	8	3.00	0
1994 Norfolk	Int.	8	12¹/₃	0	1	.000	10	6	12	4.38	3
1994 New York f	N.L.	37	47¹/₃	3	2	.600	48	13	34	2.66	2
1995 New York	N.L.	12	16	1	2	.333	14	6	18	7.87	0
1995 New York g-h-i	A.L.	11	17¹/₃	0	0	.000	11	9	19	2.08	0
1996 Taiwan			NO DATA AVAILABLE								
1997 Memphis j	Southern	2	3	0	0	.000	6	0	1	3.00	0
1997 Tacoma	P.C.	11	14	0	0	.000	15	8	16	6.43	1
1997 Seattle k-l	A.L.	16	18¹/₃	0	1	.000	18	17	19	5.40	0
1997 New Orleans m	A.A.	11	14¹/₃	0	0	.000	11	6	17	4.40	0
1998 Durham	Int.	19	85¹/₃	7	6	.538	61	30	93	4.64	1
1998 Norfolk n-o	Int.	13	77²/₃	4	4	.500	72	31	77	3.24	1
1999 New York p-q	N.L.	12	18²/₃	0	0	.000	25	4	19	5.79	0
2000 Nashville	P.C.	15	23¹/₃	0	2	.000	23	6	19	2.70	0
2000 Pittsburgh r	N.L.	43	58²/₃	2	2	.500	39	32	50	3.38	0
Major League Totals	7 Yrs.	148	206¹/₃	7	8	.467	177	103	191	4.41	3

a On disabled list from June 8 to September 1, 1987.
b On disabled list from April 8 to September 1, 1988.
c Filed for free agency, March 24, 1992, signed with Kansas City Royals organization, April 3, 1992.
d Filed for free agency, October 15, 1992, signed with Milwaukee Brewers, November 20, 1992.
e Traded to New York Mets for outfielder Wayne Housie, June 12, 1993.
f On disabled list from July 27 to October 1, 1994.
g Claimed on waivers by New York Yankees, June 5, 1995.
h On disabled list from July 6 to October 1, 1995.
i Filed for free agency, October 16, 1995, signed to play in Taiwan for 1996.
j Signed with Seattle Mariners organization, December 21, 1996.
k On disabled list from April 9 to May 6 and May 25 to July 1, 1997.
l Released by Seattle Mariners, July 17, 1997, signed with Houston Astros organization, July 27, 1997.
m Filed for free agency, October 15, 1997, signed with Tampa Bay Devils Rays organization, December 18, 1997.
n Released by Tampa Bay Devil Rays, July 1, 1998, signed with New York Mets organization, July 3, 1998.
o Filed for free agency, October 15, 1998, re-signed with New York Mets organization, December 18, 1998.
p On disabled list from June 21 to September 1, 1999.
q Filed for free agency, October 4, 1999.
r Signed with Pittsburgh Pirates organization, February 9, 2000.

MARTINEZ, PEDRO JAMIE

Born, Manoguyabo, Dominican Republic, July 25, 1971.
Bats Right. Throws Right. Height, 5 feet, 11 inches. Weight, 170 pounds.

Year	Club	Lea	G	IP	W	L	Pct	SO	BB	H	ERA	SAVES
1988 Santo Domingo	Domin. Sum.	8	49¹/₃	5	1	.833	28	16	45	3.12	0
1989 Santo Domingo	Domin. Sum.	13	85²/₃	7	2	.778	63	25	59	2.75	1

Year	Club	Lea	G	IP	W	L	Pct	SO	BB	H	ERA	SAVES
1990 Great Falls	Pioneer	14	77	8	3	.727	82	40	74	3.62	0	
1991 Bakersfield	California	10	61⅓	8	0	1.000	83	19	41	2.05	0	
1991 San Antonio	Texas	12	76⅔	7	5	.583	74	31	57	1.76	0	
1991 Albuquerque	P.C.	6	39⅓	3	3	.500	35	16	28	3.66	0	
1992 Albuquerque	P.C.	20	125⅓	7	6	.538	124	57	104	3.81	0	
1992 Los Angeles	N.L.	2	8	0	1	.000	8	1	6	2.25	0	
1993 Albuquerque	P.C.	1	3	0	0	.000	4	1	1	3.00	0	
1993 Los Angeles a	N.L.	65	107	10	5	.667	119	57	76	2.61	2	
1994 Montreal	N.L.	24	144⅓	11	5	.688	142	45	115	3.42	1	
1995 Montreal	N.L.	30	194⅔	14	10	.583	174	66	158	3.51	0	
1996 Montreal	N.L.	33	216⅔	13	10	.565	222	70	189	3.70	0	
1997 Montreal b-c	N.L.	31	241⅓	17	8	.680	305	67	158	*1.90	0	
1998 Boston	A.L.	33	233⅔	19	7	.731	251	67	188	2.89	0	
1999 Boston d-e	A.L.	31	213⅓	*23	4	*.852	*313	37	160	*2.07	0	
2000 Boston f-g	A.L.	29	217	18	6	.750	*284	32	128	*1.74	0	
Major League Totals	9 Yrs.	278	1576⅓	125	56	.691	1818	442	1178	2.68	3	
Division Series												
1998 Boston	A.L.	1	7	1	0	1.000	8	0	6	3.86	0	
1999 Boston	A.L.	2	10	1	0	1.000	11	4	3	0.00	0	
Division Series Totals		3	17	2	0	1.000	19	4	9	1.59	0	
Championship Series												
1999 Boston	A.L.	1	7	1	0	1.000	12	2	2	0.00	0	

a Traded to Montreal Expos for second baseman Delino DeShields, November 19, 1993.
b Traded to Boston Red Sox for pitcher Carl Pavano and player to be named later, November 18, 1997. Montreal Expos received pitcher Tony Armas to complete trade, December 18, 1997.
c Selected Cy Young Award Winner in National League for 1997.
d On disabled list from July 19 to August 3, 1999.
e Selected Cy Young Award Winner in American League for 1999.
f On disabled list from June 26 to July 12, 2000.
g Selected Cy Young Award Winner in American League for 2000.

MARTINEZ, RAMON JAIME

Born, Santo Domingo, Dominican Republic, March 22, 1968.
Bats Right. Throws Right. Height, 6 feet, 4 inches. Weight, 176 pounds.

Year	Club	Lea	G	IP	W	L	Pct	SO	BB	H	ERA	SAVES
1985 Bradenton Dodgers	Gulf C.	23	59	4	1	.800	42	23	57	2.59	1	
1986 Bakersfield	California	20	106	4	8	.333	78	63	119	4.75	0	
1987 Vero Beach	Fla. St.	25	170⅓	16	5	.762	148	78	128	2.17	0	
1988 San Antonio	Texas	14	95	8	4	.667	89	34	79	2.46	0	
1988 Albuquerque	P.C.	10	58⅔	5	2	.714	49	32	43	2.76	0	
1988 Los Angeles	N.L.	9	35⅔	1	3	.250	23	22	27	3.79	0	
1989 Albuquerque	P.C.	18	113	10	2	.833	127	50	92	2.79	0	
1989 Los Angeles	N.L.	15	98⅔	6	4	.600	89	41	79	3.19	0	
1990 Los Angeles	N.L.	33	234⅓	20	6	.769	223	67	191	2.92	0	
1991 Los Angeles	N.L.	33	220⅓	17	13	.567	150	69	190	3.27	0	
1992 Los Angeles a	N.L.	25	150⅔	8	11	.421	101	*69	141	4.00	0	
1993 Los Angeles b	N.L.	32	211⅔	10	12	.455	127	104	202	3.44	0	
1994 Los Angeles c	N.L.	24	170	12	7	.632	119	56	160	3.97	0	
1995 Los Angeles d-e-f	N.L.	30	206⅓	17	7	.708	138	*81	176	3.66	0	
1996 San Antonio	Texas	1	2⅔	0	0	.000	1	3	0	0.00	0	
1996 Vero Beach	Fla. St.	1	7	1	0	1.000	10	0	5	0.00	0	
1996 Los Angeles g	N.L.	28	168⅔	15	6	.714	133	86	153	3.42	0	
1997 Los Angeles h	N.L.	22	133⅔	10	5	.667	120	68	123	3.64	0	
1998 Los Angeles i-j	N.L.	15	101⅔	7	3	.700	91	41	76	2.83	0	
1999 Sarasota	Fla.St.	3	12	1	0	1.000	9	7	11	3.00	0	
1999 Lowell	N.Y.-Penn.	1	2	0	0	.000	3	0	0	0.00	0	
1999 Pawtucket	Int.	2	9	0	1	.000	7	6	10	9.00	0	
1999 Red Sox	Gulf Coast	4	13	1	0	1.000	15	3	9	1.38	0	
1999 Boston k	A.L.	4	20⅔	2	1	.667	15	8	14	3.05	0	
2000 Pawtucket	Int.	2	11⅔	1	0	1.000	10	4	8	2.31	0	
2000 Boston l-m	A.L.	27	127⅔	10	8	.556	89	67	143	6.13	0	
Major League Totals	13 Yrs.	297	1880	135	86	.611	1418	779	1675	3.62	0	
Division Series												
1995 Los Angeles	N.L.	1	4⅓	0	1	.000	3	2	10	14.45	0	
1996 Los Angeles	N.L.	1	8	0	0	.000	6	3	3	1.13	0	
1999 Boston	A.L.	1	5⅔	0	0	.000	6	3	5	3.18	0	
Division Series Totals		3	18	0	1	.000	15	8	18	5.00	0	
Championship Series												
1999 Boston	A.L.	1	6⅔	0	1	.000	5	3	6	4.05	0	

a Appeared in one additional game as pinch runner.
b Suspended five games for June 15 intentionally hitting batter with pitch from July 8 to July 12, 1993.
c Declared restricted free agent under Major League Baseball implemented labor proposal, December 23, 1994.
d Pitched no-hit, no-run game against Florida Marlins, July 14, 1995.
e Filed for free agency, November 12, 1995.
f Re-signed with Los Angeles Dodgers, November 20, 1995.
g On disabled list from April 7 to May 14, 1996.
h On disabled list from June 15 to August 20, 1997.
i On disabled list from June 15 to September 28, 1998.
j Not offered 1999 contract, October 26, 1998. Signed with Boston Red Sox, March 11, 1999.
k On disabled list from April 1 to September 2, 1999.
l On disabled list from August 1 to September 1, 2000.
m Not offered 2001 contract, October 31, 2000.

MATHEWS, TIMOTHY JAY (T.J.)

Born, Belleville, Illinois, January 9, 1970.
Bats Right. Throws Right. Height, 6 feet, 2 inches. Weight, 200 pounds.

Year	Club	Lea	G	IP	W	L	Pct	SO	BB	H	ERA	SAVES
1992 Hamilton	N.Y.-Penn.	14	86²/₃	10	1	.909	89	30	70	2.18	0
1993 Springfield	Midwest	25	159¹/₃	12	9	.571	144	29	121	2.71	0
1994 St. Petersburg	Fla. St.	11	66¹/₃	5	5	.500	62	23	52	2.44	0
1994 Arkansas	Texas	16	97	5	5	.500	93	24	83	3.15	0
1995 Louisville	A.A.	32	66²/₃	9	4	.692	50	27	60	2.70	1
1995 St. Louis	N.L.	23	29²/₃	1	1	.500	28	11	21	1.52	2
1996 St. Louis	N.L.	67	83²/₃	2	6	.250	80	32	62	3.01	6
1997 St. Louis a	N.L.	40	46	4	4	.500	46	18	41	2.15	0
1997 Oakland	A.L.	24	28²/₃	6	2	.750	24	12	34	4.40	3
1998 Oakland	A.L.	66	72²/₃	7	4	.636	53	29	71	4.58	1
1999 Vancouver	P.C.	1	1	0	0	.000	0	0	1	9.00	0
1999 Oakland b	A.L.	50	59	9	5	.643	42	20	46	3.81	3
2000 Sacramento	P.C.	3	3²/₃	0	0	.000	5	1	2	0.00	0
2000 Oakland c	A.L.	50	59²/₃	2	3	.400	42	25	73	6.03	0
Major League Totals	6 Yrs.	320	379¹/₃	31	25	.554	315	147	348	3.80	15
Division Series											
1996 St. Louis	N.L.	1	1	1	0	1.000	2	0	1	0.00	0
Championship Series											
1996 St. Louis	N.L.	2	0²/₃	0	0	.000	2	1	2	0.00	0

a Traded to Oakland Athletics with pitcher Eric Ludwick and pitcher Blake Stein for first baseman Mark McGwire, July 31, 1997.
b On disabled list from July 1 to July 24, 1999.
c On disabled list from August 12 to August 31, 2000.

MAYS, JOSEPH EMERSON (JOE)

Born, Flint, Michigan, December 10, 1975.
Bats Both. Throws Right. Height, 6 feet, 1 inch. Weight, 160 pounds.

Year	Club	Lea	G	IP	W	L	Pct	SO	BB	H	ERA	SAVES
1995 Mariners	Arizona	10	44¹/₃	2	3	.400	44	18	41	3.25	0
1996 Everett	Northwest	13	64¹/₃	4	4	.500	56	22	55	3.08	0
1997 Wisconsin	Midwest	13	81²/₃	9	3	.750	79	23	62	2.09	0
1997 Lancaster a	California	15	96¹/₃	7	4	.636	82	34	108	4.86	0
1998 Fort Myers	Fla.St.	16	94²/₃	7	2	.778	83	23	101	3.04	0
1998 New Britain	Eastern	11	57²/₃	5	3	.625	45	21	63	4.99	0
1999 Minnesota	A.L.	49	171	6	11	.353	115	67	179	4.37	0
2000 Salt Lake	P.C.	3	15²/₃	2	0	1.000	18	2	16	1.72	0
2000 Minnesota	A.L.	31	160¹/₃	7	15	.318	102	67	193	5.56	0
Major League Totals	2 Yrs.	80	331¹/₃	13	26	.333	217	134	372	4.94	0

a Traded by Seattle Mariners to Minnesota Twins to complete trade in which Mariners received outfielder Roberto Kelly, October 8, 1997.

McELROY, CHARLES DWAYNE (CHUCK)

Born, Galveston, Texas, October 1, 1967.
Bats Left. Throws Left. Height, 6 feet. Weight, 195 pounds.

Year	Club	Lea	G	IP	W	L	Pct	SO	BB	H	ERA	SAVES
1986 Utica	N.Y.-Penn.	14	94²/₃	4	6	.400	91	28	85	2.95	0
1987 Spartanburg	So. Atl.	24	130¹/₃	14	4	.778	115	48	117	3.11	0
1987 Clearwater	Fla. St.	2	7¹/₃	1	0	1.000	7	4	1	0.00	0
1988 Reading	Eastern	28	160	9	12	.429	93	70	172	4.50	0
1989 Reading	Eastern	32	47	3	1	.750	39	14	39	2.68	12

Year	Club	Lea	G	IP	W	L	Pct	SO	BB	H	ERA	SAVES
1989 Scranton	Int.	14	15⅓	1	2	.333	12	11	13	2.93	3
1989 Philadelphia	N.L.	11	10⅓	0	0	.000	8	4	12	1.74	0
1990 Scranton	Int.	57	76	6	8	.429	78	34	62	2.72	7
1990 Philadelphia a	N.L.	16	14	0	1	.000	16	10	24	7.71	0
1991 Chicago b	N.L.	71	101⅓	6	2	.750	92	57	73	1.95	3
1992 Chicago	N.L.	72	83⅔	4	7	.364	83	51	73	3.55	6
1993 Iowa	A.A.	9	15⅔	0	1	.000	13	9	19	4.60	2
1993 Chicago c	N.L.	49	47⅓	2	2	.500	31	25	51	4.56	0
1994 Cincinnati	N.L.	52	57⅔	1	2	.333	38	15	52	2.34	5
1995 Cincinnati d	N.L.	44	40⅓	3	4	.429	27	15	46	6.02	0
1996 Indianapolis	A.A.	5	13⅓	1	1	.500	10	4	11	2.70	0
1996 Cincinnati	N.L.	12	12⅓	2	0	1.000	13	10	13	6.57	0
1996 California e-f	A.L.	40	36⅔	5	1	.833	32	13	32	2.95	0
1997 Anaheim-Chicago g-h-i	A.L.	61	75	1	3	.250	62	22	73	3.84	1
1998 Colorado	N.L.	78	68⅓	6	4	.600	61	24	68	2.90	2
1999 Colorado-New York j-k	N.L.	56	54	3	1	.750	44	36	60	5.50	0
2000 Baltimore	A.L.	43	63⅓	3	0	1.000	50	34	60	4.69	0
Major League Totals	12 Yrs.	605	664⅓	36	27	.571	557	316	637	3.74	17

a Traded to Chicago Cubs with pitcher Bob Scanlan for pitcher Mitch Williams, April 7, 1991.
b Appeared in one game as pinch runner.
c Traded to Cincinnati Reds for pitchers Larry Luebbers and Mike Anderson and catcher Darron Cox, December 10, 1993.
d On disabled list from June 7 to June 23, 1995.
e On disabled list from August 11 to August 28 and April 1 to April 28, 1996.
f Traded to California Angels for pitcher Lee Smith, May 27, 1996.
g Traded to Chicago White Sox with catcher Jorge Fabregas for outfielder Tony Phillips and catcher Chad Kreuter, May 18, 1997.
h Selected on expansion draft by Arizona Diamondbacks, November 18, 1997.
i Traded to Colorado Rockies for outfielder Harvey Pulliam, November 19, 1997.
j Traded to New York Mets with outfielder Darryl Hamilton for outfielder Brian McRae, outfielder Thomas Johnson and pitcher Rigo Beltran, July 31, 1999.
k Traded to Baltimore Orioles for pitcher Jesse Orosco, December 11, 1999.

MEADOWS, MATTHEW BRIAN (BRIAN)
Born, Montgomery, Alabama, November 21, 1975.
Bats Right. Throws Right. Height, 6 feet, 4 inches. Weight, 210 pounds.

Year	Club	Lea	G	IP	W	L	Pct	SO	BB	H	ERA	SAVES
1994 Marlins	Gulf Coast	8	37	3	0	1.000	33	6	34	1.95	0
1995 Kane County	Midwest	26	147	9	9	.500	103	41	163	4.22	0
1996 Brevard City	Fla.St.	24	146	8	7	.533	69	25	129	3.58	0
1996 Portland	Eastern	4	27	0	1	.000	13	4	26	4.33	0
1997 Portland	Eastern	29	175⅔	9	7	.563	115	48	204	4.61	0
1998 Florida a	N.L.	31	174½	11	13	.458	88	46	222	5.21	0
1999 Florida b	N.L.	31	178½	11	15	.423	72	57	214	5.60	0
2000 San Diego	N.L.	22	124⅔	7	8	.467	53	50	150	5.34	0
2000 Kansas City c	A.L.	11	71⅔	6	2	.750	26	14	84	4.77	0
Major League Totals	3 Yrs.	95	549	35	38	.479	239	167	670	5.31	0

a On disabled list from July 28 to August 13, 1998.
b Traded to San Diego Padres for pitcher Dan Miceli, November 16, 1999.
c Traded to Kansas City Royals for pitcher Jay Witasick, July 31, 2000.

MECHE, GILBERT ALLEN (GIL)
Born, Lafayette, Louisiana, September 8, 1978.
Bats Right. Throws Right. Height, 6 feet, 3 inches. Weight, 180 pounds.

Year	Club	Lea	G	IP	W	L	Pct	SO	BB	H	ERA	SAVES
1996 Mariners	Arizona	2	3	0	1	.000	4	1	4	6.00	0
1997 Everett	Northwest	12	74⅔	3	4	.429	62	24	75	3.98	0
1997 Wisconsin	Midwest	2	12	0	2	.000	14	4	12	3.00	0
1998 Wisconsin	Midwest	26	149	8	7	.533	168	63	136	3.44	0
1999 New Haven	Eastern	10	59	3	4	.429	56	26	51	3.05	0
1999 Tacoma	P.C.	6	31	2	2	.500	24	13	31	3.19	0
1999 Seattle	A.L.	16	85⅔	8	4	.667	47	57	73	4.73	0
2000 Tacoma	P.C.	3	14	1	1	.500	15	10	10	3.86	0
2000 Wisconsin	Midwest	1	5	0	0	.000	6	2	1	0.00	0
2000 Everett	Northwest	1	1	0	0	.000	0	0	3	9.00	0
2000 Seattle a	A.L.	15	85⅔	4	4	.500	60	40	75	3.78	0
Major League Totals	2 Yrs.	31	171⅓	12	8	.600	107	97	148	4.25	0

a On disabled list from May 29 to June 24 and July 31 to October 1, 2000.

MECIR, JAMES JASON (JIM)

Born, Bayside, New York, May 16, 1970.
Bats Both. Throws Right. Height, 6 feet, 1 inch. Weight, 195 pounds.

Year	Club	Lea	G	IP	W	L	Pct	SO	BB	H	ERA	SAVES
1991 San Berndno	......	California	14	70⅓	3	5	.375	48	37	72	4.22	1
1992 San Berndno a	....	California	14	61⅔	4	5	.444	53	26	72	4.67	0
1993 Riverside	....	California	26	145⅓	9	11	.450	85	58	160	4.33	0
1994 Jacksnville	....	Southern	46	80⅓	6	5	.545	53	35	73	2.69	13
1995 Tacoma	....	P.C.	40	69⅔	1	4	.200	46	28	63	3.10	8
1995 Seattle b	....	A.L.	2	4⅔	0	0	.000	3	2	5	0.00	0
1996 New York	....	A.L.	26	40⅓	1	1	.500	38	23	42	5.13	0
1996 Columbus	....	Int.	33	47⅔	3	3	.500	52	15	37	2.27	7
1997 New York	....	A.L.	25	33⅔	0	4	.000	25	10	36	5.88	0
1997 Columbus c-d	....	Int.	24	27	1	1	.500	34	6	14	1.00	11
1998 Tampa Bay	....	A.L.	68	84	7	2	.778	77	33	68	3.11	0
1999 Tampa Bay e	....	A.L.	17	20⅔	0	1	.000	15	14	15	2.61	0
2000 Tampa Bay-Oakland f-g	.A.L.		63	85	10	3	.769	70	36	70	2.96	5
Major League Totals	....	6 Yrs.	201	268⅓	18	11	.621	228	118	236	3.62	5
Division Series												
2000 Oakland	....	A.L.	3	5⅓	0	0	.000	2	0	1	0.00	0

a On disabled list from June 25 to August 25, 1992.
b Traded to New York Yankees with infielder Tito Martinez and pitcher Jeff Nelson for infielder Russ Davis and pitcher Sterling Hitchcock, December 7, 1995.
c Sent to Boston Red Sox as player to be named later for designated hitter Mike Stanley and infielder Randy Brown, September 29, 1997.
d Selected in expansion draft by Tampa Bay Devil Rays, November 18, 1997.
e On disabled list from May 12 to November 8, 1999.
f On disabled list from April 27 to May 22, 2000.
g Traded to Oakland Athletics with pitcher Todd Belitz for pitcher Jesus Colome and player to be named later, July 27, 2000.

MENDOZA, RAMIRO

Born, Los Santos, Panama, June 15, 1972.
Bats Right. Throws Right. Height, 6 feet, 2 inches. Weight, 154 pounds.

Year	Club	Lea	G	IP	W	L	Pct	SO	BB	H	ERA	SAVES
1993 Yankees	....	Gulf Coast	15	67⅔	4	5	.444	61	7	59	2.79	1
1993 Greensboro	....	So. Atl.	2	3⅔	0	1	.000	3	5	3	2.45	0
1994 Tampa	....	Fla. St.	22	134⅓	12	6	.667	110	35	133	3.01	0
1995 Norwich	....	Eastern	19	89⅔	5	6	.455	68	33	87	3.21	0
1995 Columbus	....	Int.	2	14	1	0	1.000	13	2	10	2.57	0
1996 Columbus	....	Int.	15	97	6	2	.750	61	19	96	2.51	0
1996 New York	....	A.L.	12	53	4	5	.444	34	10	80	6.79	0
1997 Columbus	....	Int.	1	6⅓	0	0	.000	4	1	7	5.68	0
1997 New York	....	A.L.	39	133⅔	8	6	.571	82	28	157	4.24	2
1998 New York	....	A.L.	41	130⅓	10	2	.833	56	30	131	3.25	1
1999 New York	....	A.L.	53	123⅔	9	9	.500	80	27	141	4.29	3
2000 Tampa	....	Fla.St.	2	5	0	2	.000	7	0	9	7.20	0
2000 New York a	....	A.L.	14	65⅔	7	4	.636	30	20	66	4.25	0
Major League Totals	....	5 Yrs.	159	506⅓	38	26	.594	282	115	575	4.27	6
Division Series												
1997 New York	....	A.L.	2	3⅔	1	1	.500	2	0	3	2.45	0
Championship Series												
1998 New York	....	A.L.	2	4⅓	0	0	.000	1	0	4	0.00	0
1999 New York	....	A.L.	2	2⅓	0	0	.000	2	0	0	0.00	1
Championship Series Totals	......		4	6⅔	0	0	.000	3	0	4	0.00	1
World Series Record												
1998 New York	....	A.L.	1	1	1	0	1.000	1	0	2	9.00	0
1999 New York	....	A.L.	1	1⅔	0	0	.000	0	1	3	10.80	0
World Series Totals	....		2	2⅔	1	0	1.000	1	1	5	10.13	0

a On disabled list from June 25 to July 27 and July 30 to October 1, 2000.

MERCEDES (SANTANA), JOSE MIGUEL

Born, El Seibo, Dominican Republic, March 5, 1971.
Bats Right. Throws Right. Height, 6 feet, 1 inch. Weight, 180 pounds.

Year	Club	Lea	G	IP	W	L	Pct	SO	BB	H	ERA	SAVES
1990 Balt/Chi Ws	....	Domincan	15	68	2	7	.222	42	36	81	5.96	1
1991 Balt/Chi Ws	....	Domincan	10	66⅓	5	2	.714	24	19	86	4.48	0
1992 Orioles	....	Gulf Coast	8	35⅓	2	3	.400	21	13	31	1.78	0

Year	Club	Lea	G	IP	W	L	Pct	SO	BB	H	ERA	SAVES
1992 Kane County	Midwest	8	47⅓	3	2	.600	45	15	40	2.66	0
1993 Bowie a	Eastern	26	147	6	8	.429	75	65	170	4.78	0
1994 El Paso	Texas	3	9²/₃	2	0	1.000	8	4	13	4.66	0
1994 New Orleans	A.A.	3	18¹/₃	0	0	.000	7	8	19	4.91	0
1994 Milwaukee	A.L.	19	31	2	0	1.000	11	16	22	2.32	0
1995 Milwaukee	A.L.	5	7¹/₃	0	1	.000	6	8	12	9.82	0
1996 Milwaukee	A.L.	11	16²/₃	0	2	.000	6	5	20	9.18	0
1996 New Orleans	A.A.	25	101	3	7	.300	47	28	109	3.56	1
1997 Milwaukee	A.L.	29	159	7	10	.412	80	53	146	3.79	0
1998 El Paso	Texas	1	3¹/₃	0	0	.000	0	0	9	10.80	0
1998 Milwaukee b	N.L.	7	32	2	2	.500	11	9	42	6.75	0
1999 Norfolk	Int.	6	32	2	1	.667	19	11	36	2.53	0
1999 Calgary	P.C.	4	26	1	2	.333	13	3	30	3.12	0
1999 Las Vegas c-d-e	P.C.	15	88	2	6	.250	57	20	110	4.30	0
2000 Baltimore f	A.L.	36	145²/₃	14	7	.667	70	64	150	4.02	0
Major League Totals	6 Yrs.	107	391²/₃	25	22	.532	184	155	392	4.34	0

a Selected by Milwaukee Brewers from Baltimore Orioles in Rule V draft, December 13, 1993.
b On disabled list from May 5 to September 28, 1998.
c Released by Milwaukee Brewers, December 16, 1998, signed with San Diego Padres organization, March 19, 1999.
d Released by San Diego Padres, June 24, 1999, signed with Florida Marlins organization, June 30, 1999.
e Released by Florida Marlins, July 30, 1999, signed with New York Mets organization, August 6, 1999.
f Filed for free agency October 15, 1999, signed with Baltimore Orioles organization, January 3, 2000.

MERCKER, KENT FRANKLIN
Born, Dublin, Ohio, February 1, 1968.
Bats Left. Throws Left. Height, 6 feet, 2 inches. Weight, 195 pounds.

Year	Club	Lea	G	IP	W	L	Pct	SO	BB	H	ERA	SAVES
1986 Bradenton Braves	Gulf C.	9	47¹/₃	4	3	.571	42	16	37	2.47	0
1987 Durham a	Carolina	3	11²/₃	0	1	.000	14	6	11	5.40	0
1988 Durham	Carolina	19	127²/₃	11	4	.733	159	47	102	2.75	0
1988 Greenville	Southern	9	48¹/₃	3	1	.750	60	26	36	3.35	0
1989 Richmond	Int.	27	168³/₃	9	12	.429	*144	*95	107	3.20	0
1989 Atlanta	N.L.	2	4¹/₃	0	0	.000	4	6	8	12.46	0
1990 Richmond b	Int.	12	58¹/₃	5	4	.556	69	27	60	3.55	1
1990 Atlanta	N.L.	36	48¹/₃	4	7	.364	39	24	43	3.17	7
1991 Atlanta c-d	N.L.	50	73¹/₃	5	3	.625	62	35	56	2.58	6
1992 Atlanta	N.L.	53	68¹/₃	3	2	.600	49	35	51	3.42	6
1993 Atlanta	N.L.	43	66	3	1	.750	59	36	52	2.86	0
1994 Atlanta e-f	N.L.	20	112¹/₃	9	4	.692	111	45	90	3.45	0
1995 Atlanta g-h	N.L.	29	143	7	8	.467	102	61	140	4.15	0
1996 Buffalo	A.A.	3	16	0	2	.000	11	9	11	3.94	0
1996 Baltimore-Cleveland i-j-k	A.L.	24	69²/₃	4	6	.400	29	38	83	6.98	0
1997 Cincinnati l-m-n	N.L.	28	144²/₃	8	11	.421	75	62	135	3.92	0
1998 St. Louis o	N.L.	30	161²/₃	11	11	.500	72	53	199	5.07	0
1999 St. Louis	N.L.	25	103²/₃	6	5	.545	64	51	125	5.12	0
1999 Boston p-q-r	A.L.	5	25²/₃	2	0	1.000	17	13	23	3.51	0
2000 Lake Elsinore	California	1	4	0	0	.000	3	0	0	0.00	0
2000 Anaheim s-t	A.L.	21	48¹/₃	1	3	.250	30	29	57	6.52	0
Major League Totals	12 Yrs.	366	1069¹/₃	63	61	.508	713	488	1062	4.31	19
Division Series											
1995 Atlanta	N.L.	1	0¹/₃	0	0	.000	0	0	0	0.00	0
1999 Boston	A.L.	1	1²/₃	0	0	.000	1	3	3	10.80	0
Division Series Totals		2	2	0	0	.000	1	3	3	9.00	0
Championship Series											
1991 Atlanta	N.L.	1	0²/₃	0	1	.000	0	2	0	13.50	0
1992 Atlanta	N.L.	2	3	0	0	.000	1	1	1	0.00	0
1999 Boston	A.L.	2	7²/₃	0	1	.000	5	4	12	4.70	0
Championship Series Totals		10	16¹/₃	0	2	.000	10	9	16	3.31	0
World Series Record											
1991 Atlanta	N.L.	2	1	0	0	.000	1	0	0	0.00	0
1995 Atlanta	N.L.	1	2	0	0	.000	2	2	1	4.50	0
World Series Totals		3	3	0	0	.000	3	2	1	3.00	0

a On disabled list from April 2 to August 1, 1987.
b On disabled list from March 30 to May 6, 1990.
c On disabled list from August 9 to August 24, 1991.
d Pitched first six innings of no-hit, no-run game completed by Mark Wohlers (7th and 8th innings) and Alejandro Pena (9th inning) against San Diego Padres, winning 1-0, September 11, 1991.

e Pitched no-hit, no-run game against Los Angeles Dodgers, winning 6-0, April 8, 1994.
f Declared restricted free agent under Major League Baseball implemented labor proposal, December 23, 1994.
g Re-signed with Atlanta Braves, April 27, 1995.
h Traded to Baltimore Orioles for pitcher Joe Borowski and Rachaad Stewart, December 17, 1995.
i Traded to Cleveland Indians for desigated hitter Eddie Murray, July 21, 1996.
j Filed for free agency, November 4, 1996.
k Signed with Cincinnati Reds, December 10, 1996.
l On disabled list from August 17 to September 1, 1997.
m Filed for free agency, October 27, 1997.
n Signed as free agent with St. Louis Cardinals, December 16, 1997.
o On disabled list from June 14 to July 1, 1998.
p Traded to Boston Red Sox for catcher David Benham and pitcher Mike Matthews, August 24, 1999.
q On disabled list from September 7 to September 23, 1999.
r Filed for free agency, November 8, 1999. Signed with Anaheim Angels organization, January 26, 2000.
s On disabled list from May 14 to August 11, 2000.
t Filed for free agency, November 8, 2000, signed with Boston Red Sox organization, January 5, 2001.

MESA, JOSE RAMON

Born, Azua, Dominican Republic, May 22, 1966.
Bats Right. Throws Right. Height, 6 feet, 3 inches. Weight, 225 pounds.

Year	Club	Lea	G	IP	W	L	Pct	SO	BB	H	ERA	SAVES
1982 Bradenton Blue Jays	G.C.		13	83⅓	6	4	.600	40	20	58	2.70	1
1983 Florence	So. Atl.		28	141⅓	6	12	.333	91	93	153	5.48	0
1984 Florence	So. Atl.		7	38⅓	4	3	.571	35	25	38	3.76	0
1984 Kinston a	Carolina		10	50⅔	5	2	.714	24	28	51	3.91	0
1985 Kinston	Carolina		30	106⅓	5	10	.333	71	79	110	6.16	1
1986 Ventura	California		24	142⅓	10	6	.625	113	58	141	3.86	0
1986 Knoxville	Southern		9	41⅓	2	2	.500	30	23	40	4.35	0
1987 Knoxville b	Southern		35	*193⅓	10	*13	.435	115	104	*206	5.21	0
1987 Baltimore	A.L.		6	31⅓	1	3	.250	17	15	38	6.03	0
1988 Rochester c	Int.		11	15⅔	0	3	.000	15	14	21	8.62	0
1989 Hagerstown d	Eastern		3	13	0	0	.000	12	4	9	1.38	0
1989 Rochester	Int.		7	10	0	2	.000	3	6	10	5.40	0
1990 Hagerstown e	Eastern		15	79	5	5	.500	72	30	77	3.42	0
1990 Rochester	Int.		4	26	1	2	.333	23	12	21	2.42	0
1990 Baltimore	A.L.		7	46⅔	3	2	.600	24	27	37	3.86	0
1991 Rochester	Int.		8	51⅓	3	3	.500	48	30	37	3.86	0
1991 Baltimore f-g	A.L.		23	123⅔	6	11	.353	64	62	151	5.97	0
1992 Balt.-Cleveland h	A.L.		28	160⅔	7	12	.368	62	70	169	4.59	0
1993 Cleveland i	A.L.		34	208⅔	10	12	.455	118	62	232	4.92	0
1994 Cleveland	A.L.		51	73	7	5	.583	63	26	71	3.82	2
1995 Cleveland	A.L.		62	64	3	0	1.000	58	17	49	1.13	*46
1996 Cleveland	A.L.		69	72⅓	2	7	.222	64	28	69	3.73	39
1997 Cleveland	A.L.		66	82⅓	4	4	.500	69	28	83	2.40	16
1998 Cleveland	A.L.		44	54	3	4	.429	35	20	61	5.17	1
1998 San Francisco j-k	N.L.		32	30⅓	5	3	.625	28	18	30	3.52	0
1999 Seattle	A.L.		68	68⅔	3	6	.333	42	40	84	4.98	33
2000 Seattle l	A.L.		66	80⅔	4	6	.400	84	41	89	5.36	1
Major League Totals	12 Yrs.		556	1096⅔	58	75	.436	728	454	1163	4.42	138
Division Series												
1995 Cleveland	A.L.		2	2	0	0	.000	0	2	0	0.00	1
1996 Cleveland	A.L.		2	4⅔	0	1	.000	7	0	8	3.86	0
1997 Cleveland	A.L.		2	3⅓	0	0	.000	2	1	5	2.70	1
2000 Seattle	A.L.		2	2	1	0	1.000	2	1	0	0.00	0
Division Series Totals			8	12	1	1	.500	11	4	13	2.25	1
Championship Series												
1995 Cleveland	A.L.		4	4	0	0	.000	1	1	3	2.25	1
1997 Cleveland	A.L.		4	5⅓	1	0	1.000	5	3	5	3.38	2
2000 Seattle	A.L.		3	4⅓	0	0	.000	3	3	5	12.46	0
Championship Series Totals			11	13⅔	1	0	1.000	9	7	13	5.93	3
World Series Record												
1995 Cleveland	A.L.		2	4	1	0	1.000	4	1	5	4.50	1
1997 Cleveland	A.L.		5	5	0	0	.000	5	1	10	5.40	1
World Series Totals			7	9	1	0	1.000	9	2	15	5.00	2

a On disabled list from August 27 to end of 1984 season.
b Traded by Toronto Blue Jays to Baltimore Orioles with pitcher Oswald Peraza for pitcher Mike Flanagan, August 31, 1987.
c On disabled list from June 29 to end of 1988 season.
d On disabled list from May 27 to end of 1989 season.
e On disabled list from April 6 to April 25, 1990.

f On disabled list from August 21 to September 6, 1991.
g Appeared in one additional game as pinch runner.
h Traded to Cleveland Indians for outfielder Kyle Washington, July 14, 1992.
i Suspended three games by American League for March 30 fight from April 5 to April 8, 1993.
j Traded to San Francisco Giants with pitcher Alvin Morman and infielder Shawon Dunston for pitcher Steve Reed and outfielder Jacob Cruz, July 24, 1998.
k Filed for free agency, October 23, 1998, signed with Seattle Mariners, November 13, 1998.
1 Not offered 2001 contract, November 2, 2000, signed with Philadelphia Phillies, November 17, 2000.

MICELI, DANIEL

Born, Newark, New Jersey, September 9, 1970.
Bats Right. Throws Right. Height, 6 feet, 1 inch. Weight, 185 pounds.

Year Club	Lea	G	IP	W	L	Pct	SO	BB	H	ERA	SAVES
1990 Baseball City Royals ..	Gulf C.	*27	53	3	4	.429	48	29	45	3.91	4
1991 Eugene	Northwest	25	33²/₃	0	1	.000	43	18	18	2.14	10
1992 Appleton	Midwest	23	23¹/₃	1	1	.500	44	4	12	1.93	9
1992 Memphis	Southern	32	37²/₃	3	0	1.000	46	13	20	1.91	4
1993 Mem.-Carolina a ...	Southern	53	71	6	6	.500	87	43	65	4.69	17
1993 Pittsburgh	N.L.	9	5¹/₃	0	0	.000	4	3	6	5.06	0
1994 Buffalo	A.A.	19	24	1	1	.500	31	6	15	1.88	2
1994 Pittsburgh	N.L.	28	27¹/₃	2	1	.667	27	11	28	5.93	2
1995 Pittsburgh	N.L.	58	58	4	4	.500	56	28	61	4.66	21
1996 Carolina	Southern	3	9	1	0	1.000	17	1	4	1.00	1
1996 Pittsburgh b	N.L.	44	85²/₃	2	10	.167	66	45	99	5.78	1
1997 Detroit c	A.L.	71	82²/₃	3	2	.600	79	38	77	5.01	3
1998 San Diego	N.L.	67	72²/₃	10	5	.667	70	27	64	3.22	2
1999 San Diego d	N.L.	66	68²/₃	4	5	.444	59	36	67	4.46	2
2000 GC Marlins	Gulf Coast	2	3	0	0	.000	3	1	0	0.00	0
2000 Brevard County	Fla.St.	5	6	1	0	1.000	7	0	3	3.00	0
2000 Florida e	N.L.	45	48²/₃	6	4	.600	40	18	45	4.25	0
Major League Totals	8 Yrs.	388	449	31	31	.500	401	206	447	4.71	31
Division Series											
1998 San Diego	N.L.	3	3¹/₃	1	1	.500	4	0	2	2.70	0
Championship Series											
1998 San Diego	N.L.	3	0²/₃	0	0	.000	1	0	4	13.50	0
World Series Record											
1998 San Diego	N.L.	2	1²/₃	0	0	.000	1	2	2	0.00	0

a Traded by Kansas City Royals to Pittsburgh Pirates organization with pitcher Jon Lieber for pitcher Stan Belinda, July 31, 1993.
b Traded to Detroit Tigers for pitcher Clint Sodowsky, November 1, 1996.
c Traded to San Diego Padres with pitcher Donne Wall and infielder Ryan Balfe for pitcher Tim Worrell and outfielder Trey Beamon, November 19, 1997.
d Traded to Florida Marlins for pitcher Brian Meadows, November 16, 1999.
e On disabled list from May 30 to July 18, 2000.

MILLER, TRAVIS EUGENE

Born, Dayton, Ohio, November 2, 1972.
Bats Right. Throws Right. Height, 6 feet, 3 inches. Weight, 205 pounds.

Year Club	Lea	G	IP	W	L	Pct	SO	BB	H	ERA	SAVES
1994 Fort Wayne	Midwest	11	55¹/₃	4	1	.800	50	12	52	2.60	0
1994 Nashville	Southern	1	6¹/₃	0	0	.000	4	2	3	2.84	0
1995 New Britain	Eastern	28	162²/₃	7	9	.438	151	65	172	4.37	0
1996 Salt Lake	P.C.	27	160¹/₃	8	10	.444	143	57	187	4.83	0
1996 Minnesota	A.L.	7	26¹/₃	1	2	.333	15	9	45	9.23	0
1997 Salt Lake	P.C.	21	125²/₃	10	6	.625	86	57	140	4.73	0
1997 Minnesota	A.L.	13	48¹/₃	1	5	.167	26	23	64	7.63	0
1998 Salt Lake	P.C.	34	57²/₃	3	4	.429	65	31	60	4.84	9
1998 Minnesota	A.L.	14	23¹/₃	0	2	.000	23	11	25	3.86	0
1999 Salt Lake	P.C.	16	18	1	2	.333	19	6	16	2.50	1
1999 Minnesota	A.L.	52	49²/₃	2	2	.500	40	16	55	2.72	0
2000 Minnesota	A.L.	67	67	2	3	.400	62	32	83	3.90	1
Major League Totals	5 Yrs.	153	214²/₃	6	14	.300	166	91	272	5.11	1

MILLER, WADE T.

Born, Reading, Pennsylvania, September 13, 1976.
Bats Right. Throws Right. Height, 6 feet, 2 inches. Weight, 185 pounds.

Year	Club	Lea	G	IP	W	L	Pct	SO	BB	H	ERA	SAVES
1996	Astros ....Gulf Coast		11	57	3	4	.429	53	12	49	3.79	0
1996	Auburn .........N.Y.-Penn.		2	9	1	1	.500	11	4	8	5.00	0
1997	Quad City ....Midwest		10	59	5	3	.625	50	10	45	3.36	0
1997	Kissimmee ....Fla.St.		14	100	10	2	.833	76	14	79	1.80	0
1998	Jackson a ....Texas		10	62	5	0	1.000	48	27	49	2.32	0
1999	New Orleans .........P.C.		26	162⅓	11	9	.550	135	64	156	4.38	0
1999	Houston .............N.L.		5	10⅓	0	1	.000	8	5	17	9.58	0
2000	New Orleans .........P.C.		16	105⅓	4	5	.444	81	38	95	3.67	0
2000	Houston .............N.L.		16	105	6	6	.500	89	42	104	5.14	0
Major League Totals ....2 Yrs.			21	115⅓	6	7	.462	97	47	121	5.54	0

a On disabled list from June 1 to September 1, 1998.

MILLS, ALAN BERNARD

Born, Lakeland, Florida, October 18, 1966.
Bats Right. Throws Right. Height, 6 feet, 1 inch. Weight, 192 pounds.

Year	Club	Lea	G	IP	W	L	Pct	SO	BB	H	ERA	SAVES
1986	Salem a ....Northwest		14	83⅔	6	6	.500	50	60	77	4.63	0
1987	Prince William ......Carolina		35	85⅔	2	11	.154	53	54	102	6.09	1
1988	Prince William ......Carolina		42	93⅔	3	8	.273	59	43	93	4.13	4
1989	Ft. Lauderdale ....Fla. St.		22	31	1	4	.200	24	9	40	3.77	6
1989	Prince William ......Carolina		26	39⅔	6	1	.857	44	13	22	0.91	7
1990	Columbus ....Int.		17	29⅓	3	3	.500	30	14	22	3.38	6
1990	New York .............A.L.		36	41⅓	1	5	.167	24	33	48	4.10	0
1991	Columbus ....Int.		38	113⅔	7	5	.583	77	75	109	4.43	8
1991	New York b ...........A.L.		6	16⅓	1	1	.500	11	8	16	4.41	0
1992	Rochester ....Int.		3	5	0	1	.000	8	2	6	5.40	1
1992	Baltimore .............A.L.		35	103⅓	10	4	.714	60	54	78	2.61	2
1993	Baltimore c ...........A.L.		45	100⅓	5	4	.556	68	51	80	3.23	4
1994	Baltimore .............A.L.		47	45⅓	3	3	.500	44	24	43	5.16	2
1995	Rochester ....Int.		1	2⅔	0	1	.000	2	5	2	0.00	0
1995	Orioles ....Gulf Coast		1	2	0	0	.000	1	2	3	0.00	0
1995	Baltimore .............A.L.		21	23	3	0	1.000	16	18	30	7.43	0
1996	Baltimore d ...........A.L.		49	54⅔	3	2	.600	50	35	40	4.28	3
1997	Baltimore e ...........A.L.		39	38⅔	2	3	.400	32	33	41	4.89	0
1998	Baltimore f ...........A.L.		72	77	3	4	.429	57	50	55	3.74	2
1999	Los Angeles ...........N.L.		68	72⅓	3	4	.429	49	43	70	3.73	0
2000	Los Angeles g ........N.L.		18	25⅔	2	1	.667	18	16	31	4.21	1
2000	Frederick ....Carolina		1	2	0	0	.000	1	0	2	4.50	0
2000	Baltimore h ...........A.L.		23	23⅔	2	0	1.000	18	19	25	6.46	1
Major League Totals ....11 Yrs.			459	622	38	31	.551	447	384	557	3.99	15
Division Series												
1997	Baltimore .............A.L.		1	1	0	0	.000	1	0	1	0.00	0
Championship Series												
1996	Baltimore .............A.L.		3	2⅓	0	0	.000	3	1	3	3.86	0
1997	Baltimore .............A.L.		3	3⅓	0	1	.000	3	2	1	2.70	0
Championship Series Totals 6				5⅔	0	1	.000	6	3	4	3.18	0

a Traded by California Angels to New York Yankees organization to complete December 19, 1986 trade in which New York acquired pitcher Ron Romanick and player to be named for catcher Butch Wynegar, June 22, 1987.
b Traded to Baltimore Orioles for two players to be named, February 29; New York Yankees acquired pitchers Francisco de la Rosa, March 5, and Mark Carper to complete trade, June 8, 1992.
c Suspended four games by American League for June 6 fight from June 26 to June 29, 1993.
d On disabled list from April 1 to May 11, 1996.
e On disabled list from April 10 to June 15, 1997.
f Filed for free agency, October 23, 1998, signed with Los Angeles Dodgers, November 13, 1998.
g Traded to Baltimore Orioles with cash for pitcher Al Reyes, June 13, 2000.
h On disabled list from August 5 to August 30, 2000.

MILLWOOD, KEVIN AUSTIN

Born, Gastonia, North Carolina, December 24, 1974.
Bats Right. Throws Right. Height, 6 feet, 4 inches. Weight, 205 pounds.

Year	Club	Lea	G	IP	W	L	Pct	SO	BB	H	ERA	SAVES
1993	Braves ....Gulf Coast		12	50	3	3	.500	49	28	36	3.06	0
1994	Macon ....So. Atl.		12	32⅔	0	5	.000	24	32	31	5.79	1

Year	Club	Lea	G	IP	W	L	Pct	SO	BB	H	ERA	SAVES
1994 Danville	Appal.	13	46	3	3	.500	56	34	42	3.72	1
1995 Macon	So. Atl.	29	103	5	6	.455	89	57	86	4.63	0
1996 Durham	Carolina	33	149⅓	6	9	.400	139	58	138	4.28	1
1997 Greenville	Southern	11	61⅓	3	5	.375	61	24	59	4.11	0
1997 Richmond	Int.	9	60⅔	7	0	1.000	46	16	38	1.93	0
1997 Atlanta	N.L.	12	51⅓	5	3	.625	42	21	55	4.03	0
1998 Atlanta	N.L.	31	174⅓	17	8	.680	163	56	175	4.08	0
1999 Atlanta	N.L.	33	228	18	7	.720	205	59	168	2.68	0
2000 Atlanta	N.L.	36	212⅔	10	13	.435	168	62	213	4.66	0
Major League Totals	4 Yrs.	112	666⅓	50	31	.617	578	198	611	3.78	0
Division Series											
1999 Atlanta	N.L.	2	10	1	0	1.000	9	0	1	0.90	1
2000 Atlanta	N.L.	1	4⅔	0	1	.000	3	3	4	7.71	0
Division Series Totals		3	14⅔	1	1	.500	12	3	5	3.07	1
Championship Series											
1999 Atlanta	N.L.	2	12⅔	1	0	1.000	9	1	13	3.55	0
World Series											
1999 Atlanta	N.L.	1	2	0	1	.000	2	2	8	18.00	0

MILTON, ERIC ROBERT
Born, State College, Pennsylvania, August 4, 1975.
Bats Left. Throws Right. Height, 6 feet, 3 inches. Weight, 200 pounds.

Year	Club	Lea	G	IP	W	L	Pct	SO	BB	H	ERA	SAVES
1997 Tampa	Fla.St.	14	93⅓	8	3	.727	95	14	78	3.09	0
1997 Norwich	Eastern	14	77⅔	6	3	.667	67	36	59	3.13	0
1998 Minnesota a	A.L.	32	172⅓	8	14	.364	107	70	195	5.64	0
1999 Minnesota b	A.L.	34	206⅓	7	11	.389	163	63	190	4.49	0
2000 Minnesota	A.L.	33	200	13	10	.565	160	44	205	4.86	0
Major League Totals	3 Yrs.	99	578⅔	28	35	.444	430	177	590	4.96	0

a Traded by New York Yankees to Minnesota Twins with pitcher Danny Mota, infielder Christian Guzman and outfielder Brian Buchanan and reported $3 million in cash for infielder Chuck Knoblauch, February 6, 1998.

b Pitched no-hit, no-run game against Anaheim Angels, September 11, 1999.

MLICKI, DAVID JOHN
Born, Cleveland, Ohio, June 8, 1968.
Bats Right. Throws Right. Height, 6 feet, 4 inches. Weight, 190 pounds.

Year	Club	Lea	G	IP	W	L	Pct	SO	BB	H	ERA	SAVES
1990 Burlington	Appal.	8	18	3	1	.750	17	6	16	3.50	0
1990 Watertown	N.Y.-Penn.	7	32	3	0	1.000	28	11	33	3.38	0
1991 Columbus	So. Atl.	22	115⅔	8	6	.571	136	70	101	4.20	0
1992 Canton	Eastern	27	172⅔	11	9	.550	146	80	143	3.60	0
1992 Cleveland	A.L.	4	21⅔	0	2	.000	16	16	23	4.98	0
1993 Canton a	Eastern	6	23	2	1	.667	21	8	15	0.39	0
1993 Cleveland	A.L.	3	13⅓	0	0	.000	7	6	11	3.38	0
1994 Charlotte b	Int.	28	165⅓	6	10	.375	152	64	179	4.25	0
1995 New York	N.L.	29	160⅔	9	7	.563	123	54	160	4.26	0
1996 New York	N.L.	51	90	6	7	.462	83	33	95	3.30	1
1997 New York	N.L.	32	193⅔	8	12	.400	157	76	194	4.00	0
1998 New York-Los Angeles c	N.L.	30	181⅓	8	7	.533	117	63	188	4.57	0
1999 Los Angeles	N.L.	2	7⅓	0	1	.000	1	2	10	4.91	0
1999 Detroit d	A.L.	31	191⅔	14	12	.538	119	70	209	4.60	0
2000 West Michigan	Midwest	1	6	1	0	1.000	6	1	1	0.00	0
2000 Toledo	Int.	1	5⅔	0	1	.000	3	0	11	7.94	0
2000 Detroit e	A.L.	24	119⅓	6	11	.353	57	44	143	5.58	0
Major League Totals	8 Yrs.	206	979	51	59	.464	680	364	1033	4.41	1

a On disabled list from April 4 to August 4, 1993.

b Traded by Cleveland Indians to New York Mets with pitchers Jerry DiPoto and Paul Byrd and player to be named for outfielder Jeremy Burnitz and pitcher Joe Roa, November 18; New York organization acquired second baseman Jesus Azuaje to complete trade, December 6, 1994.

c Traded to Los Angeles Dodgers with pitcher Greg McMichael for pitcher Hideo Nomo and pitcher Brad Clontz, June 4, 1998.

d Traded to Detroit Tigers with pitcher Mel Rojas and cash for pitcher Rick Roberts, pitcher Robinson Checo and pitcher Apostol Garcia, April 16, 1999.

e On disabled list from July 23 to September 4, 2000.

MOEHLER, BRIAN MERRITT

Born, Rockingham, North Carolina, December 31, 1971.
Bats Right. Throws Right. Height, 6 feet, 3 inches. Weight, 225 pounds.

Year	Club	Lea	G	IP	W	L	Pct	SO	BB	H	ERA	SAVES
1993 Niagara Fls	N.Y.-Penn.		12	58²/₃	6	5	.545	38	27	51	3.22	0
1994 Lakeland	Fla. St.		26	164²/₃	12	12	.500	92	65	153	3.01	0
1995 Jacksnville	Southern		28	162¹/₃	8	10	.444	89	52	176	4.82	0
1996 Jacksnville	Southern		28	173¹/₃	15	6	.714	120	50	186	3.48	0
1996 Detroit a	A.L.		2	10¹/₃	0	1	.000	2	8	11	4.35	0
1997 Detroit a	A.L.		31	175¹/₃	11	12	.478	97	61	198	4.67	0
1998 Detroit	A.L.		33	221¹/₃	14	13	.519	123	56	220	3.90	0
1999 Detroit	A.L.		32	196¹/₃	10	*16	.385	106	59	229	5.04	0
2000 West Michigan	Midwest		1	6¹/₃	0	1	.000	4	1	5	4.26	0
2000 Detroit b	A.L.		29	178	12	9	.571	103	40	222	4.50	0
Major League Totals	5 Yrs.		127	781¹/₃	47	51	.480	431	224	880	4.50	0

On disabled list from August 7 to August 22, 1997.
On disabled list from April 17 to May 18, 2000.

MORGAN, MICHAEL THOMAS

Born, Tulare, California, October 8, 1959.
Bats Right. Throws Right. Height, 6 feet, 2 inches. Weight, 220 pounds.

Year	Club	Lea	G	IP	W	L	Pct	SO	BB	H	ERA	SAVES
1978 Oakland	A.L.		3	12	0	3	.000	0	8	19	7.50	0
1978 Vancouver	P.C.		14	92	5	6	.455	31	54	109	5.58	0
1979 Ogden	P.C.		13	101	5	5	.500	42	49	93	3.48	0
1979 Oakland	A.L.		13	77	2	10	.167	17	50	102	5.96	0
1980 Ogden a-b	P.C.		20	115	6	9	.400	46	77	135	5.40	0
1981 Nashville c	Southern		26	169	8	7	.533	100	83	164	4.42	0
1982 New York d	A.L.		30	150¹/₃	7	11	.389	71	67	167	4.37	0
1983 Toronto e	A.L.		16	45¹/₃	0	3	.000	22	21	48	5.16	0
1983 Syracuse	Int.		5	19	0	3	.000	17	13	20	5.59	1
1984 Syracuse f	Int.		34	*185²/₃	13	11	.542	105	*100	167	4.07	1
1985 Seattle g	A.L.		2	6	1	1	.500	2	5	11	12.00	0
1985 Calgary	P.C.		1	2	0	0	.000	0	0	3	4.50	0
1986 Seattle	A.L.		37	216¹/₃	11	*17	.393	116	86	243	4.53	1
1987 Seattle h	A.L.		34	207	12	17	.414	85	53	245	4.65	0
1988 Rochester	Int.		3	17	0	2	.000	7	6	19	4.76	0
1988 Baltimore i-j	A.L.		22	71¹/₃	1	6	.143	29	23	70	5.43	1
1989 Los Angeles	N.L.		40	152²/₃	8	11	.421	72	33	130	2.53	0
1990 Los Angeles	N.L.		33	211	11	15	.423	106	60	216	3.75	0
1991 Los Angeles k	N.L.		34	236¹/₃	14	10	.583	140	61	197	2.78	1
1992 Chicago	N.L.		34	240	16	8	.667	123	79	203	2.55	0
1993 Chicago l	N.L.		32	207²/₃	10	15	.400	111	74	206	4.03	0
1994 Chicago m	N.L.		15	80²/₃	2	10	.167	57	35	111	6.69	0
1995 Orlando	Southern		2	10²/₃	0	2	.000	5	7	13	7.59	0
1995 Chicago-St. Louis n-o-p	N.L.		21	131¹/₃	7	7	.500	61	34	133	3.56	0
1996 St. Petersburg	Fla. St.		1	5²/₃	1	0	1.000	4	1	4	0.00	0
1996 Louisville	A.A.		4	23	1	3	.250	10	11	29	7.04	0
1996 St. Louis-Cincinnati q-r-s	N.L.		23	130¹/₃	6	11	.353	74	47	146	4.62	0
1997 Cincinnati t-u-v	N.L.		31	162	9	12	.429	103	49	165	4.78	0
1998 Minnesota	A.L.		18	98	4	2	.667	50	24	108	3.49	0
1998 Chicago w-x-y	N.L.		5	22²/₃	0	1	.000	10	15	30	7.15	0
1999 Texas z-aa	A.L.		34	140	13	10	.565	61	48	184	6.24	0
2000 Arizona	N.L.		60	101²/₃	5	5	.500	56	40	123	4.87	5
Major League Totals	20 Yrs.		537	2700¹/₃	139	185	.429	1366	912	2857	4.22	8

Division Series

Year	Club	Lea	G	IP	W	L	Pct	SO	BB	H	ERA	SAVES
1998 Chicago	N.L.		2	1¹/₃	0	0	.000	1	0	0	0.00	0

On disabled list from May 14 to June 27, 1980.
Traded by Oakland Athletics to New York Yankees organization for infielder Fred Stanley and Brian Doyle, November 3, 1980.
On disabled list from April 9 to April 22, 1981.
Traded to Toronto Blue Jays with infielder Fred McGriff and outfielder Dave Collins for pitcher Dale Murray and outfielder Tom Dodd, December 9, 1982.
On disabled list from July 2 to August 23, 1983.
Drafted by the Seattle Mariners from Toronto Blue Jays organization, December 3, 1984.
On disabled list from April 17 to end of 1985 season.
Traded to Baltimore Orioles for pitcher Ken Dixon, December 9, 1987.
On disabled list from June 9 to July 19 and from August 12 to end of 1988 season.
Traded to Los Angeles Dodgers for outfielder Mike Devereaux, March 13, 1989.
Filed for free agency, October 28; signed with Chicago Cubs, December 3, 1991.
On disabled list from June 14 to June 29, 1993.

m On disabled list from May 9 to May 25, June 5 to June 22, and July 28 to end of 1994 season.
n On disabled list from April 25 to May 25 and July 4 to July 24, 1995.
o Traded to St. Louis Cardinals with infielder Paul Torres and catcher Francisco Morales for infielder Todd Zeil June 16, 1995.
p Filed for free agency, November 12, 1995; re-signed with St. Louis Cardinals, December 7, 1995.
q On disabled list from April 1 to May 18, 1996.
r Released by St. Louis Cardinals, August 28, 1996.
s Signed with Cincinnati Reds, September 3, 1996. On disabled list from June 8 to June 24, 1997.
u Filed for free agency, October 28, 1997.
v Signed as free agent by Minnesota Twins, December 15, 1997.
w On disabled list from June 27 to July 13 and July 15 to August 16, 1998.
x Traded to Chicago Cubs for player to be named later and cash, August 25, 1998. Minnesota Twins received pitcher Scott Downs to complete trade, November 3, 1998.
y Filed for free agency, October 30, 1998. Signed with Texas Rangers organization, January 26, 1999.
z On disabled list from May 24 to June 8, 1999.
aa Filed for free agency, November 8, 1999. Signed with Arizona Diamondbacks, January 14, 2000.

MORRIS, MATTHEW CHRISTIAN

Born, Middletown, New York, August 9, 1994.
Bats Right. Throws Right. Height, 6 feet, 5 inches. Weight, 210 pounds.

Year	Club	Lea	G	IP	W	L	Pct	SO	BB	H	ERA	SAVE
1995 New Jersey	N.Y.-Penn.	2	11	2	0	1.000	13	3	12	1.64	0
1995 St. Petersburg	Fla. St.	6	34	3	2	.600	31	11	22	2.38	0
1996 Arkansas	Texas	27	167	12	12	.500	120	48	178	3.88	0
1996 Louisville	A.A.	1	8	0	1	.00	9	1	8	3.38	0
1997 St. Louis	N.L.	33	217	12	9	.571	149	69	208	3.19	0
1998 Arkansas	Texas	1	4	0	0	.000	2	0	4	0.00	1
1998 Memphis	P.C.	4	14	1	0	1.000	21	4	16	4.50	0
1998 St. Louis a	N.L.	17	113²/₃	7	5	.583	79	42	101	2.53	0
1999 St.Louis b	N.L.	INJURED - Did Not Play									
2000 Arkansas	Texas	2	7	0	0	.000	7	4	8	6.43	0
2000 Memphis	P.C.	3	14²/₃	1	2	.333	8	6	20	7.98	0
2000 St. Louis c	N.L.	31	53	3	3	.500	34	17	53	3.57	4
Major League Totals	3 Yrs.	81	383²/₃	22	17	.564	262	128	362	3.05	4
Division Series												
2000 St. Louis	N.L.	2	2	0	0	.000	0	1	0	0.00	0
Championship Series												
2000 St. Louis	N.L.	2	3²/₃	0	0	.000	2	2	3	4.91	0

a On disabled list from March 31 to April 11 and April 12 to July 10, 1998.
b On disabled list from March 26 to November 8, 1999.
c On disabled list from March 25 to May 27, 2000.

MOYER, JAMIE

Born, Sellersville, Pennsylvania, November 18, 1962.
Bats Left. Throws Left. Height, 6 feet. Weight, 170 pounds.

Year	Club	Lea	G	IP	W	L	Pct	SO	BB	H	ERA	SAVE
1984 Geneva	N.Y.-Penn.	14	*104²/₃	*9	3	.750	*120	31	59	1.89	0
1985 Winston-Salem	Carolina	12	94	8	2	.800	94	22	82	2.30	0
1985 Pittsfield	Eastern	15	96²/₃	7	6	.538	51	32	99	3.72	0
1986 Pittsfield	Eastern	6	41	3	1	.750	42	16	27	0.88	0
1986 Iowa	A.A.	6	42¹/₃	3	2	.600	25	11	25	2.55	0
1986 Chicago	N.L.	16	87¹/₃	7	4	.636	45	42	107	5.05	0
1987 Chicago	N.L.	35	201	12	15	.444	147	97	210	5.10	0
1988 Chicago a	N.L.	34	202	9	15	.375	121	55	212	3.48	0
1989 Charlotte Rangers	Gulf C.	3	11	1	0	1.000	18	1	8	1.64	0
1989 Tulsa	Texas	2	12¹/₃	1	1	.500	9	3	16	5.11	0
1989 Texas b	A.L.	15	76	4	9	.308	44	33	84	4.86	0
1990 Texas c	A.L.	33	102¹/₃	2	6	.250	58	39	115	4.66	0
1991 Louisville	A.A.	20	125²/₃	5	10	.333	69	43	125	3.80	0
1991 St. Louis d-e	N.L.	8	31¹/₃	0	5	.000	20	16	38	5.74	0
1992 Toledo f	Int.	21	138²/₃	10	8	.556	80	37	128	2.86	0
1993 Rochester	Int.	8	54	6	0	1.000	41	13	42	1.67	0
1993 Baltimore	A.L.	25	152	12	9	.571	90	38	154	3.43	0
1994 Baltimore	A.L.	23	149	5	7	.417	87	38	158	4.77	0
1995 Baltimore g-h	A.L.	27	115²/₃	8	6	.571	65	30	117	5.21	0
1996 Boston-Seattle i-j-k	A.L.	34	160²/₃	13	3	*.813	79	46	177	3.98	0
1997 Tacoma	P.C.	1	5	1	0	1.000	6	0	1	0.00	0
1997 Seattle l	A.L.	30	188²/₃	17	5	.773	113	43	187	3.86	0
1998 Seattle	A.L.	34	234¹/₃	15	9	.625	158	42	234	3.53	0

Year Club	Lea	G	IP	W	L	Pct	SO	BB	H	ERA	SAVES
1999 Seattle	A.L.	32	228	14	8	.636	137	48	235	3.87	0
2000 Seattle m	A.L.	26	154	13	10	.565	98	53	173	5.49	0
Major League Totals .... 14 Yrs.		372	2082$\frac{1}{3}$	131	111	.541	1262	620	2201	4.30	0
Divisional Series											
1997 Seattle	A.L.	1	4$\frac{2}{3}$	0	1	.000	2	1	5	5.79	0

a Traded to Texas Rangers with outfielder Rafael Palmeiro and pitcher Drew Hall for infielders Curtis Wilkerson and Luis Benetiz, pitchers Mitch Williams, Paul Kilgus and Steve Wilson, and outfielder Pablo Delgado, December 5, 1988.
b On disabled list from May 31 to September 1, 1989.
c Released, November 13, 1990; signed with St. Louis Cardinals organization, January 10, 1991.
d Became free agent, October 15, 1991; signed with Chicago Cubs organization, January 8, 1992.
e Released by Chicago Cubs, March 30; signed with Detroit Tigers organization, May 24, 1992.
f Became free agent, October 15; signed with Baltimore Orioles organization, December 19, 1992.
g Filed for free agency, November 12, 1995.
h Signed with Signed with Boston Red Sox, January 2, 1996.
i Traded to Seattle Mariners for outfielder Darren Bragg, July 30, 1996.
j Filed for free agency, October 29, 1996.
k Re-signed with Seattle Mariners, November 20, 1996.
l On disabled list from April 1 to April 29, 1997.
m On disabled list from April 15 to June 1, 2000.

MULDER, MARK ALAN

Born, South Holland, Illinois, August 5, 1977.
Bats Left. Throws Right. Height, 6 feet, 6 inches. Weight, 200 pounds.

Year Club	Lea	G	IP	W	L	Pct	SO	BB	H	ERA	SAVES
1999 Vancouver	P.C.	22	128$\frac{2}{3}$	6	7	.462	81	31	152	4.06	0
2000 Sacramento	P.C.	2	8$\frac{1}{3}$	1	1	.500	6	4	15	5.40	0
2000 Oakland	A.L.	27	154	9	10	.474	88	69	191	5.44	0

MULHOLLAND, TERENCE JOHN

Born, Uniontown, Pennsylvania, March 9, 1963.
Bats Right. Throws Left. Height, 6 feet, 3 inches. Weight, 215 pounds.

Year Club	Lea	G	IP	W	L	Pct	SO	BB	H	ERA	SAVES
1984 Everett	Northwest	3	19	1	0	1.000	15	4	10	0.00	0
1984 Fresno	California	9	42$\frac{2}{3}$	5	2	.714	39	36	32	2.95	0
1985 Shreveport	Texas	26	176$\frac{2}{3}$	9	8	.529	122	87	166	2.90	0
1986 Phoenix	P.C.	17	111	8	5	.615	77	56	112	4.46	0
1986 San Francisco	N.L.	15	54$\frac{2}{3}$	1	7	.125	27	35	51	4.94	0
1987 Phoenix	P.C.	37	172$\frac{1}{3}$	7	12	.368	94	90	200	5.07	1
1988 Phoenix	P.C.	19	100$\frac{2}{3}$	7	3	.700	57	44	116	3.58	0
1988 San Francisco a	N.L.	9	46	2	1	.667	18	7	50	3.72	0
1989 Phoenix	P.C.	13	78$\frac{1}{3}$	5	4	.444	61	26	67	2.99	0
1989 S.F.-Philadelphia b	N.L.	25	115$\frac{1}{3}$	4	7	.364	66	36	137	4.92	0
1990 Scranton	Int.	1	6	0	1	.000	2	2	9	3.00	0
1990 Philadelphia c-d	N.L.	33	180$\frac{2}{3}$	9	10	.474	75	42	172	3.34	0
1991 Philadelphia e	N.L.	34	232	16	13	.552	142	49	231	3.61	0
1992 Philadelphia	N.L.	32	229	13	11	.542	125	46	227	3.81	0
1993 Philadelphia f	N.L.	29	191	12	9	.571	116	40	177	3.25	0
1994 New York f-g	A.L.	24	120$\frac{2}{3}$	6	7	.462	72	37	150	6.49	0
1995 Phoenix	P.C.	1	4	0	0	.000	4	1	4	2.25	0
1995 San Francisco h-i-j	N.L.	29	149	5	13	.278	65	38	190	5.80	0
1996 Philadelphia	N.L.	21	133$\frac{1}{3}$	8	7	.533	52	21	157	4.66	0
1996 Seattle k-l-m	A.L.	12	69$\frac{1}{3}$	5	4	.556	34	28	75	4.67	0
1997 Chicago-San Francisco n-o	N.L.	40	186$\frac{2}{3}$	6	13	.316	99	51	190	4.24	0
1998 Chicago p	N.L.	70	112	6	5	.545	72	39	100	2.89	3
1999 Chicago-Atlanta q	N.L.	42	170$\frac{1}{3}$	10	8	.556	83	45	201	4.39	1
2000 Atlanta r	N.L.	54	156$\frac{2}{3}$	9	9	.500	78	41	198	5.11	1
Major League Totals .... 14 Yrs.		469	2146$\frac{2}{3}$	112	124	.475	1124	555	2306	4.28	5
Division Series											
1998 Chicago	N.L.	2	2$\frac{1}{3}$	0	1	.000	2	2	2	11.57	0
1999 Atlanta	N.L.	2	0$\frac{2}{3}$	0	0	.000	0	0	3	27.00	0
2000 Atlanta	N.L.	3	3$\frac{1}{3}$	0	0	.000	1	2	1	5.40	0
Division Series Totals		7	6$\frac{1}{3}$	0	1	.000	3	4	6	9.95	0
Championship Series											
1993 Philadelphia	N.L.	1	5	0	1	.000	2	1	9	7.20	0
1999 Atlanta	N.L.	2	2$\frac{2}{3}$	0	0	.000	2	1	1	0.00	0
Championship Series Totals		3	7$\frac{2}{3}$	0	1	.000	4	2	10	4.70	0

Year Club	Lea	G	IP	W	L	Pct	SO	BB	H	ERA	SAVES
World Series Record											
1993 Philadelphia	N.L.	2	10²/₃	1	0	1.000	5	3	14	6.75	0
1999 Atlanta	N.L.	2	3²/₃	0	0	.000	3	1	5	7.36	0
World Series Totals		4	14¹/₃	1	0	1.000	8	4	19	6.91	0

a On disabled list from August 1 to end of 1988 season.
b Traded to Philadelphia Phillies with pitcher Dennis Cook and infielder Charlie Hayes for pitcher Steve Bedrosian and player to be named, June 18; San Francisco Giants acquired infielder Rich Parker to complete trade, August 6, 1989.
c On disabled list from June 9 to June 28, 1990.
d Pitched no-hit, no-run game against San Francisco Giants, winning 6-0, August 15, 1990.
e Appeared in one additional game as pinch runner.
f Traded to New York Yankees with player to be named for pitchers Bobby Munoz and Ryan Karp and infielder Kevin Jordan, February 9; New York acquired pitcher Jeff Patterson to complete trade, November 8, 1994.
g Filed for free agency, October 27, 1994.
h Signed with San Francisco Giants, April 8, 1995.
i On disabled list from June 6 to July 4, 1995.
j Filed for free agency, November 12, 1995. Signed with Philadelphia Phillies organization, February 17, 1996.
k Traded to Seattle Mariners for infielder Desi Relaford, July 31, 1996.
l Filed for free agency, October 28, 1996.
m Signed with Chicago Cubs, December 9, 1996.
n Claimed on waivers by San Francisco Giants, August 8, 1997.
o Filed for free agency, October 27, 1997.
p Filed for free agency, October 28, 1998, re-signed with Chicago Cubs, November 6, 1998.
q Traded to Atlanta Braves with infielder Jose Hernandez for pitcher Micah Bowie, pitcher Ruben Quevedo and player to be named later, July 31, 1999. Chicago Cubs received pitcher Joey Nation to complete trade, August 24, 1999.
r Filed for free agency, October 31, 2000, signed with Pittsburgh Pirates, December 8, 2000.

MUSSINA, MICHAEL COLE

Born, Williamsport, Pennsylvania, December 8, 1968.
Bats Right. Throws Right. Height, 6 feet, 2 inches. Weight, 185 pounds.

Year Club	Lea	G	IP	W	L	Pct	SO	BB	H	ERA	SAVES
1990 Hagerstown	Eastern	7	42¹/₃	3	0	1.000	40	7	34	1.49	0
1990 Rochester	Int.	2	13¹/₃	0	0	.000	15	4	8	1.35	0
1991 Rochester a	Int.	19	122¹/₃	10	4	.714	107	31	108	2.87	0
1991 Baltimore	A.L.	12	87²/₃	4	5	.444	52	21	77	2.87	0
1992 Baltimore	A.L.	32	241	18	5	*.783	130	48	212	2.54	0
1993 Bowie	Eastern	2	8	1	0	1.000	10	1	5	2.25	0
1993 Baltimore b	A.L.	25	167²/₃	14	6	.700	117	44	163	4.46	0
1994 Baltimore	A.L.	24	176¹/₃	16	5	.762	99	42	163	3.06	0
1995 Baltimore	A.L.	32	221²/₃	*19	9	.679	158	50	187	3.29	0
1996 Baltimore	A.L.	36	243¹/₃	19	11	.633	204	69	264	4.81	0
1997 Baltimore	A.L.	33	224²/₃	15	8	.652	218	54	197	3.20	0
1998 Baltimore c	A.L.	29	206¹/₃	13	10	.565	175	41	189	3.49	0
1999 Baltimore	A.L.	31	203¹/₃	18	7	.720	172	52	207	3.50	0
2000 Baltimore d	A.L.	34	*237²/₃	11	15	.423	210	46	236	3.79	0
Major League Totals . . . . 10 Yrs.		288	2009²/₃	147	81	.645	1535	467	1895	3.53	0
Division Series											
1996 Baltimore	A.L.	1	6	0	0	.000	6	2	7	4.50	0
1997 Baltimore	A.L.	2	14	2	0	1.000	16	3	7	1.93	0
Division Series Totals 3			20	2	0	1.000	22	5	14	2.70	0
Championship Series											
1996 Baltimore	A.L.	1	7²/₃	0	1	.000	6	2	8	5.87	0
1997 Baltimore	A.L.	2	15	0	0	.000	25	4	4	0.60	0
Championship Series Totals 3			22²/₃	0	1	.000	31	6	12	2.38	0

a On disabled list from May 5 to May 12, 1991.
b On disabled list from July 22 to August 20, 1993.
c On disabled list from April 17 to May 3 and May 15 to June 6, 1998.
d Filed for free agency, October 27, 2000, signed with New York Yankees, November 30, 2000.

MYERS, MICHAEL STANLEY

Born, Cook County, Illinois, June 26, 1969.
Bats Left. Throws Left. Height, 6 feet, 3 inches. Weight, 200 pounds.

Year Club	Lea	G	IP	W	L	Pct	SO	BB	H	ERA	SAVES
1990 Everett	Northwest	15	85¹/₃	4	5	.444	73	30	91	3.90	0
1991 Clinton	Midwest	11	65¹/₃	5	3	.625	59	18	61	2.62	0
1991 Giants	Arizona	1	3	0	1	.000	2	2	5	12.00	0
1992 Clinton	Midwest	7	37²/₃	1	2	.333	32	8	28	1.19	0
1992 San Jose a	California	8	54²/₃	5	1	.833	40	17	43	2.30	0

Year	Club	Lea	G	IP	W	L	Pct	SO	BB	H	ERA	SAVES
1993 Edmonton		P.C.	27	161²/₃	7	14	.333	112	52	195	5.18	0
1994 Brevard City		Fla. St.	3	11¹/₃	0	0	.000	15	4	7	0.79	0
1994 Edmonton		P.C.	12	60	1	5	.167	55	21	78	5.55	0
1995 Charlotte		Int.	37	36²/₃	0	5	.000	24	15	41	5.65	0
1995 Toledo		Int.	6	8¹/₃	0	0	.000	8	3	6	4.32	0
1995 Florida		N.L.	2	2	0	0	.000	0	3	1	0.00	0
1995 Detroit b-c		A.L.	11	6¹/₃	1	0	1.000	4	4	10	9.95	0
1996 Detroit		A.L.	*83	64²/₃	1	5	.167	69	34	70	5.01	6
1997 Detroit d		A.L.	*88	53²/₃	0	4	.000	50	25	58	5.70	2
1998 Milwaukee		N.L.	70	50	2	2	.500	40	22	44	2.70	1
1999 Milwaukee f		N.L.	71	41¹/₃	2	1	.667	35	13	46	5.23	0
2000 Colorado		N.L.	78	45¹/₃	0	1	.000	41	24	24	1.99	1
Major League Totals	6 Yrs.		403	263¹/₃	6	13	.316	239	125	253	4.31	10

a Selected by Florida Marlins from San Francisco Giants in Rule V draft, December 7, 1992.
b Buddy Groom was traded to Florida Marlins for player to be named later, August 7, 1995.
c Detroit Tigers received pitcher Mike Myers to complete trade, August 9, 1995.
d Traded to Milwaukee Brewers with pitcher Rick Greene and infielder Santiago Perez for pitcher Bryce Florie and player to be named later, November 21, 1997.
f Traded to Colorado Rockies for pitcher Curtis Leskanic, November 17, 1999.

NAGY, CHARLES HARRISON

Born, Bridgeport, Connecticut, May 5, 1967.
Bats Left. Throws Right. Height, 6 feet, 3 inches. Weight, 200 pounds.

Year	Club	Lea	G	IP	W	L	Pct	SO	BB	H	ERA	SAVES
1989 Kinston		Carolina	13	95¹/₃	8	4	.667	99	24	69	1.51	0
1989 Canton		Eastern	15	94	4	5	.444	65	32	102	3.35	0
1990 Canton		Eastern	23	175	13	8	.619	99	39	132	2.52	0
1990 Cleveland		A.L.	9	45²/₃	2	4	.333	26	21	58	5.91	0
1991 Cleveland		A.L.	33	211¹/₃	10	15	.400	109	66	228	4.13	0
1992 Cleveland		A.L.	33	252	17	10	.630	169	57	245	2.96	0
1993 Canton		Eastern	2	8	0	0	.000	4	2	1	1.13	0
1993 Cleveland a		A.L.	9	48²/₃	2	6	.250	30	13	66	6.29	0
1994 Cleveland		A.L.	23	169¹/₃	10	8	.556	108	48	175	3.45	0
1995 Cleveland		A.L.	29	178	16	6	.727	139	61	194	4.55	0
1996 Cleveland		A.L.	32	222	17	5	.773	167	61	217	3.41	0
1997 Cleveland		A.L.	34	227	15	11	.577	149	77	253	4.28	0
1998 Cleveland		A.L.	33	210¹/₃	15	10	.600	120	66	250	5.22	0
1999 Cleveland		A.L.	33	202	17	11	.607	126	59	238	4.95	0
2000 Akron		Eastern	2	9	1	0	1.000	10	2	4	1.00	0
2000 Buffalo		Int.	3	14²/₃	1	1	.500	5	4	12	4.30	0
2000 Cleveland b		A.L.	11	57	2	7	.222	41	21	71	8.21	0
Major League Totals	11 Yrs.		279	1823¹/₃	123	93	.569	1184	550	1995	4.32	0
Division Series												
1995 Cleveland		A.L.	1	7	1	0	1.000	6	5	4	1.29	0
1996 Cleveland		A.L.	2	11¹/₃	0	1	.000	13	5	15	7.15	0
1997 Cleveland		A.L.	1	3²/₃	0	1	.000	1	6	2	9.82	0
1998 Cleveland		A.L.	1	8	1	0	1.000	3	0	4	1.13	0
1999 Cleveland		A.L.	2	10	1	0	1.000	6	2	11	7.20	0
Division Series Totals			7	40	3	2	.600	29	18	36	5.18	0
Championship Series												
1995 Cleveland		A.L.	1	8	0	0	.000	6	0	5	1.13	0
1997 Cleveland		A.L.	2	13	0	0	.000	5	5	17	2.77	0
1998 Cleveland		A.L.	2	9²/₃	0	1	.000	6	1	13	3.72	0
Championship Series Totals			5	30²/₃	0	1	.000	17	6	35	2.64	0
World Series Record												
1995 Cleveland		A.L.	1	7	0	0	.000	4	1	8	6.43	0
1997 Cleveland		A.L.	2	7	0	1	.000	5	5	8	6.43	0
World Series Totals			3	14	0	1	.000	9	6	16	6.43	0

On disabled list from May 17 to October 1, 1993.
On disabled list from May 17 to September 13 and September 25 to October 1, 2000.

NATHAN, JOSEPH MICHAEL (JOE)

Born, Houston, Texas, November 22, 1974.
Bats Right. Throws Right. Height, 6 feet, 4 inches. Weight, 195 pounds.

Year	Club	Lea	G	IP	W	L	Pct	SO	BB	H	ERA	SAVES
1997	Salem-Keizer	Northwest	18	62	2	1	.667	44	26	53	2.47	2
1998	Shreveport	Texas	4	15⅓	1	3	.250	10	9	20	8.80	0
1998	San Jose	California	22	122	8	6	.571	118	48	100	3.32	0
1999	Shreveport	Texas	2	8⅔	0	1	.000	7	7	5	3.12	0
1999	Fresno	P.C.	13	74⅔	6	4	.600	82	36	68	4.46	0
1999	San Francisco	N.L.	19	90⅓	7	4	.636	54	46	84	4.18	1
2000	San Jose	California	1	5	0	1	.000	2	1	4	3.60	0
2000	Bakersfield	California	1	5⅓	1	0	1.000	6	7	2	5.06	0
2000	Fresno	P.C.	3	14⅓	0	2	.000	9	7	15	4.40	0
2000	San Francisco a	N.L.	20	93⅓	5	2	.714	61	63	89	5.21	0
Major League Totals	2 Yrs.		39	183⅔	12	6	.667	115	109	173	4.70	1

a On disabled list from May 13 to June 5 and July 14 to August 18, 2000.

NEAGLE, DENNIS EDWARD JR. (DENNY)

Born, Prince Georges County, Maryland, September 13, 1968.
Bats Left. Throws Left. Height 6 feet, 4 inches. Weight, 217 pounds.

Year	Club	Lea	G	IP	W	L	Pct	SO	BB	H	ERA	SAVES
1989	Elizabethton	Appal.	6	22	1	2	.333	32	8	20	4.50	1
1989	Kenosha	Midwest	6	43⅔	2	1	.667	40	16	25	1.65	0
1990	Visalia	California	10	63	8	0	1.000	92	16	39	1.43	0
1991	Orlando	Southern	17	121⅓	12	3	.800	94	31	94	2.45	0
1991	Portland	P.C.	19	104⅔	9	4	.692	94	32	101	3.27	0
1991	Minnesota a-b	A.L.	7	20	0	1	.000	14	7	28	4.05	0
1992	Pittsburgh c	N.L.	55	86⅓	4	6	.400	77	43	81	4.48	2
1993	Buffalo	A.A.	3	3⅓	0	0	.000	6	2	3	0.00	1
1993	Pittsburgh	N.L.	50	81⅓	3	5	.375	73	37	82	5.31	0
1994	Pittsburgh	N.L.	24	137	9	10	.474	122	49	135	5.12	0
1995	Pittsburgh	N.L.	31	*209⅔	13	8	.619	150	45	*221	3.43	0
1996	Pittsburgh-Atlanta d	N.L.	33	221⅓	16	9	.640	149	48	226	3.49	0
1997	Atlanta	N.L.	34	233⅓	*20	5	.800	172	49	204	2.97	0
1998	Atlanta e	N.L.	32	210⅓	16	11	.593	165	60	196	3.55	0
1999	Indianapolis	Int.	3	17⅓	2	0	1.000	9	2	11	4.67	0
1999	Cincinnati f	N.L.	20	111⅔	9	5	.643	76	40	95	4.27	0
2000	Cincinnati g	N.L.	18	117⅔	8	2	.800	88	50	111	3.52	0
2000	New York h	A.L.	16	91⅓	7	7	.500	58	31	99	5.81	0
Major League Totals	10 Yrs.		320	1520	105	69	.603	1144	459	1478	3.92	3
Championship Series												
1992	Pittsburgh	N.L.	2	1⅔	0	0	.000	0	3	4	27.00	0
1996	Atlanta	N.L.	2	7⅔	0	0	.000	8	3	2	2.35	0
1997	Atlanta	N.L.	2	12	1	0	1.000	9	1	5	0.00	0
1998	Atlanta	N.L.	2	7⅔	0	0	.000	9	2	8	3.52	0
2000	New York	A.L.	2	10	0	2	.000	7	7	6	4.50	0
Championship Series Totals			10	39	1	2	.333	33	16	25	3.46	0
World Series Record												
1996	Atlanta	N.L.	2	6	0	0	.000	3	4	5	3.00	0
2000	New York	A.L.	1	4⅔	0	0	.000	3	2	4	3.86	0
World Series Totals			3	10⅔	0	0	.000	6	6	9	3.38	0

a On disabled list from July 28 to August 12, 1991.
b Traded to Pittsburgh Pirates with outfielder Midre Cummings for pitcher John Smiley, March 17, 1992.
c Appeared in one additional game as pinch runner.
d Traded to Atlanta Braves for infielder Ron Wright, outfielder Corey Pointer and pitcher Jason Schmidt, August 29, 1996.
e Traded to Cincinnati Reds with outfielder Michael Tucker and pitcher Rob Bell for infielder Bret Boone and pitcher Mike Remlinger, November 10, 1998.
f On disabled list from March 24 to April 21 and May 20 to July 30, 1999.
g Traded to New York Yankees with outfielder Mike Frank for infielder Drew Henson, outfielder Jackson Melian, pitcher Ed Yarnall and pitcher Brian Reith, July 12, 2000.
h Filed for free agency, October 31, 2000, signed with Colorado Rockies, December 4, 2000.

NELSON, JEFFREY ALLAN
Born, Baltimore, Maryland, November 17, 1996.
Bats Right. Throws Right. Height, 6 feet, 8 inches. Weight, 235 pounds.

Year	Club	Lea	G	IP	W	L	Pct	SO	BB	H	ERA	SAVES
1984	Great Falls	Pioneer	1	0²/₃	0	0	.000	1	3	3	54.00	0
1984	Bradenton Dodgers	G.C.	9	13¹/₃	0	0	.000	7	6	6	1.35	0
1985	Bradenton Dodgers	G.C.	14	47¹/₃	0	5	.000	31	32	72	5.51	0
1986	Bakersfield a	California	24	71¹/₃	0	7	.000	37	84	80	5.74	0
1986	Great Falls	Pioneer	3	2	0	0	.000	1	3	5	13.50	0
1987	Salinas	California	17	80	3	7	.300	43	71	80	5.74	0
1988	San Bernardino	California	27	149¹/₃	8	9	.471	94	91	163	5.54	0
1989	Williamsport b	Eastern	15	92¹/₃	7	5	.583	61	53	72	3.31	0
1990	Williamsport	Eastern	10	43¹/₃	1	4	.200	14	18	65	6.44	0
1990	Peninsula	Carolina	18	60	2	2	.500	49	25	47	3.15	6
1991	Jacksonville	Southern	21	28¹/₃	4	0	1.000	34	9	23	1.27	12
1991	Calgary	P.C.	28	32¹/₃	3	4	.429	26	15	39	3.90	7
1992	Seattle	A.L.	66	81	1	7	.125	46	44	71	3.44	6
1992	Calgary	P.C.	2	3²/₃	1	0	1.000	0	1	0	0.00	0
1993	Calgary	P.C.	5	7²/₃	1	0	1.000	6	2	6	1.17	1
1993	Seattle	A.L.	71	60	5	3	.625	61	34	57	4.35	1
1994	Calgary	P.C.	18	25¹/₃	1	4	.200	30	7	21	2.84	8
1994	Seattle	A.L.	28	42¹/₃	0	0	.000	44	20	35	2.76	0
1995	Seattle c	A.L.	62	78²/₃	7	3	.700	96	27	58	2.17	2
1996	New York	A.L.	73	74¹/₃	4	4	.500	91	36	75	4.36	2
1997	New York	A.L.	77	78²/₃	3	7	.300	81	37	53	2.86	2
1998	Tampa	Fla.St.	2	2	0	0	.000	4	1	1	0.00	0
1998	New York d	A.L.	45	40¹/₃	5	3	.625	35	22	44	3.79	3
1999	Tampa	Fla.St.	3	3	0	0	.000	5	2	1	0.00	0
1999	GC Yankees	Gulf Coast	2	2	0	0	.000	3	1	1	0.00	0
1999	New York e	A.L.	39	30¹/₃	2	1	.667	35	22	27	4.15	1
2000	New York f	A.L.	73	69²/₃	8	4	.667	71	45	44	2.45	0
Major League Totals		9 Yrs.	534	555¹/₃	35	32	.522	560	287	464	3.29	17
	Division Series											
1995	Seattle	A.L.	3	5²/₃	0	1	.000	7	3	7	3.18	0
1996	New York	A.L.	2	3²/₃	1	0	1.000	5	2	2	0.00	0
1997	New York	A.L.	4	4	0	0	.000	0	2	4	0.00	0
1998	New York	A.L.	2	2²/₃	0	0	.000	2	1	2	0.00	0
1999	New York	A.L.	3	1²/₃	0	0	.000	3	1	1	0.00	0
2000	New York	A.L.	2	2	0	0	.000	2	0	0	0.00	0
Division Series Totals			16	19²/₃	1	1	.500	19	9	16	0.92	0
	Championship Series											
1995	Seattle	A.L.	3	3	0	0	.000	3	5	3	0.00	0
1996	New York	A.L.	2	2¹/₃	0	1	.000	2	0	5	11.57	0
1998	New York	A.L.	3	1¹/₃	0	1	.000	3	1	3	20.25	0
1999	New York	A.L.	2	0²/₃	0	0	.000	0	0	0	0.00	0
2000	New York	A.L.	3	3	0	0	.000	6	0	5	9.00	0
Championship Series Totals			13	10¹/₃	0	2	.000	14	6	16	7.84	0
	World Series Record											
1996	New York	A.L.	3	4¹/₃	0	0	.000	5	1	1	0.00	0
1998	New York	A.L.	3	2¹/₃	0	0	.000	4	1	2	0.00	0
1999	New York	A.L.	4	2²/₃	0	0	.000	3	1	2	0.00	0
2000	New York	A.L.	3	2²/₃	1	0	1.000	1	1	5	10.13	0
World Series Totals			13	12	1	0	1.000	13	4	10	2.25	0

a Drafted by Seattle Mariners from Los Angeles Dodgers organization in minor league draft, December 9, 1986.
b On disabled list from July 16 to end of 1989 season.
c Traded by Seattle Mariners to New York Yankees with infielder Tino Martinez and pitcher Jim Mecir for infielder Russ Davis and pitcher Sterling Hitchcock, December 7, 1995.
d On disabled list from June 25 to September 4, 1998.
e On disabled list from May 3 to May 20 and June 3 to August 11, 1999.
f Filed for free agency, October 31, 2000, signed with Seattle Mariners, December 4, 2000.

NEN, ROBERT ALLEN (ROB)
Born, San Pedro, California, November 28, 1969.
Bats Right. Throws Right. Height, 6 feet, 4 inches. Weight, 200 pounds.

Year	Club	Lea	G	IP	W	L	Pct	SO	BB	H	ERA	SAVES
1987	Sarasota Rangers	Gulf C.	2	2¹/₃	0	0	.000	4	3	4	7.71	0
1988	Gastonia	So. Atl.	14	48¹/₃	0	5	.000	36	45	69	7.45	0
1988	Butte	Pioneer	14	48¹/₃	4	5	.444	30	45	65	8.75	0

Year	Club	Lea	G	IP	W	L	Pct	SO	BB	H	ERA	SAVES
1989 Gastonia	So. Atl.	24	138⅓	7	4	.636	146	76	96	2.41	0
1990 Charlotte a	Fla. St.	11	53⅔	1	4	.200	38	36	44	3.69	0
1990 Tulsa	Texas	7	26⅔	0	5	.000	21	21	23	5.06	0
1991 Tulsa b	Texas	6	28	0	2	.000	23	20	24	5.79	0
1992 Tulsa c	Texas	4	25	1	1	.500	20	2	21	2.16	0
1993 Oklahoma City	A.A.	6	28⅓	0	2	.000	12	18	45	6.67	0
1993 Texas d-e	A.L.	9	22⅔	1	1	.500	12	26	28	6.35	0
1993 Florida	N.L.	15	33⅓	1	0	1.000	27	20	35	7.02	0
1994 Florida	N.L.	44	58	5	5	.500	60	17	46	2.95	15
1995 Florida	N.L.	62	65⅔	0	7	.000	68	23	62	3.29	23
1996 Florida	N.L.	75	83	5	1	.833	92	21	67	1.95	35
1997 Florida f	N.L.	73	74	9	3	.750	81	40	72	3.89	35
1998 San Francisco	N.L.	78	88⅔	7	7	.500	110	25	59	1.52	40
1999 San Francisco	N.L.	72	72⅓	3	8	.273	77	27	79	3.98	37
2000 San Francisco	N.L.	68	66	4	3	.571	92	19	37	1.50	41
Major League Totals 8 Yrs.		496	563⅔	35	35	.500	619	218	485	3.08	226
Division Series											
1997 Florida	N.L.	2	2	1	0	1.000	2	2	1	0.00	0
2000 San Francisco	N.L.	2	2⅓	0	0	.000	3	1	2	0.00	0
Division Series Totals		4	4⅓	1	0	1.000	5	3	3	0.00	0
Championship Series											
1997 Florida	N.L.	2	2	0	0	.000	1	0	0	0.00	2
World Series Record											
1997 Florida	N.L.	2	4⅔	0	0	.000	7	2	8	7.71	2

a On disabled list from March 28 to April 26 and May 6 to May 24, 1990.
b On disabled list from April 18 to June 10, June 29 to July 8 and July 9 to end of 1991 season.
c On disabled list from April 29 to end of 1992 season.
d On disabled list from June 13 to July 17, 1993.
e Traded to Florida Marlins with pitcher Kurt Miller for pitcher Cris Carpenter, July 17, 1993.
f Traded to San Francisco Giants for pitcher Joe Fontenot, pitcher Mike Villano and pitcher Mick Pageler, November 18, 1997.

NITKOWSKI, CHRISTOPHER (C. J.)

Born, Suffern, New York, March 9, 1973.
Bats Left. Throws Right. Height, 6 feet, 2 inches. Weight, 185 pounds.

Year	Club	Lea	G	IP	W	L	Pct	SO	BB	H	ERA	SAVES
1994 Chattanooga	Southern	14	74⅔	6	3	.667	60	40	61	3.50	0
1995 Chattanooga	Southern	8	50⅓	4	2	.667	52	20	39	2.50	0
1995 Cincinnati	N.L.	9	32⅓	1	3	.250	18	15	41	6.12	0
1995 Indianapolis	A.A.	6	27⅔	0	2	.000	21	10	28	5.20	0
1995 Detroit a-b	A.L.	11	39⅓	1	4	.200	13	20	53	7.09	0
1996 Toledo	Int.	19	111	4	6	.400	103	53	104	4.46	0
1996 Detroit c-d	A.L.	11	45⅔	2	3	.400	36	38	62	8.08	0
1997 New Orleans	A.A.	28	174⅓	8	10	.444	141	56	183	3.98	0
1998 New Orleans	P.C.	5	15	0	1	.000	18	7	22	6.00	1
1998 Houston e	N.L.	43	59⅔	3	3	.500	44	23	49	3.77	3
1999 Detroit	A.L.	68	81⅔	4	5	.444	66	45	63	4.30	0
2000 Detroit	A.L.	67	109⅔	4	9	.308	81	49	124	5.25	0
Major League Totals 5 Yrs.		209	368⅓	15	27	.357	258	190	392	5.42	3

a Traded by Cincinnati Reds to Detroit Tigers with pitcher David Tuttle and player to be named later for pitcher David Wells, July 31, 1995.
b Detroit Tigers received infielder Mark Lewis to complete trade, November 16, 1995.
c On disabled list from August 11 to August 29, 1996.
d Traded to Houston Astros with catcher Brad Ausmus, pitcher Jose Lima, pitcher Trever Miller and infielder Daryle Ward for outfielder Brian Hunter, infielder Orlando Miller, pitcher Todd Jones and pitcher Doug Brocail, December 10, 1996.
e Traded to Detroit Tigers with catcher Brad Ausmus for pitcher Dean Crow, pitcher Mark Persails, pitcher Brian Powell, catcher Paul Bako and infielder Carlos Villalobos, January 14, 1999.

NOMO, HIDEO

Born, Osaka, Japan, August 31, 1968.
Bats Right. Throws Right. Height, 6 feet, 2 inches. Weight, 210 pounds.

Year	Club	Lea	G	IP	W	L	Pct	SO	BB	H	ERA	SAVES
1990 Kintetsu	Japan Pac.	29	235	18	8	.692	287	109	...	2.91	0
1991 Kintetsu	Japan Pac.	31	242⅓	17	11	.607	287	128	...	3.05	1
1992 Kintetsu	Japan Pac.	30	216⅔	18	8	.692	228	117	150	2.66	0
1993 Kintetsu	Japan Pac.	32	243⅓	17	12	.586	276	148	201	3.70	0

ar	Club	Lea	G	IP	W	L	Pct	SO	BB	H	ERA	SAVES
94 Kintetsu	Japan Pac.	17	114	8	7	.533	126	86	103	3.63	0
95 Bakersfield	California	1	5⅓	0	1	.000	6	1	6	3.38	0
95 Los Angeles a-b	N.L.	28	191⅓	13	6	.684	*236	78	124	2.54	0
96 Los Angeles c	N.L.	33	228⅓	16	11	.593	234	85	180	3.19	0
97 Los Angeles	N.L.	33	207⅓	14	12	.538	233	92	193	4.25	0
98 Los Angeles-New York d	.N.L.	29	157⅓	6	12	.333	167	94	130	4.92	0
99 Huntsville e-f	Southern	1	7	1	0	1.000	7	1	5	0.00	0
99 Iowa g	P.C.	3	17	1	1	.500	18	12	12	3.71	0
99 Milwaukee h	N.L.	28	176⅓	12	8	.600	161	78	173	4.54	0
00 Detroit i-j	A.L.	32	190	8	12	.400	181	89	191	4.74	0
jor League Totals	6 Yrs.	183	1150⅔	69	61	.531	1212	516	991	3.97	0
Division Series											
95 Los Angeles	N.L.	1	5	0	1	.000	6	2	7	9.00	0
96 Los Angeles	N.L.	1	3⅔	0	1	.000	3	5	5	12.27	0
vision Series Totals	2	8⅔	0	2	.000	9	7	12	10.38	0

Signed with Los Angeles Dodgers organization, February 13, 1995.
Selected Rookie of the Year in National League for 1995.
Pitched no-hit, no-run game against Colorado Rockies, winning 9-0, September 17, 1996.
Traded to New York Mets with pitcher Brad Clontz for pitcher Dave Mlicki and pitcher Greg McMichael, June 4, 1998.
Outrighted by New York Mets, March 24, 1999.
Signed with Chicago Cubs organization, April 1, 1999.
Released by Chicago Cubs, April 23, 1999, signed with Milwaukee Brewers organization, April 29, 1999.
Filed for free agency, November 1, 1999. Signed with Detroit Tigers, January 21, 2000.
On disabled list from July 30 to August 17, 2000.
Not offered 2001 contract, November 2, 2000, signed with Boston Red Sox, December 15, 2000.

NUNEZ, VLADIMIR

Born, Havana, Cuba, March 15, 1975.
Bats Right. Throws Right. Height, 6 feet, 4 inches. Weight, 235 pounds.

ar	Club	Lea	G	IP	W	L	Pct	SO	BB	H	ERA	SAVES
96 Visalia	California	12	53	1	6	.143	37	17	64	5.43	0
96 Lethbridge	Pioneer	14	85	10	0	1.000	93	10	78	2.22	0
97 High Desert	California	28	158⅓	8	5	.615	142	40	169	5.17	0
98 Tucson	P.C.	31	95⅓	4	4	.500	78	37	103	4.91	2
98 Arizona	N.L.	4	5⅓	0	0	.000	2	2	7	10.13	0
99 Tucson	P.C.	3	2⅔	1	0	1.000	3	0	5	6.75	0
99 Arizona-Florida a	N.L.	44	108⅔	7	10	.412	86	54	95	4.06	1
00 Calgary	P.C.	15	89⅔	6	7	.462	95	38	92	4.12	0
00 Florida	N.L.	17	68⅓	0	6	.000	45	34	88	7.90	0
ajor League Totals	3 Yrs.	65	182⅓	7	16	.304	133	90	190	5.68	1

Traded to Florida Marlins with pitcher Brad Penny and player to be named later for pitcher Matt Mantei, July 9, 1999. Florida Marlins received infielder Abraham Nunez to complete trade, December 13, 1999.

OHKA, TOMOKAZU

Born, Kyoto, Japan, March 18, 1976.
Bats Right. Throws Right. Height, 6 feet, 1 inch. Weight, 180 pounds.

ar	Club	Lea	G	IP	W	L	Pct	SO	BB	H	ERA	SAVES
94 Yokohama	Japan Cent.	15	28	1	1	.500	18	18	29	4.18	0
95 Yokohama	Japan Cent.	3	9⅓	0	0	.000	6	13	3	1.93	0
96 Yokohama	Japan Cent.	14	18	0	1	.000	11	14	26	9.50	0
98 Yokohama a ...	Japan Cent.	2	2	0	0	.000	1	2	2	9.00	0
99 Pawtucket	Int.	12	68⅓	7	0	1.000	63	11	60	1.58	1
99 Trenton	Eastern	12	72	8	0	1.000	53	25	63	3.00	0
99 Boston	A.L.	8	13	1	2	.333	8	6	21	6.23	0
00 Pawtucket	Int.	19	130⅔	9	6	.600	78	23	111	2.96	2
00 Boston	A.L.	13	69⅓	3	6	.333	40	26	70	3.12	0
ajor League Totals	2 Yrs.	21	82⅓	4	8	.333	48	32	91	3.61	0

Sold to Boston Red Sox, November 20, 1998.

OLIVARES (PALQU), OMAR

Born, Mayaguez, Puerto Rico, July 6, 1967.
Bats Right. Throws Right. Height, 6 feet, 1 inch. Weight, 193 pounds.

Year	Club	Lea	G	IP	W	L	Pct	SO	BB	H	ERA	SAVE
1987	Charleston, SC	So. Atl.	31	170⅓	4	14	.222	86	57	182	4.60	0
1988	Charleston, SC	So. Atl.	24	185⅓	13	6	.684	94	43	166	2.23	0
1988	Riverside	California	4	23⅓	3	0	1.000	16	9	18	1.16	0
1989	Wichita a	Texas	26	*185⅔	12	11	.522	79	61	175	3.39	0
1990	Louisville	A.A.	23	159⅓	10	11	.476	88	59	127	2.82	0
1990	St. Louis	N.L.	9	49⅓	1	1	.500	20	17	45	2.92	0
1991	Louisville	A.A.	6	36⅓	1	2	.333	27	16	39	3.47	0
1991	St. Louis b-c	N.L.	28	167⅓	11	7	.611	91	61	148	3.71	1
1992	St. Louis b-c	N.L.	32	197	9	9	.500	124	63	189	3.84	0
1993	St. Louis d-e	N.L.	58	118⅔	5	3	.625	63	54	134	4.17	1
1994	Louisville	A.A.	9	47⅓	2	1	.667	38	16	47	4.37	0
1994	St. Louis f	N.L.	14	73⅔	3	4	.429	26	37	84	5.74	1
1995	Colorado Springs	P.C.	3	11⅔	0	1	.000	6	2	14	5.40	0
1995	Scranton-Wilkes Barre	Int.	7	44⅓	0	3	.000	28	20	49	4.87	0
1995	Colo.-Philadelphia g-h-i	N.L.	16	41⅔	1	4	.200	22	23	55	6.91	0
1996	Toledo	Int.	1	5⅓	1	0	1.000	5	3	4	8.44	0
1996	Detroit j	A.L.	25	160	7	11	.389	81	75	169	4.89	0
1997	Detroit-Seattle k-l	A.L.	32	177⅓	6	10	.375	103	81	191	4.98	0
1998	Anaheim	A.L.	37	183	9	9	.500	112	91	189	4.03	0
1999	Anaheim-Oakland n-o	A.L.	32	205⅔	15	11	.577	85	81	217	4.16	0
2000	Modesto	California	2	6	0	0	.000	3	1	3	1.50	0
2000	Sacramento	P.C.	1	6	0	0	.000	3	2	3	0.00	0
2000	Oakland p	A.L.	21	108	4	8	.333	57	60	134	6.75	0
Major League Totals	11 Yrs.		304	1481⅔	71	77	.480	784	643	1555	4.53	3

a Traded by San Diego Padres to St. Louis Cardinals organization for outfielder Alex Cole and pitcher Steve Peters, February 27, 1990.
b On disabled list from May 25 to June 13, 1992.
c Appeared in on additional games as pinch runner and three additional games as pinch hitter.
d On disabled list from June 4 to June 19, 1993.
e Appeared in one additional game as pinch hitter and one game as pinch runner.
f Appeared in one additional game as pinch hitter.
g Signed with Colorado Rockies, April 9, 1995.
h Claimed on waivers by Philadelphia Phillies, July 11, 1995.
i Designated for assignment by Philadelphia Phillies, July 27, 1995.
j On disabled list from April 16 to May 30, 1996.
k Traded to Seattle Mariners with pitcher Felipe Lira for pitcher Scott Sanders and pitcher Dean Crow, July 18, 1997.
l Filed for free agency, October 30, 1997.
m Signed as free agent with Anaheim Angels, December 11, 1997.
n Traded to Oakland Athletics with infielder Randy Velarde for pitcher Elvin Nina, outfielder Jeff DaVanon and outfielder Nathan Haynes, July 29, 1999.
o Filed for free agency, October 29, 1999. Re-signed with Oakland Athletics, January 8, 2000.
p On disabled list from June 17 to August 11, 2000.

OLIVER, DARREN CHRISTOPHER

Born, Rio Linda, California, October 6, 1970.
Bats Right. Throws Left. Height, 6 feet. Weight, 200 pounds.

Year	Club	Lea	G	IP	W	L	Pct	SO	BB	H	ERA	SAVE
1988	G.C. Rangers	Gulf C.	12	54⅓	5	1	.833	59	18	39	2.15	0
1989	Gastonia	So. Atl.	24	122⅓	8	7	.533	108	82	86	3.16	0
1990	G.C. Rangers a	Gulf C.	3	6	0	0	.000	7	1	1	0.00	0
1990	Gastonia	So. Atl.	1	2	0	0	.000	2	4	1	13.50	0
1991	Charlotte b	Fla. St.	2	8	0	1	.000	12	3	6	4.50	0
1992	Charlotte	Fla. St.	8	25	1	0	1.000	33	10	11	0.72	2
1992	Tulsa c	Texas	3	14⅓	0	1	.000	14	4	15	3.14	0
1993	Tulsa	Texas	46	73⅓	7	5	.583	77	41	51	1.96	6
1993	Texas	A.L.	2	3⅓	0	0	.000	4	1	2	2.70	0
1994	Oklahoma City	A.A.	6	7⅓	0	0	.000	6	3	1	0.00	0
1994	Texas	A.L.	43	50	4	0	1.000	50	35	40	3.42	2
1995	Texas d	A.L.	17	49	4	2	.667	39	32	47	4.22	0
1996	Charlotte	Fla. St.	2	12	0	1	.000	9	3	8	3.00	0
1996	Texas	A.L.	30	173⅔	14	6	.700	112	76	190	4.66	0
1997	Texas	A.L.	32	201⅓	13	12	.520	104	82	213	4.20	0
1998	Oklahoma	P.C.	1	5	0	0	.000	1	1	2	0.00	0
1998	Texas	A.L.	19	103⅓	6	7	.462	58	43	140	6.53	0
1998	St. Louis e-f-g	N.L.	10	57	4	4	.500	29	23	64	4.26	0
1999	St. Louis h	N.L.	30	196⅓	9	9	.500	119	74	197	4.26	0
2000	Tulsa	Texas	1	4⅔	0	1	.000	5	2	10	11.57	0
2000	Oklahoma	P.C.	7	32	2	1	.667	28	14	22	1.97	0

ear	Club	Lea	G	IP	W	L	Pct	SO	BB	H	ERA	SAVES
00 Texas i	....	A.L.	21	108	2	9	.182	49	42	151	7.42	0
ajor League Totals	.... 8 Yrs.		204	942	56	49	.533	564	408	1044	4.88	2
	Division Series											
96 Texas	....	A.L.	1	8	0	1	.000	3	2	6	3.38	0

On disabled list from April 6 to August 9, 1990.
On disabled list from May 1 to end of 1991 season.
On disabled list from July 1 to end of 1992 season.
On disabled list from June 27 to October 2, 1995.
On disabled list from June 11 to June 26, 1998.
Traded to St. Louis Cardinals with infielder Fernando Tatis and player to be named later for infielder Royce Clayton and pitcher Todd Stottlemyre, July 31, 1998.
St. Louis Cardinals received infielder Mark Little to complete trade, August 9, 1998.
Filed for free agency, October 29, 1999. Signed with Texas Rangers, January 12, 2000.
On disabled list from June 17 to July 19 and July 31 to August 31, 2000.

ORTIZ, DIOGENES (RAMON)
Born, Cotui, Dominican Republic, March 23, 1976.
Bats Right. Throws Right. Height, 6 feet. Weight, 165 pounds.

ear	Club	Lea	G	IP	W	L	Pct	SO	BB	H	ERA	SAVES
995 California	....	Dominican	16	97	8	6	.571	100	54	79	2.23	0
996 Angels	....	Arizona	16	68	5	4	.556	78	27	55	2.12	1
996 Boise	....	Northwest	3	19²/₃	1	1	.500	18	6	21	3.66	0
997 Cedar Rapids	....	Midwest	27	181	11	10	.524	225	53	156	3.58	0
998 Midland	....	Texas	7	47	2	1	.667	53	16	50	5.55	0
999 Erie	....	Eastern	15	102	9	4	.692	86	40	88	2.82	0
999 Edmonton	....	P.C.	9	53¹/₃	5	3	.625	64	19	46	4.05	0
999 Anaheim	....	A.L.	9	48¹/₃	2	3	.400	44	25	50	6.52	0
000 Lake Elsinore	...	California	1	6	1	0	1.000	7	2	8	3.00	0
000 Edmonton	....	P.C.	15	89	6	6	.500	76	37	74	4.55	0
000 Anaheim a	....	A.L.	18	111¹/₃	8	6	.571	73	55	96	5.09	0
ajor League Totals	.... 2 Yrs.		27	159²/₃	10	9	.526	117	80	146	5.52	0

On disabled list from March 25 to April 10, 2000.

ORTIZ, RUSSELL REID
Born, Van Nuys, California, June 5, 1974.
Bats Right. Throws Right. Height, 6 feet, 1 inch. Weight, 200 pounds.

ear	Club	Lea	G	IP	W	L	Pct	SO	BB	H	ERA	SAVES
995 Bellingham	....	Northwest	25	34¹/₃	2	0	1.000	55	13	19	0.52	11
995 San Jose	....	California	5	6	0	1	.000	7	2	4	1.50	0
996 San Jose	....	California	34	36²/₃	0	0	.000	63	20	16	0.25	23
996 Shreveport	....	Texas	26	26²/₃	1	2	.333	29	21	22	4.05	13
997 Shreveport	....	Texas	12	56²/₃	2	3	.400	50	37	52	4.13	0
997 Phoenix	....	P.C.	14	85	4	3	.571	70	34	96	5.51	0
998 Fresno	....	P.C.	10	50²/₃	3	1	.750	59	22	35	1.60	0
998 San Francisco	....	N.L.	22	88¹/₃	4	4	.500	75	46	90	4.99	0
999 San Francisco	....	N.L.	33	207²/₃	18	9	.667	164	*125	189	3.81	0
000 San Francisco	....	N.L.	33	195²/₃	14	12	.538	167	112	192	5.01	0
ajor League Totals	.... 3 Yrs.		88	491²/₃	36	25	.590	406	283	471	4.50	0
	Division Series											
000 San Francisco	....	N.L.	1	5¹/₃	0	0	.000	4	4	2	1.69	0

OSUNA, ANTONIO PEDRO
Born, Sinaloa, Mexico, April 12, 1973.
Bats Right. Throws Right. Height, 5 feet, 11 inches. Weight, 160 pounds.

ear	Club	Lea	G	IP	W	L	Pct	SO	BB	H	ERA	SAVES
991 Dodgers	....	Gulf Coast	8	11	0	0	.000	13	0	8	0.82	4
991 Yakima	....	Northwest	13	25¹/₃	0	0	.000	39	8	18	3.20	5
992 Mexico	....	Mexican	28	167	13	7	.650	129	74	181	4.04	0
993 Bakersfield a	.....	California	14	18¹/₃	0	2	.000	20	5	19	4.91	2
994 San Antonio	....	Texas	35	46	1	2	.333	53	18	19	0.98	19
994 Albuquerque b	....	P.C.	6	6	0	0	.000	8	1	5	0.00	4
995 San Berndno	.....	California	5	7	0	0	.000	11	5	3	1.29	0
995 Albuquerque	....	P.C.	19	18¹/₃	0	1	.000	19	9	15	4.42	11
995 Los Angeles c	....	N.L.	39	44²/₃	2	4	.333	46	20	39	4.43	0

Year	Club	Lea	G	IP	W	L	Pct	SO	BB	H	ERA	SAVES
1996 Albuquerque	...........P.C.		1	1	0	0	.000	1	0	2	0.00	0
1996 Los Angeles	...........N.L.		73	84	9	6	.600	85	32	65	3.00	4
1997 Albuquerque	...........P.C.		13	14	1	1	.500	26	4	9	1.93	6
1997 Los Angeles	...........N.L.		48	61²/₃	3	4	.429	68	19	46	2.19	0
1998 Los Angeles d	.......N.L.		54	64²/₃	7	1	.875	72	32	50	3.06	6
1999 San Bernardino	....California		13	19¹/₃	0	0	.000	27	6	19	2.33	0
1999 Los Angeles e	.....N.L.		5	4²/₃	0	0	.000	5	3	4	7.71	0
2000 San Bernardino	....California		3	7¹/₃	0	2	.000	11	3	4	4.91	0
2000 Albuquerque	...........P.C.		3	5²/₃	0	0	.000	7	5	2	0.00	0
2000 Los Angeles f	.........N.L.		46	67¹/₃	3	6	.333	70	35	57	3.74	0
Major League Totals	...6 Yrs.		265	327	24	21	.533	346	141	261	3.28	10
Division Series												
1995 Los Angeles	...........N.L.		3	3¹/₃	0	1	.000	3	1	3	2.70	0
1996 Los Angeles	...........N.L.		2	2	0	1	.000	4	1	3	4.50	0
Division Series Totals	....		5	5¹/₃	0	2	.000	7	2	6	3.38	0

a On disabled list from April 8 to July 17, 1993.
b On disabled list from April 8 to June 6, 1994.
c On disabled list from May 19 to June 16, 1995.
d On disabled list from September 9 to September 28, 1998.
e On disabled list from March 25 to April 16 and April 18 to May 3 and May 17 to November 17, 1999.
f On disabled list from March 27 to May 5, 2000.

PADILLA, VICENTE DE LA CRUZ
Born, Chinandega, Nicaraqua, September 27, 1977.
Bats Right. Throws Right. Height, 6 feet, 2 inches. Weight, 200 pounds.

Year	Club	Lea	G	IP	W	L	Pct	SO	BB	H	ERA	SAVES
1999 Tucson	...............P.C.		18	93²/₃	7	4	.636	58	24	107	3.75	0
1999 High Desert	.......California		9	50²/₃	4	1	.800	55	17	50	3.73	0
1999 Arizona	...............N.L.		5	2²/₃	0	1	.000	0	3	7	16.88	0
2000 Tucson	...............P.C.		12	18¹/₃	0	1	.000	22	8	22	4.42	0
2000 Arizona-Philadelphia a	-...N.L.		55	65¹/₃	4	7	.364	51	28	72	3.72	2
Major League Totals	........2 Yrs.		60	68	4	8	.333	51	31	79	4.24	2

a Traded to Philadelphia Phillies with infielder Travis Lee, pitcher Omar Daal and pitcher Nelson Figueroa for pitcher Curt Schilling, July 26, 2000.

PAINTER, LANCE TELFORD
Born, Bedford, England, July 21, 1967.
Bats Left. Throws Right. Height, 6 feet, 1 inch. Weight, 195 pounds.

Year	Club	Lea	G	IP	W	L	Pct	SO	BB	H	ERA	SAVES
1990 Spokane	........Northwest		23	71²/₃	7	3	.700	104	15	45	1.51	3
1991 Waterloo	...........Midwest		28	200	14	8	.636	201	57	162	2.30	0
1992 Wichita a	...........Texas		27	163¹/₃	10	5	.667	137	55	138	3.53	0
1993 Colo Sprngs	..........P.C.		23	138	9	7	.563	91	44	165	4.30	0
1993 Colorado	...........N.L.		10	39	2	2	.500	16	9	52	6.00	0
1994 Colorado	...........N.L.		15	73²/₃	4	6	.400	41	26	91	6.11	0
1994 Colo Sprngs	..........P.C.		13	71¹/₃	4	3	.571	59	28	83	4.79	0
1995 Colo Sprngs	..........P.C.		11	25²/₃	0	3	.000	12	11	32	5.96	0
1995 Colorado b	...........N.L.		33	45¹/₃	3	0	1.000	36	10	55	4.37	1
1996 Colorado c-d	.......N.L.		34	50²/₃	4	2	.667	48	25	56	5.86	0
1997 Louisville	...........A.A.		18	20²/₃	1	0	1.000	22	4	18	5.23	0
1997 St. Louis e	...........N.L.		14	17	1	1	.500	11	8	13	4.76	0
1998 St. Louis	...........N.L.		65	47¹/₃	4	0	1.000	39	28	42	3.99	1
1999 St. Louis	...........N.L.		56	63¹/₃	4	5	.444	56	25	63	4.83	1
1999 Arkansas f-g	........Texas		1	2	0	0	.000	4	0	1	0.00	0
2000 Dunedin	...........Fla.St.		1	1	0	0	.000	0	0	0	0.00	0
2000 Toronto h	...........A.L.		42	66²/₃	2	0	1.000	53	22	69	4.72	0
Major League Totals	........8 Yrs.		269	403	24	16	.600	300	153	441	5.14	3

a Selected in expansion draft by Colorado Rockies from San Diego Padres, November 17, 1992.
b On disabled list from April 17 to May 6, 1995.
c On disabled list from August 6 to September 30, 1996.
d Claimed on waivers by St. Louis Cardinals, December 2, 1996.
e On disabled list from April 5 to May 12 and May 20 to June 20, 1997.
f On disabled list from June 14 to June 29, 1999.
g Traded to Toronto Blue Jays with catcher Alberto Castillo and pitcher Matt DeWitt for pitcher Pat Hentgen and pitcher Paul Spoljaric, November 11, 1999.
h On disabled list from May 17 to June 5, 2000.

PANIAGUA, JOSE LUIS

Born, San Jose De Ocoa, Dominican Republic, August 20, 1973.
Bats Right. Throws Right. Height, 6 feet, 2 inches. Weight, 185 pounds.

ar Club	Lea	G	IP	W	L	Pct	SO	BB	H	ERA	SAVES
91 Montreal	Dominican	13	33	2	2	.500	19	17	24	2.18	0
93 Expos	Gulf Coast	4	27	3	0	1.000	25	5	13	0.67	0
94 Wst Plm Bch	Fla.St.	26	141	9	9	.500	110	54	131	3.64	0
95 Harrisburg	Eastern	25	126⅓	7	12	.368	89	62	140	5.34	0
96 Harrisburg	Eastern	3	18	3	0	1.000	16	2	12	0.00	0
96 Ottawa	Int.	15	85	9	5	.643	61	23	72	3.18	0
96 Montreal	N.L.	13	51	2	4	.333	27	23	55	3.53	0
97 Wst Plm Bch	Fla.St.	2	10	1	0	1.000	11	2	5	0.00	0
97 Ottawa	Int.	22	137⅔	8	10	.444	87	44	164	4.64	0
97 Montreal a	N.L.	9	18	1	2	.333	8	16	29	12.00	0
98 Tacoma	P.C.	44	68⅓	3	1	.750	61	22	66	2.77	5
98 Seattle b	A.L.	18	22	2	0	1.000	16	5	15	2.05	1
99 Seattle	A.L.	59	77⅔	6	11	.353	74	52	75	4.06	3
00 Seattle	A.L.	69	80⅓	3	0	1.000	71	38	68	3.47	5
ajor League Totals	5 Yrs.	168	249	14	17	.452	196	134	242	4.16	9
Division Series											
00 Seattle	A.L.	2	2⅓	1	0	1.000	3	2	1	0.00	0
Championship Series											
00 Seattle	A.L.	5	4⅓	0	1	.000	4	1	4	4.15	0

Selected in expansion draft by Tampa Bay Devil Rays, November 18, 1997.
Claimed on waivers by Seattle Mariners, March 26, 1998.

PARK, CHAN HO

Born, Kong Ju City, South Korea, June 30, 1973.
Bats Right. Throws Right. Height, 6 feet, 2 inches. Weight, 185 pounds.

ar Club	Lea	G	IP	W	L	Pct	SO	BB	H	ERA	SAVES
994 Los Angeles	N.L.	2	4	0	0	.000	6	5	5	11.25	0
994 San Antonio	Texas	20	101⅓	5	7	.417	100	57	91	3.55	0
995 Albuquerque	P.C.	23	110	6	7	.462	101	76	93	4.91	0
995 Los Angeles	N.L.	2	4	0	0	.000	7	2	2	4.50	0
996 Los Angeles	N.L.	48	108⅔	5	5	.500	119	71	82	3.64	0
997 Los Angeles	N.L.	32	192	14	8	.636	166	70	149	3.38	0
998 Los Angeles	N.L.	34	220⅔	15	9	.625	191	97	199	3.71	0
999 Los Angeles	N.L.	33	194⅓	13	11	.542	174	100	208	5.23	0
000 Los Angeles	N.L.	34	226	18	10	.643	217	124	173	3.27	0
ajor League Totals	7 Yrs.	185	949⅔	65	43	.602	880	469	818	3.88	0

PARQUE, JIM VO

Born, Norwalk, California, February 8, 1975.
Bats Left. Throws Right. Height, 5 feet, 11 inches. Weight, 165 pounds.

ear Club	Lea	G	IP	W	L	Pct	SO	BB	H	ERA	SAVES
997 Winston-Sal	Carolina	11	61⅔	7	2	.778	76	23	29	2.77	0
997 Nashville	A.A.	2	10⅔	1	0	1.000	5	9	9	4.22	0
998 Calgary	P.C.	8	48	2	3	.400	31	25	49	3.94	0
998 Chicago	A.L.	21	113	7	5	.583	77	49	135	5.10	0
999 Chicago	A.L.	31	173⅔	9	15	.375	111	79	210	5.13	0
000 Chicago	A.L.	33	187	13	6	.684	111	71	208	4.28	0
ajor League Totals	3 Yrs.	85	473⅔	29	26	.527	299	199	553	4.79	0
Division Series											
000 Chicago	A.L.	1	6	0	0	.000	2	1	6	4.50	0

PARRIS, STEVEN MICHAEL (STEVE)

Born, Joliet, Illinois, December 17, 1967.
Bats Right. Throws Right. Height, 6 feet. Weight, 190 pounds.

ear Club	Lea	G	IP	W	L	Pct	SO	BB	H	ERA	SAVES
989 Batavia	N.Y.-Penn.	13	66⅔	3	5	.375	46	20	69	3.92	0
990 Batavia	N.Y.-Penn.	14	81⅔	7	1	.875	50	22	70	2.64	0
991 Clearwater	Fla.St.	43	93	7	5	.583	59	25	101	3.39	1
992 Reading	Eastern	18	85⅓	5	7	.417	60	21	94	4.64	0
992 Scranton-WB	Int.	11	51⅓	3	3	.500	29	17	57	4.03	1

Year	Club	Lea	G	IP	W	L	Pct	SO	BB	H	ERA	SAVES
1993 Scranton-WB ....Int.			3	5$\frac{2}{3}$	0	0	.000	4	3	9	12.71	0
1993 Jacksnville a-b-c .. .Southern			7	13$\frac{2}{3}$	0	1	.000	5	6	15	5.93	0
1994 Salem d ....Carolina			17	57	3	3	.500	48	21	58	3.63	0
1995 Carolina ....Southern			14	89$\frac{2}{3}$	9	1	.900	86	16	61	2.51	0
1995 Pittsburgh ............N.L.			15	82	6	6	.500	61	33	89	5.38	0
1996 Augusta ....So.Atl.			1	5	0	0	.000	6	1	1	0.00	0
1996 Carolina ....Southern			5	26$\frac{2}{3}$	2	0	1.000	22	6	24	3.04	0
1996 Pittsburgh e ..........N.L.			8	26$\frac{1}{3}$	0	3	.000	27	11	35	7.18	0
1997 Chattanooga ......Southern			14	80$\frac{2}{3}$	6	2	.750	68	29	78	4.13	0
1997 Indianapols f-g ........A.A.			5	35$\frac{1}{3}$	2	3	.400	27	11	26	3.57	0
1998 Indianapols ....Int.			13	84$\frac{1}{3}$	6	1	.857	102	26	74	3.84	0
1998 Cincinnati ............N.L.			18	99	6	5	.545	77	32	89	3.73	0
1999 Indianapolis ....Int.			6	35$\frac{2}{3}$	0	2	.000	31	9	39	4.04	0
1999 Cincinnati h ...........N.L.			22	128$\frac{2}{3}$	11	4	.733	86	52	124	3.50	0
2000 Cincinnati i ...........N.L.			33	192$\frac{2}{3}$	12	17	.414	117	71	227	4.81	0
Major League Totals ....5 Yrs.			96	528$\frac{2}{3}$	35	35	.500	368	199	564	4.49	0

a Claimed on waivers by Los Angeles Dodgers from Philadelphia Phillies, April 19, 1993.
b Claimed on waivers by Seattle Mariners, April 26, 1993.
c On disabled list from May 12 to June 23 and July 17 to July 31, 1993.
d Released, July 31, 1993, signed with Pittsburgh Pirates organization, June 24, 1994.
e On disabled list March 6 to July 11 and August 18 to September 10, 1996.
f Released, signed with Cincinnati Reds organization, May 6, 1997.
g Filed for free agency, re-signed with Cincinnati Reds, October 27, 1997.
h On disabled list from July 26 to September 1, 1999.
i Traded to Toronto Blue Jays for pitcher Clayton Andrews and pitcher Leo Estrella, November 22, 2000.

PATTERSON, DANNY SHANE
Born, San Gabriel, California, February 17, 1971.
Bats Right. Throws Right. Height, 6 feet. Weight, 170 pounds.

Year	Club	Lea	G	IP	W	L	Pct	SO	BB	H	ERA	SAVES
1990 Butte ....Pioneer			13	28$\frac{1}{3}$	0	3	.000	18	14	36	6.35	1
1991 Rangers ....Gulf Coast			11	50	5	3	.625	46	12	43	3.24	0
1992 Gastonia ....So. Atl.			23	105$\frac{1}{3}$	4	6	.400	84	33	106	3.59	0
1993 Charlotte ....Fla. St.			47	68	5	6	.455	41	28	55	2.51	7
1994 Charlotte ....Fla. St.			7	13$\frac{2}{3}$	1	0	1.000	9	5	13	4.61	0
1994 Tulsa ....Texas			30	44	1	4	.200	33	17	35	1.64	6
1995 Tulsa ....Texas			26	36$\frac{1}{3}$	2	2	.500	24	13	45	6.19	5
1995 Okla City ............A.A.			14	27$\frac{1}{3}$	1	0	1.000	9	9	23	1.65	2
1996 Okla City ............A.A.			44	80$\frac{1}{3}$	6	2	.750	53	15	79	1.68	10
1996 Texas ...............A.L.			7	8$\frac{2}{3}$	0	0	.000	5	3	10	0.00	0
1997 Tulsa ....Texas			2	2	0	0	.000	0	0	5	4.50	0
1997 Texas a .............A.L.			54	71	10	6	.625	69	23	70	3.42	1
1998 Tulsa ....Texas			2	4	0	0	.000	4	0	3	4.50	0
1998 Oklahoma ............P.C.			1	2	0	0	.000	2	1	4	4.50	0
1998 Texas b .............A.L.			56	60$\frac{2}{3}$	2	5	.286	33	19	64	4.45	2
1999 Oklahoma ...........P.C.			2	3	1	0	1.000	4	1	1	0.00	0
1999 Texas c .............A.L.			36	60$\frac{1}{3}$	2	0	1.000	43	19	77	5.67	0
2000 Detroit d .............A.L.			58	56$\frac{2}{3}$	5	1	.833	29	14	69	3.97	0
Major League Totals ....5 Yrs.			228	257$\frac{1}{3}$	19	12	.613	179	78	290	4.20	3
Division Series												
1996 Texas ...............A.L.			1	0$\frac{1}{3}$	0	0	.000	0	0	1	0.00	0
1999 Texas ...............A.L.			1	1	0	0	.000	0	0	1	0.00	0
Division Series Totals			2	1$\frac{1}{3}$	0	0	.000	0	0	2	0.00	0

a On disabled list from May 17 to June 14, 1997.
b On disabled list from March 31 to April 17, 1998.
c Traded to Detroit Tigers with outfielder Juan Gonzalez and catcher Greg Zaun for pitcher Justin Thompson, pitcher Francisco Cordero, pitcher Alan Webb, outfielder Gabe Kapler, catcher Bill Haselman and infielder Frank Catalanotto, November 2, 1999.
d On disabled list from July 22 to August 6, 2000.

PAVANO, CARL ANTHONY
Born, New Britain, Connecticut, January 8, 1976.
Bats Right. Throws Right. Height, 6 feet, 5 inches. Weight, 228 pounds.

Year	Club	Lea	G	IP	W	L	Pct	SO	BB	H	ERA	SAVES
1994 Red Sox ....Gulf Coast			9	44	4	3	.571	47	7	31	1.84	0
1995 Michigan ....Midwest			22	141$\frac{1}{3}$	6	6	.500	138	52	118	3.44	0
1996 Trenton ....Eastern			27	185	16	5	.762	146	47	154	2.63	0

Year	Club	Lea	G	IP	W	L	Pct	SO	BB	H	ERA	SAVES
997 Pawtucket a	Int.	23	161²/₃	11	6	.647	147	34	148	3.12	0
998 Jupiter	Fla.St.	4	15	0	0	.000	14	3	20	6.60	0
998 Ottawa	Int.	3	18²/₃	1	0	1.000	14	7	12	2.41	0
998 Montreal	N.L.	24	134²/₃	6	9	.400	83	43	130	4.21	0
999 Ottawa	Int.	2	5	0	1	.000	3	0	7	9.00	0
999 Montreal b	N.L.	19	104	6	8	.429	70	35	117	5.63	0
000 Montreal c	N.L.	15	97	8	4	.667	64	34	89	3.06	0
Major League Totals	3 Yrs.	58	335²/₃	20	21	.488	217	112	336	4.32	0

Traded by Boston Red Sox to Montreal Expos with player to be named later for pitcher Pedro Martinez, November 18, 1997. Montreal Expos received pitcher Tony Armas to complete trade, December 18, 1997.
On disabled list from July 12 to September 11, 1999.
On disabled list from June 25 to November 13, 2000.

PENNY, BRADLEY WAYNE (BRAD)
Born, Broken Arrow, Oklahoma, May 24, 1978.
Bats Right. Throws Right. Height, 6 feet, 4 inches. Weight, 200 pounds.

Year	Club	Lea	G	IP	W	L	Pct	SO	BB	H	ERA	SAVES
996 Diamondbcks	Arizona	11	49²/₃	2	2	.500	52	14	36	2.36	0
997 South Bend	Midwest	25	118²/₃	10	5	.667	116	43	91	2.73	0
998 High Desert	California	28	164	14	5	.737	207	35	138	2.96	0
999 El Paso a-b-c	Texas	17	90	2	7	.222	100	25	109	4.80	0
999 Portland	Eastern	6	32¹/₃	1	0	1.000	35	14	28	3.90	0
2000 Brevard County	Fla.St.	2	8	0	1	.000	11	4	5	1.13	0
2000 Calgary	P.C.	3	15	2	0	1.000	16	10	8	1.80	0
2000 Florida d	N.L.	23	119²/₃	8	7	.533	80	60	120	4.81	0

On disabled list from April 20 to 30, 1999.
Traded by Arizona Diamondbacks to Florida Marlins with pitcher Vladimir Nunez and player to be named later for pitcher Matt Mantei, July 9, 1999.
Florida Marlins received outfielder Abraham Nunez to complete trade, December 13, 1999.
On disabled list from July 20 to September 1, 2000.

PERCIVAL, TROY EUGENE
Born, Fontana, California, August 9, 1969.
Bats Right. Throws Right. Height, 6 feet, 3 inches. Weight, 200 pounds.

Year	Club	Lea	G	IP	W	L	Pct	SO	BB	H	ERA	SAVES
991 Boise	Northwest	28	38¹/₃	2	0	1.000	63	18	23	1.41	12
992 Palm Springs	California	11	10²/₃	1	1	.500	16	8	6	5.06	2
992 Midland	Texas	20	19	3	0	1.000	21	11	18	2.37	5
993 Vancouver	P.C.	18	18²/₃	0	1	.000	19	13	24	6.27	4
994 Vancouver	P.C.	49	61	2	6	.250	73	29	63	4.13	15
995 California	A.L.	62	74	3	2	.600	94	26	37	1.95	3
996 California	A.L.	62	74	0	2	.000	100	31	38	2.31	36
997 Lk Elsinore	California	2	2	0	0	.000	3	0	1	0.00	0
997 Anaheim a	A.L.	55	52	5	5	.500	72	22	40	3.46	27
998 Anaheim	A.L.	67	66²/₃	2	7	.222	87	37	45	3.65	42
999 Anaheim	A.L.	60	57	4	6	.400	58	22	38	3.79	31
2000 Lake Elsinore	California	2	2	0	0	.000	1	1	1	4.50	0
2000 Anaheim b	A.L.	54	50	5	5	.500	49	30	42	4.50	32
Major League Totals	6 Yrs.	360	373²/₃	19	27	.413	460	168	240	3.16	171

a On disabled list from April 7 to May 16, 1997.
b On disabled list from August 5 to August 25, 2000.

PEREZ, CARLOS GROSS
Born, Nigua, Dominican Republic, April 14, 1971.
Bats Left. Throws Left. Height, 6 feet, 3 inches. Weight, 195 pounds.

Year	Club	Lea	G	IP	W	L	Pct	SO	BB	H	ERA	SAVES
1990 Expos	Gulf Coast	13	35²/₃	3	1	.750	38	15	24	2.52	2
1991 Sumter	So. Atl.	16	73²/₃	2	2	.500	69	32	57	2.44	0
1992 Rockford	Midwest	7	9¹/₃	0	1	.000	8	5	12	5.79	1
1993 Burlington	Midwest	12	16²/₃	1	0	1.000	21	9	13	3.24	0
1993 San Berndno	California	20	131	8	7	.533	98	44	120	3.44	0
1994 Harrisburg	Eastern	12	79	7	2	.778	69	18	55	1.94	1
1994 Ottawa	Int.	17	119	7	5	.583	82	41	130	3.33	0
1995 Montreal	N.L.	28	141¹/₃	10	8	.556	106	28	142	3.69	0

Year	Club	Lea	G	IP	W	L	Pct	SO	BB	H	ERA	SAVE
1997	Montreal	N.L.	33	206 2/3	12	13	.480	110	48	206	3.88	0
1998	Expos	Gulf Coast	1	5	1	0	1.000	2	1	5	0.00	0
1998	Montreal-Los Angeles a	N.L.	34	241	11	14	.440	128	63	244	3.59	0
1999	Los Angeles	N.L.	17	89 2/3	2	10	.167	40	39	116	7.43	0
1999	Albuquerque b	P.C.	6	38	3	3	.500	14	10	46	5.92	0
2000	Los Angeles	N.L.	30	144	5	8	.385	64	33	192	5.56	0
Major League Totals	5 Yrs.		142	822 2/3	40	53	.430	448	211	900	4.44	0

a Traded to Los Angeles Dodgers with infielder Mark Grudzielanek and outfielder Hiram Bocachica for infielder Wilto Guerrero, outfielder Peter Bergeron, pitcher Ted Lilly and infielder Jonathan Tucker, July 31, 1998.
b On disabled list from September 7 to November 17, 1999.

PERISHO, MATTHEW ALAN (MATT)

Born, Burlington, Iowa, June 8, 1975.
Bats Left. Throws Right. Height, 6 feet. Weight, 175 pounds.

Year	Club	Lea	G	IP	W	L	Pct	SO	BB	H	ERA	SAVE
1993	Angels	Arizona	11	64	7	3	.700	65	23	58	3.66	0
1994	Cedar Rapds	Midwest	27	147 2/3	12	9	.571	107	88	165	4.33	0
1995	Lk Elsinore	California	24	115 1/3	8	9	.471	68	60	137	6.32	0
1996	Lk Elsinore	California	21	128 2/3	7	5	.583	97	58	131	4.20	0
1996	Midland	Texas	8	53 1/3	3	2	.600	50	20	48	3.21	0
1997	Midland	Texas	10	73	5	2	.714	62	26	60	2.96	0
1997	Vancouver	P.C.	9	52 1/3	4	4	.500	47	29	68	5.33	0
1997	Anaheim a	A.L.	11	45	0	2	.000	35	28	59	6.00	0
1998	Tulsa	Texas	1	3	0	0	.000	1	3	3	6.00	0
1998	Oklahoma	P.C.	15	90 1/3	8	5	.615	60	42	91	3.89	0
1998	Texas b	A.L.	2	5	0	2	.000	2	8	15	27.00	0
1999	Oklahoma	P.C.	27	156 1/3	15	7	.682	150	78	160	4.61	0
1999	Texas	A.L.	4	10 1/3	0	0	.000	17	2	8	2.61	0
2000	Texas c	A.L.	34	105	2	7	.222	74	67	136	7.37	0
Major League Totals	4 Yrs.		51	165 1/3	2	11	.154	128	105	218	7.29	0

a Traded to Texas Rangers for infielder Mike Bell, October 31, 1997.
b On disabled list from June 29 to July 25, 1998.
c Traded to Detroit Tigers for pitcher Kevin Mobley and pitcher Brandon Villafuerte, December 15, 2000.

PERSON, ROBERT ALAN

Born, Lowell, Massachusetts, October 6, 1969.
Bats Right. Throws Right. Height, 5 feet, 11 inches. Weight, 180 pounds.

Year	Club	Lea	G	IP	W	L	Pct	SO	BB	H	ERA	SAVE
1989	Burlington	Appal.	10	34	0	1	.000	19	17	23	3.18	1
1990	Kinston	Carolina	4	16 2/3	1	0	1.000	7	9	17	2.70	0
1990	Indians	Gulf Coast	8	7 1/3	0	2	.000	8	4	10	7.36	2
1990	Watertown	N.Y.-Penn.	5	16 1/3	1	0	1.000	19	7	8	1.10	0
1991	Kinston a	Carolina	11	52	3	5	.375	45	42	56	4.67	0
1991	Bend	Northwest	2	10	1	1	.500	6	5	6	3.60	0
1991	South Bend	Midwest	13	76 1/3	4	3	.571	66	56	50	3.30	0
1992	Sarasota b-c-d	Fla. St.	19	105 1/3	5	7	.417	85	62	90	3.59	0
1993	High Desert e	California	28	169	12	10	.545	107	48	184	4.69	0
1994	Binghamton	Eastern	31	159	9	6	.600	130	68	124	3.45	0
1995	Binghamton	Eastern	26	66 2/3	5	4	.556	65	25	46	3.11	7
1995	Norfolk	Int.	5	32	2	1	.667	33	13	30	4.50	0
1995	New York	N.L.	3	12	1	0	1.000	10	2	5	0.75	0
1996	Norfolk	Int.	8	43	5	0	1.000	32	21	33	3.35	0
1996	New York f	N.L.	27	89 2/3	4	5	.444	76	35	86	4.52	0
1997	Syracuse	Int.	1	7	1	0	1.000	5	2	4	0.00	0
1997	Toronto g	A.L.	23	128 1/3	5	10	.333	99	60	125	5.61	0
1998	Syracuse	Int.	20	59	3	3	.500	55	29	38	2.29	6
1998	Toronto	A.L.	27	38 1/3	3	1	.750	31	22	45	7.04	6
1999	Dunedin	Fla.St.	1	3	0	0	.000	3	1	4	3.00	0
1999	Toronto	A.L.	11	11	0	2	.000	12	15	9	9.82	2
1999	Philadelphia h-i	N.L.	31	137	10	5	.667	127	70	130	4.27	0
2000	Clearwater	Fla.St.	1	2 2/3	0	0	.000	2	1	3	6.75	0
2000	Reading	Eastern	1	4 2/3	1	0	1.000	7	3	3	5.79	0
2000	Philadelphia j	N.L.	28	173 1/3	9	7	.563	164	95	144	3.63	0
Major League Totals	6 Yrs.		150	589 2/3	32	30	.516	519	299	544	4.62	8

a Traded by Cleveland Indians to Chicago White Sox for pitcher Grady Hall, June 27, 1991.
b On disabled list from April 10 to May 13, 1992.

d Filed for free agency, December 19, 1992, re-signed with Florida Marlins organization, January 8, 1993.
e Traded to New York Mets for pitcher Steve Long, March 30, 1994.
f Traded to Toronto Blue Jays for first baseman John Olerud, December 21, 1996.
g On disabled list from May 8 to May 27 and September 9 to September 29, 1997.
h On disabled list from March 25 to April 12, 1999.
i Traded to Philadelphia Phillies for pitcher Paul Spoljaric, May 5, 1999.
j On disabled list from June 19 to July 21, 2000.

PETERS, CHRISTOPHER (CHRIS)
Born, Fort Thomas, Kentucky, January 28, 1972.
Bats Left. Throws Right. Height, 6 feet, 1 inch. Weight, 170 pounds.

Year Club	Lea	G	IP	W	L	Pct	SO	BB	H	ERA	SAVES
1993 Welland	N.Y.-Penn.	16	27²/₃	1	0	1.000	25	20	33	4.55	0
1994 Salem	Carolina	3	3¹/₃	1	0	1.000	2	1	5	13.50	0
1994 Augusta	So.Atl.	54	60²/₃	4	5	.444	83	33	51	4.30	4
1995 Lynchburg	Carolina	24	144²/₃	11	5	.688	132	35	126	2.43	0
1995 Carolina	Southern	2	14	2	0	1.000	7	2	9	1.29	0
1996 Carolina	Southern	14	92	7	3	.700	69	34	73	2.64	0
1996 Calgary	P.C.	4	27²/₃	1	1	.500	16	8	18	0.98	0
1996 Pittsburgh	N.L.	16	64	2	4	.333	28	25	72	5.63	0
1997 Calgary	P.C.	14	51¹/₃	2	4	.333	55	30	52	4.38	1
1997 Pittsburgh	N.L.	31	37¹/₃	2	2	.500	17	21	38	4.58	0
1998 Pittsburgh	N.L.	39	148	8	10	.444	103	55	142	3.47	0
1999 Nashville	P.C.	11	49¹/₃	3	1	.750	34	15	54	2.19	0
1999 Pittsburgh	N.L.	19	71	5	4	.556	46	27	98	6.59	0
2000 Nashville	P.C.	11	51²/₃	2	4	.333	31	26	70	5.57	0
2000 Pittsburgh a-b	N.L.	18	28¹/₃	0	1	.000	16	14	23	2.86	1
Major League Totals	5 Yrs.	123	348²/₃	17	21	.447	210	142	373	4.57	2

a On disabled list from August 7 to October 1, 2000.

b Not offered 2001 contract, December 21, 2000, signed with Montreal Expos organization, January 10, 2001

PETKOVSEK, MARK JOSEPH
Born, Beaumont, Texas, November 18, 1965.
Bats Right. Throws Right. Height, 6 feet, 1 inch. Weight, 185 pounds.

Year Club	Lea	G	IP	W	L	Pct	SO	BB	H	ERA	SAVES
1987 Rangers	Gulf Coast	3	5²/₃	0	0	.000	7	2	4	3.18	0
1987 Charlotte	Fla. St.	11	56	3	4	.429	23	17	67	4.02	0
1988 Charlotte	Fla. St.	28	175²/₃	10	11	.476	95	42	156	2.97	0
1989 Oklahoma City	A.A.	6	30²/₃	0	4	.000	8	18	39	7.34	0
1989 Tulsa	Texas	21	140	8	5	.615	66	35	144	3.47	0
1990 Oklahoma City	A.A.	28	151	7	14	.333	81	42	187	5.25	0
1991 Texas	A.L.	9	9¹/₃	0	1	.000	6	4	21	14.46	0
1991 Oklahoma City a	A.A.	25	149²/₃	9	8	.529	67	38	162	4.93	0
1992 Buffalo b	A.A.	32	150¹/₃	8	8	.500	49	44	150	3.53	1
1993 Buffalo c	A.A.	14	70²/₃	3	4	.429	27	16	74	4.33	0
1993 Pittsburgh d	N.L.	26	32¹/₃	3	0	1.000	14	9	43	6.96	0
1994 Tucson e-f	P.C.	25	138¹/₃	10	7	.588	69	40	176	4.62	0
1995 Louisville	A.A.	8	54¹/₃	4	1	.800	30	8	58	2.32	0
1995 St. Louis	N.L.	26	137¹/₃	6	6	.500	71	35	136	4.00	0
1996 St. Petersburg	Fla. St.	3	6	0	0	.000	5	0	6	4.50	0
1996 Louisville	A.A.	2	3	0	1	.000	4	1	5	9.00	0
1996 St. Louis g	N.L.	48	88²/₃	11	2	.846	45	35	83	3.55	0
1997 St. Louis	N.L.	55	96	4	7	.364	51	31	109	5.06	2
1998 St. Louis h	N.L.	48	105²/₃	7	4	.636	55	36	131	4.77	0
1999 Anaheim	A.L.	64	83	10	4	.714	43	21	85	3.47	1
2000 Lake Elsinore	California	2	2²/₃	0	0	.000	3	3	3	3.38	0
2000 Anaheim i-j	A.L.	64	81	4	2	.667	31	23	86	4.33	2
Major League Totals	8 Yrs.	335	633¹/₃	45	26	.634	316	194	694	4.50	5
Division Series											
1996 St. Louis	N.L.	1	2	0	0	.000	1	0	0	0.00	0
Championship Series											
1996 St. Louis	N.L.	6	7¹/₃	0	1	.000	7	3	11	7.36	0

a Filed for free agency from Texas Rangers, October 16, 1991 signed with Pittsburgh Pirates organization, Jan 22, 1992.

b Filed for free agency, October 15, 1992, re-signed with Pittsburgh Pirates organization November 9, 1992.

c On disabled list from July 4 to July 23, 1993.

d Filed for free agency, October 12, 1993, signed with Houston Astros organization, March 4, 1994.

e On disabled list from July 20 to August 12, 1994..

f Filed for free agency, October 15, 1994, signed with St. Louis Cardinals organization, November 18, 1994.
g On disabled list from April 1 to April 19, 1996.
h Traded to Anaheim Angels for player to be named later, December 14, 1998. St. Louis Cardinals received pitcher Matt Garrick to complete trade, December 18, 1998.
i On disabled list from May 17 to June 11, 2000.
j Filed for free agency, November 1, 2000, signed with Texas Rangers, December 10, 2000.

PETTITTE, ANDREW EUGENE

Born, Baton Rouge, Louisiana, June 15, 1972.
Bats Left. Throws Left. Height, 6 feet, 5 inches. Weight, 235 pounds.

Year	Club	Lea	G	IP	W	L	Pct	SO	BB	H	ERA	SAVES
1991	Yankees	Gulf Coast	6	36²/₃	4	1	.800	51	8	16	0.98	0
1991	Oneonta	N.Y.-Penn.	6	33	2	2	.500	32	16	33	2.18	0
1992	Greensboro	So. Atl.	27	168	10	4	.714	130	55	141	2.20	0
1993	Prince William	Carolina	26	159²/₃	11	9	.550	129	47	146	3.04	0
1993	Albany	Eastern	1	5	1	0	1.000	6	2	5	3.60	0
1994	Albany	Eastern	11	73	7	2	.778	50	18	60	2.71	0
1994	Columbus	Int.	16	96²/₃	7	2	.778	61	21	101	2.98	0
1995	Columbus	Int.	2	11²/₃	0	0	.000	8	0	7	0.00	0
1995	New York	A.L.	31	175	12	9	.571	114	63	183	4.17	0
1996	New York	A.L.	35	221	*21	8	.724	162	72	229	3.87	0
1997	New York	A.L.	35	240¹/₃	18	7	.720	166	65	233	2.88	0
1998	New York	A.L.	33	216¹/₃	16	11	.593	146	87	226	4.24	0
1999	Tampa	Fla.St.	1	5	1	0	1.000	8	2	4	0.00	0
1999	New York a	A.L.	31	191²/₃	14	11	.560	121	89	216	4.70	0
2000	New York b	A.L.	32	204²/₃	19	9	.679	125	80	219	4.35	0
Major League Totals		6 Yrs.	197	1249	100	55	.645	834	456	1306	3.99	0
Division Series												
1995	New York	A.L.	1	7	0	0	.000	0	3	9	5.14	0
1996	New York	A.L.	1	6¹/₃	0	0	.000	3	6	4	5.68	0
1997	New York	A.L.	2	11²/₃	0	2	.000	5	1	15	8.49	0
1998	New York	A.L.	1	7	1	0	1.000	8	0	3	1.29	0
1999	New York	A.L.	1	7¹/₃	1	0	1.000	5	0	7	1.23	0
2000	New York	A.L.	2	11¹/₃	1	0	1.000	7	3	15	3.97	0
Division Series Totals			8	50²/₃	3	2	.600	28	13	53	4.62	0
Championship Series												
1996	New York	A.L.	2	15	1	0	1.000	7	5	10	3.60	0
1998	New York	A.L.	1	4²/₃	0	1	.000	1	3	8	11.57	0
1999	New York	A.L.	1	7¹/₃	1	0	1.000	5	1	8	2.45	0
2000	New York	A.L.	1	6²/₃	1	0	1.000	2	1	9	2.70	0
Championship Series Totals			5	33²/₃	3	1	.750	15	10	35	4.28	0
World Series Record												
1996	New York	A.L.	2	10²/₃	1	1	.500	5	4	11	5.91	0
1998	New York	A.L.	1	7¹/₃	1	0	1.000	4	3	5	0.00	0
1999	New York	A.L.	1	3²/₃	0	0	.000	1	1	10	12.27	0
2000	New York	A.L.	2	13²/₃	0	0	.000	9	4	16	1.98	0
World Series Totals			6	35¹/₃	2	1	.667	19	12	42	3.82	0

a On disabled list from March 26 to April 17, 1999.
b On disabled list from April 8 to April 25, 2000.

PICHARDO, HIPOLITO ANTONIO

Born, Jicome Esperanza, Dominican Republic, August 22, 1969.
Bats Right. Throws Right. Height, 6 feet, 1 inch. Weight, 185 pounds.

Year	Club	Lea	G	IP	W	L	Pct	SO	BB	H	ERA	SAVES
1988	Royals	Gulf Coast	1	1¹/₃	0	0	.000	3	1	3	13.50	0
1989	Appleton	Midwest	12	75²/₃	5	4	.556	50	18	58	2.97	0
1990	Baseball Cy	Fla.St.	11	45	1	6	.143	40	25	47	3.80	0
1991	Memphis	Southern	34	99	3	11	.214	75	38	116	4.27	0
1992	Memphis	Southern	2	14	0	0	.000	10	1	13	0.64	0
1992	Kansas City	A.L.	31	143²/₃	9	6	.600	59	49	148	3.95	0
1993	Kansas City a	A.L.	30	165	7	8	.467	70	53	183	4.04	0
1994	Kansas City	A.L.	45	67²/₃	5	3	.625	36	24	82	4.92	3
1995	Kansas City b	A.L.	44	64	8	4	.667	43	30	66	4.36	1
1996	Kansas City	A.L.	57	68	3	5	.375	43	26	74	5.43	3
1997	Omaha	A.A.	5	4²/₃	0	0	.000	3	3	5	5.79	1

298

Year	Club	Lea	G	IP	W	L	Pct	SO	BB	H	ERA	SAVES
1997 Kansas City c-d	....	A.L.	47	49	3	5	.375	34	24	51	4.22	11
1998 Lansing	....	Midwest	1	1	0	0	.000	0	0	0	0.00	0
1998 Kansas City e	....	A.L.	27	112⅓	7	8	.467	55	43	126	5.13	1
1999 Kansas City f-g	....	A.L.			INJURED - did not play							
2000 Sarasota	....	Fla.St.	7	13	1	1	.500	12	0	9	1.38	0
2000 Pawtucket	....	Int.	3	4⅔	0	0	.000	4	0	2	0.00	0
2000 Boston	....	A.L.	38	65	6	3	.667	37	26	63	3.46	1
Major League Totals	.... 8 Yrs.		319	734⅔	48	42	.533	377	275	793	4.39	20

a On disabled list from August 14 to September 1, 1993.
b On disabled list from August 15 to September 1, 1995.
c On disabled list from July 5 to August 26, 1997.
d Filed for free agency, October 31, 1997, re-signed with Kansas City Royals, December 4, 1997.
e On disabled list from May 6 to May 23 and August 21 to September 28, 1998.
f On disabled list from April 5 to November 1, 1999.
g Filed for free agency, November 11, 1999, signed with Boston Red Sox organization, February 16, 2000.

PLESAC, DANIEL THOMAS
Born, Gary, Indiana, February 4, 1962.
Bats Left. Throws Left. Height, 6 feet, 5 inches. Weight, 215 pounds.

Year	Club	Lea	G	IP	W	L	Pct	SO	BB	H	ERA	SAVES
1983 Paintsville	....	Appal.	14	82⅓	*9	1	*.900	*85	57	76	3.50	0
1984 Stockton	....	California	16	108⅓	6	6	.500	101	50	106	3.32	0
1984 El Paso	....	Texas	7	39	2	2	.500	24	16	43	3.46	0
1985 El Paso	....	Texas	25	150⅓	12	5	.706	128	68	171	3.97	0
1986 Milwaukee	....	A.L.	51	91	10	7	.588	75	29	81	2.97	14
1987 Milwaukee	....	A.L.	57	79⅓	5	6	.455	89	23	63	2.61	23
1988 Milwaukee	....	A.L.	50	52⅓	1	2	.333	52	12	46	2.41	30
1989 Milwaukee	....	A.L.	52	61⅓	3	4	.429	52	17	47	2.35	33
1990 Milwaukee	....	A.L.	66	69	3	7	.300	65	31	67	4.43	24
1991 Milwaukee a	....	A.L.	45	92⅓	2	7	.222	61	39	92	4.29	8
1992 Milwaukee b	....	A.L.	44	79	5	4	.556	54	35	64	2.96	1
1993 Chicago	....	N.L.	57	62⅔	2	1	.667	47	21	74	4.74	0
1994 Chicago c	....	N.L.	54	54⅔	2	3	.400	53	13	61	4.61	1
1995 Pittsburgh	....	N.L.	58	60⅓	4	4	.500	57	27	53	3.58	3
1996 Pittsburgh d-e	....	N.L.	73	70⅓	6	5	.545	76	24	67	4.09	11
1997 Toronto	....	A.L.	73	50⅓	2	4	.333	61	19	47	3.58	1
1998 Toronto	....	A.L.	78	50	4	3	.571	55	16	41	3.78	4
1999 Toronto	....	A.L.	30	22⅔	0	3	.000	26	9	28	8.34	0
1999 Arizona f	....	N.L.	34	21⅔	2	1	.667	27	8	22	3.32	1
2000 Arizona g	....	N.L.	62	40	5	1	.833	45	26	34	3.15	0
Major League Totals	.... 15 Yrs.		884	957	56	62	.475	895	349	887	3.65	154
Division Series												
1999 Arizona	....	N.L.	1	0⅓	0	0	.000	0	0	3	54.00	0

a On disabled list from April 22 to May 12, 1991.
b Filed for free agency, October 27; signed with Chicago Cubs, December 8, 1992.
c Filed for free agency, October 14; signed with Pittsburgh Pirates, November 8, 1994.
d Traded to Toronto Blue Jays with outfielder Orlando Merced and infielder Carlos Garcia for pitcher Jose Silva, pitcher Jose Pett, infielder Brandon Cromer and players to be named later, November 14, 1996.
e Pittsburgh Pirates received pitcher Mike Halperin, infielder Abraham Nunez and catcher Craig Wilson to complete trade, December 11, 1996.
f Traded to Arizona Diamondbacks for infielder Tony Batista and pitcher John Frascatore, June 12, 1999.
g Filed for free agency, October 30, 2000, signed with Toronto Blue Jays, December 8, 2000.

POLITTE, CLIFFORD (CLIFF)
Born, Kirkwood, Missouri, February 27, 1974.
Bats Right. Throws Right. Height, 5 feet, 11 inches. Weight, 185 pounds.

Year	Club	Lea	G	IP	W	L	Pct	SO	BB	H	ERA	SAVES
1996 Peoria	....	Midwest	25	149⅔	14	6	.700	151	47	108	2.59	0
1997 Pr William	....	Carolina	19	120⅓	11	1	.917	118	31	89	2.24	0
1997 Arkansas	....	Texas	6	37⅔	4	1	.800	26	9	35	2.15	0
1998 Memphis	....	P.C.	10	50⅔	1	4	.200	42	24	71	7.64	0
1998 Arkansas	....	Texas	10	67	5	3	.625	61	16	56	2.96	0
1998 St. Louis a	....	N.L.	8	37	2	3	.400	22	18	45	6.32	0
1999 Reading	....	Eastern	37	109	9	8	.529	97	33	112	3.63	0
1999 Philadelphia	....	N.L.	13	17⅔	1	0	1.000	15	15	19	7.13	0
2000 Scranton-WB	....	Int.	21	112⅔	8	4	.667	106	41	94	3.12	0

Year	Club	Lea	G	IP	W	L	Pct	SO	BB	H	ERA	SAVES
2000 Philadelphia		.N.L.	12	59	4	3	.571	50	27	55	3.66	0
Major League Totals	.3 Yrs.		33	113²/₃	7	6	.538	87	60	119	5.07	0

a Traded to Philadelphia Phillies with outfielder Ron Gant, pitcher Jeff Brantley and cash for pitcher Ricky Bottalico and pitcher Garrett Stephenson, November 19, 1998.

PONSON, SIDNEY ALTON
Born, Noord, Aruba, November 2, 1976.
Bats Right. Throws Right. Height, 6 feet, 1 inch. Weight, 220 pounds.

Year	Club	Lea	G	IP	W	L	Pct	SO	BB	H	ERA	SAVES
1994 Orioles		.Gulf Coast	12	73	4	3	.571	53	17	68	2.96	0
1995 Bluefield		.Appal.	13	77²/₃	6	3	.667	56	16	79	4.17	0
1996 Frederick		.Carolina	18	107	7	6	.538	110	28	98	3.45	0
1997 Bowie		.Eastern	13	74²/₃	2	7	.222	56	32	77	5.42	0
1997 Orioles a		.Gulf Coast	1	2	1	0	1.000	1	0	0	0.00	0
1998 Rochester		.Int.	1	5	1	0	1.000	3	1	4	0.00	0
1998 Baltimore		.A.L.	31	135	8	9	.471	85	42	157	5.27	1
1999 Baltimore		.A.L.	32	210	12	12	.500	112	80	227	4.71	0
2000 Baltimore		.A.L.	32	222	9	13	.409	152	83	223	4.82	0
Major League Totals	.3 Yrs.		95	567	29	34	.460	349	205	607	4.89	1

a On disabled list from June 13 to July 15, 1997.

POTE, LOUIS WILLIAM (LOU)
Born, Evergreen Park, Illinois, August 27, 1971.
Bats Right. Throws Right. Height, 6 feet, 3 inches. Weight, 190 pounds.

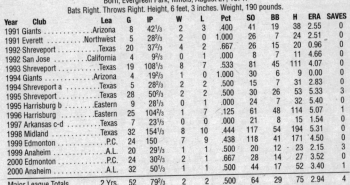

Year	Club	Lea	G	IP	W	L	Pct	SO	BB	H	ERA	SAVES
1991 Giants		.Arizona	8	42¹/₃	2	3	.400	41	19	38	2.55	0
1991 Everett		.Northwest	5	28²/₃	2	0	1.000	26	7	24	2.51	0
1992 Shreveport		.Texas	20	37²/₃	4	2	.667	26	15	20	0.96	0
1992 San Jose		.California	4	9²/₃	0	1	.000	8	7	11	4.66	0
1993 Shreveport		.Texas	19	108¹/₃	8	7	.533	81	45	111	4.07	0
1994 Giants		.Arizona	4	19²/₃	1	0	1.000	30	6	9	0.00	0
1994 Shreveport a		.Texas	5	28²/₃	2	2	.500	15	7	31	2.83	0
1995 Shreveport		.Texas	28	50²/₃	2	2	.500	30	26	53	5.33	3
1995 Harrisburg b		.Eastern	9	28¹/₃	0	1	.000	24	7	32	5.40	0
1996 Harrisburg		.Eastern	25	104²/₃	1	7	.125	61	48	114	5.07	1
1997 Arkansas c-d		.Texas	7	23¹/₃	0	0	.000	21	8	15	1.54	0
1998 Midland		.Texas	32	154¹/₃	8	10	.444	117	54	194	5.31	0
1999 Edmonton		.P.C.	24	150	7	9	.438	118	41	171	4.50	0
1999 Anaheim		.A.L.	24	29¹/₃	1	1	.500	20	12	23	2.15	3
2000 Edmonton		.P.C.	24	30²/₃	2	1	.667	28	14	27	3.52	0
2000 Anaheim		.A.L.	32	50¹/₃	1	1	.500	44	17	52	3.40	1
Major League Totals	.2 Yrs.		52	79²/₃	2	2	.500	64	29	75	2.94	4

a On disabled list from April 8 to July 31, 1994.
b Traded by San Francisco Giants to Montreal Expos for pitcher Luis Aguino, July 24, 1995.
c Released by Montreal Expos, March 28, 1997, signed with St. Louis Cardinals organization, August 7, 1997.
d Filed for free agency, October 17, 1997, signed with Anaheim Angels organization, December 15, 1997.

PROKOPEC, KENNETH LUKE (LUKE)
Born, Blackwood, Australia, February 23, 1978.
Bats Left. Throws Right. Height, 5 feet, 11 inches. Weight, 166 pounds.

Year	Club	Lea	G	IP	W	L	Pct	SO	BB	H	ERA	SAVES
1997 Savannah		.So.Atl.	13	42	3	1	.750	45	12	37	4.07	0
1998 San Berndno		.California	20	110¹/₃	8	5	.615	148	33	98	2.69	0
1998 San Antonio		.Texas	5	26	3	0	1.000	25	13	16	1.38	0
1999 San Antonio		.Texas	27	157²/₃	8	12	.400	128	46	172	5.42	0
2000 San Antonio		.Texas	22	128²/₃	7	3	.700	124	23	118	2.45	0
2000 Los Angeles		.N.L.	5	21	1	1	.500	12	9	19	3.00	0

QUANTRILL, PAUL JOHN
Born, London, Ontario, Canada, November 3, 1966.
Bats Left. Throws Right. Height, 6 feet, 1 inch. Weight, 185 pounds.

Year	Club	Lea	G	IP	W	L	Pct	SO	BB	H	ERA	SAVES
1989 Sarasota Red Sox		Gulf C.	2	5	0	0	.000	5	0	2	0.00	2
1989 Elmira		N.Y.-Penn.	20	76	5	4	.556	57	12	90	3.43	2
1990 Winter Haven		Fla. St.	7	45²/₃	2	5	.286	14	6	46	4.14	0
1990 New Britain		Eastern	22	132²/₃	7	11	.389	53	23	149	3.53	0
1991 New Britain		Eastern	5	35	2	1	.667	18	8	32	2.06	0
1991 Pawtucket		Int.	25	155²/₃	10	7	.588	74	29	165	4.45	0
1992 Pawtucket		Int.	19	119	6	8	.429	56	20	143	4.46	0
1992 Boston		A.L.	27	49¹/₃	2	3	.400	24	15	55	2.19	1
1993 Boston		A.L.	49	138	6	12	.333	66	44	151	3.91	1
1994 Boston a		A.L.	17	23	1	1	.500	15	5	25	3.52	0
1994 Scranton		Int.	8	57	3	3	.500	36	6	55	3.47	0
1994 Philadelphia		N.L.	18	30	2	2	.500	13	10	39	6.00	1
1995 Philadelphia b		N.L.	33	179¹/₃	11	12	.478	103	44	212	4.67	0
1996 Toronto		A.L.	38	134¹/₃	5	14	.263	86	51	172	5.43	0
1997 Toronto		A.L.	77	88	6	7	.462	56	17	103	1.94	5
1998 Toronto		A.L.	82	80	3	4	.429	59	22	88	2.59	7
1999 Dunedin		Fla.St.	5	6	0	1	.000	2	1	5	4.50	0
1999 Syracuse		Int.	2	2	0	0	.000	1	0	1	0.00	0
1999 Toronto c		A.L.	41	48²/₃	3	2	.600	28	17	53	3.33	0
2000 Toronto		A.L.	68	83²/₃	2	5	.286	47	25	100	4.52	1
Major League Totals	9 Yrs.		450	854¹/₃	41	62	.398	497	250	998	3.97	16

a Traded to Philadelphia Phillies with outfielder Billy Hatcher for outfielder Wes Chamberlain and pitcher Mike Sullivan, May 31, 1994.
b Traded by Philadelphia Phillies to Toronto Blue Jays for infielder Howard Battle and pitcher Ricardo Jordan, December 6, 1995.
c On disabled list from March 27 to June 15, 1999.

QUEVEDO, RUBEN EDUARDO
Born, Valencia, Venezuela, January 5, 1979.
Bats Right. Throws Right. Height, 6 feet, 1 inch. Weight, 190 pounds.

Year	Club	Lea	G	IP	W	L	Pct	SO	BB	H	ERA	SAVES
1996 Braves		Gulf Coast	10	55	2	6	.250	49	9	50	2.29	0
1997 Danville		Appal.	13	68¹/₃	1	5	.167	78	27	46	3.56	0
1998 Macon		So.Atl.	25	112	11	3	.786	117	31	114	3.13	0
1998 Danville		Carolina	6	32²/₃	0	2	.000	35	13	28	3.58	0
1999 Richmond		Int.	21	105²/₃	6	5	.545	98	34	112	5.37	0
1999 Iowa a-b		P.C.	7	44¹/₃	3	1	.750	50	21	34	3.45	1
2000 Iowa		P.C.	13	74²/₃	7	2	.778	77	31	68	4.22	0
2000 Chicago		N.L.	21	88	3	10	.231	65	54	96	7.47	0

a Traded by Atlanta Braves to Chicago Cubs with pitcher Micah Bowie and player to be named later for pitcher Terry Mulholland and infielder Jose Hernandez, July 31, 1999.
b Chicago Cubs received pitcher Joey Nation to complete trade, August 24, 1999.

RADKE, BRAD WILLIAM
Born, Eau Claire, Wisconsin, October 27, 1972.
Bats Right. Throws Right. Height, 6 feet, 2 inches. Weight, 180 pounds.

Year	Club	Lea	G	IP	W	L	Pct	SO	BB	H	ERA	SAVES
1991 Twins		Gulf Coast	10	49²/₃	3	4	.429	46	14	41	3.08	1
1992 Kehosha		Midwest	26	165²/₃	10	10	.500	127	47	149	2.93	0
1993 Ft. Myers		Fla. St.	14	92	3	5	.375	69	21	85	3.82	0
1993 Nashville		Southern	13	76	2	6	.250	76	16	81	4.62	0
1994 Nashville		Southern	29	186¹/₃	12	9	.571	123	34	167	2.66	0
1995 Minnesota		A.L.	29	181	11	14	.440	75	47	195	5.32	0
1996 Minnesota		A.L.	35	232	11	16	.407	148	57	231	4.46	0
1997 Minnesota		A.L.	35	239²/₃	20	10	.667	174	48	238	3.87	0
1998 Minnesota		A.L.	32	213²/₃	12	14	.462	146	43	238	4.30	0
1999 Minnesota		A.L.	33	218²/₃	12	14	.462	121	44	239	3.75	0
2000 Minnesota		A.L.	34	226²/₃	12	*16	.429	141	51	261	4.45	0
Major League Totals	6 Yrs.		198	1311²/₃	78	84	.481	805	290	1402	4.32	0

RAIN, STEVEN NICHOLAS (STEVE)

Born, Los Angeles, California, June 2, 1975.
Bats Right. Throws Right. Height, 6 feet, 6 inches. Weight, 250 pounds.

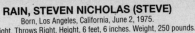

Year	Club	Lea	G	IP	W	L	Pct	SO	BB	H	ERA	SAVES
1993	Cubs	Gulf Coast	10	37	1	3	.250	29	17	37	3.89	0
1994	Huntington	Appal.	14	68	3	3	.500	55	19	55	2.65	0
1995	Rockford	Midwest	53	59¹/₃	5	2	.714	66	23	38	1.21	23
1996	Orlando	Southern	35	38²/₃	1	0	1.000	48	12	32	2.56	10
1996	Iowa	A.A.	26	26	2	1	.667	23	8	17	3.12	10
1997	Iowa	A.A.	40	44¹/₃	7	1	.875	50	34	51	5.89	1
1997	Orlando	Southern	14	14²/₃	1	2	.333	11	8	16	3.07	4
1998	Iowa a	P.C.	29	103²/₃	4	6	.400	83	64	118	6.68	0
1999	Iowa	P.C.	8	9	0	1	.000	9	4	7	2.00	0
1999	West Tenn	Southern	40	45¹/₃	3	1	.750	55	16	32	1.59	0
1999	Chicago	N.L.	16	14²/₃	0	1	.000	12	7	28	9.20	0
2000	Iowa	P.C.	28	31¹/₃	0	2	.000	34	6	31	3.45	0
2000	Chicago b	N.L.	37	49²/₃	3	4	.429	54	27	46	4.35	0
Major League Totals	2 Yrs.		53	64¹/₃	3	5	.375	66	34	74	5.46	0

a On disabled list from June 24 to July 6, 1998.
b Not offered 2001 contract, December 20, 2000.

RAMSAY, ROBERT ARTHUR

Born, Vancouver, Washington, December 3, 1973.
Bats Left. Throws Right. Height, 6 feet, 5 inches. Weight, 230 pounds.

Year	Club	Lea	G	IP	W	L	Pct	SO	BB	H	ERA	SAVES
1996	Red Sox	Gulf Coast	2	3²/₃	0	1	.000	5	3	5	4.91	0
1996	Sarasota	Fla.St.	12	34	2	2	.500	32	27	42	6.09	0
1997	Sarasota	Fla.St.	23	135²/₃	9	9	.500	115	63	134	4.78	0
1998	Trenton	Eastern	27	162²/₃	12	6	.667	166	50	137	3.49	0
1999	Pawtucket	Int.	20	114¹/₃	6	6	.500	79	36	114	5.35	0
1999	Tacoma	P.C.	5	33¹/₃	4	1	.800	37	14	20	1.08	0
1999	Seattle a	A.L.	6	18¹/₃	0	2	.000	11	9	23	6.38	0
2000	Tacoma	P.C.	3	16	0	1	.000	6	6	16	4.50	0
2000	Everett	Northwest	1	2	0	0	.000	4	0	2	0.00	0
2000	Seattle b	A.L.	37	50¹/₃	1	1	.500	32	40	43	3.40	0
Major League Totals	2 Yrs.		43	68²/₃	1	3	.250	43	49	66	4.19	0
Championship Series												
2000	Seattle	A.L.	2	1²/₃	0	0	.000	1	0	2	0.00	0

a Traded by Boston Red Sox to Seattle Mariners for outfielder Butch Huskey, July 26, 1999.
b On disabled list from August 14 to August 28, 2000.

RAPP, PATRICK LELAND (PAT)

Born, Jennings, Louisiana, July 13, 1967.
Bats Right. Throws Right. Height, 6 feet, 3 inches. Weight, 205 pounds.

Year	Club	Lea	G	IP	W	L	Pct	SO	BB	H	ERA	SAVES
1989	Pocatello	Pioneer	16	73	4	6	.400	40	29	90	5.30	0
1990	Clinton	Midwest	27	167¹/₃	14	10	.583	132	79	132	2.64	0
1991	San Jose	California	16	90	7	5	.583	73	37	88	2.50	0
1991	Shreveport	Texas	10	60¹/₃	6	2	.750	46	22	52	2.69	0
1992	Phoenix	P.C.	39	121	7	8	.467	79	40	115	3.05	3
1992	San Francisco a	N.L.	3	10	0	2	.000	3	6	8	7.20	0
1993	Edmonton	P.C.	17	107²/₃	8	3	.727	93	34	89	3.43	0
1993	Florida	N.L.	16	94	4	6	.400	57	39	101	4.02	0
1994	Florida b	N.L.	24	133¹/₃	7	8	.467	75	69	132	3.85	0
1995	Charlotte	Int.	1	6	0	1	.000	5	1	6	6.00	0
1995	Florida	N.L.	28	167¹/₃	14	7	.667	102	76	158	3.44	0
1996	Charlotte	Int.	2	11	1	1	.500	9	4	18	8.18	0
1996	Florida	N.L.	30	162¹/₃	8	*16	.333	86	91	184	5.10	0
1997	Phoenix c-d	P.C.	3	15	2	0	1.000	6	9	16	3.60	0
1997	Florida-San Francisco	N.L.	27	141²/₃	5	8	.385	92	72	158	4.83	0
1998	Kansas City e-f	A.L.	32	188¹/₃	12	13	.480	132	107	208	5.30	0
1999	Boston g	A.L.	37	146¹/₃	6	7	.462	90	69	147	4.12	0
2000	Baltimore h	A.L.	31	174	9	12	.429	106	83	203	5.90	0
Major League Totals	9 Yrs.		228	1217¹/₃	65	79	.451	743	612	1299	4.67	0
Championship Series												
1999	Boston	A.L.	1	1	0	0	.000	0	1	0	0.00	0

a Selected by Florida Marlins in expansion draft, November 17, 1992.

b Appeared in one additional game as pinch runner.
c Traded to San Francisco Giants for pitcher Brandon Leese and pitcher Bobby Rector, July 18, 1997. On disabled list from July 20 to August 6, 1997.
d Released by San Francisco Giants, December 19, 1997.
e Signed with Kansas City Royals organization, January 22, 1998.
f Not offered 1999 contract, December 19, 1998. Signed with Boston Red Sox, January 11, 1999.
g Not offered 2000 contract, November 2, 1999. Signed with Baltimore Orioles, January 28, 2000.
h Not offered 2001 contract, October 23, 2000, signed with Anaheim Angels, December 11, 2000.

REAMES, WILLIAM BRITT (BRITT)

Born, Seneca, South Carolina, August 19, 1973.
Bats Right. Throws Right. Height, 5 feet, 11 inches. Weight, 175 pounds.

Year	Club	Lea	G	IP	W	L	Pct	SO	BB	H	ERA	SAVES
1995	New Jersey	N.Y.-Penn.	5	29²/3	2	1	.667	42	12	19	1.52	0
1995	Savannah	So.Atl.	10	54²/3	3	5	.375	63	15	41	3.46	0
1996	Peoria Midwest		.25	161	15	7	.682	167	41	97	1.90	0
1997	Peoria a	Midwest		INJURED - did not play								
1998	Peoria b	Midwest		INJURED - did not play								
1999	Potomac	Carolina	10	36²/3	3	2	.600	22	21	34	3.19	0
2000	Memphis	P.C.	13	75	6	2	.750	77	20	55	2.28	1
2000	Arkansas	Texas	8	39²/3	2	3	.400	39	18	46	6.13	0
2000	St. Louis c	N.L.	8	40²/3	2	1	.667	31	23	30	2.88	0
	Division Series											
2000	St. Louis	N.L.	2	31/3	1	0	1.000	2	3	0	0.00	0
	Championship Series											
2000	St. Louis	N.L.	2	61/3	0	0	.000	6	4	5	1.42	0

a On disabled list from April 4 to September 8, 1997.
b On disabled list from April 10 to September 15, 1998.
c Traded to Montreal Expos with infielder Fernando Tatis for pitcher Dustin Hermanson and pitcher Steve Kline, December 14, 2000.

REDMAN, MARK ALLEN

Born, San Diego, California, January 5, 1974.
Bats Left. Throws Right. Height, 6 feet, 5 inches. Weight, 220 pounds.

Year	Club	Lea	G	IP	W	L	Pct	SO	BB	H	ERA	SAVES
1995	Fort Myers	Fla.St.	8	32²/3	2	1	.667	26	13	28	2.76	0
1996	Ft. Myers	Fla.St.	13	82²/3	3	4	.429	75	34	63	1.85	0
1996	New Britain	Eastern	16	106¹/3	7	7	.500	96	50	101	3.81	0
1996	Salt Lake	P.C.	1	4	0	0	.000	4	2	7	9.00	0
1997	Salt Lake	P.C.	29	158¹/3	8	15	.348	125	80	204	6.31	1
1998	New Britain	Eastern	8	47¹/3	4	2	.667	51	17	40	1.52	0
1998	Salt Lake a	P.C.	19	99¹/3	6	7	.462	88	41	111	5.53	0
1999	Salt Lake	P.C.	24	133²/3	9	9	.500	114	51	141	5.05	0
1999	Minnesota b	A.L.	5	12²/3	1	0	1.000	11	7	17	8.53	0
2000	Minnesota	A.L.	32	151¹/3	12	9	.571	117	45	168	4.76	0
Major League Totals		2 Yrs.	37	164	13	9	.591	128	52	185	5.05	0

a On disabled list from August 1 to 8, 1998.
b On disabled list from July 25 to August 10, 1999.

REED, RICHARD ALLEN (RICK)

Born, Huntington, West Virginia, August 16, 1965.
Bats Right. Throws Right. Height, 6 feet, 1 inch. Weight, 195 pounds.

Year	Club	Lea	G	IP	W	L	Pct	SO	BB	H	ERA	SAVES
1986	Pirates	Gulf Coast	8	24	0	2	.000	15	6	20	3.75	0
1986	Macon	So. Atl.	1	6¹/3	0	0	.000	1	2	5	2.84	0
1987	Macon	So. Atl.	46	93²/3	8	4	.667	92	29	80	2.50	7
1988	Salem	Carolina	15	72¹/3	6	2	.750	73	17	56	2.74	0
1988	Harrisburg	Eastern	2	16	1	0	1.000	17	2	11	1.13	0
1988	Pittsburgh	N.L.	2	12	1	0	1.000	6	2	10	3.00	0
1988	Buffalo	A.A.	10	77	5	2	.714	50	12	62	1.64	0
1989	Buffalo	A.A.	20	125²/3	9	8	.529	75	28	130	3.72	0
1989	Pittsburgh	N.L.	15	54²/3	1	4	.200	34	11	62	5.60	0
1990	Pittsburgh	N.L.	13	53²/3	2	3	.400	27	12	62	4.36	1
1990	Buffalo	A.A.	15	91	7	4	.636	63	21	82	3.46	0
1991	Pittsburgh	N.L.	1	4¹/3	0	0	.000	2	1	8	10.38	0
1991	Buffalo	A.A.	25	167²/3	14	4	.778	102	26	151	2.15	0

Year	Club	Lea	G	IP	W	L	Pct	SO	BB	H	ERA	SAVES
1992	Omaha a-b	A.A.	11	62	5	4	.556	35	12	67	4.35	1
1992	Kansas City	A.L.	19	100⅓	3	7	.300	49	20	105	3.68	0
1993	Omaha	A.A.	19	128⅓	11	4	.733	58	14	116	3.09	0
1993	Okla City	A.A.	5	34⅓	1	3	.250	21	2	43	4.19	0
1993	Kansas City-Texas c-d	A.L.	3	7⅔	1	0	1.000	5	2	12	5.87	0
1994	Okla City	A.A.	2	11⅔	1	1	.500	8	0	10	3.86	0
1994	Texas e-f	A.L.	4	16⅔	1	1	.500	12	7	17	5.94	0
1994	Indianaplis	A.A.	21	140⅓	9	5	.643	79	19	162	4.68	0
1995	Cincinnati	N.L.	4	17	0	0	.000	10	3	18	5.82	0
1995	Indianapols	A.A.	22	135	11	4	.733	92	26	127	3.33	0
1996	Norfolk g	Int.	28	182	8	10	.444	128	33	164	3.16	0
1997	New York	N.L.	33	208⅓	13	9	.591	113	31	186	2.89	0
1998	New York	N.L.	31	212⅓	16	11	.593	153	29	208	3.48	0
1999	Binghamton	Eastern	1	5	0	0	.000	5	1	1	1.80	0
1999	Norfolk	Int.	1	3	0	1	.000	2	2	10	27.00	0
1999	New York h	N.L.	26	149⅓	11	5	.688	104	47	163	4.58	0
2000	New York i-j	N.L.	30	184	11	5	.688	121	34	192	4.11	0
Major League Totals	12 Yrs.		181	1020⅓	60	45	.571	636	199	1043	3.93	1
Division Series												
1999	New York	N.L.	1	6	1	0	1.000	2	3	4	3.00	0
2000	New York	N.L.	1	6	0	0	.000	6	2	7	3.00	0
Division Series Totals			2	12	1	0	1.000	8	5	11	3.00	0
Championship Series												
1999	New York	N.L.	1	7	0	0	.000	5	0	3	2.57	0
2000	New York	N.L.	1	3⅓	0	1	.000	4	1	8	10.80	0
Championship Series Totals			2	10⅓	0	1	.000	9	1	11	5.23	0
World Series Record												
2000	New York	N.L.	1	6	0	0	.000	8	1	6	3.00	0

a Released by Pittsburgh Pirates organization, April 3, 1992.
b Signed as free agent with Kansas City Royals organization, April 4, 1992.
c Released by Kansas City Royals, August 5, 1993.
d Signed as free agent by Texas Rangers, August 11, 1993.
e Released by Texas Rangers, May 13, 1994.
f Signed as free agent with Cincinnati Reds organization, May 13, 1994.
g Signed by New York Mets as a minor league free agent, November 20, 1995.
h On disabled list from April 12 to May 3 and August 9 to September 4, 1999.
i On disabled list from June 30 to July 16, 2000.
j Filed for free agency, November 8, 2000, re-signed with New York Mets, December 6, 2000.

REED, STEVEN VINCENT

Born, Los Angeles, California, March 11, 1966.
Bats Right. Throws Right. Height, 6 feet, 2 inches. Weight, 205 pounds.

Year	Club	Lea	G	IP	W	L	Pct	SO	BB	H	ERA	SAVES
1988	Pocatello	Pioneer	31	46	4	1	.800	49	8	42	2.54	*13
1989	Clinton	Midwest	60	94⅔	5	3	.625	104	38	54	1.05	26
1989	San Jose	California	2	2	0	0	.000	3	1	0	0.00	0
1990	Shreveport	Texas	45	60⅓	3	1	.750	59	20	53	1.64	8
1991	Shreveport	Texas	15	21⅔	2	0	1.000	26	3	17	0.83	7
1991	Phoenix	P.C.	41	56⅓	2	3	.400	46	12	62	4.31	6
1992	Shreveport	Texas	27	29	1	0	1.000	33	0	18	0.62	23
1992	Phoenix	P.C.	29	31	0	1	.000	30	10	27	3.48	20
1992	San Francisco a	N.L.	18	15⅔	1	0	1.000	11	3	13	2.30	0
1993	Colorado Springs	P.C.	11	12⅓	0	0	.000	10	3	8	0.00	7
1993	Colorado	N.L.	64	84⅓	9	5	.643	51	30	80	4.48	3
1994	Colorado	N.L.	*61	64	3	2	.600	51	26	79	3.94	3
1995	Colorado	N.L.	71	84	5	2	.714	79	21	61	2.14	3
1996	Colorado	N.L.	70	75	4	3	.571	51	19	66	3.96	0
1997	Colorado b-c	N.L.	63	62⅓	4	6	.400	43	27	49	4.04	6
1998	San Francisco	N.L.	50	54⅔	2	1	.667	50	19	30	1.48	1
1998	Cleveland d	A.L.	20	25⅔	2	2	.500	23	8	26	6.66	0
1999	Cleveland	A.L.	63	61⅔	3	2	.600	44	20	69	4.23	0
2000	Cleveland	A.L.	57	56	2	0	1.000	39	21	58	4.34	0
Major League Totals	9 Yrs.		537	583⅓	35	23	.603	442	194	531	3.69	16
Division Series												
1995	Colorado	N.L.	3	2⅔	0	0	.000	3	1	2	0.00	0
1998	Cleveland	A.L.	2	0⅔	1	0	1.000	1	1	1	40.50	0
1999	Cleveland	A.L.	2	2⅓	0	0	.000	1	1	9	30.86	0
Division Series Totals			7	5⅔	1	0	1.000	5	3	12	17.47	0

Year	Club	Lea	G	IP	W	L	Pct	SO	BB	H	ERA	SAVES
	Championship Series											
1998 Cleveland	A.L.	3	1²/3	0	0	.000	0	1	0	0.00	0	

a Selected by Colorado Rockies in expansion draft, November 17, 1992.
b Released by Colorado Rockies, December 22, 1997.
c Signed as free agent with San Francisco Giants, December 24, 1997.
d Traded to Cleveland Indians with outfielder Jacob Cruz for pitcher Jose Mesa, pitcher Alvin Morman and infielder Shawon Dunston, July 24, 1998.

REICHERT, DANIEL ROBERT (DAN)
Born, Monterey, California, July 12, 1976.
Bats Right. Throws Right. Height, 6 feet, 3 inches. Weight, 175 pounds.

Year	Club	Lea	G	IP	W	L	Pct	SO	BB	H	ERA	SAVES
1997 Spokane	Northwest	9	38	3	4	.429	39	16	40	2.84	0
1998 Wichita	Texas	8	36	1	4	.200	24	29	52	9.75	0
1998 Lansing	Midwest	13	35²/3	1	1	.500	35	20	25	3.28	0
1998 Wilmington	Carolina	2	14	2	0	1.000	10	4	13	3.21	0
1998 Omaha	P.C.	3	17¹/3	1	1	.500	11	2	14	4.67	0
1999 Omaha	P.C.	17	111²/3	9	2	.818	123	50	92	3.71	0
1999 Kansas City a	A.L.	8	36²/3	2	2	.500	20	32	48	9.08	0
2000 Kansas City	A.L.	44	153¹/3	8	10	.444	94	91	157	4.70	2
Major League Totals	2 Yrs.	52	190	10	12	.455	114	123	205	5.54	2

a On disabled list from August 24 to November 16, 1999.

REKAR, BRYAN ROBERT
Born, Oaklawn, Illinois, June 3, 1972.
Bats Right. Throws Right. Height, 6 feet, 3 inches. Weight, 205 pounds.

Year	Club	Lea	G	IP	W	L	Pct	SO	BB	H	ERA	SAVES
1993 Bend	Northwest	13	75	3	5	.375	59	18	81	4.08	0
1994 Central Valley	California	22	111¹/3	6	6	.500	91	31	120	3.48	0
1995 New Haven	Eastern	12	80¹/3	6	3	.667	80	16	65	2.13	0
1995 Colorado Springs	P.C.	7	48¹/3	4	2	.667	39	13	29	1.49	0
1995 Colorado	N.L.	15	85	4	6	.400	60	24	95	4.98	0
1996 Colo Sprngs	P.C.	19	123	8	8	.500	75	36	138	4.46	0
1996 Colorado	N.L.	14	58¹/3	2	4	.333	25	26	87	8.95	0
1997 Colorado a	N.L.	2	9¹/3	1	0	1.000	4	6	11	5.79	0
1997 Colo Sprngs	P.C.	28	145	10	9	.526	116	39	169	5.46	0
1998 St. Pete	Fla.St.	4	13	0	0	.000	15	2	6	0.69	0
1998 Durham	Int.	3	11	0	1	.000	9	2	10	3.27	0
1998 Tampa Bay b	A.L.	16	86²/3	2	8	.200	55	21	95	4.98	0
1999 Tampa Bay	A.L.	27	94²/3	6	6	.500	55	41	121	5.80	0
1999 Durham	Int.	6	35	4	1	.800	26	8	29	3.86	0
2000 Durham	Int.	4	22	3	0	1.000	18	4	16	2.05	0
2000 Tampa Bay c	A.L.	30	173¹/3	7	10	.412	95	39	200	4.41	0
Major League Totals	6 Yrs.	104	507¹/3	22	34	.393	294	157	609	5.41	0

a Selected in expansion draft by Tampa Bay Devil Rays, November 18, 1997.
b On disabled list from March 31 to July 6, 1998.
c On disabled list from March 31 to April 29, 2000.

REMLINGER, MICHAEL JOHN
Born, Middletown, New York, March 26, 1966.
Bats Left. Throws Left. Height, 6 feet. Weight, 195 pounds.

Year	Club	Lea	G	IP	W	L	Pct	SO	BB	H	ERA	SAVES
1987 Everett	Northwest	2	5	0	0	.000	11	5	1	3.60	0
1987 Clinton	Midwest	6	30	2	1	.667	43	14	21	3.30	0
1987 Shreveport	Texas	6	34¹/3	4	2	.667	51	22	14	2.36	0
1988 Shreveport a	Texas	3	13	1	0	1.000	18	4	7	0.69	0
1989 Shreveport	Texas	16	90²/3	4	6	.400	92	73	68	2.98	0
1989 Phoenix	P.C.	11	43	1	6	.143	28	52	51	9.21	0
1990 Shreveport	Texas	25	147²/3	9	11	.450	75	72	149	3.90	0
1991 Phoenix	P.C.	19	108²/3	5	5	.500	68	59	134	6.38	0
1991 San Francisco b	N.L.	8	35	2	1	.667	19	20	36	4.37	0
1992 Calgary	P.C.	21	70¹/3	1	7	.125	24	48	97	6.65	0
1992 Jacksonville	Southern	5	26	1	1	.500	21	11	25	3.46	0

Year Club	Lea	G	IP	W	L	Pct	SO	BB	H	ERA	SAVES
1993 Calgary ..............P.C.		19	84²/₃	4	3	.571	51	52	100	5.53	0
1993 Jacksonville c ......Southern		7	39²/₃	1	3	.250	23	19	40	6.58	0
1994 Norfolk ....Int.		12	63	2	4	.333	45	25	57	3.14	0
1994 New York ............N.L.		10	54²/₃	1	5	.167	33	35	55	4.61	0
1995 Indianapolis ..........A.A.		41	46²/₃	5	3	.625	58	32	40	4.05	0
1995 New York-Cincinnati d-e .N.L.		7	6²/₃	0	1	.000	7	5	9	6.75	0
1996 Indianapolis ..........A.A.		28	89¹/₃	4	3	.571	97	44	64	2.52	0
1996 Cincinnati ............N.L.		19	27¹/₃	0	1	.000	19	19	24	5.60	0
1997 Cincinnati ............N.L.		69	124	8	8	.500	145	60	100	4.14	2
1998 Cincinnati f ...........N.L.		35	164¹/₃	8	15	.348	144	87	164	4.82	0
1999 Atlanta g .............N.L.		73	83²/₃	10	1	.909	81	35	66	2.37	1
2000 Atlanta h .............N.L.		71	72²/₃	5	3	.625	72	37	55	3.47	12
Major League Totals ....8 Yrs.		292	568¹/₃	34	35	.493	520	298	509	4.15	15
Division Series											
1999 Atlanta ...............N.L.		2	3²/₃	0	0	.000	4	3	4	9.82	0
2000 Atlanta ...............N.L.		3	3¹/₃	0	0	.000	3	0	6	2.70	0
Division Series Totals		5	7	0	0	.000	7	3	10	6.43	0
Championship Series											
1999 Atlanta ...............N.L.		5	5²/₃	0	1	.000	4	3	3	3.18	0
World Series Record											
1999 Atlanta ...............N.L.		2	1	0	1	.000	0	1	1	9.00	0

a On disabled list from April 30 to end of 1988 season.
b Traded to Seattle Mariners with outfielder Kevin Mitchell for pitchers Bill Swift, Mike Jackson and Dave Burba, December 11, 1991.
c Became free agent, October 15; signed with New York Mets organization, November 22, 1993.
d Traded to Cincinnati Reds for outfielder Cobi Cradle, May 11, 1995.
e Traded to Kansas City for outfielder Miguel Mejia. Cincinnati Reds then sent Mejia and infielder Luis Ordaz to St. Louis Cardinals for outfielder Andre King, December 4, 1995.
f Traded to Atlanta Braves with infielder Bret Boone for pitcher Denny Neagle, outfielder Michael Tucker and pitcher Rob Bell, November 10, 1998.
g On disabled list from April 3 to April 18, 1999.
h On disabled list from June 23 to July 12, 2000.

REYES, DENNYS
Born, Higuera De Zaragoza, Mexico, April 19, 1977.
Bats Left. Throws Left. Height, 6 feet, 3 inches. Weight, 246 pounds.

Year Club	Lea	G	IP	W	L	Pct	SO	BB	H	ERA	SAVES
1994 Vero Beach ....Fla. St.		9	41²/₃	2	4	.333	25	18	58	6.70	0
1994 Great Falls ....Pioneer		14	66²/₃	7	1	.875	70	25	71	3.78	0
1995 Mexico ....Mexican		17	58²/₃	5	5	.500	44	41	76	6.60	0
1995 Vero Beach ....Fla. St.		3	10	1	0	1.000	9	6	8	1.80	0
1996 San Berndno .....California		29	166	11	12	.478	176	77	166	4.17	0
1997 San Antonio ....Texas		12	80¹/₃	8	1	.889	66	28	79	3.02	0
1997 Albuquerque ..........P.C.		10	57¹/₃	6	3	.667	45	33	70	5.65	0
1997 Los Angeles ..........N.L.		14	47	2	3	.400	36	18	51	3.83	0
1998 Albuquerque ..........P.C.		7	43²/₃	1	4	.200	58	18	31	1.44	0
1998 Indianapols ....Int.		4	24	2	0	1.000	27	14	20	3.00	0
1998 Los Angeles-Cincinnati a .N.L.		19	67¹/₃	3	5	.375	77	47	62	4.54	0
1999 Cincinnati ............N.L.		65	61²/₃	2	2	.500	72	39	53	3.79	2
2000 Cincinnati b ..........N.L.		62	43²/₃	2	1	.667	36	29	43	4.53	0
Major League Totals ....4 Yrs.		160	219²/₃	9	11	.450	221	133	209	4.18	2

a Traded to Cincinnati Reds with infielder Paul Konerko for pitcher Jeff Shaw, July 4, 1998.

REYNOLDS, RICHARD SHANE
Born, Bastrop, Louisiana, March 26, 1968.
Bats Right. Throws Right. Height, 6 feet, 3 inches. Weight, 210 pounds.

Year Club	Lea	G	IP	W	L	Pct	SO	BB	H	ERA	SAVES
1989 Auburn ..........N.Y.-Penn.		6	35	3	2	.600	23	14	36	2.31	0
1989 Asheville ....So. Atl.		8	51¹/₃	5	3	.625	33	21	53	3.68	0
1990 Columbus ....Southern		29	155¹/₃	9	10	.474	92	70	181	4.81	0
1991 Jackson ....Texas		27	151	8	9	.471	116	62	165	4.47	0
1992 Tucson ...............P.C.		25	142	9	8	.529	106	34	156	3.68	1
1992 Houston .............N.L.		8	25¹/₃	1	3	.250	10	6	42	7.11	0
1993 Tucson ...............P.C.		25	139¹/₃	10	6	.625	106	21	147	3.62	1
1993 Houston .............N.L.		5	11	0	0	.000	10	6	11	0.82	0
1994 Houston .............N.L.		33	124	8	5	.615	110	21	128	3.05	0

Year	Club	Lea	G	IP	W	L	Pct	SO	BB	H	ERA	SAVES
1995 Houston	....	N.L.	30	189⅓	10	11	.476	175	37	196	3.47	0
1996 Houston	....	N.L.	35	239	16	10	.615	204	44	227	3.65	0
1997 New Orleans	....	A.A.	1	5	1	0	1.000	6	1	3	0.00	0
1997 Houston a	....	N.L.	30	181	9	10	.474	152	47	189	4.23	0
1998 Houston	....	N.L.	35	233⅓	19	8	.704	209	53	257	3.51	0
1999 Houston	....	N.L.	35	231⅔	16	14	.533	197	37	250	3.85	0
2000 Houston b	....	N.L.	22	131	7	8	.467	93	45	150	5.22	0
Major League Totals	.9 Yrs.		233	1365⅔	86	69	.555	1160	296	1450	3.85	
Divisional Series												
1997 Houston	....	N.L.	1	6	0	1	.000	5	1	5	3.00	0
1998 Houston	....	N.L.	1	7	0	0	.000	5	1	4	2.57	0
1999 Houston	....	N.L.	2	11	1	1	.500	5	3	16	4.09	0
Division Series Totals	....		4	24	1	2	.333	15	5	25	3.38	0

a On disabled list from June 10 to July 14, 1997.
b On disabled list from July 30 to October 1, 2000.

REYNOSO (GUTIERREZ), MARTIN ARMANDO

Born, San Luis Potosi, Mexico, May 1, 1996.
Bats Right. Throws Right. Height, 6 feet. Weight, 196 pounds.

Year	Club	Lea	G	IP	W	L	Pct	SO	BB	H	ERA	SAVES
1988 Saltillo	....	Mexican	32	180	11	11	.500	92	85	176	4.30	2
1989 Saltillo	....	Mexican	27	160⅓	13	9	.591	107	64	155	3.48	0
1990 Saltillo a	....	Mexican	27	200⅔	*20	3	*.870	*170	73	174	2.60	0
1990 Richmond	....	Int.	4	24	3	1	.750	15	7	26	2.25	0
1991 Richmond	....	Int.	22	131	10	6	.625	97	39	117	*2.61	0
1991 Atlanta	....	N.L.	6	23⅓	2	1	.667	10	10	26	6.17	0
1992 Richmond	....	Int.	28	169⅓	12	9	.571	108	52	156	2.66	0
1992 Atlanta b	....	N.L.	3	7⅔	1	0	1.000	2	2	11	4.70	1
1993 Colorado Springs	....	P.C.	4	22⅓	2	1	.667	22	8	19	3.22	0
1993 Colorado c	....	N.L.	30	189	12	11	.522	117	63	206	4.00	0
1994 Colorado d	....	N.L.	9	52⅓	3	4	.429	25	22	54	4.82	0
1995 Colorado Springs	....	P.C.	5	23	2	1	.667	17	6	14	1.57	0
1995 Colorado e	....	N.L.	20	93	7	7	.500	40	36	116	5.32	0
1996 Colorado f	....	N.L.	30	168⅔	8	9	.471	88	49	195	4.96	0
1997 St. Lucie	....	Fla.St.	2	10	1	1	.500	6	1	9	2.70	0
1997 New York g	....	N.L.	16	91⅓	6	3	.667	47	29	95	4.53	0
1998 St. Lucie	....	Fla.St.	4	12	0	1	.000	6	1	14	3.75	0
1998 Norfolk	....	Int.	2	9⅓	0	2	.000	8	4	14	10.61	0
1998 New York h-i	....	N.L.	11	68⅓	7	3	.700	40	32	64	3.82	0
1999 Arizona	....	N.L.	31	167	10	6	.625	79	67	178	4.37	0
2000 Arizona j	....	N.L.	31	170⅔	11	12	.478	89	52	179	5.27	0
Major League Totals	.... 10 Yrs.		187	1031⅓	67	56	.545	537	362	1124	4.68	1
Division Series												
1995 Colorado	....	N.L.	1	1	0	0	.000	0	0	2	0.00	0

a Purchased by Atlanta Braves organization from Saltillo Sarape Makers of Mexican League, August 15, 1990.
b Selected by Colorado Rockies in expansion draft, November 17, 1992.
c Appeared in one additional game as pinch runner.
d On disabled list from May 21 to end of 1994 season.
e On disabled list from April 25 to June 18, 1995.
f Traded to New York Mets for pitcher Jerry DiPoto, November 27, 1996.
g On disabled list from April 1 to April 15 and July 17 to September 29, 1997.
h On disabled list from March 31 to July 24, 1998.
i Filed for free agency, October 26, 1998, signed with Arizona Diamondbacks, November 25, 1998.
j Not offered 2001 contract, November 1, 2000, re-signed with Arizona Diamondbacks, December 6, 2000.

RHODES, ARTHUR LEE

Born, Waco, Texas, October 24, 1969.
Bats Left. Throws Left. Height, 6 feet, 2 inches. Weight, 206 pounds.

Year	Club	Lea	G	IP	W	L	Pct	SO	BB	H	ERA	SAVES
1988 Bluefield	....	Appal.	11	35⅓	3	4	.429	44	15	29	3.31	0
1989 Erie	....	N.Y.-Penn.	5	31	2	0	1.000	45	10	13	1.16	0
1989 Frederick	....	Carolina	7	24⅓	2	2	.500	28	19	19	5.18	0
1990 Frederick	....	Carolina	13	80⅔	4	6	.400	103	21	62	2.12	0
1990 Hagerstown	....	Eastern	12	72⅓	3	4	.429	60	39	62	3.73	0
1991 Hagerstown a	.....	Eastern	19	106⅔	7	4	.636	115	47	73	2.70	0

Year	Club	Lea	G	IP	W	L	Pct	SO	BB	H	ERA	SAVES
1991 Baltimore	....	A.L.	8	36	0	3	.000	23	23	47	8.00	0
1992 Rochester	....	Int.	17	101²/₃	6	6	.500	115	46	84	3.72	0
1992 Baltimore	....	A.L.	15	94¹/₃	7	5	.583	77	38	87	3.63	0
1993 Rochester	....	Int.	6	26²/₃	1	1	.500	33	15	26	4.05	0
1993 Baltimore b	....	A.L.	17	85²/₃	5	6	.455	49	49	91	6.51	0
1994 Frederick	....	Carolina	1	5	0	0	.000	7	0	3	0.00	0
1994 Rochester	....	Int.	15	90¹/₃	7	5	.583	86	34	70	2.79	0
1994 Baltimore c	....	A.L.	10	52²/₃	3	5	.375	47	30	51	5.81	0
1995 Baltimore	....	A.L.	19	75¹/₃	2	5	.286	77	48	68	6.21	0
1996 Baltimore	....	A.L.	28	53	9	1	.900	62	23	48	4.08	1
1997 Baltimore	....	A.L.	53	95¹/₃	10	3	.769	102	26	75	3.02	0
1998 Rochester	....	Int.	1	2	0	0	.000	1	1	3	4.50	0
1998 Baltimore d	....	A.L.	45	77	4	4	.500	83	34	65	3.51	4
1999 Baltimore e	....	A.L.	43	53	3	4	.429	59	45	43	5.43	3
2000 Seattle	....	A.L.	72	69¹/₃	5	8	.385	77	29	51	4.28	0
Major League Totals	....	10 Yrs.	310	691²/₃	48	44	.522	656	345	626	4.80	9
Division Series												
1996 Baltimore	....	A.L.	2	1	0	0	.000	1	1	1	9.00	0
1997 Baltimore	....	A.L.	1	2¹/₃	0	0	.000	4	0	0	0.00	0
2000 Seattle	....	A.L.	3	2²/₃	0	0	.000	2	2	0	0.00	0
Division Series Totals	....		6	6	0	0	.000	7	3	1	1.50	0
Championship Series												
1996 Baltimore	....	A.L.	3	2	0	0	.000	2	0	2	0.00	0
1997 Baltimore	....	A.L.	2	2¹/₃	0	0	.000	2	3	2	0.00	0
2000 Seattle	....	A.L.	4	2	0	1	.000	5	4	8	31.50	0
Championship Series Totals	......		9	6¹/₃	0	1	.000	9	7	12	9.95	0

a On disabled list from May 13 to June 5, 1991.
b On disabled list from May 10 to July 31, 1993.
c On disabled list from May 2 to May 21, 1994.
d On disabled list from July 5 to August 17, 1998.
e Filed for free agency, November 1, 1999. Signed with Seattle Mariners, December 21, 1999.

RIGDON, PAUL DAVID
Born, Jacksonville, Florida, November 2, 1975.
Bats Right. Throws Right. Height, 6 feet, 5 inches. Weight, 210 pounds.

Year	Club	Lea	G	IP	W	L	Pct	SO	BB	H	ERA	SAVES
1996 Watertown	....	N.Y.-Penn.	22	39²/₃	2	2	.500	46	10	41	4.08	6
1997 Watertown a	.....	N.Y.-Penn.		INJURED- did not play								
1998 Kinston	....	Carolina	24	127¹/₃	11	7	.611	97	35	126	4.03	0
1999 Buffalo	....	Int.	19	103¹/₃	7	4	.636	60	28	114	4.53	0
1999 Akron	....	Eastern	8	50	7	0	1.000	25	10	20	0.90	0
2000 Buffalo	....	Int.	12	71	6	1	.857	41	18	72	3.30	0
2000 Cleveland	....	A.L.	5	17²/₃	1	1	.500	15	9	21	7.64	0
2000 Milwaukee b-c-d	....	N.L.	12	69²/₃	4	4	.500	48	26	68	4.52	0
Major League Totals	....	1 Yrs.	17	87¹/₃	5	5	.500	63	35	89	5.15	0

a On disabled list from June 17 to September 15, 1997.
b On disabled list from May 22 to June 6, 2000.
c Traded to Milwaukee Brewers with infielder Richie Sexson, pitcher Kane Davis and player to be named later for pitcher Bob Wickman, pitcher Steve Woodard and pitcher Jason Bere, July 28, 2000.
d Milwaukee Brewers received infielder Marcus Scutaro to complete trade, August 30, 2000.

RITCHIE, TODD EVERETT
Born, Portsmouth, Virginia, November 7, 1971.
Bats Right. Throws Right. Height, 6 feet, 3 inches. Weight, 205 pounds.

Year	Club	Lea	G	IP	W	L	Pct	SO	BB	H	ERA	SAVES
1990 Elizabethtn	....	Appal.	11	65	5	2	.714	49	24	45	1.94	0
1991 Kenosha	....	Midwest	21	116²/₃	7	6	.538	101	50	113	3.55	0
1992 Visalia	....	California	28	172²/₃	11	9	.550	129	65	193	5.06	0
1993 Nashville	....	Southern	12	46²/₃	3	2	.600	41	15	46	3.66	0
1994 Nashville	....	Southern	4	17	0	2	.000	9	7	24	4.24	0
1995 New Britain	....	Eastern	24	113	4	9	.308	60	54	135	5.73	0
1996 New Britain	....	Eastern	29	82²/₃	3	7	.300	53	30	101	5.44	4
1996 Salt Lake	....	P.C.	16	24²/₃	0	4	.000	19	11	27	5.47	0
1997 Minnesota	....	A.L.	42	74²/₃	2	3	.400	44	28	87	4.58	0
1998 Salt Lake	....	P.C.	36	60²/₃	1	3	.250	62	31	55	4.15	4

Year Club	Lea	G	IP	W	L	Pct	SO	BB	H	ERA	SAVES
1998 Minnesota a	A.L.	15	24	0	0	.000	21	9	30	5.63	0
1999 Nashville	P.C.	1	5	0	0	.000	2	1	6	1.80	0
1999 Pittsburgh b	N.L.	28	172²/₃	15	9	.625	107	54	169	3.49	0
2000 Pittsburgh c	N.L.	31	187	9	8	.529	124	51	208	4.81	0
Major League Totals	4 Yrs.	116	458¹/₃	26	20	.565	296	142	494	4.32	0

a Filed for free agency, September 30, 1998, signed with Pittsburgh Pirates organization, November 3, 1998.
b On disabled list from August 21 to September 5, 1999.
c On disabled list from July 24 to August 10, 2000.

RIVERA, MARIANO

Born, Panama City, Panama, November 29, 1969.
Bats Right. Throws Right. Height, 6 feet, 4 inches. Weight, 170 pounds.

Year Club	Lea	G	IP	W	L	Pct	SO	BB	H	ERA	SAVES
1990 Yankees	Gulf Coast	22	52	5	1	.833	58	7	17	0.17	1
1991 Greensboro	So. Atl.	29	114²/₃	4	9	.308	123	36	103	2.75	0
1992 Ft. Lauderdale	Fla. St.	10	59¹/₃	5	3	.625	42	5	40	2.28	0
1993 Yankees	Gulf Coast	2	4	0	1	.000	6	1	2	2.25	0
1993 Greensboro	So. Atl.	10	39¹/₃	1	0	1.000	32	15	31	2.06	0
1994 Tampa	Fla. St.	7	36²/₃	3	0	1.000	27	12	34	2:21	0
1994 Albany	Eastern	9	63¹/₃	3	0	1.000	39	8	58	2.27	0
1994 Columbus	Int.	6	31	4	2	.667	23	10	34	5.81	0
1995 Columbus	Int.	7	30	2	2	.500	30	3	25	2.10	0
1995 New York	A.L.	19	67	5	3	.625	51	30	71	5.51	0
1996 New York	A.L.	61	107²/₃	8	3	.727	130	34	73	2.09	5
1997 New York	A.L.	66	71²/₃	6	4	.600	68	20	65	1.88	43
1998 New York a	A.L.	54	61¹/₃	3	0	1.000	36	17	48	1.91	36
1999 New York	A.L.	66	69	4	3	.571	52	18	43	1.83	*45
2000 New York	A.L.	66	75²/₃	7	4	.636	58	25	58	2.85	36
Major League Totals	6 Yrs.	332	452¹/₃	33	17	.660	395	144	358	2.63	165
Division Series											
1995 New York	A.L.	3	5¹/₃	1	0	1.000	8	1	3	0.00	0
1996 New York	A.L.	2	4²/₃	0	0	.000	1	1	0	0.00	0
1997 New York	A.L.	2	2	0	0	.000	1	0	2	4.50	1
1998 New York	A.L.	3	3¹/₃	0	0	.000	2	1	1	0.00	2
1999 New York	A.L.	2	3	0	0	.000	3	0	1	0.00	2
2000 New York	A.L.	3	5	0	0	.000	2	0	2	0.00	3
Division Series Totals		15	23¹/₃	1	0	1.000	17	3	9	0.39	8
Championship Series											
1996 New York	A.L.	2	4	1	0	1.000	5	1	6	0.00	0
1998 New York	A.L.	4	5²/₃	0	0	.000	5	1	0	0.00	1
1999 New York	A.L.	3	4²/₃	1	0	1.000	3	0	5	0.00	2
2000 New York	A.L.	3	4²/₃	0	0	.000	1	0	4	1.93	1
Championship Series Totals		12	19	2	0	1.000	14	2	15	0.47	4
World Series Record											
1996 New York	A.L.	4	5²/₃	0	0	.000	4	3	4	1.59	0
1998 New York	A.L.	3	4¹/₃	0	0	.000	4	0	5	0.00	3
1999 New York	A.L.	3	4²/₃	1	0	1.000	3	1	3	0.00	2
2000 New York	A.L.	4	6	0	0	.000	7	1	4	3.00	2
World Series Totals		14	20²/₃	1	0	1.000	18	5	16	1.31	7

a On disabled list from April 6 to April 24, 1998.

ROCKER, JOHN LOY

Born, Statesboro, Georgia, October 17, 1974.
Bats Right. Throws Right. Height, 6 feet, 4 inches. Weight, 210 pounds.

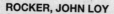

Year Club	Lea	G	IP	W	L	Pct	SO	BB	H	ERA	SAVES
1994 Danville	Appal.	12	63²/₃	1	5	.167	72	38	50	3.53	0
1995 Macon	So.Atl.	16	86	4	4	.500	61	52	86	4.50	0
1995 Eugene	Northwest	12	59¹/₃	1	5	.167	74	36	45	5.16	0
1996 Macon	So.Atl.	20	106¹/₃	5	3	.625	107	63	85	3.89	0
1996 Durham	Carolina	9	58¹/₃	4	3	.571	43	25	63	3.39	0
1997 Durham	Carolina	11	35¹/₃	1	1	.500	39	22	33	4.33	0
1997 Greenville	Southern	22	113	5	6	.455	96	61	119	4.86	0
1998 Richmond	Int.	9	19	1	1	.500	22	10	13	1.42	1
1998 Atlanta	N.L.	47	38	1	3	.250	42	22	22	2.13	2
1999 Atlanta	N.L.	74	72¹/₃	4	5	.444	104	37	47	2.49	38

Year	Club	Lea	G	IP	W	L	Pct	SO	BB	H	ERA	SAVES
2000 Richmond	....	Int.	3	3	0	0	.000	6	1	3	3.00	0
2000 Atlanta	....	N.L.	59	53	1	2	.333	77	48	42	2.89	24
Major League Totals	.... 3 Yrs.		180	163$\frac{1}{3}$	6	10	.375	223	107	111	2.53	64
	Division Series											
1998 Atlanta	....	N.L.	2	1$\frac{1}{3}$	0	0	.000	2	0	1	0.00	0
1999 Atlanta	....	N.L.	2	3$\frac{1}{3}$	1	0	1.000	5	2	0	0.00	1
2000 Atlanta	....	N.L.	1	0$\frac{2}{3}$	0	0	.000	0	1	0	0.00	0
Division Series Totals	....		5	5$\frac{1}{3}$	1	0	1.000	7	3	1	0.00	1
	Championship Series											
1998 Atlanta	....	N.L.	6	4$\frac{2}{3}$	1	0	1.000	5	1	3	0.00	0
1999 Atlanta	....	N.L.	6	6$\frac{2}{3}$	0	0	.000	9	2	3	0.00	1
Championship Series Totals	......		12	11$\frac{1}{3}$	1	0	1.000	14	3	6	0.00	1
	World Series Record											
1999 Atlanta	....	N.L.	2	3	0	0	.000	4	2	2	0.00	0

RODRIGUEZ, FELIX ANTONIO

Born, Montecristi, Dominican Republic, December 5, 1972.
Bats Right. Throws Right. Height, 6 feet, 1 inch. Weight, 180 pounds.

Year	Club	Lea	G	IP	W	L	Pct	SO	BB	H	ERA	SAVES
1993 Vero Beach	....	Fla. St.	32	132	8	8	.500	80	71	109	3.75	0
1994 San Antonio	....	Texas	26	136$\frac{1}{3}$	6	8	.429	126	88	106	4.03	0
1995 Los Angeles	....	N.L.	11	10$\frac{2}{3}$	1	1	.500	5	5	11	2.53	0
1995 Albuquerque	....	P.C.	14	51	3	2	.600	46	26	52	4.24	0
1996 Albuquerque a	....	P.C.	27	107$\frac{1}{3}$	3	9	.250	65	60	111	5.53	0
1997 Indianapolis	....	A.A.	23	26$\frac{2}{3}$	3	3	.500	26	16	22	1.01	1
1997 Cincinnati b	....	N.L.	26	46	0	0	.000	34	28	48	4.30	0
1998 Diamondbcks	....	Arizona	3	4$\frac{1}{3}$	0	0	.000	5	2	3	4.15	0
1998 Tucson	....	P.C.	1	1	0	0	.000	0	2	1	9.00	0
1998 Arizona c-d	....	N.L.	43	44	0	2	.000	36	29	44	6.14	5
1999 San Francisco	....	N.L.	47	66$\frac{1}{3}$	2	3	.400	55	29	67	3.80	0
2000 San Francisco	....	N.L.	76	81$\frac{2}{3}$	4	2	.667	95	42	65	2.64	3
Major League Totals	.... 5 Yrs.		203	248$\frac{2}{3}$	7	8	.467	225	133	235	3.87	8
	Division Series											
2000 San Francisco	....	N.L.	3	4$\frac{1}{3}$	0	1	.000	6	1	6	6.23	0

a Released by Los Angeles Dodgers organization and signed as free agent by Cincinnati Reds organization, December 23, 1996.
b Traded to Arizona Diamondbacks for player to be named later, November 11, 1997. Cincinnati Reds received pitcher Scott Winchester to complete trade, November 18, 1997.
c On disabled list from June 21 to July 30, 1998.
d Traded to San Francisco Giants for player to be named later and outfielder Chris Van Rossum, December 8, 1998. Arizona Diamondbacks received pitcher Troy Brohawn and to complete trade, December 21, 1998.

RODRIGUEZ, FRANCISCO (FRANK)

Born, Brooklyn, New York, December 11, 1972.
Bats Right. Throws Right. Height, 6 feet. Weight, 175 pounds.

Year	Club	Lea	G	IP	W	L	Pct	SO	BB	H	ERA	SAVES
1992 Lynchburg	....	Carolina	25	148$\frac{2}{3}$	12	7	.632	129	65	125	3.09	0
1993 New Britain	....	Eastern	28	170$\frac{2}{3}$	7	11	.389	151	78	147	3.74	0
1994 Pawtucket	....	Int.	28	186	8	13	.381	*160	60	182	3.92	0
1995 Pawtucket	....	Int.	13	27	1	1	.500	18	8	19	4.00	2
1995 Boston-Minnesota a-b	...	A.L.	25	105$\frac{2}{3}$	5	8	.385	59	57	114	6.13	0
1996 Minnesota	....	A.L.	38	206$\frac{2}{3}$	13	14	.481	110	78	218	5.05	2
1997 Minnesota	....	A.L.	43	142$\frac{1}{3}$	3	6	.333	65	60	147	4.62	0
1998 Salt Lake	....	P.C.	16	96$\frac{1}{3}$	5	7	.417	79	35	97	4.67	0
1998 Minnesota	....	A.L.	20	70	4	6	.400	62	30	88	6.56	0
1999 Boise	....	Northwest	1	5	1	0	1.000	6	1	3	5.40	0
1999 Salt Lake	....	P.C.	9	43	3	4	.429	33	14	40	6.70	0
1999 Seattle c	....	A.L.	28	73$\frac{1}{3}$	2	4	.333	47	30	94	5.65	3
2000 Tacoma	....	P.C.	9	35$\frac{1}{3}$	2	1	.667	26	11	30	4.84	0
2000 Seattle d-e	....	A.L.	23	47$\frac{1}{3}$	2	1	.667	19	22	60	6.27	0
Major League Totals	.... 6 Yrs.		177	645$\frac{1}{3}$	29	39	.426	362	277	721	5.45	5

Record as Position Player

Year	Club	Lea	Pos	G	AB	R	H	2B	3B	HR	RBI	SB	Avg
1991 Winter Haven Red Sox	..	Gulf C.	SS	3	14	3	7	0	1	0	3	0	.500
1991 Elmira	....	N.Y.-Penn.	SS	67	255	46	69	5	3	6	31	3	.271

a Traded to Minnesota Twins with player to be named later for pitcher Rick Aquilera, July 6, 1995.

b Minnesota Twins received outfielder Jermane Johnson to complete trade, October 11, 1995.
c Claimed on waivers by Seattle Mariners, May 26, 1999.
d On disabled list from July 1 to August 31, 2000.
e Released by Seattle Mariners, December 18, 2000.

RODRIGUEZ, RICHARD ANTHONY (RICH)

Born, Downey, California, March 1, 1963.
Bats Left. Throws Left. Height, 6 feet. Weight, 205 pounds.

Year	Club	Lea	G	IP	W	L	Pct	SO	BB	H	ERA	SAVES
1984 Little Falls	N.Y.-Penn.	25	35⅓	2	1	.667	27	36	28	2.80	0
1985 Columbia	So. Atl.	49	80⅓	6	3	.667	71	36	89	4.03	6
1986 Jackson	Texas	13	33	3	4	.429	15	15	51	9.00	0
1986 Lynchburg	Carolina	36	45⅓	2	1	.667	38	19	37	3.57	3
1987 Lynchburg	Carolina	69	68	3	1	.750	59	26	69	2.78	5
1988 Jackson a	Texas	47	78⅓	2	7	.222	68	42	66	2.87	6
1989 Wichita	Texas	54	74⅓	8	3	.727	40	37	74	3.63	8
1990 Las Vegas	P.C.	27	59	3	4	.429	46	22	50	3.51	8
1990 San Diego	N.L.	32	47⅔	1	1	.500	22	16	52	2.83	1
1991 San Diego b	N.L.	64	80	3	1	.750	40	44	66	3.26	0
1992 San Diego c	N.L.	61	91	6	3	.667	64	29	77	2.37	0
1993 San Diego-Florida d-e	N.L.	70	76	2	4	.333	43	33	73	3.79	3
1994 St. Louis f	N.L.	56	60⅓	3	5	.375	43	26	62	4.03	0
1995 St. Louis g-h-i	N.L.	1	1⅔	0	0	.000	0	0	0	0.00	0
1996 Omaha j-k-l	A.A.	47	70	2	3	.400	68	20	75	3.99	3
1997 San Francisco m-n-o	N.L.	71	65⅓	4	3	.571	32	21	65	3.17	1
1998 San Francisco	N.L.	68	65⅔	4	0	1.000	44	20	69	3.70	2
1999 San Francisco p	N.L.	62	56⅔	3	0	1.000	44	28	60	5.24	0
2000 New York q	N.L.	32	37	0	1	.000	18	15	59	7.78	0
2000 Norfolk	Int.	14	20⅔	0	1	.000	16	6	17	3.05	0
Major League Totals	10 Yrs.	517	581⅓	26	18	.591	350	232	583	3.75	7

Division Series

Year	Club	Lea	G	IP	W	L	Pct	SO	BB	H	ERA	SAVES
1997 San Francisco	N.L.	2	1	0	0	.000	0	0	1	0.00	0

a Traded by New York Mets to San Diego Padres organization for infielders Brad Pounders and Bill Stevenson, January 13, 1989.
b Appeared in one additional game as pinch runner.
c Entered one game as pinch hitter and remained in game as pitcher.
d Traded to Florida Marlins with infielder Gary Sheffield for pitchers Trevor Hoffman, Andres Berumen and Jose Martinez, June 25, 1993.
e Released, March 29; signed with St. Louis Cardinals, April 3, 1994.
f Declared restricted free agent under Major League Baseball implemented labor proposal, December 23, 1994.
g Re-signed with St. Louis Cardinals, April 5, 1995.
h On disabled list from April 27 to October 2, 1995.
i Released by St. Louis Cardinals, November 21, 1995.
j Signed as free agent by Cincinnati Reds, January 2, 1996.
k Released by Cincinnati Reds, March 23, 1996.
l Signed by Kansas City Royals, April 9, 1996.
m Signed as free agent by San Francisco Giants, November 14, 1996.
n Filed for free agency, October 30, 1997.
o Re-signed with San Francisco Giants, December 7, 1997.
p Filed for free agency, October 28, 1999. Signed with New York Mets, January 21, 2000.
q Designated for assignment by New York Mets, July 29, 2000.

ROGERS, KENNETH SCOTT (KENNY)

Born, Savannah, Georgia, November 10, 1964.
Bats Left. Throws Left. Height, 6 feet, 1 inch. Weight, 205 pounds.

Year	Club	Lea	G	IP	W	L	Pct	SO	BB	H	ERA	SAVES
1982 Sarasota Rangers	Gulf C.	2	3	0	0	.000	4	0	0	0.00	0
1983 Sarasota Rangers	Gulf C.	15	53⅓	4	1	.800	36	20	44	2.36	1
1984 Burlington	Midwest	39	92⅔	4	7	.364	93	33	87	3.98	3
1985 Daytona Beach	Fla. St.	6	10	0	1	.000	9	11	12	7.20	0
1985 Burlington	Midwest	33	95	2	5	.286	96	61	87	2.84	4
1986 Tulsa a	Texas	10	26⅓	0	3	.000	23	18	39	9.91	0
1986 Salem	Carolina	12	66	2	7	.222	46	26	75	6.27	0
1987 Charlotte b	Fla. St.	5	17	0	3	.000	14	8	17	4.76	0
1987 Tulsa	Texas	28	69	1	5	.167	59	35	80	5.35	2
1988 Tulsa c	Fla. St.	8	35⅓	2	0	1.000	26	11	22	1.27	1
1988 Tulsa	Texas	13	83⅓	4	6	.400	76	34	73	4.00	0
1989 Texas	A.L.	73	73⅔	3	4	.429	63	42	60	2.93	2
1990 Texas	A.L.	69	97⅔	10	6	.625	74	42	93	3.13	15

Year	Club	Lea	G	IP	W	L	Pct	SO	BB	H	ERA	SAVES
1991 Texas	A.L.	63	109²/₃	10	10	.500	73	61	121	5.42	5
1992 Texas	A.L.	*81	78²/₃	3	6	.333	70	26	80	3.09	6
1993 Texas	A.L.	35	208¹/₃	16	10	.615	140	71	210	4.10	0
1994 Texas d-e-f	A.L.	24	167¹/₃	11	8	.579	120	52	169	4.46	0
1995 Texas g-h	A.L.	31	208	17	7	.708	140	76	192	3.38	0
1996 New York	A.L.	30	179	12	8	.600	92	83	179	4.68	0
1997 New York i	A.L.	31	145	6	7	.462	78	62	161	5.65	0
1998 Oakland	A.L.	34	238²/₃	16	8	.667	138	67	215	3.17	0
1999 Oakland J	A.L.	19	119¹/₃	5	3	.625	68	41	135	4.30	0
1999 New York k	N.L.	12	76	5	1	.833	58	28	71	4.03	0
2000 Texas	A.L.	34	227¹/₃	13	13	.500	127	78	257	4.55	0
Major League Totals	12 Yrs.	536	1928²/₃	127	91	.583	1241	729	1943	4.11	28
Division Series											
1996 New York	A.L.	2	2	0	0	.000	1	2	5	9.00	0
1999 New York	N.L.	1	4¹/₃	0	1	.000	6	2	5	8.31	0
Division Series Totals		3	6¹/₃	0	1	.000	7	4	10	8.53	0
Championship Series											
1996 New York	A.L.	1	3	0	0	.000	3	2	5	12.00	0
1999 New York	N.L.	3	7²/₃	0	2	.000	2	7	11	5.87	0
Championship Series Totals		4	10²/₃	0	2	.000	5	9	16	7.59	0
World Series Record											
1996 New York	A.L.	1	2	0	0	.000	0	2	5	22.50	0

a On disabled list from April 12 to April 30, 1986.
b On disabled list from March 28 to April 30, 1987.
c On disabled list from March 20 to May 15, 1988.
d Pitched perfect no-hit, no-run game against California Angels, winning 4-0, July 28, 1994.
e Filed for free agency, October 19, 1994; ruled ineligible by Player Relations Committee due to insufficient service time.
f Declared restricted free agent under Major League Baseball implemented labor proposal, December 23, 1994.
g Re-signed with Texas Rangers, April 7, 1995.
h Filed for free agency, November 12, 1995. Signed with New York Yankees, December 30, 1995.
i Traded to Oakland Athletics for player to be named later, November 7, 1997. New York Yankees received infielder Scott Brosius to complete trade, November 18, 1997.
j Traded to New York Mets for outfielder Terrence Long and pitcher Leoner Vasquez, July 23, 1999.
k Filed for free agency, October 29, 1999. Signed with Texas Rangers, December 29, 1999.

ROMERO, JUAN CARLOS (J.C.)
Born, Rio Pedras, Puerto Rico, June 4, 1976.
Bats Both. Throws Right. Height, 5 feet, 11 inches. Weight, 193 pounds.

Year	Club	Lea	G	IP	W	L	Pct	SO	BB	H	ERA	SAVES
1997 Elizabethtn	Appal.	18	24	3	2	.600	29	7	27	4.88	3
1997 Ft. Myers	Fla.St.	7	12¹/₃	1	1	.500	9	4	11	4.38	0
1998 New Britain	Eastern	51	78	6	3	.667	79	43	48	2.19	2
1999 Salt Lake	P.C.	15	19²/₃	4	1	.800	20	14	18	3.20	0
1999 New Britain	Eastern	36	53	4	4	.500	53	34	51	3.40	0
1999 Minnesota	A.L.	5	9²/₃	0	0	.000	4	0	13	3.72	0
2000 Salt Lake	P.C.	17	65¹/₃	4	2	.667	38	25	60	3.44	0
2000 Ft.Myers	Fla.St.	2	4²/₃	0	0	.000	3	1	4	1.93	0
2000 Minnesota	A.L.	12	57²/₃	2	7	.222	50	30	72	7.02	0
Major League Totals	2 Yrs.	17	67¹/₃	2	7	.222	54	30	85	6.55	0

ROSADO, JOSE ANTONIO
Born, Jersey City, New Jersey, November 9, 1974.
Bats Left. Throws Left. Height, 6 feet. Weight, 175 pounds.

Year	Club	Lea	G	IP	W	L	Pct	SO	BB	H	ERA	SAVES
1994 Royals	Gulf Coast	14	64²/₃	6	2	.750	56	7	45	1.25	0
1995 Wilmington	Carolina	25	138	10	7	.588	117	30	128	3.13	0
1996 Wichita	Texas	2	13	2	0	1.000	12	1	10	0.00	0
1996 Omaha	A.A.	15	96²/₃	8	3	.727	82	38	80	3.17	0
1996 Kansas City	A.L.	16	106²/₃	8	6	.571	64	26	101	3.21	0
1997 Kansas City	A.L.	33	203¹/₃	9	12	.429	129	73	208	4.69	0
1998 Kansas City	A.L.	38	174²/₃	8	11	.421	135	57	180	4.69	1
1999 Kansas City	A.L.	33	208	10	14	.417	141	72	197	3.85	0
2000 Kansas City a	A.L.	5	27²/₃	2	2	.500	15	9	29	5.86	0
Major League Totals	5 Yrs.	125	720¹/₃	37	45	.451	484	237	715	4.27	1

a On disabled list from May 1 to October 1, 2000.

ROSE, BRIAN LEONARD
Born, New Bedford, Massachusetts, February 13, 1976.
Bats Right. Throws Right. Height, 6 feet, 3 inches. Weight, 215 pounds.

Year Club	Lea	G	IP	W	L	Pct	SO	BB	H	ERA	SAVES
1995 Michigan ....Midwest	21	136	8	5	.615	105	31	127	3.44	0
1996 Trenton ....Eastern	27	163²/₃	12	7	.632	115	45	157	4.01	0
1997 Boston ..............A.L.	1	3	0	0	.000	3	2	5	12.00	0
1997 Pawtucket ....Int.	27	190²/₃	17	5	.773	116	46	188	3.02	0
1998 Boston ..............A.L.	8	37²/₃	1	4	.200	18	14	43	6.93	0
1998 Pawtucket a ....Int.	6	17²/₃	0	3	.000	17	4	24	7.64	0
1999 Pawtucket ....Int.	7	28	2	1	.667	30	8	28	2.89	0
1999 Boston ..............A.L.	22	98	7	6	.538	51	29	112	4.87	0
2000 Pawtucket ....Int.	5	31	4	1	.800	20	13	28	3.19	0
2000 Boston ..............A.L.	15	53	3	5	.375	24	21	58	6.11	0
2000 Colorado b ..........N.L.	12	63²/₃	4	5	.444	40	30	72	5.51	0
Major League Totals ....4 Yrs.	58	255¹/₃	15	20	.429	136	96	290	5.67	0

a On disabled list from May 13 to September 28, 1998.

b Traded to Colorado Rockies with pitcher John Wasdin, pitcher Jeff Taglienti and infielder Jeff Frye for pitcher Rolando Arrojo, pitcher Rick Croushore and infielder Mike Lansing, July 27, 2000.

RUETER, KIRK WESLEY
Born, Hoyleton, Illinois, December 1, 1970.
Bats Left. Throws Left. Height, 6 feet, 3 inches. Weight, 195 pounds.

Year Club	Lea	G	IP	W	L	Pct	SO	BB	H	ERA	SAVES
1991 Bradenton Expos ....Gulf C.	5	19	1	1	.500	19	4	16	0.95	0
1991 Sumter ....So. Atl.	8	40²/₃	3	1	.750	27	10	32	1.33	0
1992 Rockford ....Midwest	26	174¹/₃	11	9	.550	153	36	150	2.58	0
1993 Harrisburg ....Eastern	9	59²/₃	5	0	1.000	36	7	47	1.36	0
1993 Ottawa ....Int.	7	43¹/₃	4	2	.667	27	3	46	2.70	0
1993 Montreal ............N.L.	14	85²/₃	8	0	1.000	31	18	85	2.73	0
1994 Ottawa ....Int.	1	2	0	0	.000	1	0	1	4.50	0
1994 Montreal ............N.L.	20	92¹/₃	7	3	.700	50	23	106	5.17	0
1995 Ottawa ....Int.	20	120²/₃	9	7	.563	67	25	120	3.06	0
1995 Montreal ............N.L.	9	47¹/₃	5	3	.625	28	9	38	3.23	0
1996 Ottawa ....Int.	3	15	1	2	.333	3	3	21	4.20	0
1996 Phoenix .............P.C.	5	25²/₃	1	2	.333	15	12	25	3.51	0
1996 Montreal-San Francisco a-b N.L.	20	102	6	8	.429	46	27	109	3.97	0
1997 San Francisco ........N.L.	32	190²/₃	13	6	.684	115	51	194	3.45	0
1998 San Francisco ........N.L.	33	187²/₃	16	9	.640	102	57	193	4.36	0
1999 San Francisco ........N.L.	33	184²/₃	15	10	.600	94	55	219	5.41	0
2000 San Francisco ........N.L.	32	184	11	9	.550	71	62	205	3.96	0
Major League Totals ....8 Yrs.	193	1074¹/₃	81	48	.628	537	302	1149	4.16	0
Division Series										
1997 San Francisco ........N.L.	1	7	0	0	.000	5	3	4	1.29	0
2000 San Francisco ........N.L.	1	4¹/₃	0	0	.000	1	1	3	0.00	0
Division Series Totals	2	11¹/₃	0	0	.000	6	4	7	0.79	0

a On disabled list from May 10 to May 26, 1996.

b Traded to San Francisco Giants with pitcher Tim Scott for pitcher Mark Leiter, July 30, 1996.

RUPE, RYAN KITTMAN
Born, Houston, Texas, March 31, 1975.
Bats Right. Throws Right. Height, 6 feet, 6 inches. Weight, 240 pounds.

Year Club	Lea	G	IP	W	L	Pct	SO	BB	H	ERA	SAVES
1998 Hudson Valley ....N.Y.-Penn.	3	13¹/₃	1	0	1.000	18	2	8	0.68	0
1998 Chston-Sc ....So.Atl.	10	56¹/₃	6	1	.857	62	9	33	2.40	0
1999 Orlando ....Southern	5	26¹/₃	2	2	.500	22	6	18	2.73	0
1999 Tampa Bay ...........A.L.	24	142¹/₃	8	9	.471	97	57	136	4.55	0
2000 Durham ....Int.	5	19¹/₃	0	1	.000	18	7	24	6.52	0
2000 Tampa Bay a ..........A.L.	18	91	5	6	.455	61	31	121	6.92	0
Major League Totals ....2 Yrs.	42	233¹/₃	13	15	.464	158	88	257	5.48	0

a On disabled list from September 11 to October 10, 2000.

313

RUSCH, GLENDON JAMES
Born, Seattle, Washington, November 7, 1974.
Bats Left. Throws Right. Height, 6 feet, 2 inches. Weight, 170 pounds.

Year	Club	Lea	G	IP	W	L	Pct	SO	BB	H	ERA	SAVES
1993	Royals	Gulf Coast	11	62	4	2	.667	48	11	43	1.60	0
1993	Rockford	Midwest	2	8	0	1	.000	8	7	10	3.38	0
1994	Rockford	Midwest	28	114	8	5	.615	122	34	111	4.66	1
1995	Wilmington	Carolina	26	165²/₃	14	6	.700	147	34	110	1.74	0
1996	Omaha	A.A.	28	169²/₃	11	9	.550	117	40	177	3.98	0
1997	Omaha	A.A.	1	6	0	1	.000	2	1	7	4.50	0
1997	Kansas City a	A.L.	30	170¹/₃	6	9	.400	116	52	206	5.50	0
1998	Omaha	P.C.	3	14²/₃	1	1	.500	14	6	20	7.98	0
1998	Kansas City b-c	A.L.	29	154²/₃	6	15	.286	94	50	191	5.88	1
1999	Omaha	P.C.	20	114	4	7	.364	102	33	143	4.42	0
1999	GC Royals	Gulf Coast	2	6	0	0	.000	9	3	3	1.50	0
1999	Kansas City	A.L.	3	4	0	1	.000	4	3	7	15.75	0
1999	New York d	N.L.	1	1	0	0	.000	0	0	1	0.00	0
2000	New York	N.L.	31	190²/₃	11	11	.500	157	44	196	4.01	0
Major League Totals	4 Yrs.		94	520²/₃	23	36	.390	371	149	601	5.13	1
Division Series												
2000	New York	N.L.	1	0²/₃	0	0	.000	2	0	0	0.00	0
Championship Series												
2000	New York	N.L.	2	3²/₃	1	0	1.000	3	0	3	0.00	0
World Series Record												
2000	New York	N.L.	3	4	0	0	.000	2	2	6	2.25	0

a On disabled list from June 16 to July 1, 1997.
b On disabled list from May 31 to June 1, 1998.
c On disabled list from August 9 to September 4, 1998.
d Traded to New York Mets for pitcher Dan Murray, September 14, 1999.

RYAN, ROBERT VICTOR (B.J.)
Born, Bossier City, Louisiana, December 28, 1975.
Bats Left. Throws Right. Height, 6 feet, 6 inches. Weight, 230 pounds.

Year	Club	Lea	G	IP	W	L	Pct	SO	BB	H	ERA	SAVES
1998	Billings	Pioneer	14	18²/₃	2	1	.667	25	5	15	1.93	4
1998	Chstn-Wv	So.Atl.	3	4¹/₃	0	0	.000	5	1	1	2.08	2
1998	Chattanooga	Southern	16	16¹/₃	1	0	1.000	21	6	13	2.20	4
1999	Rochester	Int.	11	14¹/₃	0	0	.000	20	4	8	2.51	0
1999	Chattanooga	Southern	35	41²/₃	2	1	.667	46	17	33	2.59	0
1999	Indianapolis	Int.	11	9	1	0	1.000	12	3	9	4.00	0
1999	Cincinnati	N.L.	1	2	0	0	.000	1	1	4	4.50	0
1999	Baltimore a	A.L.	13	18¹/₃	1	0	1.000	28	12	9	2.95	0
2000	Rochester	Int.	14	24²/₃	0	1	.000	28	9	23	4.74	0
2000	Baltimore	A.L.	42	42²/₃	2	3	.400	41	31	36	5.91	0
Major League Totals	2 Yrs.		56	63	3	3	.500	70	44	49	5.00	0

a Traded by Cincinnati Reds to Baltimore Orioles with pitcher Jacobo Sequea for pitcher Juan Guzman, July 31, 1999.

SANCHEZ, JESUS PAULINO
Born, Nizao, Dominican Republic, October 11, 1974.
Bats Left. Throws Right. Height, 5 feet, 10 inches. Weight, 153 pounds.

Year	Club	Lea	G	IP	W	L	Pct	SO	BB	H	ERA	SAVES
1992	Mets	Dominican	15	81²/₃	5	5	.500	72	38	86	4.19	0
1993	Mets	Dominican	16	82¹/₃	7	3	.700	94	36	63	2.40	0
1994	Kingsport	Appal.	13	87¹/₃	7	4	.636	71	24	61	1.96	0
1995	Columbia	So.Atl.	27	169²/₃	9	7	.563	177	58	154	3.13	0
1996	St. Lucie a	Fla.St.	16	92	9	3	.750	81	24	53	1.96	0
1997	Binghamton	Eastern	26	165¹/₃	13	10	.565	176	61	146	4.30	0
1998	Florida	N.L.	35	173	7	9	.438	137	91	178	4.47	0
1999	Calgary	P.C.	4	9¹/₃	0	0	.000	14	5	8	5.79	1
1999	Florida	N.L.	59	76¹/₃	5	7	.417	62	60	84	6.01	0
2000	Florida	N.L.	32	182	9	12	.429	123	76	197	5.34	0
Major League Totals	3 Yrs.		126	431¹/₃	21	28	.429	322	227	459	5.11	0

a On disabled list from April 4 to May 28, 1996.

SANTANA, JOHAN ALEXANDER

Born, Tovar, Venezuela, March 13, 1979.
Bats Left. Throws Right. Height, 6 feet. Weight, 195 pounds.

Year	Club	Lea	G	IP	W	L	Pct	SO	BB	H	ERA	SAVES
1996 Houston/Bos	.....Dominican		23	40	4	3	.571	51	22	26	2.70	3
1997 Auburn	.........N.Y.-Penn.		1	4	0	0	.000	5	6	1	2.25	0
1997 Astros	.........Gulf Coast		9	36⅓	0	4	.000	25	18	49	7.93	0
1998 Quad City	........Midwest		2	6⅔	0	1	.000	6	3	14	9.45	0
1998 Auburn	.........N.Y.-Penn.		15	86⅔	7	5	.583	88	21	81	4.36	0
1999 Michigan a-b	.......Midwest		27	160⅓	8	8	.500	150	55	162	4.66	0
2000 Minnesota	...............A.L.		30	86	2	3	.400	64	54	102	6.49	0

a Selected by Florida Marlins from Houston Astros in Rule V draft, December 13, 1999.
b Traded to Minnesota Twins with cash for pitcher Jared Camp, December 13, 1999.

SANTANA, JULIO FRANKLIN

Born, San Pedro De Macoris, Dominican Republic, January 20, 1973.
Bats Right. Throws Right. Height, 6 feet. Weight, 175 pounds.

Year	Club	Lea	G	IP	W	L	Pct	SO	BB	H	ERA	SAVES
1993 Rangers	........Gulf Coast		26	39	4	1	.800	50	7	31	1.38	7
1994 Charlstn-Sc	.........So. Atl.		16	91⅓	6	7	.462	103	44	65	2.46	0
1994 Tulsa	...............Texas		11	71⅓	7	2	.778	45	41	50	2.90	0
1995 Okla City	...............A.A.		2	3	0	2	.000	6	7	9	39.00	0
1995 Charlotte	...........Fla. St.		5	31⅓	0	0	.000	27	16	32	3.73	0
1995 Tulsa	...............Texas		15	103	6	4	.600	71	52	91	3.15	0
1996 Okla City	...............A.A.		29	185⅔	11	12	.478	113	66	171	4.02	0
1997 Okla City	...............A.A.		1	3	0	0	.000	1	2	9	15.00	0
1997 Texas a	...............A.L.		30	104	4	6	.400	64	49	141	6.75	0
1998 Texas-Tampa Bay b	......A.L.		35	145⅔	5	6	.455	61	62	151	4.39	0
1999 Tampa Bay c-d-e-f	......A.L.		22	55⅓	1	4	.200	34	32	66	7.32	0
2000 Pawtucket	...............Int.		12	65	5	3	.625	55	23	61	4.71	0
2000 Montreal g-h	...............N.L.		36	66⅔	1	5	.167	58	33	69	5.67	0
Major League Totals	........4 Yrs.		123	371⅔	11	21	.344	217	176	427	5.71	0

a On disabled list from July 15 to August 10, 1997.
b Claimed on waivers by Tampa Bay Devil Rays, April 27, 1998.
c On disabled list from May 3 to May 24, 1999.
d Traded to Boston Red Sox for player to be named later, July 19, 1999.
e On disabled list from July 22 to November 16, 1999.
f Not offered contract, December 21, 1999. Re-signed with Boston Red Sox organization, February 2, 2000.
g Signed with Montreal Expos, June 18, 2000.
h Filed for free agency, October 10, 2000.

SANTIAGO, JOSE RAFAEL

Born, Fajardo, Puerto Rico, November 5, 1974.
Bats Right. Throws Right. Height, 6 feet, 3 inches. Weight, 200 pounds.

Year	Club	Lea	G	IP	W	L	Pct	SO	BB	H	ERA	SAVES
1994 Royals	.........Gulf Coast		10	19	1	0	1.000	10	7	17	2.37	2
1995 Spokane	....Northwest		22	48⅔	2	4	.333	32	20	60	3.14	1
1996 Lansing	...........Midwest		54	77	7	6	.538	55	21	78	2.57	19
1997 Wilmington	...........Carolina		4	3⅔	1	1	.500	1	1	3	4.91	2
1997 Lansing	...........Midwest		9	13	1	0	1.000	8	6	10	2.08	1
1997 Kansas City	...............A.L.		4	4⅔	0	0	.000	1	2	7	1.93	0
1997 Wichita	...............Texas		22	27	2	1	.667	12	8	32	4.00	3
1998 Wichita	...............Texas		52	72⅓	3	4	.429	31	27	79	3.61	22
1998 Kansas City	...............A.L.		2	2	0	0	.000	2	0	4	9.00	0
1998 Omaha	...............P.C.		4	7⅔	0	0	.000	2	0	10	7.04	1
1999 Wichita	...............Texas		4	9	0	1	.000	4	5	10	2.00	0
1999 Omaha	...............P.C.		1	1⅔	0	0	.000	0	0	8	0.00	0
1999 Royals	.........Gulf Coast		3	5	0	0	.000	4	0	3	1.80	0
1999 Kansas City a	.........A.L.		34	47⅓	3	4	.429	15	14	46	3.42	2
2000 Omaha	...............P.C.		11	17	0	1	.000	14	3	19	3.18	0
2000 Kansas City	...............A.L.		45	69	8	6	.571	44	26	70	3.91	2
Major League Totals	........4 Yrs.		85	123	11	10	.524	62	42	127	3.73	4

a On disabled list from June 20 to September 13, 1999.

SASAKI, KAZUHIRO
Born, Tokyo, Japan, February 22, 1968.
Bats Right. Throws Right. Height, 6 feet, 4 inches. Weight, 209 pounds.

Year	Club	Lea	G	IP	W	L	Pct	SO	BB	H	ERA	SAVES
1990 Yokohama	.....	Japan Cent.	16	47²/₃	2	4	.333	44	30	49	5.85	2
1991 Yokohama	.....	Japan Cent.	58	117	6	9	.400	137	55	72	2.00	17
1992 Yokohama	.....	Japan Cent.	53	87²/₃	12	6	.667	135	40	47	2.46	21
1993 Yokohama	.....	Japan Cent.	38	55	3	6	.333	84	23	35	3.27	20
1994 Yokohama	.....	Japan Cent.	31	46	3	1	.750	59	15	27	2.15	10
1995 Yokohama	.....	Japan Cent.	47	56²/₃	7	2	.778	78	17	30	1.75	32
1996 Yokohama	.....	Japan Cent.	39	49²/₃	4	3	.571	80	17	37	2.90	25
1997 Yokohama	.....	Japan Cent.	49	60	3	0	1.000	99	18	25	0.90	38
1998 Yokohama	.....	Japan Cent.	51	56	1	1	.500	78	14	32	0.64	45
1999 Yokohama a	...	Japan Cent.	23	23¹/₃	1	1	.500	34	16	19	1.93	23
2000 Seattle b	.....	A.L.	63	62²/₃	2	5	.286	78	31	42	3.16	37
Division Series												
2000 Seattle	.....	A.L.	2	2	0	0	.000	5	0	1	0.00	2
Championship Series												
2000 Seattle	.....	A.L.	2	2²/₃	0	0	.000	3	1	3	0.00	1

a Signed by Seattle Mariners, December 18, 1999.
b Selected Rookie of the Year in American League for 2000.

SAUERBECK, SCOTT WILLIAM
Born, Cincinnati, Ohio, November 9, 1971.
Bats Right. Throws Right. Height, 6 feet, 3 inches. Weight, 190 pounds.

Year	Club	Lea	G	IP	W	L	Pct	SO	BB	H	ERA	SAVES
1994 Pittsfield	...	N.Y.-Penn.	21	48¹/₃	3	1	.750	39	19	39	2.05	1
1995 St. Lucie	...	Fla.St.	20	26²/₃	0	1	.000	25	14	26	2.03	0
1995 Columbia	...	So.Atl.	19	33	5	4	.556	33	14	28	3.27	2
1996 St. Lucie	...	Fla.St.	17	99¹/₃	6	6	.500	62	27	101	2.27	0
1996 Binghamton	...	Eastern	8	46²/₃	3	3	.500	30	12	48	3.47	0
1997 Norfolk	...	Int.	1	5	1	0	1.000	4	4	3	3.60	0
1997 Binghamton	...	Eastern	27	131¹/₃	8	9	.471	88	50	144	4.93	0
1998 Norfolk a	...	Int.	27	160¹/₃	7	13	.350	119	68	178	3.93	0
1999 Pittsburgh	...	N.L.	65	67²/₃	4	1	.800	55	38	53	2.00	2
2000 Nashville	...	P.C.	2	2	0	0	.000	0	0	1	0.00	0
2000 Pittsburgh b	...	N.L.	75	75²/₃	5	4	.556	83	61	76	4.04	1
Major League Totals	...	2 Yrs.	140	143¹/₃	9	5	.643	138	99	129	3.08	3

a Selected by Pittsburgh Pirates from New York Mets in Rule V draft, December 14, 1998.
b On disabled list from June 15 to July 2, 2000.

SCHILLING, CURTIS MONTAGUE
Born, Anchorage, Alaska, November 14, 1966.
Bats Right. Throws Right. Height, 6 feet, 4 inches. Weight, 225 pounds.

Year	Club	Lea	G	IP	W	L	Pct	SO	BB	H	ERA	SAVES
1986 Elmira	...	N.Y.-Penn.	16	93²/₃	7	3	.700	75	31	92	2.59	0
1987 Greensboro	...	So. Atl.	29	184	8	*15	.348	*189	65	179	3.82	0
1988 New Britain a	...	Eastern	21	106	8	5	.615	62	40	91	2.97	1
1988 Charlotte	...	Southern	7	45¹/₃	5	2	.714	32	23	36	3.18	0
1988 Baltimore	...	A.L.	4	14²/₃	0	3	.000	4	10	22	9.82	0
1989 Rochester	...	Int.	27	*185¹/₃	*13	11	.542	109	59	176	3.21	0
1989 Baltimore	...	A.L.	5	8²/₃	0	1	.000	6	3	10	6.23	0
1990 Rochester	...	Int.	15	87¹/₃	4	4	.500	83	25	95	3.92	0
1990 Baltimore b	...	A.L.	35	46	1	2	.333	32	19	38	2.54	3
1991 Tucson	...	P.C.	13	23²/₃	0	1	.000	21	12	16	3.42	3
1991 Houston c	...	N.L.	56	75²/₃	3	5	.375	71	39	79	3.81	8
1992 Philadelphia	...	N.L.	42	226¹/₃	14	11	.560	147	59	165	2.35	2
1993 Philadelphia	...	N.L.	34	235¹/₃	16	7	.696	186	57	234	4.02	0
1994 Reading	...	Eastern	1	4	0	0	.000	4	1	6	0.00	0
1994 Scranton	...	Int.	2	10	0	0	.000	6	5	6	1.80	0
1994 Philadelphia d	...	N.L.	13	82¹/₃	2	8	.200	58	28	87	4.48	0
1995 Philadelphia e	...	N.L.	17	116	7	5	.583	114	26	96	3.57	0
1996 Clearwater	...	Fla. St.	2	14	2	0	1.000	17	1	9	1.29	0
1996 Scranton-W.B.	...	Int.	2	13	1	0	1.000	10	5	9	1.38	0
1996 Philadelphia f	...	N.L.	26	183¹/₃	9	10	.474	182	50	149	3.19	0
1997 Philadelphia	...	N.L.	35	254¹/₃	17	11	.607	*319	58	208	2.97	0
1998 Philadelphia	...	N.L.	35	*268²/₃	15	14	.517	*300	61	236	3.25	0

Year Club	Lea	G	IP	W	L	Pct	SO	BB	H	ERA	SAVES
1999 Philadelphia g ........N.L.		24	180⅓	15	6	.714	152	44	159	3.54	0
2000 Clearwater ....Fla.St.		4	20⅔	1	0	1.000	23	2	10	1.31	0
2000 Scranton-WB ....Int.		1	5	0	0	.000	7	1	9	3.60	0
2000 Philadelphia-Arizona h-i .N.L.		29	210⅓	11	12	.478	168	45	204	3.81	0
Major League Totals ....13 Yrs.		355	1902	110	95	.537	1739	499	1687	3.43	13

Championship Series

Year Club	Lea	G	IP	W	L	Pct	SO	BB	H	ERA	SAVES
1993 Philadelphia ...........N.L.		2	16	0	0	.000	19	5	11	1.69	0

World Series Record

Year Club	Lea	G	IP	W	L	Pct	SO	BB	H	ERA	SAVES
1993 Philadelphia ...........N.L.		2	15⅓	1	1	.500	9	5	13	3.52	0

a Traded by Boston Red Sox to Baltimore Orioles organization with outfielder Brady Anderson for pitcher Mike Boddicker, July 29, 1988.

b Traded to Houston Astros with pitcher Pete Harnisch and outfielder Steve Finley for first baseman Glenn Davis, January 10, 1991.

c Traded to Philadelphia Phillies for pitcher Jason Grimsley, April 2, 1992.

d On disabled list from May 17 to July 25, 1994.

e On disabled list from July 19 to October 2, 1995.

f On disabled list from April 1 to May 14, 1996.

g On disabled list from August 8 to September 3, 1999.

h On disabled list from March 25 to April 29, 2000.

i Traded to Arizona Diamondbacks for infielder Travis Lee, pitcher Omar Daal, pitcher Vicente Padilla and pitcher Nelson Figueroa, July 26, 2000.

SCHMIDT, JASON DAVID

Born, Kelso, Washington, January 29, 1973.
Bats Right. Throws Right. Height, 6 feet, 5 inches. Weight, 185 pounds.

Year Club	Lea	G	IP	W	L	Pct	SO	BB	H	ERA	SAVES
1991 Braves ....Gulf Coast		11	45⅓	3	4	.429	44	23	32	2.38	0
1992 Macon ....So. Atl.		7	24⅔	0	3	.000	33	19	31	4.01	0
1992 Pulaski ....Appal.		11	58⅓	3	4	.429	56	31	55	4.01	0
1993 Durham ....Carolina		22	116⅔	7	11	.389	110	47	128	4.94	0
1994 Greenville ....Southern		24	140⅔	8	7	.533	131	54	135	3.65	0
1995 Richmond ....Int.		19	116	8	6	.571	95	48	97	2.25	0
1995 Atlanta ..............N.L.		9	25	2	2	.500	19	18	27	5.76	0
1996 Greenville ....Southern		1	2	0	0	.000	2	0	4	9.00	0
1996 Richmond ....Int.		7	45⅔	3	3	1.000	41	19	36	2.56	0
1996 Atlanta-Pittsburgh a-b .N.L.		19	96⅓	5	6	.455	74	53	108	5.70	0
1997 Pittsburgh ...........N.L.		32	187⅔	10	9	.526	136	76	193	4.60	0
1998 Pittsburgh ...........N.L.		33	214⅓	11	14	.440	158	71	228	4.07	0
1999 Pittsburgh ...........N.L.		33	212⅔	13	11	.542	148	85	219	4.19	0
2000 GC Pirates ....Gulf Coast		1	4	0	0	.000	1	1	4	2.25	0
2000 Pittsburgh c ..........N.L.		11	63⅓	2	5	.286	51	41	71	5.40	0
Major League Totals ....6 Yrs.		137	799⅓	43	47	.478	586	344	846	4.58	0

a Traded to Pittsburgh Pirates with infielder Ron Wright and outfielder Corey Pointer for pitcher Denny Neagle, August 29, 1996.

b On disabled list from July 15 to August 28, 1996.

c On disabled list from April 15 to May 1 and June 10 to November 17, 2000.

SCHOENEWEIS, SCOTT DAVID

Born, Long Branch, New Jersey, October 2, 1973.
Bats Left. Throws Right. Height, 6 feet. Weight, 186 pounds.

Year Club	Lea	G	IP	W	L	Pct	SO	BB	H	ERA	SAVES
1996 Lk Elsinore ....California		14	93⅔	8	3	.727	83	27	86	3.94	0
1997 Midland ....Texas		20	113⅓	7	5	.583	94	39	145	5.96	0
1998 Vancouver ...........P.C.		27	180	11	8	.579	133	59	188	4.50	0
1999 Anaheim .............A.L.		31	39⅓	1	1	.500	22	14	47	5.49	0
1999 Edmonton ............P.C.		9	35⅓	2	4	.333	29	12	58	7.64	0
2000 Lake Elsinore ....California		1	4⅔	0	0	.000	3	3	3	1.93	0
2000 Edmonton ...........P.C.		1	7	0	0	.000	6	1	2	0.00	0
2000 Anaheim a ..........A.L.		27	170	7	10	.412	78	67	183	5.45	0
Major League Totals ....2 Yrs.		58	209⅓	8	11	.421	100	81	230	5.46	0

a On disabled list from June 17 to July 25, 2000.

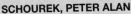

SCHOUREK, PETER ALAN

Born, Austin, Texas, May 10, 1969.
Bats Left. Throws Left. Height, 6 feet, 5 inches. Weight, 205 pounds.

Year	Club	Lea	G	IP	W	L	Pct	SO	BB	H	ERA	SAVES
1987	Little Falls	N.Y.-Penn.	12	78⅓	4	5	.444	57	34	70	3.68	0
1988	Little Falls a	N.Y.-Penn.		INJURED—Did Not Play								
1989	Columbia	So. Atl.	27	136	5	9	.357	131	66	120	2.85	1
1989	St. Lucie	Fla. St.	2	4	0	0	.000	4	2	3	2.25	0
1990	St. Lucie	Fla. St.	5	37	4	1	.800	28	8	29	0.97	0
1990	Tidewater	Int.	2	14	1	0	1.000	14	5	9	2.57	0
1990	Jackson	Texas	19	124⅓	11	4	.733	94	39	109	3.04	0
1991	New York	N.L.	35	86⅓	5	4	.556	67	43	82	4.27	2
1991	Tidewater	Int.	4	25	1	1	.500	17	10	18	2.52	0
1992	Tidewater	Int.	8	52⅔	2	5	.286	42	23	46	2.73	0
1992	New York b	N.L.	22	136	6	8	.429	60	44	137	3.64	0
1993	New York c	N.L.	41	128⅓	5	12	.294	72	45	168	5.96	0
1994	Cincinnati	N.L.	22	81⅓	7	2	.778	69	29	90	4.09	0
1995	Cincinnati	N.L.	29	190⅓	18	7	.720	160	45	158	3.22	0
1996	Cincinnati d	N.L.	12	67⅓	4	5	.444	54	24	79	6.01	0
1997	Cincinnati e-f-g	N.L.	18	84⅔	5	8	.385	59	38	78	5.42	0
1998	Kissimmee	Fla.St.	2	8⅓	0	0	.000	9	4	8	1.08	0
1998	Houston	N.L.	15	80	7	6	.538	59	36	82	4.50	0
1998	Boston h-i	A.L.	10	44	1	3	.250	36	14	45	4.30	0
1999	Pittsburgh j	N.L.	30	113	4	7	.364	94	49	128	5.34	0
2000	Pawtucket	Int.	1	3	0	0	.000	1	1	1	0.00	0
2000	Sarasota	Fla.St.	1	4⅓	0	0	.000	5	0	2	2.08	0
2000	Boston k-l-m	A.L.	21	107⅓	3	10	.231	63	38	116	5.11	0
Major League Totals		10 Yrs.	255	1118⅔	65	72	.474	793	405	1163	4.59	2
	Division Series											
1995	Cincinnati	N.L.	1	7	1	0	1.000	5	3	5	2.57	0
1998	Boston	A.L.	1	5⅓	0	0	.000	1	4	2	0.00	0
Division Series Totals			2	12⅓	1	0	1.000	6	7	7	1.46	0
	Championship Series											
1995	Cincinnati	N.L.	2	14⅓	0	1	.000	13	3	14	1.26	0

a On disabled list from March 29 to end of 1988 season.
b Appeared in one additional game as pinch runner.
c Claimed on waivers by Cincinnati Reds, April 7, 1994.
d On disabled list from June 1 to August 22 and July 2 to September 30, 1996.
e On disabled list from June 14 to July 18 and July 31 to September 2, 1997.
f Released by Cincinnati Reds, October 10, 1997.
g Signed with Houston Astros organization, January 9, 1998.
h Sold to Boston, August 6, 1998.
i Filed for free agency, October 23, 1998. Signed with Pittsburgh Pirates, December 17, 1998.
j On disabled list from August 17 to September 1, 1999.
k Released by Pittsburgh Pirates, March 29, 2000, signed with Boston Red Sox, April 2, 2000.
l On disabled list from July 21 to September 1 and September 20 to October 31, 2000.
m Not offered 2001 contract, October 31, 2000, re-signed with Boston Red Sox organization, December 7, 2000.

SELE, AARON HELMER

Born, Golden Valley, Minnesota, June 25, 1970.
Bats Right. Throws Right. Height, 6 feet, 5 inches. Weight, 205 pounds.

Year	Club	Lea	G	IP	W	L	Pct	SO	BB	H	ERA	SAVES
1991	Winter Haven	Fla. St.	13	69	3	6	.333	51	32	65	4.96	1
1992	Lynchburg	Carolina	20	127	13	5	.722	112	46	104	2.91	0
1992	New Britain	Eastern	7	33	2	1	.667	29	15	43	6.27	0
1993	Pawtucket	Int.	14	94⅓	8	2	.800	87	23	74	2.19	0
1993	Boston	A.L.	18	112⅔	7	2	.778	93	48	100	2.74	0
1994	Boston	A.L.	22	143⅓	8	7	.533	105	60	140	3.83	0
1995	Sarasota	Fla. St.	2	7	0	0	.000	6	1	6	0.00	0
1995	Trenton	Eastern	2	8	0	1	.000	9	2	8	3.38	0
1995	Pawtucket	Int.	2	5	0	0	.000	1	2	9	9.00	0
1995	Boston a	A.L.	6	32⅓	3	1	.750	21	14	32	3.06	0
1996	Pawtucket	Int.	1	3	0	0	.000	4	1	3	6.00	0
1996	Boston b	A.L.	29	157⅓	7	11	.389	137	67	192	5.32	0
1997	Boston c	A.L.	33	177⅓	13	12	.520	122	80	196	5.38	0
1998	Texas	A.L.	33	212⅔	19	11	.633	167	84	239	4.23	0
1999	Texas d	A.L.	33	205	18	9	.667	186	70	244	4.79	0
2000	Seattle	A.L.	34	211⅔	17	10	.630	137	74	221	4.51	0
Major League Totals		8 Yrs.	208	1251⅓	92	63	.594	968	497	1364	4.46	0

318

Year	Club	Lea	G	IP	W	L	Pct	SO	BB	H	ERA	SAVES
	Division Series											
1998 Texas		A.L.	1	6	0	1	.000	4	1	8	6.00	0
1999 Texas		A.L.	1	5	0	1	.000	3	5	6	5.40	0
2000 Seattle		A.L.	1	7⅓	0	0	.000	1	3	3	1.23	0
Division Series Totals			3	18⅓	0	2	.000	8	9	17	3.93	0
	Championship Series											
2000 Seattle		A.L.	1	6	0	1	.000	4	0	9	6.00	0

a On disabled list from May 24 to October 2, 1995.
b On disabled list from August 14 to September 1, 1996.
c Traded to Texas Rangers with pitcher Mark Brandenburg and catcher Bill Haselman for catcher Jim Leyritz and outfielder Damon Buford, November 6, 1997.
d Filed for free agency, November 5, 1999. Signed with Seattle Mariners, January 10, 2000.

SERAFINI, DANIEL JOSEPH (DAN)
Born, San Francisco, California, January 25, 1974.
Bats Both. Throws Left. Height, 6 feet, 1 inch. Weight, 185 pounds.

Year	Club	Lea	G	IP	W	L	Pct	SO	BB	H	ERA	SAVES
1992 Twins		Gulf Coast	8	29⅔	1	0	1.000	33	15	27	3.64	0
1993 Ft. Wayne		Midwest	27	140⅔	10	8	.556	147	83	117	3.65	0
1994 Ft. Myers		Fla. St.	23	136⅔	9	9	.500	130	57	149	4.61	0
1995 New Britain		Eastern	27	162⅔	12	9	.571	123	72	155	3.38	0
1995 Salt Lake		P.C.	1	4	0	0	.000	4	1	4	6.75	1
1996 Minnesota		A.L.	1	4⅓	0	1	.000	1	2	7	10.38	0
1996 Salt Lake		P.C.	25	130⅔	7	7	.500	109	58	164	5.58	0
1997 Salt Lake		P.C.	28	152	9	7	.563	118	55	166	4.97	0
1997 Minnesota		A.L.	6	26⅓	2	1	.667	15	11	27	3.42	0
1998 Salt Lake		P.C.	9	53⅓	2	4	.333	39	21	56	3.71	0
1998 Minnesota a		A.L.	28	75	7	4	.636	46	29	95	6.48	0
1999 Chicago		N.L.	42	62⅓	3	2	.600	17	32	86	6.93	1
1999 Iowa b		P.C.	2	13	0	0	.000	11	5	12	2.77	0
2000 Las Vegas		P.C.	26	51	2	4	.333	45	23	74	6.88	0
2000 Nashville		P.C.	7	47	4	3	.571	22	18	39	2.68	0
2000 San Diego-Pittsburgh c		N.L.	14	65⅓	2	5	.286	35	28	79	5.51	0
Major League Totals	5 Yrs.		91	233⅓	14	13	.519	114	102	294	6.06	1

a Sold to Chicago Cubs, March 31, 1999.
b Traded to San Diego Padres for outfielder Brandon Pernell, December 22, 1999.
c Traded to Pittsburgh Pirates for player to be named later, June 28, 2000.

SHAW, JEFFREY LEE
Born, Washington Court House, Ohio, July 7, 1966.
Bats Right. Throws Right. Height, 6 feet, 2 inches. Weight, 200 pounds.

Year	Club	Lea	G	IP	W	L	Pct	SO	BB	H	ERA	SAVES
1986 Batavia		N.Y.-Penn.	14	88⅔	8	4	.667	71	35	79	2.54	0
1987 Waterloo		Midwest	28	184⅓	11	11	.500	117	56	192	3.52	0
1988 Williamsport		Eastern	27	163⅔	5	*19	.208	61	75	*173	3.63	0
1989 Canton		Eastern	30	154⅓	7	10	.412	95	67	134	3.62	0
1990 Colorado Springs		P.C.	17	98⅔	10	3	.769	55	52	98	4.29	0
1990 Cleveland		A.L.	12	48⅔	3	4	.429	25	20	73	6.66	0
1991 Colorado Springs		P.C.	12	75⅔	6	3	.667	55	25	77	4.64	0
1991 Cleveland		A.L.	29	72⅓	0	5	.000	31	27	72	3.36	1
1992 Colorado Springs		P.C.	25	155	10	5	.667	84	45	174	4.76	0
1992 Cleveland a-b		A.L.	2	7⅔	0	1	.000	3	4	7	8.22	0
1993 Ottawa		Int.	2	4	0	0	.000	1	2	5	0.00	0
1993 Montreal		N.L.	55	95⅔	2	7	.222	50	32	91	4.14	0
1994 Montreal		N.L.	46	67⅓	5	2	.714	47	15	67	3.88	1
1995 Montreal		N.L.	50	62⅓	1	6	.143	45	26	58	4.62	3
1995 Chicago c		N.L.	9	9⅔	0	0	.000	6	1	12	6.52	0
1996 Cincinnati d		N.L.	78	104⅔	8	6	.571	69	29	99	2.49	4
1997 Cincinnati		N.L.	78	94⅔	4	2	.667	74	12	78	2.38	*42
1998 Cincinnati-Los Angeles e		N.L.	73	85	3	8	.273	55	19	75	2.12	48
1999 Los Angeles		N.L.	64	68	2	4	.333	43	15	64	2.78	34
2000 Los Angeles f		N.L.	60	57⅓	3	4	.429	39	16	61	4.24	27
Major League Totals	11 Yrs.		556	773⅓	31	49	.387	487	216	758	3.54	160

a Refused assignment to minor leagues and became free agent, October 8; signed with Kansas City Royals organization, November 8, 1992.
b Traded by Montreal Expos with catcher Tim Spehr for pitchers Mark Gardner and Doug Piatt, December 9, 1992.

c Traded to Chicago White Sox for pitcher Jose DeLeon, August 27, 1995.
d Signed with Cincinnati Reds organization, January 2, 1996.
e Traded to Los Angeles Dodgers for infielder Paul Konerko and pitcher Dennys Reyes, July 4, 1998.
f On disabled list from June 27 to July 12, 2000.

SHUEY, PAUL KENNETH

Born, Lima, Ohio, September 16, 1970.
Bats Right. Throws Right. Height, 6 feet, 3 inches. Weight, 215 pounds.

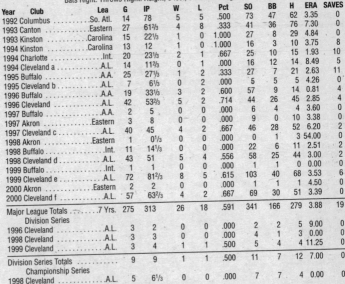

Year	Club	Lea	G	IP	W	L	Pct	SO	BB	H	ERA	SAVES
1992 Columbus	So. Atl.	14	78	5	5	.500	73	47	62	3.35	0
1993 Canton	Eastern	27	61²/₃	4	8	.333	41	36	76	7.30	0
1993 Kinston	Carolina	15	22¹/₃	1	0	1.000	27	8	29	4.84	0
1994 Kinston	Carolina	13	12	1	0	1.000	16	3	10	3.75	8
1994 Charlotte	Int.	20	23¹/₃	2	1	.667	25	10	15	1.93	10
1994 Cleveland a	A.L.	14	11²/₃	0	1	.000	16	12	14	8.49	5
1995 Buffalo	A.A.	25	27¹/₃	1	2	.333	27	7	21	2.63	11
1995 Cleveland b	A.L.	7	6¹/₃	0	2	.000	5	5	5	4.26	0
1996 Buffalo	A.A.	19	33¹/₃	3	2	.600	57	9	14	0.81	4
1996 Cleveland	A.L.	42	53²/₃	5	2	.714	44	26	45	2.85	4
1997 Buffalo	A.A.	2	5	0	0	.000	6	4	4	3.60	0
1997 Akron	Eastern	3	8	0	0	.000	9	0	10	3.38	0
1997 Cleveland c	A.L.	40	45	4	2	.667	46	28	52	6.20	2
1998 Akron	Eastern	1	0¹/₃	0	0	.000	0	1	3	54.00	0
1998 Buffalo	Int.	11	14¹/₃	0	0	.000	22	6	11	2.51	2
1998 Cleveland d	A.L.	43	51	5	4	.556	58	25	44	3.00	2
1999 Buffalo	Int.	1	1	0	0	.000	1	1	0	0.00	0
1999 Cleveland e	A.L.	72	81²/₃	8	5	.615	103	40	68	3.53	6
2000 Akron	Eastern	2	2	0	0	.000	1	1	4	4.50	0
2000 Cleveland f	A.L.	57	63²/₃	4	2	.667	69	30	51	3.39	0
Major League Totals	7 Yrs.	275	313	26	18	.591	341	166	279	3.88	19
Division Series											
1996 Cleveland	A.L.	3	3	0	0	.000	2	2	5	9.00	0
1998 Cleveland	A.L.	3	3	0	0	.000	4	1	3	0.00	0
1999 Cleveland	A.L.	3	4	1	1	.500	5	4	4	11.25	0
Division Series Totals		9	9	1	1	.500	11	7	12	7.00	0
Championship Series											
1998 Cleveland	A.L.	5	6¹/₃	0	0	.000	7	7	4	0.00	0

a On disabled list from June 27 to July 21, 1994.
b On disabled list from May 4 to May 22, 1995.
c On disabled list from April 25 to May 18 and June 19 to July 4 and July 11 to August 1, 1997.
d On disabled list from April 11 to June 16, 1998.
e On disabled list from April 26 to May 11, 1999.
f On disabled list from May 21 to June 26, 2000.

SILVA, JOSE LEONEL

Born, Tijuana, Mexico, December 19, 1973.
Bats Right. Throws Right. Height, 6 feet, 5 inches. Weight, 210 pounds.

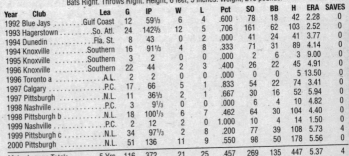

Year	Club	Lea	G	IP	W	L	Pct	SO	BB	H	ERA	SAVES
1992 Blue Jays	Gulf Coast	12	59¹/₃	6	4	.600	78	18	42	2.28	0
1993 Hagerstown	So. Atl.	24	142²/₃	12	5	.706	161	62	103	2.52	0
1994 Dunedin	Fla. St.	8	43	0	2	.000	41	24	41	3.77	0
1994 Knoxville	Southern	16	91¹/₃	4	8	.333	71	31	89	4.14	0
1995 Knoxville	Southern	3	2	0	0	.000	2	6	3	9.00	0
1996 Knoxville	Southern	22	44	2	3	.400	26	22	45	4.91	0
1996 Toronto a	A.L.	2	2	0	0	.000	0	0	5	13.50	0
1997 Calgary	P.C.	17	66	5	1	.833	54	22	74	3.41	0
1997 Pittsburgh	N.L.	11	36¹/₃	2	1	.667	30	16	52	5.94	0
1998 Nashville	P.C.	3	9¹/₃	0	0	.000	6	4	10	4.82	0
1998 Pittsburgh b	N.L.	18	100¹/₃	6	7	.462	64	30	104	4.40	0
1999 Nashville	P.C.	2	12	2	0	1.000	10	4	14	1.50	0
1999 Pittsburgh c	N.L.	34	97¹/₃	2	8	.200	77	39	108	5.73	4
2000 Pittsburgh	N.L.	51	136	11	9	.550	98	50	178	5.56	0
Major League Totals	5 Yrs.	116	372	21	25	.457	269	135	447	5.37	4

a Traded to Pittsburgh Pirates with pitcher Jose Pett, infielder Brandon Cromer, and players to be named later for outfielder Orlando Merced, infielder Carlos Garcia and pitcher Dan Plesac, November 14, 1996. Pittsburgh received pitcher Mike Halperin, infielder Abraham Nunez and catcher Craig Wilson to complete trade, December 11, 1996.
b On disabled list from June 17 to September 10, 1998.
c On disabled list from April 5 to April 23, 1999.

SIMAS, WILLIAM ANTHONY (BILL)

Born, Hanford, California, November 28, 1971.
Bats Left. Throws Right. Height, 6 feet, 3 inches. Weight, 220 pounds.

Year	Club	Lea	G	IP	W	L	Pct	SO	BB	H	ERA	SAVES
1992	Boise	Northwest	14	70²/₃	6	5	.545	39	29	82	3.95	1
1993	Cedar Rapids	Midwest	35	80	5	8	.385	62	36	93	4.95	6
1994	Midland	Texas	13	15¹/₃	2	0	1.000	12	2	5	0.59	6
1994	Lake Elsinor	California	37	47	5	2	.714	34	10	44	2.11	13
1995	Vancouver	P.C.	30	38	6	3	.667	44	14	44	3.55	6
1995	Nashville	A.A.	7	11²/₃	1	1	.500	12	3	12	3.86	0
1995	Chicago a	A.L.	14	14	1	1	.500	16	10	15	2.57	0
1996	Chicago	A.L.	64	72²/₃	2	8	.200	65	39	75	4.58	2
1997	Chicago b	A.L.	40	41¹/₃	3	1	.750	38	24	46	4.14	1
1998	Calgary	P.C.	5	9	1	0	1.000	11	1	2	0.00	1
1998	Chicago	A.L.	60	70²/₃	4	3	.571	56	22	54	3.57	18
1999	Chicago	A.L.	70	72	6	3	.667	41	32	73	3.75	2
2000	Chicago	A.L.	60	67²/₃	2	3	.400	49	22	69	3.46	0
Major League Totals	6 Yrs.		308	338¹/₃	18	19	.486	265	149	332	3.83	23
				Division Series								
2000	Chicago	A.L.	2	1¹/₃	0	0	.000	2	1	0	6.75	0

a Traded to Chicago White Sox with outfielder McKay Christensen, pitcher Andrew Lorraine and pitcher John Snyder for pitcher Jim Abbott and pitcher Tim Fortugno, July 27, 1995.
b On disabled list from July 20 to August 5 and August 15 to September 29, 1997.

SIROTKA, MICHAEL ROBERT (MIKE)

Born, Houston, Texas, May 13, 1971.
Bats Left. Throws Left. Height, 6 feet, 1 inch. Weight, 190 pounds.

Year	Club	Lea	G	IP	W	L	Pct	SO	BB	H	ERA	SAVES
1993	White Sox	Gulf Coast	3	5	0	0	.000	8	2	4	0.00	0
1993	South Bend	Midwest	7	10¹/₃	0	1	.000	12	6	12	6.10	0
1994	South Bend	Midwest	27	196²/₃	12	9	.571	173	58	183	3.07	0
1995	Birmingham	Southern	16	101¹/₃	7	6	.538	79	22	95	3.20	0
1995	Nashville	A.A.	8	54	1	5	.167	34	13	51	2.83	0
1995	Chicago	A.L.	6	34¹/₃	1	2	.333	19	17	39	4.19	0
1996	Nashville	A.A.	15	90	7	5	.583	58	24	90	3.60	0
1996	Chicago	A.L.	15	26¹/₃	1	2	.333	11	12	34	7.18	0
1997	Nashville	A.A.	19	112¹/₃	7	5	.583	92	22	115	3.28	0
1997	Chicago	A.L.	7	32	3	0	1.000	24	5	36	2.25	0
1998	Chicago	A.L.	33	211²/₃	14	15	.483	128	47	255	5.06	0
1999	Chicago	A.L.	32	209	11	13	.458	125	57	236	4.00	0
2000	Chicago a	A.L.	32	197	15	10	.600	128	69	203	3.79	0
Major League Totals	6 Yrs.		125	710¹/₃	45	42	.517	435	207	803	4.31	0
				Division Series								
2000	Chicago	A.L.	1	5²/₃	0	1	.000	0	2	7	4.76	0

Traded to Toronto Blue Jays with pitcher Kevin Beirne, pitcher Mike Williams and outfielder Brian Simmons for pitcher David Wells and pitcher Matt DeWitt, January 14, 2001.

SLOCUMB, HEATHCLIFF

Born, Jamaica, New York, June 7, 1966.
Bats Right. Throws Right. Height, 6 feet, 3 inches. Weight, 220 pounds.

Year	Club	Lea	G	IP	W	L	Pct	SO	BB	H	ERA	SAVES
1984	Kingsport	Appal.	1	0¹/₃	0	0	.000	0	1	0	0.00	0
1984	Little Falls	N.Y.-Penn.	4	9	0	0	.000	10	16	8	11.00	0
1985	Kingsport	Appal.	11	52¹/₃	3	2	.600	29	31	47	3.78	0
1986	Little Falls a	N.Y.-Penn.	25	43²/₃	3	1	.750	41	36	24	1.65	1
1987	Winston-Salem	Carolina	9	27¹/₃	1	2	.333	27	26	26	6.26	0
1987	Peoria	Midwest	16	104	10	4	.714	81	42	97	2.60	0
1988	Winston-Salem	Carolina	25	119²/₃	6	6	.500	78	90	122	4.96	1
1989	Peoria	Midwest	49	55²/₃	5	3	.625	52	33	31	1.78	22
1990	Charlotte	Southern	43	50¹/₃	3	1	.750	37	32	50	2.15	12
1990	Iowa	A.A.	20	27	3	2	.600	21	18	16	2.00	1
1991	Iowa	A.A.	12	13¹/₃	1	0	1.000	9	6	10	4.05	1
1991	Chicago	N.L.	52	62²/₃	2	1	.667	34	30	53	3.45	1
1992	Iowa	A.A.	36	41²/₃	1	3	.250	47	16	36	2.59	7
1992	Chicago	N.L.	30	36	0	3	.000	27	21	52	6.50	1
1993	Iowa	A.A.	10	12	1	0	1.000	10	8	7	1.50	7
1993	Chicago b	N.L.	10	10²/₃	1	0	1.000	4	4	7	3.38	0
1993	Charlotte	Int.	23	30¹/₃	3	2	.600	25	11	25	3.56	1
1993	Cleveland c	A.L.	20	27¹/₃	3	1	.750	18	16	28	4.28	0

Year	Club	Lea	G	IP	W	L	Pct	SO	BB	H	ERA	SAVES
1994 Philadelphia		N.L.	52	72⅓	5	1	.833	58	28	75	2.86	0
1995 Philadelphia d		N.L.	61	65⅓	5	6	.455	63	35	64	2.89	32
1996 Boston		A.L.	75	83⅓	5	5	.500	88	55	68	3.02	31
1997 Boston-Seattle e		A.L.	76	75	0	9	.000	64	49	84	5.16	27
1998 Seattle f		A.L.	57	67⅔	2	5	.286	51	44	72	5.32	3
1999 Memphis		P.C.	2	2	0	0	.000	2	0	3	4.50	0
1999 Baltimore g		A.L.	10	8⅔	0	0	.000	12	9	15	12.46	0
1999 St. Louis h-i		N.L.	40	53⅓	3	2	.600	48	30	49	2.36	2
2000 St. Louis-San Diego j-k		N.L.	65	68⅔	2	4	.333	46	37	69	4.98	1
Major League Totals	10 Yrs.		548	631	28	37	.431	513	358	636	4.08	98
Division Series												
1997 Seattle		A.L.	2	2	0	0	.000	0	1	3	4.50	0

a Drafted by Chicago Cubs from New York Mets organization in minor league draft, December 9, 1988.
b Traded to Cleveland Indians for shortstop Jose Hernandez, June 1, 1993.
c Traded to Philadelphia Phillies for outfielder Ruben Amaro, November 2, 1993.
d Traded to Boston Red Sox with pitcher Larry Wimberly and outfielder Rick Holyfield for outfielder Lee Tinsley, outfielder Glenn Murray and pitcher Ken Ryan, January 29, 1996.
e Traded to Seattle Mariners for catcher Jason Varitek and pitcher Derek Lowe, July 31, 1997.
f Filed for free agency, October 23, 1998. Signed with Baltimore Orioles, January 15, 1999.
g Released by Baltimore Orioles, April 30, 1999, signed with St. Louis Cardinals organization, May 15, 1999.
h On disabled list from June 23 to July 16, 1999.
i Filed for free agency, November 10, 1999, re-signed with St. Louis Cardinals, November 24, 1999.
j Traded to San Diego Padres with outfielder Ben Johnson for catcher Carlos Hernandez and infielder Nathan Tebbs, July 31, 2000.
k Designated for assignment by San Diego Padres, January 5, 2001.

SLUSARSKI, JOSEPH ANDREW (JOE)

Born, Indianapolis, Indiana, December 19, 1966.
Bats Right. Throws Right. Height, 6 feet, 4 inches. Weight, 195 pounds.

Year	Club	Lea	G	IP	W	L	Pct	SO	BB	H	ERA	SAVES
1989 Modesto		California	27	184	13	10	.565	160	50	155	3.18	0
1990 Huntsville		Southern	17	108⅔	6	8	.429	75	35	114	4.47	0
1990 Tacoma a		P.C.	9	55⅔	4	2	.667	37	22	54	3.40	0
1991 Tacoma		P.C.	7	46⅓	4	2	.667	25	10	42	2.72	0
1991 Oakland		A.L.	20	109⅓	5	7	.417	60	52	121	5.27	0
1992 Tacoma		P.C.	11	57⅓	2	4	.333	26	18	67	3.77	0
1992 Oakland b		A.L.	15	76	5	5	.500	38	27	85	5.45	0
1993 Oakland		A.L.	2	8⅔	0	0	.000	1	11	9	5.19	0
1993 Tacoma c		P.C.	24	113⅓	7	5	.583	61	40	133	4.76	0
1994 Tacoma		P.C.	7	37⅓	2	3	.400	24	11	45	6.03	0
1994 Reading		Eastern	5	23⅓	1	2	.333	17	5	25	4.63	0
1994 Scranton-WB d		Int.	10	38	2	3	.400	29	10	50	7.82	0
1995 Buffalo		A.A.	4	15⅔	1	1	.500	9	4	18	6.32	0
1995 New Orleans		A.A.	33	48⅓	1	1	.500	30	11	37	1.12	11
1995 Milwaukee e-f		A.L.	12	15	1	1	.500	6	6	21	5.40	0
1996 New Orleans g-h		A.A.	40	60	2	4	.333	36	24	70	4.95	1
1997 Sinon i		Taiwan	25	71	2	4	.333	31	24	76	4.94	2
1998 Jackson		Texas	9	21⅓	2	2	.500	13	2	22	6.33	0
1998 New Orleans j-k		P.C.	31	49⅓	1	4	.200	32	9	53	5.11	2
1999 New Orleans		P.C.	40	64⅓	1	4	.200	40	13	71	3.64	0
1999 Houston l		N.L.	3	3⅔	0	0	.000	3	3	1	0.00	0
2000 New Orleans		P.C.	13	20	2	1	.667	21	7	14	2.25	0
2000 Houston m-n		N.L.	54	77	2	7	.222	54	22	80	4.21	3
Major League Totals	6 Yrs.		106	289⅔	13	20	.394	162	121	317	4.97	3

a On disabled list from May 18 to 25, 1990.
b On disabled list from August 2 to 11, 1992.
c On disabled list from July 22 to August 11, 1993.
d Released by Oakland Athletics; signed with Philadelphia Phillies organization, June 3, 1994.
e Filed for free agency, October 15, 1994, signed with Cleveland Indians organization, January 20, 1995.
f Released by Cleveland Indians, April 24, 1995, signed with Milwaukee Brewers organization, May 19, 1995.
g Filed for free agency, October 16, 1995, signed with California Angels organization, February 26, 1996.
h Released by California Angels, April 4, 1996, signed with Milwaukee Brewers organization, May 12, 1996.
i Released by Milwaukee Brewers, signed to play in Taiwan for 1997.
j Signed with Houston Astros organization, May 4, 1998.
k Filed for free agency, October 16, 1998, re-signed with Houston Astros organization, December 17, 1998.
l On disabled list from July 9 to July 24, 1999.
m Filed for free agency, October 20, 1999, re-signed with Houston Astros organization, January 3, 2000.
n Not offered 2001 contract, December 21, 2000, signed with Atlanta Braves organization, January 11, 2001.

SMITH, CHARLES EDWARD (CHUCK)

Born, Memphis, Tennessee, October 21, 1969.
Bats Right. Throws Right. Height, 6 feet, 1 inch. Weight, 185 pounds.

Year Club	Lea	G	IP	W	L	Pct	SO	BB	H	ERA	SAVES
1991 Astros	Gulf Coast	15	59⅓	4	3	.571	64	37	56	3.49	0
1992 Asheville	So.Atl.	28	132	9	9	.500	117	78	128	5.18	1
1993 Quad City	Midwest	22	110⅔	7	5	.583	103	52	109	4.64	0
1994 Jackson	Texas	2	6	0	0	.000	7	5	6	4.50	0
1994 Osceola a	Fla.St.	35	84⅔	4	4	.500	60	49	73	3.72	0
1995 South Bend	Midwest	26	167	10	10	.500	145	61	128	2.69	0
1996 Pr William	Carolina	20	123⅓	6	6	.500	99	49	125	4.01	0
1996 Birmingham	Southern	7	30⅔	2	1	.667	30	15	25	2.64	1
1996 Nashville	A.A.	1	0⅔	0	0	.000	1	1	2	27.00	0
1997 Birmingham	Southern	25	62⅔	2	2	.500	57	27	63	3.16	0
1997 Nashville	A.A.	20	31⅔	0	3	.000	29	23	39	8.81	0
1998 Sioux Falls b-c	Northern	8	55	5	3	.625	70	21	44	2.62	0
1999 Oklahoma d-e	P.C.	32	85	5	4	.556	76	28	73	2.96	0
2000 Oklahoma	P.C.	11	66⅔	5	3	.625	73	38	73	3.78	0
2000 Florida f-g	P.C.	19	122⅔	6	6	.500	118	54	111	3.23	0

a Selected by Chicago White Sox from Houston Astros in Rule V draft, December 6, 1994.

b Filed for free agency, October 17, 1997, signed with Sioux Falls, Northern League, May 1998.

c Sold to Colorado Rockies, December 15, 1998.

d Released by Colorado Rockies, April 2, 1999, signed with Texas Rangers organization, April 9, 1999.

e On disabled list from July 22 to August 5, 1999.

f Traded to Chicago Cubs for outfielder Dave Martinez, June 9, 2000.

g Traded to Florida Marlins for pitcher Brant Brown, June 9, 2000.

SMOLTZ, JOHN ANDREW

Born, Detroit, Michigan, May 15, 1967.
Bats Right. Throws Right. Height, 6 feet, 3 inches. Weight, 185 pounds.

Year Club	Lea	G	IP	W	L	Pct	SO	BB	H	ERA	SAVES
1986 Lakeland	Fla. St.	17	96	7	8	.467	47	31	86	3.56	0
1987 Glens Falls a	Eastern	21	130	4	10	.286	86	81	131	5.68	0
1987 Richmond	Int.	3	16	0	1	.000	5	11	17	6.19	0
1988 Richmond	Int.	20	135⅓	10	5	.667	115	37	118	2.79	0
1988 Atlanta	N.L.	12	64	2	7	.222	37	33	74	5.48	0
1989 Atlanta	N.L.	29	208	12	11	.522	168	72	160	2.94	0
1990 Atlanta b	N.L.	34	231⅓	14	11	.560	170	*90	206	3.85	0
1991 Atlanta c	N.L.	36	229⅔	14	13	.519	148	77	206	3.80	0
1992 Atlanta d	N.L.	35	246⅔	15	12	.556	*215	80	206	2.85	0
1993 Atlanta	N.L.	35	243⅔	15	11	.577	208	100	208	3.62	0
1994 Atlanta e	N.L.	21	134⅔	6	10	.375	113	48	120	4.14	0
1995 Atlanta f	N.L.	29	192⅔	12	7	.632	193	72	166	3.18	0
1996 Atlanta g-h	N.L.	35	*253⅔	*24	8	*.750	*276	55	199	2.94	0
1997 Atlanta	N.L.	35	*256	15	12	.556	241	63	*234	3.02	0
1998 Greenville	Southern	3	14	0	1	.000	16	3	11	2.57	0
1998 Macon	So.Atl.	2	10	0	0	.000	14	1	7	3.60	0
1998 Atlanta i	N.L.	26	167⅔	17	3	*.850	173	44	145	2.90	0
1999 Greenville	Southern	2	4	0	0	.000	7	1	5	4.50	0
1999 Atlanta j	N.L.	29	186⅓	11	8	.579	156	40	168	3.19	0
Major League Totals .... 12 Yrs.		356	2414⅓	157	113	.581	2098	774	2092	3.35	0
Division Series											
1995 Atlanta	N.L.	1	5⅔	0	0	.000	6	1	5	7.94	0
1996 Atlanta	N.L.	1	9	1	0	1.000	7	2	4	1.00	0
1997 Atlanta	N.L.	1	9	1	0	1.000	11	1	3	1.00	0
1998 Atlanta	N.L.	1	7⅔	1	0	1.000	6	0	5	1.17	0
1999 Atlanta	N.L.	1	7	1	0	1.000	3	3	6	5.14	0
Division Series Totals		5	38⅓	4	0	1.000	33	7	23	2.82	0
Championship Series											
1991 Atlanta	N.L.	2	15⅓	2	0	1.000	15	3	14	1.76	0
1992 Atlanta	N.L.	3	20⅓	2	0	1.000	19	10	14	2.66	0
1993 Atlanta	N.L.	1	6⅓	0	1	.000	10	5	8	0.00	0
1995 Atlanta	N.L.	1	7	0	0	.000	2	2	7	2.57	0
1996 Atlanta	N.L.	2	15	2	0	1.000	12	3	12	1.20	0
1997 Atlanta	N.L.	1	6	0	1	.000	9	5	5	7.50	0
1998 Atlanta	N.L.	2	13⅔	0	0	.000	13	6	13	3.95	0
1999 Atlanta	N.L.	3	8⅔	0	0	.000	8	0	8	6.23	1
Championship Series Totals		15	92⅓	6	2	.750	88	34	81	2.92	1
World Series Record											
1991 Atlanta	N.L.	2	14⅓	0	0	.000	11	1	13	1.26	0
1992 Atlanta	N.L.	2	13⅓	1	0	1.000	12	7	13	2.70	0

Year	Club	Lea	G	IP	W	L	Pct	SO	BB	H	ERA	SAVES
1995 Atlanta	N.L.	1	$2\frac{1}{3}$	0	0	.000	4	2	6	15.43	0
1996 Atlanta	N.L.	2	14	1	1	.500	14	8	6	0.64	0
1999 Atlanta	N.L.	1	7	0	1	.000	11	3	6	3.86	0
2000 Atlanta k	N.L.	INJURED - did not play									
World Series Totals		8	51	2	2	.500	52	21	44	2.47	0

a Traded by Detroit Tigers to Atlanta Braves organization for pitcher Doyle Alexander, August 12, 1987.
b Appeared in four additional games as pinch runner.
c Appeared in two additional games as pinch runner.
d Appeared in one additional game as pinch hitter.
e Suspended eight games by National League for May 14 hitting batter with pitch, June 20 to June 28, 1994.
f Selected Cy Young Award Winner in National League for 1996.
g Filed for free agency, October 31, 1996.
h Re-signed with Atlanta Braves, November 20, 1996.
i On disabled list from March 31 to April 15 and May 24 to June 20, 1998.
j On disabled list from May 17 to June 1 and July 5 to July 24, 1999.
k On disabled list from April 2 to October 30, 2000.

SNYDER, JOHN MICHAEL
Born, Southfield, Michigan, August 16, 1974.
Bats Right. Throws Right. Height, 6 feet, 3 inches. Weight, 185 pounds.

Year	Club	Lea	G	IP	W	L	Pct	SO	BB	H	ERA	SAVE
1992 Angels	Arizona	15	44	2	4	.333	38	16	40	3.27	3
1993 Cedar Rapids	Midwest	21	99	5	6	.455	79	39	125	5.91	0
1994 Lake Elsnor	California	26	159	10	11	.476	108	56	181	4.47	0
1995 Midland	Texas	21	$133\frac{1}{3}$	8	9	.471	81	48	158	5.74	0
1995 Birmingham a	Southern	5	$20\frac{1}{3}$	1	0	1.000	13	6	24	6.64	0
1996 White Sox	Gulf Coast	4	$16\frac{1}{3}$	1	0	1.000	23	4	5	1.65	0
1996 Birmingham b	Southern	9	54	3	5	.375	58	16	59	4.83	0
1997 Birmingham c	Southern	20	$114\frac{1}{3}$	7	8	.467	90	43	130	4.64	0
1998 Calgary	P.C.	15	97	7	3	.700	63	34	112	4.36	0
1998 Chicago	A.L.	15	$86\frac{1}{3}$	7	2	.778	52	23	96	4.80	0
1999 Charlotte	Int.	3	17	3	0	1.000	9	5	17	4.24	0
1999 Chicago d	A.L.	25	$129\frac{1}{3}$	9	12	.429	67	49	167	6.68	0
2000 Huntsville	Southern	2	$12\frac{1}{3}$	1	1	.500	6	5	6	2.19	0
2000 Indianapolis	Int.	1	7	0	1	.000	5	0	6	2.57	0
2000 Milwaukee e	N.L.	23	127	3	10	.231	69	77	147	6.17	0
Major League Totals	3 Yrs.	63	$342\frac{2}{3}$	19	24	.442	188	149	410	6.01	0

a Traded by California Angels to Chicago White Sox with pitcher Andrew Lorraine, pitcher Bill Simas and outfielder McKay Christensen for pitcher Jim Abbott and pitcher Tim Fortugno, July 27, 1995.
b On disabled list from July 21 to September 1, 1996.
c On disabled list from April 3 to May 4, 1997.
d Traded to Milwaukee Brewers with pitcher Jaime Navarro for pitcher Cal Eldred and infielder Jose Valentin, January 12, 2000.
e On disabled list from March 25 to May 19, 2000.

SPARKS, STEVEN WILLIAM
Born, Tulsa, Oklahoma, July 2, 1965.
Bats Right. Throws Right. Height, 6 feet. Weight, 180 pounds.

Year	Club	Lea	G	IP	W	L	Pct	SO	BB	H	ERA	SAVE
1987 Helena	Pioneer	10	$57\frac{2}{3}$	6	3	.667	47	20	68	4.68	0
1988 Beloit	Midwest	25	164	9	13	.409	96	51	162	3.79	0
1989 Stockton	California	23	164	13	5	.722	126	53	181	2.41	0
1990 El Paso	Texas	7	$30\frac{1}{3}$	1	2	.333	17	15	43	6.53	0
1990 Stockton	California	19	$129\frac{1}{3}$	10	7	.588	77	31	136	3.69	0
1991 El Paso	Texas	4	17	1	2	.333	10	9	30	9.53	0
1991 Stockton	California	24	$179\frac{2}{3}$	9	10	.474	139	98	160	3.06	0
1992 El Paso	Texas	28	$140\frac{2}{3}$	9	8	.529	79	50	159	5.37	1
1993 New Orleans	A.A.	29	$180\frac{1}{3}$	9	13	.409	104	80	174	3.84	0
1994 New Orleans	A.A.	28	$183\frac{2}{3}$	10	12	.455	105	68	183	4.46	0
1995 Milwaukee	A.L.	33	202	9	11	.450	96	86	210	4.63	0
1996 New Orleans	A.A.	11	$57\frac{2}{3}$	2	6	.250	27	35	64	4.99	0
1996 Milwaukee	A.L.	20	$88\frac{2}{3}$	4	7	.364	21	52	103	6.60	0
1997 Milwaukee a	A.L.	INJURED - Did Not Play									
1998 Midland	Texas	7	$40\frac{2}{3}$	0	4	.000	34	15	49	7.08	0
1998 Vancouver	P.C.	4	28	0	0	.000	19	6	23	2.89	0
1998 Anaheim	A.L.	22	$128\frac{2}{3}$	9	4	.692	90	58	130	4.34	0

Year	Club	Lea	G	IP	W	L	Pct	SO	BB	H	ERA	SAVES
1999 Anaheim b	....	A.L.	28	147²/₃	5	11	.313	73	82	165	5.42	0
2000 Toledo	....	Int.	16	90²/₃	5	7	.417	44	41	86	3.77	0
2000 Detroit c	....	A.L.	20	104	7	5	.583	53	29	108	4.07	1
Major League Totals .... 5 Yrs.			123	671	34	38	.472	333	307	716	4.92	1

a Filed for free agency, October 17, 1997, signed with Anaheim Angels organization, April 1, 1998.
b Filed for free agency, October 15, 1999, signed with Philadelphia Phillies organization, February 2, 2000.
c Released by Philadelphia Phillies, signed with Detroit Tigers organization, March 26, 2000.

SPEIER, JUSTIN JAMES
Born, Daly City, California, November 6, 1973.
Bats Right. Throws Right. Height, 6 feet, 4 inches. Weight, 200 pounds.

Year	Club	Lea	G	IP	W	L	Pct	SO	BB	H	ERA	SAVES
1995 Williamsprt	..... N.Y.-Penn.		30	36¹/₃	2	1	.667	39	4	27	1.49	12
1996 Daytona	.... Fla.St.		33	38¹/₃	2	4	.333	34	19	32	3.76	13
1996 Orlando	.... Southern		24	26¹/₃	4	1	.800	14	5	23	2.05	6
1997 Orlando	.... Southern		50	78¹/₃	6	5	.545	63	23	77	4.48	6
1997 Iowa	.... A.A.		8	12¹/₃	2	0	1.000	9	1	5	0.00	1
1998 Iowa	.... P.C.		45	51²/₃	3	3	.500	49	19	52	5.05	12
1998 Chicago-Florida a	...... N.L.		19	20²/₃	0	3	.000	17	13	27	8.71	0
1999 Richmond	.... Int.		27	41²/₃	2	4	.333	39	22	51	5.62	0
1999 Atlanta b-c	.... N.L.		19	28²/₃	0	0	.000	22	13	28	5.65	0
2000 Buffalo	.... Int.		13	13	0	0	.000	12	3	13	4.15	0
2000 Cleveland	.... A.L.		47	68¹/₃	5	2	.714	69	28	57	3.29	0
Major League Totals .... 3 Yrs.			85	117²/₃	5	5	.500	108	54	112	4.82	0

a Traded to Florida Marlins with infielder Kevin Orie and pitcher Todd Noel for pitcher Felix Heredia and infielder
Eve Hoff, July 31, 1998.
b Traded to Atlanta Braves for player to be named later, April 1, 1999. Atlanta Braves received pitcher Matt Targac
to complete trade, June 11, 1999.
c Claimed on waivers by Cleveland Indians, November 23, 1999.

SPRADLIN, JERRY CARL
Born, Fullerton, California, June 14, 1967.
Bats Both. Throws Right. Height, 6 feet, 7 inches. Weight, 240 pounds.

Year	Club	Lea	G	IP	W	L	Pct	SO	BB	H	ERA	SAVES
1988 Billings	.... Pioneer		17	47²/₃	4	1	.800	23	14	45	3.21	0
1989 Greensboro	.... So. Atl.		42	94²/₃	7	2	.778	56	23	88	2.76	2
1990 Cedar Rapds	...... Midwest		5	12	0	1	.000	6	5	13	3.00	0
1990 Chston-Wv	.... So. Atl.		43	74¹/₃	3	4	.429	39	17	74	2.54	17
1991 Chattanooga	...... Southern		48	96	7	3	.700	73	32	95	3.09	4
1992 Cedar Rapids	...... Midwest		1	2¹/₃	1	0	1.000	4	0	5	7.71	0
1992 Chattanooga	...... Southern		59	65¹/₃	3	3	.500	35	13	52	1.38	34
1993 Indianapolis	.... A.A.		34	56²/₃	3	2	.600	46	12	58	3.49	1
1993 Cincinnati	.... N.L.		37	49	2	1	.667	24	9	44	3.49	2
1994 Cincinnati	.... N.L.		6	8	0	0	.000	4	2	12	10.13	0
1994 Indianapolis a	.... A.A.		28	73¹/₃	3	3	.500	49	16	81	3.68	3
1994 Edmonton	.... P.C.		6	10²/₃	1	0	1.000	3	4	12	2.53	1
1995 Charlotte	.... Int.		41	59¹/₃	3	3	.500	38	15	59	3.03	1
1996 Indianapolis b	.... A.A.		49	100	6	8	.429	79	23	94	3.33	15
1996 Cincinnati c	.... N.L.		1	0¹/₃	0	0	.000	0	0	0	0.00	0
1997 Philadelphia	.... N.L.		76	81²/₃	4	8	.333	67	27	86	4.74	1
1998 Philadelphia d	.... N.L.		69	81²/₃	4	4	.500	76	20	63	3.53	1
1999 Cleveland e	.... A.L.		4	3	0	0	.000	2	3	6	18.00	0
1999 San Francisco f	.... N.L.		59	58	3	1	.750	52	29	59	4.19	0
2000 Kansas City	.... A.L.		50	75	4	4	.500	54	27	81	5.52	7
2000 Chicago g-h	.... N.L.		8	15	0	1	.000	13	5	20	8.40	0
Major League Totals .... 7 Yrs.			310	371²/₃	17	19	.472	292	122	371	4.75	11

a Claimed on waivers by Florida Marlins organization, August 4, 1994.
b Released by Florida Marlins and signed by Cincinnati Reds as free agent, February 11, 1996.
c Signed as minor league free agent by Philadelphia Phillies, December 5, 1996.
d Traded to Cleveland Indians for pitcher Chad Ogea, November 13, 1998.
e Traded to San Francisco Giants for outfielder Dan McKinley and player to be named later, April 23, 1999.
Cleveland Indians received pitcher Josh Santos to complete trade, June 27, 1999.
f Traded to Kansas City Royals for player to be named later, December 13, 1999. San Francisco Giants received
pitcher Ken Ray to complete trade, January 7, 1999.
g Released by Kansas City Royals, August 30, 2000, signed with Chicago Cubs, September 8, 2000.
h Released by Chicago Cubs, November 27, 2000.

SPRINGER, RUSSELL PAUL

Born, Alexandria, Louisiana, November 7, 1968.
Bats Right. Throws Right. Height, 6 feet, 4 inches. Weight, 195 pounds.

Year	Club	Lea	G	IP	W	L	Pct	SO	BB	H	ERA	SAVES
1990	Tampa Yankees	Gulf Coast	4	15	0	2	.000	17	4	10	1.20	0
1990	Greensboro	So. Atl.	10	56⅓	2	3	.400	51	31	51	3.67	0
1991	Fort Lauderdale	Fla. St.	25	152⅓	5	9	.357	138	62	118	3.49	0
1991	Albany	Eastern	2	15	1	0	1.000	16	6	9	1.80	0
1992	Columbus	Int.	20	123⅔	8	5	.615	95	54	89	2.69	0
1992	New York a	A.L.	14	16	0	0	.000	12	10	18	6.19	0
1993	Vancouver	P.C.	11	59	5	4	.556	40	33	58	4.27	0
1993	California b	A.L.	14	60	1	6	.143	31	32	73	7.20	0
1994	Vancouver	P.C.	12	83	7	4	.636	58	19	77	3.04	0
1994	California	A.L.	18	45⅔	2	2	.500	28	14	53	5.52	2
1995	Vancouver	P.C.	6	34	2	0	1.000	23	23	24	3.44	0
1995	California	A.L.	19	51⅓	1	2	.333	38	25	60	6.10	1
1995	Philadelphia c-d	N.L.	14	26⅔	0	0	.000	32	10	22	3.71	0
1996	Philadelphia	N.L.	51	96⅔	3	10	.231	94	38	106	4.66	0
1997	Jackson	Texas	1	1	0	0	.000	2	0	2	9.00	0
1997	Houston e-f	N.L.	54	55⅓	3	3	.500	74	27	48	4.23	3
1998	Arizona-Atlanta g-h	N.L.	48	52⅔	5	4	.556	56	30	51	4.10	0
1999	Richmond	Int.	11	15⅓	1	0	1.000	13	1	9	1.17	2
1999	Atlanta i-j	N.L.	49	47⅓	2	1	.667	49	22	31	3.42	1
2000	Arizona	N.L.	52	62	2	4	.333	59	34	63	5.08	0
Major League Totals	9 Yrs.		333	514	19	32	.373	473	242	525	5.01	7
Divisional Series												
1997	Houston	N.L.	2	1⅔	0	0	.000	3	1	2	5.40	0
1999	Atlanta	N.L.	1	1	0	0	.000	1	1	2	0.00	0
Division Series Totals			3	2⅔	0	0	.000	4	2	4	3.38	0
Championship Series												
1999	Atlanta	N.L.	2	2	1	0	1.000	1	1	0	0.00	0
World Series Record												
1999	Atlanta	N.L.	2	2⅓	0	0	.000	1	0	1	0.00	0

a Traded to California Angels with first baseman J. T. Snow and pitcher Jerry Nielsen for pitcher Jim Abbott, December 6, 1992.
b On disabled list from August 2 to end of 1993 season.
c Kevin Flora was traded to Philadelphia Phillies with player to be named later for outfielder Dave Gallagher, August 9, 1995.
d Philadelphia Phillies received pitcher Russ Springer to complete trade, August 15, 1995.
e On disabled list from June 17 to July 10, 1997.
f Selected in expansion draft by Arizona Diamondbacks, November 18, 1997.
g Traded to Atlanta Braves for pitcher Alan Embree, June 22, 1998.
h On disabled list from August 6 to August 21, 1998.
i On disabled list from April 3 to May 17, 1999.
j Filed for free agency, November 2, 1999, signed with Arizona Diamondbacks, November 23, 1999.

STANTON, WILLIAM MICHAEL (MIKE)

Born, Galena Park, Texas, June 2, 1967.
Bats Left. Throws Left. Height, 6 feet, 1 inch. Weight, 190 pounds.

Year	Club	Lea	G	IP	W	L	Pct	SO	BB	H	ERA	SAVES
1987	Pulaski	Appal.	15	83⅓	4	8	.333	82	42	64	3.24	0
1988	Burlington	Midwest	30	154	11	5	.688	160	69	154	3.62	0
1988	Durham	Carolina	2	12⅓	1	0	1.000	14	5	14	1.46	0
1989	Greenville	Southern	47	51⅓	4	1	.800	54	31	32	1.58	19
1989	Richmond	Int.	13	20	2	0	1.000	20	13	6	0.00	8
1989	Atlanta	N.L.	20	24	0	1	.000	27	8	17	1.50	7
1990	Atlanta a	N.L.	7	7	0	3	.000	7	4	16	18.00	2
1990	Greenville	Southern	4	5⅔	0	1	.000	5	3	7	1.59	0
1991	Atlanta	N.L.	74	78	5	5	.500	54	21	62	2.88	7
1992	Atlanta	N.L.	65	63⅔	5	4	.556	44	20	59	4.10	8
1993	Atlanta	N.L.	63	52	4	6	.400	43	29	51	4.67	27
1994	Atlanta b	N.L.	49	45⅔	3	1	.750	35	26	41	3.55	3
1995	Atlanta	N.L.	26	19⅓	1	1	.500	13	6	31	5.59	1
1995	Boston c-d-e	A.L.	22	21	1	0	1.000	10	8	17	3.00	0
1996	Boston-Texas f-g	A.L.	81	78⅔	4	4	.500	60	27	78	3.66	1
1997	New York	A.L.	64	66⅔	6	1	.857	70	34	50	2.57	3
1998	New York	A.L.	67	79	4	1	.800	69	26	71	5.47	6
1999	New York h	A.L.	73	62⅓	2	2	.500	59	18	71	4.33	0
2000	New York	A.L.	69	68	2	3	.400	75	24	68	4.10	0
Major League Totals	12 Yrs.		680	665⅓	37	32	.536	566	251	632	4.00	65

Year	Club	Lea	G	IP	W	L	Pct	SO	BB	H	ERA	SAVES
	Division Series											
1995 Boston		.A.L.	1	2⅓	0	0	.000	4	0	1	0.00	0
1996 Texas		.A.L.	3	3⅓	0	1	.000	3	3	2	2.70	0
1997 New York		.A.L.	3	1	0	0	.000	3	1	1	0.00	0
2000 New York		.A.L.	3	4⅓	1	0	1.000	3	1	5	2.08	0
Division Series Totals			10	11	1	1	.500	13	5	9	1.64	0
	Championship Series											
1991 Atlanta		.N.L.	3	3⅔	0	0	.000	3	3	4	2.45	0
1992 Atlanta		.N.L.	5	4⅓	0	0	.000	5	2	2	0.00	0
1993 Atlanta		.N.L.	1	1	0	0	.000	0	1	1	0.00	0
1998 New York		.A.L.	3	3⅔	0	0	.000	4	1	2	0.00	0
1999 New York		.A.L.	3	0⅓	0	0	.000	0	1	1	0.00	0
Championship Series Totals			15	13	0	0	.000	12	8	10	0.69	0
	World Series Record											
1991 Atlanta		.N.L.	5	7⅓	1	0	1.000	7	2	5	0.00	0
1992 Atlanta		.N.L.	4	5	0	0	.000	1	2	3	0.00	1
1998 New York		.A.L.	1	0⅔	0	0	.000	1	0	3	27.00	0
1999 New York		.A.L.	1	0⅓	0	0	.000	1	0	0	0.00	0
2000 New York		.A.L.	4	4⅓	2	0	1.000	7	0	0	0.00	0
World Series Totals			15	17⅔	3	0	1.000	17	4	11	1.02	1

a On disabled list from April 27 to end of 1990 season.
b Not offered 1995 contract, December 23, 1994.
c Re-signed with Atlanta Braves, April 12, 1995.
d Traded to Boston Red Sox for player to be named later and outfielder Marc Lewis, July 31, 1995. Traded to Boston Red Sox with player to be named later for two players to be named later, July 31, 1995.
e Boston Red Sox received pitcher Matt Murray and Atlanta Braves received pitcher Michael Jacobs and outfielder Marc Lewis to complete trade, August 31, 1995.
f Traded to Texas Rangers with player to be named later for pitcher Mark Brandenberg and pitcher Kerry Lacy, July 31, 1996. Texas Rangers received outfielder Dwyane Hosey to complete trade, November 4, 1996.
g Filed for free agency, October 27, 1996. Signed with New York Yankees, December 11, 1996.
h Filed for free agency, November 5, 1999, re-signed with New York Yankees, November 29, 1999.

STEIN, WILLIAM BLAKE (BLAKE)

Born, McComb, Mississippi, August 3, 1973.
Bats Right. Throws Right. Height, 6 feet, 7 inches. Weight, 210 pounds.

Year	Club	Lea	G	IP	W	L	Pct	SO	BB	H	ERA	SAVES
1994 Johnson City		.Appal.	13	59⅔	4	1	.800	69	24	44	2.87	0
1995 Peoria		.Midwest	27	139⅔	10	6	.625	133	61	122	3.80	0
1996 St. Pete		.Fla.St.	28	172	16	5	.762	159	54	122	2.15	1
1997 Arkansas		.Texas	22	133⅔	8	7	.533	114	49	128	4.24	0
1997 Huntsville a		.Southern	7	34⅔	3	2	.600	25	20	36	5.71	0
1998 Edmonton		.P.C.	5	23⅓	3	1	.750	31	11	22	3.47	0
1998 Oakland		.A.L.	24	117⅓	5	9	.357	89	71	117	6.37	0
1999 Vancouver		.P.C.	19	109⅔	4	2	.667	111	43	94	4.10	0
1999 Oakland-Kansas City b		.A.L.	13	73	1	2	.333	47	47	65	4.56	0
2000 Wilmington		.Carolina	2	5⅓	0	0	.000	12	2	6	6.75	0
2000 Wichita		.Texas	2	8⅔	1	0	1.000	12	1	10	6.23	0
2000 Omaha		.P.C.	2	12⅓	2	0	1.000	14	2	9	0.73	0
2000 Kansas City c		.A.L.	17	107⅔	8	5	.615	78	57	98	4.68	0
Major League Totals	...3 Yrs.		54	298	14	16	.467	214	175	280	5.32	0

a Traded by St. Louis Cardinals to Oakland Athletics with pitcher T.J. Mathews and pitcher Eric Ludwick for infielder Mark McGwire, July 31, 1997.
b Traded to Kansas City Royals with pitcher Brad Rigby and pitcher Jeff M. D'Amico for pitcher Kevin Appier, July 31, 1999.
c On disabled list from March 24 to July 4, 2000.

STEPHENSON, GARRETT CHARLES

Born, Takoma Park, Maryland, January 2, 1972.
Bats Right. Throws Right. Height, 6 feet, 4 inches. Weight, 185 pounds.

Year	Club	Lea	G	IP	W	L	Pct	SO	BB	H	ERA	SAVES
1992 Bluefield		.Appal.	12	32⅓	3	1	.750	30	7	35	4.73	0
1993 Albany		.So.Atl.	30	171⅓	16	7	.696	147	44	142	2.84	1
1994 Frederick		.Carolina	18	107⅓	7	5	.583	133	36	91	4.02	0
1994 Bowie		.Eastern	7	36⅔	3	2	.600	32	11	47	5.15	0
1995 Bowie		.Eastern	29	175⅓	7	10	.412	139	47	154	3.64	0
1996 Baltimore		.A.L.	3	6⅓	0	1	.000	3	3	13	12.79	0
1996 Rochester a		.Int.	23	121⅔	7	6	.538	86	44	123	4.81	0

Year	Club	Lea	G	IP	W	L	Pct	SO	BB	H	ERA	SAVES
1997	Scranton-WB	.Int.	7	29	3	1	.750	27	12	27	5.90	0
1997	Philadelphia	.N.L.	20	117	8	6	.571	81	38	104	3.15	0
1998	Scranton-WB	.Int.	13	73²/₃	1	8	.111	48	16	81	5.25	0
1998	Philadelphia b	.N.L.	6	23	0	2	.000	17	19	31	9.00	0
1999	Arkansas	.Texas	1	5¹/₃	0	0	.000	2	1	8	3.38	0
1999	Memphis	.P.C.	4	25²/₃	1	1	.500	19	7	22	3.16	0
1999	St. Louis	.N.L.	18	85¹/₃	6	3	.667	59	29	90	4.22	0
2000	St. Louis	.N.L.	32	200¹/₃	16	9	.640	123	63	209	4.49	0
Major League Totals ....5 Yrs.			79	432	30	21	.588	283	152	447	4.44	0
Division Series												
2000 St. Louis		.N.L.	1	3²/₃	0	0	.000	2	2	3	2.45	0a

Sent to Philadelphia Phillies with outfielder Calvin Maduro as players to be named later to complete trade for infielder Todd Zeile and outfielder Pete Incavliglia, September 4, 1996.

b Traded to St. Louis Cardinals with pitcher Ricky Bottalico for outfielder Ron Gant, pitcher Jeff Brantley, pitcher Cliff Politte and cash, November 19, 1998.

STOTTLEMYRE, TODD VERNON
Born, Yakima, Washington, May 20, 1965.
Bats Left. Throws Right. Height, 6 feet, 3 inches. Weight, 200 pounds.

Year	Club	Lea	G	IP	W	L	Pct	SO	BB	H	ERA	SAVES
1986	Ventura	.California	17	103²/₃	9	4	.692	104	36	76	2.43	0
1986	Knoxville	.Southern	18	99	8	7	.533	81	49	93	4.18	0
1987	Syracuse	.Int.	34	186²/₃	11	*13	.458	143	*87	189	4.44	0
1988	Syracuse	.Int.	7	48¹/₃	5	0	1.000	51	8	36	2.05	0
1988	Toronto	.A.L.	28	98	4	8	.333	67	46	109	5.69	0
1989	Syracuse	.Int.	10	55²/₃	3	2	.600	45	15	46	3.23	0
1989	Toronto	.A.L.	27	127²/₃	7	7	.500	63	44	137	3.88	0
1990	Toronto	.A.L.	33	203	13	17	.433	115	69	214	4.34	0
1991	Toronto	.A.L.	34	219	15	8	.652	116	75	194	3.78	0
1992	Toronto a-b	.A.L.	28	174	12	11	.522	98	63	175	4.50	0
1993	Toronto c	.A.L.	30	176²/₃	11	12	.478	98	69	204	4.84	0
1994	Toronto d	.A.L.	26	140²/₃	7	7	.500	105	48	149	4.22	1
1995	Oakland e-f	.A.L.	31	209²/₃	14	7	.667	205	80	228	4.55	0
1996	St. Louis	.N.L.	34	223¹/₃	14	11	.560	194	93	191	3.87	0
1997	St. Louis	.N.L.	28	181	12	9	.571	160	65	155	3.88	0
1998	St. Louis	.N.L.	23	161¹/₃	9	9	.500	147	51	146	3.51	0
1998	Texas g-h-i	.A.L.	10	60¹/₃	5	4	.556	57	30	68	4.33	0
1999	Diamondbacks	.Arizona	3	17	2	0	1.000	25	1	11	0.53	0
1999	Arizona j	.N.L.	17	101¹/₃	6	3	.667	74	40	106	4.09	0
2000	AR Diamondbacks	.Arizona	2	10	1	1	.500	10	1	10	3.60	0
2000	Arizona k	.N.L.	18	95¹/₃	9	6	.600	76	36	98	4.91	0
Major League Totals ....13 Yrs.			367	2171¹/₃	138	119	.537	1575	809	2174	4.25	1
Division Series												
1996	St. Louis	.N.L.	1	6²/₃	1	0	1.000	7	2	5	1.35	0
1998	Texas	.A.L.	1	8	0	1	.000	8	4	6	2.25	0
1999	Arizona	.N.L.	1	6²/₃	1	0	1.000	6	5	4	1.35	0
Division Series Totals			3	21¹/₃	2	1	.667	21	11	15	1.69	0
Championship Series												
1989	Toronto	.A.L.	1	5	0	1	.000	3	2	7	7.20	0
1991	Toronto	.A.L.	1	3²/₃	0	1	.000	3	1	7	9.82	0
1992	Toronto	.A.L.	1	3²/₃	0	0	.000	1	0	3	2.45	0
1993	Toronto	.A.L.	1	6	0	1	.000	4	4	6	7.50	0
1996	St. Louis	.N.L.	3	8	1	1	.500	11	3	15	12.38	0
Championship Series Totals 7			26¹/₃	1	4	.200	22	10	38	8.54	0
World Series Record												
1992	Toronto	.A.L.	4	3²/₃	0	0	.000	4	0	4	0.00	0
1993	Toronto	.A.L.	1	2	0	0	.000	1	4	3	27.00	0
World Series Totals 5			5²/₃	0	0	.000	5	4	7	9.53	0

a On disabled list from June 20 to July 16, 1992.

b Suspended by American League for August 5 umpire bumping from September 23 to September 27, 1992.

c On disabled list from May 25 to June 12, 1993.

d Filed for free agency, October 17, 1994.

e Signed with Oakland Athletics, April 11, 1995.

f Traded to St. Louis for pitcher Bret Wagner, pitcher Jay Witasick, pitcher Carl Dale and outfielder Allen Battle January 9, 1996.

g Traded to Texas Rangers with infielder Royce Clayton for pitcher Darren Oliver, infielder Fernando Tatis and playe to be named later, July 31, 1998.

h St. Louis Cardinals received infielder Mark Little to complete trade, August 9, 1998.

i   Filed for free agency, October 22, 1998, signed with Arizona Diamondbacks, November 19, 1998.
j   On disabled list from May 18 to August 20, 1999.
k   On disabled list from May 30 to June 14 and June 26 to August 31, 2000.

STRICKLAND, SCOTT MICHAEL

Born, Houston, Texas, April 26, 1976.
Bats Right. Throws Right. Height, 5 feet, 11 inches. Weight, 180 pounds.

Year	Club	Lea	G	IP	W	L	Pct	SO	BB	H	ERA	SAVES
1997	Vermont	N.Y.-Penn.	15	61$\frac{1}{3}$	5	2	.714	69	20	56	3.82	0
1997	Cape Fear	So.Atl.	3	5$\frac{2}{3}$	0	1	.000	8	1	8	6.35	1
1998	Cape Fear	So.Atl.	15	36$\frac{1}{3}$	0	3	.000	53	12	36	4.46	4
1998	Jupiter	Fla.St.	22	69	4	3	.571	51	20	64	3.39	2
1999	Ottawa	Int.	19	27$\frac{2}{3}$	3	0	1.000	34	11	23	1.63	0
1999	Harrisburg	Eastern	14	29	1	1	.500	36	10	25	2.48	0
1999	Jupiter	Fla.St.	12	25$\frac{2}{3}$	1	1	.500	33	4	21	3.51	0
1999	Montreal	N.L.	17	18	0	1	.000	23	11	15	4.50	0
2000	Ottawa	Int.	3	4	0	0	.000	4	0	1	0.00	0
2000	Montreal a	N.L.	49	48	4	3	.571	48	16	38	3.00	9
Major League Totals	2 Yrs.		66	66	4	4	.500	71	27	53	3.41	9

a On disabled list from May 3 to July 2, 2000.

STURTZE, TANYON JAMES

Born, Worcester, Massachusetts, October 12, 1970.
Bats Right. Throws Right. Height, 6 feet, 5 inches. Weight, 190 pounds.

Year	Club	Lea	G	IP	W	L	Pct	SO	BB	H	ERA	SAVES
1990	Athletics	Arizona	12	48	2	5	.286	30	27	55	5.44	0
1991	Madison	Midwest	27	163	10	5	.667	88	58	136	3.09	0
1992	Modesto	California	25	151	7	11	.389	126	78	143	3.75	0
1993	Huntsville	Southern	28	165$\frac{2}{3}$	5	12	.294	112	85	169	4.78	0
1994	Huntsville	Southern	17	103$\frac{1}{3}$	6	3	.667	63	39	100	3.22	0
1994	Tacoma a-b	P.C.	11	64$\frac{2}{3}$	4	5	.444	28	34	73	4.04	0
1995	Chicago	N.L.	2	2	0	0	.000	0	1	2	9.00	0
1995	Iowa	A.A.	23	86	4	7	.364	48	42	108	6.80	0
1996	Chicago	N.L.	6	11	1	0	1.000	7	5	16	9.00	0
1996	Iowa c	A.A.	51	72$\frac{1}{3}$	6	4	.600	51	33	80	4.85	4
1997	Texas	A.L.	9	33$\frac{2}{3}$	1	1	.500	18	18	45	8.27	0
1997	Okla.City	A.A.	25	114$\frac{2}{3}$	8	6	.571	79	47	133	5.10	0
1998	Rangers	Gulf Coast	3	7	0	1	.000	10	4	12	7.71	0
1998	Charlotte	Fla.St.	1	3	0	1	.000	3	1	2	6.00	0
1998	Tulsa	Texas	1	1$\frac{2}{3}$	1	0	1.000	3	2	2	5.40	0
1998	Oklahoma d-e	P.C.	13	35	3	1	.750	31	18	33	3.34	0
1999	Charlotte	Int.	33	104$\frac{1}{3}$	9	4	.692	107	41	83	4.05	1
1999	Chicago	A.L.	1	6	0	0	.000	2	2	4	0.00	0
2000	Chicago-Tampa Bay f-g	A.L.	29	68$\frac{1}{3}$	5	2	.714	44	29	72	4.74	0
Major League Totals	5 Yrs.		47	120	7	3	.700	71	55	139	5.92	0

a On disabled list from April 7 to 16, 1994.
b Selected by Chicago Cubs from Oakland Athletics in Rule V draft, December 6, 1994.
c Filed for free agency, October 15, 1996, signed with Texas Rangers, November 20, 1996.
d Released by Texas Rangers, March 6, 1998, re-signed with Texas Rangers organization, March 11, 1998.
e Filed for free agency, October 15, 1998, signed with Chicago White Sox organization, November 23, 1998.
f Traded to Tampa Bay Devil Rays for infielder Tony Graffanino, May 31, 2000.
g On disabled list from August 27 to October 1, 2000.

SULLIVAN, WILLIAM (SCOTT)

Born, Tuscaloosa, Alabama, March 13, 1971.
Bats Right. Throws Right. Height, 6 feet, 4 inches. Weight, 210 pounds.

Year	Club	Lea	G	IP	W	L	Pct	SO	BB	H	ERA	SAVES
1993	Billings	Pioneer	18	54	5	0	1.000	79	25	33	1.67	3
1994	Chattanooga	Southern	34	121$\frac{1}{3}$	11	7	.611	111	40	101	3.41	7
1995	Cincinnati	N.L.	3	3$\frac{2}{3}$	0	0	.000	2	2	4	4.91	0
1995	Indianapolis	A.A.	44	58$\frac{2}{3}$	4	3	.571	54	24	51	3.53	1
1996	Indianapolis	A.A.	53	108$\frac{2}{3}$	5	2	.714	77	37	95	2.73	1
1996	Cincinnati	N.L.	7	8	0	0	.000	3	5	7	2.25	0
1997	Indianapolis	A.A.	19	27$\frac{2}{3}$	3	1	.750	23	4	16	1.30	2
1997	Cincinnati	N.L.	59	97$\frac{1}{3}$	5	3	.625	96	30	79	3.24	1
1998	Cincinnati	N.L.	67	102	5	5	.500	86	36	98	5.21	1

Year	Club	Lea	G	IP	W	L	Pct	SO	BB	H	ERA	SAVES
1999 Cincinnati	....	.N.L.	79	113²/₃	5	4	.556	78	47	88	3.01	3
2000 Cincinnati	....	.N.L.	79	106¹/₃	3	6	.333	96	38	87	3.47	3
Major League Totals	....	.6 Yrs.	294	431	18	18	.500	361	158	363	3.70	8

SUPPAN, JEFFREY SCOT

Born, Oklahoma City, Oklahoma, January 2, 1975.
Bats Right. Throws Right. Height, 6 feet, 1 inch. Weight, 200 pounds.

Year	Club	Lea	G	IP	W	L	Pct	SO	BB	H	ERA	SAVES
1993 Red Sox	....	.Gulf Coast	10	57²/₃	4	3	.571	64	16	52	2.18	0
1994 Sarasota	......	.Fla. St.	27	174	13	7	.650	173	50	153	3.26	0
1995 Trenton	....	.Eastern	15	99	6	2	.750	88	26	86	2.36	0
1995 Pawtucket	....	.Int.	7	45²/₃	2	3	.400	32	9	50	5.32	0
1995 Boston	....	.A.L.	8	22²/₃	1	2	.333	19	5	29	5.96	0
1996 Pawtucket	....	.Int.	22	145¹/₃	10	6	.625	142	25	130	3.22	0
1996 Boston a	....	.A.L.	8	22²/₃	1	1	.500	13	13	29	7.54	0
1997 Pawtucket	....	.Int.	9	60²/₃	5	1	.833	40	15	51	3.71	0
1997 Boston b	....	.A.L.	23	112¹/₃	7	3	.700	67	36	140	5.69	0
1998 Arizona	....	.N.L.	13	66	1	7	.125	39	21	82	6.68	0
1998 Tucson c	....	.P.C.	13	67	4	3	.571	62	17	75	3.63	0
1998 Kansas City	....	.A.L.	4	12²/₃	0	0	.000	12	1	9	0.71	0
1999 Kansas City	....	.A.L.	32	208²/₃	10	12	.455	103	62	222	4.53	0
2000 Kansas City	....	.A.L.	35	217	10	9	.526	128	84	240	4.94	0
Major League Totals	....	.6 Yrs.	123	662	30	34	.469	381	222	751	5.15	0

a On disabled list from August 25 to September 30, 1996.\
b Selected in expansion draft by Arizona Diamondbacks, November 18, 1997.
c Sold to Kansas City Royals, September 3, 1998.

SUZUKI, MAKOTO (MAC)

Born, Kobe, Japan, May 31, 1975.
Bats Right. Throws Right. Height, 6 feet, 3 inches. Weight, 195 pounds.

Year	Club	Lea	G	IP	W	L	Pct	SO	BB	H	ERA	SAVES
1992 Salinas	....	.California	1	1	0	0	.000	1	0	0	0.00	0
1993 San Berndno	......	.California	48	80²/₃	4	4	.500	87	56	59	3.68	12
1994 Jacksnville	....	.Southern	8	12²/₃	1	0	1.000	10	6	15	2.84	1
1995 Mariners	....	.Arizona	4	4	1	0	1.000	3	0	5	6.75	0
1995 Riverside	....	.California	6	7²/₃	0	1	.000	6	6	10	4.70	0
1996 Port City	....	.Southern	16	74¹/₃	3	6	.333	66	32	69	4.72	0
1996 Seattle	....	.A.L.	1	1¹/₃	0	0	.000	1	2	2	20.25	0
1996 Tacoma	....	.P.C.	13	22¹/₃	0	3	.000	14	12	31	7.25	0
1997 Tacoma	....	.P.C.	32	83¹/₃	4	9	.308	63	64	79	5.94	0
1998 Tacoma	....	.P.C.	28	131²/₃	9	10	.474	117	70	130	4.37	0
1998 Seattle	....	.A.L.	6	26¹/₃	1	2	.333	19	15	34	7.18	0
1999 Seattle-Kansas City a-b		.A.L.	38	110	2	5	.286	68	64	124	6.79	0
2000 Kansas City	....	.A.L.	32	188²/₃	8	10	.444	135	94	195	4.34	0
Major League Totals	....	.4 Yrs.	77	326¹/₃	11	17	.393	223	175	355	5.46	0

a Traded to New York Mets with player to be named later for pitcher Allen Watson and cash, June 18, 1999.
 New York Mets received pitcher Justin Dunning to complete trade, September 14, 1999.
b Claimed on waivers by Kansas City Royals, June 22, 1999.

SWINDELL, FOREST GREGORY (GREG)

Born, Houston, Texas, January 2, 1965.
Bats Right. Throws Left. Height, 6 feet, 3 inches. Weight, 225 pounds.

Year	Club	Lea	G	IP	W	L	Pct	SO	BB	H	ERA	SAVES
1986 Waterloo	....	.Midwest	3	18	2	1	.667	25	3	12	1.00	0
1986 Cleveland	....	.A.L.	9	61²/₃	5	2	.714	46	15	57	4.23	0
1987 Cleveland a	....	.A.L.	16	102¹/₃	3	8	.273	97	37	112	5.10	0
1988 Cleveland	....	.A.L.	33	242	18	14	.563	180	45	234	3.20	0
1989 Cleveland b	....	.A.L.	28	184¹/₃	13	6	.684	129	51	170	3.37	0
1990 Cleveland	....	.A.L.	34	214²/₃	12	9	.571	135	47	245	4.40	0
1991 Cleveland c	....	.A.L.	33	238	9	16	.360	169	31	241	3.48	0
1992 Cincinnati d-e	....	.N.L.	31	213²/₃	12	8	.600	138	41	210	2.70	0
1993 Houston f	....	.N.L.	31	190¹/₃	12	13	.480	124	40	215	4.16	0
1994 Houston	....	.N.L.	24	148¹/₃	8	9	.471	74	26	175	4.37	0
1995 Houston	....	.N.L.	33	153	10	9	.526	96	39	180	4.47	0
1996 Houston g	....	.N.L.	8	23	0	3	.000	15	11	35	7.83	0

Year	Club	Lea	G	IP	W	L	Pct	SO	BB	H	ERA	SAVES
1996 Cleveland h-i-j-k	A.L.	13	28²/₃	1	1	.500	21	8	31	6.59	0	
1997 Minnesota	A.L.	65	115²/₃	7	4	.636	75	25	102	3.58	1	
1998 Minnesota-Boston l-m	A.L.	81	90¹/₃	5	6	.455	63	31	92	3.59	2	
1999 Arizona n	N.L.	63	64²/₃	4	0	1.000	51	21	54	2.51	1	
2000 Arizona	N.L.	64	76	2	6	.250	64	20	71	3.20	1	
Major League Totals .... 15 Yrs.		566	2146²/₃	121	114	.515	1477	488	2224	3.80	5	
Division Series												
1998 Boston	A.L.	1	1¹/₃	0	0	.000	1	1	0	0.00	0	
1999 Arizona	N.L.	3	3¹/₃	0	0	.000	1	3	1	0.00	0	
Division Series Totals		4	4²/₃	0	0	.000	2	4	1	0.00	0	

a On disabled list from July 2 to end of 1987 season.
b On disabled list from July 26 to August 30, 1989.
c Traded to Cincinnati Reds for pitchers Jack Armstrong, Scott Scudder and Joe Turek, November 15, 1991.
d On disabled list from August 23 to September 7, 1992.
e Filed for free agency, October 26; signed with Houston Astros, December 4, 1992.
f On disabled list from July 6 to July 25, 1993.
g Waived by Houston Astros, June 3, 1996.
h Signed with Cleveland Indians, June 15, 1996.
i On disabled list from July 4 to July 21 and April 20 to May 22, 1996.
j Designated for assignment by Cleveland Indians, August 28, 1996.
k Filed for free agency, August 3, 1996. Signed with Minnesota Twins organization, December 18, 1996.
l Traded to Boston Red Sox with infielder Orlando Merced for pitcher Matt Kinney, pitcher Joe Thomas and outfielder John Barnes, July 31, 1998.
m Filed for free agency, October 27, 1998, signed with Arizona Diamondbacks, November 11, 1998.
n On disabled list from June 13 to June 28, 1999.

TAM, JEFFREY EUGENE (JEFF)

Born, Fullerton, California, August 19, 1970.
Bats Right. Throws Right. Height, 6 feet, 1 inch. Weight, 202 pounds.

Year	Club	Lea	G	IP	W	L	Pct	SO	BB	H	ERA	SAVES
1993 Pittsfield	N.Y.-Penn.	21	40¹/₃	3	3	.500	31	7	50	3.35	0	
1994 Columbia	So.Atl.	26	28	1	1	.500	22	6	23	1.29	18	
1994 St. Lucie	Fla.St.	24	26²/₃	0	0	.000	15	6	13	0.00	16	
1994 Binghamton	Eastern	4	6²/₃	0	0	.000	7	5	9	8.10	0	
1995 Mets	Gulf Coast	2	3	0	0	.000	2	1	2	3.00	0	
1995 Binghamton	Eastern	14	18	0	2	.000	9	4	20	4.50	3	
1996 Binghamton	Eastern	49	62²/₃	6	2	.750	48	16	51	2.44	2	
1997 Norfolk	Int.	40	111²/₃	7	5	.583	67	14	137	4.67	6	
1998 Norfolk	Int.	45	64	3	3	.500	54	6	42	1.83	11	
1998 New York	N.L.	15	14¹/₃	1	1	.500	8	4	13	6.28	0	
1999 Buffalo	Int.	16	26	2	2	.500	13	8	23	2.08	0	
1999 Norfolk	Int.	16	20¹/₃	0	1	.000	10	3	24	3.10	0	
1999 St.Lucie	Fla.St.	2	2²/₃	0	0	.000	3	0	4	3.38	0	
1999 Cleveland	A.L.	1	0¹/₃	0	0	.000	0	1	2	81.00	0	
1999 New York a-b-c-d-e	N.L.	9	11¹/₃	0	0	.000	8	3	6	3.18	0	
2000 Oakland	A.L.	72	85²/₃	3	3	.500	46	23	86	2.63	3	
Major League Totals .... 3 Yrs.		97	111²/₃	4	4	.500	62	31	107	3.39	3	
Division Series												
2000 Oakland	A.L.	3	2	0	0	.000	1	1	3	0.00	0	

a On disabled list from March 21 to May 16, 1999.
b Claimed on waivers by Cleveland Indians, June 18, 1999.
c On disabled list from July 23 to August 1, 1999.
d Claimed on waivers by New York Mets, August 10, 1999.
e Filed for free agency, October 15, 1999, signed with Oakland Athletics organization, November 23, 1999.

TAPANI, KEVIN RAY

Born, Des Moines, Iowa, February 18, 1964.
Bats Right. Throws Right. Height, 6 feet. Weight, 188 pounds.

Year	Club	Lea	G	IP	W	L	Pct	SO	BB	H	ERA	SAVES
1986 Medford	Northwest	2	8¹/₃	1	0	1.000	9	3	6	0.00	0	
1986 Modesto	California	11	69	6	1	.857	44	22	74	2.48	0	
1986 Huntsville	Southern	1	6	1	0	1.000	2	1	8	6.00	0	
1986 Tacoma	P.C.	1	2	0	1	.000	1	1	5	15.43	0	
1987 Modesto a	California	24	148	10	7	.588	121	60	122	3.76	0	
1988 St. Lucie b	Fla. St.	3	19	1	0	1.000	11	4	17	1.42	0	
1988 Jackson	Texas	24	62¹/₃	5	1	.833	35	19	45	2.74	3	
1989 Tidewater	Int.	17	109	7	5	.583	63	25	113	3.47	0	

Year	Club	Lea	G	IP	W	L	Pct	SO	BB	H	ERA	SAVES
1989 New York c	N.L.	3	7⅓	0	0	.000	2	4	5	3.68	0
1989 Portland	P.C.	6	41	4	2	.667	30	12	38	2.20	0
1989 Minnesota	A.L.	5	32⅔	2	2	.500	21	8	34	3.86	0
1990 Minnesota d	A.L.	28	159⅓	12	8	.600	101	29	164	4.07	0
1991 Minnesota	A.L.	34	244	16	9	.640	135	40	225	2.99	0
1992 Minnesota	A.L.	34	220	16	11	.593	138	48	226	3.97	0
1993 Minnesota	A.L.	36	225⅔	12	15	.444	150	57	243	4.43	0
1994 Minnesota e	A.L.	24	156	11	7	.611	91	39	181	4.62	0
1995 Minnesota	A.L.	20	133⅔	6	11	.353	88	34	155	4.92	0
1995 Los Angeles f-g	N.L.	13	57	4	2	.667	43	14	72	5.05	0
1996 Chicago h-i-j	A.L.	34	225⅓	13	10	.565	150	76	236	4.59	0
1997 Orlando	Southern	1	4	0	0	.000	2	2	3	4.50	0
1997 Daytona	Fla. St.	1	4⅔	0	0	.000	4	2	5	3.86	0
1997 Rockford	Midwest	2	11	1	0	1.000	7	0	5	0.82	0
1997 Iowa	A.A.	1	9	0	1	.000	4	1	5	4.00	0
1997 Chicago k	N.L.	13	85	9	3	.750	55	23	77	3.39	0
1998 Chicago	N.L.	35	219	19	9	.679	136	62	244	4.85	0
1999 Chicago l	N.L.	23	136	6	12	.333	73	33	151	4.83	0
2000 Chicago m	N.L.	30	195⅔	8	12	.400	150	47	208	5.01	0
Major League Totals 12 Yrs.		332	2096⅔	134	111	.547	1333	514	2221	4.34	0
Division Series											
1995 Los Angeles	N.L.	2	0⅓	0	0	.000	1	4	0	81.00	0
1998 Chicago	N.L.	1	9	0	0	.000	6	3	5	1.00	0
Division Series Totals		3	9⅓	0	0	.000	7	7	5	3.86	0
Championship Series											
1991 Minnesota	A.L.	2	10⅓	0	1	.000	9	3	16	7.84	0
World Series Record											
1991 Minnesota	A.L.	2	12	1	1	.500	7	2	13	4.50	0

a Traded by Oakland Athletics to New York Mets organization as part of a three-team trade in which New York also acquired pitchers Wally Whitehurst from Oakland and Jack Savage from Los Angeles Dodgers, Oakland acquired pitchers Bob Welch and Matt Young from Los Angeles and Los Angeles acquired pitcher Jay Howell and short stop Alfredo Griffin from Oakland and pitcher Jesse Orosco from New York, December 11, 1987.

b On disabled list from March 28 to May 7 and June 3 to June 24, 1988.

c Traded to Minnesota Twins organization with pitchers Tim Drummond, Rick Aguilera and David West and player to be named for pitcher Frank Viola, July 31; Minnesota acquired pitcher Jack Savage to complete trade, October 16, 1989.

d On disabled list from August 17 to September 11, 1990.

e Declared restricted free agent under Major League Baseball implemented labor proposal, December 23, 1994.

f Re-signed with Minnesota Twins, April 5, 1995.

g Traded to Los Angeles Dodgers with pitcher Mark Guthrie for pitcher Jose Parra, pitcher Greg Hansell and infielder Ron Coomer, July 31, 1995. Minnesota Twins received outfielder Chris Latham to complete trade, October 30, 1995.

h Signed with Chicago White Sox, February 3, 1996.

i Filed for free agency, October 29, 1996.

j Signed with Chicago Cubs, December 13, 1996.

k On disabled list from April 1 to July 22, 1997.

l On disabled list from April 13 to May 1 and August 26 to September 25, 1999.

m On disabled list from September 18 to October 10, 2000.

TAVAREZ (CARMEN), JULIAN
Born, Santiago, Dominican Republic, May 22, 1973.
Bats Left. Throws Right. Height, 6 feet, 2 inches. Weight, 165 pounds.

Year	Club	Lea	G	IP	W	L	Pct	SO	BB	H	ERA	SAVES
1990 Cleveland	Dominican	2	4⅔	0	1	.000	1	7	6	11.57	0
1991 Cleveland	Dominican	19	121⅓	8	2	.800	75	28	95	2.67	0
1992 Burlington	Appal.	14	87⅓	6	3	.667	69	12	86	2.68	0
1993 Kinston	Carolina	18	119	11	5	.688	107	28	102	2.42	0
1993 Canton-Akrn	Eastern	3	19	2	1	.667	11	1	14	0.95	0
1993 Cleveland	A.L.	8	37	2	2	.500	19	13	53	6.57	0
1994 Cleveland	A.L.	1	1⅔	0	1	.000	0	1	6	21.60	0
1994 Charlotte	Int.	26	176	15	6	.714	102	43	167	3.48	0
1995 Cleveland	A.L.	57	85	10	2	.833	68	21	76	2.44	0
1996 Buffalo	A.A.	2	14	1	0	1.000	10	3	10	1.29	0
1996 Cleveland a-b	A.L.	51	80⅔	4	7	.364	46	22	101	5.36	0
1997 San Francisco	N.L.	89	88⅓	6	4	.600	38	34	91	3.87	0
1998 Fresno	P.C.	1	2⅓	0	0	.000	1	0	6	19.29	0
1998 San Francisco c	N.L.	60	85⅓	5	3	.625	52	36	96	3.80	1
1999 Fresno	P.C.	4	8	0	0	.000	9	3	3	2.25	0
1999 San Jose	California	1	4	0	0	.000	3	1	1	0.00	0
1999 San Francisco d-e	N.L.	47	54⅔	2	0	1.000	33	25	65	5.93	0
2000 Colorado f	N.L.	51	120	11	5	.688	62	53	124	4.42	1

Year	Club	Lea	G	IP	W	L	Pct	SO	BB	H	ERA	SAVES
Major League Totals . . . . .8 Yrs.			364	552²/₃	40	24	.625	318	205	612	4.41	2
Division Series												
1995 Cleveland	. . . . .A.L.		3	2²/₃	0	0	.000	3	0	5	6.75	0
1996 Cleveland	. . . . .A.L.		2	1¹/₃	0	0	.000	1	2	1	0.00	0
1997 San Francisco	. . . . .N.L.		3	4	0	1	.000	0	2	4	4.50	0
Division Series Totals			8	8	0	1	.000	4	4	10	4.50	0
Championship Series												
1995 Cleveland	. . . . .A.L.		4	3¹/₃	0	1	.000	2	1	3	2.70	0
World Series Record												
1995 Cleveland	. . . . .A.L.		5	4¹/₃	0	0	.000	1	2	3	0.00	0

a Traded to San Francisco Giants with infielder Jeff Kent, infielder Jose Vizcaino and player to be named later for infielder Matt Williams and player to be named later, November 13, 1996.

b Cleveland Indians received outfielder Trenidad Hubbard and San Francisco Giants received pitcher Joe Roa to complete trade, December 16, 1996.

c On disabled list from July 13 to August 7, 1998.

d On disabled list from May 1 to June 1, 1999.

e Claimed on waivers by Colorado Rockies, November 16, 1999.

f Filed for free agency, October 31, 2000, signed with Chicago Cubs, November 16, 2000.

TELFORD, ANTHONY CHARLES

Born, San Jose, California, March 6, 1966.
Bats Right. Throws Right. Height, 6 feet, 1 inch. Weight, 180 pounds.

Year	Club	Lea	G	IP	W	L	Pct	SO	BB	H	ERA	SAVES
1987 Newark	. . . . .N.Y.-Penn.		6	17²/₃	1	0	1.000	27	3	16	1.02	0
1987 Hagerstown	. . . . .Carolina		2	11¹/₃	1	0	1.000	10	5	9	1.59	0
1987 Rochester	. . . . .Int.		1	2	0	0	.000	3	3	0	0.00	0
1988 Hagerstown	. . . . .Carolina		1	7	1	0	1.000	10	0	3	0.00	0
1989 Frederick	. . . . .Carolina		9	25²/₃	2	1	.667	19	12	25	4.21	1
1990 Frederick	. . . . .Carolina		8	53²/₃	4	2	.667	49	11	35	1.68	0
1990 Hagerstown	. . . . .Eastern		14	96	10	2	.833	73	25	80	1.97	0
1990 Baltimore	. . . . .A.L.		8	36¹/₃	3	3	.500	20	19	43	4.95	0
1991 Rochester	. . . . .Int.		27	157¹/₃	12	9	.571	115	48	166	3.95	0
1991 Baltimore	. . . . .A.L.		9	26²/₃	0	0	.000	24	6	27	4.05	0
1992 Rochester	. . . . .Int.		27	181	12	7	.632	129	64	183	4.18	0
1993 Baltimore	. . . . .A.L.		3	7¹/₃	0	0	.000	6	1	11	9.82	0
1993 Rochester a	. . . . .Int.		38	90²/₃	7	7	.500	66	33	98	4.27	2
1994 Richmond b-c	. . . . .Int.		38	142²/₃	10	6	.625	111	41	148	4.23	0
1995 Edmonton b-c	. . . . .P.C.		8	36¹/₃	3	2	.600	17	16	47	7.18	0
1995 Canton-Akrn.	. . . . . . .Eastern		2	11	2	0	1.000	4	4	6	0.82	0
1995 Buffalo d	. . . . .A.A.		16	39	4	1	.800	24	10	35	3.46	0
1996 Ottawa e	. . . . .Int.		30	118¹/₃	7	2	.778	69	34	128	4.11	0
1997 Montreal	. . . . .N.L.		65	89	4	6	.400	61	33	77	3.24	1
1998 Montreal	. . . . .N.L.		77	91	3	6	.333	59	36	85	3.86	1
1999 Montreal	. . . . .N.L.		79	96	5	4	.556	69	38	112	3.94	2
2000 Montreal f	. . . . .N.L.		64	78¹/₃	5	4	.556	68	23	76	3.79	3
Major League Totals . . . . .7 Yrs.			305	424²/₃	20	23	.465	307	156	431	3.94	7

a Released by Baltimore Orioles and signed as free agent with Atlanta Braves organization, November 23, 1993.

b Signed by Oakland Athletics organization, November 17, 1994.

c Signed by Cleveland Indians organization, June 15, 1995.

d Released by Cleveland Indians organization, October 15, 1995.

e Signed as free agent with Montreal Expos organization, February 22, 1996.

f On disabled list from May 19 to June 2, 2000.

THURMAN, MICHAEL RICHARD (MIKE)

Born, Corvallis, Oregon, July 22, 1973.
Bats Right. Throws Right. Height, 6 feet, 4 inches. Weight, 190 pounds.

Year	Club	Lea	G	IP	W	L	Pct	SO	BB	H	ERA	SAVES
1994 Vermont	. . . . .N.Y.-Penn.		2	6²/₃	0	1	.000	3	2	6	5.40	0
1995 Albany	. . . . .So. Atl.		22	110¹/₃	3	8	.273	77	32	133	5.47	0
1996 Wst Plm Bch	. . . . .Fla. St.		19	113²/₃	6	8	.429	68	23	122	3.40	0
1996 Harrisburg	. . . . .Eastern		4	24²/₃	3	1	.750	14	5	25	5.11	0
1997 Harrisburg	. . . . .Eastern		20	115²/₃	9	6	.600	85	30	102	3.81	0
1997 Ottawa	. . . . .Int.		4	19²/₃	1	3	.250	15	9	17	5.49	0
1997 Montreal	. . . . .N.L.		5	11²/₃	1	0	1.000	8	4	8	5.40	0
1998 Ottawa	. . . . .Int.		19	105²/₃	7	7	.500	76	49	107	3.41	0
1998 Montreal	. . . . .N.L.		14	67	4	5	.444	32	26	60	4.70	0
1999 Montreal	. . . . .N.L.		29	146²/₃	7	11	.389	85	52	140	4.05	0

Year Club	Lea	G	IP	W	L	Pct	SO	BB	H	ERA	SAVES
2000 Jupiter ....Fla.St.		3	13	1	1	.500	6	0	14	2.08	0
2000 Harrisburg ....Eastern		1	4⅓	0	0	.000	1	3	4	4.15	0
2000 Ottawa ....Int.		4	16⅓	0	3	.000	8	9	23	7.71	0
2000 Montreal a ...........N.L.		17	88⅓	4	9	.308	52	46	112	6.42	0
Major League Totals ....4 Yrs.		65	313⅔	16	25	.390	177	128	320	4.91	0

a On disabled list from March 23 to May 11 and May 25 to July 20, 2000.

TIMLIN, MICHAEL AUGUST (MIKE)
Born, Midland, Texas, March 10, 1966.
Bats Right. Throws Right. Height, 6 feet, 4 inches. Weight, 210 pounds.

Year Club	Lea	G	IP	W	L	Pct	SO	BB	H	ERA	SAVES
1987 Medicine Hat ....Pioneer		13	75⅓	4	8	.333	66	26	79	5.14	0
1988 Myrtle Beach ....So. Atl.		35	151	10	6	.625	106	77	119	2.86	0
1989 Dunedin ....Fla. St.		33	88⅔	5	8	.385	64	36	90	3.25	7
1990 Dunedin ....Fla. St.		42	50⅓	7	2	.778	46	16	36	1.43	22
1990 Knoxville ....Southern		17	26	1	2	.333	21	7	20	1.73	8
1991 Toronto a ..............A.L.		63	108⅓	11	6	.647	85	50	94	3.16	3
1992 Dunedin ....Fla. St.		6	10	0	0	.000	7	2	9	0.90	1
1992 Syracuse ....Int.		7	11⅓	0	1	.000	7	5	15	8.74	3
1992 Toronto b ..............A.L.		26	43⅔	0	2	.000	35	20	45	4.12	1
1993 Dunedin ....Fla. St.		4	9	0	0	.000	8	0	4	1.00	1
1993 Toronto ................A.L.		54	55⅔	4	2	.667	49	27	63	4.69	1
1994 Toronto c ..............A.L.		34	40	0	1	.000	38	20	41	5.17	2
1995 Syracuse ....Int.		8	17⅓	1	1	.500	13	4	13	1.04	0
1995 Toronto d ..............A.L.		31	42	4	3	.571	36	17	38	2.14	5
1996 Toronto ................A.L.		59	56⅔	1	6	.143	52	18	47	3.65	31
1997 Toronto-Seattle e .......A.L.		64	72⅔	6	4	.600	45	20	69	3.22	10
1998 Seattle f ..............A.L.		70	79⅓	3	3	.500	60	16	78	2.95	19
1999 Baltimore .............A.L.		62	63	3	9	.250	50	23	51	3.57	27
2000 Baltimore .............A.L.		37	35	2	3	.400	26	15	37	4.89	11
2000 St. Louis g-h ..........N.L.		25	29⅔	3	1	.750	26	20	30	3.34	1
Major League Totals ....10 Yrs.		525	626	37	40	.481	502	246	593	3.59	111
Division Series											
1997 Seattle ................A.L.		1	0⅔	0	0	.000	1	1	3	54.00	0
2000 St. Louis .............N.L.		2	1⅔	0	0	.000	2	1	5	10.80	0
Division Series Totals		3	2⅓	0	0	.000	3	2	8	23.14	0
Championship Series											
1991 Toronto ................A.L.		4	5⅔	0	1	.000	5	2	5	3.18	0
1992 Toronto ................A.L.		2	1⅓	0	0	.000	1	0	4	6.75	0
1993 Toronto ................A.L.		1	2⅓	0	0	.000	2	0	3	3.86	0
2000 St. Louis .............N.L.		3	3⅓	0	1	.000	0	2	1	0.00	0
Championship Series Totals		10	12⅔	0	2	.000	8	4	13	2.84	0
World Series Record											
1992 Toronto ................A.L.		2	1⅓	0	0	.000	0	0	0	0.00	1
1993 Toronto ................A.L.		2	2⅓	0	0	.000	4	0	2	0:00	0
World Series Totals 4			3⅔	0	0	.000	4	0	2	0.00	1

a On disabled list from August 1 to August 15, 1991.
b On disabled list from March 27 to June 12, 1992.
c On disabled list from May 25 to June 9, 1994.
d On disabled list from June 22 to August 18, 1995.
e Traded to Seattle Mariners with pitcher Paul Spoljaric for outfielder Jose Cruz Jr., July 31, 1997.
f Filed for free agency, October 22, 1998, signed with Baltimore Orioles, November 13, 1998.
g On disabled list from April 2 to April 16, 2000.
h Traded to St. Louis Cardinals for outfielder Chris Richard and pitcher Mark Nussbeck, July 29, 2000.

TOLLBERG, BRIAN PATRICK
Born, Tampa, Florida, September 16, 1972.
Bats Right. Throws Right. Height, 6 feet, 3 inches. Weight, 195 pounds.

Year Club	Lea	G	IP	W	L	Pct	SO	BB	H	ERA	SAVES
1994 Chillicothe ....Fron.		13	94⅔	7	4	.636	69	27	90	2.85	0
1995 Beloit ....Midwest		22	132	13	4	.765	110	27	119	3.41	0
1996 El Paso ....Texas		26	154⅓	7	5	.583	109	23	183	4.90	0
1997 Mobile a ....Southern		31	123⅓	6	3	.667	108	24	123	3.72	0
1998 Mobile ....Southern		6	41	3	2	.600	45	4	31	2.41	0
1998 Las Vegas ..............P.C.		33	110	6	6	.500	109	27	138	6.38	3
1999 Las Vegas ..............P.C.		5	29⅔	1	2	.333	23	6	34	4.85	0

Year	Club	Lea	G	IP	W	L	Pct	SO	BB	H	ERA	SAVES
1999 AR Padres	Arizona	2	4	0	0	.000	6	0	4	4.50	0
2000 Las Vegas	P.C.	13	76⅓	6	0	1.000	60	11	72	2.83	0
2000 San Diego	N.L.	19	118	4	5	.444	76	35	126	3.58	0

a Traded by Milwaukee Brewers to San Diego Padres for infielder Antonio Fernandez, March 13, 1997.

TOMKO, BRETT DANIEL
Born, Cleveland, Ohio, April 7, 1973.
Bats Right. Throws Right. Height, 6 feet, 4 inches. Weight, 215 pounds.

Year	Club	Lea	G	IP	W	L	Pct	SO	BB	H	ERA	SAVES
1995 Chston-Wv	So. Atl.	9	49	4	2	.667	46	9	41	1.84	0
1996 Chattanooga	Southern	27	157⅔	11	7	.611	164	54	131	3.88	0
1997 Indianapolis	A.A.	10	61	6	3	.667	60	9	53	2.95	0
1997 Cincinnati	N.L.	22	126	11	7	.611	95	47	106	3.43	0
1998 Cincinnati	N.L.	34	210⅔	13	12	.520	162	64	198	4.44	0
1999 Indianapolis	Int.	2	12⅔	2	0	1.000	9	1	15	4.97	0
1999 Cincinnati	N.L.	33	172	5	7	.417	132	60	175	4.92	0
2000 Tacoma	P.C.	2	12⅔	1	0	1.000	8	5	13	2.84	0
2000 Seattle a-b	A.L.	32	92⅓	7	5	.583	59	40	92	4.68	1
Major League Totals	4 Yrs.	121	601	36	31	.537	448	211	571	4.40	1
Division Series											
2000 Seattle	A.L.	1	2⅔	0	0	.000	0	1	1	0.00	0
Championship Series											
2000 Seattle	A.L.	2	5	0	0	.000	4	4	3	7.20	0

a Traded to Seattle Mariners with outfielder Mike Cameron, infielder Antonio Perez and pitcher Jake Meyer for outfielder Ken Griffey, February 10, 2000.
b On disabled list from June 7 to June 23, 2000.

TRACHSEL, STEPHEN CHRISTOPHER
Born, Oxnard, California, October 31, 1970.
Bats Right. Throws Right. Height, 6 feet, 3 inches. Weight, 185 pounds.

Year	Club	Lea	G	IP	W	L	Pct	SO	BB	H	ERA	SAVES
1991 Geneva	N.Y.-Penn.	2	14⅓	1	0	1.000	7	6	10	1.26	0
1991 Winston-Salem	Carolina	12	73⅔	4	4	.500	69	19	70	3.67	0
1992 Charlotte	Southern	29	191	13	8	.619	135	35	180	3.06	0
1993 Iowa	A.A.	27	170⅔	13	6	.684	135	45	170	3.96	0
1993 Chicago	N.L.	3	19⅔	0	2	.000	14	3	16	4.58	0
1994 Iowa	A.A.	2	9	0	2	.000	8	7	11	10.00	0
1994 Chicago a	N.L.	22	146	9	7	.563	108	54	133	3.21	0
1995 Chicago	N.L.	30	160⅔	7	13	.350	117	76	174	5.15	0
1996 Orlando	Southern	2	13	0	1	.000	12	0	11	2.77	0
1996 Chicago	N.L.	31	205	13	9	.591	132	62	181	3.03	0
1997 Chicago	N.L.	34	201⅓	8	12	.400	160	69	225	4.51	0
1998 Chicago	N.L.	33	208	15	8	.652	149	84	204	4.46	0
1999 Chicago b	N.L.	34	205⅔	8	*18	.308	149	64	226	5.56	0
2000 Tampa Bay-Toronto c-d	A.L.	34	200⅔	8	15	.348	110	74	232	4.80	0
Major League Totals	8 Yrs.	221	1347	68	84	.447	939	486	1391	4.42	0

a On disabled list from July 20 to August 4, 1994.
b Filed for free agency, October 28, 1999. Signed with Tampa Bay Devil Rays, January 13, 2000.
c Traded to Toronto Blue Jays with pitcher Mark Guthrie for infielder Brent Abernathy and player to be named later, July 21, 2000.
d Filed for free agency, October 31, 2000, signed with New York Mets, December 11, 2000.

TROMBLEY, MICHAEL SCOTT
Born, Springfield, Massachusetts, April 14, 1967.
Bats Right. Throws Right. Height, 6 feet, 2 inches. Weight, 208 pounds.

Year	Club	Lea	G	IP	W	L	Pct	SO	BB	H	ERA	SAVES
1989 Kenosha	Midwest	12	49	5	1	.833	41	13	45	3.12	2
1989 Visalia	California	6	42	2	2	.500	36	11	31	2.14	0
1990 Visalia	California	27	176	14	6	.700	164	50	163	3.43	0
1991 Orlando	Southern	27	*191	12	7	.632	*175	57	153	2.54	0
1992 Portland	P.C.	25	165	10	8	.556	138	58	149	3.65	0
1992 Minnesota	A.L.	10	46⅓	3	2	.600	38	17	43	3.30	0
1993 Minnesota	A.L.	44	114⅓	6	6	.500	85	41	131	4.88	2
1994 Salt Lake City	P.C.	11	60⅔	4	4	.500	63	20	75	5.04	0
1994 Minnesota	A.L.	24	48⅓	2	0	1.000	32	18	56	6.33	0

Year Club	Lea	G	IP	W	L	Pct	SO	BB	H	ERA	SAVES
1995 Salt Lake	P.C.	12	69⅔	5	3	.625	59	26	71	3.62	0
1995 Minnesota	A.L.	20	97⅔	4	8	.333	68	42	107	5.62	0
1996 Salt Lake	P.C.	24	36⅔	2	2	.500	38	10	24	2.45	10
1996 Minnesota	A.L.	43	68⅔	5	1	.833	57	25	61	3.01	6
1997 Minnesota	A.L.	67	82⅓	2	3	.400	74	31	77	4.37	1
1998 Minnesota	A.L.	77	96⅔	6	5	.545	89	41	90	3.63	1
1999 Minnesota a	A.L.	75	87⅓	2	8	.200	82	28	93	4.33	24
2000 Baltimore	A.L.	75	72	4	5	.444	72	38	67	4.13	4
Major League Totals ....9 Yrs.		435	713⅔	34	38	.472	597	281	725	4.43	38

a Filed for free agency, October 29, 1999, signed with Baltimore Orioles, November 17, 1999.

URBINA, UGUETH URTAIN

Born, Caracas, Venezuela, February 15, 1974.
Bats Right. Throws Right. Height, 6 feet, 2 inches. Weight, 185 pounds.

Year Club	Lea	G	IP	W	L	Pct	SO	BB	H	ERA	SAVES
1991 Expos	Gulf Coast	10	63	3	3	.500	51	10	58	2.29	0
1992 Albany	So. Atl.	24	142⅓	7	13	.350	100	54	111	3.22	0
1993 Burlington	Midwest	16	108⅓	10	1	.909	107	36	78	1.99	0
1993 Harrisburg	Eastern	11	70	4	5	.444	45	32	66	3.99	0
1994 Harrisburg	Eastern	21	120⅔	9	3	.750	86	43	96	3.28	0
1995 West Palm Beach	Fla. St.	2	9	1	0	1.000	11	1	4	0.00	0
1995 Ottawa	Int.	13	68	6	2	.750	55	26	46	3.04	0
1995 Montreal	N.L.	7	23⅓	2	2	.500	15	14	26	6.17	0
1996 Wst Plm Bch	Fla. St.	3	14	1	1	.500	21	3	13	1.29	0
1996 Ottawa	Int.	5	23⅔	2	0	1.000	28	6	17	2.66	0
1996 Montreal	N.L.	33	114	10	5	.667	108	44	102	3.71	0
1997 Montreal	N.L.	63	64⅓	5	8	.385	84	29	52	3.78	27
1998 Montreal	N.L.	64	69⅓	6	3	.667	94	33	37	1.30	34
1999 Montreal	N.L.	71	75⅔	6	6	.500	100	36	59	3.69	*41
2000 Montreal a	N.L.	13	13⅓	0	1	.000	22	5	11	4.05	8
Major League Totals ....6 Yrs.		251	360	29	25	.537	423	161	287	3.43	110

a On disabled list from May 9 to November 13, 2000.

VALDES, ISMAEL

Born, Victoria, Tamaulipas, Mexico, August 21, 1973.
Bats Right. Throws Right. Height, 6 feet, 3 inches. Weight, 185 pounds.

Year Club	Lea	G	IP	W	L	Pct	SO	BB	H	ERA	SAVES
1991 Kissimmee Dodgers	Gulf C.	10	50⅓	2	2	.500	44	13	44	2.32	0
1992			Played in Dominican Summer League								
1993 San Antonio	Texas	3	13	1	0	1.000	11	0	12	1.38	0
1994 San Antonio	Texas	8	55⅓	2	3	.400	55	9	54	3.38	0
1994 Albuquerque	P.C.	8	45	4	1	.800	39	13	44	3.40	0
1994 Los Angeles	N.L.	21	28⅓	3	1	.750	28	10	21	3.18	0
1995 Los Angeles	N.L.	33	197⅔	13	11	.542	150	51	168	3.05	1
1996 Los Angeles	N.L.	33	225	15	7	.682	173	54	219	3.32	0
1997 Los Angeles a	N.L.	30	196⅔	10	11	.476	140	47	171	2.65	0
1998 Vero Beach	Fla.St.	1	3	0	0	.000	3	1	2	0.00	0
1998 San Berndno	California	1	6⅓	1	0	1.000	4	1	7	2.84	0
1998 Los Angeles b	N.L.	27	174	11	10	.524	122	66	171	3.98	0
1999 Los Angeles c	N.L.	32	203⅓	9	14	.391	143	58	213	3.98	0
2000 Daytona	Fla.St.	1	5	1	0	1.000	5	3	3	1.80	0
2000 Chicago-Los Angeles d-e-f	N.L.	21	107	2	7	.222	74	40	124	5.64	0
Major League Totals ....7 Yrs.		197	1132	63	61	.508	830	326	1087	3.59	1
Division Series											
1995 Los Angeles	N.L.	1	7	0	0	.000	6	1	3	0.00	0
1996 Los Angeles	N.L.	1	6⅓	0	1	.000	5	0	5	4.26	0
Division Series Totals 2			13⅓	0	1	.000	11	1	8	2.03	0

a On disabled list from July 6 to July 28, 1997.

b On disabled list from July 27 to September 1, 1998.

c Traded to Chicago Cubs with infielder Eric Young for pitcher Terry Adams, pitcher Chad Ricketts and player to be named later, December 12, 1999. Los Angeles Dodgers received pitcher Brian Stephenson to complete trade, December 16, 1999.

d On disabled list from March 20 to May 4, 2000.

e Traded to Los Angeles Dodgers for pitcher Jamie Arnold and outfielder Jorge Piedra, July 26, 2000.

f Filed for free agency, October 30, 2000, signed with Anaheim Angels, January 4, 2001.

VALDES, MARC CHRISTOPHER

Born, Dayton, Ohio, December 20, 1971.
Bats Right. Throws Right. Height, 6 feet. Weight, 170 pounds.

Year	Club	Lea	G	IP	W	L	Pct	SO	BB	H	ERA	SAVES
1993	Elmira	N.Y.-Penn.	3	9²/₃	0	2	.000	15	7	8	5.59	0
1994	Kane County	Midwest	11	76¹/₃	7	4	.636	68	21	62	2.95	0
1994	Portland	Eastern	15	99	8	4	.667	70	39	77	2.55	0
1995	Charlotte	Int.	27	170¹/₃	9	13	.409	104	59	189	4.86	0
1995	Florida	N.L.	3	7	0	0	.000	2	9	17	14.14	0
1996	Portland	Eastern	10	64¹/₃	6	2	.750	49	12	60	2.66	0
1996	Charlotte	Int.	8	51	2	4	.333	24	15	66	5.12	0
1996	Florida a	N.L.	11	48²/₃	1	3	.250	13	23	63	4.81	0
1997	Montreal	N.L.	48	95	4	4	.500	54	39	84	3.13	2
1998	Montreal b	N.L.	20	36¹/₃	1	3	.250	28	21	41	7.43	0
1999	Durham	Int.	9	40	1	2	.333	23	12	39	5.17	0
1999	Orlando c-d	Southern	2	7²/₃	0	1	.000	5	2	7	5.87	0
2000	Durham	Int.	9	47²/₃	5	2	.714	25	17	52	4.15	0
2000	Houston e-f	N.L.	53	56²/₃	5	5	.500	35	25	69	5.08	2

Major League Totals .... 5 Yrs. 135 243²/₃ 11 15 .423 132 117 274 4.88 4

a Claimed on waivers by Montreal Expos, December 12, 1996.
b On disabled list from May 27 to June 11 and June 23 to September 28, 1998.
c Filed for free agency, December 21, 1998, signed with Tampa Bay Devil Rays, January 20, 1999.
d Filed for free agency, October 15, 1999, re-signed with Tampa Bat Devils Rays organization, December 14, 1999.
e Traded to Houston Astros for infielder Russ Johnson, May 27, 2000.
f Not offered 2001 contract, December 21, 2000, signed with Atlanta Braves organization, January 11, 2001.

VAN POPPEL, TODD MATTHEW

Born, Hinsdale, Illinois, December 9, 1971.
Bats Right. Throws Right. Height, 6 feet, 5 inches. Weight, 210 pounds.

Year	Club	Lea	G	IP	W	L	Pct	SO	BB	H	ERA	SAVES
1990	Sou Oregon	Northwest	5	24	1	1	.500	32	9	10	1.13	0
1990	Madison	Midwest	3	13²/₃	2	1	.667	17	10	8	3.95	0
1991	Huntsville	Southern	24	132¹/₃	6	13	.316	115	90	118	3.47	0
1991	Oakland	A.L.	1	4²/₃	0	0	.000	6	2	7	9.64	0
1992	Tacoma a	P.C.	9	45¹/₃	4	2	.667	29	35	44	3.97	0
1993	Tacoma	P.C.	16	78²/₃	4	8	.333	71	54	67	5.83	0
1993	Oakland	A.L.	16	84	6	6	.500	47	62	76	5.04	0
1994	Oakland	A.L.	23	116²/₃	7	10	.412	83	89	108	6.09	0
1995	Oakland	A.L.	36	138¹/₃	4	8	.333	122	56	125	4.88	0
1996	Oakland-Detroit b-c	A.L.	37	99¹/₃	3	9	.250	53	62	139	9.06	1
1997	Omaha	A.A.	11	37	1	5	.167	27	24	50	8.03	0
1997	Charlotte	Fla.St.	6	35²/₃	0	4	.000	33	10	36	4.04	0
1997	Tulsa d-e	Texas	7	46²/₃	3	3	.500	26	15	53	5.06	0
1998	Tulsa	Texas	1	4	0	0	.000	2	4	2	4.50	0
1998	Oklahoma	P.C.	15	87	5	5	.500	69	25	88	3.72	0
1998	Texas	A.L.	4	19¹/₃	1	2	.333	10	10	26	8.84	0
1998	Pittsburgh f	N.L.	18	47	1	2	.333	32	18	53	5.36	0
1999	Nashville g-h	P.C.	27	163²/₃	10	6	.625	157	62	173	4.95	0
2000	Iowa	P.C.	10	40²/₃	3	4	.429	52	10	37	3.10	0
2000	Chicago	N.L.	51	86¹/₃	4	5	.444	77	48	80	3.75	2

Major League Totals .... 7 Yrs. 186 595²/₃ 26 42 .382 430 347 614 5.88 3

a On disabled list from May 28 to September 11, 1992.
b Claimed on waivers by Detroit Tigers, August 6, 1996.
c Claimed on waivers by California Angels, November 12, 1996.
d Released by Anaheim Angels, March 26, 1997, signed with Kansas City Royals organization, April 17, 1997.
e Released by Kansas City Royals June 6, 1997, signed with Texas Rangers organization, June 11, 1997.
f Traded to Pittsburgh Pirates with infielder Warren Morris for pitcher Esteban Loaiza, July 17, 1998.
g Filed for free agency, October 15, 1998, re-signed by Pittsburgh Pirates organization, January 2, 1999.
h Filed for free agency, October 15, 1999, signed with Chicago Cubs organization, November 22, 1999.

VAZQUEZ, JAVIER CARLOS

Born, Ponce, Puerto Rico, June 25, 1976.
Bats Right. Throws Right. Height, 6 feet, 2 inches. Weight, 180 pounds.

Year	Club	Lea	G	IP	W	L	Pct	SO	BB	H	ERA	SAVES
1994	Expos	Gulf Coast	15	67²/₃	5	2	.714	56	15	37	2.53	0
1995	Albany	So.Atl.	21	102²/₃	6	6	.500	87	47	109	5.08	0
1996	Delmarva	So.Atl.	27	164¹/₃	14	3	.824	173	57	138	2.68	0
1997	Wst Plm Bch	Fla.St.	19	112²/₃	6	3	.667	100	28	98	2.16	0
1997	Harrisburg	Eastern	6	42	4	0	1.000	47	12	15	1.07	0

337

Year	Club	Lea	G	IP	W	L	Pct	SO	BB	H	ERA	SAVES
1998 Montreal		N.L.	33	172 1/3	5	15	.250	139	68	196	6.06	0
1999 Ottawa		Int.	7	42 2/3	4	2	.667	46	16	45	4.85	0
1999 Montreal		N.L.	26	154 2/3	9	8	.529	113	52	154	5.00	0
2000 Montreal		N.L.	33	217 2/3	11	9	.550	196	61	247	4.05	0
Major League Totals	3 Yrs.		92	544 2/3	25	32	.439	448	181	597	4.96	0

VENAFRO, MICHAEL ROBERT (MIKE)

Born, Takoma Park, Maryland, August 2, 1973.
Bats Left. Throws Right. Height, 5 feet, 10 inches. Weight, 170 pounds.

Year	Club	Lea	G	IP	W	L	Pct	SO	BB	H	ERA	SAVES
1995 Hudson Val		N.Y.-Penn.	32	50 2/3	9	1	.900	32	21	37	2.13	2
1996 Chston-Sc		So.Atl.	50	59	1	3	.250	62	21	57	3.51	19
1997 Charlotte		Fla.St.	35	44 2/3	4	2	.667	35	21	51	3.43	10
1997 Tulsa		Texas	11	15 2/3	0	1	.000	13	12	13	3.45	1
1998 Tulsa		Texas	46	52 1/3	3	4	.429	45	26	42	3.10	14
1998 Oklahoma City		P.C.	13	17	0	0	.000	15	10	19	6.35	0
1999 Oklahoma City		P.C.	6	11 2/3	0	0	.000	7	0	16	5.40	1
1999 Texas		A.L.	65	68 1/3	3	2	.600	37	22	63	3.29	0
2000 Texas		A.L.	77	56 1/3	3	1	.750	32	21	64	3.83	1
Major League Totals	2 Yrs.		142	124 2/3	6	3	.667	69	43	127	3.54	1
Division Series												
1999 Texas		A.L.	2	1	0	0	.000	0	1	2	0.00	0

VERES, DAVID SCOTT

Born, Montgomery, Alabama, October 19, 1966.
Bats Right. Throws Right. Height, 6 feet, 2 inches. Weight, 195 pounds.

Year	Club	Lea	G	IP	W	L	Pct	SO	BB	H	ERA	SAVES
1986 Medford		Northwest	15	77 1/3	5	2	.714	60	57	58	3.26	0
1987 Modesto		California	26	148 1/3	8	9	.471	124	108	124	4.79	0
1988 Modesto		California	19	125	4	11	.267	91	78	100	3.31	0
1988 Huntsville		Southern	8	39	3	4	.429	17	15	50	4.15	0
1989 Huntsville		Southern	29	159 1/3	8	11	.421	105	83	136	4.69	1
1990 Tacoma a		P.C.	32	151 2/3	11	8	.579	88	88	160	4.47	5
1991 Albuquerque b		P.C.	57	100 2/3	7	6	.538	81	52	89	5.30	0
1992 Tucson		P.C.	29	52 2/3	2	3	.400	46	17	60	4.90	5
1993 Tucson		P.C.	43	130 1/3	6	10	.375	122	32	156	4.90	1
1994 Tucson		P.C.	16	24	1	1	.500	19	10	17	1.88	1
1994 Houston		N.L.	32	41	3	3	.500	28	7	39	2.41	1
1995 Houston c		N.L.	72	103 1/3	5	1	.833	94	30	89	2.26	1
1996 Montreal		N.L.	68	77 2/3	6	3	.667	81	32	85	4.17	4
1997 Montreal d-e		N.L.	53	62	2	3	.400	47	27	68	3.48	1
1998 Colorado		N.L.	63	76 1/3	3	1	.750	74	27	67	2.83	8
1999 Colorado f		N.L.	73	77	4	8	.333	71	37	88	5.14	31
2000 St. Louis		N.L.	71	75 2/3	3	5	.375	67	25	65	2.85	29
Major League Totals	7 Yrs.		432	513	26	24	.520	462	185	501	3.32	75
Division Series												
2000 St. Louis		N.L.	2	2	0	0	.000	4	0	1	0.00	0
Championship Series												
2000 St. Louis		N.L.	3	2 1/3	0	0	.000	3	0	2	0.00	0

a Traded by Oakland Athletics to Los Angeles Dodgers organization for pitcher Kevin Campbell, January 15, 1991.
b Became free agent, October 15; signed with Houston Astros organization, May 28, 1992.
c Traded to Montreal Expos with catcher Raul Chavez for infielder Sean Berry, December 20, 1995.
d On disabled list from August 18 to September 17, 1997.
e Traded to Colorado Rockies with player to be named later for outfielder Terry Jones and player to be named later, December 10, 1997. Montreal Expos received pitcher Mark Magnum to complete trade, June 5, 1998.
f Traded to St. Louis Cardinals with pitcher Darryl Kile for pitcher Manuel Aybar, pitcher Jose Jimenez, pitcher Rich Croushore and infielder Brent Butler, November 16, 1999.

VILLONE, RONALD THOMAS (RON)

Born, Englewood, New Jersey, January 16, 1970.
Bats Left. Throws Right. Height, 6 feet, 3 inches. Weight, 230 pounds.

Year	Club	Lea	G	IP	W	L	Pct	SO	BB	H	ERA	SAVES
1993 Riverside		California	16	83 1/3	7	4	.636	82	62	74	4.21	0
1993 Jacksnville		Southern	11	63 2/3	3	4	.429	66	41	49	4.38	0
1994 Jacksnville		Southern	41	79 1/3	6	7	.462	94	68	56	3.86	8
1995 Seattle		A.L.	19	19 1/3	0	2	.000	26	23	20	7.91	0

Year	Club	Lea	G	IP	W	L	Pct	SO	BB	H	ERA	SAVES
1995 Tacoma	.P.C.	22	29²/₃	1	0	1.000	43	19	9	0.61	13
1995 San Diego a	.N.L.	19	25²/₃	2	1	.667	37	11	24	4.21	1
1996 Las Vegas	.P.C.	23	22	2	1	.667	29	9	13	1.64	3
1996 San Diego	.N.L.	21	18¹/₃	1	1	.500	19	7	17	2.95	0
1996 Milwaukee b	.A.L.	23	24²/₃	0	0	.000	19	18	14	3.28	2
1997 Milwaukee c	.A.L.	50	52²/₃	1	0	1.000	40	36	54	3.42	0
1998 Buffalo	.Int.	23	22¹/₃	2	2	.500	28	11	20	2.01	7
1998 Cleveland d	.A.L.	25	27	0	0	.000	15	22	30	6.00	0
1999 Indianapolis	.Int.	18	19	2	0	1.000	23	13	9	1.42	1
1999 Cincinnati	.N.L.	29	142²/₃	9	7	.563	97	73	114	4.23	2
2000 Cincinnati e	.N.L.	35	141	10	10	.500	77	78	154	5.43	0
Major League Totals . . . . .6 Yrs.		221	451¹/₃	23	21	.523	330	268	427	4.67	5

a Traded to San Diego Padres with outfielder Marc Newfield for pitcher Andy Benes and a player to be named later. July 31, 1995. Mariners received pitcher Greg Keagle to complete trade, September 16, 1995.

b Traded to Milwaukee Brewers with pitcher Bryce Florie and outfielder Marc Newfield for outfielder Greg Vaughn and a player to be named later, July 31, 1996. Padres received outfielder Jerry Parent to complete trade, September 16, 1996.

c Traded to Cleveland Indians with pitcher Mike Fetters and pitcher Ben McDonald for pitcher Jeff Juden and outfielder Marquis Grissom, December 8, 1997.

d Released by Cleveland Indians, April 2, 1999, signed with Cincinnati Reds organization, April 5, 1999.

e Traded to Colorado Rockies for two players to be named later, November 8, 2000. Cincinnati Reds received pitcher Jeff Tahlienti and pitcher Justin Carter to complete trade, December 20, 2000.

WAGNER, WILLIAM EDWARD
Born, Tannersville, Virginia, July 25, 1971.
Bats Left. Throws Left. Height, 5 feet, 10 inches. Weight, 180 pounds.

Year	Club	Lea	G	IP	W	L	Pct	SO	BB	H	ERA	SAVES
1993 Auburn	.N.Y.-Penn.	7	28²/₃	1	3	.250	31	25	25	4.08	0
1994 Quad City	.Midwest	26	153	8	9	.471	204	91	99	3.29	0
1995 Jackson	.Texas	12	70	2	2	.500	77	36	49	2.57	0
1995 Tucson	.P.C.	13	76¹/₃	5	3	.625	80	32	70	3.18	0
1995 Houston	.N.L.	1	0¹/₃	0	0	.000	0	0	0	0.00	0
1996 Tucson	.P.C.	12	74	6	2	.750	86	33	62	3.28	0
1996 Houston a	.N.L.	37	51²/₃	2	2	.500	67	30	28	2.44	9
1997 Houston	.N.L.	62	66¹/₃	7	8	.467	106	30	49	2.85	23
1998 Jackson	.Texas	3	3	0	0	.000	7	0	1	0.00	0
1998 Houston b	.N.L.	58	60	4	3	.571	97	25	46	2.70	30
1999 Houston	.N.L.	66	74²/₃	4	1	.800	124	23	35	1.57	39
2000 Houston c	.N.L.	28	27²/₃	2	4	.333	28	18	28	6.18	6
Major League Totals . . . . .6 Yrs.		252	280²/₃	19	18	.514	422	126	186	2.73	107
Division Series											
1997 Houston	.N.L.	1	1	0	0	.000	2	0	3	18.00	0
1998 Houston	.N.L.	1	1	1	0	1.000	1	0	4	18.00	0
1999 Houston	.N.L.	1	1	0	0	.000	1	0	0	0.00	0
Division Series Totals		3	3	1	0	1.000	4	0	7	12.00	0

a On disabled list from August 23 to September 7, 1996.

b On disabled list from July 16 to August 7, 1998.

c On disabled list from June 18 to November 5, 2000.

WAKEFIELD, TIMOTHY STEPHEN
Born, Melborne, Florida, August 2, 1966.
Bats Right. Throws Right. Height, 6 feet, 2 inches. Weight, 204 pounds.

Year	Club	Lea	G	IP	W	L	Pct	SO	BB	H	ERA	SAVES
1989 Welland	.N.Y.-Penn.	18	39²/₃	1	1	.500	42	21	30	3.40	0
1990 Salem	.Carolina	28	190¹/₃	10	14	.417	127	85	187	4.73	0
1991 Buffalo	.A.A.	1	4²/₃	0	1	.000	4	1	8	11.57	0
1991 Carolina	.Southern	26	183	15	8	.652	123	51	155	2.90	0
1992 Buffalo	.A.A.	20	135¹/₃	10	3	.769	71	51	122	3.06	0
1992 Pittsburgh	.N.L.	13	92	8	1	.889	51	35	76	2.15	0
1993 Carolina	.Southern	9	56²/₃	3	5	.375	36	22	68	6.99	0
1993 Pittsburgh	.N.L.	24	128¹/₃	6	11	.353	59	75	145	5.61	0
1994 Buffalo	.A.A.	30	175²/₃	5	15	.250	83	98	197	5.84	0
1995 Pawtucket	.Int.	4	25	2	1	.667	14	9	23	2.52	0
1995 Boston a-b	.A.L.	27	195¹/₃	16	8	.667	119	68	163	2.95	0
1996 Boston	.A.L.	32	211²/₃	14	13	.519	140	90	238	5.14	0
1997 Boston c	.A.L.	35	201¹/₃	12	*15	.444	151	87	193	4.25	0
1998 Boston	.A.L.	36	216	17	8	.680	146	79	211	4.58	0

Year Club	Lea	G	IP	W	L	Pct	SO	BB	H	ERA	SAVES
1999 Boston	A.L.	49	140	6	11	.353	104	72	146	5.08	15
2000 Boston d	A.L.	51	159⅓	6	10	.375	102	65	170	5.48	0
Major League Totals .... 8 Yrs.		267	1344	85	77	.525	872	571	1342	4.47	15
Division Series											
1995 Boston	A.L.	1	5⅓	0	1	.000	4	5	5	11.81	0
1998 Boston	A.L.	1	1⅓	0	1	.000	1	2	3	33.75	0
1999 Boston	A.L.	2	2	0	0	.000	4	4	3	13.50	0
Division Series Totals		4	8⅔	0	2	.000	9	11	11	15.58	0
Championship Series											
1992 Pittsburgh	N.L.	2	18	2	0	1.000	7	5	14	3.00	0

a Released by Pittsburgh Pirates, April 20, 1995.
b Signed by Boston Red Sox, April 27, 1995.
c On disabled list from April 15 to May 6, 1997.
d Filed for free agency, October 31, 2000, re-signed with Boston Red Sox, December 7, 2000.

WALKER, KEVIN MICHAEL
Born, Irving, Texas, September 20, 1976.
Bats Left. Throws Right. Height, 6 feet, 4 inches. Weight, 190 pounds.

Year Club	Lea	G	IP	W	L	Pct	SO	BB	H	ERA	SAVES
1995 Padres	Arizona	13	71⅔	5	5	.500	69	12	74	3.01	0
1996 Idaho Falls	Pioneer	1	6	1	0	1.000	4	2	4	3.00	0
1996 Clinton	Midwest	13	76	4	6	.400	43	33	80	4.74	0
1997 Clinton	Midwest	19	110⅔	6	10	.375	80	37	133	4.88	0
1998 Clinton	Midwest	2	14⅔	2	0	1.000	10	7	11	1.23	0
1998 Rancho Cuca	California	22	121⅓	11	7	.611	94	48	122	4.15	0
1999 Rancho a-b	California	27	39	1	1	.500	35	19	35	3.46	0
2000 Mobile	Southern	4	4	0	1	.000	6	1	1	2.25	0
2000 San Diego	N.L.	70	66⅔	7	1	.875	56	38	49	4.18	0

a On disabled list from April 8 to 24, 1999.
b On disabled list from June 19 to July 30, 1999.

WALL, DONNELL LEE (DONNE)
Born, Potosi, Missouri, July 11, 1967.
Bats Right. Throws Right. Height, 6 feet, 1 inch. Weight, 180 pounds.

Year Club	Lea	G	IP	W	L	Pct	SO	BB	H	ERA	SAVES
1989 Auburn	N.Y.-Penn.	12	65⅓	7	0	1.000	69	12	45	1.79	1
1990 Asheville	So. Atl.	28	132	6	8	.429	111	47	149	5.18	1
1991 Burlington	Midwest	16	106⅔	7	5	.583	102	21	73	2.03	0
1991 Osceola	Fla. St.	12	77⅓	6	3	.667	62	11	55	2.09	0
1992 Osceola	Fla. St.	7	41	3	1	.750	30	8	37	2.63	0
1992 Jackson	Texas	18	114⅓	9	6	.600	99	26	114	3.54	0
1992 Tucson	P.C.	2	8	0	0	.000	2	1	11	1.13	0
1993 Tucson	P.C.	25	131⅔	6	4	.600	89	35	147	3.83	0
1994 Tucson	P.C.	26	148⅓	11	8	.579	84	35	171	4.43	0
1995 Tucson	P.C.	28	177⅓	17	6	.739	119	32	190	3.30	0
1995 Houston	N.L.	6	24⅓	3	1	.750	16	5	33	5.55	0
1996 Tucson	P.C.	8	52⅓	3	3	.500	36	6	67	4.13	0
1996 Houston	N.L.	26	150	9	8	.529	99	34	170	4.56	0
1997 Houston a-b	N.L.	8	41⅔	2	5	.286	25	16	53	6.26	0
1997 New Orleans c	A.A.	17	110	8	7	.533	84	24	109	3.85	0
1998 Las Vegas	P.C.	3	15	2	0	1.000	12	8	11	4.80	0
1998 San Diego	N.L.	46	70⅓	5	4	.556	56	32	50	2.43	1
1999 San Diego	N.L.	55	70⅓	7	4	.636	53	23	58	3.07	0
2000 Las Vegas	P.C.	2	2	0	0	.000	1	2	3	0.00	0
2000 San Diego d-e	N.L.	44	53⅔	5	2	.714	29	21	36	3.35	1
Major League Totals .... 6 Yrs.		185	410⅓	31	24	.564	278	131	400	4.01	2
Division Series											
1998 San Diego	N.L.	1	1	0	0	.000	2	0	2	9.00	0
Championship Series											
1998 San Diego	N.L.	3	3	0	0	.000	4	4	3	3.00	1
World Series Record											
1998 San Diego	N.L.	2	2⅔	0	1	.000	1	3	3	6.75	0

a Claimed on waivers by Cincinnati Reds, October 7, 1997.
b Traded to Detroit Tigers with catcher Paul Bako for outfielder Melvin Nieves, November 11, 1997.
c Traded to San Diego Padres with pitcher Dan Miceli and infielder Ryan Balfe for pitcher Tim Worrell and outfielder Trey Beaumon, November 19, 1997.
d On disabled list from June 1 to June 30, 2000.
e Traded to New York Mets for outfielder Bubba Trammell, December 11, 2000.

WASHBURN, JARROD MICHAEL

Born, LaCrosse, Wisconsin, August 13, 1974.
Bats Left. Throws Right. Height, 6 feet, 1 inch. Weight, 190 pounds.

Year	Club	Lea	G	IP	W	L	Pct	SO	BB	H	ERA	SAVES
1995	Boise	Northwest	8	46	3	2	.600	54	14	35	3.33	0
1995	Cedar Rapids	Midwest	3	18⅓	0	1	.000	20	7	17	3.44	0
1996	Lk Elsinore	California	14	92⅔	6	3	.667	93	33	79	3.30	0
1996	Vancouver	P.C.	2	8⅓	0	2	.000	5	12	12	10.80	0
1996	Midland	Texas	13	88	5	6	.455	58	25	77	4.40	0
1997	Midland	Texas	29	189⅓	15	12	.556	146	65	211	4.80	0
1997	Vancouver	P.C.	1	5	0	0	.000	6	2	4	3.60	0
1998	Midland	Texas	1	8⅔	0	1	.000	8	2	13	6.23	0
1998	Vancouver	P.C.	14	91⅔	4	5	.444	66	43	91	4.32	0
1998	Anaheim	A.L.	15	74	6	3	.667	48	27	70	4.62	0
1999	Edmonton	P.C.	11	59	1	5	.167	55	17	50	4.73	0
1999	Anaheim	A.L.	16	61⅔	4	5	.444	39	26	61	5.25	0
2000	Lake Elsinore	California	1	3	0	0	.000	7	2	3	6.00	0
2000	Edmonton	P.C.	5	30⅔	3	0	1.000	20	13	35	3.52	0
2000	Anaheim a	A.L.	14	84⅓	7	2	.778	49	37	64	3.74	0
Major League Totals	3 Yrs.		45	220	17	10	.630	136	90	195	4.46	0

a On disabled list from March 25 to April 8 and July 22 to August 6 and August 8 to October 1, 2000.

WEATHERS, JOHN DAVID

Born, Lawrenceburg, Tennessee, September 25, 1969.
Bats Right. Throws Right. Height, 6 feet, 3 inches. Weight, 205 pounds.

Year	Club	Lea	G	IP	W	L	Pct	SO	BB	H	ERA	SAVES
1988	St. Catharines	N.Y.-Penn.	15	62⅔	4	4	.500	36	26	58	3.02	0
1989	Myrtle Beach	So. Atl.	31	172⅔	11	*13	.458	111	86	163	3.86	0
1990	Dunedin	Fla. St.	27	158	10	7	.588	96	59	158	3.70	0
1991	Knoxville	Southern	24	139⅓	10	7	.588	114	49	121	2.45	0
1991	Toronto	A.L.	15	14⅔	1	0	1.000	13	17	15	4.91	0
1992	Syracuse a	Int.	12	48⅓	1	4	.200	30	21	48	4.66	0
1992	Toronto b	A.L.	2	3⅓	0	0	.000	3	2	5	8.10	0
1993	Edmonton	P.C.	22	141	11	4	.733	117	47	150	3.83	0
1993	Florida	N.L.	14	45⅔	2	3	.400	34	13	57	5.12	0
1994	Florida c	N.L.	24	135	8	12	.400	72	59	166	5.27	0
1995	Brevard City	Fla. St.	1	4	0	0	.000	3	1	4	0.00	0
1995	Charlotte	Int.	1	5	0	1	.000	0	5	10	9.00	0
1995	Florida d	N.L.	28	90⅓	4	5	.444	60	52	104	5.98	0
1996	Charlotte	Int.	1	2⅓	0	0	.000	0	3	5	7.71	0
1996	Florida e	N.L.	31	71⅓	2	2	.500	40	28	85	4.54	0
1996	Columbus	Int.	3	16⅔	0	2	.000	7	5	20	5.40	0
1996	New York	A.L.	11	17⅓	0	2	.000	13	14	23	9.35	0
1997	Columbus	Int.	5	36⅔	2	2	.500	35	7	35	3.19	0
1997	Buffalo f-g	A.A.	11	68⅔	4	3	.571	51	17	71	3.15	0
1997	New York-Cleveland h	A.L.	19	25⅔	1	3	.250	18	15	38	8.42	0
1998	Cincinnati-Milwaukee i	N.L.	44	110	6	5	.545	94	41	130	4.91	0
1999	Milwaukee j	N.L.	63	93	7	4	.636	74	38	102	4.65	2
2000	Milwaukee k	N.L.	69	76⅓	3	5	.375	50	32	73	3.07	1
Major League Totals	10 Yrs.		320	682⅔	34	41	.453	471	311	798	5.12	3
Division Series												
1996	New York	A.L.	2	5	1	0	1.000	5	0	1	0.00	0
Championship Series												
1996	New York	A.L.	2	3	1	0	1.000	0	0	3	0.00	0
World Series Record												
1996	New York	A.L.	3	3	0	0	.000	3	3	2	3.00	0

a On disabled list from May 11 to July 31, 1992.
b Selected by Florida Marlins in expansion draft, November 17, 1992.
c Appeared in two additional games as pinch runner.
d On disabled list from June 26 to July 13, 1995.
e Traded to New York Yankees for pitcher Mark Hutton, July 31, 1996.
f Traded to Cleveland Indians for outfielder Chad Curtis, June 9, 1997.
g Outrighted by Cleveland Indians, August 8, 1997.
h Signed as free agent with Cincinnati Reds, December 19, 1997.
   Claimed on waivers by Milwaukee Brewers, June 24, 1998.
   Filed for free agency, October 29, 1999, re-signed with Milwaukee Brewers, December 2, 1999.
   On disabled list from August 2 to August 21, 2000.

WEAVER, JEFFREY CHARLES (JEFF)

Born, Northridge, California, August 22, 1976.
Bats Right. Throws Right. Height, 6 feet, 5 inches. Weight, 200 pounds.

Year	Club	Lea	G	IP	W	L	Pct	SO	BB	H	ERA	SAVES
1998 Jamestown	......	N.Y.-Penn.	3	12	1	0	1.000	12	1	6	1.50	0
1998 W Michigan	....	Midwest	2	13	1	0	1.000	21	0	8	1.38	0
1999 Jacksonville	....	Southern	1	6	0	0	.000	6	0	5	3.00	0
1999 Detroit	....	A.L.	30	163²/₃	9	12	.429	114	56	176	5.55	0
2000 Toledo	....	Int.	1	5¹/₃	0	1	.000	10	1	5	3.38	0
2000 Detroit	....	A.L.	31	200	11	15	.423	136	52	205	4.32	0
Major League Totals	....	2 Yrs.	61	363²/₃	20	27	.426	250	108	381	4.88	0

WELLS, DAVID LEE

Born, Torrance, California, May 20, 1963.
Bats Left. Throws Left. Height, 6 feet, 4 inches. Weight, 225 pounds.

Year	Club	Lea	G	IP	W	L	Pct	SO	BB	H	ERA	SAVES
1982 Medicine Flat	......	Pioneer	12	64¹/₃	4	3	.571	53	32	71	5.18	0
1983 Kinston	....	Carolina	25	157	6	5	.545	115	71	141	3.73	0
1984 Kinston	....	Carolina	7	42	1	6	.143	44	19	51	4.71	0
1984 Knoxville a	....	Southern	8	59	3	2	.600	34	17	58	2.59	0
1985 Knoxville b	....	Southern		INJURED—Did Not Play								
1986 Florence	....	So. Atl.	4	12²/₃	0	0	.000	14	9	7	3.55	0
1986 Ventura	....	California	5	19	2	1	.667	26	4	13	1.89	0
1986 Knoxville c	....	Southern	10	40	1	3	.250	32	18	42	4.05	0
1986 Syracuse	....	Int.	3	3²/₃	0	1	.000	2	1	6	9.82	0
1987 Syracuse	....	Int.	43	109¹/₃	4	6	.400	106	32	102	3.87	6
1987 Toronto	....	A.L.	18	29¹/₃	4	3	.571	32	12	37	3.99	1
1988 Syracuse	....	Int.	6	5²/₃	0	0	.000	8	2	7	0.00	3
1988 Toronto	....	A.L.	41	64¹/₃	3	5	.375	56	31	65	4.62	4
1989 Toronto	....	A.L.	54	86¹/₃	7	4	.636	78	28	66	2.40	2
1990 Toronto	....	A.L.	43	189	11	6	.647	115	45	165	3.14	3
1991 Toronto	....	A.L.	40	198¹/₃	15	10	.600	106	49	188	3.72	1
1992 Toronto d	....	A.L.	41	120	7	9	.438	62	36	138	5.40	2
1993 Detroit e-f	....	A.L.	32	187	11	9	.550	139	42	183	4.19	0
1994 Lakeland	....	Fla. St.	2	6	0	0	.000	3	0	5	0.00	0
1994 Detroit g	....	A.L.	16	111¹/₃	5	7	.417	71	24	113	3.96	0
1995 Detroit	....	A.L.	18	130¹/₃	10	3	.769	83	37	120	3.04	0
1995 Cincinnati h-i	....	N.L.	11	72²/₃	6	5	.545	50	16	74	3.59	0
1996 Baltimore j-k	....	A.L.	34	224¹/₃	11	14	.440	130	51	247	5.14	0
1997 New York	....	A.L.	32	218	16	10	.615	156	45	239	4.21	0
1998 New York l	....	A.L.	30	214¹/₃	18	4	*.818	163	29	195	3.49	0
1999 Toronto m	....	A.L.	34	*231²/₃	17	10	.630	169	62	*246	4.82	0
2000 Toronto n	....	A.L.	35	229²/₃	*20	8	.714	166	31	*266	4.11	0
Major League Totals	....	14 Yrs.	479	2306²/₃	161	107	.601	1576	538	2342	4.06	13
Division Series												
1995 Cincinnati	....	N.L.	1	6¹/₃	1	0	1.000	8	1	6	0.00	0
1996 Baltimore	....	A.L.	2	13²/₃	1	0	1.000	6	4	15	4.61	0
1997 New York	....	A.L.	1	9	1	0	1.000	1	0	5	1.00	0
1998 New York	....	A.L.	1	8	1	0	1.000	9	1	5	0.00	0
Divisional Series Totals	....	5	37	4	0	1.000		24	6	31	1.95	0
Championship Series												
1989 Toronto	....	A.L.	1	1	0	0	.000	1	2	0	0.00	0
1991 Toronto	....	A.L.	4	7²/₃	0	0	.000	9	2	6	2.35	0
1995 Cincinnati	....	N.L.	1	6	0	1	.000	3	2	8	4.50	0
1996 Baltimore	....	A.L.	6	6²/₃	1	0	1.000	6	3	8	4.05	0
1998 New York	....	A.L.	2	15²/₃	2	0	1.000	18	2	12	2.87	0
Championship Series Totals	....	9	37	3	1	.750		37	11	34	3.16	0
World Series Record												
1992 Toronto	....	A.L.	4	4¹/₃	0	0	.000	3	2	1	0.00	0
1998 New York	....	A.L.	1	7	1	0	1.000	4	2	7	6.43	0
World Series Totals	....	5	11¹/₃	1	0	1.000		7	4	8	3.97	0

a On disabled list from June 24 to end of 1984 season.

b On disabled list from April 10 to end of 1985 season.

c On disabled list from July 7 to August 20, 1986.

d Released, March 30; signed with Detroit Tigers, April 3, 1993.

e On disabled list from August 1 to August 20, 1993.

f Filed for free agency, October 28; re-signed with Detroit Tigers, December 14, 1993.

g On disabled list from April 16 to June 4, 1994.

h Traded to Cincinnati Reds for pitcher C.J. Nitkowski, pitcher Dave Tuttle and player to be named later, July 31 1995. Detroit Tigers received infielder Mark Lewis to complete trade, November 16, 1995.

i Traded to Baltimore Orioles for outfielder Curtis Goodwin and outfielder Trovin Valdez, December 26, 1995.
j Filed for free agency, October 29, 1996.
k Signed with New York Yankees, December 17, 1996.
l Pitched perfect no-hit, no-run game against Minnesota Twins, May 17, 1998, winning 4-0
m Traded to Toronto Blue Jays with pitcher Graeme Lloyd and infielder Homer Bush for pitcher Roger Clemens, February 18, 1999.
n Traded to Chicago White Sox with pitcher Matt DeWitt for pitcher Mike Sirotka, pitcher Kevin Beirne, pitcher Mike Williams and outfielder Brian Simmons, January 14, 2001.

WELLS, ROBERT KIP (KIP)
Born, Houston, Texas, April 21, 1977.
Bats Right. Throws Right. Height, 6 feet, 3 inches. Weight, 195 pounds.

Year	Club	Lea	G	IP	W	L	Pct	SO	BB	H	ERA	SAVES
1999 Winston-Salem	.....Carolina		14	85²/₃	5	6	.455	95	34	78	3.57	0
1999 Birmingham	.......Southern		11	70¹/₃	8	2	.800	44	31	49	2.94	0
1999 Chicago	............A.L.		7	35²/₃	4	1	.800	29	15	33	4.04	0
2000 Charlotte	..............Int.		12	62	5	3	.625	38	27	67	5.37	1
2000 Chicago	............A.L.		20	98²/₃	6	9	.400	71	58	126	6.02	0
Major League Totals ....2 Yrs.			27	134¹/₃	10	10	.500	100	73	159	5.49	0

WELLS, ROBERT LEE
Born, Yakima, Washington, November 1, 1966.
Bats Right. Throws Right. Height, 6 feet. Weight, 180 pounds.

Year	Club	Lea	G	IP	W	L	Pct	SO	BB	H	ERA	SAVES
1989 Martinsville	.........Appal.		4	6	0	0	.000	3	2	8	4.50	0
1990 Spartanburg	........So. Atl.		20	113	5	8	.385	73	40	94	2.87	0
1990 Clearwater	..........Fla. St.		6	14²/₃	0	2	.000	11	6	17	4.91	1
1991 Clearwater	..........Fla. St.		24	75¹/₃	7	2	.778	66	19	63	3.11	0
1991 Reading	.........Eastern		1	5	1	0	1.000	3	1	4	3.60	0
1992 Clearwater	..........Fla. St.		9	9¹/₃	1	0	1.000	9	3	10	3.86	5
1992 Reading	.........Eastern		3	15¹/₃	0	1	.000	11	5	12	1.17	0
1993 Clearwater	..........Fla. St.		12	27²/₃	1	0	1.000	24	6	23	0.98	2
1993 Scranton	..............Int.		11	19¹/₃	1	1	.500	8	5	19	2.79	0
1994 Reading	.........Eastern		14	19¹/₃	1	3	.250	19	3	18	2.79	4
1994 Scranton	..............Int.		11	14²/₃	0	2	.000	13	6	18	2.45	0
1994 Philadelphia a	..........N.L.		5	5	1	0	1.000	3	3	4	1.80	0
1994 Calgary	...............P.C.		6	31²/₃	3	2	.600	17	9	43	6.54	0
1994 Seattle	...............A.L.		1	4	1	0	1.000	3	1	4	2.25	0
1995 Seattle	...............A.L.		30	76²/₃	4	3	.571	38	39	88	5.75	0
1996 Seattle	...............A.L.		36	130²/₃	12	7	.632	94	46	141	5.30	0
1997 Seattle	...............A.L.		46	67¹/₃	2	0	1.000	51	18	88	5.75	2
1998 Wisconsin	.........Midwest		1	3	0	1	.000	2	0	4	3.00	0
1998 Seattle b-c	............A.L.		30	51²/₃	2	2	.500	29	16	54	6.10	0
1999 Minnesota	............A.L.		*76	87¹/₃	8	3	.727	44	28	79	3.81	1
2000 Minnesota	............A.L.		76	86¹/₃	0	7	.000	76	15	80	3.65	10
Major League Totals ....7 Yrs.			301	509	30	22	.577	338	166	538	4.92	13
Division Series												
1995 Seattle	...............A.L.		1	1	0	0	.000	0	1	2	9.00	0
1997 Seattle	...............A.L.		1	1¹/₃	0	0	.000	1	0	1	0.00	0
Divisional Series Totals 2				2¹/₃	0	0	.000	1	1	3	3.86	0
Championship Series												
1995 Seattle	...............A.L.		1	3	0	0	.000	2	2	2	3.00	0

a Claimed on waivers by Seattle Mariners, June 30, 1994.
b On disabled list from April 16 to May 19, 1998.
c Released by Seattle Mariners, November 19, 1998. Signed with Minnesota Twins organization, January 19, 1999.

WENDELL, STEVEN JOHN (TURK)
Born, Pittsfield, Massachusetts, May 19, 1967.
Bats Both. Throws Right. Height, 6 feet, 2 inches. Weight, 190 pounds.

Year	Club	Lea	G	IP	W	L	Pct	SO	BB	H	ERA	SAVES
1988 Pulaski	.............Appal.		14	*101	3	8	.273	87	30	85	3.83	0
1989 Burlington	........Midwest		22	159	9	11	.450	153	41	127	2.21	0
1989 Greenville	.........Southern		1	3²/₃	0	0	.000	3	1	7	9.82	0
1989 Durham	.........Carolina		3	24	2	0	1.000	27	6	13	1.13	0
1990 Greenville	.........Southern		36	91	4	9	.308	85	48	105	5.74	2
1990 Durham	.........Carolina		6	38²/₃	1	3	.250	26	15	24	1.86	0

Year	Club	Lea	G	IP	W	L	Pct	SO	BB	H	ERA	SAVES
1991	Greenville	Southern	25	147²/₃	11	3	.786	122	51	130	2.56	0
1991	Richmond a	Int.	3	21	0	2	.000	18	16	20	3.43	0
1992	Iowa b	A.A.	4	25	2	0	1.000	12	15	17	1.44	0
1993	Iowa	A.A.	25	148²/₃	10	8	.556	110	47	148	4.60	0
1993	Chicago	N.L.	7	22²/₃	1	2	.333	15	8	24	4.37	0
1994	Iowa	A.A.	23	168	11	6	.647	118	28	141	2.95	0
1994	Chicago	N.L.	6	14¹/₃	0	1	.000	9	10	22	11.93	0
1995	Daytona	Fla. St.	4	7²/₃	0	0	.000	8	1	5	1.17	0
1995	Orlando	Southern	5	7	1	0	1.000	7	4	6	3.86	1
1995	Chicago c	N.L.	43	60¹/₃	3	1	.750	50	24	71	4.92	0
1996	Chicago	N.L.	70	79¹/₃	4	5	.444	75	44	58	2.84	18
1997	Chicago-New York d	N.L.	65	76¹/₃	3	5	.375	64	53	68	4.36	5
1998	New York	N.L.	66	76²/₃	5	1	.833	58	33	62	2.93	4
1999	New York e	N.L.	80	85²/₃	5	4	.556	77	37	80	3.05	3
2000	New York e	N.L.	77	82²/₃	8	6	.571	73	41	60	3.59	1
Major League Totals	8 Yrs.		414	498	29	25	.537	421	250	445	3.83	31
Division Series												
1999	New York	N.L.	2	2	1	0	1.000	0	2	0	0.00	0
2000	New York	N.L.	2	2	0	0	.000	5	1	0	0.00	0
Division Series Totals			4	4	1	0	1.000	5	3	0	0.00	0
Championship Series												
1999	New York	N.L.	5	5²/₃	1	0	1.000	5	4	2	4.76	0
2000	New York	N.L.	2	1¹/₃	1	0	1.000	2	1	1	0.00	0
Championship Series Totals			7	7	2	0	1.000	7	5	3	3.86	0
World Series Record												
2000	New York	N.L.	2	1²/₃	0	1	.000	2	2	3	5.40	0

a Traded by Atlanta Braves to Chicago Cubs organization with pitcher Yorkis Perez for catcher Damon Berryhill and pitcher Mike Bielecki, September 29, 1991.
b On disabled list from May 4 to end of 1992 season.
c On disabled list from April 25 to May 27, 1995.
d Traded to New York Mets with pitcher Mel Rojas and outfielder Brian McRae for outfielder Lance Johnson, pitcher Mark Clark and player to be named later, August 8, 1997. Chicago Cubs received infielder Manny Alexander to complete trade, August 14, 1997.
e Filed for free agency, November 3, 2000, re-signed with New York Mets, December 1, 2000.

WETTELAND, JOHN KARL

Born, San Mateo, California, August 21, 1966.
Bats Right. Throws Right. Height, 6 feet, 2 inches. Weight, 215 pounds.

Year	Club	Lea	G	IP	W	L	Pct	SO	BB	H	ERA	SAVES
1985	Great Falls	Pioneer	11	20²/₃	1	1	.500	23	15	17	3.92	0
1986	Bakersfield	California	15	67	0	7	.000	38	46	71	5.78	0
1986	Great Falls	Pioneer	12	69¹/₃	4	3	.571	59	40	70	5.45	0
1987	Vero Beach a	Fla. St.	27	175²/₃	12	7	.632	144	92	150	3.13	0
1988	San Antonio	Texas	25	162¹/₃	10	8	.556	140	*77	141	3.88	0
1989	Albuquerque	P.C.	10	69	5	3	.625	73	20	61	3.65	0
1989	Los Angeles	N.L.	31	102²/₃	5	8	.385	96	34	81	3.77	1
1990	Albuquerque	P.C.	8	29	2	2	.500	26	13	27	5.59	0
1990	Los Angeles	N.L.	22	43	2	4	.333	36	17	44	4.81	0
1991	Albuquerque b	P.C.	41	61¹/₃	4	3	.571	55	26	48	2.79	*20
1991	Los Angeles c-d	N.L.	6	9	1	0	1.000	9	3	5	0.00	0
1992	Montreal	N.L.	67	83¹/₃	4	4	.500	99	36	64	2.92	37
1993	West Palm Beach	Fla. St.	2	3	0	0	.000	6	0	0	0.00	0
1993	Montreal e	N.L.	70	85¹/₃	9	3	.750	113	28	58	1.37	43
1994	Montreal f-g	N.L.	52	63²/₃	4	6	.400	68	21	46	2.83	25
1995	New York h-i	A.L.	60	61¹/₃	1	5	.167	66	14	40	2.93	31
1996	New York j-k-l-m	A.L.	62	63²/₃	2	3	.400	69	21	54	2.83	*43
1997	Texas	A.L.	61	65	7	2	.778	63	21	43	1.94	31
1998	Texas	A.L.	63	62	3	1	.750	72	14	47	2.03	42
1999	Texas	A.L.	62	66	4	4	.500	60	19	67	3.68	43
2000	Texas n	A.L.	62	60	6	5	.545	53	24	67	4.20	34
Major League Totals	12 Yrs.		618	765	48	45	.516	804	252	616	2.93	330
Division Series												
1995	New York	A.L.	3	4¹/₃	0	1	.000	5	2	8	14.54	0
1996	New York	A.L.	3	4	0	0	.000	4	4	2	0.00	2
1998	Texas	A.L.	1	1	0	0	.000	1	1	0	0.00	0
1999	Texas	A.L.	1	1	0	0	.000	1	0	0	0.00	0
Division Series Totals			8	10¹/₃	0	1	.000	11	7	10	6.10	2

Year	Club	Lea	G	IP	W	L	Pct	SO	BB	H	ERA	SAVES
Championship Series												
1996 New York ............A.L.			4	4	0	0	.000	5	1	2	4.50	1
World Series Record												
1996 New York ............A.L.			5	4⅓	0	0	.000	6	1	4	2.08	4

a Drafted by Detroit Tigers from Los Angeles Dodgers organization, December 5, 1987; returned to Los Angeles organization, March 29, 1988.
b On disabled list from May 1 to May 8 and June 3 to June 29, 1991.
c Traded to Cincinnati Reds with pitcher Tim Belcher for outfielder Eric Davis and pitcher Kip Gross, November 27, 1991.
d Traded by Cincinnati Reds to Montreal Expos with pitcher Bill Risley for outfielder Dave Martinez, infielder Willie Greene and pitcher Scott Ruskin, December 11, 1991.
e On disabled list from April 4 to April 23, 1993.
f On disabled list from April 18 to May 3, 1994.
g Declared restricted free agent under Major League Baseball implemented labor proposal, December 23, 1994.
h Traded to New York Yankees for outfielder Fernando Seguignol and cash.
i Re-signed with New York Yankees, June 7, 1995.
j Re-signed with New York Yankees, February 13, 1996.
k On disabled list from August 13 to September 6, 1996.
l Filed for free agency, November 4, 1996.
m Signed with Texas Rangers, December 16, 1996.
n Filed for free agency, November 1, 2000.

WHITE, GABRIEL ALLEN (GABE)

Born, Sebring, Florida, November 20, 1971.
Bats Left. Throws Right. Height, 6 feet, 2 inches. Weight, 200 pounds.

Year	Club	Lea	G	IP	W	L	Pct	SO	BB	H	ERA	SAVES
1990 Expos ....Gulf Coast			11	57⅓	4	2	.667	41	12	50	3.14	0
1991 Sumter ....So.Atl.			24	149	6	9	.400	140	53	127	3.26	0
1992 Rockford ....Midwest			27	187	14	8	.636	176	61	148	2.84	0
1993 Harrisburg ....Eastern			16	100	7	2	.778	80	28	80	2.16	0
1993 Ottawa a ....Int.			6	40⅓	2	1	.667	28	6	38	3.12	0
1994 Wst Plm Bch ....Fla.St.			1	6	1	0	1.000	4	1	2	1.50	0
1994 Montreal .............N.L.			7	23⅔	1	1	.500	17	11	24	6.08	1
1994 Ottawa b ....Int.			14	73	8	3	.727	63	28	77	5.05	0
1995 Ottawa ....Int.			12	62⅓	2	3	.400	37	17	58	3.90	0
1995 Montreal c ...........N.L.			19	25⅔	1	2	.333	25	9	26	7.01	0
1996 Indianapols d .........A.A.			11	68⅓	6	3	.667	51	9	69	2.77	0
1997 Indianapols ...........A.A.			20	118	7	4	.636	62	18	119	2.82	0
1997 Cincinnati .............N.L.			12	41	2	2	.500	25	8	39	4.39	1
1998 Cincinnati .............N.L.			69	98⅔	5	5	.500	83	27	86	4.01	9
1999 Cincinnati .............N.L.			50	61	1	2	.333	61	14	68	4.43	0
2000 Cincinnati-Colorado e ....N.L.			68	84	11	2	.846	84	15	64	2.36	5
Major League Totals ....6 Yrs.			225	334	21	14	.600	295	84	307	4.10	16

a On disabled list from July 2 to 27, 1993.
b On disabled list from April 7 to May 6, 1994.
c Traded to Cincinnati Reds for pitcher Jhonny Carvajal, December 15, 1995.
d On disabled list from September 17 to October 1, 1996.
e Traded to Colorado Rockies for pitcher Manny Aybar, April 7, 2000.

WHITE, RICHARD ALLEN (RICK)

Born, Springfield, Ohio, December 23, 1968.
Bats Right. Throws Right. Height, 6 feet, 4 inches. Weight, 215 pounds.

Year	Club	Lea	G	IP	W	L	Pct	SO	BB	H	ERA	SAVES
1990 Pirates ....Gulf Coast			7	35⅔	3	1	.750	27	4	26	0.76	0
1990 Welland .........N.Y.-Penn.			9	38⅔	1	4	.200	43	14	39	3.26	0
1991 Augusta ....So.Atl.			34	63	4	4	.500	52	18	68	3.00	6
1991 Salem ....Carolina			13	46⅓	2	3	.400	36	9	41	4.66	1
1992 Salem ....Carolina			18	120⅔	7	9	.438	70	24	116	3.80	0
1992 Carolina ....Southern			10	57⅔	1	7	.125	45	18	59	4.21	0
1993 Carolina ....Southern			12	69⅓	4	3	.571	52	12	59	3.50	0
1993 Buffalo a ...........A.A.			7	28	0	3	.000	16	8	25	3.54	0
1994 Pittsburgh ...........N.L.			43	75⅓	4	5	.444	38	17	79	3.82	6
1995 Calgary ...........P.C.			14	79⅓	6	4	.600	56	10	97	4.20	0
1995 Pittsburgh b ...........N.L.			15	55	2	3	.400	29	18	66	4.75	0
1996 Pirates ....Gulf Coast			3	12	0	0	.000	8	3	8	2.25	0
1996 Carolina ....Southern			2	6⅓	0	1	.000	7	1	9	11.37	0
1997 Orlando c ....Southern			39	86	5	7	.417	65	22	93	4.71	12
1998 Durham ....Int.			9	53⅓	4	2	.667	31	11	63	4.22	0
1998 Tampa Bay ...........A.L.			38	68⅔	2	6	.250	39	23	66	3.80	0
1999 Tampa Bay ...........A.L.			63	108	5	3	.625	81	38	132	4.08	0

Year	Club	Lea	G	IP	W	L	Pct	SO	BB	H	ERA	SAVES
2000 Tampa Bay	....	A.L.	44	71⅓	3	6	.333	47	26	57	3.41	2
2000 New York d	....	N.L.	22	28⅓	2	3	.400	20	12	26	3.81	1
Major League Totals	.5 Yrs.		225	406⅔	18	26	.409	254	134	426	3.94	9
Division Series												
2000 New York	....	N.L.	2	2⅔	1	0	1.000	4	2	6	0.00	0
Championship Series												
2000 New York	....	N.L.	1	3	0	0	.000	1	1	5	9.00	0
World Series Record												
2000 New York	....	N.L.	1	1⅓	0	0	.000	1	1	1	6.75	0

a On disabled list from May 15 to July 6 and August 28 to September 4, 1993.
b On disabled list from April 14 to May 17, 1995.
c Filed for free agency on December 21, 1996, signed by Tampa Bay Devil Rays organization, January 15, 1997.
d Traded to New York Mets with outfielder Bubba Trammell for outfielder Jason Tyner and pitcher Paul Wilson, July 28, 2000.

WICKMAN, ROBERT JOE

Born, Green Bay, Wisconsin, February 6, 1969.
Bats Right. Throws Right. Height, 6 feet, 1 inch. Weight, 212 pounds.

Year	Club	Lea	G	IP	W	L	Pct	SO	BB	H	ERA	SAVES
1990 Sara. White Sox	......	Gulf C.	2	11	2	0	1.000	15	1	7	2.45	0
1990 Sarasota	....	Fla. St.	2	13⅔	0	1	.000	8	4	17	1.98	0
1990 South Bend	....	Midwest	9	65⅓	7	2	.778	50	16	50	1.38	0
1991 Sarasota	....	Fla. St.	7	44	5	1	.833	32	11	43	2.05	0
1991 Birmingham a	.....	Southern	20	131⅓	6	10	.375	81	50	127	3.56	0
1992 Columbus	....	Int.	23	157	12	5	.706	108	55	131	2.92	0
1992 New York	....	A.L.	8	50⅓	6	1	.857	21	20	51	4.11	0
1993 New York	....	A.L.	41	140	14	4	.778	70	69	156	4.63	4
1994 New York	....	A.L.	*53	70	5	4	.556	56	27	54	3.09	6
1995 New York	....	A.L.	63	80	2	4	.333	51	33	77	4.05	1
1996 New York-Milwaukee b	..	A.L.	70	95⅔	7	1	.875	75	44	106	4.42	0
1997 Milwaukee	....	N.L.	74	95⅔	7	6	.538	78	41	89	2.73	1
1998 Milwaukee	....	N.L.	72	82⅓	6	9	.400	71	39	79	3.72	25
1999 Milwaukee	....	N.L.	71	74⅓	3	8	.273	60	38	75	3.39	37
2000 Milwaukee	....	N.L.	43	46	2	2	.500	44	20	37	2.93	16
2000 Cleveland c-d	....	A.L.	26	26⅔	1	3	.250	11	12	27	3.38	14
Major League Totals	....	.9 Yrs.	521	761	53	42	.558	537	343	751	3.76	104
Division Series												
1995 New York	....	A.L.	3	3	0	0	.000	3	0	5	0.00	0

a Traded by Chicago White Sox to New York Yankees organization with pitchers Melido Perez and Domingo Jean for second baseman Steve Sax and cash, January 10, 1992.
b Traded to Milwaukee Brewers with outfielder Gerald Williams for pitcher Graeme Lloyd, pitcher Ricky Bones and infielder Pat Listach, August 23, 1996. Listach trade voided due to prior injury and New York Yankees received infielder Gabby Martinez to complete trade, November 5, 1996.
c Traded to Cleveland Indians with pitcher Steve Woodard and pitcher Jason Bere for infielder Richie Sexson, pitcher Paul Rigdon, pitcher Kane Davis and player to be named later, July 28, 2000.
d Milwaukee Brewers received infielder Marcus Scutaro to complete trade, August 30, 2000.

WILKINS, MARC ALLEN

Born, Mansfield, Ohio, October 21, 1970.
Bats Right. Throws Right. Height, 5 feet, 11 inches. Weight, 200 pounds.

Year	Club	Lea	G	IP	W	L	Pct	SO	BB	H	ERA	SAVES
1992 Welland	....	N.Y.-Penn.	28	42	4	2	.667	42	24	49	7.29	1
1993 Augusta	....	So.Atl.	48	77	5	6	.455	73	31	83	4.21	1
1994 Salem	....	Carolina	28	151	8	5	.615	90	45	155	3.70	0
1995 Carolina	....	Southern	37	99⅓	5	3	.625	80	44	91	3.99	0
1996 Carolina	....	Southern	11	24⅔	2	3	.400	19	11	19	4.01	0
1996 Pittsburgh	....	N.L.	47	75	4	3	.571	62	36	75	3.84	1
1997 Pittsburgh	....	N.L.	70	75⅔	9	5	.643	47	33	65	3.69	2
1998 Carolina	....	Southern	2	2	0	0	.000	4	0	1	4.50	0
1998 Nashville	....	P.C.	5	4⅓	1	0	1.000	4	3	3	10.38	0
1998 Pittsburgh a	....	N.L.	16	15⅓	0	0	.000	17	9	13	3.52	0
1999 Nashville	....	P.C.	8	11⅓	1	1	.500	8	3	9	0.79	0
1999 Altoona	....	Eastern	4	6	0	1	.000	5	4	4	1.50	0
1999 Pittsburgh b	....	N.L.	46	51	2	3	.400	44	26	49	4.24	0
2000 Nashville	....	P.C.	17	38	2	3	.400	33	24	34	4.97	0
2000 Pittsburgh c-d-e	....	N.L.	52	60⅓	4	2	.667	37	43	54	5.07	0
Major League Totals	....	.5 Yrs.	231	277⅓	19	13	.594	207	147	256	4.12	3

a On disabled list from April 26 to May 11 and May 23 to September 28, 1998.

b On disabled list from March 25 to May 1, 1999.
c Claimed on waivers by Oakland Athletics, October 12, 2000.
d Designated for assignment by Oakland Athletics, December 7, 2000.
e Released by Oakland Athletics, December 15, 2000.

WILLIAMS, BRIAN O'NEAL

Born, Lancaster, South Carolina, February 15, 1969.
Bats Right. Throws Right. Height, 6 feet, 2 inches. Weight, 195 pounds.

Year	Club	Lea	G	IP	W	L	Pct	SO	BB	H	ERA	SAVES
1990	Auburn	N.Y.-Penn.	3	6²/₃	0	0	.000	7	6	6	4.05	0
1991	Osceola	Fla.St.	15	89²/₃	6	4	.600	67	40	72	2.91	0
1991	Jackson	Texas	3	15	2	1	.667	15	7	17	4.20	0
1991	Tucson	P.C.	7	38¹/₃	0	1	.000	29	22	39	4.93	0
1991	Houston	N.L.	2	12	0	1	.000	4	4	11	3.75	0
1992	Tucson	P.C.	12	70	6	1	.857	58	26	78	4.50	0
1992	Houston	N.L.	16	96¹/₃	7	6	.538	54	42	92	3.92	0
1993	Tucson	P.C.	2	3	1	0	1.000	3	0	1	0.00	0
1993	Houston	N.L.	42	82	4	4	.500	56	38	76	4.83	3
1994	Tucson	P.C.	3	20¹/₃	2	0	1.000	14	9	22	2.21	0
1994	Houston a	N.L.	20	78¹/₃	6	5	.545	49	41	112	5.74	0
1995	San Diego b	N.L.	44	72	3	10	.231	75	38	79	6.00	0
1996	Toledo	Int.	3	19²/₃	1	2	.333	21	9	22	5.49	0
1996	Detroit c	A.L.	40	121	3	10	.231	72	85	145	6.77	2
1997	Rochester	Int.	22	69¹/₃	4	3	.571	78	23	68	3.89	8
1997	Baltimore d-e	A.L.	13	24	0	0	.000	14	18	20	3.00	0
1999	Houston f-g	N.L.	50	67¹/₃	2	1	.667	53	35	69	4.41	0
2000	Chicago	N.L.	22	24¹/₃	1	1	.500	14	23	28	9.62	1
2000	Cleveland h-i	A.L.	7	18	0	0	.000	6	8	23	4.00	0
Major League Totals		9 Yrs.	256	595¹/₃	26	38	.406	397	332	655	5.37	6

a Traded to San Diego Padres with infielder Ken Caminiti, outfielder Steve Finley, infielder Andujar Cedeno, infielder Roberto Petagine amd player to be named later for outfielder Phil Plantier, outfielder Derek Bell.
b San Diego Padres received pitcher Sean Fesh to complete trade, May 1, 1995.
c Filed for free agency, December 20, 1995, signed with Detroit Tigers, January 10, 1996.
d Released by Detroit Tigers, November 20, 1996, signed with Baltimore Orioles, January 21, 1997.
e Sold to Fukuoka Daiei Hawks (Japan Pacific), December 18, 1997.
f Played in Japan in 1998, signed as free agent by Houston Astros organization, January 21, 1999.
g Filed for free agency, October 28, 1999. Signed with Chicago Cubs, January 7, 2000.
h Waived by Chicago Cubs, May 27, 2000, signed with Cleveland Indians, June 5, 2000.
i Filed for free agency, October 5, 2000, signed with Boston Red Sox organization, January 4, 2001.

WILLIAMS, GREGORY SCOTT (WOODY)

Born, Houston, Texas, August 19, 1966.
Bats Right. Throws Right. Height, 6 feet. Weight, 190 pounds.

Year	Club	Lea	G	IP	W	L	Pct	SO	BB	H	ERA	SAVES
1988	St. Catharines	N.Y.-Penn.	12	76	8	2	.800	58	21	48	1.54	0
1988	Knoxville	Southern	6	28¹/₃	2	2	.500	25	12	27	3.81	0
1989	Dunedin	Fla. St.	20	81¹/₃	3	5	.375	60	27	63	2.32	3
1989	Knoxville	Southern	14	71	3	5	.375	51	33	61	3.55	1
1990	Syracuse	Int.	3	9	0	1	.000	8	4	15	10.00	0
1990	Knoxville	Southern	42	126	7	9	.438	74	39	111	3.14	5
1991	Knoxville	Southern	18	42²/₃	3	2	.600	37	14	42	3.59	3
1991	Syracuse	Int.	31	54²/₃	3	4	.429	37	27	52	4.12	6
1992	Syracuse	Int.	25	120²/₃	6	8	.429	81	41	115	3.13	1
1993	Syracuse	Int.	12	16¹/₃	1	1	.500	16	5	15	2.20	3
1993	Dunedin	Fla. St.	2	4	0	0	.000	2	2	0	0.00	0
1993	Toronto	A.L.	30	37	3	1	.750	24	22	40	4.38	0
1994	Syracuse	Int.	1	1	0	0	.000	1	0	0	0.00	1
1994	Toronto	A.L.	38	59¹/₃	1	3	.250	56	33	44	3.64	0
1995	Toronto	A.L.	23	53²/₃	1	2	.333	41	28	44	3.69	0
1995	Syracuse	Int.	5	7⅝	0	0	.000	13	5	5	3.52	1
1996	Dunedin	Fla. St.	2	7²/₃	0	2	.000	11	2	9	8.22	0
1996	St. Catharines	N.Y.-Penn.	2	7¹/₃	0	0	.000	12	4	7	3.68	0
1996	Syracuse	Int.	7	32	3	1	.750	33	7	22	1.41	0
1996	Toronto a	A.L.	12	59	4	5	.444	43	21	64	4.73	0
1997	Toronto	A.L.	31	194²/₃	9	14	.391	124	66	201	4.35	0
1998	Toronto-b	A.L.	32	209²/₃	10	9	.526	151	81	196	4.46	0
1999	San Diego	N.L.	33	208¹/₃	12	12	.500	137	73	213	4.41	0
2000	Rancho Cucamonga	California	1	5	0	0	.000	10	0	3	0.00	0
2000	Las Vegas	P.C.	1	6	0	0	.000	5	0	7	1.50	0

Year Club	Lea	G	IP	W	L	Pct	SO	BB	H	ERA	SAVES
2000 San Diego c	N.L.	23	168	10	8	.556	111	54	152	3.75	0
Major League Totals	.8 Yrs.	222	989²/₃	50	54	.481	687	378	954	4.23	0

a On disabled list from April 1 to May 31 and June 7 to July 26, 1996.
b Traded to San Diego Padres with pitcher Carlos Almanzar and outfielder Peter Tucci for pitcher Joey Hamilton, December 13, 1998.
c On disabled list from May 6 to July 1, 2000.

WILLIAMS, MICHAEL DARREN
Born, Radford, Virginia, July 29, 1969.
Bats Right. Throws Right. Height 6 feet, 2 inches. Weight, 199 pounds.

Year Club	Lea	G	IP	W	L	Pct	SO	BB	H	ERA	SAVES
1990 Batavia	N.Y.-Penn.	27	47	2	3	.400	42	13	39	2.30	11
1991 Clearwater	Fla. St.	14	93¹/₃	7	3	.700	76	14	65	1.74	0
1991 Reading	Eastern	15	100	7	5	.583	50	34	92	3.69	0
1992 Reading	Eastern	3	15²/₃	1	2	.333	12	7	17	5.17	0
1992 Philadelphia	N.L.	5	28²/₃	1	1	.500	5	7	29	5.34	0
1992 Scranton	Int.	16	92²/₃	9	1	.900	59	30	84	2.43	0
1993 Scranton	Int.	14	97¹/₃	9	2	.818	53	16	93	2.87	0
1993 Philadelphia	N.L.	17	51	1	3	.250	33	22	50	5.29	0
1994 Scranton	Int.	14	84	2	7	.222	53	36	91	5.79	0
1994 Philadelphia	N.L.	12	50¹/₃	2	4	.333	29	20	61	5.01	0
1995 Scranton-WB	Int.	3	9²/₃	0	1	.000	8	2	8	4.66	0
1995 Philadelphia	N.L.	33	87²/₃	3	3	.500	57	29	78	3.29	0
1996 Philadelphia	N.L.	32	167	6	14	.300	103	67	188	5.44	0
1997 Omaha	A.A.	20	79	3	6	.333	68	38	71	4.22	5
1997 Kansas City a-b-c	A.L.	10	14	0	2	.000	10	8	20	6.43	1
1998 Nashville	P.C.	16	37	0	2	.000	34	14	36	5.59	1
1998 Pittsburgh	N.L.	37	51	4	2	.667	59	16	39	1.94	0
1999 Burlington	Midwest	37	127¹/₃	6	7	.462	83	65	119	4.45	2
1999 Pittsburgh d	N.L.	58	58¹/₃	3	4	.429	76	37	63	5.09	23
2000 Pittsburgh	N.L.	72	72	3	4	.429	71	40	56	3.50	24
Major League Totals	.9 Yrs.	276	580	23	37	.383	443	246	584	4.50	48

a Signed with Boston Red Sox organization, February 15, 1997.
b Outrighted by Kansas City Royals, July 3, 1997.
c Signed with Pittsburgh Pirates organization, December 18, 1997.
d On disabled list from June 24 to July 9, 1999.

WILLIAMSON, SCOTT RYAN
Born, Fort Polk, Louisiana, February 17, 1976.
Bats Right. Throws Right. Height, 6 feet. Weight, 185 pounds.

Year Club	Lea	G	IP	W	L	Pct	SO	BB	H	ERA	SAVES
1997 Billings	Pioneer	13	86	8	2	.800	101	23	66	1.78	0
1998 Chattanooga	Southern	18	100	4	5	.444	105	46	85	3.78	0
1998 Indianapols	Int.	5	20²/₃	0	0	.000	17	9	20	3.48	0
1999 Cincinnati a	N.L.	62	93¹/₃	12	7	.632	107	43	54	2.41	19
2000 Cincinnati b	N.L.	48	112	5	8	.385	136	75	92	3.29	6
Major League Totals	.2 Yrs.	110	205¹/₃	17	15	.531	243	118	146	2.89	25

a Selected Rookie of the Year in National League for 1999.
b On disabled list from August 25 to September 7, 2000.

WITASICK, GERALD ALFONSE (JAY)
Born, Baltimore, Maryland, August 28, 1972.
Bats Right. Throws Right. Height, 6 feet, 4 inches. Weight, 205 pounds.

Year Club	Lea	G	IP	W	L	Pct	SO	BB	H	ERA	SAVES
1993 Johnson Cty	Appal.	12	67²/₃	4	3	.571	74	19	65	4.12	0
1993 Savannah	So.Atl.	1	6	1	0	1.000	8	2	7	4.50	0
1994 Madison	Midwest	18	112¹/₃	10	4	.714	141	42	74	2.32	0
1995 St. Pete	Fla.St.	18	105	7	7	.500	109	36	80	2.74	0
1995 Arkansas	Texas	7	34	2	4	.333	26	16	46	6.88	0
1996 Huntsville	Southern	25	66²/₃	0	3	.000	63	26	47	2.30	4
1996 Edmonton	P.C.	6	8²/₃	0	0	.000	9	6	9	4.15	2
1996 Oakland a	A.L.	12	13	1	1	.500	12	5	12	6.23	0
1997 Modesto	California	9	17¹/₃	0	1	.000	29	5	16	4.15	1
1997 Edmonton	P.C.	13	27¹/₃	3	2	.600	17	15	25	4.28	0
1997 Oakland	A.L.	8	11	0	0	.000	8	6	14	5.73	0
1998 Edmonton	P.C.	27	149	11	7	.611	155	49	126	3.87	0

Year Club	Lea	G	IP	W	L	Pct	SO	BB	H	ERA	SAVES
1998 Oakland	A.L.	7	27	1	3	.250	29	15	36	6.33	0
1999 Kansas City b	A.L.	32	$158\frac{1}{3}$	9	12	.429	102	83	191	5.57	0
2000 Kansas City c	A.L.	22	$89\frac{1}{3}$	3	8	.273	67	38	109	5.94	0
2000 San Diego	N.L.	11	$60\frac{2}{3}$	3	2	.600	54	35	69	5.64	0
Major League Totals .... 5 Yrs.		92	$359\frac{1}{3}$	17	26	.395	272	182	431	5.76	0

a Traded by St. Louis Cardinals to Oakland Athletics with pitcher Bret Wagner, outfielder Allen Battle and pitcher Carl Dale for pitcher Todd Stottlemyre, January 9, 1996.

b Traded to Kansas City Royals for player to be named later and cash, March 30, 1999. Oakland Athletics received pitcher Scott Chiasson to complete trade, June 9, 1999.

c Traded to San Diego Padres for pitcher Brian Meadows, July 31, 2000.

WOLF, RANDALL C. (RANDY)
Born, Canoga Park, California, August 22, 1976.
Bats Left. Throws Right. Height, 6 feet. Weight, 190 pounds.

Year Club	Lea	G	IP	W	L	Pct	SO	BB	H	ERA	SAVES
1997 Batavia	N.Y.-Penn.	7	40	4	0	1.000	53	8	29	1.58	0
1998 Reading	Eastern	4	25	2	0	1.000	33	4	15	1.44	0
1998 Scranton-WB	Int.	24	148	9	7	.563	118	48	167	4.62	0
1999 Scranton-WB	Int.	12	$77\frac{1}{3}$	4	5	.444	72	29	73	3.61	0
1999 Philadelphia	N.L.	22	$121\frac{2}{3}$	6	9	.400	116	67	126	5.55	0
2000 Philadelphia	N.L.	32	$206\frac{1}{3}$	11	9	.550	160	83	210	4.36	0
Major League Totals .... 2 Yrs.		54	328	17	18	.486	276	150	336	4.80	0

WOOD, KERRY LEE
Born, Irving, Texas, June 16, 1977.
Bats Right. Throws Right. Height, 6 feet, 5 inches. Weight, 225 pounds.

Year Club	Lea	G	IP	W	L	Pct	SO	BB	H	ERA	SAVES
1995 Cubs	Gulf Coast	1	3	0	0	.000	2	1	0	0.00	0
1995 Williamsprt	N.Y.-Penn.	2	$4\frac{1}{3}$	0	0	.000	5	5	5	10.38	0
1996 Daytona a	Fla.St.	22	$114\frac{1}{3}$	10	2	.833	136	70	72	2.91	0
1997 Orlando	Southern	19	94	6	7	.462	106	79	58	4.50	0
1997 Iowa	A.A.	10	$57\frac{2}{3}$	4	2	.667	80	52	35	4.68	0
1998 Iowa	P.C.	1	5	1	0	1.000	11	2	1	0.00	0
1998 Chicago b	N.L.	26	$166\frac{2}{3}$	13	6	.684	233	85	117	3.40	0
1999 Chicago c	N.L.	INJURED - Did Not Play									
2000 Daytona	Fla.St.	2	12	2	0	1.000	17	5	3	1.50	0
2000 Iowa	P.C.	1	7	0	0	.000	7	4	4	2.57	0
2000 Chicago d	N.L.	23	137	8	7	.533	132	87	112	4.80	0
Major League Totals .... 2 Yrs.		49	$303\frac{2}{3}$	21	13	.618	365	172	229	4.03	0
Division Series											
1998 Chicago	N.L.	1	5	0	1	.000	5	4	3	1.80	0

a On disabled list from May 24 to June 19, 1996.

b Selected Rookie of the Year in National League for 1998.

c On disabled list from March 31 to November 2, 1999.

d On disabled list from March 25 to May 1 and July 30 to August 21, 2000.

WOODARD, STEVEN LARRY
Born, Hartselle, Alabama, May 15, 1975.
Bats Left. Throws Right. Height, 6 feet, 4 inches. Weight, 225 pounds.

Year Club	Lea	G	IP	W	L	Pct	SO	BB	H	ERA	SAVES
1994 Brewers	Arizona	15	$82\frac{2}{3}$	8	0	1.000	85	13	68	2.40	0
1995 Beloit	Midwest	21	115	7	4	.636	94	31	113	4.54	0
1996 Stockton	California	28	$181\frac{1}{3}$	12	9	.571	142	33	201	4.02	0
1997 El Paso	Texas	19	$136\frac{1}{3}$	14	3	.824	97	25	136	3.17	0
1997 Tucson	P.C.	1	7	1	0	1.000	6	1	3	0.00	0
1997 Milwaukee a	A.L.	7	$36\frac{2}{3}$	3	3	.500	32	6	39	5.15	0
1998 Milwaukee	N.L.	34	$165\frac{2}{3}$	10	12	.455	135	33	170	4.18	0
1999 Milwaukee b	N.L.	31	185	11	8	.579	119	36	219	4.52	0
2000 Milwaukee	N.L.	27	$93\frac{2}{3}$	1	7	.125	65	33	125	5.96	0
2000 Cleveland c-d	A.L.	13	54	3	3	.500	35	11	57	5.67	0
Major League Totals .... 4 Yrs.		112	535	28	33	.459	386	119	610	4.83	0

On disabled list from August 28 to September 29, 1997.

On disabled list from August 12 to September 10, 1999.

Traded to Cleveland Indians with pitcher Bob Wickman and pitcher Jason Bere for infielder Richie Sexson, pitcher Paul Rigdon, pitcher Kane Davis and player to be named later, July 28, 2000.
Milwaukee Brewers received infielder Marcus Scutaro to complete trade, August 30, 2000.

WORRELL, TIMOTHY HOWARD (TIM)

Born, Pasadena, California, July 5, 1967.
Bats Right. Throws Right. Height, 6 feet, 4 inches. Weight, 200 pounds.

Year	Club	Lea	G	IP	W	L	Pct	SO	BB	H	ERA	SAVES
1990	Charleston SC	So. Atl.	20	110⅔	5	8	.385	68	28	120	4.64	0
1991	Waterloo	Midwest	14	86⅓	8	4	.667	83	33	70	3.34	0
1991	High Desert	California	11	63⅔	5	2	.714	70	33	65	4.24	0
1992	Wichita	Texas	19	125⅔	8	6	.571	109	32	115	2.86	0
1992	Las Vegas	P.C.	10	63⅓	4	2	.667	32	19	61	4.26	0
1993	Las Vegas	P.C.	15	87	5	6	.455	89	26	102	5.48	0
1993	San Diego	N.L.	21	100⅔	2	7	.222	52	43	104	4.92	0
1994	San Diego a	N.L.	3	14⅔	0	1	.000	14	5	9	3.68	0
1995	Rancho Guca	California	9	22⅔	0	2	.000	17	6	25	5.16	1
1995	Las Vegas	P.C.	10	24	0	2	.000	18	17	27	6.00	0
1995	San Diego b	N.L.	9	13⅓	1	0	1.000	13	6	16	4.72	0
1996	San Diego	N.L.	50	121	9	7	.563	99	39	109	3.05	1
1997	San Diego c-d	N.L.	60	106⅓	4	8	.333	81	50	116	5.16	3
1998	Detroit-Cleveland-Oakland e-f-g	A.L.	43	103	2	7	.222	82	29	106	5.24	0
1999	Modesto	California	1	2	0	0	.000	5	0	0	0.00	0
1999	Oakland h-i	A.L.	53	69⅓	2	2	.500	62	34	69	4.15	0
2000	Baltimore j	A.L.	5	7⅓	2	2	.500	5	5	12	7.36	0
2000	Iowa	P.C.	6	10⅔	2	0	1.000	7	5	9	5.06	0
2000	Chicago k	N.L.	54	62	3	4	.429	52	24	60	2.47	3
Major League Totals	8 Yrs.		298	597⅔	25	38	.397	460	235	601	4.29	7

Division Series

Year	Club	Lea	G	IP	W	L	Pct	SO	BB	H	ERA	SAVES
1996	San Diego	N.L.	2	3⅔	0	0	.000	2	1	4	2.45	0

a On disabled list from April 19 to end of 1994 season.
b On disabled list from April 25 to October 2, 1995.
c Selected in expansion draft by Arizona Diamondbacks, November 18, 1997.
d Traded to Detroit Tigers with outfielder Trey Beamon for pitcher Dan Miceli, pitcher Donne Wall and outfielder Ryan Balfe, November 17, 1997.
e Traded to Cleveland Indians with outfielder Dave Roberts for outfielder Geronimo Berroa, June 22, 1998.
f Traded to Oakland Athletics for player to be named later, July 12, 1998.
g Cleveland Indians received infielder Aaron Robinson to complete trade, July 28, 1998.
h On disabled list from July 20 to August 8, 1999.
i Filed for free agency, October 29, 1999. Signed with Baltimore Orioles organization, February 4, 2000.
j Released by Baltimore Orioles, May 3, 2000, signed with Chicago Cubs organization, May 8, 2000.
k Traded to San Francisco Giants for infielder Bill Mueller, November 19, 2000.

WRIGHT, JAMEY ALAN

Born, Oklahoma City, Oklahoma, December 24, 1974.
Bats Right. Throws Right. Height, 6 feet, 6 inches. Weight, 205 pounds.

Year	Club	Lea	G	IP	W	L	Pct	SO	BB	H	ERA	SAVES
1993	Rockies	Arizona	8	36	1	3	.250	26	9	35	4.00	0
1994	Asheville	So. Atl.	28	143⅓	7	14	.333	103	59	188	5.97	0
1995	Salem	Carolina	26	171	10	8	.556	95	72	160	2.47	0
1995	New Haven	Eastern	1	3	0	1	.000	0	3	6	9.00	0
1996	New Haven	Eastern	7	44⅔	5	1	.833	54	12	27	0.81	0
1996	Colo Sprngs	P.C.	9	59⅔	4	2	.667	40	22	53	2.72	0
1996	Colorado	N.L.	16	91⅓	4	4	.500	45	41	105	4.93	0
1997	Salem	Carolina	1	1	0	1	.000	1	1	1	9.00	0
1997	Colo Sprngs	P.C.	2	11	1	0	1.000	11	5	9	1.64	0
1997	Colorado a	N.L.	26	149⅔	8	12	.400	59	71	198	6.25	0
1998	Colorado	N.L.	34	206⅓	9	14	.391	86	95	235	5.67	0
1999	Colorado Spgs	P.C.	17	100⅓	5	7	.417	75	38	133	6.46	0
1999	Colorado b	N.L.	16	94⅓	4	3	.571	49	54	110	4.87	0
2000	Huntsville	Southern	2	12⅓	2	0	1.000	10	5	7	0.00	0
2000	Indianapolis	Int.	1	5	0	0	.000	7	3	8	1.80	0
2000	Milwaukee c	N.L.	26	164⅔	7	9	.438	96	88	157	4.10	0
Major League Totals	5 Yrs.		118	706⅓	32	42	.432	335	349	805	5.22	0

a On disabled list from May 15 to June 8, 1997.
b Traded to Milwaukee Brewers with catcher Henry Blanco and pitcher Justin Miller for infielder Jeff Cirillo and pitcher Scott Karl, December 13, 1999. Miller was then traded to Oakland for pitcher Jimmy Haynes as part of a three-club deal, December 13, 1999.
c On disabled list from March 28 to May 22, 2000.

WRIGHT, JARET SAMUEL

Born, Anaheim, California, December 29, 1975.
Bats Right. Throws Right. Height, 6 feet, 2 inches. Weight, 220 pounds.

Year	Club	Lea	G	IP	W	L	Pct	SO	BB	H	ERA	SAVES
1994 Burlington	....	Appal.	4	13$^{1}/_3$	0	1	.000	16	9	13	5.40	0
1995 Columbus	....	So. Atl.	24	129	5	6	.455	113	79	93	3.63	0
1996 Kinston	....	Carolina	19	101	7	4	.636	109	55	65	2.50	0
1997 Akron	....	Eastern	8	54	3	3	.500	59	23	43	3.67	0
1997 Buffalo	....	A.A.	7	45	4	1	.800	47	19	30	1.80	0
1997 Cleveland	....	A.L.	16	90$^{1}/_3$	8	3	.727	63	35	81	4.38	0
1998 Cleveland	....	A.L.	32	192$^{2}/_3$	12	10	.545	140	87	207	4.72	0
1999 Buffalo	....	Int.	1	3	0	0	.000	4	0	0	0.00	0
1999 Akron	....	E.L.	1	5	1	0	1.000	6	0	3	0.00	0
1999 Cleveland a	....	A.L.	26	133$^{2}/_3$	8	10	.444	91	77	144	6.06	0
2000 Buffalo	....	Int.	1	2	0	0	.000	1	1	0	0.00	0
2000 Akron	....	Eastern	2	8	0	0	.000	5	3	4	3.38	0
2000 Cleveland b	....	A.L.	9	51$^{2}/_3$	3	4	.429	36	28	44	4.70	0
Major League Totals	.... 4 Yrs.		83	468$^{1}/_3$	31	27	.534	330	227	476	5.03	0
Division Series												
1997 Cleveland	....	A.L.	2	11$^{1}/_3$	2	0	1.000	10	7	11	3.97	0
1998 Cleveland	....	A.L.	1	4$^{1}/_3$	0	1	.000	6	2	7	12.46	0
1999 Cleveland	....	A.L.	1	2	0	1	.000	1	1	4	22.50	0
Division Series Totals	....		4	17$^{2}/_3$	2	2	.500	17	10	22	8.15	0
Championship Series												
1997 Cleveland	....	A.L.	1	3	0	0	.000	3	2	6	15.00	0
1998 Cleveland	....	A.L.	2	6$^{2}/_3$	0	1	.000	4	8	7	8.10	0
Championship Series Totals	......		3	9$^{2}/_3$	0	1	.000	7	10	13	10.24	0
World Series Record												
1997 Cleveland	....	A.L.	2	12$^{1}/_3$	1	0	1.000	12	10	7	2.92	0

a On disabled list from July 19 to August 3 and August 9 to September 10, 1999.
b On disabled list from May 12 to May 26 and June 3 to October 31, 2000.

WUNSCH, KELLY DOUGLAS

Born, Houston, Texas, July 12, 1972.
Bats Left. Throws Right. Height, 6 feet, 5 inches. Weight, 192 pounds.

Year	Club	Lea	G	IP	W	L	Pct	SO	BB	H	ERA	SAVES
1993 Beloit	....	Midwest	12	63$^{1}/_3$	1	5	.167	61	39	58	4.83	0
1994 Beloit	....	Midwest	17	83$^{1}/_3$	3	10	.231	77	47	88	6.16	0
1994 Helena	....	Pioneer	9	51	4	2	.667	37	30	52	5.12	0
1995 Beloit	....	Midwest	14	85$^{2}/_3$	4	7	.364	66	37	90	4.20	0
1995 Stockton a-b	......	California	14	74$^{1}/_3$	5	6	.455	62	39	89	5.33	0
1997 Stockton	....	California	24	143	7	9	.438	98	62	141	3.46	0
1998 El Paso	....	Texas	17	101$^{1}/_3$	5	6	.455	70	31	127	5.95	0
1998 Louisville c	....	Int.	9	51$^{2}/_3$	3	1	.750	36	15	53	3.83	0
1999 Louisville	....	Int.	16	41$^{2}/_3$	2	1	.667	20	14	52	4.75	0
1999 Huntsville d-e	......	Southern	22	50$^{2}/_3$	4	1	.800	35	23	40	1.95	0
2000 Chicago	....	A.L.	*83	61$^{1}/_3$	6	3	.667	51	29	50	2.93	1
Division Series												
2000 Chicago	....	A.L.	3	0$^{2}/_3$	0	1	.000	0	0	2	0.00	0

a On disabled list from April 4 to May 13, 1996.
b On disabled list from June 19 to September 10, 1996.
c On disabled list from April 8 to May 7, 1998.
d On disabled list from Jluy 10 to 17, 1999.
e Filed for free agency from Milwaukee Brewers, October 15, 1999, signed with Chicago White Sox organization, November 15, 1999.

YAN, ESTEBAN LUIS

Born, Campina Del Seibo, Dominican Republic, June 22, 1974.
Bats Right. Throws Right. Height, 6 feet, 4 inches. Weight, 230 pounds.

Year	Club	Lea	G	IP	W	L	Pct	SO	BB	H	ERA	SAVES
1993 Danville	....	Appal.	14	71$^{1}/_3$	4	7	.364	50	24	73	3.03	0
1994 Macon	....	So. Atl.	28	170$^{2}/_3$	11	12	.478	121	34	155	3.27	0
1995 Wst Plm Bch	....	Fla. St.	24	137$^{2}/_3$	6	8	.429	89	33	139	3.07	1
1996 Bowie	....	Eastern	9	16	0	2	.000	16	8	18	5.63	0
1996 Baltimore	....	A.L.	4	9$^{1}/_3$	0	0	.000	7	3	13	5.79	0
1996 Rochester	....	Int.	22	71$^{2}/_3$	5	4	.556	61	18	75	4.27	1
1997 Rochester	....	Int.	34	119	11	5	.688	131	37	107	3.10	2
1997 Baltimore a	....	A.L.	3	9$^{2}/_3$	0	1	.000	4	7	20	15.83	0
1998 Tampa Bay	....	A.L.	64	88$^{2}/_3$	5	4	.556	77	41	78	3.86	1

Year	Club	Lea	G	IP	W	L	Pct	SO	BB	H	ERA	SAVES
1999 St. Petersburg	Fla.St.	2	4	0	0	.000	0	1	3	0.00	0
1999 Tampa Bay b	A.L.	50	61	3	4	.429	46	32	77	5.90	0
2000 Tampa Bay	A.L.	43	137²/₃	7	8	.467	111	42	158	6.21	0
Major League Totals	5 Yrs.	164	306¹/₃	15	17	.469	245	125	346	5.76	1

a Selected in expansion draft by Tampa Bay Devil Rays, November 18, 1997.
b On disabled list from June 17 to July 15, 1999.

YOSHII, MASATO

Born, Osaka, Japan, April 20, 1965.
Bats Right. Throws Right. Height, 6 feet, 2 inches. Weight, 210 pounds.

Year	Club	Lea	G	IP	W	L	Pct	SO	BB	H	ERA	SAVES
1985 Kintetsu	Japan Pac.	2	3	0	1	.000	1	3	6	21.00	0
1986 Kintetsu	Japan Pac.	2	2¹/₃	0	0	.000	2	2	10	23.14	0
1987 Kintetsu	Japan Pac.	13	36	2	1	.667	23	12	45	4.75	24
1988 Kintetsu	Japan Pac.	50	80¹/₃	10	2	.833	44	27	76	2.69	20
1989 Kintetsu	Japan Pac.	47	84¹/₃	5	5	.500	44	37	77	2.99	15
1990 Kintetsu	Japan Pac.	45	741/3	8	9	.471	55	30	80	3.39	2
1991 Kintetsu	Japan Pac.	21	26¹/₃	2	1	.667	13	6	30	3.42	0
1992 Kintetsu	Japan Pac.	9	11²/₃	1	0	1.000	4	2	10	2.31	0
1993 Kintetsu	Japan Pac.	22	104²/₃	5	5	.500	66	25	100	2.67	0
1994 Kintetsu a	Japan Pac.	21	97	7	7	.500	42	37	118	5.47	0
1995 Yakult	Japan Cent.	25	147¹/₃	10	7	.588	91	39	127	3.12	0
1996 Yakult	Japan Cent.	25	180¹/₃	10	7	.588	145	47	177	3.24	0
1997 Yakult b	Japan Cent.	28	174¹/₃	13	6	.684	104	48	149	2.99	0
1998 New York	N.L.	29	171²/₃	6	8	.429	117	53	166	3.93	0
1999 New York c	N.L.	31	174	12	8	.600	105	58	168	4.40	0
2000 Colorado	N.L.	29	167¹/₃	6	15	.286	88	53	201	5.86	0
Major League Totals	3 Yrs.	89	513	24	31	.436	310	164	535	4.72	0
Division Series											
1999 New York	N.L.	1	5¹/₃	0	0	.000	3	0	6	6.75	0
Championship Series											
1999 New York	N.L.	2	7²/₃	0	1	.000	4	3	9	4.70	0

a Traded to Yakult Swallows, October, 1994.
b Signed as a free agent with New York Mets, January 13, 1998.
c Traded to Colorado Rockies for pitcher Bobby M. Jones and pitcher Lariel Gonzalez, January 14, 2000.

ZIMMERMAN, JEFFREY ROSS (JEFF)

Born, Kelowna, British Columbia, Canada, August 9, 1972.
Bats Right. Throws Right. Height, 6 feet, 1 inch. Weight, 200 pounds.

Year	Club	Lea	G	IP	W	L	Pct	SO	BB	H	ERA	SAVES
1997 Winnipeg a	Northern	18	118	9	2	.818	140	35	94	2.82	0
1998 Charlotte	Fla.St.	10	14¹/₃	2	1	.667	14	1	10	1.26	0
1998 Tulsa	Texas	41	63	3	1	.750	67	20	38	1.29	9
1999 Oklahoma	P.C.	2	3²/₃	1	0	1.000	2	0	0	0.00	1
1999 Texas	A.L.	65	87²/₃	9	3	.750	67	23	50	2.36	3
2000 Texas	A.L.	65	69²/₃	4	5	.444	74	34	80	5.30	1
Major League Totals	2 Yrs.	130	157¹/₃	13	8	.619	141	57	130	3.66	4
Division Series											
1999 Texas	A.L.	1	1	0	0	.000	1	0	1	0.00	0

a Signed by Texas Rangers from independent Winnipeg, January 6, 1998.

ZITO, BARRY WILLIAM

Born, Las Vegas, Nevada, May 13, 1978.
Bats Left. Throws Right. Height, 6 feet, 4 inches. Weight, 205 pounds.

Year	Club	Lea	G	IP	W	L	Pct	SO	BB	H	ERA	SAVES
1999 Vancouver	P.C.	1	6	1	0	1.000	6	2	5	1.50	0
1999 Midland	Texas	4	22	2	1	.667	29	11	22	4.91	0
1999 Visalia	California	8	40¹/₃	3	0	1.000	62	22	21	2.45	0
2000 Sacramento	P.C.	18	101²/₃	8	5	.615	91	45	88	3.19	0
2000 Oakland	A.L.	14	92²/₃	7	4	.636	78	45	64	2.72	0
Division Series											
2000 Oakland	A.L.	1	5²/₃	1	0	1.000	5	2	7	1.59	0

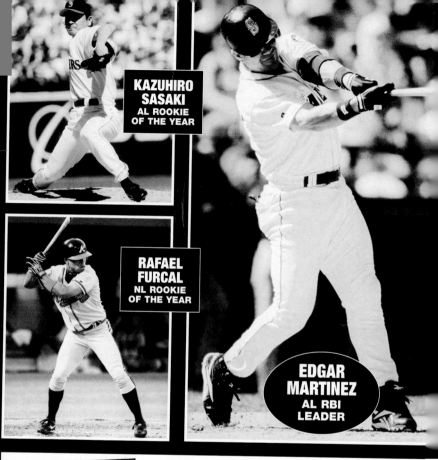

KAZUHIRO SASAKI
AL ROOKIE OF THE YEAR

RAFAEL FURCAL
NL ROOKIE OF THE YEAR

EDGAR MARTINEZ
AL RBI LEADER

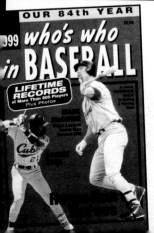

OUR 84th YEAR

'99 who's who in BASEBALL

LIFETIME RECORDS of More Than 800 Players Plus Photos

Who's Who in Baseball

BACK ISSUES

ORDER NOW WHILE OUR STOCK LASTS

EDITIONS AVAILABLE   **COST** (Per Copy)

2000, 1998, 1997, 1991 ....$15.00
1989, 1988, 1987, 1986, 1985 ....$25.00
1984, 1983, 1982, 1981, 1980 ....$35.00
1978, 1977, 1976, 1974, 1971 ....$50.00
1967, 1965, 1963, ...$75.00

(Include $2.00 per copy to cover postage & handling.)

Send check or money order to:

WHO'S WHO IN BASEBALL MAGAZINE CO.
1115 BROADWAY, DEPT. W
NEW YORK, NEW YORK 10010

Make sure to list editions wanted. Allow 8 to 10 weeks for delivery

FRONT ROW: (L–R) Coach Bob Didier, Coach Mel Stottlemyre, Coach Tony Cloninger, Coach Don Zimmer, Manager Joe Torre, Coach Lee Mazzilli, Coach Chris Chambliss, Coach Willie Randolph, Bullpen Catcher Mike Borzello.

SECOND ROW: (L–R) Team Physician Dr. Stuart Hershon, Equipment Manager Rob Cucuzza, Head Trainer Gene Monahan, Asst. Strength and Conditioning Coach Brian McNamee, Luis Sojo, Clay Bellinger, Mike Stanton, David Cone, Video Coordinator Charlie Wonsowicz, Shane Spencer, Chuck Knoblauch, Nick Testa, Traveling Secretary David Szen.

THIRD ROW: (L–R) Asst. Traveling Secretary Eddie Robinson III, Randy Choate, Luis Polonia, Jose Vizcaino, Chris Turner, David Justice, Tino Martinez, Derek Jeter, Bernie Williams, Mariano Rivera, Scott Brosius, Massage Therapist Rohan Baichu, Strength and Conditioning Coach Jeff Mangold, Asst. Trainer Steve Donohue, Clubhouse Manager Lou Cucuzza Jr.

BACK ROW: (L–R) Ramiro Mendoza, Allen Watson, Denny Neagle, Glenallen Hill, Paul O'Neill, Jason Grimsley, Andy Pettitte, Jeff Nelson, Roger Clemens, Jose Canseco, Dwight Gooden, Orlando Hernandez, Jorge Posada, Roberto Kelly. **BATBOYS:** (Seated L–R) George Brown, John Viola,

ISBN 0-910692-20-3

Who's Who presents ISSUE #16

0 09281 02736 2

Printed in U.S.A.